SECRET GERMANY

SECRET GERMANY
STEFAN GEORGE AND HIS CIRCLE

ROBERT E. NORTON

Cornell University Press   Ithaca & London

Copyright © 2002 by Cornell University

All rights reserved. Except for brief quotations in a review, this book, or parts thereof, must not be reproduced in any form without permission in writing from the publisher. For information, address Cornell University Press, Sage House, 512 East State Street, Ithaca, New York 14850.

First published 2002 by Cornell University Press

Printed in the United States of America

All of the photographs in this book are reproduced by permission of the Stefan George Foundation, Frankfurt am Main, Germany.

Library of Congress Cataloging-in-Publication Data

Norton, Robert Edward, 1960–
  Secret Germany : Stefan George and his circle / Robert E. Norton.
    p. cm.
Includes bibliographical references and index.
  ISBN 0-8014-3354-1 (cloth : alk. paper)
  1. George, Stefan Anton, 1868–1933—Friends and associates. 2. George, Stefan Anton, 1868–1933—Political and social views. 3. Poets, German—20th century—Biography. 4. Germany—Politics and government—20th century. 1. Title.
  PT2613.E47 Z7557 2002
  831'.8—dc21
                        2001007823

Cornell University Press strives to use environmentally responsible suppliers and materials to the fullest extent possible in the publishing of its books. Such materials include vegetable-based, low-VOC inks and acid-free papers that are recycled, totally chlorine-free, or partly composed of nonwood fibers. For further information, visit our website at www.cornellpress.cornell.edu.

Cloth printing   10 9 8 7 6 5 4 3 2 1

The great poet, in writing himself, writes his time.
T. S. Eliot

Nothing becomes reality in the political life of a nation that was not present in its literature as spirit.
Hugo von Hofmannsthal

contents

Preface ix

I. POET: 1868–1899

1. Beginnings 3
2. School 15
3. First Travels 32
4. Paris 43
5. Berlin 57
6. *Hymns* 68
7. *Pilgrimages* 85
8. A Child in Pale Blue Clothes 95
9. *Algabal* the Decadent 108
10. *Pages for Art* 122
11. Forging Alliances 134
12. Becoming German 144
13. A Group Is Formed 149
14. Schwabing 164
15. A Usable Past 176
16. *The Year of the Soul* 189
17. Going Public 211
18. *The Tapestry of Life* 222
    Illustrations 241

II. PEDAGOGUE: 1900–1908

19. The Disciple 265
20. The Anthologies 278
21. The Cosmic Circle 292

22. Boys: Good, Bad, and Divine 311
23. Maximin 335
24. *The Seventh Ring* 351
Illustrations 373

III. POLITICIAN: 1909–1918

25. Admission to the Order 395
26. The *Führer* and His *Reich* 405
27. The Globe Room 417
28. Secret Germany 428
29. After the *Yearbook* 443
30. Heidelberg 457
31. *The Star of the Covenant* 472
32. Legends of Summer 502
33. The War and Secret Germany 513
34. Surviving 529
Illustrations 555

IV. PROPHET: 1919–1933

35. Revolution I 571
36. Treason 594
37. Regrouping 618
38. Revival 630
39. The Time of Tents 641
40. Stupor Mundi 660
41. *The New Reich* 675
42. Fame 687
43. Apotheosis 698
44. Revolution II 713
45. Epilogue 743

Abbreviations 747
Notes 753
Selected Bibliography 815
Acknowledgments 821
Index 825

arrogance, and economic opportunism, the National Assembly resolved in 1792 to export the ideals of *liberté, fraternité, egalité* to its benighted German brethren, whom they perceived, not a little self-servingly, as still toiling under the yoke of the old regime. For two decades, from 1794 to the final defeat of Napoleon in 1814, the entire left bank of the Rhine, from Speyer to Cleves, remained firmly under French administration.

Not everyone appeared overly troubled that the noble aspirations of the French were enforced by the less exalted means of invading armies and prolonged military occupation. On the contrary, along the west bank of the Rhine, sympathies for France ran high. With few exceptions, the people living in the Rhineland tended to give credit to Napoleon for having at least freed them from the old system of feudal privileges that had paralyzed the German states for centuries. A schoolmaster from a small town near Bingen expressed a prevalent view when he confided to his journal that Napoleon had performed "a necessary cleansing on the Rhine with his iron broom." In any case, he went on, Napoleon presented the lesser of two evils, for it was agreed that the nature of the Rhinelanders had far more in common with their Catholic western neighbors than with the cold, northern, Protestant "Prussian character."

When the twenty-two-year-old Johann Baptist George left his home town in 1804 and traveled on the heels of Napoleon's army to Büdesheim, he must have done so in the hope of capitalizing on the new opportunities made available in the newly conquered territories to someone who spoke both French and German fluently. Obviously, the French administrators posted in the Rhineland could not manage the enormous business of the occupation by themselves. They were forced to enlist the services of local officials to aid in the gathering and distribution of goods, in the overseeing of the new customs and tariff posts set up along the Rhine, and — inevitably — in the collection of taxes. Taxes represented the greatest, and most resented, burden placed on the backs of the people the French claimed to have liberated. One citizen of Burtscheid complained bitterly: "What a difference between the taxes we pay now and those we used to pay! Then, even the leading firm here did not pay more than 60 crowns all told, while today it pays 600 and more in direct taxes alone, not counting indirect taxes." Not accidentally, Johann Baptist, who had tilled the fields as a simple farmer in Rupeldingen, ventured east to start a new life as a tax collector.

Evidently he met with some success in his role as the grasping hand on the fiscal arm of the French occupational government, for he soon bought land in Büdesheim, built a house there, and settled into what was clearly a reasonably prosperous existence. He had a brother, Jakob, likewise a farmer and a custom tailor on the side, who had elected to stay in Rupeldingen. But Jakob's two sons, Etienne and Anton, followed their uncle eastward to Büdesheim to try their luck there as well, probably attracted by the prospects of the fertile Rhineland's natural wealth and by the new economic possibilities afforded by the French occupation, and perhaps, too, by the hope of receiving the benefaction of an unmarried and affluent relative. Etienne, the older of the two and listed in the family registry as Stephan George I, ended up enjoying the rights of the first born. He became Johann Baptist's legal heir, eventually expanding his inherited property holdings to include a sizable and profitable vineyard. Bolstered by such economic fortune, Etienne went on to win the mayor's seat of Büdesheim and was even elected as a member of the regional diet. His brother, Anton, less ambitious politically, practiced trade as a cooper, which allowed him to make an easy transition into the wine business. In time Anton bought and ran a little winepub in Büdesheim, aptly, though dully, named the "Tavern of the Grape" — Wirtschaft zur Traube. It was here that he made a living with his wife, Maria Anna, whom he had married in 1828 and where his only son, Stephan George II, the father of the poet, was born three years later.

The French influence in Alsace-Lorraine, and in fact throughout the whole Rhineland, left a permanent mark on the people who lived and worked there. Having originally provided to many the means for social and professional advancement, French culture continued to enjoy a kind of vitality and prestige that could be maintained only through widespread popular sympathy. In a youthful letter he wrote to a school friend, George himself openly acknowledged and even defended the debt the region owed to France. "Despite all of the invasions," he explained to his skeptical Prussian classmate, "the Rhine-Hessians not only suffered, but also profited the most, and, say what you will, I will prove to you in minute detail that the French rule (as short as it was) was not an unimportant moment in the formation of our people's spirit." Indeed, the George household itself was in many ways typical of that spirit. French was freely intermixed with German in their private conversations (George later told a friend that "French is my second native language"); one of the uncles had studiously translated a verse drama by the seventeenth-century writer Fénelon, *Les Aventures de Télémaque;* a statuette of Napoleon graced the grandparents' mantelpiece in Büdesheim; and until well after his twentieth year George was known to his family and friends not as "Stefan," but, like his great uncle, as "Etienne," and he pronounced his last name in the French manner as well, softening the hard German *g*s to the gentler Gallic sibilants. Even in later life, when he had become famous far beyond the confines of Bingen, local residents, rather puzzled by all the commotion but nevertheless proud of their brilliant native son, still referred to him familiarly as "Herr Shorsh."

Bingen itself sits nestled against the hilly left bank of the Rhine where the river Nahe empties into its stream, facing sloping vineyards draped across a steep incline that rises up from the opposite eastern shore. Located at a point almost equidistant from Lake Constance and Rotterdam, Bingen is thus situated on the ancient axis that joins, or divides, the major geographic regions of Europe, sitting squarely on the crossroads between Latin and Germanic culture. But even though Bingen has been continuously inhabited since the beginning of recorded history, the town can boast of no more than a moderately distinguished past. Not long after the birth of Christ, Drusus, Augustus's most trusted general and the second son of Nero, built a bridge over the Nahe to enable access through Bingen (founded as Bingium) to two main Roman roads. One led west up over the Hunsrück ridge to Augusta Treverorum (now Trier), and the other traced the lower left shore of the Rhine northward to Colonia Agrippinensis (Cologne). To defend Bingium, the Romans had built a fortress on a hill overlooking the river, and in his day George liked to take friends on walks up to the terrace of the medieval castle, Burg Klopp, which rests on the ancient foundations, to enjoy its commanding view of the river valley below.

During the intervening centuries, Bingen was burned and rebuilt numerous times, repeatedly beset by Germanic tribes attacking the Roman invaders, by Carolingian princes seeking to expand or regain their sphere of influence, by the Swedes during the Thirty Years' War, and by the French on any number of occasions, most recently by the troops of Louis XIV. Four years after the last Hohenstaufen Emperor, Frederick the Second, had died in 1250, Bingen had received the title of Free Imperial City and joined the medieval trade organization of the Hanseatic League. By the time the George family took up residence there in 1873, Bingen still mainly reflected the middle-class values of the burghers who quietly went about making their living through wine-making, shipping, and mercantile exchange.

While never expressing any great fondness for the town or its inhabitants, which the poet once dismissively described as being "entirely unliterary," Stefan George nevertheless regularly returned to the parental house in Bingen, where his rooms were always kept ready for him. But the town made no particular claim to cultural aspirations: the prolific German abbess and visionary mystic Saint Hildegard, who lived from 1098 to 1179, was a notable but distant exception. Six hundred and fifty years later, Goethe had found enough interest in the feast of Saint Rochus, in whose name a chapel had been built commemorating the town's salvation from the plague in the fourteenth century, to include in his collected writings a lengthy and engaging account of the annual event. Otherwise there was little in Bingen to stimulate the imagination of a precocious and lonely boy. Most citizens of Bingen — stolid, thrifty, focused on the practical affairs of life — would have viewed art, and especially poetry, with an uneasy suspicion, and would have mainly ignored it altogether. To convey his impression of the provincial mulishness that George thought was native to Bingen's river-faring residents, he once told the story of someone riding a bicycle through a muddy street and taking a spill on the slippery cobblestones. A man who witnessed the incident stood leaning complacently in his doorway, making no move to lend a hand. Instead, he offered the helpful observation, "You would have done better to stay on board!"

Still, George always looked back on the years he spent in Bingen as "the time of concentration and the completion of works." Perhaps bespeaking a more conflicted attitude than he wanted to admit, George even went so far as to call Bingen and its environs "the most expressive region in Germany." It was, after all, the site of his earliest memories and experiences, even if they were not all uniformly happy. As a child, he recollected, he almost drowned in the Nahe when the block of ice he was using as a raft capsized. So that no one would learn of this humiliating and dangerous escapade, he surreptitiously retired to the garden to dry off in the sun. Perhaps mindful of this narrow escape, George thereafter frequently used images of water and of the strange creatures that inhabit the depths to convey ideas of danger, dissolution, and violent death. Even in old age he still said that he had an aversion to "everything fishy, aquatic." Another traumatic episode, also involving the river, actively haunted him into adulthood as well. When the forty-eight-year-old George arrived in the Swiss resort of Klosters during the summer of 1916, he refused to move into the Villa Fliana, which his travel companion had selected for their stay. He later revealed that the house, which stood next to a torrential mountain stream, reminded him of another terrifying event in his childhood, and he told the story of a dreadful flood that had once inundated his home town. Fueled by this ancient yet still frightening memory, his fear was so acute that they had to find other lodgings for him that night in a nearby boarding school for boys.

Not all of George's youthful reminiscences entailed such anxiousness, though. In one of the few autobiographical fragments he chose to make available to the public, he evoked a nostalgic, mythologizing image of Büdesheim, where his grandparents had stayed behind. There he described

> the antiquated village where our ancestors lived and where they lie buried in a row along the ivy-covered wall of the cemetery. A few people whom I had never seen before greet me on the lanes paved with graystone, and on the way to the church I meet an old woman, who recognizes me with ancestral joy and stops to chat. Dimly they rise up before me again: the wooden portal with a rounded arch and carved heads at the foot of the stairs and the old-fashioned furniture that makes one feel at home, like the outdated honest hospitality of the occupants.

There, in the garden behind his grandparents' home, Etienne often played as a child. But these were solitary games. He delighted in concealing himself in the thick foliage of the garden hedges, especially when his hiding place went undiscovered by the search party sent out to look for him. One time, when his parents were absent and he found himself alone in the house, he locked all of the rooms and buried the keys in the garden, thus making himself sole master of the domain.

Probably induced by his mother's distant austerity, and by his father's benign inattention, the young boy soon grew accustomed to a degree of autonomy that bordered on abandonment. With no one else to give him what he needed, he soon learned to take care of himself. In a telling instance, he related how, when he was eight, someone predicted a dire future for him after he had revealed a defiant selfishness. One Christmas day, after the obligatory sweets were handed out, with all of the children receiving three pieces each, they were asked what they would do if they were given ten pieces instead. The first one answered he or she "would give four to my parents and eat the rest." The second dutifully responded that he or she "would give them to my parents for safekeeping." The third coolly said, "I would eat up all ten." This last child was George himself.

On another occasion, when he was about the same age and attending a school for boys and girls in Bingen, he got into some mischief in the town's market square on the way to class one morning and had to flee the scene of the crime. Although it was winter, a thaw had set in, and Etienne slipped and fell down in his haste to escape, covering himself in filth. When he arrived at school, a girl he had befriended came up and asked, "What did you do? What's the matter? You can tell me. I won't tell anyone, not a single child, not one teacher." George continued: "So I told her, and she pulled out her little handkerchief, as I did mine, and with the help of these rags she cleaned me up as best she could, so that when the teacher came in I looked quite presentable. But as soon as the hour was over, she had nothing more pressing to do than to go to the teacher and tell her everything down to the last detail. Then I knew enough." Being well enough acquainted with George to suspect his likely reaction to such a traitorous act, the person listening to this tale guessed that "she was then no doubt duly punished with disdain." "By no means," George answered, "I wouldn't have done her the favor. I acted as before; but now I knew!" It is hard to say what exactly he had learned, but the memory of this juvenile betrayal stayed with him for the rest of his life.

A final recollection, even more prophetic of George's later tendencies, comes from a boyhood acquaintance named Julius Simon. When he and Etienne, as Simon knew him, were both nine years old, they founded their own imaginary kingdom, which they gave the exotic sounding name "Amhara" and for which Etienne even designed special postage stamps. Every day after school, Julius hurried over to Etienne's grandparents' house, where they both presided either in the expansive attic or down by the river among the dense reeds. They had agreed to alternate in the roles of king and prime minister; there were no vassals, and they made no effort to recruit any. After four weeks, when Julius was scheduled to assume the royal dignity and Etienne was supposed to step down to occupy the ministerial seat, Etienne refused: he did not wish to relinquish the throne of Amhara. Since there were no other subjects to call upon, taking a survey of public opinion proved impossible, and no alternative solution presented itself. Little Julius, put off by Etienne's oligarchic obstinacy, drew the necessary consequence and went into voluntary exile. "I had already longed to return to my playmates for some time," the adult Simon recalled, "and I gladly gave up our empire for more amusing games with my other comrades. Stefan almost never joined in our games during the school recess either, that wasn't for him! Even then he was the odd man out." Significantly, this was also the period when Etienne made his first halting forays into verse.

He obsessively evoked this boyhood realm in his later works, and most fully in a poem called "A Child's Kingdom," which he wrote in the early 1890s when he was in his mid-twenties. It is an astonishing production, not just for the humorless lack of irony with which he memorializes — and fictionalizes — his own early past, but also, and perhaps more remarkable, for the degree to which it foreshadows the person he would later become.

> You were already chosen when you sought
> Precious stones amidst the gravel in your
> Father's garden for a throne and a crown
> In whose brilliance your head found fortune's favor.
>
> You created there among the shallows
> In the mysterious thickets your state ·
> In their shadows you heard the song
> Of desire for strange splendor and distant deed.
>
> Comrades whom your glance enflamed for you
> You rewarded with gold and lands ·
> They believed in your plans · in your office
> And that it would be sweet to die for you.
>
> They were nights of your most glorious delights
> When your entire people knelt round you

In a hall full of boughs colors sun
Listening to wonders as they were revealed only to you.

But, aside from schoolwork and boyish games, the rhythm of George's childhood days conformed to the ancient pattern set down by the church and the ecclesiastical calendar. "True Catholicism," he said just after the First World War, when a new wave of religious sentiment was washing over a dazed and defeated Germany, "is something venerable, pure, and right. I myself lived in it until my eighteenth year." Yet even after his loss of faith, the hierarchical forms of the Catholic Church, its rituals, assumptions, and vocabulary, its temporal richness, and its inherent Latinity all continued to exert a deep influence on George's imagination and art. How could it not? Nothing escaped its compass. The natural cycle of the seasons, the major events of the year, indeed all human interaction, took on shape and meaning within the broad embrace of the church. In the weeks following the birth of the Lord, around the time of Candlemas, one began to hear about the lengthening of the days and the hope for winter's end. Shrovetide brought the colorful and strange costumes of Carnival, where men dressed as women and human beings were mysteriously transformed into bizarre animals. At mid-Lent, on Laetare Sunday, the vintners went out again to inspect their vines, and as the sap rose in the tree trunks, the children sat among the willow thickets and whittled pipes and flutes from the loosened bark. During Good Friday, the faithful lay stretched out in the chancel and kissed the holy cross as it was placed before them. After Low Sunday, toward the end of April, the regular trips out into the meadows and mountains resumed once again. On Corpus Christi, the Holiest of Holies was led in a great procession through the decorated streets smelling of incense, and the high bright voices of the children intermingled with the bass notes of the elders singing the Te Deum. The beginning of summer came at Whitsuntide, with extended excursions into the forest and long evening meals among the pines, enlivened by the heavy earthen jugs of wine left to cool in shaded streams. In mid-August, the whole town accompanied a sculpture of Bingen's patron, Saint Rochus, leading it out of the church and up to a chapel on the hill standing high above the river. Thus the weeks passed in regular succession, until finally, to the thankful relief of the children, Advent arrived once again.

Circumscribed by these familiar rituals, George's childhood thus unfolded within a framework validated by tradition and bound by obeisant ceremony. Yet his talents, or merely his unusualness, which his companions perceived or perhaps only dimly felt, cannot have escaped his parents either. Even as a youth, he made it clear that he had no intention of becoming Stefan George III, Wine Commissioner at Bingen. Fortunately for the boy, late-nineteenth-century German families, particularly those with social pretensions, viewed academic or intellectual achievement with a level of respect that rivaled and often surpassed regard for fiscal prowess. The educated bourgeoisie, or *Bildungsbürgertum,* invested heavily in the trappings of culture, making a piano and a large library of leather-bound books the requisite tokens of reputability and upward mobility. Although the Georges did not belong to this largely urban elite, they must have envisioned such a prospect, possibly even a university career, for their bright, studious, and willful son. Having proved himself at the parochial school in Bingen, Etienne was thus sent off in 1882, at the age of fourteen, to the prestigious Ludwig-Georg-Gymnasium located in Darmstadt, the principal city of the grand duchy of Hesse-Darmstadt.

CHAPTER 2
School

When Etienne George arrived in the residential seat of Grand Duke Ludwig IV, the attractive, well-ordered town still exuded the staid calm that had sat like a benign fog over the numerous provincial capitals that dotted pre-imperial Germany. The newer section of the city had been designed and built under the supervision of the town planner Georg Moller during the long stable years following the Vienna Congress in 1815. The plan rigorously adhered to the Roman scheme, with straight, perpendicular streets overlaid on a rational grid. The tidy houses and solemn palaces, interspersed by well-tended gardens and parks, all lent Darmstadt, with some forty thousand inhabitants, a charming but decidedly sleepy air. Someone who grew up there said that "one could have taken a nap on the carriageway of the Rheinstrasse at any time of the day or night without running the slightest risk of bodily harm."

Henry James, an inveterate and loquacious traveler, briefly visited the town in September of 1873 during one of his European jaunts. More attuned to the moldering enchantments of Italy and France, James made a perceptive but not especially indulgent tourist of Darmstadt. He described how "you walk into the town through the grand, dull, silent street which leads from the railway station" to reach the ducal Schloss, which rose up in the center of town above the tiled roofs of the lower-lying structures surrounding it. "Picturesquely, the palace is all it should be — very huge, very bare, very ugly, with great clean courts, in which round-barrelled Mecklenburg coach-horses must often have stood waiting for their lord and master to rise from table. The gateways are adorned with hideous sculptures of about 1650, representing wigged warriors on corpulent charges, cork-screw pilasters, and scroll-work like the 'flourishes' of a country writing-master — the whole glazed over with brilliant red paint." Turning his attention to the official houses lining the square in front of the Schloss, James was similarly underimpressed. "All around Duke Louis's huge red pedestal rises a series of sober-faced palaces for the transaction of the affairs of this little empire. Before each of them is a striped red-and-white sentry-box, with a soldier in a spiked helmet mounting guard. These public offices all look highly respectable, but they have an air of sepulchral stillness."

There were, however, political reasons for this civic somnolence. The reigning grand duke's father, Ludwig III (1806–1877), had made the ill-advised decision, prodded mainly by his conservative prime minister, Baron Reinhard Dalwigk zu Lichtenfels, to side with Austria in the war against Prussia in 1866. It had seemed at the time a fair gamble. Few could have predicted that the Prussian army, untried in real combat since the Napoleonic wars, could have prevailed against the massive Austrian forces, until then feared as the mightiest in Middle Europe. But the humiliating defeat of the Austrian army at Königgrätz enabled Prussia to assume an unrivaled dominance in German politics and ultimately allowed the Prussian state to dictate the terms of German unification five years later. Having hoped for a broader European conflict to force an advantageous realignment of power, even willing to enlist the aid of France in its struggle against Bismarck's increasingly aggressive pan-German designs, Hesse-Darmstadt found itself isolated and marginalized after the disastrous seven-week conflict.

The political significance of the war and especially of the Austrian — and thus Hessian — defeat was immediately obvious. Johann Droysen, a historian partial to the Prussian cause, made that meaning explicit: "The war of 1866 has made it finally possible for us to launch a truly national German policy. The German nation which has been politically dead since the fall of the Hohenstaufens has now the opportunity of making its national greatness effective." On January 18, 1871, two and a half years after George was born, that opportunity came to fruition. Capping the swift and stunning Prussian victory over France, the second German Reich came into being in the Palace of Versailles when the Prussian king, Wilhelm I, was proclaimed emperor of a united Germany. For the first time since the middle of the thirteenth century, Germany was finally no longer an abstract noun, an informal aggregate composed of scores of independent duchies, principalities, and protectorates, but a political reality standing as a unified nation. Having been, as the Austrian Prince Metternich once memorably quipped, no more than a geographical designation for over six hundred years, the new German empire under Prussian rule lost no time in its bid to catch up with the established European nations.

Throughout the 1870s and 80s, Count Otto von Bismarck, the real architect of the empire, worked single-mindedly to consolidate the gains won in the Franco-Prussian War and set the fledgling empire on a course that soon led to extraordinary growth in both economic and political might. Within forty years, by the beginning of the First World War, the German population grew by an astonishing fifty percent; France by comparison added only ten percent to the number of its inhabitants. And the possibilities latent in such an expanded pool of labor did not go untapped either: during this period most of the country's leading manufacturing firms were formed or consolidated, especially those concerned with the production of steel, machine tools, electrical engineering equipment, and chemicals. In little more than a generation, Germany would manage to transform itself from a loose confederation of largely independent agrarian states into the industrial and military powerhouse of Europe.

Not everyone was overjoyed at the spectacle. The other major European powers, and especially the battered Austria-Hungary and France, all viewed the emergence of the German empire with wary and thoroughly understandable mistrust. But even within Germany there were those who had grounds to be nervous. One of the first official acts carried out after the founding of the Reich was the reannexation of Alsace-Lorraine, parts of which had by then rested in French hands for close to two centuries. Although the majority of the people who lived in these territories were still German-speaking, they felt themselves to be French in almost every other respect. After nearly two hundred years of acculturation, it was only understandable that the political, religious, and cultural affinities of the Rhinelanders ran toward the Republic of France, and not toward the new German Empire, which was widely viewed as merely a cover for Prussia's driving ambitions for political and cultural dominance. Predictably, there were tensions, and many "new" citizens in the re-annexed lands protested against what they considered occupation by a foreign power. Bismarck was unmoved. Referring to the "basically German" nature of the inhabitants of Alsace-Lorraine, he confidently announced that "we shall succeed through German patience and German benevolence in winning our countrymen there — perhaps in less time than is now expected." The threat, veiled though it was by the lofty appeal to nationalist sentiment, was clear enough. Cooperation was preferable, but one way or the other the Iron Chancellor would prevail in making all of Germany German.

To the George family, whose connections to the Lorraine were old and still strong, as well as to many others living on the west bank of the Rhine, Bismarck's determination to promote specifically German interests by quelling all foreign, and particularly French, attachments seemed an intolerable intrusion into their lives. One thing is certain: Stefan George nurtured a passionate and abiding antipathy toward Bismarck and his Reich. "I was an enemy of

Bismarck as of my fifteenth year," George once said, and he never changed his mind. In a conversation as late as 1916, he contemptuously asserted that the absence of any mention of either the statesman or his state in his poems proved that there was "nothing positive" about either one. But it was a feeling that was broadly shared in the south, where up until the unifying fervor of the Great War people saw themselves as Hessians, Alsacians, or Bavarians first, and as "Germans" second. George enjoyed telling the story of a school superintendent in Darmstadt who would gleefully ask his pupils, "Who is the external enemy?" Only too happy to supply the answer himself, he would then shout out, "The French. — The internal one? — The Prussians!"

But Bismarck's concerns about the integration and loyalty of the empire's "Frenchified" subjects paled in comparison to his almost visceral fear and distrust of Catholicism, which he spent the better part of the 1870s trying to eradicate as a political and cultural force in Germany. Although Bismarck made every effort to portray his aims of national unification as reflecting a universal "German" agenda, in reality his vision conformed to specifically Prussian and, in confessional terms, Protestant values. For their part, the predominantly Catholic populations in southern and southwestern Germany harbored deep and justified suspicions about the motives of the politically ascendant Prussians. Essentially conservative in both social and political terms, the Catholics sought to protect their interests by organizing themselves in opposition to the government and portraying their cause as a viable alternative to the liberal, materialistic, and hegemonic north. Both sides saw the other as the aggressor, while viewing their own actions as legitimate measures of self-defense. It was a conflict waiting to happen. Once the empire had been established, it did.

The reasons for the Catholics' initial apprehensions are obvious. A strong, centralized Protestant state would, they feared, constitute a potentially overpowering threat to a numerically much smaller minority. The decision of Hesse-Darmstadt to cast its lot with Austria in 1866 had arisen in part at least from the desire to shield its Catholic constituency from predictable and unwanted Prussian interference. Seeing Catholic opposition as a potential obstacle to his goals, and possessing an unforgiving political memory, Bismarck resolutely responded to the challenge. As early as 1868, he had written to Count Harry Arnim, the Prussian envoy to Rome, that "given the way things have worked out in southern Germany, we cannot deny that those people are right who see the Catholic Church as it exists there as a danger to Prussia and northern Germany and warn strongly against anything that might foster or promote that church or in any way increase its influence." It was only a short step from this defiant posture toward the Catholic Church to the adoption of active, interventionist policies designed to diminish its real and perceived influence.

The decisive event in the deterioration of relations between Catholics and Prussia was the first Vatican Council of 1870. Fearing a creeping evisceration of faith in religious doctrine, Pope Pious IX convened his bishops in Rome early that year and officially declared papal infallibility as dogma. To many Protestants and even some liberal Catholics throughout Europe, it seemed that the church was attempting to return to the Middle Ages, and specifically that it was trying to assume a position of supreme authority not just in ecclesiastical, but in political matters as well. If — so went the argument — the Pope were infallible and issued injunctions that conflicted with national duties, the loyalty of Catholic subjects to their secular state might be fatally compromised. The subsequent formation of the so-called Center Party in Germany, representing primarily Catholic concerns, heightened the sense that the church was adopting an active and intrusive role in the political affairs of the state. Immediately after the Reich was formed, Bismarck and his deputies thus sought to frame the issue in the most dramatic way possible. They argued that the struggle with the Catholics did not just concern the separation of powers in the empire, but potentially compromised its very integrity. Franz Schenk von Stauffenberg declared before the Reichstag in April 1871 that "the conflict between church and state has now passed from theory into reality." Driving the point home more forcefully, Robert Römer stated that the question went to the heart of one's ultimate loyalty. "The issue today is: Rome or Germany."

The *Kulturkampf,* as the conflict between Bismarck and the Catholics during the 1870s and 80s is generally known, was thus more than simply a "cultural struggle." It entered deeply into the fabric of ordinary experience, affecting the daily lives of everyone in the southern Catholic states. All institutions that might have been subject to "ultramontane" manipulation were placed under secular direction. Previously, the administration of secondary schools had been largely under the jurisdiction of religious authorities. Bismarck passed laws wresting control over education out of the hands of the church and had it passed to state supervision. Secular authority was likewise assumed over other aspects of everyday life, such as in the introduction of compulsory civil marriages that had to complement church ceremonies. Priests were also legally forbidden from speaking out on public or political issues. The antagonism deepened with the adoption of the so-called May laws in 1873. These stipulated, insultingly, that all priests must be "Germans," by which was meant that they must have graduated from a German Gymnasium, studied for at least three years at a German university, and have absolved a sequence of courses in German history, German philosophy, and German literature. Of course, the insinuation was that Catholics were not really German at all but rather covert agents of the Pope.

Although the effectiveness, indeed the necessity, of Bismarck's campaign is debatable — his punitive measures even alienated many Protestants, who realized that their own religious freedom now depended solely on the capricious good will of a single, all-powerful state — his actions nevertheless reinforced a deep rift in German society that was felt for many decades thereafter. Even though most of the laws were repealed by the end of the 1880s, the suspicion that Catholics were somehow foreign, or at least not wholly German, lingered on. The *Kulturkampf* had a decisive effect on the life of Stefan George, whose attitudes toward art, culture, and the German nation itself first took shape within a poisonous atmosphere of deep religious conflict and acrimony.

No doubt justifiably concerned about their son's spiritual welfare at school in Darmstadt, George's parents deposited their boy at the home of a Catholic primary school teacher named Philip Raab. He and his wife ran a boarding house on Riedeselstrasse, a broad boulevard bounded on one side by a large public park and at the end of which rose up St. Ludwig's, the town's principal Catholic church. But the Raab household provided a generously ecumenical environment. Three other boys were also boarded there: another Catholic, a Protestant, and a Jew. George's catechism teacher in the Gymnasium assumed the semi-official responsibility of monitoring his church attendance and ensuring that his charge observed his other religious devotions.

In old age, George still spoke kindly of Raab, saying that he had shielded him from otherwise unspecified "complaints" emanating from the school or from home. Raab also appears to have recognized, if darkly, that the boy from Bingen fell out of the normal range. "One day," Raab predicted, "he will become someone very great or nothing at all!" At the Gymnasium, his fellow pupils noticed more tangible qualities. An early acquaintance remembered him as "a lean, lanky chap, with conspicuously thick dark-blond hair above a high forehead, an unusually strong, prominent jaw, but distinguished above all by a pair of brightly glistening blue eyes that had a cunning stare. He was a wild, pugnacious lad, who often engaged in scuffles on the school yard, preferably against an entire horde of opponents." This combativeness, whatever the immediate catalyst, soon found other, less physical channels of expression. Still, he also enjoyed the more benign fruits of youthful liberty. Released from parental surveillance, the teenage George is also said to have initially displayed an exuberant temperament, joining in long sessions of the popular card game, "Skat," engaging in late night bouts of beer drinking and in general adhering to the regimen expected of young and energetic scholars.

But he did not neglect his schoolwork. The Ludwig-Georg-Gymnasium, like most such institutions, preserved the traditional classical curriculum. Unlike the other two branches of the German secondary school system, the Realgymnasium and the Oberrealschule, the Gymnasium was intended solely to prepare students to attend university. Unconcerned about, even hostile toward, practical training, the teachers thus saw their primary mission in funneling the ancient Greek and Roman authors into the minds of their pupils. In Bingen, George had already begun to learn Latin at the Realschule in 1879, and two years later he seems to have taken up the study of Greek as well. Owing at least in part to this early preparation, he excelled. Throughout his Gymnasium career he remained a model student, regularly receiving Ones and Twos in languages, history, German composition, and even in mathematics. A grade card he preserved from the summer of 1883 testifies to "especially competent performance." As a result, when he returned from summer recess, he was allowed to transfer into the top form.

On the first day of the new school term in 1884, the "newcomers" were subjected to critical scrutiny by their peers. "One among them stands out," an older student recalled that day in vivid present tense; "it must be a foreigner, many think, because he just doesn't look like the others. His sharply profiled, bony, sallow, closed face, which already suggests the later 'Dante type,' under a dark, unkempt mane created a sickly impression. The long gaunt fingers of his fleshless hands clenched together, the gray, indefinable eyes, not deigning to look at anyone, fixed on the window — thus he utterly rejected us all." The description reaches for literary effect and is colored perhaps more by an awareness of the person George became than by a sober appreciation of the boy he was. But much rings true. Above all, his "foreignness" and reserved distance — perhaps necessary defense mechanisms for a provincial Catholic in embattled times — strike most forcibly.

In time, reacting to the taunts and cruelties in which children can perversely excel, Etienne did cultivate a protective air of superiority. (Even in old age, we are told, he did not like to be stared at by children because he considered them "unfeeling," and he emphasized that even Plato had noticed their "natural cruelty.") Singled out by his non-German name, by his religious assumptions, and by his notable accomplishments in school, he began to seem even more a stranger to his fellow pupils. His French teacher from Bingen, Dr. Gustav Lenz, a sprightly gentleman who enjoyed a good jest, had also been transferred that year to the Gymnasium in Darmstadt. On his first day at the new school, Lenz turned to George and, in front of the entire class, said good-naturedly, "En avant! I know: you will be my best one in French here, too." It was offered as a well-meaning compliment, but one can imagine how the other boys — already finely attuned to the differences setting him apart from the rest of them — responded.

Having grown up accustomed to hearing and speaking French at home, he naturally handled the language with ease. But he soon developed a proficiency in foreign languages that went far beyond this effortless fluency in a familiar idiom. Even in Bingen the thirteen-year-old had begun to teach himself Italian, laboriously copying out and translating sonnets by Petrarch, and in Darmstadt he continued his study of the language by reading, among others, the Renaissance poet Torquato Tasso. He also learned English, plowing through Daniel Defoe's *Robinson Crusoe* in the original, as well as all of Walter Scott. "There was a set of his books standing around," he later casually remarked, "one simply read through them." At the same time, of course, he expanded his acquaintance with German authors. He was chiefly captivated by the elevated pathos of Schiller's plays and by Heine's elegant and melodious rhymes. The florid, rather recherché wit of the novelist, Jean Paul, whom George would do much to rehabilitate from obscurity later on, did not yet strike a chord with the boy. "I had no understanding of humor," he said of himself at this age. "That came only at thirty." Soon he added the masters of modern Russian prose, Gogol and Turgenev, to his reading list.

Most remarkably, however, Etienne set about inventing his own language. He had already begun to experiment with language as a young boy, and he had even created something like an official idiom for his childhood empire, "Amhara." He had not made much progress in these first attempts, but it signaled an early tendency that continued to preoccupy him for several years. Once he was in Darmstadt, he elaborated on the linguistic rudiments set down in Bingen and fit them out with a more complex grammar and vocabulary. Much later, in the cycle of poems collected in *The Year of the Soul,* he also memorialized this innovation in words of pronounced self-stylization:

> The seer's word is common to few:
> Even when the first bold wishes came
> Grave and lonely in rare and strange dominion
> He invented new names for things —

Such linguistic experimentation, while suggestive of deeper needs peculiar to Etienne, was not in itself uncommon. Although based heavily on ancient Greek, his newest creation, which he called "Imri," was in fact in many ways a product of the time. During the late nineteenth century, a succession of idealistic visionaries, earnest internationalists, and harmless cranks, emboldened by the advances taking place in virtually every arena of science and technology, generated a profusion of artificial languages intended to foster communication, so they dreamed, among the greater brotherhood of man. The most famous of these linguistic Frankensteins, the aptly named Esperanto ("hopeful"), came into being in 1887 as the brainchild of a Polish ophthalmologist, Dr. Ludwik Lejzer Zamenhof. A few years before, in 1880, Johann Martin Schleyer, a German cleric, had given the world Volapük, which like its better known successor was also largely dependent on the structure and vocabulary of Romance languages. But progress even here did not go unchecked. In

1907, a French logician named Louis de Beaufront offered an improvement of Esperanto called Ido (from the suffix in Esperanto meaning, appropriately, "derived from") to the Delegation for the Adoption of an International Auxiliary Language. For Etienne, however, the motivation in bringing Imri to life was not to enable greater understanding among the mass of humanity, but just the opposite. It sprang from the urge to make language itself, the mutual, indeed defining possession of humanity, bend under his private rule. Not satisfied with a vulgar instrument that could be learned, and thus violated, by the uncomprehending mob, the boy had fashioned a secret medium to be revealed only to those of his choosing.

Wrapping himself in a veil of self-imposed exclusivity, trying even to create a linguistic realm he could call exclusively his own, the adolescent George increasingly shunned the society of the other boys. Most responded, sensibly enough, by avoiding him as well. One of his few confederates at the time recalls that during recess between classes he often stood leaned against the wall of the schoolyard, arms folded, "always with a sharp, arrogant smile on his thin, harsh lips." In retrospect, George himself admitted that he frequently sneered disdainfully at his fellow pupils, more than once provoking the taunt that he was a "conceited fool." Even those benevolently disposed toward him were struck by his precocious claim to exceptional rank. One of the other boys living at the Raab household, Wendelin Seebacher, reminisced after George's death that the poet-to-be had once said to him that "the welfare of millions of people will one day depend on me." Seebacher added that he and Etienne "usually worked on our Latin homework together." "Once, when we were preparing the ode by Horace in which he sings 'exegi monumentum aere perennius' (I have erected a monument more permanent than granite), he said prophetically: 'I will do that too.'"

Again, to what extent Etienne's attitude really sprang from an arrogant self-confidence, or the fear of rejection, or simply from the desire for some sort of revenge for the slights he had to endure — and to what degree these feelings can ever be separated — remains uncertain. Tellingly, the few companions he did solicit in Darmstadt were for one reason or another outsiders like himself. Most were Catholics who no doubt also felt defensive and alienated by the lingering effects of Bismarck's *Kulturkampf*. He thus sought out the other Catholic boarder at the Raab house, Johannes Gärtner, who would go on to become a parson, and two boys at the Gymnasium from the Hessian town of Friedberg, Arthur Stahl and Hermann Weigel; symptomatically, the only Darmstadt locals who were close to him, Philipp Wahl, Georg Fuchs, and Carl Rouge, did not sit in the same classes with him. Whenever they met outside of school it occurred in Etienne's own room — and only there: he never visited them where they lived — and he fastidiously insisted they be punctual. (To the end of his life, George took particular delight in the saying, "Punctuality is the courtesy of kings.")

But those few he did admit into his private preserve witnessed a genuine if peculiar intensity behind the haughty exterior. Georg Fuchs, who would later encounter George again several times in Munich and Berlin, retained a vivid memory of the circumstances under which he entered into that privileged association. Fuchs recalled how class had ended early one day because a teacher had fallen ill. He and the sixteen-year-old Etienne extended their usual walk home, venturing into the outskirts of town, lost in animated conversation about religion. Suddenly, before the open door of a bowling alley next to a beer-garden, Etienne stopped short and said, "So let's assume that this is the sanctum we were talking about. If you can seriously believe that, if you are blessed with so much power of faith, then it really is a holy place. Do you have the courage to go in with me and resist the powers I will summon?" Fuchs laughed at first, thinking his friend was merely pulling his leg. But when he saw Etienne's stern face, he fell silent. Not wanting to allow the challenge to his courage go unmet, Fuchs declared with boyish bravado that he was ready for anything. Entering the low dark hall, George began mumbling indistinct words in his secret language while they slowly moved down the sandy strip bordering the wooden lane, all the while making bows and rhythmic genuflections. On reaching the middle of the course, Fuchs had to cover his face with the hood of his cape and blindly follow George until he was told to stop. Once at the head of the room, George set about constructing a makeshift altar out of their schoolbooks and circled around the kneeling Fuchs while continuing his nasal, singsong liturgy. Finally, after George ceremoniously repeated a certain phrase three times, Fuchs felt sand trickling down over him. On removing his hood, it took a few seconds for Fuchs to realize, after some initial bewilderment, that the bowling alley had not actually been transformed into a consecrated temple.

Between the tedium of classroom exercises and the growing sense of estrangement from the pursuits of the other pupils, the teenage Etienne awakened to the stirrings of new needs. In later life, he said he remembered from his Darmstadt days only "the handsome, prematurely deceased son of the seneschal as one who attracted him more deeply." But there were others. Fuchs relates how George, repulsed by the enthusiasms his pubescent colleagues displayed for their dance-school flames, devoted himself to a passionate friendship with the son of a wealthy merchant. The bond seemed incomprehensible to Fuchs, "because it was not a matter of common intellectual interests, since the person in question had no appreciation of what moved us." Nevertheless, "it was he alone, of all people, with whom George spoke and corresponded in the secret language he created and to whom he also addressed verses in this language." Soon, however, the other boy "began to tire of this fanatically strict, mysterious person's desire for total exclusivity, it was also he who, without imagining that it would be viewed so tragically, declared him to be 'meschugge' in front of the others and sacrificed his 'fantasies' to the laughter of his class-mates." It was a painful, degrading experience. But it was not the first, nor would it be the last, rebuff George received to his solicitations of restrictive affection.

As would become typical of the older poet, even now Etienne sought refuge from the uncontrollable forces of reality by creating a realm that responded more pliantly to his own desires. His first extant poem, written just after he arrived at the Gymnasium in 1882, reveals with disarming clarity the painful struggle the fourteen-year-old had already begun to wage with his feelings and hopes. It is in the main, as one would expect, a derivative, immature piece, strongly reminiscent of Heine's romances, and giving no hint of the formal mastery he later achieved. But it resonates with purely Georgean themes. Set in an exotic, mythical Oriental realm he called Golkonda, "Prince Indra" narrates the premature return of a beautiful young shahzada to his father's palace after having received instruction in princely virtues and wisdom from a pious hermit living in a "holy penitential forest." Though unhappy to leave behind his beloved master and his "sweet sojourn" in the woods, Prince Indra yearns for a life of noble deeds and he departs hopeful of future glory. Greeted by the jubilant cheers of the gathered throng gathered to welcome him home, the prince joins a festive procession that winds through the city streets, accompanied by fanfares of trumpets, drums, and flutes. Yet, in the midst of the joyous celebrations marking his arrival, the prince dejectedly wanders alone in the garden one evening, reflecting how to reconcile his teacher's most fervent wish for him — "that God may allow you to find / A friend at the right hour" — with the great numbers of cheerful people that surrounded him. Just then he hears a gentle song, and following the sound of the enchanting, beckoning voice, he sees next to a fountain bathed in moonlight "a water nymph, desirous / And resplendent in all her charms." It turns out to be Aspara, considered the most beautiful girl in the palace, who had "often sought to ensnare him / with fiery glances of love." Vainly battling against his awareness of "impending sin," Prince Indra finally succumbs to her seductive wiles in a moment of passionate abandon.

Following this first section of the poem, ominously titled "The Fall," the prince is tortured by remorse and guilt in the next segment, no less balefully called "The Consequences" — "Die Folgen." Thinking he has betrayed his master's teachings, the prince dismally roams the corridors of the palace full of self-reproach, seeking some form of deliverance from his pangs of conscience; he even considers relinquishing his royal station and returning forever to his mentor in the forest of atonement. His father, the Rajah, notices the change in his son and summons him. Unable to extract from his son what troubles him, the Rajah bleakly concludes that the prince is merely anxious to assume the throne and sees his own father as an obstacle to his ambitions. Prince Indra, realizing that now he has lost even his father, despairs.

Rescue comes unexpectedly in the next part of the poem, "The Savior." Slipping out of the palace disguised in commoner's clothes, the prince comes upon another singer, this time a young boy, "beautiful, even though in simple dress," sitting in front of a hut in the middle of a palm grove, playing a lyre.

> Never, it seemed, had a fairer image
> Appeared before the prince —
> A mighty, ardent longing
>
> Pulled him toward the lad
> Who was so lovely and so glad.

Tentatively, the disguised prince approaches the boy, who bids him to sit and listen to his song. Placing his trust in the winsome youth, the prince pours out a confession and is rewarded by a tender embrace in the arms of his new friend, who tells him he "must find true work / You must combine both body and soul." Heartened by this admonition to seek worthy labor and thus overcome the demons pursuing him, Prince Indra goes back to the palace with the promise they will meet again in ten months' time. There he undertakes an ambitious building campaign, successfully resists the girl Aspara's "vile temptations," and soon regains his inner equilibrium. On the appointed day, he rushes to the grove. Reunited with his friend, Prince Indra never wants to part with him again, saying:

> Come my savior, my advisor
> Let us hasten to my father
>
> He shall gladly embrace you
> His second, dearest son
> Who gave his first one, almost lost,
> A new life and a new birth.
>
> Come and see my works
> See me in my fullest happiness!
> Stay always at my side
> As a friend for all time.

Adumbrated in this relatively brief narrative poem are some of the principal concerns and motifs that return in countless works by George. Although the identification with an aristocratic figure who is a misunderstood and lonely stranger in a strange land is a familiar enough topos in adolescent poetic outpourings, George never abandoned it. Hinted at, almost buried, is an equally familiar conflict with the father — the mother merits no mention — and the painful issue of growing up to assume his place. Too, the injunction to sublimate unruly desires in productive work — another Freudian motif that George would never articulate in those terms — surfaces on several occasions in subsequent poems. Most important, though, is the identification of female sexual enticements, and of heterosexual liaisons more generally, with something vile and debased that is to be resisted and subdued at all costs. This theme occurs repeatedly, almost obsessively, in the poems he writes for the next ten years; then it disappears altogether, as if the issue had been finally resolved. Similarly, the search for a friend, and specifically for a male friend and comrade, the longing for a companion and confidant, someone who is handsome, devoted, and loyal, continues to recur again and again — until George discovered that, instead of equals "at my side," he actually preferred subordinates.

Despite the relative lethargy of Darmstadt, the town was not entirely devoid of amusements. The principal attraction came in the form of the old Hoftheater. In his fairly peevish report of the town, Henry James did not overlook "the theatre, which stands close beside the Schloss, with its face upon the square and its back among the lawns and bowers." Not unusual for such regional stages, the theater, James explained, "is quite an affair of state, and the manager second only in importance to the prime minister or the commander-in-chief. Or rather the Grand-Duke is manager himself, and the leading actress, as a matter of course, his morganatic wife. The present Grand-Duke of Hesse-Darmstadt, I believe, is a zealous patron of the drama, and maintains a troupe of comedians, who doubtless do much to temper the dulness of his capital." The Hoftheater, though an extension of the court, liberally opened its doors to all, and since the price of a ticket was a reasonable forty pfennigs during the week (and fifty on Sundays), even schoolboys could afford to go as often as they wished.

And go they did. Etienne rarely missed any of the performances at the "Olympus," as the ducal theater was rather grandly but affectionately known. Competent productions of plays by the standard German classical writers, primarily Lessing, Goethe, and Schiller, were interspersed with works by Shakespeare and even the occasional Wagnerian opera. But when the generally staid Hoftheater ventured beyond its safely conservative repertoire and presented *The Pillars of Society* by Henrik Ibsen, it caused a minor sensation. During the 1870s the Norwegian dramatist had aroused increasing attention on the Continent with his disarmingly frank probings beneath the shroud of privacy that was politely — or, as Ibsen would have had it, disingenuously — thrown over domestic affairs. The controversy generated by *A Doll's House* in 1879, which struck an early and powerful blow for the modern feminist movement, was quickly superseded by the scandal and outrage surrounding *Ghosts* two years later, in which Ibsen dared to explore the ravages of syphilis on the life of a young man. One anonymous critic for the London *Daily Telegraph* regarded it "a wretched, deplorable, loathsome history," and another called it "revoltingly suggestive and blasphemous." More witty observers dryly commented on the wave of "Ibsenity" washing over Europe.

Etienne was enthralled. For most bright young people in the 1880s, Ibsen represented a refreshing blast of honesty that challenged bourgeois hypocrisy and self-satisfied, middle-class smugness. Although the name of Nietzsche was just beginning to make the rounds in fashionable salons in the capital cities of Europe, he had not yet reached the provinces, and Ibsen was the next best thing. A short time after seeing *The Pillars of Society*, Etienne had already mastered Norwegian well enough to render selections from Ibsen's earlier works into German, such as *Catiline* (1850) and *The Vikings at Helgeland* (1858), with the aid of existing translations. Characteristically, he preferred these older tragedies, with their emphasis on heroic hubris — *Catiline*, for example, is based on the life of the eponymous Roman aristocrat turned demagogue who attempted to overthrow the senate in a violent coup — while he eschewed the modern social dramas. In his zeal, Etienne tried to persuade his small circle of friends to learn Norwegian as well and encouraged them to read precisely those plays which enjoyed little favor with the public. Soon they had eagerly consumed them all, if not in the original, then at least in the available German translations: *Lady Inger of Østråt, Love's Comedy, The Pretenders, Brand, Peer Gynt,* and *The Emperor and the Galilean.*

In the meantime, Etienne continued to test his hand at his own poetic endeavors. Later collected in a volume published at the turn of the century called *The Primer* (*Die Fibel*), the short verses written between 1886 and 1887 also reveal none of the unsettling originality that mark his poetry at the height of his powers. Most in fact hark back to the subjects already sounded in "Prince Indra": they evoke the youthful desire for bold and meaningful action, yet the simultaneous fear of creative impotence; reminiscences of a childhood spent in bucolic and lonely reveries; melancholy meditations on early death and immortality; and, most especially, a longing for the love of a friend, coupled with the equally urgent need to withstand and forget female allurements, which usually appear in the threatening and mysterious guise of beckoning naiads, sirens, and nymphs. Whether there was a biographical source for these latter fears is unknown. If George had a relationship with a girl during these years, all record of it, apart from the poems, has entirely disappeared. What remains is merely a distillate, but the story it tells is clear enough.

When his school friends gathered in his room during their regular conventicles, Etienne often recited these first hesitant rhymes to his guests, while they drank the hot chocolate that had been carefully prepared by the host. Many of the other boys also composed their own verses, but not all of them did. Carl Rouge mentioned that some of the regulars lacked any poetic inclination whatsoever, and that several never wrote a single line; they owed their inclusion instead to other qualities. "George probably believed," Rouge suggested, "that there had to be not just poets, but also readers and listeners." But it is important not to exaggerate the significance of these early experiments. The young George was still searching, trying to find an appropriate form to harness and express his energies. "At that time, he by no means believed that he was called upon to be a poet," Georg Fuchs reminds us. "He felt himself instead destined to be an ordained priest." In time, the role of the poet and the priest merged in George's person as he more or less explicitly sought to combine the sacred function of the one with the creative authority of the other.

Nevertheless, it was poetry, and Etienne's forceful personality, that provided the principal cement holding the band of boys together. To be sure, there were other "literary" groups in Darmstadt, such as the one collected around the now forgotten writer Wilhelm Walloth (1854–1932). In 1885, Walloth published *Oktavia: Historical Novel from the Time of Emperor Nero,* a work that soon became notorious for its enthusiastic depictions of the love of two boys for each other. In 1889 the Imperial Supreme Court in Leipzig ordered the confiscation of Walloth's works, and the following year, in the so-called Realist Trial, Walloth, along with another author and a publisher, were all convicted of disseminating indecent literature. Walloth may well have been the unnamed "older man" whom George later recalled as having approached him indirectly through an intermediary in 1887: "He asked someone," George said of the episode, "to invite me to give him poems for publication." Perhaps instinctively obeying an inner voice cautioning prudence, Etienne declined the offer, just as he would stay away from all other literary clubs not of his own making. But the episode may have also inspired him to take the next logical and momentous step. On June 20 of the same year, he along with four or five of his friends assembled their choicest works and issued them in a literary review, which they painstakingly reproduced using a hectograph, and gave it a name redolent with adolescent preoccupations: *Roses and Thistles: An Illustrated Journal.*

All of the contributors used synonyms: Etienne George signed himself as Edmund Delorme, a name he would use again in a subsequent publication; Georg Böttcher wrote verses in French under the name G. Tonnelier; Arthur

Stahl, in honor of a promenade in his hometown of Friedberg known as the "Rumania," assumed the pen name Rumanophile, while Rouge debuted as Crispus in recognition of his curly head of hair. Hermann Weigel, whose usual nickname was Fips, decided for inexplicable reasons to adopt the literary persona of Mo. And although the nicknames themselves announced the satirical intentions of the authors, there was a serious substratum underlying the project, which the editors announced in their introduction:

> To our readers:
>
> The review, which today comes into existence, expresses its goal in its title. Strictly eliminating articles of religious or political content, it will seek to instruct and entertain its readers through novels, short stories, essays (of varying content), and epic, lyric, and dramatic poems. In order also to accommodate the taste for wit and humor, we will publish anecdotes and illustrated jokes in a separate section.
>
> Since our publication grew from the need to provide a stimulating and refreshing occupation in exchange for the often tiresome and deadening activity of school, this mood will sometimes be expressed here. Should a local coloration be occasionally apparent, we ask that you make allowance for the place of residence and the education of the authors, especially since we will always strive to offer our readers the best.
>
> The Editors

Thanks to their enthusiasm for Ibsen, drama seemed to enjoy the greatest prestige, and most of the contributors were working on plays of their own to include in the review. Rouge, probably the most gifted and ambitious of the group, wrote a Roman tragedy called *Sartorius,* on a subject drawn from Plutarch, and he had drafted extensive plans and sketches for a work entitled *Eudoxia.* Etienne also tried his hand on the genre and fragments survive of a play called *Manuel,* and of two other dramatic works titled *Phraortes* and *Bothwell.* Uncertain for some time whether his own path would lead toward the theater, Etienne continued to work on these sketches for several years until he finally rejected drama altogether. Although the title page confidently announced that "an issue will appear every other Monday," another number never materialized. Whether for financial reasons, differences of opinion, or simple inertia, *Roses and Thistles* thus had a brief run. Short-lived though it may have been, it contained the seeds of future projects.

Gradually the time approached for Etienne to take his final exams at the Ludwig-Georg-Gymnasium and return home to an uncertain future. The topic assigned for his matriculation essay in German fortunately dealt with his favorite subject — drama — but it was formulated with such mind-numbing dreariness that he responded in equally unimaginative prose. Asked to trace "the dramatic development of Schiller's *The Bride of Messina,*" he trotted out all of the empty fillers beloved by countless generations of beleaguered students. After dutifully rehearsing the plot of the play, Etienne concluded by assuring his examiners that "the beautiful poetic language and the masterful development and joining together of the individual scenes make the *The Bride of Messina* a work of art of the first order." Well versed in the pedantic expectations of his schoolmasters, he did not neglect to qualify his praise, however, by pointing out that "the introduction of choruses into the drama is to be seen as a regression and this antique conception of the tragic is no longer condoned in our time." For this diligent but dull performance, Etienne was rewarded with the equally undistinguished but acceptable mark, "quite good" — likewise for history and geography. French and Religion remained his strongest suits, earning him the higher "good." The other disciplines were deemed only "satisfactory." All in all, a lackluster performance, but a passable one. The main thing was that he was free.

Before Etienne left Darmstadt for good, he called his friends together in his chamber for a final ceremonial act. The room he had occupied for the past six years at the Raabs' boarding house was scheduled to be completely refurbished after his departure. Since the old wallpaper was thus to be consigned to oblivion, the boys decided to send it off in dignity. In high spirits, they all congregated at the Raabs, with each one taking up a brush and a pot of paint, and soon the chamber radiated with garish designs. The middle of one wall featured a huge, fanciful escutcheon, depicting the sun, the moon, and various obscure symbols. Surrounding this central emblem were various rhyming mottoes in several ancient and modern languages, including the obligatory quotation from Ibsen, which was drawn from the Norwegian text of *Brand* and more or less read, "I do my duty with conviction, but only in my jurisdiction." Another maxim of their own invention announced, "Here we paint 'al fresco,' and though it's not endearing: There's method to our madness and art is in our smearing." When they had applied the final brushstroke to their masterpiece, Frau Raab came in and good-naturedly shook her head at the "beautified" room of "her" departing Etienne.

CHAPTER 3
First Travels

Back in Bingen just before Easter of 1888, Etienne was relieved but irresolute. He knew what he did not want. Just seeing his father again smiling and scraping before his customers reminded him of that. Yet the greater question still loomed. On his exit certificate from the Gymnasium he had indicated his intention to go to university and study jurisprudence. But his friends more accurately assumed that, with his extraordinary facility in languages, he would devote himself instead to modern philology. His indecision, though not unusual in a nineteen-year-old, was actually the outward sign of an even deeper restiveness. In a conversation with Ernst Robert Curtius several decades later, George placed his youthful ambivalence within a broader context. "Germany was intolerable then," he insisted. "Think of Nietzsche! I would have thrown a bomb if they had forced me to stay here — or I would have been destroyed like Nietzsche. My father was glad to be rid of me since he suspected the danger."

Throwing bombs seemed in fact a viable solution to any number of ills felt by disaffected and angry young men throughout Europe during the late 1880s and 90s. Anarchism, as this incendiary form of political action was known, posed an alarming threat at the turn of the century to social stability in most major European capitals. By 1890, individuals acting either on their own or in concert with like-minded confederates had attempted to assassinate the king of Italy, the German emperor, the king of Spain, and the Russian czar. Nor did the danger abate in subsequent years: on September 10, 1898, Empress Elisabeth of Austria was stabbed to death in Geneva by an Italian anarchist named Luigi Leccheni, and less than two decades later, in Sarajevo, the murder of another member of the Habsburg house helped to light the fuse of world war. But the anarchist revolt represented less an assault on the superstructure of the state than a remorseless attack on the broad, soft middle of society known as the bourgeoisie. And the anarchists did not so much seek to change or improve what they saw as a complacent society infected by corruption, soulless materialism, and oppressive class divisions. Rather, they simply wanted to destroy it.

The movement found an especially strong foothold in France, particularly in Paris, where the centralization of political and social life enabled the anarchists to achieve an unparalleled concentration of organizational effort and activity. In the first four years of the 1890s, at least eleven major explosions occurred in Paris alone. The most notorious, and lethal, of the anarchists was Emile Henry, who was responsible for two murderous attacks. In one he threw a bomb into the crowded Café Terminus, killing one person and injuring twenty more; in another, he planted a bomb that killed five policemen at the station in the Rue des Bons Enfants. During his trial he expressed no remorse for his deeds and the resultant loss of innocent lives. On the contrary, in his statement before the court he defiantly declared, "We wish neither to show mercy nor to stumble, and we shall always march onwards until the revolution, the final aim of our efforts, shall have come at last to crown our work by freeing the world." To erase any doubt about the object of his "efforts," and to demonstrate his willingness to die for his beliefs, he added that "in this war without pity which we have declared on the bourgeoisie, we ask for no pity." In another celebrated case, Auguste Vaillant had detonated a powerful bomb, packed with nails, in the French Parliament; he was publicly guillotined to set a preventive example. Vaillant himself remained unrepentant to the end, and as he was led to his execution, he shouted out, "Death to bourgeois society and long live anarchy!"

The teenage Etienne George had probably not yet completely translated his own feelings of distaste for his father's occupation into an ideological indictment of the greater social structure he represented. But, in time, he too developed a profound hatred of the bourgeoisie and expressed it in terms that explicitly harked back to the political atmosphere of his youth. Just prior to the First World War, in September 1910, when such talk could no longer be dismissed as a merely harmless intellectual exercise, he described to one of his associates his view of the cultural life of Germany in drastic and highly provocative language. "He explained that today he thought, just as he had earlier, that the situation and people generally were abysmally bad. 'If you want to characterize me, then only as the worst kind of anarchist.' " Taken aback by the violence these words implied, his interlocutor recoiled: "But you can't call for dynamite!" George calmly replied: "Preferably, yes. I just don't know how. These people live under the earth." Later still, in 1922, he continued to praise "the first Russian anarchists, Bakunin and Alexander Herzen," saying that "what these men had written was still absolutely valid and true today."

For the moment, though, in the early spring of 1888, the conflicts besetting Etienne were more narrowly focused. And while they may have been potentially explosive, he managed to keep them safely hidden beneath his austere demeanor. Unsuspectingly, Frau Raab had sent her outwardly placid boarder home with a letter to his father saying how much she regretted "having lost such an upright soul." It might have been an intentionally ambiguous comment, but she almost certainly meant it in a harmless sense. In fact, however, had the good woman really known about the state of Etienne's soul, it may very well have given her pause. His raging self-doubt, coupled with the intense, if diffuse, ambition he had begun to articulate while at the Gymnasium, now grew stronger and more insistent in the absence of classroom distractions. But there was another kind of turbulence besieging him, a growing and increasingly distressing realization about the nature and direction of his physical desires and how others would view them if they were revealed. Gradually, what had been only a dim awareness was turning into an undeniable certainty, and it was that fact itself which produced the greatest anxiety. These worries found their way into a poem called "The Pupil," which he wrote soon after leaving Darmstadt. Recounting how previously "my days flowed by in devout exercise / Within gloomy halls," the poetic voice recalls that, while safely ensconced in school, "I received as reward / Far from the sinful, vain striving of humanity / The peace of the pious." That inner quiet was, as such things usually are, a false calm. Suddenly, unexpectedly, everything changes:

> What brings now this transformation? Surely not just
> My roaming in the abandoned alcoves
> Where, next to many a strange device,
> I discover the mirror of glistening metal
> Before which I first learned to consider
> The secret of my own body, and that of others.
> And it would be wicked sacrilege to believe any longer
> That the blond child, the youngest pupil there,
> Who often seeks me out with his large eyes,
> Could so utterly shake my soul.

Brought on by the objectifying recognition of his own body reflected in the mirror, the entrance of his physical being into his consciousness came, as it typically does, at the cost of the placid stability of youthful innocence. But this sexual awakening is even more fraught than usual. Unable or unwilling to believe that the unnamed blond boy could have stirred such violent emo_ in him, and acknowledging the moral censure hanging over such an attach_ ment, he tries to deny what he feels. Puberty marks a crisis at the best of times; when it is complicated by the sense that one's longings may be evil or corrupt, it can be devastating. Tortured by uncertainty about his inclinations, no doubt keenly aware of the disgrace and humiliation — or worse — his feelings might cause him if they were openly expressed, and unsure more generally of the direction his life would take, Etienne felt trapped, confused, and frightened. The only solution seemed to be flight.

Thankfully freed of the obligation to remain in Bingen and assist his father — who, perhaps resignedly, called on his younger son, Fritz, to assume that role — Etienne quickly made preparations for travel. Perhaps not quite an anarchist, he could at least feel he was rejecting bourgeois existence by avoiding it. Still, he stressed there was a pragmatic pretext for his trip. If he were indeed going to realize his aim of studying modern languages, so went the thinking, it made sense to gain a firmer grasp on the spoken medium. French posed no real difficulty, of course, so that could wait. Feeling weakest in colloquial English, he thus decided to go first to London. Writing back to one of his comrades in Darmstadt in mid-March, he asked Carl Rouge to procure a certain language textbook for him, somewhat unreassuringly called *Do You Speak English?* Two weeks later, Rouge reported that he had looked all over town, including Schlapp's and two other stores, and had been unable to find a single copy of the book. No matter: unarmed, but undeterred, Etienne took leave of his family toward the end of April 1888 and embarked on a river boat, making his way down the Rhine through Holland before sailing across the English Channel.

With nearly four million inhabitants, London was then the largest city in the world, the center of a vast and still expanding empire, and the site of revolutionary changes taking place in virtually every realm of human experience. Sprawling, vibrant, mighty, and industrious, the English capital embodied a world power at the crest of its dominion. Of more immediate interest to the German traveler, London was also a dynamic cultural mecca. At one end of the spectrum, and one of decided consequence for George, there was the still irrepressible Oscar Wilde, then at the height of his popularity within London society. Stepping lightly over the foundations laid in the 1850s by the Pre-Raphaelite school — represented chiefly by Dante Gabriel Rossetti, Edward Burne-Jones, and Algernon Charles Swinburne — and closely following the example of Walter Pater, whose book *The Renaissance* he revered, Wilde promoted a view of art that ostentatiously repudiated any value save that of beauty itself. Breaking with a tradition that sent roots into classical antiquity, exercise of democratic muscle to the supercilious observation: "Such a meeting is an exquisite thing."

He stayed at a boarding house run by a family acquaintance in Stoke Newington, one of the newer industrial suburbs north of the city center that had sprung up in the first half of the century. There Etienne found himself in an environment where English was "spoken almost exclusively." English was the common language but not the native one for most of the international clientele. His friends back home were especially eager to hear about the women he encountered, a curiosity he somewhat dutifully satisfied, such as when he mentioned to Stahl that "recently I was also in Hyde Park. My, what ladies on foot, in carriages, on horseback. From now on I won't hear anything bad about English ladies. By the way, I am being introduced to them by the dozen here in the family where I am living." The "dozens" of female acquaintances he made, although confined for the most part to other guests of the household, did include some exotic figures. Again, he told Stahl a little later on, for example,

> that just about all nationalities are represented in our house. We were recently visited by a Dutch woman, a very robust type, and imagine whom I had the honor of being introduced to recently — a — princess, an Indian princess. That is not an uninteresting acquaintance. She is, by the way, black as pitch but otherwise not ugly (her mother was an Englishwoman) and herself speaks the purest English. Now we have a woman from Ireland (her father, incidentally, was an Italian) and I truly have an excellent opportunity here to meet not just English women, but *women* generally.

He relayed similar reflections to Rouge, who excitedly demanded that he "bring back photographs of *all* the ladies you know," roguishly adding in his own rather adventurous English, "That is pleasant to me!" In contrast to Rouge's enthusiasm, though, Etienne's descriptions of the women he met sound notably clinical, detached, and perfunctory.

Most likely because his own English was still relatively rough, Etienne also appears not yet to have discovered contemporary poetry. For that he would have to wait until Paris. He did read novels, and he singled out for particular praise Bulwer Lytton's *Rienzi* and Thackeray, and he seems to have shown some interest in current English literary affairs. Yet, unlike Paris, London was not an especially hospitable place for aspiring but socially ill-placed writers. George Moore, who published his chatty, autobiographical *Confessions of a Young Man* the year Etienne arrived in the English capital, remarked that "it is said that young men of genius come to London with great poems and dramas in their pockets and find every door closed against them." For the German visitor, there were also more specific reasons he might have felt unwelcome. George later mentioned to a friend that during his stay in London he had sensed "that the English were not well disposed toward the Germans, and were especially envious of their economic, industrial and trade successes." Being German was bad enough, but being Catholic was in some ways even worse. Moore himself expressed an unapologetic religious bigotry of a kind that Etienne must have encountered in one form or another. "England is Protestantism, Protestantism is England," Moore confidently proclaimed. "Protestantism is strong, clean, and westernly, Catholicism is eunuch-like, dirty, and Oriental." Not everyone subscribed to such sentiments, obviously. Oscar Wilde himself flirted with the idea of converting to Catholicism all his life. But Moore, and others who thought like him, might have said that was precisely the point.

Mainly, during his time in London, he was preoccupied by the same concerns that had begun to manifest themselves in Darmstadt. Early on in Etienne's stay, Stahl expressed his hope "that you are well and content and that your cosmopolitan, insistent, and raging spirit will be tamed somewhat under a foreign clime." Etienne confirmed that, indeed, "I am becoming more and more cosmopolitan in England." But what he meant by that evidently caused him some concern. "I thus ask you to conceal my letters with any offensive remarks so that some Prussian snoop-nose won't smell a rat through your closet or chest of drawers." Not surprisingly, his central worry continued to be focused on his future vocation, not so much in terms of his profession, but with regard to his writing. He anguished to Stahl "whether I should write drama? If not — I will not write any more poetry in my entire life. — My 'Manuel,' which I see finished before me, and which *prior* to its completion had encouraged me so much, now gives me no encouragement whatsoever." "To be sure," he continued, "it can't be denied now any longer that I have written a drama, which of course tastes and smells entirely like me (I told exactly the same thing to C. Rouge) and which was conceived a year ago and was finally born in England. I gave no one any more precise information and perhaps it will be its fate to die a death of flames without ever being heard by human ears. 'So much for the great plan.' " Sensitive about keeping his inner life well shielded from public view, in addition to wishing to avoid any run-ins with the distrusted Prussians, Etienne again implored Stahl to store his letters in a safe place. "Imagine what a disgrace it would be to me if at some later date someone would recall this letter apart from you!!! Someone who would have read these lines of mine and remember some time later how this creature, who wrote about poetry and drama, who was plagued by poetic delusions, and with clipped wings as — ugh! — I don't want to finish the sentence — — ."

On the whole, however, Etienne proved relatively uncommunicative, at least as far as his faltering attempts at writing went, while demanding that his friends remain forthcoming with their own projects. Symptomatically, even when he did write, he withheld specific details about himself. "I can't enter into descriptions," he told Stahl. "That's too boring to me, and then they usually don't come up to reality anyway." But he imperiously demanded that Stahl and Rouge send him copies of their latest work. Even when he was trying to be congenial, his tone could take on a condescending ring, as if he were an older mentor encouraging hopeful but slightly undisciplined charges. "C. Rouge," he officiously informed Stahl, "is a promising young man, and the whole world will be surprised when they read in his biography: Even at the age of sixteen he completed a tragedy called 'Sartorius.' I don't mean that ironically." Yet Etienne's general reticence, as well as his somewhat patronizing importunity, also drew an occasional reproach from his correspondents. "I don't understand why or how you conceal your productions so much," Stahl replied a little testily in July. "You demand openness from your friends, yet don't give it yourself. And if you then write: 'of course after I have told you everything so freely, I hope that I will also hear of all the poetic works that you are planning and executing,' then that almost sounds like irony, or we both have a completely different notion of openness."

In the meantime, Etienne did seem to be attending to the main purpose of being in London. On June 4, he sent a dutiful letter to his father thanking him for the regular transfers of money and prudently not forgetting to include a report of the strides he was making in learning English. His father responded in the stiff, ungainly style of someone unaccustomed to expressing himself on paper, unable to refrain from using the kinds of economic metaphors that must have made his son shudder: "It is very pleasing to hear that you are making good progress; for that pile of money one must turn the time to good account in order to derive a substantial profit from it." If Etienne had needed further incentive, it was precisely such parental admonitions that cemented his resolve never to stand behind a cash register. That he was thinking along these lines emerges from a "rhymed letter" he sent to Stahl a few months later, in September, in which he confessed that, with the prospect of going home looming before him, his "cosmopolitanism / Which almost borders on anarchism / Is coming under massive pressure."

As October approached, Etienne made ready to leave London. He intended to return briefly to Bingen and then immediately resume his travels, this time to Montreux. While stopping at home, he remained in contact with a few of his London acquaintances. In the middle of October, someone he had met named Tom Wellsted sent him a cheery note, saying, "I suppose you are now invigorating your flagging energies with a deep draught of the 'good Rhinewine' and I wish I could keep you company" And, testifying to his ability to conceal his interior from unwanted inspection, Caroline Mess, his hostess in London, also told him, "We miss you very much; we have never had a more quiet and in every respect more gentlemanly behaved boarder than you." Obviously informed of his itinerary, Mess added that "the next time you return home it will be the French accent they will have to laugh at. That ought to come naturally to you considering your genealogy."

But before departing for Switzerland, he summoned his friends to Bingen for a meeting, or what he called a "congress," where, in addition to the pleasantness of seeing one another again, they would all have the chance to discuss in person various unresolved issues, read aloud from the works they had produced in the interim, and, above all, make concrete plans to revitalize their literary journal. Mention of the "portfolio-plan," as they took to calling it, recurred repeatedly in their letters to one another after Etienne had left again, but it was clear that he was the driving force behind its conception.

At one point Etienne asked Stahl what he thought of the "portfolio-plan" and whether he believed it could be carried out in the way he had proposed it to Rouge. Hoping to find kindred souls in Switzerland, he wrote in December that he "could perhaps engage a few French poets here, too, I will at least give it my best." It was a sign of Etienne's "cosmopolitanism" — but also of the still fairly limited circle of acquaintance and talent on which he might draw — that he even considered inviting the decidedly unpoetic Tom Wellsted to participate. "I will ask my English friend for contributions," he confided to Stahl, "so that our portfolio would be, so to speak, the first 'international' institution of its kind." Nothing came of the "portfolio plan" until several years later, when the first issue of the *Blätter für die Kunst* (*Pages for Art*) appeared in 1892, and in which only one of the friends from Darmstadt, Carl Rouge, was represented among the contributors. But it was here, in the conversations in Bingen during the autumn of 1888, that the idea for such a venture was conceived.

After forwarding his things and packing away various books and papers, Etienne finally left at the end of October for Verneux-Montreux. Ostensibly part of his scheme to secure a surer footing in the spoken forms of modern languages, this itinerancy sprang from a more complex set of motives. "I have to satisfy my drive to wander," he had already told Stahl in August. Once in Montreux, he elaborated the reasons for his travels a little more fully. Chiding Stahl for his decision to become a soldier, he explained in early January 1889 that "in order to learn practical things and to show oneself to be quick-witted and able to cope with various situations in life one doesn't need to go into the military; I simply want to tell you, go *on travels,* as I am going to England, to France and to Switzerland, etc., and I guarantee you that you will then be capable in all of life's circumstances." This still seems a little too utilitarian, a little too pat, even a little too bourgeois. Traveling, in Etienne's mind, still had to serve a positive end, entail a concrete purpose. He even told Stahl that he now felt capable of *"earning a living*. There is a place everywhere for me if I only want to accept it."

In a relatively short time, he felt he had gained confidence and flexibility, a sure-footedness, which he thought gave him more options and even potentially liberated him from parental dependence. "If I want to study in Germany, I can do that," he told Stahl. "If I want to stay abroad I would find the resources to live on my own. That's a very nice feeling, no?" Much later, in the self-stylization of his maturity, George portrayed these youthful journeys as forming part of a deliberate plan. "One has to know the world," he said in 1916, "if one wants to master it."

Having found his winter lodgings at a private hotel run by a Mme de Lespaul, Etienne felt generally more comfortable in a linguistic and cultural atmosphere closer to the one he was used to at home. Writing in French, he said as much to Stahl: "One cannot imagine a greater difference than that between my surroundings here in Switzerland and my surroundings in England. On the one hand the dignity, the most ceremonious tranquility, on the other hand the vivacity and agility that never lull." He gained entrance to a lively circle of theater enthusiasts, and he described putting on a performance of Molière's *The Misanthrope* featuring himself, appropriately enough, in the title role of Alceste. "I wish you could hear me parleying French, in a Louis XIV costume, surrounded by a circle," he continued to Stahl. "Can you imagine anything more rich in contradiction than me, the socialist, communard, atheist, with a German Herr Baron, in the house of a professor of theology, surrounded by a whole row of 'highlife' ladies playing in a comedy?" His account does evoke a curious image, laden with multiple ironies. And while he may have been using the words "socialist, communard, atheist" a little loosely, they convey accurately enough his sense of estrangement from the pursuits of the people he encountered.

Despite Etienne's regular and condescending jibes about Stahl's military life, the loyal soldier continued to send long, cheery missives to his friend. But a note of caution began to appear in Stahl's communications that may have had its origin in the events surrounding the congress that had taken place in the fall — and which Stahl had been the only one to miss. In one long letter from the beginning of January, Stahl attempted to summarize a conversation or perhaps an argument he had recently had with Rouge "and indeed about a subject that we had already previously discussed in Darmstadt." The "subject," and the way in which Stahl laid out the debate, gives an indication of the kind of attachment the young men had formed to one another, and of the slightly troubled undercurrents they were trying to clarify for themselves. In his letter, Stahl fastidiously organized the "subject" of their debate in quasi-syllogistic order, as if to render the highly subjective issue more objective and thus more manageable form:

> I. Love (the tender affection of *two individuals*) is not *necessarily* connected with *desire*.
>
> II. Love between *two individuals of different sexes* also does not necessarily have to be connected with *desire*.
>
> IIa. Proof for I from the love between father and son and *vice versa*, between mother and daughter and *vice versa*, between friends, love of one's country.
>
> IIb. Proof for II from the love between brother and sister, between cousins, uncle and niece, nephew and aunt.
>
> Accordingly, the proof is delivered for I and II, love is not desire but *devotion* and it should not be morally condemned when a man loves the wife of his neighbor (*not desires*). If we just replace "love" with "friendship," which in this case is exactly the same thing, nobody thinks a thing about it.

It is unclear who had initially expressed "love" for whom, or even how the subject had come up, but obviously the word had arisen and had caused some anxiety among the young men. Stahl, perhaps in concert with Rouge, had decided that "love" between two people of the same or different gender did not have to entail a physical or sexual component, but the possibility that it *might* had been sufficient cause to prompt him to define the word more precisely. Yet whether he was fully conscious of it or not, by finally substituting "love" with "friendship," which despite his reassurances do not of course mean exactly the same thing, Stahl was repeating the age-old rejection given to urgent suitors whose feelings we do not wish to hurt. Indirectly, tactfully, but firmly nevertheless, Stahl was telling Etienne he just wanted to be friends.

Still restless, in search of something he himself probably could not yet define or even identify, Etienne left Montreux at the end of February. Adhering to the example set by countless other German writers before him, he traveled farther south into Italy. In a postcard from the middle of March he reassured his father: "Today I left Ponte Tresa and have arrived in Milan. I have found a very good 'Roman' family here where they speak a fine Italian and is otherwise also very respectable." Then he got to the real point of writing: "Since my cash balance has been reduced to almost nothing (I lived amazingly cheaply in Ponte Tr.) I ask you to send reinforcements *immediately*. More in a letter. EG." He stayed in Milan two more weeks, but he felt out of place there, too. A poem about the journey describes a "dark, starless sky" over the "spires of the Cathedral," and abruptly concludes: "I sigh and don't know why / It is not good for me to stay here." At the beginning of April he returned to Montreux and took long, solitary walks along the alpine meadows and lakes. By the end of the month he was in Paris for the first time.

CHAPTER 4
Paris

Before Etienne had entered the French capital in late April of 1889, just shy of his twenty-first birthday, he had never actually met a genuine poet, or indeed any writer of note. His knowledge of modern literature was unusually far-ranging but spotty and confined mostly to drama and prose. Moreover, he was still uncertain about whether he had the ability or even the desire to write at all. He had, it is true, composed a number of verses that revealed a certain talent for translating his experience into linguistic form. But there had been nothing so far in his background or his writing that even hinted that one day he would become the most important and influential German poet of his time — even, some would think, of all time. The paradox is that he awakened to his calling as a poet, and more generally became aware of possibilities he had never known existed before, in Paris.

Or perhaps it was not so paradoxical after all. For centuries, young men — and more recently women — have gone to Paris and returned transformed, bringing home a gospel they first heard proclaimed on the banks of the Seine. Following that familiar pattern, George's life, too, changed utterly as a result of the few months he first spent in Paris. Partly, this response was predictable. Paris provided a far more hospitable environment to someone of his upbringing and tastes than any of the cities he had previously visited. He felt virtually as comfortable speaking French as he did his native tongue, and there had never been any substantive challenge to Catholicism in France. There one was either religious — which by default meant Catholic — or not: no third option had ever really prevailed. And the kinds of questions that had pursued the young man about his sexual yearnings were being explored in Paris with unparalleled and unapologetic exuberance. Most critically for George at this stage, however, it was there during the two decades prior to his arrival that a new understanding of poetry had arisen, one that made extraordinary claims both for and of the poet. Here he learned that poetry was not something that one wrote casually, that its main function was not merely to please or to entertain. From now on, George would understand poetry as a supreme office, as the consummate expression of creative energy, as the highest form of art, and by extension, as the summit of human culture. And the poet, the maker of the absolute, would stand henceforth in his mind at the pinnacle of humanity.

For such a momentous sea change in his life, the Parisian sojourn started out on a rather prosaic plane. After returning from Milan, he had made plans to meet his French teacher from Darmstadt, Dr. Lenz, who knew Paris well from his own student days and seemed eager to share his knowledge with his young protégé. Like everyone else, though, Lenz had also become caught up in the heady excitement of the Universal Exposition that year, timed to coincide with the centennial of the Revolution in July and already drawing tens of thousands of curious visitors to the city. Celebrating a century of accomplishments under the banner of liberty — or, depending on one's perspective, engaging in a pompous display of imperialistic self-congratulation — France sought to give tangible evidence of the power of the human spirit, or at least of French ésprit, and to show the world what it had achieved. Enormous palaces, pavilions, statues, arches, colonnades, and bannered booths proclaimed in fantastic and whimsical designs the fecundity of invention unleashed by freedom and science. The fact that most were only temporary structures built of plaster and papier-mâché was not lost on some of the more skeptical observers. One of Etienne's acquaintances from London, Miss Helen Kain, wrote to ask what he thought of the fanciful centerpiece of the Exposition, a 984-foot-tall steel tower designed by a well-known engineer. "I have seen some pictures of it," Miss Kain dubiously noted, "and don't think it looks strong enough to be of much use."

But Lenz was also careful to discharge his professorial duty toward Etienne by including the chief historical sights of Paris in their perambulations. Armed with his Baedecker guidebook, the indispensable reference to all nineteenth-century travelers, and fueled by his considerable enthusiasm, Lenz accompanied Etienne on extended strolls through the city's streets and boulevards, fastidiously dispensing dates, names, and detailed information about historical events connected to the stations they encountered along the way. Lenz conscientiously took his charge to the column marking the spot where the Bastille tower had stood and been gleefully dismantled exactly one hundred years before, and he drew up an ambitious itinerary that included visits to the Louvre and the city's other principal museums and sights.

Had Lenz prevailed in his intentions, George might have left Paris with a few gaudy souvenirs in his suitcase and a mind filled with dead and useless facts. Probably more by chance than design, however, circumstances took matters out of his zealous chaperone's hands. They had taken lodgings at a small hotel called the Pension des Américains on the rue de l'Abbé de l'Epée, nestled between the rue Saint-Jacques and the Boulevard Saint-Michel in middle of the Latin Quarter. As it happened, this little family-run establishment served as an informal meeting place to a succession of some of the most brilliant figures of the Parisian avant-garde: the hotel was favored by a remarkable concentration of poets, critics, dramatists, and journalists in a city that suffered no shortage of talent in any of the fields they represented. Among the guests, at the time Lenz and his protégé occupied their rooms, was the lively but now forgotten poet Albert Saint-Paul, a "dark, handsome southerner" from Toulouse, seven years George's senior, and who reputedly possessed one of the best and most beautiful voices in Paris at the time for reading poetry aloud. In addition to his frequent contributions for the symbolist periodicals *Ecrits pour l'art, L'Ermitage,* and later the *Mercure,* Saint-Paul was also closely associated with the journal *La Wallonie,* which was edited by two Belgians, Henri de Régnier and Albert Mockel, and which proudly proclaimed itself to be a "revue symboliste." Indeed, following its inception in 1886, *La Wallonie* became the most significant French-language symbolist mouthpiece, until it folded in 1892. Saint-Paul and Mockel, in turn, had close connections to Jean Moréas, who had delivered his famed definitions of symbolism in 1886 in the pages of *Le Figaro.* They were also acquainted with Gustave Kahn, the French-speaking American poets Stuart Merrill and Francis Vielé-Griffin, as well as Villiers de l'Isle-Adam, Edouard Dujardin, and, most importantly, Paul Verlaine and Stéphane Mallarmé.

Saint-Paul had already met "Herr doctor Lenz" during one of his prior journeys to Paris. Saint-Paul plainly enjoyed the company of the amiable and gregarious scholar, describing him as "always smiling and affable, blond and rosy, taking pleasure in gay conversation." Playing on the literal meaning of *Lenz* in German — "spring" — Saint-Paul jested that "his name suited him well." But Saint-Paul was struck by the contrast between Dr. Lenz and his somber companion, who "despite his young age, bent a grave brow under an abundant head of golden-brown hair." "George was anything but communicative, perhaps timid," Saint-Paul observed, "but next to the merry Monsieur Lenz, he slowly thawed out."

At first, the Frenchman knew only that the silent, earnest young man wanted to be a student of philology and was considering enrolling in the university at Strasbourg. He had no idea that Etienne had any interest in poetry. But they both seemed sympathetic to one another, and soon they hatched a little plan. Etienne confessed that he did not relish the prospect of visiting the museums with his loquacious and overly diligent guide, and he asked Saint-Paul to act as intermediary to help deliver him from Lenz's well-meant but rather burdensome attentions. To their mutual surprise, Saint-Paul easily gained permission from the good doctor to accompany George, unescorted, into the wilds of the city. Soon enough, even though the younger German discretely refrained from asking prying questions, Saint-Paul revealed that he wrote for some of the progressive literary journals, and he noticed that his remarks about the new poets and their work piqued George's interest. Seeing a potential comrade-in-arms, Saint-Paul resolved to initiate his new friend into the "French poetic movement."

Just as Paris was the unrivaled cultural center of France, the heart of the new "poetic movement" was located in the city's storied Latin Quarter. With the Sorbonne situated in its midst and an abundance of cheap rooms available for rent, the Latin Quarter provided a generous and forgiving haven to students, impoverished or disaffected artists, eccentrics, prostitutes, and political dreamers. But it also attracted people in search of escape from precisely the sort of materialistic excess which the Universal Exposition loudly flaunted. For the representatives of the new "poetic movement" in particular, the delicate filigree of the Eiffel Tower reminded them of nothing so much as the latticework of an iron cage from which there increasingly appeared no hope of escape.

The Latin Quarter, with its Bohemian largesse, offered not escape, perhaps, but a refuge of sorts. And it seemed then, in the late spring of 1889, that a kind of golden age was breaking. In May, Paul Verlaine, who held melancholy court at the Café François Premier not far from George's hotel on the rue de l'Abbé de l'Epée, published the second edition of his confessional collection of poems, *Sagesse,* which Saint-Paul urged George to read. The famous and beloved Café Vachette hosted Moréas's regular assemblies. Mallarmé occasionally stepped into the Voltaire, also nearby; and in the basement of the Café Soleil d'Or in the neighboring Place Saint-Michel, Léon Deschamps, founder and editor of *La Plume* (which had been inaugurated only a month before, in April) conducted his rambunctious "soirées" every second Saturday night until his death in 1899. During his stay, George went to several of these occasions in the Soleil d'Or, when as many as two hundred people, some dressed in the long capes and broad-brimmed felt hats that were then in fashion, crowded into the smoke-filled basement where they were rewarded by impromptu songs and poetry recitals performed on a tiny, makeshift stage.

Predictably, the desire for intellectual and personal freedom from the constraints of the modern bourgeois world sought out by the habitués of the Latin Quarter was no less strong in their political beliefs. Most of the writers and poets who identified themselves with symbolism also took a sympathetic stance toward anarchism, and many put their names on the subscription list of the most influential and widely read anarchist journal in Paris, *La Révolte,* edited by Jean Grave, an autodidact leather-worker turned revolutionary. Another periodical called *L'En Dehors,* which was run by a man who gave himself the exotic name Zo d'Axa, frequently provided a forum for anarchist treatises and manifestos. *L'En Dehors* counted among its regular contributors some of the most artistically progressive poets of the day, including René Ghil, Emile Verhaeren, Henri de Régnier, and the American Vielé-Griffin. The latter's compatriot, Stuart Merrill, likewise lent financial support to Grave's *La Révolte*. Even Deschamps's *La Plume,* which otherwise published nothing but literary pieces, devoted a special issue to anarchist ideas. Critics quickly picked up on the cozy relationship that had formed between the political revolutionaries and the literary innovators. Hippolyte Fierens-Gevaert, a conservative historian, decried the situation as the symptom of a larger social crisis: "Every philosopher, writer, poet, dramatist, artist is today a latent anarchist," he claimed. "And very often they boast of being one. Anarchy is even fashionable in the salons where it should terrify the most. Avant-garde authors have adopted the theories of Kropotkin and Jean Grave."

This fusion of the instruments of protest offered a seductive and powerful arsenal, and its effect was not lost on the young George. But it was poetry, and not politics, that interested him most at this point. While directing Etienne to the works of the symbolist poets, and especially those of Baudelaire, Saint-Paul had also lost no time introducing his new friend to Albert Mockel, his collaborator and co-editor at *La Wallonie*. Mockel later remembered the German as being "serious without pedantry, and with a rather melancholy expression, tempered by the keen light of his blue eyes — he still maintained in his bearing a hint of hesitancy that later became transformed into an elegant reserve. He fought an unacknowledged timidity through a resolve that was already very determined." Mockel and Saint-Paul decided that he fulfilled the criteria — namely, disinterestedness, a pure fervor, and obedience to the cult of beauty — for being admitted into the presence of Stéphane Mallarmé, the most revered poet in Paris and "Maître" before whom every other poet bowed in devoted veneration, and who was widely considered "a priest of the Word."

Mockel reported that when he and Saint-Paul asked Mallarmé for permission to present the German visitor to one of the celebrated weekly meetings that took place in Mallarmé's apartment in the rue de Rome, the older poet first wanted to know something about him. After mentioning that Etienne was thinking of translating Baudelaire's *Fleurs du mal* into his native language, they assured Mallarmé that "he reminds one of the young Goethe, of Goethe before *Werther*." "Very well," Mallarmé said, smiling, "I will expect him Tuesday evening, your young Goethe. But inform him of the vanity of shooting oneself over Charlotte." With that, their host underscored one of his favorite themes, one that had not just aesthetic, but also veiled political undertones: "The ideal is not to die for an emotion, for an idea," Mallarmé said on another occasion, "but, on the contrary, to live in order to exalt them with beauty."

The *Mardistes*, as the regulars at Mallarmé's Tuesday evening gatherings were known, had included among their number at one time or another virtually every major literary and cultural figure of the day. It was a diverse and cosmopolitan group, mirroring the international character of the symbolist movement itself. Painters such as James Whistler, Paul Gauguin, Odilon Redon, Edouard Manet, Berthe Morisot and Auguste Renoir were as welcome in the rue de Rome as were the English writers Oscar Wilde, Arthur Symons, Lord Alfred Douglas, the Belgian poets Maurice Maeterlinck and Emile Verhaeren, the Americans Merrill and Vielé-Griffin and most of the native representatives of the new symbolist mode. And they all went to Mallarmé's diminutive fourth-floor apartment as pilgrims who traveled to a holy shrine. "No one who has ever climbed those four flights of stairs," Symons wrote, "will have forgotten the narrow, homely interior, elegant with a sort of scrupulous Dutch comfort; the heavy, carved furniture, the tall clock, the portraits, Manet's, Whistler's, on the walls." Making room for his guests by folding up the dining room table and pushing it against a wall, Mallarmé brought in twelve chairs — no more could fit into his cramped quarters — and he ceremoniously placed a Chinese bowl filled with fragrant loose leaf tobacco on a stand next to fine cigarette wrappers, shrouding the gas lamps with Japanese crêpe paper to lend the room a subdued and hieratic air. At nine o'clock, the first *Mardistes* began to appear.

Accounts vary somewhat about the particular details of these sessions, but they all agree in their broad outlines. Symons called Mallarmé "one of the best talkers of our time," and Mockel also delighted in his "veiled and captivating voice, alternately cheerful and grave." Everyone praised Mallarmé's courtesy, his solicitous generosity to younger poets and artists, and above all his absolute, uncompromising devotion to poetry. With a single-mindedness that made a powerful impression on George, Mallarmé banned, more by example than injunction, any subject from the general conversation that did not concern the fundamental or essential questions of art. But it went beyond mere aesthetic temporizing: for Mallarmé, art took on the role and function of a religion. "Here was a house," Symons eulogized, "in which art, literature, was the very atmosphere, a religious atmosphere; and the master of the house, in his just a little solemn simplicity, a priest." In the temple he created out of his unassuming apartment, Mallarmé performed the rites of a sacred ceremony before the devout company of adepts. As Symons put it:

> The attitude of those young men, some of them no longer exactly young, who frequented the Tuesdays, was certainly the attitude of the disciple. Mallarmé never exacted it, he seemed never to notice it; yet it meant to him, all the same, a good deal; as it meant, and in the best sense, a good deal to them. He loved art with a supreme disinterestedness, and it was for the sake of art that he wished to be really a master. For he knew he had something to teach, that he had found out some secrets worth knowing, that he had discovered a point of view which he could to some degree perpetuate in those young men who listened to him.

While the atmosphere of the Tuesday evenings was usually genial and relaxed, there were certain guidelines that had to be observed. Those who dared to contradict the "Master" soon found that the rules of the evening were strictly enforced, if not directly by Mallarmé himself, then all the more vigilantly by his attendants. Camille Mauclair, for example, retained precise and painful memories of his first evening with the poet. Permitting himself at one point to contest, however respectfully, a minor point in one of Mallarmé's pronouncements, Mauclair found that the Master himself remained unruffled by this intervention, but that the others present shot scandalized glances at the impudent guest. At the end of the evening, as everyone gathered on the landing outside before leaving, the censure of his behavior became more manifest: they all underlined their severe disapproval of Mauclair's selfish profanation by treating him with measured coldness. After descending to the second floor, Pierre Louÿs took Mauclair to one side and, attempting simultaneously to scold and console him, he explained the rituals to the inexperienced newcomer: it is better to listen than to speak; it is preferable to be attentive than to argue; and experience had shown that the contribution of the guests is, or ought to be, negligible and that a sustained monologue from the master assured a dazzling and thoroughly enjoyable evening. For his part, Mauclair, who nursed a rather foul humor for some time after this rebuke, later took revenge by objecting that "I always found it slightly ludicrous that they imposed on him this air of a Buddha, of a prophet enveloped by cigarette smoke. . . . They were embalming him while he was still alive." Not coincidentally, it was a criticism that not long afterward others began to make of George and his own followers.

Perhaps aided by better advance preparation, or simply protected by his own natural reticence, George did not make the same mistake as Mauclair.

Mockel recalled that, on the contrary, he was "very silent." "But," Mockel admitted, "we were all more or less silent in that temple consecrated by meditation. That expansive joy of expressing oneself, which young people feel so strongly, disappeared before that of listening to the marvelous Word."

What George heard there must have seemed marvelous indeed. Mallarmé may have radiated kindness and a certain avuncular benevolence toward his loyal admirers, but he displayed remorseless hostility, even contempt, for everything that threatened to desecrate his cherished idols. Art, Mallarmé repeatedly said, has no need to be experienced by the masses, and in fact ought to be well concealed from the importunate gaze of the crowd. In an early essay from 1862, characteristically titled "Artistic Heresies: Art for Everyone" ("*Hérésies Artistiques:* L'Art pour tous"), but which remained representative of his later views, he proclaimed that "every thing that is sacred and which wishes to remain sacred wraps itself in mystery. Religions retreat behind the shelter of mysteries revealed only to an elect. Art has them, too." Mallarmé vehemently rejected the demand being raised by writers representing the Naturalist school — most prominently by the novelist and physician Emile Zola — that art should not just reflect the everyday lives and concerns of average working people, but that it should be made accessible to them as well. Mallarmé wanted, instead, to shield art from what he called "hypocritical curiosity" and to protect it from the self-satisfied "smile and grimace of the ignorant and of the enemy."

The "enemy" for Mallarmé was, of course, as it had also been for Baudelaire, the bourgeoisie. Not that he always resorted to such inflammatory language to describe his stance. Writing to Villiers de L'Isle Adam in 1867, for instance, he indulged in a little heavy-handed levity on the subject, remarking that he was working on a book on "Beauty": "Indeed," he said, "it's called 'The Aesthetics of the Bourgeois,' or 'The Universal Theory of Ugliness.'" The taste of the bourgeoisie, Mallarmé thought, was the direct and inevitable result of their attitude toward the world more generally. The philistine bourgeois, who viewed material success as proof of social worthiness, wanted to validate that success with external signs of prestige. But they believed that culture, like iron or grain, could be purchased and consumed in the same way as any other commodity. In Mallarmé's mind, art was, on the contrary, not an acquisition, but a charge, and he detested the presumption that poetry, or any other form of art, could be treated as an object that could be bought and sold. Again, the political significance of this stance was not just implied: it was overt. Like many other symbolist writers, Mallarmé subscribed to Jean Grave's *La Révolte,* and he too felt generally sympathetic to the anarchists and their struggle against bourgeois values. Detractors also recognized the intimate association linking symbolism with anarchist ideas, and they deplored the consequent rejection of art intelligible to the multitudes. "The art of today in its highest, or at least, its most original expressions," Fierens-Gevaert complained, "is essentially anarchist. It ceases to address the crowd." Mallarmé did not just refuse to address the crowd, but actively wanted to prevent the masses from coming into any contact with art whatsoever.

But Mallarmé was preeminently, and exclusively, a poet, not a political pamphleteer. He expressed his contempt for the bourgeoisie not by throwing bombs, but by denying them access to the realm he regarded as his own. Making a comparison to the printed notes of music, which remain incomprehensible and meaningless to the untutored onlooker, Mallarmé regretted that poetry had no similar means of shutting out the intrusions of unqualified readers. And for Mallarmé, poetry was the supreme art, not merely the one that transcended all others, but the only one that truly mattered. In another letter from 1867, this time to his friend Henri Cazalis, he insisted that "there is nothing but Beauty — and Beauty has only one perfect expression, Poetry. All the rest is a lie — ."

Just as art, which Mallarmé repeatedly defined as "a mystery that is accessible to rare individuals," should withdraw into an esoteric domain so as not to be contaminated or defiled by contact with the unwashed multitudes, the artist too must preserve an absolute purity. This did not mean that an artist must live in total isolation, cut off from all worldly contact; Mallarmé himself was an overworked and underpaid schoolteacher. But he insisted that artists, as distinct from their status as human beings, must be uncompromising in their high-minded devotion to their task. "The man may be a democrat," he conceded, but "the artist splits himself in two and must remain an aristocrat." Calling the modern species of writer, or what he termed the "worker poet" who was interested and actively participates in the affairs of the day, a "grotesque" and "sad" spectacle in the eyes of a purebred poet, Mallarmé exhorted his peers to renounce the vain and debasing urge to engage the world with their works. "Let the masses read works on ethics, but for pity's sake do not give them our poetry to ruin." "O Poets," he exclaimed, "you have always been proud; be more, become disdainful."

With remarkable tenacity, Mallarmé adhered to his unyielding principals, forsaking even the normal avenues for disseminating his own poetry. As he wrote to his friend, Henry Cazalis, "I'll need twenty years during which I'll remain cloistered within myself, renouncing all publicity other than readings to friends." To publish a volume of poetry meant, virtually unavoidably, permitting the incompetent multitudes to penetrate and defile the holy sanctum. As a result, Mallarmé could never bring himself to complete what he called "The Book," which was his great project, the definitive summation of what he knew and represented as a poet. George himself would find his own solution to this particular conundrum. Much later he once commented on Mallarmé's final inability to produce his book by saying, quite ungenerously, that "il est devenu célèbre à force de ne rien faire." To say that Mallarmé became famous by doing nothing was putting it too strongly, and George knew it. Mallarmé was by no means prolific, but he did much more than nothing. Indeed, he had given to George, as he had to his other adherents, no less than the model for the life of a poet. In a more magnanimous moment George admitted as much. Asked whether he had been influenced by the French, he responded, "Yes — by Mallarmé and Verlaine very much so." Pressed to be more specific, he went on to make the telling, if slightly disingenuous, distinction that they "didn't influence him with regard to language, but very much in the most profound sense in the conduct of life." That, finally, was true. Mallarmé did no less than teach George how to conduct his life as a poet.

Although George may have said little himself during the Tuesday evening congregations, he obviously drank in and absorbed everything he saw and heard. Sitting in the cramped and darkened living room, drinking tea and rolling cigarettes, he listened in engrossed silence to the Master talk about poetry as if it were a holy sacrament and he, the Poet, an anointed priest performing rites before faithful acolytes. Of course, for the young Catholic from Bingen, who had himself performed quasi-religious ceremonies with his school mates, and had shown an early taste for hierarchical structures with his friends, the example of Mallarmé only validated and enforced what he had long held to be true in his own experience. But the effect of these sessions on George, as it was on many of those whom Mallarmé called his friends, was still nothing less than intoxicating. Saint-Paul remembered the late-spring evenings spent strolling along the brightly lit boulevards. George, he said,

> was enchanted. Toward midnight, returning from the rue de Rome back to the Luxembourg garden, we walked through Paris in the company of Ferdinand Herold, André Fontainas, Achille Delaroche, and sometimes Vielé-Griffin and Mockel. We chatted about poetry, about techniques of verse. George listened to us with a passionate curiosity. The Saint-Lazare train station, the Opera, the Seine, the Sorbonne were for him the magnificent stages of a dreamlike path which the magic of the night sky prolonged. And sometimes, on the Boulevard Saint-Michel, we encountered Moréas or Retté, both impenitent noctambulists.

Back in the Latin Quarter, on the other side of the Seine, the reigning monarch of the café society was the simultaneously majestic and pitiful figure of Verlaine. Addicted to absinthe and brandy, suffering from a variety of ills stemming from his alcoholism — but also from a severe, if undiagnosed, case of gonorrhea that manifested itself in a painful and euphemistically labeled "rheumatism" — and lacking any steady means of subsistence, Verlaine was instantly recognizable in his tattered, threadbare clothes, with his reddish, unruly beard imperfectly tamed by a thick woolen scarf and a soiled yellow cravat peeking through his coat, as if to remind him of other, better days. But Verlaine could also write verses of both exquisite beauty and alarming immediacy, suffused with an emotional, often sensual directness matched only by a profundity of genuine feeling. An American visitor to Paris, Vance Thompson, noted this contrast between the brutish man, often drunk and perpetually broke, and the brilliant radiance of his poetry: "We were all worshippers of Verlaine," Thompson wrote. "We had read *Sagesse*. We had lent the poet five-franc pieces, had bought him absinthe, had helped him up the hospital steps when his diseases were too many for him. He sat among us there, this old man, with the dirty neckerchief and the ribald and unclean speech. And is it thus that I remember him? No. I remember him best when, with his glowing eyes half-closed, he recited some new sonnet or unforeseen verses — splendid as golden coins. His art was at once subtle, refined, difficult, and inveterately young. His was the subtle simplicity of the Middle Ages."

Verlaine espoused an ardent if naive Catholicism. Someone once said that "Verlaine abandons himself to the Church as a child to a fairy tale" — which he had done apparently when he fervently re-embraced religion while serving the jail sentence that had resulted from his violent affair with Arthur Rimbaud. Whatever its source, the religiosity of Verlaine's poetry, and its specifically Catholic themes of sin, remorse, repentance, and ultimate forgiveness appealed to George. No less, the ill-fated relationship that had prompted Verlaine's revived interest in religion may have been instructive to George about the possibilities — and dangers — of similar liaisons. George had in fact met Verlaine at one of Mallarmé's *mardis* and he sometimes saw the older man wobbling down a street or huddled over a drink in a café. But the taciturn German probably did not make much of an impression on a man increasingly distracted by growing numbers of admirers and cultural curiosity seekers, and on a mind progressively benumbed by Bacchanalian excess.

Thus George passed the first two months of summer in Paris with Saint-Paul reading to him in the morning from the works of the poets he met by night, spending the afternoons strolling through museums or the Tuileries and the Luxembourg gardens, and filling his evenings with the heady conviviality of the cafés. He also made a point of attending a recitation by the adulated Sarah Bernhardt, who, George later attested, "read poems well." But he engaged in other explorations, too. It would have proved irresistible to anyone in Paris in 1889 not to try one's hand at the new poetic forms being heralded there, and George, who had arrived already equipped with a powerful but undirected urge to write, was no exception. Yet the poems he wrote during this time betray a preoccupation not so much with poetry per se as with another, more common experience of visitors to Paris: the tumult and insistent longings of the flesh. In a series of poems later collected under the title *Drawings in Gray* (*Zeichnungen in Grau*), George paints a picture of a young man consumed by conflicting, and conflicted, desires. In one, evocatively called "Poison of Night," the poetic voice describes himself lying alone in bed, unable to fall into restful slumber as a nearby bell tolls midnight. During this nocturnal reverie, he recalls himself as a boy, "who did not know the penalty / For wild desires." Now he sees that he remained an innocent far beyond his boyhood years, shielded by his Catholic schooling, which he visualizes as embodied in "the smoke of candles / And the haze of incense." He realizes that it was for this reason — because of his belated entry as an adult into the world — that he had now so urgently sought out someone who would initiate him in profane knowledge:

> And thus I wanted to find
> The wise Wicked one
> With the arts of destruction:
> Wanted to run into my ruin
> With open arms
> To love like a madman
> Deprave myself completely
> And die a rapid death.

The conflation of sex, disease, and death had been familiar enough in French poetry not just since Baudelaire, and George treads a well-worn path in these fairly derivative lines. Nevertheless, nothing even resembling these poems was being written in Germany at the time, and even the formal looseness of the verses marked a dramatic departure from his own stiffly metrical earlier productions. Despite their thematic dependency, they demonstrate their own peculiar intensity, betraying an almost prurient fascination with sensual experience coupled with a self-debasing condemnation of sexuality as vile, sinful, and deadly. In another poem from the same collection, provocatively titled "Priests," George similarly sketches an image of two lovers, hurrying through the dissipating early morning mists, "Both showing the unmistakable signs / Of pleasures enjoyed beyond measure." They are, the poet writes, like

> Priests who offer themselves for sacrifice
> Deliver themselves, without prudent restraint,
> To orgies that destroy and kill!
> Their foreheads mirrors of desire!

With that undeniable ugliness
Which is the majesty of vice.

Probably because of the inescapable identification of sex with heterosexual liaisons, George remained suspicious of pure physicality, and even later on his poetic evocations of sexuality are never entirely free of a certain hesitancy and, frequently, open revulsion. The degree of George's growing alienation — from his upbringing, from his native country, even from his own body — is further underscored by the language in which he wrote these poems. The published German version is actually a translation from another one of his linguistic inventions, which this time he more scientifically named "lingua romana" and which he later described as "resembling Spanish." Proudly, he took especial pains to emphasize, however, that "it stands in no relation to the invented languages of my childhood." But it did represent yet another, and by no means the last, attempt to establish a space, and a medium of expression, that he could claim entirely as his own, that would provide a barrier between himself and the real or imagined dangers of the external world.

Toward the end of the summer, in August, George began to think about traveling again. His Iberian "lingua romana" seems to have been not simply the outgrowth of his desire to forge a private language, but also the reflection of a personal attachment. He had met three Mexicans in Paris, Antonio Peñafiel and his two sons, Porfirio and Julio, with whom he had spoken almost solely in Spanish. The Peñafiels apparently inspired him not just to invent a new language, but also to travel to Spain. In his own memoirs, Saint-Paul claimed that he had accompanied his German friend to Burgos, Madrid, and Toledo, but George himself insisted he had gone alone. Spain was in some ways an odd choice. Ever since Goethe's equally impetuous Italian journey in the late eighteenth century, the "South" had been synonymous with Italy, which connoted to the educated German's mind escape, flight, and above all an idealized notion of sensuous abundance and bucolic simplicity, all set amidst a pleasingly melancholy landscape, presenting a poignant memento of imperial grandeur achieved and then squandered. But here, too, George would brook no predecessors. Later forgetting, or suppressing, his brief venture in Milan the year before, George once claimed, rather obliquely, that his "daemon had not driven him to Italy, but to Spain."

George's Spanish journey was marked by several stations — he apparently visited Aranjuez, Elche, Murcia, Cartagena, and San Sebastian — and he never forgot the stark impression made on him by the brooding, craggy palaces jutting out of the dry, empty landscape. "Toledo is the most extraordinary city I know," he once told a friend many years later. "It lies on a mountain, the train goes no farther than to its foot, and then one has to climb up on winding paths into the city. Everything there is strange and exotic. The south of Spain is already completely African — for vast stretches a desert, in which only occasionally a palm tree emerges, now and again an oasis." Comparing Spain to Italy, George said that the Italians had always lived in and among the ancient monuments that bear witness to their own great past, giving them a sense of uninterrupted continuity and a vital connection with their history. Spain was more barren and remote, both geographically and historically. For that reason, too, George thought, "we have a closer relationship to Italy and feel more easily at home there. Not so in Spain, where everything remains foreign to us." George later interpreted his foray into the ancient Moorish outpost of Murcia in the southeastern tip of the Iberian peninsula as representing a peril he had successfully evaded. "I was once drawn to Syrian and Arabic culture," he confided, "but I fought it. The Dionysian element is entirely lacking there." More prosaically, but more accurately, he subsequently revealed that he had indeed wanted to continue from Cartagena across the Mediterranean to Tunis, but had simply missed the ship.

Whatever the "daemon" was that pursued him in the summer of 1889, George in fact felt foreign everywhere. Although he never returned to Spain again (despite continuing to talk into old age of going to Ibiza), he did bring back with him a memento of the journey that he kept with him for the rest of his life. For the next forty years, particularly whenever he traveled, George could often be seen wearing a dark blue wool Basque beret he had acquired on his Spanish journey, rakishly slanted to the left, almost as if it were an emblem and reminder of those wondrous, magical summer months when he had first discovered what a poet could be.

CHAPTER 5
Berlin

Stopping briefly in Paris again in September on his way back from Spain to take leave of his new friends, the nineteen-year-old Etienne displayed a resurgent indecision about his future course. Abandoning the idea of studying in Strasbourg, he now planned to enroll in the Friedrich-Wilhelm University in Berlin, then the most prestigious institution of higher learning in Germany, to pursue his interests in modern philology on a more formal level. Located in the center of the capital, the university lies close to the river Spree and occupies a palatial, colonnaded edifice fronting the broad leafy boulevard Unter den Linden, the rather sober German answer to the Champs Elysées. But George, envisioning a frigid northern outpost occupied by dour Prussian Protestants, felt uncertain. Saint-Paul related that "he confided in me the anxiety he had about going to Berlin. He did not yet know the city. He hesitated to make the voyage and almost decided to write in French and stay in Paris."

In 1889, Berlin presented a spectacle that would have daunted its most determined advocate, not to speak of someone of George's constitution. Like Germany itself, Berlin was a newcomer to international prominence, and it displayed all the familiar qualities of the parvenu. Brash, energetic, restless, and aggressive, the city left many thinking it was merely vulgar, sorely lacking the dignified self-assurance of older European capitals. At the time of George's arrival, the city was in the midst of the convulsive *Gründerjahre,* or "founding years," fueled in large part by the military victory over France two decades earlier. As the residence of the ruling Hohenzollern monarchy, and as the official capital of the fledgling Reich, Berlin had sustained an unparalleled, almost frenzied expansion, ever since the mid-1870s. Flush with the windfall infusion of capital from the Franco-Prussian War — the indemnity exacted from the French finally amounted to some five billion francs — Berlin had been propelled out of a sleepy provincial existence into serious contention as one of Europe's major industrial centers. Lured by glittering promises of swift and easy success, or simply by the prospect of abundant jobs, people streamed into the city from all over the northern empire. In 1865, there were 657,690 Berliners, but ten years later that number had already grown to 964,240. By no later than 1910, the two million mark had been passed.

Although George came to spend more time in Berlin during the 1890s than in any other German city apart from Munich, and continued to return to the capital for frequent and extended stays until the end of his life, it was a marriage based more on convenience than affection. Given the economic upswing there, and the generally expansive mood, Berlin clearly offered opportunities not available elsewhere in Germany. But they came at a high price. Writing to Saint-Paul in 1895, George lamented that he was again in "this terrible city," and his complaints about the sordidness, noise, and banality of Berlin never ceased, despite his yearly pilgrimages there. As late as 1927, he still groaned about "the unpleasant life in Berlin" to his companions, who reported "now that he has been here for two weeks, he feels truly miserable." Occasionally, George was able to find some consolation by casting his sufferings in a sardonic light. During a conversation with some friends a few years before the war, he archly proclaimed that "the really grandiose, the truly beautiful thing is the complete artlessness of the city." When someone mildly pointed out that there were a few choice examples of Rococo and Gothic architecture in the older central section along the Spree, he objected: "That's precisely the awful thing. That shouldn't even be seen. Berlin is beautiful only by being completely bad, uniformly artless." It was this, the perceived absence of any beauty or art in Berlin, and of people who noticed the lack, that aroused his most severe displeasure. Sabine Lepsius, a committed, if not abundantly gifted, painter who worked in the impressionist mode, was a Berliner who later became one of George's most devoted admirers — and one of his few longtime female friends. She similarly found that "it is impossible for anyone seeking out beauty to feel at home in Berlin, unless one possesses the strength to retreat deliberately to solitary labor and to set up a life on an island in the Spree where one can ignore the insipidity that surrounds one."

There are echoes here of the doctrines George had imbibed in Paris, and it was above all the contrast to the luminous weeks and months experienced there that seemed most painful at first. At the beginning of November, 1889, just after George had installed himself in his new quarters in Berlin, Saint-Paul sent word that "M[allarmé] asked me about news of you," and the message sent a pang of nostalgia through Etienne. "Oh, this Berlin, and oh that Paris!" he sighed and requested that Saint-Paul duly convey his greetings to "Mr. Mallarmé one of these Tuesdays." Alone, in unfamiliar surroundings, far away from the sultry splendor of those summer days and evenings in Paris spent reading and discussing poetry, George felt cut off, marooned, exiled in a cold and hostile land. He could hardly have expected to find many people in Berlin who shared his enthusiasm for French poetry and culture. In those days, *Franzos* was a word of derision, mockery, and no little suspicion. To make matters worse, he, a Catholic in all but belief and instantly identifiable as a Southerner by his marked Rhenish accent, found himself in the stronghold of the belligerent Prussian nationalism Bismarck had fanned for more than a decade. Although, as a political program, the *Kulturkampf* had lost most of its momentum and support during the 1880s, the underlying suspicion of Catholicism that motivated it continued to pervade Northern German cultural attitudes for much longer. This deep-seated antagonism gained an institutional voice, and one of great eloquence and persuasiveness, at the place that had been founded by the Prussian state to promulgate its own cultural orthodoxy: the university.

George enrolled in the Friedrich Wilhelm University in late October and began attending lectures on French linguistics, philosophy, Shakespeare, and modern German drama. The latter course was taught by Erich Schmidt, the immediate successor and disciple of Wilhelm Scherer, who had come to Berlin in 1877 to occupy the first university chair created for German literary history. Originally trained as a philologist, Scherer devoted his first book to the grammarian Jacob Grimm, which was quickly followed by the monumental *History of the German Language* in 1868. Scherer had thus set the tone for the study of philology and the history of literature in Germany that prevailed for decades after his premature death in 1886. Turning away from the idealist speculation that had dominated German scholarship during the first half of the century under the heavy hand of Hegel, Scherer had sought to inject the objective spirit of English empiricism and scientific positivism into the study of history. In other words, he believed "that the goals of the historical sciences were essentially related to those of the natural sciences."

Having just returned from a place where poetry was regarded as a sacred commission and the poet as a holy priest, George felt repelled by this desire to treat literature as an object one should dissect and examine dispassionately in search of mechanical causes and effects, like a polyp or a rock. This was not what he had expected when he had decided the previous year to devote himself to philology. But there were other, more direct conflicts at the university that deepened his sense of alienation from the academic climate. Although Scherer had been a native Austrian, he had aligned himself early on with nationalist cultural goals, first of Prussia and then of the newly established Germany. And, as had been the case in the political realm, the spiritual or cultural values of the nation were likewise considered to be synonymous with those of Protestantism. Without seeing any contradiction in overtly pursuing an activist agenda while simultaneously advocating a "scientific" method of history, Scherer explicitly put his scholarship in the service of the political and social objectives of the reborn Empire. In his *History of the Intellectual Life of Germany and Austria,* published in 1874, Scherer had bluntly stated that "Luther's Bible was the decisive act toward the establishment of a unified German culture and language. It was the act of creation of that which we now call our nation. We attribute to Luther our national unity as Italy attributes its unity to Dante. Luther's Bible is our *Divina Commedia*. It is the foundation stone of the temple which surrounds us." The Reformation, in other words, had initiated a process that achieved its logical conclusion in Bismarck's Reich. For George, who detested Bismarck only slightly less than he hated Luther ("that monk of doom," as he liked to call him), Scherer's words, and the form of intellectual culture he represented, implicitly called into question George's very status as a German.

It is thus no surprise that Etienne George responded, as he had done in Darmstadt, by seeking out the company of others who, like himself, were strangers in the Prussian capital. As luck would have it, the Mexican family he had met in Paris, Señor Antonio Peñafiel and his two sons Porfirio and Julio, were staying in Berlin as tourists, and George accompanied them on many excursions through the city and to nearby Potsdam, where they visited the formal gardens and palace of Sanssouci, built in the eighteenth century by the francophile King Frederick the Great. In fact, George's intimacy with these friends was so close, especially with the elder boy Porfirio, and his estrangement from his own countrymen so great, that during these first few months in Berlin he spoke almost nothing but Spanish.

He made another acquaintance in Maurice Muret, a French-speaking Swiss student from Morges, a town that overlooks Lake Geneva. Approaching Muret after one of the lectures they were both attending at the university, George, dressed entirely in the fashionable black costume favored by the symbolist poets, introduced himself by announcing his own feelings of dislocation, saying darkly, "Je suis de la même race que vous." George described himself to Muret as stemming from a family of French origin, that he retained a love for his "native land," and indeed that he had just spent several months in Paris. Proudly, he told Muret that there, on the banks of the Seine, he had become the friend of "a brilliant older poet named Stéphane Mallarmé." Longing to recreate the camaraderie he missed from Paris, and now himself playing the role he had learned from Saint-Paul, George took Muret to his room and read from the works not only of Mallarmé, but also of Verlaine, Merrill, and Vielé-Griffin. Later, he revealed his "secret language" to Muret and gave him copies of his own poems composed in his "lingua romana." They also frequented the theater, and George made sure that they were present for the German premiere of Ibsen's youthful work, *The Lady from the Sea.* When Muret, who was visibly disappointed by the performance, asked what George thought of it, he replied in what seemed to Muret a very "Germanic" fashion. "I will tell you my opinion in a few days," George deferred. "Give me time to reflect on it."

Muret, though a foreigner, seemed more familiar, less alien, to George than the Prussian students. Yet George did cultivate the acquaintance of a fellow German in the unsettled and unsettling person of Carl August Klein, a volatile, erratic young man who tended toward bizarre extremes in both behavior and expression. George's official biographer, couching the matter in typically veiled terms, explained that Klein had a "strong male drive and a delicate, almost over-refined soul." But Klein himself never seems to have articulated or even understood the source of his inner unrest. Anecdotes survive that he liked to provoke the indignation of the stolid burghers of Berlin by dressing up in dandyish outfits and parading on the boulevards wearing powder and makeup, or that in a fit of sudden agitation one night he stripped off his clothes and rode a horse bareback out into the moonlit countryside. There is a photograph depicting Klein and George standing facing one another, both clad in formal attire, decked out in dark heavy overcoats, stiff white collars and high cylindrical top hats. On their youthful and diminutive frames, the costumes occasioned bemused responses. "One meter man and two meters oven pipe," a market woman was once heard to say as the young gallants sauntered by. Klein, a native of Darmstadt, had also attended the Ludwig-Georg-Gymnasium at the time George was there, but they had somehow never crossed paths. Yet their belated acquaintance in Berlin was, for Klein at any rate, a momentous and fateful occasion, for he came to be George's earliest collaborator and ally, the one who first put his energy, indeed his entire being, in the service of George's "mission." Klein viewed it as proof of the impenetrable workings of destiny that both he and George had sat on the same school bench, but did not meet until they noticed one another in the same lecture course in which George had found Muret.

Recalling how "our eyes met" in the spartan auditorium where they listened to the history of French syntax during the Winter term, Klein said that George came up to him after one lecture and offered his hand. Klein is vague about the details of their meeting, but not about its effect. "Something that I was as yet unable to account for rose slowly within me, expanded mysteriously, suddenly shot up and turned into a wordless bliss." Even after the passage of forty years, when he wrote these frothy recollections, Klein still insisted that the origin of the violent and strange sensations he experienced when he met George stemmed only from his own frustrated desire for intellectual companionship. But his words belie a more elemental disturbance. The night following their meeting was, Klein wrote, "horrible." "A maelstrom of the most contradictory feelings raged within me. Out of dark chasms I was jerked up into dizzying heights. I plummeted from raptures for which there is no name into devastating despair. Penetrating doubts assailed me. I raved in the jubilation of redemption, moaned in the agony of madness, twisted under the torture of doubt." "And yet," Klein assured us, "it was a night of tremulous happiness, of happiness over the revolution that had shaken up everything inside me, of trembling at the thought that such a blessing, which I considered undeserved, which had been handed to me like a holy vessel, could be taken away from me again." Going to George the next morning, Klein confessed the inward strife he had undergone. George "gently stroked with a soft hand over the wounds that so pained me," Klein wrote. "He spoke simply and with meaning. He said he vouched for my trial. He said that he always knew what he was doing and that the people he chose had never disappointed him."

Even while making allowances for his supersaturated rhetoric, it seems improbable that Klein actually foresaw already that his own life would change so radically after meeting George and even more doubtful that this turmoil had to do with his subsequent decision to serve as the selfless herald and champion of the poet's work. Rather, he more likely felt the insistent tug of George's equally powerful desire for companionship — albeit on his own terms — and Klein realized, however dimly, that friendship would entail the tacit but irrevocable recognition of George's claim to dominance. Clearly, Klein was also troubled, if unconsciously, by the strong pull of erotic attraction that forever remained unacknowledged between them. Yet in the end, after his struggle with forces — and feelings — he was unable to tame, Klein freely elected to subordinate himself and in so doing become George's first true disciple.

If George noticed the upheaval taking place in Klein, he gave no indication of it, and he certainly showed no sign of a similar disquiet. "He never revealed to me," Klein admitted, "what I meant to him. It remained unsaid and wisely concealed, even to the last day." As he would do with countless others, George simply accepted Klein's devotion as if it were his natural right, the inevitable and proper recognition of his own superiority. In any case, he had other, more pressing worries of his own. Even with the small circle of friends he had acquired in Berlin, he still felt displaced and isolated, disconnected from what he now recognized as his proper sphere. Summoning the energy or will to write at all, much less compose poetry, seemed increasingly difficult, if not impossible, in the constrictive environment of the capital. After spending Christmas at home in Bingen — he was accompanied there by his Swiss friend Muret — George had returned to Berlin by the beginning of 1890. Just after New Year's Day, he sent a long, rambling letter to Arthur Stahl that began symptomatically with a few lines in his made-up "lingua romana." He addressed Stahl as the "amico de meo cor" and mentioned — but did not exactly apologize for — "nostra corespondencia longamente interrompida." But George soon dropped the linguistic mask. A little further on he revealed, this time in German:

> Now a further confession that I find difficult to write down: the idea, which has plagued and pursued me since childhood, which has forced itself on me again and again during certain periods, has recently taken hold of me once more: I mean the idea of creating, out of clear Romanic material, a literary language for my own use that would be as easy on the ear as it would be to understand. I can't explain to you in such a brief space the reasons why I don't like to write in my German language. (At the beginning of this letter you have a sample.) Therein also lies the reason why I haven't written anything for many moons, because I very simply don't know in which language I should write. I sense that this idea will either vanish from my mind or make me into a martyr.

Cautious, reserved, and distant even when making what he regarded as a "confession," Etienne did not tell everything to Stahl. Something of a crisis was building within him, much more severe than his previous bouts of uncertainty about his future. Trying to decide what language to write, indeed to speak, although serious enough in itself, was only emblematic of his general state of mind. He had already been deeply put off by the official culture of the Protestant Prussian state, which now aggressively identified itself with — and as — the German nation as a whole. But George now felt that simply by speaking or writing in German he was allowing himself to be assimilated or co-opted by a regime he did not recognize, and one that, moreover, viewed his own cultural assumptions with suspicion and even open hostility. His earliest attempts to forge his own language had been, somewhat less urgently, the expression of his will to exert absolute control over all aspects of his life. Now the external world, concentrated in the frenetic Moloch of Berlin, seemed to pose a genuine, immediate threat to everything he valued. Even the relatively placid field of philology had been turned in Scherer's hands into a tool to promote a political and intellectual ideology that directly opposed George's experience and beliefs. In addition, despite having found a few companions who shared his interests — he went on in his letter to Stahl to say that, although he was leading a "rather retired" life, he had formed "a circle of friends" in Berlin, "among them Frenchmen, Italians, Mexicans, etc." — the memory of the vital summer in Paris grew more painful as the cold, gray winter weeks and months in Berlin wore on. True, Klein must have responded to certain needs. But he had an essentially receptive nature and was incapable of fully giving George what he required. Once more, he saw the only answer in finding some means of physical escape.

Temporary release came in March, at the end of the first term of university, when he returned home to Bingen, this time joined by Porfirio and Julio Peñafiel. But George had bigger plans. Just before leaving Berlin, the two brothers, together with Klein and George, had gone to the train station to bid farewell to Maurice Muret, who went back to Switzerland for the semester break. Apparently Muret had been no happier in Berlin than his German friend. The month before, in February, Muret and Etienne had begun seriously discussing the possibility of emigrating to Mexico with the Peñafiels. It would, of course, be a radical, tumultuous move, and one that had to be carefully prepared. Since Etienne was still dependent on his father for financial support, he had to approach the issue diplomatically. Staying with the George family for two weeks, Porfirio and Julio served as a kind of living argument for his intentions. But it still cannot have been easy. During the second week of March, Klein, who was in on the scheme, tentatively inquired into the state of negotiations. "So how high is the atmospheric pressure you are placing on your parents?" he cautiously inquired; "I hope that an all-too strong one isn't necessary and that they will agree more easily to the emigration of their son."

In the end, George did not take the extreme step of leaving Germany for good, but it was a sign of how profoundly miserable he was in his native country that he had even considered it. In fact, he continued to view expatriation, or at least some form of emigration, as a viable option for some time. Later in the same year, in another letter to Stahl that he intended as a farewell in several respects, he wrote that "this is perhaps the last year that I can still remain in Germany." Even as late as January 1892, he was still thinking about going permanently "abroad." Again, these plans never materialized, or at any rate not in this form. But for the rest of his life, he would also never remain in one place for more than a few months, at first traveling at regular intervals to France, Holland, Belgium, Austria, and Denmark, then gradually limiting his sphere to a familiar circuit within Germany, Switzerland, and occasionally Italy, ceaselessly moving about and living for short periods in rooms reserved for him at the houses of friends or in modest hotels. Even when, much later, he became the representative, or rather the incarnation, of a new German culture, George never accepted the Germany that claimed him as its own. It was as if, by refusing to be bound to any particular geographical place, he was able not just to maintain the supreme independence he coveted but also to create his own version of Germany while — or by — physically rejecting the one that actually existed.

As April approached, Etienne resigned himself to a further semester at university and prepared his return to Berlin. Writing to Muret, who had finally decided that the city was unbearable and that he would rather continue his studies in Munich, George explained that, as alluring as the prospect was of avoiding the malignancies of the capital, he needed a larger context for his own aims. "That's just the way it is with us big-city eels, who no longer feel comfortable in a provincial goldfish pond. To be sure, I am quite snug here in Bingen, but I can stand it only for a limited amount of time there. I am therefore going back day after tomorrow to my dear — oh, God — to my dear Berlin." He also chided Muret for failing to keep up his end of the correspondence, saying "how much I regretted that you were not here on the Rhine during those wonderfully beautiful early spring days in the company of our friends the Peñafiels! It would have been so delightful, we spoke so often of you (ingrate!) on all of our outings and you never once let your thoughts ascend to our circle." It was a fairly gentle reprimand, but clear enough: if Muret was to be his friend, he had to observe some basic rules.

One person George could always count on was Klein. In fact, it may very well have been this fragile, unstable, yet fanatically loyal young man who ultimately persuaded him not only to stay in Germany, but also to press forward with his poetic plans. George had obviously told him of his writings, but, displaying typical wariness, he had withheld them. From his home in Darmstadt, Klein grew more insistent, pleading to see his works. Referring to a poem written in the "lingua romana," Klein beseeched George in early April: "I am aching for your 'Cognicion.'" Sensing that Klein would respond to its message, George finally relented and sent a handwritten copy of the poem.

The German version of "Cognicion," one of three "Legends" ("Legenden") he had completed the year before in Paris, is called in German "Erkenntnis" or "knowledge," and reflects again the deep ambivalence he was feeling toward female blandishments and the kind of knowledge they represent. The poem contains several motifs familiar from George's earlier works, not least the identification of sexual desire, especially heterosexual attraction, with a morbid conclusion. But it is also the clearest evocation yet in his poetry of the paranoid logic that underlies extreme self-love. Set in an idyllic, vaguely Grecian landscape of clear brooks, "virginal flowers," and shady groves, the poem introduces a Narcissus-like figure stretched out in languorous repose, gazing into a stream. A detached poetic voice narrates how this handsome ephebe, having grown weary of his lonely reveries, searches desperately for a mate and finally finds "the Woman dreamt of, the Divine One." Together they retreat to his isolated dwelling, where he rejoices — significantly — in his complete possession of the woman, telling himself, "You have her entirely — seen only by you — / Only for you does she blossom and smile." But no sooner do they arrive at his refuge than he is afflicted by doubts about whether he is indeed the sole owner of her virtue and whether "she came as a pure priestess?" As he sits, brooding over his "bitter pain," she approaches him softly and, unaware of his unfounded suspicions, kisses him on the head. He reacts violently: "Did I summon you, woman? / Come near me only when I require you!" She recoils, silently, and he becomes more convinced that her supplications are false and her apparent modesty the product of dissimulation and hypocrisy:

> While I twist myself in knots of anguish
> She wants to conquer me with easy effort . .
> She pretends to be dismayed at my wrath
> Perhaps she really is because her beguiling wiles
> Do not work as easily on me as on others.
> It is precisely the tender, flattering ways
> Which are supposed to substantiate her oaths
> That betray her by their subtlety and art:
> They are revealed by the test . .
> Her childlike naiveté is mere trickery.

As a psychological portrait, this delusional eruption is convincing — and chilling — enough. But there is more. With faltering hopes that his fears may yet be proven groundless, the man waits until they consummate their bond before making a definitive judgment. After this night — and giving the poems its title — he "knows":

> Now Foolish Man you have certainty!
> Ruinous knowledge! vile test!
> I was a criminal from the moment
> That I stepped to her side in union
> With a foul deed did I purchase the answer.

Feeling debased and humiliated by the discovery he had made through what he sees as loathsome "animal spasms," he runs back to the stream — now swollen and turbid from stormy downpours, so that "it throws back to me an ugly image" — and throws himself into the roiling depths.

Instead of being repelled or warned off by this sordid tale of ferocious narcissism and raving possessiveness, Klein was enraptured. He submitted it on his friend's behalf to a small journal to be considered for publication. In mid-July, Klein received a disappointing response from the editor of the journal, M. G. Conrad, who had rejected the poem, but for a telling reason. Conrad admitted that "the poem is an impressive test of talent, but it would be perhaps be better if — in view of the outcome of the Leipzig trial — we refrained from publication." Conrad was referring to the Realist Trial in Leipzig, in which the novelist Wilhelm Walloth, among others, was convicted of producing "indecent literature" — the same Walloth who had possibly approached George when he was in school in Darmstadt. The trial thus produced the desired effect: fearing similar reprisals, Conrad retreated while giving cautious and fairly ambiguous encouragement to the young poet. "Why don't you send — in spite of the prudes — something really energetic," he suggested, quickly adding, "but not at all erotic!"

But George was already moving in different directions. The poem, particularly in its original linguistic form, was partly an expression of the conflicts that had led up to the aborted decision to emigrate in March. Now he needed to discover some new means of combating and overcoming the crisis. He found it in the form of his first book of poetry.

CHAPTER 6
Hymns

At the conclusion of the summer semester in mid-July of 1890, George left Berlin to return to Bingen. But before going home, he made a short detour by way of Copenhagen. There was a young Dane of Polish descent there by the name of Stanislaus Rozniecki who later became a professor of Slavic philology at the university and with whom George would later exchange a few letters about symbolist poetry. Whether George had met him earlier in Berlin or only after he arrived in Copenhagen is unclear, but there would seem to be no other obvious reason he would have gone to Denmark except to visit someone there he already knew. Although he stayed for only a few days, it proved to be an intensely productive time, giving rise to some of his most sensual and affirmative verses to date. But as it turned out, he never returned to Copenhagen again. For Rozniecki soon made the kind of mistake that George could never forgive, at least not in someone who would figure as a friend.

Others were about to make the same error. After gathering some things in Bingen, George set out once again for Paris. It was as if, during the year that had elapsed, a kind of poetic gestation had occurred. Now it seemed as if he wanted to return to his literary place of origin to bring forth there what had germinated during the silent crisis of winter. In April, while still in Berlin, he had already begun to write the initial drafts of the poems that would form the introductory sequence to his first book of poetry. But it was not until summer, first during the brief fruitful interlude in Denmark and then finally that August in Paris, that the torrent broke. In rapid succession the eighteen poems that comprise George's first book, *Hymns* (*Hymnen*), assumed their definitive shape.

After the struggles of the past year, the tumultuous doubts about his feelings, his ambitions, his country, even his language, the verses that now came forth offered an eloquent testimony of their own. Through their very existence, they made an argument for the validity of the contest he had been fighting within and against himself. But the change he experienced went beyond an affirmation of his literary calling. It convinced him that he now belonged to the company of those who could genuinely call themselves poets.

Every authentic poet experiences a kind of awe before his own gift, a reverence for his art that seems strangely objective. Once externalized and given the permanence of form, true poetry seems to have been inevitable, as if it had merely waited patiently for concrete expression. Often the verses give us the peculiar sense of possessing a kind of preordained rightness, or at least that they had not so much been invented as simply found. Poetry of this order enters into the very fabric of language, becomes an indelible part of our linguistic reality, and thus participates in a larger dialogue that is indeed no longer merely subjective. There is no accounting for this phenomenon, no way to predict when it may occur or to whom. But when it does, the poet who feels that he has thus become a mouthpiece for a force greater than himself will often find it impossible not to believe that he has left the narrow boundaries of individual striving and passed into a broader, greater, impersonal realm of almost infinite scope.

Of course, there was much in Etienne's personality that predisposed him to such a belief. Outwardly detached, marked by a somber, even morose reserve, and clearly in possession of an uncommon sensibility, he already seemed to have largely removed himself from the mundane preoccupations consuming most of his peers. Even more, the estrangement caused by the inner upheavals besetting him since his adolescence made him susceptible to the idea that his proper place existed outside the compass drawn by the concerns of ordinary people. But it was not until he had met Mallarmé during the previous summer that he discovered a stable medium, a context that would grant him some steady purchase, something external he could embrace without forfeiting his absolute requirements for sovereignty, independence, and meaningful work. Henceforth Etienne would regard poetry as his legitimate province and the role of the poet, as revealed to him by the master in Paris, as his sole and proper office.

What is peculiar about this transformation is that it happened virtually instantaneously, before he had published a word or even before his works had passed any qualified review. The act of writing itself seemed to provide proof enough for George, apparently delivering all the evidence he needed to support his conviction that he now counted among the elect. Not surprisingly, his newfound confidence, not to say presumption, elicited ambivalent reactions from his friends.

In August, before he had left again for Paris, Etienne had met with Carl Rouge and read aloud to him one of the poems he had completed in Denmark, together with some others he had written earlier in Berlin. In a long letter Rouge wrote at the end of August, we gain a clear picture of the changed tone that had already emerged in George's conception of himself and his writing. Rouge told Etienne he found it odd that he was not willing to show his most recent work to Stahl, who after all had been one of the founding editors of their school review and for many years one of their closest mutual friends. The reason for Etienne's reticence, it turns out, was that he did not believe that Stahl belonged to the "sphere" that would allow him to understand his new poetry. "Since," Rouge wrote to Etienne in August, recapitulating the argument, "in your view apparently, the people of the 'sphere' are *born* as such (I conclude from this that you seem to believe that they cannot be *educated*), then it may be possible that Stahl belongs to these 'born ones': so why exclude him? On the contrary: I *demand* on his behalf the communication of your 'opera,' since literary property is the possession of everyone." Obviously, Stahl had not told Rouge everything about his correspondence with Etienne, neither about the persistent taunts he was forced to bear concerning his military career, nor about his own demure retraction from anything stronger than mere friendship between himself and George. Ignorant of these private reasons for a cooling of their relationship, and inspired by a democratic desire to defend literary openness, Rouge took it upon himself to describe in a letter to Stahl the meeting he had had with Etienne, a copy of which he then sent to George himself.

> He [i.e. Etienne] has this *idée fixe* — or perhaps it is more than an *idée fixe* — that every work of art is created for a particular sphere and can be properly appreciated only by that sphere. This is no doubt partially entirely correct, but on the other hand probably ridiculously exaggerated, for then where would the place of *criticism* be? Thus it perhaps would have been better had George given his poems to me to *read* without any prior comment than to read them *aloud* to me with several preambles, a method of communicating that sacrifices a lot. Now that I have Etienne's works written out in front of me, they no longer look at all as "new" as he had trumpeted, not so very different from his earlier manner. — "Consecration," "In the Park," "Invitation," are, I think, as accessible to you as to Etienne's particular "sphere."

Knowing Etienne well enough to be able to predict how he would receive this fairly critical but evenhanded appraisal, and now addressing George directly again, Rouge carefully admixed some praise with his assessment. Strikingly, Rouge had already identified certain characteristics within these first few works that would later become known as some of the most distinctive hallmarks of George's mature poetry. "I will say right away," Rouge wrote, "that something truly *new* appears in your poems, however: that is the perfection of form! In some spots inversions or strange words produce an unpleasant effect: but in any case this form is original and entirely your own. This is vividly demonstrated, for example, if one memorizes a few poems after reading them over once (e.g. 'Consecration,' 'In the Park,' 'Newland Love Feasts'), owing to their pregnant, unique form." But, apart from recognizing the technical merits of the poems, and their "original" form, Rouge seemed generally underimpressed, and he said so. He certainly did not accept Etienne's dark pronouncements about there being a separate realm to which only a privileged few had access, nor did Rouge think that his only reaction to Etienne's poetry should be unquestioning veneration. "Now, you write that I can't 'feel for or sympathize with a sphere that is unknown to me,'" Rouge wrote, but then objected, "I must say I don't find any unknown sphere in your poems! Further, I disagree with you saying: 'often superior to our classical writers with respect to purity.' What sort of purity must it be that you mean by that? [. . .] In short I say to you: I will judge your works on their own merits, not according to what you say about them." After asking a few questions about individual poems, he then concluded, "Apart from these and the questions above, your poems seem clear to me: usually they can be made even more so by precise punctuation. You can prove your friendship by precisely enlightening me: but don't come to me with explanations from the special 'sphere'!! Even though that is certainly easier! — "

In any other circumstance, and by anyone else, this would have been regarded as a relatively harmless missive, an honest but essentially well-meaning expression of opinion from one aspiring writer to another — indeed, as a letter from a friend to someone he considered his equal. Even a year ago, George may have taken it that way. But another lesson he learned from Maître Mallarmé was that criticism was not to be tolerated. The day after Rouge's letter arrived, Etienne sat down to draft a response, but everything had changed. Beyond the words themselves, even the stylistic idiosyncrasies George began to use in this letter — the clipped, abbreviated syntax, the formal, even stilted phrasing, and the studied neglect of conventional punctuation — all herald the conversion that had taken place in his view of himself and of his station, and indeed they anticipate what became the characteristic epistolary mode of his maturity.

Thanks be to your exultant underscored critique.

But the challenge is: receiving and taking above all else, the Master will always find his masterer.

And now forget — please — what I recently wrote to you as the last confused unwise transitional note to sounds in which we once understood one another. They will not come again.

Do not be so surprised that in turning my pages they became familiar and less new to you. If you are indeed as much a master of words as I and, after your astonishment, you lend them a meaning — then: does there not cling to every revolution a stigma of the old order and was it so long ago that we sang fervently and often in the same rhythms?

Thus, finding a certain meaning for the intention of the poet was not preposterous even for a deaf man.

Thus, what you found was the old.

For I want to build on what you consider bad, casting off your good as childish for ever and ever. And the perfection of the man in Art will strive after this: That his work shall be such that you will find fault with it from the first to the last sound.

How wasted therefore your hints, improvements and above all effort.

It was a deliberately brusque, insulting message, a slap in the face, an insolent dismissal. Rouge cannot but have felt hurt and offended, but most of all he must have been bewildered by the abrupt change in Etienne's behavior. During his short stop in Bingen, George had already let Rouge know that he thought of himself as belonging to a domain, a "sphere," that was inaccessible to those not born to it. Now he was telling Rouge in no uncertain terms that the door to that "sphere" was closed to him.

This, too, would become a distinctive trait of the older George: throughout his life he was capable of discarding friends, and not a few of them of very long standing, with brutal swiftness. He would jettison them for a perceived injury or slight, for the failure to observe proper form when speaking to or of the poet, and sometimes for no apparent reason at all. And once he had banished someone from his sight, there was almost always no recourse or return to favor.

It was obvious that the rift between Etienne and his school friends was unbridgeable, if only because George insisted that it was. In the following spring of 1891, he sent an elliptic postcard to Stahl — it would be one of his last communications with him — on which he had drawn a thick black line around the border in a grim parody of formal obituaries and death announcements. "Why the black border?" George rhetorically wrote, "because of the literary death of the poet and friend C[arl] R[ouge]." Soon thereafter, all contact between them ceased. Almost four decades later, in November 1929, Stahl's widow wrote a note to George with the news that her husband had died the previous month, adding that Stahl had never forgotten their youthful friendship and had often warmly spoken of the now famous poet. But, for George, Stahl had ceased to exist long before.

Although George placed an absolute premium on the originality of his work, even in his first emergence as a poetic voice, it was that very claim and the way in which he made it that most closely aligned him with those he owed the most. For their part, his French mentors not only recognized the affinity, they enthusiastically celebrated it. When the *Hymns* appeared in December, George's first act was to send three copies to Paris: one destined for Saint-Paul, along with a letter containing instructions for the disposal of the other two. "The second, my good solicitor, you should give to Delaroche, and the third, following the advice you once gave me, I ask you to have the goodness to place, together with the enclosed letter, in the hands of Monsieur Stéphane Mallarmé." Saint-Paul was exuberant:

> My dear, my dear, my very dear George, what a pleasure you have given me! how happy I am with your shipment! with what joy do I congratulate you! The volume is superb and very much gives the impression of one of ours. You must have sought that. That is excellent. But, for heaven's sake! send me a translation — otherwise it is cruel of you. Yesterday evening I took the volume to Delaroche, to the café Voltaire, where we meet every Monday. It passed from hand to hand and some attempted a few translations, which, aided by my explanations of the personality of the poet, thereupon enthroned you. From now on you are the symbolist poet of Germany.

But it was not until early March of the following year that the most important, and no doubt anxiously awaited, reaction came. Making polite apologies for the delay, Mallarmé began his note with a salutation that must have made George tremble with joy:

Paris 89 rue de Rome
28 February 1891
My dear poet

I initially lacked your address, hence my silence: for no sooner received your book was read, translated around me. I was enraptured by the unspoiled and proud strain, the brilliance and reverie of those *Hymns* (no title could be more beautiful); but also, my dear exile (yes, I would almost like to put it thus) by the fact that your handiwork, so fine and rare, should make you one of us and of today.
With fondest regards,
Stéphane Mallarmé

George was jubilant. "Imagine," he excitedly told Saint-Paul, "I received a letter from M." Momentarily forgetting his usual reserve, he even admitted to "my ecstasy." Yet the generosity of spirit Mallarmé displayed, the charitable and perhaps even sincere praise of a novice's poems, and most of all the unhesitating willingness to embrace George within the fold, all stand in marked contrast to his own cold rejection of his longtime friends, whom he had deemed insufficient and unworthy, and whom he had roughly excluded from the same "sphere" into which Mallarmé now officially and warmly welcomed *him*. Apart from everything else, the difference in Mallarmé's attitude and George's presents a striking example of the way the German poet could absorb external influences and still place his own very personal stamp on them, making them somehow more rigid, formal and, above all, more answerable to his own will — and to his alone.

When Mallarmé proclaimed George to be "one of us," he was primarily referring of course to the loose but self-aware group of writers known as the symbolists. Perhaps he, unlike the less circumspect Saint-Paul, had refrained from actually using the word itself, because, then as now, it seemed to create more confusion than real clarity. Indeed, like almost every other literary or artistic movement, symbolism is notoriously difficult to pin down, and rivers of ink have been spilled in the attempt. But for many of its practitioners, and this would be true of George as well, its obscurity was precisely one of its attractions. Much of symbolism itself represented an explicit, unrelenting critique of that very urge for rational clarity and objective certainty, a desire the symbolists, with their anarchist sympathies, equated with the easy superficiality and acquisitiveness of the bourgeois society they so vociferously detested. The symbolists were convinced that the modern, scientific age had not improved but rather impoverished the world by reducing it to what was merely calculable and quantifiable, and in the process stripping it of any transcendental meaning. Not the material "thing" but the metaphysical "idea," not the concrete specificity of the senses but the evanescent fluidity of the spirit, stood at the center of the symbolists' preoccupations. In Jean Moréas's vigorous defense of symbolism, which appeared in 1886 in *Le Figaro,* he had sententiously declared that "symbolist poetry seeks to clothe the Idea in a sensible form that, nevertheless, is not itself its end, but which, while serving to express the Idea, remains its subject. The Idea, in turn, must at no point allow itself to be seen deprived of its sumptuous robes of external analogies. For the essential character of symbolic art consists in never arriving at the conception of the Idea in itself. Thus, in this art, portraits of nature, human actions, all concrete phenomena would not know how to manifest themselves: they are sensible materializations intended to represent their esoteric affinities with the primordial Ideas."

This is heady fare, and one may well wonder whether much of the poetry ostensibly written according to these precepts could ever live up to such lofty aspirations. But the ambition, if in fact unrealized, indeed impossible to fulfill, was nonetheless quite genuine — and ancient. The thought that one has to pierce the veil of the visible to enter into a concealed, but more real, more true sphere, inaccessible and unknown to the multitudes, has never ceased to obsess the European imagination. From Plato's Forms, to the Christian Mysteries, to the Kantian "Thing in itself," the True has always been thought to exist in a domain that stood beyond reason, unattainable by our ordinary senses, lying forever outside our comprehension. The most we can ever have are intimations of the True, which we can never directly perceive but which we know must lie hidden behind the pale reflections and poor copies of its nature. What the symbolists imagined they were doing, paradoxically, was turning these inescapable limitations to their positive advantage. If all we have are imperfect derivatives of the Real, if objects, language, indeed all matter itself is but an inferior mask of the True, then emphasizing this fact will inevitably divert attention away from the distractions of mere surface ephemera and toward the contemplation, if not actual apprehension, of the eternal beyond.

It is a frankly mystical program, but it was pursued with supreme sobriety. The central paradox — the articulation of the ineffable, expressing the inexpressible — inherently defies description. Mallarmé himself best articulated the seemingly contradictory goals of symbolism by contrasting them with those of the previous generation of poets, the Parnassians. In 1891, just a few months after George's *Hymns* appeared, Mallarmé was interviewed by Jules Huret, a journalist for the *Echo de Paris*, who was writing a series of vignettes about the modern literary scene in France. Asked to characterize the content of the new poetry, Mallarmé responded that

> the contemplation of objects, the image floating up from the reveries aroused by them, that makes a poem: the Parnassians, on the other hand, take a thing in its entirety and show it; that way they lack mystery; they deprive our minds of that delicious joy of believing that they are creating. To *name* an object is to suppress three quarters of the pleasure of a poem, which is made of the joy of guessing little by little; to *suggest,* that is the dream. It is the perfect use of this mystery that constitutes the symbol: to evoke, bit by bit, an object in order to show a mood, or, conversely, to choose an object and to extricate from it a mood through a series of decipherments.

Again, it is useful to remember that the underlying conceptions propping up the symbolist creed all boasted a venerable, or at least recondite, past.

Many of the ideas expressed here can be traced, more or less directly, to the German Romantic writers, whom the symbolists all professed to have read, to Christian mystics such as Swedenborg, the theories of Schopenhauer and of his fervent disciple Richard Wagner, and to various occult doctrines made fashionable in the 1860s and 1870s by such figures as the prolific but errant Alphonse Louis Constant, known better by the pseudonym Eliphas Levi, and the hugely popular Josephin Péladan, who adopted the flamboyant title Sâr Mérodack. These and many other sources all combined to form the common stock of ideas shared by the symbolist writers and artists, inevitably exerting a profound effect on George as well.

But above all others towered the saturnine form of Baudelaire — that "extraordinary and pure genius," as Mallarmé once extravagantly called him — who in both his critical essays and poems had established what were universally recognized as the basic tenets of the symbolist doctrine. His theory of "correspondences" acquired its definitive expression in a poem of the same name near the beginning of *Fleurs du Mal,* which George would begin to translate into German later that spring.

It is usually said — and the symbolists themselves, including George, liked to say it as well — that the primary enemy, the foe they sought to beat back with their works, was naturalism. Like all polemical weapons, this assertion owes its effectiveness to its bluntness; further refinement, while perhaps yielding greater accuracy, would also diminish its potency. Certainly, the symbolists derided the naturalist belief that it was desirable or even possible to capture the tangible world in all of its obvious and more submerged complexities with the flawed instrument of language. Too, they scorned the political agenda of many naturalist writers, who with their liberal sensibilities wanted to depict the ordinary lives of working people in a way that would be accessible to them. Through unflinching depictions of the hard reality of their circumstances, the naturalists also claimed to be intervening on behalf of the less fortunate and thus helping to improve their lot. By contrast, the symbolists scornfully believed that literature, and especially poetry, had nothing to do with such trivial and base concerns. The proper task of the poet was to commune with the universal, not to wallow in the particular. On a more philosophical level, they also considered it naive to think that literature could stand in any immediate relation to reality, as if the nature of either one were clear or obvious to anyone. Mallarmé was eloquent and unyielding in this regard as well. Asked by the journalist of the *Echo de Paris* what he thought of "naturalism," he answered by way of an illustrative example:

> The infantalization of literature up until now has been to believe, for example, that to choose a certain number of precious stones and to put their

names on paper, even very well, means one *makes* those precious stones. Well, no! Poetry consists in *creating,* one must take moods from the human soul, gleams of a purity so absolute that, if they are sung well and well illuminated, it indeed constitutes the joys of man: it is here that there is symbol, there is creation, and the word poetry finds its meaning here: it is, finally, the only possible human creation. And, truly, if the precious stones with which one adorns oneself do not manifest a mood, then one adorns oneself wrongfully with them.

Yet symbolism's real opponent, if it must be framed in such adversarial terms, was not naturalism at all, or solely, but in a sense the traditional Western view and practice of art as a whole. Ever since antiquity, art had always fundamentally been thought to represent a reflection of the external world. The imitation of nature, understood, to be sure, in countless ways and to as many ends, had nevertheless always remained the stated origin and purpose of art. Faithfully reproducing nature — or at least the firm belief that one was doing so — was thought, variously, to celebrate the glory of God's creation; to give evidence of human mastery over the world; to serve as a vehicle for imparting useful knowledge about that world; to preserve the past from total oblivion; or, more simply, to augment the pleasure we take in our senses by depicting certain things for no other reason than that we enjoy the experience. But, over the course of those two and a half millennia, there was never any serious question that the business of art was to seize hold of the shapes, colors, sounds, even the movements that surround us and then to present them back to us in recognizable form.

For the symbolists, however, art had a much greater and more difficult task. Since, most symbolists believed, the external world — Nature — was nothing but a shimmering figment or thin veneer obscuring the true invisible inner realm, the evocation of natural objects would then take on a decidedly secondary, auxiliary role. Objects become "symbols" of otherwise hidden realities, visible tokens to take the place of what cannot strictly be represented. Even when speaking of the natural world, a symbolist is always talking of something else. The phrase Mallarmé used to describe the effect of a symbol, the "mood" he said it renders, means literally "state of soul" (*état d'âme*). But by saying that it elicits a "state of the soul," Mallarmé did not mean that the work of the poem stops at, or even consists in, the awakening of a certain psychological or affective response. The words of a poem act, rather, as a kind of conduit, leading not to an appreciation of the things they describe, or even to a specific emotion they might evoke, but through an ultimately inexplicable alignment the poem makes possible to a sort of spiritual attunement to the poet's vision, and, ultimately, an encounter with what was variously called the

"Idea," the "Infinite," or the "Absolute." And it is the poet, and the poet alone, who can supply the medium enabling this encounter to occur.

The proximity of this conception of art, and of the artist, to religious attitudes is both obvious and highly deliberate. Mallarmé clearly regarded himself as a kind of secular priest, and it was not lost on the regulars of his Tuesday evenings that he regarded those sessions as a form of temporal mass. But it was a view widely shared by many other symbolists as well. They saw the artist, and specifically the poet, as occupying a privileged position before the rest of humanity, privy to esoteric knowledge, engaged in rituals performed in a language that only the initiated could — and should — comprehend, and acting as a intermediary to a force that is invisible, mysterious, and, for that reason, vaguely frightening to ordinary mortals. The symbolists consciously and deftly exploited these beliefs, which were familiar from the Catholic background many of them shared and drew upon.

It was an intoxicating mixture: the fantasy of seemingly unlimited power over the phenomenal world — no matter that it was a purely imaginary power — combined with an exaltation of one's person that bordered on self-deification. For George, who saw in it not only a means of conquering his own uneasy relations with the world, but also, and most crucially, a way finally of subjecting it entirely to his control, it was a formula that proved irresistible. Having always tended to seek out all available means of maximizing his authority over his physical and intellectual environment, George discovered in symbolism a system of belief that seemed to grant him unrestricted supremacy over more than he had ever thought possible. But it is important to emphasize that, for George, this achievement of dominion over the world, indeed over life, was not a matter of metaphor, a mere figure of speech: it was a conviction that quite literally shaped the rest of his life. There is an anecdote that rings too true to be apocryphal in which George, some two decades later, heard someone say that Napoleon had once exclaimed, "J'aime le pouvoir comme artiste," to which George immediately shot back, "J'aime l'art comme pouvoir."

That was it: in the end, beyond all other aesthetic considerations — and they were not negligible — he loved art for the power he thought it conferred on him to shape and define the world. True, he admitted once in a conversation in 1919 that "the poet did not make the world, he only expresses it." But that was less of a concession than might appear at first glance. For he was also convinced, as he had tersely put it a few years earlier, that "to write poetry is a form of rule." The original German, more compact and more forceful, is even more direct: *Dichten ist ein Herrschen*.

Naturally, when George brought out his first book of poetry, all of these ideas were as yet largely unformed, more latent than conscious. But they were there, buried among the lines of verse, implied in the stance they took toward the subjects they address. As even the title of the collection suggests, the *Hymns* conjure forth an atmosphere of quasi-religious experience, a sense sustained by the first poem of the book, whose title, "Weihe," contains the multiple associations of consecration, dedication, and formal ordination. Yet, even though the vocabulary is the same, the initiation here is not of a priest or official into the Catholic church, but of a poet to his calling.

Addressing himself in the second person, the poetic voice describes venturing out into the warm night air, down to a river, and lying in the grass on the water's edge, "without the disturbance of thought." While staring out over the glimmering reflection of the stars on the calm surface of the stream, a strange transformation begins to take place: "The flight of time loses its old names / And space and being remain only in the image." It is an arresting moment: here, at the very beginning of the book, indeed at the inception of George's poetic career, the whole of reality — space, time, all "being" — is said to undergo an elemental change. Everything has shed its old designation — to be renamed, one assumes, by the poet himself like a latter-day Adam — and the whole of existence, already seen to be chimerical, will henceforth endure only in and through his words, the "images" he deploys. And it is in this otherworldly state, in which the universe has been metamorphosed into a glimmering mirage, that the "consecration" itself occurs:

> Now you are ready · now the goddess floats down ·
> Embraced by misty veils the color of the moon
> Her dream-heavy eyes half open
> Bent down over you to perform the blessing:
>
> While her mouth trembled on your face
> And seeing you so pure and holy
> She did not try to elude the kiss
> You bring to your lip with guiding hand.

Although the "goddess" has been the subject of much earnest and searching speculation, it is not really so important to identify who or what she represents. It could be a figure for inspiration, a private muse, an allegorical personification of poetry itself, or even a vision of hoped-for fame. What is telling, however, is that the "kiss," the conferral of distinction, the sign of benediction she administers making him a poet, is as much taken as it is given. Even here, that is, in the magical instant in which the poet would receive the blessing of poetic agency, there is a conveyed sense of coercion, as if he felt compelled to take forcible possession of what was already being freely offered.

"Weihe," or "Consecration," is arguably the strongest and most successful poem of the *Hymns,* setting a distinctive tone for the rest of the collection and deftly establishing a mood that any alert symbolist would have recognized and savored. Nature denaturalized, ordinary objects veiled in a strange and unworldly aspect, the evocation of mysterious, ethereal realms, all delivered in unconventional, highly stylized language: these are all familiar symbolist conceits, used to indicate won mastery over the material world, even hinting at a kind of potential transcendence. Reinforcing this impression is the fundamental rhetorical mode of the poems, which is not description but solemn declamation. When the poet addresses himself in the subsequent verses, he often uses words referring to regal majesty: in one poem, he remembers (and this is not the least of the autobiographical resonances) "as if in a magic well / The early time when I was still king." In another, the Muse reappears and similarly congratulates him for "royally forbidding your body / To the lowly maids who brazenly desire it." Most obviously, though, the overriding concern with the task of the poet, with his station and mission, makes it clear that the central interest lies not with the external sphere but precisely and preeminently with the poet himself.

Not all of the poems that follow respond directly to this set of concerns, but there is a thematic unity linking the second poem, called "In the Park," to this same constellation. Here, George employs images of inorganic materials or the products of human industry to destabilize the natural scene announced in the title, again with the purpose of asserting the priority of the poet's consciousness over the base reality of the things themselves. In the first two stanzas of the poem, for instance, he uses the names of hard gems and precious jewels to evince the effect of water drops falling from a fountain; he compares the grass below the basin to a green silk rug; and the rows of surrounding tree trunks become the columns of a "shadowy hall." In other poems, too, the blue of someone's eyes is likened to "a turquoise," or a sunlit hillside is evoked as a "smooth cast of heavengreen glass." Yet the conquest enacted in "Consecration" had to be constantly repeated, the blessing had to be perpetually won anew, and "In the Park" ends with the lament that, on this day, the poet "has to govern the stylus that resists." Similarly, in the concluding poem of the cycle, "The Gardens Close," the question is raised: "Has your hope become your possession?" It is a layered issue: the poet asks himself whether he has fulfilled the promise expressed at the outset of the book, whether his dream of becoming a poet has indeed been realized. But at the heart of that desire, in fact synonymous with it, is the urge to take possession, to seize hold of the world and to claim it entirely as his own. To become a poet, for George, essentially meant to preside over the triumph of art — and of the artist — over life itself.

The apotheosis of this victory of artifice over nature comes toward the very end of the book, in a poem titled "An Angelico." Its ostensible subject is a painting by the Italian Renaissance artist Fra Angelico depicting the coronation of the Virgin, a work George had seen in the Louvre during his first trip to Paris. But the real object is to draw attention to the achievement of the artist himself. Calling the picture a "gloriously great deed," the poem celebrates how the artist appropriated the materials he needed from the world around him, wringing colors from familiar objects and putting them to his own purposes:

> He took the gold from holy chalices ·
> For blond hair the straw of ripening wheat ·
> The pink from children who draw with brick ·
> From the washerwoman at the stream the indigo.

Not art in the service of nature is being admired here, but nature placed in the service of art. Indeed, the poem ends with a refined ambiguity, which read one way might well be considered blasphemous. Calling forth the image of Mary at the moment she receives her crown, the poem leaves open who is actually performing the act itself: God or the artist.

> The bride with eternally still childish breast
> Full of humility but glad of her reward
> Receives from his hand the first crown.

It was an old idea that both the Romantics and symbolists shared: that the artist, endowed with the power of creation, seemed like a "second maker" under God, indeed appeared himself almost divine. The suggestion here, though, is that the first — and most important — distinction may belong to the painter: it is his hand that bestows the golden crown we see. Not satisfied with seeing the artist in a position of parity with God, George seems to want to usurp his place.

Even in those poems of the *Hymns* which do not overtly engage in such self-reflexive meditation on the essence of art and the artist, there is still the feeling that a single, prevailing consciousness is never far from the center, making it seem that all existence is sustained and validated only by the poet's own experience. In "Strand," one of the several love poems in the book that George wrote while visiting Stanislaus Rozniecki in Copenhagen, the poetic voice urges his lover that they leave the shore by the tempestuous sea, which, itself "wild in desire and with dark undulations," tolerates only "shy gulls" and the "chaste sky" in its presence. He suggests that they travel instead to calmer inland lakes, where dense green vegetation creates a kind of permanent night, forming a secluded natural "altar" where they can perform their private rites undisturbed. The poet imagines being led there by swans "full of secret mystery." Then comes the most remarkable transformation of all: enraptured by this fanciful seduction, the poet envisages their physical transport in figurative terms by picturing it as a further flight, symbolized by the names of exotic plants found only in warmer southern climes.

> Desire carries us off away from the pale north:
> Where your lips burn strange calyxes blossom –
> And your body stretches out like a bed of flowers
> Then all the shrubs and bushes rustle in accord
> Now becoming aloe tea and laurel.

Read straightforwardly as a love poem, the lines possess a genuine power, an erotic fervor that became one of George's poetic hallmarks. But the poem lacks innocence in another way, too. If we look again we find that it is the mirror image of the procedure we traced in the other poems: here George draws on images taken from the natural realm, but in order to banish the present reality by eliciting a vision that opposes it. Yet nature here is not just used to eradicate nature, for by comparing the body of his lover to a bed of flowers — as familiar as the image may be — the poet even manages to erase the boundaries marking out the human form itself.

Another example of this urge to evoke and simultaneously delete the features of the beloved, leaving only the poet to contemplate the vacant scene, comes in the poem, "Of an Encounter." The title is in fact a misnomer, for no meeting takes place at all. It describes instead a missed opportunity. It recounts how the poet, sitting by himself in a colonnade, suddenly sees someone appear — the poem, like the previous one, is addressed to an otherwise nameless and genderless "you" — and, while stealing surreptitious glances at the stranger's "velvety white cheek white temple," the poet yearns to make eye contact. But, not daring to stare too long at the "sweet body," he looks away before any exchange, even of glances, can take place. As the days pass, the poet wishes for providence to arrange another "encounter," since he feels that, even though he has spent long nights painting in his mind each feature of "your portrait," time is erasing the sharpness of detail in his memory so that now he can no longer even remember "how was your hair and how your eye?" In the end, the poet is left alone to himself, with nothing more — or nothing less — than his verses to give him solace.

Throughout all of the *Hymns*, the characteristic emotional note of the verses — the "mood" or "state of soul" they convey — is thus restricted to a fairly narrow register. Every effort is made to foreground the accomplishment of the poet, who seeks either to assimilate or to suppress everything that lies outside of himself. Not just inanimate objects and things are submitted to this process: other human beings appear only in vague outline, rendered in the most general terms, only to disappear altogether without ever achieving individual identity or substance. As we will see, with regard to the targets of the poet's affection, there were some very pragmatic reasons for avoiding specifics, and his exclusive use of the second-person pronoun was part of that strategy as well. It is one of the oldest and least dangerous ways of referring to lovers of the same sex, neatly sidestepping the necessity — and consequences — of saying either "he" or "she." But there is more here than coyness or caution. The entire book is suffused by the unmistakable will to negate every natural phenomenon, to dissolve the world into usable material, with the result that every mention of seemingly well-known things is made to seem like a kind of private victory of the artist. Nothing exists — or nothing has value — that does not owe its very being to the poet and his words.

This is an extreme attitude to adopt, and the threat of solipsistic self-imprisonment it entails is perhaps the least worrisome of its implications. Indeed, later on George himself clearly understood and openly expressed what some of those deeper consequences were. "If I had had 20,000 soldiers when I was twenty," he once revealed, "I would have got rid of all the potentates of Europe." But to the young man who saw in poetry a way — no: *the* way — of overcoming his own feelings of alienation and loneliness while satisfying his hunger for power and authority, any potential danger that desire entailed fell away into insignificance before the immediate rewards. We should no doubt be grateful that the twenty-year-old George did not in fact have an army at his disposal, but to him poetry was no less a means of achieving domination.

Again, it would be a mistake to imagine that this agenda already appeared to him with anything approaching the clarity and focus implied by the preceding discussion of his poems. Nor should the impression arise that they are all accomplished works: several are weak, some are painfully trite or maudlin, and in not a few does the solemn, sacramental tone strike one as merely pompous and hollow. The *Hymns* were, after all, the effort of a neophyte. But it would be no less of an error to think that George, even at this earliest stage, did not invest his entire being in a conception of poetry that was anything less than unlimited. Put positively, art and poetry in particular, had now become for George the absolute means of exerting mastery over himself and the world.

Nevertheless, it should also not be forgotten — as much as, in George's hands, it became a peculiarly German doctrine and a singularly German fate — that it was from the French symbolists and above all from Stéphane Mallarmé that George first learned to believe in the awesome possibilities of poetry and in whom he saw the validation of that faith. In was in recognition of this debt, a gesture of homage and sincere thanks, but also an announcement of his own new and distinct beginning, that the title page of the *Hymns* was not signed "Etienne," but by another form of the same name, similar to yet sufficiently different from that of the French Maître. Henceforth he was called, in public and in private: "Stefan."

CHAPTER 7
Pilgrimages

George may have found a way to conquer the world, but, for the time being, the world seemed wholly unaware of its subjugation. Not that he was making it especially easy for anyone to notice. As would be his practice for most of the remaining decade, the *Hymns* were printed privately, in a very limited number — the first edition counted a mere one hundred copies — and distributed among a carefully selected circle of intimates and literary colleagues. In December 1890, just before the book appeared, he outlined to Stahl his motives for taking this course.

> I also wanted to say about my book: I have diligently avoided the noise of publication and promotion. It is above all intended for my friends. — If I want to make it available in Berlin Munich Darmstadt it is to enable distant acquaintances and those who are particularly interested to acquire it. If you will trouble yourself to visit my brother, Marfeldstrasse 13, you may receive your copy there and five others and if it is not too much trouble give them to your bookstore in Amalienstrasse — I leave it entirely to you and the bookseller to reach an agreement I say only that I don't wish it to be sold for under five marks. Perhaps not a single copy will be sold but what does it matter, the main thing is that it will have been there and you can take them back. Forgive me I am just going to Bremen where I am accompanying a family to the harbor.

The unnamed "family" — early on George developed the habit of maintaining a strict separation among his friends, revealing their identity and even their existence to one another only when, and if, it suited him — were the Peñafiels, finally returning home to Mexico. Apparently they assumed George would soon follow. In early January, Porfirio sent a card from New York saying that he would return the favor shown to them in Berlin and act as Etienne's "cicerone" when he came to the American metropolis. But they had all expressed "great astonishment" when at their departure in Bremen he presented them with a copy of the *Hymns:* evidently George had never even mentioned that he wrote poetry. This reticence, by now a familiar trait, sprang from sources other than mere private reserve when it came to his writing. Most likely, it was again under the direct influence of his cherished idol, Mallarmé, that he expressed such disdain for the mechanisms of publishing. Mallarmé often repeated similar sentiments, as he did in letters to his confidant, Henri Cazalis, where Mallarmé reminded him, "You know I have no desire for publicity, accepting it only on condition that I publish works which can assure for me a reputation of perfection." In Mallarmé's case, supreme fastidiousness mixed in with no small measure of contempt for the reading public rendered him comparatively mute. George, too, initially seemed to view publishing as a necessary evil, as a distasteful but inescapable aspect of a poet's existence, with the only other alternative being the relative silence of private publication.

In fact, however, and understandably enough, given the enormous psychological investment he had already made in poetry, George was more than eager to have his poems read and disseminated: but only among the right people, that is, within the proper "sphere." He thus hit upon an elegant compromise solution. By publishing his works privately, and in such small numbers, he had the luxury of having it both ways. He could enjoy the satisfaction of keeping his hands clean of the marketplace — and above all maintain absolute control over the entire process — and still make his poems accessible, but again strictly in a way and to people of his own choosing. George did not shun the promulgation of his work; on the contrary. And he harbored as much craving for recognition and even fame as any other even moderately ambitious writer. But it had to be on his own terms.

In this way, too, George made certain that he got the response he wanted, and the only one, even now, he would tolerate. The reaction of his English friend, Tom Wellsted, was jaunty but otherwise not of much use: he thanked George for the "nice book of poems, which I like 'muchly.' I have shewn them to a literary friend and he says they are much after the style of Walt Whitman." George's Swiss friend, Maurice Muret, after receiving his copy sent back a more substantive appreciation that must have met with George's approval. "If I'm not mistaken," Muret astutely ventured, "I believe I recognize in your verses our love of the symbolist poetry of Mallarmé and Verlaine, the subject of which we discussed so often last year. What captivates me the most at the moment in your verses is your language, which is so original and personal, your vocabulary, which is so colorful and so extensive, so full of suggestive words that say more by themselves than long phrases." That was fine, a little vague perhaps, slightly tentative, but certainly acceptable. Entirely inadmissible, on the other hand, was the reaction he got from his Danish acquaintance, Stanislaus Rozniecki. Here a much more measured tone generally prevailed, but, most objectionably, the letter from his Danish friend ended on a thoroughly unpleasant, which is to say, negative note. Rozniecki admitted that, considered as a whole, "much gave me pleasure, some things delighted me, and nothing left me cold," and he also noted the "close connection to the French symbolist school." Likewise, it did not escape him that George's poems "are written only for a small circle of friends, and I certainly understand that they will not be able to find favor with the public, that many-headed and fickle beast. And yet I must confess that it was often difficult for me to discover the correct meaning, indeed in some cases it was entirely impossible. Although I regret this and hold the firm conviction that the mistake does not lie with me, I was still unable to refrain from telling you my opinion." It was no more than a whiff of reproof but it did not take much to offend George. After a few more exchanges, with each correspondent becoming more defensive and prickly, they never wrote again.

More important were the echoes from Paris. But even here George was not making things simple. Understandably, he was anxious to have his book distributed among the opinion makers there, and his friend, Saint-Paul, seemed more than willing to help. The problem was that few people knew George's language well enough to grasp the subtleties of the poems, and most had no German at all. Saint-Paul, wanting to publish a French version of the *Hymns* in *La Wallonie,* had already prodded George to send translations, but strangely, George continued to drag his feet. Finally in January he grudgingly complied but sent only a couple of samples. Resorting to a telegraphic style in order to convey the urgency of the situation, Saint-Paul became more insistent: "Received translation. Many thanks. That's just what we need. But I need everything, everything — everything! you jealous father are keeping your children all to yourself! Did you send copy to Mockel? Do it. Useful. (102 rue Manderville — Liège). And I await complete translation. Don't deprive me of enjoying everything, now that I have so exquisitely excited the palace."

George did not like to be pushed. "To my dear friend Saint-Paul," he began in response, which sounded more like a pointed reminder than a greeting, "your postcards and your incessant pleas disturb me, I did for you what I was able to do, would that you could convince yourself that the difficulties I mentioned are not exaggerated." George made it sound as if only the technical challenges of translation were holding him back. "Consider, for example: the word 'esprit' has many meanings, if you open a French-German dictionary you will find them, maybe half, but the one you choose will never substitute for exactly the same sense — Take 'Gemüt' in German, to explain to a Frenchman what 'Gemüt' is would take an entire page of explanatory prose. If you translate the English 'how do you do' into French you have 'comment faites-vous faire' which means nothing, if you translate 'comment vous portez-vous' into German, one would understand 'how do you carry your own weight' and so on [. . .] and how can you hope to see my artistic and above all innovative ideas through a translation? very few of them would remain in one for you French."

Generally speaking, it was a fair enough point, but it seems an odd stance for someone to take who, only two months later, and turning again to Saint-Paul, asked, "What do you say to my plan to give the Germans a taste of some translations of Baudelaire? I have already done a few pieces. They have to be translated precisely, with all of their rhythmical melody (that's the main thing) and chiseled as if they were the originals." With characteristic good grace, Saint-Paul replied that "you are right to translate Baudelaire and it will undoubtedly be very good." Knowing — or sensing — George's predilections, Saint-Paul also obligingly sent a copy of Baudelaire's notorious "Lesbos" poem, which the French censors still banned from appearing in public editions of the *Fleurs du Mal*. But, if Saint-Paul noticed it or even cared, he was too tactful to draw attention to the discrepancy in George's behavior. Perhaps the German poet felt that, compared to the works of the French masters he revered, his own efforts would seem derivative in translation; he had openly hinted that this was the case. No doubt, a more complex set of feelings kept him from obeying Saint-Paul's requests. The fear of exposing possible weakness before a discriminating and influential audience was only natural. But to George, in the face of his preternatural craving for unquestioning adulation, coupled with the equally strong desire to preserve control over where and how his poems were published, it proved an insurmountable barrier.

In any case, he probably knew that he could count on his Parisian friends to champion his book even without the aid of translations. In the summer, Mockel published a friendly but generic review in his journal, *La Wallonie*, and in the October 1891 issue of *L'Ermitage* "Deux Poèmes de Stefan George" appeared, with French versions next to the German originals, accompanied by a well-meaning but rather hesitant introduction by Saint-Paul. Of necessity, it too was slight on detail, but Saint-Paul did not let the opportunity pass to claim the German author as an ally against their common foe. "One will see," he hopefully wrote, "whether Herr Stefan George is influenced by

French poets, if at all. He seems to stand under the stars of Baudelaire, of whom he is planning a translation, and of Mallarmé and Verlaine. Symbolism exerts its power of attraction on him. Thus, like the French symbolists, he awakens in Germany the same countermovement against the predominance of Naturalism."

Although George, with his remarkable linguistic gifts, would eventually translate some of the greatest works of European literature into his native tongue — including all of Shakespeare's sonnets and significant portions of Dante's *Divine Comedy,* as well as numerous works by contemporary poets from Italy, Poland, England, Denmark, Holland, and Belgium — it was primarily to the French, and in particular to Baudelaire that he initially devoted his best energies of poetic transposition. Over the next ten years he continued to modify and refine his renditions of Baudelaire's *Fleurs du Mal.* In the process he made his German equivalents more fluid and graceful but also gradually less beholden to the original text. At first, they were exact, scrupulous, even pedantic in their adherence to Baudelaire's words. In time, though, they became less a strict translation than a kind of variation on the same theme, remaining a tribute to Baudelaire while also becoming a deliberate assertion of George's own poetic personality. Even in its physical aspect, George's "translation" betrays the signs of an intervening will. Including only 118 of the 151 poems that make up the complete *Fleurs du Mal,* George's *Die Blumen des Bösen* actually constitutes a selection, an anthology, or, less charitably, an expropriation, a literary annexation. In the forward to the first printed edition of the translations in 1901, George openly admitted as much. There he somewhat truculently announced he had intentionally created "less an accurate reproduction than a German monument." He also explained, or rather emphatically did not explain but imperiously declared, which poems were not included and why. "Today there is hardly any necessity to mention that it was not the repulsive and disgusting images that had attracted the Master for a time which have earned him the great veneration of the entire younger generation but rather the zeal with which he conquered new regions for poetry and the ardent spirituality with which he penetrated even the most obdurate matter." This is a forced and a patently false representation of Baudelaire's work and of his historical impact. But that was a matter of utter indifference to the older George. In the end, his German version of Baudelaire, and of the other poets he translated, became only one more of the means by which he sought to take possession of the world, to render it his by making it conform to his own image of himself.

At the moment, however, still in deferential awe of his French masters and keen to receive and sustain their approval, George reigned in his urge to assert any personal or national prerogatives. In any event, he had other concerns. After shepherding the *Hymns* through the press in December and finishing out the winter term in Berlin, he set out on travels again, this time heading south. Making his way first to Munich in late February, where he stopped to visit his brother Fritz, he continued on into Italy, through Verona and finally to Venice. By early April he was back in Vienna. He had decided that three semesters in Berlin were enough, preferring to exchange it with the more venerable and hospitable institution in the Austrian capital. But he does not seem to have gone very often to university lectures, choosing to spend his time instead in the richly stocked court library, reading the German Romantic poets — and thereby making useful discoveries about the symbolists themselves — visiting the city's many theaters and spectacular new museums, and generally enjoying an atmosphere more congenial to his sensibilities than Berlin — pugnacious, Prussian, Protestant Berlin — could ever be. Presided over for what already seemed like an eternity by the grandfatherly Emperor Franz Josef, Vienna seemed in the spring of 1891 to exemplify everything Berlin was not: gracious, tradition bound, elegant, and confidently restrained. The Habsburg dynasty, in power for almost seven hundred years, stood as a living bond to medieval forms of rule. This, next to the undiminished role of the Catholic church in the Austrian monarchy, lent the city a pervasive air of seemingly unassailable tranquility and stability.

But within George there was anything but calm, and not even the relative languor of Vienna seemed to be of any use in restoring his inner equilibrium. Although he had been writing poetry continuously since the beginning of the year, the exultant victory he thought the *Hymns* had represented appeared to be slipping away, vanishing before a renewed onslaught of doubt, worry, even despair over his poetic vocation. The overweening optimism he had felt, the perception of himself as a kind of omnipotent demiurge who possessed the power to create or at least refashion the world, receded like a beautiful dream, threatening to be replaced once more by a vacant loss of faith in himself and his art. Or perhaps it was more like the morning after a drunken binge, with the dull sobriety of day painfully taking the place of the intoxicating reveries from the night before. Notably, George himself used a related image in one of the poems he wrote during this year of unabated inner upheaval. It is, like most of the verse he wrote during this period, still in the manner of Mallarmé: syntactically choppy, compact and allusive, with most of the connective tissue pared away. But the story it tells is nevertheless clear. The dissatisfaction, even disillusionment with accepting the shadowy constructs created by the poetic imagination as substitutes for the actual world gives way to the prospect that something more "real" and more "tangible" might emerge, that "true meadows" might be attained, as opposed to the chimerical fields he had previously conjured forth:

Mighty dream in which I believed
That I would prefer its daughters as loyal companions
To a single one from this world:
Long did I gaze at them.

Gleaming seductive peacocks of the night ·
Agents of avidly desired terror ·
In the morning the larks beat strongly

But with dignity like the clear day ·
Could there be in the pleasure in intelligible sounds
Which have resounded in my mouth now for months
The seed of a new epiphany?

Will I now return home to true meadows?

    This poem captures the fundamental question George addressed in his second book, the *Pilgrimages* (*Pilgerfahrten*), which appeared at the end of 1891. Like the *Hymns,* it was also privately published in a small edition, and, as its title indicates, it likewise still drew on a familiar store of images suffused with a distinctive, if unspecified, religious coloration. Although the tenor of this poem, which appears almost exactly midway through the *Pilgrimages,* is chiefly affirmative, albeit subdued, the emotional scale of the *Pilgrimages* as a whole wildly fluctuates.

    At the center of the book is the issue of what had really been gained in the poetic struggle of the previous year. It was a problem that George may have thought he had resolved, but which continued to rankle — precisely because, for him, the stakes were so high. In their entirety, the poems gathered in the *Pilgrimages* chronicle the renewed fight George was waging with himself and his work. In one, the poet reproaches himself for his earlier delusions of grandeur, now assuming the aspect of an empty achievement: "Was this then really the land you fought to gain?" he asks, implying that if so, it was not much. At the same time, he admonishes himself for succumbing to feelings of weakness, as if to imply that, although the promise of the *Hymns* is now felt to be hollow, there is no need to think he has been vanquished: "And do not say that your pain has become your guide / And do not exchange an honorable gown." In yet another, both notes register at once: that is, a tenacious desire to conquer, if not the world, at least himself, by means of poetry, coupled with the despondent sense that he is not fit even for this task.

Lament be silent!
Which envy too
Aligned with your gifts.

> Seek and bear
> And over suffering
> The song will prevail!
> . . . .
>
> At the foot of an oak
> He dug out a grave
> For his coat and staff ·
> They became a corpse:
> Now I am preparing a journey
> Of a joyful kind.
>
> Then the dam broke
> Holding back floods ·
> His eye became moist
> He moaned . . . I think
> I too should dash
> My lyre on the tree-trunk.

Following hard on this doleful reflection is another admonition to "leave the garment and expression of sorrow," even if he now avoids new forms of consolation, poetic or otherwise. And referring back to the earlier expression of hope for the advent of just such a departure, the poet now declares:

> You old images now slumber with the dead ·
> I lack the power to awaken you ·
> The true meadows were forbidden to me ·
> Now I am indulging in depraved splendor.

Not all of the poems in the *Pilgrimages* are concerned so exclusively with the role of the poet, or better, with George's understanding of his own poetic mission. Nor is the ambience as different from the *Hymns* as these lines might lead one to believe. Here, too, the natural world serves at best as a backdrop or quarry, and it is usually rendered in hazy, abstract outline. The poetic protagonist, as is obvious from the foregoing, is also ferociously lonely, disdaining yet also longing for companionship, searching for physical distraction and comfort (except, that is, when offered by women, and the poet reprimands himself at one point by saying to himself: "Forget your tears / For a woman / Your imaginings are false / Be still and stay!"). Also reminiscent of the artificial and highly wrought cast found in *Hymns* is the frequent mention of exquisite or rare objects, including "tourmaline," "coral pearl diamond and emerald," "heavy velvet," "morocco," and "fiery-red gold." But gone, or at least severely challenged, is the belief that the world can be vanquished simply by effacing its contours in a poem. This is not to say that the desire to harness reality had left George, or that he no longer believed in the power of the word to accomplish that goal. He merely realized that so far he had employed inadequate means, or at least that his resources were as yet too limited.

Pilgrimages is an uneven book, a work of transition, bearing as many traces of what the twenty-three-year-old had left behind as of what he was about to undertake. The veiled allusion to the poet's having "indulged in depraved splendor" was only one of the signs it contains of the direction in which George would soon head. Another comes in the penultimate poem of the book, like many without a title, but separated from the preceding one by a blank page, as if to emphasize its importance, or perhaps to indicate a temporal distance between it and its predecessors. It projects an autumnal scene, where leaves turning "red-yellow" and a "speckled brown" are mixed in with "scarlet and a strange green." Into this dusky setting, redolent of decay and ebbing life, a late arrival enters in the form of a youth — once again the gender is indeterminate — but the figure represents less a hope for renewed vigor than a final, pallid resurgence of waning vitality before the lowering darkness descends.

> Who approaches the nameless one
> Who grieves far from the crowd?
> A child in pale blue clothes . .
> Thus rustles a cautious wind
> Thus do dying roses smell
> Warmed by departing rays.

The afflicted "nameless one" — that is to say, the pilgrim, the poet — approaches the youth, and the poem concludes: "We lead one another by the hand / Like siblings in a fairy tale / Enraptured and with hesitant gait."

It is not known when precisely George wrote this poem or whether he had any particular person or event in mind when he did. Its somber twilight mood, while common enough in the works of other artists gloomily contemplating the end of the century, was also rooted in personal experience for George. For months he had seemed even more restless than usual, as if his inner turmoil would not allow him to stay in one place for very long (and perhaps also prompting the peregrinatory title of the collection of poems that were the fruit of that year). In July he had already left Vienna again, passing through Munich, alighting briefly in Bingen and then setting out for an ill-starred visit to London in September, which lasted only six days and ended unexpectedly in a hurried and turbulent departure. The next month, after a short visit to Berlin, he was in Vienna once more. Again, whether the "child" envisioned in the poem was the distillate of an actual encounter remains uncertain. What we do know is that all his life he had yearned for a comrade, a friend, a companion, and this almost manic itinerary may be a reflection of some kind of growing, panicky desperation. He had expressed the wish for intimate fellowship in verse as early as "Prinz Indra," and it had recurred in various forms ever since. Of course, the fact that George coupled friendship with blind obedience or at least uncritical approbation may have contributed to his difficulty in finding a suitable soul mate.

In any event, he already had a devoted admirer, but the association seemed less satisfying than he may have imagined it could be. At the beginning of the year, coinciding with the publication of the *Hymns,* Carl August Klein had taken to calling him "you great hero" and "your Majesty" in his letters to George, and he signed them as "Your Prince." Although these were partly no more than playful salutations, Klein was also acutely aware of what was expected of him as a reader and a "friend." In March, he deferentially congratulated George on his ongoing poetic "fertility," but when Klein dared to express a mild reservation about one of the new poems, George sent back a terse, cool note, prompting Klein to stammer in reply: "Rigorous criticism in the sense of the word is further from my mind than ever. I don't dare before your regal poetic figure. Dear Master!" But, at least for Klein, the attachment to George went deeper than a mere literary alliance. In another letter, again hailing him as "my lord and master," Klein, in the overblown, sexually charged language that was peculiar to him, bemoaned his own inability to produce. "I request that you disown your impotent disciple at any time and anywhere. This morning I dreamt of you. We were together: You so great and regal and I so small and weeping on your mighty breast." For his part, George also occasionally sent encouraging signals to Klein, including a postcard from Venice that quotes some lines by the poet August von Platen (a minor writer in the German literary canon who more or less openly expressed his love of men) and contains, for George, the highly unusual exclamation, "Oh, if you could only ride with me on the Canale grande." George had even gone so far as to dedicate the *Hymns* to Klein, memorializing him, slightly misleadingly, as "the true and faithful one since my youth."

But this was not really the relationship George had in mind. He was, at this point, still looking for someone he considered his intellectual equal, someone who shared his interests and ambitions, and above all someone who also viewed poetry both as the supreme expression of human action and as the privileged instrument for harnessing — and wielding — its power. That winter, in Vienna, he thought he had finally found him.

CHAPTER 8
A Child in Pale Blue Clothes

The coffee house was one of the many gifts Vienna has seemed to bestow in such lavish abundance on civilization that was really a gift to itself. The café was, as Stefan Zweig memorably described it, an institution of a special kind, "actually a sort of democratic club, open to everyone for the price of a cheap cup of coffee, where every guest can sit for hours with this little offering, to talk, write, play cards, receive post, and above all consume an unlimited number of newspapers and journals." In the best coffee houses one could find, Zweig said, "all of the Viennese papers and not just the Viennese ones, but also those from the entire German Empire and the French, English, Italian, and American ones as well, in addition to all of the important literary and artistic magazines of the world, the *Mercure de France* no less than the *Neue Rundschau, Studio,* and the *Burlington Magazine.*" And anyone was welcome: old, young, men, women, aristocrat, bourgeois, and revolutionary. Here, thanks to the rich daily diet of diverse and current information, anyone who cared to — or had the time — could find out about virtually anything of consequence taking place anywhere in the world. Zweig in fact attributed a good measure of Vienna's cosmopolitan air to its existence. "Nothing perhaps contributed as much to the intellectual mobility and international orientation of the Austrians," he proposed, "as the opportunity the coffee house provided of informing oneself so comprehensively about all of the events in the world and at the same time discussing them within a friendly and familiar circle."

One of the most famous institutions was the Café Griensteidl, occupying the ground floor of the Palais Herberstein on the Michaelerplatz across from the Hofburg and favored especially in the early 1890s by actors, writers, editors, and journalists. The young turks of the Viennese literary establishment met under its dimly lit vaulted ceiling, sitting and talking animatedly at the large round tables strewn with papers, magazines, periodicals, illustrated journals — and of course the cups of coffee that were the ostensible reason one came. The establishment became so closely identified with its argumentative, opinionated, and highly articulate clientele that it was informally known as Café Größenwahn, or "Café Megalomania."

Hermann Bahr, an influential critic and essayist and a regular of the Café Griensteidl, often spent his afternoons there, reading and writing letters, meeting friends, and catching up on the latest news. In April 1891, Bahr, just having returned from a six-week trip to St. Petersburg, hurried to the cafe to find out what he had missed during his absence. As he pored over the pages, he began to see it had not been much: just the usual tirades, polemics, scandals, and sensational chatter. In one of the journals there was also a long review of one of his own pieces, which he casually began to read, expecting that it too would produce no more than a little stimulation to the nerves and probably only a yawn. The name of the author certainly did not awaken any great hope: "Loris." "What kind of name is that?" Bahr thought, slightly bemused. "That's what you would call a poodle, or a delightful little coquette, but to be sure an elegant, very well-combed poodle." Chuckling to himself, he began to read.

"Then something strange happened to me, after only two sentences. I don't quite know what to call it. It suddenly gave me a violent smack — I can't put it any other way. My soul blinked from unexpected light. This, I imagined, was what the famous 'coup de foudre' was like that all the novels talk about. In great consternation, I threw my spoon aside and never touched my coffee again." As he read on, Bahr became convinced that the author, who had plucked and dissected him with such consummate finesse and judicious tact, could only be a Frenchman of exquisite culture, an experienced man of letters who had somehow previously escaped Bahr's notice. Wanting to know the identity of the author, he immediately ran over to interrogate the editor of the magazine where the review had appeared, but he would reveal no more than that the writer was in fact a Viennese, a local, perhaps even someone Bahr knew. Rereading the article, Bahr tried to form a mental image of the man: no doubt mature in years, probably between forty and fifty, clearly of old nobility, of refined and exacting intellect, widely traveled, learned but not pedantic, no, just the opposite: someone who had lived a great deal, and was now returning to a more contemplative existence, wiser, more sober and consciously resigned, maybe even slightly melancholy. The next day, sitting as usual in the cafe, he was startled by someone darting across the room toward his table. A young man, a mere boy really, came up and extended his hand, "a soft, stroking, unconsciously caressing hand of the great 'amoureuses,' like the soft, heavy blandishment of faded silk, and says soothingly: 'You see, I'm Loris.' " In reaction to this revelation, Bahr confessed, "I must have made the dumbest face of my entire life."

"Very young, hardly over twenty, and entirely Viennese," Bahr continued, describing his impressions after the initial shock had worn off. He thought the youth had

> the profile of Dante, only a little softened and blurred, in more gentle, supple traits, as Watteau or Fragonard would have painted it, except for the nose with strong, rigid, motionless nostrils under the short, narrow brow, as if made of marble, so hard and decisive, topped by smooth bangs. Brown, merry, trusting eyes of a girl, in which there was something reflective, hopeful, and quizzical mixed in with a naive coquetry, the kind that loves wry, sidelong glances; short, thick, shapeless lips, malicious and cruel, the bottom one turned inside out and hanging down so that one sees the gum. A fine, slender, pageboy body of gymnastic grace, flexible as a willow switch, and preferring to bend forward slightly in round lines, with the falling shoulders of those of sophisticated culture.

At a stroke, Hugo von Hofmannsthal became famous, for it was he who was hiding behind the precious pseudonym "Loris." In fact, Hofmannsthal was even younger than Bahr had thought, only seventeen then and still attending school. The old and illustrious Akademisches Gymnasium forbade its pupils from appearing in print, making the conceit of a pen name necessary for those who published anyway. And to say merely that Hofmannsthal became famous does not fully capture the nature of the phenomenon: old enemies who normally agreed on nothing, cynical critics who had seen everything, and aspiring young writers whose view of their rivals' success was sharpened by jealousy and spite, all concurred in this one instance. But they also all had the same unsettling experience as Bahr, finding it difficult to reconcile the stunning technical mastery of his work with the incongruous body of a teenager. At about the same time, the writer Arthur Schnitzler had also met Hofmannsthal by chance. Hearing the young man had written a little playlet in verse, Schnitzler invited him to his apartment, where he suggested Hofmannsthal read aloud before a few friends. On the appointed day, "Loris" appeared in knee britches and, visibly self-conscious and slightly nervous, he began to read. "After a few minutes," Schnitzler recalled, "we suddenly sat up straight with a start and exchanged astonished, almost frightened glances. We had never heard verses of such perfection, such flawless plasticity, such intense musical feeling from a living person, indeed had hardly thought it possible since Goethe. But even more miraculous than this singular mastery of form (and one subsequently never again attained by anyone in the German language) was the knowledge of the world, which could have only come from magic intuition in a boy who sat on a school bench during the day."

Late one evening in December 1891, as Hofmannsthal was sitting in the Griensteidl, leafing through an English literary review, someone walked up to his table, a "person of very strange appearance," he later recalled, "with an arrogant, passionate expression on his face (someone who seemed *much* older than I was, as if he were already in his late twenties) and asked me if I were this and that person — said that he had read an essay of mine and that what people had otherwise told him about me indicated that I was among the few in Europe (and here in Austria the only one) with whom he would seek contact: it was a matter of an association of those who had some idea of what the Poetic was." Hofmannsthal had already heard some people in the café say that there was a new "poet" in town "who came from the circle of Mallarmé" and he now realized that this must be the Stefan George they had been talking about.

For George, the effect of the meeting can only have been overwhelming. The initial impression he had received while reading Hofmannsthal's work was confirmed and intensified by the encounter with the author. In person, Hugo von Hofmannsthal exceeded even his most extravagant hopes. As they conversed, George noticed that Hofmannsthal spoke with ease and familiarity about the poets he revered: the names of Verlaine, Baudelaire, Swinburne, Rossetti, Shelley were naturally woven into Hofmannsthal's conversation, as were those of d'Annunzio and, of course, Mallarmé. Here, George thought, was a kindred spirit at last, a fellow poet who surely understood what moved him, who must feel what he felt, think what he thought. But George was also probably completely disarmed, as was everyone else, by Hofmansthal's extreme youth, his slender, athletic figure, his soulful eyes, and his bashful yet eerily composed demeanor. Our language is poor in words to describe our most individual experiences, those most laden with private significance, those which seem most unique and unrepeatable. Perversely, in such moments we always have to resort to the old familiar phrases, the worn-out cliches, the tired and trivial stammerings, uttered daily in countless different contexts by countless numbers of people to express, in each case, something entirely unique and very much our own. It may not have been said on this occasion, but there is only one word to describe what George felt when he first met the young Hugo von Hofmannsthal, and it was a feeling that he would increasingly make no effort to hide. For the first time in his adult life, Stefan George had fallen helplessly, totally and irreversibly in love.

For his part, Hofmannsthal at first pretended that he thought George was interested only, or primarily, in poetry. But soon enough he was forced to acknowledge that the German had much more in mind. Hofmannsthal had done nothing to give George the idea that his feelings were reciprocated, but Hofmannsthal was also too polite, too discreet, to give any sign they were not. Not that Hofmannsthal was put off by the fact that his suitor was male. He had earlier felt similar feelings for some boys he had known, but he had always suppressed those dark stirrings before or kept them to himself. Trying to come to terms with the unsettling aspects of his new acquaintance, Hofmannsthal wrote a brief, three-verse poem, which he sent to George. It began "you reminded me of things / that lie secretly within me / you were for the strings of my soul / the nighttime whispering wind." The lines are ambiguous, but they most likely refer to Hofmannsthal's own sense of detachment from the poetic endeavors of his contemporaries — few people in Vienna at the time knew of, let alone understood, the aims of the French symbolists — and he saw in the older poet the promise that he may not have to continue working in total isolation. Curiously, however, the little poem is titled, as if conveying a not-so-hidden hope, "To one who passes by."

On December 22, George responded, thanking Hofmannsthal for the poem but not failing to remark on the slightly off-putting title. "Your beautiful confession gave me great delight — only he who admires is able to create admirable things. But am I to you nothing more than 'one who passes by'? If by chance I do not see you this evening in the cafe could you indicate another place and time?" Over the next few days, a series of brief written exchanges were sent back and forth, short notes that conveyed a kind of nervous excitement, with both of them setting and then abruptly canceling meetings, until the Christmas holidays intervened, forcing a temporary respite. On the 26th, George, who had initially said that he planned to stay in Vienna only a short while, now wrote to Hofmannsthal, somewhat ominously, that "for the moment there can be no thought of my departure and when are you coming?" George, too, tried to harness the powerful surge of emotion he was feeling by putting them into poetic form, and, now becoming more insistent, he sent the lines to Hofmannsthal, beseeching him to "reflect and say soft words / To the stranger whom your broad gaze has moved." But mere words would not suffice. Soon, George began showing up at the Akademisches Gymnasium to walk Hofmannsthal home after school, which George ceremoniously took to calling "our academic conversations." One afternoon, abandoning all caution, George sent a messenger wearing a red cap to the Gymnasium to deliver a large bouquet of roses to the twelfth grader while he was still in class.

Clearly things had taken an unexpected and alarming turn. Hofmannsthal was becoming not just embarrassed but frightened as well. He noted in his diary that he felt a "growing fear; the need to revile him in his absence." Once more he turned to verse in the attempt to sort out his feelings, resulting in another poem inspired by the encounter with George, this one called "The Prophet." Notably, it is not addressed directly to its subject but describes him in the more distant, and distancing, third person.

> He received me in a long high hall
> That mysteriously frightens me with violence
> Sweet odors swirl repulsively about
> Strange birds hang there, colorful snakes,
>
> The gate slams shut, the sound of life dies down
> The soul's breath is hampered by a dull dread
> A magic potion holds the senses hostage
> And everything flees, helplessly, without restraint.
>
> But he is not as he always was.
> His eye entrances, strange his brow and hair.
> From his words, so inconspicuous and soft,
>
> Emanates a ruler's will and a seduction
> He makes the empty air swirl and seem stifling
> And he can kill without even touching.

It seems astonishing that Hofmannsthal could intuit, after only a fleeting encounter, essential moments of Stefan George's character. Yet there it all is: the sickly sweet scent of violence and aggression, the erotic energy, the hypnotic effect on others and the suffocating will. Although Hofmannsthal never sent this poem to George, the older poet began to sense that something was wrong. On Monday, January 4, he began to express impatient puzzlement over Hofmannsthal's refusal to answer his messages. "I don't understand your continued silence (are you forgetting already?) · or did you not receive my letter?" That Saturday, acting as if everything were normal, George sent both of his books of poems, the *Hymns* and the recently published *Pilgrimages,* along with a poem by Mallarmé, which he had painstakingly copied out in dark blue ink on heavy, yellow paper and held together by a cord with a tassel on the end. He also requested another meeting on the following day.

Hofmannsthal agreed to see George at 5 P.M. on Sunday in the Griensteidl but did not mention that he had asked another friend, Felix Salten, to accompany him. Not only did he no longer want to be alone with George, he now wanted to obtain a release from the increasingly unwanted and ever more vehement attention being bestowed on him. That Sunday, although no doubt surprised to find Hofmannsthal being escorted by Salten, George nevertheless handed him a sealed envelope and asked that the letter be returned to him after Hofmannsthal had read it. The letter is a long, rambling, and wholly unprecedented baring of himself, and as George himself recognized, he poured out everything that he had never said to anyone over the last few years. It was not so much a confession or a plea as the offer of a glimpse into himself.

> Don't let yourself be frightened by the secretive exterior! but you see even if we would conduct our academic conversations a dozen more times, the following would never be said.
>
> Silence would be better but further below you will find the reason why I broke it.
>
> Fortunately you can't entirely understand since you don't yet know the great affliction. You will still come to know it later since you are a true artist — I wish with all my heart that it is much later.
>
> For a long time I have yearned for that being of critical penetrating and refined intellectual powers who forgives understands appreciates everything and who would fly with me above things and appearances — and strangely this being should nevertheless have something of a nebulous veneer and stand under the constraint of a certain romantic conception of nobility and honor from which it can't free itself somewhat like Johannes in Rosmersholm.
>
> That being would have given me new impulses and hopes (for what I shall write after Halgabal is incomprehensible to me) and would have stopped me from the path that leads straight to nothingness. O the sentence that I wrote yesterday — no I will not mention it since to the other they are only so much paper ink pens whereas to me it means boiling gushing immaterial blood. . . .
>
> I have ceaselessly looked for and never found this superman just like the Other undiscoverable thing in the universe.
>
> But you can guess that from my books
>
> The great crisis of the soul was threatening.
>
> And finally! what? yes? a hope — a premonition — a flicker — a hesitation — oh, my twin brother —
>
> But let's become reasonable again — that is now past. I now see more clearly and know: At our age the significant great intellectual alliance is already impossible. Each one has already entered a certain circle of life in which he is stuck and from which he can never free himself · only small changes and adjustments are permissible. The great and important thing has already been taken care of and whoever wanted to give it another form (outside of the circle) would be an interloper . . .
>
> I am trying to suppress it and revile myself for having spoken · for why? perhaps the usual calm after one has smashed clinking rattling things such

as glasses windows vases and I want you to give the sheet back to me or destroy it immediately (along with those verses). Be silent. You are the only one who has ever heard such confessions from me. In this I blindly trust you. One who passes by.

As a declaration, George's stammering, half-concealing, half-revealing interior monologue left much to be desired, but it served its purpose well enough.

The same day, Hofmannsthal responded to George's tortured avowal with a no less opaque model of discretion,

> What should I say to you? how may I respond to you? I, who have heard your half-veiled confession, a confession to yourself and for yourself, something more overheard by chance than a present or a gift.
>
> And me? I can give only myself . . I cannot do otherwise, my being pours out the wine of its young life . . whoever can take, takes.
>
> I believe that a person can be a great deal to the other: light, key, seed, poison . . but I see no fault and no merit and no will that can help where Tyche acts mysteriously. The great crisis shall end, for that is its will.
>
> If you, who already know where the path goes from here, mean to bedeck me with the features of a savior: he may if must and he must if he can. I would like to able to support you, to thank you for showing me depths but you like to stand where you become dizzy and proudly love the abyss that few can see.
>
> *I* can *also* love what frightens me.

That evening, after Hofmannsthal had mailed his letter but before George had received it, they inadvertently ran into one another in the cafe again. Both were in a state of extreme emotional agitation. Hofmannsthal sought some pretext to excuse himself again quickly but not before witnessing George, who was being pestered by a stray dog, kick viciously at the beast, uttering, "Sale voyou," as it yelped and scampered away. For Hofmannsthal, burdened with such a finely tuned sensibility that, as a young boy, he often imagined he could feel his way into the soul of an animal, this was the final confirmation that he must avoid this person at all costs.

On the following Tuesday, having heard nothing for two days, George wrote again, his wounded pride and hurt feelings now expressing themselves in sarcasm and biting irony:

> How much longer this hiding game? If you want to speak freely (which is now also my intention) I invite you once again to appear on neutral ground. Your letter, which was so diplomatic — but was it my fault that of all places you came into that accursed cafe on Sunday? So please be so big and kind enough I want to keep the trouble and waste of time for you as

small as possible: Say (you do know my hours) when I can expect you on the Kärnthnerring (city side) · we can then go into a nearby cafe of your choice.

I will explain my tactless pressing demands.

Hofmannsthal made no motion to see George at the indicated place, and on the following day, without any accompanying explanation, he returned the *Hymns* and the *Pilgrimages* to their author, hoping that this mute gesture would be a sufficiently clear indication of his own intentions. On receiving the books, George appeared unannounced at Hofmannsthal's house. It is unknown what passed between the two young men, but it could not have been a very enjoyable encounter for either one.

This last confrontation prompted another letter that very evening from Hofmannsthal, which he had delivered by courier to George's hotel. The letter does not survive, but it seems to have been uncharacteristically direct and, perhaps in Hofmannsthal's desperation to make the stranger stop tormenting him, deliberately insulting. After reading it, George also immediately sat down again, obviously in great distress, and wrote something like an ultimatum, attaching a separate note with the dark warning: "Please read this letter to prevent the most unpleasant consequences — as I already said I expect an immediate answer in my apartment." George also engaged a messenger to take the missives to Hofmannsthal that same evening as well. When Hofmannsthal read the contents of the second envelope, he must have blanched:

Yesterday the books — then today your words . . .

To be sure, if I had considered I would receive such a letter I would not have come this evening to you. Rather I believed it was the last thing I could expect.

So in response to something and God knows what something 'that you believe to have understood' you hurl a bloody insult at a gentleman who was about to become your friend. How could you have been so careless and thoughtless, even common criminals are judged according to obvious facts. You see I am speaking very soberly and when you calmly think in a few days or in several years then you (along with your esteemed parents whose only child you are!) will be very grateful to me that I maintained my composure so well and am not immediately undertaking what will end with your or my death.

I must of course refuse any further explanation until you take back the content of your letter.

I must speak with you immediately: do not play rashly with your life.

George also indicated that his messenger would wait for Hofmannsthal's answer. Under the pressure of time, and taking the threat seriously, Hofmannsthal hastily jotted down only a brief reply: "Excuse my nerves and great agitation for any perceived slight. I hope you will be satisfied with this explanation." He must have known that George would not, could not, be satisfied with this response. The next day, George once more pressed for a conversation, saying that "your lines from yesterday were sufficient — socially. You did not get any further . . . I hate bargaining and posing and I would not have pushed your hand away although your blow still burns in my face." Even though he said he did not like negotiating, George closed by making a bizarre proposition: "I therefore say: either you seek to regain fully my respect and my affection (which you so despicably interpreted) or: we establish a 'status terribilis.' One of us leaves the city namely me — for you cannot. Thus I must speak to you without delay. I will follow your when and where."

Hofmannsthal never responded to this letter or its renewed demand for a meeting. In the meantime, he had informed his parents of the escalating situation, and they had understandably become, as Hofmannsthal already was, "very frightened" as well. Two days later, on January 16, Hofmannsthal's father intervened and took "the unpleasant story in his own hands" by writing a letter to the violent young man who was threatening the life of his son. Hofmannsthal *père* asked George not to force the association and to refrain from contacting his son in any form. He also declared that he was prepared to explain the reasons for this request orally. Apparently, George accepted the offer. On the same day, George felt it was still necessary to explain himself further. The tone of this letter is much more placid, conveying mainly regret and a little embarrassment, but the aggressive, threatening tone is gone.

> Since I am now thinking of departing — from Vienna quite possibly for ever — I have to turn once more to you despite how much my pride resists being importunate. I would have wished for a reconciliation, not one at twenty paces but one face to face, but now I feel that I am not entitled to search for reasons and I accept that. — the following is for the future: If your son and I do not want to know one another for the rest of our lives, if he turns away, I turn away. For me he will always remain the first person on the German side who, without having previously been close to me, understood and appreciated my work — and that at a time when I was beginning to tremble on my lonely cliff; it is difficult to explain to a non-poet how tremendously significant that was. It could hardly be surprising that I threw myself on the heart of this person (Carlos? Posa?) and I found absolutely nothing indecent in it.
>
> What occurred has long been forgotten; forgiven I am more cautious and for me a favorable turn of events has occurred.

Furthermore, I exposed my soul in extreme detail to your son (there are only two people in the world who have been allowed to see as far) and it is understandable that I feel great shame at the thought that He is now a complete stranger to me.

Finally, there is such a great connection between my thinking and that of your son (my Algabal his Andrea are despite everything different children of the same spirit) and this separated-ness from the artistic directions in our native countries is and will remain a bond for us, even if he should stay in Europe and I go abroad.

I thus believe that I am not asking too much if I request that you (especially once I am over there) send me word now and then about your son's work since you wish that he does not do so himself.

Shortly after sending this letter, George left Vienna — not quite for ever, but he would never spend a significant amount of time there again and mainly avoided the city entirely. He went as far as Munich, where he probably spent time simply recovering from the ordeal. All in all, from the time he first met Hofmannsthal to the tumultuous climax of their association, only a month had elapsed.

Although George had promised to leave the boy alone, he already sent another letter to Hofmannsthal's father in early February pressing again for direct communication from his son: "I thought a word from him would also be essential — if for no other reason than for the chance that we might encounter one another somewhere. Should I need to resume my stay in Vienna I will inform you before doing so." George also demanded that Hofmannsthal return "a letter (it was explicitly requested)." The elder Hofmannsthal, mistakenly thinking that George had made the request of him, responded that neither he nor his son knew which letter he meant, but perhaps if George could say why he wanted it and describe it, it could be located. Put on the spot, George evaded saying directly what the contents of the letter were that he meant. "I would also like to explain why I want it back although it will be difficult — now after such a long time." Only a few weeks had passed since George had written his "confession," but it may have indeed seemed like an eternity to him, and describing it would only reopen the still fresh wounds. And it seemed as if the younger Hofmannsthal — to whom George referred only as "He" — was deliberately trying to make him suffer by pretending to have forgotten what George was talking about. "So if He cannot remember," George said, "how should I explain to you which letter I mean? since I don't remember the date (probably without a date) no identifying characteristic . . . end . . . beginning." For George, it was a painful and humiliating exercise. "I never doubted the 'good faith' of our discussions," he wrote, "but don't you feel how awkward things are when one speaks with a person one knows only superficially about something that is more than superficial?"

Apparently, the very fact that George had written and asked to hear from Hofmannsthal directly had upset the young man again and caused his father to repeat the agreement he had reached with George in Vienna. George had to explain his motives again.

> I would not have demanded a few lines from the hand of your son if I had thought it possible that I would thereby provoke any agitation — since I am now hundreds of kilometers away — I did after all understand you perfectly well during our discussion. I would have thought it would be much more embarrassing (although the possibility is slight in such a large city as Vienna) to encounter one another in the street or somewhere else. Should we look at one another — avoid one another — greet one another? just to put it in very bourgeois terms for a moment — — .

These last lines must have sounded as if George were planning to return to Vienna and perhaps was even planning a "chance" encounter. Once more, Hofmannsthal's father felt it necessary to remind George that such a meeting would not be welcome. George responded with a final, aggrieved letter to Hofmannsthal senior, no longer even trying to conceal his wounded pride. The entire affair, he wrote, may have seemed trivial to the older man, and perhaps as no more than an annoyance to his son, but "all of this was no small matter for me. You need not have the slightest fear that *I* will ever take the first steps toward an approach. For that I am, despite your pacifying elaborations, too deeply offended." But George assured Herr Hofmannsthal that "you should not expect any further annoyance from me in either oral or written form."

Although George and the younger Hofmannsthal reestablished written contact with one another later that same year and continued to communicate frequently thereafter, they did not meet again in person again until seven years later, in 1899, when they accidentally ran into each other in a Berlin cafe. It did not go well. In 1902, Hofmannsthal reminded George of the incident, saying, "You were estranged from me at that time in a way that was almost incomprehensible, and is today still difficult to grasp." Four years later, in 1906, after a several more attempts at a rapprochement, all more or less unsuccessful, the relationship finally and decisively ended.

To the last, George and his associates always claimed they admired Hofmannsthal as a poet, but they habitually ridiculed all of the work he produced as a librettist during his fruitful collaboration with Richard Strauss. Shortly before the First World War, when a young initiate in George's circle naively expressed enthusiasm for the *Rosenkavalier,* which had just premiered in Munich, and said a few admiring words about the author of the text, an older friend of George's said, "Oh, you're speaking about the poet Hofmannsthal! He was enormous. But he died in 1906. The libretto is by a cousin of the same name." Confused and chagrined, the young man initially fell for the jest. But even Karl Wolfskehl, who would become one of George's most loyal friends, recognized the extraordinary talent of Hofmannsthal, and once even went so far as to say that "Hofmannsthal's *natural* gift, especially that of the young Hofmannsthal, surpassed George's own. A mellifluousness of a sort that no German poet had in his beginnings (even Goethe's Leipzig songbook lacked it). Such mellifluousness is always unforgettable. Naturally, the old civilization of Vienna. Old culture and of course just as much weariness."

George himself viewed the break between Hofmannsthal's early accomplishments and later work, the supposed decline of his talent into the triviality of popular art, more bleakly and in more intensely personal terms. Asked once to explain how such a promising poet could have deteriorated so completely, George obliged by relating a story handed down by Tactitus concerning Nero. In George's version, the Roman historian claimed that Nero had governed superbly as long as his teacher had stayed near him. But when Nero was released from his teacher's supervision, he became worse, and when his mentor eventually died, the entire monstrousness of Nero's character finally manifested itself.

The comparison between the bloodthirsty and deranged exploits of the psychopathic emperor and the exquisite reserve, the sensitive humanity that marked Hofmannsthal throughout his life is so grotesque, so incongruent, that it succeeds in throwing far more light on George than he intended to shed on Hofmannsthal. But it is also an indication of the lengths to which George would go to punish anyone who denied him what he wanted.

CHAPTER 9

Algabal *the Decadent*

When George summoned the image of Nero, with its unsavory associations of moral degeneracy and unhinged folly, to describe Hofmannsthal's later apostasy, he actually evoked precisely the right mood animating their initial encounter; he just attributed it to the wrong person. As he had revealed to Hofmannsthal in the winter of 1891–92, George was already working on his third book of poetry, and even then he had worried that he did not know what to write "after Halgabal." *Algabal,* as he eventually called it, does indeed leave the impression of a conclusion, an absolute end, or, if not quite that, the reaching of some extreme limit. It is in its entirety an astonishing work that is unprecedented in George's career, because it is the first one that achieves a formal level that can be measured against his best verse. Yet the book is most remarkable not so much for what it positively says, as for what it indirectly implies. Much later, when he no longer needed his former French friends and allies and could thus afford to forsake them, George himself said of that time: "In France I found people with whom I could live and whom I could like. Of course, they did not understand my true nature. Many think that there is only something artistic in my first books, not the will toward a new humanity. Totally wrong! *Algabal* is a revolutionary book."

George left it to others to figure out what he meant by "revolutionary," but *Algabal* has always made people feel slightly uneasy. This was especially true of his later adherents, the members of his "circle," who were more than a little concerned that it might give his readers the wrong idea. Friedrich Gundolf, one of George's most gifted and most devoted followers, expended a good deal of energy insisting on what George was *not* doing in the book. "Neither the exotic nor the abnormal," Gundolf assured his readers in 1920, "neither vice nor riddle, neither psychology nor history attracted him" in writing it. Similarly, George's appointed biographer, Friedrich Wolters, categorically announced a decade later that "*Algabal* has nothing of the unmistakable Parisian perfume of the Baudelaire poems, nothing of the particular odor of French decay." Wolters declared outright that "whether the historical image of the late Roman emperor Elagabalus corresponds more or less, or not at all, to the poet's created symbol is of no importance." Saying what George *was* up to in the book, however, proved to be rather more difficult. Gundolf and Wolters, as well as many others, largely took refuge in abstract, and thus safe, generalizations about the book's aims and provided at best one-sided commentary on the individual poems. But in the face of their bullying assertions, which were calculated to stifle and silence anyone who was impudent enough to object, an "official," sanitized, dehistoricized view of the book long prevailed. As a result, *Algabal* was often shorn of its real significance, in terms of both its historical and literary origins as well as its larger meaning for George's life.

Seen from a certain perspective, the fears of his followers would appear to be wholly justified. Certainly the subject of the volume would tend to raise some questions — and not a few eyebrows. It was inspired by the life of the late Roman emperor Elagabalus, who assumed power in A.D. 218 at the tender age of fourteen and who was violently deposed and murdered only four years later. Elagabalus, or Heliogabalus as he was also known, is sometimes mentioned in the same breath with other, more famous Roman rulers such as Tiberius, Caligula, and Nero, who all presided over years of spectacular debauchery and inventive cruelty. But Elagabalus seems to have surpassed even these notorious reprobates in both the extent and sheer imaginativeness of his crimes. Elagabalus was in fact considered so detestable that after his assassination his body was mutilated and contemptuously tossed into the Tiber, all trace of his reign was expunged from senate records, and public monuments bearing his name were defaced or completely destroyed. The three main sources of information about the emperor — Cassius Dio, Herodian, and Lampridius — all vilify him, outdoing one another in painting a picture of unrelieved infamy and bestiality. Admittedly, each of these historians either had an ax to grind or interests to protect or was simply motivated by the desire to curry favor with the reigning emperor by placing one of his predecessors in an unflattering light. But whatever George's own view of the reliability of these sources, he assiduously studied their works, and it was against the lurid and scabrous backdrop erected by the historians that he raised his own *Algabal*.

The salient details of Elagabalus's life are quickly told. Born in the Syrian city of Emesa in A.D. 204, raised by his mother and grandmother, he took his name from the sun god he had learned to worship there as a boy. Once in Rome, his Oriental name was modified to Invictus (or Deus) Sol Elagabalus. He was proclaimed emperor while still in Syria, and when he embarked on the arduous voyage to the imperial capital, he took along a sculpture representing the deity that he planned to install along with his religion in Rome. It was not a conventional, realistic statue, but an abstract, symbolic icon, a huge black stone, or betilos, in the shape of a massive cone, gradually tapering off at the top. The phallic connotations of the object were lost on no one, least of all the teenage emperor.

Once in Rome in 219, he immediately took a wife from one of the leading aristocratic families but quickly tired of her and cast her off, forcing her to return in disgrace to common life. He is also said to have robbed a vestal virgin from her temple, forcing her to break her sacred vow of chastity; he soon became bored with her as well and casually abandoned her to her fate. Another wife followed, and another, all of whom suffered the same treatment. But then Elagabalus began to demonstrate broader interests. We are told that he had always shown an inordinate taste for elaborate adornment and luxurious vestments. "He wore the most expensive clothes," Herodian chuffed, "woven of purple and gold, and adorned himself with necklaces and bangles. On his head he wore a crown in the shape of a tiara, glittering with gold and precious stones." Shunning the wool and cotton clothes of ordinary Romans and Greeks, the Syrian emperor allowed nothing but the most costly garments to touch his body: "Only seric silk was good enough for him." His shoes, also made of the choicest materials, were covered with gems, pearls, and silver or gold. Romans, however, "considered this kind of finery more appropriate for women than men." This impression, that Elagabalus was effeminate, or at least not unequivocally masculine, was strengthened by his habit of going "out with painted eyes and rouge on his cheeks." Another historian mentioned that in "the public baths he always bathed with the women, and he even treated himself with a depilatory ointment, which he applied also to his own beard."

All this seemed bad enough. Most offensive to his later chroniclers, though, was that the presumptive master of the Roman world assumed the role of a woman in sexual terms as well — or, as Edward Gibbon gingerly phrased it, he "preferred the distaff to the sceptre." It was noted — and deplored — that even during his long journey to Rome he had been "living in a depraved manner and indulging in unnatural vice with men." Lampridius, who offered the most salacious version of the emperor's life and is the source George appears to have consulted most carefully, went on to say that Elagabalus installed a public bath in the imperial palace so that "by this means he might get a supply of men with unusually large organs." Couching his description in pseudo-evasive language, Lampridius suggested that the emperor also publicly engaged in sexually illicit behavior: "such was his passion for Hierocles" — a former slave and palace favorite — "that he kissed him in a place which it is indecent even to mention, declaring that he was celebrating the festival of Flora." Soon Hierocles was replaced by another paramour, this time a Greek athlete named Zoticus and "with this man Elagabalus went through a nuptial ceremony and consummated a marriage, even having a bridal matron." Dio tells us that, wanting to consummate the bond in every way, Elagabalus asked his physician to give him, by means of an anterior incision, an artificial vagina. Kissing his "husband" after the vows were exchanged, Elagabalus thereupon pronounced himself "Empress."

These were, for later observers and commentators, the most unwholesome but also the most characteristic aspects of Elagabalus's life and reign. Otherwise, his résumé reads like that of any other decadent emperor of the late Roman period: he is variously accused of performing ritual human sacrifices, of slicing open children to examine their entrails for useful portents, of harnessing naked women to a chariot and, while likewise naked, driving them about the imperial palace, and generally of engaging in a life oscillating between luxuriant profligacy and savage bestiality. It is said that he enjoyed having the path in front of him strewn with gold dust as he strolled about, that he surrounded himself with exquisite scents and flowers, including roses, lilies, violets, hyacinths, and narcissus, that he had his dogs fed on goose livers, and served himself and his guests rare and exotic aliments such as camels' heels, tongues of peacocks and nightingales, flamingo brains, and partridge eggs. He is also supposed to have held extravagant banquets in which the emperor, to amuse himself, would indulge in puerile pranks such as inviting twelve people who were bald, or only those who were fat, or blind, and so on. Sometimes he would have his guests served not actual food, but elaborate imitations made of wood, marble, terra cotta, or glass. While the emperor complacently sampled the very real delicacies set before him, he would inquire with mock solicitousness about the meal and receive stammered assurances about the excellence of his kitchen from his bewildered and slightly frightened guests. Afterward, as tigers and leopards roared in the torch-lit darkness of the palace grounds, bloody contests were waged among gladiators and wild animals, while the bejeweled and painted adolescent emperor idly watched on, surrounded by his doting entourage of eunuchs, slaves, well-endowed athletes, and vacant-eyed prostitutes picked up from Rome's back alleys.

Although the name of Elagabalus has remained relatively obscure, it has never disappeared entirely. In modern France especially, the memory of his misdeeds lived on, no doubt in part because of their appealingly subversive quality. Not surprisingly, during the previous century the Marquis de Sade had already mentioned his name approvingly in his *Justine et Juliette,* next to those of Nero and Tiberius. In the nineteenth century he even became something of a cult figure. The decisive impetus came from Théophile Gautier, whose novel *Mademoiselle de Maupin* of 1834 enflamed generations of writers, not least of all the symbolists. Gautier was consumed by the notion that the culture of his own time, like that of the Late Roman Empire, was corrupt, enervated, depleted, its possibilities exhausted, and generally on an inexorable path of decline and self-destruction. As a tonic to the pervasive sense of dreary sameness, to escape the numbing boredom with a world that no longer offered any surprises or enchantment, the characters of Gautier's works obsessively engage in a search for ever more bizarre forms of amusement. The protagonist of *Mademoiselle de Maupin,* Chevalier d'Albert, racked by ennui and yet still desiring new sensations and experiences, often fantasizes about what he calls "the impossible": "I am afflicted," d'Albert groans at one point, "by that illness that attacks powerful peoples and men during their old age." He soon reveals what this means concretely: "I have dreamt of igniting cities to illuminate my celebrations; I have wished to be a woman to taste new sensual pleasures . . . Nero . . . Heliogabalus." This was, as one student of the time has observed, a veiled but reliably unsubtle way of signaling homosexual, or "inverted," tendencies or desires. And, indeed, in all of Gautier's works homosexuality is a constant and central theme, along with the related phenomena of androgyny and hermaphroditism.

For Gautier's numerous ardent admirers — most notably among them Baudelaire, for whom Gautier wrote a laudatory introduction to the *Fleurs du Mal,* and Joris-Karl Huysmans, a long-time friend of Gautier whose novel *À Rebours* of 1884 was hailed as the "breviary of the Decadence" — the name of Elagabalus thus became indelibly fixed with the association not just of excess and vice, but also specifically, as it was then known, of sexual inversion. To be sure, it was not simply prurient interest or the private wish to confess secret longings that prompted all writers to dwell on the offenses attributed to Elagabalus or to similar representatives of the "decadent" late Roman empire. The predilection for topics deemed "unnatural" and "artificial," which easily translated into the associated notions of what was considered shocking, perverse, morbid, and evil, was only another expression of the greater effort in which all symbolists were engaged. It was a way of rejecting the values of the bourgeois society they uniformly loathed; it was seen as a generalized instrument of revolt, a convenient means of asserting their will over a world they perceived as adversarial or simply intransigent. As we know, this protest against nature was not solely, or even primarily, an artistic gesture, and the political undercurrents were well understood by those on both sides of the ideological divide. It was thus no coincidence, but rather yet another sign of the specific and enduring potency of this compound mixture that as many as forty years after George wrote *Algabal,* Antonin Artaud could still count on its continued resonance when in 1934 he called his book *Heliogabalus or the Anarchist Crowned.*

For George in 1892 the unification of aesthetic, political, and social subversion — which the figure of Elagabalus neatly synthesized to form a kind of symbolist, anarchic, and psychosexual amalgam — also made the boy-emperor virtually irresistible. But it bears repeating, if only because his later exegetes labored so mightily to insist otherwise, that each one of these elements is an essential and, on George's part, very much a consciously chosen part of the whole. Nor were the attractions associated with Elagabalus merely abstract interests of recent vintage, but issues that had pursued him for most of his adult life. As early as 1888, when he was in London for the first time, his friend Carl Rouge, harking back to a conversation they had already conducted in Darmstadt, had reminded Etienne that "you once spoke to me in reference to 'Julian' about the beauty of sin in antiquity (for which, however, you never gave a real example)." Unconvinced, Rouge had countered, equally unpersuasively, that "I have to admit that I don't see this beauty of sin at all in Antiquity," and he asserted that "the Ancients themselves didn't see it." What the younger George had meant by "the beauty of sin" remains obscure, but the fact that he was already thinking along those lines before he had ever set foot in Paris would indicate a more than merely scholarly involvement with the subject.

But the question of Elagabalus's sexuality, and its possible significance for the poet, has long remained hidden behind a veil of enforced secrecy and uncomfortable silence. It is surely no accident, however, that Karl Heinrich Ulrichs, one of the pioneers of nineteenth-century "scientific" attempts to account for homosexuality, and who openly identified himself as homosexual, also claimed Elagabalus as one of his own. Ulrichs, who lived from 1825 to 1895, insisted of himself and of those like him that, as he first put it in 1862: "We are spiritually women, that is sexually, namely in the direction of our sexual love." Ulrichs remained convinced that "Uranians" had the body of a male, but the soul and sexual nature of a woman, representing a physical and spiritual "middle" or "third sex" that should be recognized and accepted as such. (The word "homosexual" was not coined until 1869, and Ulrichs always preferred his own term, "Uranian," derived from the mythological Greek figure Uranus who was castrated by Cronus.) "The Uranian is a species of manwoman," Ulrichs proposed. "Uranism is an anomaly of nature, a game of nature of which we see a thousand examples throughout Creation." He even thought that "Uranism is a species of hermaphroditism, or perhaps a coordinated variant of it." For the rest of his public career, Ulrichs indefatigably sought to compile data attesting to "the presence of the female nature in Uranians," not neglecting to look to science, literature, and history for evidence to support his theory. It made perfect sense, then, that in his first publication in 1864, Ulrichs singled out the precedent offered by the Roman Emperor, Heliogabalus, by viewing "Heliogabalus as incontrovertible proof of his theory — and of the naturalness of the Uranian condition. For it was that emperor," Ulrichs reminded his readers with a little literary flourish, "who had once enjoined to his beloved to: 'Call me not Lord, but Lady.'"

Whether George ever read Ulrichs is not known, but it is quite likely, since he was certainly aware of his work and was unquestionably interested in the subject. A few years after the publication of *Algabal*, Richard M. Meyer, a professor of literature in Berlin and the author of the first — and positive — evaluation of George's poetry to appear in Germany, reported back to George the results of some research he had conducted on the poet's behalf. "My informant," Meyer wrote, "writes the following: 'I personally know nothing about the publishing house "Kreisende Ringe," but I hear from a well-informed (and I believe trustworthy) source the following: owner of the firm is Max Spohr, an extraordinarily wealthy man who is making an enormous profit with books on sexual matters of all kinds, who signs with *his* name, and on the side also publishes occult works, as well as novels, stories, etc.'" Meyer added that his "informant" further revealed that "the firm is quite respectable, it seems to me, but by virtue of the aforementioned main branch not first-class." Writing in his own words, Meyer concluded: "The assessment of this assessment I must now leave to you. As regards the 'aforementioned main branch,' I would say: an author has no sexe!" The last phrase, which in the original is in English, is odd, but it appears to be a euphemistic reference to the "main branch" in which the publisher profiled himself.

Max Spohr, whose firm was based in Leipzig, did not merely specialize in books on sexual matters in general, but specifically in works pertaining to the growing field of research into homosexuality. Spohr was also an activist in the nascent homosexual rights movement and on May 15, 1897, he founded the so-called Wissenschaftlich-Humanitäres Komitee together with Magnus Hirschfeld and a ministerial official named Erich Oberg. The purpose of the committee was to work toward the abolishment of Paragraph 175 and increasing public enlightenment about the nature of homosexuality. In 1896, one year prior to Meyer's letter to George, Spohr had published *Sappho and Socrates: How to Explain the Love of Men and Women for Persons of the Same Sex?* by his friend and collaborator Magnus Hirschfeld, soon to become the most widely recognized — and controversial — researcher and advocate in the emerging field of sexology. Max Spohr also published the influential *Yearbook for Intermediary Sexual Stages*. Edited by Hirschfeld from its inception in 1899 until the Nazis forced it to close down in 1933, its subtitle proclaimed that it gave "special consideration to homosexuality." And it was also Spohr's firm that in 1898 published the collected works of Karl Heinrich Ulrichs, who had died three years earlier. Spohr's name — intriguingly, in connection with that of the Darmstadt writer Wilhelm Walloth — also occurs in another letter to George, from Alfred Schuler, in 1899. Finally, George owned a scholarly article about Heine and Platen — in his *The Baths of Lucca,* Heine had viciously attacked Platen for his homosexuality — in which Ulrichs's works are extensively cited and discussed. If George was ignorant of current research on homosexuality, it was obviously not because of any lack of information or opportunity.

Ultimately, however, it was not decisive for George to know the work of Ulrichs to be aware of the intimate connection between the figure of Elagabalus and contemporary notions concerning the nature of homosexuality. It was so widely assumed among the French writers he admired, and it so permeated their works, that he could hardly have escaped its almost ubiquitous presence. One of the most impressive and widely noted retellings of the story came in the form of a popular historical novel, *L'Agoni,* published by Jean Lombard in 1888, the year before George had first gone to Paris. Set during the reign of Elagabalus and informed by extensive research — most of Lombard's information about the emperor was gleaned from Dio and Lampridius — the novel is a not very thinly disguised portrait of the late nineteenth century dressed in Roman garb. The program, if one can call it that, of Lombard's work is the "Révolution sexuelle" of the late Roman world, whose stated goal was to establish "l'universalisation de l'Amour Androgyne." What this entailed is explained by one of the novel's central characters. The new cult imported to Rome by Elagabalus, he opines, based on "the relentless pursuit of the male sex by the male sex, would not need the female sex, or rather human bisexuality, and would aid in the creation of the ANDROGYNE, the being that is sufficient unto itself because it includes both sexes." Like several other prominent figures of the Parisian avant-garde, Lombard was also an autodidact with a checkered past — he had worked his way up from simple laborer to successful *littérateur* through hard work, perseverance and guile — and he maintained strong anarchist sympathies. What set him apart, though, is his apparent belief that the path to salvation was paved by the elimination of sexual differences, or at least that, to his mind, the anarchic state was synonymous with an androgynist one.

While this may all sound like a self-serving plea for pederastic license, androgynism was a favorite and frequent subject in countless and otherwise unrelated works of the time. Probably no one helped promote the popularity of androgynism with more success than the charismatic but outlandish figure of

Joséphin Péladan, who adopted the royal Assyrian title "Sar," assumed the name of the ancient Babylonian king Merodach Baladan, donned fanciful costumes consisting of heavy dark robes and complicated hats, and espoused a promiscuous mélange of notions cobbled together from the occult teachings of Zoroaster, Pythagorus, Orpheus, the Knights Templar, and the Rosicrucians. Péladan promulgated his bizarre vision in a series of enormously successful novels known collectively as *La Décadence latine*, which began to appear in 1884, the year in which Huysmans's *À Rebours* was also published. All of the individual works in the *Décadence latine series* — each one decked out with such lubricious titles as *Curieuse!*, or *L'Androgyne*, as well as its transposition *Gynandre*, and so on — contain countless scenes of sexual aberrancy, with Péladan's interest predominantly fixed on androgynism. He pretended to deplore the symptoms of modern moral turpitude he described — it is not by accident that Max Nordau, that implacable critic of cultural decline and stout defender of middle-class values, quite liked Péladan — and the author of the *Décadence latine* insisted that the series was meant to serve as both a warning and preventive tonic. Whatever his intent, the number and vivacity of his detailed descriptions of all manner of sexual experiment certainly did not hurt sales of his books. Ever resourceful, Péladan also presided over a succession of art exhibitions during the 1890s — grandiosely dubbed the Salons of the Rosy Cross — that drew huge crowds: the first Salon, which opened on March 10, 1892, attracted over eleven thousand curious or perhaps merely bemused visitors. George, too, appears to have been fascinated for a time by this strange apparition, who combined in equal measure the role of magician, impresario, preacher, and confidence man. At the end of the following year, he made a point of going to one of Péladan's lectures in Brussels — and where, as it happened, he also ran into Verlaine.

When George said *Algabal* was a "revolutionary" book, then, he meant it in a way that encompassed but also went beyond Lombard's quasi-anarchic promotion of a "sexual revolution" as a means of hastening universal androgynism, not to speak of Péladan's disingenuous protestations that he was preaching the opposite. Still, they and their renderings of the enterprising boy-emperor cannot have been very far from George's mind when he sat down to create the comparably richer and darker figure of Algabal. In all probability, George simply took the association linking Elagabalus and various permutations of an "unnatural" sexuality for granted, knowing that it would serve as a dependable and effective shorthand for one part of his overall design. Yet when his official biographer makes a point of saying that "the poet appears in *Algabal* only in a suprapersonal image of himself, in a symbolic figure," then we should by all means take him at his word, not just in the spirit, but also in the letter. Algabal is not George, obviously, just as little as Algabal is identical with Elagabalus. But it is no less true that for George, who poured his very being into his poetry, to assert that he strove for anything other than a total immersion of himself in his art would be a trivialization or a lie.

With a concerted intensity unmatched by his previous two books, *Algabal* marks out the outermost boundaries — and hidden dangers — of George's burgeoning conception of himself and his work. In fact, in an almost uncanny way, the "symbolic figure" he chose to represent his ambitions and fears encompasses an enormously wide range not just of his poetic aspirations, but also of his private experience. Unlike either the *Hymns* or the *Pilgrimages*, *Algabal* is a sustained, coherent exploration of a single image, or symbol, rather than a series of thematically linked but ultimately disparate episodic portraits. Many of the same earlier concerns as before are still operative here as well, but they are drawn together by a tauter, more unified organization and, above all, by the central controlling presence of the titular character.

The book is divided into three main parts called "In the Lower Realm," "Days," and "Memories." The first section already presents a magnificent fusion of the elements underwriting George's view of his poetic task. For the subterranean "realm" or "empire" it evokes (the German word, *Reich*, rich in connotations, will repeatedly return in varying contexts throughout George's career) is not simply one entirely of the emperor's making, it also is emphatically and flamboyantly contrived. Referring to the emperor for the moment in the third person as "he," we read that "the landscape by the shore does not entice the master," who has instead built an alternative sanctuary for himself according to his own plan, with "the houses and courtyards how he conceived them." The underground grottos, lakes, hills, and fountains that make up this world are constructed not of their natural materials, but of exquisite stones, precious gems, and choice woods — rubies, diamonds, crystal, pearls, alabaster, opals, topaz, ivory, cypress, and beaten gold comprise Algabal's building materials — all illuminated by the flickering, artificial light of candles. In this, his private creation, "where no will governs apart from his own," and where he even "commands light and weather," Algabal has fashioned a self-made sphere that responds to, because it quite literally mirrors, his every wish.

There are several proximate literary models for this secret buried domain, where the elaboration of an alternative reality acts as an antidote to or substitute for the less than perfect one we know. Baudelaire's poem, "Le rêve Parisien" (*Les Fleurs du mal*), evokes a related world of hard, brilliant surfaces, dead and denatured vistas, and solipsistic silence. The tale, "Duke of Portland," which Villiers de l'Isle-Adam included in the collection *Contes cruels* of 1883, similarly describes a concealed dungeon, its vaults covered by Venetian glass, the floor tiled with marble and fantastic mosaics, where the story's protagonist, Lord Richard, lives in solitary splendor. The following year gave birth to the most famous of these reclusive master builders in Huysmans's *À Rebours*. Its central character is Duc Jean des Esseintes, the overrefined scion of an ancient and noble family, educated by Jesuits, and connoisseur of the Latin "decadent" period. Not incidentally, he is an avowed and knowledgeable admirer of Elagabalus. Des Esseintes is possessed of a complex, highly wrought sensibility. He locks himself away in his house, awakes only at sunset, and in lonely midnight reveries he devotes himself to "extravagant caprices" in rooms he has had made to resemble ships' cabins, monastery cells, and torture chambers. Des Esseintes never travels. In fact he hardly goes out, "since he believed that the imagination could provide a more-than-adequate substitution for the vulgar reality of actual experience." "Nature, he used to say, has had her day."

These and other literary parallels are obvious enough not to require much interpretive massaging. The worlds they depict, like Algabal's underground realm, act as concrete images of rebellion. Yet it was a rebellion not simply against a particular time or place, but against Nature itself. The artificial realms contrived by the symbolists are meant to embody, in tangible form, the effort to subdue and overthrow a physical world considered irretrievably debased, tawdry, and malignant — in short, too bourgeois. And in its place they install their own creation. Ultimately, they signify the attempt to assume the role of God himself. In one of Des Esseintes's monologues, for instance, he flatly states that "man has done as well as the God in whom he believes." As we know, this is a central tenet of the symbolist credo, and George subscribed to it as well. The emperor Algabal is not just a kind of alter ego, he is the fantasy fulfillment of George's long-held wish-dream: an omnipotent ruler presiding unchallenged over a world beholden to him, and to him alone, because it is completely of his own manufacture. Algabal and the world he governs are, moreover, also fairly transparent equivalents of his vision of the poet and his purpose.

But there was a problem. The heightened, vaguely sinister sheen of Algabal's underworld, with its petrified veneers and dampened, frigid glow, highlight its predominant feature: it is a dead zone. Apart from the emperor himself, this private reserve contains nothing that lives. At first, he seems proud of this fact, as if it meant he had prevailed over life itself. But soon he realizes that this infertility will finally threaten his own sovereignty. In the concluding poem of the first section, perhaps the most monumental and finely chiseled of the entire book and the first in which Algabal speaks in his own voice, this dilemma is directly addressed in the form of a dawning realization:

Neither air nor warmth my garden needs ·
The garden that I built for myself
And its lifeless swarms of birds
Have never witnessed a spring.

Of coal the trunks · Of coal the branches
And dark fields against a darkening slope ·
The unbroken weights of eternal fruits
Gleam like lava in the grove of pine.

. . . .

But how do I engender you in my sanctuary
 — Thus did I ask when I traversed it deep in thought
And forgot my care in pondering bold constructions —
Great dark black flower?

It seems the perfect, if vaguely repellent emblem of George's contradictory aims at this point: the "black flower" Algabal wants to cultivate has of course no equivalent in nature, but in conventional poetic iconography the flower is the symbol par excellence of a natural, benevolent fecundity, with no obvious purpose outside of itself other than to be beautiful. But the primary color of Algabal's underworld, with its landscape constructed of obsidian and coal — which is of course, not incidentally, the color of ink as well — is black, the shade of death. His "black flower" would thus be not just one more addition to Algabal's subterranean realm. It would be its crowning achievement, the quintessential artifice: a man-made contrivance that is simultaneously vital, somehow both inanimate, patently inorganic yet also strangely alive. It represents a kind of botanical analog to the vampire or, perhaps better, to Frankenstein's monster. It would be the ultimate clone: not just the creation of life out of inert matter, it would perform a fusion of life and death itself.

Even the most chary of George's followers recognized that the black flower was also, as Gundolf put it in unusually direct terms, "the sensuous-dark symbol for the secret of procreation." Somewhat more specifically, Ernst Morwitz, who was close to George for almost thirty years, understood the image within the context of a particular notion of sexuality. "Only softly does the wish for perpetuation and progeny assert itself in the 'Lower Realm,'" Morwitz suggested. "The emperor does not wish to be a father, he wants to give birth. Physical birth is not possible. Only the mind can shape the form of existence in reverse. Thus the emperor seeks to lead the life of a woman, as the history of Elagabalus reports." But we can be more precise still. In one of the poems in the middle section of the book, Algabal recalls how he would shut himself away from the crowd and gaze at himself in a looking glass: "And the mirror returned to the viewer / The face almost of a sister." Elsewhere, Algabal is described celebrating in the temple he had built to house the towering black monolith representing his God. But in George's version, in variance to what we know about his historical namesake, the massive idol does not possess only the stylized attributes of the male sex, but is explicitly said to have a "double form," which is to say it appears as an androgyne or hermaphrodite. The emperor, the high priest of the cult, seeks to model himself after his duo-form God, to assume its multiple attributes, even to take his place. Narcissus wants to become Salmacis, the dual-natured offspring of Hermes and Aphrodite, whose new name, merging those of both parents into a single term, symbolizes his/her double identity. And the black flower — that supreme hybrid, encompassing an even greater range of opposites than its maker — would be Algabal's signature creation.

At first glance, Algabal and his underworld would appear to offer a symbolic fulfillment of George's long cherished desire for absolute dominion in a realm entirely of his own making. Not only does the book adumbrate a counter-reality that answers to Algabal's every wish, but, by uniting both sexes in himself and his works, the emperor also seems to portend the divine ability to reproduce, to engender new life, to overcome even the death threatened by solipsistic asphyxiation. Except that the pall of sterility is merely held off, not permanently lifted. The hermaphrodite might solve certain problems, but it also evades others. Like flowers, which frequently possess both the male and female reproductive organs — the stamens and the pistil — but are unable to pollinate themselves, so too the hermaphrodite enjoys an abundance of riches but is still unable to bring life out of itself alone. Both, without external aid, are impotent and barren.

Significantly, the dominant temper throughout the rest of the book is not jubilation, or even contentment, but a heavy dread. A pervasive atmosphere of violence infects many of the following poems, and Algabal himself seems indifferent, desensitized, cold in the face of death. A slave who inadvertently startles the emperor as Algabal walks by announces he will commit suicide for having unintentionally given his master alarm. Algabal accepts this self-sacrifice as a fitting tribute to his sovereignty: "A broad dagger already projected from his chest · / The green tile is tinged by the red pool. / The emperor recedes with a scornful gesture." Likewise, in an episode based on the recorded life of the historical Elagabalus, his brother makes an attempt to usurp his power, to which Algabal responds by arranging to have him murdered. As the emperor descends a marble staircase, he sees below "A corpse without a head lying in the middle · / There seeps my dear, dear brother's blood · / I merely softly gather up my purple train." In another scene — also handed down in the chronicles — guests at a banquet are asphyxiated under a mass of roses dropped from the ceiling. And his savagery is not confined to his immediate circuit, but extends to the inhabitants of the whole empire. Algabal admits to himself that in his darkest days he had often decreed that "I want the people to die and groan / And anyone who laughs shall be nailed to the cross." Eventually, he begins to have premonitions of his own demise, but he announces his resolve to kill himself before giving anyone else the satisfaction of doing so. The book ends, however, uneventfully, not with an armed and angry uprising, or grisly scenes of self-immolation, but with the emperor quietly indulging in private reminiscences of his childhood and former glory — although this too represents yet another way of defying the power of the present.

Whether he realized it now or not, George had yet again reached a critical impasse. In practice, the promises held out by the symbolist doctrine increasingly appeared to be partial, empty, or worse. The attempt to subsume, indeed to replace, the world with the poet's word seemed to lead inexorably to precisely what the symbolists sought to escape: a kind of suffocating death, a forced silence imposed by a tacit acknowledgement of the futility, or rather impossibility, of the venture. Paradoxically, no matter how much the symbolists protested to the contrary, they at last fell into the same trap they thought the naturalists blindly walked into. The endeavor to erase reality by means of language actually gave language as much, and arguably more, power as did the allegedly naive faith in the ability of words to reproduce it. The symbolist poetic gospel, like the black flower and like Algabal himself, hubristically wanted to be everything and everyone: man and woman, beginning and end, totality and nothingness, life and death — only to succumb in the end to its own self-administered poison.

In September 1892, the first ten copies of the advance edition of *Algabal* appeared in Paris, identical in design, layout and typographical austerity to its two predecessors, and, unvarying in this too, numbering only one hundred copies in the final print run that finally occurred in November. But in the meantime, a severe illness had taken hold of George and had forced him to return to Bingen, a condition so grave that he did not fully recuperate until the following spring. Caution is warranted in attributing psychic origins to these kinds of physical maladies. Yet the coincidence is too tantalizing not to entertain the idea that the disorder afflicting Algabal came perilously close to destroying his author as well.

CHAPTER 10
Pages for Art

It was not necessary for George to fall acutely ill at the end of 1892 to make it plain that *Algabal* meant more to him than a simple literary exercise. Next to his clumsy, garbled disclosures to Hofmannsthal earlier that year, the book represented the most public admission of his most personal yearnings to date. The fact that the two revelations occurred more or less simultaneously and that they were both, albeit in different ways, overshadowed by humiliating failure and defeat, and that, even more disastrously, they had both nearly ended in George's death, only lent a gloomier cast to the whole episode. True, in neither instance had George articulated the nature of his sexual leanings in clear and unambiguous terms. He never did, and he never would. For that he was too proud, too secretive — and too wary. In Germany, as opposed to the relatively more liberal and tolerant France, the legal penalties for same-sex liaisons, quite apart from the inevitable social stigma they incurred, were severe and potentially ruinous. In 1871, under the watchful guidance and tacit encouragement of Bismarck, the existing Prussian edict outlawing homosexuality had been adopted into the new German penal code as Paragraph 175, which metallically stated: "Unnatural lewdness committed between persons of the male sex or by persons with animals is to be punished by prison. Loss of civil rights may also be imposed." If the equation of male-male attachments with acts of bestiality did not convey with sufficient force how the Prussian authorities regarded such matters, the consequent threat of imprisonment or even total disenfranchisement surely did.

This was, in addition to everything else, undoubtedly yet another reason for George's less than warm feelings toward Prussia. He was, and always remained, extraordinarily discreet about his physical experiences, and, given such strictures, it is small wonder that he was. But in his poetry he exercised much less caution, as if he felt that too much was at stake not to be as candid and truthful as possible. In an early essay on George, Hofmannsthal, perhaps in reference to this relative literary frankness, made the cloaked remark that "whoever lies makes bad metaphors." That there were perils in George's policy of poetic disclosure is obvious. And with *Algabal* a new level of risk had been reached.

In 1878, to cite only one example, a certain Friedrich Berthold Loeffler, who had written a manual for medical students preparing for the state examination in Prussia, took the opportunity to indulge in a vituperative digression while discussing medical details pertaining to Paragraph 175. He singled out for particular consideration the work of none other than Karl Heinrich Ulrichs, by then the most visible and prolific defender in the German empire of what would now be called gay rights. "Paederasty has been seen from time immemorial as the most shameful and unnatural vice," Loeffler intoned, "even in the time of the lowest dissolution of Roman emperors." Yet, he noted with rhetorical incredulity, there was someone in his own day who perversely tried to argue that "pederasty" was natural. Loeffler reasoned that the only way to explain how "today a man can have the audacity, in opposition to the whole civilized world, to present man-love as justified" would be, quite simply, to conclude "that this man is not in complete possession of his senses." "This man is the former Hanoverian Amtsassessor Ulrichs, who," Loeffler darkly warned, "takes on the risk of defending man-love and putting us back to the times of a Nero, Caligula, those disgraceful monuments to human immorality."

Such pronouncements by a public official would have given anyone pause. Ulrichs himself prudently heeded the warning and emigrated to Italy two years later in 1880. In George's case, having just published a book that seemed to celebrate precisely what Loeffler had condemned, also made him potentially vulnerable to similar attacks. Naturally, the hazard of being singled out as a contributing factor in the moral decline of civilization was comparatively low for the still unknown author. Too, George had taken the precaution of having his work published in Paris, in an infinitesimally small number, and he had even subtly altered the name of the book's historical archetype in a way that would have thrown all but the most determined pursuer off the trail. But, for anyone with enough imagination, patience, and prosecutorial zeal, the story *Algabal* told provided evidence enough. And, as the scandalous trial against Oscar Wilde in London would demonstrate with brutal effectiveness less than three years later, one could never be too careful.

While George retreated to Munich in February 1892, perhaps mulling over these and related matters, and also while nursing his bruised pride and battered feelings over the Hofmannsthal fiasco, his brother Fritz was making awkward overtures of his own to a young lady back at home in Bingen. One evening that month, as Fritz was escorting his companion to her door after a dance, he tentatively broached a delicate subject: "Fräulein Ida," he timidly began, "I would like to confide something to you. My brother Shtefan" — Fritz had evidently been instructed that his brother was no longer to be called "Etienne," but he was still having trouble with the new name — "well, our Shtefan writes poetry! And just imagine, his first poems have now been printed, and we can't understand them, not a single one of us, and I am convinced that you would understand them." Fräulein Ida Coblenz, the recipient of this flattering confidence, gamely declared her willingness to act as literary interpreter, and the next day she duly received a copy of the *Hymns*.

"The miracle occurred that I, a twenty-year-old, ignorant of the world, after having read the first poems, knew, not just felt, what I had in my hands. I gave myself absolutely and entirely to the sounds I had never heard before; I had become a Georgean; the first one there was." Ida Coblenz's claim to have been the first "Georgean" is almost certainly correct, but only in the original linguistic form in which she made it. For she had naturally added to the German word meaning a follower or adherent or simply an admirer of George — namely, "Georgianer" — the conventional suffix used to signify a feminine subject in German. Fräulein Coblenz, that is, was indeed the first "Georgianer*in*," and therein lies a story.

When Ida — or, as she was known to her family and friends, "Isi" — next met Fritz, she gushed with enthusiasm about his brother's poems. A week later she received a laboriously composed letter from Fritz — written, as if to emphasize the importance of the communication, on his father's business stationery — in which he related that he had told his brother in Munich about both her and her excitement over his poems. But he had not really been able to reproduce exactly what she had said to him, and his brother wanted to know if she would be so kind as to repeat what she had said to Fritz in a letter, which he would then in turn convey to "Shtefan." Apparently unruffled by this oddly roundabout way of communicating, she complied. After the passage of a further week, another letter from Fritz arrived and, adding a thousand apologies, he wrote how his brother urgently requested that she now write down more specifically what she thought of a certain poem in the *Hymns*, the one titled "Gespräch" or "Conversation." Good-naturedly, Fräulein Isi fulfilled this demand as well.

This, too, foreshadowed a future habit of George's: he liked to test possible acolytes by having them read aloud a poem on sight — usually one of his own, but it might also be one by Goethe or Hölderlin — and, based on the quality of the performance, the candidate would be judged worthy of further consideration or summarily dismissed. Isi's exegesis, while not evincing a particularly penetrating insight, was creditable enough. She at least did not commit the categorical error of confusing the Muse evoked in the poem with a real, flesh-and-blood woman, and that, to George, was probably the main thing. Granted, in her "examination letter" to him, she did write hopefully that "I am convinced, however, that the poet will some day find the embodiment of his Muse." But one could magnanimously overlook that as the romantic whimsies of an unmarried young woman. Overall, she passed the test.

Her reward was a visit from the author himself. "A short time thereafter," Isi later recalled, "I saw from afar, while I was sitting in the garden, a youth come up the steps in front of our house in a very light-colored suit, with a huge forest of hair that stood up so high in the back that the small round straw hat sat angled over his brow: Stefan George. The first time he called on me it lasted two hours, and that was the measure for all of his future visits — always a bit too much of a good thing. For George spoke very quickly in a very even, rather thin voice — it overtaxed me to listen to him for such a long time."

They talked — or rather he talked — about poetry, of course, and George told her that "he spent his time in Berlin, Munich, or Paris; among the French he had found artists with whom he felt a kinship: Verlaine, Baudelaire, Mallarmé." The only contemporary German artists he professed any admiration for were Max Klinger and Arnold Böcklin — symptomatically, both were painters, not poets. "He hated Berlin writers," Isi remembered him saying. "And it was one of the instinctive responses that intimidated and frightened me when he spoke of those 'naturalists' and at the same time bent down the corners of his mouth forming an indescribably contemptuous arc." Over the next few months, through the spring and summer as George traveled almost maniacally back and forth among the European capitals in search of . . . what? Friendship, companions, fellow poets, peace of mind and body, respite from nameless torments — he made a point of regularly returning to Bingen to see his neighbor and new friend. They took long walks along the Rhine and the Nahe rivers, following the broad, well-paved paths for hours, lost in conversation or amicable silence, sometimes without encountering another soul along the way.

What is one to make of this relationship? Photographs of George apparently taken during this time, possibly even in the garden behind the Coblenz family's house, show him, uncharacteristically, smiling. Someone who met George a little later in Munich recalled, "I believed that during those years a hopeless passion for a woman filled his soul." In 1898, in Berlin, another female friend, Sabine Lepsius, reported that one evening George reminisced about his younger years, about the time he had hardly known anyone in the city. " 'Except for One,' " he exclaimed, " 'and she was my world!' When we fell silent, moved, he continued: 'Nice, isn't it, if one can still say that about a person.' Much later," Lepsius continued, "I learned, without seeking to do so, who this wonderful woman 'Isi' had been." Someone who met George many years later also insisted that "the great love of the poet was Ida Coblenz." Even decades after George had died, Robert Boehringer, who became his legal heir and his loyal if sober biographer, stated more simply: "Frau Isi was, I think, the only woman who gained such importance in his life."

If all this is true, George managed to keep his emotions well concealed from their putative object. Ida Coblenz, by then Frau Dehmel, lived to see the publication of Sabine Lepsius's memoirs, which appeared in 1935. After reading the passage concerning herself, Frau Isi divulged that "it contains a word by George about me that I would never have believed of him, so that I was deeply shaken." The "word" that moved her so was presumably George's claim that she had meant the "world" to him. Yet Isi maintained that during their earliest conversations "he revealed himself entirely to me, we became friends. I write the word 'friends' hesitantly; what is most personal cannot be expressed. We meant a great deal to one another, each in his own way something unique — but we had a completely different meaning for each other. George, with his parchment-like skin, whose permanently cold hands I slightly dreaded, retained something lifeless. As much as I enjoyed every time I was with him — the monk-like aspect of his being deeply impressed me." Elsewhere she admitted to feeling a sort of physical aversion toward George, an instinctive repulsion from this person who she felt had manifested a "hint of a cold lifelessness which a radiant young woman would have had to perceive as being almost repulsive." Generously, she explained his own restrained behavior toward her as gracious and knowing tact: "He probably felt himself that even the slightest suggestion of any inclination would have broken our alliance." For his part, George wrote several poems to and for her, and he originally planned to dedicate *Das Jahr der Seele* (*The Year of the Soul*) to her, although he changed the wording of the dedication at the last moment. But he never seems to have revealed to Isi herself, by word or gesture, that anything more than a sincere friendship — warm, affectionate, even tender, but only a friendship nonetheless — united them.

Another possibility, less orthodox, less reverent, and yet equally plausible, emerges from an encounter that took place two years after Ida Coblenz first read the *Hymns*. In February 1894, George, once more in Munich, made the acquaintance of Leopold von Andrian, a friend of Hugo von Hofmannsthal and a poet of notable talent with whom George collaborated for some time.

The evening after they had first met and spoken in a cafe, Andrian went home and entered into his diary that he had met "Stefan George," noting that the experience had been "creepy and eerie." Andrian described George as having an "hermaphroditic exterior, such a sickly sweet, gliding glance, very Darmstadt-ish accent when speaking." It struck Andrian as being especially "strange that he, the twenty-seven-year-old" — actually, George was not yet twenty-six, but he always looked older than his years — "speaks entirely like someone who is in decline. About the poetic potency that is strongest when one is twenty to twenty-five, and that one then has to force oneself with more difficulty. — He says he can no longer endure all of the traveling — he says he needs peace and quiet, and everything depends on mere accidents. And that it would be good to have a woman or wife who would take care of one — and on account of the food." A few days later, Andrian wrote a letter to his friend Hofmannsthal that related the meeting in virtually identical terms, saying there as well that George reminded him of "an aging hermaphrodite."

Even allowing for the fact that this account may be tinged by Andrian's stronger feeling of fealty toward an old school chum than by a commitment to strict historical fidelity, the author of *Algabal* emerges much more believably from Andrian's description than from the slightly hackneyed narratives of unrequited, or even unrequitable, love subsequently offered by George's anxious and protective disciples. Admittedly, it is not an especially charming picture Andrian painted, but it is arguably the more accurate one: George, already appearing prematurely aged, felt exhausted, lonely, slightly defeated, and perhaps understandably in need of a little domestic comfort, if for nothing else, as he had told Andrian, then only "on account of the food." That this scenario bears all the hallmarks of a bourgeois existence for which George, as a practicing symbolist and closet anarchist, could have nothing but contempt is only an additional reason why he ended up rejecting it. But, in the spring of 1892, when he grasped the soft, warm hands of Isi Coblenz with his own cold and bony fingers, he was not looking for love; he was looking for a cook.

Meanwhile, more serious plans were underway. Ever since his first trip to Paris, where he had seen what an enormous influence such things could have, George had harbored the desire to found his own literary journal.

Following the adolescent experiment in Darmstadt, when he, Carl Rouge, Arthur Stahl and the others had put together the first, and only, number of *Roses and Thistles,* George had frequently returned to the idea of establishing a forum for "poetic and critical" works, as he had said to Stahl in early January 1890. He had apparently also conveyed something similar to Carl August Klein. That April, when there still seemed to be a chance George might emigrate to Mexico, Klein had worriedly inquired, "What is now to become of our journal?" Later the same year, Klein now wondered aloud to George "if it is not too risky to start a paper with [only] two men in place." But George appeared to have changed his mind, or at least to have formed a new notion about what his role in such an enterprise should be. "You understood my words 'I want to direct a publication' from an unintended angle," he corrected Klein. "I meant by 'directing a publication' submitting a book to be published. You see, I have not the slightest interest in journalistic trifles. Let's leave that to others!" Klein, ever sensitive to the slightest reproof, did not bring up the subject again for almost two years.

But what George had meant by leaving such "trifles" to others was not that he was averse to participating in a journal; far from it. He meant only that he did not want to bother himself with the mundane details it would involve. Luckily, he knew there was someone he could count on who was more than willing to shoulder the onerous burden of overseeing the necessary financial arrangements, negotiating with the publishers, assembling manuscripts, correcting proofs, organizing distribution, fielding direct inquiries, and conducting the time-consuming correspondence with contributors. George was a poet, not a businessman. For that, fortunately, he had Klein.

After George had "directed the publication" of his three books of poetry, the time seemed right to revisit the project of putting out a journal. Apparently, before the blow-up with Hofmannsthal had occurred, George had told the Viennese poet of his hope to inaugurate such a venture, clearly with the intention of winning the support and collaboration of the extraordinarily gifted young writer. Despite their estrangement, George remained convinced that Hofmannsthal was the only person writing in German who both understood and shared his convictions — and the only one with whom George would tolerate any comparison. Now, however, as he obliquely put it to Klein, a "certain agreement prevented him" from directly approaching Hofmannsthal himself. At that point, the exchange with Hofmannsthal's father was only five months past, and George had intimated something like a promise to him to stay away from his son. It would thus take some fancy footwork to woo the skittish Hofmannsthal as an ally and not provoke another paternal intervention. Dutifully, Klein assumed the role of intermediary, and in June 1892, he sought to reestablish communication by stiffly informing Hofmannsthal that "for the moment I am overseeing the business side of the journal plan of which Herr S. George informed you." Asking whether he was still interested in joining such an undertaking, Klein emphasized that it would maintain a "strictly exclusive character." "From what I know of you from your writings," he surmised, "I suspect the wish is alive in you not to immortalize your name and your words in those tasteless (so-called modern) journals that would only besmirch you." Klein further assured him "that I hardly need to say that no fixed program or school is being formed here: everyone who has the right to the name of artist shall have a voice here."

For close to three decades thereafter, until 1919, the *Blätter für die Kunst* (*Pages for Art*) would form the nucleus around which George constructed his life, indeed in some ways represent his central achievement. Over the years, many of the poems he later collected and issued as independent books were first published in the *Blätter,* and the energy he devoted to recruiting new talent to its pages was only the most external indication of its importance to him. Like everything else relating to his work, however, the *Blätter für die Kunst* meant much more to him than merely a literary enterprise. It was to become for a time the most visible, and the most successful, instrument of his relentless will to exert power over people and things, to set his stamp on the world. Conceived at first as a place for promulgating his own version of the "new art" he had absorbed in Paris, it gradually took on the role of an official organ, parcelling out the elements of a doctrine that only gradually became more explicit and refined. In time, to be connected with the *Blätter* was to involve far more than being a contributor to the journal; it meant that one subscribed to an entire system of belief, to a set of specific values, and above all that one recognized George as a spiritual, and not just poetic, mentor and guide. When George would meet a young man for the first time, he would often gaze at him attentively and ask: "How did you come into contact with the *Blätter*?" But more was implied by the question than meets the eye: for George the word *Blätter* became synonymous with what soon began to be called his "circle." In fact, it became so closely identified with the person of George and the movement he inspired that Friedrich Wolter's canonical biography of 1930 virtually merged the two into a single entity. *Stefan George und die Blätter für die Kunst* its title announced, followed by the subtitle *Deutsche Geistesgeschichte seit 1890* (The history of the German spirit since 1890), more than implying that one and the same phenomenon was being described.

Not that any of this could be foreseen in the summer of 1892, of course, especially since George, disdainful of dirtying his hands with printer's ink, was more than happy to have Klein sign himself as "the editor" of the *Blätter.* But there can be no doubt that, even at the very beginning, Klein was basically a front man — and a gratifyingly hardworking, compliant and unassuming one at that. All of the strings, therefore remained firmly in George's hands. The first order of business was gathering a viable cadre of contributors. Even the most gifted general needs reliable lieutenants. If Hofmannsthal suspected anything, he demonstrated his customary discretion by not letting on that he did. But he may have succumbed to a ruse all the same. He responded very positively to Klein's initial inquiry, indicating that "everything that you say about the lack of a program and exclusivity is very welcome to me." Klein must have known — because George would have told him so — that Hofmannsthal was almost as fastidious as George was about the company he kept. Hofmannsthal's friend, Leopold von Andrian, once claimed that "apart from George, Hofmannsthal recognized very few contemporary writers, especially German authors, as his equals." "I remember," Andrian added to illustrate the point, "his indignation when he found the name of a novelist who was then famous cited in an essay next his own as if they were of the same rank." While George was not accustomed to using flattery to get his way, when it came to the weighty matter of recruiting Hofmannsthal to his cause, an appeal to the younger man's vanity may not have seemed too high a price to pay.

Before he committed himself fully, Hofmannsthal did want to know a little more about the journal as a whole. How large would it be? How many contributors were envisioned? Would there be only poetry, or were critical and theoretical essays planned? But, unwittingly, he had already overstepped his bounds. To someone of George's sensitivity, these questions might have sounded like an implied judgment. Hofmannsthal's services, and good name, were desired, not his advice, much less his criticism. Adopting a condescending tone, Klein frostily replied that "the size of the journal will depend entirely on whether we will have enlisted four six eight twelve participants. There can be no question of popular critical essays." Obviously somewhat taken aback by this unprovoked rebuff but couching his surprise in diplomatic terms, Hofmannsthal assured him that "I am completely agreed with everything you say; I also have no concern for the 'paper,' nor for publicity, rather I am concerned solely about coming into contact with a necessarily small circle of people searching as I am and to get to know related works of art that are otherwise inaccessible." Responding to Klein's brusque dismissal of his innocent query, he clarified that "by prose essays I had imagined much less popular critical essays than rather reflections about technical questions, contributions on the theory of the color of words, and similar by-products of the artistic work process, the communication of which would, I think, certainly allow one person to aid the other." If this was a courtship, one could only shudder to think what the marriage would be like.

A further bombshell broke only a few days later. In June 1892, an essay by Hermann Bahr devoted to the "new" literary movement called symbolism had appeared in the Berlin periodical *Die Nation*. Instead of engaging in a long-winded disquisition on what the word meant, Bahr produced two previously unpublished poems that would serve, he wrote, "as convenient textbook examples." Especially the second poem, Bahr proposed, "contains, purely and distinctly, all of Symbolism and it contains nothing that is not Symbolism." Both were, he almost forgot to mention, by "Loris."

On July 10, Klein sent a stern reprimand to "Loris": "Herr G. has given me to understand that a circumstance has recently shaken confidence in you. He speaks of names which you have unfortunately begun to associate with yours and which we cannot possibly introduce into our undertaking." Klein further said that he had asked "Herr G." to take up the matter directly with Hofmannsthal but got the answer that he was constrained by that "certain agreement." Once again forced into a position of having to explain himself, Hofmannsthal replied, in measured words, that "I hope and presume" that a misunderstanding had occurred and that it was "above all a misconception that any arrangement prevents Herr George from writing directly to me and sending any inquiry etc. to me; our last conversation ended after all with the exchange of our postal addresses." Feigning ignorance of what Klein was otherwise referring to, he professed his innocence of any literary crime and insisted that he knew no "writer with whom I stand in anything more than a personal relationship, which one can hardly be called an 'association of names.'"

One should keep in mind that Hofmannsthal was still only eighteen, that he detested nothing more than open conflicts and thus avoided them whenever he could, and that he protected his fragile psyche by scrupulously adhering to the ritualized forms of politesse. But this seemed too disingenuous for George to bear. Dispensing with his proxy, he readily accepted the offered invitation: "I read your letter to H. Klein. We both shouldn't fool ourselves. Our last discussion in Vienna was only to satisfy a form · nothing lifted nothing new happened · you felt that to be true as well and acted accordingly · or did you ever write to me? I did everything to explain myself and the way I acted · if we go through life with mistrust and squinting at each other then it is because you wish it so." After thus clearing away, or in any case acknowledging, the larger obstacles, George then turned to the particular item of dispute: "the minor matter (which you did not guess) which recently made an unpleasant impression on me: when I bade you for poems you had none, but then a little later you did, only to have them printed in an arbitrary paper as 'textbook examples.' That's not much · but do think of the former, won't you, before you enter into regular contact with me (even if on the oh-so professional level)."

It was the first time he had communicated directly with Hofmannsthal since their rupture, and although George's passion had cooled, the wounds were still fresh enough to smart. Hurt pride tends to want company, and George's letter, while more candid than Hofmannsthal's, was calculated to sting. It did. "We agreed very clearly and calmly," Hofmannsthal calmly and clearly explained — it seemed all he was doing was explaining — "to write to one another as soon as one was in a position of receiving something worth knowing." As for the "expression 'textbook examples,'" he averred, it "characterizes very precisely what I intended in letting Herr Bahr have two poems of very minor importance." Hofmannsthal then sought to defend his position by going on the counterattack: "And is it not better, even in common literary circles, to help spread superficial but essentially correct accounts of the externalities of our views of art than none at all or misleading ones? One can certainly keep private opinions secret but not theories of art."

Perhaps it was simply the pleasure of having successfully reestablished contact, however charged, or perhaps it was a more malicious joy at seeing that his words had had the intended effect, or perhaps he actually believed — or wanted to believe — Hofmannsthal's version of events. Whatever the reason, George now responded in an expansive, even conciliatory vein, going so far as to address him as "dear friend": "We are both right. In a couple of things our feeling is simply different. But I decidedly disagree with you that your two poems (especially 'My Garden') are of 'minor importance.' I and those to whom I showed them were full of praise. And when would an artist such as you ever let something out of his hand of which he was convinced that it is of minor importance?" This was fine indeed. George had pulled off the trick of wrapping censure within a very seductive, and probably sincere, compliment. Even more generously, although still laced with an undertone of mild reproach, George continued: "You surely could not have seriously entertained the idea that I doubted your work whereas on the contrary I honestly pay tribute to everything you write. It was merely the how, with whom, the way in which things were done that I dared describe as being unpleasant to me. You are also mistaken when you allude to my wanting to keep views of art secret, the plan of the journal indeed proves just the opposite. But here too it matters to me 'how' things are done. You think otherwise. I: better not at all than halfway or a quarter."

Now it was George's turn to be disingenuous. What he really meant was: he would prefer not to do something at all rather than not do it exactly the way he wanted. And what he most wanted was for the journal to go forward. Sensing that the entire project was being jeopardized by these tiresome recriminations, rebuttals, and renewed allegations, George held out an olive branch: "Forgive me · I was a little combative. Now to the journal." The peace offering, rarely made by George and explicable only by the genuine admiration he felt for Hofmannsthal's gift — and perhaps by deeper residual feelings he could not openly acknowledge — actually worked. Over the next two months, the letters exchanged among Hofmannsthal, Klein, and George remained remarkably cordial and matter-of-fact, containing little of the peevish rancor that had marked the beginning of their negotiations. This is not to say that the fundamental basis of their relationship was not in serious jeopardy. As it turned out, it had sustained irreparable damage. The personalities of the two poets were simply too different, too incompatible, for a long-term truce ever to hold. Not long afterward, Hofmannsthal began to voice new objections, raise new concerns, only to try to distance himself entirely from George once again. They would perform this complicated, long-distance dance for more than a decade, breaking off their correspondence, letting months, sometimes years pass until one or the other made a hesitant gesture of reconciliation, which the other would just as gingerly accept, thus setting the whole cycle in motion once more. But not once did they personally meet again until the end of the century.

This time, though, the compromise lasted long enough for George to achieve his principal goal. In October, as George already lay in bed recuperating from the illness that struck him down after the publication of *Algabal*, the first number of the *Blätter für die Kunst* appeared, containing excerpts from George's own three books and Hofmannsthal's masterful, hauntingly melodic dramatic fragment, *Der Tod des Tizian* (The death of Titian). George's will had prevailed, yet again, after all.

CHAPTER II
Forging Alliances

As the foundation stone for the construction of an empire, the first issue of the *Blätter* seems an unsubstantial basis indeed. Besides the contributions from George and Hofmannsthal, it otherwise contained only two poems from George's school friend Carl Rouge — it was the one and only time his name would appear there — three short verses by a Flemish writer, Paul Gérardy, who was equally at home in both German and French, and the poem "Erkenntnis" (Knowledge), mysteriously signed by one Edmund Lorm. This latter was, we may remember, a slight variation of the pseudonym George had donned in the Darmstadt production, *Roses and Thistles,* and he used it here to give the impression of a larger group of contributors than really existed. Years later, George joked about this early necessity, saying that "there were no poets then; one had to divide oneself like a lower organism to increase in number." Five men masquerading as six, and only two who could make any legitimate claim to the title of poet: an unlikely inauguration to a new literary movement, but it was a beginning nonetheless.

Moreover, one of the most interesting items in the volume was not even a poem at all, but the laconic introduction, actually a kind of aesthetic mini-manifesto, which was signed solely by "the editor." In all likelihood, it was cobbled together from programmatic outlines supplied by all three main players. But it seamlessly joins many of George's most characteristic views, and even its diction has a distinctly Georgean ring. The name of the journal, it solemnly proclaims, already states its intention: "to serve art particularly poetry and literature, excluding all political and social matters." To elucidate what that meant, and to underscore its significance, the "editor" put into majuscules that the central desire was to promote a "SPIRITUAL ART" — *geistige Kunst* — "on the basis of the new sensibility and manner — an art for art." This latter phrase, a direct translation of *l'art pour l'art*, which we, of course, normally render as "art for art's sake," was an open acknowledgment of the journal's intellectual paternity. More explicit still was the claim that the *Blätter für die Kunst* stood "in opposition to that exhausted and inferior school that sprang from a false conception of reality." So great was the contempt for this unidentified "school," apparently, that its name was not even deemed worthy of mention, as if doing so would have irredeemably defiled the unblemished purity of the pages dedicated to Art.

Privately, George dropped this overly scrupulous mien. In August 1892, he had already alerted Mallarmé to the imminent publication of the journal, describing it as being "perfectly free of any naturalistic ties." George knew that Mallarmé would understand this remark in the way he had meant it: as a simple declaration, stating more or less that "we are one of you." In the same fashion, the introduction would have signaled to anyone with even a passing knowledge of contemporary literary affairs that it was as much a declaration of what the authors were for as what they were against. Yet subsequent and less than impartial interpreters of George's achievement and of the place of the *Blätter* within German cultural history have instead stressed that its real originality is to be found here, in its resolve to combat the pernicious influence of the debased, sick, and thoroughly unliterary movement called "naturalism." Klein, for motives not just peculiar to himself, especially enjoyed calling attention to the disparity between the formal cleanliness of George's poems and what he derided as the "pseudo-poetry" being passed off as literature by filthy and decadent "naturalists." In their low-minded scribblings, Klein tells us, we can read of a cow "that dreams of a wonderful time digging in dung," or that "the sun spits its starry entrails into the night," or that the sun is again compared to a "rotten orange that splats open and stinks" and the sky, somewhat less obviously, is likened to a "hairy lout." This is all amusing enough. The not very subtle message of these and similar perorations, though, was that as opposed to this kind of fetid hideousness, George and the *Blätter für die Kunst* represented the rejuvenation of an art worthy of the name. Or, as the introduction to the inaugural number phrased it, "We believe in a brilliant renascence in art."

What was often overlooked, however, is that by the time the first issue of the *Blätter* came out, naturalism itself was already showing unmistakable indications of its impending exodus. Even as early as 1890, the indefatigable Hermann Bahr had announced, in an essay called "The Crisis of Naturalism," that "the signs have long been there, strange harbingers and warnings, that literature is approaching a change, heading toward new drives, away from an aging naturalism." And in the essay on symbolism two years later that had included Hofmannsthal's two poems and caused such great affront to Klein and George, Bahr stated even more categorically that "art wants to leave naturalism and is looking for something new." No one could yet say what that "new" thing might be — Bahr himself presciently suggested it might emerge from the movement variously called "Décadence" or "Symbolismus" — but in any case the prognosis for naturalism was not good. It would be unfair to say that the *Blätter* was engaged in flogging a dead horse — not an image Klein would have appreciated — but they were certainly vigorously whipping one already tottering on its last legs.

Possibly because the new journal preached a negative doctrine that many already agreed with, but had not yet clearly formulated what the journal positively stood for, the first few numbers of the *Blätter* were either dismissed or totally ignored. In December 1892, Hofmannsthal dejectedly reported to Klein that "I am having nothing but trouble with the reception of the *Blätter f. d. Kunst* in Vienna; we are really more lonely than I would have ever thought." Nearly two weeks later, the news was no better, in fact in some ways even worse: "What I have to report about the success of the *Blätter f. d. K.* in Vienna is in general rather depressing and for me in particular almost embarrassing to relate. I must have lent roughly fifty people the copies I have," he complained, "and from these fifty people I heard the usual, conventional, socially expected praise of my own contribution to the issue, whereas they reacted to the other poems with blank incomprehension or tactless derision (in the way in which Herr Max Nordau casually writes in his book 'Degeneration'). In fine, I can count on four to five completely sympathetic readers here."

Naturally, the argument could also be made that this response was merely the logical result of the ambivalent, not to say schizophrenic attitude the *Blätter* took toward its own publication. On the front page stood the peculiar formulation that the journal was available to a "closed readership on the invitation of its members." At the same time, and just below this odd announcement, were the names and addresses of three bookstores in Berlin, Vienna, and Paris where "individual numbers" of the publication were readily obtainable. One could easily buy the *Blätter,* but the implication seemed to be that unless one was explicitly invited to *read* it, to do so constituted a gross indiscretion, almost the equivalent of opening someone else's mail. This sense was underscored by the introduction to the volume, which justified the existence of the journal in words that made the whole thing sound like an unfortunately necessary, purely pragmatic, but decidedly nonpublic affair: "If we distribute these pages then it occurs in order to discover and recruit scattered still unknown like-minded people." Just to read the *Blätter,* therefore, was a delicate matter. To do so would tacitly assert an allegiance, or something even more intimate; yet failing either one of these conditions irrevocably meant that one was an intruder, an interloper, an uninvited guest in a domain that was none of one's business. No wonder Hofmannsthal found less than half a dozen people who were well-disposed toward the *Blätter* in all of Vienna: the rest, with their ingrained bourgeois manners and sturdy sense of propriety, were probably too polite to read it.

That this reaction — or rather nonreaction — to the *Blätter* sprang at least partially from such complications emerges from a communication sent to George that November. Isi Coblenz remembered that, during one of their conversations that winter, he had mentioned that "I received a strange letter today from a young man in Darmstadt, Karl Wolfskehl is his name." Through a fellow student, this "young man" — he counted twenty-three years against George's twenty-four — had found out about the journal and had been lent a copy to read. "I must apologize," the poet's newest admirer confessed, "for having looked into pages meant for the eyes of friends who are kindred spirits, for having been intoxicated by blossoms and noble treasures that are not meant for me. I can say in my defense only that I respectfully and knowingly welcome the leap in the history of art with the most ardent zeal and that poetry in particular is the area that — to be sure not in a productive fashion — enflames my enthusiasm." He also humbly asked for permission to make a copy to keep as his own. George, as had no doubt been Wolfskehl's intention, was duly charmed and could hardly have resisted the humbly submitted request. "You have no need to apologize for your candid letter," George magnanimously answered, "still less for the fact that you had someone give you my works and that they give you pleasure. I am happy about every discerning reader. I cannot object if you make a copy, particularly since my books are now all available in the Press for Art."

Although they would not meet in person for another year, this brief, rather stiff exchange laid the groundwork for what became one of the longest lasting friendships of George's life, ending only when he died in 1933. Spanning four decades, the relationship to Wolfskehl was nearly unbroken, if not entirely unmarred, during that entire time, so that not only the longevity but also the continuity of the friendship remained unparalleled by any other of George's attachments. No small part of this extraordinary endurance is attributable to the degree of devotion Wolfskehl brought to George, a dedication one can only call fanatical: not just unquestioning but irrational, ferocious, and unwavering. A friend from Wolfskehl's university days named Georg Edward, who had emigrated in the early 1890s to Chicago, returned on a visit in 1911 to find Wolfskehl unchanged except in one important respect. "Only once did he seem strange to me," Edward recalled, "namely when I expressed the view that I liked a substantial number of his poems better than Stefan George's poems. At that, he jumped up from his chair, paced in giant strides from one corner of the room to the other and declared that this was a 'temple-desecrating judgment,' that his own things were not worthy of being compared to those of the Master, there was not a single person, not one poet, no artist who came close to him, he, who like 'the epitome of humanity, belongs to no time, to no country, to no world, appears only once in centuries.' " By that time, just before the Great War, this was by no means a unique perception of George; indeed, it was fairly common both within and outside the "circle." But Wolfskehl never changed his mind, nor did George ever see any serious reason to distance himself too greatly from his trusty lieutenant.

Close to six feet tall, stoutly planted on size thirteen feet, sporting a bristly, dark reddish beard and so severely shortsighted that he was nearly blind in one eye, Wolfskehl cut an imposing, even slightly theatrical figure. Given to eruptive outbursts of the sort Georg Edward witnessed, he was a passionate bibliophile, possessing an agile mind stuffed with arcane learning, a barbed wit, and wielding a dense, florid prose style so convoluted and allusive as to be sometimes impenetrable, all of which fit snugly together with his unabashedly mystical leanings. Born in 1869 in Darmstadt, he was thus only one year younger than George, but otherwise worlds separated them. The Wolfskehls were one of the oldest Jewish families in Germany, whose history could be traced back to 870, when his ancestor Moses ben Calonymus the Old, living in the Tuscan town of Lucca, introduced the Cabala to Europe. The family name Wolfskehl first appeared during the 1600s, but it was not until the early part of the nineteenth century that the banking firm, Heyum Wolfskehl & Sons, was established that created what soon became a considerable family fortune.

By the time Karl was born, the name Wolfskehl was one of the most prominent and respected not just in Darmstadt but throughout all of Hesse and far beyond. His father, Otto, was head of the bank his grandfather had created until it merged with a larger entity in 1881, but his political activity provided most of his name's luster. From 1875 until his death in 1907 Otto Wolfskehl occupied the post of city councilor for the National-Liberal Party, in which he additionally served as chairman of the finance committee. Before Wolfskehl's father died, he had even founded another bank, the Hessische Hypotheken-Bank, which implemented modern and innovative accounting practices.

Given the advantages bestowed on him by his patrician background, complemented by a prodigious intellect, Karl Wolfskehl became not just an unfaltering friend and formidable ally — as well as an unforgiving foe to their mutual enemies — but he also provided a welcome and much needed source of material support. The cost of publishing the *Blätter* was not exorbitant, but it was not negligible either, and, in the face of its dismal reception, it was uncertain whether they could keep it afloat. Even Hofmannsthal had expressed perplexity about this hard fact. "The financial side of our undertaking is incomprehensible to me," he had written in October to Klein, who he knew was responsible for all such pedestrian matters; "in what way can I do something for its maintenance?" Typically, Hofmannsthal tactfully — one might also say passively — avoided coming out and making a blunt offer of money. In case his euphemistic proposition fell on deaf ears, he offered an alternative by wondering if he should seek subscribers — provided, of course, they were suitably "qualified" — or attract buyers of individual issues. But he needed more information: "Please orient me a little." Klein, as usual, sent back a strained reply: "I have certainly informed you what the subscription price amounts to effective from this moment on — semiannually three marks." Wolfskehl took a more direct approach. In November 1895, for example, he sent a letter to George, asking if "I may permit myself to offer you a fifty-mark contribution each for this and the following two months toward the costs of the *Blätter*?" It was a sizable sum of money, totaling fifty times what Klein had originally set as the subscription fee for half a year. Wolfskehl knew that George would never accept an outright gift. But they both could keep up appearances and still attain their objectives by preserving the fiction that Wolfskehl was merely making a "contribution." However phrased, the infusion of cash from Wolfskehl's purse was as welcome as it was necessary. It is entirely conceivable that, had it not been for his deep pockets and unfailing, discreet generosity, the *Blätter* may well have withered on the vine.

For the moment, however, money worries were not foremost on George's mind. Sometime after Christmas 1892, Isi Coblenz, who had been sent the *Blätter* and knew of George's wish to recruit suitable contributors, wrote with what she thought was a capital suggestion: "Do you know Richard Dehmel's *Erlösungen*, published in Stuttgart? He could become a collaborator for you — there is a grand strain flowing through his works." Well-intentioned though her proposal may have been, Fräulein Isi could not have picked a worse person to put forward as a possible colleague. "Your recommendation of Herr Dehmel astonishes me somewhat," George wrote in response the following January. "A 'grand strain' does indeed go through the so-called song of humanity, which does not prevent the same from being one of the most doughy and most talentless creations." These were strong words, but normally he used even stronger ones to describe anything associated with Dehmel. Several years later, when Hofmannsthal and George were in the midst of a fairly stable entente, Hofmannsthal inadvertently committed a serious blunder by admitting that "of all the more recent productions in the German language nothing has really affected me except perhaps the poems of

Dehmel." Worse, Hofmannsthal found that "not a few" contained "great beauty, deeply exciting turns of phrase," and he even thought some were "unsurpassed." To say the least, George was not pleased. "What you furnish with considerable praise," he curtly responded, not deigning to set the hated name on paper or even to indicate he was talking about a human being, "for me counts among the worst and most revolting things that have come into my hands." Nothing, but absolutely nothing could redeem such a "complete lack of artistic talent" coupled, as it was, with such "artistic poverty and baseness of soul." On another occasion, after stepping into the room of a younger friend, George spied one of Dehmel's books lying on the bedside table. He immediately seized it and threw it to one side with the comment, "What poetic filth!"

What is curious is not the vehemence, even the violence of his feelings toward Dehmel — George was capable of searing, crushing hatred — but that he had them at all. On the surface, they seem wholly unfounded and disproportionate to their cause. Dehmel was not a particularly good poet, but he was not an unredeemably bad one either, certainly nothing of the order to elicit the wholesale denunciations George reserved for the slightest mention of his name. Clearly something else was at work. In February 1893, just after Isi Coblenz had commended Dehmel to George, the *Mercure de France* published a review by one Henri Albert, who lavished praise on a recently published translation into German of two poems by Verlaine. The translator was none other than a young poet by the name of Richard Dehmel. "Such a venture," Monsieur Albert announced, "undertaken by one of the best poets of the youngest generation in Germany, cannot help but be interesting, and M. Dehmel has applied here his subtle lyrical talent with extreme skill, which excels in the nuances and tender intonations of the 'Lied.' "

The most galling thing was not so much the assertion of Dehmel's rank, together with the inevitable and intolerable comparison it implied, but rather precisely the French critic's failure to compare Dehmel's translation with another one that had just appeared. The previous December, the second number of the *Blätter* had been printed, containing among other things three poems by Verlaine rendered into German. All were unsigned, but they stemmed from George himself, who had included in the issue further translations of works by Mallarmé, Jean Moréas, and Henri de Régnier. George had been meticulous about obtaining the permission of the authors before publishing his translations of their poems. A short preface explicitly, if rather grandiloquently, thanked all four "for their approval of our plan and the approbation with which they blessed us by their counsel." As he wrote to Saint-Paul in February, while complaining about the near total lack of encouraging noises from Paris: "Of course it is I who translates everything — only I did not sign my name so as not to have it on every page. As for Klein, one has to leave him a vote, that is, the decision to say yes or no, since he is the principal." It was useful to have Klein to fill out the roster, but no one should be under the mistaken impression that he did much more than lend his name.

Klein did have other uses. In March, at the behest of George, he composed an indignant letter to the *Mercure de France* taking exception to the article by Albert praising Dehmel's translations. "In the February issue under 'Journals and Review' you speak of a German translation" — Klein inserted an addition above the line as an afterthought specifying that it was an "extremely mediocre" translation — "of Verlaine by a gentleman whom I know personally and whom I judge absolutely incapable of translating Verlaine. Besides, this translation is illegitimate without the consent of the poet, without the consent of the editor." Despite all of his efforts during the last two years — the three books of poetry and now the journal — it seemed to George that he was not receiving the recognition he felt he had earned and more than deserved, whereas Dehmel was being praised of all places in the Parisian press. His scathing repudiations of Dehmel, then, were not composed of purely aesthetic judgments but were entangled with more mixed motives. It would appear that at least one component of his ferocious antipathy originated in the all-too-human emotions of professional envy and gnawing resentment stirred by the success of a rival George considered his inferior and within an area he regarded as strictly his own.

More irritations awaited him from what was quickly becoming a familiar quarter. The fragile accord among the principal contributors to the *Blätter* that had allowed the first numbers to materialize was already starting to fray again. In November, Klein had begun pressing Hofmannsthal to write a review of the journal for publication in a newspaper or literary journal to attract wider attention to their endeavor. Hofmannsthal, who disliked being coerced almost as much as George did, stiffened at the suggestion. "What for?" he asked, "Why not then go ahead and have my things printed somewhere else among strangers? Then I have apparently misunderstood the entire nature of the foundation." It was not, Hofmannsthal hastened to add, that he was apprehensive about "compromising" himself somehow; in all matters concerning his art he was, he assured Klein, fearless and resolute. "But please tell me clearly what you want and why you want it."

The rapport between Hofmannsthal and Klein — even apart from the clouded issue of the degree to which Klein was merely the mouthpiece for George in these sallies — had never been especially cordial. But now relations were rapidly breaking down entirely, approaching a nadir from which they, and the *Blätter,* might not ever recover.

In June, George intervened. Affecting ignorance of the skirmish taking place, he feigned wonderment that Hofmannsthal had remained silent for so long and asked if anything was wrong. Hoping to coax Hofmannsthal into a more cooperative mood, George also made what he probably thought would be another irresistible gambit on the younger man's amour-propre. Claiming he was acting on a suggestion made by several collaborators of the *Blätter,* George proposed appending a page to the next issue that would bear photographs of the poets who had appeared in the journal. Assuming the answer could only be positive, he asked Hofmannsthal both to give his assent and send a suitable photograph to use in the group portrait. Here, too, however, Hofmannsthal remained intransigent. "For my part," he wrote back at the beginning of July, "I would not like to include myself in the plan of a collective portrait; with poets it is precisely their faces that hold very little interest for me; in addition, such things are very typical among the publicity hungry journals from which we stand so far apart; incidentally I do not even own a single photograph of myself, nor a reproduction of an oil painting, nothing other than a terra-cotta relief."

It was as if each one were trying to outdo the other in the extent of his discrimination, as if to prove that he were the more refined, the more punctilious, the more pure. But matters had already deteriorated so far that the petty bickering was beginning to crowd out any substantive debate. Obviously something had to be done. George tried to take the high road again, saying that "in reference to the unfortunate portrait I regret not being able to comprehend any of your reasons, least of all, however, that you weave in the word 'publicity,' whereas it is only a question of distributing a souvenir to our members as the members of a family." It was a nice touch to compare the poets of the journal to a family — and soon enough George would make it clear that, if it was a family, then he was the paterfamilias. But he was being less than sincere to claim that he thought of the *Blätter* only as a private memento. Yet George also realized that a debilitating deadlock had been reached, that their energies were being dissipated in pointless squabbling, that the journal — *his* journal — was being endangered by this unrelenting and unproductive contentiousness. It was with evident regret, even some sadness, but perhaps also with the intention of presenting Hofmannsthal with an honorable way out, that he closed his letter by assuring him that "I hardly need to say to you that the loss of an artist whom I highly esteem and continue to admire would be irreplaceable to me." It was as if he were saying: I want you to stay, but you may go if you must.

A week later, on July 17, 1893, Hofmannsthal accepted the extended offer of escape. "Since it is impossible for me, probably through my own fault, to communicate with you, I would thus like to have my relationship to the *Blätter für die Kunst* definitively understood in such a way that whenever a contribution sent in by me is deemed suitable I am viewed as an occasional collaborator, otherwise as a neutral component of a favorably disposed readership." Apart from making a failed attempt to arrange a meeting in Vienna the following summer, George did not correspond with him again for nearly two years.

CHAPTER 12
Becoming German

Amid all these vexations, crises and tedious imbroglios, George never lost sight of his main objective. He was constantly seeking new contributors to the journal — he may have anticipated the loss of Hofmannsthal even before the open break occurred, which made filling the ranks more imperative than ever — ceaselessly traveling between Berlin, Paris, Munich, Darmstadt, and Bingen, and shrewdly sending copies of the *Blätter* to well-placed and influential writers throughout the rest of Europe. The great Belgian symbolist, Maurice Maeterlinck, for instance, gracefully thanked George for sending him a volume of translations by declaring that "I would never have believed such transpositions were possible." Likewise, the swashbuckling Italian poet Gabriele d'Annunzio, three of whose poems George had translated for the third issue of the *Blätter* in March, sent his own *Eligie Romane* by way of acknowledgment, inscribing it with a dedication to George, gushingly calling him "the most elect creator, dear brother." But these were isolated voices, hardly the clamorous recognition George repeatedly said he did not want even as he tirelessly strove to attain it. His single-minded tenacity, his unflagging resolve in the face of adversity — yet another extension of his indomitable will — was a quality that would serve him well in the years to come, when far greater difficulties threatened to destroy all he had worked to achieve. No such peril confronted him in the spring and summer of 1893, but there seemed every reason to feel discouraged.

Perhaps owing to some related sentiment if not of defeat, then at least of persistent frustration, the twenty-four-year-old George now began to effect a momentous shift in the way he saw and presented himself as a poet. Up to this point, there was little that would have differentiated him, on the surface anyway, from a progressive Parisian symbolist — except that he wrote in German. His poetic aims, his political beliefs — or what passed for them — his social pretensions, his cultural biases, his manner of dressing, even his sexual leanings: the entire ensemble could have been imported from the Left Bank. Of course, given his family background and his religious education, this uninhibited embrace of the French seemed only natural, even instinctive. Moreover, and for the same reasons, he was treated virtually like a stranger in his native country, whereas his French friends reacted to his wholesale adoption of them by cheerfully regarding him as one of their own.

He thus figured he could count on sympathy and a maybe even a little solace when, in January of the same year, during the dead of winter, he wrote to Saint-Paul from Bingen, lamenting that he felt as if he were "exiled in this dreary country." As often happened to him during the cold dark season, a depressing gloom had descended over George. Augmented by the lingering illness following the publication of *Algabal* and the apparent failure of the *Blätter,* his despondency grew to the point where he once again returned to the idea of leaving Germany forever. But now that he had embarked on his course as a poet and resided in a world entirely composed of words, leaving the country would have also meant forfeiting the one thing he had managed to bring under his control: language, and more particularly the German language. The looming question was whether he could do the same with French. In the same letter to Saint-Paul, although not revealing the full extent of his designs, George included a poem he had composed in French and asked him "what do you honestly think of these verses? Germany is beginning to disgust me."

Bravely, Saint-Paul took George at his word and he frankly, though still rather gently, gave his honest opinion. It was not that the poems were bad, but they would need a lot of work. "Everything could be completely fixed," he reassured George, "I don't want to discourage you — on the contrary, try again, and then we will see when we are together." Saint-Paul did not mean to be patronizing, and he probably did not suspect how much rested on his evaluation. But for George, this diagnosis would have amounted to a blanket condemnation, a declaration of his utter failure. His French was very good, virtually native, but writing poetry demanded an unconscious mastery of the language, a deep, almost prelinguistic feel for it that he simply did not possess. Rather than risk further humiliation and possibly total ruin, he instead realistically drew the necessary consequences and performed an abrupt about-face. At least it was now clear which road he had to take, even if it would be a treacherous and arduous one. "The winter spirits, which always inspire wild and grandiose things, drove me to French poetry," he half confessed to Hofmannsthal in April 1893, suppressing the part about Saint-Paul. "Now that plan is abandoned and I want to travel home again on a golden boat."

The weighty decision to commit himself entirely to Germany, or at least to the German language, was actually longer in the making than the mortifying exchange with Saint-Paul would suggest. In the second issue of the *Blätter* from the previous December, Klein had published an essay titled "On Stefan George, A New Art." It is not so much the attempt to explain this "new art" as it was an effort to ward off any suspicion that it may not, in fact, be as "new" or as original as Klein desperately wanted it to be. While expressing appropriate gratitude for Saint-Paul's selfless efforts to promulgate George's poetry through his translations and favorable notices in *L'Ermitage*, Klein did take issue with the general tendency of the Frenchman's appraisal. "He relates all phenomena to similar ones in his own country," Klein miffed, "and he calls Stefan George a descendent of Baudelaire, Verlaine, and Mallarmé." This was an unendurable notion to Klein: it was impossible that his "great hero" could in any way be derivative, dependent, or weak. He thus offered an alternative explanation, one that was much more congenial to his own views and more acceptable to him on an emotional plane: "In view of the brief period the young movement has been effective," he proposed, "one should speak rather of a meeting of minds on the same journey than of a following."

This was patent nonsense, of course: George owed virtually everything to all three of the poets mentioned by name, and he knew it, even if Klein found the idea unbearable. Klein himself perhaps felt a little uneasy about making such a bold and bald-facedly inaccurate assertion, and he sought to lend his claim a kind of retrospective legitimacy by writing, seemingly as an aside, that, "incidentally, the original sources of the 'Nouvelle Poésie' — almost all of its representatives make a distinct swing toward Germanic territory — lie in Germany, in German Romanticism." The logic does not work, even if the motive is obvious: Klein wanted George to stand free of any influence by French writers; but if, for the sake of argument, one were to entertain the hypothesis that he *was* influenced by them, then the lineage would still be German, not French. Klein also left open the question whether this meant that George was thus to be regarded as a German Romantic poet. In any event, the essay concludes, "We also have representatives of a new art and do not need to rely on other countries." Having eliminated all foreign contenders, Klein had to identify a befittingly illustrious pool of indigenous talent alongside — but not behind — which he could place his "Master": "Richard Wagner the composer Friedrich Nietzsche the orator the painter Arnold Böcklin and the draftsman Max Klinger. Joining them is a poet." It was indeed good company, and while not every one of the choices made immediate sense, most striking was that the list ostentatiously excluded other poets — and non-Germans.

This brief essay thus began the determined effort to make George into an unequivocally German affair. It was an undertaking that would be pursued by many of his other subsequent disciples, most of whom were far more subtle, far more resourceful — and some far less benign in their intentions — than Klein ever was. The motivations for this increasingly chauvinistic campaign were varied and complex, and as time went on the extraliterary implications of George's professed Germanness would become more evident and explicit, but also more disturbing. Here, however, in its first appearance, it had more to do with George's powerful desire to set himself apart, so as to set himself above, anyone he saw as a competitor. It was only later — vociferously abetted by his followers — that he transferred this private, psychological need into a larger ideological framework.

Still, that he shared — and was perhaps the real source of — the views expressed in Klein's essay emerges from an exchange he conducted with Stuart Merrill. As an American, he was a foreigner writing in French who, unlike George, did manage to write quite respectable poetry in a non-native idiom. In February 1893, Merrill wrote from Paris that "people here have too often said that you are inspired by Baudelaire or by Verlaine. Yet, in the *Pilgrimages*, I noted pieces of a most pure Germanic symbolism." Quite apart from the tenability of his analysis — one would be hard pressed to find evidence of a specifically "Germanic symbolism" in the *Pilgrimages* — Merrill's letter clearly came at an opportune moment. Even better, Merrill had also generously offered to write an appreciation of George that might address these and related questions more fully. George's response is unusual for its fulsomeness and detail, especially in a letter to a stranger, suggesting that he was particularly invested in the subject:

> I would be delighted if you wished to devote some lines to me in a review and to remove some errors circulating on my account. Errors that are easy to comprehend. For the French who speak about me have inexact ideas about our literature and the Germans know only very little about the most recent literature in France. Previously one called everything one did not understand 'decadent' now one says 'symbolist' tomorrow it will be something else . . Similarly, they used to call me a disciple of Baudelaire, today I am a disciple of Verlaine and tomorrow I will be a disciple of Mallarmé! Minor ignorances that amuse me. But, seriously, what has earned me the title of 'non-German' is the rarely used orthography (which is however that of the Brothers Grimm, the most German of men and the greatest of scholars) . . If I would recognize the influence of the French in my work

then it would have to be of the most vague and broad sort: the general rule that in poetry one must reach for the greatest beauty, purity, sublimity. Otherwise, in the *Hymns,* simple 'plein air' scenes, I see nothing foreign, on the contrary a sentimentalism reigns there that can only be German. In *Pilgrimages* you yourself found a very German soul. Most certainly, the entire book is conceived like a gothic structure. And finally *Algabal* I tried hard to find a trace of Baudelaire in it. No, if one absolutely has to go back to an influence, one would have to recall the fatal luxury of the Royal Palaces, of the most decadent king disguised as a Roman emperor as painted by Herodian, Zonaras. Baudelaire: but where?

It is hard to know what exactly to make of this self-description. One hesitates to accuse George of out-and-out lying. But the alternative, no less unappealing, would be that he fundamentally misunderstood his own poetry. A more lenient account, though still not without its unsavory aspects, would suggest that George, feeling underappreciated and neglected by his French colleagues and completely passed over at home, saw in Merrill's inquiry an opportunity to target two objectives at once. By repudiating any overt or specific French influence in his works, and by thus distancing himself from his teachers and friends, he could imagine he was punishing them for their failure to grant him what he thought was his due. Moreover, and related to this act of retribution for goods he deemed owed to him but withheld, he might thereby be able to assume a place within his native culture in what was perhaps the only way available to him. As a southerner and a Catholic, George had two major strikes against him; being perceived as essentially French, or "non-German," may have sidelined him forever. The Republic of Letters was an ecumenical state, but it still had national regions. If George were going to establish himself as a poet, he had to make a choice. Actually, a choice had already been made for him: he knew, perhaps even before Saint-Paul had told him so, that he could never contend as a writer in France. It was now Germany or nothing.

CHAPTER 13
A Group Is Formed

George's decision to cast his lot with Germany, to give up the quixotic notion of seeking his fortune, poetic or otherwise, on foreign shores, appears fraught with contradiction, even laced with a certain irony. All of his cognizant life he had been trying to escape the native grasp, either through actual physical flight, plans for permanent emigration, or more lately through his incessant peregrinations. His will to flee surfaced most eloquently in his conception of poetry as the realization of a surrogate and superior reality, as the creation of a separate realm in which the poet enjoyed an unchallenged supremacy. Even the boy's attempts to forge a private language had been in no small part expressions of his consuming desire to remove himself from the reach of hostile external forces — which in their collective guise had almost always gone by the name of Prussia, and later of Germany itself. After spending most of his adolescence and all of his adult life thus far trying to turn a mute and contemptuous back to his own country — a country, moreover, that so far seemed quite happy to return the favor — he now seemed to be prepared to assume the role of prodigal son.

The difference was that in this, as in everything else, George would make his return in his own way and on his own terms. For one thing, just because he could not be a French poet in France did not mean that he could not preach the same gospel to his benighted brethren back home. He may have disavowed his French masters in name, but in spirit he was still very much part of the fold. Henceforth he would thus speak in the vernacular, but the words would be a translation, an interpretation of an original French text for those who were otherwise unable to comprehend its message. His newfound commitment to Germany thus bore less of a resemblance to a hearty embrace than to a rather guarded attempt to keep it, and his fellow countrymen, at arm's length. He would devote himself to Germany but at most in the way a teacher devotes himself to his pupils or a priest to his congregation: he was not asking to be accepted but attentively listened to. "How long it takes," he still groaned a few years later, in 1896, "and how difficult it is to teach the Germans a little taste." All he needed was a pulpit and a place to erect it.

But there was no Paris in Germany, no single center of intellectual and cultural ferment, no one city where all of the bright and ambitious young writers and artists congregated to form a critical mass. Berlin he detested and frequented for purely utilitarian purposes; Vienna was out of the way and tainted by too many painful associations. The best and perhaps only viable option was to choose some other place that answered to as many of his needs as possible — and was as far away from Prussia as feasible — and to create there what did not yet already exist. As early as February 1893, Hofmannsthal had responded to a letter in which Klein, who lived in Berlin, had apparently hinted at such a plan. "The intimated intention of moving to a southern German artistic center seems very good to me," Hofmannsthal wrote, whose favorable endorsement of the idea no doubt partially grew from his relief that the contemplated move was to a German location and not an Austrian one. In October of the same year, at the beginning of the winter semester, George began his final term as a student at the University of Munich — he would never receive a degree — and his first longer period of residence in the Bavarian capital.

"Here life is simply livable," George later wrote from Munich to one of his collaborators, "for there are still minds and spirits here, something that has been entirely chased away from the skies of Berlin." He often contrasted the two cities but always to the detriment of the imperial capital. Not everyone was convinced that Munich was really preferable, and some dubbed it "Beer City" in snide reference to its perceived provincialism and sleepy pace — as well as for the well-known predilection of its citizens for the beverage. "Why do you begin [your letter] with a criticism of the beer city?" he reprimanded the same correspondent four years later. "*I see nothing of the kind. Munich is the only city on earth without 'the bourgeois' here there is only the Volk and youth. No one says that these are always pleasant · but a thousand times better than this Berlin mish-mash of petty bureaucrats jews and whores!*" This last fulmination uncovers at least one quality of Munich that it shared with Berlin: a pandemic and toxic strain of anti-Semitism, propagated not only by ignorant beer-drinking louts, but also by cultivated if highly eccentric visionaries such as Alfred Schuler and Ludwig Klages, both of whom George met in Munich in the waning months of 1893 and who remained close to him for the next ten years.

Klages, born in 1872 in the northern German city of Hanover, was studying in Munich and living in the same pension on Hesstrasse in which George had taken a room. A tall, lean, fair-haired young man, he must have soon caught George's eye, who introduced himself — still pronouncing his last name in the French manner — over dinner one evening. For his part, Klages registered that George possessed "a bony face with a strong lower jaw, a jutting chin, coarse cheek bones, somewhat overhanging nose, broad, flat, fleeing forehead, deeply furrowed by 'worry lines' " — this last was something George would describe to Klages as "un héritage de notre famille" — "strongly developed bulges over the eyes, flaccid cheeks, wan color, extinguished glance, and a relatively huge mop of hair." To Klages's question about what he did for a living, George regally replied he was "un poète maudit." Even though Klages was initially put off by this pretentious apparition, George persisted, visiting him in his room and delivering copies of his three books of poems, each fitted out with a solemn dedication. "The first time I read them I didn't understand a fifth" of it, he admitted to a friend in January 1894. But when George persuaded him to read aloud from some of Klages's own work, George's unrestrained enthusiasm for the verses led Klages to agree to have them published in the *Blätter*.

Close to the same time, Klages's friend Alfred Schuler, who had already heard of George elsewhere, asked to borrow the books from Klages. To the latter's astonishment, Schuler thought he had discovered in George not so much a poet but particularly in *Algabal* the proclamation of a kindred disposition. Three years George's senior, Schuler himself presented a physical appearance that was the diametrical opposite but every bit as distinctive as that of the poet. Short, pudgy, preceded by a gently protruding belly, he had a round beardless face, with large, bulging, slightly watery blue eyes, closely cropped hair, and even then the beginnings of a double chin. His tripping gait and sartorial style reminded some of an eighteenth-century French abbé, others of a Buddhist lay brother, and still others of a Catholic monk. He could always be seen wearing a black or dark blue habit, closed by a single row of buttons running up to the neck, and complemented on rainy days by a robe-like vestment topped by a pointed cowl.

As peculiar as Schuler's outward appearance was, his ideas were even more bizarre. A perpetual student of law, history, and ancient archaeology, he possessed a formidable if jumbled knowledge of the late Roman period and of Hellenistic and Byzantinian paleography, and he was a connoisseur of ornamental symbols, rites, and liturgical forms. But he was no scholar. Indeed he was defiantly anti-intellectual, refusing to take part in any scientific endeavors such as excavations, museological research, or grave explorations. For Schuler truly believed that he experienced the world from the perspective of a Roman from the time of Nero, and that in a previous existence he had actually lived during the reign of the Caesars. Everything assumed a vital, Roman reality to him, so that dilapidated stone cisterns, old gates, and abandoned copper utensils all provoked ardent rhapsodies from Schuler that were ignited by their evocative glow. Someone who knew him well said that "he was unable to eat any food of even the most obviously contemporary provenance, such as Bavarian dumplings or veal sausage, without immediately viewing this food in, as it were, transubstantiated form, as if it had been served at a Roman feast."

Schuler's great contemporary heroes were Nietzsche and the Swiss historian, Johann Jakob Bachofen, whose *Mutterrecht* (Matriarchy) of 1861 provided his principal inspiration. Schuler would have denied he had a theory, or a method, but in so far as one might formulate his technique for conjuring up the times of Nero, it would be something like the following: the ardor of life had burned most brightly among the ancient heathen peoples, a fervor that had been largely quenched by Christianity and then completely extinguished by the later Reformation. Thus, in his own day, only those people were still capable of the ardor of life in whom the old heathen fires still burned in what Schuler called a "blood light" (*Blutleuchte*). Scorning the exacting, methodical investigations of professional historians and archaeologists, whom he dismissed as blind and plodding pedants, he styled himself as a kind of oracle or medium who could afford direct access to distant times and places through his own experience of them. He treated ancient cultic objects, statues, fibulae, lamps, and tools as conduits to the world from which they sprang, insisting that his archaic revelations were the undistorted truth — more true, because more vitally experienced than the impoverished bookish knowledge of university professors. He actually went to Rome only once, and then for no more than a few days. But he returned claiming that by virtue of his hereditary blood memory, he had mentally reconstructed with clairvoyant certainty all of the structures and temples of the oldest parts of Rome, saying he had even received instructions from Pan in one such reconstituted temple.

The blatantly mystical, antirational, even psychotic bent of Schuler's mind was disturbing enough. But his hatred of reason, modernity, and especially of Christianity was fed by other, poisoned springs that made those delusions seem relatively harmless. Schuler was what one might call an unfocused anti-Semite. Anyone he deemed responsible for the historical dimming of the "heathen fires" earned the epithet "Jew" from Schuler. Luther, he thought, had certainly stood in league with the enemies of life, since he had violently banned everything that had survived within the Christian Church from heathen times, such as the cult of Mary. More generally, the Augustinian friar stood guilty of having initially caused the disastrous rift within the German people when he split the Christian church and thus the nation itself into two. Because of this supposed attack on the "vital substance," Schuler thus always referred to Luther, perversely, as a "Jew." Others who attracted his ire for related reasons, such as Charlemagne and even Bismarck, were likewise accorded this distinction. It was a blanket term of abuse, applicable as well to those within closer range. "Klages comes from Hanover," he once said, "the Phoenicians made it to Hanover, thus Klages is also a Jew?" But the evident preposterousness, even lunacy, of these indiscriminate expostulations should not deceive us about their malignancy, nor obscure the earnest reception they were granted by his numerous admirers. It would not be the only connection that tied him to later events, but it is surely not an insignificant fact that it was Schuler who deserves the credit — or the blame — for having unearthed an ancient symbol that had long lain dormant in dusty tomes, a symbol he therefore helped to popularize. For it was Schuler who in the 1890s resurrected a decorative motif often found on Greek vases and in Roman mosaics, and which at one point he even wanted to substitute for his own name: the swastika, or "hooked cross," as it is called in German.

Given his fervor for Nero, Schuler's interest in *Algabal* should come as no surprise. But here, too, the currents ran deeper, if no less muddy. One of his acquaintances characterized Schuler as "the clearest type of the hermaphroditic double nature" he had ever known. In this case, as well in others we have seen, "hermaphrodism" was simply the customary euphemism for what was otherwise called "sexual inversion" or "Uranism." Schuler's disdain for conventional morality was explicable, the same person went on, "by his homo-eroticism, which was feminine and primitive, fascinated only by male strength, by young soldiers and sailors, boxers and wrestlers, by muscle-bound workers in overalls and by strapping farm boys in lederhosen." Someone else referred to him, not entirely in jest, as being "half Nero and half woman." Yet, even if his personal inclinations tended in a single direction only, in intellectual terms he was mesmerized by all forms of human sexuality. If everything shone with symbolic import for Schuler, the specific content of the symbol was most frequently, and explicitly, sexual. He could hold lectures on the meaning of the virginal hymen, which he saw as the incorporation of the will to suffering and death connected to all sensual pleasure; or he could wax lyrical about the symbolic value of the uterus. In fact, he was convinced that much of ancient culture mirrored the shapes of the phallus and cunnus, citing as evidence the Circus Maximus in Rome, whose elliptical shape he thought followed the contour of the female genitalia, whereas the two upright, perpendicular metae at either end around which the chariots turned represented the male genitals. Countless other examples proved to Schuler that the ancient world had been suffused with erotic energy, embodied in its myths, religions, and artifacts, only to have been subsequently suffocated and annihilated by "Jewish Christianity." Again, he regarded these subjects with utmost seriousness, and it is reported that it was only with great effort that he was able to contain his furious aggression when a guest once indulged in a tart witticism about a phallic symbol in his extensive private collection.

Many of the people in Munich who knew this odd creature and lent an attentive ear to his rantings viewed him as an entertaining but basically innocuous "character," embodying a mixture of charlatan and genius, buffoon and fantast, while others justifiably thought he was simply insane. Years later, George himself claimed that he met Schuler through a psychiatrist who was studying him as "a lunatic." There is no corroboration verifying that Schuler ever sought or received any such treatment, although it sounds plausible enough. True or not, however, George's account does reveal his subsequent wish to dissociate himself from someone who played a substantial role in his life for well over a decade and together with Klages formed his most intimate ties to the Bavarian capital. Paradoxically, the nucleus of the Munich circle was completed by none other than Karl Wolfskehl, and it was partly over the presence of this unapologetic — and genuine — Jew in their midst that George's ultimate break with Klages and Schuler finally took place over a decade later, in 1904.

The noxious theories about Jews were of course not original to Klages or Schuler, but reflected instead larger forces shaping the rest of German and European society. Ever since the disastrous collapse of the Frankfurt stock market in 1873, many Germans who had lost their fortunes or jobs, or who merely saw in it a new cause for more long-standing miseries, searched for an answer to explain what had happened and found instead a scapegoat. Naturally, ill feelings toward Jews, born of an unholy amalgam of suspicion, ignorance, envy, and spite, were also nothing new to the nineteenth century, nor were they indigenous to Germany alone. But the word "anti-Semitism" did not exist until 1879, which is when it was invented — perhaps not entirely coincidentally, by a German. In the following years, several political parties sprouted up in Germany and Austria espousing anti-Jewish platforms, and hundreds of books and articles appeared with such unappetizing titles as *The Victory of Judaism over Germanic Culture* by Wilhelm Marr, or *The Jewish Question as Racial, Moral and Cultural Question,* published in 1881 by the notorious Eugen Dühring.

A professor at the Berlin university, Dühring became famous through the controversy that erupted following the publication of his book and carried out a series of polemical exchanges he conducted with Friedrich Engels, who objected to his portrayal of Jewish "characteristics" as being rooted in biology, that is, as being racially and genetically fixed and thus unalterable. For it was owing to the Jews' unchangeable nature, Dühring proposed, that the only way to solve the "Jewish question" was to expel the Jews. Other luminaries at the university voiced similar opinions, thus lending them a sheen of intellectual respectability. Most notable among them was perhaps the nationalistic historian Heinrich von Treitschke, who in the 1890s coined the unforgettable phrase repeated millions of times until 1945, that "the Jews are our misfortune."

With subtle differences stemming from their private obsessions, Schuler's and Klages's pronouncements about Jews mainly conformed to a depressingly familiar pattern. Presumably so as not to be forced to utter the loathsome sounds too frequently, Schuler even devised an alternative to the word "Jewish," preferring to say instead "Molochitic," formed after the name of the Old Testament god of the Ammonites and Phoenicians to whom children were said to be ritually sacrificed. Klages, who possessed the more analytic and discursive temperament of the two, took the time to expound his view that "the critical and intellectual principle, which conceals the growing barrenness of the soul and impoverishment of the instincts and is the actual parasite and cancerous growth on life, *that* is the principle which one most correctly designates with words such as: Judaism, Semitism, Jehovism and whose historical carriers are the 'Jewish people.' " One could go on. Suffice it to say that here, in Klages's words of hate dressed up in a travesty of reasoned argument, we have all of the essential elements of a doctrine that, only a few decades later, would take on a terrible reality.

George's own stance toward Jews was ambiguous and fluid, much less hostile and uniform than that of either Klages or Schuler, but also not free of its distasteful elements. It is true — though this is the classic and not very convincing form of exculpation for all kinds of prejudice and bigotry — that many of George's closest friends and associates throughout his life were Jews. It is also true that there is no record of his having uttered anything approaching Klages's or Schuler's vile beliefs. But something must have caused Hofmannsthal's friend Leopold von Andrian, when he met George in Munich in February 1894 during the first flush of George's relationship with both Klages and Schuler, to note in his diary that George was "entirely doctrinaire in art, which I hate, anti-realist, anti-Semite." In later years, George took care to moderate his language, giving the impression of a more tolerant standpoint. When one of his less liberal adherents complained that he was surrounded by too many Jews, he shot back: "I could have ten more Jews of the kind that I have around me, wouldn't hurt me in the slightest." It is admittedly a fairly equivocal retort, layered with ambiguity, but conventionally anti-Semitic it is not. Yet George was also capable of saying at times that "we" — meaning his circle of friends — "have too many Jews," or that "one Jew is very useful, but as soon as there are more than two of them, the tone becomes different and they tend to their own business." Similarly, in 1911, he said that "Jews are the best conductors. They are good at spreading and implementing values. To be sure, they do not experience life as deeply as we do. They are in general different people. I will never allow them to be in the majority in my community or in the *Yearbook*." A few years later, however, George also said that it did not matter if a person were a Catholic, Protestant, or Jew; it mattered only whether he belonged to him and his friends. That, in the end, was the most important thing for George: the external world was only a foil, a blackened but necessary backdrop, against which his own realm would shine forth in the bright, calm light that he alone, as its maker and master, supplied. There the only measure that counted, the only value he acknowledged, was the one he represented himself.

But that was yet to come. And, in any case, what most preoccupied him during these precarious first years was not the Jewish question but the German one. "As far as the Germans are concerned," someone heard him say in 1916, "there was an earlier time when he felt as foreign as, for instance, we feel Jews are foreign to us." There were specific reasons why the Jews felt alienated, of course, and not all of them had to do with their own sense of a separate identity. Yet the comparison is telling. We know how "foreign" George felt — and was made to feel — throughout his life. And, like any other member of a minority group who is faced with the extreme choice between assimilation or ostracism, George obviously felt the pressure to conform. He found a way out of the dilemma by taking neither one of the two conventional routes, but by embarking on a far more difficult path. Rather than integrating himself into Germany, he resolved instead to make Germany itself yield to the image of what he thought it should be.

To be sure, the image of Germany George had in mind at this point was to all appearances more or less exclusively an aesthetic one. His goals, that is, still seemed to be confined solely to the sphere of art and particularly poetry — so much so that it stirred the first chords of dissent among his new friends in Munich. "The others pressed for some anarchic deed," he said of that time, whereas "I only continued to make poems." Schuler accused George of squandering his natural, or rather his supernatural resources: "George has at his disposal all of the daemonic powers, and what did he use them for? Art." Klages made a comparable protest: "Everything he, George, and his people did was only art; [*we*] wanted to found a religion." One could respond by saying that, for George, art *was* a religion, and that he wanted to be its head priest.

Every religion needs a catechism, and the *Blätter für die Kunst* seemed the most appropriate place to formulate it. In the March 1894 issue, the journal contained, alongside the usual poems and fragments of dramas and prose, an introductory section composed of short, aphoristic, almost decretal statements addressing more general artistic and cultural matters. These gnomic pronouncements would later become a fixture of the *Blätter,* and for many years they would form the only public and nonpoetic expression of what George and his associates stood for. Since they are never signed, it is impossible to know with certainty who wrote them. But what is certain is that George would never have allowed anything to be published in the *Blätter* that had not received his explicit approval. For that reason, the introductory maxims to the *Blätter,* if not always from George's pen, were an undeniable — and official — expression of his views.

In conformity with his wish to bring the "new art" — the word "French" was now assiduously avoided — to a German readership hopelessly mired in the "old," the maxims stake out a territory that is by now quite familiar but with an added new twist. Each short paragraph treats individual words or concepts that were being used to designate the new poetic movement, and each maxim seeks to bend these slogans to a particular, which is to say indigenous, purpose. Most striking is the declared intention to replace all "foreign words, even those that have taken root" with those of Germanic origin. The stated rationale was that, in so doing, "much empty talk would remain unsaid. if a sentence that cannot do without such a word is omitted then neither language nor society would thereby experience a loss."

Unlike English, German had remained closer to its linguistic roots, with the Latin influence coming much later and with far less widespread effect. As recently as the seventeenth century, when numerous so-called language societies sprouted up in the effort to reform and regularize German grammar, there had even been earnest attempts to "translate" Latin words into their Germanic equivalents. Many of these coinages stuck — the verb *abhängen,* literally "to hang from" is a direct translation of *dependere,* and is now the normal German word for "to depend" — whereas more fanciful constructions met a swift and merciful end. The suggestion to supplant the Latinate *Nase,* or "nose," with the more Germanic-sounding *Gesichtserker,* meaning "face gable," failed to convince even the most fervent partisans of standardization. But the idea of "purifying" the German language of its "foreign" or non-Germanic elements continued to resurface from time to time. Given the rich inflectional possibilities inherent in the language and its nuanced prepositional system, it was not as far-fetched as it may seem, even if the aims that drove the effort were usually more than questionable.

An explanation of motives did not belong to the style of the *Blätter.* They did not say why they took this or that position: they simply took it, and left the whys to others. Indeed, the very first aphorism — again, in the peculiarly apodictic mode that would become the journal's trademark — we are informed it is "not merely in times of transition" — the German word is *Übergang*, literally "crossing over" — that "sweeping piercing suggestive sentences are preferable to pedantically fixed ones: they are the sibylline signs from which youth receives its deepest stimulus." The passing reference to "youth" is the first specific mention of the kind of readers the *Blätter* envisioned as its proper audience. But it also nicely adumbrates one of the key paradoxes of the entire endeavor: the "transition" from "old" to "new" art is also a generational shift, a passing of the torch from the old guard to younger standard bearers. Yet this transfer of power is headed as much toward the past as the future: the desire to eliminate foreign words from the poetic and critical vocabulary stood even then under a slightly reactionary nimbus, signifying a conservative wish to return to a prior state of linguistic innocence and purity which in reality had never existed. The very first issue of the *Blätter* had brashly announced that "in art we believe in a brilliant renascence." It is apparently the fate of all renaissances that, in the effort to renew a culture held to be decrepit and moribund, one has to reach back to an earlier time of imagined youth and energy to generate the rejuvenation to come.

The following maxims accordingly take up slogans associated with the "new art" and translate them into German terms and a German context. Playing on the common root shared by *Übergang* and *Untergang*, with the latter meaning "decline," the next maxim reads: "Decline (decadence) is in several respects a phenomenon that people unwisely wanted to make into the sole product of our time — [a phenomenon] that someday may certainly admit artistic treatment by the right hands but otherwise belongs in the realm of medicine." Again, the English version does not do justice to the flavor of the original: although the Latinate *Medizin* was, and is, a perfectly normal and acceptable term, a German word is used here instead: *Heilkunde*, a more archaic, less scientific-sounding, and above all a native locution. More broadly, though, the obvious point of relegating the treatment of decadence to medical journals was to distance the *Blätter* from any suspicion that it was engaged in such sickly, unwholesome pursuits, whether they were practiced by native naturalist writers or frivolous Frenchmen. Just to hedge all bets, however, another apothegm declared that "every appearance of decline also bears witness to higher life." We repudiate all decadence, the editors seemed to be saying, but if there is any decadence to be found in these pages, it is merely the symptom of its own overcoming. In like manner, another aphorism addresses the other major catchword connected to the new poetry and proclaimed that, despite its fashionable status, "the image (symbol) is as old as language and poetry itself." Once more, one is forced to acknowledge the truth of the statement, but not without having a nagging feeling that one is conceding more than is immediately apparent. It is as if the editors were saying that it is erroneous to think that *Blätter* is a "symbolist" organ, but if it does exhibit traits that might be seen as "symbolic," then it is for the simple reason that all language is composed of "symbols" or linguistic "images." In any case, as the subsequent maxim reads, "to think symbolically is the natural result of intellectual maturity and depth." It is hard to argue with that. But the impression lingers that the *Blätter* — or rather George — always wanted to have it both ways.

While most of the introductory maxims to the *Blätter* rely as much, if not more, on innuendo than on explicit amplification to communicate their message, there are moments of relative clarity. "Between older art and that of today," we read for instance, "there are to be sure several differences: We do not want invention of stories but the rendering of moods not examination but representation not entertainment but impression." Ever since the first number of the *Blätter* had appeared, all nonpoetic, and in particular all political concerns had been expressly excluded from the enterprise. The introduction to the first issue had asserted that the "spiritual art" it envisioned could not "occupy itself with improvements of the world and dreams of universal happiness"; these were all well and good, it allowed, "but belong to a different realm than that of poetry." The overriding emphasis on the emotional, nonrational effect to which this new art aspired, and above all its liberation from extraliterary ends — its status, that is, as an "art for art's sake" — emerges even more clearly in the definition of a "the poem" as being "there for the highest spiritual enjoyment. There is as little a purpose-poetry as little as there is a purpose-painting or a purpose-composition. [A] Poem is not [a] rendering of a thought but of a mood." The point of orientation this time was not generically Latin but specifically French: the *Stimmung,* or "mood," said to constitute the purposeless concern of a poem was, of course, the German version of the *état d'âme,* the evocation of which Mallarmé had designated as the sole task of poetry. But it did not fit with George's current plan to recognize his prior indebtedness; in fact, as we have seen, he was already actively denying it. He now wanted to be regarded as a German poet writing for German readers, and incidental details involving literary influence — from France or anywhere else — would merely get in the way of that larger, more important mission.

At the very end of the introductory section, the journal hints at what that larger mission was. "We have noticed now for years," it sententiously observed, that "in no other adjoining state — not even in the ancestrally related netherlandish or northern countries — may the same level of readers be offered such products as poetry as here in Germany. From that fact arises the difference of our artistic task for the next few years from that of our neighbors."

Although one initially has the impression that a substantive difference is being described here between the endeavor on which the *Blätter* had embarked and that of its unnamed "neighbors," what in fact is said to set them apart has more to do with form than with content. The *Blätter,* that is, would be more pedagogical, more insistently educational in nature than its counterparts abroad, because it had to be. German standards were so abysmally low, they insisted, that a good deal of remedial work would have to be done just to raise them to a level comparable to that of other countries. What remained unspoken, of course, was that the measure against which the Germans were being held was precisely the one — the foreign one — that the authors of the *Blätter,* and principally George himself, had disclaimed as a point of orientation.

This odd doublespeak surfaces elsewhere, too. As much as the *Blätter* overtly disavowed any nonliterary "purpose" for itself or its contents, it is evident that from the very beginning the journal pursued an agenda that implied a political, or at least cultural-political, program. At no time, not even in its infancy, did the *Blätter für die Kunst* actually adhere to the purely aesthetic, strictly nonpolitical platform it claimed it was advancing. Even without knowing what we do about George's personal background, it does not take much imagination to see that the intensity with which the *Blätter* condemned the external world, and specifically modern German reality, was in itself already a deeply political gesture. This is not to suggest that the strategy was free of inconsistencies. On the contrary, it teems with them. A modern movement that turns to the past for inspiration; a German journal espousing a French literary creed, which it loudly repudiates; a private venture with the express intention of improving the taste of an indigenous public readership, which it holds in open contempt and from which it tries to stay as far away as possible while simultaneously courting its favor — one would not think this would be exactly a recipe for success.

In 1894, however, George still measured success by other criteria. Slowly but steadily the journal was attracting more and better writers to its pages. Yet here, too, not all the signs were auspicious. Since the end of the previous year, Klein had been in contact with Leopold von Andrian, which had eventually culminated not just in George's meeting with him in February, but more crucially in the publication of one of Andrian's poems in the January number of the *Blätter.* George's admiration for the lyrical talent of this son of an aristocratic Austrian family was extraordinarily high; indeed, many years later he said that Andrian's "poems were after Hofmannsthal the best thing there was at the time." The comparison to Hofmannsthal was apt not just with regard to the quality of his poetry.

Born in 1875 only a few months after his friend, Andrian was thus seven years younger than George and also like Hofmannsthal wary of being consumed by the older poet's appetite for talented and pliant accessories. Not that he had not been forewarned. In January 1894, breaking a six-month silence, Klein had sent an insulting letter to Hofmannsthal, loftily informing him that he intended to announce that Hofmannsthal was no longer affiliated with the journal. "As a former collaborator of our *Blätter,*" Hofmannsthal deserved to know, Klein told him, that "in the next number in the 'news' section I will place a neutral notice that we must dispense with your participation since you have turned to other literary activities and that we do this with the greatest regret." Hofmannsthal sent a dignified response to Klein, saying that "however the notice about my exit will read, in your hands it will do justice to every requirement of tact and I take the liberty of approving of it in advance." Klein had not requested his approval, which made the noble act of granting it all the more satisfying. But to his friend Andrian, Hofmannsthal fumed: "For your entertainment I am giving you this impertinent letter from our mutual friend. These people are completely unbearable."

In his own dealings with those "people," Andrian quickly ran into difficulties as well. After the issue of the *Blätter* featuring his verse had appeared, Klein forwarded a copy containing the poem to Andrian himself, mentioning off-handedly that "nothing in it needed to be changed regarding its expression, only a few undesirable rhythmic irregularities were evened out." Half apologizing for this gross and previously unannounced intervention, Klein sought to put at least part of the blame on Andrian: "Next time we will communicate beforehand, which because of the short time you left us was impossible this time." Undoubtedly shocked by the high-handed manner in which Klein felt free to make unauthorized "improvements" to his work but inexperienced in such things, Andrian graciously thanked Klein for the consignment and added fairly meekly that "as concerns the printing of my poem, I would have almost preferred, I think, the original version." Yet Andrian also sent several more poems to be considered for publication in the next number of the *Blätter,* although this time not without making sure to ask Klein to let him know if he had "any wishes concerning changes," so they could be discussed before going to press.

When Andrian finally received his copy of the August issue, he flew into a rage. On September 3, he wrote to Hofmannsthal: "I have had a falling out with the *Bl. f. d. K.*, that is, I have written them a very rude letter; they made an *unbelievable* mess of one of my poems in the last number. I am furious." The letter he had written to Klein was not quite as rude as he had boasted, but it was sufficiently direct to convey the state of his feelings. Pointing to the agreement he had thought they had reached in January about notifying him about any changes to be made before publication, Andrian reminded Klein that he had consented to only a single alteration, and even that he had done unwillingly. "Although I considered it a coarse worsening in terms of meaning and rhythm," Adrian said he had acquiesced and allowed the change to stand so as not to cause any unnecessary friction, believing that he had at least thus protected himself against any further unwanted meddling with his words. "Now I find to my astonishment the second strophe entirely rearranged; the expression: 'to envision Eros for himself' not only seems vapid and clumsy, it is an outgrowth of St. George's manner of writing, not mine." This was simply unacceptable: "You will understand that it must be upsetting to me to see my name under the words of another artist; I must therefore in future relinquish the pleasure of finding my verses in your pages, of which I am so fond." Assuming — or pretending to assume — that Klein really was the one who had performed the surgery on his work, Andrian wrote to George a few days later informing him of his intention not "to publish any more verses in the *Bl. f. d. K.* in the future. I do not need to justify this decision to you who are an artist." Still, he professed unbroken admiration for George himself. "I would only like to say to you that this necessary step has as little effect on my sympathy for the *Blätter* as on my affection for you."

What Andrian could not have known was that the reason the changes to his poem were so much in the manner of "St. George" was that it was George himself, and only he, who could have made them. Klein would never have presumed to trespass into a territory that he knew the "Master" regarded as his alone. Moreover, Klein was the "editor" but not a poet. Only rarely, in the three decades of its existence, did verses by Klein appear in the pages of the *Blätter,* and no one would have confused him with George himself. Or perhaps Andrian did suspect that the fiction of Klein's single-handed tampering with his words was just that: a convenient pretense that not only allowed George to act freely in the background and to speak or remain silent as he wished, but a mask that, strangely, permitted a greater candor among the contributors than might have otherwise been possible. In any case, it was difficult to tell which was the more painful to George: Andrian's harsh characterization of the emendations George had unilaterally performed or his angry and apparently irrevocable defection from the journal.

It was a blow, but one George could absorb — if not forgive. He now had a larger and growing number of contributors to the *Blätter,* including Ludwig Klages, Karl Wolfskehl, whom he had met and befriended in the meantime, Waclaw Lieder, a Polish poet he greatly admired, and Paul Gérardy, the reliable Belgian workhorse. That September, following the dispute with Andrian, George announced to Saint-Paul, with visible pride, that "our little group is formed." But the loss, and under such ignoble circumstances, of the second most gifted poet he had managed to recruit thus far was not something George took lightly. Despite his abiding regard for Andrian's poems, George later emphasized that "personally, however, he disappointed me so much that I was not able to make a secret of my disappointment. He tried to make it up by being charming, but I was already closed shut, I couldn't take it any more." This is not an entirely accurate portrayal of the sequence of events surrounding their breakup, but that was not really the point. The essence remained true: George could tolerate — though not forever — considerable boisterousness, aberrant personal idiosyncrasies, even questionable poetic talent among his friends, but one thing he would never endure was a direct or implied disparagement of himself or of his poetry. The penalty for committing such a crime varied, but it was always immediate and usually permanent. Had Andrian ever actually seriously tried to reingratiate himself with George after their split, in all probability he would have found a locked and silent door.

CHAPTER 14
Schwabing

Apart from a few brief interruptions, George lived in Munich for more than half a year, from October 1894 through the following April, residing in the northern district of Schwabing. In the wake of the ambitious urban reconstruction campaigns undertaken by the Wittelsbach kings Ludwig I and Maximilian II during the first half of the century, Munich had become familiarly known as the *Kunststadt*, the "city of art" — or rather with the word "Art" writ large. For what Munich embodied was a kind of official, authorized, and highly formal Art realized on a grand scale. Great numbers of recently constructed neoclassical monuments, temples to sculpture and painting such as the Glyptothek and the Pinacothek, the new opera house and private villas built according to painstakingly precise Hellenistic designs, all served to lend Munich the somewhat eerie appearance of an enormous open-air museum but one with a decidedly Greek accent. "Athens on the Isar" was another, perhaps inevitable nickname applied to the Bavarian capital. We may remember that Berliners also liked to call their city the "Athens on the Spree." But this self-appraisal involved even more wishful thinking, as well as a healthy dose of Prussian self-promotion, than the Bavarians' claim, which, given their southern heritage and more pleasure-seeking nature, made it more plausible that they were the authentic heirs of ancient Greek cultural and civic virtues. The residents of Munich were proud of their city and self-conscious about asserting their cultural attainments as a foil against the political dominance of the new northern rulers, whom they often perceived as crass and pretentious *arrivistes*. In a guide book published in 1905, the gentleman visitor to Munich was given the practical advice that, while in the city, he "should entirely refrain from wearing jewelry made of gold and precious stones; one's reputation is not enhanced by them. It is for ladies to decorate themselves, but only in the salon." For good measure, tourists from the north were also pointedly informed that in Munich "when shaking hands one avoids the jerky Prussian elbow."

Schwabing, however, was something else again. There anything went. Although it would not reach the apogee of its notoriety until the end of the decade, Schwabing was already attracting an alarming number of misfits, outcasts, malcontents, and troublemakers, in short, artists, but not necessarily of the variety sanctioned by the royal house. Adjoining the university, Schwabing had an immense quantity of affordable apartments for rent. At the turn of the century, the entire city of Munich, with a total population of about half a million, still had ten thousand empty flats available for rent, and many were located in Schwabing. It thus fulfilled approximately the same role as the Latin Quarter in Paris, offering a sanctuary for the dispossessed and culturally restless, providing a forgiving and inexpensive environment for radical experiments in art, politics, and sexual protocols. Schwabing easily assimilated the likes of Schuler and Klages, while still remaining attractive to such disparate figures as Thomas Mann, Frank Wedekind, Rainer Maria Rilke, or the anarchist Erich Mühsam, but also Paul Klee, Wassily Kandinksy, Alfred Kubin, and Vladimir Ilyich Lenin. Painters, poets, sculptors, composers from all over Germany and the rest of Europe — they were all embraced as "Schlawiner," a name punningly derived from the word for Slovenians or Slovaks. A Schlawiner was "anyone who painted behind the thousand atelier windows in Schwabing, who kneaded clay, wrote poetry in the garrets, sang or wrote music, amassed debts in the little inns and proclaimed Nihilism or Aestheticism in the cafés. The only prerequisite was that the artist had to appear unbourgeois in both clothing and behavior. If he did this, then, even though a born Mecklenburger, Frenchman, Rhinelander, Norwegian or Thuringian, he was a Schwabing 'Schlawiner.' "

In addition to the general atmosphere of unchecked liberty, not to say libertinage, Paris provided other parallels. The most important employer in Schwabing was the publishing house of Albert Langen and the satiric journal, *Simplicissimus,* which the firm launched in 1893 and had candidly modeled after the popular French magazine, *Gil blas illustré.* But it was the café, and a particular kind of café culture, that most recalled of the French capital. The most celebrated was the Café Luitpold, which had opened to much fanfare and excitement in the late 1880s, and had already become a fixture of Schwabing life by the time George arrived. On any given night, one could find there French, Flemish, Dutch, Polish, and even some German patrons, "all clothed with the greatest of care in long, dark frock coats 'created' by exclusive tailors in London or Paris; gleaming top hats and evening jackets worked in silk in the latest fashion hanging on the golden bronze coat stand, stylishly patterned shirtfronts with profoundly symbolic lapel pins: nephrite scarabs, Medusa heads, and Abraxas — everything testified to the fact that the *dernier cri* of the Parisian 'Parnassiens' set the tone here." That other rules held sway than in downtown Munich was also evident in the way in which the waitresses, selected more for their looks than their waiting skills, glided among the red plush sofas, attending to the various needs of the customers. Many of the young women had "diamond-studded bracelets, brooches, earrings, watches, and rings: all presents from rich admirers" among the clientele. Although George would have had an eye for other attractions, he also became a regular at the "Luitpold," where he could often be seen, "his young defiant head thrown back, walking, no, striding through the café like a bishop through the middle of Saint Peter's."

In the first part of 1895, a friend of Klages named Theodor Lessing, who had recently published a little book of poetry, came to Munich and, like countless other aspiring writers, found modest but adequate quarters in Schwabing. Klages, always on the lookout for new recruits to the *Blätter,* took both Lessing and his tome to George for approval. "He leafed through it, smiling," Lessing recalled, "and complained about the poor quality of the paper." In return, Lessing received copies of George's exquisite, if austere books, as if to show him how it ought to be done. Even though Lessing was visibly put off by this implied criticism of his own effort, and even more by the confusing lack of conventional punctuation and capital letters he found in these new acquisitions, George still wanted to know if Lessing was willing to contribute a few lines to his "museum," as he now sometimes took to calling the *Blätter.* Lessing noticed that George "set great store by formality and clothing. He carefully tied his ruff in front of a mirror — something we ladykillers had no inclination for — he looked at fashion magazines, studied new jewelry patterns, commended fabrics and silks, attentively examined the sit of his tie in the mirror." Unswayed by the invitation to join forces with George, and perhaps alarmed by what the association might imply — "George and probably most of those in his circle were men-loving," he explained — Lessing blurted out that he was a living human being, and not an apprentice wallpaper-hanger for the bourgeois world of luxury. Needless to say, Lessing's name did not appear in the *Blätter.*

Lessing gives us a snapshot of George as he was in the mid-1890s: a twenty-six-year-old "melancholy prince in exile," as Lessing described him, projecting an aura that was both "imperious and careworn." Although George regarded himself and his work with deadly seriousness, there was of course no guarantee he could convince — or force — others to treat him with the deference he clearly expected. Should he fail, his entire life would appear to have been nothing better than a slightly sour farce. But he equated victory with absolute conquest, total domination. It was a high-stakes gamble, an all-or-nothing wager. "Simultaneously odd and impressive," was how Lessing described the effect of this spectacle, "simultaneously foolish and commanding respect. For if he remained without success, then he was only one of the many unrecognized geniuses identified by their long manes and beautiful ties who drank tea in droves in Schwabing at the time." Externally, there was indeed little that separated George from hundreds of other rhyming aesthetes, inoffensive poetasters who dressed according to the latest Parisian fashion, spent long hours idling in the cafés and who viewed their principal triumphs in successfully wooing young women — or, if their tastes ran in a different direction, seducing handsome boys. But George, while not indifferent to these diversions, was consumed by a more powerful urge, a craving for complete mastery that eventually set him apart from everyone else.

His will to rule was still primarily concentrated on poetry, and here he admitted no challengers, at most recognizing equals. After a tentative rapprochement, he and Lessing frequently met, and the topic of their conversation almost always concerned the one subject that truly interested George, but only within certain bounds. "Bad address," George would interrupt Lessing when he would enthuse about this or that writer who did not meet with George's approval, or he would silence Lessing by saying: "I have no organ for literature." In George's vocabulary, "literature" encompassed everything that was not poetry and was therefore trivial, insignificant, and worthless. Similarly, the word "writer" entailed a negative definition, that is, someone he did not consider a poet, someone who wrote mere "literature." "That is a writer," was thus one the most damning words he could pronounce over another laborer in the field. When the editor of an anthology of contemporary German poetry wrote to ask whether George might care to participate by submitting a few of his poems, he had one of his friends reply that "Herr George regrets having no interest in German literature." This was not literally true, since he was keenly interested in German poetry, even in German "literature." But he would be the person to decide what belonged to these categories — and what did not — and he alone.

Yet, as time went on, George's claims were beginning to expand beyond the limits of "mere" literature or even poetry. Lessing recalled an excursion they undertook to visit a friend in the countryside outside Munich. On the way home a thunderstorm broke. The others clasped their woolen capes more tightly about themselves and pulled their hats down over their ears, but George seemed to view the violent weather as a personal insult, making bitter comments about the unnecessary discomfort it was causing, all the while cursing such great nature worshipers as Tolstoy and Rousseau. Lessing, who fancied himself both a nature lover and a red-blooded adventurer, found George's imprecations against the elements highly amusing, not realizing, perhaps, that George's professed hatred of nature fed on deeper springs. Once, when walking together through a village, George stopped in front of a dung heap and made the acid remark: "Look here, a pile of manure! That must appeal to Herr Lessing!" In self-defense, Lessing argued that it was just as grotesque to imagine that a poet would sing about lion hunts, desert storms, Viking voyages, burning cities, murder, and triumph while lounging in a garden chair, clutching a stylus in pale hand. "A poet," was the cool reply, "can also go on a lion hunt in the Luitpold." In any case, George sneeringly added, "The fauteuil is more comfortable than a tree trunk." Whereas countless poets have seen nature as a source of inspiration, solace and wonder, George seemed to regard it mainly as a rival.

Inevitably, others also noticed, and some were frightened by, this hostility toward nature in George. His Berlin friend, Sabine Lepsius, whom he met the following year, remembered a walk she once took with him in the woods near Darmstadt. "I have completely forgotten what we talked about," she later reported, "because another, stronger impression than words seized me and has remained unforgettable: I had never experienced Stefan George in natural surroundings, in which I was now strolling with him in complete isolation. A sudden, uncanny, I would even say evil force emanated from him, which made me perceive him as inhuman. Pretending to feel tired, I urged for us to return home because fear aroused me and drove me away from him." Having no appreciation for the blooming yellow gorse all around them, George suddenly appeared to her as "a dangerous daemon" from whom she now only wanted to escape. But whatever it was in George that had so frightened her, appeared to linger on after they returned indoors, remaining visible to others as well. After they had arrived back at home, Sabine Lepsius's son was brought to them. George turned to the boy, "whereupon the child was overcome with such mortal terror that we could only quickly carry him away amidst loud shrieking." This disturbing scene was followed by a final one. It was the practice in the Lepsius family for guests to plant a young tree instead of signing a guest book to commemorate their stay. Before he left, George was asked to perform the established ritual. "For the third time I was gripped by secret horror as the pale man wielded the spade with an unaccustomed arm. Again, I thought innocence was lacking in his relationship to nature. He did not dig like a gardener, he dug like someone looking for buried treasure." In the first draft of this passage, Sabine Lepsius had originally written, and perhaps more accurately reflecting her real impression, that he seemed to her to wield the shovel like a "gravedigger."

There is more here than the simple affectation of someone who has adopted the French symbolists' disdain for nature, or the decadent's disdain for everything else. George's antagonistic attitude toward the natural realm is not a superficial air but, at least in part, another expression of his inability to abide by the idea that there was some external power he could not completely dominate, that something could resist his efforts to control it. Whatever he could not subsume under his will, whatever withdrew itself from his authority, met with unremitting antagonism — until he either won the contest, or had eliminated the source of aggravation. There was already a considerable number of irritants on George's slate, ranging from individual people, artistic tastes, social mores, and political beliefs, even entire countries — including his own. Adding the vastness of nature to the list made for a rather daunting foe. But its placid imperviousness to his enmity only made it seem all the more infuriating, and his desire to conquer it all the stronger.

Of course, though perhaps not nature itself, there was still a good deal else over which he could prevail. It seemed that, with each passing month, the *Blätter* was finding a larger and more responsive readership, thus bringing an ever widening circle of potential collaborators within George's purview. Even the signals from France were improving. After a two-year lull, during which he had refashioned himself into a German poet, George resumed contact with Mallarmé in April 1895, sending him a bound copy of the second year's issues of the journal along with a photograph of himself. Characteristically, Mallarmé responded warmly: "Thank you, my dear Poet, for sending, as a whole, all of those beautiful new things, close to us and very free, which the second volume of the *Blätter für die Kunst* contains, verse, prose, also providing a friendly reminiscence of your features. You are conducting the delicate fight there that is necessary, entirely avant-garde." Publicly, Mallarmé was even more supportive. That same month, he participated in a survey that had been jointly carried out by the *Mercure de France* and the *Neue Deutsche Rundschau*. Prominent figures in both Germany and France were asked to express their views on the desirability of a closer relationship between their two countries following the thawing of relations enabled by the death of the bellicose French war minister, General Boulanger. As one of the invitees, Mallarmé wrote: "Regarding the intellectual exchange, to me, in my field, it seems to have been fervent in the last few years — since Paris has exalted Wagner and Berlin, in the *Blätter für die Kunst*, has recently translated Baudelaire. I applaud." It was the first time George and his group had been placed in such august company by someone other than themselves. Better yet, similar sentiments were also being aired in *La Plume* and other Parisian publications, and George no doubt felt confident and gratified that the winds were finally changing. But now, partly as a way of placing greater distance between himself and France, he was setting his sails not toward the French capital, but rather in the direction of the lowland states of Belgium and Holland.

Actually, he had already been attracted to Belgium for some time. One of his first acquaintances, Albert Mockel, had been Belgian. George had first traveled to Belgium in the summer of 1892, where he stayed in the town of Tilff, probably at the suggestion of Paul Gérardy. He had met there a number of leading poets and artists, including Léon Paschal, the brothers Edmond and Armand Rassenfosse, as well as the painters James Ensor, Fernand Khnopff, and August Donnay. Later trips to Brussels and Lüttich (Liège) brought him together with the poets Emil Verhaeren and Charles van Lerberghe; it is possible that he even met Maurice Maeterlinck. His connection to Belgium would remain strong for the next couple of years, as he sought to expand the reach of the *Blätter* beyond the confines of Germany and give it a truly international scope. He had even managed to persuade Donnay and Khnopff to contribute two drawings to the August 1894 issue, which concluded with a note about this seeming departure in format that read: "If we primarily wished to serve the new efforts in poetry we have resolved to open these pages as well to like-minded composers and pictorial artists. May the example of our Belgian friends, the eminent men Fernand Khnopff and August Donnay, who have placed selections from their work at our disposal, motivate our younger German masters to collaborate in our endeavor." The last clause revealed what the underlying intention really was: not so much to enlist foreign aid for its own sake as to help ferret out native talent. It was a strategy that would soon bear fruit in the figure of the Berlin artist and designer, Melchior Lechter.

But not only artistic ties attached him to Belgium. He was closest to Edmond Rassenfosse, who, six years George's junior, possessed a fragile, unstable psyche and who leaned heavily on George for emotional sustenance and reassurance. He wrote long, painfully sentimental letters in French to George, pouring out his vague sorrows in cloying entreaties for understanding and consolation. "I would like, instead of writing to you, to come be close to you, to take your hands and press myself against your heart," one such lachrymose missive begins. "You would then see that I love you and you would understand that you mustn't judge ill of my silence." Pleading with George that "whatever may happen you will believe in me," Rassenfosse revealed that "I am afraid of becoming weak; I have a horrible anguish of losing myself in the unconscious crowd." "I am afraid," he elaborated, "of never being anything and of having deceived all those who have loved my soul. . . . My ignorance crushes me, my nullity suffocates me. I know that these are confessions that one doesn't make. Thus you understand how much you are my friend! Oh, that you are not here to take me on your shoulder!" The letter ends — much later — with the plaintive cry, "I am lonely, desperately lonely!"

George knew what was troubling the young man, even if Rassenfosse himself appeared perhaps willfully ignorant of the source of his woes. In a remarkable letter — remarkable for its length, for its candor, and even for its generosity — George tried to lend him tactful aid by engaging in discreet circumlocutions, offering at the same time an analysis, some encouragement, and a little friendly counsel:

> If a young man of your age says he is profoundly unhappy there is always a *single* cause. Everyone of us has had in his youth such a crisis. It is impossible to remove the pain but one must think of keeping it *pure,* you understand me — that is my only advice. The great silent grief ennobles one's character, vehemence destroys one's character, and in this case as well — love. When I was almost twenty I also suffered the same way from an immense love — even as far as wanting to die. Today these past pains remind me of an elevated life, a superhuman life — the years have taught me that there is an even stronger grief, namely this one: to look over the vast plain of life — everything covered with ashes — where all pains all joys all emotions slowly go to sleep and die. . . . And that is my only consolation for you: that there is a much stronger pain than yours and that your friend suffers from it. Yes! much stronger, much more acute precisely because one doesn't die from it. You understand that I can only say general things in a drama of the soul in which I know the actors too little, and that one cannot always write what one can easily say. There are sublime and cold divinities that are called duty and friendship. Often they succeed in healing the injuries of passion. I would be happy if these lines would give you some courage and the will to avoid a reconciliation that would crush a life that is still so young!

That was about as much as he would ever be able — or willing — to write in a letter, but for George it was a lot. In no other surviving letter would George ever again speak so openly of love or of his own experience of it or its loss. Yet if these unusually direct and heartfelt words helped Rassenfosse any, it did not show. In another typical refrain, from April 1896, he again complained of unrelenting, if always unspecified, torments. "Believe at least that everything I have left I give to you entirely, tenderly, piously," Rassenfosse wrote, his unfocused feelings uncontrollably welling up. "But don't reproach me for not being able to give you more, since that is my sorrow. It is my great and intimate suffering, my humiliation of every day, every moment! Have pity for me and love, my friend, and help me so that what is tottering within me doesn't die away." After exchanging several more letters of this general tenor over the next few years, interspersed with the occasional meeting in Brussels or Liège, George finally grew tired, or bored, of propping up the labile Belgian and ceased to heed his hand-wringing calls for assistance.

While the Belgian friendships were intensive but relatively short-lived, his bond with Holland was less sexually charged and of much longer duration. In May 1895, the Dutch poet Albert Verwey published a review of the first two years of the *Blätter* in the journal he edited, called the *Tweemaandelijksch Tijdschrift,* accompanied by a largely benevolent consideration of George's *Pilgrimages* and *Algabal*. This review would lay the groundwork for what soon became "the most manly friendship of George's life," as Robert Boehringer curiously put it, that is, "a friendship with an adult man and poet." Three years George's senior, Verwey was independent and firmly established in his own country, solidly self-confident, emanating a calm self-assurance that, quite apart from the semi-hysterical Rassenfosse, very few of George's other acquaintances displayed. Married and the father of several children, Verwey fell out of the mold George generally preferred in his friends in other ways as well. Sporting a scruffy mustache, later expanded to include an untidy beard, topped by a head of bristly hair, and the owner of a generously proportioned nose, Verwey was arguably the least physically attractive of all of George's confederates. But a genuine regard united the two, founded on sincere respect for the very different conceptions of poetry they each had. (George's affection did not extend to Verwey's wife, Kitty, however, who the poet thought "dominated her husband too much.") Over the next decade they frequently visited one another in their respective homes, with George staying sometimes for weeks in Noordwijk aan Zee and in turn hosting Verwey for slightly shorter periods in Bingen. As soon as George began to transform himself into something more than, or instead of, a poet, however, Verwey discovered, with no little regret, that where real sympathy had previously grown, only a cold, rather dutiful acknowledgement remained.

The contacts with the lowlands meant that George was not utterly dependent on France for an informed and receptive audience. But things finally appeared to be picking up back home in Germany as well. In March 1895, a young professor of philosophy named Max Dessoir at the University of Berlin wrote to Klein to ask if back issues of the *Blätter* were available. Dessoir was preparing his lectures on the history of aesthetics and the theory of art for the summer semester, and he wanted to address the most recent pertinent developments in the field, although he candidly advised Klein that what he had to say may not be uniformly positive. This, too, was unprecedented: never before had a member of the official cultural elite in Germany, much less in

Berlin, and even less at the university, shown the slightest interest in their undertaking. Klein jumped at the opportunity, uncharacteristically accepting in advance the criticism Dessoir had announced may be forthcoming. "Since just at this moment," Klein wrote back in his customary pompous style, "an artistic and aristocratic drive is asserting itself against the naturalistic and plebeian one and is beginning to imitate the works of our collaborators, we would find ourselves much obliged to you if you wished to say a few conscientious honest words about our movement." This was also a first: later referring to George as the poet "who has called the entire movement into existence," Klein now identified the *Blätter für die Kunst* not simply as a literary journal, but as the embodiment and herald of an entire movement, with George as its inspiration and guide. This had, of course, always been its latent message, so much so that it almost seemed unnecessary to express it. Once formulated, though, the idea would gain its own momentum, eventually outgrowing the *Blätter* itself to assume an even greater and unforeseeable magnitude.

For the moment, though, Professor Dessoir's inquiry was a welcome sign that, despite the miniscule publication runs, despite the aura of forbidding exclusivity the journal deliberately cultivated, and despite the echoing silence that had mainly greeted the first two years of the *Blätter,* a turn-around in its fortunes might be in sight. Decidedly unwelcome, however, were other reverberations from Berlin. That year, in April 1895, a new journal had been founded in the capital, with the bold and broadminded intention of bringing international avant-garde art and literature "to the people." It was conceived, in other words, as a kind of democratically based *Blätter für die Kunst*. The journal was named *Pan,* after the Polish word for "gentleman," but the association with the goatish Greek god of the woods proved to be stronger, enforced by the emblem that appeared on its title page: the head of a faun drawn by Max Klinger. Big, attractively produced, and emphatically not esoteric — nor inexpensive: the first issue cost seventy-five marks — it was an instant success. And serving as one of the two principal literary editors for *Pan* was none other than the reviled Richard Dehmel.

Isi Coblenz, now Frau Ida Auerbach — she had been given away in a marriage arranged by her father in April that year — was living in Berlin with her new husband, miserable in a loveless union of convenience, and looking for ways to distract herself. In August 1895, after reading an article by Dehmel on contemporary German literature in the newly inaugurated magazine he edited, she felt the need to write to the author. "Why do you too ignore," she crossly wrote Dehmel, "you who unreservedly mention everything good that you found, why do you also ignore this entire group of young artists who have gathered in the *Blätter für die Kunst* around their leader: Herr Stefan George? I cannot understand it."

Soon thereafter, Frau Isi and Dehmel met in person, and together they hatched a little plot. Having already made the mistake of commending Dehmel to George, Frau Isi knew better than to mention him by name when she told George of her scheme. Fibbing that she had recently attended an event where contemporary art had been discussed, she declared that "to my joy one of the gentlemen spoke with great enthusiasm about your works, regretting that they are available only to such a small circle." The others present had never heard of George — "they were painters and musicians," she hastily offered as an excuse — which had prompted her to offer to bring his books to the next meeting. "The gentlemen," she said almost as an aside, "belonged to the board of *Pan*." She sought to reassure him that the journal was not, as George had feared, a "collecting place of Naturalism," and that room would be given to such unobjectionable poets as Verlaine, Maeterlinck, and Rossetti. Following a meeting with "one of the board members," she now disclosed that she had made two additional promises to this unnamed gentleman: "First, to ask you for your three books: *Hymns, Algabal,* and *Pilgrimages* so that one of the gentlemen is in a position to write in detail about Stefan George, but second, and this is definitely the more important: a contribution from your pen."

George obviously saw through the masquerade, but he graciously thanked his well-meaning promoter for "your steadfastly friendly stance and your efforts on my behalf." Even though he loathed Dehmel personally, Dehmel was not the only member of *Pan*'s editorial board, which would thus dilute his contaminating effect. More pragmatically, the high profile of the magazine would guarantee the kind of exposure George increasingly realized would be necessary to achieve his own ends. But he was not going to make it easy. It was to be all or nothing. "I will be able to appear in *Pan* only if the principal collaborators of the *Blätter f. d. Kunst*, namely: Hofmannsthal Gérardy and Wolfskehl appear as well. The unmistakable peculiarity of these poets has the one common trait that THEIR works cannot be seen next to other German poetic contributions in *Pan*." Like the cuckoo, which lays its eggs in the nests of other birds, George was prepared to use *Pan* as a kind of surrogate vessel, smuggling in his own brood with the intention of fostering his own journal, which was not yet ready to stand on its own. But there would be no miscegenation, no unseemly commingling of what he insisted were two separate breeds.

In the end, however, after several rounds of negotiations, in which Dehmel finally acquiesced to all of his demands, the deal fell through. Differences of opinion and taste among the members of the editorial board of *Pan* — and, it appears, a flagrant misuse of the journal's expense account — led to Dehmel being summarily fired in September. In the aftermath, various agreements Dehmel had made were scotched and the magazine was hastily reorganized. George, who in the meantime had returned to Berlin himself, wrote to a friend in October — interestingly repeating many of the words Klein had used in his letter to Dessoir — that "here in Berlin our young movement is making only slow progress, which is probably largely caused by the press which is now already starting to talk about the imitations and excrescences before it is capable of discussing what is original and genuine. Great confusion was also caused within our writing as well because a few very mediocre and insipid minds (*Pan*!) mixed their products among the works of first-rate artists and foreign masters. An error that is possible only here in Germany." The whole affair, which had never been entirely palatable to begin with, thus ended on a thoroughly distasteful note. But it was an indication of how keenly George was interested in reaching a wider audience at this point, now that the first stirrings of public recognition were making themselves felt, that he was prepared to think that any means, even those most corrupt and debased in his eyes, could be justified by the greater goal.

CHAPTER 15

A Usable Past

At the beginning of September 1895, just before Dehmel suddenly became unemployed and it still looked as if George was about to step into the harsh glare of the limelight for the first time in his life, he outlined his vision of the future — or rather of his future — to Frau Isi Auerbach. "I am again standing at a turning point," he told her, "and am looking back over an entire life that will I feel be replaced by an entirely different one."

It may sound slightly absurd, or merely precious, to hear a twenty-seven-year-old speak of his experience as encompassing "an entire life." But it was a habit of viewing himself that George acquired early on and never abandoned. More realistically, and less dramatically, though, he had also suggested that he was simply bringing one stage of his life to an end and preparing to embark on another. The transition would be marked, as always at critical junctures, by a publication, the passage from one phase to the next given a physical permanence in the form of a book — or in this case, of several books. "I would like to conclude it," he continued, referring to the life he said he was now leaving behind, "with the publication of my books. I would like to unify *Hymns, Pilgrimages,* and *Algabal* in the first, the *Eclogues Legends and Songs and Hanging Gardens* in the second, and the last poems as *Annum animae* or *Year of the Soul* in the third. Thus my sung, my painted and my spoken works are together."

This was indeed a departure in several ways. First, the word George used for "publication" was *Herausgabe,* a perfectly normal term in German, but one that also retains its literal meaning of "handing over," or "surrendering," or, more strongly, "renouncing." For George, whose relationship to the public was anything but cozy, publication did seem to involve a kind of relinquishment or forfeiture. Giving up one's works for general perusal would seem the natural price one had to pay if the goal was to reform the public's taste, but it was a sacrifice George still made with great reluctance. And, although the plan to go public with a more widely available edition of his works was not realized until the end of the decade, it is noteworthy that he was already considering it so early on in his career. Yet it was also clear that he was also no longer thinking in terms of single works only, but now with a view toward larger patterns, greater structures that were beginning to take on an identifiable identity. It is not completely obvious what he meant by the distinction between the works in which he had "sung," "painted," and "spoken." But the fact that he was beginning to see his work as forming an abstract or ideal unity composed of disparate yet related parts also pointed to future trends.

In December 1895, George published the middle volume of the projected trilogy, with the ungainly title *Books of Eclogues and Eulogies · of Legends and Songs and of the Hanging Gardens* (*Die Bücher der Hirten- und Preisgedichte · der Sagen und Sänge und der Hängenden Gärten*). There was another novelty in that the print run numbered two hundred copies instead of the usual one hundred: as a concession it might appear negligible, but progress is also made by taking small steps. At any rate, as the title more than amply indicates — it would be the longest and least euphonious of all his titles — the book as a whole is composed of three separate parts. Each of the three sections of the *Books* is in fact inspired by a different historical period and in each case by a different cultural context. The first one "paints" a portrait of ancient Greece, the second one evinces a medieval world of pageantry and heroism, and the third conjures forth, as the name suggests, the Oriental splendor of Babylon. But it is the Greece of Böcklin, the Middle Ages of the Pre-Raphaelites, and the Orient of the French symbolists that the three books evoke, rather than a more immediate vision of the original sources. They are thus doubly, even triply "false" images, copies of copies, or at least imitations of already highly idiosyncratic interpretations of past times and distant places. This aura of intense artificiality was a quality much prized by George, of course, but it is not the only connection, or even the most important one, to his previous works. The preface to the book states merely that "in these three works there was no intention to draw the picture of an historical or developmental period: they contain the reflections of a soul that temporarily fled to different times and localities and sought shelter there." The external world figured only in so far as it provided a foil, at most the usable material, for the poet's inner experience, his "mood," his *état d'âme,* which the poem then commemorates and, ideally, reproduces again in the soul of the reader.

But that was only half, and perhaps less, of the story. In the vague, allusive language that was coming to typify his public pronouncements, the preface went on to admit that, "understandably," the poet had benefited from "inherited notions," as well as from "real surroundings" in creating his portrayals. Again, this statement also says less than first meets the eye. For, when George specified what he meant by a "real" environment, it was "on the one hand our still undesecrated valleys and forests · on the other, our medieval rivers · and further the heady air of our beloved cities." It is ambiguous who the "our" refers to, but given George's determination to be regarded as a — indeed, as *the* — German poet, it was probably not meant in a broadly inclusive sense. While there is much in all of the *Books* that strongly reminds one of Henri de Régnier, Maeterlinck, and Dante Gabriel Rossetti, George impatiently waved away any such association. If there was any external aid of a "real" or "natural" kind, he seemed to be saying, it was a German nature, a German past, and German culture that provided it.

This desire to appropriate the past, and different cultures, as domestic — which is to say as German — possessions is one more way in which the three *Books* announce a new phase in George's conception of himself and his task. As before, however, and as the preface also demonstrated, this change or shift of emphasis is more implied than openly stated. Most of the poems that make up the introductory section describe scenes that do not, at first appearance, go beyond the evocation of a particular emotion, and it is usually a rather muted, attenuated sentiment at that. There we read, for instance, of two women — the setting is an abstract "antique" landscape — who regularly meet on the anniversary of their lovers' deaths to commiserate over each other's loss; in another of a simple shepherd's joy at the waning of winter, which causes him to break into a jubilant song (hinting at the mythical origins of poetry itself); and in still another, of an aging satyr who bemoans his creeping inability to tempt laughing young girls with his pipe.

But these are all disconnected images, setting a wistful, faintly melancholy frame, to be sure, yet one without any binding urgency. It is not until later that something like a program or unifying idea emerges. In one poem, describing the departure of young warriors from their homes to uncertain fates — which means to early graves for many — we read that "we go happily: we are certain of a beautiful goal." In a similar vein, another poem describes how "we" embarked on a voyage, ignoring the pleas to stay made by "blond" and "lovely" suitors: "Your happiness does not move us," they sing. "We heard the booming call / That draws us on / To the temple to the service / Of the Beautiful: the Highest and Most Supreme."

"Beauty" may be called the highest good, but as the following poems make clear, it was beauty of a certain sort being praised. Throughout, the human physical form is celebrated, and most often it is the male body that is singled out for special mention. "His arm — astonishment and admiration — rests / On his right hip," a poem called "The Wrestler" begins; "the sun plays / On his strong body and on the laurel / On his brow." In another, the "divine nakedness" of marble statues is celebrated, or in yet another, varying the same theme, a dark Oriental palace is described, built of massive, rough-hewn stones, into which thin rays of light fall, illuminating the naked bodies within, which are all of different hues: "Bodies of the white of marble with bluish veins / Of the lush yellow of berries beginning to ripen — / Bodies bright red like blossoms and deep red like blood." This last passage, which is found not surprisingly in the third section of the book, "Of Hanging Gardens," also sets the stage for some of George's most ardently erotic poetry to date. A series of fifteen poems, all in this last, third part and thematically connected with one another, narrates the story of two lovers, recounting a series of events that culminates in their physical union. Leading up to this climax is much fervid petitioning on the part of the poetic voice. "If I do not touch your body today," we learn in one particularly evocative passage, "The fiber of my soul will tear / Like a string drawn too taut." At last, the long-awaited moment of fulfillment comes, but it goes by as if in a dream:

> When, behind the flower-covered gate,
> We finally felt only one another's breath
> Did we attain the bliss we had imagined?
> I remember that we both began to tremble
> Silently like frail reeds
> When we only softly touched each other
> And that our eyes began to run over —
> Thus you remained long at my side.

One of George's critics has written, rather demurely, that "the love poems in the *Hanging Gardens* are the only artistic record of a satisfactory relationship with the other sex" — with the "other" supposedly being, in this case, female. But there is reason to doubt the soundness of this judgment. It is true that the cycle begins with the lover, who wants to arrange a "chance" encounter with the object of his affection, wondering on which path "she will pass by today." Yet the gender of the beloved is never mentioned again, not even hinted at, either through pronouns or adjectives or definite articles. We have seen George employ this technique before, and here the intention can have been no different. The poem that immediately follows the one just cited strengthens the assumption that at the very least George wanted to keep his options open. Following the consummation of their passion, the two lovers — their gender, as previously, is undeclared here as well — lie entwined in each other's arms, but one of them seems unnaturally and inexplicably afraid of being discovered, a discovery, we gather, that might well lead to their deaths:

> When our hands nestle against our temples
> While lying in deep mats in holy calm
> Veneration relieves the burning of our limbs:
> So do not mind the shapeless shadows
> That sway up and down along the wall ·
> Nor the guards who may quickly separate us
> Nor that the white sand lying just beyond the city
> Is ready to gulp down our warm blood.

The threat of violence, of state-sanctioned murder and savage cruelty, familiar enough from *Algabal* and here serving to accentuate the penalties awaiting the exposure of forbidden love, in fact pervades the entire book. This is perhaps to be expected in the "Oriental" segment, which describes how a nameless "Conqueror," wandering "over the corpses" in the "city of ruins" that he has just crushed, walks into a temple of the defeated people and defiantly raises his "steaming blade" at the image of their god. Elsewhere, we are told of another ruler bearing more than a passing resemblance to the emperor Algabal who, facing the impending loss of his kingdom to an invading enemy, engages in solitary reminiscences about the "last time I was a hero," namely, when he could look unflinchingly at those "who did not show me obedience / Lying on the ground and at every one of my nods / A head rolled off a smooth and slender trunk."

But the predominance of a similar atmosphere of warfare and random bloodshed and other similarly "heroic deeds" in the middle, medieval section is more worrisome. References abound in these central pages to the "whistling of spears," "warriors bridling their steeds," "flaming swords," "legions of knights" and "fighters" engaged "in the good war" who deliver "the testimony of true heroic worth." The most revealing, and not incidentally the most sanguinary, is a poem titled "The Deed." Tellingly, it memorializes not an actual occurrence or a real "deed" but an imaginary one; it reproduces the daydream of a young boy. Walking by a field of flowers — they are ominously likened to a "silent and modest army" — the youth throws a stone into a well, and while staring absently at the concentric rings forming in the water, he fantasizes about his future glory, "perhaps seeing himself therein covered with fame and blood." In a scene stolen straight out of the *Nibelungenlied,* the boy dreams how he would "set out avid for death and wounds," bravely enter into a gloomy forest where a terrifying dragon-like beast lives, and "before his hand armed with a bare sword / The monster lies vanquished plunged in poison and fire." The boy, victorious, would then "follow his path illuminated by torchlight / His beautiful gaze still and straight fixed on the horizon."

To a Christian, and particularly to a Catholic, this scenario might also suggest the story of Saint George who according to legend bravely dispatched a fearsome dragon. The fact that the common abbreviation of the saint's name — St. George — was also a favorite one used by the poet for himself highlights only one of the more playful of the poem's several autobiographical allusions. What is more disturbing is that George's desire for conquest seems to have taken a decidedly darker turn in this book, that he equated victory over the world with martial, or at least physical, prowess, and no longer simply with poetic appropriation. Admittedly, this last poem told of a mere lad enthralled by nothing more than a harmless reverie, and of a sort to which, for better or worse, little boys everywhere are prone. But George was no longer a boy, and his own dreams of dominance were not just innocuous wishful thinking. Too, the images deployed in all three sections of the *Books* — of strong and silent youthful "heroes" performing great "deeds" illuminated by the bare flickering light of open flames — continue to recur in George's writing to the end.

Once more, it is important to stress how implicit much of what is presented here as being conclusive actually is, how faintly drawn what appears here, in retrospective analysis, to stand out with garish clarity, and how colored our understanding is by the inescapable knowledge of what eventually became of George and his legacy, instead of how he appeared to those who knew him at the end of 1895. The poems collected in *Books of Eclogues and Eulogies · of Legends and Songs and of the Hanging Gardens* are not rabid calls to arms: far from it. But they were the expression of his fierce and unrelenting will to make everything, and everyone, submit to his rule — or at least to his word. This fundamental trait, always active, reveals itself in more subtle ways in the book as well. There is a separate section appended to the first "Grecian" part, which even has its own title, "Eulogies for Several Young Men and Women of This Time." Each poem in this section is addressed to a particular person, but the names are either Greek or Greek-sounding: Damon, Menippa, Callimachus, Sidonia, Phaon, Kotytto, Antinous, and Apollonia. As it turns out, these were all masks for people George knew — hence the reference to "men and women of this time." They are poetic portraits of his friends, including Albert Saint-Paul, Isi Auerbach, Waclaw Lieder, Ludwig Klages, Frieda Zimmer-Zerny (a singer he had met in Munich), and Edmond Rassenfosse (not accidentally, it was he to whom George gave the pseudonym of the Roman emperor Hadrian's beloved and ill-fated Antinous). George carried over this practice of dedicating poems to his friends into subsequent books, often devoting large portions of them to these tributes. In his next work, *The Year of the Soul,* their identities are no longer hidden behind fictional guises, but only their initials appear. Finally, in *The Seventh Ring* of 1907 they emerge wearing their full names, and in his last book, *The New Reich* (1928), both the first and last names and the initials of friends are used seemingly at random. But, in all of these instances, one has the nagging sense that by incorporating them into his private sanctuary George wanted as much to eulogize his friends as to absorb them.

George's attempt to commandeer an issue of *Pan* as a vehicle for promoting his own cause may have failed, but increasingly others were obliging him in his efforts by taking care of his publicity for him. In March 1896, Hofmannsthal wrote a lengthy essay for the Viennese daily, *Die Zeit,* on the three *Books* called simply "Poems by Stefan George." It was the first major notice his work had received and among the most perceptive ever to appear. Noting the peculiar ambiguity inhabiting George's stance toward publication, Hofmannsthal suggested that the poems "neither offer themselves to the public nor are they held back from it." They were simply there, like some natural phenomenon, not seeking out attention, but hard to overlook. Or rather, since natural phenomena were not exactly George's strong suit, they could be said to exude a slightly alien, almost benumbing, physical presence. "Although weaving in a rich expanse of internal and external experience," Hofmannsthal astutely saw, "life is so completely tamed, so subjugated in these three books of poems that our senses, accustomed to confused noise, are wafted by an incredible calm and the coolness of a deep temple." Hofmannsthal also noted, no doubt mindful of George's own effect on him, that "here and there, among their muted measures, the tone of the poems becomes violent, almost threatening." The basic attitude they convey, he acutely recognized, was the desire "to remain superior to life," and that the last section especially, "Of Hanging Gardens," is "full of the concept of a highly personal sovereignty and full of dim and cruel experiences." The essay ends with a virtuoso flourish, in which Hofmannsthal perfectly captured the poet in his poems. "The innate royalty of a soul in possession of itself is the subject of the three books. Nothing is more alien to our time, nothing is more valuable to the few. Our time will have to be satisfied to find a strange appeal in the spare tyrannical gestures, in the words frugally uttered by narrow lips, in this lightly striding humanity with head held high and the world seen in the uncertain light of the early morning hours. A small number of people believe, however, that they now know more about the value of existence than before."

It was a subtle performance, one that could be taken a number of ways, and not all of them positive. Far from feeling exposed or ill treated, George was delighted. "Your analysis of my pastoral poems of praise is so sensitive and fine," George wrote in acknowledgement, adding it was a review "as a poet would wish it. An understanding word is a warm spring rain for the dry soul. Remain loyal to me." This last injunction, which under the best of circumstances was demanding, sounded even more importunate in the context of their perennially rocky relationship. For a year, since March 1895, George had again been trying to patch things up with Hofmannsthal, sending sometimes cajoling, sometimes scolding, sometimes sweetly flattering letters. In most of them, George more or less insistently returned to the vexing question of Hofmannsthal's participation in the *Blätter,* repeatedly enjoining him to return to the fold. George had initially tried to lure him with the prospect of a new beginning, telling him that "our *Blätter* shall undergo a small external change (perhaps I'll take everything in hand!) and I hope for your assistance." Thus far, however, Hofmannsthal had politely, but resolutely, demurred. He wanted to stay only "in a certain proximity to the circle," he said on one occasion, or to remain merely "in a certain relationship to your artistic efforts," as he put it on another. Never one to give up easily, George tried another tack. "You can hardly write a strophe that does not enrich one with a new thrill, indeed a new way of feeling" he cooed in February 1896. He even credited Hofmannsthal, not quite straightforwardly, for having drawn him back to Germany, telling him "who knows if I — had I not found you or Gérardy as poets — would have continued writing in my mother tongue!" All to no avail. Impervious to George's constant inveigling and browbeating, Hofmannsthal persisted in maintaining a safe distance.

Hofmannsthal's reluctance to commit himself to what George had called the "good cause" was, as we know, based less on principled skepticism about the worth of the enterprise itself than on the legitimate fear that George would use it as a pretext to consume him. George had by then already refined what was to become one of his favored means of enmeshing his friends and associates within an intricate net of obligation and implicit subservience. He would have them carry out little tasks, undertake minor errands for him — such as writing letters on his behalf, acting as his intermediary by performing visits to troublesome third parties, or simply by having them submit a potential new contributor to the journal for his approval — that created a subtle but palpable hierarchical division between them. It was George who gave the orders others carried out. As long as one was happy to serve as a messenger, scribe, or patsy, everything was fine. But as soon as a wish went unfulfilled or a command was disobeyed, George would register his disappointment, displeasure, or worse. This was what lay behind his appeal for Hofmannsthal's "loyalty," and Hofmannsthal knew it.

Although Hofmannsthal seemed to be causing him nothing but grief, George could take comfort in the allegiance of others. He was, for example, confident of Wolfskehl's faithfulness because, as opposed to the unruly Hofmannsthal, the big, propulsive, and fanatically devoted Hessian never gave him serious reason to doubt his allegiance. Yet even here George thought the best policy was to trust but verify. Wolfskehl's voracious appetite for human contact, his passion and gift for free-ranging conversation, and his spontaneous, expansive nature did make George occasionally wonder if he was truly committed to George's singular cause. Earlier that year, in March 1896, George had experimentally voiced reservations at Wolfskehl's perhaps too energetic embrace of the frenetic pleasures — and potential dangers — of Berlin. George hoped this did not mean that he had become untrue to his most important calling. "My dear and venerated Master," Wolfskehl effusively assured him, "how could I have ever been permitted to call myself your disciple if I were now capable of wavering. But you know me and my hunger for people and you won't take it amiss if I strive to know life to the fullest. I have chosen for today and forever. You must remain in the temple — but let us outside rapturously bring tidings from the streets and the marketplace. It is no less the case that we know where we owe worship, truly!" In any case, Wolfskehl went on, it was not that he was happy in the Prussian capital. "Berlin is only the concentrated expression, the extract, as it were, of our awful age." Wolfskehl seemed genuinely to suffer in the city, to feel out of place and ill at ease there. But it is possible that his protest was made a little sharper by his knowledge that it conformed to official doctrine. As if to reward him for having thus demonstrating his fealty, George wrote back saying that "the fact that your stay in this city of heroes heathens and w[hore]s is becoming unbearable is a good sign you see that you still belong entirely to us." "You belong to us": it was a phrase that George had inherited from Mallarmé, but George used it with a characteristic shift of emphasis. Whereas the French Maître meant it more as a badge of confraternal affiliation, in which the second pronoun was truly plural, the German Meister intended it in a more singular sense. "You belong to us," in other words, meant more and more for George, "You belong to me."

But no amount of suasion, wheedling, or intimidation seemed to be capable of moving Hofmannsthal into that desired category. In April, when George briefly thought that he had finally managed to induce him to come to Bingen, George triumphantly wrote to the steadfast but afflicted Wolfskehl, who now felt marooned up in Berlin: "May the pleasant news brighten you up that Hugo Hofmannsthal intends to come here in September. I will then invite you, too, Lieder and Gérardy to the first German Poets' Conference." In the end, as we know, Hofmannsthal did not attend the meeting. But his absence at the congress did not prevent George from making one last attempt at winning the Austrian's cooperation. In mid-September 1896, George wrote to him to report on "what has recently taken a new turn in our literature, especially what closely concerns you yourself." Reminding him about the meeting in Bingen he had just missed, George told him that their discussions mainly centered on their future plans for the journal. "I already made intimations to you about expanding our *Blätter für die Kunst* and strengthened by many encouraging signs I believe the time will soon be nigh to publish a monthly German review which as you know does not yet exist. To be sure we would then be addressing the masses." To Hofmannsthal, who almost certainly knew nothing of the *Pan* debacle and thus of George's newfound willingness to risk soiling the hem of his gown by venturing out into the mud of the marketplace, this revelation must have seemed a bolt out of the blue. Equally startling would have been what followed. "The artistic direction would probably remain the same but the aesthetic section would increase considerably by the addition of some truly outstanding young scholars. Thus the editorial board would consist of two poets and one scholar." Just to be clear, George added that "I think it essential to suggest to you that you offer yourself as one of these poets. You are the first person I am approaching."

From the beginning, Hofmannsthal had pressed for the inclusion of more analytic and discursive essays, and his requests had been consistently ignored or rebuffed, often accompanied by the condescending rationale that the *Blätter* had no part in such crude, popularizing undertakings. Now, not only would the journal include an "aesthetic" section, and invite "scholars" to participate (George seems to have had in mind the Berlin professor Max Dessoir), but it would also explicitly and deliberately seek to appeal to the "masses." Moreover, George implied that he would also dispense with the fiction of having Klein sign himself as the editor, which would allow him, standing next to Hofmannsthal, to step out into the open for the first time. In a draft of a letter probably written that October but which was never sent, George in fact revealed what many had long suspected. He admitted that "for almost six years," while "not the sole person tending to and executing matters, I nevertheless was the guiding spirit of every element, even the smallest internal and superficial concern, in our *Blätter f. d. Kunst* — thus my complete knowledge." The fact that the new plan would mean jettisoning Klein did not seem to distress George particularly. He had already more or less dispensed with him anyway. "Are you dead or alive? I have some interest in knowing it," Klein wrote to him — oddly, in English — that same month. "The matter of mere business is almost exhausted between us — very well — but has it to imply cessation of interchanging friendly subjects?" Although Klein was later permitted to assume some secretarial duties again, and despite his name continuing to appear on the cover page of the *Blätter* as the editor to the end, his active participation, both in the journal and George's life, had thus ceased at the latest by the fall of 1896.

George would not relinquish Hofmannsthal so easily. Having had enough experience to be able to anticipate Hofmannsthal's probable reaction to his offer of coeditorship, George had impressed upon him to think carefully about it before giving his answer. "Since this journal can have enormous significance for your life as well as for mine, I ask you to examine yourself diligently before you send an objection." The expectation of a rejection turned into a self-fulfilling prophecy. Waiting a month to reply, Hofmannsthal framed his refusal within a self-indictment, cleverly blaming his own weakness for his inability to accept George's invitation. "I feel myself to be so uncertain in my work, so far away, not from maturity, but even from individual confidence and cheerfulness, that the thought of appearing to promulgate my writings before people fills me with a kind of dread." Given this professed lack of self-confidence, this almost morbid insecurity about his place in the world, how could he pretend to teach others? "For which ideas, for whose views of art and whose philosophy, for whose poetry would I be able to stand up with confidence and faith as long as I, doubting myself, have to wait for every new day, hesitant and fearful, for confirmation that I am not entirely unqualified even to take the words into my mouth which we use to designate values, as long as every bad day can deny me this confirmation, as long as every proof of an inner or outer inadequacy is capable of robbing me for months of my composure, even of language altogether?"

Although he did not mention it to George, these were concerns that Hofmannsthal was genuinely wrestling with at the time, a growing distrust in the efficacy of language as a whole to capture and convey anything at all. This suspicion that language was a permanently damaged instrument, capable of referring only to itself, that it was forever caught within a sterile, solipsistic prison of its own making, culminated in Hofmannsthal's famous and paradoxically eloquent "Lord Chandos Letter," which fictionalizes this linguistic crisis. Not accidentally, George was also confronted by a similar dilemma, and the ways they both approached the problem says as much about their respective characters as do their direct exchanges with one another. Hofmannsthal, the more frail of the two, initially saw the only way to escape the inherent emptiness of language was to take the drastic route of completely avoiding it and falling mute. (Indeed, not long afterward he actually stopped writing poetry entirely and turned exclusively to other genres.) George, however, took another path, one equally in line with his own constitution. If words would not do the work he expected of them, he was soon to conclude, then deeds would have to step in their place.

Hofmannsthal — and he would not be the only one — wondered what the nature of these deeds was supposed to be. Concluding the letter in which he rejected George's proposal, he urged him "now to let me have some sort of general idea what is being planned. For I cannot imagine that my inability to make of myself what would be valuable to you and perhaps extremely welcome to me would have to sever all connections between you and me." As usual in his communications with George, the tone here is civilized, courteous, even mildly deferential. To others, he showed his real feelings. In November 1896, Clemens von Franckenstein innocently asked Hofmannsthal about news concerning the journal and received a rough reply from his friend. Hofmannsthal said that he no longer wanted to hear anything about the "stupid *Blätter,* which have both annoyed and taken even me aback by the entirely unexpected, sudden publication of my poems, and with which I have, by the way (I think) already had another falling out, and which will soon disappear and transform itself into a weekly review or some other mysterious thing." Yet again, their fragile, tentative bond — with one vigorously pushing and pulling, the other coyly drawing back — broke asunder with Hofmannsthal saying, somewhat wearily, that he just wanted to be left alone.

George never responded to the rebuff. Hofmannsthal's intransigent refusal of his advances was obviously a bitter disappointment, and not just on the personal level. No doubt partially because of this failure, the *Blätter* never did remake itself in the way he had outlined to Hofmannsthal. And not until a decade and a half later, with the appearance of the first *Yearbook for the Spiritual Movement (Jahrbuch für die geistige Bewegung)* in 1910, did anything like the critical journal George had envisioned come into being.

But George was to suffer yet another loss that winter. As usual, he spent part of the season in Berlin. He had begun to frequent the house of the painters Sabine and Reinhold Lepsius there, who had first heard of him during a trip to Rome when someone had described George to them as "an uncrowned king" and as "one of the greatest spirits alive." Naturally, their interest was piqued, and when George presented himself at their spacious apartment and studio on Kantstrasse in the autumn of 1896, Sabine Lepsius was immediately certain that she had before her "an exceptional, powerful personality." "His glance distant and yet also charming. His speech, without being loud, of vigorous force." Also finding his "southern German dialect" pleasing, the only discordant notes she registered were the top hat in his hand and the monocle stuck to one eye. Soon George was a regular visitor at the Lepsius home, and the couple remained among his closest friends in Berlin for a considerable time. Most usefully, over the next two years, Sabine arranged for George to give several carefully staged readings of his works to select members of the Berlin intelligentsia in their salon, which she would decorate with laurel for the occasion and darken with muted lighting, giving the scene a solemn, almost consecrated air.

One afternoon in November, shortly after arriving in the city, George also stopped by the apartment of an older friend, Isi Auerbach, now deeply anguished in a marriage she never wanted and with a man she never loved. She received him, reclined in a chaise longue in her parlor, suffering from chronic dispiritedness. After trying to lend her whatever comfort or solace he could, George rose to go. Just as he was about to leave the room, however, another concerned well-wisher was ushered in. With a start, George saw himself face to face with Richard Dehmel. They both silently passed by each other, with lowered glances. George appears to have taken this as a deliberate attempt on Isi's part to bring the two men together. In a strange, stiffly ceremonious gesture, almost as if he were issuing a challenge to the poor woman for satisfaction to repair his damaged honor, he called on her again later. This time, he came in the company of the dark, towering Wolfskehl, who, acting like a second in a duel, wordlessly handed her a sealed envelope, which she opened only after they had both just as silently taken their leave. "Do not revile *friendship*," the delivered letter admonished her. "Between us it occurs when one is able to carry what is great and noble within him into the other — grows and thus diminishes — then disappears entirely when what seems great and noble to one is coarse and vile to the other." She appeared to realize that an irreparable rift had opened up between them. She replied, despondently, that "the tone of your card confirms that my feeling was not wrong. I want to issue neither questions nor reproaches to you. I am gradually beginning to believe that people need friends for themselves. They do not want to be friends to others. I want to be very still. Good-bye."

Even in her sad, remorseful farewell, Frau Isi — who George only a little later would claim had once been "his world" — had managed to put her finger on a deep truth about her now former friend. He needed friends for himself, for his own purposes, and not the other way around. Whereas Hofmannsthal seemed to be caught in a perpetual retreat, Isi Auerbach had tried too hard to reconcile two incompatible beings, perilously ignoring George's repeated warnings that Dehmel meant less than nothing to him. Both were made to feel the penalty for disregarding his will. But Hofmannsthal, granted special status because of his exquisite gifts, kept benefiting from repeated, if unasked for, acts of clemency. Ida Auerbach née Coblenz he never saw or wrote to again.

Chapter 16
The Year of the Soul

One of the more impressive things about George during this period, and indeed throughout his entire life, was his sheer capacity for work. His poetic output had been constant and prodigious ever since the beginning of the decade, with a book initially coming out every year. Only after the inception of the *Blätter für die Kunst* in 1892 — which alone required a major investment of time and energy — did the pace slacken to a volume every two years. Traversing the continent looking for kindred spirits, which again could have been a full-time occupation in itself, appears not to have dampened his creative fires through fatigue or distraction but on the contrary only to have stoked them. Too, the management of his increasingly diverse and far-flung friendships, which often called for hastily arranged on-site visits, did not appear to have caused him undue distress or adversely affected his ability to concentrate. It is a wonder how George — who seemed to be always on the move, one week presiding in the Café Luitpold in Munich, the next checking in at Bingen, only to set out the following day for some destination in Belgium or Holland, finally to end up for a slightly more extended stay in Berlin — could ever find the time to write, much less write poetry of a kind that had never been heard in German before.

Part of it was that George followed a rigorous daily regimen for most of his life. One of his friends revealed that, until he was about fifty, he usually stayed up late conversing with friends. Typically he worked during the quiet hours between five and eight in the morning, when he would take a light breakfast and then go back to sleep. At ten he would go on an extended walk, eat lunch at twelve, sleep until four in the afternoon and then receive his friends. In later years he would retire at nine in the evening but otherwise retained this division of his days. But that did not really explain his fertility. Adding to the mystery was his practice of never letting anyone see him work or view his desk in anything but a pristine state. When someone commented on this disconcerting habit, he offered in explanation that "one also doesn't show the preparation of a meal or the leftovers to guests." A tactful consideration of the sensibilities of others played only a small part, if any, in George's overly fastidious attempt to conceal the tools of his trade. He was well aware that the very fact that few people had ever actually caught him working only heightened the sense of awe many felt before his output. This covertness regarding the means of poetic production was thus yet another facet of his calculated self-dramatization. But it remains undeniable that, especially in view of the irregular circumstances of his life, George's continued faculty for sustained and productive work is nothing short of astonishing.

Nowhere were the benefits of this determination more evident than in the *Blätter für die Kunst*. Despite the seemingly endless tug-of-war with Hofmannsthal, whose participation George had tried to portray as the sine qua non of its existence, the journal was positively flourishing. In all, five issues were published in 1896, with the first appearing in January and continuing to come out on a bruising bimonthly schedule through October. Since Klein had been temporarily shunted aside, most of the drudgery work would have fallen on George's own shoulders, although he must have unloaded some of it on the broad willing back of Wolfskehl. And, if anything, the journal was becoming more complex, more wide-ranging, more ambitious — and thus more time-consuming — than ever before. At stake was how George would transform himself, and the "movement" he now claimed to lead, into something more than, or truly different from, simply a German version of a familiar French model. He had already declared his independence from foreign influence; now he had to establish the limits of his own domain. Over the course of 1896, the first outlines of what George would eventually become begin to make themselves faintly visible. Initially, the boundaries are still blurred. But gradually the contours assume a more definite form, forced into a recognizable shape by the pressure of internal criticism, friendly prodding, and the growing need to defend ground already won.

The introductory maxims of the *Blätter,* which accompanied every number but one in this year, had already crystallized into the forum where its aims, and always foremost those of George himself, found their most prominent and concentrated articulation. But clear they are not. In January, for instance, apparently responding to the perfectly reasonable question "*what* kind of art was represented in these pages," the not very helpful answer was offered that "essential is the artistic transformation of a life — which life? is of no importance for the time being." Realizing that matters could not really be left there, George allowed for a bit more specificity about his conception of art, or at least for some expansion on this fairly cryptic declaration, at the end of the introduction. "Simply put what we partly sought partly perpetuated: an art free of any service: above life after it has penetrated life," or in other words, "an art out of the joy of contemplation out of ecstatic transport of sound and sun."

That was also not exactly helpful: it merely restated, but without adding much by way of precision or freshness, the *l'art pour l'art* thesis. But next to an essay by Wolfskehl, contained in the same issue, these pronouncements seem the model of perspicuity. Entitled "The Priest of the Spirit" ("Der Priester vom Geiste"), the short, two-page sketch is in actuality a veiled, ideal biography of George himself, tracing in extremely abstract, indirect terms his intellectual and artistic itinerary. But only an initiate would get even that far. "The easy victory! All being had become a mirror to you and you laughed." This is how Wolfskehl described George's own imagined reaction to his first book of poetry, the *Hymns;* his dissatisfaction that followed, which led to his second book, is expressed thus: "Small goal! Small goal! Thus your lips resounded, your soul however bled. You enwrapped yourself in the pride of your sorrow to which you paid no heed." This is not the language of someone whose first concern is to elucidate or explain. And, indeed, Wolfskehl wanted neither to analyze nor evaluate but to exhort. The essay was not just about George, it was aimed at him. Seizing hold of "life in the realm of the real" is what Wolfskehl was advocating. At bottom, Wolfskehl wanted to urge George to leave the ethereal plane of pure poetry and take part in active life, to cast off the mantle of the isolated and lonely poet, whose "victories" are victories, quite literally, in name only, and to take up greater goals in the real world. "Swept away the fearful selfishness, that timid soul! that always clings to the ephemeral and is averse to all becoming. A new priesthood has arisen to proclaim a new realm [*Reich*] to the faithful. The soul feels the thunderous inexpressible ecstasy of creation, true creation." "The path to life is found, the holy way on which every step is as a song of triumph."

But the transition from esoteric symbolist to sacerdotal conqueror is even harder than it sounds. First, to erect a "new realm," the perimeters of the old one had to be perceptibly marked out. In the next issue, in March, the introduction faced this issue head-on. "To approach art with gravity and holiness: that was unknown to the entire generation of poets that preceded us." Obviously, the maxim refers specifically to German poets, and a few lines later it draws on the authority of Goethe and Nietzsche — both of whom also never wasted an opportunity to lambaste their own people and culture — in order to bolster claims concerning the Germans' backwardness and cultural deficiencies. "The fact," another maxim read, "that there can be no artistic or poetic event in our country proves that we find ourselves in a second-class cultural state." (Again illustrating the close proximity of the ideas expressed in these aphorisms to George's own views, a letter he wrote to Hofmannsthal in April mentions his desire to publish an article in a "major foreign paper," "where artistic events are considered to be events at all.") Even the traditional German "gothic" typeface called *Fraktur* used in most published books in the nineteenth century was seen both as symptomatic of and contributing to the generally dire state of affairs. "The Germans will not achieve taste until they have disabused themselves of this tasteless so-called German script."

We know that this relentless disparagement of German poetry, German culture, and of the entire German state had, for George, deeply personal roots and was not only, or even mainly, the outgrowth of his artistic proclivities. But it was an odd spectacle to behold nonetheless. For here was someone, almost totally unknown to the wider reading public in Germany, who had taken it upon himself to reform the allegedly abysmal taste of his fellow citizens, not just in poetry but in all of the arts. And he seemed to believe that the quickest way to rouse his sluggish compatriots from their barbaric slumber was through a bracing harangue. If the Germans could only be convinced how awful they really were, he seemed to believe, then they could not fail to try to improve. It hardly seemed like a winning strategy for gaining widespread sympathy and cooperation for the cause. But, as time would show, it turned out there were plenty of people willing to be told how worthless they were so long as they were able to venerate someone they believed their flawless superior.

One person who seemed disinclined to make that sacrifice was Ludwig Klages. The previous December of 1895, Klages — a northern German and a Protestant — had written to George saying he was thinking of quitting the *Blätter* on the grounds that he felt it was becoming "too personally oriented and too soft, symbolic, southern, harmonious." He wanted to stick to what he called "the northern element" instead. Although George sent a carefully worded rejoinder to him privately, the real response appeared as one of the maxims to the journal. "The reproach has been leveled at us," the March 1896 issue reads, "that our entire artistic movement in the *Blätter* is too southern, not German enough. But it is perhaps the most outstanding and most natural of all the German tribal peculiarities: to seek completion in the south, in the south of which our ancestors took possession, to which our emperors descended to receive the essential benediction, to which we poets make pilgrimage to find light to accompany depth: the eternal rule in the Holy Roman Empire of the German Nation."

Whether he was swayed by this argument or not, Klages finally decided not to distance himself from George for almost another decade. Yet, whatever its effect on Klages himself, the greater import of the passage is far-reaching. It was the first time George had ever enunciated what he positively identified with Germany, as opposed to what he tirelessly repudiated. Fundamentally, the Germany he claimed as his own was not the new nation formed in 1871, but instead the area roughly circumscribed by the ancient Roman Limes. This, too, is a typical if complicated gesture: by defining the Holy Roman Empire as his point of reference in demarcating his idea of Germany — that is, by rekindling the memory of a political entity that began when the pope had crowned German king Otto I emperor in 962 and which had officially ceased to exist almost a thousand years in 1806 when the German empire dissolved itself after Napoleon had crushed Austria and Prussia the year before — George was also, and not very subtly, rejecting the German state that factually existed in both temporal and geographical terms. The end of the Holy Roman Empire was indelibly associated in most people's minds with Prussian humiliation and disgrace, and evoking its long and storied history inescapably recalled the time prior to the Prussian dominance of Germany as a whole. In addition, and in an obviously related consideration, the confessional framework that the older nation presupposed stood as a silent protest against the belligerently Protestant Prussian state. As its name implied, the Holy Roman Empire existed when there was no split in the Church, no schism caused by northern rebels, selfish dissidents and hypocritical heretics, but only the one, all-embracing, universal home, a transcendent power even the medieval Emperors had acknowledged by traveling to Rome to receive the Pope's blessing of their rule.

No less important, of course, was the assertion in the *Blätter* that Germans achieved a kind of cultural completion in the south, that they found a cheerful "light" to complement their meditative "depth" only in Mediterranean climes. Here, as well, the associations multiply. George meant, and knew his readers would understand, not simply Goethe's Italian journey and everything it had entailed, namely the attainment of a classical serenity, along with furnishing a kind of spiritual template for successive generations of German wanderers — including George himself. But he had also gestured toward another long-standing German preoccupation with the south, this time not of Roman but of Greek provenance. The contrast between "light" and "depth," the brilliant radiance of sunlit surfaces and the dark, brooding, vaguely menacing interior, suggests the opposite but mutually indispensable categories of the Apollonian and Dionysian that Nietzsche elaborated in *The Birth of Tragedy*. The German infatuation with ancient Greece, initiated during the previous century by the ardent Grecophile Johann Joachim Winckelmann and advocated by countless others, still burned brightly in George's day. Hence many Germans believed they saw in Greece everything they lacked and desperately wanted. The Greeks represented to them the pinnacle of physical prowess, unsurpassed artistic achievement, the realization of beauty in all of its forms; in short, the ancient Greeks embodied perfection. In a strange kind of doublethink, educated Germans truly thought that they could achieve their own authentic cultural identity by refashioning themselves after the Greeks — or after the idealized image of the Greeks they had manufactured.

In an introductory paragraph to the following year's issue, in November 1897, this connection was finally made explicit. "That a ray from Hellas fell on us," it read, "that our youth is now beginning to view life passionately and no longer basely: that it seeks beautiful proportions in the physical and intellectual sphere: that it is liberated from both the enthusiasm for shallow general culture and happiness as well as worn-out militaristic barbarism: that it shuns the stiff uprightness and the bent-over burdensomeness of those living around them as ugly and wishes to stride through life beautifully with unencumbered head: that it finally conceives of its national character [*Volkstum*] in grand terms and not in the limited sense of a tribe: here one will find the complete change in German nature at the turn of the century." German youth will become most quintessentially German, in other words, when it has cast off everything that makes it — German.

But what may at first appear to be an agreeably cosmopolitan, even openminded, sentiment reveals on closer inspection a more disquieting strain. For, as we must keep reminding ourselves, George and his friends always intended several things by the words German or Germany. When used negatively, they almost always referred, as we know, to the official state and culture of Prussia, together with all that implied. In the rarer though increasingly more frequent instances in which the words were mentioned affirmatively, they alluded not to an existent entity but rather to an imaginative construction composed of historical fantasy, religious idealism, and both ancient and modern mythology. The "Germany" George endorsed resided entirely in his imagination, either because it had long ago ceased to be a historical reality — provided one assumes that the glorified Germanic past he envisioned had ever existed at all — or because it beckoned as a future but remote possibility to come. The result was that George was asking his readers to form an allegiance to a Germany — or, more precisely, to *his* Germany — that was wholly unreal, an immaterial phantasm assembled from disparate and often purely illusory elements, and to reject the concrete political and legal body that actually existed.

What kind of deleterious consequences this stance could engender is made plain in the experience recorded by an acquaintance George made in early 1897. A young composer from England by the name of Cyril Scott had come to Frankfurt the previous year to round out his musical studies. Before long, he became attached to Clemens von Franckenstein — the same friend of Hugo von Hofmannsthal that had been the pretext for the latest tiff with George. Tall, thin, blond, and arrestingly handsome, Scott achieved an early success (he, together with the Australian composer Percy Grainger and several others, were later dubbed the "Frankfurt Group" in England), but Scott ultimately failed to live up to his initial promise. "As a composer," his obituary read in 1970, "he had every gift except that of a strong character to impress his audience." Strong character or not, personally he was exceedingly likeable. Charming, confident, and energetic, he exuded an attractive vivacity. One afternoon, in the rooms of Franckenstein, Scott was introduced to George who took an immediate shining to the young English musician. Born in 1879, Scott was eleven years junior to the poet, and George soon invited him to come to Bingen, which Scott gladly accepted. "Both in appearance and manner," he later recalled, "Stefan George was the most striking and unusual personality I have ever encountered." At least as far as the seventeen-year-old Englishman's own appearance was concerned, Scott evidently aroused a similar animation in George. He remembered how, when the English lad once visited Bingen with some of his friends, a local fisherman was moved to exclaim in admiration, "My, ain't those beautiful boys!"

To Scott himself, George was unusually direct. "We took many walks together," Scott confided in his memoirs, "and I recall that it was during one of these rambles that Stefan George confessed that his attachment to me was no ordinary one." Apparently, George did not harbor any great hopes that his affection would be answered in kind. As Scott went on inform us, George had told him that "he had guessed from the very beginning that I was not of the type who would reciprocate his feelings." Even though Scott found "the confession and its cause extremely embarrassing" and felt "distressed to think he should have propensities which in those days most people regarded with loathing and disgust," Scott did not break off the relationship. "If I had not admired and liked Stefan George so much," he explained, and "had not felt proud to be seen walking in the street or sitting in cafés with so striking and magnetic a personality, I would have contrived to let the friendship cool off and so end what must have been for him a painful association." As it happened, their "association," albeit punctuated by several long abeyances, lasted another quarter century. But it always had to remain, as Scott once gingerly put it in a letter to George, strictly "platonic."

Significantly, George could accept this arrangement on personal grounds but most emphatically not because he bowed to any external tribunal or higher authority. "I remember another remark," Scott continued, "that I made to George one fine morning as we were sitting together and looking out over the Rhine. I said that I disapprove of every form of conducting one's life that contradicts the laws of the land. He smiled derisively at this and declared that if these laws would be vigorously enforced then many prominent personages in various countries would be affected. Thus the police would have to think carefully more than once before taking any measures." This disdain for the law is perhaps not particularly surprising in George, especially given its source and jurisdiction. How could he have recognized a law that denied and vilified an essential part of his being, a law, moreover and more offensively, that was passed and implemented by meddlesome, small-minded, and odious Prussian bureaucrats?

Yet George's scorn for legal customs or restraints was not limited to such fatuous prohibitions placed on his private life, nor was Scott alone in witnessing its expression. The following year, in July 1898, George received an unexpected letter from Leopold von Andrian. Saying that he, Andrian, had only just learned that a sonnet he had sent to Klein in 1893 had appeared in the November issue of the *Blätter,* Adrian demanded an explanation why he had not been asked for his permission to publish the poem after the passage of so much time. The poem, written more than five years ago, no longer reflected his feelings or the person he had subsequently become. Still pretending that he believed Klein was the actual editor of the journal, he pitched his letter as an appeal to George — "you who probably knew nothing of the publication" — to intervene on his behalf and to communicate to the renegade Klein both his severe displeasure and an open threat. Pointing to the copyright law that had been adopted by Austria and the German empire in 1894, which specified that an editor's right to print work submitted for publication extended only two years after receipt, Andrian emphasized "how much more flagrant the editor's offense, which the law already punishes, is in my particular case." "I hope," Andrian pompously concluded, "that you will recommend somewhat greater caution and consideration to the gentleman who so little understands his own office. I would finally like to request that you communicate to him only that I will take legal action against him if he publishes another old poem of mine."

George realized there was probably more bark than bite in Andrian's words. But he had no desire to become entangled in a court case, however remote the chance it would ever get that far, and his response was providently calibrated to cool Andrian's ire. Assuring him that his poem had been published with no other intention than to "do honor to you," George regretted that the affair had caused him such annoyance, and he promised not to print any more of his verses in the future without permission. But in reaction to the threat of legal proceedings, George's tone became frigid. "I advise you as a friend of many years to resort only in the most extraordinary cases to what one calls the 'law.' You would at most give the defendant pleasure in doing so as well as a number of idle spectators and listeners." It is an alarming remark, not made any less so by the quotation marks around the word "law." George was not simply telling Andrian that he would be indifferent to any prosecution aimed at either Klein or himself, but also that he did not even acknowledge the basis of the complaint as legitimate. George had no use for "what one calls the 'law.'" The only law he recognized, he seemed to be implying, was the one he represented himself.

But as Cyril Scott told it, George's contempt for legal strictures spilled over into his attitude toward the state more generally. "Being an artist-aristocrat of the most pronounced type, he roughly divided mankind into two categories," Scott explained. "Under one heading the artists and intellectuals, and under the other, the *bourgeois,* who counted as 'nobodies.' The latter needed laws and religions to rule them and regulate their conduct, the artists ruled themselves by their aesthetic feelings and so were above laws and regulations." Like many others, Scott imbibed this heady doctrine in greedy draughts. Wanting desperately to count among the elect and avoid at all costs being relegated among the "nobodies," he soon became happily accustomed to thinking of himself as standing far above the law as well.

From the sober perspective of older age, Scott was clear-eyed about the effect this hubris had produced on him. "What it did, of course, in a youth of my age," he later wrote in self-recrimination, "was to foster arrogance and subdue all feelings of democracy." Here, in a few words, we are confronted by the final implication, the ultimate danger of George's renunciation of the Germany that existed in favor of one of his own creation. It bred and encouraged a haughty disregard for the rule of law, a dismissal of the legal government as illegitimate or, at most, as pertaining only to those too stupid or too unreliable to govern themselves. It nourished the sense that there were certain unalterable, hierarchically fixed differences setting people apart, and that the crude mechanism of an artificial, abstract, and purely arbitrary invention such as "the law" remained powerless in the face of those supposedly deeper and more lasting truths.

Cyril Scott also made the acquaintance of another friend of George's that year in the person of the Berlin painter and designer Melchior Lechter. "He had," Scott wrote, "a round cherubic face with a complexion like that of a woman, very small twinkling eyes, longish light-coloured hair, with a plump physique. He dressed with great elegance but in a manner quite peculiar to himself, and he spoke with a slight lisp." Born in 1865, in the Westphalian capital of Münster — and a stronghold of northern Rhenish Catholicism — Lechter had grown up in extremely simple circumstances, and at age fourteen he had apprenticed himself to a stained-glass window maker. Four years later, he ran away to Berlin, where he enrolled in the Academy of Fine Arts. There, to support his studies, Lechter worked in the mornings and nights in a glass factory. "Yes, I was not bedded on roses," Lechter said of his early days. "When other young academics were getting up and relaxing over their breakfast, I had already earned my bread for the day!" Not having had the privilege of attending a "classical" Gymnasium and thus never forced to learn Latin and Greek, Lechter nevertheless possessed the kind of formidable, if slightly disjointed, learning often encountered in autodidacts. He had read and memorized great works of world literature — as long as they were available in German translations — and he was especially enamored of Dante, Shakespeare, and Goethe. But he was also drawn to more recent writings, such as the novels by Huysmans and the still popular Péladan. Even decades later, when he mentioned *À Rebours* to a younger friend and saw that the title produced a blank, Lechter urged him to read the novel, saying it had made a "strong impression in my youth."

Lechter had first written Klein in March 1894 to inquire about how he might obtain a copy of the "Baudelaire translation" announced in the most recent issue of the *Blätter*. As Lechter told it, he often stopped by the sole book shop in Berlin that sold the journal, on Unter den Linden, to ask if a new issue had yet appeared. The proprietor told George of his persistent admirer, and soon enough George wanted to "meet the only person in Berlin who read the *Blätter*." Curiously, when they finally did meet, George presented himself as Carl August Klein — apparently the masquerade was not confined to the literary sphere — and "Herr Klein" listened to Lechter describe how much he liked George's poems, especially *Algabal*. Only as he was leaving and already on the stairs did Lechter's visitor, who had occasionally given an odd smile during their conversation, call out and say, "By the way, I am Stefan George myself."

Once begun, their collaborative association proved hearty and immensely fruitful. The January 1896 number of the journal included a printed reproduction of one of Lechter's stained-glass windows as a supplement. And, in December of the same year, Lechter's first major exhibit was held in the fashionable Gurlitt gallery in Berlin, featuring works depicting images of Tristan and Isolde — Lechter was a passionate and lifelong devotee of Wagner — and illustrations of aphorisms by Nietzsche. George, ever resourceful in expanding his stable, was said to have visited the exhibit daily for several hours not only for its own sake but also because he thought "that the people who would be receptive to this art would also be his people." To his Dutch colleague Albert Verwey, George enthusiastically commented on the "exhibit of Melchior Lechter, our collaborator [. . .] for many he was a revelation and — strange to say — he also had a resounding success in broader circles as well. There wasn't a single major paper in all of Berlin that did not attempt to devote itself extensively to his works. His importance lies primarily in that he is the first person to strive to imbue his entire life (apartment furniture ornamentation) down to the smallest detail with Art . . . he thus forms a welcome addition to us in literature and poetry."

What George meant when he said Lechter aimed to infuse his entire life with "Art" was made more concrete in Scott's recollections. "Lechter lived in a top flat which, apart from his studio, he had furnished almost exactly like a chapel. The furniture, of his own design, was ecclesiastical in every detail, and even his bedroom was arranged to look like a mediaeval picture. In both his rooms were beautiful stained-glass windows, which produced such a very holy atmosphere that one felt one ought never to speak above a whisper, and that to laugh would be sacrilegious." Scott even thought he could detect the scent of incense in the air. Lechter's custom of wearing long velvet robes in the form of a monk's habit and a ring engraved with *Om,* the holy syllable of the Veda, added to the sense that he would be more comfortable in a cathedral than a cafe. To the Englishman's relief, however, Scott discovered that "far from being sanctimonious, he turned out to be a most humourous individual, fond of a ribald joke, and always highly amused whenever I made a 'bloomer' in German." Soon, they were on the best of terms. "His child-like manner, his equally child-like impatience, and his resemblance to a well-nourished priest — although he is a strict vegetarian — endear him to the hearts of all his friends." But about his art Lechter was uncompromising, and he saw in George the only person in Germany who, like himself, viewed art as a religion and the artist as a priest.

George also grew fond of Lechter, and they worked closely on numerous projects over the next fifteen years. (Scott assured his readers that, although he had initially jumped "to the conclusion that [Lechter] was a homosexual like his friend," he later learned that "I was greatly mistaken.") But what drew George to Lechter were not so much his stained-glass windows and interior designs but rather Lechter's elaborate book decorations. In early 1896, Lechter had begun sending sample sketches to George of title pages to illustrate the poet's previously published books. Although these drawings were never realized, they already contain the germs of what became his characteristic visual style: ornate borders displaying gothic motifs, ivy tendrils encircling thin fluted columns, organ pipes encased within high pointed arches, and outsized candelabra. For a full decade and more Lechter would use these elements to give George's works their most distinctive physical appearance, a material vocabulary that, as much as the poetry itself, spoke a strongly idiosyncratic language instantly recognizable as belonging to George. But Lechter's contribution went far beyond providing designs and mere ornament. "I don't decorate a book," he once testily said, "I make a book!" Or, as he insisted on another occasion, his entire artistic credo was contained in the sentence, "Content is animated form."

The art of bookmaking had languished in Germany during most of the second half of the nineteenth century as newer and faster printing techniques led to increased numbers and reduced quality. Time and money-saving innovations such as the rotating press, the introduction of paper made of wood pulp, and the invention of photogravure had led to an explosion of print. But this progress had also resulted in the production of poorly printed, hastily assembled books that quickly fell apart or whose pages became yellowed and brittle even after only one or two years of use. As Otto Grautoff, a contemporary historian of bookmaking, complained, this chapter of its history presented a "miserable and shameful picture," a period that "in view of the profusion of ugliness and dreary examples of bad taste" would deserve to be called "the saddest and most corrupt era in the history of art." That was no doubt putting it too strongly. But this disparagement of the state of publishing in Germany at the end of the century bears a more than passing resemblance to George's own views of German culture at large.

Things began to change during the 1890s. Inspired by the pioneering example of the Englishman William Morris, who founded the Kelmscott Press in 1891 with the intent of reviving dormant artisinal traditions and values, people throughout Europe also began to look anew at books as cultural artifacts and not simply as ordinary merchandise. Morris involved himself in every step of the process: he drew and cut his own type, designed the initials, created the decorative borders and ornaments, made his own woodcuts for the illustrations, used the finest paper available — slightly rough handmade stock — and he personally directed the printing of the works. His books had a strong, harmonious, and distinctively individual character, and they were much praised for the perfection and beauty of their finish. George, too, was well aware of Morris, and in August 1896 he had written to Hofmannsthal that he wanted to publish "after the manner of the Kelmscott Press not only the more modern poets but also the Good Old Ones in a tasteful edition (one more fit for human beings than up to now)." And the person who would help him realize that desire was the mystically inclined, monkish Melchior Lechter.

Yet George's decision to collaborate with Lechter was motivated by more than just the concern to make beautiful or "tasteful" objects. George later said that he admired a well-made book not so much for its aesthetic appeal as for the technical proficiency it revealed. When someone pointed out that most of the examples of competent bookmaking he mentioned were French, he explained that it was because France was the only country to have preserved a tradition of craftsmanship, which had kept alive an appreciation for art throughout a broad segment of the population. But there was hope, he added, that the resuscitated arts and crafts movement would gradually bring about an improvement of workmanship in Germany as well. By calling attention to the physical quality of the book — which George had always done, although less obviously, through his unorthodox punctuation and orthography — he thus meant to stress, even in concrete terms, the difference setting him and his works apart from the cultural context they were forced to inhabit. Naturally, such handcrafted works could not be produced in great quantity and would not come cheap, thus even materially limiting the number of copies one could publish and, not incidentally, thereby enhancing their esoteric appeal. It was also no accident that the visual style he and Lechter chose to communicate this oppositional stance toward their age was derived from the period when the arts in Germany experienced their first great blossoming. The thirteenth century, before the Hohenstaufen emperor Frederick II died, when the Holy Roman Empire — which, looking backward, was also known as the first German *Reich* — stood as a cultural zenith, a time when poetry, music, architecture, and the decorative arts had achieved a coherent balance of purpose and idiom unmatched since.

As was increasingly becoming the case with George, here too the line dividing cultural and more properly political themes became blurred to the point of disappearing. "The Gothic is probably like no other artistic style a beautiful and wonderful expression of Germanic sensibility," the book historian Grautoff had thought; "nowhere is the Gothic so much an outgrowth of the soul of the people, nowhere is it so deeply intertwined with the people's sentiment than in Germany." It was this belief, that the gothic style was somehow archetypically German, that it possessed a mysterious, vital, almost organic bond with the German soul, that gave it its peculiar power and resonance. This, coupled with its historical remoteness, its religious or at least its spiritual connotations, coupled with its formal purity, made the gothic purely in instrumental terms almost irresistibly appealing to George. For he could now establish himself within an authentic, culturally superior "Germany" without having to align himself with the modern and decidedly deficient state that went by the same name.

At the beginning of October 1897, Lechter wrote his sister informing her that "Stefan George is now also in Berlin again for awhile to have his new book the *Year of the Soul* printed," adding that "it is precious rich full of deep sounds!" It was the first of the books he and George were to make together, resulting in a volume that Grautoff himself, in 1902, proclaimed was "indisputably one of the most beautiful books that has appeared in Germany in recent times." Others were of the same opinion. George's fellow student from Darmstadt, Georg Fuchs, wrote a friendly article devoted to the book that winter for the periodical *German Art and Decoration,* asserting that "German printers have not produced anything for a long, long time that could be compared to this book." Fuchs emphasized the attention paid to the smallest detail: "Thus, when choosing the paper, he even considered 'how it felt' and what the relationship to the cover was for both the hand and the eye." Fuchs noted that

> the transition from the exterior to the interior of the Japanese cover and then to the paper of the text was chosen with the finest taste for *The Year of the Soul*. The cover alone is furnished with pictorial decoration. — In the text, lead-red initials were chosen for the beginning of each strophe, and blue ones for the beginning of each verse, which then also alternate in the almost pathetic sounding titles. All of the other letters of each line are deep black. The pages have very narrow margins: thus the entire book appears compact, harmoniously unified, artistic page for page, merely through the tasteful handling of what was *necessary,* without ostentation, without images: a new master work.

Everything about the book's physical aspect bespoke the resolve to recapture the imagined virtues of a gothicized past. To begin with, the exquisite workmanship and choice materials acted as a tangible protest against mass production. But the woodcut image adorning the title page depicting a winged angel in a long, trailing gown and seated in front of a pipe organ, and the blue and red capital initials at the beginning of each line of verse were also suggestive of a medieval manuscript. Finally, the small print run of only 206 copies completed the impression that *The Year of the Soul* breathed the spirit of a different and implicitly better age. (George had originally wanted to call the book *Annum animae,* which would have been even more consonant with a mediaeval ambience but not very good Latin: *annus* is the correct, although admittedly less attractive, form of the noun.)

Whatever George thought all this meant, however, he preferred to keep it to himself. Years later, he claimed that "Mallarmé praised the alternation of red and blue and saw a deeper significance in it." It would have been the only significance the French poet, who knew no German, would have been able to glean from the volume. In his letter from January 1898 thanking George for the book, Mallarmé did not in fact mention its color scheme, saying only that he was honored to be counted "among your faithful even though I may only half divine the marvel of your" book. He also praised its "nobility" and the "ingenuity of your dream and of the supreme imaginative music. You attribute here seasons to your soul; excellently, since all poetry, even of an intimate sort, plays out the spectacle of some ideal year." Despite Mallarmé's good intentions, it was obvious that he could not follow his pupil. It would also be the last time they communicated with each other: the great French master, who eight years before had taught George how to be a poet, died later that year, on September 9, at his country house in Valvins. But if the passing of Mallarmé had any affect on George, he kept his own counsel on that score as well.

While he was in Berlin, George did more than simply supervise the publication of his new book. In early November, he began to meet regularly with Sabine Lepsius to plan what became the first of several semipublic readings held in their spacious apartment at Kantstrasse 162. The guest list was assembled with extreme care and finalized only after repeated consultations with the poet, with Frau Lepsius making sure to give George the opportunity to vet each new addition or change. Most of those invited seemed chosen for their ability, and willingness, to convey a favorable report of the session to as broad an audience as possible. Several were professors at the university, others wrote for the literary pages of newspapers, and still others were simply well known and therefore listened to. As word spread of the impending affair, Sabine Lepsius was surprised to discover that an invitation to the reading was quickly becoming a desirable commodity. "So," she wrote George four days before the reading took place, "Erich Schmidt is, unless you have a decided aversion toward him, almost unavoidable. We have run into him twice in the meantime and he always begins speaking about you with us. — I hope you won't exercise your veto here." This was the same person who had held the lectures on modern German drama that George attended in the fall of 1889 when he first arrived in Berlin, but it is unlikely Schmidt ever knew that the poet he was so keen to meet was a former student. Richard M. Meyer, another professor of literature at the university, was also invited, along with his wife Estella, probably owing to an agreeable article on George and the *Blätter* Meyer had published that April in the *Preussische Jahrbücher,* auspiciously entitled "A New Circle of Poets." Yet another professor counted among those present, the sociologist and philosopher Georg Simmel, who was becoming an increasingly prominent figure within Berlin's intellectual circles and already one of the most popular lecturers at the university (he attracted so many students to his courses — there were 269 in one — that he had to use the largest auditorium available). Also included were Lou-Andreas Salomé, then best known for her connection to Nietzsche, accompanied by her young escort, the as-yet-unpublished Rainer Maria Rilke. Among the remaining listeners were Karl Wolfskehl, Gertrud Kantorowicz, a new member of the *Blätter* confraternity by the name of Karl Gustav Vollmoeller, the composer Conrad Ansorge, and his wife, Margarethe, as well as several others. All in all, an illustrious and dignified group, one that could be counted on to represent the poet in the kind of light in which he now wanted, and expected, to be shown.

A final addition was one Marie von Bunsen, a painter and occasional journalist. "I had already spoken with you about Fräulein M. v. Bunsen," Frau Lepsius told George. "She is a bad artist, or rather not an artist at all — but she is receptive — and in any case harmless." Sabine Lepsius, a generous and conscientious hostess, could be privately catty when describing those she saw as competitors; she also never warmed to Melchior Lechter — notably absent at the evening's festivities — for the same reason. But it was to the allegedly "bad artist" Ms. Bunsen that we owe the most vivid account of the reading, which appeared two months later in the paper, *Vossische Zeitung*. "It was a late afternoon in November," she wrote, evocatively setting the scene, "indefinite gray masses of houses, dark silhouettes of people rushing by, the white glow of electric light and a yellowish green dying sky, one of those mystically beautiful moments which the metropolis affords to those who have the nerves for it. Our host was the finest, most subtle portrait painter in Berlin." (Bunsen was referring not to Sabine but to her husband, Reinhold Lepsius, who did indeed enjoy the respect of his colleagues, even though he has now been almost wholly forgotten.) Bunsen continued:

> We sat in rooms dimly lit by veiled lamps, seated on armchairs worked in Florentine style, covered in faded brocade. Well-known people were present. They spoke only in hushed voices. Then a man slid in through a side door and sat down after a bow next to the yellow enshrouded light: behind him a Japanese embroidery in dark gold, not far from him branches of laurel and red-orange blossoms in a beaten copper vessel. Never in my entire life have I been confronted by such a strange face: pale, worn, with tired heavy eyelids, a mouth vibrating with a severe expression. The cheek bones are strongly pronounced, the forehead is massively domed, from which heavy, dark masses of hair rise. His features, emaciated by thought and inner battles, look much, much older than his twenty-eight years. His profile has a preoccupying similarity to the portrait of Dante in the Bargello. The entire head, the thin nervous hands strangely remind one of the young Liszt. He read with a soft, even voice, with fine, distinct intonation. Now and again his Rhenish accent was disturbing. Although I knew most of the poems, it was not easy to follow the already unusual associations of images and ideas. But we were progressively hypnotized, entranced by the mood. At the end, he got up, recited one more poem and for the first time opened his eyes: dull, slightly red lids, dark, fixed, not large pupils. Then he bowed and left.

Almost all of the poems George read that afternoon were from his new work, *The Year of the Soul,* which appeared, adorned with Lechter's lavish creation, in the middle of the same month. However, the poems themselves were not new, with some having been written as long as three years before and many published in various numbers of the *Blätter* throughout 1896. But, next to *Algabal,* the new book is the most tightly organized and thematically unified work George had yet produced. It is also, as its title might suggest, the most intensely personal, the most lyrically plangent, he had ever written. To this day it remains his most popular cycle of poetry, the one thought to be most accessible, most available to an emotional response because it seems to be such a open expression of the poet's own emotions, a frank disclosure of his own "soulful" experience. Here the poet does not engage in fantasies of medieval or Byzantine blood sports, nor is there much overt evidence of an overweening urge to subjugate and conquer the world by whatever means necessary. Instead, a kind of melancholy wash appears to have been spread over the interior landscape of the poet's mind, giving everything a slightly faded, somewhat elegiac cast, mournful, sometimes even morose. Heightening the sense that the poet is speaking directly out of the depths of his own soul, that we have been made privy to the intimate colloquy of the poet with himself, is the bizarrely contradictory preface to the book, which simultaneously affirms and denies its autobiographical relevance. Saying that the preface is in response to questions about whether "identifying certain people or places" would aid in understanding the individual poems, the poet advises that it is "unwise" to look for "the human or natural original" in all poetry, including his own. "It has experienced such a transformation through art," he explains, "that it has become insignificant for the creator himself and any knowledge of it for others would confuse rather than enlighten." We are told that where the names of people do occur — actually none do: only initials appear — they were meant only as a "tribute" or "gift" to those so honored. Most important, the preface ends, is to remember that "seldom are I and you so completely the same soul as in this book."

 The assertion that the poetic voice and the addressee — the "I" and the "you" — are virtually identical in *The Year of the Soul* must be taken with a grain of salt, as does the claim that the biographical origin of the verses is insignificant or merely distracting. It is true that a familiarity with the particulars of George's life is not crucial to an understanding of the poems; the story they tell on their own, while not exactly unambiguous, is comprehensible enough even on a fairly general plane. But never before had he inscribed so much of himself, and in such an unconcealed way, into his work. He obviously no longer felt the need to take refuge behind the mask of Roman emperors or traveling minstrels to project his feelings into mythical or historical characters who resided in faraway times and places, or to use an allusive, indirect language no one else spoke for fear of saying too much to the wrong people. For the first time, George places his poetic persona in the middle of his own world — many of the poems take place along a river that can only be the Rhine and within a natural setting that likewise evokes the hills and valleys around Bingen — and he choreographs a complicated shadow dance with figures that are the recognizable, if faint, distillates of various people he knew — and some of whom he had loved.

The book, like its predecessor, is divided into three main parts. The first section is, in many ways, the most dramatic and most easily grasped, for it tells of a failed relationship soon followed by a more successful and fulfilling one. This first part is itself broken into three separate segments and, in adherence to the governing temporal motif of the collection — the "year" the soul traverses is marked out by the consecutive passing of the seasons — each group of poems is gathered within a seasonal cluster: "After the Harvest," "Pilgrims in the Snow," and the "Victory of Summer." In the first, George exploited the common symbolic values of autumn and winter to convey a sense of growing emotional darkness and cold, of exhausted life and the approach of death. But the object of this symbolic death is the poet's attachment to a woman or, perhaps better, to Woman in general. Not that the bond being severed was particularly strong to begin with: the poet says to the female companion in the autumnal first sequence that he "will learn gentle tender words for you," as if it will cost him no small effort to do so, and as if he were forcing on himself an unpleasant but necessary duty. Long walks are described, beneath the colorful fall foliage of beeches and almond trees, along ponds and through parks and gardens. But their conversation is subdued, tempered, almost hushed, and often punctuated by long silences. As they sit on a bench, each one lost "in dreams," they "only gaze and listen when in pauses / The ripe fruit thumps down onto the ground."

It is a beautiful image, to be sure, but not one that conveys much passion. Rather, the opposite is implied: it evokes a spent flame, waning light, dissipating heat. Finally, the poet says he has put into words what he and his female companion both already know, and he writes a letter to her and then retreats to watch from a distance as she reads it:

> I wrote it down: no longer will be concealed
> What I cannot banish from my mind
> What I don't say · you don't feel: a great span
> Stands between the two of us and happiness.
>
> Next to a high and withered flower
> You unfolded it · I stand apart and think . .
> It was the white sheet that fell from your hand
> The brightest color upon the pallid surface.

It is difficult not to read these lines without envisioning George's tentative approaches toward Isi Coblenz-Auerbach and the epistolary end to their own relationship. This connection is especially hard not to make if one knows that he had originally planned to dedicate the entire book to her, which he then abruptly changed to his sister's name after the unexpected encounter with Richard Dehmel at Frau Auerbach's apartment in Berlin the previous winter. But the frame of reference here is much wider, having less to do with a single person or event, and more to do with her entire gender. The first section ends with the poet, having bid his female companion farewell, saying that "I feel that no sooner has time separated us / Then you will no longer inhabit my dream." In *The Year of the Soul* George was not just saying goodbye to Frau Isi; he was saying that women would never find a meaningful place in his world.

The second section, "Pilgrims in the Snow," serves mainly to underscore this break, and in one poem the image of the flower — so frequently a symbol of sexuality in George's work — is again used to express the finality of the rupture. The poet describes a potted plant on his window ledge that he had long faithfully tended but which has now begun to wilt and become hateful to his sight:

> To eradicate from my mind the memory
> Of its earlier blossoming fortunes
> I choose sharp tools and I snip off
> The pale flower with the diseased heart.

Capping this rather dramatic caesura, and leading into the triumphant "Victory of Summer," the poet constructs a "pyre," which he says he builds for his "memories" and "for you," and sets it alight. Walking away from the flames, he climbs into a waiting boat and sees that "Yonder on the shore a brother / Waves and swings the happy banner." And it is with this "brother" that the poet celebrates the exuberant summer solstice.

In this segment, "The Victory of Summer," the "happiness" that eluded the poet in the preceding two now appears within reach. "The air stirs as if moved by new things," we read, an arousal that heralds "a new adventure." Here the language becomes bright, unencumbered, almost rhapsodic. In the poems that follow, the poet indulges in descriptions of his companion and their "adventures." But the "victory" is a substantial one. For the first time in George's work the beloved is no longer hidden behind the neutral pronoun "you," but he receives a definite sex. Not only that, George becomes as explicit about the nature of the relationship between the two lovers as he had ever been:

> Are you still reminded of the beautiful image of him
> He who boldly grabbed the roses on cliffs' edge ·

> He who forgot the day in hot pursuit ·
> He who supped the full nectar from umbels?

The last word — "umbel" — is strange in German, too. George used the unusual term *Dolde*, which generically refers to a class of flowering plant in which the individual stalks arise from the same point or bulb, such as the geranium, milkweed, onion, or, most suggestively, the leek. In addition, the word he chose for "nectar" — *Seim* — is equally abstruse, and it bears a strong similarity to the common word in German for "seed" or "semen" — namely *Same*. Even given what we know about George's habit of saying it with flowers, as it were, the phallic connotations of this last line, although still well-camouflaged, mark a startling relaxation of his policy of refusing to call a thing by its name.

Or perhaps, taking into account George's own experiences over the past year, his newfound candor — if one can really call it that — should not seem so very astonishing after all. His revelations to Scott indicated a new willingness to drop the facade of indirect disclosures, and his letters to his Belgian friend, Edmond Rassenfosse, likewise signaled that he was prepared to discuss — for George, at extraordinary length and in unprecedented detail — affairs of the heart openly, or as openly as George would ever do. Indeed, it has been surmised that the poems in this section of the book do in fact commemorate his liaison with one, or both, of the young men. But here, as well, the biographical prototype is important only insofar as it confirms what the poems already, albeit abstractly, express with sufficient clarity. For that message is straightforward: in the place ceded by Woman, to whom he had long felt forced to utter hollow words of tenderness and feigned affection, will henceforth stand the Brother, the Man, and the Boy.

Another reason for George's unwonted directness was related to Wolfskehl's admonitions in the *Blätter* to quit the symbolist ivory tower, to take up residence in the material world and to embrace, as Wolfskehl had put it previously, "life in the realm of the real." Accordingly, in one of the poems from the "Victory of Summer," the poet reminds as much himself as his lover to take joy in the here and now, hoping "that this sweet life may satisfy us · / That we live here as thankful guests!" Similarly, in a syntactically complicated strophe, the poetic voice envisions a time when the ideal and the actual coincide. But, until that day arrives, he says one should not condemn the desire to flee into history and the imagination as a way of experiencing, or at least of anticipating, love:

> And call it foolish to reject as evil
> That you already kissed distant images in yourselves
> And that you never knew how to reconcile
> Receiving a kiss in a dream and a real one.

Yet eventually the summer ends, as all summers must, and the poet again finds himself lonely and bereft of the sensual plenitude he has just extolled. Apart from the middle section of tributes to George's friends — and most of these poems were written earlier than the two parts coming before and after — the rest of the book is dominated by an oppressively dark and somber mood, thematically enunciated by the general title of the concluding part, "Sorrowful Dances." A single poem will suffice to give an idea of the dismal pall resting over these last few pages of *The Year of the Soul*. Employing the image of a cold hearth, filled only with the charred remnants of a now extinguished fire, the poem has an almost funereal resonance:

> You stepped up to the hearth
> Where all embers have died ·
> The only light on the earth
> Was the moon's cadaveric color.
>
> You dipped your pallid fingers
> Deep into the ashes
> Searching feeling groping —
> That there may be a glow again!
>
> See what the moon advises you
> With a gesture of consolation:
> Step away from the hearth ·
> It has become late.

Friedrich Gundolf, who had particular reasons for doing so, claimed that this was "in every 'sense' an incomprehensible poem." Certainly the poem is not reducible to a single meaning, but the radius of its "sense" can be drawn. The image of dead or dying embers faintly illuminated by a wan crepuscular light was, at the turn of the century, so common as to risk becoming hackneyed. Nations, entire cultures, even the whole world seemed bathed in a kind of twilight glow, spent of all vitality, cooling to the touch, and emitting an audible death rattle. This was how George saw the German empire: externally seemingly vigorous and hale, but inwardly corrupt, worm-eaten, and irreparably moribund. Yet the poem is not jubilant but resigned, and there is no indication that the extinction is desired; quite the reverse. For — and this is typical of George's tendency to see the world as an extension of himself — the poet's own dreams are mixed in with the ashes, his hope to rekindle the flame an expression of his wish to relive the high days of summer, now no more than the dead gray residue running through his fingers — or the black ink flowing through his pen. That is, the poem, and indeed all of *The Year of the Soul,* also eulogizes — and renounces — the earlier ambitions of the poet to challenge the world by creating a substitute realm solely within poetry itself, of fashioning, alchemist-like, an alternate universe — or at least a surrogate Germany — out of the chimerical lifeless stuff of language alone. Poetry would continue to play a crucial role in the construction of George's realm, but increasingly as a means to another end, and not as an end in itself.

CHAPTER 17
Going Public

The period immediately following the publication of *The Year of the Soul* initiated one of the major turning points in George's life, perhaps even the most important one. The effects of the change would not become visible for some time yet, but the course he would take had been inalterably set. After spending much of the previous decade in self-imposed obscurity, George now began to assert a place in the public consciousness that he would come to occupy for the rest of his life. Increasingly the claims of dominance he made for and of himself were becoming recognized outside of his small circle of friends as well, making them seem less like megalomaniacal delusions and more like reasonable statements of fact. Victory seemed well within grasp, and others were beginning to sense that, too. In January 1898, Albert Verwey reviewed the most recent issue of the *Blätter* in his own *Tweemaandelijksch Tijdschrift*, saying that "George has reason to be content. The public pressure for a greater distribution of his works and journal is already growing stronger. Now it is his turn to make clear that he has reached his goal of assembling all of the good writers in Germany. [. . .] Yet there are signs that the movement will soon achieve greater public prominence." Soon it became not just impossible to ignore George — however one rated his achievement — but it also began to be difficult to assess him by any other measure than the one he had created himself.

To what extent this development reflected a conscious strategy on his part is hard to judge. To one critic, Stefan George during the 1890s "rather resembled a general who — for a relatively brief period — gathers his forces in secret till he knows he can attack with advantage." The martial analogy would no doubt have pleased George, who liked to fancy himself the spiritual kin of Caesar and Napoleon. What is true is that, for at least two years prior to *The Year of the Soul,* he had been considering various ways of bringing both the *Blätter* and his own books to the notice of a larger audience without compromising the principles on which they rested. His decision to don an identifiably German coat (or to insist that the one he was wearing was originally of German design), his abortive effort to stage a coup on the pages of *Pan;* his plans, also fruitless so far, to step up the publishing schedule and widen the scope of the *Blätter* so as to embrace philosophy, painting, and music; the "public" readings at the Lepsius's home; and finally the ornate, highly stylized quality of his own most recent work: these were all not exactly the actions of a man who wanted to avoid drawing attention to himself. We know that George had long maintained an almost antagonistic attitude toward the "public," and in many ways his stance would forever remain distanced and disdainfully wary. Now he seemed pragmatically prepared to drop or at any rate to soften his scruples and to do what was necessary to achieve his other aims. But once he had made the decision to go public, George would ensure that there would be only one possible outcome. In mid-October, 1897, just before Sabine Lepsius began compiling her guest list for the reading, he told Hofmannsthal that "nothing accidental may occur that could prevent success. For as you know not to seek success is great — to seek it and not have it indecent."

Clearly, the reading itself had been a resounding success, but George had meant more than that. It was not enough to win over a small number of already well-disposed admirers. He needed to extend his reach beyond the relatively narrow circle of personal acquaintances that until now had formed nearly the entire scope of his readership and influence. He wanted to expand into a larger orbit. In a sense, *The Year of the Soul* had been the expression of that wish in literary form, signaling the final turn away from the symbolist preoccupation with negating the world through language toward the related but essentially different desire to reign over both. But George knew he could not do it alone. He had always recognized that he had to have like-minded champions and allies by his side, and his incessant though unsuccessful wooing of Hofmannsthal sprang at least partly from that realization. So far, however, no one else had emerged who possessed anything approaching the same keenness of judgment, the sureness of taste, or the subtle pliancy of expression that seemed to come so effortlessly to Hofmannsthal. For a brief moment, though, one exception appeared to be Georg Simmel.

Born in Berlin in 1858, Simmel was a full decade older than George and in many other respects not exactly the poet's type. "He was considered ugly," was how Frau Lepsius, who had been a friend of the philosopher since childhood, bluntly put it. Yet it was not so much his physical appearance that gave him that reputation. On the contrary, she thought that "his head was well-shaped and very distinctive and his forehead almost handsome with its thought-induced furrows, his eyes small but immensely expressive. His nose was generally Jewish, the mouth quite finely formed, and his frame also well proportioned." What made some consider Georg Simmel unattractive was his almost demonic intensity, an intellectual vehemence that produced long, brilliant, but ultimately exhausting waves of convoluted, abstract reflections on anything from Italian Renaissance art to door handles to the social significance of offering someone a chair to sit down in. No one disputed that Simmel possessed an extraordinarily nimble and profound mind. Even his anti-Semitic detractors, who could never forgive him his Jewish parentage (he was a baptized Protestant), were forced to acknowledge his protean genius. But his intellectual restlessness, born of a kind of compulsive mental agitation, manifested itself in an edgy, ceaseless fidgetiness that many found off-putting. "I saw Simmel's face, which was in constant, lively motion when he spoke, only once in a state of complete calm," an acquaintance remembered. "It was while listening to the music of Bach." Sabine Lepsius also identified this nervous physical disquiet as the source of the less than pleasing effect he had on some observers. "The only truly unattractive part of him were his thin, veined hands, with which he gesticulated far too much."

At the university, where Simmel spoke before large and ever growing crowds of students and curious onlookers, his eccentricities did not count against him, and in fact probably made him even more compelling to his listeners. Relying on no more than a few scribbled notes on a sheet of paper for his lectures, Simmel gave the enthralling impression of actively thinking out loud, developing his ideas as they came to him in a kind of frenzied trance, weaving his vast knowledge of European philosophical and cultural history into his monologues on the origin of evil, say, or on the psychology of Dante. As he visibly wrestled with the subject, pushing and stretching it to its limits, exploring all of its subtle complexities, it seemed, as someone who witnessed several of these remarkable performances described them, as if "his entire body was involved, participating in the creation." Simmel's style of lecturing was so idiosyncratic that his auditors even coined a verb to describe it, calling his full-body oratory *simmeln,* or "simmeling." The following anecdote is representative: "Everyone who knew him experienced the surprising hand gestures and contortions of his upper body that accompanied his own discourses when he got caught up in intense intellectual excitement. It thus happened that while making a concluding point to one of his lectures in our circle he moved back and forth in such an agitated fashion that his frock coat became stuck between the arm rest and the cushion of his chair. When he did not immediately succeed in freeing himself, one of the listeners said with a smile: 'Herr Professor, I believe you have simmeled yourself to your seat.'"

George, who forever maintained a suspicious distance between himself and all theoretical speculation, likewise occasionally indulged in playful puns on the professor's name. As early as 1901, for instance, he cautioned Wolfskehl about the dangers of "simmelfication" — *Versimmelung* — by which he appeared to mean the intellectual dissolution of everything into no more than a sum of abstract relations. Even though they had become acquainted soon after the first reading in the Lepsius house, which the restless professor had attended with his wife, Gertrud, and despite the fact that Simmel devoted two penetrating essays to his poetry, George never warmed entirely to his pyrotechnics. George was a poet, not a philosopher, and he thus had little use for the complicated analyses that Simmel wrung from both his body and mind. Indeed, George insisted that he often did not even know what Simmel was talking about. When the subject arose during a conversation, George once said of Simmel's writing: "I don't understand a word of it." In a literal sense, that was patently untrue; but on a more subjective level, it well enough conveyed George's distrust of purely abstract reasoning. And, to George, Simmel personified such bloodless rigors to an extreme degree. One of George's later friends even invented a particular torment that would await Simmel in hell: there below he would be consumed by a terrible hunger for corporeality and eternally embrace only the patterns of concepts. Yet George's private misgivings about Simmel did not prevent him from appreciating the value of such a persuasive, forceful, and widely admired advocate in furthering his own agenda.

In February of 1898 Simmel published "Stefan George: An Art-Philosophical Consideration." It was far and away the most intelligent and far-reaching appraisal of George's work to date. Not incidentally, the essay was also the most favorable treatment he had yet received, containing words of acclaim that would soon become standard fare in accounts of the poet. More keenly than anyone before, Simmel not only perceived the distinctive character of his poetry, but he also understood what was ultimately, and deeply, at stake for George. Beginning with general reflections about the nature of human experience, Simmel asserted that it was "feeling," instead of reason or understanding, that constituted the most fundamental, the most authentic, the most immediately "real" sense of ourselves as living, human beings. Yet, he continued, there are two basic kinds of "feeling": the common but by no means insignificant sensations of love and hate, rage and humility, delight and despair, and so on, which form the bedrock on which all personal experience rests. But, as opposed to these purely "subjective" feelings, there is another category in which the solely personal, the merely individual feeling cedes to an almost transpersonal or "objective" sentiment, as if our own ego were merely the conduit for a larger reality. It is this second kind of "feeling," the sense of being moved by a power greater than oneself, when our sentiments seem to form part of a universal continuum, that, according to Simmel, underlies both the creation and enjoyment of all true art.

Although Simmel was nothing if not eclectic, his neo-Kantian sympathies are clearly in evidence in this outline of our aesthetic response. But his argument serves a decidedly non-Kantian purpose: pursuing the idea that art consists in the refinement and universalization of "feeling" in the defined subjective sense, Simmel was in effect claiming that art eventually, and paradoxically, resulted in the negation of its origin. That is, the "natural," "subjective" feelings that make up the basis of all human experience have no importance as such in art where they become, in Simmel's idiosyncratic version, "objective." Otherwise, he reasoned, there would be no need for art at all. If a painting or poem could be reduced to, or were merely identical with, its emotional content, then it would be simpler and less time-consuming to communicate that content by more direct means. Simmel states this point with vigorous clarity: "Not some content is supposed to be presented in poetic form, but rather a poetic work of art shall be created for which the content has no other significance than marble has for a statue." An art work takes on an absolute value of its own and becomes a measure unto itself, serving no master beyond itself. Or, as Simmel wrote in a clever variation on a theme already becoming a little tiresome, "for the first time, here poetry has fundamentally entered the stage of *l'art pour l'art* and left behind that of *l'art pour le sentiment*." And Simmel left no doubt about how meaningful he thought this development was. "Although in fact the works of all great poets are located on the path from the primary, or as it were naturalistic feeling, to the objective one that is rescued from the violation of the primitive impulse, it seems to me that, ever since Goethe's late poems, it was not until the poetry of Stefan George that this foundation on the transsubjective quality of feeling, this holding back from its unmitigated assault, has become the unequivocal principle of art."

Simmel rarely made it easy on either his readers or his listeners, and this last passage is a fairly typical example of his densely intricate prose. But the import is obvious enough: George was, in his view, the first German poet since Goethe to have understood the true essence of art and to have given that understanding concrete form in his poems. The primary distinction shared by both Goethe and George, Simmel thought, was that they had managed to transform what had commonly been considered the end of poetry — namely, the expression and excitation of an immediate, all-embracing, but narrowly subjective feeling — into the reverse. In George's poems, "feelings" (*Gefühle*) have become, rather, the building material, the formal means to another, higher end: that of art itself. Simmel used an arresting image to convey more precisely what he meant. He said he realized that from the standpoint of everyday humanity this turn away from the "first warmth of feeling" would appear strange and alienating as long as one did not understand that the opposite to this "warmth" is not coldness, "but the autocratic rule of the feeling of art." "Feeling has, to be sure, left behind its youth, not to become old but rather timeless." Leaving conventional reality behind lifted the poem, and the poet, into a sphere governed by its own laws, unaffected by ordinary concerns, removed even from the influence of time.

Simmel also finely discerned the consequences involved in this elevation of the poet over the substratum of simple existence. "With this turn, the power of the poet over the world is complete," Simmel concluded; "thus the artist has become absolute ruler." Given Simmel's own resolutely modernist stance and his unconcealed affinity with the symbolist conception of an art that supposedly eschewed any purpose outside of itself, it is perhaps no wonder that he identified and applauded the self-contained, almost hermetic universe George had created by and within his poems. But Simmel had felt out the deeper wish to be a "ruler" that had animated George from the very beginning. He saw that George wanted not just to fashion an alternative to the world with his poetry, but, moreover, thereby to assert his authority over it. He recognized that George intended nothing less than to take possession of the world and submit it to his control. Not that Simmel judged this desire negatively: he unreservedly and enthusiastically admired its boldness. In fact, his estimation of George was so unqualified that he even thought that George embodied more than simply a poet. "As great as I consider the purely poetic genius of Stefan George, one could nevertheless concede that his importance as an artist transcends his specific importance as a poet." Thanks to the strength of his insistence on the autonomy of poetry, George, in Simmel's eyes, had in effect performed a restitution of art to itself and installed himself as its supreme and representative master.

Appearing only months after the publication of *The Year of the Soul*, Simmel's essay was at once part symptom and part stimulus of George's now rapidly growing success, both reflecting and prompting the momentous turnaround in his fortunes. It is hard now to appreciate the full weight of Simmel's assessment, most particularly his having placed George next to Goethe. Among many well-educated Germans at the end of last century, Goethe was the object of a veneration that quite literally bordered on deification: seen as much more than a poet, Goethe was regarded as a mighty Olympian sage, a universal genius, a cultural hero on a par with figures no less than Homer,

Dante, or Shakespeare. For Simmel to liken George to Goethe was thus tantamount to ushering him into a pantheon where few mortals were ever admitted. It must have given George a delicious sense of ironic satisfaction that he, so much an outsider within the official Germany that he often felt himself to be a stranger in a strange land, was now being favorably compared to one of its most cherished idols. But one would be mistaken to imagine that George was awed, or even noticeably impressed, by the comparison. Almost two decades later, when he casually mentioned Simmel's essay to a friend, George lauded the philosopher "for having seen that his poems were more Art than earlier poetry," but he faulted Simmel "for not having drawn the conclusion that all earlier poetry was therefore not true poetry; for only one of two things is possible: either the old poetry was poetry, in which case his own was not, or his is, and the old was not." George lived in a world made up of strong contrasts, strict divisions, and permanent absolutes. In later life, the idea that there might be two or more kinds of "true" poetry was as unthinkable to him as the notion that there could ever be more than one "true" poet. Simmel may have thought he was paying George a compliment by aligning him next to Goethe. But as far as George was concerned the compliment went only one way.

Of course, not everyone was as taken by George's poetry as Simmel — not to speak of George himself. One of the first, and by no means the last, hostile reviews he received came from the pen of one Fritz Mauthner, who secured himself a minor place in the history of thought for having written a ponderous, three-volume philosophy of language that subsequently caught the eye of Ludwig Wittgenstein. In a series of articles Mauthner wrote for a literary magazine, he reported in April of the following year that he had taken on "the thankless task" of trying to gain an accurate picture of the current situation regarding German poetry. The news, as Mauthner gave it, was not good. Correctly identifying the impetus for the most recent poetry in Germany as coming out of France, Mauthner thought that the young German poets who sought to imitate "the eccentric Mallarmé" and the whole "Parisian clique" did so only to their own detriment. To his credit, Mauthner based his argument not so much on nationalist grounds as on the less belligerent observation that the cultural traditions in Germany and France were simply vastly different. For Mauthner, too, Goethe remained a touchstone, but here Goethe's name was used more as a cudgel than as a commendation. The "currently recognized leader" of the young German upstarts, Mauthner explained, was "Stefan George" who "is a poet, a real one; he has the gift of saying what ails him in the secret language of his school; to betray his secrets in our native German language, with which Goethe did not after all fare so badly, is unfortunately not one of his gifts."

Elsewhere in the review Mauthner did not hesitate to formulate his objections in deliberate contrast to the language cultivated by the targets of his attack in direct and simple terms. Arguing, not without reason, that this new "school" wrote its poetry solely for and to itself — Mauthner declared the *l'art pour l'art* slogan to be "nonsense": art is made by people for people, he insisted, but this was *l'art pour les artistes* — he decried the sectarian, elitist attitude struck by these "new-fashioned poets." "Every one of them writes not for the people, but only for his congregation." The habit of leaving out commas and periods, which Mauthner also deplored as being "copied from the terrible Mallarmé," did not just make comprehension difficult; it gave rise to the uncomfortable feeling of being an uninvited and improperly dressed guest at a fancy ball. With heavy sarcasm, Mauthner verified that "Stefan George remained resolutely loyal to all of these principles in the first edition of his *Year of the Soul*. No comma to allow the reader to catch his breath. A democratic, plebeian hand like mine even found touching the hairy paper of the cover to be a nuisance, which would lead one to conclude that aristocratic hands received the inexpressible charm of a refined personality from the same paper."

Still, "despite everything," Mauthner admitted that "something of a poet" undeniably resided in George. But Mauthner found that overall the ratio of intelligibility to formal accomplishment remained tilted decidedly, and damningly, toward the latter. After a good deal of strenuous puzzling through some verses that had baffled him, Mauthner sarcastically confessed that his "plebeian mind" finally managed to decipher the "probable meaning" of a few poems. But it seemed too much labor for too little result. George, he quipped, "offers inedible fruits on a silver platter." Or, borrowing the words of the eighteenth-century aphorist Georg Christoph Lichtenberg, Mauthner concluded with the rhetorical question: "When the heads of a poet and a reader collide and there is a hollow sound, does it always have to have been the reader who made it?"

Whereas George took the time to correct and amplify the generous praise of someone like Simmel, anyone who displayed less than courteous respect toward him was simply ignored. His English friend Cyril Scott remembered that he had once told him that "no true artist must ever be swayed by either the praise or the blame of the masses. As for the critics, they were even more 'stupid' than the public, and the futility of newspaper criticism could be proved by the fact that quite frequently one review flatly contradicted another." Theodor Lessing had heard a similar view from George, who informed him that "as a matter of principle, one should teach the people that it has no business babbling about art." Good reviews were tolerated because they were at most useful, but bad ones only proved once again that art was an affair for artists — or more precisely for George — alone.

Although George was unprepared to accept advice, much less criticism, from "the people" about art, he was more than happy to dispense his own views on the subject to anyone willing to listen. The problem so far had been that so few people had fallen into that latter category. In April 1898 he finally set the plan into motion that he had harbored since the autumn of 1895 for rectifying that increasingly bothersome state of affairs. That spring, while traveling through Italy, he met a gentleman in Rome by the name of Georg Bondi who had been following his career from afar with considerable interest for over a year. Ever since Bondi had heard Richard M. Meyer's lecture on "A New Circle of Poets," held under the auspices of the Society for German Literature in Berlin in early 1897, he had been captivated by Stefan George's poems. More specifically, since Bondi was also the owner and executive editor of a small but discriminating publishing firm, he was, he said, irresistibly moved by "the wish to publish them." He asked someone who knew George for the poet's address but was told that his "address is completely unknown," and Bondi was given that of Klein instead. Klein also responded that "George is unreachable by mail at the moment," but that he, Klein, looked favorably on Bondi's proposal and would communicate it to the poet at the next opportunity.

Bondi heard nothing more until he happened to run into George by chance in Italy at the home of a German artist living in Rome named Ludwig von Hofmann. George had befriended Hofmann, no doubt in part because he painted almost exclusively "youthfully beautiful figures in rhythmic motion, either nude or in ideal costume" after the manner of Böcklin, Puvis de Chavannes, and Hans von Marées. At any rate, Bondi agreed to George's suggestion that they both meet later that afternoon in the popular Café Aragno to discuss the terms of Bondi's offer. They subsequently met again every two or three days until the details of a contract had been worked out to their mutual satisfaction. George's demands were relatively simple: he wanted to publish three volumes of his own poetry — the *Hymns, Pilgrimages,* and *Algabal* would appear together in the first, with the *Books* and *The Year of the Soul* forming the second and third volumes — and to put out a separate anthology of selected poetry and prose from the previous issues of the *Blätter für die Kunst*. Understandably, Bondi cheerfully accepted the terms, and in June he spelled out his own obligations regarding compensation.

Bondi was an honorable, straightforward businessman with somewhat exotic tastes in literature but with a sound head for the nuts and bolts of his trade. And by today's standards, he was more than fair. Writing to Klein, Bondi said that, if desired, he would gladly share part of the "net profit" from all sales of the books: "This procedure, which is often chosen in England, is however not the usual one in Germany. Yet, since I am of the opinion that it is more equitable, I have already signed a series of contracts on this basis and have repeatedly received the thanks of the respective authors for this suggestion." But Bondi cautioned that, given that he did not think George's books of poetry were exactly best-seller material, he feared that profits from sales may not ever amount to much. "Thus the agreement seems much more proper to me that every edition would entail a certain royalty, for example 20 percent of the *retail price* of the entire edition, that is, approximately one third of the bookseller's price (the trade rebate usually amounts to 33.3 percent for cash payment and for every eight books one free copy). One half of this royalty could then be paid on publication, and the other half after the sale of one half of the edition." This way, Bondi reasoned, George was guaranteed to receive at least fifty percent of the agreed-upon amount, as opposed to conceivably nothing at all according to the first method of payment should the books fail to sell. Money had never been a central consideration for George; indeed, he saw writing to earn money as a positive evil. But there was no reason not to accept it when it was being freely offered.

There was one sticking point. "George wanted," Bondi recalled, "for the name *Blätter für die Kunst* to appear together with the publisher's name, next to the firm Georg Bondi, since he wanted from the outset to distinguish the publications of his circle from all other literary works." Bondi said that he had grave reservations about this request, since any addition to the firm's officially registered name was forbidden by the German laws governing commerce and trade. We know what George thought about "laws," but Bondi would not be swayed. Then he had an idea: "I suggested that George should ask his friend Melchior to design a publisher's vignette that would contain the words 'Blätter für die Kunst.' A brilliant solution; George immediately agreed and Lechter designed the beautiful gothic vignette that adorned and still adorns the title page of all of George's poetry in my editions."

Thus was forged a relationship that would endure until George's death. From now on, George published all of his works with the firm of Georg Bondi in Berlin, all instantly identifiable not only by Lechter's gothic ornament but also by their characteristic shape, color, and typographic design. In time, Bondi would publish the works of George's friends and followers, as well, in a special series that stood under George's personal supervision. It was a partnership in only a limited sense, however, for everything George wanted he got, and he never accepted compromises or half measures. To be sure, as the fame of George and his circle grew, adding extraordinary prestige to Bondi's house and no small amount of lucre to his coffers, Bondi had every reason to make his most prized author happy. Although Bondi remained immune to the most violent excesses of unchecked adulation that George would come to inspire in some of his admirers, the good-natured publisher did feel genuine esteem, even deep respect for the poet and to the end regarded him as a friend. When George's parents died and he finally had to sell the family house in Bingen, George no longer had a permanent legal residence. Since he needed an official address for bureaucratic reasons (among others, in order to keep and renew his passport), George indicated, with Bondi's assent, his publisher's home in the shady Berlin suburb of Grunewald as his fixed abode until the end of his life.

CHAPTER 18
The Tapestry of Life

With a neat symbolic punctuality, the final year of the old century also brought the first chapter of George's life to a close. No one could have predicted the extraordinary things that were still to come. But then again no one could have foreseen, a decade before, the events that had transformed George from a virtually anonymous poet who wrote skillful but not particularly original verses after the model of the French symbolists into a writer some were beginning to suspect might be the most important German poet to appear in a hundred years or more. Soon he would be seen as something far greater than that, assuming the role of mentor, leader, and guide. And it was now, on the threshold of a new era, almost as if at the strike of some strange cosmic clock, that George began to undergo a fateful metamorphosis.

Actually, given the benefit of hindsight, it is possible to discern the faint shadow cast by later developments even here at their inception. From the beginning, and unlike most poets who usually prefer to work in solitude, George had desired and tirelessly sought out the company of like-minded writers and artists, comrades in arms who shared his convictions and could help promote his cause. This, like so much else, may have also been part of Mallarmé's handsome legacy to his German colleague, who had experienced firsthand at the rue de Rome what a powerful role the members of the Tuesday night *cénacle* played in disseminating the poet's word. Yet, from the start it was equally true that the need for companionship in George did not stem solely from purely literary concerns or merely from a shrewd understanding of cultural politics, although his hunger for comrades was stimulated by both of those considerations. Rather, it formed part of his more fundamental need to assert his will over his environment, to control it and shape it according to his own design. His poetry had always been an expression of that urge, and even his earliest dealings with the collaborators to the *Blätter,* who were in theory supposed to be his partners and equals, had never been entirely free from his assumption of his own superiority. But what had previously been an unspoken postulate now began to crystallize into an explicit doctrine. Whereas, at least officially, George had up to this point been a kind of *primus inter pares*, henceforth he would define the center of his world as its sole and undisputed master.

The word *Meister* in German has as many resonances as does its English equivalent. The original frame of reference for George and his associates, though, was close to the medieval guild tradition of master artisans, skilled craftsmen who passed on their expertise by training young apprentices in their workshops. The hierarchical relationship was as unquestioned as it was natural, for it presupposed a body of knowledge and technical proficiency that could be acquired only through years of dedication, self-sacrifice and patient, unstinting labor. By association, George and his friends began using the word "master" in the mid-1890s as an affectionate, familiar term of confraternal recognition, a shared emblem of respect for the other's talents and artistic commitment. Thus, George and Melchior Lechter frequently addressed one another as *Meister* in their letters, nor was it especially unusual for George to append *Meister* before the name of a poet he especially admired or liked. But around the turn of the century and thereafter, a new valuation of the term began to take hold, incorporating and going beyond this fairly loose, informal practice. As the members of the *Blätter* began to codify their ideas, behavior, and collective organization in more specific and elaborate ways, the notion that there could be, or should be, more than one "master" seemed to be an irritant. Thus, and again more in line with the model of Mallarmé, whose followers had also called him *le* Maître as a signal of his unique distinction, George came to be called "*the* Master" — "der *Meister*" — as if to differentiate him from any false pretenders. In time, it became the preferred way both to address George and to speak of him to others. Among the initiates, *der Meister* meant only one person, and later still it became shortened simply to *d. M.* "I have been meaning to stop by your place," one of George's disciples thus typically wrote to Lechter in 1916, "to ask you something at the behest of t. M."

Running parallel to this development, indeed giving it the context and content it required, was the gradual systematization of the so-called circle in which George presided as the "Master." At first limited to, in fact synonymous with, the contributing writers of the *Blätter für die Kunst,* the "circle" also slowly assumed a more articulated and complex structure, eventually becoming disengaged from the journal and taking on an independent existence of its own. As George and the movement he headed began to enjoy an increasing visibility in the German cultural landscape, speculation about the composition and nature of the "circle" by those who stood outside of it also intensified. As one might predict, the inferences some people drew about its nature did not always conform to the image that George or the members of the circle wanted to convey, either of it or of themselves. But specifying what the circle *was* never came easy even to those who professed allegiance to the Master, and the issue occasionally flared up into a touchy problem. Friedrich Gundolf, one of George's most brilliant, eloquent, and impassioned spokesmen and one of his most loyal adherents, put it this way in 1920:

> As concerns the 'circle,' it like everything else that seems strange today is often abused by rogues and fools. A sure sign that someone does not belong to it is if he boasts about belonging to it and discreetly or indiscreetly makes himself appear important with his knowledge. The circle is neither a secret society with statutes and regular meetings, nor a sect with fantastical rites and articles of faith, nor a writers' club (publishing with the *Blätter für die Kunst* is in itself not a sign of belonging). Rather, it is a small number of individuals joined by certain attitudes and convictions, unified by the spontaneous and involuntary veneration of a great human being and who endeavor to serve the idea that he embodies (not dictates) to them in their everyday life or through public service in a simple, practical, and serious fashion. All of the rumors flying around on the outside is the gossip of imbeciles, pranksters, swindlers, and slanderers.

The vitriol is impressive, but the intensity of Gundolf's invective conspicuously stands in inverse proportion to the clarity of the description. Given such accounts of what the circle was or ought to be, it is no wonder that many felt mystified. Even how one became a subscriber to the *Blätter* had always been seemingly shrouded in secrecy. At the end of the November 1897 issue, for instance, a short notice had appeared under the rubric reserved for "news" stating that "we are refraining from making admission into our circle of collaborators easier since experience has taught us that not a single serious and valuable participant has yet been put off by the effort to find the way to us." It was hard to tell if that was an invitation or a brush-off. In fact, it was both. The following month, immediately after the reading at the Lepsius house, Rainer Maria Rilke, who had been present as Lou Andreas-Salomé's guest, accordingly wrote to the poet with a particular request. Careful to address him as "Meister Stefan George," Rilke, then twenty-two, expressed the wish "to follow everything that is connected with your art, with faithful interest." He indicated that he already owned and esteemed *The Year of the Soul*. "Yet I believe that I can recognize the paths of your disciples only if I am permitted to follow every step to you and the artistic goals of your circle. To belong to the inner circle of readers of the *Blätter für die Kunst* that is selected by its members is the distinction I am requesting of you." In response, George — who addressed Rilke as "Dear Poet"; the title of *Meister* was already consciously being kept in reserve — explained that since "membership in the circle" consisted in "participation, reading, and further distribution of the *Blätter*," Rilke's wish was fulfilled merely by having been expressed. It was a cryptic nonresponse, which probably left Rilke feeling more than a little confused. Although their paths crossed once more — they met by chance in the Boboli Gardens in Florence six months later and spoke for two hours — Rilke did not publish any poetry in the *Blätter* or become a member of the circle, except in the vague, noncommittal sense George had left open to his younger colleague.

It was natural that the pages of the *Blätter* provided the place where the idea of the circle began to find a more explicit formulation. The *Blätter* were, after all, not simply the most concrete manifestation of the circle and its ostensible reason for existence. They also offered a kind of semipublic forum, providing a communal place for the members to speak both to themselves and to the outside world about their objectives, plans, and common constitution. In the November 1897 number, the introductory maxims had expressly taken up the notion of the circle for the first time. Revealingly, the idea of the circle was also coupled from the start with the issue of hierarchy and the relative standing of its constituent members. "We well know that the most beautiful circle cannot produce great minds," one states with disarming candor, "but also that many of their works are possible only from within a circle." Clarifying this somewhat cryptic pronouncement is the claim that "it is a mistake [to imagine] that only great minds are able to promote an undertaking with a great idea. Of supreme importance is educating the smaller ones and leading them so that they create the atmosphere in which the great idea can breathe." The notion that "smaller" minds are important insofar as they are useful to the "greater" ones is also the subject of the subsequent reflection. "Significant consolation for the smaller ones: if you have understood the higher life of your leaders [*Führer*] then you are necessary not only to keep the field fresh and well-ploughed but you often gather flowers and fruits which — if you are not able to do so yourself — a greater one will later weave into his wreath." What the equally florid metaphors in this passage seem to be implying is that the less gifted members of a circle should take comfort in the notion that the products of their labors, lowly though they might in themselves be, may ultimately find an ennobling use in the works of their superior, whose "higher life" they have "understood" and absorbed. In this way, then, the meaning of one's life would be contained and fulfilled in the life and works of one's master — or, to use the word employed above, one's *Führer*.

From the outset, then, the idea of the "circle" involved much more than a group of people merely united by common interests, as Gundolf would disingenuously insist two decades later. It was not just a neutral designation, nothing more than a convenient name. Instead, the circle was always presupposed a center that gave stability, direction, and purpose to the whole. Every component of the circle was vital to its integrity, but that did not mean that every one was equal. The circle was not a democratic institution; rather, each member occupied an assigned place and value within the overall structure. But in the middle, giving the circle its coherence and form, was the final, in fact the real reason for its existence. For what held it together was the belief in the elevated status of the one who stood at its core.

Going hand in hand with this total immersion of the lesser being's self within the greater destiny of the master, or at least the implied abrogation of individual identity in favor of the larger communal whole, was a resolute attack on the power and value of reason or rationality. To a certain degree, this seems to be a self-evident evolution: the critical faculty is an isolating mechanism, creating doubts, calling things into question, refusing to acknowledge sanctioned authority. Belief, on the other hand, is best nurtured and sustained in the absence of rational probing. In an essay aptly titled "On Darkness" that had already appeared in the last issue of the *Blätter* in 1896, Karl Wolfskehl had extolled the virtues of "holy darkness holy night." Cobbling together ideas culled from the works of his two great heroes, Nietzsche and Bachofen, Wolfskehl saw himself as elaborating the fundamentals of a neoheathen, nonrational, mystical theology. As we have seen before, he eschewed the language of logical demonstration and proof, preferring to use metaphors, allegories, and hidden allusions to convey his meaning. "Never has a consecrated bond been entered under a bright sun." Claiming that mere concepts had never, on their own, brought two "souls" together, Wolfskehl rhapsodized about the opposite wonders of "darkness trembling with secrets." For "as the wise men from the lands of the rising sun teach us the divine is unveiled only to loving devotion: thus we know that the goddess of beauty beckons with her round dance only in the twilight." Playing on the literal Greek meaning of "Pan," or "all" (which in German also means the "universe"), the essay ends with a tribute to the Greek god who presides over creation in an ecstatic celebration that erases all distinctions among individual beings: "What knowledge of ourselves makes us richer and deeper, the silent secret of heavy words and distant sounds, is what causes the shrouds to fall from foreign and strange life. Only when we grasp ourselves do we grasp the universe. Pan, however, the great light, extinguishes all individual flames."

A good deal of this is nonsensical or hopelessly muddled, but the basic point is important for understanding the emerging ideology of the circle. The hostility to rationality would play an enormous role in later contexts as well, particularly in the attempt to delineate and defend the conception of a specifically German — that is to say non-French and hence non-Enlightenment — cultural tradition, which became a prominent intellectual hallmark of George's circle of followers. Here, Wolfskehl seemed to be making the more limited argument — if that is the word — that what the rational mind is able to apprehend pales in significance to the deeper, unconscious springs of exultant joy that can come only when one is released from the fetters of individual consciousness and merges with the divine, universal Presence, symbolized by the figure of Pan. On a more prosaic level, it might be also seen as a plaidoyer for forfeiting one's petty, isolated existence to join ranks with the happy few, headed by someone who was, perhaps, not a divinity, but was at least, as another of Wolfskehl's essays had put it earlier, a "Priest of the Spirit."

Wolfskehl was by no means alone with his distrust of reason in his efforts to unearth the buried strata of human nature. Not just Nietzsche and Bachofen, but the entire generation of Romantic writers, philosophers, and poets that preceded them had likewise suspected that the rational mind was really just a self-protective and thus falsifying bulwark against the unknown and unknowable, shielding us from potentially destructive forces — and truths — beyond our control or comprehension. Closer to home, and much more famously, Sigmund Freud was also on the verge of making his own troubling discoveries, which seemed to reduce the rational mind to a thin crust laid over a deep and roiling sea of churning, unconscious drives. But among the contributors to the *Blätter,* the challenge to the predominance of reason in the explanation and governance of human affairs had begun to advance to a central article of faith. It is, for instance, a controlling thesis in a short essay by Ludwig Klages called "On the Creative One," which is, ironically enough, a comparatively clear and carefully structured expository piece of writing. Beginning with the thesis that "the rich understanding alone is insufficient for the production of a work," Klages offers the proposal that "enthusiasm," not reason, drives the artist: "Creative natures are characterized by the deep love of life. From it flows enthusiasm — that is the power of self-sacrifice, of dissolving into the object of veneration. Belief and adoration are in the soul of the creative one." Art is not created out of objective knowledge, but out of an enthusiastic embrace of illusions and dreams. Klages goes on to list various other necessary qualities of the artist, or of the "creative one," such as his ambition, self-control, and technical proficiency. But he ends with a series of questions, or "doubts," about the current age: "Is it possible that our art is the sad glow of an evening twilight over a day of humanity that is coming to an end? Is understanding the hostile power and capable of extinguishing the fire of the will? Will all the passions finally disappear in a fanaticism of knowledge and this itself in an apathetic omniscience?"

The apocalyptic pathos, as well as much of the vocabulary, strike one as a thin imitation of Nietzsche. Too, broodings on the imminent end of civilization, dark premonitions of universal catastrophe and doom, formed no small part of the shared intellectual baggage carted around by turn-of-the-century intellectuals. Yet Klages, along with most of the other *Blätter* members, were deadly serious about their visions of disastrous collapse, heralding a new era of barbarism and chaos, which they saw occurring, paradoxically, as a result of the rational principle making its unchallenged ascendancy. And they were just as serious about combating rationality at any cost. To counter the advance of sober realism, no measure seemed too excessive. For they, like the anarchist symbolists who inspired them, equated it with the social and cultural dominance of a dull and pragmatically minded bourgeoisie. Not by accident, comparisons to warfare were often used to evoke the nature of their struggle against the soulless materialism, the crude, lowbrow tastelessness, and a bleary-eyed indifference to anything that did not immediately appeal to the senses. In his essay "On the Creative One," Klages asserted that creative energy expressed itself in numerous ways. But there was always the same fundamental impulse, or "movement," at work, whether "the movement be directed toward universal comprehension, toward great deeds of war, or some other kind of shaping and forming."

This glorification of war was no isolated incident. In another prose sketch by Klages, titled "The Conqueror" and which he published in the only issue of the *Blätter* to appear in 1899, he indulged in a fantasy portrait of a fearsome Germanic warrior leading his troops to military victory. After carefully setting the scene — Klages evokes a cold, dark, windswept plain punctuated only by the "metallic" reflection of the stars on the watery surface of dead marshes — he introduces us to his hero: "In stony motionlessness the conqueror waits on his stationary horse. His traits have the splendor of weathered dolomite. In his glance there is the cold glow of the northern light. On his head he wears a ring of bluish steel. Disconsolate sadness has molded with an iron hand the face of this man." Although followed by faithful hordes, the Conqueror is separated from happiness by a deep abyss of loneliness. "Storms broke down over him, and in the white fire of lightening he forged the unsparing sword of his hate. He has already subdued *one* half of the globe, he would also place his victorious sole on the other one." Suddenly, the news comes that the remains of the vanquished armies that opposed him have now banded together, threatening with their combined strength to overpower his own forces. The Conqueror, reanimated by this new challenge, rallies his flagging troops:

"The certainty of murderous victory flames up in his eyes and seizes the graying warriors with intoxication." As they set out, the warlord keeps a steady eye trained on the distant "slumbering palaces and domes. The shadows of future conflagrations seem to flicker ahead of him, and behind him lumbers the thudding might of the mass pregnant with power which his destroyer's will lent a soul." It has been suggested that this was a veiled portrait of Napoleon, but the figure of Attila more quickly springs to mind.

Either way, it is a chilling performance. Notwithstanding the fact that "the Conqueror" is clearly an allegorical rendering of George and his own crusade — and, again, despite the patent indebtedness to Nietzsche, particularly to his notorious vision of the "blond beast" — the piece gives one more than momentary pause. It is true that the figure of the lonely knight traveling through a gloomy and hostile landscape had long been a stock figure in northern Christian iconography, appearing most memorably in the writings of Erasmus and in the famous print of the *Knight, Death and the Devil* by Albrecht Dürer. But the evident relish with which Klages evoked the brutal warlord, his delight in the hard metaphors of death and destruction — steel, iron, stone, fire, and flames — and his eager embrace of a kind of ennobling violence, all send a shiver down one's spine. It might have been a purely symbolic conflagration Klages was envisioning. Soon enough, however, it would become hard to distinguish the symbolic from the real.

We recall that a number of poems in George's *Books of Eulogies and Eclogues* had also sounded the martial drum, and that elsewhere the poet was not averse to resorting to images of organized mayhem to convey his intentions. In addition, George had frequently identified himself with merciless despots, with *Algabal* being only the most concentrated expression of that tendency. But it was not until 1899, with the publication of his sixth book of poetry, *The Tapestry of Life,* that he managed to harness his autocratic proclivities, which had so far found an outlet only within the abstract realm of the poetic word, within a framework that could also be transposed back onto reality itself. To be sure, the advantage of concentrating his powers on poetry alone was that it gave him the satisfaction, and limitless authority, of reigning supreme over his own creation. But in the meantime his ambition had grown. He was no longer content to hold sway merely over insubstantial phantoms. He wanted to lay his hands on real beings, bodies of flesh and blood, to mold them, shape them according to his own plan, just as he had previously arranged the words of his verses to respond to his desires and aspirations. The instrument that would allow him to take that leap, the vehicle for transferring his formative appetite from the figurative to the literal, was the idea and reality of the circle itself.

To be effective, however, that idea had to be spelled out. As we saw, the notion of a "circle" had been implicit for some time in the way the *Blätter* was first conceived and organized. But it was one thing to recognize that the members of the journal composed a unified, self-contained group. Both before and after George, there have been countless artistic "circles" and "schools" of all stripes held together by common assumptions and practices. It was quite another matter to elaborate a behavioral code, so to speak, a system of values that stood apart from, although was intimately related to, the artistic program that had brought its adherents together in the first place. And it was even less self-evident that there should be one controlling agency, a single inviolable will that should exert mastery over the whole. Yet this is precisely what George envisioned — with, of course, himself in that central role — and it was here that his expectations concerning the conduct and duties of his subordinates harked back to the fantasies of domination from his earliest youth. Now, though, those dreams were on the brink of becoming reality.

The Tapestry of Life bears a number of parallels to *The Year of the Soul,* which had appeared two years before. Like its immediate forerunner, *The Tapestry of Life* was again the product, at least in its physical dress, of a close collaboration with Melchior Lechter. The visual language was familiar as well: the title page, framed on either side by the images of two seven-armed candelabras, encloses the poet's name at the top, under which a haloed dove, with wings spread, is shown facing downward, as if mediating between the poet and the title of the book. Here, once more, the heavy, slightly coarse paper was carefully chosen, the type, based on George's own handwriting, cut to specification. What is new are the book's dimensions: almost three times the size of George's previous works, it measures a foot and a half from top to bottom. The binding, with the title of the book deeply embossed on the front cover and the letters colored with deep blue ink, is held together by two massive wooden boards in front and back, each almost half an inch thick and covered in a rough dark green linen that George himself selected. Its heft and size, its sacramental opulence, the grave, muted colors, everything combined to make it clear that this book, even more than the others, was intended to be read not casually, not to be tucked under the arm or into a pocket and taken to the park or a restaurant and absently leafed through between other distractions. It was meant to be the sole focus of attention, the object of devotion, to be read — and even better, to be read aloud — as an act of observance. It had the feel, and indeed the purpose, of a prayer book, a book of orders. "How is work progressing on the construction of the temple?" George asked Lechter in late May 1899, and he was being only half ironic. Another friend similarly called the book "cathedral-like."

Fittingly, if somewhat startlingly, in the opening poem of *The Tapestry of*

Life an angel appears. In what might be described as an inverted annunciation scene, the poet describes himself being visited by a heavenly herald bringing him tidings of new things to come.

> I searched with pale zeal for the treasure
> For strophes in which my deepest grief
> Made a muffled and uncertain sound —
> Then a naked angel stepped through the door:
>
> Toward my lowered mind he carried
> The burden of the richest flowers and no less
> Than almond blossoms did his fingers seem
> And roses, roses encircled his chin.
>
> No crown rose up on his head
> And his voice seemed similar to mine:
> The beautiful life sends me to you
> As a messenger: while he said this, smiling
>
> He dropped lilies and mimosas
> And as I bent over to pick them up
> HE also knelt · delighted I bathed
> My entire face in the fresh roses.

George was capable of pulling off grand gestures in his poetry, and this one ranks among his most spectacular. It is a highly complex moment, at once a concentrated synthesis of his poetic journey thus far that also alludes to his future course, as well as a synoptic distillation of some of the principal themes of his verse. With near perfect economy, the four strophes exploit the overdetermined symbolic value of the flowers. Joining sensuous gratification with rhetorical excess, signaling both poetic and sexual fulfillment, they reveal a by now familiar narcissistic fixation on the poet's self (the word "I" is not accidentally the first one in the poem, just as the angel's voice is not casually said to be a mirror image of the poet's own). Finally, the lines enact the final, open conquest of the naked male body — the angel is explicitly masculine — as an object of delight and inspiration. But it is the figure of the angel himself, and the message of the "beautiful life" he has been sent to convey, that stand as the poem's most audacious bid. This, too, is an extraordinary feat of poetic control, for it was precisely ten years before, in the very first poem of his first book — "Consecration" in the *Hymns* — that George had introduced a similar, and equally mysterious, "goddess" descending down to bestow her blessing on the poet. There, it marked the inauguration of his poetic career; here, the angel announces yet another new beginning. The two obviously related figures thus serve to enclose this segment of George's poetic life as if between two ideal bookends. Not the least significant of the transformations that had taken place in the intervening decade was the change of his paragon's gender. But the most important difference between them is that, as opposed to that earlier apparition, the angel is not a harbinger of a way to escape the world. Rather, the angel proclaims a way to reside within this world. It is not the beautiful poem he announces but the beautiful life.

There is another similarity between this new book and *The Year of the Soul*. *The Tapestry of Life* is a tightly structured work, but it takes systematic rigor to unprecedented lengths. No other work by George, apart from *The Star of the Covenant* in 1914, would be as carefully constructed. The book is divided into three main sections that have their own heading — "Prologue," "The Tapestry of Life," and "The Songs of Dream and Death" — and each one consists of exactly twenty-four poems. Each poem, in turn, has precisely four stanzas, and each four-line stanza has alternating rhymes and adheres to a relentless iambic pentameter. The result is a kind of liturgical cadence, an almost ritualistic rhythmic uniformity that, together with the book's sumptuous exterior, reinforces the air of a sacred text.

But of course it was the content, more than these comparatively superficial elements, that was mainly responsible for its sacramental character. The rather generic nature of the angel corresponds to the equally general aura of religiosity that suffuses the language and images of the first section of the book. In the second poem of the "Prologue," for example, the poet implores the angel to lend him the "great solemn breath" of inspiration and to enclose him in "your sanctuary." When the angel calmly informs him that his "glorious gift" cannot be forcibly gained, the poet, recalling the biblical words of Jacob wrestling with his own angel, wraps his arm around the divine messenger's knee and says, "I will not let go unless you bless me." In another verse, the angel pulls the poet back from the temptation to leave his chosen vocation with a look that is said to be like Jesus Christ's — also called here, interestingly, "the Master" — when the Lord tested the loyalty of his apostles at the Sea of Galilee: "with the long melancholy glance which / Resembled that of the Master at the homeland sea / When he asked the disciples: do you love me?"

More by association than by direct comparison, then, George established a link in these poems with the language and forms of Christian, and specifically Catholic, ceremony and belief. But he was not concerned with creating religious poetry, or at least not in any ordinary sense. Here, as elsewhere, George sought instead to co-opt the inherent power of the Catholic ritual and apply it to his own ends. It is a private gospel he would preach but one that seemed validated by the ancient formulas that partially served as its model and source.

Above all, it is the figure of the angel — the mediator between the divine and the human realms, the bringer of the doctrine of "the beautiful life," the poet's protector and counselor — who serves as a sort of liaison between the conventional imaginary repertoire of Christian motifs and George's own more idiosyncratic vision.

The most important lesson the angel teaches the poet, it appears, is the value and importance of submitting to a superior being. "Now a good spirit is holding the balance straight," another verse reads, comparing this state of inner equilibrium with the unspecified "terrible days" he had experienced in his life before. "Now I will do everything the angel wants," the poet promises. Elsewhere, the angel assures him that "I am friend and guide [*Führer*] and pilot to you," but this oath comes with the implied proviso that he will be all these things only so long as the poet unquestioningly obeys his injunctions. Crucially, the angel also gives him the courage, or the leave, to assume a similarly commanding position toward his own followers and takes the poet to the top of a mountain from where he can survey potential candidates. From his high vantage point, he sees

> A small flock going quietly along its way
> Proudly remote from the working bustle
> And on their flags the slogan stands:
> To Hellas forever our love.

Although we have seen earlier declarations of fidelity to the Greek idea in the *Blätter,* it had not yet congealed for George into a coherent doctrine, as it later would. But even in approximate terms, the allegiance to Hellas already acted as a rallying point, allowing the poet to use it as a means of identifying those who might be susceptible to his message. One poem, still in the first section, gives an idea of how seductive George knew to make his offer. The poet, already grown in the self-confidence that the angel has been sent to awaken in him, has begun to formulate the reasons why others should follow him and abandon their accustomed lives to join him in his pursuit:

> If you dwell in the most wretched regions
> Where ingloriously the deeds of the strong and of the pale
> Are buried then my call will direct you to action —
> As the body inexorably does to every pleasure.
>
> The clear answer rises with my sun
> If you ask yourself: toward which wind to turn
> Where to reach when all the threads are entangled
> Where to draw water when every well spills over?

> And if you suffer from the hesitant timidity of the fathers
> So that you are confused by the changing colorful swirling
> Of forms and their excessive number:
> If you are crushed by the number of worlds in the firmament:
>
> Then come to the place where we form a union!
> In my grove of consecration you hear the reverberating roar:
> Even if there are countless forms of things
> There is only One for you — Mine — to proclaim it.

If you feel yourself caught a world of transience and confusion, the poet is saying to an unnamed potential disciple, if you do not know which way to turn or if find you have utterly lost your way among the myriad possibilities of life, then I invite you to come to my own realm, "consecrated grove," where I promise the shelter of meaning and certainty, to provide the comfort of a single truth, namely, "Mine." The only thing the poet asks in return from the person who enjoys this privilege is absolute fealty, total adherence to his word, and the willingness to promulgate it.

Actually, that was not quite the only requirement. Later on in the "Prologue," we find a poem in which the poet envisions his disciples, now a sizeable group, as speaking in a single voice in what one of George's followers likened to a "marching song." (The suggestion that George was a sort of spiritual drill sergeant is not as far-fetched as it might at first sound. In a candid moment, he once said with some emphasis to Albert Verwey that "what I like doing best of all is drilling."):

> We are the same children who gather amazed
> But not despondently before your ruler's gait
> When a soldier sounds the signal
> For your banner to tower over the open field.
>
> We march at the side of our severe lord
> Who carefully examines his fighters
> No weeping keeps us back from following our star
> No friend's arm and no bride's kiss.
>
> Rejoicing, we read in his glance
> What he has foreseen for us in his waking dream
> Whether his raised or down-turned thumb
> Will command honor or dark retreat.
>
> We receive as a loan from his hand
> What delights glorifies and delivers us

And if he gives the sign: we are strong and proud and ready
To go out into night and death for his glory.

Not only are the disciples ready to foreswear all other social bonds — neither "friend" nor "bride" shall hold them back — but they are also prepared to make the ultimate sacrifice, a complete forfeiture of the self, symbolized (or, perhaps better, exemplified) by the willingness to give one's life in the interests of the master's greater renown. In a poem from the middle section of the book, titled "The Disciple" ("Der Jünger"), the attitude toward the master — here called *Herr*, which encompasses the semantic range of the English words "Lord," "sir," and "gentleman," as well as "master" — is portrayed as less turbulent but not as less absolute. In this poem, the disciple is speaking of his feelings for his *Herr* to others who do not understand him:

You speak of delights that I do not desire
In me love resides for my Master
You know only the sweet love · I the noble one ·
I live for my noble Master.

Other verses of the poem speak, in the same repetitious, incantatory vein, of how the Disciple's *Herr* is "mild," "wise," and, naturally, "the greatest": "My reward is in the glances of my Master. / If others be richer: my Master is the greatest / I follow my greatest Master." Further underscoring the proximity of this conception of human relationships to more traditional forms of religious behavior, another poem, "The Monastery," outlines what the communal life of the poet's disciples might look like. He enjoins his small band "to flee the loud hordes with a few brothers" — like its historical model, this virtual "monastery" would exclude "sisters" — and to find a place "in a quiet valley for your order." There, occupied by edifying work, they live together chastely, "without avid desire." Instead, they should form "pious pairs" and "in the evening flee sobbing word and kiss" — that is, avoid expressions of physical or verbal emotion — to lead a life of "dedicated striving most divine renunciation." The quasi-sacramental implications of this arrangement are obvious and deliberate, reinforced by the tenor of the whole book. Like monks who take sacred vows and turn their back on the world forever, the poet's disciples would also commit themselves to a bond that was severable only by death.

How literally George conceived of the disciple's preparedness to die for the master is open to debate. Certainly George valued loyalty as a supreme good, and he bitterly condemned those who weakened the bond between master and disciple, or worse, dared to break it. His opinion of Nietzsche, who distanced himself from Richard Wagner after an early period of intense admiration, is instructive. "Nietzsche betrayed Wagner," George once categorically said to one of the philosopher's admirers. "Do you wish to justify this treason?" Bravely, George's interlocutor tried to respond to this challenge by arguing that in removing himself from the overpowering gravitational pull of Wagner's star, Nietzsche had been able to "see through" his operas, and only then did Nietzsche turn against him. George, who disliked Wagner even more than he mistrusted Nietzsche, rejected this argument as irrelevant, saying that Nietzsche's behavior touched on a matter of principle. Attacking Nietzsche did not mean he took Wagner's side. "Do you really think I would speak on behalf of that bad actor and of his Valhalla swindle?" George said indignantly. "This is about something else. Wagner, who is disgustingly false and insincere on the stage, honestly took up the fight against the nineteenth century in his youth, and Nietzsche was his companion. And Wagner was Nietzsche's master! No *Birth of Tragedy,* no Nietzsche without being awakened by Wagner! No, no — Nietzsche betrayed Wagner! If he really grew beyond him, then he could have gone silently from him. But this ruckus, this supposed unmasking! Nietzsche himself knew perfectly well that the case of Wagner was also the case of Nietzsche." While Nietzsche's apostasy was bad enough, though in the end perhaps forgivable, nothing could excuse his disloyalty. For George, the union between disciple and master, even if it grew weak or strained over time, was in and of itself a consecrated one. Even if both move inwardly apart, the disciple had a duty to maintain the memory of his master in grateful homage. Once bound, one was bound for life.

In reality, George had not been principally speaking about Nietzsche or Wagner at all but about himself and his own past and future followers. Not a few of them would give him cause to invoke the example of Nietzsche's "faithlessness," and George always reacted remorselessly to their "treachery" and "betrayal" by cutting them off without a word, never to see or speak with them again. As far as George was concerned, they were in fact already dead. That George was quite happy to consider the idea of consigning those closest to him to at least a metaphorical death is the subject of a poem from the middle section of *The Tapestry of Life*. Called "Der Täter" — we have no handy equivalent in English for the German noun meaning the "doer of the deed"; "perpetrator" comes closest perhaps — the title recalls the violent imagery in the poem, "The Deed," from the *Books of Eclogues and Eulogies*. Here, instead of presenting us with a young boy fantasizing about deeds of glory, the poet tells of someone contemplating a foul crime on the eve of its execution. We learn neither who the victim of the intended act will be, nor what the infraction itself was that will be punished. But there is little reason to doubt that the "deed" being planned is murder. Oddly, the "perpetrator" justifies his deed-to-be with the following reflection:

> He who has never measured the spot on his brother where he would plunge the dagger
> How easy is his life and how thin the thoughts
> Of him who has never eaten the deadening grains of hemlock!
> Oh if you only knew how I slightly despise you all!

There are few people who have not been so angry or so hurt by someone that they have not contemplated murdering their offender, no matter their relation. What is disturbing here is that, whereas such a violent act of passion or rage may be comprehensible, if not excusable, the "perpetrator" in the poem is obviously not at the mercy of some uncontrollable emotion. He is, instead, coldly calculating, plotting a vicious deed as if he were planning a Sunday outing. He is aware that his actions will be met with the shock and condemnation of the burgers now placidly asleep in their beds, but he expresses only contempt for what he regards as their hypocrisy and self-delusions.

Such considerations also place the third and last part of *The Tapestry of Life*, "The Songs of Dream and Death," within a revealing light. Most of this section contains poems that are devoted to individual people, including Albert and Kitty Verwey, Reinhold and Sabine Lepsius, Carl August Klein, Leopold von Andrian, Clemens von Franckenstein, and others. As we know, this practice was not new with George, because in both of his preceding books he had done the same thing, with the difference that in the *Books of Eclogues and Eulogies* he had hid his friends behind ancient Greek pseudonyms, and in *The Year of the Soul* he had indicated only their initials. Here, however, and for the first time, he reproduced their entire names. But it was not an innocent gesture. Ernst Morwitz, who knew George for close to thirty years, explained that "according to the poet's view of life, this attests to the fact that his experience with the dedicatees had already ended. If he would have thought a further development of his experience with them were possible, he would have concealed their names or only hinted at them." Morwitz went on to say that "by naming them by their full names, he is gathering them together, and he is aware that they will no longer accompany him on his future path."

Not that George openly revealed his intentions. Instead of viewing themselves as outcasts, the friends George named in these dedications in all likelihood felt genuinely honored. In October 1899, for example, Leopold von Andrian learned of George's intention to publish his name in *The Tapestry of Life*. He wrote to the poet to communicate his "surprise and joy" that only a "few hours of being together" had sufficed to earn this distinction, "despite a five-year separation." "I am a little proud of the fact that our connection even prompted you to write verses that belong to me and thus shall speak to your readers about both of us at the same time." Andrian would probably have been slightly less thrilled had he known that George meant the poem less as a tribute to the living than as an epitaph to the dead — at least to George himself. George may have wanted the verses concluding *The Tapestry of Life* to stand as lasting monuments to his friends, but for him to do so in this way was equivalent to burying them alive.

George viewed his book as a cenotaph or sepulcher in more than just a loosely figurative sense. Unlike Andrian, Sabine Lepsius appeared to sense that something had changed in her relationship to the poet, and she said so in a letter to her husband in early May 1899. Until then, however, all three had enjoyed a close and regular intimacy, with George making almost daily visits to the couple's apartment during his now annual autumnal sojourns in Berlin. He had also continued the practice of holding readings there, and just before one such occasion, on November 24, 1898, a young man by the name of Richard Perls died in Munich. Three years before, George had met Perls, then twenty-two and by all accounts extraordinarily handsome. "A young man of great beauty," was how Theodor Lessing remembered him. "His supple body carried the joyful Apollonian head of a young Roman." Sabine Lepsius, who owed her acquaintance with George to Perls, also knew no better way to describe him than by reference to classical models, saying his "delicate head resembled a beautiful Greek cameo." Perls was also blessed by a quick and active mind, equally gifted in the sciences and mathematics as well as in the plastic arts and music. At seventeen he was attending lectures on physics by Hermann Helmholtz at the University of Berlin, and then he went on to Munich to study psychology with Theodor Lipps. It was there Perls met George and discovered morphine.

At first, Perls used the drug as a means of heightening and intensifying his experiences, self-consciously emulating Des Esseintes, the self-indulgent hero of Huysmans's still popular novel. As time went on, though, the morphine became not the means of enhancing his ardor for life but an insistent end in itself. Increasingly, Perls's behavior turned erratic and unpredictable. Despite attempts by his family to save Perls from himself by sending him to a series of doctors and sanatoriums, he always returned to the drug's welcome embrace. As the ghastly course of his addiction played itself out, Perls's friends watched in helpless horror as he systematically destroyed himself. Toward the end, after Perls had to be confined to bed, he showed signs of a lowering insanity, his once lithe body became wasted and frail, and only his weakness prevented him from putting an end to his sufferings with a pistol. At last, his caretaker relented to his constant pleas for release and mercifully administered a final, massive overdose.

George was severely shaken by the news of Perls's death. Besides having been a contributor to the *Blätter* — among his other talents, Perls had also been a respectable poet — he had formed a tender attachment to the older man. In April 1896, for instance, he had written to George from Paris, wondering "how would it be if we set up house together in a small town in central Italy or in Belgium? Buried in solitude and love, radiant in the fire of an art whose soul has drunk all of the melancholy of our departing world, ought not we be able to live out days that would be exemplary to those who must suffer more in this the best of all worlds?" At the beginning of May, George had gone to Brussels for a week to be with him, but what he saw made him fear for the worst. Telling Wolfskehl about the visit, George wrote that "I met our dear Richard Perls there in a physical and mental condition that raises the most serious concerns."

Whatever George had been unable to do for Perls while he was alive, he resolved to make up for by at least providing a suitable memorial to mark his passing. Writing to Wolfskehl five days after Perls died, George asked him to contribute a few words to the effort. "Behind this DEAD MAN march sadly the poets who loved him, if *you* also find a few lines that are devoted to him and honor him — then they will form part of the wreath I want to weave for him and will add to the next volume of the *Blätter*, and also on *Sunday* (when you unfortunately will be away and when I will again read before a larger circle at the home of our friends) I will remember Him." Wolfskehl complied with the request and, even though he was not present, his words, along with a few poems by Perls himself, were used to introduce the recitation.

The reading was held on the afternoon of December 4, 1898. As usual, the guests were led from the entrance foyer of the Lepsius home into the dimly lit living room. Immediately adjacent, connected by broad double doors, was the music room, now shrouded in darkness except for two piano lamps that would cast their strong, white light on the poet as he read. Standing in the middle of the passageway was a music stand that held the large unwieldy volume; vases of flowers also stood by the side, and in the music room one could make out a copper vessel containing sprigs of laurel. Among those invited was the socialite and tireless diarist Count Harry Kessler. Having seen only photographs of the poet before, Kessler noted that George's face was "harder and bonier" than he had expected; "the jawbones and the skull have, in their width and power, something brutal." At the same time, Kessler observed, "he reads with a voice that alternates between a rasping sound and a nasal preacher's tone, but rhythmically not unattractive." Strangest of all, he noted, was the way George introduced the recitation. "To begin," George had announced, "we will read from the work of a brother who has passed away and beheld with us the dream, Richard Perls." Somewhat nonplused by the whole event, Kessler wrote that "the nasal tone [was] exactly like the beginning of a sermon."

Consciously or not, Count Kessler had put his finger not just on the intended mood of the reading but also on the very essence of George's self-understanding at this critical juncture in his life. George was no longer satisfied with being simply a poet — although there had never been anything simple about being a poet to George. Performing the Office of the Dead for Richard Perls before a selected congregation was more like it, since this validated the sacred function of the poet in a realm other than the merely literary. But dirges are a dreary business, and George, for all of his sympathy for fin-de-siècle lugubriousness, did not see himself presiding over a mass funeral — at least not yet. He would publish only three more books — *The Seventh Ring* in 1907, *The Star of the Covenant* in 1914, and *The New Reich* in 1928 — but they would be as much, and arguably more, esoteric elaborations of his peculiar vision of life than works of poetry in any traditional sense. Despite all of his reservations about his country, his people, and his time, George, now vested with a greater power and authority than ever before, gathered new hope from what he had called, in *The Tapestry of Life,* "divine youth." From now on, he would concentrate his best formative powers on creating a cadre of ardent, devoted, and able young men who would embody his word even more truly than his poetry ever could. He would not stop writing verse, of course, but in some ways it became demoted to something like a supporting role. Now his principal concern would be consolidating the circle of people to whom he would be Master.

Stephan George II, the father of the poet, as a young man

George's father

George's mother, née Eva Schmitt

Wirtschaft zur Traube (Tavern of the Grape) in Büdesheim, where George was born

Bingen on the Rhine

House in Bingen where the Georges lived after 1873 (destroyed in World War II)

Ludwig Georgs-Gymnasium, Darmstadt

Stefan George sitting in a window looking onto the garden in Bingen

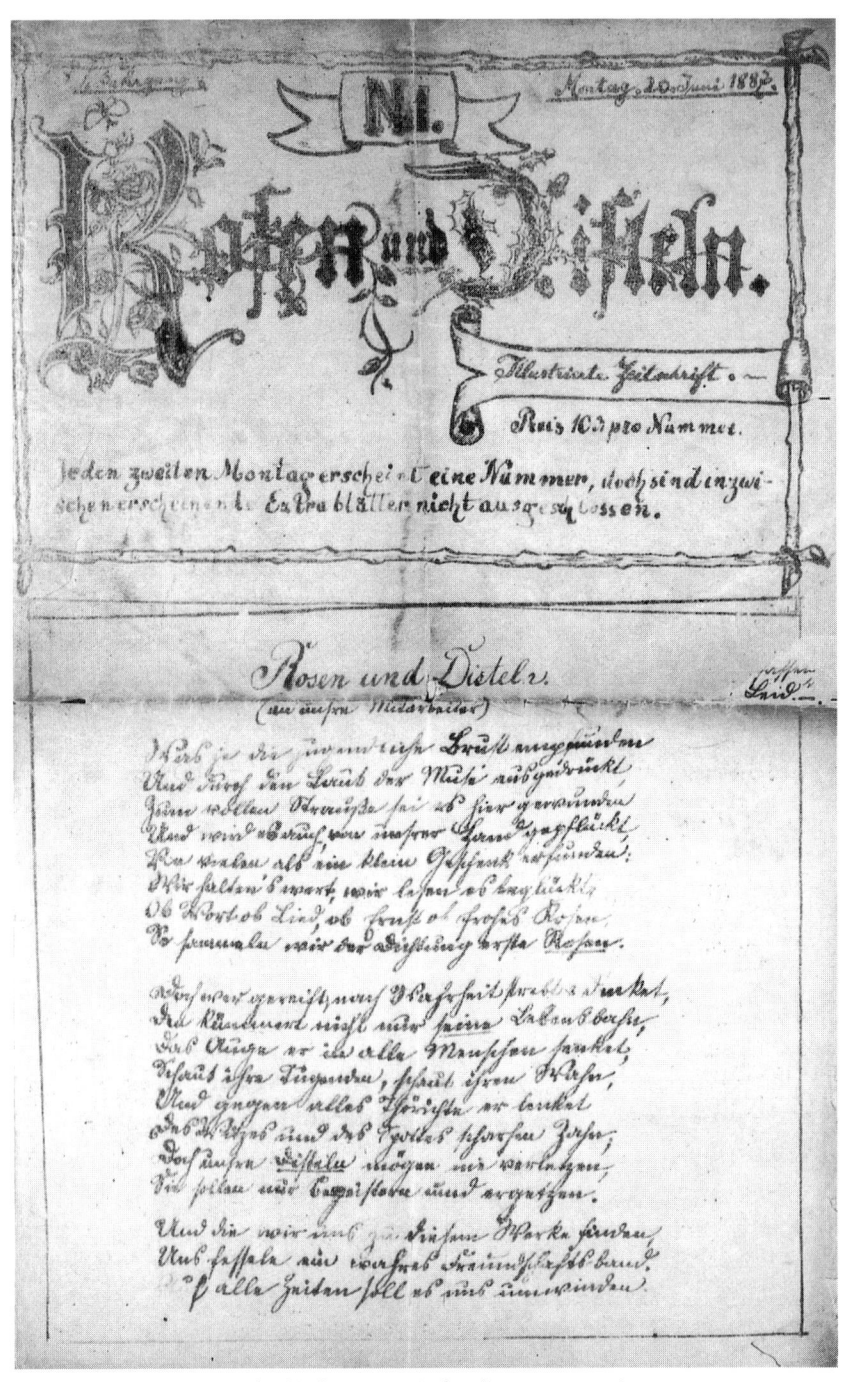

Roses and Thistles, *George's first literary magazine, 1887*

Carl Rouge

Arthur Stahl

George around 1890

Albert Saint-Paul

Paul Verlaine in his favorite haunt, the Café François Ier

Stéphane Mallarmé

Exterior of Café Griensteidl in Vienna where George met Hofmannsthal

Interior of Café Griensteidl

Hugo von Hofmannsthal

Leopold von Andrian

George and his Belgian friends, Edmond Rassenfosse and Paul Gérardy

Ida "Isi" Coblenz

George in the garden of Ida Coblenz's house

George in his favorite beret, around 1893

George and a friend, 1896

Albert Verwey

The indiscreet Cyril Meir Scott

Melchior Lechter

Title page of The Year of the Soul, *1897, designed by Melchior Lechter*

Sabine Lepsius

Reinhold Lepsius

Part ii
PEDAGOGUE + 1900–1908
YOUTH + EROS + MYTH

CHAPTER 19

The Disciple

In March 1899, shortly before George turned thirty-one, Karl Wolfskehl sent his friend an early birthday present. "I am able to share a happy experience with you, namely the verses I am enclosing. A young eighteen-year-old compatriot wrote them, and you will love the glances, the glances of life in them, as you will perhaps love him, the ephebe, when you see him." Wolfskehl admitted that the author was indeed still quite young, "but since he is deep and passionate and full of love we may take joy in him and place our hopes in him."

Wolfskehl was in the habit of sending George young boys for his evaluation. A year and a half later, for example, Wolfskehl wrote (although he appears to have been speaking about a photograph rather than an actual person), "Dearest friend, may this tender boy bring you the tribute of my greeting! He crossed my path and I grabbed hold of him — I hope to your pleasure. It's almost grotesque how the stiffly collared neck and the conservative cut of the clothes support his charming face, and how boyish still his lips and already heavy with life his eye." Over the following decade and more, Wolfskehl — like many other solicitous friends of George — procured a sizable number of adolescent boys and young men for the poet, who would then personally examine them to determine their suitability for admission. At first the fiction was upheld that they were being drafted merely for the *Blätter*. In this there was at least a precedent to fall back on. In the waning years of the 1890s, the number of contributing members to the journal had steadily risen while their average age had just as consistently sunk. In the only issue to come out in 1897 (none appeared in the following year), three poets had made their debuts:

Ernst Hardt, Karl Gustav Vollmoeller, and August Mayer-Oehler. The oldest of the three was Hardt, born in 1876. The youngest was Mayer-Oehler, who, having been born in 1881, was only sixteen and thus almost half George's age when he was presented to the public in the *Blätter*. For various reasons, all three soon fell out of sight again. But a distinct pattern had already begun to emerge.

As time went on, the pretext of looking for undiscovered poetic talent was gradually dropped. And as George's sphere of influence grew, it became evident that he was physically unable, and anyway was not temperamentally inclined, to do all the searching himself. His friends would thus obligingly scour their own circles of acquaintance, scrutinize passersby on the street, and cast discerning glances over the crowds gathered at theaters, restaurants, cafés, and public houses hunting for a face or a bearing they knew would please the Master. Naturally, those who were in some way attached to a university enjoyed the advantage of having access to a constant flow of attractive, bright, usually socially advantaged seventeen- and eighteen-year-old candidates to review. Edgar Salin, who taught in Heidelberg and met George just before the war, relates a typical incident. Having unsuccessfully sifted through the large numbers of students at the beginning of a new semester, Salin was despairing of finding a single person worthy of being presented to George, when a long-limbed youth suddenly walked into the seminar room. He was wearing short pants that exposed his bare knees, but his graceful height seemed only accentuated by this sporty, boyish outfit. He had a shapely noble head, steel-blue eyes with a bright, piercing gaze, and waves of blond hair. The next day, hoping to bring the happy news to George, who was recovering from a nagging illness and would, Salin imagined, be invigorated by such a catch, he was greeted instead by a stern reprimand. "You just saw this boy for the first time? What do you have eyes for, anyway? Does such a miracle have to blow into your room before you notice it?"

It turned out that this "miracle," the son of an admiral, had lived in Heidelberg all his life. George thought it unforgivable that Salin had not spotted him before, as George himself obviously had. And George had only derisive scorn for Salin's stammered explanation that the boy's family resided on the opposite bank of the Neckar and was thus outside of his normal circuit. "That's supposed to be an excuse?" George chided him. "How many times do you go every week in the afternoon and the evening to the Gotheins?" (Eberhard Gothein, another professor at the university and a common friend, lived in Neuenheim, which is also on the other side of the river.) To George, it was as unfathomable as inexcusable that the boy had never caught Salin's eye. "Have you never watched the children playing ring-around-the-roses on the large meadow in Werderstrasse," George incredulously asked him, "never admired the blond ringleader who sets the pace and keeps the little pairs in motion?" The storm soon abated — although George would mockingly turn to Salin when a new face appeared and sneer, "And you never noticed him either?!" — but it was a lesson not to be forgotten. How and where one chose the fresh young things George hungrily consumed was almost as important as the acquisition itself. For the Master judged not just the new recruit, he also saw it as an opportunity to take the measure of the recruiter.

But the eighteen-year-old "ephebe" Wolfskehl offered to George in the spring of 1899 was different. In the first place, when Wolfskehl had called him a "compatriot," he had meant it in a narrow sense. The young man's father, Sigmund Gundelfinger, was a respected professor of mathematics in Darmstadt and an active member of the city's Jewish community, where he had made the acquaintance of Wolfskehl's own father, the banker and politician Otto Wolfskehl. In the fall of 1898, when young Friedrich Gundelfinger was still attending Gymnasium in Darmstadt — the same one the poet had left behind only a decade before — he had attracted the younger Wolfskehl's attention, who then asked the boy's father if he would be permitted to introduce him to Stefan George. Since Herr Gundelfinger insisted that his son first complete his studies and embark on his university career before he involve himself in such distractions, the meeting had to wait until the following spring in Munich, where Friedrich had matriculated the previous winter semester. Finally, on April 15, 1899, Wolfskehl sent young Gundelfinger an urgent message: "George, the Master, has been here for two days. Come at once!!! *He is staying only a little longer.*"

Although the encounter predictably had a much more considerable impact on the sensitive teenage student than on the thirty-year-old poet, it changed both of their lives forever. After this first visit not even the younger man's name would be the same. Although he already revered George's poetry and had long yearned to meet the poet in person, he was so overcome by shyness when the great moment came that he was hardly able to utter a word. George, however, felt free enough to give his new acquaintance a new name. Disliking the sound of Gundelfinger — he gave no reason why it aroused his displeasure, hinting only that he thought it was "ugly" — George called him instead "Gundolf," and it was as Friedrich Gundolf that he was thereafter known to the world. George often used nicknames when addressing his friends in private: he sometimes referred, for instance, to Reinhold Lepsius as "the Apollonian" and his wife Sabine as "the Dionysian," and both together went under the sobriquet "the Divine Pair." Women's names aroused George's particular antipathy, and he preferred to use generic designations in place of their real names. Gertrud Kantorowicz, a friend of Georg Simmel and the only woman ever to publish in the *Blätter für die Kunst* — albeit under the masculine-sounding pseudonym Gert Pauly — was never addressed by her given name by George, who instead liked to call her *Dottoressa* or *Huldin*, the latter an ironic coinage derived from the antiquated German word for graciousness. But in no other case did the name that George invented for one of his friends become, as it were, the official one. Gundolf wore it like a badge of honor. Henceforth, to his friends and family, in his letters, and in his many books and essays, he appeared wearing the mantle George had laid upon him. It was literally a rechristening, a second baptism, the most visible sign that Friedrich Gundolf né Gundelfinger had crossed a threshold and entered a new stage of life.

As usual, George kept silent about whatever effect the meeting might have had on himself. One may hazard a few reasonable guesses about his reaction, though. Tall, elegantly thin, with an oval face, a fine tapered nose seated above a full, expressive mouth, and with large inward-looking eyes that were surmounted by a clear well-formed forehead, Friedrich Gundolf struck everyone who saw him the first time not just as handsome but as disorientingly attractive. "His beautiful appearance enchanted us all," Sabine Lepsius wrote, who met him the following year. "His classically modeled head, surrounded by dark hair, was carried by a tall and slender frame." George soon took Gundolf around to meet his other Berlin contacts, including the Simmels, Melchior Lechter, and his publisher Georg Bondi, who also reported that "everyone noticed his beauty." Bondi was even put upon by curious guests pressing him for more details of the liaison, perhaps titillated by an exciting whiff of impropriety in seeing the older poet with his arresting young companion perpetually in tow. (Even Sabine Lepsius daringly referred to Gundolf as George's "page.") "Everyone," Bondi complained, "wanted to know more from me about this extraordinary appearance." Even in his maturity, Gundolf's good looks were legendary. The story is told that visitors to Heidelberg, where he went in 1911 to teach German literature to packed auditoriums, would sometimes see him on the street and stop and stare, even pointing at him with their fingers.

One element of Gundolf's attractiveness was that none of this appeared to make much of an impression on him. It was not uncommon for female admirers to send him bouquets of flowers, which he would absently toss into a corner, saying he had no time to unpack them and in any case had nowhere to put them. But it was by virtue of his stupendous intellectual gifts, his supple encyclopedic mind, and an almost elemental power of expression, all coupled with a demeanor of earnest sincerity and modest simplicity, that his physical charms seemed, if anything, only heightened. Gundolf could talk about anything at all and make it fascinating. Later, as a professor at Heidelberg, it would happen in conversation with his colleagues and friends, among them men of such caliber as Max Weber and Eberhard Gothein, that, even if they disagreed with his views, they sometimes would fall in admiring silence in the face of Gundolf's formative, almost plastic handling of language. As George had done with Simmel, he coined a verb for this dynamic linguistic virtuosity as well, calling it "gundeling" — *gundeln* — but he was never quite so enamored of these shows of verbal brilliance as everyone else. Even though Gundolf became one of the most prolific and influential literary scholars of his time, George always vaguely seemed to disapprove of his work. When someone was reading the book Gundolf wrote on Goethe in 1916 and pointed out a particularly fine passage to George, he acerbically responded, "Yes, yes, every inch a genius." Suspicious of purely intellectual pursuits and regarding them as something of a wasteful self-indulgence, George was often exasperated by Gundolf's erudition. Not even the radiance of his mind could fully persuade George of the merits of what he essentially saw as nothing better than highbrow dalliances.

But Gundolf was not all work and no play. Everyone who knew him remarked on his love of jokes and funny stories — with no obvious effort, he could toss off extemporaneous comic jingles, burlesque rhyming couplets and impromptu limericks — and his letters teem with puns and playful, witty allusions. This almost impish delight in word play and frivolous good-natured games never abandoned him, which further added to his boyish allure. Even well into middle age, Gundolf struck some as an Ariel-like figure, as someone who had never fully grown up. "Like a child," was how a later member of the circle once described him. He was also an accomplished mimic. He was known to pacify restive infants in their cradle by making soothing bird sounds, and George told the story of how Gundolf was so good at imitating the bawling of a baby that once, when they were in Switzerland together and Gundolf delivered one of his more convincing performances, all of the good nannies within earshot came rushing to console the wailing child.

Beautiful, brilliant, boyishly youthful, Gundolf must have seemed the answer to George's dreams. Yet the only glimpse George gave of his own feelings after their first meeting comes in a short letter to Albert Verwey. At the beginning of 1899, Karl Wolfskehl had moved to Munich and taken up residence in a large apartment in the wilds of Schwabing. The previous October, Wolfskehl had transferred out of the hated Prussian capital and settled in more congenial southern climes — for reasons not solely related to Munich's cultural attractions. On December 28, 1898, he had married Hanna de Haan, and he now needed room for the expected family to follow. Indeed, one year later, on December 23, the first of his two daughters, Renate, was born. The following April, six days after he had met Gundolf, George wrote to Verwey from the new house in Munich, saying he was residing "where Karl Wolfskehl has established his headquarters in rooms where masters and disciples stroll searching for wisdom and loving beauty — a premonition of new hellenic days and nights." It was unclear whose disciple George regarded Gundolf to be at this point — the young man was, after all, Wolfskehl's find — but the "presentiment" of some Greek experience, however envisioned, is notable. So far, talk of "Hellas" and all that it entailed had been confined to poems and the introductory postulates to the *Blätter*. This was the first time he had ever spoken of such things as being possible in real life.

Toward Gundolf himself, George initially appeared to adopt a posture of cool reserve, even aloofness. Perhaps mindful of the mistakes he had made eight years ago in his behavior toward Hofmannsthal, and perhaps, too, having been made chary by the sorrow he felt at the recent loss of Richard Perls, he let Gundolf take all the first steps. It was thus the younger of the two, some two months after they had become acquainted, who initiated written communication. Addressing him already as his "esteemed Master," Gundolf wrote a brief note explaining that he was sending some of his own poems along with translations of six sonnets by Shakespeare and Rosetti. A few days later George answered, thanking him for the original poems, "a number of which," he surmised, "you would probably like to find in the *Blätter*." The translations, too, he thought were "good in tone." "Perhaps your industry will one day fill a gap." George closed with the perfunctory, nonbinding wish "to hear something good from you again."

As praise goes, it was tepid to the point of insult, and in general not exactly encouraging. Far from feeling rebuffed, Gundolf was ecstatic. "Your letter, the most beautiful fulfillment and the richest promise that could be bestowed on my wishes and hopes, embolden me to send a few more verses to you in respect." Looking on the bright side of George's leaden reception of his translations, Gundolf explained that he had an insufficient command of either German or English to do the originals justice, but he added that "should I perhaps have successfully translated some of the sonnets that did not seem foreign to my mood then I know that from the first to the last I have you alone, esteemed Master, to thank for it." It was signed, "in deep reverence and fervent gratitude, your devoted Friedrich Gundolf."

Whatever George had expected, it probably was not this display of almost abject veneration. He must have been even more surprised by another letter he received from Gundolf only six days later. "The great task you have brought home to me," he revealed, "did not let me rest: in the last few days I have translated as well as I was able approximately sixty sonnets, and of those the first fifty in consecutive order." On average, Gundolf had thus rendered ten of Shakespeare's sonnets a day into German and had done so under the pressure of the knowledge they would have to pass George's muster. By any measure, it was an incredible feat, and the first indication of Gundolf's ability to perform almost herculean labors. Over the next decade, albeit benefiting from the advice and practical help of George, he translated all of Shakespeare's plays, or "revised" the famed versions by Schlegel and Tieck, sometimes putting in sixteen hours at a stretch. In 1910 he wrote what became his first book, *Shakespeare and the German Spirit,* in just two months, amassing the manuscript of 490 folio pages at breakneck speed. In the case of the sonnets, it was as if he were trying to win George's approval, if not by the quality of his translations, then at least by their sheer mass as evidence of his industry.

Once more, George chose to remain mute. It was not that he was unaware of what effect a word from him would have on his zealous admirer. Shortly after George had sent his first letter to Gundolf, Wolfskehl had told George that the "words written in the Master's own hand have made our young Gundolf endlessly happy. He glowed with joy and pride when he repeated them to me." George had never been particularly forthcoming in his letters, preferring, for any number of reasons, to say anything that was important in face-to-face meetings. "You have to forgive my matter-of-fact brevity," he had apologized to a friend in 1897. "You belong to those who already know that my letters never contain anything other than factual matters." That was not quite literally true, as we know, but in general it was accurate enough. Nor was it entirely correct when George had written to Wolfskehl in March, just before he met Gundolf, that "writing is not my way of communicating." But, with Gundolf, he was being even more reticent than usual, seeming deliberately to hold back, silently watching and waiting.

Not allowing himself to feel disheartened, Gundolf decided to go on the offensive again. Having bided his time patiently for a month and a half without any response, he worked up the courage to ask George directly for what he described to Wolfskehl as an "audience." Reminding George of a vague offer to that effect which he had extended at the conclusion of their first encounter, Gundolf wrote from his home in Darmstadt on a Wednesday in early August of 1899 that "I now dare to inquire if I may call on you in Bingen." The same day the reply he longed for was sent, although the way it was formulated may have unnerved someone less starstruck. "It is convenient to me that you visit me now," George regally wrote, giving precise instructions about the date and time of the "audience," which he set for that same Friday. "I have much to discuss with you about your translations and about final matters concerning your new poems before they are published in the *Blätter.*"

Either by accident or by design, however, Gundolf was not granted the luxury of seeing his Master alone. Albert Verwey, who had arrived a few days earlier, was spending the week with his old friend and so became acquainted with both the Rhineland and George's new companion. After Verwey met

Gundolf, he wrote home to his wife Kittey about the event, remarking with consummate understatement that George "likes to have such young people around him and this was not one of the worst." On the same day, Gundolf gave his own impression of the encounter to Wolfskehl, bestowing the slightly ambiguous praise on Verwey as being "a wonderfully solid and securely grounded and as far as I could tell intelligent man." But the main, indeed the only attraction for Gundolf was of course George himself. "The Master was extremely charming and kind and great; [he] seemed, by the way, much younger than the last time." To George himself, Gundolf immediately wrote back to "thank you again from the bottom of my heart for all of your kindness, which made yesterday one of the most beautiful and unforgettable." Three days later, Gundolf wrote again, including a photograph of himself that he had had specially made for the purpose, more translations, and the repeated wish for George's opinion about his own latest poems. "You are the first person to know all of these poems and I would like to know in each case whether I am on the right path; I am too young and dim. If you would personally be my guide [*mein Führer*], as your works and words have already been for some time, then, esteemed Master, no one would be more grateful to you."

Perhaps this was what George had been waiting for: a declaration of absolute devotion and an uncategorical recognition of himself not solely as a poet, but, moreover, as a mentor and guide. Significantly, he reacted to this entreaty by sending Gundolf a short, four-line poem — the first of what would be several verses dedicated to him — that was at once a reprimand and an invitation. As significant as the poem itself is the use of the intimate, familiar pronoun *du* instead of the formal *Sie* that they would both continue to use in their letters to one another for the next six months.

> Why study distant people so much and read in legends
> When you can invent a word yourself so that one day they'll say
> Straightaway I was this to You and thus you to me
> Is that not light and answer above all industry

Gundolf must have understood that the first line was not only a reproach of his feverish diligence but also of his connected failure to appreciate present, living pleasures as opposed to digging around in those entombed in books. But he either misread or chose to disregard the subsequent and unambiguous words of courtship, the offer George was extending in compensation for the loss of dead knowledge. "Your admonition shall be beneficial to me," Gundolf answered, suddenly become uncharacteristically taciturn, and he promised to write again soon.

If George's poetic solicitation caused Gundolf any major reservations about the path he had embarked on, they quickly dissolved. A little over a week after he had received the poem, Gundolf wrote again to ask if he would be allowed visit the poet at his home on August 21. George not only gave his permission, he invited Gundolf to come a day early so that they could celebrate the feast of Saint Rochus together, commemorating Bingen's patron saint and savior. "It was so rich, so delightful," Gundolf told Wolfskehl after he had arrived back in Darmstadt, "I spent two days with the Master. Rhine excursions, golden days with silver vistas over joyous meadows among friendly conversations. On the first day we wandered six to seven hours along the banks and through the gorges of the most intimate parts of the Rhine. At eleven at night we were together and the Master feasted with me in the upper living room (no one was home). 'Few have enjoyed such intimacy' (sic fere dixit). It was truly magnificent — and I was in the most reverential and affectionate mood. After the meal, we marveled at Jean Paul's divine Germanness, and the Master read aloud the most marvelous parts in a marvelous way. He showed me his archive and drawings etc." George also gave him a photograph of himself — Gundolf thought it "by far the best photograph of George, characteristic and strong" — and he seems to have made his feelings toward Gundolf more specific. "I believe the Master is very fond of me and says that he esteems me not a little. And the way I venerate and love Him allows me to consider myself with more solemnity than before, and since I feel the kisses and handshakes of Him whom I revere, the dusty present will no longer touch me with slimy fingers."

The metaphors in this last clause may have skidded a bit out of control, but the fundamental emotional tenor of the whole passage tracks a steady, if jubilant course. Gundolf, feeling honored to be the privileged recipient of George's undivided attention and obvious affection, was experiencing, quite simply, the giddy happiness of love. Somewhat in awe of himself for deserving this extraordinary distinction, and filled with the exhilarating sense that the entire world had been transformed, he was experiencing that ancient, familiar delight that always regards itself as new, unique, and unprecedented because it forgets everything else. But there was something else mixed in with Gundolf's love for George from the very beginning, something that went beyond the esteem or reverence normally reserved for the object of our devotion. The day before he had sent the discreetly detailed account of the visit in Bingen to Wolfskehl, he had written to George himself asking him to accept his "heartfelt thanks for all of the splendors" he had been shown there. Oddly, Gundolf also asked him not to spurn his expression of gratitude, as if he expected that George would. "Do not reject it: I know that I am above all indebted to you if I have learned to see for the first time, if I have a content to my life, a path and a goal; every moment that I am granted in your proximity and the constant reminder of these most beautiful moments constantly remind me how much I owe you, dear Master."

It is no exaggeration to say that, from now on, George formed the center of Gundolf's existence. Everything he did, said, or wrote during the next three decades was sustained by the meaning George held for him. For many years, he was George's most frequent travel companion, his amanuensis, his closest apostle, and his confidant. Yet, as much as George meant to Gundolf — which was close to everything — it is far more difficult to say what Gundolf was to George. One reason for this difficulty is, banally, George's own uncommunicativeness. In September 1899, replying to Gundolf's seemingly endless outpourings of gratefulness, he sent a note of caution that appears to border on a challenge. Thanking Gundolf for his "words and parcels," George also chided him for his self-deprecating effusiveness. "It seems to me that you bring me almost too much GRATITUDE . . I have as much reverence for your beginning life as you do for my half-fulfilled one. I can certainly illuminate much for you but you can also be a great help to me. Yet — do I have the right and do you have the strength to cut a deeper channel? Let time decide. Speak to me — I ask you — of your plans and work as often as you feel the urge. But count on few words in response from me without being discouraged. I express myself almost exclusively in motion and figure." Through the fog of studied self-mystification, the message sounded loud and clear: give but do not expect to receive.

Attesting to his resilience, or at least to his appetite for punishment, Gundolf was not thrown off by this new reproach or the prospect of forever being the more openhanded partner. Saying that the letter had made him "exceedingly happy," Gundolf resolutely focused on the positive. Pledging not to overtax George anymore with burdensome words of thanks — "yet is not reverence the most beautiful right and the purest duty of youth!" — Gundolf assured him that "henceforth your admonition shall teach me to show my gratitude in silence by trying, as far as my strength will permit it, to stride along your path, the path of pure art, immersing myself into your works with increasingly fervent love and veneration." If this was Gundolf's idea of curbing his outbursts of appreciation, one can understand George's desire for a little less of a good thing.

But what was finally behind George's efforts to dampen, or at least tone down, the fire of Gundolf's zeal was his by now familiar mechanism of bending people to fit his own designs. George knew, or perhaps only instinctively felt, that the most expedient way to exercise his will over people was to bind them in a relationship of dependence, particularly through a strong emotional attachment. Once the bond was established, and for as long as it held, he enjoyed virtually unlimited power over those who relied on his affirmation and who thus wanted to preserve it at all costs. To work, naturally, it had to be George who dispensed approbation or dissatisfaction, and his authority could never be challenged. Too, people with a vital sense of themselves, a sturdy ego, and a fair degree of self-confidence were less susceptible to this kind of manipulation and hence tended not to count among the majority in George's entourage. Those, however, who were more labile or tentative, who felt socially alienated and in need of external recognition to bolster their sense of self-worth — especially common traits, not incidentally, among the young and intellectually gifted — were more prone to seeing George as providing the real purpose and significance to their lives. This put them, paradoxically, in an even more precarious position, for what can be won can just as easily be lost. The most severe penalty one could incur, one we have seen George impose before and which he would also strategically dispense in the future, was the complete withholding of himself, the irrevocable expulsion of the offending party from all contact with his person. The effect of this retraction of himself could be, and sometimes was, devastating to the victim. But even in smaller, more subtle doses — such as his laconic, "factual" letters, or the refusal to answer a letter at all, or his growing secretiveness about his physical whereabouts — George's proffering or withholding of himself and his affections formed one of the most potent weapons in his arsenal. The notion of the circle, with its sustaining hierarchical structure composed of a master and devoted disciples, only further served to lend this psychological indenture a kind of external validity.

Obviously, in addition to pulling the fine threads of psychological suasion, George did not hesitate to engage in the less delicate art of direct action to get his way. It was not long before Gundolf irritated George by something more serious than his fawning letters. In November, at the urging of Wolfskehl, Gundolf published a critique in the Viennese journal *Wiener Rundschau* of contemporary drama, decrying in particular certain practices in stage direction, and singling out one W. von Scholz for a sound drubbing. When George learned of the existence of the article, he became infuriated. A similar incident several years ago no doubt immediately forced itself on his mind. On that occasion, unannounced and without his sanction, Hugo von Hofmannsthal had allowed Hermann Bahr to publish two of his poems, likewise in a Viennese rag. Not wanting to repeat history, George was perhaps also fearful that his newest "collaborator" might go the way of the eternally fickle Austrian. His reaction was swift and, in contrast to his elusive communiqués to Gundolf, exceptionally direct. "To be frank," he told Wolfskehl, "what affected me quite unpleasantly was that I saw *Friedrich Gundolf,* still warm from coming out of the *Blätter*, jumping into this novelty-obsessed hybrid journal *Wiener Rund-*

schau. I would have thought he would be more 'chaste.' " George never liked the contributors to the *Blätter* to have already published elsewhere when he took them in; they had to be unblemished, untarnished — in a word, virginal. And once they had become a collaborating member, he insisted that they remain monogamous. It was not only that Gundolf was being indecently promiscuous, George felt that others were also poaching on his territory, and he thought Wolfskehl should have done more to hold off the marauders. "As soon as we have some new name these people immediately reach out for it with their sticky fingers." Since Wolfskehl was still Gundolf's protector, George held him personally responsible for this transgression: "Did you have no say at all in the matter?"

Wolfskehl realized that the only defense was to confess, try to put everything in the most positive light, and hope for the best. "That Gundolf's words are in the WR," Wolfskehl admitted, "is my fault alone." Explaining that he had merely intended to put a stop to Herr von Scholz's "vile presumptions," Wolfskehl revealed that the same person had recently written an article about George that had been less than flattering. "In addition to his simpleminded baring of teeth at St. G. this summer (which you know about), I will no longer conceal that a short while ago this bandit allowed himself to indulge in exceedingly despicable shamelessness in a longer essay that had to be censured in one way or the other." The opportunity thus seemed ripe to strike back, and, he assured George, the journal in which Gundolf had published the riposte was, contrary to the Master's objections, "*not an unconsecrated* place!" Now changing tack, Wolfskehl tried to make a virtue out of necessity. He reminded George of the suspended plan to broaden the scope of the *Blätter* to include essays on philosophical, cultural, and even political subjects — a plan that had been discussed at the conference in Bingen in September 1896, which Hofmannsthal had conspicuously missed, even though the idea of expanding the journal had been his all along. In the continuing absence of such an organ, Wolfskehl reasoned, one was forced to do combat under a foreign flag. "As long as the very desirable *journal* of a wider format, which now should be considered more essential than ever, and for which a brilliant circle of collaborators is assured" — Wolfskehl, whose sentences could get sometimes away from him, took a breath and started again — "as long as it still waits in the background, we simply have no other choice but to fight in foreign service, for fight we must. G. seems (I recently already indicted this) capable in due course of becoming a necessary warrior for the good cause, and he is too pure for the arena to be able to soil him, and his weapons are good and of noble construction." "I would say that he proved himself and did not mar his *Blätter*-chastity in the slightest. It was his armed sentry duty and a war against nocturnal ghosts and fabrications."

Apart from Wolfskehl's rather alarming readiness to play fast and loose with martial metaphors in framing literary debates (three years later, he similarly greeted the publication of one of George's prose volumes with the exclamation, "With you Master victory forever!"), his equally unabashed willingness to contradict, or at least disagree with, George seems remarkable. If there was a reply to Wolfskehl's insubordination, it has not survived. Anyway, the real target of the rebuke was Gundolf. Wolfskehl was virtually George's contemporary and by now a seasoned veteran. But the eighteen-year-old neophyte, Gundolf, could not afford to incur the Master's wrath and thereby risk everything. Whether he had astutely picked up that obedience and loyal submission were a necessary condition for maintaining George's favor, or whether his constitution naturally tended in that direction, Gundolf never seriously crossed any of George's wishes again — except once, and for that he paid the ultimate price.

"Love is after all the best education," George was heard to say on more than one occasion. There is no question that he inspired such a profound and complex emotion in Gundolf, as he would do in many other young men thereafter. And, as time passed and George began to make good on his vision of "new hellenic days and nights" by reading and reinterpreting the ancient Greek authors, and foremost among them Plato, something like an educational or pedagogical program did indeed begin to emerge. But, while love, or "eros," is indisputably a powerful spur, it was more often through the careful management of his affection and the implied threat that it might be withdrawn that George achieved his ends. The underlying objective of his pedagogical ambitions, the intended outcome of this "education through love," was not to set the individual minds of his protégés free, nor to make them fit to take their place in the state — unless, that is, it was George's own — nor even to give them a reliable guide — apart from himself — for negotiating the perils and disappointments of life. In fact, these were all "bourgeois" values or goals that George explicitly rejected. What his pedagogical mission would consist in, and what he first realized in practical form with Gundolf, was to secure for himself a band of adherents bound to him by the irrational force of an unquestioning devotion. George did not want to redeem his followers; he wanted to enthrall them.

CHAPTER 20
The Anthologies

In defending Gundolf from George's ire, Wolfskehl himself did not escape entirely unscathed. On the surface, he appeared to be nearly invulnerable. His active association with George was now entering its seventh year. In that time the imposing Hessian had emerged as the chief stalwart of the *Blätter,* beating back impertinent critics, canvassing for new recruits, supplying a stream of poems and prose pieces of his own, and even occasionally making opportune financial contributions to fatten the journal's war chest. He was also on the brink of making his most daring raid to date, a series of books that would integrate representative works by the German literary forebears George and the *Blätter* would choose to acknowledge as their own. More than just anthologies, they were intended to stake out a territory that George and his collaborators wanted to claim for themselves. It would be a brazen act of cultural annexation, a conscious bid for literary expropriation. And the most audacious part of the ploy was that it was not a grab for foreign holdings but rather a rearguard action conducted on and within the German patrimony itself.

The stratagem had been a long time in the making. In 1896, we recall, George had informed Hofmannsthal that Wolfskehl intended to issue an edition of older and more recent German poets in the "tasteful" style of William Morris's Kelmscott Press. In the meantime, such an edition had become desirable for more than merely aesthetic reasons. In conjunction with George's growing desire to establish himself as a specifically German presence, and allied with his seemingly incompatible rejection of anything having to do with the contemporary German empire, there was the dawning realization of the need to redefine and reconstruct the Germany he wanted to incorporate. Initially, he thought he might be able to effect this repossession through and in his poetry alone. After all, he had always regarded his poems as having the power to absorb and transform reality. Given the symbolic potency of the Rhine, both in personal terms and with regard to its larger historical significance, he thought he might start there. Albert Verwey remembered how, during his visit to Bingen in the summer of 1899 when he had met Gundolf, George had told him that he had "an image of a great poem he would like to write: the Rhine, from its source to its end, and in which he would like to unify all of his German feeling and striving. It would be a legacy for the younger ones and be a guide to them in both poetic and statesmanlike terms." The last adjective is arresting, clearly indicating how George's thinking had already begun to shift onto a larger plane that can only be called political. "There lives in him now," Verwey continued, "the attempt to establish himself and his endeavor as having an historically demonstrable origin. A book about Jean Paul is the beginning. He feels in many ways the urge to consolidate himself."

Verwey's memory failed him slightly, for the inaugural volume of the anthology series would be not a book "about" Jean Paul but rather a choice selection of passages from his works. Jean Paul, the pen name of the unclassifiable Friedrich Richter, lived from 1763 to 1825 and was a native of the southern German duchy of Franconia. Although his life thus spanned the periods of German Classicism and Romanticism, he was neither a Classicist nor a Romantic. His sprawling, mammoth, rather ploddingly humorous novels had never been terribly popular, although Thomas Carlyle had manfully translated huge slabs of text into English in the 1820s before finally losing steam. Nineteenth-century German literary historians, who liked to place things in tidy, well-defined categories, never really knew what to do with him. By the end of the century, Jean Paul had thus all but disappeared from the German consciousness. That he had been forgotten was not a liability in George's eyes. On the contrary: it made him especially attractive, for it had left Jean Paul's unwieldy corpus untainted, undisturbed by the greedy, "sticky fingers" of scrounging *littérateurs* and thus ripe for the picking.

Several times in the *Blätter*, George had publicly expressed interest in Jean Paul before. In the March 1896 number of the journal, a lengthy encomium had appeared, also accompanied by several extracts from his writings. The tribute had referred to Jean Paul as "one of the greatest and most forgotten" poets. It praised his ability to wring "infinitely delicate shades" of meaning from words, thus revealing "their mysterious invisibly rustling and captivating undercurrent." This, it asserted, made him "a father of the entire impressionistic art of today." (Curiously, it went on to say how astonishing and humbling it was to behold in his works "such an exquisite sensibility, such a womanly attentiveness, such a wealth of feelings.") Indeed, although Jean Paul was almost exclusively a novelist, his language is lyrical, multilayered, and dense — which was one more reason why his works had never caught fire. Gradually, however, the attraction of these perceived qualities receded before another more pressing concern: what Gundolf, following his two-day sojourn in Bingen in August during which George had read aloud from the poet's work, had called "Jean Paul's divine Germanness." George's recapture of Germany would thus commence not with the powerful Rhine but with an obscure and neglected Franconian novelist.

As was becoming customary, George enlisted Melchior Lechter to tailor a suitable outfit for the planned book. As second-in-command, Wolfskehl was entrusted with overseeing the purely textual side of things. But here problems soon began to arise. There was no doubting Wolfskehl's commitment to the cause; it was his ability to deliver, and do so on time, that had often caused George no little exasperation. Wolfskehl's tremendous energy, enthusiasm, and increasingly complicated social life in Munich had often led him, quite simply, to overextend himself. In early 1897, George had already alluded to his growing reluctance to overburden Wolfskehl with too many assignments, "which your spirit willingly receives but your flesh is incapable of carrying out." In December 1899, when the first proofs of the Jean Paul text arrived, George worried about whether Wolfskehl would manage to summon the will to perform the painstaking labor of proofreading with sufficient care or alacrity. Fortunately, a new, eager, and demonstrably hardworking conscript had just been signed up. "Indicate to the poet *Friedrich Gundolf*," George instructed Wolfskehl, "that he can earn great credit for himself by reading the J.-P. proofs."

Another difficulty, and one that made the task of combing through the proofs looking for typographical errors, omissions, broken type, and so on even more arduous for Wolfskehl was the miserable and deteriorating state of his vision. From birth the sight in his left eye had been so bad that it was almost useless, and his right eye was only marginally better. In 1895, a severe illness had nearly rendered him totally blind. A pair of glasses with thick, bulging lenses helped but did not eliminate the problem. One casualty of Wolfskehl's appallingly poor vision were his correspondents. Apart from Gundolf, who developed something like a paleographic expertise in decoding Wolfskehl's letters, almost no one else could make out his sprawling, hieroglyphic handwriting. In August 1901, Melchior Lechter, normally the soul of good-natured patience, responded to an unreadable message from Wolfskehl by writing, "My dear friend: thank you for your card. Unfortunately I could not decipher its contents!" Not long afterward, Gundolf informed Wolfskehl "that there is a conspiracy afoot among your admirers and friends not to answer your letters anymore until they shine forth clearly on large sheets of paper." A support group of fellow sufferers had even formed, dubbed the "Berlin Society of Recipients of Wolfskehl Letters." Just so Wolfskehl would know that the matter was not all in jest, however, Gundolf added that "the Master says that this too belongs to the sphere that is not in fact superficial." When George himself bothered to respond personally, he was even less forgiving. He once returned one of Wolfskehl's scrawls to its author with a curt note written in pencil at the top: "Completely illegible. Stefan."

Whereas illegible letters were an annoying but ultimately trifling affair, the work to be done on the anthologies was a serious business. In April 1900 George received a copy of the first corrected proofs after they had ostensibly been vetted by Gundolf and Wolfskehl. He was shocked. Writing to Gundolf, George said that he had discovered "disturbing gaps" on the initial pass, and now "I am working almost day and night" on them "since they still teem with (in the first half, several HUNDRED) defective wrong and particularly missing words." He paternalistically chided Gundolf for his sloppiness, saying that "this is a more laborious business than you both think." It was certainly no way to begin a campaign. Moreover, George felt it was bitterly ironic that he, of all people, had to remind them, of all people, of the importance of paying meticulous attention to seemingly pedantic details. "That I the least scholarly one am preaching vigilance + conscientiousness to you the German scholars!!"

Mainly, though, he held Wolfskehl responsible for the mess. Telling him that the matter was "very serious," George announced that "Gundolf, obliging but still inexperienced, assumed the corrections as far as he was able. I myself have spent *many* days on them and still find the text imprecise. Pleasantly rummaging around is a very far cry from a thorough correction and makes my workload more difficult than it lightens it." He impressed upon Wolfskehl the importance of taking greater care with the "*second* reading" in a way that would do justice to the "nobility and beauty of the task." "For your *name* stands next to mine as organizer of the collection and on *yours* falls the most blame for a slapdash and faulty version." At the end of this rebuke George added what he probably regarded as a word of conciliation. "Do not read anger into these heavily underlined words but rather only the effort to remind you in unambiguous terms of the duties in the great task you have assumed." Conciliatory, maybe, but ambiguous it was not.

Compounding George's frustrations with Wolfskehl and Gundolf over the Jean Paul text were inexplicable delays from Melchior Lechter. Since the beginning of the year, George had been pressing Lechter to speed up his work on the project, and despite repeated entreaties for some word about his progress, many weeks passed without any sign. "All of my decisions are being inhibited by your last words of 'letter to follow' for which I have been waiting for 8 days," George had written in February. A month later, he asked again, "But when O MASTER will you finish the J — P — work?" Another month passed, and still no word. In April, George delivered an ultimatum: "For the seventh and last time I must turn to you because the publication of the J-P-work is now at risk." Finally, at the eleventh hour, Lechter announced at the end of the month that "all of the drawings are finished!" But still he did not send them for George's approval. This time, however, instead of venting his anger, George tried a different approach. Lacing his words with sarcasm, he painted a depressing scenario. "Imagine that I in my misfortune had (which is truly the case) ten books at the ready then I would be faced with only two equally wretched possibilities: either I would have to have the books produced in my modest way and thus have to put up with your censure and scolding my entire life — or *you* oversee the production and then I have to be prepared to receive perhaps the fifth or sixth of those books on my deathbed."

When in late June George at long last received the entire set of final proofs, accompanied by Lechter's illustrations, his petulance melted away. He brimmed over with expressions of "my astonishment and my admiration." "The work is great and simple: the final piece to the introduction that is repeated in blue on the final page belongs among the most free and beautiful decorations you have devised." He singled out for special acclaim the "raised urn," a smoking monstrance upheld by two slender hands against a dark starlit background and surrounded by a wreath of flowers. It was genuine praise: George liked it so much that it came to be used as the insignia on his private stationery and for all of the books published by Bondi in the *Blätter für die Kunst* series, until it later became replaced by another vignette. Overall, George was so pleased with the outcome that all of his previous reservations and recriminations faded from memory. "How fortunate that the task fell to you," he purred to Lechter, "to present our German poets for the first time in a worthy garment."

Before he closed, George added a note of caution. "Now, however, forearm yourself against the arrows that will be hurled against me as well as you or bathe in the lindworm-blood of contempt!" George had never forgotten that the Jean Paul book was much more than a literary exercise. It was to be the first strike in an all-out war of conquest and, now that it was being launched, they had to expect to encounter some armed resistance. The predicted response was not long in coming. That August, in the inaugural number of the literary magazine, *Die Insel,* one of its founding editors, the twenty-two-year-old Rudolf Alexander Schröder, went on the counterattack. Objecting to the appropriateness of presenting a necessarily slanted view of Jean Paul by offering only short excerpts from his work, Schröder found the high-handed tailoring of the writer's legacy an "unforgivable lack of taste." The editors, Schröder wrote, "are apparently trying to stamp Jean Paul as a kind of classical writer in their sense by leaving everything out that does not fit with the principles espoused by the *Blätter* or the aims they strive for." Saying that he felt compelled to "energetically protest" this "violation and mutilation of an important author," Schröder also took aim at the "quite empty introduction" that preceded the collection, which justified the selection of texts by claiming that Jean Paul's "being" had suffered a "rift." "A psychology that operates with these kinds of clichés and superficial notions," Schröder mockingly wrote, "would resemble a geology that would be satisfied with the superficial observation that he sun circles around the earth." As for Lechter's contribution, he had nothing but derision. The illustrations seemed "even more repulsive than the *Tapestry of Life*, which was already revolting enough with its cast-iron gothic and its unutterably affected triviality." Schröder had thought Lechter's work on *The Year of the Soul* had been all right; "all the more regrettable that he [now] demonstrates a positively astonishing incompetence."

Schröder was a young writer, anxious to make a mark, but his assault could not go unretaliated. Gundolf immediately sat down to write a furious rejoinder. George, who had gone to Holland in July to recuperate from the travails of bringing the volume to fruition, read the draft, disapproved of it, and forbade Gundolf from publishing it. Sometimes, he apparently thought, discretion truly is the better part of valor. Even though they were denied a public outlet to their indignation, both Gundolf and Wolfskehl took their private revenge. In a deft rearrangement of the first letters of Rudolf Alexander Schröder's name, they took to referring to him in their correspondence as the "ARSch" — modeled after the German word that closely resembles the Anglo-Saxon one for the same rearmost part of human anatomy — and they gleefully renamed *Die Insel* the "ARSCH-enal."

The Jean Paul book was of course not an isolated potshot but formed part of a sustained and concerted salvo. Ever since his collaboration had begun with the firm of Georg Bondi in 1898, George had been busy putting together "popular" editions of his previously published works and assembling completely new ones. For purely pragmatic reasons, these books had to forfeit Lechter's rich ornamentation, thus allowing Bondi both to make them affordable and to increase the number of copies that could be produced. In July 1898 Bondi had agreed to a print run of five hundred to eight hundred copies of each book he published, which, though still relatively small, represented a fourfold expansion of George's customary number. That same November, George was putting the finishing touches on the second editions of *The Year of the Soul,* as well as the *Hymns, Pilgrimages* and *Algabal,* which were unified within a single volume, and a selection of poetry and prose from the *Blätter,* and outfitting each one with a new introduction. The year 1900, less than a year after the first edition, saw the trimmed-down version of the *Tapestry of Life* that had already come out, in addition to the Jean Paul book that was first issued with Lechter's ornate designs and bound in costly vellum (though even it appeared in an unprecedented edition of 403 copies). The following year was even more frenetic, giving birth to George's translation of Baudelaire, a collection of George's juvenilia called *The Primer* (*Die Fibel*), and finally the second volume in the anthology series that was devoted entirely to the poetry of Goethe.

As if all that were not enough, in 1901 the fifth number of the *Blätter für die Kunst* appeared, the largest and most extensive one yet. Instead of dividing up the issue into individual numbers, which had been the typical procedure until then, George decided to combine everything in an omnibus issue. The number of contributors had also risen to thirteen, the most ever included in a single issue. The volume contains the usual poems and poem cycles, along with several lengthy dramatic scenes, but there seemed to be a greater spirit of consistency or uniformity holding everything together. For one thing, apart from the introductory maxims, there were no prose pieces at all, only verse, thus lending it a kind of formal coherence missing from previous numbers. Also new were translations of passages from Dante's *Divine Comedy,* which George had been working on for the past year and would profoundly affect his changing view of himself as a poet. Even in visual terms, however, the *Blätter* presented a tauter, more consolidated appearance. Instead of mixing various typefaces in the titles and main body of the text, as had been the case until then, only one type was used throughout, giving the surface impression of an unbroken harmonious whole, as if it were the work of a single mind or will and not the assemblage of disparate individual parts it really was.

Unified it may have appeared, but harmonious — or at least pacific — it was not. There seems to have been the deliberate effort to make the maxims more direct and intelligible, but they had lost nothing of their polemical bite; if anything, they had become even more acerbic. Most notable, though, is the widening scope of critique. It had always been a characteristic of the *Blätter*'s maxims to offer more in the form of harsh repudiations than in the elaboration of a positive platform. But earlier issues had largely stuck to round scoldings of contemporary Germans' literary tastes and, at most, recitations of their cultural failings. Now the ambit was broadened to encompass more far-reaching intellectual, social, and even political subjects. Once more adopting the disconcerting form of responding to a question, and thus a conversation, to which we as outside readers are not privy, one of the maxims states that "it is a cheap pretense" to claim that "formal purity is something inappropriate to the German spirit and is more proper to the south." Citing the example of Hans Holbein as a clear refutation of such an assertion — i.e. a German painter who was as formally rigorous as his Italian colleagues working at the same time — the maxim insists that it was only the traditional emphasis on the one side of the German character that made us forget the other one existed. "To be sure, after the political and religious turmoil of the sixteenth century, a predilection began to make itself felt among Germans for everything that is vacuous, fitful, and shallowly intellectualistic."

Two things are going on here that deserve notice. First, the discussion of Holbein and his work is being conducted not solely as a means of understanding the art itself but to make a larger cultural-historical point. The fiction that one practiced "art for art's sake," in other words, was beginning to erode in the face of the temptation to use art for the sake of something else, namely, as a polemical weapon in extra-artistic debates. Second, for the first time, George's own personal agenda and not simply his poetic views is being raised here to the status of dogma. For the reference to the upheaval of the 1500s, though vaguely expressed, was in fact focused on the very specific historical episode of the Reformation and its instigator, the abominable Martin Luther. After having dispatched one of his great nemeses, George then turned toward another. "When we speak of the influence of the Prussian character," the subsequent maxim begins, then every "sensible" person should realize that the *Blätter* were not protesting against an individual or even an entire "tribe," "but rather against an admittedly very effective system but one hostile to all art and culture." "Prussia" had of course long been a major bogeyman in George's private lexicon, but from now on its vilification would form part of the official creed of the circle as a whole. The next target was also a favorite. Called the "The confusion (perversity) of the bourgeoisie," it mocked the fact that the bourgeois "often reproves artists for their perverse inclinations" — interestingly, the maxim makes no effort to refute the criticism — "but we stand in astonishment before the many great and trivial things that the bourgeois loves." Without being more precise, the maxim finds that it is "the burgher," and not the artist, who demonstrates true "depravity and perversity" by surrounding himself with "inauthentic conglomerations."

Protestantism, Prussia, the bourgeoisie: it is a familiar litany by now. But this willingness to mix social, cultural and political themes with "purely" artistic matters marks a significant departure from the *Blätter*'s previous stance. We know that it merely gave voice to the large-scale campaign George had already been orchestrating over the last few years, but it signaled a conspicuous deviation nonetheless. A telling expression of this newfound inclination to combine poetry with politics comes in yet another dictum. "That the German finally acquires a gesture: the German gesture — that is more important for him than ten conquered provinces." It is unclear what was meant by the "gesture" that would be preferable to captured territory — it could be "style," or "comportment," or "attitude," or any number of things — but the point of comparison, by contrast, is explicitly stated. Yet, most remarkable is that the comparison was made at all. It was still the case that something as abstract as a "gesture," however defined, was considered superior to more tangible victories. Soon enough, in George's mind, the one would be seen as the necessary precondition, indeed the precursor, of the other.

Not all of the maxims address such extraneous topics. Most of them still adhere to the familiar *Blätter* canon but with a distinctly new twist. In one, the declaration is offered that a development, coming out of "a small circle," has begun in Germany that had heretofore been observable "only in neighboring lands," namely, the formation of "an intellectual and artistic society that feels united by very particular rejections and affirmations by a certain feeling of life." Responding to the reproach that the writers associated with the journal had "turned away from life," another apothegm claims that the reason for this fatuous perception was simply that "the writing of yesterday is palpably plebeian that of today palpably aristocratic." Contrasted with the "intellectual scum" that characterized modern literary opinion makers, it concluded, "every higher form of life" — meaning naturally themselves — "must appear artificial and lifeless" in the eyes of others. In the final aphorism, titled "New Dreams," a vision of the future is drawn that merges all of the motifs mapped out thus far into a panoramic vista. "The youth we see before us permits us to believe in a proximate future with a higher conception of life more noble leadership and a more fervent desire for beauty. If however great revolutions and eruptions should occur, then we know that these have to be of an entirely different nature than the political and economic skirmishes that fill people's minds today."

The repetitive emphasis on "life," as opposed to mere "art," that runs through all of the maxims is only the most obvious sign of the new direction in which George, and hence the entire *Blätter,* were headed. It is also symptomatic that, in the list of the three anticipated developments projected in the last axiom, the need for beauty brings up the rear. Most salient is the evocation of possible convulsions and radical transformations to come, unspecified though they are. For all pretense of speaking about strictly literary or even cultural affairs had thus been definitively dropped, replaced by an overt motion toward an all-embracing policy. To be sure, the content of that policy had not yet been explicitly articulated, much less formulated. But the space had been created for a future program, a course of action that would be carried out not so much in poetry as in "life" itself. Here too, however, the maxims had provided a guideline, or at least a justification for the apparently adamant refusal to be forthcoming about particulars. "A new culture arises," one of them asserts, "when one or more primal spirits [*Urgeister*] reveal their life-rhythm which was first adopted by a body of followers then by a larger social class. The primal spirit [*Urgeist*] works not through his doctrine but rather through his rhythm: the disciples make the doctrine." Again, the word "rhythm" is a calculated obfuscation, although it is easy to imagine that the cadenced language of poetry is principally implied. But there could be no doubt who the "primal spirit" was, and his "disciples" wasted no time in fulfilling the implicit order.

Perhaps the most important event to occur in 1901, and one that went some way toward detailing the advertised "doctrine," did not, as predicted, stem immediately from the *Urgeist* himself. At the end of that year but with a printed publication date of 1902, the first book-length appreciation of George appeared, likewise published by Georg Bondi and written by Ludwig Klages. Judged solely by the number and variety of his contributions, Klages had been one of the most valuable and productive collaborators among the members of the *Blätter* throughout most of its early existence. And aside from the occasional note of dissension, he had also been one of its most reliable mainstays. Still, he had always been an independent mind, not inclined to subjugate himself blindly to George, seeing him instead for the most part as an equal. Klages never, for example, called him "Master," and in general he viewed the whole idea of the "circle" with a reserved suspicion. In 1895, we remember, he had even considered distancing himself from the journal entirely, claiming it was "too personally oriented," only to allow himself to be appeased and return to the fold. But he always carefully guarded his autonomy and almost defiantly engaged in activities that fell outside the normal range of the circle's interests. One of the most peculiar was graphology, which Klages began to practice professionally in early 1899 and about which he later wrote several lengthy studies.

Klages's uneasy relationship with George, one composed of equal parts of admiration and skepticism, of initial fervid hope and subsequent rancorous disappointment, left discernable traces in his book, which documents both the high point of his association with the poet and the first step toward his final defection. In some ways, it is surprising that he even bothered to write it at all. In the preface, and mirroring the *Blätter*'s long-standing ambivalence about wanting to go public and to stay private simultaneously, Klages insisted that his book was not written to enlighten those who had no prior inner connection to Stefan George: "The 'many' will find our explanations just as foreign as the matter to be explained itself." In addition, the preface went on, the author had no intention of explicating George's poems in such a way that would produce what "is considered to be 'clarity' in philosophical writings." Nor would he discuss any "personal tendencies" regarding the poet — here Klages's reservations about George achieved a kind of principled utterance. Indeed, "even important aspects of content remained untouched insofar as they were unable to deepen our insight into the transpersonal sphere." Klages even stated that in his disdain for the communication of mere "facts," he deliberately did not shy away from using certain "esoteric formulae." No, what he was after was something else, something greater, something that might be called the "metaphysical content" of George's poetry "although we ourselves would prefer another name for it. May it be taken as the first attempt at a reconciliation between living mysticism and the necessarily dead formulas of science."

That was a tall order. But Klages was nothing if not dedicated to the belief that such a feat was possible. True to his promise, he offered not so much an interpretation of George's poetry as a declaration of the new era it was ushering in. "We call artistic a direction of life that is fulfilled in works," Klages categorically announced. "Among German poets George is the lonely reviver of a faith that had been lost since the days of Romanticism." What follows is a blistering attack on the intervening period, covering pretty much the whole of the nineteenth century and its supposed achievements, and against which Klages portrays George as the sole salutary antidote. Uppermost in the catalogue of ills Klages diagnosed were the "soul-killing forced labor called 'progress'"; a pernicious and shallow version of "reality" and its advocates, whom he referred to as those "rash heralds of truth who were just on the verge of brewing life out of atoms"; and the divisive notion that people were or could be individuals: "Seldom has a more pitiless heresy dazed minds more than the blasphemous word individualism." Under the cover of generalized abstractions, then, Klages was assailing the same bugbears that had previously gone by various names, such as rationality, materialism, and pragmatism, in short, the ideology of the "bourgeoisie" that had provided the negative foil against which George and his cohorts had always tried to define themselves. The difference was that Klages would try to sketch in something like a positive complement to this familiar negative image.

"Here," Klages confidently affirmed, pointing to George's poetry, "we stand before the complete reversal of what has come before." At this juncture, where he steps up to an enunciation of how George differed from the desiccated world view he opposed, Klages's language becomes dark, dithyrambic, almost impenetrably opaque. "The world taken to be real fades and dissolves in the glowing ring of a more powerful reality. Consumed before the purple core the hallucinatory veil of thought falls." Although he did not say so directly — for how could he? — Klages wanted to imply that George's poetry partakes of this vast nonrational, intangible realm. More: that it induces a kind of ecstatic reverie, a release from the constraining fetters of consciousness, volition, and even identity. "The wave of intoxication does not well up in the brain, the seat of consciousness, but in the blood." A mind that does not exist in this state of intoxication, Klages writes, "speaks a dead language, in which sounds have withered away into conceptual mummies." Thus George, much more than giving us poetry, puts us in touch with these profound verities, a function that can go by only one name. "His poems are the linguistic-formative realization of a religiously tuned fundamental condition." Like a priest, George stands between the dead region of mere matter and the font of true life, and his poems serve as the conduit allowing us to pass from one to the other. "Deep art is the bridge between 'nous' and 'hyle,' between Helios and Gaea; the mediator's soul is androgynous, an umbilical cord stretched between the dark primal middle and the point of light torn away from the circle: Spirit."

Or at least that was the theory. And Klages had more than hinted at what that theory was. The references to the "androgyny" of the artist and the negotiation art performs between "Helios" and "Gaea" were explicit, if heavily cloaked, allusions to the sustaining context of his ideas. Likewise, a passing mention of "a time that told the history of the universe in cosmogonic images of wonder, that revered numbers, that wove fateful decisions on the basis of entrails and the flights of birds," was another frank nod in the direction of Klages's intellectual indebtedness. But there were few people, in 1901, who would have had more than a faint glimmer of what Klages was really talking about. Part of his message was familiar enough: his assault on the soulless vapidity of the nineteenth century was becoming old hat, and he had offered nothing in that respect that Nietzsche had not already said, and said much better. Yet beneath or behind Klages's vituperations was another, even older and more obscure strain, and one that would play a momentous role in George's life over the following years.

Despite his murky oratory, Klages did occasionally cast some illuminating light on how he understood George's poems. At one point, while considering the sensitive issue of George's literary and cultural forebears, Klages reminded his readers "that in the Rhenish tribes the thread of tradition that links us with Antiquity never tore so completely as in Germany's Protestant regions." For Klages, who was a confirmed Protestant, to make that kind of argument involved a substantial concession; or perhaps it merely proved that he was concentrating on the "transpersonal" element as regarded himself as well and was all but excluding private interests, even his own, from his account. In any case, he had thus made the way clear to claim that "one and a half thousand years of Roman-Christian spiritual culture are the soil out of which the golden fruit of George's poetry grows." Elsewhere, Klages again specified the temporal boundaries of George's reach. "He begins in the twilight of paganism and Christianity and stops at the banks of the machine age." In other words, "his train of images reaches into the eighteenth century," but goes no further, as if in mute protest to what came after. The outer limit of George's sphere was thus marked by "the end of the culture that fell under the guillotine." From classical antiquity to Roman Catholicism to even the Ancien Régime, the entirety of Western European culture up to the French Revolution was the orbit in which George moved and could properly call his own. This is not to say that Klages forgot to stress George's Germanness. When he identified other figures as points of reference, they are exclusively German, even though they were drawn from the *Blätter*'s official register of approved precursors. Goethe, Jean Paul, Holbein, Nietzsche, Böcklin, and Hölderlin all make an appearance. But where others had been content to measure George against Goethe — in most Germans' eyes, already an unsurpassable standard — as a way to evaluate George's merit, Klages had raised the stakes considerably higher. Now George would be seen in the context of the whole sweep of European civilization and not viewed solely as a poet but as its agent.

Klages's book was greeted by a tumultuous reception among the small band of the faithful. Gundolf informed Wolfskehl that Frau Lepsius, who had passed through Munich returning from a trip Italy on her way back home to Berlin, "had spent several marvelous hours with Klages and is full of admiration." Gundolf also reported that "the book has aroused the greatest enthusiasm among all the top minds: above all M. L[echter] and R. L[epsius]. Only the half-pints are carping somewhat. The youth is in ecstasy." After having had the chance to read it, Wolfskehl also found that he was no less enthused. "How unbelievably rich Klages's book is!" Letting his metaphors slip away from him a bit, Wolfskehl pronounced that every "sentence is the tip of a vineyard in which the critical laborers and miners of our time would have to burrow for the rest of their lives!" Albert Verwey also showered the book with praise, telling George personally how highly he thought of it. George himself was also more than delighted. "I was very happy to hear," he wrote back to Verwey, "that you liked the book by Klages. A lot of people are talking about it. How few works there are today that are able to divulge something to us about the deepest and most secret powers! How few there are that have a 'tone'!" Coming from George, this seems high praise indeed. On second thought, though, his approval of the book takes on a slightly different hue. Anyone who did not know what Klages's book was about would have had trouble guessing that, in George's unselfconscious words of admiration for the way Klages had revealed the "deepest and most secret powers," George was talking about himself.

Klages was more circumspect about all the commotion. "Thank you for your pleasant and enthusiastic letter," he wrote to Gundolf, who had sent his congratulations to the author. "But you OVERESTIMATE my effort. In my book I was only the VOICE and speaking tongue of an entire CIRCLE, and any knowledge that speaks from my pages was not given to ME alone but born of the collision of spirits, and if I deserve any merit, then it is this: to have lent it EXPRESSION. Above all, however, my book sought to erect a monument to GEORGE that was WORTHY of him." While he was prepared to stand by what he wrote, Klages still did not want to be identified too closely with its import, or at any rate with its object. That would have entailed abandoning one of the book's central tenets: that an "individual" — either himself as author or George as subject — counted for very much, or was even anything more than the false abstraction of a spurious ideology. Primarily, though, Klages wanted to shift attention away from a narrow focus on the person of the poet and onto what he considered the poet's greater significance. Indeed, Klages again said as much publicly. In a short advertisement for the book that Klages wrote for the journal *Die Zukunft,* he declared, referring to himself in the third person, "In his book he was more concerned with the higher forces working through the poet than with the person of the poet George." Klages, in other words, had bigger, "cosmogonic" fish to fry, and he did not want George to get in the way of that greater goal.

Klages may have felt that, through the medium of George, he was unveiling the secrets of the universe, but others remained steadfastly earthbound in their estimation of the poet. In the "New Year's Oracle" for 1901, a humorous outlook on the coming year's attractions that the daily *Berliner Tageblatt* published on December 31, one of the forecasts took aim at a poet who was beginning to attract a fair degree of notoriety. The anonymous prankster who wrote the piece was clearly not an insider — for one, he misspelled the poet's name — but that only made the whole thing more amusing. "Stephan George," the article predicted for the next year, "will finally make his peace with the rules of punctuation, against which he has revolted with a noble rebel's fury until today, and he will refund free of charge to the owners of his books all of the punctuation marks that he has obstinately withheld until now. If he has so far only published poems without commas, then he will now publish a volume of commas without poems, and people even maintain that it will be his most satisfying publication."

CHAPTER 21
The Cosmic Circle

In October 1900, after having transferred from Munich and spent the previous spring semester at the university in Heidelberg, Friedrich Gundolf moved to Berlin. He had officially gone there to write his dissertation under Erich Schmidt, the professor of German literature who had crossed paths with George several times over the years. Unofficially, however, Gundolf had been sent to replace Wolfskehl as George's point man in the capital. Whereas Wolfskehl had been afflicted by his sojourn in what he felt was the cold, cheerless north, making him sullen and even less responsive to George's directives, Wolfskehl positively flourished down in the more congenial climate of Schwabing. But the post in Berlin, as hard as it was to bear, was too important to be left vacant. The nineteen-year-old Gundolf, at first captivated by the amusements and bustle of the city, also quickly developed a distaste for the imperial colossus that could have only made both of his mentors proud. "Nothing great will ever stick to Berlin," he was telling Wolfskehl by December. "It will never be able to have any history or its own atmosphere because no one feels respect for anything there: the most unreal complex of lifeless things." The only thing that could redeem it, he mused, were its "vices," for in that department Berlin had undeniably developed something like a world-class status. More seriously, Gundolf thought back on a brief visit he had recently made to Weimar — the tiny Thuringian town that had been home to such giants as Goethe, Schiller, Herder, Jean Paul, Wieland, and Liszt — and he mentally compared the two experiences. "I would not trade the two hours in Weimar," Gundolf said, "for a year in Berlin."

That was just what Wolfskehl was waiting to hear. Ever since he had established himself in Munich in early 1899, his large accommodating apartment in Leopoldstrasse 87 had become a nucleus of Schwabing's frenetic social and intellectual life. He seemed to know or want to meet everyone who was anyone, and the looming, bearded, semiblind, preternaturally loquacious Wolfskehl had himself quickly become a fixture among the countercultural elite collected there: the "Zeus of Schwabing," someone once called him. But, too much was never enough for Wolfskehl, and he aimed to make Schwabing into something more just than the gathering place for artists and social outsiders it already was. He wanted to create a new countercapital there, a kind of anti-Berlin, a surrogate cultural center that would serve as the base and staging area for the rebellion he and the other members of the *Blätter* were preparing. He was thus delighted that Gundolf was showing signs of disaffection with his life in the north. "Dear Gundolf, do come as soon as possible back to Munich country! that you would not know up from down up there was to be expected and that is just as well. If only all those who are valuable to us would come with you or at least away from Berlin." Enumerating the "valuable" ones by name — foremost among them Lepsius, Lechter, George, and Klages — Wolfskehl envisioned them forming a community in Munich that could achieve great things. "Such an assembly," Wolfskehl pressed home to Gundolf, "sure of its goal and deeply united, could change the working process, I am sure of it. For salvation [*Heil*] goes outward from the smallest centers, the inner ring — be it that of the Curetes with froth and swastika, which is incidentally truer than you know — is the basis of life."

Of all of George's paladins, no one had pressed more insistently or more eloquently than Wolfskehl — if not always with perfect clarity — for leaving the gossamer regions of poetry behind and stepping directly into the battleground of life. In Munich, or more precisely in Schwabing, he thought the place had been found to put those more concrete plans into action. He even had a chief ideologue in Alfred Schuler. In one of Gundolf's letters to Wolfskehl, he made the mistake of mentioning Schuler's name in less than reverential terms, calling his ideas a "delusional construction." Wolfskehl wasted no time setting Gundolf straight, saying that the "remark recently about Schuler took me aback. After all, you know my and Ludwig's estimation of this unique pathfinder, who gave us innumerable new things, above all a basic knowledge. How could you talk of a delusional construction where we admire!" It was Schuler and his theories of a pagan "blood light" who sought to rekindle the ancient Roman world in frenzied, trance-like states, who believed that he had established an inner psychic link to the time of Nero, and who held the Jewish-Christian — he preferred to say "Molochitic" — tradition responsible for having quenched the heathen fires: it was this disturbed and unstable character that Wolfskehl looked to as providing the bedrock of "basic knowledge" on which a new world order would be based.

Here we enter into one of the strangest chapters of George's life, and yet one that is of profound importance to understanding his future course. It is difficult for us now to imagine, much less believe, how earnestly he and his closest followers and friends at the time engaged in the events we are about to witness. But to them it was no mere game, no idle pastime. In fact, many were convinced it was a matter quite literally of life and death, and for some of the participants that ultimate outcome seemed vividly, terrifyingly real. As farcical, or even incredible, as much of the Schwabing disorder may now appear, it would be a grave error to discount its effect either on George himself or on the movement he headed. For it was here, in the midst of almost phantasmagoric excess and self-induced deliriums, that the order George envisaged was successfully defended, many of its rites and symbols solidified, and its ground firmly consolidated. Even more momentous, it was also here, arising out of the smoldering cauldron of the so-called Cosmic Circle — as the small group of friends in Schwabing became known — that George's new religion found its god.

As Wolfskehl had said, at the center of the Cosmic Circle, lending it not just a vocabulary but a paragon, was Alfred Schuler. Ever since George had met him through Klages at the end of 1893, Schuler had been constantly refining his wayward theories of ancient culture and history, eagerly offering his wisdom to anyone who cared to listen. In the interim, George's contact with Schuler had been sporadic, though cordial, but it was not until Wolfskehl had taken up permanent residence in Munich that George resumed their acquaintance on a more regular basis. That summer there even seems to have been the attempt to move Schuler to contribute something of his own to the *Blätter*. Schuler harbored a deep-seated aversion to anything that might resemble traditional scholarship. That would have been too rational, too analytical, too "Molochitic." As a result he wrote little, published almost nothing, and chose instead to perform delirious monologues in semiformal settings. In June 1899, though, Wolfskehl seemed to have made progress in persuading Schuler to waive his reservations about committing his thoughts to paper. But there was a catch, Wolfskehl told George, in "that under no circumstances does he want to use his 'bourgeois name,' at which he snorts in rage. After a prolonged hesitation, he decided that he would also refrain from a pseudonym and instead of which he shall perhaps indicate the secret of his porphyrogenesis only by the swastika." To illustrate Schuler's wishes, Wolfskehl drew the crooked, four-armed figure, adding that he himself was not averse to the suggestion, since "it is after all typographically easy to make." Only a few days later, however, Schuler wrote George to inform him that "I have decided against my intention to sign with a" — and here Schuler also traced the unpronounceable symbol — "instead of my name and have nothing against my full name." Yet he did insist that "the typesetter should employ the genuine Roman V in place of the barbaric U in the Latin headings."

In the end, Schuler published only one of his works in the *Blätter,* a short poem dedicated to Leopold von Andrian that appeared in the 1904 edition. Instead of going the conventional route of sending another work to a printer, he elected to create a lavish manuscript by himself. Set on three heavy cardboard tablets, each covered in a deep reddish purple ink that served as the background color, Schuler painstakingly hand-lettered the text in gold using his own, specially devised script. Schuler sometimes referred to the three tablets as the "Odin Trio," after the Norse god of wisdom, war, art, culture, and the dead, who was venerated as the supreme deity and creator of the cosmos, and whose name appears in the first segment of the work. He also illustrated it with the symbol that possessed a mystical, quasi-divine significance for him. Separating the paragraphs of the text, and employed as a kind of emblem at the top of each sheet, set against a white background and also drawn in gold, was the swastika he had wanted to substitute for his own name. And it was this work that he presented to George as a Christmas present for the year 1899.

The swastika was, for Schuler, the preeminent symbol of his vision of "life" and very much at the center of his theories. The origins of the swastika are obscure, but we know that it was commonly used in ancient India, and during Heinrich Schliemann's excavations of Troy in the 1870s it was discovered on numerous artifacts there as well. Yet Schuler cared little for archaeological findings and was more interested in what he thought was the inherent vital power residing in the symbol. For the swastika formed the centerpiece, the visible emblem of his pansexual, anti-Semitic rantings, and he explicitly set it in opposition to the Christian cross, which, in deliberate provocation, he habitually called a "castrated swastika." The swastika was an unspeakable mantric symbol for Schuler, the spinning, flashing hinge on which his private cosmography turned.

Although Schuler either ignored or poured scorn on academic classical scholarship, he did look up to one figure with something approaching the awe he felt for the ancient world itself. Indeed, with the exception of his adoption of the swastika as his private insignia, he owed virtually everything of substance in his thinking to the Swiss historian Johann Jakob Bachofen, whose works Schuler once expansively called "immortal." Immortal they may be, but well known or even well regarded they are not. Bachofen, who had begun as a promising student of the great legal scholar Friedrich Carl von Savigny, had written several works on the history of law in the 1840s that established him as a conscientious, if not quite brilliant historian. Following a sort of epiphany Bachofen experienced in Rome in 1851, his life changed completely, and he turned away from the secure but dusty path of legal scholarship to embrace a highly idiosyncratic interpretation of ancient cultures. Aiming to treat myth, legend, symbols, even poetic texts as legitimate sources of knowledge about the past, Bachofen felt that he had discovered previously hidden truths about the very basis of civilization. The first articulation of his theory came in 1859 with the publication of his *Essay on the Funerary Symbolism of the Ancients*. At a stroke, he had thereby destroyed his professional reputation, with one of the leading classicists of the day dismissing the book as a ludicrous mélange, calling it nothing more than "high-flown nonsense." Deeply wounded but undeterred, Bachofen pressed on, and two years later, in 1861, he delivered his magnum opus, *Matriarchy* (*Das Mutterrecht*). Whatever vestige of credibility he may have still had was entirely wiped away by this new offering. Poorly printed, cluttered, badly organized, and seemingly formless, the huge tome came out in only fifty copies and was greeted with stony silence by the scholarly world. Not a single review of the book was ever published. When Bachofen died in 1887, at the age of seventy-two, his passing was barely registered.

Bachofen's fundamental idea, the core of his thought, was that all manifestations of culture could be traced back to the relationship, or better the conflict, between the two sexes. All of our conceptions of morality and religion, all of our social and political structures are deeply informed by this primal constellation. Indeed, history itself, according to Bachofen, took shape as a struggle between the female and male principles. And at the beginning, lying at the origins of humanity, embodied in what Bachofen alternately called a "matriarchy" or "gynococracy," the female principle initially reigned supreme, only to be subsequently overthrown by "patriarchy," or the "male-phallic principle." Each had, as one might imagine, distinct qualities in Bachofen's mind, but they largely conform to nineteenth-century stereotypes governing gender roles. The primal, originary, gynococratic era signified a time of maternal benevolence, conditioned by the specifically female ability to give physical birth to new life, and served as the cradle of the virtues of love, peace, justice, and harmony: in short, it generated humanity itself. In time, the "phallic master" rose up to challenge and defeat the dominance of the "matriarchal" principle. As opposed to the earthbound nature of the "gynococracy," the patriarchal element was intellectual, abstract, rational. "The Mother Right is the law of material life, the law of the earth from which it derives its origin," Bachofen explained. "In contrast, the Father Right is the law of our immaterial, non-corporeal nature." In purely temporal terms, the Father Right ultimately emerged as the victor, but only by dominating, and thus eliminating, the prior sovereignty of the Mother Right.

In the constant clash of these two primal forces, then, Bachofen saw the course of human civilization unfold. Canvassing ancient Greek, Indian, Egyptian, and even Mayan cultures, and making free use of all available data — as well as his overly active imagination — Bachofen attempted to argue that the same, basic pattern always held true: a chthonic or tellurian matriarchal substratum in each case preceded, and was eventually replaced by, the male intellectual or spiritual *ratio*. One might suppose that, given the altruistic character he ascribed to the rulers of gynococracies, Bachofen would have deplored this inexorable development. But he was more ambivalent than one might think. Citing the example of the Amazons, he stated in typical fashion that "Woman, bloody and pernicious when in power, becomes a blessing to humanity in the subordination to Man." Repeatedly he pointed to the inherent "weakness" of the female "sex," and portrayed the "cosmic harmony and intellectual perfection" of the male as intrinsically superior, if necessarily one-sided. If Bachofen imagined some ideal state, a period of relative calm and accord between the two sexes and hence a model of culture, it would have been the time in Greek history when the religion of Dionysus was dominant. In Bachofen's view, the cult of Dionysus represented a positive synthesis of the two competing principles. At once orgiastic, sensuous, and beholden to the tangible truth of the body, through the authority of his divine masculine rule, Dionysus also kept the congenitally chaotic and thus dangerous female tendencies in check by enforcing "woman's return to her destiny as mother and the recognition of the eminent magnificence of his own male, phallic nature." On balance, Bachofen's own sympathies thus swung decidedly in favor of the rational Father Principle that put Mother Right in its place.

Having been stung by the cold reception of his previous work, Bachofen knew that his grand psycho-sexual, mytho-poetic history would probably also meet with disbelief or worse. Not very convincingly, he tried to preempt objections simply by brushing them aside. "The subordination of the spiritual to physical laws, the dependence of human development on cosmic forces appears so strange," he admitted, "that one feels tempted to consign them to the realm of philosophical dreams or to portray them 'as feverish visions and high-flown nonsense.'" Obviously the criticism of his first book had rankled, but Bachofen insisted that his ideas were "not a theory at all but rather, if I may express it thus, objective truth, simultaneously empiricism and speculation, a philosophy revealed in the historical development of the ancient world itself." Bachofen did not seem to appreciate fully that anyone who equated "objective truth" with "speculation" would have a lot of explaining to do.

One person he did not need to persuade was Schuler. But with friends like

Schuler, Bachofen hardly needed enemies. Having rescued *Das Mutterrecht* from its ignoble, though perhaps well deserved obscurity, Schuler attempted to validate it in a way that its author, who had still rather pathetically clung to the language of science and truth, would have only found discouraging. For Schuler did not merely want to know about the deepest layers of human experience; he wanted to relive them, literally to bring them back to life. And Schuler thought the most expedient way to resurrect the ancient world was to reenact it. During the early years of the 1900s, he thus arranged and attended lavish costume balls in which the participants dressed as Dionysus, Euridice, and Orpheus; and as Bacchants, Phrygians and Thracians. Men and women wrapped in togas appeared wearing crowns of ivy or laurel, with revelers wielding scepters and staffs in the shape of the phallic thyrsus and engaging in nightlong orgies of ecstatic abandon in the attempt to recapture and relive the spirit Bachofen had only wanted to understand and describe.

Ludwig Curtius, later to become a respected classical archaeologist, had the chance as a student to be an eyewitness to one of Schuler's performances. In February 1903, a Greek festival in celebration of Carnival was arranged by Curtius and his friends, including Schuler. Everyone enthusiastically planned their costumes, using a Greek vase as a source of inspiration. They sought out tailors to fashion elaborate garments, procured silver helmets, they made ready precious gems and strands of pearls, and they manufactured mock lyres of tortoise shell and horn. They also leased the court theater for the occasion and overlaid the parterre seats with a parquet floor to create an enormous stage. In the background arose an Attic landscape with the Acropolis visible at the top. Of all of the celebrants, however, Schuler had shown the most zeal in the preparations, throwing himself at the task of painting the scenery and sewing the costumes and tirelessly offering his suggestions and help to the others. "He was also the only one of us," Curtius remembered, "who appeared at the festival wearing a wig with reddish brown locks and in makeup, whereby his old face became even older." The others seemed mainly interested in the buffet table and the ample quantities of champagne on offer. But Schuler became increasingly agitated and began insisting that "we had to perform a Greek dance on the stage." Curtius calmly said that would undoubtedly be very nice, but since such a dance had not been originally planned, it would be difficult to pull off extemporaneously. "He then came a second time and repeated his suggestion more urgently. When I again refused I watched to my horror as he stepped into the middle foreground of the stage and there began to dance by himself, if one wants to call the clumsy tossing of his head, waving his arms in the air, his stamping and jumping and turning around on his own axis 'dancing,' for which his ungainly, plump figure was in no way suited." At this point, one of the others present yelled out, " 'What does this clown think he's doing?' and I had to tear Schuler out of his rapture and lead him off the stage. He really felt he was an Orphic." There are similar tales about Schuler making plans to go to Weimar before the end of the century to cure Nietzsche of his insanity by performing an orgiastic dance in front of the ill philosopher.

Had Schuler limited himself to dancing wildly on stage or in private ceremonies, he might have been more easily discounted as the madman many reasonably thought he was. But between these bouts of exuberant self-surrender, and drawing on the rich repertoire of symbolic lore he found in Bachofen, Schuler sketched the outlines of what he materially hoped to achieve through his more spectacular antics. To speak of Schuler's ideas as constituting a "theory" would be stretching the limits of common usage beyond comfort, but they do have a certain consistency and aim toward an identifiable goal. Following Bachofen's suggestions that human culture is composed of an incessant clash between the male and female principles, Schuler sought deliverance from this perpetual strife in what one might call universal hermaphrodism. Citing as additional support the theories of bisexuality recently formulated by Wilhelm Fliess, the troublesome early collaborator of Sigmund Freud, Schuler concluded that there was always a "mixture of the male and female substance in the individual." This finding had certain practical consequences, Schuler thought. "Naturally, every individual is thus actively and passively charged; for life consists in and propagates itself as this interplay. A purely male, purely female being would be dead." Schuler averred that "the agent of evolution" was certainly Man, the male "substance" or, in Schuler's coinage, the "spermatikos Logos of the Stoa." Man was, in other words, "the creative, world-creating principle." But that, according to Schuler, was the problem: the male principle was based on expansion, individuation, division, and discord, eventually stifling and snuffing out the opposing "female substance." What was therefore needed, he said, was a complete "transformation of the sexes," which would inaugurate a new "harmonious merging of the two substances within the individual being." His ideal would be "neither male nor female," but rather "a new human being" that, he said, "combined both sexes within it."

As we know, similar thoughts about the emancipatory potential of hermaphrodism or androgyny circulated widely throughout Europe during the last decades of the century. George's *Algabal* had participated in the same network of preoccupations, and it was no accident that Schuler most admired this book among the poet's works. We also know — and this holds true for Schuler as well — that the championing of hermaphrodism often served as much, and arguably more, as a cover for advancing the cause of same-sex unions as it was used merely to argue against the constraints of conventional sexuality. Thus, when Schuler turns to consider his favorite historical epoch, the "Imperium Romanum," as a way to legitimate his own undertaking, his attention is largely focused on the "vast numbers of boys" he claimed populated ancient Rome and on their putative cultural significance. When he discussed eating rituals in Rome, for example, he singled out for particular comment the silver salt cellars, the ceremonial middle point of the "Cena Romana." According to Schuler, salt symbolized the "sperm of the ancestors," and its use gave the departed a symbolic new lease on life, figuratively releasing them from the realm of the dead. And the young boys who acted as servers on these festive occasions also personified a symbolic victory over death. "The transfiguring conception of the bloom of youth is in the final analysis an erotics of the dead," Schuler explained. Similarly, when he examined the ubiquity of public bathing in Rome, he noted that "it was well known in the ancient world that warm water was the symbol of sperm in general." By extension, "the sprinkling of warm water on slaves on the part of the dominus is to be described as an ideal sexual act." (Schuler saw another such "ideal act of procreation" in the Corybants' beating of their swords against their shields while dancing around the infant Zeus, for, of course, "the sword is nothing other than a symbol of the phallus.") But it was the boy, and especially the boy child, that most greatly excited Schuler's interest. And it is this context, while trying to link his promotion of hermaphrodism with his keen regard for adolescent boys, that he made his most startling assertion. "Humanity has never recognized the child as a little boy, the innermost thing, the most precious host there is and possesses life, in any other form except that of a hermaphroditic boy. In the most ancient times girls were totally unknown." It seemed that, in the end, the cosmic reconciliation in hermaphroditic concord that Schuler sought came with the condition that a sufficient number of boys stood in the ready; girls were not part of the plan.

As one might expect, many of Schuler's notions were granted a favorable reception by George and clearly contributed to the shape of his own views on the same subjects. Sabine Lepsius recalled a conversation she had with the poet in October 1901 during his seasonal residence in Berlin. When their discussion touched on the question of religion, George yet again took the opportunity to voice his continuing reservations toward Protestantism and especially toward Luther but with an added dimension to his complaints. "Original Christianity, as long as it still contained heathen elements, was close to him," he told her in words that could have been borrowed from Schuler. George went to say that "one could cite the Christian Church in Rome that is built on the remains of an ancient temple, 'Santa Maria sopra Minerva,' as a symbol" of his standpoint. A little later, George brought up another issue. Sabine Lepsius diplomatically recounted that "the supersexual love of Plato,

Dante, and Shakespeare was considered in our conversations"; that is, they discussed "the love that is not dependent on sex because it is not directed at *it,* but at the whole person, whose spirit, soul, and body is loveable, no matter in what form. We agreed that the more developed a person is, the more profoundly he will be inclined toward love without purpose or goal." Through the tactful veil of Frau Lepsius's rendering emerge the contours of a candid confession, and one that easily dovetailed with Schuler's own inclinations.

The notion of "supersexual love" would play the central role in George's subsequent explorations of the subject. Not incidentally, it had also featured large in Bachofen's thinking. "The male eros," he had written, "stands in close connection with the overcoming of the lowest stage of physical life." In line with his general contention that the male "principle" tended toward ever increasing degrees of abstraction and immateriality, Bachofen saw the "male eros" as issuing from the desire to rise above the morass of carnality and hence above earthbound Woman. "Not the sensuality of love," therefore, "but the elevation above it, the replacement of the common eros with the higher one, the creation of moral modesty is the idea of love between men in its original purity." Of course, these are all ideas that Plato had famously expressed in one form or another before, but Bachofen was not making any claims to original insight. Accordingly, he gave credit to Socrates as having identified this conception of eros as "the first elevation of humanity, in it he recognizes the liberation from the power of matter, the transition from the body to the soul, in which love raises itself above the sexual drive; he thus declares it to be the best means of approaching perfection." While Bachofen himself may have preferred to see perfection as resulting from an appeasement of body and soul, matter and mind, woman and man, he had provided more than enough material for a less symmetrical reading.

Given the radical, even explosive nature of the theories espoused by Schuler, it would have been nearly impossible for disagreements, tensions, even open antagonism not to occur. The four main players within the Cosmic Circle, namely Schuler, Klages, Wolfskehl, and George himself, were all powerful personalities, and each had his own complex agenda that was not in every way compatible with the others. Plus, in the hothouse atmosphere of Schwabing, minor squabbles easily took on the proportions of major incidents. It was really only a matter of time before the lines of division became apparent and finally insurmountable. Although George's association with Schuler, as well as with Klages, lasted in total for more than a decade, notes of dissension had been audible fairly early on. While George was more than happy to entertain the suggestion that salvation may be attained through an ideal hermaphroditic pederasty, and was not averse to Schuler's rejection of modernity as a sump of soulless materialism and dead rationality, he was less certain of Schuler's belief that the answer lay in a magical return to a previous state of being. At bottom, George was too much of a pragmatist, and too dedicated to the notion that unforeseen possibilities still lay in the future, to surrender himself entirely to Schuler's desire to cancel the present by voyaging into the past. This, George came to think, was not only an unattainable goal, quite apart from being objectionable, it also dangerously verged on insanity.

In the second, "popular" edition of *The Year of the Soul,* which had appeared in late 1898, George had already expressed his advancing skepticism in a poem dedicated to "A. S." The imagery George used — the "red" denoting the all-important blood, a heaven-sent boy, and ritualistic contrivances — are all recognizable components of Schuler's repository of pseudo-ancient "Cosmic" wisdom.

> So was it real this round? when the torches
> Illuminated the pale faces · when vapors rose
> From bowls around the divine boy and with your words
> Elevated us into delusional worlds dazzling red?

The question marks, unusual in George's poetry — as were almost all other forms of conventional punctuation — signal as strongly as do the words themselves the degree of his growing distance from the Cosmic world. If Schuler needed such confirmation, he would have realized at the latest after reading this poem that he could no longer count on George's unconditional support within the alliance. True to form, Schuler thus decided that the only remaining option was to take forcible possession of George's soul.

Several months later, on April 29, 1899, Schuler invited George, Wolfskehl and his wife, Hanna, and Klages to his apartment for what he had advertised as a Roman meal. In reality, it was a spiritual ambush. Everyone was seated at a long table covered with various edibles, illuminated by candles and Roman-style oil lamps, decorated with a replica of a statue standing on a pedestal, and strewn with laurel and other greens; surrounding every plate was a wreath of flowers and burning incense. After the meal, Schuler began to read from his fragments. He was an accomplished, even captivating speaker. Wolfskehl once told Gundolf of another occasion on which Schuler read aloud from Goethe's *Faust:* "He recited everything to us in such a way that we were all overwhelmed and carried away and were overcome by a rare enthusiasm." Wolfskehl said, "It was stupendous!" Schuler must have given a similarly mesmerizing performance that evening. Klages said that everyone seemed gripped by "a magic field, assimilating related things, exorcising and driving out everything foreign." Yet while the others present seemed to be enjoying the spectacle, George "fell into a mounting, and in the end barely controllable agitation. He had stood up behind his chair; more pale than pale, he seemed about to lose his composure." Meanwhile, Schuler was reaching the climax of his oration, and "from the roar of his voice a volcano was growing that was spitting burning lava, and out of the embers arose purple images, robbing consciousness, transporting." Then, abruptly, it was all over. "Suddenly I was standing on the darkened street alone with George," Klages recounted. "Then I felt him seize my arm: 'This is madness!' " George said. " 'I can't bear it! What have you done to lure me into there! This is madness! Take me away; take me to a pub where upright burghers, where plain, ordinary people smoke cigars and drink beer! I can't stand it!' " Klages fulfilled George's demand and took him to an "ordinary" bar where people sat nursing their beers, while George, who was still visibly "strained, churned up, inwardly restless," recovered only gradually.

In principle, as this episode attests, George was not resistant to the suggestion that there were mysterious forces in the world that escaped normal comprehension, and he believed that the rational mind perceived only what it had been trained to accept as reality. Indeed, in the late 1890s, this antirationalism, or at least the readiness to view reason with skepticism and distrust, had begun to crystallize into the formal platform, even the official philosophy, of the *Blätter*. Nor was it an especially uncommon stance at the time: séances, esoteric sessions devoted to summoning spirits and ghosts, even the attempt to photograph revenants counted among the more popular forms of highbrow entertainment at the turn of the century throughout Europe. Although the episode at Schuler's home had evidently shaken up George, he had sufficiently regained his equanimity to have considered an invitation to a séance later that year, in November. In 1909, he and Karl Wolfskehl participated in some "spiritistic sessions," and in September of that year George debated with Lechter and a few other friends about "mysticism and occultism." And as late as 1916, when he happened to learn of a large exhibition of magic phenomena imported from America, he became very animated and talked about it at length. "Ah," he sighed, "I want to go to that. I am mad about supernatural phenomena." The conversation that followed this rather startling revelation, however, put the matter in a more nuanced perspective. George said that he firmly believed that "miraculous powers existed, they could not be denied, but their development is insignificant and one-sided, indeed is licentiousness and dissipation of the spirit." It is difficult not to think that George had Schuler at least in the back of his mind when added the last qualification.

Still, George was even prepared to think that madness, too, had its proper place in the general order of things. During the conversation with Sabine Lepsius in which he had spoken of "supersexual love," he had also made the bold assertion that "the great actions in the world originate in the insanity (mania) of individuals." When Frau Lepsius looked understandably puzzled by this pronouncement, George offered by way of clarification: "'Love thy neighbor' — is that *not* insane!" Behind this attack on the late Christian ideal of meekness and charity — virtues that had been, not coincidentally, favorite targets of Nietzsche's invective as well — the shade of Schuler stands as a glowering, if invisible presence. Supersexual love was accorded a prominent place in the Cosmic universe, but that did not mean it did not also have ample room for hate.

Ultimately, it was not Schuler's real or suspected insanity that caused the final break among the principal protagonists of the Cosmic Circle. Rather, it was the intense and escalating hatred of Jews that he shared with Klages that forged the rift with George and Wolfskehl and that eventually drove them all apart. What is astonishing is that it did not happen sooner. Neither Klages nor Schuler had ever attempted to hide their anti-Semitism. If anything, they flaunted it, concocting intricate theories of history and culture that always turned, in some essential way, on what they deemed to be the nefarious intervention of the Jews. Schuler's institution of the "blood light" and his recreative invocations of the past represented, in addition to everything else, the attempt to go back to a period that antedated and was thus free of any "Molochitic" influence. But just as Klages and Schuler were willing to condemn some people as Jews who obviously were not, they also conceded that some people who were considered Jews might not be. Apparently, they initially included Wolfskehl and Gundolf, as well as numerous other Jewish denizens of Schwabing in this latter category; they tolerated their presence as honorary non-Jews, if not by "blood," then by conviction. Moreover, those granted immunity were not only happy to accept their special status, they appeared convinced that, as adherents to the Cosmic faith, they could not possibly be counted as Jews in Klages's or Schuler's sense. After all, they reasoned, they completely shared a common outlook, for they were united in their opposition against a common enemy, and they even rejected "Molochitic" thought just as strenuously as the others. Some even distanced themselves from Judaism altogether and expressed views that were hardly distinguishable from those held by anti-Semites. In 1903, for example, Gundolf wrote to Hanna Wolfskehl that "I am more anti-Zionist than ever, so that the dissolving of Jewry seems desirable to me. The most noble races are not the ones that live forever. I myself want to serve Shakespeare and not Yahweh or Baal."

Of course, this was a widespread view among assimilated Jews in Germany and elsewhere in Europe at the time and sprang from a densely interwoven set of motives. We may now consider this posture as hopelessly, even self-destructively naïve. But it remains a fact that before 1933 innumerable German Jews were more passionately, more wholeheartedly "German" than many of their non-Jewish compatriots. And, as we will soon see, at the outbreak of the Great War in 1914, many Jews counted among the most fervently patriotic, indeed often bloodcurdlingly nationalistic supporters of the German cause, even after the atrocities in Belgium began to come to light. But Gundolf's reference to his "anti-Zionistic" stance had a specific origin.

Ever since the turn of the century, Karl Wolfskehl had become increasingly involved in the nascent Zionist movement. He had met its charismatic leader, Theodor Herzl, shortly after the publication of Herzl's epoch-making book, *The Jewish State* (*Der Judenstaat*) in 1896. Impressed and eager to lend a hand, Wolfskehl became a cofounder of the regional Zionist group in Munich the following year. Naturally, his activities did not go unnoticed by the other members of the Cosmic Circle — Klages himself said that "Wolfskehl never concealed from us that he was a Zionist" — and they soon made their displeasure over his association known. In mid-1901 Wolfskehl asked Gundolf to test the temperature of Schuler's feelings toward him. Asking Gundolf to employ due discretion in this "diplomatic mission," Wolfskehl requested that he "please try as inconspicuously as possible to find out from the cosmic Alfred, who has descended on Berlin, how he inwardly stands toward me." There had been some unnamed trouble down in Schwabing that spring, Wolfskehl said, and ever since then "I think he considers me a Molochite in disguise, and I would like to know more about that."

Somehow, Wolfskehl managed to assuage Schuler's suspicions, but he became more fully dedicated to the Zionist effort than ever before. Well aware of Gundolf's own misgivings, he even tried — unsuccessfully — to win him over to the cause as well. In June 1902, Wolfskehl wrote Gundolf that "I have to talk to you at length about Zionism. There's a lot of noise in it, smugness, empty phrases and yet the voice of the depths. At least it seems to me. To be sure, whether I am the person to lend the voice a purer sound, whether I should, whether I can? I'll talk to you about that." Throughout 1903, Wolfskehl even half-jokingly toyed with the idea of becoming King of Damascus. The high point of his active participation in Zionism came in the middle of that year. Between August 23 and 28, 1903, he was an official representative attending the sixth Zionist Congress, the so-called Uganda conference, that was held in Basel.

To Schuler and Klages the Zionist movement as a whole can only have seemed like an open declaration of war by the "Molochites" against their own Cosmic designs. Worse still, it appeared to them that an agent of the enemy had infiltrated their midst. Their paranoid delusions of a Jewish conspiracy suddenly assumed an immediate, objective certainty in the form of none other than Karl Wolfskehl. As Klages described it much later, in 1940, "the signs that Schuler and I were in a *trap of Judas* had increased." As irrefutable proof of this treachery, Klages pointed to the "ambiguous-unambiguous figures crossing the stage: a shady Rabbi — a dreadful Galician Jewess — a Jewish 'mystic,' the representative apparently of a secret society. The dependence of the *Blätter* on a Jewish central office was certain." Further evidence for the insidious plot unfolding beneath their noses was that "the international press, which had until then had adopted a brusquely negative stance, began to fall into line, and the advocates that now came forward publicly here and there were Jews, nothing but Jews. Secret control became recognizable and the leader's name was — Wolfskehl."

Things quickly took a critical turn. The members of the Cosmic Circle regarded their shared beliefs as a sacred affair. Franziska von Reventlow, who wrote a thinly disguised and well informed roman à clef of the Schwabing escapades, had one of her characters say that "we have sworn, quite literally sworn, that the betrayal of cosmic secrets is punishable by death." That Schuler's and Klages's "cosmic secrets" appeared not just to have been betrayed but revealed to their mortal enemy, seemed a particularly flagrant form of sedition. And there were elements within the group that took the Cosmic vow of silence, and the threat of punishment for any disclosure, very seriously indeed. Roderich Huch, a friend of Gundolf who had introduced him to the Cosmic Circle, revealed himself to be indiscreet, freely regaling outsiders with tales from the inner council. When Huch was banished into exile for his infractions, he decided to take revenge. In an article Huch submitted sometime that fall to an informal newsletter that was widely read in Schwabing, called the *Schwabing Observer,* he revealed that extensive research had brought the sensational news to light that Ludwig Klages was actually a Jew. Descending from an old Hebrew rabbinical family, Klages was actually called "Kageles," and Huch added that "Herr Louis Kageles" would soon be leaving Schwabing to return to the land of his fathers and continue his efforts in Jerusalem.

The night after this rather unpleasant but essentially harmless prank was published, Huch was walking home over a dark, open field known as the "cosmic meadow" on the edge of town. Out of nowhere, he was suddenly grabbed from behind by his arms and thrown to the ground. As Huch struggled back to his feet, he recognized his attacker was one Albert Hentschel, nicknamed "the Panther," another associate of the Cosmic Circle and someone who was occasionally called upon to do Klages's dirty work for him. Instinctively, Huch tried to flee, not knowing what fate was in store for him but certain that "what was intended for me if they seized me, was surely something terrible. Fortunately my flight was successful; leaving behind my suit, my coat, vest, collar, tie and even parts of my pants, I was able to wrest myself free of the strong grip of the 'Panther' and reach the streetcar in front of the Schwabing brewery." Disheveled and distraught, Huch managed to make it to the house of his sister, who offered him sanctuary for the night. The next morning, he found his clothes in front of a friend's house, carefully folded and neatly laid out, acting as a warning that they knew where to find him.

Naturally, Wolfskehl immediately learned of the incident, and, beginning to fear for his own safety, he wrote to George for help in mid-December. George had attended several "Jours" at Wolfskehl's house over the last few years, daylong celebrations in which the crème de la crème of Schwabing society participated, including Schuler, Klages, and many others, and in which everyone donned the costume of their favorite ancient notable. At the same time, however, George's skepticism had intensified not just about Schuler's soundness of mind but, more importantly, about his intentions. As early as 1901, George had left a mysterious note on Wolfskehl's desk with the dark admonition:

> Do not set the fakir in the place of the priest
> the magus in place of the vates
> ghosts in place of spirits.

Quite apart from George's equation of himself with a "priest," "vates," and "spirit," the cryptic warning served as evidence that he was also concerned about Wolfskehl's loyalty. As the assaults on George's "soul" and Roderich Huch's person had made clear, their opponents were willing to use all means available to protect their interests. Schuler represented a threat to George's authority on any number of levels, and George seemed more and more determined to defend himself against these mounting incursions. Now that the attacks appeared to be descending from the spiritual to the physical plane, he realized that the time had come to act, and act decisively.

Rushing to Munich a few days after receiving word from Wolfskehl, George arranged a meeting with Klages in early January 1904. What was said is unknown, nor do we know whether Wolfskehl was present during this confrontation, although it seems likely that he was. Either way, it cannot have been a pleasant interview. Klages maintains that he asked George the provocative question: "What binds you to Judas?" Whatever George said in response, it did not assuage Klages's suspicions. Apparently, after repeated prodding, Klages did not ever receive a satisfactory reply. With nothing resolved, the parties broke up. Soon thereafter, Klages asked again for a meeting, but this time he wanted "to see him one-on-one." George refused, and sent a letter explaining his decision. Saying that he thought a further meeting would be fruitless given that the "basic moods" of the two camps were so different, George indicated that even during the previous year, "I had the certain feeling of alienation." Tactfully, or strategically, stepping over Klages's and Schuler's central concern, George framed the matter in more general terms. "I would reject it as hurtful and offensive if you again impute to me allowing human preferences and extra-artistic motivations to influence me in the selection of contributions for the *Blätter*." George may have believed his version of events was true, but he was under no circumstances ready to engage in a conversation with Klages that would only end up in their making mutual accusations: "You would describe verses that I have accepted as wretched, amateurish, etc." George explained, and "I would counter by declaring that I consider the verses you promote to be far more amateurish and insincere. You would call people with whom I associate dreadful, I would name those of your acquaintance who are even more repugnant to me!" Still hoping, apparently, that something might be saved of their association, George wanted to avoid an encounter in which "each one believes he is right and the worst: that phrases could be used that would make any further human relationship impossible."

It was a remarkably diplomatic tactic. Even though he did not articulate it directly, George knew what lay at the bottom of Klages's protest and that he was faced with an all-or-nothing gambit. But he had ceded no ground to Klages's demands and at the same time had forced his opponent's hand. Klages had been skillfully maneuvered into a corner and had been left with only two equally disagreeable alternatives: either knuckle under George's will or go his own way. As George probably predicted, Klages settled on the latter course. The day after he received George's letter, he solemnly announced that "the personal connection" between them would henceforth "be regarded as *broken*." Schuler, always the more flamboyant of the two, took a slightly different route. Somewhat later, he engaged a soldier in full military uniform to deliver an envelope closed with a black seal to "Herr Dr. Wolfskehl." The contents of the envelope were lost or destroyed, but Klages cited another fragment from around the same time in which Schuler wrote, "The time is here. Sign after sign is coming to me. Also those of great personal danger."

There has been a temptation to trivialize the frantic events that brought the Cosmic Circle to a close as amounting to no more than the overheated high jinks of a borderline schizophrenic, the foaming rage of an unregenerate but impotent anti-Semite, and the ingenuous, perhaps gullible involvement of the rest of the participants in a self-indulgent amusement that merely got out of hand. Claude David, usually one of the more perceptive, and least partisan, of George's readers, casually remarked that "everyone talked a lot of blood but hesitated to let it flow." In fact, David almost derisively concluded, "in the end, nothing happened at all." But those who were involved did not take such a sanguine view. Genuinely alarmed by the menace of bodily harm, Karl Wolfskehl acquired a revolver, and even two years after Schuler had sent the soldier to his door he was still carrying the pistol around with him, tucked in his back pocket. Not only did he keep it loaded, he also kept the safety off, and while returning home late one night he stumbled in his garden and accidentally shot himself in the leg. It was only a flesh wound, but it sent him to the hospital; it took several weeks for Wolfskehl to recover fully. The day after the mishap, Wolfskehl's wife, Hanna, wrote a letter to George that revealed how acute her own distress was. "Just imagine," she told him, "last night I dreamt that the Cosmics had invited us to a reconciliation party and Karl accepted and finally we all went to renew the old ties. We climbed a high tower and found the whole assembly happy and enjoying themselves. But then all of a sudden I am seized by fear and think: it was just pretense and they are going to murder us! I try to stifle the thought, but suddenly the cry comes from the mouth of my neighbor, 'The revolver, the revolver!'"

Again, it would be mistaken to let the rather comic denouement of the Cosmic Circle's heyday cloud our view of either its contemporary effect or its future repercussions. Klages and Schuler may have distanced themselves from George, but they did not disappear from the scene. Until his death in April 1923, Schuler continued to hold his lectures before sympathetic listeners in Munich, spinning out his visions of "Molochitic" perfidy, heathen reawakening, and hermaphroditic utopia, all standing under the banner of his cherished symbol, the swastika. One of his venues was the house of the prominent publisher Hugo Bruckmann. The Bruckmann firm specialized in conservative cultural criticism and popular history, and one of its best known works was the poisonously anti-Semitic — and hugely successful — tract by Houston Stewart Chamberlin, *The Foundations of the Nineteenth Century*. Bruckmann's wife, Elsa, a rich Romanian countess, also presided over a salon in which she welcomed intellectuals, artists, politicians, and other society figures into their spacious home on the Karolinenplatz. The relationship to Schuler had been so close that Frau Bruckmann even became one of Schuler's literary executors, a natural choice given her husband's business. Only half a year after Schuler had died, plans were already under way to publish his collected fragments and transcribed lectures.

Although one wants to avoid imputing guilt by association, one guest at the Bruckmann house deserves particular mention. Later the following year, in December 1924, Adolf Hitler, who had served as an officer in the disastrous war and had just been released from serving a term in prison for having engaged in activities against the state, entered the Bruckmann household for the first time. Although Schuler was dead, his legacy most assuredly was not, and it is possible, even likely that the newcomer to the Bruckmann residence was at least told of Schuler's ideas and perhaps even shown the writings that were just then being assembled for publication. They would have found in the Bruckmanns' guest an attentive admirer, someone who would have responded sympathetically to Schuler's message of hate disguised as historical truth, someone who would assimilate that message, and its symbol, and lend them an unforeseen virulence. Of course, if Hitler did indeed learn of Schuler's theories at the Bruckmann house, they by no means constituted the only or even the most important source for the tangled, contradictory web of prejudice, hatred, and a readiness for violence that was beginning to coagulate into a political movement. But for all of the caution that is warranted in drawing such historical connections, as speculative as they must remain, it is no less noteworthy, if ironic, that Elsa Bruckmann, a female representative of the haute bourgeoisie, stands as the first tangible link between the two forces that would alter Germany, and the world, forever.

CHAPTER 22
Boys: Good, Bad, and Divine

At the height of the Cosmic troubles, Gundolf tried to console George with a soothing note. "That the Cosmic world would burst sooner or later like a big, beautiful, shimmering soap bubble was foreseeable even to unprophetic minds." Gundolf regretted losing Klages, he said, but felt more ambivalent about Schuler, whom he belittlingly dubbed the "violet-ring Nero," and now insisted that Karl Wolfskehl had "often followed him only out of fear." Knowing George's own dissatisfaction with Wolfskehl's halting rate of production, Gundolf ventured that perhaps the breakup was ultimately for the better. "If only K. would finally record his wisdom and create — no one knows more — and give us the often promised Sauls, Moseses, and Psalms." And as far as George himself was concerned, Gundolf saw the rupture as an unequivocally positive gain, for he thought it would allow George to return his full attention once more to his poetry. "What is now left over is hopefully the notorious Mere-art, which was supposed to carry the train of the bloated Cosmic Semiramis as a gray Cinderella and had to breathe the foul-smelling dust it stirred up. — "

But Gundolf could not help feeling slightly smug about the final turn of events, for he had always been more than a little skeptical about the whole Cosmic affair. "Sometimes I have to laugh," he added to George, "when I think how I was reprimanded a year ago when I doubted Schuler's omniscience!" Even after Wolfskehl had upbraided him at late 1900 for daring to suggest that Schuler's ideas were "delusional," Gundolf had persisted in letting his unease with the Cosmic Circle be known. In mid-1902, he had tried again to locate the source of his discomfort. "What bewilders me about the Klages-Schuler world," he had told Wolfskehl, "is that they have received a revolutionary knowledge outside of themselves and have to make it known with and for organs in this world. Spirit and earth insert themselves between them and their knowledge, and the annihilators of individualism are, whether they like it or not, individuals themselves as soon as they make pronouncements and take all of their arms from the world they combat." It was a sound argument, difficult to refute, and yet Gundolf was willing to exempt Klages from the heaviest brunt of his criticism, reserving his most unqualified indictment for Schuler alone. Gundolf said he simply could not follow him down the same path, especially "when Schuler's most uncanny wisdom, set into words, becomes (or seems — no matter) terrible and enticing insanity."

Nevertheless, the gratification Gundolf savored at having been proven right paled before his happiness that his Master had escaped from the clutches of the Cosmics. For not only did he feel that Schuler and Klages had been distracting George from his true calling and pushing him in directions Gundolf regarded with dismay, they had also seemed, more distressingly, to have displaced him in George's attentions. Ever since Gundolf had been sent up to Berlin in October 1900, he had been writing nearly daily letters to George, telling him about everything he was doing, seeing, reading, the people he met, even offering to undertake little tasks he knew would please George, such as procuring his favorite tobacco and running useful errands, all the while reminding him, repeatedly and at considerable length, how much his Master meant to him. For the most part George received this uninterrupted stream of devotion and reverence in complete silence. "Please write once to me soon," Gundolf finally begged him, "so that I also know that all of my letters and packages are arriving." For weeks, sometimes months, there was virtually no response. In the face of George's apparent apathy, Gundolf soldiered on, but he began to close his letters with a miserable plea. Using the abbreviation for another affectionate nickname George had given him — "Dolf" — Gundolf took to writing, "Don't forget your loyal D." Later, he simply asked, "Don't forget me entirely!" When George did answer, it was usually in the terse, telegraphic style he liked to use in written communications. "Thanks for your news," one of those rare missives began in February 1901. "Console yourself! for I hope that next year will bring us all together in Munich!" It was not much, but it was all Gundolf had to go on.

Or, rather, he did have some other signs that George was not totally indifferent to his existence, yet these signals could not give him much solace either. For George's thirty-third birthday in July 1901, Gundolf sent a dramatic fragment he had composed called "King Kophetua and the Beggar Woman." It was based on an old English ballad that told the story of a monarch who, insensitive to feminine charms, was languishing away in loneliness and sorrow. The subject was a favorite one at the time, achieving its most famous contemporary expression in the painting of the same name by the Pre-Raphaelite artist Edward Burne-Jones. The original poem, which had been included in Percy's *Reliques of Ancient English Poetry,* states the King's situation clearly: "From nature's laws he did decline [. . .] / He cared not for woman-kind / But did them all disdain." One day, however, while peering through his window the king spies a "beggar all in gray" and, in an instant, he is smitten, shot through by Cupid's, or Eros's, arrow. "The blinded boy, that shoots so trim / From heaven down did hie / He drew a dart and shot at him / In place where he did lie." The king summons the one who enflamed him and to his no small surprise discovers the beggar is actually a woman. Yet, overcome by love, he takes her in and makes her his queen.

It seems unlikely, though certainly possible, that Gundolf was intimating to George that a disinterest in the opposite sex was a temporary condition that could be remedied if only the right person came along. If that was the case, Gundolf could have meant it as an oblique explanation, or excuse, for his own disappointing proclivities. Whatever Gundolf's intention, George's reaction was swift and categorical. The next day, he wrote back irritably that "King Kophetua" had "greatly disturbed me in that it was difficult for me to place myself in any relationship to it." George said he would go over the more serious details "later" and for the moment intended to confine himself instead to more formal issues of composition. Even here, though, the verdict was no less severe. George singled out that "the sudden changes in meter seem to me to be like the stumbling of a horse during a nice carriage ride," and in general the piece as a whole felt "unwashed." Yet the most eloquent testimony to the depth of George's discontent was his simultaneous return of the photograph that Gundolf had gone to some trouble to have made of himself the summer before and had given to his Master. In a model of disingenuous cruelty, George acted as if the photograph had merely been on loan and, in sending it back, he thanked Gundolf for having let him borrow the image, "which is so dear to me — you know . . but which in my opinion ought better to return to your possession which I'm sure it left with difficulty."

Gundolf bore this fresh injury with dignity, nobly answering that "my picture is yours wherever it may hang." If anything, however, George's intermittent messages now became even more infrequent and perfunctory, and were usually larded with words of reproach for some perceived failing or lapse. To Wolfskehl, Gundolf lamented that "I receive news from the Master almost only when I have committed some stupidity." Six months later, in January 1902, Gundolf implored George to "be kind just once and write one or two sentences even if there is nothing you want me to do or censure me for." It was almost as if George were putting him through some sort of endurance test, measuring Gundolf's ability to withstand extremes, probing for the point at which his constancy would cave in. Through it all, Gundolf faithfully wrote on, clinging to the hope, or pretending to believe, that George's silence meant only that the Master was too preoccupied or busy to respond.

Finally, on the occasion of Gundolf's twenty-second birthday on June 20, 1902, George rewarded him for his patience. Only three days before, Gundolf had again bemoaned George's continuing "silence," and for that reason alone, when the large envelope addressed by the unmistakable hand arrived at his home in Darmstadt, it must have caught him off guard. When Gundolf opened it, he was overcome. "My one and only Master," he gushed in reply. "Since I could not thank you in any other way but by everything that I am and do and by the delight in existence that you have bestowed on me I would have to remain in shamed silence before this new indescribable joy which you, who are Inexhaustible always Surprising, have now given to me again." As much as he may have wanted to be, Gundolf was not one to remain silent for long, and in the same breath he declared, "I will thus no longer take anything piecemeal and try to respond to your entire life with mine in the full knowledge that all of its worth belongs to you and depends on your estimation."

The catalyst of this renewed outburst were seven poems written out by George on heavy paper bound in a dark red cover, with large hand-lettered initials in the style of Melchior Lechter that began each poem. Reflecting his ongoing involvement with the Cosmics, the poems were richly decorated with swastikas. Although George had written the poems two years earlier and published most of them in the omnibus issue of the *Blätter* in 1901, Gundolf seems not to have previously applied them to himself. All the stranger since they overtly trace the ideal course of their relationship and rank among the most candid love poetry George would ever write. Like most of George's love stories, however, this too was an unhappy one. The poems chronicle the progression from the first, rapturous encounter, the joy the poet experiences in thinking that the lover for whom he had long yearned had unexpectedly arrived, then yielding to a growing feeling of uncertainty, then disillusionment, and then fading out in the last, mournful farewell after the fires of passion had been extinguished. In the opening poem of the cycle, the older poet, already feeling worn and weak, is oppressed by the fear that his young beloved will be suffocated or repulsed by his insistent longing:

When my desires envelope you
My ailing breath surrounds you —
A groping and craving and grieving:
Then it seems that in the waning day

> As if a rough tendril were entwining
> The youthfully supple tree ·
> As if fingers grown cold
> Were gliding over cheeks of sunny down.

But his apprehensions prove unfounded, and the poem ends in a first consummation: "Now his devouring fever is quenched / My mouth in the blossoming mouth." The next several verses describe the poet's elation — "I want to rejoice" one line reads — and they evoke blissful nighttime reveries: "In those nights full of giving / Your cheek rested upon my knees." Another, also set in a nocturnal scene, celebrates the transformation this love has wrought within the poet, who now sees the world, and himself, with different eyes:

> With all my thoughts in you I see as if changed
> Room and city and silvery avenue.
> Foreign to myself I am filled with you and wander
> Enraptured the nights over the blue snow.

If the beloved had initially demurred in coy refusal, all resistance is eventually broken down, and they both finally submerge in an amorous embrace:

> You relented in amazement willingly sinking down
> Moaning at the sudden overabundance ·
> You stood up blinking in a pure glorious halo ·
> You were benumbed by the breathless kiss.

> And an hour came: the intertwined ones rested there
> Still flushed from the wild sweep of the lip.

Yet, no sooner is the poet's hunger sated than new doubts begin to assail him. With an anxiety growing into panic, he senses that there is some dividing element, something that prevents them from maintaining their perfect union. "Trembling I feel today as if I could read in you / Amidst our happiness still much of a foreign spirit." To George, love always meant total possession, indeed absorption of the other in himself, and the idea that he could not completely merge the other's identity with his own, that the other may not — or may not want to — fully surrender his autonomy to George's being was unbearable to him. The poet thus asks, "Can you not soak up within yourself what is spent for you?" But the damage is already done, and the poet, knowing that the divide is unbridgeable, begins the process of inward separation. The paths they once wandered in unconscious bliss now seem "as if they led to a graveyard." His companion, who still notices nothing, rejoices at the natural spectacle of spring blooming around them, but the poet perceives it as a "hollow field of rubble" and hears only "funeral bells" ringing down the slopes. The poet even begins to think that his lover had misled himself about his own desires, and he silently accuses him of a self-deception that fooled the poet as well, while resolving to preserve the memory of their previous triumph:

> Already my strength is fading to bleed to death in silence
> That you deceived yourself to your benefit and to my demise . .
> I will still be thankful to you for some time for the minutes
> In which you seemed beautiful to me and moved me . . .
> Farewell!

It is difficult to imagine that these poems left Gundolf feeling exactly overjoyed, but at least they helped explain George's prolonged and painful silence. In that way, though, nothing changed. In early 1903, Gundolf was again forced to put on a brave face and surmise that "your silence is owing to the days full of pleasure in Munich and Karl's joyous insatiable appetite for the Master." Yet, remarkably, unlike other friends of George whom he had ceremoniously buried in his poetry after they no longer interested him or satisfied his needs, Gundolf did not suffer the terrible fate of irrelevance and preemptory dismissal. Perhaps George was impressed by his doggedness, or was persuaded that he may have made an error by writing him off too quickly, or perhaps he had begun to suspect that the Cosmic Circle's days were numbered and that he might soon be robbed of a sizeable portion of his coterie. Whatever the reason, in the late spring of 1903, George suddenly began to send more encouraging signals to Gundolf. "Dear Gundolf," one letter begins (George had previously taken to simply writing "D. G.", so that spelling out Gundolf's full name was in itself a hopeful sign), "apart from a few small metrical gaffes your poems in the *Blätter* are first rate. In reading them I again had the impression as if of very great things." If one overlooked the little slap on the wrist that George could never fully refrain from administering even when he offered praise, these were the most positive words Gundolf had heard from him in almost two years. In a similar vein, George wrote again in October about another one of Gundolf's poems. Saying he had read it with "feverish excitement," George judged it to be "extraordinarily talented." Yet, almost as a reflex, he again added a deflating qualification, observing that "unfortunately here and there the 'gundeling' peeks through," making the poem seem "a little sloppy and uncleaned."

But it was not until just before the final confrontation with Klages in Munich in January 1904 that George completely changed the tone of his communications with Gundolf. Apologizing for an earlier "irritable" message, which he attributed to "the often depressing events of the last weeks," he more or less asked for Gundolf's forgiveness. "My general condition is no longer as unfavorable as it has been in the last few days," George cryptically revealed, "but the heights of the last months have sunk alarmingly, and at the moment I still see no way out." But, George went on, even if the Cosmic Circle should be broken, that was not the main thing. What was important was that Gundolf should know that "you will remain from now on my Gundolf my friend my beloved!" It was surely no coincidence that George's change of heart occurred just as his association with Schuler and Klages was coming to a dramatic end. But no matter: Gundolf's banishment in the desert had at long last been lifted.

So there would be no misunderstanding as to the terms of his reinstatement, however, in the same letter George appended a comment about a new female acquaintance, Manja Steinberg, whom Gundolf had recently met. George, who had a mixed opinion about Fräulein Steinberg, indicated that he would tolerate the affair but only provided that it did not develop beyond an innocuous fling.

Manja Steinberg was the first of several girlfriends Gundolf would attract over the years who, in one way or the other, George would find either unworthy or threatening or for some reason simply unacceptable. The "deception" of which George had accused his young lover in the poems he had sent Gundolf was undoubtedly related to Gundolf's early confusion about his own sexuality. Gundolf had been, after all, only eighteen when he had first encountered the overpowering figure of George, and he may have been genuinely ambivalent or uncertain about himself. But Gundolf had discovered in the meantime that he preferred women to men as lovers. After a long period of resentment and ill will, George had obviously decided he could accept Gundolf's inclinations provided that he still maintained the right of veto regarding their object. And George exercised this privilege with a vengeance, perhaps motivated at a deep level by the urge to deprive Gundolf of the happiness that George felt he himself had been forced to relinquish. And every time George said no, Gundolf always obeyed and let go of the woman he loved. Only once, many years later, did he override the Master's wishes, and he paid the ultimate price for his defiance.

For now, though, the sacrifice seemed negligible compared to what Gundolf was getting in return. He was so elated at the prospect of being drawn back into the fold that he considered no toll too great. Only two days after receiving George's halfhearted endorsement of the romance with Manja Steinberg, Gundolf wrote to him and conceded that "I see complications coming and even before your letter reached me I had written to her myself that I am now afraid of seeing her again in Munich, which could only disappoint us." And with that, the affair was over. But Gundolf had his Master back.

Whereas Gundolf was restored to grace, others would not fare so well. In the spring of 1902, after a four-year absence, Hugo von Hofmannsthal suddenly appeared on the scene again. The external impetus was a minor confusion about an offer extended to George to translate Gabriele d'Annunzio's *Francesca di Rimini,* which George said he would consider only if the invitation came from the poet himself. Wanting to clarify matters, George wrote directly to d'Annunzio about the issue, who then informed his German publisher, Samuel Fischer, of George's inquiry and asked for his advice on how to handle the matter. On the face of it, Fischer told d'Annunzio, he had nothing against the proposal, but he did have some concerns. Fischer made it clear that, as opposed to George's practice, he had no intention of limiting the edition of the translations to only three or four hundred copies. But there were other questions. "I am not at all certain that Herr George, with his rather pale lyrics," Fischer cautioned, "will be the right man for your sumptuous and powerful verse form." D'Annunzio, who admired George's translations of some of his earlier works, prevailed upon the publisher to overlook his reservations, and Fischer, though still with some reluctance, approached George with the offer. Somehow the wires got crossed, d'Annunzio failed to answer George's request for an elucidation, George became suspicious of maneuverings behind his back, and, with things at an impasse and about to unravel, Hofmannsthal was contacted as an intermediary to salvage the deal.

With many years of experience in dealing with George behind him, Hofmannsthal, who would soon turn thirty, thought he knew the right approach to take. In his letter, he assured George that it was d'Annunzio's explicit wish that George translate his work and that nothing untoward had transpired. Yet Hofmannsthal also realized that in view of their common past he was obliged to address, even if indirectly, how he now personally stood toward George, or at least toward his poetry. He thus spoke of the "deep relationship that forms within me to every one of your works — often only after possessing the book for years," and how he sought to convey to others "the feeling of the uniqueness of your works." In case there might be some remaining doubt in George's mind about Hofmannsthal's inward stance, he stated his position explicitly: "You may rest assured that the past years have not alienated me from you but rather brought me closer." Hofmannsthal even acknowledged that he had occasionally shown poor judgment in his literary tastes, "including that Herr Richard Dehmel about whose possible development and purification I admit to have been mistaken." He went so far as to extend an invitation to George to visit him in his home in Rodaun, outside of Vienna. So as to leave no means untried, he even closed with the pledge that George may "be sure of my interest and admiration for the entirety of your artistic existence."

Hofmannsthal could not have dreamt what transformations George had been going through since their last correspondence. But he must have been aware that even the George he had come to know — and fear — would have immediately seen through this fairly thinly disguised attempt to butter him up. Some time in the same month of May 1902 George acknowledged the overture. After ironically thanking Hofmannsthal for his letter so "full of friendly words," George came straight to the point: "I cannot answer it the same way after a silence that lasted for years and was interrupted only by chance or for business reasons." Trampling over Hofmannsthal's measured niceties, he minced no words about his own attitude toward Hofmannsthal: "If I wish to respond to you today with every friendly intention what I think about you, then I am not enough of a philosopher to conceal from you what I have *against* you." After this preparatory volley, George then specified what he had against Hofmannsthal: "Ever since our first closeness in the *Blätter f. d. Kunst* I felt you working more against me · consciously or unconsciously · even though it was a matter of nothing more than the unambiguous struggle of the good against what was acknowledged to be bad." Further, and more gravely, George accused him of privately disowning his connection to the *Blätter* and of perversely refusing to be open in his dealings with him, even though he, George, insisted he had always striven to be as candid as possible. George also deplored Hofmannsthal's distressing tendency to allow his name to appear in print next to those of "arbitrary" hacks. And, owing to Hofmannsthal's inexplicable "reserve and timidity," whenever George had tried to meet with him to discuss mutual plans, "you were always the evasive one," all these years frustrating his repeated attempts to have nothing more than a normal, human exchange.

But as much as Hofmannsthal had been a personal disappointment, it was, George said, on the more significant level of what they could have achieved together in the cultural sphere that stirred his greatest regrets. Here George not only used his most blunt language yet toward Hofmannsthal, he also employed a phrase to describe how he conceived of what their thwarted effort might have accomplished that casts a bright light on the true direction of his own ambitions. "I was of the firm belief," George declared, "that we · you and I · could have exercised for years a very salutary dictatorship over our literature · that it did not come to that is something for which I hold you alone responsible." On the surface, this might appear to be a surprising admission, a frank avowal of George's intense desire to influence, indeed to dominate the German literary world. In fact, however, in George's mind, to equate his actions with establishing a dictatorial rule merely stated the obvious and was, moreover, an accurate way to portray what he and the *Blätter* had been pursuing all along. But as far as Hofmannsthal was concerned, recognizing that this fierce drive for total control propelled George's exertions must have been reason enough to stand clear. For Hofmannsthal undoubtedly understood that there could be no more than one dictator in a dictatorship, and that it was unlikely to be him.

Once George had cleared the air by venting his pent-up anger, frustrations and feelings of sadness at opportunities lost, he felt he could afford to be more generous regarding the "human" element between them. Alluding to their first, tumultuous encounter in Vienna a decade before, and insisting that it continued to form the "immutable" basis of their relationship, George claimed that "what you meant and still mean to me as a person was I trust revealed to you by my movements and words when we were together." And George insisted that his estimation of Hofmannsthal's poetic gift was equally unaffected: "The zeal with which I reach for every published line from you shows my great interest and the deep impression that your poems made on me." But George could not, after the passage of so much time and after Hofmannsthal's repeated rebuffs of his own invitations to come to Bingen, simply go to Vienna as if everything were normal. George thus offered to make a deal: "If after a period of a more lively correspondence we have created a good foundation: then I will come to you."

Overall, it was a bracing, somewhat patronizing summation of his standpoint, frank to the point of rudeness. Hofmannsthal seems to have recoiled from the unexpectedly acidulous tone of George's response and let several weeks go by before he again set pen to paper. When he finally did, it also took the form of a general inner stock-taking, as if he were trying to explain to George why he had acted in the past as he had done. "In the first years," Hofmannsthal wrote, "let's say until 1898 — I lacked, in addition to maturity, also to a strong degree precisely the overview over those people writing at the same time in German and in other languages." This inexperience led him, he explained, to turn to writers who later turned out to be unacceptable — he again apologized for having been duped by Dehmel's "tastelessness and crudity" — or who simply dulled his critical faculties. Yet, even allowing that his choice of literary companions or models had not always been defensible — which meant, in other words, that George disapproved of them — Hofmannsthal did not want to imply that he thought he had always been in the wrong. There were, he claimed, several good reasons for his decision to uphold a cautious distance between himself and George's circle. "What the *Blätter* contained apart from your and my works," Hofmannsthal admitted, "really filled me with a violent impatience. It is not entirely easy for me to locate the deeper root of this antipathy, indeed to account for it even to myself. I think that I am very reluctant to hear the expression of the mastery over life, of the nobility of spirit from the mouth of someone whose tone does not simultaneously fill me with the most genuine awe." A mediocre poet who speaks modestly, in a plain, unsophisticated manner, was more appealing to Hofmannsthal than someone who illegitimately donned the sacred robes befitting the practitioners of the "new" mode of poetry. A poem constructed according to this latter type "thus seems to me to be the greater lie, because it presupposes the feeling of being totally immersed, the victory over the whole — or, if it is not genuine, fakes it." For the rest, Hofmannsthal ran down the list of alleged faults, errors or indelicacies that George had laid at his feet — writing for popular newspapers, consorting with people who were beneath him, and so on — and defensively attempted to refute, or relativize, them all.

Hofmannsthal had never expressed anything but unmixed respect for George's own work, but this was not the first time he had openly stated his views on the quality of the other poets associated with the *Blätter,* and he could have expected the result. Also granting himself a generous pause before answering Hofmannsthal's prickly letter, George excused the delay by noting that "there is hardly a point in it where I do not feel precisely the opposite." He could overlook Hofmannsthal's own dalliances, but he would not brook any disparagement of matters relating to himself, which to George's mind encompassed the contributors to his journal. Beginning with "artists and thinkers as for example Wolfskehl and Klages," George said that he could not fathom how Hofmannsthal had failed to appreciate their abilities: "The dark passions of the one and the sharp air of the plains of the other are so unique so original that I would be unable even approximately to compare anyone from your circle (in as much as it has manifested itself) with them." Yet even as concerned the "smaller stars" circling around George, "you are greatly mistaken if you sense there the dishonesty and false serenity you mentioned — they are all people of good spiritual cultivation with whom you would live very nicely if you knew them." Among these "smaller stars," George singled out for special mention Gundolf and a recent piece he had published in the *Blätter.* But George would not permit Hofmannsthal's criticism to apply even to "the very small" members of his circle. He admitted that many of their works contained "random flourishes and ornaments." "But the fact that the most minor ones were able to produce such work: that in purely technical terms despite all of their thinness one can accuse them of less incompetence than many of those who are much praised: that seems to me viewed in terms of time and place much more important for our art and culture than all the volumes of poetry and all the dramas you previously placed your hopes on." After treating several other less serious issues, George closed by saying that "I have communicated to you as faithfully as possible my opinions and feelings so that nothing will strike you unexpectedly in a conversation." In the hope that such a conversation might take place, he suggested that "an oral discussion" would serve best to iron out any remaining ambiguities.

Yet again, it must have felt to Hofmannsthal that the old constellation was reasserting itself, with George pressing, castigating, baiting, trying to ensnare him within his embrace, leaving Hofmannsthal constantly fending off unwanted attentions, harsh recriminations, and the oppressive sense that he was being forced into something he did not want and could not fully comprehend. Although Hofmannsthal may have hoped that time had changed things for the better, it was becoming increasingly obvious that George was just the same, and in some ways even more overbearing than before. Either owing to this rather depressing realization, or perhaps stemming from a more general feeling of helplessness and spiritual lassitude that frequently plagued him, Hofmannsthal answered George's stern lecture with resigned fatigue. He was, he said, "in one of the nasty deep foul moods in which I agonizingly lose not only all luster of inward contemplation but even the clarity of thought." Even though the term did not yet exist, every indication of his psychic state pointed toward a clinical and chronic depression. Whatever one called it, the mental paralysis numbing his mind did not leave him feeling up to confronting George. It seemed only reasonable, Hofmannsthal concluded that "I would not like to see you in a condition such as my present one." Revealingly, he added that if there were not so many immovable obstacles preventing him from leaving Vienna, perhaps "I would depart tomorrow and come to you, in a region I have never set foot in, to restore myself abruptly by the strength and clarity of your mind or — how can one ever know? — to sink more deeply and gloomily into myself."

George appears not to have been particularly perturbed by the revived note of wariness in Hofmannsthal's uncertainty about whether a meeting with him would improve or worsen the younger man's own precarious mental state. In fact, George gave the impression of genuinely welcoming the opportunity to be of service and sent an immediate reply. He was reacting with unusual dispatch, George explained, "because I know of myself that in times of greatest depression one often needs only a little nudge to chase away the heavy clouds." It seemed a generous gesture, a charitable offer of aid to someone who was suffering. Although George did not know, or pretended not to realize, that he was a major contributing factor to Hofmannsthal's distress, the remaining store of affection and esteem he still felt for his fellow poet made the figurative extension of George's hand seem sincere. At the same time, he could not help lending his words of encouragement something resembling a reproach. "I believe," he confidentially told Hofmannsthal, "that hardly a single one of the ghosts weighing down on you has spared me. In my youth I was strong enough to conquer even the most adverse circumstances and without help — but later I would have certainly collapsed if I had not felt bolstered by the Ring. That is one of my greatest wisdoms — that is one of the secrets! What you most painfully suffer from is a certain rootlessness." In essence, then, while seeming to proffer comfort, George was actually making one last bid to pull Hofmannsthal within his orbit. The "rootlessness" he had diagnosed in Hofmannsthal could be repaired, in other words, if he would only come out of his detached isolation and surrender himself to the "Ring."

But it was partly due to the strain of trying to avoid doing just that and to escape George's grasp that Hofmannsthal had been thrown into his most recent, and most debilitating, funk. It was thus unlikely that he would choose as a remedy the very thing that was making him ill. In the oblique, noncommittal way he had long ago perfected in his exchanges with George, Hofmannsthal wrote back in August that "I prefer to respond to the profound and mysterious things your letter contains by way of reflection than, for now, with words. I myself have found the terrible word 'rootlessness' within me during wan hours; I have perhaps occasionally been able to sense the secret of the ring which you intimate."

But in reality Hofmannsthal was further away than ever from attaching himself to George's star. Indeed, something fundamental seems to have given way in the interim: their letters no longer contained the unfeigned assurances of mutual regard always there before, and they became increasingly limited to external matters pertaining exclusively to business. Reading them is a little like listening in on two former lovers who have realized that the fires between them have been extinguished, but neither has the courage or the will to be the first to say so. They both made halfhearted plans to see one another, which always fell through at the last minute. George again aired the possibility of reviving the long-delayed idea of producing a broader yearbook, but Hofmannsthal did not take that bait, either. And, for most of 1903, they wrangled about a book of Hofmannsthal's poetry that was to come out with George's publisher, Georg Bondi in Berlin, a book Hofmannsthal said at first he did not want but to which he finally, although reluctantly, gave his assent. In the following year, the situation began to deteriorate even more dramatically, with Hofmannsthal writing unflattering, even consciously provoking things about the *Blätter* authors, describing a piece by Gundolf as "ordinary," for example. George responded in kind by tearing into Hofmannsthal's play, *Venice Saved* (*Das gerettete Venedig*), which Hofmannsthal had dedicated to him. George told him that it reminded him of "poorly applied Shakespeare," that "your two protagonists cannot convince me," and that the plot was "implausible." Nevertheless, George bitingly added, he was certain that Hofmannsthal's art "will doubtlessly make a deep impression on the people before whom it is performed."

Their last two exchanges underscore the extent to which they had not only moved inwardly apart but had also quite simply failed to understand each other any longer. In December 1905 Hofmannsthal broke another prolonged silence by inviting George to join "40–50 of the absolutely first names of the country" and sign an open letter condemning the possibility of a German-English war, a horrifying specter that had briefly arisen in the aftermath of the Moroccan crisis during the summer. The intention was for a corresponding group of English intellectuals to do the same, and they would then have each other's declarations printed in the newspapers of their respective countries, "because," Hofmannsthal explained, "the papers are the real powder kegs." George's reply, which he never sent, was as uncompromising as ever. "If this letter had not come from someone whose mind I most highly esteem: then I would consider it a joke." He saw no purpose in making such futile attempts to influence the world directly by such crude means. Besides, he did not even think that a war between the two nations would necessarily be such a bad thing. "War is only the last consequence of a senseless headlong process over many years on both sides," George informed Hofmannsthal, "the efforts of a few people to patch things up seems to me devoid of any effect. And viewed from an even greater distance: who knows whether a true friend of the Germans should not wish them a powerful setback at SEA so that they may regain that national modesty which will enable them to create spiritual values again." But George did say that, after reading Hofmannsthal's letter, he had come to the conclusion "that there seems to be hardly a single point anymore at which we do not misunderstand one another."

Their final communication resulted from a similar misunderstanding. In early 1906, again breaking a long silence, Hofmannsthal wrote to complain that George's printer was refusing to release the rights to his own book of poetry. He demanded that George intervene on his behalf and inform the printer that the poems were "my unlimited property." Failure to comply with his wishes, Hofmannsthal warned, would prompt a legal "claim for damages." Since he cannot have been ignorant of the threats to bring a suit against Klein several years before by his friend Leopold von Andrian, he thus more than likely knew the expressions of complete contempt for the "so-called" law George had delivered then. Therefore, Hofmannsthal's act of raising the challenge of a possible lawsuit would have seemed a calculated taunt. This time, however, George did not even bother to deal with the matter himself. Engaging someone else to write the rejoinder, on which George's name was signed only by proxy, he spoke in a voice that had become formal, cold, and bitter. "In your letter," it reads, "you make assertions that exclude any personal discussion on my part." George did not even do Hofmannsthal the favor of directly mentioning the subject of the dispute. "I will have you informed in detail by the appropriate agency wherein your right consists in this matter and to what you have absolutely no right." And that, finally, was that: they never spoke or wrote to each other again. After fourteen exhausting years, Hofmannsthal was free at last.

While Gundolf doggedly struggled to recapture George's indulgence and Hofmannsthal fought just as hard to rid himself of it, another drama was unfolding in George's life that would soon far surpass these two in both emotional intensity and imaginative scope. In his own way, George had unquestionably loved both Gundolf and Hofmannsthal, and in both instances his love, mainly due to the demanding conditions under which he had offered it, had been either unrequited or rejected or both. George eventually accommodated himself to Gundolf's nonerotic devotion, which promised undeniable rewards in compensation, whereas Hofmannsthal had finally proven himself incapable of yielding anything at all. But it was beginning to appear that George, now in his mid-thirties, would never find someone who would fully respond to his needs and desires, someone who would pliantly bend in his direction, yet also offer the strengths of mind and character he demanded of his closest companions, someone who was both acquiescent but of firm disposition, someone who combined beauty and inward power, grace and dignity in equal measure. Put simply, he was despairing of finding someone he could call his own.

George was probably beginning to suspect not just that he may remain profoundly lonely all his life, that his genuine longing for love may forever go unfulfilled, but also that the person he envisioned as his ideal companion did not, indeed *could* not exist. The brute limitations of the real had never posed much of an obstacle for George, and here, too, they would prove to be less a hindrance than an inspiration to surmount them. If it was impossible to find what he was looking for in this world, then he would simply have to seek it, which is to say create it, in another. If, in other words, reality failed to meet his expectations, then so much the worse for reality. Again, this had been his method from the start. But now the stakes seemed quite a bit higher. He had moved from an awareness that poetry alone could not satisfy his wish to conquer and take possession of his environment, and he had thus come to the realization that he had to engage immediately with the world and face it more directly on its own terms. As Wolfskehl and others had repeatedly exhorted him, he now knew he had to confront "life" head-on, rather than only fashion tractable alternatives to it, if he hoped to subjugate it to his control. Yet, try as he might, he seemed unable to make progress in forcing it to deliver the one thing he most desired. Love can be neither bought nor coerced. Following the dictates of a logic that had governed his entire life, George therefore took the only course of action he could wholly rely on to provide favorable results. Lacking a suitable candidate willing to serve as the sole object of his affection, George took the decisive step of creating his ideal companion, of actually engendering his own lover. More: his ideal beloved would be not merely the compliant receptacle of his most fervent yearnings; he would also be the deity before which he would henceforth bow, the only supreme being above himself George would ever acknowledge.

In some respects, there was nothing intrinsically odd or even especially original in George's half-desperate, half-proud resolve to improve on the relatively meager offerings of nature in his search for a perfect love. Dante's Beatrice, Petrarch's Laura, and perhaps even more aptly the addressee of Shakespeare's sonnets are all prototypes of George's more recent attempt. And it is no accident that, at this very time, his involvement with both Dante and Shakespeare approached its zenith, concretely resulting in extensive translations from both poets' works during the first decade of the century. But George brought his own idiosyncratic investment to the familiar convention of transforming a mortal archetype into a blemishless paragon. For some time now, both within and outside of his "circle," various friends and followers of George as well had been portraying him as something more than merely human, as a kind of poetic priest presiding over the dawning of a new era, as a spiritual mediator standing between the sordid reality of nineteenth-century bourgeois culture and the higher reaches of a transcendent order yet to be revealed. This was, in essence, Klages's argument in his book on George, even though he had wanted to focus attention less on the poet than on his poems. But others, such as Wolfskehl, saw the issue in a more personal light. In July 1902, in one of his characteristic fits of exuberance, Wolfskehl had exclaimed, "But you Friend Master are the Leader of the New Man." There was no doubt in many minds, including George's own, about the nature or legitimacy of his calling. What was needed, and still missing, was someone to exemplify, literally embody the "New Man" George was supposed to lead. To the surprise of not a few, when he finally did appear, it was not as a "man" at all but as a boy who was proclaimed a god.

On first inspection, the chosen one did not seem a fitting aspirant for such high office. Born on April 14, 1888, Maximilian Kronberger was the son of an affluent brewer who thanks to his success had been able to withdraw from active participation in business in 1900 and settle down to a life of comfortable leisure in Munich. In March 1902, George, always on the lookout for fresh blood, spotted the not quite fourteen-year-old Maximilian at the edge of Schwabing and immediately took a keen interest in the youth. George himself later reported that he followed the boy around for days "under the spell of his charm before daring to speak to him." (This was, incidentally, a favorite technique George employed whenever he spied someone he found attractive. A decade later, just before the war, he noticed a young boy on the streets of Berlin and dispatched some of his minions to gather information about him. They followed the unsuspecting lad around for weeks, sometimes for hours at a time, thereby surreptitiously discovering his name, where he lived, who his friends were, how he behaved and so on. George often accompanied them on these reconnaissance missions and together they watched the boy from afar. For whatever reason, though, George did not pursue the matter further. "Never," reported one of George's companions at the time, "did he speak to him or approach him.")

George was not so coy with young Herr Kronberger. One day, as Maximilian was standing in front of his house with his sister Johanna, a man suddenly came up to them and, without introducing himself, announced that he found the boy's head "very interesting" and asked for permission to have a portrait made of him. Understandably somewhat bewildered, Maximilian distractedly granted the stranger's request. The next day, in the company of Johanna, they all went to a photographer and had a picture made, a copy of which was promised to the boy. On the way back home, their escort obliquely inquired whether Maximilian had "certain inclinations and tendencies." Thinking the older man meant only what his pursuits were, the boy bashfully concealed that he wrote verses and pretended instead to be interested in natural history. Only then did Maximilian dare to ask what his new acquaintance's name was and learned that he was called "Stefan George."

It was the last time he saw or heard from George for the rest of that year. After noticing the poet's name on the cover of Klages's treatise in a Munich bookstore, he asked his father to buy a copy for him, but, like most everyone else, Max confessed that "I didn't understand a single page." Soon enough, he all but forgot the whole affair. But George did not forget him. In physical appearance, Maximilian Kronberger seemed to fit most of the criteria George normally required in potential acolytes. His father, Alfred Kronberger, was Jewish but had converted to Catholicism following his marriage to Christina Buch. Although the other members of the family sported a light complexion, Maximilian had dark brown, almost black hair, and his skin was nearly olive-colored, obscuring even the reddish blush that comes so easily to the cheeks of fair-skinned adolescents. With full lips, deep-seated, almond-shaped eyes and a strong, jutting jaw, there seemed something exotic, almost slightly oriental about him. He also seemed unusually mature for his age, and even his voice changed earlier than that of his peers. And while George could not have known it yet, even if he may have surmised as much, Maximilian displayed a precocious interest in poetry and literature, revealing in his letters and diary that he was reading on his own the great medieval works in Middle High German, Goethe, and Aristotle's *Poetics*. Alongside this intellectual alertness, not entirely typical of a fourteen-year-old, Maximilian had also written a number of poems that exhibit a penchant for themes close to the hearts of mentally awake adolescents — the brevity of life, the terror and mystery of death, the existence of God, and so forth — but also demonstrate a notable facility in handling formal poetic structures.

In mid-January 1903, when George had returned to Munich for the winter and was walking down the street one afternoon with Wolfskehl, they accidentally bumped into Maximilian returning home from school. "I was overjoyed," the boy related in his memoirs. They made an appointment for the following day, and George took him to Wolfskehl's apartment and showed him the photograph taken the previous spring. In short order, Maximilian began making regular visits to George. They took long meditative walks together, and the older man expressed the wish for a few lines in the boy's hand for graphological analysis. Although Maximilian had still disclosed nothing of his poetic endeavors, he submitted one of his own poems for evaluation without identifying its author. When George next saw him, he made a wily face, eyed Max conspiratorially and announced, "What you gave me is by you." Since the youth initially understood the remark as a question, he replied "yes." George told him he thought the poem was "quite nice" and wanted to know if he had written more and, if so, whether he might be able to look at them. Maximilian then gave him a little volume of his collected works, which he had never shown to anyone else in its entirety, and George became even more enthusiastic, judging many to be "very good." It was for both of them a momentous occasion. In Maximilian's words, "a new life had now begun."

At the beginning of February, George marked the commencement of this "new life" by presenting Maximilian with the third and last volume of the anthology of German poetry he and Wolfskehl had edited, *Goethe's Century* (*Das Jahrhundert Goethes*), promising to give him the other two as a present after his Confirmation. George also gave him a poem of his own, which in slightly modified form would eventually make its way into the collection he would devote to Maximilian several years later. It reads, however, less like a celebration of his new companion than the attempt to put the feelings of abandonment occasioned by another friend into allegorical perspective.

> The disciple remained in sadness day and night
> On the mountain from which the Lord had risen toward heaven. —
> "I plead for a sign yet you wrap yourself in silence,
> Will I never hear your voice again

And kiss your hem and your feet?
Do you allow your Loyal One thus to despair?"
Then a stranger came along the way: "Brother speak!
Such torment blazes on your cheek
That I will suffer too if I cannot quench it."
"Your consolation is in vain, leave me, impoverished as I am!
I seek my Lord who has forgotten me!"
The stranger disappeared. — the disciple sank to his knees
With a loud cry, for by the heavenly radiance
That remained at the spot he realized
What in his blinding pain and wild hopes he
Had not seen: it was the Lord who had come and gone.

Only Gundolf would have known whom the wailing disciple symbolized, but the fact that George chose to give this poem to the young Kronberger throws a revealing light on his own view of the situation. Quite apart from the implications attached to the parallel drawn between the story of the unnamed "Lord" and Jesus's appearance to his apostles on the way to Emmaus after the crucifixion, the poem depicts the blame for the disciple's suffering as resting entirely on his own shoulders. George may have intended it as a veiled warning to his own newest disciple: recognize your "Lord," it seems to say, and you shall experience bliss; failure to do so will cast you, like the miserable disciple in the poem, into self-imposed and dreadful anguish.

Maximilian was a bright boy, but he probably did not extract this lesson from the poem. Anyway, there were plenty of other things to divert his attention from the darker strains of George's personality. In 1903, as the Cosmic Circle reached its peak, Max was invited to a riotous celebration held in February at Wolfskehl's apartment in observance of Carnival. In all, some seventy people attended, both women and men, all dressed in colorful costumes inspired by various ancient Greek and Roman figures: George appeared as Caesar, Wolfskehl presided as Dionysus, present as well were Persephone and Nike, and still others came decked out in the guise of hermaphrodites and hetaerae. In Franziska zu Reventlow's novelistic account of the event, which she also attended, her fictional author admits that "it would be particularly difficult to describe the fest itself since for me it was an indescribable confusion of people, costumes, music, noise, isolated incidents, conversations and so on." Perhaps the most striking appearance was Schuler: attired in a long dark robe and wearing a black wig, beret, and heavily made-up face, he impersonated the Magna Mater, acting as a kind of patron spirit presiding over the whole occasion. Not by chance, the rites associated with the worship of the Magna Mater in antiquity had been especially popular in Rome during the second and third centuries, or just during the period of Elagabalus's reign. Intended as an act of purification and initiation, the ceremony originally involved the slaughter of a bull or a ram harnessed to a perforated board slung over a pit in which the neophyte stood, who would then be bathed in the blood cascading down from the slain animal. In Elagabalus's time, the cult of the Magna Mater also encompassed orgiastic rituals in his honor, including the act of castration, magic ceremonies, and, it was said, even the sacrifice of children.

No children were put to the knife in Wolfskehl's apartment, but when Maximilian Kronberger walked in, he said he was "amazed." Photographs were taken of the participants in their festive outfits, and George made sure to give Maximilian a print of himself dressed up as the Roman emperor, which the boy had framed and placed in his room. In general, photographs were an important part of George's life, and he liked to exchange them as gifts and mementos with his friends. Of some, he had several different photos, showing them in formal poses, intimate interior settings, alone or in a group. The pictures taken at Wolfskehl's were all carefully staged, but, significantly, none preserve a vital element of the cosmic creed, and which may or may not have been featured during the Carnival festival: nudity.

Rumors had begun circulating at the end of the previous century that during a reading of *The Tapestry of Life* at the Lepsius house in 1899, the large book from which George declaimed had been "upheld by two beautiful naked boys." Sabine Lepsius dutifully scoffed at such tales, even as she repeated them, but others offer compelling corroborating evidence that they were not entirely far-fetched. Some time before the 1903 celebration, Roderich Huch, who would soon fall out of favor with the Cosmic Circle for his "indiscretions," was invited to the Wolfskehl house. Someone — Huch assumed either Klages or Wolfskehl himself — had observed him while he was swimming and noticed that Huch was the owner of an attractive, well-proportioned body. George had been duly informed, which apparently led to the summons to the Wolfskehls' apartment. Without warning, the side door to the room in which Huch was standing flew open. George came up to him and, breaking the silence that had instantly descended at his appearance, commanded, "Take off your clothes!" Flabbergasted but not wholly thrown, Huch said, "No." Not accustomed to being openly disobeyed, George turned on his heel and disappeared, while Wolfskehl stammered in Hessian dialect, "Rodi, how could you, how could you, just think, the Master!" Huch stood his ground and kept his clothes on. A few days later he was called back to the Wolfskehls. There stood the Master, who pointed to a table and said with great majesty, "There is something for you!" It was a letter from Gundolf, whom George had allowed to remain in written contact with his friend Huch. But George forbade Wolfskehl from ever bringing Huch into his own house again.

Maximilian Kronberger appears to have been more amenable to George's wishes. In addition to the photograph that had been made on the first day he had met Maximilian, George owned others. One, a detail of which served as the frontispiece to the book he later dedicated to Maximilian, shows him in rear three-quarter profile wearing a laurel wreath, displaying his bare neck and shoulders, with his left hand grasping a wooden staff. There is, however, another picture showing George, Wolfskehl, and Gundolf seated or lying around a table after a meal, all wearing long toga-like robes and crowns of laurel. On the wall above them hangs what looks to be the larger version of the same photo of Maximilian, depicting a naked youth in the identical pose, from the same side-rear angle, likewise holding an upright staff by the left hand, but cropped just at the thigh, thus revealing his nude back, arms, and buttocks

Naturally, photographs of nude boys would have had a specific appeal to George, but within the context of Schwabing and of the Cosmic Circle in particular, nudity and the challenge it represented to bourgeois notions of sexual propriety, played a larger role. If reports are to be believed, George himself was known to have disrobed for some of the festivities. Georg Fuchs relates how he once encountered George standing "almost naked" at the top of some stairs, wearing nothing but "ivy wreaths" and swinging a phallic thyrsus in Dionysian abandon. In a heated conversation between George and Schuler, who was arguing that poetry was an ineffective tool to promote change, George asked him what he suggested he do instead. Schuler leapt at the challenge and said that George should stand naked on the market square, which Schuler was convinced would produce a catalytic effect and unleash a revolutionary movement and "could be the beginning of a change in the world." George is supposed to have shrugged his shoulders and said that filling one more cell in a mental institution was not his calling.

Franziska zu Reventlow, who was notorious for her numerous extramarital liaisons (she bore one child out of wedlock and had affairs with Klages, Wolfskehl, and many others), also touched on the subject of ritual nakedness in her autobiographical novel. At one point in her story, one of the characters recommends organizing "an orgy — a pan-erotic orgy." When someone else acts surprised by this suggestion, he retorts, "Why not? Are we not just as entitled to celebrate orgies as the ancient Romans and Greeks?" In addition to its shock value, though, the Schwabing conception of nudity was invested with an explicitly pedagogical function. In an unpublished manuscript, Countess Reventlow assailed traditional "so-called good upbringing with all of its antediluvian moral concepts and views." Shot through with hypocrisy and cowardice, this sanctimonious morality, she argued, was especially loathsome for its "hiding and covering up of all questions concerning sexuality."

Most insidious, she thought, was the general attempt to "make nudity taboo." "We however see in nudity in general, both in life and in art, not only not as a 'sin,' but rather as a *positive* educational element of great importance." She therefore proposed an overtly aesthetic education, as opposed to a narrowly prudish one, advocating a physical cultivation that led "to the healthy pleasure in all beautiful things, whether they be in art or nature, nude or clothed — to the healthy abhorrence of everything that is truly not beautiful." In fine, the new pedagogy, resting on the uninhibited appreciation of the unadorned human body, would demand that "the measure of the actions (of our child) shall not be his 'moral' feeling but rather exclusively his aesthetic one."

George may have also partially seen his relationship with the pubescent Maximilian as forming part of this subversive pedagogical ethos. But, being secretive both by inclination and necessity, he carefully covered his tracks and to an almost self-contradictory degree sought to preserve a veneer of respectability in his dealings with the boy. In 1919, for instance, long after the events being described had become myth, he burned all "personal" letters relating to the Cosmic Circle and to Maximilian. And even during their friendship, George always fastidiously reminded Max of his duties toward his parents, urging him to keep up with his studies in school, and George took pains to speak often and at length with his mother and father, whom George met soon after Maximilian himself and who several times graciously invited the older man to meals at their home. George was also not averse to setting the youth straight in a way that, while conforming to his usual treatment of his associates, struck a strongly paternalistic note, schooling him in some codes of behavior that did not diverge a great deal from those observed by the bourgeoisie. When Maximilian's relatives from Vienna visited him in April 1903, for example, he proudly took them to meet the famous poet who had befriended him, but without giving advance warning of the visit. To the boy's evident surprise, George expressed sharp annoyance at the unexpected call and bluntly indicated that he was "known to be someone who generally did not accept unannounced visitors and that in the future he (Max) should not bring people into his house." A week later, George again let his irritation be known when Maximilian stood him up at a planned meeting. George said he had cancelled an appointment with another friend specially for Max's sake and that "he was not accustomed to being neglected by his friends in small things, nor did they do so." "If one expects someone," George condescended to instruct him, "it is bad manners to cancel two hours before the arranged time." Apparently, George thought that being antibourgeois did not necessarily entail being badly behaved.

Still, even despite George's efforts to adhere scrupulously to certain social conventions and never to allow even a trace of doubt to surface about his motivations, one can imagine that Maximilian's parents looked on the whole relationship with something less than undiluted joy. Apart from everything else, the difference in age between them would have caused anyone to have second thoughts. By mid-1903, George was thirty-five and Maximilian had just turned fifteen. Writing to one of his cousins, Maximilian confided that "my parents have always wished that I would not go so often to George (I have been going there every Sunday)." He did not say exactly why his parents felt uneasy, but it would not be hard to guess. A few months earlier, George had once asked him with great solemnity, "Max, do you believe that a kind of friendship exists that is higher than love?" Whether he knew what George was talking about or not, he answered affirmatively. Yet if he relayed this episode to his parents, it may have given them only one more reason to worry.

An incident in early 1904 made Maximilian wonder whether they might be right. He had let another appointment pass by the previous Sunday without alerting George with sufficient notice — Max airily explained that he had a lot of homework for school — but indicated that he would be "at his disposal" later in the week. On January 29, a Friday, he went to see George. "He kept me waiting for an unusually long time even though he was in the room next door." Following this object lesson on what it feels like to be kept waiting, George at last came in, "took my hand and looked at me for a long time." Maximilian asked him how he was but got no answer. When George finally did speak, he began reproaching the boy "with increasing vehemence," saying that Max's claim of not having had any time had been a "stupid excuse," and he especially objected to the phrase that Max was "at his disposal." George insisted that *he* could say such a thing to Maximilian but never the other way around. The boy countered that it was just a common phrase and that George had simply misunderstood it. "Then he turned around to me with a face as if I had committed who knows what kind of crime and threatened me with his finger." George then sat down at the desk and mockingly began to write, reading aloud as he went along, "that if I had no time, i.e. no desire to come when he has time, then he has neither the time nor desire to receive me. He ended with the words 'Come whenever you want.'" This little charade became too much for Maximilian, who had not expected to be given such a dressing down. Bidding him "adieu," Max extended his hand, but George ignored him. Briskly withdrawing it, Maximilian turned and left. "I told my parents everything," he informed his cousin, Oskar, "and will not put myself in such a situation a second time, but rather will never go to him again."

Having already forfeited Klages and Schuler, and with things looking progressively hopeless with Hofmannsthal, George realized that he could not afford to lose Maximilian Kronberger as well. Soon after this little spat, George hurried to mend things by going to the boy's father and apologizing for his behavior, explaining, intriguingly, that his outburst had been "induced by family circumstances." No less interestingly, when George saw Max again, he "gave me a big speech about my unjust behavior, and thus we were again reconciled with one another." By February 8, Maximilian reported that "things have more or less returned to the way they were," with the scene having left behind no more than an "unpleasant shadow." Indeed, if anything, he and George now became more intimate. A week later, there was another masquerade, this time at the house of Henry Heiseler, a German-speaking Russian who lived for a time in Munich and had sought out the Cosmic lights. Minus the Cosmics, though, the event at Heiseler's home was noticeably more sedate than the previous year's celebration. George dressed as Dante, Wolfskehl was, appropriately, the blind poet Homer, someone else came as Vergil, and Maximilian appeared in the guise of a noble Florentine boy. He was clothed almost entirely in red: he wore red tights covered by a red silk tunic; in his hand he held a red candle and on his head rested a crown of red carnations; only the belt cinched around his waist was silver. At the end of the month, Maximilian announced that, from then on, he would write like George — that is, he would dispense with capital letters in nouns and discard conventional punctuation marks — "even in my poems." In late March, he was addressing George as his *Meister* and he was writing poems that must have made his "Master's" heart beat faster. "Why do you prevent me from putting my arms around your neck?" one poem reads; another is encouragingly titled "The Death of the Female Beloved." Aside from a few normal growing pains, Maximilian was coming along very nicely.

Then the unthinkable, the unbearable happened. During a visit with his cousins in Vienna, Maximilian suddenly fell ill with meningitis. On April 10, 1904, he was taken home to Munich in a coma. At 3:30 in the morning of April 15, one day after his sixteenth birthday, he quietly died, having never regained consciousness. Gundolf had received word of the illness the day before and, fearing the worst, rushed to Bingen to be with George. After learning of the boy's death, they spent a secluded week together outside of town. But for George nothing would ever be the same again.

CHAPTER 23
Maximin

Only some time after the immediate shock caused by Maximilian Kronberger's death had begun to fade into a more muted sorrow was George able to take stock of what had happened. At first it was not clear that anything truly extraordinary had occurred — heartbreaking certainly but nothing unprecedented in George's experience. Of course, it was deeply painful that such a promising young man had been annihilated, that the handsome and increasingly responsive youth was now forever beyond his reach. But death and wrenching loss were no strangers to George. In some ways they had been, paradoxically, the most reliable constants in his life, a good deal of which he had spent in the constantly frustrated search for a companion and lover who could — or would want to — satisfy his expectations. Max's sudden death, as awful as it obviously was, only seemed to be yet another installment in an endlessly repeating cycle of short-lived plenitude swiftly followed by crushing privation.

Even George's closest friends did not initially seem to be aware that anything more than a horrible personal misfortune had taken place. Some noted a little later that he had more gray in his hair, that he seemed less interested in the raucous celebrations that had become synonymous with Schwabing. But no one thought anything like a seismic shift had shaken him. At the end of April, Gundolf, perhaps slightly overeager to see the memory of Max recede into the background, wrote George with the wish that "you are hopefully well and calm for your work in May," adding the rather naive hope that George was not too "lonely and in despair." But, as George told Wolfskehl's wife,

Hanna, in May, he was still a long way from returning to his normal routine. "The entire time I have been incapable of working or making a decision," George said; "slowly my body is recuperating · my spirit enters into another circle of suffering each week — different from the previous one only through the images." A month later, Sabine Lepsius invited him to accompany her and her husband, Reinhold, on a trip they were about to make to London. George declined the offer, explaining that he did not think he would be very good company. "You would not have very much from me. [. . .] I am mourning an incomprehensible and premature death that seemed to want to lead me into the final chasms." Since he had not specified whom he had lost or how — as usual, he had couched the entire matter, as Sabine Lepsius euphemistically put it in her memoirs, "in the form peculiar to George" — the Lepsiuses' understandably had no real inkling of the importance George attached to the event. "I read the letter and read it again," Sabine confessed, "but strangely enough I was unable to read from the restrained words what a flood of pain was now pouring over our friend." It was only with hindsight that Frau Lepsius could have thought it strange that she had failed to appreciate the enormity of the death in George's mind; after all, he had not given her much to go on. At the time, and for good reason, she could have had no idea, as she later said, of "the dreadfulness of this fate, dreadful not only for George but also for the world."

Even granted that the death of Maximilian Kronberger may have dealt a staggering blow to George himself, it is difficult to imagine how his passing could have held much significance for the rest of the world. Yet the signs had already began to accumulate in the summer following the boy's death that George saw, or wanted to see, something far greater in Max than merely a moderately gifted teenager. Having turned down the Lepsius's offer to go to England, George went instead to Holland in early June to visit his old friend Albert Verwey. He told his Dutch colleague the sad news as well, and one evening he read some of the boy's poems aloud. Verwey also knew the poem George had given to Maximilian that was inspired by Jesus's appearance on his way to Emmaus, which George had not so subtly intended as a warning to Max about the dangers of apostasy. "I found it weaker than I was used to from him," Verwey candidly admitted about the poem, "and feared that out of the need to translate a natural event into the supernatural realm he would take as reality what was no more than an intellectual reflection. All the more so when he read this poem aloud with more emotion than in my opinion it deserved." Although not stated with perfect clarity, Verwey's reservations are open enough. He knew that George, like all good symbolists (including himself), essentially sought to abrogate reality by replacing it with his own version of it. But whereas Verwey implied that he himself had always been conscious that there was ultimately a difference between one's private creation and the outside world, he began to sense that George was losing sight of that distinction. Strengthening this impression was something else George had said when describing the troubles he had been having in Munich with Klages and Schuler. "What deeply insulted George," Verwey recalled, "was the reproach that he placed his person in the foreground. He was profoundly convinced that he served a power that worked through his person."

George did believe, and as time passed became only more convinced, that he was the agent of powers greater than himself. He was, as we know, prepared to accept that any number of occult or merely mysterious forces governed both the visible and invisible realms. Likewise, he had always viewed himself as a being apart, as someone who stood out from, and above, the ordinary run of humanity. Until now, however, this feeling of exceptionalness had not really gone beyond a general sense of superiority, whether measured in terms of his work, his colleagues and peers, or even the entire culture that surrounded him. But the death of Maximilian Kronberger became the catalyst that spurred a new phase in George's own life and a new self-conception that exceeded these relatively modest assumptions — relative, that is, to the even greater claims he was soon to make of himself.

Sometime within the first year after Max had died, George had already formulated the plan to publish a book commemorating him. By April 1905, he had completed a manuscript, which he then sent to Lechter, as usual, for decoration. But the book was to be unusual in every other way. "I have wandered the entire time in the shadow of this Dead One," he told Lechter. "I have produced nothing of consequence since then. Perhaps when the book is finished I will then blossom again!" The book would thus be a monument, an epitaph to eulogize the "Dead One," but also a purgation, a cathartic act that would free him of the paralyzing depression that had been weighing on him ever since. As it turned out, the book would also become the defining statement of a new creed, the embodiment and paradigm of George's broadened ambitions. Thanking Lechter for his sympathy and understanding during the difficult period following the death, George further hinted at what the entire experience had meant to him. "What gave me great comfort was that you · my dearest friend · understood me at the time and had the right conception of this event that to me was supersensory — which the crowd will view in the best case with suspicion."

The fullest account George gave of what he intended by the dry, almost academic-sounding word "supersensory" appears not in connection with Maximilian but in the introduction to George's translation of Shakespeare's sonnets that he published five years later, in 1909. There, George contemptuously dismissed all speculation about who the addressee of Shakespeare's sonnets might have been and he blamed such unseemly, grubbing curiosity for the failure to understand the poet's true aim, namely, and simply, "the adoration in the face of beauty and the burning desire for immortality." If one still insisted on knowing who, in biographical terms, had inspired the poems, George asserted with a mixture of defiance and exasperation that "in our day" everyone "openly" agreed that "in the middle of the sequence of sonnets stands, in all registers and degrees, the passionate devotion of the poet for his male friend." Knowing what kind of reception this acknowledgement bordering on an endorsement of Shakespeare's homoeroticism would find among certain readers, George went on the offensive. There was no need to explain, defend, or applaud this fact, he wrote; rather "one should accept it even if one does not understand it and it is equally foolish to defile with criticism or with redemption what one of the greatest Mortals considered good." Further sharpening this derisive attack against the values and beliefs of his own age, George disqualified his contemporaries from even being able to have an opinion of the matter. "Materialistic and intellectualistic eras in particular have no right to make words about this subject since they cannot even have the slightest notion of the world-creating power of supersexual Love."

Supernatural, supersensory, supersexual — however one defined it, the main point is that the "love" George thought was represented in Shakespeare's poems and that he himself had felt for Maximilian was not and could not be of the common variety. We already have a fairly good sense of how George understood his own brand of love, as evidenced in his treatment of Hofmannsthal and Gundolf, as well as in his handling of many others besides. But with Maximilian — or rather with what would become the boy's etherized, transcendental alter ego — a wholly new level had been reached. For "Maximin," as George renamed him (even in death one could not escape George's forcible arrogation of the right to tamper with the basic elements of one's identity), was the first affective object he managed to assimilate entirely within himself, the first person he amalgamated fully with his own being, the first "other" he could call without residue "mine." Lifted up into an ideal sphere untouchable by time, Maximilian would stay forever young in George's memory, remain forever beautiful in his eyes, and, to a degree that would never have been possible had the boy lived, he would forever be George's sole and absolute possession. In one of the poems George wrote for the book dedicated to Maximin, aptly called "Incorporation," the poet states the case openly: "I [am] the creation of my own son." Lover and beloved are one in this "most secret marriage," as the poem goes on to describe it, subject and object are merged, not in physical union but — what was more in George's view — in a kind of all-encompassing spiritual embrace. What George had never been able to accomplish before in real terms had thus finally been realized in a realm he preferred anyway: "An image is born of you and me, indivisible, in the dream." The word "dream" here acts as a collective abstraction, symbolizing the immaterial nonrational sphere that George had always associated with genuine poetry, and it was there, in that timeless, unchanging world, that George could cleave to Maximin forever.

Although admittedly esoteric, all of this seems comprehensible enough. And since we have seen other instances of it so often before, even George's desire not just to fuse with but actually to engulf and absorb his idealized lover offers no particular surprises. What is less easy to accept or even understand is the poet's apparently straight-faced declaration of Maximin's divinity. George had long seen himself as a kind of secular priest. What had been missing was a god. With the advent of Maximin, that finally changed. In the very first poem of the cycle devoted to Maximin we read:

> To him you are a child · to him a friend.
> I see in you the God
> Whom I recognized with a shudder
> Whom I worship.

Here, with these deceptively simple, declarative words, George announced what amounts to the foundation of a private religion. This is unquestionably how he wanted others to think of it, and many did. As one of his later followers matter-of-factly observed, "The meeting with Maximin has a religious significance." Friedrich Wolters, whose biography of George was supervised, approved and in parts even ghostwritten by the Master himself, went even further. "With his coming," Wolters wrote, meaning Maximin, "the new conception of the world, which George carried within himself and gave to the people 'wrapped in song,' first broke into full bloom throughout the spheres." In his overblown style, Wolters went on to align Maximin explicitly with Jesus. "That he again closed the ring after twenty centuries as the first physical earthly son with the physical master, in which the love of the Divine, in which the loving God himself is perfected in man, that is the miracle that carries his name and again blesses all levels of earthly existence." The claim is as bold as it is blasphemous. Two thousand years after the birth of Christ, Wolters wanted us to believe, God decided to reappear in human form once more and did so in the guise of Maximilian Kronberger *alias* Maximin. George apparently thought that if it happened once it could happen again. More audacious still, since George imagined that he had completely merged his own being with that of his god — that Maximin was, as the poet had said, "the creation of my own son" — George's deification of Maximin was tantamount to a deification of himself.

Yet Wolters had only put into prosaic, if hyperbolic form what George had already proclaimed in his poetry. The language used throughout the verses glorifying Maximin is, even for George, unusually saturated with religious imagery, imbued with the Christian motifs of divine incarnation, deliberate self-sacrifice, resurrection, and the promise of eternal life. In one, we read that the "highest miracle" has occurred, that the presence of the new god is like a second creation of the world, that he "consecrates" the very air he breathes and blesses the ground he walks on. The entire earth, before seemingly lifeless and cold, now beats anew with his arrival by being pulsed through "a holy heart." In another poem, and reintroducing the figure of the angel that had made his first appearance in *The Tapestry of Life,* the poet is told by the angelic apparition that "you are chosen / To look into the new land." Outstretched before the poet lies a new landscape filled with flowers and blossoms — in particular, violets and George's favorite roses — and the warm air vibrates with light, all accompanied by the constant booming song of the angel. When the poet, standing in the midst of this Edenic perfection, receives his benediction, it is in the form of a kiss from the angel: "his mouth / On yours burns you pure · / You are on holy ground: / Kneel down and pray!"

When death steals Maximin away, the poet's first anguished response is to wish that he would have been taken in his place, and he throws himself onto the grass in despair. But a voice admonishes him to "get up from the ground as a healthy man! / Affirm and acclaim my miracle / And wait down below among the living." The world Maximin has left behind him "down below," however, having only just been reanimated by his coming, seems all the more dampened and lifeless after his departure. Instead of resounding with exultant angelic song, now only "Sorrow calls from the forest." Everywhere the poet turns, he finds that "The air is dull · the days are barren." Gradually, as he recovers from the numb paralysis of grief, the poet accepts the charge of declaring the "miracle" that has occurred. Gathering new strength from this mission, he calls to his companions, "Now raise your heads! for unto you salvation has been done": "a god appeared and stepped into your house." The poet instructs them "not to mourn any longer — for you too were chosen": "You too have heard the call of a god / And the mouth of a god has kissed you." Reverence for Maximin even leads George to make an exception to his otherwise complete rejection of his age. "Praise your city that has born a god! / Praise your time in which a god has lived!"

There follow several verses explaining, as if with an eye toward codification, the "life and death of Maximin," succeeded by three so-called "Prayers," and penultimately the already mentioned "Incorporation," which celebrates the mystical union joining the poet with his god. The final poem of the cycle is called "Entrueckung." It is a complex word that combines the meanings contained in the English "transport" and "reverie," intimating a blissful, almost otherworldly state of ecstatic, semiconscious abandon. It is a hauntingly ethereal work, in tone the poetic equivalent of the diaphanous musical nocturnes composed by the young Schoenberg or Strauss. The poet, having traversed the range of violent emotions stirred by the fortuitous discovery of Maxim and by the shattering trauma of his subsequent loss, has seemingly entered a kind of mystical trance, as if he were now able to stare out beyond, without actually crossing, the threshold dividing life from death itself. Peering out into the darkening void, the poet sees the images of people and places he has known in the past now beginning to melt away in time and space. But most of all he senses that he has become the channel of the higher power his god embodies. Judged solely on its poetic effect, this is surely one of George's most unnervingly eerie works:

> I feel the wind of another planet.
> The faces that had only just turned to me
> As friends grow pale through the darkness.
>
> And trees and paths that I loved are fading
> So that I hardly recognize them and You bright
> Beloved shade — herald of my sufferings —
>
> Are now fully extinguished in deeper fires
> To rise up, after the frenzy of conflict and turmoil
> With a pious shudder.
>
> I dissolve in sounds · circling · weaving ·
> Filled with fathomless gratitude and ineffable praise
> Giving myself over without desire to the great breath.
> . . . .
> I feel that above the most distant cloud
>
> I am swimming in a sea of crystalline brilliance —
> I am merely a spark of the holy fire
> I am merely a rumble of the holy voice.

From now on, the final lines imply, the poet will be the instrument and mouthpiece of a power higher than himself. Indeed, he has taken on a sacred commission, become the vessel of a holy force, the first servant of a god.

How do we come to terms with all this? There seems little point in pursuing the question whether George really thought Maximilian Kronberger, or rather his poetic namesake, was actually divine. In purely categorical terms, Maxim certainly occupied a position in George's imagination that had been filled and then vacated numerous times before. As a generative force, as an absolute creative power, Maximin shares certain structural similarities with the

Christian God, to be sure, but also with George's earliest conception of poetry and, more crucially, of himself as poet. More specifically, the unnamed muse of the first poem in the *Hymns,* as well as the naked angel in *The Tapestry of Life,* were obvious early harbingers of this latest arrival. Yet, as with these two precursors, the central object, the overriding concern, was not so much with supernatural belief per se but with finding some means of bridging the gap between the evanescent realm of the mind and the concrete factuality of the here and now. Maximin, the ideated version of a real, flesh-and-blood boy, represented the first time that George had managed to usurp a significant part of the real world and make it his own in some material way. The death of Maximilian Kronberger, in other words, was the necessary sacrifice so that Maximin may live. And the very fact that Maximin "lived on" in the form George had given him, which was literally in and through George himself, seemed to be proof that George had finally conquered his oldest and most intractable foe: life itself. If Maximin is a god, then he is a god to a negative religion, not one based on everlasting life but one bent on its eradication, or at least on the substitution of life by its opposite.

Indirectly, George himself admitted as much. In 1911, four years after the publication of *The Seventh Ring,* where the poems dedicated to Maximin take pride of place in the center of the book, George said in a conversation that "*Algabal* and the *Seventh Ring* — that is the same substance, only spread out over a smaller surface." It is no accident that it is *Algabal* — George's most brazen assault on organic vitality, a book that would almost seem to emanate a perceptible chill were it not for all of the warm blood spilled so amply over its pages — that George claimed is closest in spirit to the temple he built to house his god.

It is also not coincidental that in the prose foreword to the first edition of the "memorial book" (*Gedenkbuch*) to Maximin, as a way of explaining the importance of his appearance, George delivered his most devastating attack yet on modern society. Beginning with words that self-consciously hark back to the opening lines of Dante's *Inferno,* George — who increasingly disliked saying "I" in print and preferred to use the more regal "we" — announced that, on the eve of meeting Maximin, "we had just passed the midday summit of our life and we had grown anxious over the prospect of our immediate future." The source of this distress is diffuse but pervasive: confronted by a "disfigured and pallid humanity," George says he looked in vain for some sign of "the great deed" or "great love" that would redeem the miserable creatures around him who were his fellow men. In vain: humanity as a whole had become trivialized, banal, flattened, and coarse. "Masses created law and rule," he writes, "impure hands rummaged in a pile of baubles in which true gems were randomly thrown." Given the degree of abstract generality here, it is difficult to know precisely what George was condemning, but it would probably not be wrong to think it was almost everything. However, matters had come to such a dire pass, he implied — or, in his words, "Reductive arrogance concealed confused impotence and insolent laughter presaged the destruction of the Sacred" — that the only possible remedy would have to be a drastic one. "We were mature enough not to protest any longer against the fateful return of necessary sufferings." Again, it is not easy to say exactly what George meant by "necessary sufferings," much less by their "fateful return." But a plausible reading would be that he had come to believe that the only solution to the ostensible corruption of humanity was the elimination of the unwholesome portion of it. Yet it turned out, George went on, that the situation was far worse than he had first imagined: "A pestilence now seemed to rage against which no cure could help and which would end in the lifelessness of this entire race." The extinction of large segments of humanity — however depraved it may be — was bad enough; what was worse is that George seemed to welcome it.

It does not take much imaginative stretching to see the connection between this expression of hatred for the perverted and flaccid "masses," together with the explicit wish that they be excised from the smaller but healthy core, and George's early sympathy with anarchism. In this way, too, the intellectual and political assumptions, and not just the literary ones, that underlay *Algabal* in 1891 still remained topical in George's mind fifteen years later. The difference is that, then, George had not seen any way out of the conflict and had fallen into a crisis that nearly did him in. Now the answer came in the form of a handsome young boy, who conveniently bore the sacrifice himself. Tellingly, however, the first words George used to describe Maximin's appearance in the preface emphasize his supposedly martial qualities: Maximin walked, we read, "with the unwavering firmness of a young fencer and with the expression of a commander's absolute power." Elsewhere, George extolled his "heroic soul," and in comparing himself to Maximin he says, "We were the victorious warriors of the offensive: he was chosen to be ruler." Similarly, when searching for some historical parallel for such greatness in one so young, the figure who comes first to his mind is Alexander the Great of Macedonia, who, George claims, first conceived of the "vast excursions that changed the appearance of our continents" as a mere youth.

It is was this, the perceived combination of beauty, youth, and explicitly physical power to which George willingly succumbed. That it was all largely a product of his own imagination, that he was in effect falling in love with an idealized portrait of himself, was not particularly worrisome; indeed, it was all the more attractive for that very reason. For it meant that Maximin was everything he himself had always wanted to be, and since Maximin was his own creation, in a certain sense George was thereby all of those things as well, now externalized and semi-independent of himself. Remarkably, George seems to have been aware of this identification with the object of his desire and gladly embraced its implications: "We recognized in him the representative of the omnipotent youth of which we had dreamed," he wrote, "with its unbroken wealth and purity that today still moves mountains and traverses water dry of foot — a youth that could assume our legacy and conquer new realms." The last clause is decisive. Fundamentally, George wanted to propagate himself, to provide heirs who would receive his bequest, who would continue his work beyond himself. The conventional, biological means of ensuring a succession was unattractive to him on any number of levels, but this only made the problem of his legacy more acute. The desire to surmount sterility, to reproduce himself, and the difficulty of doing so autonomously, had made itself felt before and been given various guises. His invention of Algabal's black flower, his flirtations with androgyny and hermaphrodism, and his so far unsuccessful attempts to find companions who would submit to his efforts to subsume them were all expressions of the same basic urge. Now, with Maximin, that urge appeared to have found both an outlet and a medium.

What is interesting is the change George said his discovery of Maximin had wrought on his view of the world. Ever since "this truly Divine One had entered our circles," he continued in the preface, "the entire workings of our thoughts and actions experienced a shift." The "oppressive present" lost its power over him, he rediscovered inner "calm," and he realized how "trivial all of the battles among countries" were and saw "how all of the burning questions for societies dissolve into insubstantial darkness when after every eternity a redeemer reveals himself to mortals." Naturally, Maximin's death initially caused him to feel "despair" at the thought that "we would never be permitted to touch these hands again that these lips would never kiss us again." But the voice of the departed one comes to him as if in a dream, instructing him that it was an "iron fate" that prescribed "the necessity of early death to the highest nobility." Therefore, George resolved to wipe away his "selfish tears" and remember Maximin in a way befitting the god he was, "not in the icy impervious majesty of death but in the victorious, resplendent glory of the festival · adorned and with the wreath of flowers in his hair · not an image of solitary patient renunciation but of smiling and radiant beauty."

In early January 1905, George returned to Munich for the first time since Maximilian Kronberger's death not quite a year before. After paying his respects at the boy's grave, he called on the parents and received in return Max's unpublished poems. He immediately sent them to Gundolf, along with a letter that made it clear to Gundolf that he had underestimated the impact of the whole phenomenon on his Master. Gundolf acknowledged that he understood both the gesture and his own mistake. "I had to cry again," he told George after receiving the package, "not just for your sake, my Dear, that you were allowed to find and then lose this, but also for mine, who all too quickly lied consolation to myself and will only slowly understand what a Divine thing crossed my path, I, who didn't deserve it and now too late! have to mourn for my blindness." Now that George could be certain that Gundolf was beginning to appreciate the importance of what had happened, he instructed Gundolf to write out a clean copy of all of the poems he had composed in the aftermath of the death. To these were added some of Max's own poems and several by Wolfskehl, as well as some verses by two poets on the periphery named Lothar Treuge and Oskar Dietrich, and several by Gundolf himself. In April, after Gundolf had assembled all of the parts and made sure everything was in place, he dutifully sent the entire manuscript to Lechter.

With the book dedicated to Maximin out of his hands and off his mind, George could turn to other things. But first he needed to recuperate from the emotional strain of the last several months. In late June 1905, he headed for Switzerland, where he was to spend the rest of the summer. After a few weeks in Schaffhausen, where he stayed at the house of Wiesi de Haan, Karl Wolfskehl's sister-in-law, George was joined by his own sister, Anna, and then by Sabine Lepsius and her two children. George had found an inn, the only one, in the tiny village of Gadenstätt in the sparsely populated southern canton of Graubünden. Gundolf also arrived in late July, accompanied by his brother Ernst — now humorously called Gundolf II — and together they undertook long excursions through the Alps. Sabine Lepsius, who remembered having been frightened by being with George in a natural setting before, saw things now in a different light. "On a forest path, alone with George, I felt how much he belonged in this nature that was not idyllic," she wrote. "Among shaggy firs or bare rocks, next to dangerous ravines and plunging streams he seemed to be a mountain kobold — like the human expression of this impervious nature, which despite its barrenness allows the blue gentian to flower."

Even while on holiday, George, who for years now had never lived anywhere for more than a few months or even weeks at a time, and usually for less, could not stay put. "Instead of remaining another 3–4 days in ONE place," George wrote in a rare postcard to his father, "we wandered around." On foot, he and his companions traversed Sertig (near the resort of Davos, whose famed sanatorium would inspire Thomas Mann's *Magic Mountain* a few years later), on through Thusis, Walensee, and all the way to Zürich. If not exactly restful, the Swiss journey was at least distracting, and in that way appeared to fulfill its primary purpose. Mainly, it added physical distance to the growing temporal divide separating him from the sorrows of the previous year. In September, after briefly checking in at home in Bingen, George set out as usual for Berlin.

As we know, George had never found the Prussian capital very inviting, but now there was an additional reason for it to seem even less appealing than usual. Almost two years had gone by since the Cosmic Circle had burst apart, but Ludwig Klages still refused to go away. In the 1904 issue of the *Blätter,* which had been planned before their estrangement, George had included a collective photographic portrait of several of the contributing poets and other associates, among them a photograph of Klages. Worse still, Gundolf had used a few lines from one of Klages's poems as an epigraph to one of his own. In neither case had anyone bothered to get Klages's permission; it would not have occurred to anyone to do so. With the intention of either materially harming or simply embarrassing George, or both, Klages filed a lawsuit for copyright infringement. It was an absurd affair, but Klages pursued it with a grim tenacity. In April 1905, George and Gundolf were informed by the Attorney General of the Regional Court of Berlin that the suit was being acted upon. In November, the case was brought before a judge and Klages held a "flaming speech" denouncing the "betrayal of Cosmic secrets." Whatever the judge privately thought about "cosmic secrets" or their revelation, Klages won his case on copyright violation — the matter of the photograph was put aside — and the judge fined George and Gundolf fifty marks each. The two malfeasants had not given Klages the satisfaction of personally showing up in court and were represented in their absence by Paul Jonas, an attorney who worked for George's publisher. Jonas performed his professional duty by promptly appealing the verdict, but in July 1906, the appeal was rejected, and the ludicrous episode finally came to an end.

As it turned out, the public trial — gleefully snatched up by Berlin journalists who either misunderstood or willfully distorted the nature of the dispute — bore unexpected fruit. A nineteen-year-old admirer named Ernst Morwitz, a native of Danzig, had just been reading George's works and providentially discovered through one of the newspaper articles about the trial that the poet lived in Bingen. The letter Morwitz wrote to him in August 1905 laid the foundation for a friendship that lasted until George's death more than a quarter century later. Morwitz was monkish, taciturn, and, as his name presaged, earnest to the point of a dull sobriety — George teasingly called him "the mollusk" because of his closed reserve. But George also knew he could rely utterly on him — and did. Morwitz, who became a successful lawyer in Berlin, was one of George's chief legal advisors in later years. After 1933, Morwitz, who was a Jew, fled to the United States and there continued his work as a staunch defender of George's legacy. He devoted the rest of his long life to detailed if rather stodgy interpretations of every work George wrote; he published equally turgid but well-meaning translations of his poems into English; and in 1971, at the age of eighty-four, Ernst Morwitz returned to Minusio in Switzerland to die — where his Master also lies buried.

Perhaps the catastrophic losses of the previous year had made George feel the need to replenish his stock, or perhaps it was simply a coincidental increase, but 1905 turned out to be a banner year for recruiting new blood to the cause. In addition to Morwitz, that year also brought him the acquaintance of a twenty-year-old German-speaking Swabian named Robert Boehringer, then residing in Basel and a friend of Hans Oettinger, who was a distant cousin of Friedrich Gundolf. In May, Gundolf reported to George that Boehringer was said to be "very intelligent and pleasant, a little theatrical, and most of the citizens of Basel think he's insane." For three years, Boehringer had been applying himself to almost nothing but the reading of poems by Stefan George, often scanning them silently to himself and just as often reciting them out loud, to the point where the people around him were becoming, as he put it, "impatient" with his obsession. One evening when Boehringer returned home from an outing, his brother casually mentioned that "Stefan George was here." For Boehringer, this was the same as saying "the Emperor stopped by," or "the Lord just paid a visit." Boehringer insisted this was impossible: his brother must be mistaken. Stefan George did not simply go up to a house, pull the bell and visit an unknown twenty-year-old student; in fact, he did not visit anyone at all! "He was here," his brother calmly assured him, "and he had a pair of gloves in his hand."

Although his relationship with George would not be as intimate or unclouded as Morwitz's was, Boehringer became even more important in preserving his memory. For, in time, it was he who became the Master's legal heir, giving him full control over George's estate and all of his papers. Tenacious, politically stainless, and unwaveringly loyal, Boehringer made it his mission after George's death and especially after World War Two, to obtain any piece of information, especially unpublished manuscripts, related to George and his friends, a task made considerably easier by Boehringer's substantial personal fortune. For the rest of his life — he also lived to be a very old man, dying over the age of ninety in 1975 — Boehringer tirelessly devoted himself to the maintenance of George's reputation, editing and publishing the correspondences between George and some of the most important people in his life, including Hofmannsthal and Gundolf. In addition, he published his own biographical study of George in 1951 — modestly called "My Image of Stefan George" — that was the most factual and detailed study of the poet to date. And he oversaw the creation of the archive now located in the state library of Baden-Württemberg in Stuttgart that houses the largest collection of materials in existence concerning the poet.

But for Boehringer it was all a labor of love, made even more remarkable by the fact that he assumed this lifelong commitment in 1905, at the very beginning of their acquaintance, when he was only twenty. On Christmas eve of that year, after receiving a copy of George's monumental *The Tapestry of Life* from the poet himself, Boehringer wrote to convey his thanks for the present. "That you consider me worthy of this precious gift makes me very happy and will help me in difficult hours," he told George, and then he made a solemn pledge: "Let this be my motto for the next and coming years: to belong to you and to receive my life from you insofar as you want to give it to me." In essence, in return for George's gift, Boehringer offered him the greatest one he had to give — himself. Boehringer even made the extraordinary promise that "I am prepared to sacrifice friends and what is dear to me if you demand it. My desire is to be loyal like Gundolf." More astonishing perhaps than the vow itself is that over the span of seven decades Boehringer never broke it.

There were still other additions to George's circle of friends in the bountiful year of 1905. After the turn of the century, Kurt Breysig, a prolific, polymath historian who taught at the University of Berlin, sometimes hosted George during his autumn residences in the capital and introduced the poet to some of his more gifted students. One of them, Berthold Vallentin, had already met George at Breysig's home in 1902 — Vallentin, born in 1877, was thus twenty-five at the time — but they did not begin to have regular contact until the summer of 1904. Like Morwitz and many other friends of George, Vallentin had also studied law, and for several years he served as the district court judge in the provincial town of Spremberg, returning to his native Berlin to work as an attorney just before the war. An excellent Latinist with a penchant for the late Roman period, he often mischievously wrote his judgments in Roman legal language.

Berthold Vallentin's real life, however, took place outside of chambers. Besides attending to his professional duties, Vallentin also managed to write a fair amount of poetry and several substantial books — a mammoth study of Napoleon came out in 1923 and in 1931 he produced a monograph on the great German philhellene, Johann Joachim Winckelmann, both of which were published with George's imprimatur at his publisher, Georg Bondi — and he still had time to devote himself to an active social life. Vallentin was a physically large man, tending slightly toward corpulence. But he possessed an almost demonic level of energy, demonstrating a liveliness and vigor belying a person of his girth. Unlike the front guard of the circle, he relished the momentum of Berlin and it was a rare theater opening, art exhibit, or important social event where one did not spot Vallentin's stocky frame roving about among the crowd. Nor did he neglect enthusiastic investigations of Berlin's demimonde: indeed, he met his future wife, Diana Rabinowicz, when she was an actress and going by the lubricious stage name of Fanny Ritter. Although he was thoroughly urban in his tastes and manners, Vallentin was also known to set out spontaneously on brisk extended marches through the countryside surrounding the city. Wealthy, cosmopolitan, and a jovial *bon viveur,* Vallentin cultivated some flamboyant tics as well. He favored large capes and broad-brimmed hats, often sported a monocle or a black-rimmed pince-nez, which together with his long, black sideburns gave him an exotic, almost foreign air. When he once attended one of Gundolf's lectures, an observer thought he looked more like a "sheik or sultan" than a Prussian civil servant. Although Vallentin was not the man to display the kind of patient, still devotion that either Morwitz or Boehringer showed George, he, too, remained a faithful adherent of the *Meister* until Vallentin's premature death in March 1933, at the age of fifty-six.

Another student of Breysig was Friedrich Wolters, a close friend of Vallentin and his senior by half a year. In December 1905 Wolters wrote his first letter to George and before long he became part of the inner circle, where he stayed for the rest of his life. Like Vallentin, Friedrich Wolters was equipped with a stout figure, and also like his friend he possessed a seemingly inexhaustible vitality. At fifty he was still an avid sportsman, often joining in on ball games, noted as an impassioned swimmer and, when he did not have to adjust his pace for a companion who was older or infirm, he would forge ahead at a challenging clip. But to a far greater degree than Vallentin, who was more easily distracted by earthly pursuits, Wolters totally threw himself in the service of Stefan George. In 1909, he published a frothy, miasmic essay in the *Blätter* that could be said to have established the leitmotif for the rest of his life. Called "Sovereignty and Service," it projected the existence of a "Spiritual Empire" presided over by an absolute "Ruler" who enjoys the unquestioning veneration and obedience of his subjects. Over the next two decades, Wolters enacted what he had abstractly envisioned, focusing his talents, hopes, and prodigious energies on explaining and magnifying the meaning of George to the world. Wolters was perhaps the most militant of George's followers, the most radical in his national commitments, and the one most interested in the political ramifications of their shared ideology. It was Wolters who first used the word "state," borrowed from Plato, as a synonym for the group of people around George. And, principally thanks to Wolters's efforts, as time went by, the boundaries separating the "spiritual state" gathered around George from the real one seemed more and more permeable as well. Just before his untimely death following a heart attack in 1930, Wolters completed what he regarded as his chef d'oeuvre, the large-scale biography of George with the subtitle claiming that he represented the "History of the German Spirit since 1890." That same year, the National Socialist party achieved its first major victory in an election. Commenting on this coincidence, George is recorded as having said, "Wolters's seeds have sprouted." Although it was apparently meant as a rejection — George never fully shared Wolters's blinkered nationalism — it nevertheless signaled an awareness on George's part that there was, or could be, a causal connection between the activities of a political party and his own followers.

The death of Maximilian Kronberger, but also the strife within the Cosmic Circle and the final realization that Hofmannsthal would never be the ally, much less the friend, that George needed or wanted, had thus all perhaps indirectly served as a stimulus in other ways. In the aftermath of these considerable defeats, George had managed to assemble the group of people who would henceforth form the core members and mainstays of his coterie. In the future, there would always be new additions, defections, banishments, shifts of alignment and, above all, terrible losses caused by the war. But from now on, although exerting varying degrees of influence and enjoying fluctuating degrees of favor with the Master, the three main players within George's arena would be Wolfskehl, Gundolf, and Wolters. And over the next three decades it would principally be these figures with which the public would associate the mysterious and increasingly formidable phenomenon known as the George circle.

CHAPTER 24

The Seventh Ring

For a while in 1904 it had seemed that the disasters would never end. In his letters, Gundolf had taken to calling it, somewhat overdramatically, the "year of misfortune" — *das Unheilsjahr*. Hyperbole aside, it did sometimes seem that luck had permanently turned against them. As if the cup were not full to overflowing already, Karl Wolfskehl's sister, Margarete von Preuschen, fell seriously ill and died later that summer; both of Wolfskehl's daughters and his wife contracted a contagious fever they initially feared was typhoid; and Melchior Lechter, while vacationing on the island of Elba off the Italian coast, came down with an infectious form of arthritis that threatened to leave him totally paralyzed. To Wolfskehl, this series of deaths, illnesses, and the general air of adversity were no simple coincidence but clear signs of deliberate subterfuge. He became convinced that the unbroken string of calamities formed part of a sinister plot, and that Klages and Schuler in particular were somehow behind it. Gundolf, ever the more levelheaded of the two, pleaded with Wolfskehl's wife to try to talk her husband out of these "obsessions." It was just as crazy, Gundolf argued, to believe that either Klages or Schuler had such power as it had been to believe in the whole Cosmic lunacy itself, "as if overheated ideologues could ever become doers of deeds and as if an embittered omnipotent opponent, whether he be called Cosmos or Moloch, could employ a compliant fate against him." Yet Wolfskehl was not so easily persuaded. Only after he had spent most of August under the treatment and observation of Dr. Oskar Kohnstamm, an old school friend who had established a psychiatric practice in Königstein outside of Frankfurt, did Wolfskehl begin slowly to change his mind. In late August, Gundolf told George that he had seen "Karl" in Königstein and was happy to report that their friend had already made visible progress. "Hopefully this improvement will last," Gundolf rather speculatively offered, especially "as concerns the disbelief in magic."

A year later, everything, and not just Wolfskehl's agnosticism, appeared to be on the mend. (Just to be on the safe side, though, Wolfskehl continued to carry around the loaded pistol in his pocket until he had the accident in early 1906.) It was thus not only with genuine pleasure but also with no little relief that Gundolf was able to tell Wolfskehl in September 1905 about all of the new additions to George's stable. "The Master" — George now rarely wrote his letters himself, dictating them instead to Gundolf or to another ready scribe and appending only his signature in his own hand — "also does not want to withhold from you the pleasant news that recently he has been sensing a stirring and teeming from various directions consisting of letters, parcels, etc., which after the gradually thawed stagnation of late will offer agreeable hopes and material for the coming year." No doubt under instructions from George, who liked to keep things on a more general plane in letters, the normally garrulous Gundolf specifically mentioned only one person, and even then without revealing his name, saying only that George "found the notion very pleasant that a young Poet from his own, if distant clan" had recently appeared on the scene.

The reference was to one Saladin Schmitt, a cousin of George three times removed on his mother's side. Schmitt was studying in Bonn and writing a dissertation on the nineteenth-century dramatist Friedrich Hebbel. But, deeply dissatisfied with academic literary history and criticism, Schmitt had turned to George for something his professors did not, and perhaps could not, give him. In his first letter to George, he had included a few lines of verse he had written and naively asked, "Master, is this a poem?" Schmitt wanted to know if it demonstrated sufficient merit to justify his wish to become a full-time writer. George evasively praised the "height of its tone," but he encouraged Schmitt to send him more of his poetry and even to visit him in Bingen. In time, George did publish some of Schmitt's verse in the *Blätter* and for several years he enjoyed a regular intimacy with the Master. In acknowledgement of his gratitude, Schmitt later returned the favor by introducing George to a university friend, Ernst Bertram.

But Saladin Schmitt was only one among a steadily growing number of talented and bright young men such as Morwitz, Vallentin, Boehringer, and Wolters who were being attracted to George. After the fallow period that had descended following the events in Munich, George had every reason to believe that things truly were looking up again. Poetically it had been, understandably enough, an unproductive period for him. But even in private terms he had appeared to have withdrawn into a prolonged and mystifying silence. Some of his older friends complained that he was even less forthcoming about himself than ever before. Sabine Lepsius, for instance, perhaps sensing the widening estrangement between them that in fact soon led to their permanent separation, pressed him for details about his life, about his whereabouts and his thoughts, indicating she felt he was unfairly shutting her out. In April 1905, George sent a response that was meant to explain his relative impassiveness but did not fulfill her demand for the information she wanted; indeed, he warned her that she should expect to receive even less. After loftily informing her that he had only just returned to "my seat" — that is, to Bingen — "after many uncertain paths," George turned to the issue at hand. "Why should I report to all of my friends about the dangerous abysses that accompany all of my journeys?" he wanted to know, "and particularly about the especially terrible most recent ones — while they my friends can do nothing other than stand by helplessly in sympathetic distance . . . Is there anything that saves us from the worst when we despair except that no one knows of it? — I cannot live my life except in the most perfect external sovereignty. What I struggle for and suffer and bleed is for no one to know. But everything I do is also for my friends. To see me as they saw me is the greatest consolation in their life. Thus I struggle and endure and remain silent for them as well. I repeatedly go to the most extreme limits — what I give is the maximum possible . . . even when no one suspects it."

It is, for all of George's protestations to the contrary, quite an informative statement. For one thing, it reveals a greater degree of overt self-stylization than we have witnessed in him previously. He had, as we know, always been more than prepared to accept — or assert — his unique status among mortals. Here, however, the vocabulary of his singularity has reached unprecedented dimensions, with the added novelty of portraying his actions as the performance of a stoic self-sacrifice for the sake of others. Granted that his reasons for keeping his sufferings to himself seem more than valid — that in our sorrows as in our joys we are essentially alone and that the most others can really do is bear compassionate witness to our experiences but cannot in any meaningful way "share" them, much less truly assuage them — the main point of his argument lies elsewhere. While this is not necessarily an uncommon attitude for an artist to adopt, George intended his stance to encompass more than his poetry. He was implicitly claiming that not just his work but his whole existence constituted a selfless act to which he submitted for the good of his friends who, so he says, derived benefit not only from his labors but moreover from their ignorance of how much the effort cost him. This is obviously no longer the language of a poet speaking about fellow poets. The echoes of Jesus's words that he was sent to suffer so that we should be spared are distinctly audible and no doubt deliberate. But this was no mere affectation on George's part. He had always believed that he could give something of extraordinary value to those around him. The difference now was that he was consciously shifting the source of that value from his poetry to his person.

Given this change in the way George had begun to view himself and his role, it seems only natural that he now concentrated ever more on collecting new "friends" and reconnecting with certain old ones. What is less easy to understand is why these people so readily endorsed his increasingly overt assumption of a quasi-messianic status. Yet they did, and in many cases they appeared to be trying to outdo one another in their expressions of faith in George's exceptionalness.

We remember that Gundolf was not fully restored to George's good graces until early 1904, and in short order he was again assuring his Master that "every day I feel more that you are the only stable point in my life and its entire content flows through you." But Gundolf was far from alone in voicing such sentiments. After a three-year absence, the English composer Cyril Scott reemerged in November 1904. Somehow Scott had found out which way the wind was now blowing, and he composed an obsequious letter asking George "to accept me again in the celestial domain of your acquaintanceship," emphasizing that "you stand as the very greatest human being I have known." Apparently thinking that this was not quite enough, Scott added for good measure that "you [are] the noblest, greatest, and most wonderful of not only Artists but men."

Nevertheless, not wanting the nature of his esteem to be misunderstood, Scott made sure to address — tactfully — the question that had originally forced them apart. He hoped that George would agree with him "that a platonic admiration and love is the most flattering thing it were possible to have — one being for another — ." This, we may remind ourselves, is from someone who referred to George's evident homosexuality as his "friend's abnormalities." But Scott also assured George that he believed that "in comparison to the ephemeral sentiments one might entertain for a woman," the sort of attachment he had in mind "stands so infinitely higher in the scale of human emotions that I become more and more impregnated with the saying of Mallarmé 'that the friendship of one great man is worth the love of ten women.'"

Whether George was won over by the argument or simply curious, he agreed to see Scott again. The Englishman retained a vivid memory of the encounter. "It was a very cold winter's evening that I was shown into his sanctum, where I had to wait — feeling distinctly nervous — before he appeared. When he did at last appear, instead of coming forward into the center of the room where I was standing, he sat down very slowly on the extreme edge of a chair by the door, and making a wry face, contemplated me with an inscrutable expression. As he obviously did not propose to shake hands, I could merely, without the usual form of greeting, express my appreciation of his kindness in considering to receive me." Put somewhat off balance by this odd reception, Scott tried to make small talk about how the years had changed them both, "and I remember that he pointed to a broad streak of white which had appeared in his leonine mane, and which he told me was due to a bereavement he had sustained in Munich." It was only after Scott mentioned he had brought with him some translations of George's poetry into English that the Master become less severe. George, thinking the samples were quite good, asked who the translator was, not knowing that it was Scott himself. When Scott hedged and stuttered something about having to obtain permission from the author before revealing his name, George gave "me a playful slap on the cheek; 'Scoundrel!' " he said, "You translated them yourself!" And with the ice finally broken, their relationship rekindled and they saw one another off and on until the war began.

Apart from fishing for men and gradually recovering from assorted "bereavements," George was not completely idle. To begin with, the seventh number of the *Blätter für die Kunst* had come out in early 1904, the one that contained the lines of verse and the photograph that had sent Klages running to the courts. But even though this issue of the *Blätter* had been in the works before the upheavals of that year had begun, it bore unmistakable signs of the Cosmic troubles. Unlike the immediately preceding issue of the journal, the seventh installment returned to the practice of introducing the poetic works with belligerent apodictic maxims. One of them seems clearly minted — clear, that is, to the initiated — in response to the turmoil in Schwabing. It is almost identical to the veiled warning George had placed on Wolfskehl's desk in 1901, implying that Wolfskehl should not mistake the real thing — that is, George himself and what he represented — with some cheap counterfeit. Titled, approximately, "Fantasts of the Primeval Source" (the untranslatable original German word, which George coined, is *Urgrundschwärmer*), it cautions its readers not to "set an idol in place of God a ghost in place of Spirit a witch in place of the Seer." Another maxim perhaps takes oblique aim at the Cosmics' wish to use art as a vehicle for promoting their own attempt at heathen renewal. Ironically called "Merely-Art," it derides the tendency to measure art by standards outside of itself, thus denying art the freedom given to every other human activity, namely, "to become perfect in itself." Yet another contrasts the art produced in northern and southern Europe and claims that the difference between the two lies "in the soul" of their respective creators. "The northern person has the soul of the bourgeoisie that grows stronger in protestantism · the southern an aristocratic and heroic soul: that of catholicism." Klages, who was both from the north and a Protestant, may have recognized himself in this intentionally unflattering juxtaposition, just as he was the target of the tart if not exactly withering observation made in another aphorism to the effect that "conceptual aestheticians remain barbarians."

Mainly, however, as this last maxim demonstrates, the objects of attack conform to a familiar pattern. Germany and German culture come in for their usual lumps, as do "the masses" and — once more for good measure — the "mawkish bourgeoisie." On the more positive side, there is also the effort to defend the idea of the circle itself, and its supporting structure of disciples surrounding a dominant master, from external criticism. One aphorism, principally devoted to describing the relationship between "The Artist and his Time" — not surprisingly, this relationship is said to be best when the former completely rejects the latter, rendering "the intellectual and artistic person" in a state of "total detachment from the general public" — addresses the issue of the circle but only tangentially. It makes the claim, arguable but revealing, that "every fruitful · every liberating idea has come out of secret circles (cenacles)." This is not the first time the word "secret" had appeared in connection with the idea of the circle around George, but it was the first time it had been used positively. In November 1903 but bearing the publication date of 1904, a catalogue was issued listing all available titles that had appeared so far under the banner of the *Blätter für die Kunst*. The catalogue opened with the general statement that "society of the *Blätter für die Kunst* which some have erroneously seen as a secret association is only a loose collection of artists and aesthetic people." Quite apart from the accuracy of this self-description, it appears that in the meantime the members of the "society of the *Blätter für die Kunst*," whether viewed as a formal association or merely as a loose collection of like-minded poets, had decided that being a "secret" organization was not so bad after all.

Yet the members of the *Blätter für die Kunst* now wanted to be thought of as forming not just a secret society, as opposed to the all-too-public one they despised, but as representing a distinctly better one as well. In one of the introductory dictums, titled "Hero Worship (Cult of Personality)," the idea of the circle, understood explicitly as a social structure with a well-defined purpose and unity, is held up as a superior alternative to the aimless aggregations of otherwise disconnected people thrown together by chance, which they felt typified the modern world. Evoking ancient, more heroic eras in which statues were erected not solely to kings and generals but even to victorious boxers, it contemptuously concludes, "How high do they tower over a sullenly egotistical time that finds fault with disciples bowing in reverence before the master." Again, in light of the deliberately nonspecific rhetorical style of the

Blätter's utterances, it is difficult to say with complete certainty what precisely prompted this new outburst. But one thing is clear: the circle, composed of a single "master" and reverential followers, was being presented more and more as not simply an artistic fraternity but rather as a viable and superlative form of social order compared to the muddle and dross of the present.

This was a momentous step: having articulated and embodied the idea of the circle as no more — but also as no less — than a group of poets for almost a decade, George and his followers now seemed prepared to make the leap into the deeper waters of cultural and political efficacy. True, they had often toyed with the prospect of direct action in the past, and it had always been an implicit undertone in all of the *Blätter*'s criticisms of contemporary German affairs, just as a head-on confrontation with reality had increasingly arisen into an overt goal in George's own poetry. But that was precisely the point: before, George and the *Blätter* had little more than a negative program to offer, and even then it had been mainly confined to questions about poetry and art. Now, for the first time, they seemed about to extend something approaching a concrete, realizable program, one that promised not just the limited objective of providing a new way of making art but, more ambitiously, a new way of living in the world.

Or, perhaps it would be better to say, living against the world. The last maxim of the *Blätter* considers the related roles, as the aphorism is titled, of the "Artist and Warrior." It displays in vintage form that deep ambivalence about participating in a detested world which had been a central element of the *Blätter*'s posture, and of George's character, all along. "Never did the masses rule as today," it states, "never therefore [was] the deed of an individual so futile · no doubt one can imagine times and opportunities in which the Artist also considers it necessary to seize the sword of battle: but he stands above all these convulsions of the world state and society as a guardian of the eternal fire." As an expression of some real intention, much less as a helpful guideline for action, the message would appear self-contradictory to the point of nonsense — in addition to being numbingly vague. Since the world, it seems to say, is no longer governed by strong, heroic leaders but by the faceless throng, overpowering in its number and its brute mindless agency, any "deed" performed by an individual agent acting alone is as doomed as the gesture of someone who wants to stop the wind by extending his hand. This would seem to be a veiled argument for the necessity of a collective, a "circle," of confederates, who might be better able to accomplish what a single person could not. But then it is the individual, solitary "Artist" who is extolled, the mighty "Warrior" could carry aloft the "sword of battle," presumably to cut down the swarms of riffraff who get in the way of great things. Then, however, there is another about-face, and the artist is said to have nothing to do with such lowly concerns as, for instance, the "world," since he is much too occupied with tending the "eternal fire" — whatever that might be.

It was the same old problem: George knew that he could never achieve his objectives — however unfocused and unconscious they may have been — without the assistance of others. Yet he wanted to preserve his own absolute autonomy while still maintaining unqualified control over his associates and the sphere in which they all moved. Loathe to relinquish any authority, and thus power, to his subordinates, George had to convince them that it was to everyone's benefit if he, and he alone, triumphed. At the same time, and complicating this already delicate balance, the struggle they were engaged in was paradoxical to an extreme degree. The *Blätter für die Kunst,* conceived as an esoteric journal of poetry, originally founded to combat, at most, naturalism and "bad taste," had somehow metamorphosed, at least in its contributors' eyes, into a polemical weapon of social change. How the *Blätter,* with its miniscule print run and its jealously managed distribution only to a "closed circle" of invited readers, would accomplish that gargantuan task was anyone's guess. Even more perplexing was exactly what the change they proposed might look like. In some respects, George, like a true anarchist, cared little about what came after him. In 1909, he said in a conversation that "the moment when something that has been created begins to spread, his interest in it ceases. Then he has to think of something new. His task had been only to take things up to this boundary and no further." But if George and the *Blätter* regulars were unambiguous about one thing, it was their profound hatred for just about everything that was synonymous with modernity. There seemed to be no point of overlap, no room for compromise: it was either one or the other, with no middle ground. George was not a reformer. He did not want incremental improvements or progressive adjustments to the standing order. He was a radical who sought nothing less than the complete overthrow of things as they were, and if necessary their total destruction. What came after was of secondary concern. So far, the world could afford to ignore George, and largely it did. And while George could not entirely ignore the world, he did urgently want large parts of it to go away.

At the beginning of November 1906, after numerous delays related to Melchior Lechter's continuing poor health and even worse bouts of procrastination, the invitation was sent out for subscriptions to *Maximin,* which was scheduled to appear the following month. It was a lavish, rich production, befitting the commemoration of the god it proclaimed Maximin to be. The elaborately ornamented title page depicts two peacocks on each side holding in their beaks a garland that passes through a central crown which surmounts a stylized flower. There are also two figures portrayed, both naked, placed in little boxes just below the title words. One, the younger of the two, is crouched and is absently, perhaps mournfully playing what looks to be either a shawm or a flute. The other, who bears a striking resemblance to George, is winged like an angel and holds a lyre; kneeling, he appears to be gazing up in reverence to the name, "Maximin," emblazoned in large red majuscules at the top of the page. On the facing sheet is the photograph, though left unidentified, of Maximilian Kronberger in profile with bare shoulders and arms, holding a wooden staff and wearing a wreath of laurel.

By January 8, in only a matter of weeks, all two hundred copies had been snapped up. On that day, George reported to Gundolf that he was already receiving word from various quarters about "the M book." The publisher — since the first edition was still "private," it had not been Bondi who officially published it, but the printer Holten — was being besieged by a "storm of [book] dealers." But, as George smugly put it, they would all have to beat a retreat "before the gate of out-of-printness." He was especially gratified — or relieved — by the reaction from Maximilian's parents, who he had made sure got a copy of the volume. "What particularly pleased me," he told Gundolf, "were the thanks from Munich, which dispelled my little fears: What bearing and dignity from the hearts of such simple people!" Of course, it is probable that it was precisely because they were relatively simple people and would not have believed, had they understood, what George had done to their son that they were so ready to offer their undoubtedly sincere thanks. More eloquent were George's initial apprehensions about their response, for he knew better than anyone else that in his own heart he was far from innocent.

The main event of the year, however, was another work that, as George had done with Maximilian Kronberger, incorporated the poetic memorial to Maximin within itself, absorbing it to form an even greater, more complex entity. Massive, daunting, unwieldy, *The Seventh Ring,* published at the end of 1907, is George's largest and most elaborate book, his most grandiose canvas, the most daring pitch he had yet made for poetic conquest. In purely artistic terms, it is also perhaps his greatest failure. Its shortcomings were something even George himself, in his own fashion, recognized and admitted. "Life already seemed tamed in the *Tapestry,*" he later said to one of his friends, but "in the *Seventh Ring* chaos breaks out again anew, the way life is." Nowhere near as unified in formal composition and theme as his earlier or subsequent works, *The Seventh Ring* also traverses a vast psychological range, fluctuating wildly between lines drenched with unfettered sexual longing to others exuding an icy contempt for humanity; interspersed are poems that eulogize great historical figures, such as Dante, Nietzsche, Boecklin, Empress Elisabeth, and Pope Leo XIII, and others that evoke a mythical, dehistoricized world peopled by generic kings, princes, leaders — *Führer* — and roving Knights Templar. The book as a whole reminds one (it is a comparison George would have liked) of the shattered Greek temples at Selinunte or Agrigento: jumbled piles of mammoth stone blocks that convey both the horrifically violent forces that shook them to their foundations and yet at the same time, still visible through the chaotic heaps of wrecked columns and broken pediments, the faint traces of the original, intended structure. Rudolf Borchardt, a contemporary critic, and someone who was not wholly well-disposed toward him, wrote, "The *Seventh Ring* is in every respect George's most powerful book." That is unquestionably true. It is also his least benign, with much of that power emanating from the seething cauldron of black emotions that had been so far been given only indirect expression and moving them out into the open: the cold animus, the disdainful revulsion brought about by the modern world, coupled with the desire to dominate it or, since it was probably too foul to be saved, to see it largely annihilated, and to begin anew over the ashes of its ruin.

Not all of the poems in *The Seventh Ring* are so resolutely grim. In addition to the poems dedicated to Maximin, which form the physical and conceptual center of the book, George also included the collection of verses he had sent to Gundolf for his twenty-second birthday in 1902. Admittedly, both chart the doomed course of the poet's love, tracing relationships that in each case, although for different reasons, end in bitter loss and dejected misery. But along the way, both cycles do contain verses of rapturous joy, celebrating the experience of love as a heightening and intensification of existence itself. Throughout *The Seventh Ring,* in fact, there are many contrasting moments of intense physical abandon — there are far more evocations of nakedness and its aftermath in *The Seventh Ring* than in any other of his works — and simple, melodic poems, almost folk ditties, praising in unadorned language the changing of seasons or the gentle bounty of nature, which serve to offset somewhat the prevailing atmosphere of violence and gloom. There is also an entire section devoted to portraits of friends, past and present — although here, too, one has to remind oneself that George's poetic portraits were at best two-sided affairs, resembling most often entombments. The book ends with a series of poems that amount to a kind of poetic reappropriation of Germany itself. Most have titles taken from the names of German cities — Worms, Bonn, Aachen, Hildesheim, Quedlinburg, Munich, Bamberg, Darmstadt, Weimar, and Jena are all represented — and each isolates a particular moment in their history or some significant monument they house as a way of reclaiming them and repossessing them as his own. There is also a series of poems devoted to the Rhine, perhaps in belated realization of the ambition George had announced to Albert Verwey in 1899. Taken as a whole, *The Seventh Ring* is thus a summation, a recapitulation of George's poetic itinerary thus far, bringing together the diverse strands within a massive miscellany. But for that very reason it also makes the impression in parts of a bulging conglomerate, a seemingly random hodgepodge of unrelated poems expressing wildly contradictory aims and desires. Often the whole book feels as if it is ready to burst apart at the seams.

Partly holding it all together, at least in theory, are the pseudonumerological underpinnings of the book. Much earnest head-scratching has taken place over the significance of the title, beginning with the banal observation that, as George's seventh work and appearing in the year 1907, that number seemed a logical choice. Others have more imaginatively speculated that it may refer to the seventh ring of Dante's Paradiso, or perhaps to the number of letters in Maximin's name, or may simply reflect the fact that the book is composed of seven individual components. Least convincing, and wholly unconnected to anything in the book itself, is Ernst Morwitz's suggestion that the title "refers to the rings in the cross sections of trees." No one seems, however, to have yet stumbled on — or chosen to disclose — one of George's most likely sources and points of reference: namely, the bible of the Cosmic Circle, Bachofen's *Matriarchy*. Bachofen, predisposed to divining deep historical meaning in symbolic values, saw in the number seven nothing less than the epitome of the victorious male, or father, principle over the mother right, which he claimed was represented by the appropriately antecedent number five: "The victory of the father principle over the mother principle can be called a victory of the seven over the five." Beginning his demonstration with Apollo — not incidentally, the god of music, prophecy and poetry — Bachofen points out that on the seventh day of the month the singing swans of Pactolus circled the island of Delos seven times and before the eighth circuit began, Apollo's mother, Leto, had brought the sun god into the world. To commemorate this event, the boy Apollo later put seven strings on his lyre. Based on such indisputable evidence, Bachofen saw confirmation of the parallel between male supremacy and the number seven everywhere, reminding us that there are seven planets corresponding to seven celestial spheres in ancient cosmography; that God, the Holy Father himself, rested on the seventh day at the conclusion of his labors; that there are seven hills in Rome, the seat of the male law and rule. In short, Bachofen wrote, we recognize in the "number seven the principle of the father right and the idea of political power based on the *patria potestas* as opposed to the maternal law of the earth and of the lunar five and have found that the most intimate connection was categorically expressed among the concepts of solar empire, cosmic harmony and intellectual perfection." Among other things, then, *The Seventh Ring* glorifies the final ascendancy within George's own "ring," or circle, of the male principle.

One can easily imagine why George's advocates were not especially anxious to place him back into such company, particularly since by 1907 George was supposed to have definitively put his Cosmic past behind him. Yet many of the poems, and specifically the most forceful opening verses in the first section of the book condemning the modern world, were written well before the Cosmic breakup had occurred and had appeared in the three issues of the *Blätter* that came out in 1900–1901, 1902–3 and 1904. Yet the presence of the Cosmic ambiance throughout much of *The Seventh Ring* is irrefutable. One of the most striking examples of it is the neopaganistic poem "Solstice Procession," which reads like a poetic transmutation of one of the "Jours" at Wolfskehl's apartment in Schwabing. It describes how, during a nocturnal indoor celebration, the "smoking basins" lighting the interior scene and the sultry air within the apartment create an unbearable heat in the room, making the walls and floor "drip" with moisture. Suddenly, a blast of night air rushing through the windows extinguishes the torches, and everyone decides to head out into the open, nearby countryside. "Naked" now, "bare limbs" are intertwined as the celebrants cross a dark field, which makes them all "damp from dirt and trampled grass / With the dust of pollen seed." As the group disperses into smaller units, a "hunt" takes place in an adjoining grove:

> Trembling hands grope after locks
> Many there already parched
> Hot from chase and flight · bespattered with the fluid
> Of fruits squirted out ·
> Drink blood and saliva from hard lips
> And on steaming sheaves
> Others, alternatively, kiss both blossoms
> On the breast of the Chosen One.

We are now accustomed to George's habit of reaching for botanical metaphors to convey the physical realities of sexuality. Here he comes closest to identifying matters by their proper names, seeming almost to revel in the act of naming the slippery liquids of sex. (Still, it is a characteristic gesture that he described the lovers' lips not as yielding or inviting but as "hard" and somehow dangerous.) But he only gets as far as blood and saliva, and at the crucial moment he pulls back, again resorting to vegetable euphemisms for the discharge of semen and the caressing of the partner's bare nipples. Although the poem is thus identifiably Georgean in treatment, the thematics of the neoheathen observance of the solstice, together with the Schuleresque preoccupation with the particulars of male sexuality, and more generally the reliance on Bachofen's symbolic archaeology to provide a kind of overarching architectural framework, are all testaments to George's ongoing and sympathetic proximity to Cosmic concerns.

There were still other connections. The first poem in the book, which originally appeared in the *Blätter* of 1903, sets the tone for much of the succeeding segment. Its title, which gives the entire section its name, is a word George probably borrowed from Heine: "Das Zeitgedicht," literally "time-poem," but time in the sense of age or era, and the epoch being referred to was plainly his own. Not only that: the poem is a sort of condensed, idealized poetic autobiography, traversing the stages of George's own artistic and intellectual development — or rather, since the poem denies that any real evolution ever took place, of his steadfast pursuit of his aspirations. "You" — the "you" is plural and is addressed to the poet's contemporaries — "you see changes · yet I have been doing the same thing." But what the poet sees as the "same thing," and how he perceives his coevals, make the blood run cold. Speaking to them directly, he condemns them for having "measured" and "criticized me — you were wrong." In the midst of the "noise and rude greed" that fill his accusers' everyday lives, they presumed to judge his works by their own ignorant standard, approaching him with their "awkward gait" and running their "coarse finger" over the pages of his books. There they found him to be no more than a "smug anointed prince," a pale aesthete who counted out his rhyming meters "far removed from the earth." Nothing, the poet claims, could have been further from the truth. Even early on he was consumed, he says, by "dangerously bloody dreams," and as a cloaked "rebel penetrated / The house of the enemy with dagger and torch." No one perceived the "torments" that raged within him, everyone was "blind for what slumbered under the thin veil." This misapprehension was, he claims, partly by design. For a while, he admits, he cunningly seduced his readers "with flattering sweet tones" and arcadian murmurings — the allusion appears to be to the popular *Year of the Soul* — but these were deliberate feints. Now he intends to throw off the mantle of conceit, and rousing his troops to battle, he blasts a piercing "fanfare · goads the rotten flesh with his spurs," and "spreads molten fire."

As a self-analysis, the poem is remarkably perceptive, even allowing for the generous portion of self-mythologizing it contains. It is true enough that at no time in his life, even at the height of his career as a decadent aesthete, was George simply a placid versifier. He had always regarded his poetry as an immediate extension of his will and as a means of subduing internal and external foes. It is no less the case that his poetic imagination tended, from the beginning, to gravitate toward images of violent excess, even murderous mayhem, to communicate his impulse to prevail over whatever opponent he happened to be facing. But his antagonists thus far, even under the surface, had been different and somewhat diffuse: encompassing his own unruly desires, female allures, Nature, even the institutions of poetry itself. Until now his poems had been free of any overt reference to the one adversary that loomed above all others, the enemy he hated the most passionately, and the one he wanted most to see extirpated root and branch from the face of the earth: the ignorant "masses," the complacent "bourgeois," in short, all those whom he regarded as unworthy to exist in his sphere.

This, too, is partly a legacy of the Cosmic Circle. In 1903, the same year in which George's "Time-Poem" was first published, Ludwig Klages had told Gundolf what he also thought of his contemporaries. "Humanity is becoming more SORDID day by day," Klages ranted. "How could one still do anything in view of this vermin that stinks to high heaven! Rather, one has to try intensively to forget that people even exist at all: this coating of fungus on the crust of this planet that is starting to decompose. But one can dust off the mold and make the idols totter: for everything is rotten to the core. And for that reason: whoever even goes out should at least do so with a sword: but research is also a sword. And so you are right that a time of 'churnings' is beginning, as dead as this time is." To add a final flourish to this tirade, Klages mentioned that he liked reading books about Marco Polo — "for the sake of the contrast between the Occident and the Orient" — and that he found comfort in the realization these travel books gave him that at least somewhere in the world "there are still deserts and terrible barren wastes where PEOPLE are forced to die."

Gundolf was then finishing his doctoral dissertation in Berlin and for that reason perhaps Klages had likened "research" to a sword with which to do cultural battle, as if to suggest that he still considered Gundolf part of the solution and not the problem. In George's hands, poetry performed the same sword-like function, and in *The Seventh Ring* he wielded it with a grim ferocity. In almost every one of the "Time-Poems," an isolated individual is confronted by an uncomprehending and hostile mob, which is then duly punished by the poetic voice. In "Dante and the Time-Poem," for example, the great Florentine poet, disgraced and banished in exile, describes himself as taking merciless revenge on his tormentors in his great poem: "I drew a burning ember from my hearth and blew — / Thus was born hell." In a further poem inspired by another figure with whom George also liked to compare himself, the poet recalls the celebrations organized in 1899 in honor of the 150th anniversary of Goethe's birthday. Arriving in Frankfurt just after dawn and standing before the house in which Goethe was born, the poet disdains the garish banners and podiums erected for the occasion, which are thankfully still "free of people" at that early hour. Soon enough, though, "the consecrated room" in Goethe's house will be teeming with oafish cretins who need to "touch in order to believe." They know nothing of the man they pretend to honor, the poet says, nothing of his "agony and restlessness" or the "melancholy he hid behind a smile." What they prize most in him and think constituted his essence and now call their own are in reality only the lowest levels of his being, those most closely related to his "animal" nature — with the implication that like can perceive only like. Indeed, if Goethe himself were somehow able to come along that very day, the poet writes, "he would / Pass by you as an unrecognized king." Similarly, in the poem dedicated to Nietzsche, "the crowd" of admirers who acclaim him without understanding is also said to be to akin to "animals who besmirch him with praise."

Perhaps the clearest poetic expression in *The Seventh Ring* of George's truculent attitude toward his contemporaries, and of the fate he thought they deserved, comes in a narrative poem called "The Dead City":

The broad bay is filled by the new harbor
Which drains all the happiness of the land · a moon
Of glistening and rough house walls ·
Of endless streets in which with the same lust
The crowd haggles by day and carouses by night.
Only derision and pity rises up to the mother city
High up on the cliff which sits there impoverished
With blackened walls · forgotten by time.

The quiet fortress lives and dreams and sees
How strong its tower soars up into eternal suns ·
Silence protects its consecrated images
And among the weed-strewn streets
The inhabitants flourish in their worn-out clothes.
It feels no suffering · it knows the day is dawning:
Then a train of supplicants draws up the mountain
From their lavish palaces to plead:

>A dreary sorrow is cutting us down and we shall perish
If you do not help us — ailing amidst our luxury.
Grant us the pure breath of your heights
And the clear source! we would find shelter in the courtyard
And stalls and under the arch of any doorway.
Here treasures beyond your dreams — stones
As valuable as the freight of one hundred ships · brooch
And bracelet worth entire tracts of land!<

Yet the severe answer comes: >Here no purchase will avail.
The goods that seemed everything to you is dross.
Only seven are saved who once came
And to whom our children smiled.
You will all die. Your very number is sacrilege.

> Go with the false splendor that is odious
> To our boys! See how their naked foot
> Kicks it over the cliff into the sea.<

Here we are confronted by several quintessential themes of George's maturity: the "dead city" is of course the modern one, the busy commercial port inhabited by faceless throngs who are said to be consumed by greed and lust. Rising above this frenetic spectacle is the dark ancient fortress — even the word George uses, *veste,* is an archaic one — which, though materially poor and threadbare, is the more vital and pure. When a group of inhabitants from the lower city, beset by a nameless but deadly anguish, leaves their opulent palaces and ventures up the mountain in search of a remedy to their dimly felt ills, they are met with a cold rebuff. Not only are the offers to buy their way into the ancient stronghold turned aside with scorn — the valuables they proffer are dismissed as worthless debris — they are all calmly delivered to their deaths, with the justification that their very number is an intolerable profanity.

It is, on the face of it, a shocking poem. Looked at a bit more closely, it should be more off-putting still. We note that the source of the fortress's vitality is not stated; indeed, its "consecrated images," its holiest of holies, are said to be protected by silence. In fact, the poem tells us as little about itself as the inhabitants of the "fortress" tell the beseeching supplicants, which is only slightly more than nothing. The poem deliberately resists our own efforts to purchase its secret, and we suddenly realize that the more we pry, the more we are forced into the role of those miserable creatures from below who provoke revulsion and condemnation. George has thus placed us, as readers, into the same category of worthless, diseased people the poet has blithely sentenced to death.

This same malignant animosity also dominates the mood in the second section, called "Characters" or "Figures" — *Gestalten.* There one finds poems such as "The Battle," which is pretty much what one would expect it to be, as well as two poems exalting heroic *Führer* — the first one is shown to be "naked from his crown to his toe" — and another poem in which Algabal makes a cameo appearance. The entire segment ends with a frightening poem, called "Entry," depicting an apocalyptic scene of mass destruction and murder. "The time is ripe," it begins, and a bloody harvest commences:

> Cruel command
> Sweat of near death
> Impotent cry of the Possessed ·
> Helpless agony
> Monstrous mark
> The dying pleading of the Forgotten ·
> . . . .

Blast from the chasm!
Startle the air
The blaring of gleaming armies!
Snort songs of vengeance
Burn and pillage
Kill and sift · you Saviors!
. . . .
Storm and fire of the Heroes.

It is at this point, at the latest, that we realize the most important connection George wanted to establish between his book and another literary and cultural context. *The Seventh Ring* is at its heart George's imaginative reworking of the book of Revelation, Saint John's terrifying vision of the carnage and devastation that are to descend at the end of the world. The title of George's work provides an obvious clue here as well. In the final book of the Bible, we remember, the number seven plays a central if cryptic role. The number seven is constantly repeated, almost like an incantatory charm: we read of the seven churches of Asia, the seven candlesticks, the seven vials and seven lamps, the seven Spirits of God and the beast with seven heads that rises up out of the ocean. Most dire, and most important, is the book of seven seals, the script choreographing the end of days: as each of the seals is broken, it unleashes a new wave of unspeakable catastrophe and torment that washes over the earth. The fourth seal delivers a quarter of humanity to hunger and death; the fifth seal spits out the souls of those slain; at the sixth, great earthquakes destroy the cities, the sun turns "black as sackcloth of hair," the moon becomes as "blood," the stars fall to earth, and heaven itself is said to depart "as a scroll rolled together." As the seventh seal is loosened, seven angels sound seven trumpets while fire and hail mingled with blood rain down from the heavens, burning up the grass and the trees. But before the seventh and final trumpet blast, God establishes his reign on earth, and the new Jerusalem, the holy city, descends to take the place of the old one, now reduced to rubble and dust.

If there is a single purpose animating *The Seventh Ring* it is this: the book was designed to announce George's private eschatology, to herald the end of an old era and declare the dawning of the new. Immediately following the first two sections, or "rings," of the book, describing the degeneracy and corruption of humanity and the ruination of the world, and concluding finally with "Entry" in the annihilation of the depraved, is the segment containing the love poems to Gundolf, which is then succeeded by the central, mystical cycle revealing the advent of George's god, Maximin. In George's plan, Maximin would thus preside over the rejuvenation of mankind after its unwholesome elements had been eliminated. "New salvation [*Heil*] comes only from new love," a famous line reads. But it is a specific kind of love that is to bring salvation. Not incidentally, the biblical book of Revelation also depicts the destruction of the "great whore" of Babylon, "mother of harlots." The feminized city, antithesis to the masculine Jerusalem, is the epitome of impure sexuality in the form of lascivious woman: dressed in scarlet and purple, decked out in gold, precious stones and pearls, Babylon bears a golden cup "full of abominations and the filthiness of fornication." *The Seventh Ring* is meant to mark the ultimate victory of the male principle in George's realm, but it is achieved through the utter suppression of the feminine. If we accept that, like the book of Revelation, *The Seventh Ring* proclaims the second coming of the Messiah, then it would seem that George envisions as the outcome of the holocaust he invokes the return of his beloved Maximin. No wonder, then, that he wanted to accelerate the end, to promote the necessary cleansing that must precede the reawakening. The problem was that it was unclear who, besides George himself and his tiny band of followers, would survive the Armageddon.

But that a more pragmatic political lesson could be gleaned from the book was later demonstrated in a way that apparently annoyed George. Without his consent and, indeed, against his will, the Bavarian Communists, who enjoyed a short-lived success in Munich immediately after the war, adopted "Entry" as their marching song. Although George was not happy with this unauthorized appropriation of his words, and even less enchanted by its promoters, it would not be the last time that his poetry and beliefs would act as kindling in the highly combustible mixture of German postwar politics. But then again, as another poem from the end of the book indicates, George should have known that the actors on the political stage do not always come from expected precincts or even very palatable ones.

> The man! the deed! thus do the people and high council yearn ·
> Do not hope for one who ate at your tables!
> Perhaps he who sat for years among your murderers ·
> Slept in your cells: will rise up and do the deed.

Even though George primarily wanted to throw cold water on the middle-brow belief that greatness automatically equaled goodness, it also turned out to be a portentous reminder that political leadership often follows a crooked and unsavory path.

George spent most of 1907 assembling the manuscript for *The Seventh Ring* and preparing it for Lechter's attentions. As usual, he waited out the autumn months in Berlin, spent the winter and early spring in Munich, and by early summer he was in residence in Bingen. The only cloud over the season was the death of his father, Stephan George II, on May 12, 1907, at the age of sixty-five. But his passing did not seem to affect George particularly deeply. The only trace of his reaction is a fairly impersonal note he sent to Gundolf saying that "this morning poor father peacefully passed away." More important than his own physical sire was the book that he, as *its* progenitor, was about to bring forth. Yet again, however, Lechter appeared to be dragging his feet, taking longer over his part in the project than desirable or, George thought, really necessary. In reply to one of George's pointed prods — dictated to Gundolf — asking when the book would be finished, Lechter testily reminded George that he, unlike some people, did not have any "Gundolfs" to assist him: "I have to do everything myself!" It was a fair enough point, but still George poked and pulled his oppressed, overworked friend until, in November, the work was done. But it would be the last book of George's poetry Lechter would design.

That same year, Albert Verwey had invited George to pass the first part of the summer with his family in Holland. Thanking Verwey for the invitation, George postponed the visit, saying he first wanted to make what he was already calling his "annual holiday trip to Switzerland." In August, George finally took his Dutch friend up on the offer. Naturally, George told Verwey about the new book about to appear and he mentioned the enormous trouble and effort it had cost him to put it together (he tactfully omitted any reference to the leisurely pace he thought his illustrator was taking). But in person Verwey found him to be completely different. He said the change was so marked that he remembered George's words almost verbatim: "The last time I was with you," Verwey recalled him saying, "you said: it is not good not to take notice of one's time. That is true. In Germany there are now so many currents and movements of life and of the mind. One should organize them. One should show the way in which they can be effective. My way, however, is not the popular one, the modern one of today's civilization. I want another, an inward unity. With that I have confronted our world. I used to believe that the world would crush me. Now I am no longer afraid.–" Speaking more specifically about *The Seventh Ring*, George said that "everything is absorbed in my new work. Every question finds an answer there, however hidden it might be." To George, the book was less a literary text than a revelatory treatise.

Understandably, Verwey reacted somewhat quizzically to the rather disquieting transformation that had taken place in his friend and Verwey inwardly appeared to take a few steps back. Noticing this hesitancy, George tried to press Verwey into an acknowledgement of his new or newly asserted rank. Going over their relationship "of the last seven years," Verwey said George always pursued the same goal in their conversations: "to deliver the proof of his superiority." Frustrated by Verwey's continued reserve, George peevishly asked him, "How can someone be so *with* me and yet so *external* to me?" That, in George's mind, was the fundamental issue: he could never tolerate the notion that he could not completely possess, indeed assimilate, whatever he desired. Now that he had decided to take on the entire world, he wanted to annex it whole; whatever resisted was regarded as nonexistent or hostile. Verwey astutely saw that George "would have wanted to deny what was external to himself. That this was not possible disturbed him." Thus, Verwey recounted, "he criticized me and placed me among his enemies." In the end, Verwey was able to convince George that he was still an ally and a friend. But they did not see one another again for almost three years.

Another old acquaintance of George would also discover that the poet had undergone a pronounced metamorphosis. In the spring of 1908, George decided to return to Paris, the site of his poetic awakening. Apart from a brief visit at the turn of the century, he had not been back to Paris for almost a decade, nor had he kept in touch with his former friends and mentors there. This time he took along Ernst Morwitz, and together they went to the studio of Auguste Rodin — George generally disliked modern sculpture, but he made an exception in Rodin, whom he considered "the great Master, the only one who seemed to him to have style" — and George pointed out to Morwitz the house at 87 rue de Rome, where Mallarmé had lived. One evening he was invited, along with his old friend and promoter Albert Saint-Paul and André Gide, to the home of Albert Mockel, now married and settled into a comfortable existence. Mockel was astonished by the difference he saw in his German visitor when he mentally compared the diffident young man he remembered from his first Parisian sojourn almost two decades before with the imposing figure sitting before him: "What a transformation in his entire personality! What a reformation of his entire being! Yes, it was still Goethe; but the 'Goethe before *Werther*,' the awkward novice with grace and still trying out the powers of his will, had now acquired a serene assurance, a tranquil and joyful pride. In his entire manner of being he demonstrated that aristocracy which we like to see in a poet who is still young but already triumphant, in the accomplished Goethe of *Iphigenia on Taurus*. It was no longer the timid faith that hopes. It was the certainty that proudly asserts itself — proudly but without brutality for it is conscious of its victory."

For George, the French journey brought a personal epoch to a close. It would be the last time he ever set foot in France. Little by little, the genuine admiration, sympathy, and gratitude he had felt for the nation that had warmly welcomed him when he found his own country unbearable had begun to give way to feelings of mistrust and aversion. In part, his change of heart had to do with his determination to fashion himself into an exclusively German phenomenon, unalloyed with any baser metals. But the First World

War and its fallout — bringing with it the reannexation of Alsace-Lorraine and the ill-advised French occupation of the Ruhr — did the rest. In 1919, he mentioned that when he had last been to Paris ten years previously "I resolved never to go back there again." In explanation of his decision, he elliptically said, "I couldn't stand their faces." A year later, in bitter reaction to the terms imposed by the Versailles Treaty, George said to one of his companions that "these French have to be exterminated." After a long pause, he added, "Have you ever thought about what barbaric or diabolical tools fate usually chooses to carry out its verdict?" It is unclear whether this was a subtle retraction of the original oath or an even more subtle savoring of the future possibilities the idea conjured forth.

Either way, fate did impose a terrible judgment but in ways that were even more savage than anyone could have imagined. Uncannily, exactly seven years after the publication of *The Seventh Ring* — George's fearsome invocation of apocalyptic nightmare and doom — the most lethal war in history broke out, delivering some ten million men to their early deaths and with them an entire culture to its grave. To most of George's readers, these were not unrelated events. Many were convinced that he had not only prophesied the war but that he had also clandestinely promoted it, prepared its way, actively hastened its arrival. In June of 1917, after nearly three years of slaughter and with still no end in sight, Thomas Mann expressed a widely shared belief about George that it was "in a certain sense *his* war." Some would insist this was assigning him too much credit — or blame — while others would say it was not giving him enough of either. In any event, what was beyond dispute was that after *The Seventh Ring* and until the end of his life, George could no longer be regarded simply as a poet who stood aloof from the world and his time. From then on, to his detractors, to his disciples, and to himself, Stefan George increasingly seemed to embody something more than an individual destiny, to personify something like a new German culture. What kind of Germany he represented, however, and what he had in store for it, would not fully sink in for quite some time to come.

George around the turn of the century in a photograph taken by Lepsius

Georg Bondi, George's publisher

Karl Wolfskehl in front of his beloved books

Friedrich Gundolf, around 1900

Ludwig Klages

Group portrait of the Cosmic Circle. From left to right: Wolfskehl, Schuler, Klages, George, Verwey

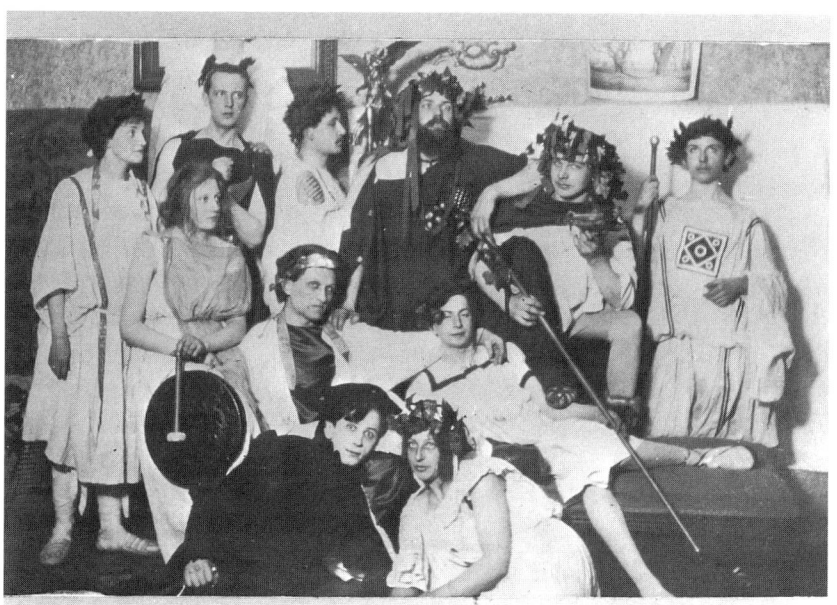

Antique Fest 1903. George as Caesar, Wolfskehl as Bacchus/Dionysus

Maximilian Kronberger

Carnival 1904. Wolfskehl as Homer, George as Dante, with his arm around Maximilian Kronberger

Carnival 1904. Maximilian Kronberger to George's left

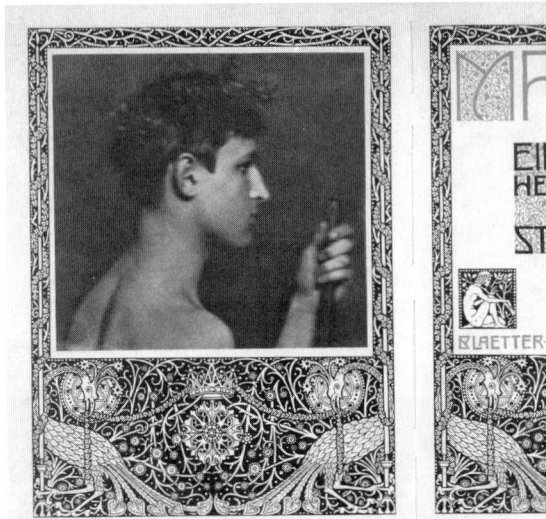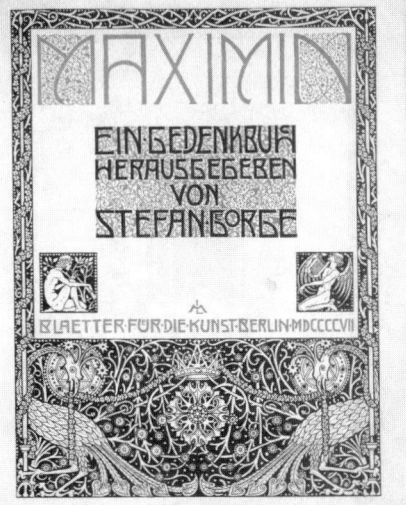

Maximin. In Memoriam *with photograph of Maximilian Kronberger*

Title page of The Seventh Ring, *1907*

Ernst Morwitz

Edgar Salin

Friedrich Wolters and Berthold Vallentin

Kurt Hildebrandt

Title page of Yearbook for the Spiritual Movement

The Globe Room (with picture of Maximin on the wall)

Edith Landmann

Julius Landmann

George in 1910

Title page of Friedrich Gundolf's translation of Shakespeare, 1908

Title page of Friedrich Gundolf's Goethe, *the first "Spirit Book" to feature the swastika signet*

Ernst Glöckner

Heinrich Friedemann

Norbert von Hellingrath

Adalbert Cohrs

Bernhard von Uxkull

George in 1917: the poet of "The War"

Part iii
POLitiCiAN + 1909–1918
MASTER + RULER + FÜHRER

Chapter 25

Admission to the Order

In September 1908, George arrived in Berlin somewhat earlier than usual to take up his fall quarters in the capital. As had been his practice since the turn of the century, he stayed for a few weeks at the home of his publisher, Georg Bondi. In 1901, Bondi had moved into a large villa in the exclusive wooded enclave of Grunewald on the southwestern skirts of the city. On Sunday mornings, Bondi liked to invite guests to come play tennis on his private court. Although not interested in the game himself, George sometimes brought along his young friend, Ernst Morwitz, who took energetic part in the matches and who frequently stayed on for lunch with Bondi and his wife; on occasion George dined with them as well. They were periodically joined by another one of George's English acquaintances, Alan H. Gardiner, whom Bondi amiably described as "an excellent Egyptologist and a brilliant tennis tournament player."

But George did not want to be the head of a private sports club. He may have had these harmless but distracting weekend contests on his mind when he met with Berthold Vallentin in January 1909 while he was still in Bingen for the holidays. Vallentin observed in his diary that George was in a "strange state of distress, in a way I have actually never seen him." Complaining about "insomnia" and other physical maladies, George revealed to Vallentin that there was also a psychic origin to his agitation. It was owing, he said, to "the instability and the lack of zeal in the circle." At first glance, his complaint seems odd, not to say somewhat out of touch with reality. Within the span of little more than twelve months, no less than eleven books would appear either by George or one of his intimates. At the end of 1908, the second, "public" edition of *The Seventh Ring* was published, and in the same year a work called "Homages" ("Huldigungen") by the elusive poet Lothar Treuge came out under the imprint of the *Blätter für die Kunst* lavishly decorated by Melchior Lechter. In 1909 Karl Wolfskehl published two dramatic fragments — "mysteries" was his name for them — entitled *Sanctus* and *Orpheus*. Plus, the third and final volume of "selections" from the *Blätter* also appeared that year, followed by George's translations of both Shakespeare's sonnets and passages from Dante's *Commedia*. It hardly seems there was a shortage of zeal.

The most important development, though, was the publication in August 1908 of the first volume of what would become a new edition of Shakespeare's collected plays in German translation. The year before, Georg Bondi had approached Gundolf to take on the task. It would be merely the first major monument to Gundolf's lifelong love affair with Shakespeare. We recall that the very beginnings of his relationship with George had revolved around the teenager's grappling with the sonnets. Gundolf's first major book, published in 1911, three years after the translation began to appear, is devoted to uncovering the deep undercurrents he saw running between *Shakespeare and the German Spirit*. And in 1928 he brought out a two-volume study, *Shakespeare: His Being and Work,* a searching, engagingly written, and deeply informed analysis of all the Bard's plays in chronological order. It might initially seem strange that an English Renaissance playwright would inspire such devotion from someone who became regarded as the preeminent historian and critic of German literature in his day. But ever since the middle of the eighteenth century, Shakespeare had enjoyed within the German cultural tradition the status of a kind of spontaneous creative force, less "English" than more broadly "natural." And "natural," in this case, meant the opposite of French. In particular, Shakespeare's use of unrhymed blank verse, his flamboyant disregard for the Aristotelian unities, his passion for the supernatural in the form of witches, ghosts, and augurs, and his taste for the violent outbursts of nature, in the form of thunder claps and raging storms, all made him seem the very antithesis of what was seen as the cold, rational, desiccated qualities of French classical drama — and by extension of Enlightenment culture as a whole. Gundolf's commitment to Shakespeare, then, was in no small measure based on the emergent ideological program of the circle more generally. To promote Shakespeare meant to ascribe to a vision of life that was irrational, uncontainable, unpredictable and, not infrequently, dangerous.

In 1909, then, everything seemed to be going George's way: the circle had fully recovered from the bloodletting stemming from the Cosmic conflicts; the number and abilities of the new additions were reaching unprecedented heights; more and better books were coming out than ever before; the previously loose, ad hoc constellation of ideas enunciated in the maxims of the

Blätter were congealing into an identifiable philosophy with real, increasingly visible consequences; and George's personal standing had never been so exalted. It was now customary for him to receive effusive letters from readers who had somehow stumbled onto his poetry and had become swept up by its power. A letter sent in the summer of 1907 by a twenty-five-year-old admirer by the name of Albert Rausch, whom Wolfskehl knew and had encouraged to write to George, is typical:

> Dear one and only master: shall I thank you again for everything that you have been and are to me? I really do not know how I could do that ... I sometimes stand so moved before the eternal signs that your hand has written into our lives that my eyes become damp — and when one spring evening as I walked with my friend through the fields and meadows behind my town and he suddenly softly said the words into my ear: 'The streets pointing into the distance are becoming paler,' I was so moved by the whole inexpressible beauty of your work ... of your being in these quiet lines — that I experienced a shudder of happiness to be young and to be kindled by such flames.

Those closer to George — Rausch himself was never admitted into the inner circle and, to his chagrin, his poems also failed to make their way into the *Blätter* — also repeatedly assured George, as Ernst Morwitz did, "how much I live in you and think in you!" "For you accompany me and know my paths and I am forever with you."

Yet, for all of these positive signs, George was, as Vallentin noted, still dissatisfied. One possible source of George's unhappiness might have had to do with the circumstances surrounding a piece he had written for the *Blätter* several years before. In the 1901 issue, a short, five-page dramatic scene, titled "The Induction into the Order," appeared to which George gave the subtitle, "An Ordination Play." The work makes no attempt at disguising itself as the literary enactment of a rite of initiation, nor was there much doubt about the identity of the "order" invoked in the title. The dramatic dialogue features a "Grand Master" standing at an altar surrounded by a monastic chorus and three "brothers" who interview a "youth" who seeks admission to the order. As the chorus announces that theirs is "The most dignified guild / And the most magnificent council! / Construction of dreams / Here they have become deed," the Grand Master informs the applicant of the rules of the order. "Here you are no longer your own here is your place: / To feel work in the circle according to your station. Here he is banned who selfishly desires." Undeterred by these warnings that joining the "circle" means accepting an assigned place and surrendering his individuality, the youth presses his bid. Impressed by his sincerity — and also, it would seem, by the "vivacity / Of his body," for the petitioning youth stands totally "naked" before his examiners — the

Grand Master tells him that he must find among those already inducted someone to act as his sponsor: "Seek the brother who will knowingly vouch for you." The only stipulation is that if he fails to find a patron after three attempts, he will be turned away. The rest of the piece is taken up by the youth approaching and then being rejected by the first two potential promoters, to be finally taken in by the third. It ends with the chorus proclaiming that "the circle is the citadel / The motive of all action."

It is not an especially subtle work, but then subtlety was not what George was after. In February 1903, just prior to the raucous Carnival celebration at Wolfskehl's apartment in Schwabing, and while Maximilian Kronberger was still alive, George and several of his intimates were already rehearsing "The Induction into the Order" as often as twice a week. Usually George read the part of the Grand Master, while the Youth and the other roles went to anyone else who happened to be present, with everyone often joining in on the chorus, the session concluding only after a few more repetitions of the whole piece. But these group recitations had more to them than the cultic reiteration of the simple formulae that held George and his band together. As much emphasis was placed on the *way* the lines were spoken as on the meaning of the words themselves — although that was certainly important as well. For George had originally envisioned nothing less than a "rebirth of drama through verse" and that "The Induction into the Order" could serve as just the model that could inaugurate such a dramatic renaissance of the genre.

Partly with this aim in view, "The Induction into the Order" became an integral part of the regular meetings with his friends over the next few years. It coincided with, and probably helped to promote, an increasingly formalized and ritualized form of interaction between George and his friends, who themselves were becoming not so much his associates as acolytes. Reading "The Induction into the Order," which after all ideally mirrored the organization of the circle and enshrined its precepts, thus served to solidify the group it defined. It almost assumed the role of a responsory, such as is typical in the Catholic ceremony, uniting the congregation through the spoken word and linking the celebrants by a shared invisible spiritual bond. George's manner of reading out loud reinforced the sense that one was reciting a liturgical text, a manner George insisted everyone else adopt as well. Robert Boehringer, who stood out for his ability to recite poetry in a way that met the Master's approval, and who later wrote an essay on the technique, described it as a "seemingly monotone reading," one that "held the middle between speaking and song; it was an intoning in which the distinctive features of poetry — rhythm, caesura, tone and rhyme — are given due attention." Boehringer likened George's manner of reading to "a solemn litany." Others similarly recounted how George read poetry "with a sonorous, restrained voice that reverberated like a bell." Less a literary performance, it was rather "a heightened recitation in a half-liturgical tone, without any raising or lowering of the melodic line to speak of, so that almost the entire poem was spoken in the same note, and the shading of soft and loud also stayed within a narrow range."

During the winter of 1909, George devoted a great deal of energy instructing his Berlin companions in the correct, which is to say his own, style of reading aloud. "We practiced reading," a typical entry in Vallentin's diary relates; "the Master praised me, [saying] how well I read now." George often went to Vallentin's home in the evening, occasionally accompanied by Wolters, where they would all dine together. But George was a relentless taskmaster: "You don't think," he abruptly said after one of these gatherings, "that we have come together here merely to live it up, to have a luxurious meal: we have to get back to some real work." Frequently this "real work" entailed repeated recitations of "The Induction into the Order," followed by a presentation of several other poems by George, and only then were the others called upon to read from their own works. Yet they were instructed to read these, too, in the same unmodulated, incantatory vein if they were to gain the Master's approval.

This ritualistic chanting was not just the social glue that helped to bind his friends together. It also served to place a unified stamp on all their poetic utterances, making it impossible, even when reading one's own work, to forget, and ever to escape, the pervasive, controlling presence of the Master. By adhering to George's singular style of reading, the injunction contained in "The Induction into the Order" to cast off all vestiges of selfishness — which is to say, all trace of individual identity — was thus carried out in practice. Or, rather, it would be more precise to say that one shed one's own personality to take on George's own through the imitation of his voice. "Stefan George is very critical in listening to verse," someone else commented who met him in February 1909. "He related that he had only once found a person who had amazed him through reading his poems aloud. He did it exactly the way he himself would have done it." That was the goal: to strive to read in a way that matched George's own practice as closely as possible, producing a near replica of the Master's voice.

At around the same time, George had also begun urging his friends and collaborators to use a typeface he had designed based on his own idiosyncratic handwriting for the publication of their works. In 1904, before the final rupture with Hofmannsthal, George had sent him some samples of the type — "my own," he proudly told Hofmannsthal, "which I have long been working to improve." Casually mentioning that "you will see it resembles my handwriting," and confidently predicting that "you will like it," George argued that in any case the type was better than all those invented by "modern designers who added some made-up curlicues to the letters that already existed." Hofmannsthal politely declined the offer. George had also tried to persuade

Verwey, though equally without success, to adopt his typeface. "I (to be sure its creator) think it is very clear," George told Verwey, "and yet the only one [that is] entirely un-bourgeois." As time went on, George won more converts and many of his later friends not only used his type, but also emulated his mannered handwriting, his unorthodox spelling and punctuation, and his stilted phraseology, often making it difficult to tell who the actual author of an unsigned manuscript was.

There was more than simple narcissism in these graphic and oral reproductions of himself. By encouraging everyone to replicate his voice and manner in their speech and writing, George was rendering them, in more than simply formal terms, into extensions of his own will, indeed of himself. In essence, it amounted to the same operation he had performed on Maximin, except in reverse. George was not incorporating his friends, absorbing them within himself, assimilating their identities into his own, but doing the opposite. He was transplanting himself, cloning the features of his personality and grafting them onto other beings. It thus represented one more way to conquer the sterility against which he had been fighting for years. The difference was that, before, the effort had been limited to the sphere of poetry alone. Now, even though poetry was still the vehicle, George's expansion of himself was actually taking place by means of and within the real world.

The act of reading aloud, apart from its implied procreative function, also became something of a yardstick by which George would measure potential admittees to the round. During his first encounter with a new young man, George would habitually inquire if the candidate knew "how poems are supposed to be read?" Ernst Morwitz remembered that the first time he met George he was also asked to choose and read a poem. Evidently, George was not wholly satisfied with Morwitz's performance. "To show me how one could do it better than I had done he thereupon read the same poem aloud, and then I heard for the first time how he slowly spoke every line separately in rhythmic uniformity with a dark, medium-loud, reverberating voice, never raising or lowering the tone."

Besides initiating the newcomer into the proper style of reading aloud, the introductory interview often resembled a general examination, and failure to live up to George's expectations could be a harrowing ordeal. Edgar Salin, who along with his university friend, Wolfgang Heyer, would be introduced to George two years later, in 1911, vividly recounted the scene of their preliminary interrogation. One evening, as was the custom, the two young men — Salin was twenty-one, Heyer twenty — were first ushered into a bare room containing a divan, a table, and a petroleum lamp that gave off a faint, smoky glow. Gundolf, who had arranged the meeting, was also present and stood to one side. After what seemed an interminable wait, the door behind them softly opened and closed. Hearing the sound of breathing behind them, they slowly turned around: "Before us stood Stefan George."

George immediately stepped up and began to grill them, wanting to know where they studied and with whom, how old they were, what their backgrounds and interests were, and then moved on to broader questions about their knowledge of literature and history. Always, George sought some connection to himself; if they mentioned a city, he asked if they knew an acquaintance of his there; the title of a book would lead to a reference to one of his own. All the while, Salin wrote, "the loud beating of our hearts seemed to be the only audible noise" in the quiet room other than George's insistent probing. Then he abruptly turned to the real point of the encounter. George asked them if they read poems out loud and, if so, why. The inspiration of the moment prompted one of them to say, "because that is the only way to enter into the spirit of a poem." George found it a passable response: "That sounds good. Why don't we go ahead and put it to the test."

To the two young men, who had come to the meeting already filled with awe for the great poet's work, this invitation sounded "like a death sentence." Salin said that "we trembled with fear" at the prospect of reading poems aloud in front of the Master. As Gundolf rummaged around for something for them to recite — he offered several suggestions, which George rejected, telling him, "No. That's too difficult for the beginning. Just look, child — you'll find something suitable" — the anxiety and apprehension of both Salin and Heyer steadily mounted. Observing their nervousness, George tried to calm them down, or distract them, by asking further questions: which books they owned, what issues of the *Blätter* they had already read or perhaps even acquired. At last, the dreaded moment came.

"The reading was completely unsuccessful," according to Salin. Even though they were both well acquainted with the chosen text — it was one of the poems in *The Year of the Soul* — George had handed them the version that had appeared in the *Blätter,* which differed slightly from the one they knew from the published book. In that tense atmosphere, with George glowering at them, faced with the unfamiliar typography used in the journal, and thrown off by the slight variation in the text, few people could have maintained their composure. Heyer, who drew the unenviable lot of being the first to read and who was normally admired by his friends for his "deep, expressive voice," flopped miserably. "George's criticism was unsparing," Salin wrote. Compared to their despair, though, the Master's disappointment "still seemed too mild confronted with the feeling of total failure, which shamed us both." Astonishingly, given his own way of reading, George mainly faulted Heyer for the "monotony" of his performance. "Where you wanted to emphasize a stressed syllable," George instructed him, "you did this too strongly so that you were incapable of any intensification of stress on the meaning."

Suddenly, George switched tracks: "And do you know what the most unpleasant thing was to me, whose voice seemed to resonate through to me?" Bafflement greeted this last question, until it turned out that George was referring to another young poet who had attempted to gain access to the Master and his friends the previous summer. For whatever undisclosed reason, George had decided that this person was a "fraud" in human, intellectual, and poetic terms, and had quickly brushed him off. As luck would have it, Salin and Heyer had also formed an attachment to the same person during that same summer and, although they had soon parted ways, too, all three had often read poems together. Now, to their distress and alarm, George claimed to have heard the voice of the banished one in Heyer's recitation, rising up like the disagreeable scent of an ex-lover's perfume emanating from a new acquaintance.

Next, it was Salin's turn. Already demoralized by his friend's debacle, and flustered by George's jealous discernment, Salin wobbled his way through another poem. George found that Salin at least avoided the error of "monotony," but the overall verdict was less than comforting. "In the end," George pitilessly told him, "you were also a disaster. The person who reads knows that best himself after all." Feeling wretched, Salin thought silently to himself, "Yes, the person who read would have preferred for the ground to swallow him up." Still, after moving over to the sofa, George — half sitting, half reclining — dispensed tips to them both on how to practice reading over the following months, "until he would have us come to him again." In the meantime, "entrust yourself to the rhythm, to the flow," he advised them. "Have courage," he admonished them, "read often in the open, not only in your room." He also told them, "Read often in the *Century of Goethe!*" — that is, the anthology of poets he and Wolfskehl had put together — "You don't know the variety of voices and rhythms enough yet!" And with that, George turned his attention to the others present and ignored both Salin and Heyer. Their first grueling audience with the Master had ended.

The eighth issue of the *Blätter,* the first to appear in five years, did not come out until February 1910, but the cover indicated that it contained works from 1908 and 1909. Departing from standard practice, the prose introduction does not consist of the usual pithy, gnomic pronouncements. Instead, it features three longish, tolerably lucid paragraphs that deal with the burning questions then preoccupying George: the relation between "The Artist and the Public," "Reciting Poetry," and "Drama." They all hold few surprises: the artist is proclaimed to be the only person, apart from someone, presumably of independent means, who is not forced to work for a living and is thus freed from society's demands, who "still has the possibility to live in a Realm [*Reich*] where the Spirit [*Geist*] gives the highest law." Reading poetry as if one were scanning liturgical psalmodies is also judged to have exemplary status: "What we have heard in reports about poetic reading proves that a poet never read otherwise and can never read otherwise." Perhaps most interesting is the section on drama, for it codifies George's reservations about that literary form in general and undergirds them with a new cultural-political argument. It claims that whereas "true" drama grows organically out of an authentic need within a society — as was the case, it asserts, in Shakespeare's time — "modern plays" are a completely different affair. They are, it claims, made simply to satisfy the desire of the masses for visual spectacle and are maintained more by habit than conviction, "to say nothing of economic necessities." They do not ripen like fruit, do not breathe any particular air or stem from any ground, but are "manufactured": "They are applied literary history." Most of all, they are cynically designed to meet "the demand of the market." "Thus dramas exist only because the expensive machines are there and because turning them sometimes generates substantial profit."

In a conversation from early 1909, when these issues were at the forefront of George's mind, he spoke at length about the theater and drama, comparing ancient Greek tragedy with Shakespeare's works, and contrasting both to the detriment of the modern stage. It was a waste of time and energy, he said, a useless enterprise for talented young people to devote themselves to the theater. Given the "disunity of our culture," he insisted, a genuine contemporary need for drama and tragedy did not, in fact could not, even exist. In 1910, George told Verwey, simply, "A drama in our time is impossible." Earlier, in 1905, he had similarly told Kurt Breysig that "drama presupposes a society, a broad circle." Breysig noted in his diary that George had said "he did not have that yet, it still had to form. He explained what difficulties he has keeping his Munich and Berlin circle together. He also needed circles around himself for his lyric art." Here, apart from all other cultural, historical or even economic arguments, we probably have the key to the real reason George finally rejected the theater. He saw it, like everything else, as something that he would either dominate or dismiss. When it became apparent that the "circle" he needed to respond to and embody his poetry could not be recreated, and as easily managed, with respect to drama, he condemned it. If George could not exercise complete and unfettered control over something — or someone — it lost all value and meaning to him; indeed, it ceased to exist. And, besides, as George more lightheartedly told Hanna Wolfskehl several years later, "As long as I have Karl, I have all the theater I need."

Still, the irritation over his inability to place the theater under his thumb, and then the protracted process of eliminating it from his catalogue of acceptable art forms, could not entirely account for the foul humor Vallentin had noticed in early 1909. George now wanted weightier opponents than the institution of the theater or "modern drama" represented. He wanted to take on modernity itself. But he was becoming impatient with the pace of things.

"Where is the path, where are the seeds," he said to someone else that winter. He wanted to discover "what has meaning for what is new, for the future." George was not interested in the past unless it had some relevance to the future. And, as far as he was concerned, he *was* the future.

CHAPTER 26

The Führer *and His* Reich

If George had been out of sorts at the beginning of 1909, unhappy with the degree of commitment he thought he detected within his circle and frustrated with the quality and tempo of its activities, by the end of the following year the picture had altogether changed. "We friends are quite pleased with the country and our life," Friedrich Wolters cheerfully announced to Lechter from Berlin in December 1910. Lechter had struck out in early October on a mystical journey to India with the similarly inclined Wolfskehl. "George is still here," Wolters continued, "and sends a hearty response to your greetings and would be very happy to hear details from the two distant travelers." Apparently, some news of Lechter's trip had already made its way to George, but the Master wanted more specifics. "That you find the people there beautiful, especially the men, delighted him greatly." George even nourished the hope, Wolters added, that Lechter might "learn to love" the "beautiful man" while abroad more than he had at home and that in the future Lechter would grant more attractive models of virility a place in his "living work," as an antidote to the "frothy and flabby bodies of our secession painters."

The prospect of finding firm, handsome male bodies depicted with greater frequency and conviction in Lechter's work must have been encouraging to George. Even more heartening was the positive development in the general atmosphere of the circle. Wolters went on to inform Lechter that "we meet often and regularly to read and a stronger feeling of unity is beginning to imbue everyone than had ever been the case before; what we have longed for in the realm [*Reich*] is beginning to come true not just, as up until now, in the work but also in the feeling of a united new life, and with the new challenges that the community is awakening, a new happiness is also forming that receives its sustenance from the self-sacrifice of each individual for the Whole."

The season of George's discontent, it appeared, had finally passed. Wolters suggested that, beyond the increased sense of harmony and solidarity among the members of the "community" surrounding George, the Master's long envisioned aim of moving the site of his operations out of the literary sphere and into the real world had at last begun to be realized and, moreover, was starting to produce tangible results. But to anyone who was not an initiate of George's "community," the rest of Wolters's letter would have probably made little sense. It was not only that his words were abstruse to the point of being unintelligible: that was, as we know, a stylistic tic shared by many of George's regulars, even though Wolters cultivated it with particular zest. But it was that he was also using a kind of code, a specialized vocabulary that depended on a common set of unspoken assumptions that provided the necessary key to decipher it. The notions of the "realm," the "leader," "new life," and "self-sacrifice" all pointed to a constellation of ideas — some indeed of Wolters's own manufacture — that had been responsible for the reinvigoration of the circle he had mentioned. At the same time, these new self-descriptions of the circle lent it a richer, more elaborate conceptual framework that further consolidated it by making its premises more explicit — if not always completely perspicuous.

By the latter part of 1910, there would be some thirty people who counted among George's friends, and many more who stood in varying degrees of closeness to him. The principle cadre consisted of Gundolf, Wolfskehl, Wolters, Lechter, Vallentin, and Morwitz, all of whom already were or would soon begin to make themselves known through their own work. Other members of the Berlin group included, most prominently, the sculptor Ludwig Thormaehlen and the physician Kurt Hildebrandt. Yet there were still others who hovered in the background, such as Friedrich Andreae, Paul Thiersch, or Erich Berger, but who still played minor though discernable roles in George's life. And as his standing friends brought in acquaintances of their own, the net was cast even wider. Around this time, Gundolf began to introduce some of his acquaintances to George, including Herbert Steiner and, most notably, Ernst Robert Curtius, who went on to achieve notable acclaim as a scholar of French and medieval literature. Wolfskehl brought him the twenty-two-year-old Norbert von Hellingrath, who was largely responsible for rescuing the poet Friedrich Hölderlin from a century of neglect by publishing a new edition of his works and, most spectacularly, by unearthing Hölderlin's lost translations of Pindar. And there was a growing number of well-known, leading intellectuals — predominantly scholars and university professors — who were showing a lively interest in George, even if they were not all entirely uncritical. Georg Simmel, although in no sense ever a "follower" of George, had as we know long been fascinated by him. In 1909 Simmel had published yet another appreciative article, devoted primarily to *The Seventh Ring,* in which he marveled on the "mysterious systematic quality" he saw as characterizing all of George's work. But new names from the intellectual elite in Germany also began to appear: the philosopher Wilhelm Dilthey had expressed his admiration for *The Seventh Ring* and followed George's career until 1911, the year of Dilthey's death. The art historian Heinrich Wölfflin also made a point of asking detailed questions about George whenever he met someone who might have any new information about him. And in 1910 George met Max Weber, then one of the most respected names in German academic circles. Weber opposed just about everything George stood for, but Weber admitted to being genuinely impressed by the power of George's poetry and by the strength of his convictions.

At the end of the century's first decade, then, George could look out over a large and constantly expanding group of talented, active, and fiercely partisan adherents, and be satisfied that he had attracted the interest and esteem of a sizable, discriminating readership. He appeared not just to have survived and surmounted the difficulties of the past several years intact, but to have emerged all that much stronger for them. More than ever before, George's implicit and increasingly overt assertions of his prerogatives as the adjudicator and emissary of his people — perhaps of the entire age — were finding affirmative, palpable resonance both within and beyond his group of devotees. And even those of his admirers who remained skeptical of his claims of personal leadership, and maintained a guarded distance from the phenomenon of the circle itself, at least possessed the significant advantage of belonging among the most brilliant and famous men of their day. With friends — even cautious friends — like that, one could almost afford to ignore one's enemies.

Almost, but not quite. Adversaries tend to become bolder when left unchallenged, and George, feeling more confident than ever before, sensed that the time had come to strike. Indeed, the last few years before the outbreak of war in 1914 marked the zenith of George's circle, its time of greatest optimism and vigor, and in many ways its most dynamic and unified period. Anything seemed possible, and much was thought to be necessary. Until then, the idea of the circle had slowly taken shape almost incidentally, never more fully articulated than in the terse, epigrammatic segments that introduced the *Blätter,* and consequently lacking the fullness and complexity of a viable ideology. Now it truly came into its own. The circle was no longer an auxiliary structure, formulated after the fact to designate the group of poets represented in the *Blätter.* Now it contained its own raison d'être. And central to the new vitality of the circle, giving it an unprecedented unanimity of purpose and direction, was the changed perception of its sustaining spirit. Before, George had represented to his advocates the preeminent champion of a certain way of making poetry. To be sure, among those who regarded him as "the Master" he had enjoyed an elevation of his person that went beyond mere professional admiration of his talents. But the focus had still primarily remained fixed on the creation of art in some recognizably conventional sense. Now, however, in the eyes of his followers — and in his own mind as well — George's role underwent another, even more radical change.

Naturally, most of the building blocks that went into the construction of this new persona and of his projected task had been fabricated earlier, in some cases even fifteen years before. The essays by Wolfskehl especially but also the various dissertations by Hofmannsthal, Simmel, and Klages had all contributed to the common project of defining who George and the *Blätter* poets were. George's own works, and most obviously his last two books, *The Tapestry of Life* and *The Seventh Ring,* had ever more insistently sounded his desire to engage the world in an open contest. Yet these were all disparate materials, unconnected with one another except in their focus on George himself. Now came the job of assembling the diverse components into a coherent whole. The goal was to provide an imposing, well-fortified edifice that could defend against a public that one could expect would be hostile, and to supply an expansive dwelling for those on the inside. As it was being expressed with increasing explicitness, the aim was to erect a citadel or fortress, an unassailable stronghold from which a war — admittedly, a war of words at first, but a war nonetheless — would be unleashed on the outlying landscape. "This war," Gundolf explained to an acquaintance a year later, in 1911, "is the father of good things, the war against barbarians, philistines, and clerics: against brutishness, servitude and narrowness." Losses were to be expected, indeed they were unavoidable and should not, Gundolf insisted, obscure the greater justness of the cause: to rescue the "living 'heritage of the Ancients'" — which is to say the Greek inheritance as embodied first and foremost in George — from internal erosion or aggressive assault. "Our common campaign, more defense than attack," Gundolf declared, "is conducted from various directions against its destruction and misinterpretation." Thus cloaked as the safeguarding of a cultural legacy, it seemed a noble and necessary enterprise, less bellicose than broadly beneficial. But, as later events would prove on a much larger and more literal plane, wars — even those said to be undertaken with the best of motives — are difficult beasts to control, often viciously turning on the very ones who unleash them from their restraints.

The first order of business was to solidify the foundations on which the circle — both as idea and as lived experience — rested. In the eighth number of the *Blätter* from early 1910, Gundolf published "Allegiance and Discipleship"

("Gefolgschaft und Jüngertum"), a short essay that almost single-handedly created the image of both George and his followers that from then on remained virtually unchanged. It is somewhat loosely organized along the lines of an apology, defending the ideals it invokes, but carried out on a relatively abstract level. Nowhere did Gundolf even mention George by name — instead, Gundolf referred only to *der Führer* — nor did he ever identify any of George's associates or "disciples," even though there could be no mistake that the entire essay was about anything else. But the rhetorical ploy had a purpose: by refusing to descend from the general to the specific, Gundolf was able to avoid soiling himself through any direct contact with the messy world of real particulars — a sphere he, as George's disciple, hated anyway. Even more important, by speaking generically, Gundolf could make his words seem more valid, less contestable, as if he were simply spelling out ancient truths instead of expressing mere opinion. Gundolf unquestionably believed in what he was writing, but for him the matter went beyond belief. The style of "Allegiance and Discipleship" says as much about his convictions as its content. Gundolf was not trying to convince himself or anyone else; he was simply revealing what was apparent to anyone with eyes to see.

The difficulty was that, according to Gundolf, most people were too blinded by vanity, prejudice, and self-interest, too dazzled by the flattering promises held out by the modern liberal ideals of individuality, independence, and self-determination to perceive the older truths he was disclosing. Small wonder, Gundolf wrote, that "the figure and concept of the 'disciple' is foreign to our time and almost ridiculous." To be a true disciple, he explained, one needed something that was in short supply in the world today: "love." Love causes a shift of perspective, it places things in a completely different light. Love knows no reasons, admits no arguments, needs no justification. "Whoever sees in the *Führer* only the representative of the cause has not understood him: whoever sees in him only a person cannot serve him." The *Führer* must be much more to the disciple than a mouthpiece for a doctrine; in fact, he must be more than merely human. The true disciple will necessarily find his leader immaculate, unrepeatable, elevated: in short, the disciple must love him as one loves a supreme being. "Whoever finds this master irreplaceable may call himself a Disciple." Disciples become the willing instruments of their master, empty vessels filled by their master's being; they offer themselves up uncategorically to the service of the one they love. "The duty of disciples is not imitation," Gundolf insisted. "Their pride is that the master is unique. They should not *make* his images · but rather *be* his work · not put on and display his petrified traits and gestures · but rather absorb into their being his blood and his breath · his light and his warmth · his music and his motion and pass them on into the still frozen or empty world." The *Führer*'s disciples,

Gundolf went on, should be "walking ovens that he has heated · matter he has animated: the realization · embodiment · replication of his great breath . . even without speaking the traces and rays and seeds of his power." Cleansed of the segregating desire to make "selfish claims" for themselves, such disciples have been liberated from the "arrogant isolation of the Ego." Genuine disciples not only relinquish the wish to be self-sufficient agents, they also would readily surrender their very beings for the sake of their master: "Where they recognize Necessity they gladly snuff out their Ego and are happy to be fuel for the higher flame."

Now, anyone who knew the inside story of Gundolf's relationship to George could justifiably claim that he had merely turned his personal brand of self-abasement into a universal maxim of behavior. Beneath the self-assured oratory one can detect Gundolf's effort to ennoble his own eagerness to please someone who hardly ever demonstrated, only received, affection as the most genuine form of love, as if he were trying to legitimate his own emotional subservience by portraying it as a universal norm. But Gundolf did not leave matters resting there. He also made an offensive assault on the antithetical prototype to his definition of the disciple: what he called the "personality." Here he heaped scorn on the notion that "the accidental · individual · limited form · the bundle of drives · desires · ideas and abilities that the little human being was given should be allowed to live life to the full · wants to be an end in itself and demands respect." Gundolf could not decide whether he found the idea that all people were equal or deserved to be treated as such was more ludicrous or repugnant. For him, there were natural and absolute divisions among people, hierarchies ratified by history and confirmed by observation, and only the modern tendency to reduce all differences to a small, interchangeable set of bland denominators had led to the perverse conclusion that everyone possessed a "personality." "Everyone is a person: personalities exist only where world substance merges into new crystals." That is, only a "master" or *Führer* can properly be said to be a "personality." Given such inescapable facts, Gundolf reasoned, the options open to the rest of us were relatively limited: "Whoever knows himself not to be a master should learn to be a servant or disciple — better than a hyperactive vanity."

One should be under no illusion about the radicality of Gundolf's conception or about the degree to which it stands in direct and intentional opposition to the basic tenets of political, moral, and even psychological liberalism. Granted, Gundolf had delivered something resembling a veiled self-diagnosis of his own private pathology, but the essay delivered more than a covert self-portrait. With it, Gundolf was consciously instituting a canon of value and conduct, ostensibly validated by an ancient, unwritten law, establishing a code that was meant to guide the actions, indeed the lives, of other people. "The reconstruction of souls is the wish or meaning of every powerful sayer and doer,"

Gundolf apodictically proclaimed. Disciples of the sort Gundolf envisioned accepted that their "souls" would be mere clay in the hands of the "doer," even that they would be dispensable fodder for his designs: "They should know that they are only material and means and should learn again to sacrifice."

Gundolf's opponent here — and by extension George's as well — was not so much contemporary Germany as it was the entire European legacy of the Enlightenment, with its emphasis on individual freedom, the fundamental right of each person to equal consideration before the law, and the inviolable worth of every human life. Gundolf's pronouncements read like a deliberate renunciation of Kant's demand that all human beings be treated as ends in themselves and never as means in some other design — the mainstay of a moral philosophy that placed human dignity at its conceptual center. We already know what George thought of his fellow man, and he was not about to grant a creature that was so contemptible and loathsome in his eyes any such lofty distinction. Other people were valuable to George only in so far as they could serve as useful tools or pliant vessels; otherwise they were less than worthless and eminently disposable. In fact, as Gundolf indicated, even those who were serviceable for a time to the *Führer* might well be discarded once their utility was exhausted. Under that category, Gundolf described various forms of "false discipleship," including those who seek out the *Führer* simply because his message is new and reserved for a small minority, priding themselves on belonging to an exclusive club. Then there are others who are truly committed but lack the depth to comprehend fully what they embrace. Both are useful, though, because they add wood to the fire — or, as Gundolf said, they draw others "onto the battlefield · they expedite the productive fight · prepare the air for the whistling of projectiles"; they are needed, that is, "to ignite the holy war." But once they have lit the spark, they are allowed to be consumed by the engulfing flame.

George thus had good reason to feel uplifted. With "Allegiance and Discipleship," Gundolf had generated a manifesto for George's current and future followers, giving them clear, unmistakable guidelines for viewing both themselves and their Master. It stipulates that his disciples should be selfless, humble, demure, and loyal but also self-sacrificing, fearless, and strong in carrying out their Master's wishes — even more: in embodying his will. And Gundolf endowed the "master" himself, the all-powerful *Führer*, with traits that would have amply satisfied any megalomaniac's most secret longings. Gundolf's style — a potent combination of haughty eloquence and bare-knuckled polemic, all clothed in choice literary attire — also did its part to make the whole ensemble even more efficacious. Although George actually never openly revealed what he thought of Gundolf's essay, he was well enough pleased with it to take it around and read it aloud to his Berlin friends. Vallentin noted in his diary that "the Master" formally presented Gundolf's treatise to them one evening with favorable results. Everyone was moved, Vallentin wrote, by the belligerent tone of the essay, "which positively enthused us with its resolute combativeness."

We have come a long way from George's beginnings as the herald of an esoteric poetic doctrine, from being a top-hatted aesthete who did not much like his beer-drinking compatriots but still thought it worth his while to teach them a little good taste. Now, encircled by a company of determined loyalists who were armed and ready to do his bidding, he stood at the center of a quasi-religious cultural crusade unabashedly calling for a "holy war." It was not a sudden transformation, but it is certainly an arresting one. As Simmel had also recognized, one of the most distinctive aspects of George's life and work was an almost uncanny single-mindedness, a seemingly unwavering purposiveness evident in everything he did. There had always been an aggressive element in both his personality and poetry, an assertive undercurrent that fed his need to dominate and control his environment. George had also tended to frame his understanding of the world in combative terms. He always principally defined himself by, and against, his enemies, real or imagined. Over time, the list of his antagonists had constantly grown and would continue to expand, eventually covering a vast range of putative villains and rogues. We hardly need to repeat the list: it included Prussians, Protestants, greedy bourgeois and gutter-minded naturalists, even nature itself. Increasingly, almost anything not immediately identified with George himself automatically fell into the category of the damned.

Perhaps the most important milestone on George's path from poet to potentate, both in the public perception of him and in the eyes of his followers, was set in 1910. In the same number of the *Blätter* in which Gundolf's "Allegiance and Discipleship" appeared, Friedrich Wolters published a portion of a work he had been laboring over for over three years called *Sovereignty and Service (Herrschaft und Dienst)*. Wolters had completed it the previous April, although sections of it had been circulating among members of the circle even earlier. In February 1909, for instance, George wrote to Wolters from Munich, where George was staying in his regular rooms at the Wolfskehls, that "people here read your lines on S[overeignty] and S[ervice] with the highest praise and interest and eagerly await the entire work." When it did appear, it was immediately perceived as signaling a turning point. Kurt Hildebrandt recalled that he and the other friends in Berlin saw it as marking the definitive rejection of the "aestheticism" of the past by establishing the guidelines for future action. "Instead of a 'circle' of readers," Hildebrandt said in defining the shift, "now a circle of disciples was to find its fulfillment in forming a spiritual state, which could gradually penetrate the outlying region in ever farther reaches. Only now did we become fully conscious of the meaning of the names Master and Disciple."

Wolters's *Sovereignty and Service*, as Hildebrandt had recognized, both complements and amplifies Gundolf's own elaborations on the Master/Disciple relation while drawing a larger circumference within which it is situated. Wolters used slightly different terms — instead of "master" or *Führer*, Wolters spoke of "the Ruler," and he also avoided the word "disciple," preferring the more active category of "servant" — but in general the phenomena they both describe are virtually identical. There are other similarities linking the two essays as well. Like Gundolf, Wolters adopted a solemn, oracular tone, but Wolters's diction is, if anything, even more opaque and diffuse. Stylistically, the language Wolters used in *Sovereignty and Service* seems in fact to fall halfway between poetry and prose. He developed a more or less coherent argument, but he did so within a highly metaphorical medium. George, who thought little of scholarly or "scientific" prose, considered such a hybrid to be ideal and viewed Wolters's work as a model of its kind. "There is an intermediary form between science and poetry," George once said. "*Sovereignty and Service* is also [such] a composite and is perfect." As time went on, this "composite" style became a hallmark of the George circle, and it was Wolters who had been among the first to refine it.

But for all of the points of agreement between Gundolf and Wolters, each one set his own distinct emphasis. Whereas Gundolf had chiefly concentrated on the psychological and emotional underpinnings of the bond between Master and Disciple, Wolters attempted to formulate the greater ideational superstructure, so to speak, in which that relation was supposed to make sense. Wolters began by drawing a parallel between what he called the "families of blood" and the "families of spirit" (*Geist*), the former designating the physical interrelations among people, and the latter the ties that come about through purely intellectual or spiritual union, free from the constraints of place and time. Thus there exists, Wolters explained, beyond or behind the material realm a "Spiritual Realm" or "Empire" (*Reich*), invisible to the eye and imperceptible to touch, but nonetheless very real. Indeed, it is the unseen forces generated within this Spiritual Empire that secretly govern the physical world, unappreciated by the dull masses, but always silently at work and evident to those able to perceive them and heed their imperatives. Collectively, the powers that covertly rule the world are what Wolters called "sovereignty" (*Herrschaft*), which is concentrated in the figure of the "Ruler" (*Herrscher*). It belongs to the nature of this spiritual power that it seeks to fashion the physical realm after its own image, to subject it to a design of its own making. "Sovereignty does not tolerate that any thing or being in the Plains of the Realm would carry any other insignia than its own," Wolters claimed. "Thus the Realm forms itself after the image of Sovereignty: but this is created and sustained by the Ruler." And it is through the so-called Spiritual Deed, in which the abstract notion is transformed into concrete form, that the Ruler exerts his influence on the world. "The Spiritual Deed is the content of Sovereignty, through which the Ruler subjects the Plains of the Empire to his formative will through inner coercion, whether he administers an inherited estate or erects one that has never been seen before, whether he exercises his fire on tried or untried substances, be it faith or clay, state or stone, language or number." Thus the "Spiritual Deed" can take on many forms, and the Ruler may also come in many guises. What remains constant is the profound, reality-changing impact the Ruler and his Deed have on the way we see ourselves and the universe.

It is here, in Wolters's conception of the constitutive power of the Ruler to shape the world, that his greatest divergence from Gundolf becomes apparent. Gundolf was so filled with aversion to what he saw as an irredeemably debased humanity that the only possible course of action he could imagine was to retreat from all contact with those outside his province or to wish their utter destruction — or, since both scenarios are not incompatible with one another, preferably both. Wolters, too, harbored no great fondness for his fellow man, but he was more interested in the Ruler's definitive ability to mold things in his own likeness, to make the world conform to his own nature. Wolters insisted that it was a matter of complete indifference how the Ruler wielded his authority or what means he employed to achieve his ends. The Ruler might be a statesman or a poet, a prophet or a physicist. What mattered was that in each case, although working through different substances, the Ruler changed the external world by imposing his particular view or understanding of things — his spiritual stamp, as it were — on it and therefore on us.

Much more obviously than Gundolf, Wolters was portraying a very specific individual as if he were rendering a universal type. And even though Wolters, like Gundolf, omitted all names to reinforce that effect, there could be no doubt that he had anyone other than George in mind. (Perhaps recognizing the futility of pretending to hide what was plain to see, Gundolf even suggested after he had read the manuscript that Wolters add the subtitle "On the Work of S[tefan] G[eorge].") Still, Wolters more or less openly admitted that his primary concern was not to consider every possible permutation in which the Ruler may manifest himself, "but rather to contemplate the Ruler, whose material is language, whose work is poetry, in his highest form as a single and unique person and through contemplation to learn to venerate him more deeply." Notably, Wolters claimed that he did see a certain advantage granted to the poet over other possible types of Ruler in that his instrument — language — permits an androgynous fusion of the male and female principles in the breast of the poet, the outcome of which — the poem — transcends in terms of its indivisibility the fruit of the bodily synthesis created by the union of man and woman. This is so, Wolters argued, because "for poetry the material is the double element of language and internal vision, whose male and female souls achieve such a unity with the formative power of the poetic spirit that its trinity in the work is less capable of being separated than even the blood of the mother, the blood of the father and creative love in the child." Thus the poet, whose creation unifies male and female, matter and spirit, does seem to occupy a privileged position in Wolters's cosmography and confirms what the reader has known all along: the quintessential Ruler is George himself, his poetry the paragon of the Spiritual Deed, and his disciples all exemplary inhabitants of the Spiritual Empire.

To anyone who had attentively followed the course of George's career and read his poetry with a sober eye, very little in Wolters's treatise would have come as a surprise. He had merely spelled out, with slightly more clarity and coherence, much of what had been there all along. What *was* new, however, and would have enormous consequences both for George and his circle as well as for Germany as a whole, is the intimate identification, even the fusion, of George and all he was seen to represent with the political realm. By using categories normally reserved for political discourse to describe the activities and goals of a poet, Wolters effectively merged the roles of politician and poet into a single office. As improbable as it would sound to the uninitiated, by the end of *Sovereignty and Service* it seemed perfectly reasonable to think of George as a "Ruler" in some meaningful sense who clandestinely governed the world. And that is precisely how George himself, as well as Wolters and the rest of his followers, saw it. Once, when a few years later someone unadvisedly criticized the prosaic description of George's poetry in Wolters's book, George vigorously defended it, placing particular emphasis on what he called the "main idea of the book [. . .] which had not been recognized until then: that to write poetry is a form of rule."

That was something George had felt, and acted on, for a long time. Wolters had simply articulated it in discursive form. From this point on, George quite literally conceived of his work, now extending well past the relatively narrow compass of his own verse, even surpassing the somewhat larger scope of the *Blätter,* as constituting a kind of secret, underground administration. To be sure, the world George ruled was still largely confined to the purely "Spiritual Empire," but he and his partisans believed that it was vastly superior to the one run by money-grubbing bourgeois. And since they were all convinced that the so-called real world took its direction from invisible dictates emanating from the spiritual realm, George's dominion was thought to be closer to the original and genuine sources of power anyway. He was, that is, a politician of the spirit, a ruler of the spiritual realm, but in instinct and ambition a politician nonetheless.

At the beginning of June 1909, George stayed briefly at the Stift Neuburg in Ziegelhausen near Heidelberg, where Karl Wolfskehl liked to spend part of the summer. Soon they were joined by other friends, including Melchior Lechter and Friedrich Gundolf. As always, it was a working holiday — George and Gundolf were in the midst of their Shakespeare translation — and George came down for breakfast every morning at seven-thirty. Punctually at eight, Gundolf would appear with his briefcase filled with the day's work, whereupon George would arise with the words: "Come, Gundel, time to govern." It was a slightly jocular comment, in flavor and tone akin to the private language often shared among close friends or family members. But George was not in the habit of mocking himself, and if he had meant it in jest, it was only just. For him, the Spiritual *Reich* over which he presided as undisputed *Führer* was as real as any other. No: it was more so.

CHAPTER 27

The Globe Room

To understand how George could make such claims of authority for himself and not be dismissed as a lunatic or a charlatan, one has to appreciate the uncanny effect he was increasingly making on the people who knew him. Alexander von Bernus, who was introduced to George when he was staying at Stift Neuburg in the summer of 1909, spoke for many when he said that "what was convincing and compelling about Stefan George was not so much his poetry [. . .] as the fascination of a great personality who had mastered his passions, but a personality that was much more that of a Roman Caesar than that of a poet." Bernus, who was writing in 1951, admitted that it was hard by then, looking back over four decades, to imagine the "magical attraction" George once exuded. But "in the years before the First World War an almost mythical nimbus surrounded him." Others, such as Edgar Salin, who met George around the same time, were similarly spellbound. "Something mysterious hovered over George," Salin recalled, "that mystery which emanates from majesty and nobility and creates a distance that only reverent love seldom bridges." A nineteen-year-old friend of Ernst Morwitz named Hans Brasch was introduced to George in the fall of 1911. "Our meetings," Brasch wrote, "almost always took place in the austere, bare rooms Morwitz had in the western part of Berlin and were borne by the indescribable solemnity of a secret center of the world, as it seemed to me."

Older acquaintances, who had known George not as a *Führer* but simply as a friend, also noticed there was something different about him now. Albert Verwey had last seen George in 1907 just before the publication of *The Seventh*

Ring. Even then Verwey had observed a disquieting tendency in his German colleague to assert prerogatives that went far beyond literature or the poet's task as Verwey understood it. In June 1910 Verwey visited George in Bingen and, as usual, they took long walks while engaging in animated conversations about literary matters that quickly turned to other issues. At one point, George took up a favorite topic and declared drama dead. Verwey realized that their argument "was not really so much about the drama question. It was about the question whether his conception of the times, which at that moment had driven him to oracular poetry, was the correct one, or mine." Actually, it was not a debate at all. George's mind was already made up that his view was the correct one and nothing could have convinced him he was wrong. Verwey felt there was no way to get through to him. "George lived at that point within a magical and prophetic propaganda which he placed far above his work. He spoke a great deal and passionately about his efficacy in this regard, about his importance, his power, his experiences. 'As time goes by, one sees in me more and more of what Wolfskehl calls the extrapersonal,'" George had told him. Verwey tried to argue that the poet who takes the extra- or super-personal element in his work and attempts to erect it as an object of veneration with the intention of forming a movement out of it was stepping outside of his poetic bounds. To no avail. George had a larger task. "What affected me in all of these speeches," Verwey wrote, "was the power of his belief. *That* the world would change was a certainty for him. Yes, I said, but *we* should only be poets."

Yet, despite Verwey's skepticism toward George's enlarged view of himself and his office, he also sensed there was something genuine, and genuinely powerful, there. To his surprise Verwey found that even he could not help occasionally succumbing to the strange allure his friend now exerted. It was almost as if, against his better judgment, Verwey were being drawn under the same spell bewitching others. "There were moments while he was speaking," Verwey revealed, "when the landscape, the hill with the towers of Bingen beyond, seemed transformed to me — as if, up on that height, I was not walking with a human being but with an angel. In his room as well, there was something in the distant gaze of his narrow, pale blue eyes, the way his large, veined hands hung down that made me think of such a divine being." Coming from such a sober and levelheaded man, it is a remarkable confession. Ultimately, though, Verwey was impressed but not persuaded. After his unsuccessful effort to make George accept that it was not the poet's role to take active part in the affairs of the world, Verwey resignedly, and presciently, contemplated the lurking danger in his friend's inflated ambitions. "I could vividly imagine what kind of influence, especially on German young people, a person such as he must have. Germany is after all the country of personal deification par excellence. And how enticing it had to be for him particularly to exercise that influence."

Verwey's apprehensions, and his sharp-eyed assessment of the prevailing temper among German youths of the day, were to be confirmed many times over in the following years. True, not everyone was equally susceptible to the forceful tug of George's personality. In 1909, when Alexander von Bernus met George at Stift Neuburg and Wolters's *Sovereignty and Service* was just going to press, the poet took Bernus to one side at one point and said with a confiding air, "I will tell you a secret: everything is achieved only by fanaticism. You are not fanatical enough by a long shot." Bernus dryly noted that "I did not make this maxim my own," and there were others who were similarly wary. Later that same year, in September, Gundolf, always on the lookout for new recruits, reported to George that Albert Rausch had visited him in Darmstadt the day before. Rausch had just returned from a trip to northern Germany, where he had apparently engaged in some eager proselytizing among his friends for what Gundolf had now habitually taken to calling "the state." Rausch was, Gundolf told George, "charming, alert, and effervescent, laden with successes for the state — he had stormed Hamburg and Lübeck and impregnated countless youths, counts and barons, with the canonical books." Even though Rausch happily drafted others, however, he was curiously hesitant to commit fully to the "state" himself. Gundolf informed George that he had chided Rausch for his obstinance, saying Rausch "was merely an individualist and extremely uncosmic, in fact too removed from any all-embracing activist passion to feel the necessity of the coming war."

It was undoubtedly just this sort of talk about an impending war and the need for fanatical devotion not just to it but also to George himself that gave some potential conscripts pause. But where the likes of Rausch and Bernus stopped short, many others were prepared to rush headlong into the breach. A twenty-six-year-old admirer named Ernst Schertel, who had met George in Munich through Wolfskehl, was a case in point. Although Schertel's own poems were not found suitable for publication in the *Blätter,* George had tolerated his presence on more than one occasion, raising hopes in the young man of a closer association. "After a long period of hesitation and despondency," Schertel wrote George in early March 1910, "I raise my glance anew to You, the great Judge yet also caring Shepherd. Take me in again, if not as a poet — who perhaps will be permitted to reach maturity only late — then as a person who drinks life from You. Allow me to breathe again in a room with You and wind the poor tendrils of my love around You. If I shall never be permitted to rise, these moments will fill my hours and drown out the torment of existence." Schertel closed by assuring George that "I await in reverent discipleship the inclination of Your masterly Goodness." In the end, George did consent to receive Schertel again but decided he could not give Schertel what he needed. "Yes, my dear," George told him at their last meeting, "you have a confused soul. I don't know how I can help you. I also don't know whether I can beget in you."

The word George used here — *zeugen,* "to beget," "engender" or "procreate" — was becoming more frequent in his descriptions of the kind of effect he wished to have on those under his tutelage. Just over a year later, in April 1911, George received a letter, not unlike others that were beginning to come his way in greater numbers, from a young man in Vienna named Hermann Bodeck. His Austrian admirer respectfully inquired whether he might be permitted to borrow a copy of *Maximin* so he could transcribe it for his private collection; everything else he already owned. "I have consecrated my life to you," Bodeck solemnly avowed. "It is true I am only seventeen years old, but I already know that salvation lies solely in the service of Greatness and in the conjoining of the soul for the highest penetration. Thus, each and every day I bow before you and live from the illumination that radiates from your books." Clearly, Bodeck had read all of George's poetry and he just as clearly knew the *Blätter* and their code. He thus made sure to tell George that "I am no aesthete and not a 'bookish' lad. I am small and insignificant before you and cannot imagine that I could ever inwardly free myself of you. [. . .] I put my trust in you and can tell you no more than that for your sake I could forego my parental house and property and wife." If George wanted to have him all to himself, Bodeck was saying, he was there for the taking.

As the number of petitioners for his attentions grew, George developed a more elaborate system of appraisal and initiation, with his own role undergoing a corresponding evolution. The communal readings continued, but they were becoming more structured and more carefully choreographed. Even what seemed to be relatively informal meetings with his friends were also beginning to take on a ritualistic air for those who were permitted to participate in them, as if every action, every word had a higher, consecrated meaning. Emblematic of this growing solemnization, or rather contributing to its rise, was the institution of the so-called Globe Room in Munich, where for more than a decade, until just after the war, George would receive his friends and scrutinize hopeful aspirants. Robert Boehringer, who could count himself among the few who experienced it, recalled in 1950, "Those who were there have retained a memory of the Globe Room as something out of the ordinary, and even after forty years I think of it as a space of rare and poetic days."

In late January 1909, Wolfskehl and his growing family had moved out of their apartment on Leopoldstrasse and into even roomier quarters in Römerstrasse 16, only a few streets away. The new apartment was chosen to accommodate not just the Wolfskehl household: the entire top floor was reserved for George during his winter residences in Munich. On either side of the upper hallway were two sets of doors, on the right leading to the unfinished attic spaces, and on the left opening into the two rooms set aside for George. The first and smaller of the two rooms served as his sleeping chamber, followed by a slightly larger space that acted as the gathering place for the Master and his friends. George had supervised its furnishing, and its spartan appointments reflected his desire to construct an asylum sheltered from the outside world. All reminders of that world, in fact, were explicitly banned from entering the room. In the hallway stood a low wooden rack with sandals that visitors had to exchange for their street shoes. There was also a large chest containing toga-like garments that guests were asked to don. George typically wore a full, long-sleeved white robe, reminiscent of the loose outer drape, or *peplos,* worn by women in ancient Greece, and others could often be seen in robes of yellow, light or dark blue, brown or a purplish red. Crowns of laurel completed the costume.

Inside the room, a simple straw mat lay on the floor and the walls were covered up to about shoulder height with a light yellow burlap. Otherwise the walls were white. Running around the perimeter of the room, just at the level of the top of the fabric wall covering, was a narrow shelf of natural, unstained wood designed to store manuscripts and page proofs, in addition to a pair of candlesticks. "There were no books in the Globe Room in Munich," George later told a friend; if a stray volume did somehow make its way in, it was fastidiously hidden away under the other papers. In the middle of the room was a table, constructed of the same blond, smoothly finished wood, with straight, untapered legs and usually covered by a plain white tablecloth. Surrounding the table were benches wide and long enough to recline on, upholstered with thin cushions covered in canvas. And, most importantly, supplementing the light coming into the room from the sole window, there hung from the ceiling a milky glass globe, made to specification, that diffused the glare from the electric bulb it concealed. The fixture gave the room its nickname. "This simple sun-like lamp which hung in the room was at that time something extremely unusual," Hans Brasch wrote, who had been introduced to the room just before the war broke out. "Today it has become a common form of illumination and probably no one has any idea who invented it in its simple functionality. At that time the globe lamp reminded one of something like the sun, cosmos, middle and circle and was like the reflection of his being."

"Those were the entire furnishings," another associate of George informs us. Actually, there was one other prominent item in the room, not mentioned in most descriptions of it, but of obvious special importance, particularly since it was the sole nonutilitarian, purely decorative article it contained. On the wall opposite the window, hanging above the manuscript shelf, was a photograph of a nude young boy, seen from a three-quarter rear view, revealing his buttocks, back, and bare shoulders. He holds a staff with his upraised left hand while his right arm hangs down by his side, and on his head sits a wreath of laurel. It was, as the one person who felt it necessary to comment on the picture's existence instantly recognized, "Maximin," in one of the photographs taken just before Maximilian Kronberger's death.

Here, then, in the Globe Room, watched over by the image of his private deity, George communed with those he summoned. As he intended, it felt as if one were stepping into a different world. "The afternoon sun fell full into [the room]," another visitor remembered. "Through the window one saw only just the roof line and the border ornamentation of the house lying opposite, and the open sky above. When the slanted glow of the sun flooded the room at an angle, one believed — far above the sounds of the street — that one was in a distant land." One of his friends said that the Globe Room was "the only true shrine of this city in which so many altars stand."

A visit to the Globe Room was obviously no casual affair, and every moment had a definite shape. On a prearranged signal at the doorbell, George himself would open the door and usher his guest into his realm. Sometimes there was only a single visitor (Hans Brasch said, "I was always alone with him, as his meetings with people close to him were in general one-on-one, in which a third person was not permitted to interfere.") More often, several people were present at the same time, even though no one knew in advance who might also be there. George referred to them only by their first names, or by one of the nicknames he liked to devise for his friends. When everyone had changed into his robe and had placed a laurel wreath on his head, they all took their place in the Globe Room, sitting or reclining on the long benches around the table.

Depending on his mood or on the people gathered, George often did not permit a conversation to disturb the initial proceedings, which normally began when he would ask one of the celebrants to read aloud, either from the Master's works or from the catalogue of official poets, or, less frequently, from verses of one's own. After this first round of reading, less structured exchanges might take place, but again George prevented them from straying too far afield and he insisted that everyone's words and thoughts be focused on the present event and above all on what was read. Another round of reading might follow in which every person would be asked to contribute in turn. As the evening wore on, they would pause for a simple meal. Pewter bowls filled with oranges, dates, and bread were laid on the table and wine was poured into pewter beakers. After the refreshment, which again could be boisterous or meditative according to the circumstances, there was more reading and either further discussion of the poems or silent reflection. Finally, the Master himself would read, often from new poems no one had heard before and always in his singular manner. "It was," another participant in these meetings described it, "an almost chant-like, tonelessly rigid magical song, stressing the rhythm all too heavily, every line a whole, every word bound to the line, certainly contrary to all theatricality, but hardly inflected, barely modulated." Following another period of mute contemplation, and as midnight approached, George would dismiss his guests into the dark and quiet streets.

We have an account of what must have been a fairly standard introduction to the poet and to the ritual of the Globe Room in the memoirs of Herbert Steiner, a native of Vienna. In early 1908, Steiner, then sixteen, had first written to Gundolf, correctly assuming one best approached the Master indirectly through an intermediary. Steiner said that he had been led to George's poetry and the entire "circle" of the *Blätter* "through Hugo von Hofmannsthal's great and praiseworthy part in the movement of the nineties." Steiner must have thought that mentioning the name of his famous compatriot would recommend him in Gundolf's and hence George's eyes. (In that assumption, Steiner was not far from wrong, but probably not in the way he imagined. A year later, in conversation with Berthold Vallentin, George said that Hofmannsthal, with whom he had ceased communicating three years prior, still continued to be valuable to him in so far as he served as a "gate" through which other people found the way to him.) Just to be on the safe side, Steiner also attempted to bolster his credentials by analyzing a few of the poems in the *Blätter,* including some of Gundolf's, and he included several verses he had written of his own, dedicated, not surprisingly, "To Friedrich Gundolf." The dedicatee responded with measured reserve, dryly thanking for the expression of Steiner's convictions and the poem — "a friendly sign of an unexpected distant impact," as Gundolf put it. A few more letters were sent back and forth, until, after the passage of several months, Steiner finally revealed what he had no doubt been burning to ask from the beginning: he wanted to know "which conditions one had to fulfill to become a member of the *Blätter für die Kunst,* or whom one should approach."

Gundolf's reply — still cool, slightly patronizing, not discouraging but not encouraging, either — adhered to the official line that the *Blätter* was not a "club" or a "closed society," but instead, "a spiritual circle whose members have found one another through a shared attitude and beliefs about art." But, Gundolf cautioned, one could not simply "declare membership" to the circle of people associated with the *Blätter,* just as little as one could declare oneself a member of the "Romantic School," say, or the Age of Goethe. Moreover, the *Blätter* — "the organ of this circle" — should not be thought of merely as an ordinary literary magazine, "but precisely the assembly point for the poetic and linguistic expression of those new beliefs and the new way of experience." Insisting that their publications were "available to anyone who reveals himself to be sympathetic," Gundolf also gave Steiner the address of Otto von Holten, the Berlin printer, who had been publishing the journal since its inception. It was a classic *Blätter* invitation: part rebuff, part reproach, a dash of hauteur and a healthy measure of disdain, all wrapped up in the apparent offer to join an organization that claimed not to be one for purposes other than what were advertised.

Despite this less than reassuring reception, and perhaps as a reward for his persistence, Steiner was given the chance to meet the Master himself only two months later, when George was briefly in Vienna. The day before their meeting was to occur, Steiner received from Gundolf the name and address of the hotel where George was staying. At the appointed hour, Steiner made his way to the poet's room. As was George's habit, he quizzed the young man about his progress in school and, while acknowledging how inadequate exams were, impressed upon Steiner how important it nevertheless was to do well in them. Then he turned to his favorite subject. He asked Steiner "if I knew how to read poems? He wanted to teach me." He also wanted to know if Steiner knew the poetry anthology he and Wolfskehl had put together and, receiving a negative answer, promised to send it to him, saying, "That will give you a standard." They exchanged a few more pleasantries and George expressed the desire to see Steiner again. But before a second meeting could take place, George abruptly left town.

Steiner must have made a favorable impression, for there were subsequently repeated attempts to arrange another encounter, but it was not until a year later that he saw George again. In mid-February of 1910, Steiner took a week's leave from school and traveled by train to Munich, where the Master was residing in his rooms at the Wolfskehl apartment. George personally went to the station to pick him up, and Steiner remembered being greeted by a figure "in the dimly lit station concourse standing at the turnstile, in a black hat and a high-necked black overcoat cut like a soutane, and I was startled by his pallid, death-like face." Back at the Globe Room, Steiner was asked to put on a camel-hair robe, while George and Gundolf, who was also present, both wore white. They were later joined by Wolfskehl and his wife Hanna and, after enjoying a light repast, everyone read aloud.

Over the next several days, George and Steiner went for almost daily morning walks together through the snowy streets of Munich. As if in outward recognition of his high spirits, George wore the blue Basque beret he had acquired twenty years before on his travels through Spain. At George's insistent prodding, his young companion tried it on, too. In general, George spoke a great deal about that early epoch in his life, regaling Steiner with stories about Mallarmé — "In that house no one ever spoke of money," George told him — the actress Eleonora Duse — an accomplished performer, George acknowledged, "but modern theater was unsalvageable" — and he retailed anecdotes about friends left behind long ago, such as Paul Gérardy, who was so disorganized, George said, that he even forgot to appear at his own wedding. George also told Steiner about his own family, about his mother and sister and his great granduncle from the Lorraine, Johann Baptist, who had followed Napoleon's troops eastward to Büdesheim.

All the while, George closely observed his new acquaintance, watching for signs that he might be responsive to his guidance and designs. Pointing to Gundolf, he said to Steiner, "See what I have made of him!" as if George were telling him that, if allowed to do so, he could perform the same transformation with Steiner as well. George more or less openly told Steiner that he wanted to take the youth of today and "form them, form them in *his* image," a desire Steiner sensibly took to be aimed at himself as well. To be the potential object of such demiurgic ambition was an overwhelming and understandably slightly frightening experience. "His tense and powerful will seldom relaxed," Steiner wrote. Reflecting back on those winter days in Munich, "his actions were systematic, aimed at the long term, those of a man who knows how to rule and makes one think that forces and secrets stand at his command." To the young man, indeed, George gave the impression of being "a secret ruler, unknown to those in power in the world, intentionally unknown, one step off the path of the visible." It was an unsettling, though oddly thrilling sensation to be in the presence of someone who seemed to live on a different plane from everyone else. During one of their conversations, George casually used the word "mahatma." Steiner had never heard the word before and asked what it meant. "I see him," Steiner wrote, conjuring up the image in his mind's eye, "his cigarette in one hand, the other playing with his monocle, I hear the calm answer, tinged with dialect: 'Mahatmas — those are the powers that stand behind life. If they need a man who fights for them, then they send him into life. I was sent by the mahatmas.'" The sense that George was somehow incognito, that he was like an exiled king, a fugitive sovereign assembling the troops of an oppositional force from some underground refuge, was reinforced during one of their walks through town. As they turned a corner they saw a regiment of soldiers marching toward them, loudly accompanied by the tingle-tangle of the band. To Steiner's bewilderment, George quickly ducked into the next side street, as if he wanted to avoid being detected.

For the moment, though, George was less concerned about falling in the hands of the enemy than capturing his own quarry. In their sessions in the Globe Room, he revealed to Steiner what he called the "secret of the ring," the mystery of the "elected filiation" — *Sohnschaft,* or literally "son-dom" — which produced the offspring whom George, who would never have physical children, could only spiritually engender. "He believed," Steiner revealed of their conversations, "in spiritual impregnation, in the resurrection and rebirth of the pupil through the master, in the implanting of the spirit, like the priest of a primitive tribe." One morning, George read aloud to Steiner from Plato's *Phaedrus* — one of the few books allowed in the Globe Room was Rudolf

Kassner's translation of the dialogue — focusing on Socrates's long speech about the mad frenzy of love.

Yet, as unambiguous as all this seems, George, guarded as ever, painstakingly avoided any direct entreaties. As the end of Steiner's stay approached, George took him one last time into the Globe Room. There he opened up the copy of the eighth number of the *Blätter,* which he had given to Steiner and contained the prose passage describing the discovery of Maximin. George gestured toward the picture hanging on the wall and said, "Here is something that I have not yet spoken a word about to you." Literally that was true. But in another sense he had spoken about nothing else. It was almost as if, by asserting that Maximin had ever entered into their conversation, George was preparing Steiner for any future inquiries about what was said or done during his visit, surreptitiously rehearsing what Steiner's responses should be. Likewise, George sent the young man off with a warning not to indulge in the presumptuous belief that he now knew everything about him or his friends: "This," George said, "was only the first initiation."

As it happened, it was also the last. Whether George sensed that he would not get very far with Steiner, or whether Steiner felt that he had gone as far as he wanted to go, they never met again. Even during his stay, George had composed a poem dedicated "To H." that indicated he had already essentially given Steiner up. George showed him the poem before he departed but since it was not yet in its finished form George did not allow him to keep it or make a copy: he said only that he did not want it to "be shown around." The poem eventually found its way into George's next book, *The Star of the Covenant,* but without any identifying marks that would reveal its actual subject. But Steiner of course recognized himself in it. He thought that the poem well documented the "playfulness and seriousness of those days, the joking that is resistance, which is elusive and hides and represses a fearful anxiety, the tension George radiated, and his courting."

It was this, George's relentless, single-minded pursuit of the young man's devotion, and Steiner's gentle rejection of his suitor's advances, that the poem plainly memorializes. As was often the case with George, he used the poem as a way to put an unsuccessful affair behind him, closing off a chapter in his life that had caused him pain or distress. In the final version, the poet, speaking to an abstract "you," indirectly expresses a vague disappointment that someone who had initially seemed so promising should have turned away from him. Yet the addressee's charms are so endearing that the poet cannot remain angry. "Who should wish you otherwise," the poet wistfully asks, "when you lower your head in that way with a smile." George even invoked his favorite floral imagery, always laden with sexual significance, to express the disparity between the apparent maturity of his departing companion in both his bearing and appearance and his actual age, comparing him to a "too full flower on too tender a stalk." Yet, the poet says he cannot wait forever for some external event to change the other's life. " 'Do not speak too severely of the weak one who separated himself,' " the poem has the object of this gentle rebuke offer in response; " 'remember how you treated me with kindness / I was a blond wonder to you — nothing more.' "

Ernst Morwitz tells us that the phrase "blond wonder" came from Friedrich Gundolf, who coined it in reference to a popular French sports figure at the time known as "the little wonder" who went by the stage name "Blondin." For George, the slightly derogatory undertone of the epithet, together with the poem's portrayal of the other's submissive assumption of blame for the failure of the relationship, and finally the claim that he had meant "nothing more" than a brief dalliance to the poet, all helped put the episode in its proper perspective. Steiner had made a choice, and he had chosen badly. Not everyone who was admitted to the sanctuary of the Globe Room and thus given the chance to be spiritually impregnated by the Master succumbed to the seduction. Those who resisted, however, were forever banished to the sterility of the outside world, a fate George equated with a living death.

CHAPTER 28
Secret Germany

As important as the ritual of the Globe Room, the published paeans to his absolute leadership, and the increasingly ceremonial, highly systematized readings in both the Munich and Berlin circles all were for the consolidation of George's persona and his power, they were still largely private affairs, reaching only a small number of selected participants and in any case mostly exercises of preaching to the converted. What was needed was a means of reaching a larger audience, a way to take the message of the Master to the world — or at least to something greater than the two dozen or so people who were the active votaries of the circle. It was a desire, as we know, that George had felt for years, and which had now assumed a kind of urgent necessity, especially given the sorts of "extrapersonal" prerogatives lately being claimed by and foisted upon him. Drama, the most dynamic and immediately effective of the literary forms, was definitely out, and few other outlets seemed either suitable or capable of delivering the required punch.

An opportunity presented itself more or less by accident at the end of 1909. One of his Berlin friends, Kurt Hildebrandt, sent George an essay that mounted a sustained attack on an eminent classical scholar at the University of Berlin, Ulrich von Wilamowitz-Moellendorff. It was a daring exploit: Wilamowitz was the undisputed giant among classical philologists not just in Germany, but in the whole of Europe, an esteemed authority on ancient Greece, and someone who wielded considerable power in the university administration. Although Hildebrandt performed a ritual bow before Wilamowitz's "erudition" and the "universality of his knowledge," his main purpose in writing his essay, he audaciously wrote, was "to convince the many who admire this philological mind of his dangerousness." George, who had several reasons of his own for reviling Wilamowitz, said he was "delighted" by the essay's polemical denunciation of the sixty-two-year-old scholar's sanitized view of Greek antiquity. He was so pleased with it that he wanted the essay to appear as a separate pamphlet with the firm of Georg Bondi. The circumspect publisher, no doubt wanting to avoid needlessly ruffling the feathers of such a highly respected and influential figure in Berlin intellectual circles, politely declined. George would never have considered asking anyone else to print the piece, so he solved the problem with characteristic aplomb. On November 3, 1909, George called together Gundolf, Wolfskehl, Lechter, Paul Tiersch, and Ludwig Thormaehlen to meet at Vallentin's house. There he announced he was founding a new journal to be called the *Jahrbuch für die geistige Bewegung*, or *Yearbook for the Spiritual Movement*, which would be published directly by the *Blätter für die Kunst* and printed by the trusty Otto von Holten.

In essence, the *Yearbook*, although born of immediate needs, was also the delayed fruition of a plan George had long nourished. As early as 1895, he had broached the notion to Hofmannsthal of expanding the *Blätter* to include, in addition to poetry, contributions of a more broadly "descriptive nature." The following year he brought up the matter again, now specifying that it would be a "monthly German review" in which "a few truly important young scholars" would be invited to participate. Owing mainly to Hofmannsthal's hesitancy to get involved in a venture he knew would only bind him closer to George than he wanted to be, the idea was temporarily shelved but not wholly abandoned. George had last mentioned the project in 1903 in two further letters to Hofmannsthal, whom he still hoped to win over to the effort and which he now envisioned not as a monthly but as an annual publication. "I wanted to speak further of the often mentioned *Yearbook*," George told him in June of that year, and in September he confidently announced that "we will finally discuss our *Yearbook* when I go to Berlin." But only four months later, the entire set of circumstances in which George had originally conceived of the *Yearbook* unexpectedly and radically changed. In January 1904, the Cosmic Circle broke apart, three months after that Maximilian Kronberger succumbed to meningitis, and soon enough Hofmannsthal himself was as good as dead as well. Months, even years passed before George was even able to begin thinking again about embarking on such a major endeavor. Yet, by the time he had recovered the strength and composure to do so, he had also undergone a transformation that had left him a different person, and with a different agenda, than before.

"The *Yearbooks*," Edgar Salin wrote, "are works of combat" — *Kampfschriften*. For George, the publication of a work, either his own or an associate, was never a straightforward issue. The books he produced had always been intended to serve a variety of purposes, one of the main ones being, paradoxically, less to invite readers into an unfamiliar domain than to strengthen and secure that domain from unbidden intruders. But most recently, George and his followers were becoming impatient with their purely defensive posture and were more and more consciously girding for attack. As the newest addition to the already formidable arsenal George had amassed for his operation, the *Yearbooks* were thus explicitly thought of as the first-line instruments of war in a battle he had been anticipating, indeed abetting, for over a decade. "Essays are weapons," George himself said, much later. "That's also the effect the *Yearbooks* had. Since then, certain people have no longer dared to be so impertinent. Now they knew: one has to be wary of them."

Thormaehlen, who was present during the spirited conversation that took place on the November evening when George launched the *Yearbook,* tells us what the primary targets of the campaign were to be. Everyone agreed that the "the spiritlessness of the time" had to be exposed and denounced, as well as "the pernicious effect of the actions and teachings" being promulgated "in the universities and among the spokesmen of daily opinion" — that is, journalists — and "above all among the advocates of so-called progress, of modern achievements, of bringing happiness to the people." The *Yearbook for the Spiritual Movement,* in other words, would take on the whole of modern German liberal culture, exposing the rot infecting its officialdom and the hollowness of the political and social structures on which it rested.

But bureaucracy is unavoidable even in war, and before the first shot could be fired, a number of practical details had to be worked out. For example: who would edit the yearbook? Someone, or several people, would have to shoulder the tedious task of prodding other contributors to finish and send in their essays, of assembling the manuscripts, clearing up the inevitable inconsistencies, errors, and stylistic infelicities, of negotiating with the printer, checking the proofs, and on and on. George, who now more then ever would never consider lowering himself to such depths, said simply he could not be an editor because he did not want his name on the title page. But someone had to assume the role. For obvious reasons, both Gundolf and Wolters seemed natural choices. Wolfskehl, with his infamous torpidity when it came to putting pen to paper or meeting deadlines, was simply too unreliable to entrust with the job. Vallentin was asked to sign himself as the third editor, making for a larger and more unified front. But Vallentin withdrew his name, fearing that it would negatively influence his pursuit of a judgeship in Berlin. Although Vallentin quickly changed his mind and said he wanted to be included after all, it was too late. George refused the request with a postcard he dictated that said, "You will have to be content with the situation you have created" and referred him to a line from the "Prologue" in *The Tapestry of Life:*

"The disciples love yet are weak and cowardly." Vallentin, bitterly disappointed but stoic, took solace in the bracing effect George's firmness had on him. "How that all hits home," was apparently all he said in response.

Kurt Hildebrandt, whose essay had been the catalyst for the entire undertaking, was subsequently offered the post, but he also hesitated. At the time, he was assistant medical director of a psychiatric clinic located in Wittenau, a district of Berlin. The clinic was known as Dalldorf, which, like the institution in London that served a similar purpose, Bedlam, had become the popular shorthand term Germans used for "madhouse." Hildebrandt, concerned that this association, once revealed, would lead to distracting and injurious witticisms, suggested that, if he signed on as an editor, he adopt a pseudonym: Kurt Florentin (the latter was actually Hildebrandt's middle name, a permanent memento of his birth in Florence). Gundolf, writing no doubt as the agent or at least with the consent of George, expressed pleasure that Hildebrandt was in principle willing to collaborate — "People in Berlin have talked a lot: now it is time to act" — but he was less happy with the idea of Hildebrandt's hiding behind a mask. "With such a strong statement of opinion as yours I also regard using your full name as necessary." It was of course the honorable position to take — anonymity is the refuge of the cowardly — but Hildebrandt, still uncertain, demurred. Like Vallentin, Hildebrandt learned that he had only once chance to consider the offer. George never asked him again.

More by default than by design, then, the *Yearbook* officially came to be edited by only Gundolf and Wolters, whose names prominently appeared on the front cover. But, as Hildebrandt said and everyone else on the inside knew, "the real editor is the Master himself." George oversaw every aspect of the *Yearbook*. He carefully read all of the articles, discussed them at length with their authors, suggested specific revisions and cuts, and he personally checked the final page proofs. Even the title of the yearbook was entirely George's doing. It was partly inspired by a similar enterprise Albert Verwey had started in 1904, which he called, simply, *De Beweging,* or "The Movement." Verwey reported that "George liked this name very much," and it was partially in homage to his Dutch colleague that George decided to incorporate the word "movement" into the title of his own publication. And when Wolters, the most hostile among the members of the circle toward rationalism in all of its guises, protested that adding the word "spiritual" — *geistig* — to the title would make it sound too intellectualistic, too conceptual, in short too rationalistic, George impatiently waived away his objections: "How do you want to have an effect today other than through spirit?" Apparently, Wolters had also forgotten that the very first issue of the *Blätter* in 1892 had declared that the journal promoted a "SPIRITUAL ART" — *geistige Kunst*. George's insistence on including the word *Geist* in the title suggested that in this way, too, he saw himself pursuing the same ends as always, just in different form. *The Yearbook for the Spiritual Movement* it was to be.

When the first issue of the *Yearbook* appeared in early March 1910, it contained only six essays: Hildebrandt's frontal assault on Wilamowitz; a short piece by Vallentin criticizing the notion and value of progress; a somewhat ill-fitting contribution by a friend of Wolfskehl named Hugo Eick on "the Legacy of the Rococo"; an essay by Wolfskehl himself on the history of the *Blätter für die Kunst;* and two works by both of the editors, with Gundolf's devoted to "George's Image," and Wolters's more nebulously proffering "Guidelines." These last three articles, by George's highest-ranking officers, formed the true core of the *Yearbook,* and they all focused more or less exclusively on revealing the Master and his meaning to the world. As the short preface signed by the editors states, all six emanated from a common intention: "to examine the legitimacy of the multiple, fragmented, confused tendencies of the time." This was an urgent task, it went on, because "the knowledge that has been indiscriminately collected has piled up to such an extent that it no longer promotes spirit and culture but rather threatens to suffocate both." It was therefore with the aim of "winnowing out" what was valuable and what was dispensable among the "tendencies of the time" that the editors put forward their views, which they openly admitted were consciously and unapologetically one-sided. They wanted, they said, not to be neutral and open to all points of view but rather "to subordinate themselves, in conscious partiality, to a comprehensive will — an Idea." Actually, it would have been more accurate to say: not to an Idea but to the Master himself.

While they may have been united in their purpose and in their allegiance to a single cause, the contributors to the first *Yearbook* do not present anything approaching a unified program. What binds them together is not so much the articulation of a positive ideology — although one could say it was implicitly present in their shared and unqualified glorification of the poet — as the total rejection of everything they collectively opposed. Yet there were certain ironies inherent to the whole enterprise. As Claude David wryly noted, the *Yearbook* "nowhere develops a coherent system," and in fact it flaunted its disdain of systematic knowledge, yet "employs a great deal of logic to celebrate illogicality." Too, even though the *Yearbook* was meant to be a vehicle on which George would ride into the consciousness of the broader public, very few readers would come away from it without thinking they were not among the majority it condemned as unfit to receive its message. On the other hand, that was partly the point. The *Yearbook* was not designed to win converts or change minds. For that the time had passed. The *Yearbook* was the opening maneuver in a conflict that would end only in ultimate victory or defeat.

As George's senior lieutenant, Karl Wolfskehl assumed the responsibility of leading the initial charge. Occupying the vanguard of the *Yearbook,* his essay performed the duty of advancing the origins, rationale, and evolution of what he programmatically called "our movement." While the picture Wolfskehl drew is expansive, it is also, as was typical for Wolfskehl, fairly short on specifics. Few names are named apart from a few conspicuous exceptions, including George himself, of course, and, notably, Nietzsche, as well as selected others. And, in general, Wolfskehl's account is suffused with the kind of murky mythographic oratory that had been the trademark of his *Blätter* essays all along. Explaining that the journal and thus the "movement" it had instigated had "been born," because "a poet ignited a flame in another poet" — presumably the reference is to George's encounter with Mallarmé — Wolfskehl insisted that the entire development followed the "organic" laws of "life itself."

After spending what seems an inordinate amount of time sketching out the prehistory of the *Blätter*, Wolfskehl finally came to Nietzsche and presented him as George's immediate precursor and as the sole positive phenomenon in what Wolfskehl a little later called "the eternally accursed nineteenth century." "With his work," Wolfskehl proclaimed, "the entire vast wealth of the German spirit that had lain underground for two generations, since the romantic world had been extinguished, was finally brought to light. With that, the great true battle began under whose sign we now stand." Nietzsche, whose fame and influence had continued their meteoric rise after his death in 1900, was an acceptable forebear for George for any number of reasons. But in this instance his primary attraction was the fact that he was German. Just as the name of Mallarmé was only alluded to but not actually mentioned, Wolfskehl goes out of his way to ridicule the notion that any external force, and in particular anything of French provenance, had ever had the slightest effect on George. After citing a lengthy passage from Nietzsche's *Human, All-Too-Human,* Wolfskehl triumphantly concludes that the sentiments expressed there and in the *Blätter* issued from the same inner and distinctly German need that "only fools or those with ill intentions could derive from the writings of the French symbolists, which were more or less contemporaneous but hardly sound the same."

Behind this shameful denigration of old colleagues and former teachers, as well as the no less problematic grasp for Nietzsche's torch, was not just Wolfskehl's desire to make George appear as a purely German character. It was also part of the intensifying effort among all of George's followers to portray him as utterly unique, as unprecedented and unrepeatable. Even Nietzsche, it is implied, ultimately could not measure up to the Master. Indeed, George himself was always ambivalent about the comparison, and he often mixed recognition of Nietzsche's importance with mitigating reservations about Nietzsche's achievement relative to his own. Somewhat later, in 1920, George said, for example, that he had long admired Nietzsche as "an orator, as a fighter who was useful." But he also added that he was uninterested in someone who still opposed Christianity. "You are still stuck in whatever you fight against. Nietzsche wasn't beyond Good and Evil, Algabal was." What essentially drove Wolfskehl's chronicle — ostensibly an historical account, though idealized, and in practice actually quite deeply antagonistic toward history — was the desire to demonstrate how George and the group of people around him represented the only viable, sanitary alternative to what he disdainfully called "our so naked and cold and repulsive reality."

In Wolfskehl's telling of the origins and rise of the *Blätter für die Kunst,* George and his circle emerge not principally, or even at all, as being united in their common understanding of art but in their shared view of life itself. As opposed to the "overheated cult of individuality of our time," which fed on the empty slogans of " 'reason,' 'freedom,' 'humanity,' " the community around Stefan George "represented the only unity of people, works, and desires to have arisen organically" during the last two decades. "Only here," Wolfskehl wrote, meaning the elect community of the circle, "where personal envy and resentment, all striving among one another, all craving to steal or swindle each other's status" were excluded, only in that choice society "could the expressions of life of an extrapersonal nature arise in at least embryonic form." Thus it was that Wolfskehl could claim "the true driving forces of the time" should be sought not in that infertile wasteland known as the modern world but somewhere else: in the constellation gathered around George that Wolfskehl here, for the first time, gave a name: "Secret Germany." "For underneath the desolate superficial scab there is beginning to stir today, still half in a dream, the *secret Germany,* the only one alive in our time, which has found expression here, only here." The fact that this "secret Germany" had managed to maintain its vigor and integrity over the years, Wolfskehl continued, "gives us deep confidence in a future that will certainly be grave, difficult, and somber, certainly full of enormous upheavals, but in which the depths shall reveal themselves for perhaps the last time."

It is hard to say exactly what Wolfskehl meant by the "depths" that would be opened up, or the "upheavals" that would overturn the existing order of things. One thing is certain, however: whatever the nature of the convulsions to come, Wolfskehl was certain they would leave devastation and ruin in their wake. And it was equally clear to Wolfskehl's mind where salvation from the impending cataclysm could be found. "Of all the peoples of Europe," he said, "we Germans are the only ones who have not yet fulfilled themselves, who may still hope." It was precisely the Germans' relative backwardness, Wolfskehl implied, that had shielded them from the worst kinds of corruption that had already rendered others irretrievably moribund. "We Germans are from yesterday," he darkly warned, "and for that reason we will be of tomorrow." It was both an honor and a weighty obligation to have the future of the world rest on one's shoulders, but it was a charge the subjects of the "secret Germany" willingly assumed. For, Wolfskehl concluded, it was obvious "that a movement out of the depths, if such a thing is still possible in Europe, can come only from Germany, from the secret Germany, for which every one of our words is spoken, from which every one of our verses draws its life and rhythm, the unceasing service of which means the happiness, necessity, and justification of our lives."

In several respects, Wolfskehl's postulate of a "secret Germany" provided a convenient solution to one of the most nettlesome difficulties that had vexed George since the mid-1890s. For it was then that he had first begun to distance himself from his French mentors and to present himself as a wholly indigenous product. Thereafter he would be an exclusively German poet, appropriating the German literary and cultural heritage as his natural birthright and divesting himself of all foreign attachments. But the problem remained that the Germany he claimed as his own had little to do with the one that really existed, which, moreover, George hated with growing intensity. By positing a "secret Germany," which unlike its all too manifest counterpart was vital, strong, and pure — and above all answerable to him alone — George could have it both ways. He could categorically reject the diseased body politic of the existent German state while exercising unlimited control over his own version of it.

It is true that the idea of an invisible or "secret" Germany had a history that predated George. To a degree, it was a fiction nurtured by the peculiar development of the real Germany it was supposed to supersede. During the first three quarters of the nineteenth century, when the German-speaking lands were the only ones among the other major European states not to have been formed into a single nation, there was no "Germany" except as an abstraction or a distant historical memory. For many German-speaking writers, whose national yearnings were unfulfilled by political reality, the only option had been to imagine a unity on some other plane. From Hölderlin to Schiller to Hebbel and Heine — all of whom, not incidentally, were sanctioned poets in George's canon — one encounters repeated invocations of a "hidden," "anonymous," "spiritual" Germany that would one day emerge and take its rightful place in the world. But for George the matter was different. His "secret Germany," with himself at the helm, was intended as a viable replacement for the flawed incarnation everyone could see. The challenge was how to get rid of that rival structure.

The next contribution in the *Yearbook*, Gundolf's essay on "The Image of George," does not so much offer the blueprint for achieving that goal as it compounds the arguments for its necessity. The body of Gundolf's article basically amounts to a lengthy book review, focusing for the most part on three previously published works with the aim of extracting the "image of George" they each present. About two of them Gundolf was unreservedly enthusiastic:

he lingered with approval over both Klages's encomium of 1902 and Wolters's even more adulatory *Sovereignty and Service*. The full weight of his opposition came down on the third work, the published version of a speech on Hofmannsthal given by the essayist, poet, and translator Rudolf Borchardt, who had been friendly with several members of the Berlin circle in 1905 but had quickly fallen out of favor. In Borchardt's original lecture, he had mentioned George in quite favorable but not hyperbolic terms and, most egregiously, had placed Hofmannsthal on equal artistic footing with George. This signaled a lack of due respect in Gundolf's eyes and unleashed a torrent of sarcasm and condescension.

But it is in what comes before and after this rather unseemly polemical exercise in character assassination that the essence of Gundolf's own "image of George" shows forth. As one might predict, that image is blemishless. Where Borchardt comes off as a desiccated philologist, parasitically sucking the lifeblood from the literary corpus, Gundolf assured us that "Stefan George sends down roots into the middle of the creative earth, inexorably bound to the *one* necessity, incapable of forming even a single word that was not forced out of the same inner necessity and consecrated by the most profound belief." "No other person," Gundolf tells us, "has taken up and led the battle against the superficial tendencies of the time and its purely temporal character as fully and extensively as Stefan George," and it is George's radical opposition to miserable condition of the contemporary world "that makes him the leader [*Führer*] in a spiritual war that can no longer be avoided." Given the role that has devolved upon him, Gundolf thought it should be self-evident that, as he wrote, "Stefan George is the most important man in Germany today."

It is an astonishing claim, astonishing as much for its audacity as for its naiveté. But Gundolf was deadly serious. For him, and not just for him, George *was* the most important person alive in Germany, and Gundolf was convinced that it was only a matter of time before others realized it as well. Yet the meaning of George's life extended well beyond his individual destiny; he represented a way of living, a system of values, to which, by recognizing him as one's Master, one could also belong. "Professing one's faith in George is not professing faith in a person," Gundolf went on. "He has no vanity and seeks no fame, much less success, to be sure, however, the power to form man and earth after the image of his god. He wields this power by creating the linguistic body of the coming spirit and forming souls for the coming faith." George, Gundolf wrote, forces us to make an absolute choice. There can be no half measures, no divided loyalties. "No inessential details should obscure the fact that there must be war between what is substantial and what is chimerical, that every being must struggle with what is foreign to it until, in the contest between the two spheres, one of the two is destroyed or converted." Naturally, Gundolf was not just confident, he was absolutely certain who the victor in this mortal contest would be. For it was George, and George alone, who "knows that the revival can come only from what is most distant, that one can extract from the poison of the time itself only relief and reprieve, but not transformation." Gundolf even hinted that the Germans were a kind of new chosen people, fortunate to have had the miracle of potential rescue dropped in their midst. Still, salvation would come to but a few even among the Germans, and the rest would perish unredeemed. "With George, those Germans who are still able to experience a poet at all are beginning to have the premonition of a new day and the lifting of an ancient anguish." For those people who were incapable of genuinely "experiencing" a poet, that new day would be a bad one.

After Gundolf's bellicose treatise, the following three essays by Vallentin, Hildebrandt and Eick seem flaccid by comparison. The weakest of the entire collection is Eick's rambling discussion of the Rococo, which Gundolf's friend Ernst Robert Curtius also recognized was "far beneath the collective niveau of the other contributions." It was so awful that Curtius wanted to know "how you and Wolters could come to accept it!" But Vallentin's promising sounding "Critique of Progress" is not much better, coming to the conclusion, after whipping up a good deal of lather, that progress is, in a word, bad. Even Hildebrandt's essay, which had got the whole ball rolling in the first place, is something of a disappointment overall. Hildebrandt had never published a word before and, as a medical doctor, had no obvious expertise in classical literature. His essay thus derived most of its piquancy from the sheer insolence demonstrated by a nobody publicly attacking someone of Wilamowitz's stature.

At issue were some translations Wilamowitz had produced of some of the greatest works of ancient Greek literature. The central accusation Hildebrandt made, and one he pressed home repeatedly, was that Wilamowitz had unconscionably distorted the true essence of the original texts. Wilamowitz had robbed them of their majesty, Hildebrandt claimed, by translating certain words or phrases with the help of deliberately anachronistic constructions or by straightening out convoluted syntax in the attempt to make his renditions more accessible to a modern readership. Wilamowitz wanted to "popularize" the Greeks by making them, in esssence, sound more like turn-of-the-century educated Germans. "It is a crime against Hellas," Hildebrandt declared, "and against any education to be hoped for, to make these works conform to bourgeois convenience and proletarian taste, to flatten what is high, to bend what is hard, to smooth out what is raw." Or, as Hildebrandt more colorfully put it elsewhere, "heroes are not bourgeois in costume." The ancient Greeks should be valuable to us precisely because they differed from the modern bourgeoisie.

Fundamentally, Hildebrandt saw Wilamowitz as yet another typical representative of the kind of middlebrow rationality that Nietzsche had ridiculed and George denounced. To Hildebrandt, and to anyone associated with George, Wilamowitz was the epitome, as Hildebrandt explained, "of the cold light of intellectualism, of will-less conceptuality." What was worse, as a scholar of Greek antiquity, Wilamowitz sought to apply his positivistic measuring stick to artifacts of supreme veneration among the members of the *Blätter*. The works of Aeschylus and Sophocles cannot — should not — be read as if they were nineteenth-century novels. And that is precisely what Hildebrandt accused Wilamowitz, with his complacent attempt to domesticate the Greeks, of trying to do. "We oppose," Hildebrandt announced, "every commentary that wants to displace the emphasis of tragedy onto an analytic examination of life, psychological interest, moralistic interpretations, and other intellectual complexities that people now make such a fuss about."

That was the official line, anyway. Privately, the hostility toward Wilamowitz was fed by a more personal antipathy. Wilamowitz's own first publication had been an infamous and rather ill-advised polemic against Nietzsche's youthful masterpiece, *The Birth of Tragedy,* of 1872. Wilamowitz, then all of twenty-four years old himself, pedantically pointed out the numerous errors of fact committed by the author, rebuked him for failing to adhere to the principles of "strict philological method," and generally objected to Nietzsche's highly tendentious interpretation of the origins of Greek tragedy. Given the sharpness of Nietzsche's pen, and the zeal of his admirers, it was a bold, if not to say foolhardy move. Generations of Nietzsche devotees have known Wilamowitz solely as the priggish fool who dared to criticize their idol. Although Nietzsche refrained from any public response to the critique, he did take to referring to Wilamowitz in his letters as "Wilam ohne Witz" — or "Wilam without Wit" — and "Wilamops" (*Mops* is the German word for "pug," the small, stout Chinese dog with a wrinkled face and curled tail, but *Mops* is also used as an abusive epithet for an overweight person, corresponding more or less to "fatty").

Defiling one icon was bad enough, but Wilamowitz did not stop there. Apparently, he had thought it would be amusing to write a parody of George's distinctive style of poetry. Some time in the late 1890s, Wilamowitz accordingly concocted a short and uninspired spoof of George and then circulated it among friends. Around the turn of the century, during a gathering at the house of Friedrich Dernburg, a prominent figure among Berlin's social elite, someone read aloud from Wilamowitz's handiwork. As parodies go, it was not an especially artful performance or even very funny — "O, stylish mouse-gray of the cover boards," it begins, "Stylish dullness of the handmade paper, / Worthy vessel into which the poet pours / The mouse-gray bounty of his stylish monotony" and so forth — but it contained a phrase that aroused indignation among those present at Dernburg's home. The poem ends with an enumeration of the various ornaments deemed suitable to adorn other celebrated poets: diamonds for Schiller, pearls for Dante, and laurel for Homer; in the case of George, however, "Only the lackluster nuance suits him / Stylishly, the mouse-gray of impotence."

The difficulty with parodies is that, to be effective, they have to be at least as good as what they mock. Even as a plain if obtuse affront, the lines were relatively tame, but they caused something of a stir nonetheless. Wilamowitz had approached, but not crossed, the line that prevented any direct mention of the taboo subject of homosexuality in polite society, yet everyone knew what "impotence" really meant. George soon found out about the affair to predictable result. From then on, he never let an opportunity pass to make some scathing remark about the great scholar. In a conversation in 1920, while discussing various other academics and how fleeting their fame and impact would be compared to that of truly creative natures (a category in which George obviously included himself), he said sarcastically: "What will remain of the entire Wilamops? Perhaps the filth he unloaded on Nietzsche's coattails." Or, that same year, when someone wondered how Wilamowitz, who had repeatedly proven he possessed a vile and ugly soul, could still be so comparatively physically attractive, George offered a novel theory. "Perhaps he excretes all that is base and mean within him, all of the offal into his books and what remains is the pure type. Books as latrine buckets!" On still another occasion, when told of the positive impression Wilamowitz had made on his English colleagues when he spoke at Oxford University, George dismissed it, saying, "Well, they don't know any German. If he spoke Latin he undoubtedly cut quite a good figure." Naturally, George's closest associates joined in on the sport. During Gundolf's first year at the University of Berlin in 1901, he had attended several lectures by Wilamowitz and had been very favorably impressed. "Among today's scholars," he had enthused then to George, "he is perhaps really the only one in whom ancient Greece has ignited a truly blazing and glowing flame." Ten years later, Gundolf had completely changed his tune. "Plato for maids," was how he described Wilamowitz's magnum opus on the philosopher. "By the way," Gundolf once joked to Hildebrandt, playing on his profession as a psychiatrist, "you also did not step out of the narrow bounds of your specialization with your 'Wilamowitz': he is the model of a 'pathography' on *dementia praecox philologica*."

Yet, in the end Wilamowitz was more a symptom than the cause — a rather sizable symptom, to be sure — of a greater malignity, the spread of which the first *Yearbook* was designed to combat. The real enemy was not Wilamowitz but scholarship and science — *Wissenschaft* — itself. From the beginning, ever since George had been a student in Berlin two decades before, he had eyed what went on in universities with a mixture of suspicion and contempt. The fact that several of his very first admirers — and, as it would turn out, many of his later friends and followers as well — were either professors or in some way associated with a university did little to change his attitude. He seemed to think universities were little better than a necessary evil, inherently corrupt institutions filled with soulless, sterile windbags who stuffed their students' minds and their own tomes with dead and useless knowledge. Yet, for better or worse, universities were also the places where the brightest and most talented youth in Germany happened to congregate, and George was thus forced to enter into a devil's pact. "Anything purely cognitive is foreign to me by nature," he told Ernst Robert Curtius in 1911. "I am interested only in what is human and vital. Knowledge is valuable and fruitful only when it is transmitted through something human." George never tired of admonishing those of his younger companions who were thinking of embarking on a university career to avoid taking the life-denying paths of their mentors. One could not, he once said, form an image of Plato's life or of his development by a dry analysis of the individual dialogues alone: "This way leads at best to a skeleton," George asserted, "not to living flesh and blood." It was not that he counseled his disciples to abandon their studies or to avoid the scholarly vocation; far from it. Apart from providing them with a respectable living, it guaranteed George access to a constantly renewed source of human capital. But the kind of work they did had to meet with his approval. When one of his young protégés was reading aloud sections from his thesis on Plato, George abruptly stopped him at one point and said, "That doesn't interest me." Chagrined, the person on the receiving end of this rebuff tried to justify his method, saying the topic demanded such a treatment. "I said nothing against your topic," George responded, "a thesis probably requires such a 'scientific question.'" What he took exception to was the way in which he was going about it. "I will gladly listen to anything that is enlivening," George told him, "but I don't want to be bored to death by empty science."

Not accidentally, the parting shot of the *Yearbook,* Wolters's essay called "Guidelines," takes direct aim at the institution and practice of *Wissenschaft* as a whole. It also carried George's explicit imprimatur. In a letter to George from December 1909, Wolters had already outlined his thoughts for the essay, indicating that he wanted to show "that an entire, larger sphere of life remains completely closed, impenetrable, unfathomable, in fact incomprehensible to science, even to occult science." "Would that correspond to the nature of the critical yearbook?" Wolters wondered. George, speaking through Gundolf who wrote the reply, confirmed that "your plan for the 'Guidelines' is excellent." Wolters's essay, more perhaps than any other in the collection and for the first time in such categorical and official terms, codifies some of George's most firmly held beliefs and articulates some of his most deeply felt animosities.

Wolters began his discussion with a basic distinction between what he called "creative power" and "organizational power." The first "power," he said, rests on the principles of life itself: it is sensuous, immediate, concrete, dynamic, undivided. The second, however, is derivative, secondary, static, and impotent. "The organizational power is logical," Wolters informs us; it "creates no inner values, but rather, as the capacity of the mind to deduce immediate and more remote causes from similarities and resemblances, sifts through substances, establishes their function relative to each other and seeks to separate and combine them according to known laws." Because "life does not come from order but from creation," the deleterious effect stemming from the ascendancy of "the organizational power" in modern society — whether one called it rationality, objectivity, pragmatism, scientific thinking, and so on — should, Wolters thought, be self-evident. Yet, as he described it, even though "many today know how ill it is making our time, how much our youth is suffering from it," it was still true that "only a few dare to grab the bull of the critical order by its own horns, which bloodies so many young brows, and say: here are your boundaries!"

Even though Wolters himself seemed to have trouble holding onto his own runaway metaphors, his meaning appears reasonably clear. The natural and human sciences, which rely on methodological exactitude, consistency, dispassionateness, and disinterestedness on the part of the researcher, stand in irreconcilable conflict with what Wolters identifies as "the life-creating powers of the body-and-mind unity, from the highest intuition to the lowest procreation." Science isolates, codifies, and pigeonholes dead things, the way a lepidopterist pins the lifeless bodies of butterflies to a board, whereas the creative force embodies and preserves the primal unity of life. Wolters's prescription then is not to think but to feel, not to analyze but to intuit. It is an appeal that he extends foremost to the youth of the day, those least corrupted by the scientific creed, who are most capable of freeing themselves from the bondage of rationality. But they need help. "What they all lack is precisely the intuition [*Anschauung*] of a world-unity; a worldview [*Weltanschauung*] does not mean to order the results, concepts, programs, desires, and goals, but in the first place to *intuit* [*schauen*], that is, *create, a world* [*Welt*]; the conceptual power can never replace intuition [*Schau*], since it only represents its logical order in a system." What was required instead was "the complete surrender of the rational conceit, the most devoted absorption in the teachings of the great heralds and the nurture of the spirit with the heartiest nourishment of sensuous blood."

It is here, in the final words of the *Yearbook,* that we come the closest to an expression of what it positively advocated instead of merely the reiteration of what the members of the *Blätter* had long opposed. "The time of logical gymnastics is over," Wolters rather optimistically concluded, "and the struggle with the angel of life has begun again." To abandon logic for creation meant to forfeit science for poetry, to choose life over death — and most immediately to embrace George as one's Master and Ruler. "That the Ordering Power so predominates in the values of this time clearly shows that its roots no longer extend into the nurturing ground; to turn away from [those values] is the maxim of everyone who loves the youth of our people; to seek the sources of the Creative Power, to act, shape, and intuit is necessary for everyone who wants to become a part of a new creation; and whoever cannot himself be such a source shall drink at it, shall serve the creative ones in selfless moderation and in the freest devotion of oneself and thus receptively have a part in what is living."

And that was that. The *Yearbook for the Spiritual Movement* closes with something resembling a summons, or at any rate a warning. The substance of the message it conveys does not differ greatly from the substance of the Master's poetry or of the maxims and essays in the *Blätter*. But now everything seemed more tangible and clear. And the circle around George now had not only its own distinct identity and doctrine, it also had its own name.

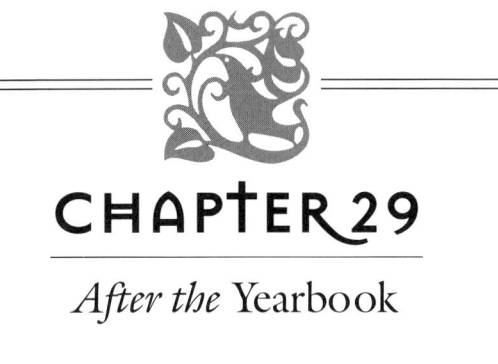

CHAPTER 29
After the Yearbook

Almost immediately after its publication, reactions to the *Yearbook* began to make themselves heard. The public response was fairly limited at first — only five hundred copies were published and even those were available only through the printer — but in its tendency satisfying nonetheless. "I just received a long lamentation in the Berlin *Tageblatt!* about the *Yearbook* right after it had appeared!" Gundolf gleefully informed George in the middle of March 1910. "Never has any praise pleased me so much as this whining: the injured are howling!" To Hildebrandt, Gundolf also had good news to report. "Your Hellas and Wilam. continues to exercise the scientific spirits," Gundolf told him that June. There had even been a brief notice about the *Yearbook* in the *Süddeutsche Monatshefte,* he added, that had singled out for special mention "the very important essay by Kurt Hildebrandt." But even among those who agreed with the gist of Hildebrandt's argument, Gundolf said, there was a certain hesitation to embrace it wholeheartedly, written as it was by someone who was not a member of the exclusive fraternity of university professors. "In general, these people are not comfortable with the fact that they have to take this assault so seriously and many who wish it on W. personally are annoyed that a 'homo novus' can and may attack a bigwig. 'Contra professorem nemo nisi professor.' " — Hildebrandt had violated the unwritten rule that the only person who may speak out against a professor is another professor — "But the effect on the youth is strong and unavoidable since the true word, once expressed, acts magically through its very existence."

Despite some misgivings about the propriety of an outsider publicly wrangling with a distinguished colleague, not everyone in the academic guild was unsympathetic to the effort as a whole. Another prominent figure at the University of Berlin, Wilhelm Dilthey, who had proven to be favorably disposed toward George and the *Blätter* several times over the years, wrote a warm letter of acknowledgement to Gundolf after receiving the copy of the *Yearbook* sent to him. Yet another fixture in the Berlin pantheon, the art historian Heinrich Wölfflin, let it be known that he was not displeased with Hildebrandt's essay either and, as Gundolf revealed to Wolfskehl, Wölfflin appeared to be "otherwise very *Blätter*-friendly as well." Even the French philosopher Henri Bergson, by then the most widely read thinker in Europe and a professor at the prestigious Collège de France, took the trouble to communicate his felicitations to Gundolf, saying he was particularly captivated by the idea of dedicating a periodical to the "spiritual movement."

But as gratifying as these and other signs of semi-official support were, it was the perceived impact the *Yearbook* had on the "unofficial" culture — the "youth" and other similarly uncorrupted souls — that most vitally interested George and his adherents. Among those close to or within the circle, the publication was unsurprisingly hailed as a triumph. Although one could hardly accuse him of impartiality, Gundolf waxed lyrical about their collective achievement. The *Yearbook,* he wrote Wiesi de Haan, "has surpassed my own boldest expectations in its richness, greatness, and depth and is full of the proud knowledge and feeling of a turning point in history." And if there was one person who stood out in Gundolf's mind — apart from George, of course — for having played the decisive part in its success, it was his own coeditor, Friedrich Wolters. "I am completely amazed by this miracle of a man," he gushed, still to Frau de Haan. "We all have unconditional admiration for him, he knows, dares, and does everything that a spiritual [*geistiger*] German of our time can achieve at the highest level." Gundolf, who was going through a Bergson phase himself, declared that Wolters's essay contained "the deepest words of the age (next to Bergson)." It was more than generous self-deprecation. To underscore the epochal importance of the event, Gundolf went so far as to draw a potentially heretical comparison between the publication of Wolters's "Guidelines" in the *Yearbook* and the appearance of George's first book of poetry, the *Hymns,* two decades before. "You see, I am full of Wolters — he has opened up new hopes and perspectives to me, established new realities, and like 1890, for us 1910 is a crossroads, as always when a new creative spirit bursts in on our world." Yet in his enthusiasm, Gundolf did not forget to mention the one person who had made it all possible in the first place. "For the Master, such a phenomenon [i.e., Wolters], which would be unthinkable without him, is the most wonderful confirmation of his work, and for us younger ones it is a new measure of what remains to do and to be."

Other "younger ones," such as the twenty-three-year-old Ernst Robert

Curtius, who despite close connections to individual members stood outside of the circle itself, expressed similar sentiments. Only three hours after reading his "fervently longed for" copy of the *Yearbook* in a single sitting — an experience Curtius described as being in a state of "continual calm astonishment and quiet rejoicing" — he sat down to convey his impressions to his friend, Gundolf. "With the appearance of the *Yearbook*," Curtius proclaimed, "a new phase begins in the transformation of the German spirit that George has inspired." He recognized that the primary purpose of the *Yearbook* was to put in prosaic form what "had been born in *The Seventh Ring* as poetry" so that it could more readily affect the thoughts and actions of its readers. "Hundreds," Curtius predicted, "who have lived without a leader and without a goal will now learn which paths lead to the future and receive an orientation whose effect cannot even begin to be calculated yet." Significantly, it was this, the potential of the *Yearbook* to influence and change the actual conduct of people that Curtius saw as its principal virtue. "For this reason," he confidently wrote, "the appearance of the *Yearbook* is of the broadest pedagogical and political importance."

Others still, however, while acknowledging the pedagogical and political ambitions of the volume, and by extension of George himself, were less certain they were an entirely good thing. Albert Rausch, who for some time had been engaged in a complicated maneuver to maintain his ties to the members of the *Blätter* while resisting the temptation, or the imperative, to be completely ensnared by them, laid out his objections in a candid and perceptive letter to George. Saying that the "tendentious statements" in the *Blätter* had already begun to leave him cold, Rausch confessed the *Yearbook* only intensified his growing feelings of alienation. Extrapolating no doubt from his own experience, Rausch protested against the insistent demand its contributors repeatedly made that one give up one's own autonomy and completely submerge oneself in the service of a greater being. Granting that the *Yearbook* contained "many fine and important things," he also thought

> it includes much that is questionable as well. When a *single* great poet sees the world as the disciples see it for him here and he realizes such poems in *his work,* that is magnificent. But in this book the disciples' vision remains *rhetoric* — and thus it lacks the deeper reality that slumbers in all that is great. The attitude of the *Yearbook* can awaken no faith in the truly spiritual. Faith can be awakened only by the work whose source nourishes this entire book. Your work, dear Master. For your work was the great redemption that came to us. Your work is a world, but the *Yearbook* is a long, long way from being a world. It is a great danger, and I wish it on no young person that he would make this view of the world his own: unless he has developed so far in his own blood and experience and knowledge, that

no such view of the world can ever take away *his* reality, the soil of his best spiritual accomplishments. It goes without saying that drawing the frontline against individualism is of great benefit: but 'only he is fit for service who feels himself a sovereign.' Before someone is in possession of himself he cannot give himself. And the most essential thing is and remains that a person must first awaken to *himself*. The homily on service that this book offers (Gundolf and Wolters) is much too much an ecstasy of giving oneself as to be able to be fruitful — and in its ecstasy unrealistic to the point of ideology.

It is a remarkably shrewd assessment. But as Rausch must have known, it revealed an attitude that was incompatible with the ideology of the circle. Even though he had been careful to confine his protest to the *Yearbook* alone, Rausch should have known that it was impossible to be selectively critical when it came to anything associated with George. For George, it was all or nothing. A victim of his own candor, Albert Rausch quickly disappeared from view.

While Rausch did not really mean much of a sacrifice, the *Yearbook* opened even deeper rifts among friends of longer standing and greater importance to George. The historian Kurt Breysig, who had introduced many of his younger Berlin associates to George when the poet was recuperating from his deprivations in Munich, was one such casualty. A proud and somewhat prickly man, Breysig was convinced that the essay by his former student, Friedrich Wolters, was not just a rejection of scientific thinking generally but more specifically, and painfully, a personal attack on himself. He took his complaint directly to the author. "I am still not getting any peace from Breysig," Wolters grumbled to Gundolf in April 1910. Wolters explained that Breysig "is profoundly hurt personally by my essay and as a defender of research, our old relationship is over and now he is looking for some remnant of common intellectual interests to permit a new one." But the breach was too wide to span. A year later, as Breysig was still trying to find a way to reconcile their differences, he told Wolters that one thing he thought was missing in Wolters's dealings with him was human warmth, kindness, or, in a word, "love." Wolters thought that was rich. "As if one had to love one's enemies," he fumed to Gundolf. "What the hell, it seems to me that we have reason enough to hate them! And we don't want peace but rather battle!"

Beyond feeling his professional dignity injured, Breysig felt betrayed by his one-time protégés, and especially by Wolters, who he had hoped would follow in his footsteps as an historian. In fact, their affiliation had already been fraying and had never really been especially intimate. Not much more than ten years' senior to Wolters, Breysig treated the younger man very much as a subordinate and regarded himself not just as Wolters's teacher but as his *Führer*. When Wolters once hazarded the word "friend" to characterize their bond, Breysig visibly stiffened and firmly rejected the implicit offer. As the younger of the two, Wolters had overstepped the bounds set by convention in making the overture, and Breysig probably considered the step inappropriate to the point of impertinence. Still, he later regretted his obstinacy — "Perhaps I made a mistake by shying away from the word friend," Breysig told his wife — but by then it was too late. But it was not Wolters he blamed for their breakup. "The mistake that had more serious consequences for my life," he regretfully concluded, was to have introduced Wolters and Vallentin to George at all. "I thus led them myself to the person to whom I then lost them."

That was the most bitter pill to swallow. The association between Breysig and George had once been quite close, and George had given him every indication of genuine affection. Once, in 1905, after a particularly long and intensive exchange — it had become five in the morning — Breysig noted that as George was leaving he showed signs of "deep emotion": "George embraces me by laying his head on my shoulder," Breysig noted in his diary, "and pressing it softly against mine." Thus it rankled all the more that now, five years later, George seemed to be turning Breysig's own former students against him. In September, 1910, some six months after the *Yearbook* had come out, Breysig confronted George about the situation, describing his previous discussions with Wolters and Vallentin: "I told them that until now they had gone my way, and still did so even now but with their head half turned toward him — George." George calmly interjected that Wolters had "told him that the friendship was unfortunately not as close as before." In any case, George assured Breysig "that he had never undertaken steps or even had the idea: now I want to make a person disloyal to Breysig." After insisting several times on his innocence of any treachery and that it had been entirely Wolters's and Vallentin's own choice to separate from Breysig — "Thirty-year-old people have to decide for themselves," George pointed out — he then changed tactics. George asserted that, if it were him, "he would no longer allow a person to remain among his friends who wanted to leave him." Breysig was either weak or desperate if he wanted to hold on to people who had obviously already turned their backs on him. George handled things differently. One could become disloyal in his books not just in deed but in thought alone, and the punishment for both offenses was equally severe. When Breysig tried to remind George that "there have been some people who have left you," George shrugged: "Only peripheral ones." Finally, perhaps wanting to save at least some face, Breysig unpersuasively announced to George that "we were never friends. We were allies and liked one another." "We were friendly," George answered. It was both a correction and a verdict.

There were more losses to come. In August 1910, George's old Berlin friend and patron, Sabine Lepsius, wrote Gundolf to say "that I am very saddened by the *Yearbook*." In a convulsion of impassioned, combative, sometimes sarcastic words, she poured forth the grounds for her agitation. Her principal grievances concerned two central issues the *Yearbook* had only tangentially broached but were among the burning questions of the day: the place and value of women in society and the more inflammatory matter of homosexuality, or pederasty, or, as she called it, literally the "love of boys" — *Jünglingsliebe:*

> *Everything* that touches on the women's question and the love of boys is *tout simplement* reprehensible.
>
> Listen to me: to want women to be enslaved again would be synonymous with the reintroduction of the ghetto. — Freedom dignifies the person, and as much as I recognize the insanity in emancipating the people, who have to be led because they are dependent and from which only the individual who has developed himself may be liberated, I just as clearly recognize the error of the view of women you all have.
>
> For you, a women should above all be 'convenient.' — But only maids and whores are convenient. Both do what they are told. A woman who has dignity (and it seems to me that you all love dignity) doesn't obey like a dog but rather communicates with a man just as a friend does with a friend. — A man needs ethical upbringing through a woman just as a woman requires intellectual education through a man, both are imperfect without the other.
>
> This is of course speaking generally. Even in school they should influence each other; there would be fewer cocks and cows and more men and women. — Again generally speaking; for: every outstanding individual can lay claim to *any* right. Such individuals carry their laws in themselves and when they live according to them they will always live well. — Woe to the person who imitates them!!! Woe to those who make the contempt of women into a program. You would then have no offspring to recruit.
>
> Gundolf, in your last letter you wrote that women are necessary and sometimes pleasant as well! — Gundolf, I laughed out loud when I read that! — We are necessary and thus you allow us to exist? — No, my dear, we are half of creation even without you finding it 'necessary.' If you are the seed and the spring, then we are the autumn and the fruit. — Our work is different from yours, but it is just as great.
>
> Culture is unthinkable without women. — Ancient Athens and the modern sapphic Paris are perversions.

It was a bracing draught, even more dismaying considering its source. Rarely were such topics spoken about so freely among George and his companions and never in such accusatory terms. One result of the "secret Germany's" going public, and presumably a consequence they had foreseen and even welcomed, was that matters that had previously been shrouded in silence would be dragged into the open and mentioned by name. But it was one thing to be harassed by enemies and quite another to be misunderstood by friends.

Initially, Gundolf pretended not to know what Sabine Lepsius was talking about. "Where for heaven's sake in the entire *Yearbook* is the issue of women's rights 'touched on' and the 'love of boys' extolled?!?" he wrote back. "Did the bookbinder perhaps switch your *Yearbook*, I search and search and don't find a single sentence that could be interpreted thus." Pointing out that "four of the *Yearbook* collaborators are fathers of families" and that the others were either "engaged to real women or in love with them with a tendency to idolize them," Gundolf conceded no ground. "What you imagine by the love of boys and by our notion of it, my dearest Frau Sabine, is partly only the bogeyman that little old maids have created who can only think sexually and fear competition, and partly the distorted image envisioned by shaggy book worms who can't imagine how they should love their ink-stained louts." Gundolf went even further, turning his defense against her accusations into an indictment of the entire society that endorsed them. He argued that her allegations were the symptom of a time in which the "feeling and intuition of the entire person as the physical expression and symbol of the divine has been lost and for which the human being has been broken down into his desacrilized elements, brain, nerves, bones, sexual organs. Wherever the body, the visible human being, no longer expresses divinity, as in the best antiquity, then everything does become problematic, psychological, physiological, sexual, and the relationships between people become, consciously or unconsciously, oriented and viewed with an eye toward material aspects, toward their purposes, toward profit and loss." Still, even though he had just condemned the culture that underwrote Sabine Lepsius's negative views of the stance toward both women and the "love of boys" in the *Yearbook* and had arrogantly dismissed her own objections as groundless and foolish, Gundolf found it necessary to repeat once more, as if through repetition he sounded more convincing, that "there is nothing about either subject in the *Yearbook*."

The most charitable word one might use to describe Gundolf's reply to Sabine Lepsius is that it was disingenuous. Technically, he was almost — but not quite — correct in saying the *Yearbook* contained no explicit reference to pederasty, or the love of boys, or to the question of women's rights. The one partial exception is Hildebrandt's essay, in which he made passing mention of Wilamowitz's own criticism of the ancient Greek treatment of women. This Wilamowitz had judged deficient compared to his own time when, as he put it, "wife and mother have found their place consecrated by nature as the equal companion of man." Wilamowitz had also characterized, and repudiated, the aristocratic culture in Greece before the time of Aeschylus, because it condoned the reprehensible "enslavement of women." Hildebrandt snorted at this as bourgeois piety but smugly refused to waste any time demonstrating "how tendentious and false everything Wilamowitz says here and elsewhere about the place of women," and left it at that. The only other place in the *Yearbook* Sabine Lepsius might have been thinking of was a brief passage in which Wolfskehl had made a characteristically oblique comment about the dissolution of "manly-erotic humanity," which was based, he wrote, on "differentiation and reverence and body and action," into the opposite form of "dissipating sound waves of their female-sexual nonworld or transworld." Although it was hard to tell what Wolfskehl might have meant by the "female-sexual nonworld," it is pretty safe to say it was not intended to be flattering to women.

But while these may have been the only parts in the *Yearbook* in which the issues troubling Sabine Lepsius overtly surfaced, they were of course only a small part of the whole story. Ever since the publication of *The Seventh Ring*, with the poems dedicated to Maximin at its core, George had been progressively less shy about revealing the direction of his inclinations, both in private conversation and in public pronouncements. Only a few weeks before the *Yearbook* appeared, for instance, the ninth number of the *Blätter für die Kunst* was also published. It featured the usual gnomic introductory paragraphs, including one titled "The Hellenic Miracle." It proclaimed Greek culture to be "something incomparable · unique and perfect," and that no effort should be spared to imitate it. The best way of going about that task, it asserted, was not by making a superficial copy of it but rather to embody it through "penetration · impregnation · a Holy Marriage." Only then will the "Greek Idea" be realized, namely, the realization that " 'the Body · the symbol of transitoriness · THE BODY IS GOD.' " It was this belief in the divinity of the body — and, it was strongly implied, of the male body, in particular — which the introduction to the *Blätter* claimed "was by far the most creative and most unimaginable · by far the greatest and most bold and most worthy of humanity · to which in terms of its sublimity every other one · even the Christian one · must necessarily be inferior."

To anyone with even an approximate familiarity with George's own work, the phrase "Greek Idea" resonated in complex but specific ways. An acquaintance of Wolfskehl by the name of Friedrich von der Leyen, a professor of literature at the University of Munich and someone regarded as a distant but reliable ally, was under no illusion about what the slogan signified. In July 1910, Wolfskehl reported that he had endured a three-hour conversation with von der Leyen in which the professor had said that the "religious allusions in the Ninth [issue of the *Blätter*] and especially the Greek Miracle were an extremely dangerous undertaking." Von der Leyen told Wolfskehl that he considered "the deification of the body, *namely the body of the beautiful boy,* also dangerous because the mystery of supersexual love is thus moved into the light out of its previous seclusion, particularly since the entire *Yearbook* dogmatically rests on this religious principle. He sees the grossest misunderstandings on the part of outsiders arising from it." In fact, even before the publication of either the *Yearbook* or the new *Blätter* volume, such "misunderstandings" in the form of gossip and rumor had already begun to crop up. Wolfskehl told George that von der Leyen had warned him, with regard to Maximin especially, that "the entire world is speaking about these matters in the most malicious way," and that "in every city to which he travels, in the various intellectual circles he enters, he says he hears the most fantastic things on this subject."

Answering for George, Gundolf responded to Wolfskehl's concerns by saying that "the Master" considered the "affair with v[on] d[er] L[eyen] not very important," and left it at that. But, despite this show of nonchalance, there was genuine reason for concern. Not only was the notorious Paragraph 175 still very much in force, which specifically outlawed sexual relations between men (and, it went without saying, with boys), the entire issue of homosexuality had also recently risen to a level of heightened national attention. In 1906, Maximilian Harden, an activist journalist who edited a Berlin weekly called *Die Zukunft* (The future), had unleashed a bombshell. In a series of articles, Harden had alleged that the members of a close-knit entourage around the German Emperor Wilhelm II were guilty of engaging in acts that were forbidden under Paragraph 175. The accusations of sexual impropriety were leveled at the so-called Liebenberg Round Table, so named because its constituents were invited every autumn to the imperial hunting grounds at the estate in Liebenberg. The regular guests included some of the leading lights of the Prussian aristocracy, men such as Helmuth von Moltke, Eberhard Count Dohna-Schlobitten, Georg von Hülsen, Emil Count von Görtz, as well as several courtiers and hangers-on, numbering as many as twenty on any given occasion.

Presiding over the festivities, acting as a kind of master of ceremonies, was Philipp Count zu Eulenburg, who had been a close friend of the emperor since 1886. A professional diplomat, Eulenburg had quickly risen to the position of Wilhelm's most trusted and influential advisor after Bismarck's fall in 1890, and Eulenburg consequently became one of the most powerful men in the new German empire. From then on Maximilian Harden, who had founded *Die Zukunft* only two years later and who detested Eulenburg's politics, worked single-mindedly to bring about his destruction. In 1906, Harden finally lit upon the instrument to do so.

Outwardly, the very idea that Eulenburg was anything but a respectable and perfectly "normal" member of the German nobility seemed preposterous. He, like most of the other members of the Liebenberg circle, was married, had children, and he gave every indication of being a doting and conscientious husband and father. But, as the historian Isabel Hull has shown, many of the letters Eulenburg exchanged with several of his friends left "little doubt about the homoerotic nature of the bond among the core members of the group."

Relying on information supplied to him by one of Eulenburg's enemies, Harden revealed in November 1906 in *Die Zukunft* that he had irrefutable evidence that the nature of the relationships between Eulenburg and various of his friends, particularly Kuno von Moltke, was anything but innocent. When the Emperor learned of the campaign Harden had initiated, he became irate and demanded that Eulenburg and Moltke mount a counteroffensive. The move badly misfired. A civil suit Moltke entered for libel against Harden led to a humiliating public trial in October 1907, which resulted, even more embarrassingly, in Harden's acquittal. Thereafter, a succession of appeals, overturned verdicts, retrials, and further revelations followed one another in rapid order, with each new disclosure bringing fresh mortification on the Emperor and his associates. As time passed — and as Harden intended — the affair began to pose a serious threat to the entire government. At the center of the growing scandal was Eulenburg himself. According to the sworn testimony of a fisherman and a laborer Harden had dug up, Eulenburg allegedly had sexual relations with the men in the late 1880s. On the strength of this new "evidence," Eulenburg, who had always rather weakly protested that he had "never done anything dirty," was placed under arrest, his estate was searched, and a date was set to try him for perjury. During the proceedings of the second tribunal in the summer of 1908, Eulenburg suffered a nervous collapse and his trial was postponed to the following year, whereupon Eulenburg delivered a repeat performance of debility. For another ten years, Eulenburg was examined every six months by court doctors to determine whether his constitution had sufficiently improved to permit a resumption of the trial, until the matter was indefinitely tabled in 1919. But Harden had achieved his goal. With Eulenburg's reputation permanently ruined, his privileges stripped, and above all his access to the Emperor forever cut off, the hapless count had been effectively eliminated from the political arena.

It could not have escaped Gundolf, or George for that matter, that anyone similarly motivated could potentially make life equally uncomfortable for the Master and his friends. The question was certainly on their minds. In 1907, as the scandal unfolded, George had discussed the Eulenburg matter with Berthold Vallentin, who noted in his diary only that they had engaged in a "conversation about Kuno Graf Moltke, Maximilian Harden." (Many years later, George also praised Georg Bondi, who had previously been on friendly terms with Harden — that "worst of the scandalmongers," as George then called him — for having severed his ties to Harden in protest over the affair.) And when Sabine Lepsius wrote her letter of complaint to Gundolf about the *Yearbook,* the second Eulenburg trial was only a year old. It is thus no surprise that in his long, detailed rebuttal Gundolf made explicit and repeated mention of the affair, expressly denying that the *Yearbook* had "anything to do" with "sexual matters, emancipation, maternity laws, Eulenburg, Paragraph 175, etc." Gundolf added that if Frau Lepsius wanted to get a better idea of what George and his clan were up to, "I advise you still to read Plato before the Harden trials." Typically, Gundolf ended on a combative note. "As concerns George himself, he says that it is a matter of indifference to him what his enemies say, but he does insist on asking his friends to fight against only what he really means and not always to pelt him, even if oh so mildly, with things that only give fresh fuel to the nefarious deeds of his enemies. He has explained dozens of times what he considers necessary *for the present* are neither women nor boys but men for the war."

Judging solely by the length and vehemence of Gundolf's denials, Sabine Lepsius had evidently hit a nerve. Noticeably, Gundolf had concentrated mostly on refuting any overlap between George's ideals and anything even remotely connected with the Harden-Eulenburg business. On the question of George's estimation of women, however, the direct evidence was less obvious and thus, it appears, not in such urgent need of a rejoinder. Perhaps for that reason Gundolf had felt it was safer to let the record speak for itself and he focussed his attention on the other, more volatile item. But with regard to the "woman question," too, as both Gundolf and Frau Lepsius well knew, the record revealed more than met the uninformed eye.

Ever since George had formally bid farewell to Woman in *The Year of the Soul* in 1897, he seems to have largely settled into a posture of bland indifference toward the female sex as a whole. George did of course still retain a few women friends, most significantly Sabine Lepsius herself, and, as Gundolf had mentioned, many of his disciples had wives as well. But women never did — and never would — answer to any of George's deeper needs and were thus fundamentally irrelevant to him. They were, it is true, often useful to have around — they conveniently cooked, cleaned, and tidied up, for instance — and thus made some aspects of life more comfortable. He also allowed those of his male companions who were so inclined to indulge in dalliances with women but only so long as it did not interfere with more important concerns. "I always say," George once announced, "you can have as many casual affairs as you want but never beyond a certain point." As time went on, however, his attitude toward women hardened, changing from his earlier benign tolerance of their presence, even his occasional enjoyment of their company, to a decided effort to exclude them from his sphere, or at least from the inner sanctum. Robert Boehringer, who knew George as well as anyone, openly admitted that George "did not want women in his state and felt the attachment to the family to be an obstacle." George would say to his friends, "If you believe that you have nothing more at all to do in the state then you can also marry."

Boehringer tells us further that George thought "marriage changes the intellectual horizon of a friend and thus would necessarily diminish the friendship." Fundamentally, marriage, and thus women, had only one purpose: to produce children, and preferably boys. In George's view, "marriage was necessary for women but was justified for men only in order to create the right progeny." When confronted once about his position on the subject — by a woman, one might add — George gave an ambiguous, not to say a deceitful answer. "When have I ever been against marriage?" he asked. "I get along splendidly with married men as well as with their wives, but they also have to be suited to it." Being suited to marriage, however, really meant being suited to his own conception of it, and that was another matter altogether. The Apostle Paul may have said that it was better to marry than to burn, but George was not so sure.

Those few women George did accept within his ambit thus had to abide by the ground rules he set and endure the knowledge that they would forever be regarded as inferior creatures, welcome in their role as hostess, handmaid, and childbearer, but barred from ever playing any substantive role in the realm of the spirit. "Women," Boehringer went on to inform us, "fulfilled the difficult task of being hospitable and placing themselves in the background." Sometimes, George would cruelly remind his female acquaintances of their subservient status. Once, when Hanna Wolfskehl, Karl's self-effacing, loyal, and hardworking wife, sat down to join the men in her house, George sneered at her, "So, now she wants to be lazy again and drink tea instead of sewing." Overall, though, women appeared to stand so far down on George's scale of values that he did not bother to give much thought to their constitution, as long as they were agreeable and pliant. "Women," he said on another occasion, "can take on any trait. Anyone can succeed in forming a woman — for a man one really needs a very strong will. To be beautiful, a man has to have character, a woman can be charming, beautiful, pleasant without it."

Beneath this surface of studied neglect and detached contempt, though, lay a profound mistrust of women and their power, based on a fear that women might, if left unchecked, attempt to wrench control from men and subjugate them to their whims. George's disdain of women was at least partly fueled by a very real sense that they posed a constant threat. George liked to tell the youngest members of retinue what he called a "symbolic story." "There was once a woman who visited her friend," he would say, "and examined the pictures he had hung on his wall. Among them was one that was especially prettily decorated. Thereupon she said: 'If you love me then destroy this.'" George saw deep meaning in this tale. "A young creature who gives herself up as an exclusive possession," he cautioned, "also wants to be the exclusive ruler." She thinks, he explained, "there should be nothing foreign about which she knows nothing and which doesn't involve her." Similarly, one of the major objections George made to the presence of women among men was their ostensible love of gossip. As one of his friends said, "there was probably not a single woman he did not think possessed this quality." It was not talkativeness as such that bothered George but the ends to which he suspected women employed it. "The poet knew that this — gossipiness, garrulousness — in women was not merely or only a weakness but rather a weapon, a weapon that was always used well and shrewdly and with cunning to control men. A woman will soon separate and divide any cohesion, any harmony among men and, after dividing and separating, by acquiring power over one easily dominates others." Loose lips, in other words, could sink the ship of state.

George's suspicions about women's designs to usurp the place and power of men only seemed confirmed by the nascent feminist movement, which had been steadily gaining momentum in Germany since the turn of the century. "He was no friend of the emancipation of women," one of his acquaintances dryly noted. And with good reason: in political and ideological terms, feminism represented the very antithesis of just about everything George and his circle stood for. "Feminists everywhere," the historian Richard Evans has written of the period, "commonly shared the ideals of bourgeois, Protestant-based liberal individualism." There was not a single article of the feminist program that George did not equate with the greater ills affecting society at large. And the entire conception of the circle and of his own role within it was fundamentally irreconcilable with the central idea on which feminism was based: the attainment of personal, individual liberty through the establishment of equality between the sexes. But in at least one respect George did hold both men and women to the same standard. Neither, he believed, should be allowed to attain complete autonomy. When Sabine Lepsius once reproached George for being against the emancipation of women, he said, "But I am also against the emancipation of men, how could I be for that of women?"

It was primarily over this smoldering question, which the *Yearbook* had finally ignited, that the fifteen-year-old friendship with Sabine Lepsius came to a blunt and hurtful end. In October 1910 she reported to her husband, Reinhold, that she had engaged in "passionate discussions about women" one evening for two hours "until half past ten." Put off by the unusually direct reprimands she was leveling at him, George began to lament to his other Berlin acquaintances, such as Georg Simmel, that Frau Lepsius was exhibiting the deplorable signs of a "development toward the unspiritual." Likewise, he mentioned to Gertrud Kantorowicz that the demands the Lepsius children made on their mother, and the distraction they caused, had produced a detrimental effect. "I love Sabine," George told her, "and will always love her, but our friendship is made impossible by the children bursting in." During one of their increasingly strained conversations, George told Sabine that her strongest quality was her "conscientiousness." She was left speechless by the comment. She knew that, far from being a compliment, George all too clearly meant it to signify that she lacked any more outstanding attributes. As an active painter who regarded herself as a dedicated and accomplished artist, she realized that his remark was equivalent to a repudiation of her credentials. The following morning, when George was leaving the house after spending the night there, he delivered in a measured voice what could only have been taken as a final goodbye. "Sabine," he told her, "you know that if you ever really need me I will always be there for you." With that he turned and went out the door.

That was the end of 1910. Three years later, in October 1913, when George paid his next visit to the Lepsius household, Sabine found him "completely changed." He hardly even looked at her and "in conversation turned almost exclusively and demonstratively to Reinhold." As George made ready to leave, he finally registered his awareness of her presence by holding out his cheek to her, asking, "Well, aren't you going to give me a kiss? I can't just say to Reinhold: would you step outside for a moment." Feeling oddly chagrined by his demand, Sabine, saying "of course," quickly performed the desired operation, fighting back tears as he left.

They saw each other only once more, in the fall of 1917. George went to offer his condolences to Reinhold and Sabine whose only son had been killed in the war. The young man's name, in honor of the poet who had once loomed so large in their lives, had been Stefan.

CHAPTER 30
Heidelberg

As the waves of indignation kicked up by the *Yearbook* began to die down again, Friedrich Gundolf made a decision that, on the face of it, seemed to contradict everything the journal — and in particular everything that he as one of its two signing editors — had espoused. "Through a certain arrangement of circumstances," he casually wrote in September 1910 to Ernst Bertram from Heidelberg, "I have allowed myself to be persuaded to habilitate here this winter." For such a major announcement, it was an oddly offhand way of making it. German universities impose a strenuous set of expectations on those who aspire to join the faculty ranks. They require not just the completion of the doctoral dissertation but a further proof of scholarly qualification in the form of another lengthy monograph — the "habilitation thesis" — which is needed in order to obtain the *venia legendi,* or the official authorization to teach. Gundolf, in other words, wanted to become a professor.

"Gundolf a lecturer?" a friend of Bertram's incredulously asked when he was told the news. "I never would have believed it." The situation did seem to strain credibility. Having just assigned no less than epochal importance to Wolters's stinging repudiation of all rationality and science, and as the most devoted and loyal follower of George — who, if possible, distrusted the scientific spirit even more, and once memorably said that "no road leads from me to science" — Gundolf now suddenly wanted to become a member of an institution in which science — *Wissenschaft* — was the defining creed. In 1902, the great historian of German universities, Friedrich Paulsen, had outlined the nature of the professor's position and task as consisting of two distinct but necessarily interrelated components. The German professor, Paulsen wrote, was at once a *"scholar* or *scientific researcher* and a *teacher of science."* Either way, science — which Gundolf had seemed to reject categorically only a few months before — was an essential and inescapable part of a professor's job description.

Still, if one absolutely had to be a professor, there were many places worse to be one than in Heidelberg. It was then, as it is today, one of the most beautiful university towns in Germany, lying picturesquely along the Neckar river, surrounded by steep verdant slopes on either side, and towered over by the majestic ruins of the Renaissance castle on the hill above. Constructed of massive reddish sandstone blocks, the castle was destroyed in the late seventeenth century by Louis XIV's army, which had rendered it only more romantic. The town itself is small and irresistibly charming. Narrow streets lead past tastefully ornate baroque buildings — Heidelberg had been razed during the Thirty Years' War in the early seventeenth century and virtually none of the medieval half-timbered houses had survived — which lend the town an attractive atmosphere of grandeur on an intimate scale. The economic upswing experienced by the entire German empire in the 1890s had left its visible mark on Heidelberg as well. Large, elegant villas had sprung up along the northern river bank, whose exposure to the southern sun had given rise to its playful nickname, "the Riviera of Heidelberg." Favored by its fortunate circumstances, in which nature and human enterprise seemed to have achieved a happy balance, the town's inhabitants had the reputation of being open, good-natured people, of humorous disposition and possessing a kind of easy, unconstrained manner. This generally carefree temperament of Heidelberg's citizens, which George would have attributed to their Catholic heritage and southern sensibility — that is to say, to the complete absence of any Prussian influence — must have been no small element of its appeal to Gundolf as well.

But it was the university that gave Heidelberg its greatest distinction. Founded in 1386, it is the third oldest German university, junior only to Vienna and Prague. Over the centuries, it had naturally undergone numerous fluctuations in the quality and vitality of its offerings. Yet, beginning in the mid-nineteenth century, the university had steadily grown in prestige until, by the time Gundolf had chosen to settle there, it was one of the leading universities in Germany, commanding respect throughout the world and drawing ever larger numbers of students to its lecture halls and seminar rooms. A single statistic will illustrate the extraordinary growth of Heidelberg's renown and appeal: during the academic year, 1899–1900, there were 1250 students enrolled; fourteen years later, at the outbreak of the war, that number had more than doubled, reaching 2,668. Among the faculty were men whose fame had spread far beyond the German borders: the philosophers Kuno Fischer and Wilhelm Windelband, the classical scholar and friend of Nietzsche Erwin Rohde, historians such as Bernhard Erdmannsdörffer and Erich Marcks, and most especially the economists Max Weber, his brother Alfred, and Eberhard Gothein, who became the rector of the university in 1919. Such was the reputation of Heidelberg that by the 1920s it enjoyed a position within the German academic hierarchy equivalent to that of Oxford in England.

Given the size of the town and the university — there were only 49 full professors in 1914, alongside 120 other associated faculty — intellectual and social interaction among both the faculty and students was not only unavoidable, it also constituted a large part of Heidelberg's allure. One student from the time asserted that "there was certainly hardly a German university town in which, as here, the professors and students met in the forest, in the gardens or in student apartments for solemn or boisterous occasions and to celebrate through the evening, and even entire days and nights." Indeed, the intensity and brilliance of the social life in Heidelberg was legendary. German professors at the turn of the century regarded themselves, and were treated, as belonging to a kind of educated aristocracy, and they ranked in both income and status among the most highly placed members of society. In Heidelberg, in particular, the life of a professor was not merely comfortable, it bordered on the luxurious. Compared to faculty elsewhere in Germany, the average Heidelberg professor was a privileged being: in Prussia, the median salary was 4,000 marks annually (those in Berlin earned 4,800), whereas the mean income in Heidelberg was almost twice that, at 7,400 marks, and it could climb as high as 10,000. Large houses with domestic servants were such a familiar part of professorial existence in Heidelberg they were taken for granted. On a trip that Max Weber and his wife, Marianne, undertook to the United States in 1904, for instance, Frau Weber was shocked to discover the difference between American and German academic households. She was astonished to see that "the highly educated wife" of a professor they visited in New York "cooks, cleans, does the washing, sewing," and that even the husband pitched in the performance of domestic tasks. That was unthinkable in Heidelberg. Extravagant dinners for a dozen guests or more were not uncommon, involving multiple courses accompanied by choice wines and often framed by a private musical recital or dramatic reading, all conducted within the spacious, tastefully decorated rooms of the professor's home and made possible by a permanent professional staff.

Not surprisingly, the social elevation of the German professorial estate, coupled with an acutely developed consciousness of their intellectual superiority, occasionally led to an excess of self-regard in a few members of the caste. Kuno Fischer, who in addition to his eminence as a philosopher was one of the wealthiest men at the university (people spoke of his house as a "millionaire's palace"), displayed a talent for making statements that revealed how he perceived himself relative to his fellow man. "Do not always call me Excellency," he is reported as having once instructed a student. "Say it only now and again." Similarly, after publicly calling his own son a "mediocrity," Professor Fischer observed, less in self-defense than by way of clarification, that "one often finds that the sons of important men don't amount to anything."

While a certain arrogance more or less came with the territory — in fact, modesty and simplicity were considered unbecoming, indeed "unprofessorial," and were thus actively frowned upon — most of the Heidelberg faculty based their solid sense of self-worth on their scholarly achievements. And in terms of both the quality and quantity of the work they produced, their self-assessment was often amply justified. "If I do not work until one in the morning, then I cannot be a professor," Max Weber once said of himself, expressing a work ethic widely shared by his colleagues. Many, like Weber, were recognized leaders in their fields, whose books and articles shaped the thinking about the subjects they touched, and whose opinions carried weight throughout the learned world. Yet the focus of their industry tended to be one-sided. "Since the university professor primarily regards himself not as a teacher but as a man of science," Friedrich Paulsen informs us, "his scientific work easily seems more important and dignified to him than instruction." The emphasis on original research and "scientific" inquiry caused many to neglect, even to resent their teaching duties, which not a few regarded as irksome interruptions to their real work. Consequently, it was not unusual for professors to fill the time they were obliged to spend lecturing by simply reading from whatever they happened to be writing at the moment, regardless of its topic or pedagogical value. Needless to say, it did not very often make for inspiring teaching.

A student who attended Heidelberg at the turn of the century recalled his first exposure to Wilhelm Braune, one of the university's most famous professors of German literature. It was a dispiriting experience. With his head buried in his manuscript, his eyes rising only intermittently to gaze vaguely out into the auditorium, Braune "seemed as if he were absent." His lecture concerned the convoluted history of manuscript sources for the *Nibelungenlied,* the medieval German national epic, a subject the student had never before given a second thought. After listening to Braune drone on for an hour in his "high, emphatic, and pinched voice" about the various manuscript traditions — designated solely by letters of the alphabet, so that he spoke of "A, B, C, etc. and their affinities" — the hopeful student felt "a horrible disillusionment and discouragement" come over him, along with a single certainty: "that if this was the path of science, I would never take it."

Not every German professor was quite so stultifying, of course — we only have to call to mind Georg Simmel's gripping displays of philosophical improvisation — and Gundolf had no intention of emulating his future colleagues in every respect. But academic life, then as now, could be treacherous, and the seemingly placid surface of quiet libraries and contemplative study often concealed dangerous rip tides of professional envy, malice, and spite. To be allowed to teach at Heidelberg, besides having to fulfill the formal requirements, Gundolf also had to win the good graces of the other Germanists there, including Wilhelm Braune himself, and to obtain the support of people within the administration who would promote him in his pursuit of a teaching position.

With diplomatic skill, substantially aided by his delightful manners, his sharp wit, and disarmingly good looks, Gundolf managed in short order to secure the backing he needed. In August 1910 he could already tell Ernst Robert Curtius that there was "it seems to me, no more external opposition" to his candidacy. "Braune expressed his good wishes to me today," Gundolf added, saying that Waldberg — another professor of literary history there and the department head — "is even supposed to be very pleased." By November, even though Gundolf was still not yet officially associated with the university, he was already informally being regarded as one of its own. To Gundolf it all seemed slightly unreal at first. "It was a strange experience," he confided to Curtius, "being addressed by Waldberg as 'Herr Colleague' (and not, as you might think, ironically or meaningfully, but rather in an entirely friendly way in passing). I positively felt as if I were growing a beard." As the time drew near for Gundolf to finalize his bid for admittance into the rarified realm of the teaching ranks, his nerves began to get the better of him. "I am already dreaming at night about seminars in which I embarrass myself," he confessed, again to Curtius, "and about Waldberg pouring nasty hatred on me!! I hope that means the opposite. . . . If he remains as well disposed and friendly toward me as he has been thus far then nothing can go wrong."

But before being given the opportunity to embarrass himself in front of students, Gundolf had to surmount one final hurdle set by his future colleagues: the habilitation thesis itself. For most people it is an arduous, painful, and protracted undertaking, sometimes stretching over several years. Gundolf completed it in eight weeks. On August 10, 1910, he began working on a manuscript that only a month later, as he wrote to Ernst Bertram, "is taking up all of my energy and concentration and has swollen into a thick book under my hands." On October 12 it was finished, all 491 pages of it. Gundolf himself was somewhat awestruck by the accomplishment, filled with an almost impersonal admiration of his feat, as if it were the work of another. Actually, he believed that in a real sense it partially was. "Now that it is lying finished before me," he told George the day it was done, "I see that I wrote it like one possessed and that it is the product of a higher necessity and of a will that extends far beyond my own paltry knowledge and ability." It was, Gundolf continued, an immediate outgrowth of everything the group of people connected to the *Blätter* and the *Yearbook* represented, a "compendium of the Spiritual Movement, as your books are its bible." But most of all, he viewed the book he had written in such a frenzy as an expression of George's own generative power on and through him, further testimony to the Master's procreative potency. "I myself," Gundolf humbly said, "am and remain the dumbest part of you, but that I was able to write this book is new proof to me that there are holy marriages and that children spring forth from them which are of divine origin, without their parents being something permanently divine. But I know that in those two months I received a new meaning and performed one of the greatest services for the 'State' that could be performed for it. I have you to thank for it, as for everything, and you should hear my happiness about it without the reservations of sociable modesty: for it is your child I am praising so, not yours alone: but its best powers come from you."

Gundolf was used to receiving no reply from George to his effusions, so he reacted in the usual way: he simply kept on effusing. Later that month, he revealed his hope that Bondi would publish the book "as a matter of 'state,' a *Blätter*-affair," seeing how it was, in his estimation, "next to Wolters's *Sovereignty and Service* the chief proclamation of a theoretical 'Imperial' nature." Gundolf, of course, knew that George would never allow any book to be brought out by "his" publisher without his express approval, so Gundolf promised in a further letter in November that, once he had finished the revisions to the manuscript — he was dictating the entire text, correcting as he went along — he would "then send it to you or to Bondi — however you decide. While dictating," Gundolf continued, "I notice that I did not overestimate this work in my initial joy and excitement over its birth. Now I am calm again and see: it is and remains good."

Finally, on November 7, George broke his silence by sending two poems, one by his own hand and one by Ernst Morwitz, and a brief note addressed to "my dearest Gundel." As was customary, the letter was laconic and factual, limited mainly to conveying the dates and destinations of his travels. Just as typically, it threw Gundolf into renewed paroxysms of devotion. Perhaps because he thought George's unresponsiveness had to do with his disapproval of the whole scientific enterprise as such, Gundolf took the opportunity not just to reaffirm his loyalty to George but also to make the case for the usefulness of his work to the cause. "Let me have ten more years of health," he vowed, "and I will be the man to make all of your primal thoughts and experiences the common possession of German culture as a whole in the best sense, that is, of German youth. I notice from numerous signs that this is my right and calling, before many other better and more original tasks. For that reason, Dear Master and Beloved, do not disdain me because of my 'intellectualism' (it now has a purpose and goal), even if it is not and does not create anything primary: for there is no better means of organizing and disseminating it in the Empire-to-be." Gundolf may have not been an original poet, but he thought he could be the spokesman for one. "Now I feel, spurred on by a new and increased love of your being and of your work, what a weapon the word can be in my mouth and in my hand. I embrace you, dear one, with thanks, reverence and fidelity."

The "habilitation thesis" itself — the trigger that had set off this fit of fresh avowals of his affection and utility — was titled *Shakespeare and the German Spirit*. It was, obviously, an outgrowth of Gundolf's intensive and ongoing engagement with Shakespeare; in October 1910 Bondi had already published the fifth volume of the translation of his plays. But in range, scope, and ambition it was unprecedented in Gundolf's prior experience as a writer. In broad terms, the book traces the spread of Shakespeare's influence in German speaking lands, a development that Gundolf largely identified with the formation of modern German culture in general. The English dramatist's works, Gundolf contended, had been instrumental in promoting the rise and growth of a specifically German spirit, or *Geist,* in the eighteenth century. They had done so by providing an antidote and alternative to the stifling rationalism ostensibly imposed by the adoption and slavish imitation of the seventeenth-century French classical mentality. This foreign intellectualism, however, was profoundly ill-suited to the German sensibility, Gundolf maintained, a sensibility that achieved its authentic expression in feeling, emotion, and by experiencing the fullness of life in its totality. And it was Shakespeare that had enabled this self-liberation, allowing the German spirit to awaken to itself.

But no brief synopsis could begin to do justice to the complexity of the book's argument, nor give an adequate sense of the almost incandescent flare of its language. Gone are the self-indulgent obscurities and mystagogic pretense that sometimes crept into Gundolf's shorter prose sketches in the *Blätter.* Instead, his prose is lucid, poised, shimmering with intelligence and enlivened by dramatic turns of phrase so finely crafted they almost sound like aphorisms. Whether one agrees with his analyses or not — and there are countless reasons to disagree — it remains an exhilarating read, offering the rare pleasure of watching an intellectual artist working at the top of his form.

When the book was published — it appeared, as Gundolf had hoped, with Bondi in April 1911 — the reaction was almost uniformly enthusiastic. His friend Ernst Robert Curtius rushed to express his "ardent admiration for your brilliant work." He said he experienced "astonishment and intellectual joy" while reading a book that would, he predicted, "itself mark an epoch in the history of the German spirit that it recounts." Curtius marveled at the "incredible surety of every step, every position, every overview" and concluded: "that comes from the extraordinary extent and clarity of your metaphysical knowledge. The entire book is in fact applied metaphysics."

Further accolades were not long in coming. Soon after Gundolf had arrived in Heidelberg, he had been introduced to the household of one of the university's luminaries, the economist and cultural historian, Eberhard Gothein, and his wife, Marie Luise. In her memoirs, she wrote that at their "first encounter I was immediately captivated by the handsome young man." When Gundolf's book appeared, her husband was similarly swept off his feet by the work. "Now that is truly something!" Professor Gothein enthused to his wife. "I have hardly ever read a literary historical treatise that is not only itself so much a work of art but also above all the expression of a strong personality and still of very solid but never showy scholarship." He could hardly believe the steadiness of Gundolf's hand, or the depth of his psychological insight. "This wonderful capacity for a sympathetic understanding of individuals and of the entire phenomenon," Gothein went on, "is, together with the vivid language the most attractive thing about this book — both are so closely linked with one another. Now I would like to begin again right away; it is a book that one would like to live with, and with the person who wrote it."

Everyone who read it was enthralled — almost everyone, that is. It was not until mid-April, after George had received his bound copy of *Shakespeare and the German Spirit*, that the person Gundolf considered the true father of the book finally acknowledged his offspring's existence. Writing from Bingen, George sent an uncharacteristically wordy letter to the author, but Gundolf knew that George's loquaciousness could be a mixed blessing. Following a few brief words of what one might take as praise — George allowed that the book "is constructed with quite extraordinary surety + and contains hidden merits above and beyond the often incredible assertions" — George's tone quickly took a more critical turn. George speculated what effect the book might have on Gundolf's future colleagues, who, George said, "must have often thought: 'What gives this young "scholar" the right to talk this way?'" And George provided the answer himself: "The reason is they do not possess the inside, 'the middle.' " In other words, George was restating in somewhat different form, and to different purposes, what Gundolf himself had repeatedly said: the "middle," the point of orientation that Gundolf enjoyed and the others lacked, was precisely George himself. It was by virtue of his attachment to his Master, George was pointedly reminding him, that had allowed Gundolf to write with such confidence and certainty in the first place. Apparently, George felt that Gundolf had forgotten what the source of his inspiration was, and he reprimanded Gundolf for even implicitly placing himself in the foreground. "In a very few places even in the section on Goethe one might have wished here + there for a bit more MODESTY of expression. You too would have NOT escaped the aberrations of the literary critics whom you rebuke so harshly merely by means of a 'spirit-SYSTEM' (I mean of the type in the best sense), but through your convictions you did." Gundolf had, in other words, managed to avoid the worst pitfalls of professorial and scientific pretensions but only because he was anchored by his beliefs. George did not feel he had to spell out what the origin and pillar of those beliefs were, obviously, but he did think it necessary to remind Gundolf again that he was merely the mouthpiece, and not the true source, of those convictions. "Otherwise," George concluded, "I am full of praise + admiration. Do you understand?"

To others, George was more direct and less lenient in his comments about Gundolf and his new book. "The professors have ruined him," George had already flatly announced to Bertold Vallentin a few months before, in January 1911. Kurt Hildebrandt, who overheard this comment and was shocked enough by it to record it, said he did not "believe my ears." It was after all Gundolf that George was talking about, "who was very much loved by the Master and his friends and was probably the most talented." Before, George had even seemed to indulge Gundolf in his irrepressible "intellectualism." Only a year and a half earlier, when the plan for the *Yearbook* was first discussed, Ludwig Thormaehlen witnessed a scene that had deeply impressed him. Gundolf became very animated during a conversation, and in the midst of his speech, George stepped behind his chair while everyone else continued to talk. As Gundolf listened intently to the next speaker, George stroked Gundolf's hair with his hand, said something encouraging to him, and quickly bent over his head and lightly pressed it with his lips. Then George went back to his place and turned his attention to the others.

Yet, increasingly there were other times when Gundolf thought he had reason to doubt whether his existence really meant all that much to his Master. In 1915, in yet another long exchange with Gundolf about *Geist,* George made no effort to conceal that the entire subject did not interest him very much. Finally, George became exasperated. "All of you," he said impatiently, "all of you *Geist* people, commit stupidities every day." What good was all that "Spirit" if it could not even improve common sense? As evidence of its shortcomings, George pointed to Wolfskehl. Gundolf resolutely defended *Geist,* saying that he could not despise what he lived by. That was the way he was, Gundolf rather pitifully said, and he might as well end it all now by hanging himself if his devotion to *Geist* were senseless. George's response was not exactly reassuring. "But I would not like it at all if you weren't there. I am quite satisfied with the fact that you exist."

Being satisfied with Gundolf's existence, though, was not the same as being satisfied with what he did. To George, it seemed that Gundolf was becoming far too enamored of Spirit for Spirit's sake. "*Geist* is a weapon," George said, also in 1915, meaning that it was not an end in itself. That had been his view at the founding of the *Yearbook,* and he still ascribed to it then. Nor did George see any conflict between this appreciation of Spirit and his poetic or artistic agenda. For, as he also appreciatively noted, "weapons are something very beautiful." But more and more it appeared to George that Gundolf was serving *Geist* rather than the other way around. Gundolf's voracious reading — he often spent whole days in the library, reading and excerpting notes, and he haunted Heidelberg's bookstores, always on the lookout for the most recent publications — suggested a pronounced bookishness that also did not help alleviate George's skepticism. "Fifty books are enough for a respectable human being," George once decided. "All the rest is 'education.' " In 1914, when Gundolf eagerly reported on a new discovery he had made in a bookstore one day after class, George interrupted him: "Why are you wasting your and my time again! Karl would have at least discovered a new elemental sound!" Eventually Gundolf became anxious about being caught reading anything that might be deemed frivolous — which encompassed almost everything. The situation sometimes assumed absurd dimensions. Whenever Gundolf sat waiting for a haircut, for example, and happened to pick up an illustrated magazine to pass the time, he would quickly set it aside when the door to the street opened out of fear it might be the Master.

Gundolf was thus uneasily suspended between two opposing principles, or at least between two spheres that viewed themselves as opposites, science and poetry, embodied in each case by the university and Stefan George. Gundolf desperately wanted to think of them not as being necessarily mutually exclusive but as potentially complementary. But George, as Gundolf himself knew better than almost anyone else, recognized only absolutes. George considered it impossible to avoid making compromises in one or the other direction, and he held up for particular scorn the notion that it was legitimate or even possible to create a "bridge" leading from poetry to science. When Gundolf heard this, he objected, saying that his own book on Shakespeare was certainly no compromise. "No," George answered. "But go ahead and ask your colleagues whether they think it is science." Whichever way Gundolf turned, he could not win. Instead of allowing him to mediate between the two worlds, George made him out as losing on both sides.

Despite his deep-seated reservations about the university and everything it represented, George was not, however, totally indifferent to all of Heidelberg's attractions. "Now, as concerns Heidelberg," he had written to Gundolf in September 1910. "You remember that when we went over the bridge last week with Ernst I called your attention to a blond boy who had a resemblance to an archaic relief so that it would be worthwhile taking a picture of him." George said he had run into the same "blond boy" again a few days later and, after asking his name, discovered he was none other than the son of Eberhard and Marie Luise Gothein. George knew that Gundolf was acquainted with the family, thus making the request to photograph their son less awkward than might otherwise have been the case. For such purposes, George liked to employ someone in Bingen named Jacob Hilsdorf, for whom he reserved a notable designation: "When our Bingen court photographer comes over again — then make the necessary arrangements — since an ordinary photographer's picture only reveals the vulgar aspects."

The boy who had awakened George's interest was Percy Gothein, then fourteen years old and already strikingly handsome. He wore his hair in a page-boy cut, which neatly framed the strong, regular features of his face. Percy had a broad high forehead, large expressive eyes, a long, thin, finely shaped nose, and full fleshy lips. His chin and jaw were also well formed, as were his slightly prominent cheekbones. He conformed, in physical type, almost perfectly to George's ideal — that is, to an idealized version of himself. Gundolf obligingly followed George's instructions and approached the family about the possibility of having a picture taken of their son. In late September, he had good news to report: "I was there and everything went well." Frau Gothein, Gundolf wrote, far from finding the request odd or off-putting, was on the contrary "visibly touched and pleased, for he is the darling of the family. In the study there is a bust of him and she showed me several sculptures that portray him in relief. The father also smiled cheerfully." The only concern his parents had voiced, Gundolf added, was that if they told their young son of the plan it might make him "vain." But about Percy himself, Gundolf agreed that he was "conspicuously beautiful, very substantial, and touchingly gawky and shy, said almost nothing (he has also not said anything of your meeting and for the time being his parents are not saying anything, either)."

In an autobiographical sketch he later wrote, Percy Gothein divulged the reason why he had not mentioned the encounter with the poet to his parents. One day, as he was coming home from classes with a group of schoolmates, he had noticed someone staring intently at him. He felt "mesmerized by the severe and imposing demeanor of this strange man." The next day, he was surprised to discover the man standing on the same spot at the same time, and again they wordlessly exchanged glances. On the third day, now expecting the man to be there, Percy looked for him in vain. As he walked on, reflecting on this peculiar train of events, he suddenly heard footsteps behind him and, turning around, recognized the strange man following him. Unsettled, he continued on, and hearing the footsteps quicken, he increased his pace as well. Just before he reached the gate to his house, now almost running, the man caught up with him. For an instant, the boy thought the man might simply rush by, but he stopped instead. Percy remembered how only recently his parents had impressed on him to be extremely reserved toward strangers who wanted to give him anything, such as sweets or money. "I rather suspiciously examined my pursuer from head to toe and when he asked me what my name was, what school I attended, who my parents were and where they lived, the thought went through my mind, as would not be unusual for a boy, that I had done something wrong." Percy even wondered whether it would not have been more prudent to outwit his interrogator "like an Indian," and give false or misleading answers to his questions. But it was already too late: the boy had truthfully delivered the requested information. The man said only, "That's fine," and Percy went home, more than slightly confused about what it all might mean.

One thing was certain, however. Percy told himself that he would not add another blunder to the one he had committed with the stranger and thus resolved to keep mum about the whole affair toward his parents. "It would have been unwise," he sensibly reasoned, "to bring fate down on my head prematurely should the incident have unpleasant consequences." Fortunately, things took a happier turn. A few days later, his mother and father blithely informed him that a letter had arrived that contained the request to photograph him "while there was still time." For, the letter writer surmised, "after two years I would probably have become as nasty to look at as most of the others." As compliments go, it was fairly leaden, but in a backhanded sort of way it was a compliment nonetheless. Percy's parents explained that the poet — whom they had not yet met — was permitted to speak that way because he knew more about such things than anyone else.

On the appointed day, Percy dressed up in his best velvet jacket, his mother instructed him to wash his hands thoroughly one last time, she combed his hair, and they all anxiously awaited their honored guest. At last the bell rang, and the strange man strode in as if he were at home, took the hostess's hand in both of his and shook it warmly. Then, placing his monocle in his eye, he instructed the boy where to stand, and in a few minutes the business was done. On leaving, George issued an invitation to Percy to visit him in Bingen the following Whitsuntide.

During the intervening fall and winter months, which George spent as usual in Berlin and Munich, he did not see young Gothein again, but he did not forget him. Occasionally, Gundolf would entice George by sending him tidbits about the boy. "I saw Percy, more handsome and stronger than ever," Gundolf wrote in early February 1911. "He is very taciturn and he shows a kind of measured boisterousness, a hieratic clumsiness in his movements that is hard to resist." Although Gundolf's assessment did not seem uniformly positive, George was entranced. He was so carried away that he let himself draw a remarkable parallel. "What you write about *Percy* greatly fascinates me," he told Gundolf, "and, as a developmental stage, easily invites the comparison with *Maximin*." George must have realized the impropriety of the juxtaposition as soon as he made it — a God can have no equal — and he quickly qualified it. "He" — that is, Maximin — "however stood ardent and fulfilled on the divine plane, with a divine knowledge Adonis-like in his completion. But P stands entirely on a humanly heroic level — full of wild urges and desires with the entire conflict already in his face that indicates someone destined to be both passive and active." Nevertheless, although perhaps no Maximin, Percy was definitely one to watch. "Whenever you see him," George told Gundolf, "write to me always only about him!"

Although Gundolf would have had every reason to feel injured by this last command — he had just completed his Shakespeare book and was preparing for his inaugural lecture at the university, both achievements that George regarded with indifference or worse — Gundolf gave no indication of his feelings if he did. He dutifully complied with George's instructions — "I hope to see *Percy* at the beginning of next week," he wrote five days later — but his own descriptions of the boy, never very effusive in the first place, became subtly more restrained and certainly less flattering than George's own in the comparisons he drew. In April, Gundolf reported that he had recently traveled to Mannheim with Percy: "He possesses something irresistibly lively and has a similarity to a young noble animal, with all of the almost amusing aspects of such a being that is still undisciplined and inchoate." Whatever animal Gundolf had in mind, at least he thought of it as noble. But that was still a far cry from likening the boy to a god.

George finally got his chance to examine Percy more minutely himself a few weeks later. In early May 1911 the boy accepted the invitation to visit him in Bingen. Decked out in a new suit his mother had bought for the purpose, Percy, excited to be on his first unchaperoned trip away from home, took the train from Heidelberg to nearby Bingen, easily found the designated house and was greeted by the poet at the garden gate. That afternoon, George showed him all of his favorite places, they took a walk up the steep paths on the slopes overlooking the Rhine, surrounded by vineyards and orchards in the full bloom of spring. "This is the landscape," George told him, gesturing toward the river valley below, "which in our Fatherland most reminds one of Greece." Since George had never been to Greece, it was an approximate comparison at best. Yet the reference had less to do with the physical reality before them than the metaphysical idea which "Greece" signified and which George saw himself as embodying. (When he was once asked whether he did not want to see Greece with his own eyes, George responded by saying that wherever he was, *was* Greece.)

Toward young Percy, imparting the Greek ideal largely meant adopting the role of Platonic mentor. It was to be a challenging assignment. The "liveliness" and "boisterousness" that both Gundolf and George had noticed frequently expressed itself in a precocious self-assurance, even in a certain insolence. Far from showing George the obsequious reverence he was used to from others, the fourteen-year-old was occasionally bold to the point of being impudent. As they became better acquainted during that first afternoon, for example, they both confessed that they had noticed each other before George had spoken to him and that they had been "friends at first glance." Letting his high spirits, and his boyish vanity, get the better of him, Percy declared: "But you would have never seen me if I had not had such long hair that caught your attention." George, surprised by this display of uncensored forwardness, halted in his tracks and laughed. "My child, that is the first daring comment you've made."

The afternoon held other experiences in store. On the hill above town there also stood an observation tower, which Percy promptly assaulted, bounding up the steps two at a time in order to reach the top first. As he caught his breath, and while waiting for George to arrive, he leaned against a pole supporting a weathervane. As luck would have it, the pole had recently received a thick coating of grease to protect it from the elements, and as George drew closer he could see that Percy's new gray pants had acquired a spot on the seat. Some consternation ensued. George asked him how he could hope to return the boy to his parents "as immaculate as possible" two days hence if such a thing happened at the very beginning of his stay. Then the poet related a story about the "disastrous effect of axle-grease," but did so only under the provision that the tale would forever remain cloaked by the veil of secrecy.

There were more intimacies as the day wore on. When darkness fell, they returned to the large house George's father had bought and in which his sister and seventy-year-old mother still lived. Not that there was any direct trace of their presence. "He seemed to be mysteriously served by invisible spirits," Percy recalled, "for now and again there would be an audible knock at the door, but no one came in, only the Poet would say loudly, 'Yes,' and then one heard nothing more. We stood up and no one was in the hall, but in the adjoining room a beautiful table had been set." Percy had learned not to ask questions that might be perceived as impertinent and, fearful he might only get a swat on the nose if he pried, he resisted the urge to satisfy his curiosity about who had prepared this marvelous feast. After the meal, they remembered the soiled pants, and George brought out a pair of his own velvet breeches, which Percy was to wear "until the invisible spirits had removed the stain from my own." Percy thrilled at the thought of slipping into the older man's pants, insensitive to the symbolic significance of the act. For George, it was yet another instance of the inventive techniques he had developed to have his friends assume the expressions of his personality as their own — by adopting the typeface designed after his handwriting, by reading poetry aloud in his manner, and so forth — as a means of replicating himself in others. To Percy, it was all just a marvelous game. "I thought of myself as nothing less than the boy in *Thousand and One Nights* who was permitted to walk about for a day in the robes of the caliph and for so long was master of all the faithful." As he sat there in George's clothes, the talk ranged over the evils of machines, progress, and modernism — how much the boy really understood of all this is debatable — until it became quite late and they finally retired. Lying in his bed, Percy heard George pass by outside his door on the way to his own room, reciting some lines of verse to himself: "Whoever does not use the riches of which he is unworthy / Must weep: not he who is poor [but] he who lost." The message, quite clearly, was that Percy had been shown unusual beneficence. It was now up to him to prove he deserved the gift generously bestowed on him, with the implied threat that, if he did not, it would be withdrawn just as swiftly as it had been offered.

George gave Percy Gothein one last present as they bid farewell: a blue Basque beret of the kind George wore when he traveled as a memento of his Spanish journey long ago and which he liked to encourage his younger friends to don as well. Back in Heidelberg, as Percy walked over the bridge toward home, with his new cap pulled low over his brow, he ran into his mother, who seemed slightly surprised by her son's new accoutrement. Asking him how things had gone in Bingen, she was perhaps no less interested to learn, as Percy described the house and its contents, that on the wall, as he said, there "also hung that unavoidable picture." He was referring to the photograph of the unclothed Maximin that also adorned the Globe Room in Munich. Frau Gothein, apparently well informed about the state of affairs with George, reprimanded her son for speaking so disparagingly of it. "You must not say that unavoidable picture," she gently scolded him, "for, you know, when someone cares for another person very much, then one puts up his image wherever one is so that one will be often reminded of him, especially when that person is no longer alive, and if a small boy such as you speaks so thoughtlessly about it, then he unintentionally hurts the person who loves the image." Still, despite the evident liberality of her sentiments, his mother thought it best to take the blue beret from Percy and lock it away. He did not see it again until seven years later, when he turned twenty-one.

CHAPTER 31

The Star of the Covenant

On May 8, 1911, the day after he delivered Percy Gothein back to his parents, George hurried to convey his delight over the visit to Gundolf. "We spent the entirety of both days together on walks and the result is that I am even more taken with him. Above all I was amazed that I got him to talk, which was hardly to be expected from the young bear I had before me in H. He even argued with me for an hour about alcohol and very skillfully and eloquently defended himself. He is also very impertinent but his presumptuousness always remains charming. When we ate dinner in the hôtel and the owner asked the usual polite questions while bowing away, Percy found that *I* had deeply disappointed HIM because I had spoken in such a friendly way to the 'bourgeois.'" George was so excited that he became positively chatty, going into detail in a way that, for him, was extremely unusual. That was the point: he was convinced Percy *was* extremely unusual. "But now the main issue: which of course I already knew: the boy is NOBLE. One can make anything out of him and every other quality is secondary by comparison. He is to be sure not unambiguous (I am thinking here of *Maximin*) and already has several very different faces and naturally enough as the son of two intellectual parents is already very conscious (critical). When you see his parents say that I am coming soon to H*eidelberg* and would speak at length with them — I would especially request that of his mother."

No one could have guessed from George's gushings that the person he was having act as his go-between with his paramour had, less than two weeks before, been granted formal permission to teach at the University of Heidelberg. On April 26, Gundolf had delivered the inaugural lecture required of all who wish to obtain that right — his address was devoted to a poem by Friedrich Hölderlin — after having effortlessly sailed through the required examination colloquium earlier in the year. Although George was present at the lecture, he assigned no great importance to it, and obviously had other things on his mind. But Gundolf himself was elated just to be there. "Heidelberg in May," he wrote to Ernst Robert Curtius just after his lecture, "is still full of its almost eerily improbable magic. I feel as if one morning, bereft and sober, I will awaken from this hopeful richness of existence." By that winter, Gundolf was already cozily referring to it as "my Heidelberg." And it was in Heidelberg that, despite an aborted attempt to woo him away to Berlin in 1920, he would stay for another two decades, until his death in 1931.

The attraction was completely mutual. In relatively short order, Gundolf became one of the most famous figures at the university, drawing steadily larger numbers of students to his lectures and constantly receiving invitations to speak at other institutions throughout Germany and the rest of Europe. In 1914, Gundolf already found to his surprise that there were "sixty to seventy people" in his class when "I had counted on twenty at the very most." And when the crowds of auditors for his university lectures became too great — after the war they averaged around two hundred, as against a total student population of three thousand — he was forced to move them into the "Aula," the university's largest auditorium. He became so popular that he could also demand — and receive — fees for his outside lectures that few others could expect. During the 1920s, Gundolf regularly earned five hundred marks for a speech, whereas a well-known writer like Stefan Zweig had to settle for a comparatively modest three hundred.

Opinions vary about how good a lecturer Gundolf really was. Edgar Salin bluntly stated that Gundolf "was not a good speaker, and never became one." Aware that he was in many respects an outsider to the academic community, Gundolf tried hard to preserve the forms of his chosen profession. "In my lecture I have now reached Hutten," Gundolf told Curtius in 1914, referring to the German Renaissance humanist, "and I always have to pull myself together so that I remain 'scientific.'" What "scientific" meant, in this instance, was a strict adherence to the typical German professor's lecture style. As Salin described it, "he read word for word from the pages he brought with him, only very rarely did he raise his eyes from the sheets and let them wander briefly and severely in the room or through the window looking out onto Ludwigsplatz." But even though Gundolf's manner at the lectern was not universally riveting, many of his listeners found that the substance of what he said more than made up for his lack of rhetorical polish. And for that reason, one had to pay attention. "Almost too rich in ideas," was how Salin characterized his style, "the sentences followed one another, without pause there accumulated profound observations that invited one to reflect on one's own — but did not allow it if the connection were not to be lost in the reader's rapid pace." (Gundolf was at least aware that he read too quickly and that his lectures were too dense, but he seemed little inclined to change. "At least," he offered by way of explanation to Curtius, "no one accuses me of offering too little, only too much.")

But for others, especially as his fame grew and the aura around him expanded, Gundolf's lectures were one of the highlights at a university that suffered no shortage of brilliant minds. "Gundolf was the star," Friedrich Sieburg wrote, who studied sociology in Heidelberg before the war. Sieburg claimed that in their overall effect Gundolf's "lectures were of incomparable intensity," indeed so powerful that they permanently colored the way Sieburg understood poetry. "I shall never forget this summer time congregation in his lecture hall with that wonderful atmosphere of intellectual curiosity and reverence."

One of the principal reasons not only for Gundolf's celebrity but also for the reverential ambience during his lectures had less to do with himself than with an awareness of his affiliation with the person who on occasion could even be seen sitting among the auditors. Edgar Salin, who along with some of his friends became Gundolf's student in 1913, recorded one such episode.

> During that time it happened that our whole group went together, as we often did, to Gundolf's lecture. Contrary to custom, we did not hear the buzz of voices from the room; instead absolute silence reigned. As we entered we saw the reason: on one of the benches toward the back sat the Master. No doubt only a few recognized him, some others may have learned his name from them, but all stood under the mighty spell of this lonely man with the expressive head, steel-hard eyes, and the firmly closed mouth. And this time, as during the other, rare hours when George came to his disciple's lectures, a tension vibrated through the room that seized even the most detached listeners: Gundolf came in, went, as always, with rapid steps to the podium and began to read his lecture from his papers. But it was not like any other lecture, to which the listener hardly paid any attention, rather in his voice there was the respectful, almost fearful excitement that overcomes a young pupil before his wise teacher, and in all of the more important sentences it sounded as if they were directed toward the poet to win his approval.

Approval was something Gundolf never fully gained from George through his "scientific" endeavors. But, through Gundolf's very presence in Heidelberg, he made accessible to George something far more valuable to him than *Wissenschaft* anyway. In the years before the war and for a short while after it ended, George could often be seen in Heidelberg, sitting in the park on the castle grounds talking to one of his friends, walking through the streets on his way to an appointment, or simply standing in one of his favorite spots: at the window of Gundolf's apartment that overlooked the path leading up to the castle above the town. George liked to stand there in the mornings and evenings, watching the youth of Heidelberg walk up and down the steps, looking to see if someone betrayed through his gait or manner — or looks — the qualities George prized. If someone caught his eye and was deemed worthy, George would sometimes signal his interest through a wave or spoken greeting, and on rare occasions he would even summon the fortunate one to him, dispensing with the usual ceremony of having an intermediary arrange an appointment with him on a particular day and time.

As George's own stature began to enlarge in the consciousness of German youths who were receptive to his message, and as word spread of his frequent residences in Heidelberg, more people began going there to study — often with Gundolf — at least in part because of the association with the poet. (Walter Benjamin, who like so many other bright young men in Germany went through a period of intense involvement with George's poetry, was one of those who made the pilgrimage to Heidelberg just to catch a glimpse of the Master. Benjamin later recorded that, even though he never met George personally, "I certainly saw him, even heard him. It was not too much for me to wait for hours on a bench reading in the castle park in Heidelberg in expectation of the moment when he was supposed to walk by.") Heidelberg thus provided a rich and self-replenishing flow of potential new recruits, and Gundolf's position at the university gave George a legitimate reason to return again and again to reap an ever bountiful harvest. With of its obvious advantages, it was no wonder that in the years leading up to 1914, Heidelberg became what Edgar Salin memorably termed "the secret capital of the Secret Germany."

Yet the irony of the whole arrangement is arresting. The person who would soon become one of the most compelling and influential forces at one of the premier universities in Germany was not even immediately connected with the university at all, in fact positively rejected the institution and all it stood for. But George, while seemingly uncompromising in almost everything, was adept at accommodating certain contradictions when it served his purposes. We find another example of what one might call his strategic flexibility in the improbable liaison, short-lived though it was, that George entertained with the other major center of gravity in Heidelberg: Max Weber.

Next to Ferdinand Tönnies and Georg Simmel, Weber was one of the great founders of modern sociology. His works on religion, economics, and politics — particularly his magisterial study, *The Protestant Ethic and the Spirit of Capitalism*, first published as a series of articles in 1904 and 1905 — are still read and widely admired today. But it was not only due to the originality and reach of his ideas that Weber stood out before his contemporaries. Born in 1864, Max Weber was four years older than George and by all accounts a powerful personality in his own right. Eloquent, grave, and robustly self-confident, Weber convinced everyone who met him that he was an extraordinary individual. "I spent an hour with Max Weber," Eberhard Gothein wrote his wife in 1908; "he was full of spirit and life, he puts everyone else in Heidelberg in the shade." When Gundolf was introduced to Weber in 1910, he was similarly impressed. "Of all the professors," he told George that November, "the two Webers" — Gundolf meant Max and his brother, Alfred — "seem to me to have most felt a shudder of the more profound life, not just like Simmel as knowledge, but rather as will." A year later, Gundolf was still saying much the same thing. "I recently had a long conversation with Max Weber about *Yearbook* questions (not about the Yb itself)," he wrote, again to George, "and I was again amazed by the abundance, seriousness, and force of this man."

Yet what was peculiar about Weber, and provided one of the bridges linking him to George, was that although he was very much present in the minds of his colleagues and friends in Heidelberg, Weber had only the slightest official connection to the university. Having assumed a chair there in 1897, he had already been forced to give it up three years later because of his fragile and unstable health. From then on he remained an almost invisible but still potent figure in the intellectual life of Heidelberg. And it seemed that the longer he worked outside of the university — through his writings and regular informal gatherings at his home — the greater his unseen prominence and leverage there became. "For the students Weber has become a myth," Gothein once said to his wife. It was a remark that cut in both directions of his standing. Both renowned and inaccessible, revered and yet practically unknown, the "myth" of Max Weber in many ways resembled that of the other unofficial fixture of Heidelberg, Stefan George.

But the differences between them were just as great. Weber was every inch the man of science: rational, deliberate, independent-minded, and congenitally skeptical. In part, it had been his strict Protestant upbringing — another factor that set him at odds with George — that had lent him a steady sobriety of character, giving him a kind of principled earnestness that was reflected not just in his intellectual pursuits but in every aspect of his life. In political terms, too, he seemed the very antithesis of George. A committed liberal with strong social democratic leanings, Weber and his wife Marianne were both devoted to a number of progressive causes that George and his followers looked on with varying degrees of indifference, such as the emancipation of women, the establishment of social justice — and the belief it was worthwhile — the achievement of personal and economic freedom, and so forth. But it was no doubt the very openness of Weber to modes of thinking and being that conflicted with his own, or at least his willingness to grant them the right to exist, that enabled him to consider a relationship with George even possible, let alone desirable.

Weber had known about George since the late 1890s, when a friend and colleague, the philosopher Heinrich Rickert, had tried to interest him in George's earliest books of poetry, especially the trilogy formed by the *Hymns,* the *Pilgrimages,* and *Algabal.* But Weber, who was then busy making his name as an economic historian of agrarian practices in ancient Rome and rural Prussia, had little time for such frivolities. After his illness, though, and more acutely around 1910, he found himself drawn to problems and experiences he had previously ignored. Weber's real admiration of George's poetry did not translate, however, into an endorsement of the poet's extraliterary aspirations, particularly as they emerged in his more recent works. While emphasizing that Weber was "extremely impressed" by George's "great artistry," his wife, Marianne, also underscored the strength of Weber's opposition to the "*religious* prophethood that the disciples ascribe to the Master," which, she said, her husband took issue with "just as he rejected every kind of cult dedicated to a contemporary, and in general any elevation of a person to the position of authority over *all* existence as the 'deification of a living creature.'" Weber was also put off by the radical repudiation of modern culture expressed in *The Seventh Ring,* and he found George's "self-segregating contempt for the masses" to be, as Marianne somewhat quaintly put it, "unbrotherly." But it was the demand for "*personal* sovereignty and *personal* service" that Weber found most objectionable. "Certainly," he said, he could consent to "service and unconditional devotion to a *cause,* to an ideal, but not to an earthly, finite human being and his limited aims, no matter how exceptional and admirable he may be." That, for Weber, was simply going too far.

Weber himself articulated his complicated stance toward George in a long letter he wrote in June 1910 to Dora Jellinek, the daughter of the great legal and political philosopher at Heidelberg, Georg Jellinek. Stressing both his genuine admiration of George's poetry and his simultaneous misgivings about George's pretensions beyond the poetic sphere, Weber said he felt that George combined "the traits of true greatness with others that almost verge on the grotesque." On the one hand, Weber thought that one would have to go as far back as Hölderlin to find a poet of comparable caliber, and he even likened George to Dante in his ability "to say things that have *never* been said." Yet, on the other hand, Weber considered the "Maximin-cult" to be "quite simply absurd." Wanting to give George the benefit of the doubt, Weber, still writing to Fräulein Jellinek, said he regarded the growing trend in his poetry toward social and cultural critique as a "foreign body" inimical to his true talents as an artist. It represented, he thought, a "derailment" from George's true path, a deviation in a direction that was, moreover, not even very original. Calling George an "ascetic," Weber keenly perceived that

George, "following the model of so many other ascetics," now wanted "to regenerate and control the 'world' he had first fled." That was certainly true. What Weber failed to realize was that it had been George's aim all along.

Finally, in September 1910, through an arrangement made by Gundolf, Weber got to meet the man who had been intriguing him from afar. To his evident surprise, Weber discovered that as soon as they stood before one another, "all of the inhibitions created by the disciple-cult instantly dissolved. The Master was entirely without affectation and acted with simple dignity and geniality." Weber found himself fascinated by the phenomenon of George as a person, even as he warily retreated from the poet's larger claims of authority. For his part, George was clearly curious enough about Weber that he not only set aside — or held back — his scruples about science, he also undertook the unusual step of going to visit Weber in his house, rather than summoning him to his own place of residence, as was normally the case, where he could regally receive his guest.

Over the next two years, through the summer of 1912, Weber and George periodically saw one another. Even in his absence, though, both George's ideas and person were the subject of frequent, and frequently heated, discussions between Weber and Gundolf, who was a regular guest in the Weber household. Predictably, many of the conversations revolved not around poetry but around political and social issues. Marianne reported that, during a series of exchanges occasioned by the *Yearbook for the Spiritual Movement,* Weber objected that his own work on the Protestant ethic had been illegitimately used to support a larger attack on "all of modern culture: rationalism, Protestantism, capitalism," and so forth. Marianne, who was active in Heidelberg circles campaigning for women's rights, also registered that during their conversations with Gundolf "the modern 'enlightened' woman, who recognizes neither authority nor God, took her lumps as the 'primary sacrilege' preventing the production of heroes." Marianne chafed at the thought that women had only a secondary role to play in George's plan, a role that closely mirrored the relationship between the disciple and the master. "The George circle," she correctly reminds us, "rejects ethical autonomy as an educational ideal and refused to recognize the value of the individual soul. Subordination to the authority of the hero, and for woman to be subordinate to man: that is their 'faith.' "

When George was in Heidelberg, he sometimes participated in these debates as well. But they often devolved into a polite though unyielding articulation of their opposing points of view. On one day in December 1911, when George came by to pay a visit, there followed a fairly typical exchange. (In her memoirs, which were published fifteen years later, Marianne carefully recorded this meeting as well, including the fact that she "assumed that he wished to see both of us and [I] was bold enough to be present" during the conversation. George, who read her book when it came out, acidly remarked when he ran across this passage: "The assumption was false.") The discussion ranged over the usual subjects, and at one point it touched on the issue of "women in general." George tried to enlist Max Weber's support "against the modern woman." Apparently, both Webers demurred. Turning to the woman of the house, George leaned "his deeply furrowed, leonine head very close to me," Marianne wrote, "his deep-set eyes shot straight ahead, and he asked: 'You believe that all people can be the judge of themselves?' " Bravely, she responded, " 'Not that they *can,* but that it is a final goal to make them mature enough to be.' — 'And *you* want to be your own judge?' " he then asked. Not precisely understanding the question, or preferring to shift the emphasis away from herself onto the cause she championed, Marianne answered, "Yes, that's what we want." That was all he needed to know. The very idea that a woman, or any other inferior creature, would presume to attain self-determination was something George could not comprehend, much less abide.

But women and their proper or improper role were not the exclusive matters of controversy among them, even though they were obviously of particular interest to Frau Weber. During a further house call, George opened up a little more than usual, dilating for example on "the blessing of war for a heroic humanity and the villainy of combat during peaceful times, about our enervation through the increasing pacification of the world, which makes it impossible for us even to slaughter a chicken." Again, either misunderstanding George's manifest glorification of war and combat or wanting to elevate it to a higher plane, Marianne ventured a conciliatory interpretation of George's words. She wondered if, regarding "the importance of the constantly escalating intellectual battles of modern man, they might perhaps produce *spiritual* heroism instead of the physical variety." That was kindly intended but not in fact what George meant. He resorted to a supercilious word of reproach to convey his disapproval of her apparently willful distortion of his words. "Miscreant, miscreant!" he scolded Frau Weber. "You always want to turn everything into spirit and in the process destroy the body." (When George later read Marianne's memoirs he also glossed this episode. Explaining his choice of words, George said, "After all, I couldn't say to her in the presence of her husband: 'Silly goose, silly goose!' The 'miscreant' was a more polite form.")

The extent to which George meant for his praise of war, physical heroism, and violent struggle to be taken literally — as well as how seriously he meant his acceptance of the inevitable toll on human life they exact — is illustrated by a comment he made many years later, in 1929. By then Max Weber had been dead for almost a decade. But he still came up in conversation from time to time, as in the following remark, which George made while discussing the relationship between overpopulation and food production. This subject evidently put him in mind of Weber's earliest scholarly work on the economics of agrarian policies. "All of England had in Napoleon's time fifteen million inhabitants," George pointed out to his listener. "Imagine: in the 1830s Berlin was a city of 200,000 inhabitants — whereas today! Quality has to diminish with such large numbers." To clarify his point, George referred to an unnamed primitive culture, saying that "when there were too many people, then so-and-so many would be put in a boat and they had to wait and see if they found any land. If not, then they drowned. Only so many were permitted to exist and no more. But if Herr Max Weber comes along, then he says: 'Nonsense, the land can feed many more.' "

To George, this kind of attitude, which failed to respect nature's presumed limits, exemplified what was wrong with modernity. The very fact that there were so many people on the planet was in itself deplorable, but, even more, it was unnatural. "If it were to please God and we were thirty million instead of seventy," George told the same person, restricting his comments this time to the population of Germany, "then all of our difficulties would be solved." It is not entirely clear which difficulties he thought would be addressed by cutting the population by more than half. But he could have no patience with someone like Weber, who saw the solution to all problems in science. Science, with its focus on what was technically possible instead of what was intrinsically appropriate, amounted in George's eyes to a perversion of nature. "Nature everywhere spreads out many more seeds than it brings to fruition," George once said and appeared to extract a larger principle from this observation. Weber, liberal democratic humanist that he was, considered human life a highest good, worth preserving no matter what the cost. George thought differently. "What people call humanism does not interest me," he said another time to some of his disciples. "I expect more from you. The way you should be is that you feel strong enough to be a match for the Greeks." Life was a contest between the strong and the weak, the few and the many, the worthy and the unworthy, and for George only one of two outcomes to the struggle was possible. One was either among the winners or losers, and death was the natural, indeed appropriate price of defeat.

In the end, the gulf that separated Weber and George could not be permanently bridged by personal sympathy or good manners alone. Unavoidably, what George had recently taken to calling his "program" caused the points of disagreement between them to overwhelm the genuine feelings of mutual regard they originally shared. More and more, during his visits with the Webers, Marianne noticed "there came a moment when George wanted to discuss the 'program,' " and it was precisely this "program" which both she and Max found impossible to accept. "The deification of mortal people," Marianne explained, "and the foundation of a religion based on George — and that, as Gundolf had let slip, was already the intention of the circle — seemed to us to be the self-deception of people who are not entirely up to modern life." On George's side, it was not the extreme nature of Weber's position that eventually put him off but that Weber was not radical enough. In a final reaction to Marianne's published portrait of her husband, George concluded that, through her eyes, "one sees what [Weber] was: a rabble-rouser, politically minded, but not a politician."

That, by contrast, was how George now saw himself: as a politician with a "program" to push through. "I will get every single point of my program endorsed," he confidently told Ernst Robert Curtius in 1911, "but never all of them together." It was certainly not for want of trying. Gundolf's installation as lecturer at Heidelberg had not brought any curtailment of his activity in the various projects he was directly involved in or oversaw. Most important of those was the *Yearbook*. Preparations for the next issue had begun in late 1910. Gundolf wrote to Curtius in November to say that Wolters and Vallentin had visited him in Heidelberg, where "we hatched the new war plans." In April 1911, during the same month in which Gundolf held his inaugural lecture, the second volume of the *Yearbook for the Spiritual Movement* was published, followed in November by what became the third and last number of the journal.

Of the two, the April issue is by far the weakest. In fact, the brief introduction to the volume, amounting to no more than a short paragraph, is one of the most interesting parts of the entire effort. There the editors ostentatiously say they refuse to comment on the "external effect" stirred up by the first issue, announcing that they would ignore "abuse of all kinds" and confine themselves merely to the observation that the only thing that might have worried them would have been no response at all. Yet, they did note that, had any one of the essays appeared separately, it would have probably provoked far less an outcry. There was a lesson in that: "It was therefore in the main the *joint action*, the *common attitude*, the *shared faith* that aroused passions. Thus all the external signs as well tell us that we are on the right path." The very fact that people had been offended or worse meant that the collaborative enterprise was working.

The second *Yearbook* may have been a group undertaking, but it was not a very compelling one. It contains several undistinguished essays: Berthold Vallentin offered a dull and predictable "Critique" of the journalistic press and the theater; Robert Boehringer delivered a plodding historical overview devoted to the art of reciting poetry; Kurt Hildebrandt reappeared with a wordy and muddled contribution on the concepts of the "romantic and dionysian"; and Paul Thiersch — an architect whose principal claim to the right of inclusion was that his wife, Fanny, was Hildebrandt's sister and his daughter, Gemma, later became Friedrich Wolters's wife — wrote an abbreviated reflection on "Form and Cult." Even the articles by the two editors, Gundolf and Wolters, do not measure up to their authors' usual standards. And perhaps most indicative of the generally low level of the volume is the lead essay ostensibly outlining the " 'Weltanschauung' of the *Yearbook*," which is signed with the name of Karl Wolfskehl — but was not actually by his own hand. Wolfskehl, who had promised to write an article on music, had been unable to overcome his natural inertia and had failed to meet the deadline for the second issue. In its place, possibly as punishment for his dereliction, a loose, disorganized compilation of quotations drawn seemingly at random from the works of Baudelaire, Alexander Herzen, Jakob Burkhardt, and Nietzsche was printed, identifying Wolfskehl as its author. If it was meant to humiliate Wolfskehl, it worked. Decades later he still expressed resentment over the incident, even though he never found out who the perpetrator had been.

The third — and as it turned out final — volume of the *Yearbook*, which appeared with a publication date of 1912, was another matter altogether. Whereas the editors had previously assumed a posture of disdainful aloofness toward the public clamor raised by the first volume, here they felt obliged to refute at least some of the objections brought against their ideas. As a result, the editors of the *Yearbook* spell out with greater clarity and candor than almost ever before what the basic tenets of their "shared faith" were. They assembled all of the points of controversy in a list — the imputed "pessimism" of the circle, the ostensible inability of its members "to come to terms with the modern world," their "contempt of science," their failure to appreciate either "humanity" or "the masses," their "contempt for women," their "cult of friendship" and their "Catholic tendencies" — and mounted a vigorous counterattack. It is not *they* who are pessimistic, they argued; the real pessimists are those who believe in a culture of progress, with its promises of ever greater riches, happiness, and ease, for that culture contains the seeds of its own inevitable destruction within itself. It is not that *they* cannot make their peace with the world that is the problem. Instead it is the world that is troubled, desperately trying to intoxicate itself with the illusions of material gain in order to hide from the truth of its inner poverty, refusing to admit that "despite all of the external improvements, enhancements and entertainments . . . things cannot continue to go on this way."

While much of the editors' indictment of the world is familiar, there is one surprise. In addition to the usual catalogue of evils — including rationalism, protestantism, liberalism, feminism, materialism, industrialism, and so on — they introduced a new villain to the rogues' gallery: the United States. Or perhaps it would be better to say that America allowed them to put a face on the world's blight. There was, to be sure, nothing especially original in the substance of the charges the contributors leveled at America and Americans. It was, by 1911, a familiar litany among many Europeans that Americans were boorish, vapid, uncultivated, egotistical, and in love with one thing only, money. Yet whatever the anti-Americanism of George's followers lacked in novelty was made up for by its intensity. In the editors' introduction to the third *Yearbook,* they even held the United States — presumably because of its puritanical heritage — to be ultimately accountable for the attacks against their "cult of friendship," in which insinuations were made of sexual impropriety in the relationships among members of the circle. "This is," they wrote, "the aversion of the American individual, having become void of passion, toward every form of heroic love." In like manner, the editors argued that their own "rejection of protestantism" was justified because "everywhere the Protestant form of Christianity becomes established, it capitalizes, industrializes, modernizes the people." In other words, Protestantism turns its unsuspecting converts into Americans.

Not surprisingly, all of these pernicious, life-threatening traits personified *en gros* by Americans found concentrated expression in "the modern woman." She had repeatedly demonstrated herself to be, the *Yearbook* claimed, "the most loyal pioneer of all progressive, inanely humanitarian, superficially rationalistic and superficially religious ideas." Not only that, and more concretely, "some of the worst [ideas] such as theosophy and the peace movement came from females." It was this, the supposedly inborn pacifistic inclination of women, that made them most suspect — and most like Americans. No one, the editors warned, should underestimate "the danger of a feminization of entire peoples," which could potentially lead "to the extinguishing of all vigorous powerful instincts in the face of the unwarlike, feminine, corrosive ones."

If things continued unchecked, the editors predicted, in another fifty years there would be nothing left of "these last remnants of old substances" and in their place "the satanically inverted, the America-world, the ant-world, will have established itself once and for all." It was a dire situation that called for dire measures. Rolling out their heaviest rhetorical guns, the editors declared that the real battle now was no longer between the sexes, the classes, or even the nations. Rather, "an entirely different battle has to be proclaimed, the battle of Ormuzd against Ahriman" — in Zorastrianism, the pre-Islamic religion of ancient Persia, Ahriman is the arch rival of Ormuzd (or Ormazd), the chief deity, the source of light, the embodiment of good, and the founder of the world, which he specifically created as a battleground on which to vanquish Ahriman — a battle, the editors continued, that would be one "of God against Satan, of World against World."

It was not the first or the last time the United States would be equated with Satan, nor would the extreme solution suggested for eliminating the evil it was thought to represent — its total annihilation — fail to find other determined advocates in the future. But the words, delivered as they are with an almost religious fervor and solemnity, bring one up short nonetheless. And they of course reflected, as did everything else in the *Yearbook,* George's own opinions. A couple of years later, for instance, George mentioned that "earlier, in the *Blätter*," it had been only Prussia and its constituents — that is, "the Imperial German, the lieutenant, the student in a dueling society" — that had stood as "the enemy of all culture." But, George said, ever since the turn of the century he had recognized something else "as the more serious enemy, which undermines life itself: the legalistic nature of the American way of thinking, which always sees nothing but antitheses, always turns things upside down." The United States represented one great antithesis to George's entire scale of values. He spoke derisively of "the entire Anglo-American deception about freedom and justice," and he never tired of disparaging "the soullessness of American civilization." Americans meant machines, masses, mediocrity and — always and again — money. During the war, in 1916, George offered the following as "an example of Americanism" and its defining obsession with money. He had seen a photograph advertising an American boarding school and under the likeness of each of its graduates were captions praising their successes that had made enough of an impression that George reproduced them in English. "G. S.: he earns 30,000 dollars a year," George recalled, reciting the advertisement from memory; "X. Y.: he earns 50,000 dollars a year, etc." George commented sarcastically that this admittedly rather unsavory practice proved once again that "the Anglo-American race demands entirely different criteria of evaluation." The word "American" even became a handy universal epithet, signifying a kind of ne plus ultra of whatever vile quality in a person he wished to disparage. When Karl Gustav Vollmoeller — once a contributor to the *Blätter* but more recently demoted to the status of a former friend — published a drama called *Mirakel* that George found wanting, the Master dismissed the man and his work by saying, "Ach, er ist ein Amerikaner!"

To accuse Americans, or Prussians for that matter, of lacking taste, decorum, and culture is one thing. To align an entire people with the forces of evil, in fact to draw no distinction between them and to recommend that they be subdued at all costs, is of course another. But that is quite openly what the *Yearbooks* do. They had been, from the beginning, explicitly conceived of as *Kampfschriften,* as issuing combat orders. They were not merely polemical exercises but works of battle, giving guidance and instructions to those who heeded the call. And there should be no illusion about the actual intentions of the *Yearbooks*. George and his followers were not talking any longer about exclusively poetic, or literary, or even cultural matters at all. They were talking about the world, the real world, as a whole. "Every decent person has to be filled with disgust just by reading the numbers that are to be expected" the editors to the third *Yearbook* wrote about the expanding population across the globe. "But the worst thing is not the material hardship that threatens but rather the deterioration of the species that steadily increases with the mass."

No one person, they add, has the courage in the present day to say that there are certain "offenses" — such, one assumes, as overpopulation — that have to be "atoned for," and that there is a means available to force that atonement: namely, "poison and fire." In a word, war.

Gundolf had always been one of the most martially inclined among George's faithful, and in his essay for the second *Yearbook* he had already found room to expound the virtues of war, in fact to argue for its necessity. "The general peace, which tolerates everything, is an old man's ideal," Gundolf proposed. "Where youth, change, creation are possible and necessary, war is necessary, too: it is a basic human form, like wandering, love, praying, and poetry: it cannot be made superfluous by any civilization." Gundolf thought that, given it was such a fundamental mode of being, war could never be engineered entirely out of existence, just as little as sex could be eliminated: "When progress will have made procreation unnecessary, then it will also make war dispensable." It is both a sad and ironic testimony to the "progress" humanity has in fact made since Gundolf's time that the one achievement he considered impossible, now attainable, has not led to the realization of the other.

In the third *Yearbook,* Friedrich Wolters also chimed in on the belligerent chorus. His essay, entitled "Person and Genus," is given over to an extended condemnation of the individual who finds "his happiness and that of humanity in the contentment and security of peaceful calm, in perpetual peace." Instead, Wolters glorifies the "dangerous person" who "does not understand this happiness and despises it, he wants to proclaim his own archetype, embody it in deeds and reproduce it in bodies: in that he is served by every strength of his body and mind, from the most swollen muscle to the most silent cunning. Peace for the sheer sake of peace is hateful to him, only a peace as a prize of battle acceptable to him." The proponents of a more tranquil existence want to convince us, Wolters warns, that "the protection of the poor the ill and the weak is the highest sole task" we face and thus, by implication, such softhearted liberals portray "what is poor, sick, and weak as the best part of humanity." We should not be deceived, he tells us, or moved by false compassion. We should esteem instead the "great man," follow him where he leads us, no matter what sacrifices he may demand. "However much great men have to destroy on their paths" was sufficient indication that whatever "great men" had destroyed was "worthy of destruction and a necessary sacrifice." Then Wolters makes a dramatic political conclusion based on these fundamental postulates. "In the state," he writes, "there must therefore be ruling men, not only officials and people who enjoy equal rights; on earth there must be ruling peoples, not only advocates of a balance of power. States and peoples that no longer produce ruling, creative men are dying structures and a vital neighbor does right to dissolve the degenerate ones and to enslave its remnants."

This is derivative Nietzsche, flattened out and brutalized, but it would be a mistake to underplay the seriousness of the message, or to imagine Wolters meant it only in a figurative sense. As an example of the real consequences he drew from his elevation of "the strong man" and his urging the subjugation, indeed enslavement, of the weak, he offered the following reflections on women. The dictates of "modern humanity," Wolters tells us, would perversely require men to renounce their "greater strength," their "male rule," and place themselves at the service of women, thus using — or rather misusing — all of their strength "for the maintenance of woman, for the pleasure of woman, in the service of woman." Allowed to abandon the only role in which they were capable of being productive — that is, Wolters implies, as mothers — women become insatiable parasites who require constant care and feeding: "Their being is entirely pleasure, pure consumption and an enormous expenditure of all technical culture only for her." It was clear to Wolters that women, and the various cultures that had let them gain the upper hand, were out to destroy men and rob them of their natural superiority. It was a struggle for survival, and Wolters felt that failure to meet the challenge would unavoidably lead to the subjection of men to the tyranny of female caprice. "Thus we are fighting not against woman but against her proliferating excrescence, 'the modern woman' — but for proper women the words of Pericles are still valid: 'you will achieve great honor when you do not disown the nature appropriate to your sex and when among men you are thought of as little as possible, neither in praise nor in censure.' " That, for Wolters — and for George — was the goal: to reduce the role of women to such a point that they would never come to mind at all.

For the lucky few — as long as they were male — a far different fate was in store. "To you therefore, boys and youths, our call goes out." Wolters urged them to "look for the man who would provide meaning and a model for your will." Specifically, they should "seek the truth in the hero, in the ruler, seek in heroically elevated men your true friends and the leaders of your youth." Above all, one should keep oneself free from all contamination of any physical or spiritual kind. "The healthy man turns his eye from suffering and keeps himself fit for battle with his enemy." "Only what is living deserves your sacrifice," Wolters told his readers, "through the sacrifice to your friend, your *Führer,* your ruler your best will partakes of the pride of a separate special being, causing there to rise within you the inner duty along with the inner right, with the gesture of physical nobility the law of the spiritual deed." If that sounded like an oath a soldier might take before plunging into battle, the similarity was not coincidental.

While the *Yearbooks* provided important elaborations of George's "program," and brought it to a wider audience in more manageable form, they were not the way he preferred to communicate. (Kurt Hildebrandt did report that George had entertained the idea of writing a contribution himself for the third issue of the *Yearbook*, but said ironically that he would first have to consult with three lawyers to make sure he would not be charged with "inciting class hatred.") Poetry was still the only vehicle, besides speech, to which George would entrust the expression of his own vision, political or otherwise, and it was verse to which he now turned to give that vision concrete form. In November 1913, first in an extremely limited private edition of only ten copies distributed among his closest friends, then followed early in the following year by a "public" printing, George published his first book in seven years since *The Seventh Ring*. Originally to be called *Songs to the Sacred Horde* (*Lieder an die heilige Schar*), George ultimately settled on *The Star of the Covenant* (*Der Stern des Bundes*). In its entirety, it comes the nearest to a full articulation of George's aims and intentions that he would ever offer himself.

It would also be the first book George produced without the collaboration of Melchior Lechter since 1896. For close to two decades Lechter had designed every volume of poetry George published. Lechter had developed insignia, colophons, type, and ornaments that were used exclusively to illustrate the works of George and members of his circle. Indeed, Lechter's characteristic style, which gave graphic form to George's repudiation of the modern mechanized world had become so closely identified with George and his "movement" that they were seen as virtually synonymous. But that was part of the problem. Lechter was one of George's oldest collaborators, someone George had even addressed as "Master" in the days when there was still more than one. They had of course both changed over the years, and they had moved in different directions. Yet it was not just that Lechter had become a relic of a time and sensibility George had since overcome and left behind. George was also no longer interested in having partners or peers. He now recognized no equal and wanted no one to share the dais with him. By their very nature, Lechter's designs called too much attention to themselves, detracted from the sense that there was but a single will at work, a single force that had found its outlet in George's poetic voice. From now on, George's books were to display an aspect entirely of his own making and thus reflect nothing extraneous to himself. Everything — the embossed covers, the title page, every line of text — was printed in the typeface based on George's handwriting, with no other decoration to spoil the effect of complete uniformity — with one exception. The only concession George made to his long history with Lechter was to include on the front page the motif he had fashioned depicting a gothic monstrance surrounded by the words, *Blätter für die Kunst*. But that, too, could be construed less as a gesture toward Lechter than as George's way to maintain a link between his own past and present, preserving a memento of his poetic origins while demonstrating how far he had come from those now distant beginnings.

George's decision to dispense with Lechter's visual aids was prompted by other considerations as well. Lechter, who had always shown a penchant for mystical experience, had become increasingly drawn to Eastern religions over the years, culminating in the trip to India he had taken in 1910 with Karl Wolfskehl, which resulted in a diffuse book based on a journal Lechter kept during the expedition. To George, Lechter's enthusiasm for such things smacked of poorly digested Romanticism. In September 1909, for example, George visited Lechter at his Berlin apartment, later joined by Wolters and Vallentin, and Lechter noted with dismay in his diary that they had "argued about mysticism and the occult." In the autumn of 1912, Ernst Morwitz similarly reported to George that he had just visited Lechter, who was about to publish his *Diary of the Indian Journey*. Morwitz pronounced the whole thing "awful: a mixture of mysticism and banality." The following day, George shared the news with Gundolf, saying that "I just heard from E[*rnst*] [there are] dreadful (literary) new births" arriving at "Kantstrasse" — Lechter's address. That same year, George told Ernst Robert Curtius, rather improbably, that "the imminent danger to the world is Indianism." As evidence of this peril he cited "Lechter's India book!" From then on, George never lost an opportunity to fulminate against the menace of "Indianism," and especially Lechter's version of it. In 1920, George announced that "mysticism and Buddhism" were, like all quietistic doctrines, "detestable." He added that when he heard of "certain acts of penance by ascetics, it makes me ill. If I have the choice," he elaborated, "between Nero, who sang the Iliad while Rome burned, and an Indian penitent who lets himself be eaten up by lice, then I'll choose Nero." But any sort of mysticism, Indian or otherwise, that did not meet with George's approval found comparable censure. Late in life, while telling a younger friend stories from his own youth, George recounted how he once accompanied Lechter and Wolfskehl on a visit to a simple peasant woman reputed to be a mystic. "She immediately got on well with Lechter, although God knows they both came from different corners. The other two of us did not understand a single syllable."

Finally, though, what motivated George to drop Lechter may have had less to do with the supernatural than with very earthly concerns. Lechter's creations were, and were intended to be, unique objects, handmade artifacts that were regarded as works of art in their own right. That, along with the fact that they were exceedingly expensive, meant that only a few copies could ever be produced or sold. Earlier, George would have had it no other way. He had once made the crack to Lechter that "I will print twelve copies of my next book, eleven for my friends, one for the broader public." It was amusing because it was only half a joke. Now, however, things had changed. George was no longer satisfied with reaching only a small number of like-minded readers: he wanted instead to form minds, motivate action, give commands, issue laws. That aim could be achieved only by appealing to a larger constituency — and by producing more and cheaper books. Even as far back as 1907, when the final preparations for *The Seventh Ring* were underway, George had not been entirely happy with Lechter's decision to make the book more lavish than originally planned. At Lechter's insistence, George finally relented but only reluctantly. "Since your heart is set on an even more elegant luxury edition," George told him in August 1907, "even though the idea does not actually completely appeal to me, I will permit you [to make] the edition in Japan paper with the silk binding and be done with it." Two years later, George was not prepared to indulge Lechter's taste for extravagance any further. In 1909, when Lechter surprised him with a deluxe edition of Wolters's *Sovereignty and Service,* George lost his temper. As he said to Gertrud Kantorowicz, "Such a book is supposed to draw the attention of young people to my poetry and lead them to it; and then they go and make an expensive showpiece out of it!"

George's fears were later confirmed, in 1917, when a young man by the name of Hans Hesse wrote to say how much the *Yearbooks* had meant to him and to tell George how they had filled him with "the belief that you can give me what I lack and what I am seeking." Hesse had also read Wolters's *Sovereignty and Service* with the same reaction, but it had been a borrowed copy: it was beyond his financial means to acquire it. "Would it not be possible," he asked, "to publish a cheaper edition — for instance like the Stefan George books for 4.50 marks?" Hesse said it was "bitter" to have found what he needed but not to be able to obtain it just because he was lacking "wretched money." "And I assume you don't want to influence aesthetes and money people who are more interested in buying the design by Melchior Lechter, but rather those who are serious about the formation of the *person.*" To let money get in the way of young men earnestly seeking out the Master was not just foolish or counterproductive, George must have thought it bordered dangerously on Americanism.

By the time his next book was ready, George was not willing to take any more chances and he chose not to involve Lechter at all. Thereafter, their relationship, once so close, gradually cooled off and eventually expired. In the winter of 1920–21, as George reminisced about Lechter, he notably compared their bond to a "marriage: a marriage that had been very good." Whether one wanted to characterize the dissolution of their partnership as a divorce or merely as a separation, the split was irrevocable. George thought there was a kind of natural cycle that all friendships experience. "When a relationship is exhausted," he explained to Robert Boehringer, referring specifically to Lechter, "then an active person turns to a new one. I am aided in that by my nature." An episode that occurred in late 1923 indicates the depth of George's later estrangement from his erstwhile friend. George was staying at the home of some Swiss acquaintances in Basel when word came that Lechter, who was on his way back from a trip to Italy and was unaware that George was in town, would be stopping there, too. George, who liked to keep his movements secret, did not want to see Lechter under any circumstances, fearing among other things that Lechter would reveal his whereabouts to others once he returned to Berlin. George therefore decided to move into different quarters until Lechter had again departed. Almost inevitably, one day, and much to his astonishment, Lechter caught sight of George crossing one of Basel's streets. Lechter grabbed the arm of his hostess, who was accompanying him on a walk, and cried, "That's Stefan!" The poor woman, torn between the unpleasant alternatives of lying to Lechter or facing even more disagreeable consequences if she did not, chose the lesser of two evils. But it was not easy. Although she repeatedly tried to assure Lechter that he must have been mistaken, he refused to let up, insistently and repeatedly asking if she really did not know whether "Stefan" was in town, thus forcing her say over and over what she knew to be untrue. When George was later informed of the incident, he showed no appreciation for the considerable sacrifice the woman had made for his sake. Instead, he only berated her, implying that contrary to their agreement she had deliberately chosen that particular route so that Lechter would see him.

Thus, *The Star of the Covenant* appeared at the end of January 1914, bare of any embellishment, with nothing but the text printed on medium-weight, cream-colored stock and bound in plain white canvas covers that featured only the title and the poet's name embossed in gold on the front, obtainable to anyone who could part with the few marks it cost. Obtainable but not necessarily accessible. Several of the poems dated from as long ago as 1907, and many had been published in the ninth issue of the *Blätter* in 1910. As he was writing the other poems, George had often read them aloud during the ceremonial gatherings in the Globe Room in Munich, during his trips to Berlin, to new recruits in Heidelberg, and to the friends he invited to Bingen. But there was always an aura of secrecy about the poems, and when they were finally presented in their permanent form as a book — as was customary, George did not permit anyone to transcribe any of the poems until they were published — it seemed that a veil had been torn aside to reveal an unadorned monument whose existence had been suspected but which had never been seen in its full majesty before.

Of all of George's books — it was his eighth — *The Star of the Covenant* yields itself the most reluctantly. More than any other previous work, it is willfully addressed to a coterie, its meaning truly available only to those who are already within the orbit it describes. But the book is so steadfastly hermetic that no one, apart from the poet, could understand every line or word, every hidden reference or every allusion. *The Star of the Covenant* thus represents the epitome of George's fraught attitude toward publication itself. Although printed in greater numbers than any previous book he had produced, it was also the least receptive to outsiders, likely to cause only confusion and frustration in readers unprepared to receive its message. As Ludwig Thormaehlen, one of the recipients of the original ten copies, put it, "We now had this book in our hands. To be sure, we had repeatedly heard a portion of the poems and through listening to them had understood the whole force, implacability and boldness, the breath, the wide sweep, the magic, the tremendously new and demanding things, how it denounced and called, judged and beseeched." Once the book was there in its entirety, however, Thormaehlen and others like him realized that they had only begun to comprehend the poems they thought they already knew. "But even now," Thormaehlen wrote, "when we had the book in our hands, parts of it remained hidden to us in their totality and their meaning, until after repeatedly reading and listening again the depth of the poetic space and the diversity and breadth of the structure of ideas little by little, only after years, fully revealed themselves." One can only imagine what the many readers must have made of it who did not have the kind of privileged access Thormaehlen had to the poet and his world. *The Star of the Covenant* could have legitimately carried the same subtitle as Nietzsche's *Zarathustra,* which is a distant cousin of George's work in tone and intent. Both were, that is, "for everyone and no one."

A large part of the new book's difficulty stems from the almost complete elimination of descriptive language in the poems. There are hardly any references to the world most of us know, and many of the words, phrases, and objects evoked in the book denote something other than what they commonly mean. And in those cases in which familiar subjects are addressed, they are often wrapped in elusive euphemisms, cloaked in indirection, hidden behind words that stand in a remote and tenuous connection to the things they normally signify. It is, in stylistic terms, the enactment, perhaps the fulfillment, of George's lifelong wish to be both visible yet undisclosed, detached yet engaged, not of this world yet covertly directing its course. In a preface added to later editions, George admitted that he had initially intended *The Star of the Covenant* to be "a secret book" — *ein Geheimbuch*. It is an apt description, not least of all regarding what it meant to his circle. For *The Star of the Covenant,* a secret book or book of secrets, is literally the testament of the Secret Germany.

Another way to put it, as Edgar Salin did, is that *The Star of the Covenant* is "the law book of the circle." Combining his roles as poet, priest, and politician, George emerges here as a lawgiver, laying down the foundations on which his realm, or empire, would come to rest. As he does so, the poet looks back over his own past as he envisions the future, pausing occasionally to contemplate — and condemn — the present. And at the center of his endeavors, forming the focus of all his desires and hopes, stands the god — unnamed but identical with Maximin — who had once appeared to him and is now portrayed as the source and guarantor of the laws the poet prescribes.

Appropriately for a book of commandments and rules, *The Star of the Covenant* is rigidly constructed, reminding one most strongly of *The Tapestry of Life* in its relentless order. There are exactly one hundred poems in the book, divided into an introductory section, reasonably enough called "Entrance," which contains nine poems, each one fourteen — or two times seven — lines long. This is followed by three "Books," each enclosing thirty verses. The volume concludes with a "Final Chorus," a single incantatory, twelve-line poem in which every line consists of precisely five words and begins with the same word: "God." The effect of this severe regularity and repetitiveness, underlined by the almost exclusive use of the iambic pentameter, is a kind of inexorable, marching gait, embodying in its very form the authoritative urgency and power of the book's internal message.

While the substance of that message would not have been entirely foreign to initiates, it still requires a good deal of excavation to bring it fully to light. The book as a whole pursues three principal aims: to describe and celebrate the advent of the god through the poet's discovery of him, to demonstrate the poverty and unworthiness of the present world, which must be eradicated before god's reign can begin, and to provide guidelines for the chosen few who will survive the cataclysm and establish his new order in place of the old. In terms of its content, *The Star of the Covenant* thus presents nothing startlingly new to anyone already immersed in George's universe. It is, instead, the insistence of its demands, the surety of its own truth, and the remorselessness of its hostility to the world at large that are in the sum staggering.

Even more astonishing, perhaps, is the degree to which George identifies himself with the god he proclaims. The book begins with an invocation of the god, who is said to encompass the full expanse of time and space: "You always still a beginning to us and end and middle." Immediately, though, it becomes clear that the poet is not just the herald of his god but in some indescribable way indivisible from him. Time and again, George has the poetic voice express his perplexity over what he calls "the power of the puzzle," namely: "How he [can be] my child I the child of my child." His god, his own creation, is also his progenitor, the one who gave him new life through the mystery of what in one of the poems earlier dedicated to Maximin in *The Seventh Ring* had been called the "most secret marriage." Here, the god is extolled for the same reason, for, the poet explains, "you delivered us from the torment of duality / You brought us the fusion become flesh." (Similarly, in a later poem, we read that, with the appearance of his god, "My dream became flesh.") Elsewhere, however, the identification goes the other way, as if the poet were the actual point of origin. "You came sprout from our own trunk," one poem reads, "Beautiful like no image and tangible like no dream / Toward us in the naked brilliance of the god." Another poem asks, "Who is your God?" and gives the answer, "The desire of all my dreams · / The closest to my archetype · beautiful and glorious." But George also suggests that in the experience of spiritual procreation he, the poet, assumed the role of both sexes, becoming mother and father to himself and to his divine offspring at once. The climax of this spiritual amalgamation occurs in an extraordinary poem, in which not just the poet and his god are assimilated in the same figure, but also the conquest of biological necessity is celebrated in the poetic realization of the hermaphroditic ideal to which George had long aspired:

> I am the One and am Both
> I am the father am the womb
> I am the dagger and the sheath
> I am the victim am the thrust
> I am the vision and am the seer
> I am the bow and am the bolt
> I am the altar and the plea
> I am the fire and the wood
> I am the rich one and the poor
> I am the sign and am the sense
> I am the shadow am the true
> I am an end and a beginning.

Having prepared us by the jarring appeal to images of combat and destruction amidst this celebration of transsexual union — the conflation of sex and violence, always an effective mixture, already takes place in the third line of the poem: the German term for "scabbard" or "sheath" (*Scheide*) is also the standard word used for "vagina" — it is toward the "end" that precedes the "beginning" that the poet then turns. God, now almost indistinguishable from the poet, after surveying the world and its inhabitants, pronounces them all unfit to live and averts his eyes from the unwholesome spectacle their extinction presents. "From purple blazes the wrath of heaven spoke: / My glance is turned away from this people." Only those who have "fled to the holy region" are spared his fury, and "all the rest is night and nothingness." The precise fate that awaits these creatures who are already plunged in abject darkness — that is, the better part of humanity — is revealed in a shocking, terrifying poem. Drawing on the biblical story of the tower of Babel to evoke the hubris and folly of modernity, George lets his poetic persona pronounce this harrowing judgment:

> You criminals build beyond measure and boundary:
> >What is high can also be higher!< yet no base
> No support or patch serves any more . . the building totters.
> And at the end of wisdom you cry to heaven:
> >What can we do before we suffocate in our own debris
> Before our own phantasms consume our brains?<
> He laughs: too late for standstill or medicine!
> Ten thousand must be struck by the holy madness
> Ten thousand must be snatched by the holy pestilence
> Ten thousands by the holy war.

There is no conceivable explanation of these lines that can get around the fact that, as unambiguously and bluntly as possible, George here is calling for the necessity of tens upon tens of thousands of people to die in what is called a "holy war." The obscenity of the poem is manifest and irrefutable. The meaning is so blatant that his later interpreters and apologists knew it would have been futile to deny what George so obviously intended. Instead, they have claimed that he only "prophesied," but did not welcome or advocate, much less should be held accountable for, the coming of later events. Whatever one thinks of George's prophetic abilities, however, we know there is a fuller story. For years, in fact for decades, George had been gratifying his appetite for strong images of martial conflict in his poetry, and scenes of violent, bloody death were no strangers to his verse. More recently, George tended to formulate his opposition to his own country, his own culture, indeed to his own time in starkly apocalyptic terms, as exemplified most grimly in *The Seventh Ring*. He appeared not just to take for granted but to want to hasten the wide-scale destruction and death he believed had to come before any hoped-for renewal. And, as many of the essays in both the *Blätter* and the *Yearbooks* document, further borne out in numerous conversations and letters, the younger members of his circle also wholeheartedly subscribed to George's politics of annihilation in the name of cultural revival. In this poem, that is, George lent the full authority and credibility of his poetic voice to what Gundolf, Wolters, Wolfskehl, and others had in public and in private long been yearning for, working toward, hurrying along: an overwhelming, devastating "holy war" that would obliterate their enemies — the list was long — to make room for the New, Spiritual Empire presided over by the Master and validated by his God.

As if to provide further justification of the need for the elimination of the sordidness of the present world, the rest of the First Book of *The Star of the*

Covenant reiterates its irreparable character. "Speak not to me about the Highest Good," the poet commands his contemporaries in one poem. "Before you are punished / You make it base the way you think and are." Simply by taking the name of the "Highest Good" in their mouths, the poet says, his fellowmen thereby defile it. Another one has the same miserable people protesting that the conflagration envisaged by the poet will consume the things he values as well as those he disdains. His reply is chilling:

> Rather, destroy them if they remain for you
> Your caustic poison and your collective grave
> As a home of rubble and maternal abyss.
> It may one day happen that from even more meager remains
> Safeguarded by ruins — from blasted wall
> Weathered stone corroded ore
> Yellowed text a life will be kindled! . .
> The way you preserve is nothing but decay.

In the coming "holy war," that is, there will be not only human casualties but cultural ones as well. George seems to have accepted that cherished objects, works of art, books, indeed whole cities, would be turned to ashes and dust. (Another poem contains the line, "He knew: no fitted stone may stand.") He even implies that the very act of preserving artifacts merely for the sake of possessing them is nothing but another expression of the same materialistic, acquisitive impulse that was synonymous with the evil of modernity. (In the same way, George frowned upon the bibliophile leanings of his friends and once said that books, like coal briquettes, had only "calorific value" according to the amount of heat they gave off when burned. Otherwise, he said, books were merely "dust-traps.") What mattered to George was not the physical object itself but the existential need it fulfilled. The very fact that museums and libraries were so easily destroyed contained in itself, George thought, a practical lesson. "Learn something from that fact for today!" he told some friends. "Copy what is important to you and learn it by heart!" The model George obviously had in mind were the handful of Byzantine humanists and anonymous monks who had salvaged what we knew of antiquity and paved the way for its subsequent rediscovery and rebirth. Yet there was a difference in, on the one hand, admiring the collective labors of nameless individuals who retrieved the fragmented records of a vanished civilization from oblivion and, on the other hand, arguing for the inevitability, even desirability, of the very forces of ruin that made that salvation necessary in the first place.

After the pestilent frenzy of the first section, the Second Book of *The Star of the Covenant* begins on a positively beatific note. The conclusion to book one had already pointed in the new direction the second one would take by announcing that: "The Deed" — the "deed" of Maximin's coming — "has rushed upward in earthly jubilation / The Image" — again, that of Maximin — "raises itself up in the light free and naked." (Maximin — the god — is always presented as nude. Earlier in the book, he is similarly apostrophized thus: "You have appeared as one unveiled / As heart of the circle as birth as image / You spirit of the holy youth of our people!") Claude David, with characteristic clear-sightedness, suggested that, in its entirety, "the second book is the book of initiation." That is undoubtedly true; but it can just as well be described, in part, as the chronicle of a seduction, or rather of multiple conquests. Although they contain no identifying details that would disclose the person in question — no names, no distinguishing physical features — we know that the first ten poems of the second book tell the story, albeit at great remove, of George's relationship with Ernst Morwitz. But, as with everything associated with George, it is no simple affair. Just as the reanimation of the world can happen only once it has been purged of all corruption, so too can the bond between the poet and his beloved be complete only when the divisive boundaries of individuality have been torn down. On the way, George proves once more that, while he might be a prophet of catastrophe, he is also a troubadour of love:

> Let me lay my mouth upon the place
> On your breast where your heart is
> So that it may suck the twitching ulcers from old fevers
> As the healing stone [does] the venom in the wound.

The "venom" here is the toxin of particularity that the poet wants to heal through the balm of unity. As we have seen, such unity, or love, for George means incorporation, absorption, appropriation of the other into himself, or, alternatively, the transference of himself — his voice, his handwriting, his spirit — into or onto the other. In another poem devoted to Morwitz, the poet thus speaks of the "wild dream" he has realized in their union, "in which I extinguish myself in you," and he likewise says that it is up to fate to determine "how I will complete myself in you."

But once the consummation has taken place, a change begins to occur. Apparently, when George considered the subtler implications of the total identification of himself with his lover, he became slightly disturbed by all that implied. In one poem, the poet seems to suggest that he backs away from the initial intense engagement because, after recognizing that he and his lover are now so alike, indeed spiritually related, continuing their intimate liaison would amount to a kind of incest:

> When my lips press on yours and
> I live wholly within your inner breath

And then loosen the embrace of your body
That envelops me and for which I am aglow
And step from you with lowered head:
It is because I intuit my own flesh —
In terrible distances that the mind will never measure
I sprang forth with you from the same royal house.

Over the years, George developed a number of different explanations — one might also say rationalizations — for his practice, now become a ritualized habit, of picking up and then fairly quickly abandoning or at least distancing himself from the young men and boys who once excited his interest. The reasons for dropping them so abruptly varied and were rarely, if ever, laid out in so many words. But it is relatively easy to imagine a typical scenario. If he was sufficiently attracted by the physical appearance of a young man, George would arrange a private meeting, be it in his borrowed quarters in Heidelberg, Munich, Berlin, or in his own house in Bingen; more rarely he would invite himself to the other's place. Then George would send him through his paces, asking questions about his tastes, his preferences and dislikes in literature, things, and people. Usually, they would read poetry together. Sometimes, if a picture of Maximin happened to be on display — if they were in the Globe Room, say, or at home in Bingen — that would also be made to serve as a wordless but unequivocal indication of what George's intentions were. All the while, he would watch and listen, looking for signs of a disposition that fit his requirements. For many, this first interview would be their last; for others, further probing was necessary before they, too, were found to be in some way unsuitable. Even those, such as Morwitz himself, who were allowed to remain in contact with the Master, discovered that after the first, ardent phase of their relationship had passed, George had placed them in a secondary category. Suddenly, with no forewarning, they realized they no longer enjoyed the privilege of being the sole or central object of his attention, that he had turned away toward yet another new conquest. Since an essential feature of George's courtship was to break down the barriers of his lover's individuality and render him utterly dependent on George for the meaning and purpose of his life, this demotion or banishment could — and in a few cases did — lead to a profound crisis. For those who manfully took the place assigned to them and obeyed the Master when and if they were called, the reward was continued, if intermittent, access to him and in some exceptional instances even a return to the inner sanctum.

To avoid incest, though, was, for George, a new pretext for distancing himself from a lover. Yet in the context of his evolving notions about "supersexual love," "elected filiation," and "spiritual impregnation" it is carried by a clear logic. Just as George was both creator of and created by Maximin, George also understood himself as entering into a "spiritual marriage" with each of his newly acquired friends. He implanted himself into them, formed them after himself, so that the "rebirth" they experienced inescapably altered their relation to him, changing them, one might say, from lovers into sons. In one poem, George explicitly draws this conclusion himself, saying that this transformation affects not solely their affiliation with him but all of their other attachments as well:

> This is the realm of Spirit: reflection
> Of my realm · grange and grove.
> Here everyone is formed anew
> And born again: the cradle and home
> Are as unto a fairy tale.
> Through the mission through the blessing
> You exchange clan, name and station
> Fathers mothers are no more . .
> From the filiation · which is elected ·
> I choose my masters of the world.

Following the poems commemorating the climax and denouement of Morwitz's extreme closeness to George, the final two-thirds of the second Book of *The Star of the Covenant* offer snapshot images of various other friends who come into George's life and undergo a comparable evolution. Some poems are devoted to people we know, including Herbert Steiner and Percy Gothein, and some eulogize friends whose identity remains shrouded in mystery, but all of them tell a similar tale. "Destroy me!" one poem has one anonymous lover cry out; "let your fire consume me! / I, free myself, freely gave myself away · ·" Another says: "What has happened that I hardly know myself anymore / Am not another and yet more than I was?" Yet another asks: "What more can I do if I grant you this? / That I nestle in your hands like clay / Attune my thoughts to the beating of your heart?" All of these poems enact scenes of a radical remaking of the self but always in the image of the other.

Throughout, hovering behind and above these scenes of inner metamorphosis, is the spirit of George's god. That god may have been conceived in and for love, but he is no languid swain. In one poem, his god is favorably compared to the Greek figure of Eros, who is rather mockingly described as having "rosy soft girlish limbs" and "thick bows in his hair." Maximin, by contrast, is "slender and firm," he is "without jewelry" and "his kiss is short and burning" (it should go without saying that he also stands "naked and free of all coverings.") As opposed to resembling the effeminate cherub of myth, he is more like a Spartan youth, hardened by an austere regimen to withstand the rigors of combat. As before, sexuality and violence are overtly connected here, too. Maximin's eyes are said to "gleam with courage and lust for battle," and the poet says the god imparts this same desire in those he "fertilizes": "Once he has inseminated from holy loins / He urges on in trouble and danger." The second book comes to a close with the poet envisioning himself going off arm in arm with a friend while being led by his god to engage in a conflict that would culminate in both of their deaths. "I thank the Guide who designated me / For the deed with you on a future day that sacrifices us / In praise of the stars · you brother in battle!" On the eve of that battle, the poetic voice looks forward to the "bloody baptism" that awaits them the next morning even as he revels in the "calm of the last night in your arms." It concludes: "With God and you toward victory! with You toward death!"

In the third and final book, George sets forth some of the rules that will govern those who are lucky enough to live through the firestorms to come and enjoy the good fortune of joining the "covenant." Here George offers injunctions, dictating codes of conduct and belief. It is not a comprehensive list, but it serves as a representative selection of the tenets underlying the circle and directing its administration. Reinforcing the sense that we are reading a book of statutes, most of the poems are not addressed to a single "you" anymore but to the plural — in German, the informal, second-person forms of *Ihr* or *Euch* — and many contain verbs in the imperative mode. "You shall spit what is rotten from your mouths," one commands; "You shall carry the dagger in the wreath of laurel," instructs another. The poet tells his followers how they will recognize one another — "you will know those of fellow birth / From the true ardor of their eyes" — and that the new pact they have entered — the covenant they have sealed — is binding: "Whoever has walked around the flame / Shall remain a satellite of the flame!" Yet another poem describes the connection as a "bond of ore."

That bond was binding, but it could be broken. In addition to regulating conduct, *The Star of the Covenant* also contains a penalty code to punish the failure to obey its directives. For minor infractions, violators are told to "go and atone silently by deed / Then come back." George hated apologies, thinking they were a sign of weakness, and he equally disliked excuses — "To beg forgiveness," the poem declares "and to forgive is loathsome" — and he preferred for those who had disappointed him to win back his favor through acts of contrition or penance. For more serious offenses, there was only one acceptable remedy: "Learn from heroes to fall on your own sword." Any transgression great enough to arouse George's ire usually resulted in the banishment of the offender — or, what was the same thing in George's mind, in his death. To commit suicide merely meant sparing the Master the trouble of carrying out the sentence himself.

Symptomatically, several of the stipulations outlined in this last section of the book concern the role and function of women in George's realm. "You shall not defile your bodies / With women of a foreign order," one poem demands of his followers; "Wait! leave the peacock to the monkey!" The members of George's new order — that is, the one projected in his book — should not take as wives women who do not know or understand their common goals. But the women who might be "worthy of carrying your seed" do not yet exist and would have to be specially instructed to learn "woman's most characteristic secret." The "secret," the task, which George saw as woman's true calling, is the bearing and raising of children. In a later poem, he puts it this way: "Woman / Bears the animal · man creates man and woman." Women are thus relegated solely to the material, domestic sphere; they fulfill a purely biological duty, and they are allowed to have no responsibility outside of the home. Everything belonging to the sphere of education, culture, and politics are matters for men alone.

The "Final Chorus" that completes the volume gathers together all of the themes enunciated in the preceding ninety-nine verses and tightly concentrates them in a single poem of tremendous force and economy. In the impervious confidence of its terrible vision, communicated with simple, lordly diction, it is surely one of George's most overpowering works:

> God's path has been shown to us
> God's land has been destined for us
> God's war has been ignited for us
> God's crown has been granted to us.
> God's calm in our hearts
> God's strength in our breast
> God's wrath on our brows
> God's ardor in our mouths.
> God's bond has embraced us
> God's fire has enkindled us
> God's good has flooded us
> God's joy has ripened us.

Here fused in perfect union with him, George and his god both speak in the same muted voice in these lines full of an awful, ineluctable certainty. For a moment, while reading them, one almost feels that God himself has rendered final judgment on the earth, a judgment to be carried out by his enflamed believers.

As if in uncanny confirmation of George's favorite number and in seemingly perverse compliance with his darkest forebodings and most fervent hopes, seven months after *The Star of the Covenant* was published, Europe exploded in war.

CHAPTER 32
Legends of Summer

From the start, the summer of 1914 promised to be a memorable one. For one thing, the weather was almost perfect. For long stretches of days and weeks, skies all over central Europe remained clear and silky blue, the air was mild and dry, and just enough rain fell to fill out the gardens, forests, and meadows with fragrant flowers and greens. Although the first few months had not been hot enough to produce the kind of vintage that had made 1911 so extraordinary, wine makers were optimistic about their prospects nonetheless. "We haven't had a summer like this in a long time," Stefan Zweig recalled one vintner telling him. "If it stays this way, then we'll have a wine of the sort we've never had. People are going to remember this summer!"

At the end of May, George was in Heidelberg after a monthlong trip to Italy. He also appreciated the benefits the friendly weather brought. Percy Gothein, now eighteen, had completed his exams and was ready to go to university. "Percy looks simply beautiful," Gundolf told George that summer. George did not need to be persuaded. Every spring since Gundolf's appointment there in 1911 — the year he also met Percy — George returned to Heidelberg just when the season reached its intoxicating zenith. But his eye was on more than the natural beauties of the place. "Every morning of that hot summer," Percy wrote in his memoirs, meaning that first year of his acquaintance with George, when he was fourteen, "we boys used to come home from school at twelve and for an hour before the noonday meal we would splash around naked in the water and blazing sun. The best thing, though, was after cooling off by swimming in the river we would stretch out on the wooden boards of the bathhouse and let our bodies get brown in the hot sun." One day, as Percy emerged from the Neckar dripping wet, his bare tanned body glistening in the heat, he saw "to my considerable surprise, just in front of me in an open changing booth lying half in the sun, half in the shade, the Poet." Feeling neither embarrassed nor self-conscious, Percy walked up to George, greeted him pleasantly and flopped down on the boards next to him. "The Poet had been there for some time already," Percy said, "and was now reclined in great leisurely abandon."

George had already been for a swim as well and had dried off in the meantime, while Percy's wet hair still gave off drops when he shook his head in response to some of George's questions. As they talked, George mentioned how enjoyable it was to be sitting there, in the sun, apparently idle and yet doing a great deal for one's body. The conversation then turned to the "ancient Greeks" whom one liked to imagine, George said, "in even greater nakedness." Percy went on to say how George "directed my attention particularly to the Spartans, whom he praised highly, telling me how they knew to curb their youth with strict discipline and how they had not shrunk from harsh corporal punishment." At this endorsement of physical chastisement, Percy inwardly jumped — he was still of the age when the issue had a more than purely theoretical significance — and he argued eloquently for the advantages of a more "humanitarian age" and against the antiquated practice of spanking. George, unmoved and impassive, merely said, "You young thing, but sometimes it seems to me to be salutary if not in fact necessary." Fortunately, there had been no transgression that required any such drastic measures and there was nothing to disturb their peaceful colloquy, which soon shifted to less alarming topics. After a while, Percy rose to his feet and stood gazing silently at the water. George later told him that at that moment he "looked like an early Greek boy," with his smooth, lithe, naked body standing erect along the riverbank, lost in thought and embodying an unconscious grace.

Perhaps in the hope of savoring similar delights, George looked forward to dividing the early part of the summer of 1914 between Heidelberg and Munich and then retreating during the hotter remaining months to the Alpine coolness of Switzerland. But Percy was not the only object of his attentions that summer. In April of the previous year, while he was in Munich, George had accidentally run into Ernst Glöckner, who was then living with his friend, Ernst Bertram. The relationship between Glöckner and Bertram was deep, intimate, and long-lasting: having met on May 3, 1906, they treated that day forever after as their anniversary, celebrating it every year for almost three decades. Their life together was even seen as exemplary by other young men who were themselves not so fortunate as to find a kindred soul. "Ah," one such acquaintance wrote to them, "I am sometimes happy to think of your vie de garçon in a single room where there are flowers, books, and pictures, where Plato and Bach bring you together, where one of you stands up from the piano and the other watches how, with a little fussiness and even awkwardness, he puts out his cigarette at the window sill and loves him because of this fussiness." When they were apart, which they frequently were, they wrote to each other at least every other day, and sometimes more often. (Bertram taught German literature in Bonn, whereas Glöckner lived more than eighty kilometers away in Weilburg, a small Hessian town north of Frankfurt, permitting them to spend only the semester breaks and the summers together). After an abortive attempt to establish himself as an art historian in Munich, Glöckner withdrew from all professional activity and with Bertram's financial support devoted himself to his extensive correspondence and to his real passion, calligraphy. Thus Bertram and Glöckner lived in relative contentment, regularly commuting between Bonn and Weilburg until Glöckner's early death in 1934. When Bertram later died in 1957, his final wishes were respected and he was also buried in the cemetery at Weilburg next to his lifelong companion.

It was in fact Bertram whom George was hoping to find when he went to their Munich apartment in the late afternoon in the spring of 1913. Bertram had written an appreciative, not to say flattering essay about George in 1908, which the Master frequently mentioned with equally extravagant praise. George had been so impressed with Bertram that he even published one of his poems — albeit with the name of the author suppressed — in the ninth issue of the *Blätter* in 1910. But Bertram steadfastly resisted George's efforts to co-opt him and he guardedly kept his distance. "I am not suited to be a disciple," he flatly told George at the very beginning of their association. Bertram always felt uneasy around George, and the first time they met left a haunting and lasting impression on Bertram. As he sat waiting in a Munich café for George to arrive, the poet's distinctive large head suddenly appeared peering through the heavy curtains hung across the doorway. Bertram's first reflexive thought was, "A werewolf!" And just to make certain George would have no illusions about where he stood, Bertram published the following poem with the title "Portrait of a Master":

The eyes · narrow and only when they rule wide ·
Were illuminated from behind as if by candles ·
The pain from some old cruelty
Etched in his cheeks.

His face fell steeply down from his dark hair
As if in princely terraces
Down to his chin · which only concealed
And was full of violence · that was deadly in hate.

> Around the immobile lips there was the trace
> Of conquered temptation ·
> And gravely his brow carried
> The noble curse like a chosen jewel.

George got the message. He retaliated by disparaging Bertram's looks — on one occasion he described Bertram, fairly harmlessly, as being "plain," but on another he complained that Bertram's physiognomy was "unbelievably unfortunate" — and by repeatedly criticizing Bertram's overactive intellectualism. "Too much *Geist*," was how he later characterized Bertram to Glöckner, with meaningful emphasis.

Ernst Glöckner, however, presented an altogether different aspect. Physically, he corresponded to the type George almost obsessively sought out: his face was long and regularly formed, and he had large, almost doleful eyes that peered out somewhat hesitantly from beneath a heavy brow. He looked elegant, noble, and yet somehow vulnerable, even delicate. Indeed, Glöckner possessed both a labile psyche and a weak constitution — one reason for his premature death was a chronic kidney ailment — and his susceptibility to wide emotional and physical swings appeared to be etched in his face, which seemed to express suspicion and a need for solace all at once. It was therefore, perhaps, on the basis of an all too acute self-knowledge that Glöckner had so far avoided meeting George. Then, one evening, as he was returning home to the apartment in Munich he and Bertram were sharing — Bertram happened to be in Rome at the time, leaving his friend by himself — Glöckner caught sight of George heading in the same direction and then finally disappearing into the very house where they lived. Glöckner later told Bertram that "after overcoming a senseless fear," he went inside as well, "trembling and agitated," and arrived at the apartment just as George was hearing from the maid that Bertram had gone to Rome. But for Glöckner it was too late. After learning who he was, George invited him to his own apartment. "And now I have only the one wish," Glöckner wrote, "that I had never met this person."

Glöckner's account of his meeting with George is remarkable, not just because it documents the event in such minute and credible detail, but also because it attests to Glöckner's own profound ambivalence, even acute distress, over the entire experience. "What I did that evening," he confessed to Bertram, "was beyond my self-control, I acted as if I were asleep, standing under his will, will-less, oh, obedient, only too obedient like a child. It was a terrible, indescribable, blissful, vile, and exalted experience, with many fine shivers of happiness, with as many glances into an infinite abyss." Once he had managed to regain his composure after the meeting had taken place, Glöckner was able to view the occurrence, as well as his and George's behavior, more objectively. But in the overpowering presence of the Master he had felt incapable of exercising his own will. "I could not act otherwise," Glöckner wrote, in almost abject honesty. "He was stronger than me. Perhaps he did wrong since he saw my weakness; perhaps he should have left me alone since he saw me being weak; for there was no more resistance in me — I only watched and cursed myself."

Realizing he was being slightly incoherent, Glöckner pulled himself together and narrated the sequence of events that had so perturbed him. That first evening, after they had introduced themselves to each other in front of the apartment door, Glöckner felt he had no choice but to invite George in. It was to be the most harrowing experience of Glöckner's life. Sitting in Glöckner's chair, George began to grill him about Bertram, what he was up to, what he was writing, what his plans were. Throughout, there was a subtle hint that, although George genuinely esteemed Bertram's undeniable talents, the Master faintly disapproved of the end to which he put them. He uttered words of mild reproach that Bertram had published some poems with a press other than the *Blätter für die Kunst* — "Terrible, terrible," George said, "where such things appear!" — all the while shaking his head, winking at Glöckner and licking his lips with his tongue. (Glöckner also made the startling discovery, confirmed by others, that George had "a forked tongue" — there was in fact a pronounced indentation at its tip — "like a snake.")

Then George turned the focus of his inquiry on Glöckner himself. He wanted to know, above all, why Glöckner had not sought him out. "He was angry," Glöckner noted with alarm, "and his eyes flared that I had left it to chance to meet him." That was not how people treated the Master. "He said it was my duty to come to him." When Glöckner stammered something about his "shyness," George dismissed it as a flimsy excuse. "One has to overcome that," he told Glöckner, "if one is allowed to get to know me. But you all have no will of your own, you are overly sensitive and fragile, you boys. Here there is still a human being" — George was referring to himself — "and you don't have enough nerve to trouble yourselves to come up to him." It was more than indignation; George felt outraged that Glöckner had failed to appreciate what a unique opportunity had almost been lost. "Am *I* supposed to do it, then?" he asked scornfully; "I'm too old now. You have to come." Glöckner tried to placate him by squeezing his hand, but George would not be appeased. "No," he said, "I can't forgive you for that so quickly."

Next came the ritual that belonged to all first encounters with George. He asked Glöckner how he occupied his time and, hearing that Glöckner did a little writing, George shot back, "Poems as well?" Glöckner's affirmative reply sealed his fate. There followed, he wrote, "one of the most ghastly moments of my life. I had to read aloud. My resistance was futile." Brushing aside all of

Glöckner's efforts to evade the performance, George kept saying, "You have to be able to." Almost panic-stricken, Glöckner nervously fumbled around in his desk, looking for his manuscripts. Witnessing Glöckner's obvious anxiety, George remained unmoved. "A young poet," he said mockingly, "who doesn't know where he keeps his verses." It was almost as if he were enjoying Glöckner's mortification as he fruitlessly searched for his poems, becoming more and more bewildered with each passing second. "Just take your time," George advised him, taking advantage of the delay to inspect the items on Glöckner's desk. His eyes lighted on a photograph of Thomas Mann. "Terrible, terrible," was his only comment. Both Glöckner and Bertram knew Thomas Mann personally and admired his works, favoring one story in particular. "Do you know 'Death in Venice'?" Glöckner hopefully asked, no doubt thinking that George would be receptive to its frank exploration of the protagonist's homoerotic awakening. Glöckner was mistaken. "There is a word," was George's stern response, "that is called silence," and he made a contemptuous gesture as if to wave away everything Thomas Mann stood for.

Meanwhile, Glöckner had finally located his manuscripts and tried to hand them to George. "No, you read," he was told. "I also want to know how you read aloud." With no other recourse available, Glöckner obeyed while George sank in a nearby armchair and covered his eyes, occasionally emitting something that to Glöckner sounded like a growl. After plowing through three or four poems, feeling increasingly humiliated and spent, Glöckner simply stopped, saying, "That's enough now."

Perhaps sensing that he may have pushed Glöckner too far, George now changed tack. He stood up, gazed at Glöckner and then spoke. "His voice was hard," Glöckner said, "and full of metal." George returned to the subject of Glöckner's attempt to evade him. "Do you know why you did not come to me?" George asked, then answered himself. "I know why. You were afraid of the gulf that lies between you and me." George again made a violent motion with his hands, as if he were severing an imaginary boundary between them. "And yet you sense that you partly belong to me." Glöckner felt totally defenseless. George's "face became that of a devil," he thought, and in the growing darkness of the room he told himself that even though "this man is doing violence to you," Glöckner felt he had no option but to succumb or risk something worse. George seized one of Glöckner's hands and what little was left of Glöckner's resolve finally broke down completely. He kissed George's hand and with failing voice whispered, "Master, what shall I do?" George's reaction was immediate and no less disconcerting. "He raised me up to his breast, embraced me and kissed me on the forehead. He held me firmly and I him. All the while, he softly said, 'Boy, dear boy. Dear.' How I was able to endure this I no longer know. I had a feeling of well-being and sweetness and yet at that moment I despised myself as I have never despised myself before. I was grateful to him and hated him with the same breath. It was awful."

Glöckner was witnessing the new George here, the poet of *The Star of the Covenant*, the father and son of his own god, the disseminator of a new order, someone who no longer saw his experience in purely personal terms but as the expression of historical necessity. The event of their meeting clearly had for George a higher significance, one that could be termed only religious. After releasing Glöckner, he said, "Do you believe that there are still miracles? You have experienced one. You were permitted to experience that! Do you know what that means?" Glöckner was so nonplused that he was now unsure whether he believed a miracle had actually occurred or not. "So," George continued, "now walk with me a while." George also counseled him to "let what you have experienced act on you," as if Glöckner had imbibed a potion that took some time to take effect. As they strolled through the dusky streets toward Wolfskehl's apartment, where George was staying in the Globe Room, he repeatedly spoke of the miracle that had taken place and how marvelous it was, even though few believed it possible, that miracles did still occur just as in other, past times when myths were formed. At his door, George invited Glöckner to come in and, on the way up the stairs, once more chastised him for not seeking him out earlier. "Even if you would have had to travel for fourteen days," George said, "then you should have done it. There are few people who had as great an opportunity as you. That you got to know me so effortlessly and easily is unparalleled. That has never happened to anyone. They all tried to obtain it. And I mean everyone! Many come, but with most of them I know that they have some personal interest." Glöckner again tried to justify his actions, and again George rejected his arguments. "There is no excuse. You *ought* to have come. You see what you would have missed if fate, if chance had not smiled on you." Glöckner was still enough in possession of his faculties to think to himself, "What presumption!" But he found that, try as he might, he was unable to find George "ridiculous."

The remainder of the evening was less eventful but no less disturbing. George ushered him into the spartanly furnished Globe Room; he told Glöckner that although the room was "bare, all of the conversations that have taken place here still linger in it. They make it warm." He instructed Glöckner to sit down on one of the benches — "you will look good against the wall," he decided — and continued his examination. At one point, George wanted to know how old Glöckner was. "Twenty-eight," came the reply. This was serious. "Terrible, terrible," Glöckner now heard George say for the third time that evening. Glöckner was well past the age George liked in his newer recruits. One of the things he repeatedly said to Glöckner was that Bertram was "already too determined" or set in his ways — or, in other words, too old — to be fully susceptible to George's formative influence. On the bright side, at least the number twenty-eight was divisible by seven, perhaps indicating to George that not all was lost. Too, George must have sensed that, although Glöckner was relatively advanced in age, he was exceedingly malleable. As they parted, George emanated confidence that their union would be fertile. "You will see," George calmly predicted, "and one day recognize that there is only one path for you and you will then go down it, blind to everything else. You will be amazed that everything is so easy." George seemed positively cheerful now, in sharp contrast to the gruff fire he had displayed earlier. "Now I know you," he said. "Let everything act on you. Come again on Saturday at 6:30. There is more I need to say to you."

It was a classic example of a Georgean seduction: the elected one — or the victim — overwhelmed by this onslaught, rendered confused, anxious, and yet strangely flattered by the unasked for attentions of this commanding personality, had no chance to assert his own prerogatives and had to accept the terms as George set them — or take flight. Symptomatically, during that first meeting in the Globe Room, when George briefly disappeared, Glöckner considered the latter course of action. "I had to wait," Glöckner remembered, and "at the same time very much felt like running away out of fear *and* cowardice." In the end, though, Glöckner stayed.

After their first meeting in early April 1913, Glöckner and George saw each other almost every day through the middle of May. Slowly Glöckner got over his initial apprehensions, but for a long time his letters to Bertram sound as if he were trying to convince himself that his decision not to keep clear of George had really been the right one. "I have trust, great trust in him," he told Bertram but hesitatingly added, " — and yet . . ." A week later, Glöckner informed Bertram that he would be unable to join him in Rome, as originally planned, because of his new obligations. "I promised George that I would come to him; and I have to keep this promise." Still, Glöckner sounded somewhat uncertain. "I don't want to flee," he wrote, for that would be "a pathetic flight away from something from which one can't flee anyway: no." After all, Glöckner said, as much for Bertram's benefit as for his own, "George means well. . . . He surely means well." By early May, however, Glöckner had fully abandoned his scruples and was telling Bertram that "I believe in George, believe in his importance." He had experienced a total conversion: "I have never felt so secure facing the world, never felt so strongly that nothing bad can ever happen to me again as when I am near him. He is a genius and also possesses the magical powers of a good physician." Not only that, Glöckner solemnly told his friend, "He knows everything; I am not exaggerating; he is a prophet."

Thus began a relationship that would endure another decade, lasting until 1924. Over the course of the intervening years, Glöckner frequently proved himself a devoted and tireless friend, sending food and tobacco to offset the difficult wartime shortages, providing constant advice about doctors and remedies when George fell ill, and generally making himself available for any requirement, wish, or service George might have needed fulfilled.

This last category of functions Glöckner performed must be thought of broadly. For Glöckner was the only person among the scores of George's companions to have left any surviving record of a physical intimacy with the poet. George was always careful to instruct his correspondents not to commit anything too personal to paper, and his own terse epistolary style was in part an expression of the extreme caution he took regarding the details of his private affairs. Late in life, George told Vallentin, with evident satisfaction, that "in general there are few letters" — meaning written by himself — "in which there was anything of importance to read about him." Thus, only a small number of relatively trivial letters and postcards from George to Glöckner survive.

The same is not true, however, of Glöckner's almost endless letters to George — Glöckner spent hours every day writing letters, and during the ten-year period of their liaison George was, next to Bertram, one of the principal beneficiaries of his epistolary exertions — and in their very number would overtax even the most vigilant guardian of George's legacy. As time went on, George himself paid increasingly close attention to what remained in his personal archive. By 1929, he had already put all the letters he had received in chronological order, and he intended to vet the more sensitive ones among them. As he told a friend, "My correspondence, the things that were sent to me, is pretty much organized, not according to the sender but according to the year. But there is also a lot of private things in there, I'd have to sift through it." Edgar Salin also reported that "Wolfskehl told Ernst Morwitz as well as me that George burned all 'personal' letters," and Salin speculated that this fate had also befallen, among many others, "the extraordinarily large number of letters that concerned the Cosmics and Maximin." Anything else that may have hinted at an aspect of his experience George wanted to keep hidden from inspection likely met the same fate.

One letter from Glöckner appears to have escaped the furnace. Writing in August 1917, at the height of their relationship, Glöckner seems not to have been able to keep his feelings for George in check any longer, and he poured out a remarkable confession. "Only he who has moaned under the weight of your body," Glöckner wrote with a candor that is startling only because it is so rare in this context, "and experienced the transformation because he saw you in your ultimate dignity will secretly give you the name, which is above all names, without being permitted to say it in your presence." The phrase "ultimate dignity" is a quotation from a poem in *The Star of the Covenant* and can mean, as it does here, several things, but one of them is nudity, and the "name" Glöckner referred to belongs to the same sphere. For he undoubtedly meant "Maximin," and the fact that he inwardly calls George by that same name indicates Glöckner understood that, at least in George's mind and presumably in his own as well, there was no longer any distinction between the Master and his god. Nevertheless, by referring to what can only have been a physical experience between them, Glöckner knew he had overstepped a boundary few were allowed to cross, and he hurried to reassure George that it would not happen again. "Master, now you know how I stand toward you. The most recent experience forced this word from my silent lips. From now on I will never speak about it again." Either Glöckner kept his promise or any record of his having broken it has disappeared.

Not all of George's time was taken up by such affairs, as pleasant as they were. There was still much serious work to be done: a new volume of the *Blätter* was in the works, plans were afoot to publish a fourth *Yearbook,* the Shakespeare translation had not yet been finished and, perhaps closest to George's heart at the moment, Friedrich Wolters was preparing a large-scale book devoted to the history of the movement George had founded. The idea of writing a history of the *Blätter* — George still liked to use this word to refer to the entire phenomenon — had been with him for several years already. In January 1909, he had mentioned in conversation with Berthold Vallentin, perhaps with the intention of sounding out Vallentin about his willingness to assume the task, that he wanted someone "to write a history of the *Blätter für die Kunst* based on his documents." For whatever reason, Vallentin failed to take the bait. Friedrich Wolters, whose *Sovereignty and Service* came out later that year and whose star had risen even higher as one of the editors of the *Yearbook,* seemed a more suitable choice anyway, and it was thus on his shoulders that the assignment fell. With George's blessing — and at his not so subtle prodding — Wolters thus became George's official historian and biographer.

During the fall of 1913, when George was in Berlin attending to the publication of *The Star of the Covenant,* he lived with Ernst Morwitz in an almost empty apartment, sleeping on an ordinary cot and working by day at the desk set up for that purpose. Apart from a few simple chairs, the room was the way the poet liked it: bare, with no reminders of the world outside. In the evenings, his Berlin friends would gather in the apartment to read aloud from various works, including the Goethe anthology, George's translations of Dante, Shakespeare's sonnets, poems by Swinburne and Rossetti, and particularly Hölderlin's translations of Pindar that had recently been discovered and published by Norbert von Hellingrath. Naturally, George's own poems were a staple of the repertoire as well. Present during these sessions, which usually lasted two hours or so, were Morwitz himself, Thormaehlen, Friedrich Gundolf's brother Ernst, in addition to Vallentin and Robert Boehringer. Wolters often attended these communal readings, too, but his main focus was on the conversations he conducted almost daily with George from late September to the end of October. In measured doses, George was giving him the version of his life he wanted Wolters to preserve for posterity. Knowing he could trust Wolters to put things in their proper light, he opened himself to the kind of questions he would never have tolerated from anyone else. George even said that the "legends" that had already formed about him — involving "purple cloaks, festivals, castles, love of boys, etc." — did not bother him at all. In fact, he thought they often "convey more truthfully the facts of the matter than a plain narrative would be able to." "For," he slyly reasoned, "even the plainest legends contain a kernel of figurative truth." (George did in fact enjoy some of the stories, or "legends," that circulated about himself and he sometimes played up to them. When he heard that someone had described a celebration at Wolfskehl's apartment as a satanic mass held under violet lights and ambergris lamps, he mischievously added, "Don't forget that a bowl of steaming blood stood before me.")

Over the next several months, Wolters traveled wherever the Master went, faithfully transcribing George's words in preparation for the commissioned book. In the early spring, Wolters journeyed to Munich for long meetings with George in the Globe Room, and that summer Wolters accompanied him to the village of Saanenmöser in Switzerland, where he hoped to complete the material gathering stage of the project. With such uninhibited access to so much first-hand information, Wolters made rapid headway. In February 1914 he was already able to tell Gundolf that "the plan for the history of the *Blätter* is now clear: I want to devote all available energy to it in the summer." He was so confident of his progress that in June the firm of Georg Bondi published a four-page pamphlet announcing several forthcoming books, including Wolters's "history" of the *Blätter für die Kunst,* which it promised would be available the following year. A month later, however, another sort of history intervened that would delay the publication of Wolters's book for another decade and a half.

CHAPTER 33
The War and Secret Germany

Just over six centuries ago, on June 28, 1389, the Turks delivered a devastating defeat to the Serbs at the battle of Kosovo. That date, with all its associations of humiliation and disgrace, has remained burned in the Serbian collective memory ever since. In 1914, five hundred and twenty-five years later to the day, a Bosnian Serb nationalist named Gavrilo Princip observed the anniversary of that trauma by assassinating both the heir to the Austrian throne, Archduke Franz Ferdinand, and his wife during a state visit to Sarajevo.

The reaction in Vienna was swift: only two hours after hearing the news, most people had returned to their usual pastimes, music was again playing in the outdoor cafes and bars, and lighthearted laughter interrupted the casual conversations that went on until late into the balmy summer evening. Many even felt a private sense of relief that the ambitious and remote Franz Ferdinand had been rather conveniently removed from the scene, making way for the much more popular Archduke Karl. Stefan Zweig remembered having seen Franz Ferdinand in the theater several times. The heir apparent would sit stiffly watching the performance, refusing to acknowledge the audience with a friendly glance or to encourage the performers with animated applause. He was never seen smiling, showed no interest in music, and — an especially grave fault in the eyes of the genial Viennese — he completely lacked a sense of humor. When the beloved Crown Prince Rudolf, the only son of Emperor Franz Josef, had committed suicide in 1889, and when his mother, Empress Elizabeth, was stabbed to death by an anarchist in 1898, the public display of grief on their behalf was genuine and prolonged. But Franz Ferdinand's death drew few tears and everyone assumed that the whole matter, like the Archduke himself, would soon be laid to rest.

What no one expected was that his murder would lead to a European war. True, there had been irresponsible talk for years as the major nations jostled each other in their bids for military and economic supremacy, grabbing up any remaining areas of the globe they could add to their collection of colonies, and generally engaging in increasingly risky shows of muscle. Germany, which had begun the race late and thus doubled its exertions to catch up, found itself being eyed with growing mistrust by its neighbors to the east and west. France, still smoldering over the loss of Alsace and Lorraine as a result of the last war to have been fought in Europe, had no reason to believe that an even more powerful German empire would have its best interests foremost in mind. Russia, an even later arrival on the international stage, was no less aware of the German desire to perform a similar operation on its western provinces, with the intention of surgically removing the remaining Polish and Baltic lands from Russian control and reuniting them with the Fatherland. And Britain, watching its industrial might and, more alarmingly, its naval superiority being seriously challenged for the first time in a century, also took a dim view of the efforts by its upstart cousin to gain, as the kaiser once famously said, its own "place in the sun." Yet over the last decade, Europe had weathered several other more severe crises, such as the two confrontations between France and Germany over Morocco in 1905 and 1911, and the clash between Austria and Russia in 1908 when the Austrians had annexed Bosnia-Herzegovina. Most people thought not unreasonably that the latest incident involving the house of Habsburg — a personal tragedy to be sure, but no cause for an international emergency — would, like the others, finally pass uneventfully.

Having enjoyed unbroken peace and prosperity on the continent since 1871 and benefited from unprecedented advances in science, technology, transportation, and communication, Europe had, if anything, grown more cosmopolitan during the last four decades. The International Court of Arbitration at The Hague, established in 1899, had been designed to settle disputes between nations by peaceful, civilized means, thus rendering the call to arms redundant. Trade agreements had made most borders equally superfluous, and it was possible for people to travel through most countries without a passport or official papers. Many artistic and political movements — symbolism and socialism, to name only two — had an explicitly international reach, appealing less to narrowly chauvinistic sentiments than to more broadly human concerns. The filiations among the European states had become so numerous and so intertwined, that a general war would have amounted to fratricide. It seemed quite simply unimaginable.

Yet there were forces in the German government and military who perceived an opportunity in the assassination at Sarajevo. Spurred on by a variety of motives — racist theories, ideological opportunism, masculine braggadocio, and plain, irrational fear — a group of advisors around Wilhelm II decided that the moment had come to put the levers in motion of a scheme already long in the making. General Chief of Staff Helmuth von Moltke, one of the most influential members of the kaiser's Cabinet, had written in a private letter, in February 1913, that "I am now as before of the opinion that in the long or the short run a European war must come, in which it will basically be a war between Germandom and Slavdom." It was the paranoid conviction of many among the German governing elite: encircled on both sides, Germany they thought was threatened, in the case of the Russians, by wild hordes of half-savage barbarians and, in the west, by envious, unscrupulous competitors who wanted to clip the unfolding wings of the ascendant Imperial eagle. To avoid falling prey to an attack on either front, an attack the German policy makers increasingly regarded as inevitable and imminent, a preventive strike was deemed necessary. In July of 1914 they felt the moment to act had come.

The nightmarish chain of events is well known: with cynical calculation, several key members of the German government prodded Austria into invading Serbia, with the intention of provoking Russia into a larger confrontation with the Hapsburg empire. To his credit, the German kaiser sought to avert a wider conflict up to the last minute, but his diplomatic skills, never very great even in times of relative calm, proved disastrously inadequate as the crisis quickened. On July 23, the Austrian ultimatum was sent to Belgrade; five days later, one month after the assassination of Archduke Franz Ferdinand, Austrian guns began firing on the Serbian capital. As anticipated, Russia ordered a full mobilization against Austria on July 30. Thinking the Russian troops would be tied up in the east by the Austrian army, the Germans immediately sprang into action to unleash the centerpiece of their strategy. Knowing that France would come to the aid of its eastern alliance partner, Germany had adopted the so-called Schlieffen Plan, named after the Prussian general who had devised it ten years before. Alfred von Schlieffen realized that the only way to win a quick, decisive victory over France was to bypass the heavily fortified frontiers to the west and invade through the north, rapididly descending through Holland and Belgium. Once France was defeated — thus went Schlieffen's scenario — Germany could then turn her attentions to Russia. The plan was seductively simple, even elegant in its design: Schlieffen was confident that the entire French campaign would be over in a matter of six weeks. On August 3, with Austria and Russia already marching against each other, Germany declared war against France.

The one variable in the plan was Britain. Germany reckoned that Britain would prefer to let its continental adversaries settle their quarrels by themselves and avoid the risks of large-scale military involvement. It proved a terrible miscalculation. The fatal flaw of the Schlieffen plan was that it forced the violation of Belgian neutrality. When German troops threatened to advance through Belgium on their way to Paris, it was in conscious and flagrant defiance of international law. Britain, which had made several demands that the neutrality of Belgium be respected at all costs, had no choice but to deliver its own ultimatum on August 4: an invasion of Belgium, the British Foreign Office bluntly stated, would not be tolerated. Ignoring the warning, German troops crossed into Belgian territory at 4 P.M. Before midnight, all the major powers of Europe were at war.

In mid-July, while the German high command prepared for a conflict it complacently thought it could control, George went to his summer retreat in Switzerland. He was joining Julius and Edith Landmann, who had rented a chalet in Saanenmöser, a hamlet not far from the famous resort of Gstaad. Julius Landmann, a professor of economics in Basel, and his wife, an independent scholar who wrote several commendable works on epistemology and aesthetics, were family friends of Robert Boehringer, then also living in Basel. Through Boehringer, the Landmanns had first met George in Berlin in 1908, but nothing came of the encounter for a number of years thereafter. (Edith Landmann speculated that their relationship to Rudolf Borchardt, which lasted until 1911, was the main obstacle preventing any closer association with George.) In the summer of 1912, which George also spent in Switzerland, he looked up the Landmanns, who were vacationing nearby, and they all found each other sympathetic. On that basis, they made a plan to meet in the Alps the following year, but Edith fell ill and could not travel, forcing George to make last-minute alternative arrangements. In 1914, it seemed that fate had finally smiled on them and they looked forward to a restful summer spent together in the Bernese Highlands.

The group eventually included the Landmanns, their two children, as well as Wolters and a new acquaintance named Balduin Waldhausen. Edith Landmann, with whom George remained befriended until his death, wrote down everything she could remember from her conversations with the poet, devoting the last few moments of every evening before she retired to recording the Master's words. She recalled, however, that, during those weeks in July, "political matters were hardly mentioned. No newspapers came to the house." The only indication of the momentous events taking place in the world around them came in such a way that considerably lessened its impact. "One day, on a page of newspaper wrapped around a piece of butter, we noticed the word printed in thick letters: Ultimatum." The following day, as they all sat at the table, a neighbor suddenly burst in. Since it was not customary that one simply walked into a room, uninvited and unannounced, in which the Master presided, they all looked dumbfounded. "It's war after all!" the intruder yelled.

Perhaps foreseeing the pandemonium to come, George decided to remain in Switzerland for the time being, although everyone else was impatient to leave. As the vacationers hastily made plans to return to their respective homes to await further developments, virtually the same scene was being repeated in every European capital. Huge throngs formed in the central squares of London, Paris, Berlin, and Vienna when the news was announced. But instead of expressing anxiety or dread, the crowds everywhere burst into jubilation, cheering at the announcement. The citizens of each nation were confident not only that the war would be of short duration but that they would emerge as the victors. In a kind of collective delirium of joy, people filled the streets as word of the war spread, "strangers shook each other's hands, laughing and crying, each man feeling, as one recalled, 'united to his fellow by a common bond of love and hate.'" Not only was everyone sure of victory, everyone predicted the armies would be back, as the German kaiser rashly told the first departing troops in Berlin, "before the leaves have fallen from the trees." Even in the smaller regional centers throughout Germany the public demonstrations of exuberance were overwhelming.

Caught up in the general excitement, many of George's associates felt similarly thankful for living at a time that allowed them to take part in such a great drama. On August 2, Gundolf admitted to feeling intoxicated by it all. Writing to Edgar Salin he said that "just to have experienced these hours is enough, come what may! We are living in a state of exhilaration that has its eternal value in itself." Gundolf also immediately drew a connection between the real war beginning to unfold and the one he and other members of the "movement" had so ardently desired for so long. Even before hostilities had broken out, Gundolf had told George that he thought that a war could take on "comprehensive significance for our 'state.'" That the war was being led almost entirely by Prussian military staff was an irony not lost on Gundolf, but such distinctions did not matter now. "I feel," he had written to George a few days before, "that (however one many have stood toward the Prussians until now) it is now a matter of our Germany . . . and I am happy that the enormous decision will now become visible for us all as well, the secret Germany, too." Friedrich Wolters, on his way back to Berlin by train, also found that their old nemesis had been somehow transformed by the galvanizing experience of mobilization. Mentioning that it was taking "forty-eight to sixty hours" to travel from Munich to Berlin, Wolters said he had seen "hundreds of trains of soldiers pass along the route" and that his "accommodation for the night" had been "three hours on top of my suitcase." Even in the rush to put the enormous numbers of canons, horses, and men at the western front, the initial ebullience had not yet worn off. "The train stations resound with songs," Wolters wrote, "there are vats and tubs full of tea, coffee, and cocoa, mountains of bread — and everyone takes and drinks from the same cups. The Prussians are unrecognizable — everyone is helpful, friendly, and everyone has time. Only the military trains don't."

Overcrowded trains were not the only impediment to travel. Literally overnight, the freedom to move about the continent that Europeans had enjoyed for a generation had been severely restricted, making the formalities of passports and visas suddenly necessary. Rumors circulated wildly about spies, infiltrators, and saboteurs on the loose, which made travel in unfamiliar territory risky and potentially hazardous. Concerned that George may have gone to Switzerland without taking adequate documents, Gundolf wrote on August 4 from his home in Darmstadt to tell him that "no one is let through without a passport or is immediately arrested. Here in particular they consider (with some justification) anyone who stands out and has no means of identification to be a spy. (That's what happened when I arrived and fortunately I had my papers with me.)"

The reason Gundolf had passed on the information was not only to save George from an embarrassing or more serious situation, but also to urge him to come to where Gundolf thought he belonged. In all of Germany, the euphoria that had swept through the country showed no signs of dissipating. Indeed, if anything the first few successes in Belgium seemed to stoke both enthusiasm and confidence. No one doubted that the troops would return home victorious by Christmas. The only regret Gundolf had was that George was missing out on it all. "I am distressed that in these days you have to be out of the country and not with us," Gundolf wrote in mid-August. "You ought to have experienced these days HERE!" Gundolf could not understand how George was able to stay away from his native country at one of its greatest historical moments. "I would not for the world want to be anything other than a German now," he raved to George. For Gundolf, the war represented an opportunity to achieve the goals he and the others had been working toward for more than a decade. Writing to a colleague in Heidelberg in late August, he explained that "the transformation of millions of people into a *single* German *Volk* that deserves this sacred name, the turn toward action of a dull bundle of forces, whose degeneration had already frightened us, will also if not already realize a new heroism, at least make it possible." What was more, the fate of the entire world, Gundolf thought, now rested on German shoulders. "There is probably no other *Volk* any longer from whom one could expect a new world to come into being if the Germans do not achieve it." Well into September, Gundolf was still saying, this time to Wolfskehl, that "to have experienced these days as a German makes up for all the yearning for the glory of the Persian Wars and Imperial victories — it is the reality of a great *Volk,* and of *our Volk.*"

While Gundolf had always been one of the most hawkish members of

George's entourage, he had never been much of an overt patriot. It is thus a little surprising to see him waxing positive over the virtues of the German *Volk* and identifying so closely with it. That seemed much more Friedrich Wolters's cup of tea, who did in fact see the conflict in terms of a battle of and for the German spirit. Once he had arrived in Berlin after his arduous journey from Switzerland, for example, Wolters told George that travelling through the length of the country had allowed him to take the measure of the popular mood. His findings were more than encouraging: "The German people seemed transformed. It is not the Prussian state that is waging this war but rather the German *Volk* has stood up like one man for perhaps the first time in its history and is conscious of its power and its worth." During his entire trip, Wolters said, he did not hear a single word of "doubt even less of despair"; rather, he saw only "an earnest optimism and certainty of victory." In words that strongly remind one of his essay, "Person and Genus" in the third *Yearbook,* Wolters pronounced that victory assured because of the intrinsic superiority of Germany over its foes, who were to a one enfeebled and corrupt. "Everyone feels the moral values [are] on Germany's side," he wrote to George on August 17, "and the means by which the enemy conducts the war in fact show from the very beginning the instincts of the weaker, indeed base: it is a battle against the existence of the German character, against that which peoples in decline feel to be stronger and more powerful, a battle of faded and hypocritical humanity — not to speak of [the] wretched Russians — against a dawning heroic element in our *Volk,* a battle of a new species against a degenerate, once brilliant world."

As these and other letters made their way to George, each one more or less expressing the same ecstatic point of view — that the war was a precious gift and that it heralded Germany's finest hour — the Master remained aloof, seemingly unmoved by the exultant tumult going on all around him. In answer to Gundolf's entreaties to return to Germany, he merely said on August 14, "I presently see no reason to leave Switzerland in haste" and he calmly assured Gundolf that the German Consulate in Bern had verified that "my identity cards also suffice to cross the border." It was as if George were content to perch high over Europe in his Alpine aerie, surveying the landscape below with dispassionate curiosity. At the end of the month, the day before he finally left for Munich and in the face of further pleas from Gundolf to come back soon, he sent an even sterner reply. "The sojourn in Switzerland also had its good aspect," he wrote, specifying that it enabled him to maintain "a nice objectivity!" It was if Switzerland's political neutrality had allowed him to keep his head clear, not to confuse what was ephemeral with what was important, something he missed in the effusions of his correspondents. "I say to all of you," he wrote Gundolf with pronounced emphasis, "whether it turns out well or badly: — the most difficult thing will come ONLY AFTERWARD!!" A few weeks later, he again sought to tamp down Gundolf's unquenched fire. "After the war everything that has made you so enthusiastic may have vanished," George darkly predicted. "You speak the language of enthusiasm; that is youthful and always beautiful and whoever speaks the language of reason seems cold and sober to the enthusiastic person. But enthusiasm alone does not do the job."

It may seem at first surprising, in light of everything we know about George's explicit and repeated invocations of a "holy war" whose coming he had so unmistakably welcomed, that he did not openly embrace this war as his own. His followers certainly understood it as his and thus as theirs. Edgar Salin tells us that even two years into the war, "George knew then very well — in March 1916 — that almost without exception the youngest among us, but also Gundolf and Wolters and even Wolfskehl, considered this first World War to be the prophesied holy war in its first months (and several still [did] then and even later as well)." But George himself was adamant on this score. A year later, in May 1917, he spoke to Vallentin about the "wrong perception of the war at the beginning: how Wolters and Erika Wolters had referred to it then as 'the greatest German event.'" George said that he had "remained silent then — as he often had to do," but that "he foresaw everything the way it happened. Today everyone saw it. Gundolf as well."

Although George never fully spelled out why this war was not, at least in his own view, the one he had predicted and wanted, it is fairly easy to guess the reasons why he did not embrace it. What his friends had momentarily forgotten was that the two Germanys they lived in were not identical, that their "secret" Germany had its own government, leader, statutes, and mandates that were distinct from, in fact opposed to, those of the other state carrying that name. The Germany ruled by Protestants and Prussians, no matter how much of a metamorphosis it may seem to have undergone, could never be confused with the new order George sought to form. "What is your entire attitude worth, then," George once impatiently asked a group of his friends, "if you can all believe that a couple of heightened moments of fate are capable of transforming a depraved people." Nothing so profound could happen so quickly. "Is the bourgeois different today than before 1914?" he rhetorically asked. This war, the one run by and for the common run of humanity he despised, was not his war, which would come only when he had radically reformed the people according to *his* plan and made them ready for the cataclysms *he* would unleash.

It may have also been that George feared — justifiably, as it would soon turn out — that this war might exact a terrible toll not only on the bourgeoisie he hated, but also on the group of young men and boys he had so lovingly cultivated in the decade since Maximilian Kronberger's death. Even if they had had a choice, none of his friends would have passed up the opportunity to participate in the grand adventure. Virtually everyone who was not conscripted signed up as a volunteer. Indeed, there was such a surplus of troops from all over Germany that many were initially sent back home. Salin, Thormaehlen, Wolters, Morwitz, Hildebrandt, Heyer, Hellingrath, both Boehringer brothers, Robert and Erich — they all eagerly enlisted, looking forward to fighting in the war they thought was theirs. Despite his worries, George did not attempt to persuade any of them not to join. "As concerns the younger ones," he told Gundolf, "I would not keep any one of them, no matter how much I loved him, from the war even if I could." (Only Wolfskehl, with his abysmal eyesight, was forced to stay behind, as he lamented to Gundolf, "as a non-combatant! If you knew how that offends me, and what desperate steps I undertook to join the rank and file!" All to no avail: "Not a single medical officer took me, my eyes are absolutely unfit.")

In September George finally decided to leave Switzerland, and he continued on to Berlin after pausing for a few days in Munich. It was as if, by following his habitual routine of spending the autumn in the German capital, he imagined he could impose some degree of normalcy on things. But nothing was normal. Some of his friends still lingered in Berlin, but many more were already at the front or about to ship out. By the middle of the month, there were already casualties and anyone could have foreseen there would be more. In Berlin, that inevitability was very much on George's mind. "Everyone is well here," he wrote to Gundolf. "Everyone's doing fine even if everyone has to be prepared for losses. R's only brother" — George was referring to Erich Boehringer — "lies wounded in Kreuznach." Of particular concern to George was Percy Gothein, who had joined the *Landsturm,* or territorial reserve. "What has become of Percy?" he insistently asked Gundolf. "Where is he now?" Gundolf reassured George that Percy was well — and that he made "an impressive soldier" besides — but George never stopped worrying about him and always wanted to keep abreast of his whereabouts. George needed everyone and could spare no one. As he told Gundolf, "who will do and say what is necessary when you all are not there?"

While George soberly brooded over the war during its first few weeks, distrustful of its legitimacy and apprehensive of its costs, his closest associates held fast to their conviction that it was the rejuvenating purgation that they, and especially he, their Master, had envisioned. The chance to express that view publicly came in early September in response to an open letter issued by the French writer Romain Rolland. On August 25, German troops heading for Paris had entered the Belgian university town of Leuven (Louvain), known as the "Oxford of Belgium" in part because of the antiquity and beauty of its buildings. That evening, as the invading German soldiers strolled through the streets lined with lovely Gothic and Renaissance facades, shots suddenly rang out, probably originating from some drunk members of the conquering army. What happened next was a revolting crime. Apparently believing they were being fired upon by snipers, or merely using that as a pretext, the Germans set out on a destructive rampage, setting houses on fire that ostensibly contained the attackers and executing anyone suspected of being a *franc-tireur*. After three days of unchecked vandalism and terror, 209 civilians had been killed, 1,100 buildings of the ancient town had been reduced to rubble, and the magnificent university library of 230,000 books and irreplaceable manuscripts had gone up in flames.

The day after the violence ended, on August 29, Rolland published a letter in the *Journal de Genève* indicting the action. It was specifically addressed to the dramatist Gerhart Hauptmann, but it appealed to the educated caste of Germany as a whole. Privately, Rolland was nauseated by what had occurred. "The news of the destruction of Leuven makes me sick," he wrote in his diary. "What madness is driving these Germans to their moral ruin? Every step they take digs an abyss of hatred." In his public response, however, he tried to maintain a pose of rational circumspection. Rolland proclaimed his continued admiration and respect for the cultural achievements of Germany, singling out for particular mention "*our* Goethe," who, Rolland asserted, far from being a strictly German possession, "belongs to the entirety of humanity." But for that very reason he called on Hauptmann and all German intellectuals to disclaim the acts being committed in Belgium. As far as Rolland was concerned, Hauptmann and his German colleagues stood at a crossroads, and their response to the savagery at Leuven would indicate the direction they and their country would take. "Are you a descendant of Goethe," he asked in pointed provocation, "or of Attila?"

A German translation of Rolland's letter appeared in the *Frankfurter Zeitung* on September 12, accompanied by Hauptmann's reply — a patronizing, unbending reiteration of the official position that the German soldiers had merely acted out of self-defense in response to a well-organized "guerilla war" — in addition to two other letters in response, one of which was by Karl Wolfskehl. Arguing that the war was neither "desired" nor caused by Germany but nevertheless inevitable and necessary, Wolfskehl placed the entire phenomenon in a context that probably perplexed Rolland and many other readers as well. "I want to tell you," Wolfskehl wrote, "that *there is another Germany,* behind the exterior where the literary champions of Europe meet with the great worlds of politics and finance. This Germany says to you in Europe's difficult hour: this unwanted war, which was forced upon us, is essential nonetheless, it had to strike for the sake of Germany and of the world of European humanity, for the sake of this world. We did not want it, but it comes from *God*. Our poet knew of it. He saw and presaged this war and its necessity and its virtues long before premonitions mounted this year — before any papers began to rustle. The *Star of the Covenant* is that book of prophecy, that book of necessity and conquest."

It is a remarkable document. Wolfskehl appears both to reject and sanction the war simultaneously, just as he also aligns it with George's most recent book while seeming at the same time to differentiate between the nation led by Wilhelm II and "another Germany" following another leader. And it was in the willingness to fight for that other, secret Germany that Wolfskehl saw the righteousness of the war. "Yes, Romain Rolland," Wolfskehl tauntingly wrote, "try, as a Frenchman, to gaze into the mystery of this time. Ask yourself, marvel at why we, the *spiritual Germans*" — *geistigen Deutschen* — "unanimously take part with body and soul in this war, this terrible war." Yet, for all of his bluster, nowhere did Wolfskehl even address the central question Rolland had raised: the barbarity of the deeds in Leuven. His silence on that issue seems in bald defiance of Rolland's challenge. In fact, Wolfskehl concluded with words that not only equate, however vaguely, the meaning of the war with George's vision, but they also imply that the kinds of events Rolland had deplored were an inescapable, even desirable consequence of realizing that vision. "Thus we stand in the midst of death and ruins under the star," Wolfskehl wrote, "one *covenant* and one *unity*. I had to say this to you whether you hear it, whether Europe has ears to hear it, or not. From now on our *deeds* will be our words."

A month later, Gundolf lent his voice to the debate. In an article published in the same newspaper in which Wolfskehl's letter had appeared, and obviously inspired both by Wolfskehl's example and in response to the same challenge, Gundolf argued in his "Word and Deed in War" that the war was a "blessing" for those strong enough to endure it. After outlining his position that the true significance of the war would emerge only after it was all over, Gundolf then turned to the matter Wolfskehl had ignored and, without mentioning either Rolland or Leuven by name, offered this breathtakingly disdainful rejoinder to the Frenchman's objections and pleas:

> Thus the whining and tantrums about destroyed artistic treasures is (insofar as it is honest) tired Romanticism and comes out of a shallow, false conception of culture, as if it consisted in collecting and the piety of observers. Culture is not a possession, not an enjoyment, it is being, acting, becoming, it is creating, destroying, changing — and Attila has more to do with culture that all the Shaws, Maeterlincks, d'Annunzios, and so on combined. Works of art do not come into being to be gazed at, esteemed, collected and paid for, but as the expression of creative forces. They are the obsolescent (and, if need be, transitory) precipitate of immortal activity and it is this activity that matters, not the precipitate. Whoever is strong

enough to create, is also permitted to destroy, and if our future were not able to create any more, then it would have no right to enjoy the past.

What is most shocking is not so much the contemptuous dismissal of Rolland's protests as nothing more than the feeble complaints of an impotent aesthete but rather Gundolf's ready acceptance, even sardonic endorsement of the total annihilation of irreplaceable works of art and, by extension, of whole cities, even of entire cultures. Or perhaps we should not really be surprised at all and see it instead as the logical conclusion of the ideas that had been formulated and repeated within the circle over the years. For it is not as if Gundolf's attitude was unprecedented. On the contrary: it had been declared many times, in many ways, and most frequently by George himself. Gundolf, too, had in fact already made essentially the same point in his essay for the third *Yearbook*, entitled "Models" (*Vorbilder*), which he had written three years before in the summer of 1911. There Gundolf had stated that it was "better that all artistic treasures be destroyed than ever to lower art to [the status of] mere decoration and enjoyment!" In countless conversations and in his own poetry, George had reiterated various versions of the same sentiment. As recently as in *The Star of the Covenant*, George had specifically damned the preservation of artworks merely for the sake of possessing them and advised they be destroyed if they had lost their vitality. And no one should have expected sympathy for the burning of the Leuven library from someone who had asserted that books had only "calorific value."

But there was a difference between making such offhand comments, and even between the more formal utterances contained in an expository essay or a poem, and taking the same stance toward actual immediate events. Before, anyone who doubted — or did not want to believe — how seriously George, Gundolf, or any other member of the circle meant everything they said could have downplayed such remarks as amounting to no more than rhetorical flourishes exaggerated for effect. Now there could be no more uncertainty in anyone's mind about where they stood. Whereas there had been only "words" before, now those words were backed and validated by real "deeds."

Nor could there be any question whether Gundolf's letter reflected George's own stance. Although Gundolf wrote and published the article without George's prior knowledge or consent, he did so thinking he was only saying what George felt. Gundolf confessed to Wolfskehl that he was slightly nervous about the essay, since "it is the first time that I am speaking publicly in the Master's name without asking him." But Gundolf considered the risk was minimal, since he was acting "for the benefit of the secret Germany." The day after the essay appeared, George sent a letter to Gundolf that allayed any remaining misgivings he may have had. George told Gundolf he was delighted by "how much everything is also my opinion: how the hammer falls on the anvil and how Spirit reveals itself: that is what is valuable and lasting in such an article." Still, George did express some irritation that Gundolf had not approached him before sending the essay to the paper, and he curtly commanded Gundolf "not to repeat something like that with the Frf. *Journal* again!" Despite the reprimand, Gundolf was clearly relieved by George's basic reaction. "I was very pleased by your sanction of my essay," he wrote, and added that "I have won enthusiastic approval from the MOST DIVERSE quarters, all the way into the more well-disposed bourgeoisie." After putting aside his annoyance at Gundolf's insubordination, George himself found that the more he thought about the essay, the more he warmed up to it. "I am liking the essay better and better," he wrote two days later. "It is like 'Fichte' only more military (militarism of the *Blätter f d K*!)." George liked it so much that he thought it presented an opportunity to formalize this "militarism" and give it concentrated form. George said he "thought it would be good to assemble the remarks on the war by the *Blätter* that already exist . . Wolfskehl Gundolf Vallentin Hildebrandt Wolters to publish a little War Yearbook that Bondi wants to issue: what do you think?"

In the end, such a "war yearbook" did not appear — Gundolf advised against it, or at least counseled prudence until the course of the war became more discernible — and in some ways a new *Yearbook* was unnecessary. The resonance of the two newspaper articles had been enormous. Several days after his had come out, Gundolf told George, "I am getting the most peculiar letters from strangers because of my essay, especially from loonies, Protestants, theosophists and suchlike." From more respectable addresses, the response was also largely gratifying. Ernst Glöckner, writing to Bertram about Gundolf's essay, rightly suspected his friend would not like "the passage about the destruction of artworks." "But," Glöckner placatively explained, "when everything's at stake, then it's a thousand times better that the greatest work of art be damaged than an entire *Volk* become ineffectual and infertile." Glöckner's and Bertram's mutual friend, Thomas Mann, also commented approvingly on the matter, saying that it was obvious to everyone "that there are important things to be said about this war from your sphere, your circle, and since the prophet is now permitted to remain silent, people are looking all the more expectantly toward the intelligent, qualified disciples. Gundolf, in the Frankfurt paper, was very good; a few sentences by Wolfskehl, too." For his part, Wolfskehl published a letter in Albert Verwey's journal, *De Beweging,* in which he emphatically declared that the two contributions in the Frankfurt newspaper embodied their official collective policy. Pointing out to those who did not know it that he belonged to "Stefan George's circle," Wolfskehl reminded his Dutch readers that the circle had led a separate existence "for more than twenty years behind the German outside world" and that it had chastely remained "as far away from politics as from all other public activities." However, "all that is past now. It is so much in the past that we have even begun speaking confessionally in public papers."

Yet for those who wanted to hear the Master's voice directly, instead of having it filtered through that of his followers, there were always the poems and now most relevantly *The Star of the Covenant* to turn to. Not only for the insiders within George's circle, but for many other readers as well, the war validated the inner truth of that book and lent it an even greater power. The mother of Percy Gothein, who would lose two of her sons to the war, wrote that "throughout the entire period of the war, the *Star of the Covenant*," as well as other poems by George, were "*the* works that could give us the greatest consolation and interpret the meaning of the terrible events." Edgar Salin took only two books with him into the trenches, for which he had pockets specially sewn into his uniform: Hölderlin's *Hyperion* and George's *The Star of the Covenant*. Indeed, George's book became for many a "war breviary," carried into battle by young soldiers, giving meaning to the maelstrom they were entering and lending a purpose to the sacrifices they would make.

George was aware that it had become a kind of cult book for the fighting youth, and he reacted with typical ambivalence. In a preface added to later editions of *The Star of the Covenant,* he felt obliged to correct what he called a "misunderstanding" that "enshrouded this work." It was not the case, he wrote, that the poet had "wanted to create a breviary of an almost popular sort .. especially for the youth on the Battlefields." Rather, he explained, the reason he had abandoned his usual practice of publishing his works in limited numbers for a select audience was purely pragmatic. It flowed, he said, from "the consideration that keeping hidden what had already been expressed was hardly possible any more today." It was only then, after the book had appeared and the war broke out, that events had "made the minds of even those in broader sections of society receptive for a book that for years could have remained a secret book." Thus the "misunderstanding" George professed wanting to set straight was not really the widespread perception that there was a deep connection between his book and the war; in fact, he comes close to affirming it. Instead, he appears only to have wanted to make sure that no one thought he had written the book in direct response to actual events. That would have been an intolerable notion to George, for it would have implied that he had passively reacted to the world rather than the other way around. And, in George's rendering of the matter, the war — whether it was "his" war or not — was merely the belated echo or confirmation of convictions he had held all along.

Then, later that year, something interesting happened. On New Year's Eve 1914, the *Neue Zürcher Zeitung* published a long review essay devoted to George's latest book, titled "Germany and the *Star of the Covenant.*" The author of the review, a literary scholar named Johannes Nohl, called the book's publication, rather startlingly, "a national German event." Like others, Nohl explicitly drew a parallel between the book and the war that was supposed to have been over by then, saying that "not one of the warring countries experienced such a great spiritual prelude as did Germany to the immense drama that is now making the world tremble. Stefan George's *Star of the Covenant* is this great prelude, a mystery play before the dark, solemn night of these times." While it was not all that unusual, as we have seen, to establish this link between the book and the war, what was noteworthy, even unprecedented, was the degree to which Nohl identified George with the fate of his nation. "The unity between poet and people," Nohl wrote, "the absence of which has been rightly recognized as a basic evil of recent times, that highest unity which sets the seal on the unity of all areas of life, has been achieved and depicted in the *Star of the Covenant* to an extent previously undreamed of." Nohl realized that it represented much more than a conventional book of poetry. It stood, he wrote, as "the first great monument of a new cultural unity and thus the guarantee of the victory of the German spirit, irrespective of how the final lots of battle are drawn." *The Star of the Covenant,* in other words, provided nothing less than "the foundation of the new German order proclaimed by the poet."

No one, not even George's boldest followers, had ever made that kind of claim before, at least not so openly. Coming from a complete stranger, it made an even greater impact. Nohl had presented George as the spiritual touchstone of Germany, even more: as offering the basis for a new way of being, not just for a small coterie, but for all of his countrymen to adopt as their own. It was as if at a single stroke George's most grandiose ambitions for power and leadership had been ratified and even, if possible, magnified. And indeed for increasingly larger numbers of readers hereafter, George's idiosyncratic version of a clandestine Germany under the leadership of an all-powerful *Führer,* a surrogate state that had originally taken shape in repudiation of virtually everything everyone else thought of as being German, would become for them the only authentic one. Although that idea had been implicit in many of the essays in the *Blätter* and the *Yearbook,* Nohl's article marks the first time that someone outside of the circle had validated what those within it believed but hardly dared to say: that George's "secret Germany" — along with everything that implied — was the real, the only true Germany. More and more, George would be seen not as pursuing a separate cause, but as embodying the cultural ideals and political model that all of Germany should — and would — embrace.

Although somewhat puzzled by its source, George was greatly pleased with the article itself. In January 1915 he sent a copy of it to Wolters, indicating that he found it "very peculiar" that an "outsider" had managed to write such things. Wolters agreed that "it is certainly very strange for an outsider," but for that very reason he felt it sent an encouraging signal. George gave the article to Glöckner to read as well, saying that he found it to be "quite good." George also told him how he had first come across it. "He had received it in Munich," Glöckner wrote in his diary. "It was in the morning just as he was getting dressed, he was standing in the room naked when the newspaper was shoved under the door. He said he was so captivated by its contents that he read it in that state. 'If the author only knew that!' he said."

It does evoke a piquant image, vaguely off-putting, yet curiously apt: the man Nohl had suggested was the unappointed sovereign of his people, the promulgator of the "Hellenic miracle" who sought to reawaken an appreciation of the virtues of the disciplined and unadorned male body, standing in what Glöckner had euphemistically called his "ultimate dignity," so engrossed in a newspaper article openly endorsing his program, and by implication himself, that he even puts off getting dressed. It is not hard to imagine how gratifying, even thrilling that moment must have been to George. But there was still a long way to go — and the matter of the war to be settled — before that program could be fully implemented.

CHAPTER 34

Surviving

By early 1915 the western front had drawn a jagged line down the length of Europe that would remain virtually stationary for the next two years. Stretching almost five hundred miles from the North Sea to Switzerland, the killing zone was limited to a long but narrow band, measuring no more than ten thousand yards in width, corresponding to the range of the heaviest artillery. On either side, the towns and countryside looked much as they had during peacetime, and only the steady crescendo of the booming guns as one approached the front indicated there was anything out of the ordinary going on.

The front itself, however, presented a hellish moonscape: the exposed earth was turned over and over by millions of exploding shells, miles of trenches had torn deep gashes in the land, with the cratered surface relieved only by blackened stumps of trees stripped of their branches and leaves. Many of the towns unlucky enough to overlap with the front line were simply erased from the earth, often leaving little more than a few fragments of brick or stone as reminders they had ever existed. In February 1915, Friedrich Wolters, who was posted in the Alsatian fortress town of Metz, described to George a scene of devastation that would be repeated up and down the entire length of the front. "The war is much more murderous than people back home think," Wolters wrote, his tone noticeably more moderate now; "I will say nothing of the necessary deaths of the men, but the way the land looks all around is terrible. Villages and small towns along the way lie completely in ruins, not a single house still standing: not one living creature in them: the fields uncultivated." It was a horrible sight, but Wolters added that "the comrades say that everything is supposed to be much worse in Belgium." Writing to Gundolf later that year, Wolters said he thought the vast, complex system of trenches, some of which burrowed more than thirty feet into the ground, would become a permanent fixture of the landscape, a ghoulish testament to the age that had made them necessary.

But it was the horrific destruction of human life on a scale never seen before that left an imprint that not even time could erase. By the end of 1914, the number of dead among the principal combatants alone was already staggering: the French had lost 306,000 in the first five months of fighting, Germany 241,000. The total, including British and Belgian fatalities, approached three quarters of a million dead by December. In the failed German offensive at Ypres conducted in mid-October, 50,000 German soldiers had died in two weeks alone, half of them volunteer university students under the age of twenty-two.

As the appalling truth of the war started to sink in, the enthusiasm everyone felt at its outbreak began to give way to a kind of grim fatalism. Ernst Robert Curtius, who was stationed in Strasbourg, wrote to Gundolf in late November to thank him for sending his newspaper article, "Word and Deed in War." Curtius assured Gundolf that he had "taken the words right out of my mouth. But now that I have seen it in its reality," Curtius continued, "I can no longer view the war as the blessing I did before moving out. What is horrifying about modern war is that human beings do not fight against other human beings, but against gruesome impersonal machines. Land mines, machine guns, artillery fire: that is the anonymous horror on which every idealistic perception of the war must founder."

That was not what Gundolf wanted to hear. Miles away in Heidelberg and untouched by the mechanical fist of modern warfare, he still clung to the notion that war was ennobling, heroic, and at the very least beneficial. "What you say about the impersonality of the war with and against machines," Gundolf replied, "seems to me to rest on a confusion of the 'romantic' with the 'idealistic' (spiritual). The meaning of this cosmic war lies in the fates, indeed precisely in its incredible ferocity, which is mercilessly destroying all Romantic lies of civilization, humanity, and even tradition." It did not occur to Gundolf that his glorification of war was itself one of the Romantic traditions that would not emerge intact from the mindless slaughter taking place. "For precisely the same reason that the war is so awful in your view," he continued, "I welcome it as a *salvation*, not because I pictured beautiful battlefields to myself — I know that it is incredibly monotonous, impersonal, and the fact that I have not seen it has not caused me to beautify it in my mind: it is the destruction of everything that was atmospherically, romantically, and soulfully 'beautiful,' and that is good." Gundolf's blind arrogance, his willful incomprehension of the unspeakable suffering and senseless waste Curtius was witnessing first hand was apparently too much for Curtius. They did not communicate again for another year.

Gundolf was of course far from alone in his ennoblement of the war. But as Curtius and many others already knew, "soulful beauty" would be the least among its mounting casualties. Some of George's other friends who, unlike Gundolf, had actually experienced the war firsthand, were much less optimistic about its effect or its outcome. "The longer the war lasts," Robert Boehringer had written to George in October, "the more Gundolf will be proven wrong." Soon enough, however, even Gundolf began to waver. The first major blow came with the death of twenty-six-year-old Heinrich Friedemann, who had been drawn to George through reading the *Yearbooks* and then introduced to the Master himself by Gundolf. After completing a doctorate in 1911 with Paul Natorp in Marburg, Friedemann turned to a book-length work on Plato inspired by his new mentors and self-consciously written in their style. When George received the manuscript he was enthralled. He told Glöckner that "he had been entirely carried away on first reading it; he read the book in two nights." To Hildebrandt, George said, "He had read it with greater excitement than a Sherlock Holmes novel." When someone imprudently suggested that Friedemann's language bore too great a resemblance to Wolters — a comparison not intended to be flattering to either one — George stiffened. "If I receive a manuscript in the evening and then read until four in the morning without interruption, then it really has to be something." George always spoke of Friedemann's book with extravagant praise, even comparing it to Nietzsche's *Birth of Tragedy,* and to the end he remained stubbornly convinced, despite all evidence to the contrary, that "all of the new studies of Plato have been influenced by this book." On February 20, 1915, just weeks after Friedemann had received a copy of his freshly printed book in the field — it was the only work of prose ever to be published separately by Georg Bondi with the smoking urn signet of the *Blätter für die Kunst* — and three months before his twenty-seventh birthday, Heinrich Friedemann was killed while fighting against Russian forces on the eastern front during the second battle of the Masurian Lakes. His book, *The Figure of Plato,* bore a dedication to "Friedrich Gundolf: *Führer* and Friend."

It was a severe jolt. More bad news quickly followed. The Gotheins lost one son, then a second; in June Percy also received a grave head wound from which he slowly recovered, only gradually regaining his speech and memory. By the autumn of 1915, Gundolf's passion for the war had dramatically cooled before the merciless bloodletting. But he was not yet ready to admit to defeat. "Here, as probably in all of Germany," he wrote to George in October, "there is a certain apprehension following upon the weeks of triumph in August and the beginning of September — not at all a dejection or even fear — because of the French Attack." Gundolf, being uncharacteristically incoherent, was referring to the ferocious Allied offensives raging that autumn in the provinces of Artois and Champagne. In both cases, it was a massacre on an enormous scale. "What one hears by way of details exceeds all the horrors of the earlier battles," he conceded. It was enough to make anyone somber. But then Gundolf made a telling revelation, telling not so much in what he relayed to George, but rather more in his reaction to it. "My very first real friend," Gundolf wrote, "from the age of six to ten, a Baron von Grancy, who was then — I hadn't seen him at all since and heard nothing of him — a handsome, gentle, fine boy, has been killed in action — I just happened to read his death notice, which left me with an incomprehensible feeling of sorrow." Only someone who had reveled in the glory of war could find the natural reaction of grief in the face of death incomprehensible.

As the lists of the dead and wounded grew longer, George himself withdrew into a posture of mute watchfulness. With a few significant exceptions, such as Gundolf and Wolfskehl, almost everyone he knew, everyone he valued was out in the field, constantly exposed to the risks of disfigurement or death. The rituals that had become central components of his life — the communal gatherings and readings, the pursuit of new companions, and the incessant travels across Germany to tend to old ones — had all been rendered practically impossible. Too, all of the circle's ambitious publication plans — a new number of the *Yearbook,* the ongoing *Blätter für die Kunst,* the Shakespeare translation, and other projects — had to be put on hold, with no certainty when or even if they could be taken up again. But the most cherished products of George's labors, his spiritual sons and lovers, were being forever taken away at a frightening rate.

The war that everyone had been sure would be concluded in a matter of months was now a year old and showed no sign of ending anytime soon. Even George had originally thought it would all be over before the summer of 1915. When it became obvious that he was wrong and that the war was only becoming more lethal, George fell into an even more profound silence. Still, anyone could have imagined what he must have been going through. "I have not heard a word from George," Glöckner wrote Bertram in May 1915, but Glöckner thought he knew the reason why. "It must be terrible for him," he speculated, to see "how his most important work" — namely, the education of the younger generation — "is being called into question by the war." That generation was not just being called into question; it was being methodically wiped out.

The toll the war seemed to be taking on George was not limited to its psychological effect alone. At the end of July 1915, he fell so seriously ill that he had to be admitted to a Heidelberg clinic, where he was confined for almost a month. It would be the first of several debilitating illnesses to strike George over the next several years. Although records about the specific nature of the ailment do not exist, it seems to have originated with a urinary tract or bladder infection. Ernst Glöckner did not find out about George's illness until October, but when he did he was genuinely alarmed, as much over George's personal well-being as for what Glöckner thought his loss, should it come to that, would mean. "George was severely ill?" he anxiously asked Bertram. "If only nothing would happen that would take him away from us one day. That would be disastrous. If we need one person now for our future then it is him. I believe that the *only* possibility for a deeper union of the best people lies in him. He *is* the German center." Glöckner felt that the entire country needed George for at least another ten years. "He is the only one who can give us our bearings. If we lack this point — then it's all over; our German fate depends on him."

In the end, George did recover, if slowly. In December he was still feeling unwell and complaining of being unable to do any work, and the lingering illness left him permanently susceptible to similar complaints. Although no precise medical information about George's condition survives, the recurring symptoms, together with what we know or can surmise about his habits, strongly suggest chronic gonorrhea.

Whatever the exact cause of his afflictions, George himself also seemed increasingly convinced that his personal fate, even his physical being was linked in some inscrutable way to the larger fortunes of his country. "I am a barometer for Germany," he said the following year, in September of 1916. "Through my illness and suffering I know what is happening to Germany's body." Reinforcing this belief were the growing numbers of people both within and outside of his coterie who thought the same thing. In February 1916, when George was still feeling the aftereffects of his sickness, Glöckner noted one evening that "he looked very poorly, tired, afflicted. If he will only stay with us! He is the most important person for the period after the war." On the same occasion, George told Glöckner that he had received a letter from a soldier in the field, who had written, "Now we are fighting for Germany, but after the war for you." The letter had deeply impressed George and gave him, Glöckner reported, "great hope for the future." Nevertheless, these expressions of faith in his transcendent significance sometimes seemed to overwhelm even George himself. During one of their conversations at that time, Glöckner registered "a moment in which [George] was amazed by his own existence as if by something great, foreign to himself." It was, Glöckner concluded, "the naïve amazement of genius at itself. 'Yes, that exists, Ernst,' was George's comment. It was as if George were saying that just because even he might have been startled by his own preeminence from time to time, this did not mean that he doubted it.

Nor did many others. In May 1916, at the height of the ghastly battle of Verdun, Josef Liegle, who would become a prisoner of war a few months later, asked George, fully expecting that George would have the answer, "Is there to be no peace soon? We out here are gradually seeing nothing anymore that could end the war." Later that year, during the even more murderous campaign of the Somme, Hans Brasch sent the plaintive appeal, "When will there be peace — oh Master?" George did not of course know when peace would return or under what terms. Just in case things turned out unfavorably for Germany, though, he began to distance himself from the idea that a German victory was inevitable or even desirable, and that a much greater task awaited him and his followers after its conclusion. In a letter to Wolters that Gundolf wrote at George's behest in April, Wolters was informed that "as concerns the war, [George]now frequently has occasion to refer to his initial opinion that as a WHOLE it cannot have anything actually 'brilliant' about it and thus a 'brilliant' victory or peace is out of the question." The war, Gundolf went on — still reproducing George's words — "is rather the prelude to later more important occurrences. The wonderful thing is that events have already slipped from the reins of all the drivers and are now rolling with a fateful rumble down their own path." In July, while summering again with the Landmanns in Switzerland, George similarly stated it was irrelevant whether there was a "victory or defeat of Germany: in both cases the indestructible spirit can win or lose." He also repeated his rejection of the views of "Wolters, who sees the victory of the spiritual Empire as depending on the victory of Germany as well." Even after many years of insisting on the distinction, George still found himself having to remind his followers that the two realms were not identical and that the decline of one did not necessarily portend the failure of the other. In fact, George was convinced that just the opposite held true.

Which is not to say that he was totally indifferent to the fate of the official Germany, or that he saw some other nation as being more deserving of triumph, military or otherwise. On the contrary: he had very definite ideas about the relative merits of the different cultures and races in the world. George held views that most would regard as racist today, but his categories were broad and, as usual, idiosyncratic. Generally speaking, George regarded those peoples who had been shaped by Christianity and had absorbed the traditions of Greece and Rome as belonging to a single, if highly diverse, cultural family that he sometimes referred to as "the white race" — *die weisse Art*. All others — Islamic, Indian, and Far Eastern cultures — were so alien that George considered them unknowable, incomprehensible and, just as important, inassimilable to the one he recognized as his own. It was not that they were inferior necessarily, just incompatible. There was, he thought, an absolute, unbridgeable difference between Europe and everything else. When a Japanese admirer visited George in 1927, the poet received him but gave him to understand that their relationship could go no further. "We are not yet so far along as the Catholic Church," George sarcastically said to Edith Landmann, "which also pronounces its blessing on yellow and black people and recently consecrated a Chinese bishop." Such a violation of boundaries was unimaginable to him. The Chinese had no business in the church or in any other European institution, for, as George cryptically said at another point, "they think yellow." Whatever that meant, it was obvious Asia as a whole represented not just an unintelligible Other to George's mind but also a potent threat. Accordingly, in 1916 he predicted there would be "terrible battles that will be waged between the white and the yellow races in the next fifty years." Only partially in jest, George also revealed what his intentions were should those battles occur during his lifetime. "If the yellow monkeys come," he vowed, "then I will grab a rifle myself."

Yet the "yellow peril" was a comparatively abstract menace. The more immediate and, as Heinrich Friedemann's recent death on the eastern front demonstrated, very real source of danger lay closer to home: Russia. For George, the Russians were the true, and truly life-threatening foe, and he loathed them with a vehemence he expressed toward no other people. (All the same, the extent to which he was prepared to throw all non-Europeans into the same pot emerges from a casual comment he made that "Asia begins at the Alexanderplatz in Berlin.") Specifically citing the atrocities committed by Ivan the Terrible, who George thought had established an unsurpassed standard of "absolute savagery," George condemned what he called "the cruelty of the Russians: this was something unparalleled, not like anything European, had no counterpart and was incapable of being humanized." Over and over, George declared that the Russians were devoid of any redeeming quality, insisting that their "kind of cruelty was a crime against life" itself. "It was a central point of his doctrine," Edith Landmann recorded him saying, "that one understood the basic difference between the Russian and European character." Nothing about the Russians escaped his indictment. When he was not denouncing their barbarity and brutishness, George accused them of being flaccid and impotent. "Just as their thinking is sterile," he said, "so, too, are the Russians' deeds." Some years later, in 1922, George became more explicit about what he meant by their sterility when he mused to Bertold Vallentin that "the Russians are by nature a receptive people. They could not produce any new form of humanity on their own. They lack the 'phallic' element." To George, these traits were in fact two sides of the same coin: their ostensible passivity, their want of fertility was merely the analog to their supposed urge to extinguish all life outside of themselves. George perceived the same qualities in Russian literature, with its emphasis on emotional turmoil and introspection, which he dismissed as amounting to no more than a "worship of rot," labeling it elsewhere a "cult of self-destruction." "I have no sympathy for that," he announced. "It just makes me feel ill."

As the war progressed — or rather refused to progress — there was much more than Russian literature to make George feel sick. Despite the horrendous losses suffered on both sides — a total of roughly 700,000 French and German soldiers were killed during the ten-month battle at Verdun that ended in December 1916, and nearly the same number of German and English troops died in half that time at the Somme the same year — the front had all but stalled. The lives of so many men had bought only a few miles of worthless terrain, and often no gains at all. Everyone was stunned by the carnage. But Germany was facing the real prospect of running out of eligible young men of recruiting age and it was forced to begin easing its enlisting criteria. Older men who had been passed over in the first two years of war were thus being reexamined. In late October, Friedrich Gundolf, now thirty-six, was reclassified as fit for service, called up and sent to basic training in the west.

George, usually so guarded with his feelings, reacted with undisguised, almost panicky distress. "My child," he wrote, "I cannot permit you to be actually exposed to the most extreme danger — what would I do without YOU?" Attempting to play down his fears with levity, George added that perhaps it was a good omen after all that Gundolf had been drafted: "I would have to be very mistaken if it were not as I always predicted: that as soon as you entered the war the entire affair would have to end — for super-terrestrial reasons." But there was no denying that the matter was very serious indeed.

George was faced with an agonizing quandary. He could not bear the thought Gundolf would be ground up like so many others in the senseless machinery of a pointless war. Too many had already been sacrificed, but Gundolf was — well, Gundolf. He was simply too invaluable, too irreplaceable; if anyone deserved to be spared, it was he. Yet George had deliberately refrained from preventing anyone else from going off to the war and it would have appeared awkward for him to interfere now. George was nothing if not consistent, and he demonstrated no inclination to deviate from the course he had always hewn to. Fortunately for Gundolf, there were others, including Alfred Weber and Eberhard Gothein, were also concerned about his welfare and were attempting to prevent him from being sent into actual combat. Gundolf even applied directly to the War Ministry himself for a transfer that would permit him to make, as he put it in a letter to Curtius, "more profitable use of my intellectual abilities." So far, however, all efforts to recall him from active duty had yielded no positive results.

At first, no doubt mindful of his earlier panegyrics on war, Gundolf appeared sanguine, even cheerful about his new station, glibly assuring George that "there is no cause for any worry whatsoever." Writing from his training post at St. Avold in the Lorraine, Gundolf even sought to portray the experience as positively educational, seeing as it allowed him to become acquainted with a segment of society that he, in his rarified Heidelberg existence, had never encountered on such intimate terms before. "Life together with my comrades is a real enrichment of my perception of the *Volk*," he told George, obviously deaf to the condescension in his own words. "They are almost all artless and uncomplicated peasants and laborers with a natural feeling for inner decency and distinctions." There was no question, Gundolf said, "that we could learn more from a real peasant than from a dozen professors."

After a couple of weeks, Gundolf had apparently learned enough. "To my observations on the *Volk* I must add that they are often not very courageous morally and more preoccupied with eating than people like us can imagine. [. . .] Metabolism in general plays an enormous role in the life and imagination of the common soldier." It was a tactful way to put it, but his meaning is clear. Gundolf must have known the old adage that an army marches on its stomach. What he had clearly not counted on was how much the entire digestive process was involved.

Whereas his "comrades" were merely crude and probably smelly, the war itself posed a genuine threat to Gundolf's continued well-being. In the middle of December 1916, he was transferred directly to the front as a sapper, charged with overseeing the digging of trenches. He described travelling "through the cold winter morning sun" toward the battle lines, passing by "destroyed villages, endless plains," and, as he drew closer, hearing "the incessant thunder of Verdun." Gundolf was awed by the "constant barrage nearby that makes the earth tremble" and compared the whole spectacle to "a dream that my mind and imagination do not yet comprehend." But it was no dream. If anything, it was a nightmare. Norbert von Hellingrath, the Hölderlin scholar, had volunteered as an artillery observer and was also serving on the frontline at Verdun. On the same day that Gundolf arrived there, December 14, Hellingrath and his unit took a direct hit from an enemy shell. There was so little left of Hellingrath's body that final confirmation of his death was delayed for almost two months. What could be identified as his remains were buried in a mass grave near Fort Douaumont. In a poem later written in his memory, George compared Hellingrath's death with that of the last Byzantine emperor: according to legend, all that could be found of Constantine XII after his final battle against the Turks were the clasps of his shoes.

At the end of December, after having spent not quite two weeks in the freezing, muddy trenches, Gundolf thought he finally had good news to relay: "I am getting indications from Berlin that I can probably be released," he told George; "People are 'interested' both in the Ministry of Culture and in the Foreign Office." Despite these encouraging signals, however, there was still no actual movement to take him away from the front. Early in the new year, Gundolf received a dispiriting telegram informing him that his request for transfer had been denied. His circumstances were becoming dire. "I am now stuck in a mass pen devoid of space and time, without sleep and light, without halfway meaningful work and without any real respite," he miserably complained to Curtius. Every day consisted of "a disgusting shuffle and din, sometimes interrupted by a numb dozing and hard labor in absolutely indescribable filth. I will not comment on the lack of any stimulation other than comradely participation in squabbling and dirty jokes." Bored, exhausted, and perpetually grimy, Gundolf was becoming frantic to get out of a situation he was finding increasingly intolerable and, although he did not say so, undoubtedly terrifying. Things were so bad that he asked Curtius to speak on his behalf to a certain Paul Clemen, a professor of art history in Bonn who had connections reaching all the way up to the kaiser. "To beg for patrons is painful to me," Gundolf admitted, but "my misery [is] greater than any efforts they may make." Conspicuously gone now was the blustery bravado of the swaggering deskbound warrior who had said he welcomed death and destruction as a necessary cleansing. In its place had moved a very common and very understandable fear. "My misery does not help the Fatherland in the *slightest,* on the contrary," he rationalized to Curtius, "but it harms me a great deal." Gundolf well knew that he was asking for special treatment, that his behavior might seem hypocritical, dishonorable, even cowardly. But he was desperate.

Just when Gundolf's hopes for rescue were beginning to fade, in February 1917 there was suddenly a breakthrough. His pleas had finally reached a sympathetic ear. He was quickly transferred to the bureau of General Hans von Haeften, who oversaw the military section of the Foreign Office in Berlin. There Gundolf's duties would be agreeably light: he was charged with the congenial task of monitoring the foreign press and periodically summarizing his findings to his superiors.

When George learned of this development, instead of expressing relief, he sent Gundolf a frosty note. "*Karl* said something about you changing your post. Why have I heard nothing about it. All of this concerns me too after all." Gundolf's unexpectedly rapid relocation had, it turned out, come about not through the intervention of Weber or Gothein or even Curtius, but from a different quarter entirely. Sabine Lepsius, who despite her estrangement from George still maintained contacts with Gundolf, also stood on a friendly footing with Walter Rathenau. An influential industrialist with political ambitions, Rathenau had held a prominent position in the government as the head of the War Raw Materials Department in the War Ministry from August 1914 to the spring of 1915. And it was Rathenau, with his continued close ties to the ruling powers, who had managed to secure Gundolf's release.

To George, who disdained Rathenau, this was an intolerable breach of protocol, a violation of his own realm by an unauthorized agent. He was incensed that something as important to him as Gundolf's fate should have been acted on without his knowledge and without his supervision. If Gundolf had been so anxious to get away from the front that he would resort to any means to do so, then he should have said something earlier to his Master. "To be sure," George wrote, "I am all for setting everything in motion in such a case." But there were limits. "It would probably have worked through the university (I spoke to Gothein myself about the matter) and would have been best. I consider the fact that the matter with L . . Rath — succeeded a mere coincidence." George evidently could not even bring himself to write out the full names of Lepsius and Rathenau. Gundolf should have waited for assistance from an approved address. By allowing Rathenau to act as his savior, Gundolf had made himself, and by association George, beholden to someone who belonged to the world they had always regarded as their foe. George tried to put this as plainly as he was able:

> In short, what I want to say is: I think one must be prepared for the fact that in these times there will be difficult situations — in which it is more dignified to stay — than to accept ANY help offered, this Rath. affair borders very closely on that — or — there can come circumstances in the course of these times in which EVERYONE of us has to ask himself whether our private life is still decent + viable in a situation in which no one helps us except our own decision to put an end to it. It is true we were never preachers of stoic principles but I read in your words something like the desire of someone who is adrift at sea to try everything — that would stand in glaring contrast to the life that we have lived so far + was the right one.

As always, George was careful not to give away too much in writing by being more explicit than absolutely necessary. But he was telling Gundolf as clearly as he ever would that preserving one's own life was not — or should not be — the highest priority if it meant compromising the ideals by which it had been previously conducted. Indeed, George seemed to imply that, if the alternative was between death and the betrayal of those ideals, it should be plain which one to choose. Not that Gundolf should have been surprised by this conclusion. After all, in *The Star of the Covenant,* which was the circle's official code of conduct, George had advised his disciples that when there was no other recourse in a given situation, they should "learn from heroes to fall on your own sword." But the fact that he was talking about Gundolf, his most loyal and selfless apostle, his dearest and most talented follower, lent George's censure even greater force. It was as if he were saying that he was prepared, if necessary, to make the sacrifice of Gundolf that Gundolf himself had been reluctant to perform.

If Gundolf was disturbed by George's apparent willingness to let him die rather than accept a favor from someone deemed unworthy, he did not reveal it. But not long afterward, he gave George an even more dramatic reason to be displeased. Ever since he had been reinstated in George's favor in 1904, Gundolf had made liberal use of the relatively tolerant policy George had adopted toward his favorite disciple's relations with the opposite sex. With Gundolf's charm, good looks, and boyish enthusiasm, he never lacked for female company. As Sabine Lepsius diplomatically put it, Gundolf "hardly let a day go by without seeking out the stimulation of intelligent and charming women." Although George was not happy with the arrangement, he pragmatically extended the same indulgence toward other members of his circle. In 1911, for instance, Hildebrandt had witnessed a conversation between George and Wolters concerning the latter's "fondness for women." The Master was concerned that at that stage of the circle's development — it was during the publication of the *Yearbooks* — Wolter's involvement with women might cause "disturbances in the activity of the state." Yet George also realized that he had to show some leniency, for, as he recognized, "if he would stubbornly insist on his rules, then no one would stay with him."

But as time passed George seemed to be growing less inclined to make even this kind of modest compromise. In February 1916, during an encounter with Ernst Glöckner, he "spoke a lot about women and about his 'state.' On this point he is becoming more and more rigid; rightly so," Glöckner felt, who agreed that "family matters should not be mixed up with the affairs of state, which is, however, what the presence of women does, as he said." Several days later, George wrote to Gundolf with the same thing obviously still on his mind: "I have to speak with you next time at some length about women-matters," he rather darkly said. Without revealing the precise cause for his agitation, George made no secret of his feelings. "This spiritual aimless and irresponsible sleeping around with that sex," he wrote, "will have more harmful consequences than the carnal variety." Whether the interaction with them was spiritual or physical, George did not want women having any part in his "state." "Women are a PRIVATE AFFAIR," he warned Gundolf, adding more ominously, "Woe to both parties if they try to make something more out of it."

A year later, Gundolf learned just how seriously George had meant his threat. In early February 1917, just after Gundolf had been transferred to Berlin and thus removed from harm's way, he had arranged to meet with an old friend, Agathe Mallachow, whom he had not seen in two years. Three months later, she was pregnant. Wanting to avoid a scandal and to prevent her from losing her job — she taught music at a secondary school — they agreed to get married. But apparently it was with the understanding that the union would be an arrangement of convenience only and would not otherwise affect their lives. Sometime in the first part of May, Gundolf communicated his intentions to George. His response was like a blast from hell.

Dear Gundolf: The way in which you announce a marriage without any warning as if it were a pleasurable excursion seems incredible and has

caused me extreme disquiet. After all of what you previously told me about the relationship I can only recognize it as an act of insanity for which you tacitly presuppose my approval. The way in which you write, especially about the later development of things, leaves the impression that you have no idea what the consequences will be of what you are about to do. If there really is a child (which after the earlier surprise attack and accepted medical practice may still be doubted) then a marriage will admittedly be difficult to avoid, but only in that case — and even then marriage is for you in every respect the worst of all forms of settlement. If difficulties arise for both parties during the wait then both parties were old enough to think about this beforehand . . But every reasonable person knows enough that one does not enter into a marriage in such haste and without having made the most precise inquiries in all respects . . Even the most lax relative does that and considers it necessary for even the most trivial lad! How much more would I do so for YOU! It would be unscrupulous of you if you were to undertake something so serious without asking me, unscrupulous of me if I simply smiled and said yes while your entire fate is at stake. The opinion you express in your letter is that of someone who is completely naïve. I will entirely refrain from mentioning other serious doubts — I will hold back serious but justified reproaches so as not to exacerbate the situation — But if you take this step without having thoroughly discussed all of the questions to be raised — then although I cannot expel you from the STATE until you have placed yourself in some untenable position there: in PERSONAL terms however everything would change in ways that you cannot imagine.
St. G.

Whatever Gundolf had expected, it cannot have been this. The threat was as unequivocal as it was pitiless: if Gundolf married Agathe Mallachow, he would be cut off from George forever. Faced with such an ultimatum, Gundolf acted in the only way he probably could, but his behavior was disgraceful nonetheless. Obeying George's injunction, he abandoned Agathe Mallachow and their child to their fate. Worse still, Gundolf did not appear to have been overly troubled by his decision. Whatever his feelings for the mother, becoming a father does not seem to have made much of an impression on him. Although George was not exactly an impartial observer, he relayed to Edith Landmann that Gundolf "had got a child from a girl he no longer loved very much." If anything, Gundolf appeared to view it all as a nuisance. "I have also became a father," Gundolf casually informed Wolfskehl in December, as if it were an afterthought, adding merely, "that belongs to the hardships of war." At the end of the year, after she had given birth to their daughter, Fräulein Mallachow brought suit against Gundolf to petition for financial support. In

January 1918 he wrote George that "concerning A[gathe], I have determined to make a one-time payment. Vallentin will represent me in court." A month later, Gundolf told his Master that, now that the whole thing was finally behind him, he had seen the error of his ways. "What a blessing that I did not consummate that incurable stupidity back then in my 'mental disturbance' — I will always be indebted to Vallentin for this first bleeding."

But it was not behind Agathe Mallachow. Forced to resign from her teaching position in Berlin, and no doubt wanting to escape the shame of bringing up an illegitimate child as a single unwed mother, she left the country and settled in Rome where she stayed for the rest of her life. She got by as well as she could, aided by occasional financial contributions from friends back in Berlin. Yet not even that was enough — in the last year of the war, inflation climbed to four times that of 1914 — and at one point there was talk among some of George's friends about coming to her assistance in some other way. But George would show no mercy. When someone once brought up the plight of the mother and daughter in a conversation and suggested ways in which one might alleviate their predicament, he brusquely cut off all discussion of the matter, saying, "God does not love the children of whores."

Even without having to bear the brunt of George's brutality, nearly everyone was finding it difficult just to get by as the war dragged on. Within months after it had begun, prices had steeply risen and some goods had become harder to find. By the summer of 1915, things were so uncertain that George wrote to Julius Landmann in advance of a planned trip to Switzerland to make sure there would be enough food when he got there. "The effects of the war in this country with respect to nutrition," Landmann assured him in May, "are evident, apart from a uniform price increase of approximately fifteen to twenty percent, in only two areas. First, for months we have not had any good bread, namely whole-wheat bread, and second, beef is occasionally unobtainable. Sometimes no steers, only cows are slaughtered, and one has to make do with veal and mutton and goat." As the Allied blockade of Germany tightened from 1916 onward, the situation became progressively worse. When the potato crop failed that year, people survived on whatever substitutes they could find, resulting in what became known as the "Turnip Winter" (*Rübenwinter*). In 1917 the daily civilian ration was reduced from 1,350 calories, already half of a normal diet, to a mere 1,000. Ernst Glöckner, writing to George in January 1917, said that "cocoa and tea, as well as coffee, can't even be found any more." Everything, not just food, was in short supply: clothing, shoes, heating fuel, even soap. As things got worse, starvation, once inconceivable in the prosperous prewar empire, began to afflict the urban centers.

When the hostilities finally ceased, some three quarters of a million people had died of hunger alone.

With the war approaching the end of its third year, with millions already dead, maimed or missing, the economy in ruins and basic commodities scarce to nonexistent, the giddy optimism felt at the outset had long since made way for the gloomy realization that a German victory was by no means inevitable. As early as November 1916, while he was in Berlin, George had one of his last meetings with Kurt Breisig. They spoke at length about the war, and George himself revealed that his views "also encompassed the possibility of a defeat, a defeat of Germany." When Breysig patriotically objected, George said that he had just spent three months in Switzerland and that on returning he had "found the mood in Germany much more depressed than before." He also told Breysig that "people in very influential circles [. . .] had asked him for his view; but he refused to express it, for if he would reveal his true (i.e., so pessimistic) opinion, then that would sound too presumptuous."

For whatever reason — avoiding the appearance of presumption did not frequently guide his actions — George also did not divulge who the "very influential" people were who had wanted to hear his observations on the state of the nation. But the fate of Germany, and his own role in the outcome, was very much in George's thoughts at the time. In an earlier conversation with Breysig, in October, he had held forth on his belief in "the aptitude of poets for politics." Breysig objected to this, too, arguing that the province of the poet is beauty, not polity. George railed at him for narrowly seeing in him a "poet only": "You would have gotten along much worse with Dante," George said. "He was even more political and much else besides. Unfortunately, I only began so late to concern myself with politics, only ten years or so ago." Whatever he may have lacked in terms of time devoted to politics George would make up for in determination. He was quite capable, he told Breysig, "of turning to politics, and of using newspapers. If everything — in the war — went badly and there was no one better for the leadership (i.e., the Office of Reichskanzler) then he would do it." Breysig could not believe his ears. He knew how much George despised anything to do with the official Germany, how he detested the entire bourgeois Prussian government apparatus that kept the Empire afloat. And now here George was apparently in all seriousness picturing himself as the Imperial Chancellor, occupying the seat that Bismarck once held. It seemed ludicrous. Breysig tried to give him an idea of what he would have to contend with if, by some turn of events, he would actually be considered for the office. "If it were ever your misfortune to be placed into practical politics," Breysig told George, "then you would learn what a crushing mill of meanness and servility it is. Within eight days people would start throwing not stones, but mud, table legs, and all sorts of things at you. Their slogan would be: Down with that guy." Listening to this, George only said, "Perhaps you are right."

What Breysig was forgetting — or did not fully comprehend — was the degree to which George's entire being was concentrated on the acquisition and exercise of power. George was not really interested in being the Chancellor of Germany per se or in holding any other traditional political office. He was only interested in ruling Germany — or, more particularly, a Germany cut out of his own cloth. Politics, like poetry, was a means to a greater end for George, and that was something Breysig — and many others as well — failed to appreciate adequately. Breysig even admitted later that there was "*one* essential feature of George's behavior that always struck me as foreign: it was what I would like to call the political aspect of his behavior." Breysig thought this element of George's being "stood in a fair amount of conflict with the nature of an artist, which I would have imagined was freer and more unfettered." Apart from offering a romantically naïve conception of the artist, Breysig's comments also reveal how little he had understood his former friend. A few years later, George mentioned Breysig in a conversation with Edith Landmann, trying to explain what he saw as the fundamental difference between the scholar and himself. "If Breysig did not have science," he said, "then he wouldn't have anything at all. If I didn't write poetry, then I would still have something else, and the poems are the means to that something else. If they were nothing other than poems, they wouldn't be worth much." And it was increasingly that "something else," which Breysig and others viewed as an irritant but which George regarded as most crucial of all.

Nevertheless, poetry still remained the instrument George wielded with greatest skill and to greatest effect. If he wanted to speak directly to the people, to act upon them and bring them under his sway, he still thought poetry would be the best way to achieve that goal. Thus far, George had said nothing about the war in print and had not even completely disclosed his stance to many of his closest associates. In mid-1917, George felt the time had finally come to speak out. That July, Bondi published a six-page pamphlet containing George's contribution to the war effort. Called simply "The War" ("Der Krieg"), it is one of the most devastating poems written in German during the four-year conflict. But, as George might have said, the work was intended to be more than just a poem. "The War," that is, represents his own continuation of politics by other means.

The poem is lengthy — it consists of twelve stanzas of twelve lines each — but tightly focused. And for most of the poem, apart from the last two stanzas, that concentration of energy is expressed in a cascade of almost unrelieved fury and contempt. It opens with a comparison of the enthusiasm at the start of the war and of the sense of common purpose shared by virtually everyone at its eruption with the reflexive herd-instinct of wild animals: when threatened by a natural catastrophe such as fire or earthquake, they, too, set aside their natural enmity and band together. The poetic voice disdains this false feeling of unity, in which everyone forgot "the cowardly years of chaos and triviality" preceding it and now "saw itself great in its poverty." Here, at the latest, we begin to realize that this is not an antiwar poem in any conventional sense at all. George was not denouncing the war, he was denouncing the people waging it.

At this point, the poet introduces himself onto the scene. Referring to himself as the "Hermit on the mountain" — one thinks of George waiting through the outbreak of the war high up in the Swiss Alps — he describes how people approach him and, overcome by their own excitement, urgently ask, "Do you still stay silent before this stupendous occasion?" His answer, like the entire poem, is merciless and unyielding:

> What convulses you has long been familiar to me.
> I have long perspired the red sweat of fear
> When people played with fire . . I cried
> My tears in advance . . today I can find no more.
> Most of it had occurred and no one saw . .
> The most dreadful things are yet to come and no one sees.
> . . . .
> I take no part in the conflict that moves you.

Like his long-standing conviction that he was the mouthpiece of higher wisdom, George's belief in his own prophetic powers had been growing in recent years. The previous summer, spent with the Landmanns in the Swiss village of Klosters, he had said that "what is written in a poem becomes truth, just as the war had to come, for it is written: I saw from afar the tumult of a battle." With these last words, George was quoting himself, citing a line from one of his poems in *The Seventh Ring*, which concludes: "I saw the small horde stand around the banner . . . / And everyone else saw nothing." On hearing this, Edith Landmann pointed out that by the same reasoning one could say the war offered proof that everything else in his poetry would also come true. George reacted as if her conclusion were painfully obvious: "Ach, that's not the issue. There's no doubt about that. What is in the spirit must be lived. Reality is the form in which it lives out its end. That is why poetry is the most dangerous thing in the world. It can lie dormant for a while, remain sunken in the earth, but it does not disappear." Whether one accepted George's claims of divinatory abilities or not, there was no question that his poetry was dangerous, as later events would more than amply show. But the danger lay less in what it augured than in what it appeared to sanction.

In the third stanza of "The War," George began to articulate more precisely the "reality" he had foreseen and now regarded as unavoidable. Changing perspective slightly by referring to the poet now in the third person, it emphasizes his prophetic abilities and the ingratitude and deafness of those who might have learned from, perhaps even have been saved by, his message: "The Seer is never thanked . . he meets scorn / And stones if he predicts disaster — rage and stones / When it strikes." Then, again suddenly shifting gears, the poet-as-prophet poses a question of his own to his unworthy auditors: "What is the murder of hundreds of thousands to HIM / Compared to the murder of Life itself?"

It is difficult to know what George meant by "Life itself." Certainly it was a phrase much bandied about at the time, when the "philosophy of life" — *Lebensphilosophie* — had reached the zenith of its popularity and was identified most closely with such figures as Nietzsche, Bergson, and Dilthey. For George, though, it presumably refers more narrowly to the system of values he and his circle had developed over the years, which he viewed, as we know, as providing the only legitimate grounds for existence. That George was willing not just to sacrifice the lives of hundreds of thousands of people who failed to measure up to or abide by those values, but also to consider their deaths comparatively paltry and insignificant, ought to be deeply shocking. But we have seen him express that opinion too many times in too many ways to find it truly surprising, however monstrous and repugnant it is in itself. In the same way, George makes it clear that the true enemy is not French or English, or even necessarily foreign. Rather, the real opponents, and the ones who carry full responsibility for the slaughter occurring on the battlefields, can be found in every town in every country:

> The woman who wails · the smug burgher ·
> The gray beard bear more guilt than the stab and shot
> Of the adversary for the glassy eyes and shredded bodies
> Of our sons and grandsons.

It was, in other words, the bourgeoisie — and women — who had over time created the conditions that had made the war inescapable. The poet thus holds the entire social order of modern Europe, and not any particular political or military policy, accountable for the butchery of its own youth.

George's catalogue of condemnation was not through yet. The poet writes that, even knowing what fate awaited his friends in battle, "he sent the youngest of the dear ones out with his blessing." It is not that he does not fear what might happen to them in the field, but "HE is seized by a deeper horror." Addressing the fighting youth directly, he spells out the grounds for that greater dread:

> >You who swing the broadsword over mounds of corpses ·
> Wish to preserve us from too easy an end

And from the worst · from blood-disgrace! < Peoples
That commit it are to be indiscriminately exterminated

This is quite possibly the nadir of George's entire poetic career in moral if not also in artistic terms. The word he used to characterize the worst thing that could befall his countrymen — worse, that is, than the deaths of millions of innocents — is "miscegenation" — *Blut-schmach* — or, literally, "blood-disgrace." Not content simply to reprove the mixing of races, the poet openly and unmistakably calls for the wholesale extermination of those who practice or allow interracial unions. It is a repulsive, abominable declaration, and it is difficult not to think that in such utterances the seeds were planted of later crimes. George had, after all, explicitly assigned prophetic significance to his own poetry, and he no less frankly acknowledged that poetry can and does do genuine harm. Read by the wrong people at the wrong time, such words can be taken not merely as a prediction but as an exhortation, fully validated by the Master's authority and seemingly preordained by his ostensible prescience. Without much effort at all, his pronouncements could be understood, that is, as furnishing a license to murder — more: as condoning the mass liquidation of entire peoples.

Even his closest followers have been troubled by what George was saying here and took pains to try to clarify his intent. Their main concern appears to have been that later readers, especially after the Nazi era, would think George's denunciation of interracial commingling went beyond straightforward racism and included an anti-Semitic component. Kurt Hildebrandt, for example, assures us as if it were somehow an exoneration that in George's understanding, "the white race encompasses the Aryan and Semitic tribes." Ernst Morwitz, who wrote a brief commentary on George's poetry just before the Master died, likewise speculated that the word "is probably to be understood as [referring to] the physical and spiritual intermingling of whites and colored people in the struggle against whites. It necessarily leads — so prophesizes the poet — to the destruction of the entire people, to the annihilation of the white race by the yellow and black ones." Morwitz tells us that George, who lived long enough to review the proofs of the book, wrote in the margin next to this passage, "Perhaps." Whether that indicated assent or uncertainty on the poet's part, what is certain, Morwitz goes on to say, is that George was outraged over the presence of African and Indian soldiers in both the French and English armies. He felt they were deployed as part of a calculated affront, a tactic designed to humiliate the Germans, forcing them to fight against "inferior" and unworthy opponents. Later, when the French stationed African soldiers in the occupied territories of the Rhineland after the war, George was deeply offended for the same reason, seeing their presence on German soil as a deliberate gesture of provocation and mockery. In June

1920, using the same violent language as in the poem, and presumably for the same reasons, George bluntly said, "These French have to be exterminated." And we know what he thought about Asians — not to speak of the Russians.

This, then, is the ultimate meaning George ascribed to the war: that it would stem the tide of racial impurities threatening to pollute the blood of the "white race," however defined. And since her enemies had already corrupted themselves, Germany stood alone as the last remaining hope for the preservation and continuance of Europe as a whole. In the poem, George was unambiguous on this score:

> oh Land
> Too beautiful that a foreign step should ravage you:
> . . . .
> Where the radiant Mother first revealed her true countenance
> To the decayed and decadent white Race . . Land that still
> Possesses much promise — that therefore will not die!

The "Mother" evoked here is Greek culture, which the Germans prided themselves on having been first to rediscover but which had not yet been fully resuscitated. The poet thus sees the surest guarantee that Germany will not become extinct in that it alone can complete the still unfinished task of reanimating the Hellenic dream. Not coincidentally, it was also just this task that George felt that he and the inhabitants of his own secret Germany were the best equipped to fulfill.

Before that could happen, however, George thought that many more still had to perish, including, for better or worse, many Germans. As another strophe states: "It is not seemly to celebrate: there will be no triumph · / Only many downfalls without dignity. ." Again, the only redeeming aspect of the war is that it quickened a process that was already underway. "Sick worlds are rushing feverishly to their end / In the melee. Only the still untainted / Spattered blood is sacred — an entire river."

When he had completed the poem in June, George wrote Glöckner to inform him that "the 'War' is finished . . Does that mean it is really over?" Glöckner, who was perhaps somewhat less persuaded by George's prophetic faculties than George himself, quoted the Master's words in a note to Bertram, adding skeptically, "Let's hope that he is right *this* time." It would be almost another year and a half before the killing finally stopped.

The response to George's poem was varied but uniformly strong. " 'The War,' " Gundolf was already able to inform him by August, "is selling well." Gundolf himself wrote a review of the poem for the *Frankfurter Zeitung,* resulting in a predictably adulatory homage. "Never have more powerful tones rung out in German poetry than his twelve strophes," Gundolf asserted. "A wise man is speaking here, profound, devout, and bold — initiated in the laws of human growth and decline like no one since Goethe, like no one since Nietzsche devoted to merit and greatness." A more restrained but no less congenial reaction came from a soldier in the field, one of the countless numbers of his adherents who were increasingly looking to him from afar as their spiritual guide. Eleven years after the poem had appeared, on the occasion of George's sixtieth birthday, Bruno Werner published a newspaper article vividly describing the circumstances in which he and his comrades first came to read the poem in the bloody summer of 1917:

> It happened that, as we were lying in the mud before Warneton in a cratered landscape in which the Canadians had destroyed one third of our small battalion with incendiary grenades at one in the morning the night before and at two had smashed in the skulls of a second third with nail-studded flails, the mail brought us a letter that contained the yellow brochure "The War" by the poet George.
>
> And we crouched in that tiny dugout, where the aroma of twenty men mingled with the odor of stagnant ground water, illuminated by the rays of a carbide lamp whose little flame was snuffed out by every detonation and had to be lit again, and suddenly we heard — and it was the first and last time during the war — the sound of a fanfare of such incredible vigor and force that it seemed a curtain was being ripped down the middle in two. It was as if what each one of us vaguely, wordlessly felt was being expressed, and in that moment — there is no need to shrink from the word — we sensed a sacred and terrible excitement. Here was someone speaking who not only seemed to be a soldier like us, but who was at the same time a leader [*Führer*] into a new world.

Throughout the war, George managed to keep up his accustomed regimen: as had been his habit now for years, he spent the fall and early winters in Berlin, where he shuttled among various residences, staying alternately in a room reserved for him in the large and comfortable house of his publisher, Georg Bondi, and in the more modest quarters offered by both Morwitz and Thormaehlen; then moving south to Munich and the Globe Room for the remainder of the winter and spring; and finally on to Switzerland in the late summer. These principal stops were punctuated by shorter excursions to Darmstadt, Heidelberg, or wherever he was needed. Some of the moves were dictated or at least accompanied by practical considerations. Food remained a constant worry, and even keeping warm had become a major preoccupation. Partly, that is, George went wherever the conditions promised some relief from the growing privations as the conflict entered it fourth year.

The cold was something almost everyone was having to bear during the last, brutal winter of the war. After the United States had entered the conflict the summer before and had sent its first troops to the Continent, the drain on German resources further increased as the Allied embargo on the Empire choked off almost all external supplies of food and energy. Severely undernourished, poorly clothed, and living in unheated apartments and houses, people in Germany were beginning to fall ill in ever larger numbers. In January 1918 Gundolf came down with a lung infection that kept him in bed for a full two months. At the end of February, his condition had improved but only marginally. "I found Gundolf to be quite weak still," Boehringer, who was then visiting him in Berlin, reported to George. "He actually had a mild case of pneumonia. He has gotten over that now. He no longer has a fever, but he is pale and feels miserable. He complains about constant headaches. He is truly afraid that his nerves may not stand up to it. In short, he is very dispirited and in my opinion needs weeks of rest and to be well looked after."

Fortunately, Gundolf was on the receiving end of the doting ministrations of yet another female admirer by the name of Elisabeth Salomon, or Elli, who had been a student of his at Heidelberg. She was an intelligent, charming, and extremely attractive, even beautiful young woman who liked to seek out the company of equally gifted men. Elli had a knack for saying and doing just the right thing, and at first even George tolerated her presence. Whenever he was in Berlin during the war, she would bring by a small container of milk for his afternoon tea. That act in itself was enough to stir admiration, for, as Thormaehlen pointed out, "God knows where she found that beverage, which was scarce in Berlin in those days." During Gundolf's long convalescence, Elli lavished the same resourcefulness on him. "At the moment he is being nursed by Elli, who is also sleeping there," Boehringer went on in his letter to George. "Everyone is trying to collect food from all corners. There is a shortage of meat and fruit."

The desire for peace, at any cost, and for a return to normal life was beginning to outweigh all other considerations. At the end of January, more than 400,000 workers had gone on strike in Berlin to protest the mounting deprivations and to press for immediate peace. Within two days, the strikes had spread to six other cities. With the Russian Revolution less than three months old, the German authorities reacted with understandable alacrity, declaring martial law and removing the striking workers from the scene by forcibly enlisting them into the army. But the fundamental problems remained. People were literally starving to death, forced to eat whatever they could find, including domestic pets — cats were sardonically referred to as "roof rabbits" — supplemented by a euphemistically named "bread" consisting of potato peelings and sawdust.

Not even the massive counteroffensive Germany launched on the western front in the spring of 1918 inspired much more than the hope that it would hasten the end. About the only thing that seemed to offer much by way of optimism, to some people anyway, was the approach of George's fiftieth birthday on July 12. But even here there was little to be very encouraged about. The war had been hard on everyone and had left its physical mark on George as well. His hair, still long and dense, had turned completely white, his skin, which had always had a darker tone, had acquired an unhealthy pallor, and the furrows on his brow had grown deeper and longer. His illness, combined with the years of poor nutrition and the psychological strain of bearing the deaths of so many loved ones, had aged him far beyond his actual years. When a physician examined him later that summer and asked one of George's friends how old the poet was, he was astonished to learn that George had just completed only his fiftieth year. "I am sure you are wrong," the doctor said. "According to his somatic condition he is an ancient person."

The public acknowledgement of George's birthday reflected the expanding scope of his reputation. Almost every daily paper in Germany, as well as those published in Switzerland and Austria, contained at least a notice of the event, and many carried longer articles. The *Karlsruher Tageblatt* called him "perhaps the greatest *artist* in modern literature." The *Berliner Tageblatt* hailed him not only as a poet, but also as a "moralist, an educator who wants to teach us where our happiness, where the meaning of our life is to be sought." In the *Fränkischer Kurier,* Oskar Walzel, a prominent Swiss literary scholar, published a lengthy and sympathetic appreciation of George's influence on his own academic discipline at German-speaking universities. Still, while George's presence, indeed his rising predominance on the German cultural landscape was undeniable, his person remained as mysterious as ever to everyone outside his narrow circle of friends. As the author of yet another newspaper article put it, even though George's works were now widely available and attentively read by a substantial readership, "one knows nothing about his life apart from a few factual details."

The private tributes from his friends were, predictably, even more extravagant. Probably the most remarkable testimonial, though, came from an anonymous letter writer who sent a long treatise entitled "My Declaration of Faith on the occasion of Stefan George's Fiftieth Birthday." After taking several critics to task for having misunderstood or misrepresented George's poetry and especially its inherent claim to have a direct "effect on life" (*Lebenswirkung*), the unidentified author claims that this "effect" has been misinterpreted because it has been grasped too narrowly:

> Whoever makes such a deep impression as George also unleashes expressions that here and there await in *others* their liberation from their fetters. These 'expressions' do not need to be only poems or formed poetry. It can

also be lived poetry. To be sure, the hacks that write such articles do not suspect what life a *poet* is able to ignite in receptive souls. And hardly know that many a poem that *transports us away from the world* contains the seeds to *move the world*. When I look at my two blond-headed boys, then I hope and yearn for them and myself for the days when we will enjoy together such a *pure* art as Stefan George has bestowed and when we will be mutually strengthened in the *faith* in *such* a custodian of the holy fire in *cold* times. Perhaps these boys will be among the most enthusiastic ones in twenty years who will pay tribute to the Great Man on his seventieth birthday. And that is not supposed to be an 'effect on life'?

Although he did not live to see it, George's seventieth birthday would have been in 1938, when his "effect on life" could no longer be challenged by literary critics or anyone else. But we cannot know whether this nameless woman, whose two sons would have just reached fighting age on the eve of the next and vastly more destructive war, ever came to regret that she had raised them in the spirit of the "custodian of the holy fire."

Yet George's influence over life had its limits. Later that month, on July 28, two young officers, Adalbert Cohrs and Bernhard von Uxkull, drove to the Dutch border and, consummating a pact they had sealed with each other, committed suicide by simultaneous revolver shots. George had known them both for several years, having been introduced to them by Morwitz. Uxkull, who would have turned nineteen in September, had been a sensitive, somewhat shy boy, not particularly handsome — his hands were slightly too large, his ears stuck out a little too far, and his eyes were somewhat too wide — but he was precociously learned. At sixteen, he was said to know the history of Byzantium as well as any scholar, his knowledge based on a familiarity with the original Greek and Latin source texts. Cohrs, two and a half years older than his friend, was just the opposite: confident, athletic, vigorous, and practical. He seemed the born soldier, a self-assured man of action. But by that summer he had already been at the front for two years as an artillery observer and had seen too many young lives dispatched in the mass butchery. Even though Cohrs had served impeccably and had obediently fulfilled his duty, privately he hated and cursed the war. With his friends, he spoke approvingly of comrades who killed themselves when they were promoted and given the command of a unit rather than be forced to send others to their inevitable and unnecessary deaths. In the summer, after enjoying a long and restful leave, Cohrs received orders to return to the front as a commanding officer. Convinced that he would meet certain death anyway and unwilling to participate any longer in the meaningless bloodshed, Cohrs decided to take his own life.

When he revealed the plan to Bernard von Uxkull, his friend refused to allow him to die alone.

George was devastated. It was, he said, as if "both of my legs had been shot off." Edith Landmann saw him shortly after he had received the news of their deaths, and she recalled him "looking so wretched I was frightened." A few weeks later, in August, George fell ill again, so seriously that he had to be readmitted to the clinic in Heidelberg. During the following month his condition worsened further and he had to be transferred to Berlin to receive specialist treatment by Dr. Caspar, a noted urologist, who found bladder stones and extensive damage to his kidneys. It was not until the first week of October that George was again well enough to leave the sanatorium. A month later, on November 9, Wilhelm II abdicated his throne and went into exile in Holland. Two days after that, the war was finally over.

George and his circle in Heidelberg, 1919

Friedrich Wolters in 1927

Friedrich Gundolf in 1925

Ludwig Thormaehlen

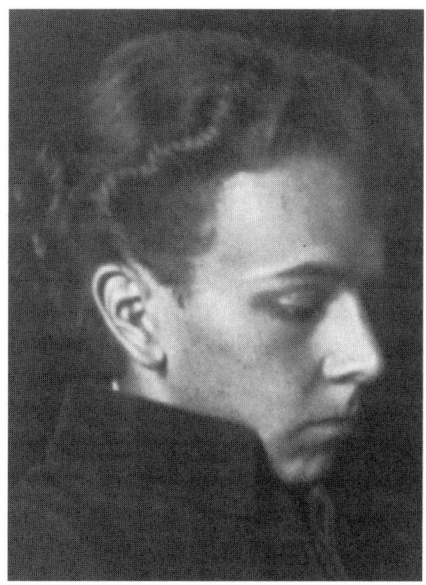

Max Kommerell

Hans Anton

Group portrait in Wolters's garden in Marburg.
From left to right: Anton, Volhard, George, Kommerell, Wolters, Elze

Claus, Berthold, and Alexander von Stauffenberg with their father

Claus and Berthold Stauffenberg in Berlin with George, just after his last and successful operation, in 1924

George in 1924

Title page of Ernst Kantorowicz's Friedrich the Second

Title page of Friedrich Wolters's history of the Blätter

Title page of Max Kommerell's The Poet as Leader

George at sixty, 1928

"Viktor" Frank Mehnert

George in 1931/32, the first winter spent in Minusio, Switzerland

George arm-in-arm with Frank Mehnert and Michael Stettler

George on the terrace of the house in Minusio with Mehnert

Part IV
PROPHET + 1919–1933
University + State + Empire

CHAPTER 35

Revolution I

The last major phase of George's life, spanning the fifteen years between the end of the war and his death in December 1933, was perhaps the most remarkable yet in an already extraordinary career. It was also the most portentous. In just under three decades he had transformed himself from an obscure poet writing in the French symbolist style, fastidiously shunning the attention of a broader public he professed to despise, into the leader of a large and growing movement in his native Germany, a movement that was being recognized as having increasingly relevant political implications for the country at large. Or rather, since George had never really wavered in his pursuit of his fundamental goal — to amass and exert maximum power over people and things — he had not so much changed as he had gradually expanded the focus of his efforts. At first satisfied to exercise his mastery over the world through the poetic word alone, George had quickly become impatient with the largely abstract authority poetry gave him. Soon he had turned his formative attentions to his fellow man, who proved to be a much more rewarding material than the dead letters of language, and finally to the larger sphere of life itself. Along the way, he and his associates had elaborated and refined their own code of values and behavior; they had devised their own rituals and symbols, and they had even discovered a new deity. What began as a purely poetic enterprise had become the catalyst for nothing less than fashioning a new mode of existence. In seeking to escape a world they detested, George and his adherents had invented an alternative universe governed by its own superior principles and laws, creating a new realm George oversaw as high priest, sovereign ruler, and anointed prophet.

But what is most arresting about this process is that, during this last phase of George's life, the separate domain he and the members of his circle had constructed for themselves began to appeal to an ever larger segment of the very German populace he had spent most of his life scorning, people who were now looking for guidance and certainty in a time short of both. The traumatic loss of the war, followed by a seemingly unending series of setbacks and failures, so seriously eroded confidence in traditional political, religious, and cultural institutions that many Germans felt disoriented and compelled to look elsewhere for substitutes. For many people during the turbulent 1920s, feeling as if they had been set adrift in a confusing and hostile environment, George's spiritual empire, his Secret Germany, came to represent the last, best refuge of confidence in the future, one of the few reliable sources of meaningfulness in life, and the only organization that preserved its inner integrity and an unfaltering sense of purpose throughout the tumult. More and more, George and his austere convictions were seen as offering a viable alternative to the inner and social aimlessness suffered by innumerable Germans, and ever larger numbers turned to him for consolation, direction, and hope.

"The disgrace and defeat and the entire baseness of my people has long since ceased to affect me," one representative petition to George reads, sent to him in late December 1918 by a young man who was returning home from captivity as a prisoner of war in Russia. "I am freed," the young man continued, "from any involvement in their external fate. Only in your pronouncements and nowhere else is Germany. The struggle of forces now taking place is of no interest to me. Nowhere is there a spiritual spark, a faith, a goal. Both the old and the new are empty husks. But everything must serve your work, even all these dreadful events, which you had foreseen long ago, will only extend the territory of your realm."

And so thought many more. During the critical years of the Weimar Republic, there were untold numbers of other bright, young, idealistic, and well-educated Germans — mainly, but not only, young men — who imagined that George's spiritual *Reich* was the more pure, the more real, the more substantial one. Those who embraced it ardently devoted themselves to its realization by internalizing his values while repudiating the reality around them. It is even in the best of times a dangerous illusion to believe that the intangible realm of ideas is the preferable, because unsullied, arena of political engagement. In periods of tremendous social instability, when clearheaded thinking and decisive action are especially needed, such dreaminess can become life-threatening, both to oneself and to others. As a political party arose in Germany that self-consciously wrapped itself in language and imagery that bore a vague but calculated affinity to George's Spiritual Empire, not a few took it to be the final consummation of his vision in real, concrete terms. For those who only subsequently awakened to their error — assuming it was one — as well as for those who never did, it would already be too late.

During the last weeks of the war, the historian Friedrich Meinecke, a political moderate and levelheaded patriot, used a letter to a friend to take stock of the national situation and to hazard his own somber prognosis for the future:

> A fearful and gloomy existence awaits us in the best of circumstances! And although my hatred of the enemy, who remind me of beasts of prey, is as hot as ever, so is my anger and resentment at those German power-politicians who, by their presumption and their stupidity, have dragged us down into this abyss. Repeatedly in the course of the war, we could have had a peace by agreement, if it had not been that the boundless demands of the Pan-German-militaristic-conservative combine made it impossible. It is fearful and tragic that this combine could be broken only by the overthrow of the whole state.

It was a bleak assessment but not an isolated one. Although nearly everyone had yearned for the war to end and had been prepared to accept almost any reasonable provision to achieve peace, few had foreseen, much less wished for, the collapse of the whole empire. When Prince Max von Baden, the last German chancellor appointed under Wilhelm II, suggested on the morning of November 9 to Friedrich Ebert, the leader of the Social Democratic Party, that Ebert take over the chancellorship, far more than a simple transfer of power took place. An entire world came crashing down.

George was jubilant. In one swift gesture, the political apparatus that had upheld the German state he had hated all his life had been swept aside, creating an unprecedented opportunity, perhaps, to establish the one he administered. It was a moment for which George had long been ready. As recently as February of that same year, Friedrich Wolters, who still had trouble always distinguishing between the fates of the official and secret Germanys, had expressed his concern to George that the probable victory of the allies over Germany, together with the demoralization a German defeat would inevitably entail, would lead to a general antagonism toward their own "state." George's followers, if not George himself, had after all made it appear as if the war were "their" war and that the expected victory would be theirs as well. Given the likelihood of defeat, however, their identification with the war might prove a liability, turning people against them and their cause. George was quick to set Wolters straight: "The conclusion is not correct that after such a victory and such a defeat the Spiritual Empire would have the entire world as its enemy. The Spiritual Empire had and has the entire world as its enemy with and without victory." Now, not just with the war over, but with the Prussian monarchy destroyed and its control over Germany abolished, there was even less reason to feel defeated. On the contrary: George experienced it as a triumph.

Indeed, during the closing months of the war, George had seemed to sense that something momentous was in the offing, and he frequently spoke of the possibility, even the desirability of severe political upheavals the end would bring. In the summer, which he had spent with the Landmanns in the Hessian resort of Bad Nauheim, he had already begun to imagine what the postwar order would — or should — look like. "You probably think," he had told Julius Landmann, "that the solders who have risked their necks will come back to be the vassals of those who meanwhile have had time to make money." While it was conceivable that there might simply be a return to the old order, George thought it would be a disaster and a terrible waste if the returning soldiers allowed themselves to be reabsorbed into the same structures that had made it necessary for them to fight in the first place. For "if they would do that, if no Revolution would come, no Bolshevism, then that would be the worst, then they would be enslaved, lifeless. There is at least chaos in Russia." George was so eager to see change, any change, occur that he appears to have been willing to take even Russia, which he normally considered beneath contempt, as a model. It was not that he viewed Bolshevism as the best course. But at least what it represented was an undeniable break with the old way.

Mainly, George just wanted something to happen. "There is a very particular impatience," he said, still to the Landmanns, "when one foresees everything from the first moment on and then events come limping along so slowly." One virtue of revolutions was that they tended to move with satisfying speed: "Through them the necessary change is achieved more quickly, the delay of which prolongs peoples' suffering." Of course, as George recognized, revolutions can also cause as much, or more, suffering as they alleviate. Nor did George shy away from the price a revolution would levy. As he saw it, Germany faced two options: "Continue muddling along or Revolution. In the former instance, everything deteriorates slowly, in the second it happens more quickly. 'I prefer that,'" George coldly declared. "'People die in that case. That is never a bad thing.'" Indeed, he regarded violence and sacrifice as integral to the political process as such. "A people that wants to attain political maturity," he said in late July 1918, "must first behead its king." What George did not say, although he surely knew, is that beheadings rarely stop there.

The insistence on the need for a revolution of whatever sort — and at whatever cost — became a kind of refrain in George's conversation during the summer and fall before the war's end. "The anarchy must become even greater," he had told a young friend in August, "otherwise the new will not be adopted." George was convinced, he added, that a "revolution or a long period of turmoil was necessary and unavoidable." Yet, when the Revolution did come in early November, George was, as always, hesitant about wholeheartedly embracing the very thing he had so actively promoted when it actually happened. To be sure, while he convalesced in Berlin from his last illness, George attentively followed developments unfolding there and in Munich. The Bavarian Socialists had preempted their northern comrades by deposing the ruling monarch — the last Wittelsbach king, Ludwig III — and proclaiming a Republic on November 7, four days earlier than the declaration in Berlin. The leader of the Bavarian movement was Kurt Eisner, who had honed his rhetorical and political skills as the editor of the agitative *Vorwärts* in Berlin. Although not himself a native of Munich — Eisner had in fact spent most of his career in the capital — he was a genuine "Schlawiner" and felt at home in the radical bohemian atmosphere of Schwabing, where he lived. And he also shared the lingering mistrust, even animosity toward Prussia that many southern Catholic Germans still felt. Thus, it was not merely political expediency, but also an expression of Eisner's own private principles that the program of the new "Bavarian People's Party" included the announcement: "Bavaria for the Bavarians! The present extreme economic and fiscal dependence of Bavaria upon the dominating north must be stopped at all costs. In all these areas we oppose unilateral, ruthless, Prussian rule because this led us to ruin in the past."

To George, all of this was very encouraging indeed. Here, finally, were politicians both declaring and acting upon ideas that he and his circle had been advancing for years, even decades. George and his followers had not been alone in urging them, naturally, but there had been a time when they were laughed at or ignored, dismissed as irrelevancies on the fringe of the cultural and political mainstream. Now, with Prussia discredited and the Empire it forged in shambles, the values George espoused suddenly had room to attain a legitimacy and currency they could never have enjoyed before. And despite the confusion and uncertainty about the future, George thought the current disarray was a thousand times preferable to the old morass. As he told a group of friends visiting him in Berlin that November, "he liked many things in Germany now better than before the war." Or, as another acquaintance recalled from the same time, George was visibly cheered by the "defeat of the German empire, which had freed the Master from a pressure he could hardly bear any longer." Still another remembered that George "viewed the defeat not as a disgrace but as deserved punishment, toward which the empty, pompous behavior of the second Empire necessarily led."

In general terms, the more chaotic the situation in Germany became, the more George seemed to like it. In January 1919, open street fighting broke out in Berlin among several competing political factions. Wolters, who was in the capital at the time, reported that traveling through the city "is more dangerous than a tour of duty in the field was, where you at least knew the enemy was only IN FRONT of you." Things had deteriorated to such an extent all over Germany, in fact, that Wolters was seriously thinking about accepting an offer to transfer to Switzerland, where Julius Landmann had arranged a position for him as the press officer at the German legation in Bern. Since this would be a significant step, Wolters first asked George for "masterly advice." George's response was measured but unambiguous. "Consider very carefully any such emigration!" he counseled, not so subtly advocating that Wolters stay put in Berlin where he was most useful. As for himself, George said that nothing could persuade him to leave the country in such promising circumstances: "Not even a golden carriage could carry *me* away now." Far from feeling threatened or apprehensive, George was in his element. Any way he viewed it, the loss of the war and the political consequences it brought were the best thing so far that had happened to Germany in his lifetime.

Nevertheless, when Karl Wolfskehl, who was impatient with standing idly by on the sidelines watching events unfold in Munich, suggested to George that the time seemed propitious to act and secure influence and power while it was still available for the taking, George hesitated. "I think the hour has not yet come for any activity," he told Wolfskehl on Armistice Day. Similarly, when Melchior Lechter inquired a week later whether he should take part in one of the political councils being formed to govern the new Republic and join a public appeal, George dissuaded him from taking that step as well. "Those are words," he said to Lechter through Gundolf, "from people who never had a clear plan before and thus cannot have one today." As late as the following summer, which George passed as usual with the Landmanns in Switzerland, Edith Landmann was still trying to press him toward some sort of political action. It seemed bizarre, she said, "when the whole world is crying out for leaders and does not know in which direction to go, the only ones who know the way are standing by and looking on." George remained impervious. "If we would emerge with a political program today," he responded, "we would not satisfy anyone. The new Empire would have to count in the thousands first."

That was it: George's hesitancy was basically motivated by pragmatic calculations. Although the conditions in Germany were more favorable to his cause than ever before, he thought the moment was not yet fully ripe. His movement was still too small, his followers still too few, and the rest of Germany still too unprepared to take his lead. George saw his role, as he had always done, as consisting in educating his audience, changing their ways of thinking and acting, and readying them for the future he was confident he foresaw. Only once his preparatory work was completed would it then be possible for his ideas to assume full political reality. "If someone seizes power one day," George elaborated to Frau Landmann, "if an Imperator will come after a Revolution, then one can perhaps follow him. Today nothing can be done." What cannot be done today, though, may well be accomplished tomorrow, and George saw his charge in making ready for the Imperator, or *Führer,* to come.

To refrain from direct political intervention did not mean, however, not to engage in any activity at all. Yet it had to be in a form George recognized and could approve of. Almost immediately after the war ended, he thus began making arrangements for a new issue of the *Blätter für die Kunst*. The last one to appear had been published in the fall of 1914, and any number of obstacles had made assembling and printing another number difficult to impossible ever since. But now, with the general sense in the air of embarking on new and uncharted waters, it seemed appropriate to mark the occasion by returning to his own point of departure. In 1917, the *Blätter* had quietly observed its twenty-fifth year of existence, and George had even considered bringing out a commemorative issue then, only to scotch the plan for obscure editorial reasons. Nothing stood in his way in late 1918, though, and he quickly set to putting the familiar machinery into motion. Even though it did not appear until December of the following year, the volume was essentially finished by June. George's desire that this issue of the *Blätter* should have a far-reaching effect is revealed not least by the number of copies printed. At its inception in 1892 the *Blätter* had had a run of only one hundred copies; for its belated anniversary twenty-six years later, two thousand were produced and widely distributed.

As it happened, it was also to be the final issue of the journal, bringing to an end the endeavor that had accompanied George throughout almost all of his poetic career, indeed that had been the central, defining focus of his ambitions for much of his adult life. But neither George nor the *Blätter* showed any indication of melancholy or weariness — both were as pugnacious as ever. And George also made certain that his motives in publishing the journal were sufficiently clear. He may have fought shy of openly advocating a particular political stance, but he still very much regarded his efforts as having a distinctly political purpose and as aimed at affecting present realities. A year later, in the winter of 1920, he happened to be in Lechter's workshop and spied the most recent *Blätter* lying on a table. George took it in his hand and, raising it triumphantly in the air, exclaimed, "*This* is Germany's victory over France!"

The last issue of the *Blätter für die Kunst* did not just have the highest production run, it is also the most massive of the series, weighing in at just over three hundred pages. (Actually, it combines two issues — what would have been the eleventh and the twelfth — in one.) It is also the most uniform in appearance and design, the purest expression of the collective spirit that the *Blätter* and its members had repeatedly professed as their ideal and goal. None of the authors of the several hundred poems it contains is identified; in fact, no personal names appear anywhere except on the title page where George is listed as the journal's founder and Carl August Klein is listed as the editor, despite the fact that he had effectively disappeared from the scene long ago. Otherwise, it is vintage *Blätter*. The volume opens with a combative unsigned introduction that situates the present endeavor within the larger historical context of the moment. But rather than making any explicit reference to the events of the day, the anonymous author haughtily directs the reader to "the earlier volumes that offer everything that is essential about the relationship between poetry and art · between life and art." Instead, he announces that he will confine himself to the observation "that beyond the individual successful poem the value of greater interconnected poetic utterances is being recognized more and more." That is to say, people have begun to realize that poetry or literature as a whole does not merely offer entertainment or diversion but contains deeper truths about life itself. Yet, while it was perhaps gratifying that growing numbers of people were beginning to understand the real power of poetry, that was something the associates of the *Blätter* had known, and said, all along. "Even if," the introduction continued, "many a public figure already admits that he would have been better informed about the 'signs of the times' and 'what is really happening in the world' from books of poetry than from newspapers: that does not mean very much! Only a few can be aware that in the poetry of a people its ultimate fate is revealed." What others were only just waking up to was an ancient truth. And poetry did not just tell the truth; it foretold the future.

What kind of fate George now thought awaited his people emerges most bleakly in one of his own poems he included in the *Blätter*. Called "The Burning of the Temple," it is a short, eight-page dramatic poem very similar in form and conception to the "The Induction into the Order" that had appeared in the fifth issue of the *Blätter* in 1901. As in that earlier piece, here too George presents us with a broadly generic religious order — the five speaking characters are all "Priests" and identified individually only as "The Elder," "The First," "The Second," and so on — and this fraternity obviously evokes associations with the "order" George himself presided over. But as the title of "The Burning of the Temple" implies, the poem documents, or rather fictionalizes, a military and cultural disaster. The temple stands at the center of a city that has been overrun by an unnamed race of giant warriors led by a conqueror with the barbaric-sounding name, "Ili." And Ili embodies a mercilessly destructive force. The opening lines of the poem describe him as laying waste in one campaign a civilization that took generations to form: "What years built," the Elder priest says, "he topples in a *single* day." Yet the conqueror does not destroy indiscriminately or out of hatred; as another priest says, he is "too cold to hate." Rather, he has set out on an almost methodical drive to obliterate a culture he dispassionately regards as sterile and obsolete. When the city's merchants appeal to him, lamenting that the high taxes he has imposed are ruining them, his only, chilling response is "Whoever cannot live under me · must die." When mothers beseech him to provide food for their starving newborns, he contemptuously compares them all to animals, saying, "It would be better to strangle the litter of the women whelping on the streets." But the conqueror seems intent not just on eliminating those elements he considers undesirable or worthless but on eradicating the entire society. He absently listens to the priests' pleas to spare their holy sanctuary and then answers them in words that not incidentally bear a close resemblance to some of the comments George himself had made at the beginning of the war. "You cannot reverse the rot of your land," the conqueror tells the priests. "What are the gods who no longer help you? / What the books, images that no longer elevate you? / Thank him who frees you from the clutter." As a last resort, a young princess goes to him, desperately begging him to show mercy for her people. After turning "his chaste clear barbarian eye" toward her, he calmly pronounces his final judgment:

> "I have been sent with torch and with steel —
> So that I may harden you all · not that you should soften me
> You know not what avails you · I must rob you ·
> Degenerate as you are · if you do not surrender that
> Which only makes you weaker. So stipulates the law."

At that, realizing that nothing would win the conqueror's leniency, the princess commits suicide. The poem ends with the Eldest priest announcing to his brethren that flames were already licking up the four corners of their refuge: "The temple is burning. One half a millennium / Must pass by before it rises anew."

Although it is uncertain what precisely the Temple is supposed to represent, George may have intended its destruction to signify the dissolution of political and social structures taking place all over postwar Europe. Given the close parallel between the conqueror's verdicts and many of George's own long-held views welcoming annihilation as the indispensable prerequisite for eventual renewal — alongside of the uncritical, almost admiring portrait he paints of the ruthless "barbarian" — one might conclude that George regarded the abolishment of the old order that the temple exemplifies as welcome or at least necessary. But in the year that elapsed between the first few exciting weeks of revolutionary unrest and the publication of the new *Blätter* in December 1919, the almost giddy optimism George had initially felt had been deflated, having given way to bitter disappointment and even a dejected gloom.

The main external cause of this dramatic shift in mood seems to have been the disastrous diplomatic failure of the Versailles Treaty. Faced with the territorial loss of Alsace-Lorraine, the French occupation of the fertile and coal-rich Rhineland, the division of East Prussia by the Danzig Corridor, the humiliation of being obliged to reduce the army to a token 100,000-man volunteer force, and burdened with reparations that would officially amount to $33 billion, countless Germans thought they were being singled out for cruel and unfair punishment. They became convinced of the injustice of the arrangements when the German delegates made the terrible miscalculation of agreeing to Article 231, which stated that Germany alone had been responsible for instigating the war. After the treaty was signed on June 28, 1919, George, like virtually every other German, angrily denounced it, saying that "Europe was sold by this peace." Ten years later, he still spoke of the deep feelings of "shame and disgrace" he had experienced under the mortifying conditions the treaty had imposed.

In addition to the peace treaty itself, which was bad enough, it was particularly galling that the Americans, under the leadership of President Woodrow Wilson, had emerged from the conflict as a new world power. Even before the war had ended it had been evident that the United States would play a major role in managing the peace. Friedrich Wolters was appalled by the very thought. As happy as he was to see the Prussian state dismantled, he shuddered at the prospect of submitting to American directives. It was "ignominious," Wolters had written Gundolf in October 1918, "that the most repulsive riffraff from across the ocean should tell us what to do and it is horrifying to think that the revenge of godless peoples should devastate and defile our sacred lands." Germans felt they were being treated as second-class citizens, forced to accept terms intentionally designed to abase and hobble their country. Not surprisingly, the anger and frustration many Germans felt over the treaty became directed toward Wilson himself, whom they held personally accountable for having permitted the French and English to carve up Germany into digestible pieces. But it was a sign of the profound disappointment over both the lost war and the lost peace that the one man who had rashly promised to save Europe from itself became widely regarded as its destroyer.

No matter who was ultimately held answerable for the final shape of the treaty (and the list of scapegoats would steadily lengthen over the years), Germans of every political persuasion reacted to its harsh stipulations with outrage, indignation — and dread. Many condemned the agreement as a form of virtual enslavement and saw in it the formalized expression of hatred toward their entire culture. Most considered it a thinly veiled attempt to take vengeance for all the real or perceived transgressions Germany had committed in the past. Indeed, not a few Germans viewed the entente as merely an insidious continuation of the war by diplomatic means and ominously predicted that sooner or later it would lead to a violent backlash.

Within George's circle it was a common conviction as well that the Versailles accord was a debacle that would result only in an even greater disaster. In May 1919, just before the treaty was finalized, Ernst Glöckner noted in his diary that "this preliminary peace means war for decades to come, Bolshevism, famine, murder, and lawlessness, mass death, misery for generations." Saying that reading over the treaty's provisions had caused him "perhaps the most dismal hours of my life," Glöckner despondently revealed a prescient foreboding. "From this day onward," he wrote, "people will later reckon a time that will belong among the most terrible the world has ever experienced." Instead of ensuring lasting peace and stability, Glöckner thought the treaty "will lay waste the entire world."

George's own formal reaction to the Versailles Treaty came in the guise of a short poem, "To the Dead," which he included in the last *Blätter*. The poem made its first appearance just as the treaty conference was coming to a close. In early June, George called his friends together to convene for a three-day meeting in Heidelberg, where he wanted to read aloud to them from his new work. Among those present were Berthold Vallentin, Ernst Morwitz, Glöckner, Thormaehlen, Woldemar Uxkull, Percy Gothein, and Erich Boehringer. Erich's brother, Robert, was unable to attend because Mainz, where he lived, lay within the French occupied territory. Friedrich Wolters was also absent owing to a lingering illness he had contracted during the concluding months of the war and still prevented him from traveling. Those who managed to attend all stayed in the rooms occupied by Gundolf on the ground floor of the Villa Lobstein, a large, elegant, neo-Renaissance structure at the top of the stairs on the hill leading up to the Heidelberg castle. Although they were happy to see one another again, some after a considerable interval, the developments of the last several months unavoidably cast a solemn pall over the proceedings, an atmosphere even discernible in some of the photographs taken of the gathering.

George's poem "To the Dead" would have done little to brighten his friends' spirits. In it, the poet appears in his full oracular guise and the prophesy he delivers — or, depending on one's view, the incitement he commits — portends not one but two more wars to come. In these future conflagrations, it promises, the German people will rise up again and, by avenging the shame visited on them by their subduers, will join the slain soldiers, now hailed as heroes, who had fallen in the first one:

> If this generation will one day have cleansed itself of disgrace
> Will have flung off the shackles of slavery
> Will only feel an innermost hunger for honor:
> Then the bloody glow will flare up on the field of battle
> Full of endless graves . . then thunderous armies will

> Swoop down on clouds then there will roar through the fields
> The most terrible terror the third of the storms:
> The return of the dead!
>
> If this people will ever arouse itself from cowardly torpor
> And remember itself its election and its mission:
> Then the divine explanation of indescribable horror
> Will be revealed to it . . then hands will be raised
> And mouths will resound in the praise of dignity
> Then the king's standard with the true sign
> Will flutter in the wind at dawn and will greet with a bow
> The Glorious Heroes!

Without going so far as to invest George with actual divinatory abilities, it is striking how much of this vision, even in its particulars, eventually came to pass. Not just that resentment over the Versailles Treaty helped propel a regime into power that promised to reverse its effects by any means necessary, but also that the trappings of that regime and the forms of behavior it inspired — the "raised hands" and "resounding mouths" — all seem disconcertingly prefigured in the poem. Even more strikingly, a "true sign" emblazoned on a banner would turn out to be the defining symbol of that future regime, to become perhaps the most recognizable and notorious emblem of all time — an emblem, moreover, that George and his companions had adopted as their own and promulgated as a sign of their movement.

Despite the shared sense of pessimism and discouragement everyone felt throughout most of 1919, however, George himself did not sink into listlessness. If anything, the very desolation that had been visited on Germany seemed to energize him, and he actively looked for ways to take advantage of the vacuum created by the downfall of the old order. When Edith Landmann asked him that summer if he would not consider spending the winter in Basel to escape the disturbances many expected would break out all over Germany, George declined the invitation, saying, "Ach, there is too little unrest there." What was needed, he thought, was not an avoidance of conflict but a little strategic prodding to further the inevitable confrontation along. But one had to be careful. "Until now we have still got away unscathed," George confided to Frau Landmann, referring to his band of followers, "but if we would emerge with a political program, the battle would come, immediately. Then the bourgeois would see how we despise them." Apparently, by the end of the year, just after the *Blätter* had appeared, George thought the time had come to set aside any remaining reservations he might have had and to go on the offensive.

In early January 1920, during his yearly sojourn in Berlin, George, accompanied by Wolters, paid a visit to Vallentin. Not wanting to lose the momentum generated by the new *Blätter,* George had decided to revive the *Yearbook for the Spiritual Movement* as well. Although originally conceived as an annual journal, the last one to appear had come out at the end of 1911. Everything had changed in the meantime, and George intended the *Yearbook* to reflect that change. In unveiling his plan to Vallentin, he specified that the introduction should deal directly with "the political." A new *Yearbook,* George elaborated, would make sense only "if it took a particular new spiritual position as its starting point. This time, it is one that pertains to the political. This time there was no way to avoid politics." Vallentin objected, saying that they had always scrupulously warded off any political contamination of the spiritual sphere by political affairs. George insisted on the contrary that, while "politics had previously left the spiritual realm untouched, it now weighs so heavily on our lives that we cannot avoid taking a stance toward it." Moreover, he continued, the circumstances had never been as propitious as they currently were. It was true that "earlier the political might of the governing powers had also been so great that one would have been unable to do something against them. Today that is no longer the case. It could be that our powers would suffice to become active in some way and in a newly created moment it becomes necessary and very promising." Well into the summer, George repeatedly spoke of his wish that the new *Yearbook* should "tackle the major political movements of the present."

With the rejuvenation of the *Yearbook* underway and the *Blätter* circulating again, George must have felt that, even though the final prospects were fairly dim, at least he was expediting the inevitable. But there was also a new weapon in his arsenal, one that would become increasingly important over the next several years and would in fact far eclipse all others in the magnitude and depth of its impact. The introduction to the *Blätter* had made oblique reference to this other vehicle for propagating the circle's ideology, pointing out that "the secondary stage of our influence has also become visible in the meantime — through significant widely admired books of knowledge and overview." Specifically, there were two such books that had recently appeared and had indeed met with great popular success as well as critical esteem. In 1916, Gundolf had published a monumental book on Goethe. Although more than eight hundred pages long, and despite the distractions of the war, it sold out instantly. Only a year later, in December 1917, Gundolf told George that Bondi was already arranging for a fourth edition "since almost all copies of the third have already been ordered before it has appeared." *Goethe* became a bestseller, and not just by academic standards: by 1931, there were fifty thousand copies in print. Even Gundolf's colleagues reacted with similar, if not uniform, enthusiasm. In 1921, the editors of *Euphorion,* a scholarly periodical dedicated to German literature that still exists today, published a special issue devoted exclusively to Gundolf's work, including articles and reviews by some of the leading scholars of German literature of the day. Not all of the contributions were positive, and some were quite critical, but the very fact that the entire volume focused on the book was in itself a testament to its perceived importance.

What allowed Gundolf's *Goethe* to appeal to such a broad public, to gain the attention, if not always the respect, of his academic peers, as well as an avid following among average, educated readers, was, first of all, his genuinely original view of the poet. It was based less on a careful analysis of individual works or of biographical details than on the premise that Goethe represented the measure and model for our existence, and that his every utterance, his every action and experience was a necessary expression of his being. Not only his poems, plays, and novels, Gundolf argued, but Goethe's entire life formed the material for his creative energy. Instead of treating the life and works as separate spheres, Gundolf regarded them as parts of a larger indivisible unity. This was a new and radical departure from the way biographies had been written before, and it came to form the conceptual or methodological basis on which modern literary biography would rest. It was the attempt to understand Goethe from this comprehensive totalizing perspective, one that focused on the dynamic forces underlying every aspect of Goethe's life — a life Gundolf saw as a seamless, almost self-sufficient whole that gave its own laws unto itself — that was especially attractive to a generation that felt it had lost nearly all other political and cultural certainties.

Too, and at least as important, Gundolf was a brilliant, almost mesmerizing writer, able to make what in less skilled hands would be dry and abstract pedantry glisten with vitality, intelligence, and wit. Even his detractors acknowledged that Gundolf was an extraordinarily gifted writer, with many even going so far as to claim that his book was less a work of scholarship than a work of art (although some intended the description as an implicit repudiation of his scholarly credentials). Thomas Mann recognized this quality and found a name for it, likening Gundolf's book to an "intellectual novel." It is an apt description: the book often reads like a highbrow adventure tale, with the hero-as-protagonist moving through a life that has all of the purposiveness and forward drive of a literary creation.

But the final and perhaps most significant reason for the enormous success of the book had little to do with either Goethe or Gundolf at all. Some of the reviewers noticed that "Gundolf does not just want to describe Goethe" but that he was animated by larger "pedagogical needs" and by "a decided inclination toward hero worship." His most perceptive readers recognized that Gundolf was interested, as his essay for the last *Yearbook* had been titled, in "models," in exemplary figures who embodied what was great, timeless, and enduring. In such men — for they were of course always men — Gundolf saw the highest expression of humanity. They healed the split between body and spirit, thinking and doing, instinct and knowledge. Or, as Gundolf himself put it, "In certain heroes the unity of culture is restored." Goethe, in Gundolf's portrait, was one such hero. But even he, the great Olympian, the sage of Weimar, the renewer of German culture, had not achieved the pinnacle reached only by a later paragon and leader. Gundolf's study of Goethe, that is, in addition to its internal objectives, was also a kind of preliminary study for a greater subject, a preparatory essay laying out the historical and methodological foundations on which his understanding of that other, even more exceptional man would rest. For the real, though esoteric subject of Gundolf's *Goethe* was none other than Stefan George himself.

Virtually without precedent, Gundolf had thus created a new genre of writing. Neither conventional biography nor literary criticism nor historical study — besides its incandescent style, the book contains no footnotes, no index, no bibliography, or any other of the usual trappings of academic research — it is anything but disinterested objective scholarship. Rather, Gundolf was consciously using the figure of Goethe as an instrument to promote the specific ideological agenda associated with George and his circle. It was, one might say with only slight exaggeration, an elevated version of agitprop. George himself was acutely aware of — and energetically endorsed — the activist character of the book, just as he obviously approved of its purpose. He even coined a word for this new form of writing, a name that signaled the relationship to the Spiritual Empire it was designed to foster. George called the works written by his followers in this vein "Spirit Books" — *Geistbücher*. And to make sure that everyone understood what their real aim was, he regularly told his listeners, "*Geistbücher* are politics."

As a further, visible sign that the books all belonged to a single class, that they were unified by a single spirit and dedicated to a single cause, George had Melchior Lechter devise a new emblem that would adorn each one in the series. Beginning in 1916, with the publication of Gundolf's *Goethe,* until 1934, a total of eighteen books would appear with Lechter's insignia embossed on the front cover in gold and printed on the title page. It is a circular design with the words "Blätter für die Kunst" running around the border. At the center, enclosed within an inner ring of stylized rays of light, is the unmistakable form of a swastika.

The swastika, we remember, had long been a part of the iconographic repertoire within George's circle. It had made its first appearance in the mid-1890s, when Alfred Schuler, who saw in it the symbolic distillation of his cosmic theories, had even considered replacing his name with the literally unspeakable sign of the "hooked cross." George briefly employed it as a decorative motif for his own works as well, using it, for example, to adorn the poems he copied out for Gundolf's twenty-second birthday in 1902. Six years later, the first volume of the Shakespeare translation was issued in a deluxe edition designed by Lechter that incorporated the swastika as a prominent ornamental feature. Each of the three *Yearbooks* had also displayed the symbol on the back cover. When Lechter thus proposed a drawing to Gundolf for his book on Goethe, which would inaugurate the planned new series, it made sense that Lechter availed himself of a character that not only boasted a twenty-year history within the circle itself, but also, given its widespread use in India, appealed to Lechter's own mystical leanings. As he wrote to Gundolf in January 1916, "It seemed to me that, as the signum for the scientific publications of the *Blätter*, the ambiguous, mysterious svastika, the rolling wheel, was quite an appropriate symbol." It was thus an intentionally enigmatic sign, attractive precisely because it had no fixed, stable meaning, allowing it to take on whatever significance George and his collaborators ascribed to it. Above all it had not been trivialized or contaminated by popular use.

In 1928, when the similarity between the *Blätter* mark and the Nazi party symbol could no longer be ignored, George had Bondi issue a formal statement. Pointing out that the sign "can be found as early as 1910 on publications of the *Blätter für die Kunst*," the pamphlet sought to validate the circle's prior claim to the swastika while making clear that it had no intention of forfeiting the vignette it felt rightfully belonged to it. "When this ancient (Indian) symbol was called *Hakenkreuz* in October 1918" the pamphlet read, "and took on its present meaning, the circle of the *Blätter für die Kunst* could not get rid of the signum it had introduced many years before." That seemed fair enough. The swastika had become a kind of brand label or logo of the *Blätter,* and George, who was much more finely attuned to such things than his aloof stance led many people to believe, did not want to surrender such a powerful trademark. But the brochure then concluded with a classic piece of *Blätter,* disingenuousness. "Whoever is even superficially familiar with the books published under this symbol," it reads, "ought to know that they have nothing to do with politics."

Although this remark has been subsequently taken as one of the "proofs" that George disavowed any connection between his realm and National Socialism, the gross equivocation of the statement should give anyone pause who wanted to stake such a large claim on it. For, as George himself said countless times and in as many contexts, not merely the books he printed under the banner of the swastika, but the whole sum of his activity over the previous two decades had been intensely, almost single-mindedly political. As always, though, it had to be politics as he understood it and under his sole direction. What George in fact meant in the Bondi brochure, then, was that the books that came out under his aegis had nothing to do with anyone else's politics but his own. Yet, by 1928, few people bothered to keep such fine distinctions in mind, especially since the areas of overlap were great enough to make worrying about a few discrepancies seem overly fastidious.

Politics aside, the extent to which George was not only the covert subject of the *Geistbücher* but also intimately involved in their writing and publication is revealed by the complicated birth of the next book in the series. In 1918, Ernst Bertram published his *Nietzsche: Essay in Mythology,* adorned with the new swastika emblem reserved for the circle's "scientific" works. Bertram's friend, Thomas Mann, who had read or listened to individual chapters of the book as it was being written, was enthralled, clearly recognizing both the programmatic affiliation to Gundolf's earlier work as well as its own substantial independent merits. "If one holds up your *Nietzsche* together with Gundolf's *Goethe,*" Mann wrote Bertram in September 1918, "then one cannot avoid thinking what a level of high culture, intuition, intelligence, and spirituality our literary history has achieved." Like Gundolf's book on Goethe, as well, Bertram's *Nietzsche* became a phenomenal success. In early 1919, only six months after its publication, it became the first recipient of the newly instituted Nietzsche Prize. By 1929, when the seventh edition appeared, there were twenty-one thousand copies of *Nietzsche* in print. So great became the influence of Bertram's book on the perception of Nietzsche during the critical two decades to follow that when Walter Kaufmann wrote a rehabilitation of the philosopher in 1950, he did so in explicit opposition to Bertram. For, as Kaufmann explained, "no other book on Nietzsche left so decisive a mark on the literature," and Kaufmann was determined to erase the stain he felt that mark had made. But, as Kaufmann also knew, Bertram — and Nietzsche — were only part of the story. The real origin and focal point of the book lay elsewhere.

Curiously, the book came into being not at George's direct instigation, but at the persistent prodding of Bertram's companion, Ernst Glöckner, who hopefully saw it as a means to bridge the gulf separating the two most important people in his life. Whereas Bertram always kept a measured distance between himself and George, Glöckner had delivered himself over entirely to the Master's service. Their relationship, while not completely free of tension, was intimate and, at least as far as Glöckner was concerned, passionate. Predictably, Bertram experienced periodic bouts of jealousy or mere petulance over his friend's seemingly divided loyalties, which Glöckner countered by attempting to enroll Bertram in the common struggle. As early as Christmas, 1914, a year and a half after Glöckner and George had met, Glöckner was trying to convince Bertram to put his considerable talents to use for the sake of

George's state. "We must become courageous and selfless if we want to live," Glöckner told him. "We ought to bring sacrifices only to the great cause, to the great God that has stepped into our midst." Bertram not only refused to acknowledge the reality of this god, he also stubbornly clung to his notions about individuality. Glöckner tried to set him straight. "Ernst, we *must* get beyond and over our little life and fate: the day does *not* belong to us anymore, but rather to the great goal. If you cannot see it alone: then see it through me. Make a sacrifice here, Ernst!"

What this sacrifice would entail Glöckner explained in another letter a few days later. "The necessity of influencing the youth — and the possibility for you to do it — the wish that you can and will do that *well*, are thoughts that have preoccupied me for a long time." In other words, Bertram should write a book, one that would impress and give instruction to the German youth. "Your abilities lie in this direction. You know a lot, you also have the form at your disposal to captivate young people and to attract them to you." The only question was: what should Bertram write about? Here, too, Glöckner was full of helpful suggestions. Although he knew Bertram was partial to Nietzsche, Glöckner preferred Novalis and particularly Hölderlin, "in whom I am *keenly* interested and whose stature is growing *un*believably, even beyond that of Nietzsche." Since it would be Bertram who would actually write the book, however, Glöckner thought it prudent to offer a compromise. "A study of Hölderlin-Nietzsche would be appropriate," he conceded, "and would certainly give you not a little pleasure." Still, Glöckner was well aware that there was an even higher test that had to be passed first. "Speak with Gundolf," he urged Bertram, in order to find out "whether such a topic is permissible." Without the go-ahead from Gundolf, which he would give only after — and if — he had secured George's blessing, the whole exercise would be a wasted effort.

George's own attitude toward Nietzsche was complex and underwent subtle changes over the course of his life. Nietzsche's name had made its first appearance in connection with George as early as 1893, when Carl August Klein mentioned him positively in an essay he wrote for the second issue of the *Blätter*. At the time, George was turning away from his French mentors and toward a more German patrimony he could embrace and appropriate as his own, and Nietzsche seemed a suitable ancestor. But even though Nietzsche was generally regarded as a worthy comrade-in-arms, George never viewed him entirely uncritically. (And most particularly never as an influence: in 1916, as Bertram was settling down to work on his book, George told Glöckner that he had become acquainted with Nietzsche's writings only "when everything essential was already settled in him; Hölderlin on the other hand very early on.") Even in the poem George devoted to Nietzsche in *The Seventh Ring,* his admiration for the mighty "Thunderer," as Nietzsche is called there, was tempered by the charge that he lacked a proper appreciation of poetry: "This new soul," the poem concludes, alluding to Nietzsche's own words in *Zarathustra,* "should have sung not spoken!" Or, as George put it somewhat more plainly in a conversation with Edith Landmann, Nietzsche "did not possess a sense for the genuinely poetic." What stirred George's deepest misgivings about Nietzsche, however, was his "betrayal" of his "master," Richard Wagner. That was something George could never forgive, neither in someone else's disciples nor in his own.

Yet this very reaction to Nietzsche's ostensible disloyalty, as well as to his presumed failure to fathom poetry, also underscores again the degree to which George understood other people, including Nietzsche, through the prism of his own life and experience, judging them by how they measured up to — or more often fell far short of — the image he had of himself. In those instances when Nietzsche's behavior or opinions corresponded to his own, George deemed them acceptable. "All of the negative things Nietzsche said about Germany in *Ecce Homo,*" George once approvingly noted, for example, "are still valid today." Likewise, while commenting on his own itinerant way of life, his incessant travels from town to town, George said of himself that he "lived nowhere. It was the same way with Nietzsche as well." But George subjected those aspects of Nietzsche's life which differed from his own to harsh censure. At the top of George's list was what he saw as Nietzsche's inability to produce disciples. In another exchange with Frau Landmann in the summer of 1919, while George was reminiscing about the Cosmic Circle, he criticized its principal members — Klages, Schuler, and Wolfskehl — for having neglected to leave a vital legacy: "They all did not know how to procreate. They did not have a single disciple, just as little as Nietzsche did." George even suggested that, had Nietzsche managed to attract followers of his own, Nietzsche might have had more of an effect on him. George said that if he had ever "heard something impressive about his life, that he had had disciples, then that would have been closer to him." As it was, Nietzsche had died bereft, with no one to carry on his spirit, leaving his life's work effectively squandered. As time went on, George became even more adamant in his criticism of Nietzsche, and in the late 1920s he had almost nothing but negative comments to make about him. "He has neither personality, nor doctrine, nor direction," George once sweepingly and rather puzzlingly said. In early 1926, when someone mentioned Nietzsche's relationship to the visual arts, George cut short the conversation by announcing, "One can say nothing about that because Nietzsche didn't have one."

No doubt, George's preoccupation with Nietzsche, his need to compare himself to Nietzsche if only to demonstrate his own superiority, bespeaks a more ambivalent posture toward him than George was prepared to admit. There was much in Nietzsche's thought that intrinsically appealed to George, both temperamentally as well as ideologically, but George could not bear the notion that he might be dependent on a forerunner or that any of his ideas were not his alone. At most, Nietzsche could be permitted to stand as a laudable, even useful pioneer but ultimately fell as a profoundly flawed character.

When George thus heard of Bertram's plan to write a book about the philosopher, it must have aroused a peculiar mixture of emotions in him. In the spring of 1917, Kurt Hildebrandt visited George in Heidelberg and the Master revealed that "someone" — it was George's congenital habit never to give away more information than he had to — was working on a new book on Nietzsche, an undertaking George said he applauded, saying it would be beneficial "to determine what still had validity in Nietzsche." This "someone's" book would be valuable because it would take stock, sift through Nietzsche to identify what could be safely discarded and what was still worth saving. And, in George's eyes, anything in Nietzsche that would serve to advance his own program had more than enough justification to survive.

Bertram's *Nietzsche* was therefore intended to perform several, and potentially conflicting, functions at once: from George's perspective, its critical contribution was to clear away the unproductive features of Nietzsche's thought — that is, those which most conflicted with George's own — and, most crucially, to show how Nietzsche had prepared the way for the advent of an even greater spirit. For Glöckner, it would ideally mediate between, and if possible bring together, his Master and his friend. But for Bertram the book had only a single purpose, one completely unrelated to George, his circle or even the outside world. In January 1918, when Bertram had finished the main body of the manuscript and sent it to Glöckner, his friend complimented Bertram with words of sincere praise. "You have really achieved something quite extraordinary," Glöckner wrote to him. "And I thus congratulate you, dear Ernst, on your first work, which will open the broader public to you, which will make you a name of the best kind." To Bertram, who suffered from recurring anxieties that Glöckner could be lured away from him by George, these words worked like balsam on his fears, triggering an outburst of gratitude and, even more, relief. "Thank you my dearest bosom friend for having given me the possibility of finishing this work and to make *you* happy with it," Bertram wrote. "You should know that the entire work, good or not good, is a gift from *you*. And that anything that can possibly come into being in the future can be accomplished solely through your love."

Labor of love it might have literally been for Bertram, but it still had to pass muster with George before it could be published by Bondi. (And Bertram was very concerned that it appear specifically with Bondi and no one else: when some other friends tried to persuade him to go to another publisher — namely to Kurt Wolff in Munich — Bertram told Glöckner that "I would *much* prefer Bondi because of the whole atmosphere.") In writing the book, Bertram thus clearly kept his principal readers — and evaluators — in mind, taking care to satisfy the criteria he knew would be applied to it. When Glöckner read the manuscript, he also recognized his friend's strategy and commended one chapter, called 'Prophecy,' in particular: " 'Prophecy' made a great impression on me, an exemplary chapter that will have a strong effect on George. It almost tells his life with a change of names, his character is elucidated in its essentials and the being of a prophetic person has probably never before been seen so clearly as in this instance." Tellingly, Bertram responded to Glöckner's enthusiasm for the tight parallel he had drawn between Nietzsche and George with pronounced coolness, even discomfort. The very fact that it would likely be positively received by George, Bertram dryly wrote, ought to be regarded "perhaps in this case as an objection." More generally, Bertram worried that "too much George has found its way into the book." When Glöckner read this, he reacted with all the fervor and conviction of a true believer. "And if there is a lot of George in the book, does that do any harm?" he rhetorically asked Bertram. "Would the book have even been possible without him? I always think: one day, everything will have to orient itself toward this unique person; whether the world wants to or not is no longer even the question. If anything at all remains of our time — including the clamor and tumult of war — then it is he and his work. Those who reached this insight earlier than the others should count themselves lucky! So no more uneasiness about that."

But Bertram's distress was just beginning. While George was in Munich during the late winter and early spring of 1918, Bertram read much of the book aloud to him, usually to unreserved applause. "He repeatedly declared my book the best possibility and way of conveying N's image today," Bertram reported to Glöckner after one such session in March. On another occasion, Bertram said that George "grunted approvingly all the way through and said afterward 'very good, very good, that is very good.' " Apparently convinced that it might qualify as an official *Blätter* publication, George instructed Bertram to send it to Gundolf for his opinion and, if it met with Gundolf's approval as well, to send it on to Bondi with the recommendation to publish it. Gundolf was largely positive, but often his compliments sound slightly backhanded — the book, he wrote Bertram, for example, was "new and nowhere, as was the danger, boring" — and Gundolf suggested various editorial revisions, factual corrections, and stylistic improvements.

At long last, after Bertram had made most of the proposed adjustments, the book finally appeared in August 1918. It bore the dedication "To my friend Ernst Glöckner" and was embellished with the swastika that signaled membership to the circle associated with George. Even though Bertram had been less than entirely happy with the wearying process, and despite the fact that even after the protracted vetting the book had undergone it still did not conform to official circle orthodoxy in every detail, the end result nevertheless bore the unmistakable traces of the atmosphere in which and for which it was written. Glöckner himself summed it up well in a letter to Bertram:

> What Gundolf achieved in a different way with his *Goethe* you have achieved with *Nietzsche* in your own: both, however, have arrived at a *single* goal: they have raised up these figures again from the depths so that they now stand there like radiant idols. A common trait occasioned them both, something that had been lacking in all previous portrayals and also distinguishes them from those earlier attempts: the respectful reverence in the service of a great human being, so that one can see the divine in them again and revere this in them once more. It is the fact that this feeling is so strong in both books which makes them appear as belonging together, and which is also made visible externally through their same attire.

Over the next decade and half, sixteen more books — all devoted to the idolization of "great" men — would be published with more or less the same intention, by roughly the same procedure and all with the same "attire." Some would find greater resonance than others, a few would fundamentally alter the way their subjects were perceived, and a number failed to generate much excitement at all. But as a group, and in their common aim, they had an impact that went far beyond the appreciation of the individual figures they treated and deeply influenced the way cultural history in general came to be written and viewed in Germany. And it was an influence that was recognized almost immediately. As early as 1921, the eminent scholar and theologian Ernst Troeltsch wrote an article titled "The Revolution of Science" ("Die Revolution der Wissenschaft") that focused on the central role George was playing in fomenting what Troeltsch called "this spiritual Revolution." Troeltsch also noticed that there was something paradoxical, even contradictory about the whole movement. "For," he wrote, "the 'revolution of science' is in truth the beginning of the great world reaction against the democratic and socialist enlightenment, against the rational self-majesty of an understanding that organizes existence without restraint and against the presupposed dogma of the equality and reasonableness of human beings." This revolution was thus different from the political one taking place, and it pursued opposite goals. Another way of putting it, Troeltsch concluded, borrowing a comment that Novalis had made about Edmund Burke, was that "these books are all basically 'revolutionary books against the revolution.'"

However one defined it, this was probably not the revolution George had originally been looking for after the war. But it was a beginning nonetheless. And, as Troeltsch himself reminded his readers, a "spiritual" revolution should not be discounted simply because it occurred in a realm invisible to the eye. Sending a warning to those who saw nothing but harmless romanticism in the intellectual convulsions he was describing, Troeltsch realized that people who took seriously only "the powerful industrial complexes and workers' organizations as well as the restructuring of the world political situation will of course see only the impotence of such romanticism. But whoever knows the simultaneous importance of doctrines and ideals will nevertheless not regard the spiritual transformation as something without significance or consequence."

To someone who had always believed that the spiritual realm was the prime mover of the physical one, this was hardly news. But George could at least take it as a sign that the rest of the world may be coming around to an awareness that its fate may not rest in the hands of those who occupy the conventional seats of power. Reality, George thought, was only the final form of what had taken shape long before in spirit. "Everything that is in the sacred books," he told Ernst Robert Curtius in April 1919, using a term he now liked to employ in order to refer to his own works, "has always come true and always will come true. That's the way it always is with sacred books. We first have to go through a period of complete disintegration. But then things will get better again. That is the one consolation I can give to everyone. Whether we live to see it is of course uncertain. But the spiritual solutions have all been found already." For George, the question was not what would happen but when.

CHAPTER 36
Treason

With all of the renewed and even intensified activity going on around him, George could afford to think that he had weathered the war with his operation more or less intact. True, the war had inflicted some considerable, even irreplaceable losses. Although none of his oldest and most valuable companions had fallen — Gundolf, Wolters, Morwitz, Hildebrandt, Vallentin, Thormaehlen, and Wolfskehl had all managed to survive one way or the other — there were many others who had not been so fortunate. Some, as we saw, had died in combat, such as Heinrich Friedemann, Norbert von Hellingrath and his university friend Wolfgang Heyer, while others had been unable to bear the torment of looking on at the endless killing any longer and had taken their own lives in despair. Less than a month before the war ended, Walter Wenghöfer, a quiet and unobtrusive man of forty-one years who had published several poems in the *Blätter* but had gradually retreated to the outer edges, committed suicide by drowning himself in the river running through the city of Magdeburg where he lived. The summer after Wenghöfer's death, George mentioned him in passing, saying only that Wenghöfer "was once in the innermost circle, only he lacked the ability to grow." Apparently, George believed that Wenghöfer had merely drawn the obvious consequence of his personal failings. Yet Wenghöfer's self-destruction, like the deaths of all the others, while regrettable, did not strike at the solid core. And with so much of what he had apparently foreseen coming to pass, George had less reason than ever to doubt that he and his "program" would finally prevail.

But the war's aftereffects did not immediately wane. One late if indirect casualty was Albert Verwey. In the years prior to 1914, Verwey, who by then had known George for almost twenty years, had become increasingly dismayed by the transformation overtaking his German friend. Verwey had never accepted George's vision of himself as the prophet of a new religion or as the founder and leader of a spiritual empire. Verwey was even less inclined to see the war as anything but a criminal bid for material profit waged by cynical power brokers. When the war erupted, Verwey at first hoped that George and his friends would join him in condemning it and was saddened by the attempts of George's followers to co-opt it as the "holy war" they thought was presaged in *The Star of the Covenant*. Verwey remained firm in his principled opposition to the conflict — "war is actually insanity," he once categorically said — and held fast to the belief that, as fellow poets and artists, they all had more in common with each other than with their respective national states. For the first two years of the war, letters, poems, and essays continued to be exchanged among Verwey and several members of George's circle, principally with Wolfskehl and Gundolf. But as the war dragged on, communication became more strained and less frequent and finally virtually ceased altogether after 1916.

When it was all over, Verwey tried to reestablish contact, believing that they were at least still connected by the bands of friendship, even if they did not agree on everything. Verwey was all the more shocked to discover in the last edition of the *Blätter* published at the end of 1919 a poem with the title "A Farewell," followed by the letters "A. V." None of the works in that issue of the *Blätter* was signed by its author, and although it was Wolfskehl who had written the poem, it clearly reflected George's own perspective. Basically, the poem tells the story of someone who had once belonged among the elect, who had been an initiate in the sanctuary, a brother poet and confederate, and who at the decisive moment turned against his former allies. Instead of placing his unqualified faith in the higher wisdom and truth of the cause to which he belonged, he questions what he does not understand and, in so doing, becomes a traitor. He — that is, "A. V." — had only to say "I don't know what is taking place · but whoever it is at work here / Is of my kind and whatever he does is right." Having failed to pass this test of absolute trust, he was to suffer the ultimate punishment. As in the poem, so in life: George and Verwey never saw one another again.

The ordeal over Verwey was evidently painful to George, and in the ensuing months he often mentioned his erstwhile Dutch colleague in conversation. George was even moved to do something he rarely did and talked about Verwey with people who had never met him. "It was otherwise not George's way," Edgar Salin explained, who was one of the privileged recipients of these confidences, "to speak to us disciples about friends we did not know." To Salin and others, George portrayed the break as being necessitated by Verwey's inability to comprehend his poetry. As Salin reported it, George had been deeply disturbed "that a poet such as Verwey no longer had an ear for the New Poetry, that a friend, whose human, warm openness even in their last meeting had affected him, yet could not and did not want to go any further on his path with him." At bottom, the reason for the rupture involved in fact not poetry but principle: George could not abide anyone within his domain who did not fully hew to his path. One either was completely for him or against him; there could be no room for subtlety or nuance.

Yet the distress George experienced over Verwey's dismissal soon shrank into insignificance compared to the trauma he was about to go through. Ever since Gundolf's aborted attempt to marry Agathe Mallachow in mid-1917, which George had prevented only by openly threatening Gundolf with terrible consequences if he went through with it, a faint shadow had descended between them. Superficially, nothing seemed to have changed. Gundolf had continued to write his regular newsy letters to the Master, and George frequently stayed in the rooms of the palatial apartment Gundolf rented in Heidelberg. But within Gundolf something appeared to have broken or come loose. Initially, Gundolf interpreted his inner disquiet as stemming from his professorial over-reliance on abstract *Geist* at the expense of the more immediate, unreflective interaction with "life," which he thought the artist, and of course George especially, exemplified. In January 1919, he told George that, uncharacteristically, "I am working slowly and without any particular satisfaction on my lectures, yearning in vain for a renewed poetic ability, I am already brooding in a Faustian mood about the meaning of life." Recalling the hero of Goethe's great drama, the universal scholar who, after having traversed the entirety of the knowable world, hungers for something more vital and concrete, Gundolf suggested his own problem was related to the Faustian urge. "The self-sufficient enjoyment of knowledge," he went on, "which the great generation of scholars possessed, and the belief in a discoverable truth in the spiritual and moral world, is no longer shared by the modern spiritual person [*Geistmensch*]." The reason, Gundolf explained, was that "spirit has arrogated too much to itself as opposed to life, whose laws it neither understood nor created, and now it stands helplessly before a pile of rubble, knowing full well that ONE THING is necessary and that its resources and means do not suffice any more to accomplish that Thing."

This was serious indeed. Although Gundolf obviously meant it as a self-criticism, it could also be taken as an expression of severe doubt about their common enterprise as a whole — and hence by extension about George — and that was a truly frightening prospect. George had, after all, always represented the epitome of a certain kind of *Geist* — to be sure, one that unified the opposing extremes of mind and body, past and present, good and evil within a larger totality — but it was *Geist* nonetheless that defined the whole movement George had formed and which Gundolf had faithfully served for two decades. Complicating the matter was that Gundolf, unlike George, did not see the defeat of Germany and the destruction of the Empire as an unreservedly good thing. It was he, after all, who had most closely aligned the war with George's vision, and if Germany had emerged as the victor, Gundolf would have unquestionably viewed it as a validation of their program. The catastrophic defeat inevitably suggested the unbearable opposite conclusion. Even though Gundolf had been cured of the most virulent symptoms of his enthusiasm by spending a few weeks at Verdun, he could hardly have regarded the military and political disasters that had since befallen Germany as matters entirely irrelevant to the future viability of the circle, or at least to his place within it. Still, Gundolf was not yet prepared to believe, or accept, that his specific difficulty — his newfound mistrustfulness of *Geist* — was more than a personal deficiency or imbalance, one that, if corrected, would restore both his confidence and his energy. As it was, although he did not appear to think the cause lay outside of himself, Gundolf felt impotent and lost. Even his fabled industry appeared to be fading. "What I *can* do," he groaned, "does not fulfill me and thus even my diligence flags. What I recognize as necessary I am unable to do and I don't want to lie. What you have told me for years about my nerves one day quitting on me never seems very far away from me." He sensed himself to be on the verge of some sort of a collapse. "In short," he grimly concluded, "it is not a very pretty state."

George realized the gravity of the situation and responded with unusual speed and solicitude. Addressing him, as he had not done in a very long time, by the affectionate nickname "Gundel" (he normally confined himself to the terse abbreviation "G." in his salutations), George sought to commiserate with him by agreeing that "your letter is admittedly not very bright . . but when does something pleasant reach one's ears these days." He tried to convince Gundolf that his perspective was too narrow and above all too negative. "It seems to me," George returned, "that you have no cause to think so poorly of 'spirit.' For YOU were + are not only 'spirit' . . but in spite of all spirit you have 'believed because I said it.'" The quotation is from Dante's *Paradise* and is a version of Tertullian's so-called rule of faith — *credo quia impossibile* — or of a similar idea expressed by St. Augustine in his *Confessions*. The point, for George, was that Gundolf should not abandon his faith in *Geist,* because to do so would be to abandon his faith in him. Instead, Gundolf should learn to make distinctions — naturally, not everything about *Geist* was good, particularly when it veered in the direction of exaggerated rationalism and lifeless abstraction — but not to give up championing Spirit itself. "That was worthwhile + and will continue to be worthwhile!" George assured him. "I am afraid, rather, that you are feeling the collapse of that part of spirit which was also in you and which was still slightly liberal and nineteenthcenturyish. That part is of course finished and hundreds of our earlier points of disagreement (including Luther + Bismarck) now take on for you as well a different hue." This last comment was a deliberate, even cruel dig: Gundolf had always admired both men, refusing to yield to the objections of George, who hated both just as vigorously. With Gundolf already down and his belief in so much else shaken, George did not want to waste the opportunity to settle a few outstanding scores. Overall, though, George's appraisal was upbeat. He advised Gundolf that, instead of allowing himself to feel downcast over Spirit's undeniable failures, he should be filled with optimism about what it and they still can and must achieve. "Everything," George exhorted him, "beginning with Antiquity + Christianity up to today must be seized ANEW by SPIRIT so that it will become right again . . Everything is to be done + said anew — There has thus never been a more brilliant and more rich time for SPIRIT than the present one!"

This was patently a pep talk, but George also believed what he was saying. Despite all of the grounds he had for feeling despondent over the general state of affairs in Germany, he still thought that comparatively speaking he was living in — and, it almost goes without saying, responsible for — a period of enormous fertility. "If later generations," he said to Edith Landmann in late 1923, "will no longer register the stuff that others are doing and only our things, then they will say: God, what a flowering during that time! And we are horrified by this time. But it was exactly the same with Goethe. He also amply moaned about his time and yet it was the greatest flowering that Germany had experienced since the Hohenstaufen." The period of German Classicism over which Goethe had reigned had been, George said, the true "German Renaissance." This time, the rebirth would be in and through the spirit of George himself.

But there was something else troubling Gundolf that he had not mentioned and had less to do with the spirit than with the flesh. On the same day in January of 1919 that he had written his agonized letter to George, he had sent a poem to Elisabeth Salomon, his former student and the woman who had nursed him back to health in Berlin during his illness in the early part of the previous year. In the interim, Gundolf had clearly grown attached to Elli, and there were signs that their relationship had advanced beyond the casual recreation Gundolf had often engaged in with other women. As Gundolf was more than aware, affairs with women, so long as they were purely physical and noncommittal, were far from ideal in George's books. But the Master had resigned himself to them as inevitable and, if carefully monitored, probably harmless. It was only when they threatened to turn into something more that he intervened. Marriage also was tolerated but only so long as all parties understood that the purpose of marriage was to ensure the perpetuation of their stock — and preferably only after the man had reached the age of forty and had done his part for the 'state.' Everything that touched on the realm of the spirit — meaningful friendship, intellectual exchange, genuine emotional communion — was reserved for male-to-male interaction alone. Had George seen the poem Gundolf wrote to Elli, he would have considered all the fretting over *Geist* a mere trifle — or a feint.

> When I despair of my own worth
> In the ashen trickle of a long fallow period
> Struggle with brittle images without words
> Battering the heart I have emptied . .
>
> When I do not dare to bring my abused soul
> Before the face of the masters
> I still perceive your womanly urging
> And kiss again and do not despair.
>
> For you are such a creature of my seed
> That just by desiring and affirming you
> I honor myself again by receiving myself from you . .
> You soar and I recuperate from my debility
>
> You smilingly take whom you have seen weak
> Into your strong hands, let him struggle with you . .
> Then my songs grow again through your song
> Then your dance is alive in my own feet.

These were sentiments that, ten years before, Gundolf would have directed toward George alone. Now, not only had the object of his tenderness changed, its gender had changed as well. Despite his astounding gifts, Gundolf had always suffered from a deeper lack of self-confidence and he had relied on George to provide him with reassurance, comfort, and guidance, while offering his unconditional love in return. In Elli, Gundolf seemed to have found someone who could supply what George had given him — and more. For all of the love Gundolf brought to George, he had often been — and of late was increasingly — unsure whether it was really reciprocated. With Elli, those anxieties melted away.

They were replaced, however, by an even greater worry. Gundolf knew that he had inwardly overstepped the boundaries George placed on such liaisons. Even though he was then thirty-nine and thus approaching the age when marriage might be allowable, he also knew he had already gone far beyond the acceptable limits in his relationship with Elli. He did not want to have her as a breeder but as a soul mate. And that, to George, would be nothing less than treason.

That Gundolf appeared to understand the weightiness of what he was contemplating, and the severity of the fallout should he carry it through, is forcefully borne out by a short dramatic dialogue he submitted a few months later for publication in what was to become the final edition of the *Blätter*. In June 1919, Gundolf sent the manuscript of the dialogue to his friend Marianne Kassner, claiming it was "perhaps the best thing I have accomplished in twenty years and is the concentrated essence of my long brooding over Caesar." Gundolf had been fascinated by Caesar for many years. His dissertation of 1904 had been devoted to an examination of Caesar's image in German literature, and Gundolf had obsessively collected anything connected with Caesar ever since: books, portraits, coins, busts, and various paraphernalia testifying to the emperor's stature and might. Naturally, Gundolf's interest in the Roman dictator was also fed in no small measure by his belief that there existed a profound affinity to the person he viewed as Caesar's rightful descendant — a conviction confirmed in Gundolf's mind by the odd coincidence that both Caesar and George shared the same birthday: July 12. Thus it was all the more significant that Gundolf did not choose one of the moments of triumph in Caesar's life as the subject of the dialogue. Rather, as the title ominously announced, "Caesar and Brutus" focused on the treachery committed by his most favored and trusted officer.

The dialogue does not address the issue besetting Gundolf directly. Instead, Gundolf framed the matter in broad circumlocution. The piece opens with Caesar greeting Brutus, strangely, as his "beloved enemy" and welcoming him back from a dangerous campaign. "I feared more *for* you," Caesar somewhat tentatively tells him, "than *from* you." Brutus, accepting Caesar's cautious embrace, responds for his part with equally ambiguous gratitude for this reception: "I do not hate you," Brutus says. "Yet I mourn for us / That I may not love you as I would wish: / Out of justice." Neither Brutus nor Caesar clarify what this "justice" is that prevents Brutus from loving Caesar in the way he would prefer. But the rest of the dialogue centers on their conflicting, and as it turns out incompatible, conceptions of what is right and lawful. Caesar recognizes only, as he says, "what affects me and what I affect" — that is, he acknowledges only the laws that he creates and that act through him. Brutus, however, argues that there are other forces even greater than those embodied in Caesar, powers that brought him into being as they did all men, and which Caesar blindly wants to usurp or deny. Realizing they have reached an unbridgeable impasse, Caesar says he cannot act otherwise even if it means sacrificing his friend. "Your law is foreign to me," he tells Brutus. "Why should I lie? / I must follow my own without haggle / And were you yourself the prize that enticed me." Brutus draws the inescapable conclusion: they must go separate ways. "You pronounce my own sentence, Brutus says. "More certainly / Than you do I feel the Law that you reject." The dialogue ends with Brutus assuring Caesar once more that "I do not hate. I do not defy . . I suffer. / Give me your hand." In response, Caesar says only, "Be as you must and have faith!"

Actually, the last word Caesar utters, and thus the final word of the entire piece, is derived from the German verb *trauen*, which means not only "to trust" or "to have faith," but also "to marry." It would appear that this was Gundolf's studied attempt to have George, through the voice of his fictional alter ego, not only to let Gundolf go in peace but also to give his consent to the union with Elli. If so, it was the worst miscalculation Gundolf ever made.

Almost immediately the situation deteriorated. Yet Gundolf, despite having cast himself in the role of Brutus, did not at first seem to appreciate the ramifications of what he was intending to do. Perhaps, initially, even George could not completely believe that his most prized pupil, his most devoted follower, indeed at one time his most beloved friend, would truly squander everything for the sake of a private inclination. However, as George realized that the attachment to Elli was not a passing fancy, he sensed that something drastic had to be done and he began to enlist others to dissuade Gundolf from taking the fateful step. In May 1919, George summoned Gundolf's former student and friend Edgar Salin to him. Even though the appointed hour was before noon, Salin was startled that "the features of the poet's face seemed tired so early in the day" and was even more disturbed when it became clear to him "that it was not physical exhaustion but rather a deeply distressing psychic gloom that had caused the change in his expression." After talking at some length about peripheral matters, which Salin could see were not what was actually preoccupying the Master, George finally broached the reason he had called on Salin. "In words of loving sorrow and concern about his first son, our teacher and *Führer* and friend," George described the liaison and his inability to make Gundolf understand that, if consummated, it would create irreparable damage. George hoped that, having failed to get through to Gundolf himself, Salin would have more success and that "a word of warning from the younger man would find a better audience." Salin felt overwhelmed by the responsibility. How, Salin wondered aloud, could he, twelve years junior to Gundolf, possibly assume the role of advisor or, worse, of judge toward his revered older mentor and friend? Adamantly, George underscored how much he was counting on Salin. "You now know your most important task," George told him. "Perhaps it will be easier for you if you bear in mind that you are supposed to help me." When Salin tried to defend Gundolf and reminded George that Elli had many admirers among their circle of friends, the Master lost his temper. "Stop it," he commanded Salin. "What concerns me is the question: what has happened with Gundolf that a female creature is able to gain such influence on him at all? — You are only to consider that Gundolf is standing at a crossroads in his life. He has retained the appearance and the form of a young man longer than is usually possible for people. Now it is a matter of whether he finds the form of a man." Had Gundolf been present at this scene, he might have said he was trying to do just that.

Throughout the rest of the year, even as George dispatched his agents to subvert Gundolf's plans, they both remained in frequent though strained contact. George stayed with him in Heidelberg and they both wrote to each other as usual — Gundolf more, George less — but their exchanges are marked by an unmistakable guardedness, limited to a kind of wary matter-of-factness. Only in gradual and almost imperceptible steps did the growing estrangement begin to show. In October, Gundolf learned that the *Blätter* was about to be published, and he rather meekly asked, "Will I receive the proofs to correct?" It was a task he had performed for two decades, one of the countless duties he routinely and cheerfully discharged as part of his service to the state. Pointedly, George had Ludwig Thormaehlen take on the assignment instead. When the *Blätter,* which contained "Caesar and Brutus," appeared in December, Gundolf received his printed copy in the mail.

Evidently, by the beginning of 1920, George's stratagems and patience were coming to an end. He had even stopped answering Gundolf's letters. Disconsolate but unwavering in his resolve, Gundolf reached out to others for sympathy and understanding. Fine von Kahler, the wife of his friend, Erich, and the person to whom he had dedicated his *Goethe,* tried to comfort him as best she could. "You are doing poorly, very poorly, as I can tell from your letter," she wrote in January. "But my dear, you must know that it is impossible, absolutely impossible, that t[he] M[aster] could have really turned away from you." She attempted to persuade Gundolf that this was simply another pedagogical tactic on George's part. "I am so certain that he is more concerned about you than ever before and that for him all of this is perhaps even darker than for you. But he probably considers this complete silence to be the only right way to say everything to you there is to say and probably — he is correct, as hard as it is." Still, she was convinced that "this is a test, it CAN only be a transition, I feel it so certainly, and as soon as you find yourself again, you will have found him again."

To others, Gundolf poured out a steady stream of misery and self-flagellation, yet he refused to do the one thing that would have restored him to George's favor. Later in the same month, he sent a rambling, overheated letter to Ernst Morwitz, who had also approached him at the Master's behest. "I have done nothing that I would have to regret," Gundolf defiantly wrote, "I AM how I should not be." That was in essence what he had adumbrated in the dramatic dialogue in the *Blätter:* Brutus and Caesar part ways over the irreconcilable "Laws" they each must obey. In less oblique terms, Gundolf was also saying that his feelings for Elli were based on his own constitution, which was as inalterable and incontrovertible as a natural law. "My affection for Elli," he continued, "is only a symptom of all of that — and it is not SHE who is costing me my peace." Gundolf had hoped, it seems, that even if George did not recognize or even approve of his disposition, he would at least tolerate it and accept him as the steadfast servant he had always been.

Yet Gundolf not only had to justify himself, he was also forced to defend Elli from attacks against her character, from suspicions about her motives, and from the growing hostility being directed toward her, it seemed, from all sides. In his memoirs, Ludwig Thormaehlen openly portrayed Elli as a sexual predator who consciously used her feminine charms to promote herself and advance her career. "She was not at all monoerotic," Thormaehlen asserted, using an unusual word to mean she was unusually promiscuous. "With enchanting uninhibitedness," he sarcastically wrote, "she would make eyes at whomever she happened to like at the moment. She also set out to run into famous men and to draw their eye to herself in a purely businesslike fashion." Thormaehlen even doubted "whether she was capable of real love." George also picked up on the "businesslike" aspect of her relations with other men and — albeit in a much later conversation — he bluntly equated Elli with a common prostitute. "She stands in all of the central train stations of Europe," he said to Edith Landmann. "In Rome, when Germans arrive, she is already there. No, I can't even describe it to you. You have not read enough bad French novels of morals. You wouldn't believe it. The psyche of such women — that's the thing, you can never know it entirely." In letters to George from his other friends, it was common to refer to Elli simply as "the whore," or, most crudely, as a "piece of shit." It was as if all of the combined feelings of distrust and aversion toward women in general that had been articulated over the years within the circle were now being trained on the individual person of Elisabeth Salomon.

Faced with such massive and organized resistance, Gundolf struggled to prove that he had not been ensnared by the wiles of some cunning Circe but that he had freely chosen someone worthy of his esteem. "You are well enough acquainted with me to know," his letter to Morwitz went on, "that I no longer pine away like a lovesick swain for a pretty face and even if 'easily enflamed' I am not dumb and young enough to be deceived by a clever or crafty sweetie." Elli was not that way at all: "Whoever has got to know her as I have over the years, in all her vicissitudes and lights, is thoroughly acquainted with her good, pure heart, her devotion, her energy, her sacrifices and the extraordinary, profound sadness that underlies all of her gaiety." He implored Morwitz "to believe me when I say that she is not calculating and does not want to tie me down." Given his conviction that Elli was kind and guileless,

Gundolf found it heartbreaking to see her so vilified and subjected to such abuse. "The thought is unbearable to me that people despise and condemn her and that I should treat her as if she were depraved. I feel as if I should fight against fate and the Master's judgments are fate, I love her, I can't change that." With no more to add, Gundolf rested his case. "Now you can imagine how I feel at the thought that I am not only supposed to leave her, but also to know she is scorned, indeed to scorn her myself, according to the judgment of the most sacred and most just mouth." He well knew and was terrified by the consequences his decision would entail, but he felt he had no choice. Over everything else, he admitted to Morwitz, "hovers the fear, the heartrending horror of not being at one with my god. That sounds empty and stupid, but I have never experienced it before in my life." He was in a miserable state. "I can hardly work and my pounding heart prevents me from sleeping."

For Elli herself, the rift can have been no easier to bear, especially since she understandably thought she was its cause and her disappearance the only way to restore calm. She must have expressed her anguish to various people who were in a position to advise her what to do, and in early March of 1920, Gundolf's brother, Ernst, obliged her with a letter that bore all the marks of an official communiqué. But what he had to say would not have gone a long way in easing her torment. "I will try once more," Ernst wrote, "to give you a clear picture from the other side so that your resolutions will at least not be determined by false conceptions." Clearly, he was familiar with her perception that she was held to be a menace to the circle itself and that her separation from Gundolf would ensure its integrity. This was a misapprehension, Ernst coldly told her, based on an exaggerated assessment of her own importance and influence. "I do not know, for example, what you are thinking by supposing that your disappearance could be desired by others. By whom, then? As far as I know, there is no party hostile toward you. On the other hand, I know several friends who consider, just as I myself do, that your temporary absence seems advisable at most in the sense that it is now perhaps the most suitable course for YOU." It was as if Ernst were saying that Elli was so insignificant that what she did or did not do was a matter of complete indifference with regard to the state. She was not an enemy, that is, because she was not considered worthy enough to inhabit that category. Instead, she needed to think only about how her decisions would affect herself. If that was not enough of a threat, Ernst made it more explicit. "You will no doubt understand that you do not pose a danger to the state, but rather that it is always only the state that poses a danger to you, since in any conceivable conflict you are from the outset the suffering party." The choice — pretending for the moment she had a choice — was hers: she could voluntarily remove herself from the scene or risk far greater injury to herself by staying on. Either way, the state — which is to say George — was impervious to her actions.

George had rarely used such heavy artillery before in waging battle, but then the stakes had rarely been so high. If Elli comprehended the forces arrayed against her, and the resolution to use whatever means necessary to predominate in the contest, she at least displayed courage in meeting her opponents. She again sought to portray the collective resistance to her relationship with Gundolf in personal terms, implying that the effort to get rid of her — and she stubbornly held on to the conviction that was their true aim — was prompted by disapproval of her as an individual. If that was so, she apparently thought, there was still a chance that she may be able to redeem herself following a period of trial. Once more, Ernst Gundolf sought to set her straight. "Your view is erroneous," he wrote later in March, "that your removal from Heidelberg (or Berlin) may be a pedagogical, let alone a punitive measure advocated by the state through me. No one wished for your removal because no one is hostile toward you. It is a matter of finding the most suitable means for maintaining and protecting human relations — above all with Gundolf — from existing conflicts." It is hard to imagine which was worse for Elli: to be treated as no more than an obstacle that stood in the way of "human relations" or to realize that she was not even regarded as belonging to that order.

Meanwhile, another development was unfolding that would put Gundolf's loyalty to a further test. On March 8, 1920, Gundolf received a letter from the minister in charge of cultural and educational affairs in Berlin, Dr. Carl Heinrich Becker, informing him that he had been appointed to a chair in German literature as the successor of his own doctoral advisor, Erich Schmidt. Gundolf, who had been given two weeks to consider the offer, duly conveyed the news to George, but, as he said with considerable understatement, "this decision causes me no little unease." Gundolf abhorred Berlin with no less vehemence than George and he shuddered at the thought of possibly having to spend the rest of his career in "the whole aggressive abomination of Berlin that stinks to high heaven and increases daily." Nothing about Berlin attracted him and moreover, he argued, he was temperamentally ill-equipped to survive, much less to flourish in the Prussian capital. "The hustle and bustle, the atmosphere of nastiness, coldness, unfriendliness, the lack of nature, all of this are more weighty negatives for me than for anyone else of us, bearable during a brief stay but certainly debilitating during a permanent one." He was afraid he would be so consumed by everyday struggles in Berlin and by the effort to stave off the effects of the poisonous environment at the university that he would have no energy left to do his own work. Heidelberg, while not without its faults, was far preferable, for there Gundolf had everything he needed: the "peace to work, NATURE and my Darmstadt holidays." His mother still lived in the house where had grown up in Darmstadt and he retreated there every weekend to relax under the umbrella of her doting attention, something that would be impossible from faraway Berlin.

There was also another consideration speaking against the move to Berlin. At the very moment the offer was extended to Gundolf, the Kapp Putsch was playing itself out there. On March 12–13, 1920, a conservative, rightist conspiracy had managed to overthrow the ruling, though wobbly Social Democratic government in a counter-revolutionary coup d'état. Although short-lived — Wolfgang Kapp and his cronies held onto power for a mere four days — the lasting effect of the insurgency went deep. Thereafter, the Social Democrats never regained a working majority again, and the young republic was dealt a blow from which it never fully recovered. In short order, the turmoil in Berlin had turned the city into a battleground of competing political factions, some of which were happy to employ any resource available to achieve their larger objectives. Anti-Semitism, long an effective tool for channeling unfocused energy, had already begun its virulent ascent in the first year of the republic. Many organizations in Berlin and elsewhere, including the forces that Kapp had inadvertently helped into prominence, ruthlessly wielded anti-Jewish resentment as a blunt but expeditious weapon for galvanizing their constituents into action. As a Jew, Gundolf would be subjected to the sort of anti-Semitic harassment that was occurring with growing frequency and left no one, not even the most distinguished professors, untouched. He thus reminded George of the "pogrom racket that now fills the lecture halls of Jews at the slightest provocation, even that of the world famous physicist Einstein." The perils to Gundolf's well-being in Berlin would be not just abstract or psychological but potentially very real indeed.

Against all of these objections, Gundolf acknowledged that there was still one reason to accept the post nevertheless. Berlin was, after all, the political and cultural center of the nation; it was the largest city in Germany and thus offered the greatest and most visible arena to promulgate the Spiritual Empire, providing an unprecedented opportunity to draw in new recruits. "Thus," Gundolf said, "INFLUENCE would be the only thing that could bring me there." Yet he was skeptical that his presence in Berlin would really be of much benefit to the state, for "with the current frenzy, the emptiness and coarseness of the student rabble there that is very doubtful." If, however, after assessing all of these factors, George still thought he should go to Berlin, he would. But Gundolf beseeched him to weigh all of the options carefully. "Master, if you advise me to say 'yes,' I will follow, but don't advise it to me lightly." Just so there would be no uncertainty about where he stood, Gundolf ended with a final plea: "My own heart and mind say with every fiber no, not because Heidelberg holds me back but because Berlin frightens me." He would go if he had to, but only if the Master told him he must.

Five days later, George sent an uncompromising response. Reverting back to the curt "G." in his greeting, George lashed out at Gundolf, mocking his reasons for wanting to turn down the position. "What especially distressed me in your letter," George wrote, "is this desire for a sinecure which I had not known in you until today . . peace quiet at your age!" As always, George refrained from directly suggesting any particular course of action while simultaneously indicating what his preferences really were. "Far be it from me to want to talk you into something that is as thoroughly frightful to you as your letter presents it — yet I strongly urge you to bear in mind that this mood may also BE SOMETHING MOMENTARY and that later you may have regrets. This idyll of H[eidelberg] you paint in such rich colors will soon lose its charms (idylls everywhere are coming to an end!). There are indications that the atmosphere of external warmer love (in the human sphere) is becoming more lukewarm there as well." This last comment is opaque, but the vaguely menacing undertone and the reference to waning human sympathies would seem to point to the smoldering dissension over Elli. If, George appeared to be saying, Gundolf thought that staying in Heidelberg among old friends might shield him from the most dire outcome should he stick to his intentions concerning her, then he was mistaken about that, too. George assured him that he would be just as isolated there as in Berlin. And on that score, George also played down Gundolf's concerns. "You exaggerate the external difficulties of Berlin," he wrote, and in any case "five more years of continuous Heidelberg at the rate you are going will take you to the brink as well . . In Berlin it is absolutely unavoidable that you would establish an external existence that would be much more rational according to the external course of things!" Whatever George precisely meant by that, he had made his position clear. Now Gundolf only had to make up his mind.

That Gundolf was once again compelled to choose between his own desires and the Master's wishes was not lost on him. Nor was he blind to the fact that George seemed prepared to sacrifice Gundolf's personal happiness and even his physical welfare to greater imperatives. But George was willing to surrender more than Gundolf's comfort. Several older friends of Gundolf, who took his apprehensions about living in Berlin more seriously than George did, decided to approach George with the hope of softening his stance. In early April, they appointed Edgar Salin, who was now functioning as a semi-official intermediary between Gundolf and George, to bring their petition to the Master. Knowing that George "inwardly hoped for acceptance of the offer," Salin called on George with the appeal that "he would induce Gundolf to decline since Gundolf's health was not up to the Berlin post."

George furiously rejected the request with derision and viciously turned on Salin. "His mother is permitted to worry about his health and so she did," George spat back. "But you, you should have known that there is something higher than mere health and that the air in Berlin is better for promoting a more manly demeanor than this greenhouse here." Hearing these words, and the hard, almost contemptuous manner in which they were spoken, stunned Salin. He was so taken aback that he did not even register that George had gone on speaking. As he regained his composure, Salin awoke to the horrifying realization that, in his fury, George had just cut him off as well. If Salin managed to persuade Gundolf to change his mind, George had been saying, he may reconsider reinstating them both, but "until then I do not want to see you anymore." George then formally extended his hand to Salin and said, "Farewell and do not lose heart. This can be atoned for." Despite many, sometimes desperate efforts to expiate his sins in the subsequent months and years, Salin never regained his place in the inner circle again.

For Gundolf himself, things momentarily appeared to have taken a slight turn for the better. Ironically, what he welcomed as a piece of good fortune would have been taken as a severe setback by anyone else. In mid-March 1920, Friedrich Wolters, who was then in Berlin, happened to speak with the minister overseeing Gundolf's appointment, who had informed Wolters that the process had hit a snag. Although Gundolf had been approved by the ministry, the university faculty had balked and declined to give its assent to his nomination. As Wolters relayed it, the grounds for refusal were based on ideological opposition to the kind of *Wissenschaft* that Gundolf — and thus the entire George circle — represented. They objected, Wolters reported to Gundolf, "in addition to the familiar reasons about your ostensible shortcomings in holding seminars and examinations, with the main (and impertinent!) justification that your works are of a more artistic than scientific nature." Provided that Gundolf was still interested, the Ministry of Culture was ready, Wolters continued, "to take up the battle against the faculty and give you a professorship in Berlin that would make you completely independent, would free you from seminars and examinations and oblige you only to lectures that are acceptable to you." Wolters, more pugnacious than Gundolf and blessed with a thicker skin — and also mindful of the unique opportunity Berlin presented for furthering their common cultural-political goals — urged Gundolf to enter the fray. "What do you think?" Wolters wanted to know. "There is much to be said for and against: I would be for accepting and even if it were only for a few years in order to show the party bosses that they have to respect the new power and can no longer do what they want."

To Gundolf, the faculty's rejection of him was an unexpected gift. He rushed to tell George about the "new facts" he had learned from Wolters:

"that the FACULTY is UNANIMOUSLY against my appointment: now that is a very weighty FUNDAMENTAL argument against acceptance (apart from the personal chicanery that can and will result for me)." Not even pretending to be disappointed, much less offended, Gundolf barely concealed his delight over this turn of events. Now it could appear that he was declining the offer on principled grounds and not because he simply did not want to go to Berlin. If he were to accept, he argued, he would thereby be recognizing the legitimacy of the university and its basic axiom: "the autonomy of the faculty before the state's claims to power." By taking the offer, that is, Gundolf would perforce be aligning himself with and, even worse, be at the mercy of the very institution that had cast fundamental doubt on his qualifications and abilities. That was hardly a solid basis on which to build a successful undertaking, either for himself or for the state. Too, he pointed out to George that what Wolters might find attractive was not necessarily equally appealing to someone of his own disposition. "Wolters possesses an enjoyment and skill for battle," he told George, "and resisting the intrigues of old men is just another thrill for him, but not for me, for I am Gundel and am courageous against ideas but very vulnerable to spiteful persons who will spoil my pleasure in work through all sorts of vexations." After a few more weeks of deliberation, at the end of April 1920, Gundolf finally wrote to the Minister for Culture in Berlin to turn down the invitation.

George was under no illusion about the import of the decision. Yet again, Gundolf had knowingly and openly defied his wishes, this time even hiding behind a transparent rationalization that was merely a convenient pretext for refusing to obey him. If George had needed further evidence that Gundolf meant to pursue his intentions with Elli, the Berlin fiasco wiped away any remaining doubts.

Nothing could cover over the fact that by now a full-blown crisis had arisen and George responded to it in what was becoming a typical fashion. Two months later, in June, he fell seriously ill again with his old complaint and he was admitted to the Heidelberg clinic under the supervision of a specialist, Professor Rudolf Krehl. Salin, who was granted a temporary reprieve by George so that he could visit the Master in his time of need, was "shaken by the suffering and grief" that was apparent "in his venerable features." After undergoing treatment in Heidelberg, George was sent to the spa at Bad Wildungen to recuperate. In early July, Salin went there as well and, as they were taking a short walk, with George holding onto Salin's arm for support, George must have seen the expression of concern and worry on Salin's face. "You are thinking of my approaching birthday and are calculating that I will be fifty-two years old," he told Salin. "But your calculation is wrong. For my years count double." Though weakened by his illness, George was still strong enough to treat Salin with undiminished rancor and bitterness. "You probably wish that I would stay in the clinic permanently," George said to him, "so that you could continue to visit me or pick me up every day."

But his savagery was not aimed at Salin alone. They had not taken a hundred steps before George broke out into a general denunciation of "this world" and "this people," which, he predicted, were headed with increasing rapidity toward the abyss. "What was the use of the warnings?" he bitterly asked. "After all, even all of you hardly hear me." Salin, at a loss about what to do or say, cautiously volunteered that prophets of all ages had experienced the same lack of appreciation and reminded George that in his poem, "The War," he himself had written, "The Seer is never thanked." George, grateful at least for this acknowledgement that he retained some authority in Salin's mind, responded, "Of course you are right. But do you also have any idea what that costs?" As they continued their walk, George stopped to point out a worker wearing blue-tinted glasses who sat on a pile of stones and, while merrily whistling to himself, pounded rocks into smaller pieces with his hammer. "Today," George dourly commented, "it is better and more valuable to be a good stonemason than a poet."

That was new. It signaled an even more dramatic breach in George's life than the conflict with Gundolf itself. Over the years, George had been through many wrenching upheavals and had suffered as many heavy defeats, but he had never faltered in his belief in the ultimate power and importance of poetry. It had been the one constant, the lodestar that had guided him out of the blackest nights. Now it seemed that even his faith in poetry, the ground on which he had staked his entire life, had begun to give way. Perhaps it was only a natural reaction. If his trust in Gundolf, of all people, could be so thoroughly betrayed, maybe there was nothing he could be sure of anymore. This conclusion seemed confirmed two days later when Gundolf came with Salin to accompany George on his constitutional walk. Although the Master appeared to be less upset than before, there was still tension in the air, which was heightened by George's obvious determination to speak almost exclusively to Salin and virtually ignore Gundolf walking on his other side. But it was clear that everything George said to Salin was actually directed at Gundolf. "George spoke sharply about the uselessness of the academic activities at universities," Salin recorded him saying, adding that George mentioned "he would therefore also not encourage anyone to write a habilitation thesis." Acutely aware who the real object of these attacks was, Salin tried to intervene by asking whether George was not still of the opinion "that the best of German youth go to the universities and that everyone of us thus has to perform the duty here of screening them and leading them to him." "Yes I am!" George replied. "Whoever feels that way is in the right place. But will you leave your place when you no longer feel that way? Will you even know at all that you have changed? And if you know it — will you not imagine that you have changed?" But that was only one danger, George said. The other one was "making compromises" and thinking it was possible to create a bridge between poetry and science. Science was at best a necessary evil, and it usually ruined more than it preserved. "How much of the best of Goethe's legacy," George fulminated, "has precisely science wasted and destroyed!" Gundolf, hearing all of this, could not have failed to apply this indictment to himself. It was as if George was repudiating everything Gundolf had done over the last twenty years.

Given the mounting intransigence on both sides, hope was fading that either one would budge. Later that month George suffered a relapse, falling even more severely ill than before. On July 22, after a doctor had discovered "the existence of a rather large bladder stone" and had advised an immediate operation, George underwent surgery under general anesthesia. In August and early September, as George slowly recovered again in Bad Wildungen, Gundolf spent his vacation with Elli in Meersburg on Lake Constance and in Munich.

Astonishingly, however, as he was wrestling with George over both his professional and personal future, Gundolf had recovered enough stamina and equanimity to begin working on a new book. Just as remarkable, it was devoted to George himself, or, as Gundolf put it in the last letter to George outlining why he could not go to Berlin: "It is a rendering of your IDEA in [the context of] the times." In mid-March Gundolf had already completed the first of the book's projected three parts, and by the end of June he had amassed, as he informed Edith Landmann, "a thick manuscript of about four hundred pages" with only thirty remaining to write. In October 1920, it was published with Bondi as part of the "scientific" series associated with the *Blätter für die Kunst* and adorned with the swastika emblem.

Anyone expecting the book, titled simply *George,* to criticize or even to equivocate about its subject would be disappointed. It is, rather, an unabashed exercise in hero worship, exalting George as an elevated figure, almost an elemental force, who had forged his own separate empire and fashioned a new type of human being. George is presented as a conqueror, ruler, and prophet, leading his people out of the morass of nineteenth-century baseness into the light of a new Hellas under the banner of a new god. In painting his portrait, Gundolf used language that is rhapsodic and combative at once, and only the few people who knew the private war he was waging against the very person extolled in its pages might have detected the faint strain of someone trying hard above all to convince himself.

Predictably, the book met with universal approval among the faithful, who saw it as yet another blow struck in the name of their cause. Wolters, also still ignorant of the disturbance between Gundolf and the Master, extravagantly exclaimed that "in it a creative dialectics has emerged again for the first time since Plato." Outside of the circle, however, the response was somewhat more mixed. Moritz Goldstein, an editor of the Berlin daily *Vossische Zeitung,* published a review of the book in February of 1921 that offered a thoughtful and astute appraisal. Goldstein began with Gundolf's assumption that George represented a world-historical figure, comparable in greatness and influence to such people as Dante, Shakespeare, or Goethe (Goldstein ignored the parallels Gundolf drew to other, nonliterary predecessors such as Caesar and Napoleon). The fact that such figures had existed before, Goldstein conceded, meant that they could arise again, and perhaps George would indeed join them in the pantheon one day. "But how may his contemporaries decide that?" Goldstein asked. "Such grandeur must stand the test of centuries. And because that is so, the premise of Gundolf's work hangs in the air. George's importance and rank cannot be proven; one can hardly debate about it. Basically Gundolf despotically dictates importance and rank. He is free to go ahead and do so if he succeeds at it! Only time will tell if he does."

On more substantive issues, Goldstein was equally trenchant. He missed, for instance, any mention of the sorts of facts about George that one normally expected from a biography, a mundanity that Gundolf's high-flown rhetoric seemed to preclude. "Thus we learn next to nothing biographical," Goldstein noted, "not the date or the place of his birth," and so forth. But it was on that score that Goldstein made his most searching criticism of all. The very language Gundolf employed, he wrote, and the hagiographic ends to which it was put, removed the book from the sphere of literary or biographical analysis and placed it instead within a far different tradition. "From here," Goldstein concluded, "it is only a step to pure mysticism; in that category belongs, among other examples, the fact that the Maximin poems are spoken of as holy texts and Maximin as a god, not metaphorically and from the uncontrolled visions of the poet, but rather understood literally, and understood by Gundolf that way, too." Apart from his doubts about the justness of the perception of Maximin — and Goldstein was more than skeptical about the claims of Maximin's divinity — he also shrewdly assessed the political hazards of endorsing such a view in a time that could ill afford confusion about where salvation might lie. "Now, it is a dangerous thing with mysticism," Goldstein elaborated. "It can indicate a very high or a very low level of the spirit and the soul. Even admitting that the first is true of Gundolf: with many of his readers, and precisely the devout ones, it is a matter precisely of the second, namely that they escape into mysticism under the pressure of mastering the intellectual and moral difficulties of life. There are already George conventicles all over the country, and even if what Gundolf says by way of warding off foolish and importunate gossip is valid for the 'circle' and the Master themselves: the mists and vapors that rise out of such subsidiary circles make the hard and sober battle that our generation has to fight only more difficult, and to encourage the cooks of these witches' brews is inappropriate for a man of Gundolf's resonance."

The last remark returned Goldstein to his point of departure. For all of his dissatisfaction with the tenor and likely impact of the book, Goldstein maintained a genuine admiration for Gundolf's talents. Indeed, it was Gundolf's very qualities that made Goldstein regret — and fear — what he regarded as their misuse. "We do not have a surplus of men of Friedrich Gundolf's consequence and authority today," he granted. "Not in the humanities generally, and still less in the study of literature. One would thus certainly prefer to agree with him than to contradict him. But I read this *George* without pleasure — and I cannot imagine that I am alone in feeling that way. Something in me resists this self-righteous wisdom that from a priestly height and dignity judges the world and the times and condemns both outright. I would wish that he would give up the pompous office of judge and would become again what he can be like no other: a loyal and fearless custodian of our literary heritage."

Had Goldstein known of the inner discord that formed the backdrop of Gundolf's book, he may have shown even more compassion for its author, even if his conclusions would have remained unchanged. For it may well have been that the very fervor with which Gundolf asserted George's supremacy, Gundolf's unquestioning insistence that George embodied an absolute measure of universal significance, actually betrayed an unconscious attempt to persuade himself that the sacrifice he was about to make would at least be laid before a worthy altar.

In November 1920, just after the *George* book appeared, Gundolf visited his friend Arthur Salz in Baden-Baden. During one of their conversations, Gundolf apparently spoke freely and, it seems, disparagingly about George's attitude toward Elli. Somehow, his words got back to George, who may have even sent Salz on a mission to sound Gundolf out. The following month, Edith Landmann saw George in Berlin, and "I heard from him the facts and the words that had been spoken — an earthquake could not have frightened me more — which made the separation necessary." Whatever Gundolf had said — and if it was ever recorded, all trace of it has been lost — George never forgave him for it. Four years later, in 1925, he still referred to the incident in terms of unrelieved enmity. Speaking of Gundolf to Frau Landmann, George said that Gundolf "had done everything imaginable, committed every conceivable stupidity right before my eyes and was permitted to do it because he knew where he had to stop. When the moment came in which he went beyond that point, once a certain word was said, then it was over." Once George had taken a stance, he rarely, if ever, changed his position, and never under pressure from others. Later still, when Edith Landmann broached the subject again and, in a hopeful gesture of conciliation, wondered if a single word might not be excused, George remained obstinate. "No. There are words that can be redressed and deeds that can be redressed, but other deeds as well as words that cannot be forgiven. Where would I be then? My word must be valid. It must stand. That is simply my rhythm. Otherwise I would have been lying in the grave long ago."

Soon after it had been uttered, George appears to have confronted Gundolf in a letter about the unknown "word" he had expressed and implied that it can only have come from someone who was mentally unstable. Referring to this communication as George's "bitter New Year's greeting," Gundolf valiantly sought to defend himself by claiming that whatever he had said to Arthur Salz that so offended George had not been intentional and that Salz had perhaps misunderstood him, or worse: that Salz had deviously laid a trap for him. "I cannot remember and convince myself," Gundolf thus told George, "that Arthur is right, but in the give and take of a conversation, which he probably conducted with a purpose in mind, but which I engaged in without having one, he may have understood me in a way that he wished to." All the same, Gundolf refused to allow his feelings for Elli to be depicted as the emanations of a confused brain that might be corrected through rehabilitation. If anything, he was more certain now than ever before that he was making the right choice. "If this condition is an illness," Gundolf continued, "then I now know for sure that it is not a delusion but a truth, not infatuation but love, and I do not believe that it will ever be curable through enlightenment or 'disenchantment.' — "

Undeterred, George continued to press the issue of the "word" Gundolf had let slip and Gundolf just as tirelessly declared his innocence of any willful insult. "In conversations that I conduct with a purpose or a plan in a matter that has been determined IN ADVANCE," he insisted, "my memory does not fail me: this matter in Baden-Baden however was not of that sort and only turned into one after the fact: it was a vague conversation and a casual question whose purpose I did not yet know, and the fact that I don't precisely remember every informal conversation does not amount to unsoundness of mind." Gundolf miserably implored George to consider that not everyone was as single-minded and deliberate in their actions as he was. "You yourself probably never say a word without a specific purpose and without a connection to action and effect," Gundolf allowed, "but you have never held me to that standard and no one apart from you has it. That many a casual word can subsequently become an important matter may warn me about speaking thoughtlessly, but thoughtlessness is not insanity." At this point, Gundolf was running out of things to say. All he could do was throw himself at George's mercy. "Don't forget that the degree of lucidity, discretion, and memory you possess is not as natural for weaker people as it is for you and don't always immediately call more frivolous and informal things by the worst names."

By now George realized that the chances for reaching a satisfactory resolution had all but vanished and he ceased communicating with Gundolf altogether, closing himself off in total silence. Gundolf made a few more attempts to contact him, but to no avail. It was as if he were writing into the void. "Solitude is harder for me than before owing to a more and more oppressive pressure of longing, grief, and sorrow," he pathetically wrote George in February 1921, "without my being able to find myself, even under the most painstaking self-examination, as guilty of blame or delusion as you, I fear, find me." But, as afraid as Gundolf was to have these assumptions confirmed, anything would have been better than the uncertainty George's silence left him in. "If I only knew to some extent whether you are angry with me or what is worse alienated from me." As always, he closed his letter with words of unbroken devotion. "In any case, dearest Master, I remain in unwavering loyalty, reverence and love Your Gundolf."

Over the next two years, as if in silent reproach of Gundolf's behavior, George's health remained precarious. In the summer of 1922 he returned to Bad Wildungen and in September he underwent a further operation. In the meantime, Gundolf had written yet another book, this time on the erratic Prussian writer Heinrich von Kleist. Like the others, it was also published with Georg Bondi, and it appeared in November with the customary emblem. But it contained something else that, had George known of it beforehand, would have surely caused him to block its publication. In the front of the book, sandwiched between the page bearing the official insignia of the circle and the introduction, was a single sheet bearing an inscription printed in large capital letters: "DEDICATED TO ELISABETH SALOMON."

That was the last straw. It seemed an act not just of flagrant disobedience but of calculated subterfuge. George, who told Ernst Glöckner that the dedication had been inserted "behind his back," was livid. He instructed Berthold Vallentin to write to Gundolf and remind him of the "responsibility" that "fate" had laid upon him, with the implicit threat of what awaited him if he neglected it. It was, in effect, an ultimatum: Gundolf had to choose between "that person" or the Master and, should he decide for the former, George's friends would have no recourse but to turn their backs on him as well. Gundolf guessed that Vallentin was acting on behalf of George and asked his brother, Ernst, if that were true. "I know nothing about Vallentin's mission, if it was one," Ernst responded. "But however it was done, he probably would not have acted on his own." As concerned the prohibition of friendly relations with other members of the circle, Ernst said he did not think "that the Master would already raise objections to encounters," but everyone was being advised that such meetings may not be prudent. "What he on no account wishes for is contact on both sides," Ernst told him. "The choice of the side is certainly up to each person — but an actual ban certainly does not exist, only a warning, which in most cases will produce the same outcome." Since he and Gundolf were brothers and it was nearly unavoidable that they would run into each other on occasion, George had made an exception in his policy and given Ernst a special allowance. All the others had to pick which side they were on.

In a final effort to explain just how serious the situation was, and perhaps with the faint hope that Gundolf would recant, Friedrich Wolters — his friend of many years, his onetime collaborator on the *Yearbooks*, and now the highest ranking member of the circle hierarchy after George himself — sent a long letter to Gundolf in early February 1923, clinically analyzing his friend's errant behavior. It was not so much that Gundolf had cast his lot with someone else, Wolters wrote, but it was rather the way in which he had done so that was "the real cause of the Master's anger toward you: you view the dedication to E. as a private matter or justify it by your defiance or by the compulsion of an absolute necessity or by the belief that it would not have such a serious effect, whereas the Master can see only the conscious concealment of an action with respect to matters of state, an intentional deception of the *Führer,* and an open disloyalty toward a friend." Gundolf still seemed to be under the mistaken impression that in dedicating the book to Elli, he had not done anything terribly wrong, or that he had merely appended an ultimately innocuous personal note to the monograph. But by publishing the book with the official seal of the circle, Gundolf had, Wolters informed him, effectively conjoined two domains that were properly distinct. "For it is not a private matter, because he cosigns as it were through the *Blätter* emblem, and because the whole world sees it that way it is no trivial matter, since it causes confusion among the younger friends and he has to warn where he should only praise, it is not a harmless matter because you have thus forced him to repudiate you before businessmen such as Bondi and thus tell them about tensions that only the innermost friends ought to know about." Gundolf had forgotten that he lived in a universe not of his own making and that he was not at liberty to act as he pleased. George would not abide, Wolters told him, that "you decide — as in the dedication matter — what to do with something that does NOT belong to you but is his work and creation." What Wolters did not mention was that, as far as George was concerned, Gundolf himself was George's own creation as well and Gundolf thus had no more freedom to dispose of himself as he had of any other part of George's realm.

On June 21, 1926, three years after Wolters's unsuccessful last-ditch effort to pull him back from the precipice, Gundolf wrote for the last time to George.

I have decided to marry Elisabeth Salomon this year as my heart and conscience command me, convinced that I am thus violating your wish, but not your law, since this creature deserves your mercy more than I do. Since I was unable to convince you, I therefore prefer to go to hell with her than to heaven without her. I know the consequences: the sorrow through you and for you, and I shall bear them. I am not deserting you even if you reject me.

    Your Gundolf

George never saw or spoke to him again.

CHAPTER 37
Regrouping

For most of 1921, as the confrontation with Gundolf reached its climax, George went into virtual seclusion. Even his whereabouts during much of the year are uncertain, and for several months there is no information about him at all. It was almost as if he had simply disappeared from the face of the earth.

Partly, George's continuing physical infirmity accounted for his keeping such a low profile. In one of the few letters from him that year — written, notably, not in his own hand but in that of Erich Boehringer, to whom he dictated it — George described to a urologist the latest bout of his illness in early May. There had been, he said, "acute pain, pus, mucus discharge as never before." George, who was in Berlin at the time, added that he "then consulted Prof. Posener here who diagnosed a very troublesome inflammation and prescribed daily treatment. However only irrigation with boron." In his desperation to rid himself of the chronic kidney and bladder ailments that had been plaguing him now for years, George had agreed to undergo an experimental therapy that involved flushing his urinary system with radium and boron-enriched mineral water. For the moment, it appeared to help, but "the pain and very uncomfortable fluid retention still continue. The muscles seem to be so weakened that in the evenings I often have to insert a catheter as well. If I were unable to do that, I would land back in the clinic."

But as painful as these afflictions were, he suffered even more from what he saw as the perfidy of the very people he had trusted most. Gundolf, though the most spectacular apostate, was not the only one. The latest statistic was Josef Liegle, a retiring native of Swabia. Liegle, who had studied the classics and was known for his ability to recite poetry well, especially Greek, had been introduced to George by his fellow Swabian Robert Boehringer before the war. George had once held him in high regard. When Liegle, who had fought in the war, was captured by the British and placed into a prisoner-of-war camp, for example, George had become alarmed and told Gundolf that "we cannot lose such people who are worth a hundred thousand!" More recently, though, Liegle had decidedly sunk in George's estimation. For reasons he never made clear, George abruptly dismissed him in early 1922. (According to Hans Brasch, Liegle was a shy, reticent man, whose "taciturnity often led to such long pauses in conversation that one felt the silence almost as a physically oppressive torment." Robert Boehringer also suspected that "the long pauses in conversation were a burden to George" and eventually led to the break.)

In an unusually lengthy speech to Edith Landmann, who for her part thought that Liegle had fallen into disgrace "undeservedly," George justified his gesture as a necessary act of political housecleaning. "Members of the state die," he declared,

> but the state lives. As long as I still have vitality there has to be a major clearing-up from time to time. One can say: why did it work until March 19 and then on March 21 it doesn't work any more? But at some point it comes to an end. It was already over earlier, but one day the opportunity comes to shake it off. Earlier there were distant relationships. Now I can't weigh things so carefully, I have to stay with those to whom I am very attached. I cannot give even those I love their full portion now because I am physically hindered. I warned him. I don't like to warn. I compromise my dignity when I warn. The others know that before I warn, but he turned a deaf ear. He doesn't listen keenly enough. I tell each person the truth only once if it's necessary. If that's no use, then a hundred times would be of no use either. It is not customary in the circle to signal with fence posts. There are too many other people for whom that would be necessary. Perhaps when everything is better, but now I am unwilling. I am explaining this to you in detail because it is also important for you that you know how I feel about it.

When Frau Landmann inquired how Liegle was supposed to endure his banishment, George shrugged. "He can prove himself. He can surprise me, I very much like to be surprised. Perhaps he will prove himself precisely by the way he bears it." But, judging from past experience, Liegle's prospects were not good. As if to underscore how unlikely any restitution of his favor was, George compared Liegle to the other person who was causing him such disappointment at the moment. "Sometimes I don't see someone for three years, but that doesn't work. Others, too, if I don't see them for a long time, then seem to me to have been left behind, entirely antiquated, I don't understand them any more; they have to live with me; even Gundolf is noticing that already."

Someone else approaching the critical three-year cutoff date was Ernst Glöckner. In November 1919 Glöckner had told Bertram that "I have wanted to write to George this whole time; but I can't think of the right thing and thus I keep putting the letter off further and further, even though that is precisely what is so extraordinarily agonizing for me." By the following March, Glöckner realized that "I have not seen him more than briefly for two years now."

At least some of the reason why they had begun to drift apart was only indirectly related to George. During that same period, Glöckner was trying to come to terms with the growing friction that had arisen between Bertram and himself over his own allegiance to the Master. If Glöckner had thought Bertram's book on Nietzsche would finally break down his friend's hostility toward George, he soon discovered that his hopes had been misplaced. More insistently than ever before, Bertram was urging Glöckner to settle the question about where he stood, but Glöckner did not want to accept Bertram's inflexible either/or. "You are right and George is right," he had bleakly told Bertram in late November 1919, "that is the terrible judgment that concerns me the most. For I, as the lover, stand between the two of you and it weighs down on me more than I have ever admitted to either one of you." Glöckner now saw that nothing would ever bring George and Bertram together, but he still hoped to keep his connections to both ends intact. "Since you are exact opposites, a coming together is basically totally impossible; the miracle would have to occur that Eros would force you onto one another, which is however impossible." Glöckner tried to argue that Bertram's view of George was one-sided and partial, and that George certainly did not harbor the same kinds of feelings about Bertram himself. "I know from a thousand comments that he esteems you and you know it yourself." And while it was true that George had let it be known that Bertram was not welcome in the circle, Glöckner explained that his exclusion was based on sound principles. That is, George "gathers only those around him whom he loves and from whom he does not have to fear apostasy." Glöckner freely acknowledged that George was no longer looking for poetic talent but rather for people who would embody his spirit, and could thus not afford to include people who might one day defect. "He wants for the block he has placed in the world to be composed only of believers and not be broken up by someone who cannot believe. And he knows that you cannot believe."

As unhappy as Glöckner was to be caught in this unstable triangle, and as much as he hoped to preserve his relationship to both, he let Bertram know that, if it came to making a choice, he would stay with him. But Glöckner warned him that such a decision would be a wrenching process and should therefore be only a last resort. He thus begged Bertram, "Do not ever accuse me of partiality anymore and don't torture me with the little malicious remarks that your language always assumes in such instances." Bertram should be confident in what he had and not demand more. "And if you say I should side with you more, you now know that this is impossible and that it would be possible only if I shattered what I worship. But I can't do that because everything in me forbids such a breach of conscience. Do I not stand on your side?" It was a delicate balance and Glöckner was doing all he could to maintain it.

Later the next year, in October 1920, Glöckner at last worked up his courage again and sent an effusive letter to George asking for a meeting with him. They had not been together at all for a year and a half. "Everything in me yearns for you," Glöckner said. "With this more than physical need I come to you today, Master, to tell you how I feel: I love you, I love you like no one can love anything earthly, so aglow and burning in the flame of love that it will consume me if its raging is not stopped by the fulfillment of my wish or a word from you. Forgive me that I beg for a small word; I would not do it . . . if I were not so at the end of my strength."

George, having by then recovered somewhat from the last operation he had undergone that summer, granted the request. At the end of the month Glöckner went to Heidelberg, where he found George "more cheerful than I expected," even though George was under "constant medical supervision." But, whether or not he recognized the motives that drove Glöckner to seek him out, George had his own agenda in receiving him. As Glöckner later described the encounter to Bertram, the main subjects of their conversation were Thomas Mann and Bertram himself. Thomas Mann had been a bone of contention between George and Glöckner from the very beginning. "Trashy writing of the lowest sort" was a fairly typical description George gave of Mann's work. Over the years, George had repeatedly sought to alienate Glöckner from Mann by disparaging Mann's character, his art, and his admirers. During this latest interview, George said he was "very furious" over a recent publication by Mann that George thought was "unbelievably bad." About Bertram, George also mentioned that a recent poem he had written was "not good and pointless." Glöckner added that George had "strongly advised against leaving the niveau established by *Nietzsche*; you would harm yourself immeasurably." Understandably, Bertram was annoyed by this unasked for criticism and advice, just as he was irritated by the renewed attack on his friend Thomas Mann. He pressed Glöckner for more details about what George had said, but Glöckner helplessly replied that "George said only what I had written to you." Glöckner did add that George had repeatedly wondered how Bertram could possibly remain friendly with a person who was so obviously unworthy of the honor: "He found and finds it incomprehensible that you still show such respect for the person you are superior to; those are his words." Bertram knew George well enough to realize that he was attempting to drive a wedge not just between Bertram and Mann, but perhaps between Bertram and Glöckner as well. Once again, George was trying to force them to take sides, this time over their mutual friend.

Toward Glöckner, Bertram felt as if he were trying to reason with someone who had been brainwashed. He even suggested to Glöckner that George must have somehow cast a spell on him or bewitched him. But Bertram was unable to shake Glöckner's conviction that he was acting under the dictate of a higher, impersonal power. As their dispute continued through the summer, Glöckner again reassured Bertram that his loyalty to the Master did not imply he was any less faithful to his friend. The question was not, Glöckner wrote in August, "George or you," for that "has been decided for years. George knows that decision. But you can't ask me to lose the closeness to this man for the sake of Th. M., to make myself despicable before myself, to win nothing for my life through such an absurd sacrifice, but rather to destroy it." As far as his relationship to Bertram was concerned, there existed no uncertainty in Glöckner's mind. He just wanted to be allowed the very freedom Bertram claimed George was preventing him from enjoying. "You know," he reminded Bertram, "that *nothing* can take me away from you as long as you guard the meaning and secret of our love. My life is your life; respect it."

As Bertram and Glöckner worked through their quarrel, George's health stubbornly failed to stabilize and he withdrew into almost complete silence. Glöckner, who likewise suffered from a persistent kidney condition, recommended a "miracle doctor" to George by the name of Zeileis who had a private practice in the town of Gallspach in upper Austria. But apart from isolated inquiries about medical issues, George barely communicated with him at all. Naturally, Glöckner took this as a sign of George's lingering disapproval. At the end of the year, in December 1921, Glöckner told Bertram that "nothing has arrived from George of course: the rift is there, I feel that so clearly! What can heal it again I do not yet know now; but I do know that I am not to blame." Without any further word from George, though, Glöckner could only speculate about where things stood.

The final rupture was caused not by any of the old disagreements but by a new irritant. The next January, Glöckner found out that a certain Professor Georg Karo, who was Jewish, had paid a visit to George. Glöckner was dismayed. "K. with George! *That* surprised me; does it always have to be the Jews again and again?" Both Glöckner and Bertram had long been dedicated anti-Semites, and the issue had been a major irritant in their relationship with George from the start. Just after Glöckner had met George, for example, he had even experienced a fleeting moment of anxiety that, as he put it, George "is perhaps a Jew after all." Naturally, Glöckner was relieved when Bertram was able to lay his concerns to rest. "Your message that he is not a Jew," Glöckner gratefully told him, "truly comforted me."

Still, for both Glöckner and Bertram the matter continued to fester, and the growing popularity of their views in many parts of Germany only aided in strengthening their beliefs. Glöckner repeatedly bemoaned the large number of Jews among George's acquaintances. "These Jews and this dependence of George's on them," he groused in 1922, "*how* painful that always is to me, because on this score I really do see more and deeper than George." There had always been, he felt, too many Jews in George's circle — some of its most prominent members, including Gundolf, Wolfskehl, and Morwitz were after all Jews — and now Karo! That was too much for Glöckner. He was convinced that as a group Jews posed an "endless danger," not just to George's state but also to the German people as a whole. In his view, Jews "all bear the same curse of sucking our blood so they can live. That George does not see this or does not want to see it, that he still tolerates and cultivates this spirit in closest proximity to himself — that is a mystery to me." Throughout the rest of 1922, Bertram and Glöckner traded numerous similarly unedifying observations. In October, Glöckner reported that "what I am hearing about George is becoming sadder and sadder, he is surrounded by nothing but Jews." A month later, when Gundolf's book on Kleist with the dedication to Elli appeared, Glöckner could not refrain from making the comment "that a Jew is not an appropriate person to treat such figures; he does not have the inner right to do so." Previously, Gundolf had mostly escaped this kind of censure, shielded by his exceptional status within George's hierarchy. In 1918, for instance, during the difficult process of publishing *Nietzsche,* Bertram floated the idea that perhaps envy on Gundolf's part was holding things up. Glöckner did not think so, "because — according to George and as we both have experienced often enough ourselves — everything Jewish in the negative sense no longer clings to him." Now, four years later, not even Gundolf could escape being tarred by the broad brush of anti-Semitism.

By January 1923, mainly because of the perceived predominance of Jewish influence within George's circle, Glöckner had already begun speaking about his attachment to George as if it belonged to the past. At first, Glöckner exempted George himself from any criticism except by association. He thus deplored "this complete submersion in Jewish intellectualism" which, he said, "is repugnant to me in the highest degree." Glöckner said he regretted this development had occurred, for it meant that he and George would have to part ways. "If *that* is his present, then he has been stranger to me than strange and I will retain only the image that I thankfully revere." Later on, though, not even the Master was absolved of responsibility for their split. When Bertram informed Glöckner in 1926 of Gundolf's ostracism in the wake of his decision to marry, Glöckner confessed that the news "made a deep impression on me — it's odd that in the long run no one can stand this tyrant."

Over the following years, as he struggled to make sense of the overpowering role George had once played in his life, Glöckner frequently returned to the label of tyrant to describe his former Master. "The highest thing that love wants is not tyranny and egoism," he told Bertram in 1928. "George serves us as a warning despite the immensity of his talents." George had misunderstood what love was about, Glöckner claimed, and it was on this single flaw that his entire project had foundered. Thus, Glöckner wrote in his diary, George had been "broken by his egoism and broke his friends as a tyrant who permitted only *his* law to be valid and destroyed his friends' natures instead of let their beings develop in beautiful freedom, completely taken care of and supported by him, the wise one. Love that destroys and only has an eye to its own advantage and is concerned only about itself is not love. The love of friends can build only where it respects the law of the friend as well as its own."

In some ways, this was what Glöckner had been saying to Bertram all along, except that until now the terms had been reversed. That is, Glöckner had been persuaded, or had convinced himself, that his own freedom lay in submitting entirely to George's will. This view did conform to the ideology of the circle, it is true, but it required a peculiar definition of freedom, to say the least. Only once Glöckner had stepped back and regarded George from a greater distance did he begin to realize that the so-called freedom he had boasted about for so long was in practice indistinguishable from servitude.

By the time Glöckner had finally wrested himself from the Master's grasp, George had long since turned his attention elsewhere. In the early 1920s, George met two new young men who would soon write works that rivaled even Gundolf's in their brilliance, originality and, in one case, enormous commercial success. Coincidentally, although they shared little else in common and perhaps never even met, they both owed it to Heidelberg that they were admitted into George's world.

Many of the soldiers returning from the war wanted to resume their interrupted studies when it ended, which occurred, happily, just in time for enrollment in the summer term of 1919. That spring, universities swelled with both new and seasoned students, many still dressed in field-gray, who were eager to forget what had happened and to find answers to the new questions that had arisen in the meantime. One of the more mature students in Heidelberg was Ernst Kantorowicz, who would complete his doctorate in history there two years later. Born in 1895 to a well-to-do German-Jewish family in the East Prussian city of Posen (Poznan), he had gone to the western front in September 1914. After being wounded in 1916, Kantorowicz returned to battle and somehow survived the next two years, receiving several commendations on the way for his skill and valor. He was, one of his superiors recalled, "an absolutely extraordinary personality, an outstanding soldier, and a truly good comrade. His military comportment and his courage were very well known." When Kantorowicz enrolled in the University of Heidelberg in the fall of 1919, at the age of twenty-four, he still had the bearing of a fighter but the manners of a gentleman. George, who met him shortly thereafter, said that "he was what the French call a chevalier, and he was entirely a chevalier of a kind one no longer sees. Lithe, yet of masculine firmness, sophisticated, elegant in dress, gesture, and speech, Kantorowicz had something of a foil fencer about him."

Although it is unknown how Kantorowicz was first introduced to George — he was a nephew of Gertrud Kantorowicz, the only woman to have published in the *Blätter für die Kunst,* but that was hardly a recommendation anymore — it is easy to imagine that he immediately found an enthusiastic reception. Physically, Kantorowicz seemed modeled on the blueprint after which so many of George's favorites appeared to have been formed: his face was ovoid, with well-proportioned features, complemented by large, thoughtful eyes and an expressive mouth. Equally visible in photographs of him is his jovial disposition, radiating an almost ironic pleasure over his own good fortune. Even years later, when he was forced to emigrate to England, Cecil Bowra noticed that he still "had an excellent sense of humour." (Bowra also thought this trait was most unusual in a German and observed that Kantorowicz "was not like any German I had met, and above all not pompous and dictatorial.") All of these qualities, along with the confidence and spring his military training had given him, lent Kantorowicz an attractive air of unpretentious self-possession. As alluring for George, though, must have been Kantorowicz's supple, penetrating mind and his beguiling verbal agility. Everyone who met Kantorowicz marveled at what Louise Gothein called his "exuberant intelligence," adding that his conversation was "always intellectually stimulating, often of a paradoxical jocularity." Although Kantorowicz is not known to have written any poetry, George, who was losing faith in poetry anyway and beginning to bet more on the "scientific" writings of his followers, would have recognized that a rich vein was waiting to be tapped in Kantorowicz and eagerly took him in.

By the summer of 1920, Ernst Kantorowicz was already among the small group of George's friends who were permitted to visit him as he convalesced in Bad Wildungen. In early 1923, their relationship had progressed to the point that George preferred to stay with Kantorowicz when he was in Heidelberg. As George wrote to Friedrich Wolters in March of that year, "I am usually NOT [at] Schlossberg" — which was Friedrich Gundolf's address —

"but rather [at] Wolfsbrunnenweg 12," where Kantorowicz lived. But as this typically condensed message suggests, in which neither name is mentioned, George treated the existence of his new friend as a closely guarded secret over the next several years. Ludwig Thormaehlen tells us that during the 1920s, "the poet did not let Ernst Kantorowicz join the circle of his younger friends in Berlin. I myself never met him in those years in Berlin or at poetry readings." As Thormaehlen explained, this behavior was not unusual for George, for he liked to keep "the groups of his friends" whose members were not already acquainted with each other "carefully separated as a matter of principle." This micromanagerial approach to the various subcircles within his sphere had already been apparent even before the war. Once, when Kurt Hildebrandt and Wolters showed up unexpectedly at Gundolf's house in Darmstadt, not knowing that George happened to be there at the time, the Master received them, Hildebrandt noted, "somewhat more coolly than usual." Hildebrandt surmised that "he was presumably irritated by our unannounced visit." They had both learned, as Wolters wrote to George on another occasion, that he did "not like such surprises," and they took care to avoid them in the future.

During the prolonged and agonizing process of separating from Gundolf, George became even more distrustful of the others than usual and he kept a vigilant watch over them. Anyone suspected of engaging in illicit activities — trying to discover his address, arriving on his doorstep unannounced, and especially seeking out other members of the circle without his explicit approval — got to feel the lash of his displeasure and risked being summarily turned out. In the autumn of 1922, Edith Landmann experienced what it was like to be at the receiving end of George's suspicions. On concluding a visit to Berlin, she had planned to stop in Heidelberg to see George on her way back to Basel. Since there was an art exhibition in nearby Darmstadt that interested her, she briefly interrupted her journey there. Thinking she was exercising due prudence, she sent word to George of her impending arrival in Heidelberg from Darmstadt. When she got to Heidelberg, he was waiting for her but greeted her "with piercing coldness. When he is angry with someone," she explained, "it is as if one had the purely physical sensation of glacial air emanating from him." Although she did not know what had provoked this treatment, she saw that George was so upset with her that "I thought now everything is over and was prepared for the worst." Only on the following day did Edith Landmann realize from his questions that George had thought she had gone to Darmstadt "without authorization" to call on Ernst Gundolf, whom she did not yet know personally. George as a rule strictly forbade, as she put it, " 'his' people from looking each other up on the basis of their common relationship to him; he wanted to reserve the right for himself of bringing them together if and when he so desired." Despite her protestations of innocence, George still did not fully believe that she had merely wanted to go to the exhibit. Only after he had obtained independent confirmation from Ernst Gundolf himself was he satisfied she had been telling the truth.

With the charming and attractive Kantorowicz, George took even greater precautions than usual to prevent any such "surprises." Made wary by all the faithlessness of late, he reserved Kantorowicz almost exclusively for himself. Thus, when Kantorowicz's first book was published a few years later — naturally, with Georg Bondi — George virtually acted as Kantorowicz's agent. He handled all of the correspondence with Bondi himself, he negotiated various financial arrangements, and he even signed the contract. Bondi did not even discover the name of the author until the book went to press.

There was one more new recruit waiting in the wings. In the summer semester of 1920, a year after Kantorowicz arrived in Heidelberg, an eighteen-year-old student by the name of Max Kommerell embarked on a doctorate in German literature there. In everything but his intellectual endowments — which were prodigious — Kommerell was the very antithesis of Kantorowicz: short and rather stocky, Kommerell had what one could only generously call a plain face. His narrow eyes, weak chin, and the downturned corners of his mouth, which seemed perpetually clenched in a defiant grimace, all bespoke the fierce ambition that, perhaps in compensation, fueled his diminutive and graceless frame. Robert Boehringer, who said only that Kommerell was "not handsome," also noted that Kommerell refused to accept even the physical limits nature had set for him. Thus, in the company of others, who were invariably taller than Kommerell, "he liked to stand on his toes and stretch himself." Edgar Salin, who neither liked nor trusted him, peevishly called him a "dwarf."

But what Kommerell lacked in physical comeliness he more than made up for by the splendor of his mind. He was quite possibly the most brilliant, the most profound, and the most exciting thinker ever to have been associated with George. Although even today still unknown in the English-speaking world, he was arguably the most original philosophical literary critic who wrote in German during the twentieth century — second only, perhaps, to Walter Benjamin, who stood on the other side of the political spectrum. Although Kommerell died young — he succumbed to cancer in 1944, at the age of forty-two — he left behind a body of work that in its scope and depth is astonishingly rich and always intellectually stirring, and many of his books and essays stand as unsurpassed highpoints of the literary culture they embody.

As a student, Kommerell began attending Gundolf's lectures immediately after settling in at Heidelberg. "Gundolf is a marvelous phenomenon of inspiring purity," Kommerell wrote to a friend in May 1920. "In his lectures I am captivated as much by his liveliness and powerful plasticity, even in the details, as I am by the sure survey of what is great and valuable, his sovereign control and oversight. The proximity to such an active force is the most refreshing thing for me I can imagine." Kommerell's private reading list seemed drawn up with the aim of immersing himself as quickly as possible in the universe Gundolf represented. Kommerell was reading, he said, "Hölderlin Novalis Schiller (*Letters on Aesthetic Education*) Gundolf George, *Yearbooks* of the *Blätter für die Kunst*, Shakespeare's sonnets," and "a lot of Nietzsche." It sounded like a syllabus for a course on George and his circle. A year later, Kommerell had still not met Gundolf personally, let alone the Master, but they were both very much at the forefront of his attention. As he told another friend in February 1921, "one can often see George now in the streets and at the university," and in August Kommerell reported that he and his companions "saw the Master walking through the park almost daily."

As it happened, when Kommerell finally did get the chance to meet his two heroes, it was not in Heidelberg but in another university town. That summer, he transferred to the University of Marburg. Located in northern Hesse about fifty miles above Frankfurt — and, fortuitously, not far from Bad Wildungen — Marburg is home to Germany's oldest Protestant university, founded in 1527. At the end of the nineteenth century, Marburg university had become renowned for its philosophical faculty and in particular for the reanimation of interest in Immanuel Kant's philosophy promoted there by Hermann Cohen and Paul Natorp. After the war, however, the neo-Kantian tradition of the "Marburg school" had largely waned, to be replaced by a younger generation of thinkers more attuned to the antirational writings of Nietzsche and Henri Bergson. In 1923, Martin Heidegger was appointed professor in Marburg and quickly became the most popular professor at the university, where he wrote his most influential work, *Being and Time,* which appeared in 1927. Heidegger also attracted other gifted young scholars, such as Karl Löwith and Hans-Georg Gadamer, who took up teaching posts later in the decade and helped to make Marburg a center of German intellectual life.

Yet Kommerell did not go to Marburg to learn philosophy. Rather, he wanted to be in the presence of another recent addition to the faculty: Friedrich Wolters, who had taken a position there as a professor of history in 1920. It turned out that Wolters's assistant was one Walter Elze, who in turn was a close friend of a young man named Ewald Volhard. The latter had gone to study history in Heidelberg, where he had also befriended Kommerell. Through this rather circuitous channel Kommerell was introduced in June of 1921 to Wolters, who subsequently took him to the people he had been admiring from afar for over a year. In August, Kommerell wrote to a friend that a "simply wonderful thing" had just taken place: he had made "the acquaintance of Gundolf. . . . You know how I have longed for that." It was not until the next February, however, that Kommerell at last met George himself.

Evidently, George was so impressed by Kommerell that he was able to overlook his not inconsiderable physical deficiencies. Soon, in fact, and not a little incongruously, George was proudly showing Kommerell around as "the new Gundolf." As with all of George's intimates, Kommerell also received a baptismal nickname to commemorate his spiritual rebirth: "Maxim." Obviously reminiscent of George's god, Kommerell's new name signaled a place of special privilege, and he soon began proudly signing his letters with it. More frequently — and more prosaically — George used another name for Kommerell that teasingly alluded to his less than imposing stature: "the Smallest (or Shortest) One" — *das Kleinste* — and, by its gender, also implicitly identified him as George's youngest "child" — *Kind* — which is a neuter noun in German. Edith Landmann, whose maiden name was Kalischer, tells the story of George noticing the monogram on a dinner knife bearing her father's initials, which were, like Kommerell's, M. K. "Ach," George said delightedly when he picked up the knife, "what familiar letters do I see here: *Mein Kleinstes!*" And it was as *das Kleinste* that Kommerell was henceforth known.

CHAPTER 38
Revival

With the new additions to his entourage, George had managed to repair most of the damage caused by the defections and dismissals that had occurred during the turbulent postwar period. Kantorowicz and Kommerell would bring the greatest benefits by far, but even Walter Elze and Ewald Volhard were valuable, if admittedly not without their drawbacks. Neither one precisely fit the physical profile George preferred, but Volhard stood out — literally — most conspicuously. He towered above all of George's other friends by a full head or more. If Kommerell was a dwarf, then Volhard was a giant. Wolters, knowing what the Master's reaction would be when he first laid eyes on Volhard, tried to soften the impact in advance of their meeting. "Even given the enormous length of his body," Wolters wrote of Volhard, "I noticed that his limbs are nevertheless well proportioned and he has enough passion to move them lightly." A photograph from the summer of 1922 shows Volhard posing with George and four other friends in the garden behind Wolters's house in Marburg. The others stand in an even row, with arms slung around each other, all more or less the same height except Volhard, who looms behind everyone else looking distinctly out of place and slightly out of sorts. George, never one to mince words, unceremoniously called him "the *Tall* One" — *der Grosse*.

As important as the added personnel were, though, was the new venue presented by Marburg itself. Although George continued to return to Heidelberg off and on for the rest of the decade — if for no other reason than to check into the clinic there — the erstwhile secret capital of the Secret Germany had obviously lost much of its appeal. Once it was clear that Gundolf would not alter his course, Heidelberg became *terra non grata*. With Wolters situated in Marburg and already attracting his own students, it thus offered a welcome and much needed substitute.

One of the immediate assets Marburg offered George was in the form of the improbably beautiful Johann Anton, a student at the university there. Born in Austria in 1900 and, like most young men of his generation, recruited to serve in the war, Johann had watched his twin brother, Karl, die next to him in France. Understandably, a veil of melancholy seemed to hang over Johann, or Hans, ever since, which only augmented his stunning good looks. When George caught sight of him, he was entranced. "The Greeks would have seen an Apollo in him," he swooned. Others would have been blind not to notice him as well. It is said that the citizens of Marburg called him "the prince," and thus his nickname was coined. When George took Hans to meet Edith Landmann, she saw that George "visibly admired" his "beauty," and he eagerly wanted to know from her whom she thought Hans resembled. Apparently, George never told her the person he had in mind and for some reason she assumed he had meant the only son of Emperor Napoleon Bonaparte. "I did not know the picture of Duc de Reichstadt," she explained, "and thus I didn't get the reference, but from then on I called him Prince Hans." Frau Landmann had made an educated guess — George was absorbed in the life and fate of Napoleon at the time — but he had not been thinking of the Duc de Reichstadt at all when he had asked her whom Hans took after. To Ludwig Thormaehlen he was more explicit. "Is Hans not similar to me," George asked him, "doesn't he look like me?" Naturally, judged strictly according to the physical evidence, the answer was clearly no. Diplomatically, Thormaehlen allowed that Johann Anton was often taken to be George's son when they walked through the streets together. But such was the strength of George's identification of himself with everyone and everything in his sphere that he really did believe that each individual component bore the unmistakable stamp of himself visible for all to see.

When Max Kommerell moved to Marburg he also fell under the spell of Hans Anton and almost instantly they became inseparable. Kommerell had never made much of a secret of his preference for male companionship, nor did he seem to be particularly concerned about justifying the fact that he did. In a letter from 1919, when he was seventeen, Kommerell had matter-of-factly revealed to a schoolmate that "until now I myself have actually never loved girls but rather only boys." Although he said he had not personally engaged in "sexual activity with the same sex," Kommerell did not think there was anything inherently wrong with it. On the contrary: it was "*better [to have] it than by suppressing sexuality also to suppress eros between man and man, boy and boy. In general I completely agree that there is no ethical standpoint* in sexual matters, that one's physical structure is a law and fate." But when he met Hans two years later it was, he wrote, like "a sweet revival of things I believed had been lost." By the summer of 1922, they were spending most of their free time together. The following January they moved into the same house in Marburg, living in rooms that faced each other across a hallway.

A letter Kommerell sent to George in August 1922 gives some insight into the nature of their relationship.

> I don't know how to compensate for how good he is to me — even in all of the matters of external comfort. I have to give the M. a description of one moment. On Sunday we were lying on deck chairs up on the hill where Hansel likes to be and from narrow meadows one can look out over all sorts of ornamental shrubbery beyond the city plain and mountains all the way to the Harz. Before sundown I roused myself to pick one more bouquet for Sunday. H. remained lying there — the search for flowers led me up and down and we sometimes waved to each other through an elder bush or hazel [tree]. Suddenly Hans jumped up to get a pencil and then I saw him gazing before himself engrossed in thought. Glowing red from pondering and the last bit of sun — and in between he waved to me very tenderly and passionately. Finally I interrupted him and lay my flowers in his lap — and since I guessed exactly what he was doing I went away and on a bench a short distance away simultaneously wrote the following:

Kommerell copied out the poem he had written down during this romantic interlude and sent it to George as well.

In many ways, then, Marburg provided an idyllic setting for George to pursue his aims. With just over twenty thousand residents, the town was small but not stiflingly so, and the university enrolled close to three thousand students, guaranteeing a constant supply of potential new enlistees. And, while not as picturesque as Heidelberg, its half-timbered houses and the thirteenth-century church of St. Elisabeth — the oldest purely Gothic structure in Germany — lent Marburg a pleasantly unmodern, even medieval character.

Yet not everything was pleasant there. Unlike Heidelberg, which was relatively liberal, the political and social atmosphere in Marburg was anything but. Notorious within certain quarters for being a "stronghold of reaction," Marburg cultivated its own defiant brand of politics that cohered largely through agreement on what to reject. And the citizens of Marburg rejected just about everything they were not. Anyone who was not Protestant, solidly middle class, a laborer or a farmer was made to feel unwelcome or worse. In particular, Marburg had a long tradition of virulent and organized anti-Semitism. In the late nineteenth century, Otto Böckel, a former Marburg university student, had founded a political movement based on anti-Semitic prejudice that gained broad support throughout North Hesse. Anti-Jewish sentiments also ran deep both in the town and at the university. Although only 2.3 percent of the student population consisted of Jews, Marburg was widely known as "*the* university of anti-Semitism." Marburg's reputation extended far beyond the borders of Hesse and was a matter of common knowledge throughout the rest of Germany. In April 1922 Georg Bondi's wife, Dora, sent a package to George from Berlin containing matzo bread in celebration of Passover, explaining that she and her husband had "presumed that the enclosed baked items are even harder to get in anti-Semitic Marburg than here — hopefully it tastes as good this year as last!"

None of George's acquaintances living in Marburg had anything directly to fear from the anti-Semitism of its inhabitants, and some, as we know, were even sympathetic to the movement. But as George and his friends became a fixture in the town — and they were hard to miss given their uniform way of dressing, their habit of walking arm-in-arm, not to mention the sight of the Master himself with his long white hair topped by his favorite blue beret cocked to one side — heads began to shake and tongues wagged. Ever since Wolters had arrived in Marburg in 1920, he had gone out of his way to canvass for the circle's common cause. He gave large public lectures devoted to George's poetry and even read poems aloud. At one particularly successful event, Wolters told George, "the four to five hundred boys listened quietly and attentively for over an hour." Somewhat mysteriously, Wolters confessed that "I was a little afraid of the experiment," but added that "now that I have done it · I am confident of casting the spell of the poetic word over any number if they are only Germans and children of the spirit." Both at the university and in private, Wolters was a tireless champion of George and the Spiritual Empire, and he seized every opportunity to expand its ranks. As Walter Elze remembered it, "for Wolters the Spiritual Empire was no mirage or fantasy, but a living and lived reality, just as George was to him the lived reality of the Master or of a ruling figure. The Spiritual Empire was an idea outside of him, around him, within him; it was reality. To describe, to praise, to demand this reality in all human interactions, to give what he had experienced voice and strength in the world around him and against the world was his desire, endeavor, and very existence." And it was in Marburg that Wolters gave free rein to his proselytizing fervor.

Not everyone applauded his efforts. A year and a half later, in April 1922, Wolters complained to George about "the depraved citizenry of professors and students" in Marburg who had turned against him. "They feel," Wolters explained, "that their 'holiest of holies' is being threatened." In other words, the members of the conservative university establishment, already finely attuned to differences setting anyone apart, had begun to see Wolters's recruiting activities as a corrupting influence on their young charges. Specifically,

Wolters told George, they objected to "the young people who they say were behaving like mating woodcocks or walking across the street embraced like bridal couples — and they hinted at even more repulsive things with their filthy looks." No doubt consciously evoking the fate of Socrates, Wolters somewhat grandiloquently said that someone had informed him, "I have become a 'danger to the youth' and the faculty is beginning to withdraw its goodwill toward me, although of course — that's how cowardly they are — no one questions my personal integrity — but the danger to the young people! etc.! The Master knows the tune."

Indeed, a few months later George himself was travestied in a local satirical magazine called the *Marburg City Spectacles*. By then, George was a regular sight in town and, since everyone readily recognized him, he was an easy target. "The Master hangs on the arms of two disciples," the article reads. "His brown velvet pants sing rhythmically. He makes a photographic face. Two disciples stroll ahead, two stroll behind. It is an eternal parade to Emmaus. Thus he walks around, so publicly hostile to publicity. Lost to the world in such a worldly way. Snow lies in the hair of the Templar. The hair waves like ripe grain on the heads of his disciples. Thus he passes through the field of corn in substantiality. Smiling like a pied piper." Four years later, when Edith Landmann reminded him of the episode, he ill-humoredly brushed it aside. "Yes, yes," he said, "then they said afterwards: the Master was going courting. That was the way it always was: they were going courting if they were seen with unfamiliar people."

In the end, though, Wolters was forced to leave Marburg not because of any political harassment or moral outrage, but — ironically enough, given the disdain for money preached among the members of the circle — for purely economic reasons. Ever since the war had ended, Germany had been plagued with recurring economic difficulties stemming from the way the war had been conducted and then lost. So convinced of a German victory that defeat was never planned for, the German empire had paid for the war by borrowing against the future rewards the inevitable triumph would shower on the nation. As a result, in 1919 Germany faced a national debt of 144 billion marks. To put this figure in perspective, the total national income the year before the war began was 40 billion marks. To make matters worse, inflation had already badly eroded the value of the German currency. At the beginning of 1920, one dollar could buy 100 marks; in 1914, by contrast, the rate of exchange had been 4.2. In 1921, Germany made its first large reparations payments, setting off panic among the general population and leading foreign investors to think that such large cash outflows would only make the situation worse. With no other choice, the German government throttled back its payments. In January 1923, the French, impatient with the slow pace of reparations deliveries, invaded the industry-rich Ruhr district, adding further to the economic and political uncertainty, which quickly sent the German currency into a free fall. That month, the exchange rate plummeted to 49,000 marks to the dollar; in August the mark was quoted at 5 million to one. On November 15, the mark was trading at a trillionth of its value in 1914. Personal savings deposited in banks evaporated, causing entire fortunes amassed over generations to vanish within weeks; the economy came to a virtual standstill, and the government, already unsteady on its feet, reeled under the staggering weight of all the worthless money it furiously printed.

In Germany, now as then, university professors are government employees or civil servants — *Beamte* — and thus paid by the state. On account of the high number of returning soldiers who entered the civil service, and confronted by salaries that ran into the trillions, the government could no longer pay its bills and did the only thing it could do. On October 27, 1923, it issued the "Decree to Reduce the Personnel Expenses of the Empire (Staff Reduction Decree)," effective immediately. For Wolters, who did not have a regular position in Marburg, the decree meant that he would almost certainly lose his job. Fortunately, though, another opportunity had presented itself at the university in Kiel, which offered Wolters a fixed appointment in history. He could have guessed that George would not like the move — a medium-sized port city on the Baltic coast, Kiel lies about forty miles south of the Danish border and is damp and gray for much of the year — so he asked for "Masterly advice" before making his decision. After waiting in vain for an answer and with time running out, Wolters went ahead and accepted the offer in early November. "In addition to other considerations," he explained after the fact to George, "I was compelled to accept the appointment above all by the new law restricting civil servants. For my nonregular position here would perhaps have been affected by the cutbacks." Kiel, then, it was to be.

Wolters's apprehensions about George's probable reaction to the move proved well-founded. George never warmed to Kiel, which he often referred to as Reykjavik, the capital of Iceland, to convey just how far north he thought it was. And George professed a dislike not just for the city and its location but for the people of Kiel as well. "They have fish eyes," he once announced as if that were explanation enough. For a long time, he flatly refused to go there. In May of 1924, Berthold Vallentin tried to persuade George to visit Kiel at least once and, as an enticement, he extolled the beauty of the surrounding landscape. George demurred, saying that "he had agreed to go to Marburg, that still belonged to his territory — it was after all almost like Darmstadt — but Kiel is already part of the north." What was more, he did not even believe in Vallentin's declarations of the area's beauty. When Vallentin pointed out that George must have found something worthwhile about that part of the world, since he had once traveled to Copenhagen, the Master evenly replied that one could not compare the two: Copenhagen was "the metropolis of the north, which as such has its own significance." And while losing Marburg was bad enough, one could not even compare Heidelberg to Kiel. "Heidelberg had been a lordly manor in a beautiful landscape," George said. Kiel, on the other hand, is merely "a friendly restaurant on the border." On the most important score — namely, what human material Kiel might offer for the state — George was not just pessimistic; he had no expectations at all. In Marburg, George admitted, Wolters had managed to gather a small group of followers around him. But in Kiel, George predicted to Vallentin, "he will have absolutely nothing. In Kiel there were only blond bread rolls."

Once Wolters was installed in Kiel, he tried to put the best face on the matter. It was obvious, he wrote to George in November 1923, "that I could hardly have continued to exist in Marburg, quite apart from the fact that the concern about the elimination or reduction of the university there appears to be being confirmed more and more." But it was the general state of things in Germany as a whole that caused him the greatest anxiety. "The total impoverishment is now slowly becoming apparent in its entire cruelty, and the German ship of state is becoming increasingly rudderless. That causes me personally little worry but very much for the free movement of our friends to and with each other."

It had always been one of the more interesting paradoxes within the circle's creed, which condemned the mechanistic character of the modern world almost as forcefully as it denounced money, that the convenience and speed of trains were essential to its maintenance. Many of the features of George's "state" — his reluctance to put in writing what he preferred to say only in person, coupled with his insistence that otherwise unconnected friends report directly to him and never to each other unless permitted to do so; his refusal to stay in one place for a couple of weeks or at most a few months at a time; and his cultivation of disparate subgroups in separate towns and cities — this was all possible only because the modern and efficient German rail system took him wherever he needed to go and brought other people wherever he happened to be. True, as Edgar Salin informs us, "George really taught his disciples to employ the technical means of the time as weapons if need be." Trains, too, could thus be regarded as "weapons" that were turned against the system that created them. Likewise, George, who owned few books and disapproved of having too many around, made an exception of the published train timetable, a copy of which he always kept handy. (In a typically witty aside, Gundolf once alluded to the central importance of trains to the existence of the circle when, in analogy to the title of *The Yearbook for the Spiritual Movement*, he called the timetable the "Traveling Book for Physical Movement.") With the catastrophic devaluation of the mark, however, and the resultant destitution to which many people had been reduced, this vital link uniting George with his friends was in danger of being put out of financial reach. That was not just an inconvenience; it threatened the very infrastructure of the circle.

For George himself the situation was somewhat less dire since his funds still adequately met his modest requirements. He had few needs apart from his medical care and transportation; he rarely stayed in hotels, relying instead on the hospitality and, of course, the meals gladly supplied by his hosts. For many others, though, the inflation was an unmitigated calamity. Gundolf, for example, whose books earned royalties equaling his salary, stood to lose a great deal. As early as February, at the suggestion of Georg Bondi, he began making ever more frequent withdrawals from his account with the publisher before the money had lost its value entirely. In May, Bondi wired 2 million marks to Gundolf and in July another 6 million. On September 23, Bondi informed him that he had "sent two billion to be credited to your bank account yesterday as an advance for honoraria. I ask that you confirm receipt of this payment, as well as the 190 million sent last week." A month later, Gundolf verified three payments totaling 29 billion, and at the beginning of December he thanked Bondi for sending the "one hundred trillion." It was and is an unimaginable figure. But by then it would have barely paid the rent.

As bad as it was, at least Gundolf still had an income. For others the inflation led to total ruin. Karl Wolfskehl, who had never had to work for a living thanks to his sizable inheritance, could only watch on as both his family trust and the life it had made possible were destroyed. As early as the end of 1921 Wolfskehl's fortune had been almost entirely wiped out by the inflation. "My economic circumstances," he wrote to Albert Verwey that December, "have become very bad." So awful, he went on, that "the terrible upheaval, devaluation of all assets forces me to provide for my own livelihood at least for myself." For the first time in his life, Wolfskehl had to earn money. His wife, Hanna, and their youngest daughter had moved to a farmhouse in the country and could get by, whereas his oldest daughter, Renate, had a secure job as a children's nurse and was able to take care of herself. Yet Wolfskehl experienced the economic disaster not just as the financial hardship it was for everyone else but also as a personal crisis, which intensified an inner unrest he had been feeling ever since the war had ended. "For two years," he confided to Verwey, "I have been determined to use any opportunity to get away, to find some distant place to recuperate, to rest. My wish to be far away for a long time has taken on the most urgent force." He was so desperate both for work and escape that he was turning to Verwey for help. "Don't you think that something could be found for me in your colonies, whether it be as a private instructor, tutor or secretary or in the public school system?" He would, he said, take anything. "I would serve in any remote school for natives in the interior of Sumatra *with pleasure*."

Besides throwing his entire family into convulsions, Wolfskehl's predicament also affected George in a very immediate and material way. Unable to afford the large apartment on Römerstrasse in Schwabing any longer, Wolfskehl was forced to move out of the house that he had occupied since 1909 and was crowned by the Globe Room. Wolfskehl asked George if he wanted to keep the room in his own name, but George was not interested in putting his name to a piece of real estate and passed on the offer. It was, however, a bitter loss. The place of so many gatherings, communal readings, shared meals, and intimate encounters was now a part of history. Superficially, George acted as if he did not care. "The furniture would all make an excellent fire," he said to Frau Landmann. "What I would really like to do is set the entire floor on fire. That would be all right. But the landlord would not put up with that." But it must have been distressing at some level, even if the Globe Room unavoidably reminded him of a brighter and now bygone time. And, on a more pragmatic note, the Globe Room would be missed if only because, with the loss of Heidelberg and Marburg, George was rapidly running out of places to stay.

Without the apartment in Schwabing there was little to hold Wolfskehl back in Munich. At the end of 1922, at the age of fifty-two, he left Germany in search of work and distraction, not to return for another three years. He did not actually go as far as Sumatra — not yet, anyway — but settled instead in Florence, where he took on a position as a tutor for the children of Baroness Münchhausen. We do not know what George thought of Wolfskehl's flight — at least, unlike Wolters, Wolfskehl had gone south — and George appears to have kept Wolfskehl in the dark about his opinion as well. In 1923, Wolfskehl asked George several times without response to give his blessing of his actions. "Master," he wrote again in October, "I have received no reply to my question. You also received my summer letter in silence." Wolfskehl assured him that only "a word that you approve of my actions would make me happy. During those weeks I went through a great deal when I did not have a word from you and waited." Desperate for some gesture, if not of approval, at least of consolation or understanding, Wolfskehl pleaded with George, "Master let me know that you have heard me. [. . .] Do not leave me alone now, thirty years of service on behalf of your work call to you, I stand by the covenant, always ready for you. I am calling, calling."

Wolfskehl, who needed stimulating, intelligent, like-minded people around him to feel happy, found life in the Tuscan capital lonely and dreary. "Florence, in general a provincial city, does not have much life," he told Verwey in the summer of 1924, after he had been there for almost two years. But that did not mean he missed Germany. "I could not and would not like to be in Germany now," Wolfskehl assured Verwey, "life in the cities, especially in those I would consider, above all Munich and Berlin, would be unbearable."

Even though his tutoring job had come to an end in the meantime and Wolfskehl had to give private lessons for hourly wages and to scrounge for odd writing jobs, he had no desire to go back any time soon. "In Germany," he wrote Verwey on another occasion, "poverty, affliction, discouragement, and moroseness seem to be raging terribly, to be turning inward and poisoning people and human relationships. There is not a single letter *from whomever it may be* in which I am not said to be fortunate to be 'outside,' not cautioned to stay away." In fact, Wolfskehl said, he had received only a single positive signal from his native land. "The best thing I have heard from Germany these days is the news of George's complete recovery, that he is fresh and resolute as in his prime."

It was true. In a dramatic turnaround, in mid-1924 George had been fully and unexpectedly delivered from his ailments. For four years he had been in an almost constant state of ill health, plagued by bladder stones, urinary tract infections, and most recently prostate trouble. In that time, he had undergone several operations, submitted to radiation therapy, and had been examined by a number of specialists, but nothing seemed to remedy the problem permanently. There had been a further operation in Bad Wildungen in September 1923, which appeared for a while to alleviate some of the symptoms. In December he had already been feeling considerably better. He had gone to Basel to convalesce under the kindly supervision of Edith Landmann, who noted that by the middle of the month "things are going uphill, the pain has become milder, and it is glorious to see how he is becoming himself again."

But at the beginning of the new year George suffered another relapse, and on February 4 he was admitted into the Basel clinic under the care of a physician named Dr. Suter. Suter was so alarmed by what he found that he recommended another operation immediately, "preferably today rather than tomorrow." Suter warned, however, that the procedure was not without risk. After receiving the diagnosis, George said he wanted to think about it and returned to the Landmanns' house and retired to bed, uttering gloomy ruminations on his own mortality and about the fate of his empire. "It has to go on without me, too," he told Frau Landmann, but even he sounded dubious. A week later, after another visit to the clinic, George revealed that he had decided he did not want to be operated on in Basel. No one, not even his closest friends, knew where he was, and he did not want to be alone, without his "state" around him, should the procedure turn out badly. "He said that if it were to be done here and it went wrong, well, then he would have disappeared for Germany." George said he could imagine what would happen. "They'll think: he's in Spain and he'll come back. If you then say what went on here," he told the Landmanns, "no one will believe you. Disappeared like Romulus." No, George did not want to have the operation in Basel, even though Dr. Suter said that he had "no concerns at all" about a positive outcome and thought a delay inadvisable. Unmoved by logic or necessity, George wanted to return to Germany.

Over the next two months, which George spent mainly in Berlin attended by various friends, inquiries were made with even more specialists. Finally, he was recommended to one of the leading urologists in Germany, Dr. Heinrich Ringleb, who had a thriving practice in the capital. In mid-May of 1924, Dr. Ringleb operated on George. Miraculously, it succeeded beyond anyone's hopes. By July, just in time for his fifty-sixth birthday, George had already regained almost all of his strength. When Edith Landmann saw him a year later in Basel, she thought he was like a "youth" and she marveled at "what a new élan there was in him." George had been given nine more years of nearly uninterrupted vitality, and there was still much to do.

CHAPTER 39

The Time of Tents

In 1916, while he was recovering from the first eruption of the illness that Dr. Ringleb had at last been able to bring under control eight years later, George had once suggested that a mysterious bond existed between his physical state and the fortunes of Germany as a whole. "Through my illness and suffering," he had said then, "I know what is happening to Germany's body."

As if in some uncanny confirmation of this belief, after George had been delivered from his physical affliction, the nation also recovered from the almost endless chaos, misery, and political tumult that had roiled its citizens ever since the war had ended. On January 15, 1924, a commission of economic experts from the United States, England, France, and Germany began meeting in Paris to discuss the German reparations. Two Americans played a leading role in the deliberations, Charles G. Dawes and Owen D. Young, who realized that Germany would be in a position to get its economy back on its feet again, and thus meet the obligations stipulated by the Versailles accord, only if it had a stable currency. One step in that direction had been the introduction in November of the previous year of the so-called *Rentenmark*, which had been devised to check the hemorrhaging of the German mark by replacing gold as security with mortgages on all the land employed in agriculture and industry. The new money, bolstered by this ingenious bit of creative accounting, soon stabilized and then held firm. Not wanting to upset this newly won but fragile balance, the Paris delegation drafted a proposal, which became known as the Dawes Plan, after the American deputy, that was specifically designed to prevent Germany from slipping into another economic tailspin. The

Dawes Plan foresaw an initial reduction in the amount of reparations payments Germany owed to a more realistic level, building in gradual increases once the economy had recovered sufficiently to bear the added financial burden. It also provided for substantial American loans at lowered rates. For the Germans, one of the most appealing aspects of the plan was that it stipulated the French withdrawal from the industrial Ruhr region, which was obviously needed to push forward with economic revitalization. Although some nationalist contrarians in Germany decried it as a "second Versailles," the Dawes Plan was quickly ratified by the four signing countries in July and August and went into effect on September 1, 1924.

If not quite overnight, conditions did improve quickly. For another five years, until the stock market crash on Wall Street in October 1929, Germany experienced a relative degree of tranquility and prosperity that it had not seen in more than a decade. New factories were built, old ones were "rationalized" — that is, made to conform with the new, more efficient American modes of manufacture — joblessness generally decreased, and wages went up. Incidents of crime also declined, as did the often violent political clashes in the larger metropolitan centers. One of the last such episodes, involving Adolf Hitler, had occurred in Munich at the end of 1923, when inflation was reaching its peak. His political faction's clumsy and disorganized coup emanated from a crowded beer hall on the evening of November 8 and ended, within a few hours, with Hitler's arrest. On April 1, 1924, he was sentenced to serve five years in prison at the fortress of Landsberg, west of Munich. Once there, he settled down to write his memoirs and was promptly forgotten.

There were certainly much more interesting things to think about. Increasing numbers of people were able to afford the conveniences of modern life, then becoming more widely available; these included the radio, telephone, and automobile. For those living in larger cities — principally in Berlin, Munich, Hamburg, Leipzig, Frankfurt, and Cologne — department stores were turning consumption from a necessity into a form of entertainment. Sporting events, movies, and dance halls competed for the attention of average Germans, while daring experimentation in painting, drama, music, and architecture occupied the cultural elite. These were the "golden" years of the Weimar Republic, the short-lived though spectacular period of cultural efflorescence that still lives on in the works of its greatest representatives. In retrospect, it appeared to be merely a brief lull in the storm.

For George and his circle, it was also an extraordinarily productive time. In 1922, Bondi published two new "Spirit Books" bearing the official insignia of the circle. One was by Wilhelm Stein, a Swiss art historian who had met

George in 1918 and had told him he was planning a work on Raphael. Stein, who was then in his early thirties, had steeped himself in the *Blätter* and the *Yearbooks* and had absorbed their murky rhetoric, trying to emulate it in his own writing. George, who took to calling Stein a "neo-Cosmic," was not entirely happy with the outcome of Stein's labors — he later told Stein that he found his writing "rather rhapsodic" — but George also recognized that Stein had his uses. "Books that are not quite right," he told Edith Landmann in 1920 while discussing Stein's plan, "have to be written quickly, and we now need spirited books more than ones that are right." When Friedrich Gundolf received his copy of the finished book in December 1922, he wrote to thank the author for the gift. Seeing how closely Stein had attempted to model the life of Raphael after precepts gleaned from his reading — Stein revealed to Gundolf that, while writing *Raphael*, he had kept Gundolf's 1910 essay on "Allegiance and Discipleship" "constantly in mind" — Gundolf tactfully acknowledged the parallel without actually endorsing it. *Raphael* was, he told Stein, "in both a good and a questionable sense a book full of secrets, a piece of applied 'secret doctrine,' a fable about the magic of Holy Youth in the form of an appreciation of art and an interpretation of life."

Of greater consequence to George was another book that appeared at the end of 1922. For at least a decade and probably longer, Berthold Vallentin had been obsessed with Napoleon. In 1911, he had written an essay for the third *Yearbook* titled "Napoleon and the Spiritual Movement" that sought to draw a line between the French emperor and George's *Reich*. In 1917, Vallentin had begun to expand it into a full-length study, and by 1919 George was eagerly telling people about the "big Napoleon book" about to appear. George also began moving levers at Bondi and in June of that year he had Gundolf solicit the publisher's cooperation. Declaring that "we are very interested in its being published by your firm," Gundolf assured Bondi that the book "in its intention and importance joins the ranks of *Goethe* and *Nietzsche* and with them forms as it were a trio of 'figure' portraits." Mindful of Bondi's business instincts — and of the dismal market for books after the war — Gundolf said he was confident the book would do well: "I believe I am not promising too much when I assign a place for the work within the literature on Napoleon that is the same as that of its two 'prize-winning' siblings within the literature on Goethe and Nietzsche. It would be very nice if a printing could be arranged soon despite or rather precisely because of the bad times so that people will see that at least we are not on strike."

Apparently, Gundolf's arguments persuaded Bondi — or the politic publisher did not want to risk alienating some of his most valuable authors — and he took a gamble on Vallentin's enormous book, which when finally published in late 1922 came to over five hundred densely written and closely printed pages. George was delighted by the result. That November he told Vallentin that he thought it "was very revolutionary, much more revolutionary than the other books of the circle, than *Goethe* and *Nietzsche*," and he said why. "Even with Gundolf's *Goethe*," George explained, "one could still say that he was a German affair. *Napoleon* is not German, not French and not Italian, but rather something that is of concern to the world." Vallentin's *Napoleon,* in other words, had managed for the first time to apply the circle's ideology to a phenomenon that was not constrained by parochial interests. It thus implicitly made the case that the ideas and values associated with George were not peculiar to any one nation or cultural group, much less to an individual, but were instead universal and timeless. Of course, since the secret agenda of Vallentin's book was, like those by Gundolf and Bertram, to identify and secure a lineage that culminated in George himself, his admiration of Vallentin's achievement was in no small sense admiration of himself. Like Napoleon, George would not be a matter that involved his countrymen alone. The whole world would feel the effect of his being.

Undoubtedly, George's high praise of Vallentin's book at the expense of those by Gundolf and Bertram was not unrelated to the changed nature of their relationship to him. But, whatever motivated George's opinion of *Napoleon,* it was not shared by the reading public. Both it and Wilhelm Stein's *Raphael* sank virtually without a trace. As Stein rather coyly put it, despite his own efforts to make it more accessible — such as retaining the capitalization of nouns, which is standard in German and which George disliked — "the book nevertheless remained esoteric with regard to its effect as well as to its sales." Only one review of *Raphael* ever appeared, and it was lengthy, detailed — and damning. Vallentin's *Napoleon,* on the other hand, was totally ignored. Neither book went beyond the first edition and neither one came anywhere close to selling out.

As disappointing as this nonresponse was, and whatever their actual merits might be, the two books were admittedly the victims of extraordinarily bad timing. Issued at the end of 1922 but with a publication date of the following year, they entered the market just at the moment the German mark began its plunge into the abyss. No one was in the position, much less the mood, to buy books in Germany throughout most of 1923. (Symptomatically, the sole critique of Stein's *Raphael* appeared in an Austrian publication.) Once the currency had been stabilized in 1924, it was already too late. New books once again began to tumble out of the presses temporarily silenced by the inflation at an even greater rate than before, and readers thus had their hands full without turning back to the products of a year that most just wanted to forget anyway.

On the bright side, the better economic situation meant new opportunities for anyone prepared to take advantage of them. Shrewdly, Bondi remembered that Wolters had announced a decade ago that he was completing a history of the *Blätter für die Kunst* but that he had heard nothing of the project ever since. Interest in George had certainly not waned in the meantime. If anything, the war and the ensuing turmoil had seemed only to validate George's vision and heighten an already widespread sense of his significance for the fate of Germany at large. Such a book, Bondi probably reckoned, might well find a very broad resonance indeed. Wasting no time, Bondi thus wrote Wolters in early January 1924 to inquire whether the book "can be published within the foreseeable future. Since the economic conditions are now of a sort that one can again have a little more confidence for a time, I would set great store in beginning publication as soon as possible."

Wolters, who was in the process of finalizing his move to Kiel, was not then in the frame of mind to tackle such a huge and all-consuming undertaking. He had made no progress on the book since the war had broken out and, in any case, he would have had to rethink and rewrite the portions he had already completed. For that he would need both time and inner calm, both of which were in short supply at the moment. Too, he was already involved in several smaller projects that occupied whatever leisure he did have. Always more patriotic, not to say nationalistic, than most of George's other companions, Wolters had been outraged by the French occupation of the Ruhr. He had thus set out on a personal crusade against France, using every possible occasion to rail against the French and to expose their wickedness in public speeches, in his classroom lectures, and in occasional publications, while simultaneously trying to whip up national sentiment among his audience. Together with Walter Elze, he thus assembled an anthology of patriotic texts and in 1923 had published it with the Breslau firm of Hirt. The title — *Voices of the Rhine: A Reader for Germans* — pretty well conveys its tendency. At the same time, he began an even larger endeavor, called *The German: A Reader,* which ultimately came to fill five volumes. But Wolters also began participating in various political demonstrations, such as a ceremony in the late spring of 1924 held in the memory of Albert Leo Schlageter. During the Ruhr occupation the French had accused Schlageter of engaging in sabotage and summarily executed him. The following year, Wolters held a speech at an event honoring Schlageter and, as he told Vallentin, "He thinks he notices a unified German attitude among the youth. From this point of view he is not unsympathetic to the sometimes extreme comments and spectacles [made by] these youths."

George, hearing this report from Vallentin in late May, was not pleased. It reminded him of the almost fanatical patriotism Wolters had displayed at the outbreak of the war, and everyone knew where that had led. George told Vallentin that "Wolters was deceiving himself again. In general, there is the danger for him that he gets involved with things of the second order instead of doing what is essential." At first, George suggested he meant this remark only in a more general sense, saying, "It is regrettable that Wolters has not yet created one first-rate work, as would be worthy of him — a great book, for which he possesses all the qualifications and which no one else could do the way he could — in the manner of Gundolf's *Goethe*." Given Wolters's evident abilities, George added that he found it all the more "astonishing that Wolters gets nothing done." But then George became more explicit, making it apparent that what was really "essential" for Wolters to do was to complete the book he had begun on their movement. He "rather bitterly said that Wolters had been working for so and so many years on the history of the *Blätter* and still has not finished." When Vallentin tartly suggested that Wolters probably only needed "an energetic remark" to focus his attention, George exasperatedly voiced skepticism. "There has been no lack of such remarks," he replied, "but Wolters always lets himself be diverted by other things, he has to do Rhine-books and readers and for that reason doesn't get to this work." It was all simply too frustrating. The time had perhaps never been better to present the "true" story of George to the world, which was now perhaps more ready than ever to hear the Master's word, and Wolters, George thought, was frittering away his energy on frivolous enterprises.

In his own defense, Wolters tried to explain to George that what the Master termed his "dissipation" should be understandable, if not excusable, in light of the events that had taken place over the last few years. The uncertainty of his professional existence, together with his own delicate health — during the war Wolters had contracted a severe articular rheumatism that had permanently damaged and weakened his heart — had combined to make shouldering such a daunting task next to impossible. Still, Wolters swore that he would eventually return to the book and that he had never lost "even for an instant the will and the intention to do it." But, at the same time, Wolters could not refrain from making a pitch for his other projects as well. Saying that his "amazement at the wealth and the magnitude of the German spirit" was growing daily, Wolters insisted that his editorial efforts were not in vain, even if one looked at them from the Master's point of view. "If it will, in addition, still be possible to spread the best examples of prose among broad sections of the youth, then I believe I am thus working according to Masterly intentions."

Until it was finally completed at the end of 1929, George repeatedly hectored, cajoled, and prodded Wolters to bring the history of the *Blätter* to a close. When Wolters visited Vallentin in late 1924, George was there and he again castigated Wolters for squandering his time on the prose collections, pointing out that he had "truly better things to do." Wolters mildly protested, claiming he could not just drop his other projects in medias res, as it were, because it was in his nature to finish what he began. It was, in hindsight, not the most judicious thing for Wolters to say. Knowing that he had of course meant his anthologies and not the history of the *Blätter,* George responded sarcastically that he did not doubt Wolters's resolve to bring things, once started, to a conclusion. But, he said, "he wanted to live to see it and he was not so young anymore that he could wait so long." In 1927, Wolters was still engaged in unapproved activities, including the publication of a book containing four lectures he had given between 1923 and 1926. *Four Speeches on the Fatherland* contained such uplifting titles as "The Rhine our Fate," "On the Meaning of Sacrificing One's Life for the Fatherland," and "Goethe as Educator toward Patriotic Thinking." Even Wolters's other friends thought he was misusing his talents and some, such as Edgar Salin, openly objected to his escalating chauvinism. Salin, who said he had "severe reservations" about the piece on the Rhine, was appalled by the essay on Goethe, which paints Goethe, the most European of Germans, as a raving nationalist. This Salin found not only wrong but also "disturbing and offensive," and he told Wolters so. George, however, did not take Wolters's patriotic fervor or his speechifying very seriously — he regarded them as no more than "pranks" — and he was more concerned that Wolters was not getting on with the more important job. Instead of doing that, he was, as George grumbled to Edith Landmann, "writing patriotic speeches on *my* time!"

Whereas George had to do everything short of lashing Wolters to his chair to get him to write the book he really wanted, he must have found it even more galling that Friedrich Gundolf continued to churn out book after book with seemingly effortless ease. In the middle of 1924, Gundolf had already managed to finish yet another sizable manuscript, and that summer, he informed Wolters, who was now the senior contact person in the circle, that he had completed a study on his great hero, Julius Caesar. Wolters relayed the news to George while indicating that Gundolf "hoped to receive the masterly commendation for it." That is, Gundolf wanted Bondi to publish his new book with the circle's insignia, which could happen only if George authorized it. Since George did not wish for any direct contact with Gundolf, communication among all the involved parties proved somewhat tricky. Gundolf thus wrote to Bondi in early July to alert him to the imminent receipt of the manuscript, giving the publisher the chance to make necessary arrangements. (Few people ever knew at any given moment where George was and finding out an address where he could be reached often took some time.) Bondi himself was ecstatic that Gundolf, one of his best-selling authors, had managed to write a full-scale monograph on his other great hero and had thus realized his ambition to give full formal expression to his long-term fixation on the Roman dictator. "I congratulate you," Bondi heartily told him a day after he received the news, "that your old wish of publishing a book about Caesar (apart from your dissertation) is now being fulfilled. I hardly need to say that I am looking forward to it with extraordinary eagerness, more perhaps than I ever have for a book before." Bondi was so excited he told Gundolf that he had been the subject of office gossip recently. The female staff of the publishing house apparently found Gundolf as irresistibly attractive as everyone else did. "I hear," Bondi confidentially told him, "that Siegfried in the Nibelungen movie that is very successful here, but which I have not yet seen, is supposed to bear a resemblance to you. The secretary who saw the film last night said: especially with regard to the eyes."

On a more sober note, however, there was the issue of the emblem. Bondi was well aware of the estrangement between George and Gundolf. If he wanted to avoid another uproar like the one surrounding the Kleist book, Bondi needed to obtain official permission from George before he could proceed. Although the manuscript had been immediately sent to George, no decision had yet been announced by the end of August. Finally, in mid-September, Bondi was able to let Gundolf know, with noticeable relief, that "as I have just been informed by telephone from my office, Morwitz was there to relay the message that St. G. has approved the printing of the vignette."

What Morwitz did not reveal was what George really thought of Gundolf's new manuscript. As George had told Vallentin, since "the book contains nothing harmful there was no cause to withhold the *Blätter* symbol from it." But the very fact that George considered the book harmless was in itself an overwhelming indictment. Books were weapons, according to George, or should be, but Gundolf's latest work contained, he said, "nothing interesting." When Vallentin offered the suggestion that Gundolf had at least satisfied his Caesar "tic," George rejected even this attempt to find some merit in the book. After all, he told Vallentin, "everyone has an individual tic and that was to a certain extent a prerequisite, but fertilizer still had to be added, the impregnation by something higher and Gundolf and his book now lack that."

No doubt, even if George thought Gundolf's book was basically benign, George had to concede that it could not hurt to have another work published by the person who, as far as the reading public knew, was still George's closest disciple. Nevertheless, George also wanted to prevent a repetition of the Kleist incident. He thus made sure he saw the proofs of the book before it went into press so that he could confirm that another rogue dedication to some undesirable personage had not been furtively slipped in at the last minute.

Skeptical though George himself was about the new book, Gundolf's *Caesar: History of his Fame* demonstrates all of the qualities that had made its author one of the most widely read and influential writers of the day. Tracing the growth and trajectory of Caesar's reputation from his death up to the end of the nineteenth century, the book is less about the Roman emperor per se as about the evolution of a mythical figure that had gripped the European imagination for two millennia. Caesar has always been synonymous with absolute power; the very word in German for emperor — *Kaiser* — was derived from his name. Gundolf showed how the example of Caesar had never been far from the minds of later rulers who wanted to measure themselves not only against their contemporary opponents but against the giants of history as well. But no one since had compared in both the glory and the menace that made Caesar so enduringly fascinating. Written in Gundolf's best, most electrifying style, the book communicates that magnetism even in the narration of it, making it hard to put down. Bondi, who still belonged to that generation of publishers who actually had more than a commercial interest in the books they sold, brimmed with enthusiasm after he had read it. Explaining that he had been ill and thus unable to concentrate on anything "serious" until then, Bondi wrote in late September that "I am now done reading it. I think your Caesar belongs among the most profound things that have ever been said about the nature of historical development. One comes closer to the character of the ages and admires the 'monumental sense' that you praise in Bossuet."

Yet Gundolf had ultimately not been so much concerned with the past as he had been preoccupied with the present — and, even more, with the future — meaning and possibility of great, inspiring leadership. In the opening paragraph Gundolf made this focus explicit. Indeed, it seems hardly accidental that the very first word of *Caesar* points to the present.

> Today when the need for the strong man has become audible, when we, weary of others who merely carp and prattle, make do with sergeants instead of leaders, when particularly in Germany anyone with a conspicuous military economic bureaucratic or literary talent is thought capable of governing the people and now social pastors, now unsociable generals, now commercial and industrial giants, now rabid petits bourgeois are viewed as statesmen, we would like to remind all those who are impatient and rash of the great man to whom the highest power has owed its name and idea through the centuries: Caesar.

At such a time — that is, "today" — it is especially urgent, Gundolf told his readers, to reconsider the prototype and standard against which all supreme rulers have always been judged. And while it was true that history does not repeat itself and knowledge of the past does not in itself create the new, Gundolf did think that the historian still had a vital function to perform in and for the present. Admittedly, Gundolf acknowledged, "one knows what the future master or savior will look like only once he prevails." But we *can* know what he does *not* look like, and therein lies the historian's charge. The historian cannot take the reins of power themselves in hand, "yet he can help stir the air in which fitting deeds flourish and recruit minds for coming heroes. In this sense he summons the powers of history and its materials, [namely,] peoples and leaders."

Here, articulated more clearly than ever before, was the way in which, as George often said, "Spirit Books are politics." They could help shape or even create a larger intellectual atmosphere among their readers, promote a psychological climate hospitable to their shared values and beliefs. They could form opinion, mold thoughts, and thus make their audience more receptive to their message and, most important, more ready to accept, indeed to welcome and even to work toward the fulfillment of their vision in reality. Gundolf's book on Caesar, then, is deliberately intended to prepare the path for the advent of a new leader in the future and to allow the people he will lead to recognize in him their true and only salvation.

This overt attempt to influence public sentiment in the service of a particular ideological program was perfectly understood by the book's readers. In a review published in the *Neue Zürcher Zeitung* by a critic named Eduard Korrodi in March of 1925, the reviewer stated outright that "Gundolf's writings from the last few years have left artistic questions far behind. They have a German-political accent, they are the history of the German spirit." Korrodi clearly saw that Gundolf, as well as other members of George's circle, were engaged in something far different from disinterested scholarship and historical research conducted for its own sake. "History is channeled into the present by this circle," Korrodi elaborated, "it becomes political will. In the first period the circle was sensual and aesthetic, in the current one it is usurping spiritual and political power in Germany." And while some, like Korrodi, seemed to applaud or at least to accept the political aims of the circle, as well as its choice of "heroes" and role models, others were more dubious.

One person who was not just cautious about holding the likes of Caesar up for unqualified admiration, but who also shuddered at the prospect that his spirit might perhaps rise again, was Moritz Goldstein. He was the same editor of the *Vossische Zeitung* who had reviewed Gundolf's *George* four years before with such discernment and lucidity, critical attributes also fully on display in his discussion of *Caesar*. So as to begin his assessment on a positive note, Goldstein professed having unalloyed respect, even awe for Gundolf's formidable knowledge and irrefutable accomplishments. Goldstein admitted that, as an observer, he stood "in complete silence before the phenomenon that Gundolf had the time to absorb all of Europe within himself, the Middle Ages and the present, in German, in Latin, in Greek, French, English, Italian,

Spanish. That is no longer human. I would like to know, and entirely without irony, how someone feels who not only knows all of that, but at the same time also delivers his judgment on everything and everyone, on Caesar, Dante, Petrarch, Luther, all the way to Napoleon." That was a good question, and even if it had not been framed, as Goldstein had protested, entirely without irony, it did pay tribute to Gundolf's incontestable authority. The real issue, though, was not whether Gundolf's facts were right or wrong; the real question was whether Gundolf had exercised good judgment in his evaluation of those facts.

And on that account, Goldstein wrote, "we do have to criticize just a little after all. What," he thus asked, "does the new Caesar-cult mean"? Obviously it entailed "hero worship, a yearning for heroes." Perceiving Nietzsche to have been the instigator, or at any rate the ratifier, of the modern passion for the superhuman hero, Goldstein himself briefly played the part of the historian. "Nietzsche dreamt of him in an all too tame world, our all too wild present hopes he will bring dominion and redemption. Does it not hope and wish rashly?" Goldstein provided his own answer.

> Alexander, Caesar, Napoleon, and a few more of the same sort, stand radiant above the history of humanity. We cannot withhold from them our admiration of their natures. But who measures the value of a human being? Success speaks in their favor and is a partial advocate. Acts of violence without mercy, ravaged land, blood and tears are not taken into account by their learned admirers, in the midst of their libraries, or they flatter themselves in the role of an imperial severity with their pens, a role that it is very doubtful would become them in life. We can imagine a figure who feels equal to world domination, but who refuses to obtain it so as not to increase suffering. Who knows in whose name Alexander, Caesar, or Napoleon would come if they were to rise again and whether we [. . .] including Gundolf, would not see ourselves compelled sooner to give up our lives than to grant them victory.

Goldstein's brooding, prescient reservations went largely unheeded by a people so anxious for decisive leadership and national renewal that they were willing to overlook some of the sacrifices it might necessitate. Gundolf's book, unlike those by Vallentin and Stein, went on to post yet another remarkable success for its author. A second printing with an edition of thirteen thousand copies occurred a year later, and it was even translated into English in 1928, with the evocative title *The Mantle of Caesar.* Reviews, almost all positive, some even adulatory, rained down from all quarters, with most affirmatively underlining its overt political message. One critic said he thought it was "Gundolf's most beautiful book," while pointing out it was also "a truly 'topical book.' " The same reviewer approvingly noted its conformity to circle doctrine — "above all there resonates from the book, in genuine Georgean fashion, 'the call to act' " — and again the critic emphasized its contemporary relevance. "It is not unintentional that the images of the *great doers* [*Täter*]" — this word recurs again and again — "are conjured forth just now." In every way, its readers thought, Gundolf's book was of and for the times.

Caesar was so well and extensively received that reviews of it appeared even on the front pages of many newspapers, together with articles on other noteworthy political events of the day. In one, a journalist named Conrad Wandrey offered his considered thoughts on Gundolf's latest work in a notice published on the front page of the afternoon edition of the *Münchener Neueste Nachrichten* on December 20, 1924. The headlines above Wandrey's essay were devoted to another event that had taken place that afternoon, at 12:15 P.M. After serving only slightly more than eight months of his already light five-year sentence, Adolf Hitler and a co-conspirator in the putsch, Hermann Kriebel, were released on early parole from Landsberg prison. "Hitler and Kriebel Set Free," the banner read, "Probationary Periods Commence."

History is full of odd coincidences, flukes of circumstance so improbable they would be preposterous if only they had not actually occurred. On a late December evening in 1924, as readers mulled over Conrad Wandrey's intelligent and sympathetic discussion of the book heralding the new Caesar, extolling the hoped-for coming of an omnipotent *Führer,* the advent of a ruthless *Täter* who would lead his people to recapture greatness, the very man who would soon claim Caesar's mantle for himself had that same afternoon walked out of jail into freedom.

Although George had not of course collaborated directly with Gundolf in the making of *Caesar,* he had still overseen the final stages of the book's production, approving the manuscript and reading proofs, and to that degree the process was no different from the approach George took to all the other publications of the circle. And while he claimed not to have found anything of significance in the book, the very fact that he let it appear with the swastika signet of the *Blätter* would indicate that he saw no fundamental contradiction between the book's larger aims and his own. Had there in fact been any basic disagreement between George's vision and Gundolf's portrait, the book would never have been allowed to go forward. For that, the Spirit Books were too important to George, too closely tied to his image of himself. Indeed, George saw them in some real sense as his intellectual or "spiritual" grandchildren, extensions of his own being spawned in others and through them given concrete expression. He once said to Michael Landmann, son of Edith and Julius, that his disciples "see with his eyes, which he had lent them, in regions into which he otherwise did not see — for that reason their works actually belonged to him. He lives with many bodies." George conceived of the "spiritual marriage" he consummated with every one of his disciples as potentially leading to a "spiritual birth" embodied in that follower's work. In early 1925, George expressly used this metaphor in a conversation with Edith Landmann. He suddenly announced that "after 1927 [. . .] no more Spirit Books may appear." When she asked why he had made this rather surprising decision, he replied, "A marriage that produces a child, good, it was fruitful; a marriage with two, three children, good, it was fruitful; a marriage with seven children, well, it was very fruitful; a marriage with ten children, that is already the utmost limit, and with thirteen, fifteen, twenty children, that is simply revolting. It is even the same with poems if someone makes too many."

This last remark, tossed off apparently so lightly, confirmed that a monumental shift had taken place within George. After his recovery from his illness in the summer of 1924 and until his death, George wrote virtually no more poetry, putting the major portion of his energy into the works of his closest followers and into the maintenance of his friendships. Partly, he stopped writing poetry because he no longer believed in its efficacy. Even as early as February of 1923, he had told Ernst Glöckner that he would "not publish anything at the moment. Everything has been said that there is to say; the worst is yet to come." Three years later, he was still saying much the same thing to Edith Landmann. "Now it is no longer so urgent to write poetry," he observed. "So much has been said that has not yet been understood. Then it's not necessary anymore." The times had also changed. He believed he now lived in a more prosaic world, one in which poetry, and literature more generally, did not occupy the place they once did when he was younger. As he said on another occasion, this time to Michael Landmann, "There was a time when it was not possible for someone in the state not to write poetry. Today that is possible, but they are all poetically impressionable. Perhaps some will come one day who have not read a line — I find it hard to believe, but it is still possible." Too, George was now approaching old age and felt his creative powers ebbing and that he had exhausted the wellspring that had fed his artistic imagination. To Ernst Morwitz he simply declared that he did not want "the resignation of old age to fall on his work. He had explored the full circle of his possibilities and did not wish to repeat himself." Even more bluntly he proclaimed to someone else that "after the age of sixty one does not *write* poems anymore!"

It seems, even still, incredible. George, for so many — not least to himself — the poet par excellence, on whom the poetic word had once bestowed all imaginable power and prestige, was abandoning poetry altogether. Yet it was true: George now no longer felt he needed to write poetry. His poems, even his best verses, had always been a means to other ends, and now he was convinced that he could achieve those ends in other, perhaps even better ways. What was crucial anyway were not the poems but the poet. "If one takes away a professor's work," George once said, "then nothing at all remains. If one takes away my work from me, Stefan George remains intact." Of course, one could object that it was originally because of his poetry that he had been able to advance to a position where he no longer thought he required it. But George now viewed the Spirit Books — for the time being anyway — as the best instruments for accomplishing his goals. In the same conversation with Glöckner in which he had announced his own retirement from writing, he had underscored the even greater significance that thereby befell the *Geistbücher*. For, George said, they alone now "had the task either to lead or to act like dynamite." Ideally, they might do both.

For the rest of the decade, then, George would be principally engaged as advisor, editor, sounding board, and critic, and even as financial backer for those ventures Bondi considered too risky to underwrite himself. It was in some ways a return to his own origins, for George had after all begun his career as an editor and literary entrepreneur. Now, though, he preferred to work almost entirely behind the scenes, letting others speak on his behalf and implicitly in his name.

One thing that did not change was George's restlessness. Throughout the mid-1920s, he kept up his regular itinerary, constantly moving among Basel, Munich, Heidelberg, Königstein (where his sister lived), Berlin, and, albeit reluctantly, Kiel. But, especially after his illness and the many operations that had left him weakened and susceptible to the effects of his environment, George increasingly shunned the cold and dark of the north, preferring the warmer southern climes. In February 1926, he thus traveled for the first time to Locarno on Lake Maggiore, just above the Italian border, where the Alps fall away and nothing more stands in the way of the sun. Yet even then, he stayed only a few weeks and once again set off on his ceaseless peregrinations. He valued each place he stopped for different reasons: the Landmanns in Basel, with their normal family life and obedient children, allowed him to relax in comfortable surroundings with people who revered him but placed no demands on him. But soon enough, he would abruptly announce his departure by saying, "Now the gypsy life begins again."

Traveling — the "gypsy life" — had indeed been his way for almost four decades now, ever since he had first gone to London in 1888, and he never lost his relish for it. When Wolters once returned from a long trip he had taken in 1920 and said he was tired from the journey, George scoffed at the very idea. "There's no such thing," he said. "One never becomes tired from traveling. I become more tired from not traveling." But it was more than a need for stimulus and change that drove George's perpetual odyssey. By leading a nomadic existence, by refusing to become too attached to any one place, to be identified with a particular city or region or even country, George could better maintain the sense that his real home was the invisible realm he had created, the Spiritual Empire that had, as yet, no physical equivalent. Another motive was more mundane: given the nature of his state, with its citizens spread out in distant cities and towns, traveling from one to the other was an inescapable necessity. Later on, as he grew older and his energy began to wane, even George implied that his incessant moving from place to place was taxing. But since they were unavoidable, he increasingly confined his travels to official visits, dispensing with all purely touristic journeys. "Now," he said in 1929, "one no longer goes somewhere to be stimulated by the countryside. One makes state trips and that's it." Either way, the ideal dwelling for George was not a house or a room, with their immovable walls and solid roof, but rather, as he often said himself, something more akin to a tent. "A tent," he once told Percy Gothein, "can be taken down when you want and pitched somewhere else." Tents, George thought, were the best form of shelter in a time of transition and impermanence. "Later times may again live in palaces," George allowed, but "ours is the founding time, the time of tents. It makes no sense to build palaces today, since no people exist for whom it would be appropriate to live in them." Only after the right conditions had been established, a firm foundation laid, would it be possible to think again about setting up more permanent arrangements. Until then, as he also said to Edith Landmann in 1927, it would remain "the time of tents."

Yet George did feel the need for some permanent base of operations, for one place that could serve as his headquarters or as a central staging area. Many of his favorite stations in the past had become untenable for one reason or another and he was now faced with the problem of finding a new home base. In late 1925, when he arrived in Basel to spend Christmas with the Landmanns, he stopped on the train station platform and breathed in deeply. "Ah, the cantonal air!" he said to Frau Landmann and then broke into a lament about what he called "the three hostile corners of fairytale land." (Referring, as he often now did, to Germany — *Deutschland* — as "fairytale land" — *Märchenland* — was another way for George both to repudiate everything taking place there and to suggest that the real Germany lay elsewhere.) The three inhospitable enclaves were, George said, "the *Geist* corner in Heidelberg, the cosmic one on the Bayrischer Platz in Berlin and the northern one in Kiel." Gundolf had made Heidelberg unpalatable, Lechter's rampant mysticism had spoiled the only part of Berlin he had ever liked, and Kiel was, well, Kiel. On his return from Locarno in March 1926, George brought up the subject again of finding some fixed abode, even raising the prospect of moving outside of Germany altogether. He spoke with Julius Landmann about "possibly settling in Switzerland: he said he had to have a permanent residence;

Bingen was over, nothing could be found in Munich, Heidelberg had been dashed, Königstein could be given up at any moment; perhaps the best thing was Basel." George also considered other options that would put him closer to his friends in the north, but the choices were obviously more limited there. In a conversation with Vallentin, he broached the issue of "moving the 'state' again," but he eliminated several locations from consideration right away: Berlin was out, Kiel was never in, and with that the already short list was quickly running out of alternatives. "In any event," he firmly told Vallentin, he "could not move it to Copenhagen; it is too watery there." But the problem of finding somewhere he *could* move to remained.

The work of the state could not wait, however, until the question of the Master's domicile had been resolved. George thus used whatever space his friends could provide to push his various projects forward, but he did insist on certain requirements. Some were practical: his surgery had made it difficult for him to climb stairs, necessitating quarters that were on ground level. This meant that, in Berlin, Thormaehlen's attic studio, which had served George as a shelter and workspace for over a decade, was no longer accessible. A Swiss friend of Thormaehlen and fellow sculptor by the name of Alexander Zschokke conveniently rented a spacious parterre workshop in the center of the city. Once Ernst Morwitz had ascertained that both the room and its occupant were acceptable — Thormaehlen also gave Zschokke precise instructions about what temperature should be maintained in the room, the form of address to be used and the "tone of conversation" he should observe — the Master himself appeared. Everything was as he liked it: walls bare of superfluous "bourgeois" decoration and furniture that was purely utilitarian in form. There was more than a faint resemblance to the Globe Room in its disposition: along the walls were long, low benches made of spruce that held up to twelve to fourteen people, and in the middle was a plain table that provided a surface to work and eat. A stove did double duty for heating and cooking, and otherwise the room contained only sculpting materials and various utensils.

The regular gatherings George held at Zschokke's studio during the 1920s were also largely businesslike in nature and focused on a specific project or task. Zschokke remembered that "in the months George spent in Berlin we usually worked a lot." Everyone there was expected to participate, for "George did not like onlookers who were not involved." Sitting at the table, they all would read and correct manuscripts, they checked proofs, occasionally recited poetry, and "after one to two hours everything was over." Zschokke noted that "we almost never spoke about poems, as in general speeches or conversations about literary or artistic matters never took place in this context. It was about facts, correcting proofs, works and labor, but all within a cheerful ambiance, sometimes accompanied by caustic humor and roaring, merciless laughter." As an example of the kind of comments that were exchanged during these sessions, George told Edith Landmann that someone had recently said something "enormously nasty about Wolters." Alluding to Wolters's weakness for patriotic subjects, one of George's younger friends had maliciously proposed — not, one assumes, in Wolters's presence — that "he should write a book some time about the Germanic kitchen." George, whose own skepticism about Wolters's extracurricular activities was well known, pretended he disapproved of the comment, observing only, "Unbelievably nasty, that."

With the communal assemblies being organized again, ambitious publications once more underway, and even places to congregate that reminded one of the sites that had since become legendary, it almost seemed as if the effects of the war and all it had entailed had finally been surmounted, indeed somehow erased. It was like a magical return to the brief but exhilarating period just before August 1914, when everyone was emboldened by the belief that anything was possible, that it was only a matter of time before George's true meaning would be revealed to the people and he would assume the role he was destined to fill. There were even several new recruits to the circle that lent it a radiance that outshone some of its brightest stars. In 1923, while in Marburg, George had been introduced to an eighteen-year-old student of law by the name of Berthold von Stauffenberg and his twin brother, Alexander. Perhaps at the same time, or shortly thereafter, George also met their younger brother Claus, two years their junior. They belonged to one of the oldest and most distinguished noble families in Germany — their father, Alfred Schenk Count von Stauffenberg, was the first chamberlain and seneschal of King Wilhelm II of Württemberg, and their mother, Countess Uxkull, was lady-in-waiting and friend to his Queen Charlotte — and whose ancestors first made their appearance in history during the thirteenth century.

All three of the Stauffenberg brothers, like many other young men of their age, had been reading George's poems since their early teens and stood entirely under their spell. Meeting the poet only heightened their reverence for the man they now regarded as their personal Master. A few weeks after Alexander had been brought before George, he said he had "seen and lived through things" that "have made [me] tremendously rich · in fact are decisive for my entire life so that I know that I will one day have great inner security." Later that year, in September 1923, Alexander referred to becoming acquainted with the Master as the "greatest experience" of his life. His twin brother Berthold likewise wrote poems to George extolling him in extravagant terms. One exclaims, "You have been sent as the savior of this world." For all three, the acquaintance with George marked a turning point in their lives, which until the end were conducted faithfully and explicitly in his service.

For his part, George was overjoyed to embrace them. Each of the Stauffenberg brothers was strong, handsome, and athletically vigorous, confident and worldly in bearing, yet untainted by the cynicism or hauteur that a privileged upbringing can sometimes induce. No less appealingly, all three were also intellectually alert and lively. Most of all, they were genuinely, thrillingly aristocratic; there was no trace of bourgeois pettiness about them. George liked to tell the story of when, during a two-week stay in Munich during the summer of 1924, he received a visit from Berthold Stauffenberg. Suddenly, the landlady, instead of using the normal porcelain service for the afternoon tea, sent up her best gilded formal ware. It turned out that she thought Berthold looked similar to the deceased son of the Crown Prince of Bavaria and suspected her guest had "high connections." When Edith Landmann remarked to George on the increased number of people in his entourage from noble backgrounds — besides the Stauffenbergs, there was also their cousin Woldemar von Uxkull and their mutual friend Albrecht von Blumenthal — George proudly acknowledged that "since the Revolution one comes by them more often." But it was not mere snobbery that made these young noblemen so attractive to George. Rather, he believed that their nobility was merely the outward manifestation, or perhaps better the inbred maintenance, of those qualities he most wanted his disciples to develop in themselves. In George's estimation, as he explained it to Frau Landmann, the aristocracy essentially consisted in that "which excluded resentment and envy because they already had sufficient self-confidence not to desire something else." What was more, he went on, he thought that "reverence and education toward service rests on self-confidence" and he saw "not being able to revere, wanting to have everything equal" as a "lack of nobility and strength: rickets of the soul." In other words, in George's mind, the more aristocratic one was, the more effortlessly one was able to obey. The nobleman's sense of self-worth is not tied to his individual person, but to his place within a hierarchy, making the recognition of a higher authority less a conscious decision than a natural expression of the system of values in which he lived. The aristocrat, in George's eyes, provided the perfect disciple.

All of this meant that George did not overtly treat the Stauffenbergs any differently from the others. They also received their requisite nicknames: Berthold was called "Adjib," or the "Miraculous," after the prince in a *Thousand and One Nights;* Alexander was known as "Offa," in honor of the son of a king in an ancient legend. Only Claus kept his proper name. In explanation of this anomaly, Ludwig Thormaehlen offered the theory that Claus was so uniquely himself that no other designation would do.

Apart from a few more additions — and a few late desertions — George now had the group of people gathered around him who would accompany him until the end of his life. They followed him wherever he went and whenever he wanted them to come, ready to do his bidding and grateful just to be in his presence. To them, he was literally everything. He was their leader, their father, their ruler, their priest, their wise man, prophet, king, and creator. He was their god; he was their Master.

CHAPTER 40

Stupor Mundi

George's excitement over the Stauffenberg brothers went beyond his appreciation for their personal qualities, as substantial as they were. For in them George saw a living connection to one of the most magnificent rulers Europe had ever witnessed and the one he probably admired the most: Frederick II of Hohenstaufen. Of German descent but born in Italy in 1194, Frederick had been elected king of Germany at the age of three, was made king of Sicily a year later and went on to crown himself king of Jerusalem and finally become Holy Roman Emperor in 1220. At the height of his power, Frederick II reigned over all of middle Europe, with his vast empire extending from the Baltic to the Strait of Sicily in the Mediterranean Sea. To his enemies he was a cruel despot, an apocalyptic monster, the Antichrist; to his defenders he was a second David, the Messiah, the benevolent Savior of the world. One of his contemporaries, the English monk Matthew Paris of St. Albans, recorded the passing of Frederick in 1250 by calling him "the greatest of the princes of the earth, wonder of the world" — *stupor mundi*. Whether one regarded him as a friend or a foe, Frederick eclipsed in everyone's eyes the categories reserved for ordinary men.

His death was all the more a shock. To many he had hardly seemed mortal. Legends soon formed about him after he died and many people throughout Europe, refusing to accept that he had gone forever, expected him to return again, more powerful and glorious than before. Especially in the northern German lands, the belief even took hold that "he is still alive and will remain alive until the end of the world; there has been and shall be no proper emperor but he." For centuries, false Fredericks appeared, emboldened by the popular myth that he would one day return to redeem his people. But Frederick did not return and with his death more than just the Hohenstaufen dynasty ended. It also led to the collapse of the whole German *Reich,* leaving it splintered in a patchwork of competing kingdoms, principalities, and autonomous fiefdoms. Not for another six centuries, long after the other European states had evolved into strong and unified nations, was there another German empire that integrated the lands that had once bowed under Frederick's scepter. Now, in the early 1920s, that second empire — forged by Bismarck and forfeited by Wilhelm II — had fallen apart as well, leaving almost as much disorder and chaos in its train as the destruction of the first. Hopes for yet another, third *Reich,* one that would outlast the previous two and even surpass them in grandeur and might, had begun to stir again among some Germans as they tried to regain their footing after the war. For George, the Stauffenberg name, with its ancient associations — the family itself believed, accurately or not, that they belonged to the Hohenstaufen lineage — rang with the kind of deep, pure sound that stirred his own dreams of conquest and triumph.

George had long looked to Frederick II as the epitome of a monarch. In 1902 he had taken Gundolf to inspect the newly reopened imperial crypt in the cathedral at Speyer. In it are buried eight German kings and emperors along with several of their consorts, including Beatrix, second wife of Frederick's grandfather, Frederick Barbarossa. The visit inspired a poem that George had included in *The Seventh Ring,* "The Graves in Speyer," which ends with the poet standing in front of the burial vault of Beatrix. In the poet's mind, she has summoned the spirit of her grandson, Frederick II, whose remains lie in Palermo and who appears before her accompanied by his own natural son, Enzo (or Enzio). Even in the presence of such exalted peers, the shade of Frederick stands resplendent:

> But before all the others, called to visit from the south
> By the ancestral mother of the Staufer
> With the beautiful Enzio at his side,
> Shines forth the Greatest Frederick · longing of true people ·
> Aiming to realize the plans of the Charles and Ottos
> The magnificent dream of the Orient
> Wisdom of the Cabala and Roman dignity
> The feasts of Agrigento and Selinunte.

The poet calls him the "Greatest Frederick" because he had sought to assimilate all of Europe within his realm, as opposed to the merely "great" eighteenth-century Frederick of Hohenzollern, who was doubly questionable for preferring French to German culture and, even worse, for having been Prussian. Besides bringing all of the German-speaking peoples under a single roof — something the poem says the Carolingian and Ottonian kings before him had tried and failed to do — the greater Frederick had harnessed both north and south, joining Italy with Germany, as well as merging the cultures of East and West. As king of Jerusalem, he united in his person Judaism and Christianity, even as he combined Hellenic civilization — symbolized by the Greek temples in Sicily at Agrigento and Selinunte — with the Roman form of rule he had inherited with the title of emperor. Frederick had been, in George's estimation, all things to all people, the pinnacle of humanity, the essence of majesty, the supreme and omnipotent ruler.

Over the years, George often referred to Frederick, sometimes in poems but even more frequently in conversation, and always in terms of great esteem. In 1920, for instance, he had tried to convince Berthold Vallentin of Frederick's preeminence by having Wolters read some of his extant letters aloud to him. Vallentin, partial naturally to Napoleon, felt that the medieval sovereign was too distant, too far removed historically to allow the kind of immediate emotional response he thought the French emperor could still elicit. George argued, on the contrary, that "the German emperors of the middle ages were not such pale, shadowy figures or as intangible" as Vallentin seemed to imply, whereupon Vallentin weakly objected that "Frederick II was after all an exception." Evidently, George must have thought that Vallentin had a point about the medieval period itself, but he was not prepared to capitulate. The difficulty, he thought, was not that Frederick was so irretrievably remote, but that no one had yet successfully brought him closer. Four years later, George was still worrying about the problem of how to make the image of Frederick more vibrant for the present. Things would be different, he told Edith Landmann, had the whole period been the subject of more literary works. "German history has not been adequately treated and developed further in literature," he said in early 1924, but he was at a loss to explain why that was so. One thing was certain: "There is no lack of greatness. The others don't have such brilliant figures as the Staufer nor ones that emerge in such three-dimensional, visible form. But they haven't been poeticized." Later the same year, in another exchange with Vallentin, he brought up the issue of "German imperial history" again, saying that "one really ought to give it visible expression one day." As he had to Frau Landmann, George similarly emphasized the unique character of the German past and particularly that of the Staufer. "What splendor the Staufer display!" he said to Vallentin. "The history of no other people presents anything like it. In all of German history some ideal factor is always the driving and decisive element; in England and France it is entirely different." Clearly, by the middle of the decade the task of reanimating Frederick had become an urgent necessity in George's eyes. All he needed was someone to perform the resurrection.

Coincidentally or not, at that very time almost all of George's closest friends and associates were heading south to Italy. In the spring and early summer of 1924, Berthold and Alexander Stauffenberg, together with several friends from university, traveled via Milan, Verona, Padua, Venice, and Ravenna to Rome before continuing on to Naples, Paestum, Capri, and finally by ship to Palermo. Vallentin and his wife, Diana, went on their own trip to Italy as well, as did Friedrich and Erika Wolters and Ernst Kantorowicz. The previous fall, Max Kommerell and Johann Anton had also made the voyage together, and of course Wolfskehl was still exiled in Florence. Even Friedrich Gundolf had gone to Italy in early 1924, where he had completed most of his book on Caesar. To be sure, an Italian journey was considered a requisite experience in the life of every educated German since Goethe, and George often sent his youngest followers to Italy to give them a final polish. But George was no romantic. He was always critical of what he perceived as the backwardness and disorder of Italy, and he liked to tell how Wolfskehl would say that "as soon as he had crossed the border in Ala and saw the filth there and received the first counterfeit notes when changing money, he felt: now I am free." Likewise, when conditions in Germany had reached their nadir in the early twenties and George was thinking about making a trip to Italy, he reflected that from one perspective the journey had been rendered superfluous. "Germany is becoming so dilapidated," he said, "that one of the main attractions of Italy has already been achieved here." Yet, more seriously, he knew that the experience of Italy had become a vital part of German culture and nothing could substitute for going there. And, whatever the faults of the Italians, he said, "one likes them nevertheless, that can't be denied. They are the custodians of old treasures. They sit in our Italy."

"Our Italy": it was a loaded phrase, particularly now that George was thinking so intensively about the last ruler the two countries had shared. With so many of those closest to him going to Italy simultaneously, it almost appears they had been sent on some sort of mission, as if they were making an official "state" visit. Even more suggestive is that all of George's friends did not just stop in Rome or Naples as most tourists did. Rather, they all made the more arduous journey to Sicily with the express purpose of visiting the many sites on the island associated with Frederick II. Berthold Stauffenberg, Albrecht von Blumenthal, and their companion Maria Fehlig thus went in April to the Palazzo Reale in Palermo where Frederick spent his childhood, and they paid their respects at the sarcophagus in the Cathedral where he is entombed. Frederick was also on the mind of Erika Wolters, who wrote to George in the middle of the same month from Agrigento. "I was looking for one thing and found something else," she said, specifying that "I was looking for Frederick II and found the Master. [. . .] I don't know if the Master has ever been here, but I can so well imagine that He walked on the hot white paths to the temples and sat high up there." Yet another visitor to Sicily who saw the landscape through the Master's eyes and was in search of the medieval emperor's traces was Ernst Kantorowicz. Writing from Naples on his way back home to Heidelberg, he told George that he noticed how his travels were different now that he knew George, that he saw things through him in a new light. "Thus I always feel some shame over my earlier blindness mixed in with the sense of happiness to be sharing in everything beautiful and really to be able to absorb it." Like the others, Kantorowicz had focused on the various stations along the way that had some connection with the medieval emperor. Indeed, Kantorowicz appears to have already decided to devote himself to some kind of work about Frederick and had spent much of his time conducting research for the project. To that end, he told George that he would remain a little longer than originally planned in Naples:

> That I have learned a great deal for my purposes, that is, for my work, goes without saying and that is also the reason why I am staying here until the beginning of May. For on the third is the seven-hundredth anniversary of the University of Naples, which Frederick II founded, and all of the newspapers are already full of hymns to the great emperor who — like Mussolini (!) — wanted to erect an Italia imperiale — in short, Frdr. II is being turned into the initiator of the fascist dream.

The Italian Fascists were not the only ones claiming Frederick as their rightful ancestor. As Kantorowicz also reported, during the commemorative festivities held in Naples that month, someone — no one knows for certain who — had laid a wreath at the foot of Frederick's sarcophagus in Palermo bearing the inscription: TO ITS EMPERORS AND HEROES FROM THE SECRET GERMANY.

In Kantorowicz, then, George had finally found the person who would bring Frederick back to life. After returning to Heidelberg, Kantorowicz worked steadily on the project for the next two years. George, to whom the subject was so dear, stayed with Kantorowicz whenever he was in Heidelberg, and he actively participated in the book's creation as it was being written. He was also intimately involved in its publication. On July 12, 1926 — not insignificantly the day of his birthday — George wrote to Bondi with what he called a "proposal": "A person close to me has completed a manuscript on the history of Frederick II. I have read it and found it important enough to secure it immediately for myself (so that it will not fall into the hands of other all too nimble publishers)." George did not assume that Bondi would bite — the publisher had after all turned down several offers in the past and a book about the Middle Ages did not on the face of it promise to be best-seller material —

and George thus presented him with an alternative. There was one condition, though, that was non-negotiable: the book had to be published with the swastika. "Since the work may appear only under the emblem of the state," George told him, "I would have it published by the *Blätter* if you considered it unsuitable to your needs. If, however, you were basically inclined to publish it I would send the first four books to you in typewritten copy."

Ten days later, Bondi had already received and read the chapters. He was entranced. "The work completely captivated me by the magic exercised by the great Hohenstaufen emperor but also by the portrayal. I am prepared to publish it with pleasure." But first, as always, several practical details had to be worked out. Perhaps because George was so heavily invested in the subject of the book, he had decided that he would sign the contract in place of the author. Bondi was uneasy about this unorthodox procedure, claiming that it would be "without precedent." But George refused to back down, and Bondi was forced to conduct all of the correspondence pertaining to the book with George alone. Too, George had expressed confidence that the book would generate the kind of enthusiasm that the best publications in the series had attracted. Bondi, having been stung by such recent flops as *Napoleon* and *Raphael*, greeted this declaration with caution, saying he naturally hoped "for success, but unfortunately I cannot share your optimism that failure in this series and with this emblem is impossible. The times have unfortunately changed very much and book sales are so poor that one would not believe it possible."

During the following months, they exchanged numerous letters concerning the project, some rather testy, discussing all aspects of the book's production, ranging from questions about the typeface, paper quality, the title, and so forth, all amidst constant complaints from George about the slow pace of the proceedings. One of the greatest controversies was over the decoration of the title page. George had commissioned Ernst Gundolf to make a line drawing incorporating Romanesque architectural elements for the title page and cover of the book. On inspecting it, Bondi pronounced the drawing "dilettantish" and insisted that, if George really wanted to add an illustration, it would have to be executed by a professional. Mainly, though, Bondi thought the whole idea of an illustration was "rather playful" and misplaced in a work of scholarship. Predictably, George bristled at this criticism and sent back a stiff response. Undeterred, Bondi repeated his reservations about the appropriateness of such a drawing on the cover of a scientific book. Bondi considered the plan, he wrote, "extremely risky," for it might "awaken the impression that it was one of those so-called popular-scientific works. I hardly need to tell you what dreadful junk has shot up like weeds in this field during the past few decades. If, say, Gundolf's name were on the title page, then this method of indicating the publisher would be less dangerous since Gundolf's scientific character is recognized. With a completely unknown author this method has to be seen as misleading." George's reaction to Bondi's reservations is revealing. (In his irritation, George no longer wrote his letters to Bondi himself but dictated them in the third person.) "St. G. insists that the external accentuation of its scientific character would be deleterious to its success: it is meant to attract entirely different — much larger — circles." And, as far as Gundolf went, George professed to be unimpressed by Bondi's arguments. "In the case of G's books St. G. is of the opposite opinion as you: their success was not caused by 'science,' but [the public] applauded only when it could not do otherwise." Not only was George optimistic that Kantorowicz's book would reach a wide readership, he was doing everything in his power to ensure that it would.

As it turned out, Bondi's fears were groundless. The first edition of *Kaiser Friedrich II*, which appeared in March of 1927, sold out before the end of the year. By the time the fourth edition was printed in 1936, ten thousand copies had already been bought. After Gundolf's *Goethe* and Bertram's *Nietzsche*, it was the most successful Spirit Book ever to appear. And, like the other two, it also bridged the divide between "science" and more popular writing, appealing to nonspecialist readers as well as to fellow academics, many of whom remained dubious precisely because the book had attracted such a large following, but who were impressed all the same by the learning displayed by the author. Although Kantorowicz, undoubtedly at George's prompting, had suppressed the vast technical apparatus he had employed in writing the book — he had consulted all the available sources in Latin, Greek, Hebrew, English, French, Italian, and Spanish, but it contains not a single footnote or bibliographic reference — it was obvious to anyone familiar with the historical documents that Kantorowicz had thoroughly mastered them. Not only that: he had infused the story the sources told with a vitality and narrative brilliance that made them seem to come alive for the very first time. Even today, over sixty years after *Frederick II* first appeared, it has lost little of its original allure. In 1991, the medieval historian Norman Cantor asserted that Kantorowicz "wrote the most exciting biography of a medieval monarch produced in this century." And, while not uncritical of the book's overall tendency, Cantor also confirmed that the scholarship remained impeccable. If one were to reissue the book retaining Kantorowicz's original assumptions and goals, Cantor claimed, one "would have very little to do in bringing out a revised edition — maybe change about seventy-five of the seven hundred pages."

This was of course exactly the kind of impact George had intended the book to have. From the beginning, he had wanted someone to tell the life of the man he regarded as the greatest leader that Germany had ever known — and possibly the greatest in all of Europe — in a way that made him matter to the present. Both George and Kantorowicz knew that to be taken seriously and withstand the scrutiny the book would inevitably attract, it would have to rest on an unshakable scholarly foundation. But too many historians, George thought, confused that foundation with the edifice itself, which by contrast often seemed to have been carelessly or indifferently assembled as an afterthought. Most readers are interested in the text itself and have little use for the dense infrastructure of notes and references on which it rests. In seeking to satisfy both audiences at once, Kantorowicz's *Frederick II* is a genuine hybrid: a work of meticulous scholarship that does not parade its credentials and is written with a captivating brilliance and verve. As one reviewer put it, in addition to all of its other virtues, the book is "on the whole extraordinarily well written; individual sections even display a truly remarkable descriptive artistry."

But there was even more at work than first meets the eye. For the effect the book produces was designed to be not merely a scholarly or even an aesthetic end in itself but rather transformed into actual, political energy. Indeed, that was the final aim of the book: it was meant both to endorse George's vision of absolute power as embodied in a single, heroic figure and to instill in its readers an active enthusiasm for its forms and expressions. Although George may not have liked hearing it, this made *Frederick II* a first cousin to Gundolf's books, and in particular to *Caesar*. As the same reviewer also noticed, by presenting Frederick as "the model of the world ruler" and by placing "the great individual in the middle of historical action as its motivating force," Kantorowicz had done more than simply offer up the medieval ruler for our detached admiration. Instead, Kantorowicz had let "a need that he feels within himself and is prompted by the contemporary situation audibly come through as a decisive element in historical representation." In other words, Kantorowicz, just like Gundolf, had deliberately placed his ideological convictions, which were defined more by present-day concerns rather than by thirteenth-century conditions, in the service of his appraisal of Frederick's life and its significance. It was not just that Kantorowicz's interpretation was subjectively colored; it was overtly and intentionally political.

Other critics, especially those less well disposed toward the author, recognized this trait as well and were deeply troubled by it. Albert Brackmann, one of the most prominent medieval scholars of the time, published a lengthy discussion of the book in 1929 that was based on a lecture he had given before the Prussian Academy in Berlin. Brackmann, who was a professor of history at Berlin, had also devoted several sessions of his university seminar during the previous semester to a critical discussion of *Frederick II*. Such extensive treatment by one of the most established figures in his discipline of a book by a previously obscure neophyte was in itself a further sign of the perceived importance and likely influence of Kantorowicz's work. In Brackmann's review, after dutifully acknowledging "the enormous success of the book" and admitting that no other work "about a topic in medieval history has recently made a stronger impression," he bluntly stated his belief that its "basic conception of the personality of the emperor was gained by methodologically false means." Although Brackmann did not yet elaborate what he meant, the very next sentence has the force of implying guilt by association: "Kantorowicz comes from the George-Circle." Although Brackmann clearly thought that simply identifying Kantorowicz's association with George was a sufficient indication of the book's tenor, what is even more interesting is that he made that assumption in the first place. For it demonstrates that by 1929 the notion of the "George-Circle" had become such common knowledge, its principles and constituency so well known, that one had merely to refer to it to evoke a specific and familiar worldview. And it was a worldview that Brackmann thought had no business in the scholarly investigation of the past.

Like most of his colleagues, Brackmann viewed history as a strictly scientific enterprise, and he accordingly saw himself as a sober man of science, someone who approached the historical record in much the same way a chemist looked upon a compound or a biologist a cell. History was not a tool or a weapon for him but simply an object to be examined and understood; the product of study should not be social change but truth. Any attempt to use the past for purposes other than gaining more and better knowledge about it and at most about ourselves was, Brackmann believed, a corruption of the historian's office and a threat to the discipline as a whole. Brackmann thus saw *Frederick II* not as the only, but certainly as one of the most dangerous recent assaults on the integrity of history as a scientific practice, and he warned that "it is a very serious situation in which our science finds itself." Precisely because Kantorowicz's book was not the work of an amateur or a fool it was, Brackmann said, "a visible sign of the dangers that imperil us." For he felt that *Frederick II* presented nothing less than an "endeavor resting on serious research to base our science on dogma rather than on working hypotheses." Interpreting the past through the lens of some doctrine distorts our vision rather than sharpens it, Brackmann believed. Notably, he concluded his essay with an exhortation that comes close to the kind of interested plea he deplored in others, insisting "that one can write history neither as a George disciple nor as a Catholic or as a Protestant or a Marxist, but rather only as a person seeking the truth." What Brackmann did not seem to realize fully was that Kantorowicz *did* affirm the importance of seeking the truth. But only part of the truth he was committed to pursuing was historical.

Kantorowicz formally responded to Brackmann's criticisms in the next issue of the journal in which they had first appeared. But his most comprehensive rejoinder came in the form of a lecture he gave the following year. Three years after its publication, Kantorowicz's book was still provoking spirited debate, and he was therefore invited to deliver a speech at the seventeenth annual German Historians Conference in April of 1930. Despite Kantorowicz's youth and inexperience, his speech was eagerly anticipated — one conference attendee reported that it stood at the "center of interest" — and drew so many listeners that the organizers had to move the lecture into a larger auditorium at the last minute. If Kantorowicz found the gathered assembly of professional historians seated before him intimidating — almost all of them were at least two decades older than he was, and many were regarded as commanding authorities in their fields — he did not display any trepidation. With greater specificity than had been possible in *Frederick II* itself, which was designed as an example rather than a description of his method, he laid out in his address the principles of historiography as he — and by implication George — viewed it. He rejected out of hand the argument that history was a science and that it should or can be ideologically neutral. What is more, Kantorowicz felt that history must be, and indeed inevitably always is, an expression of one's national identity: "For in its essence and as an art historiography absolutely belongs to [the category] of national literature; it is conceived and understood from the standpoint of being a German, no matter if the subject itself concerns the history of the Fatherland or not." As such, history thus "addresses the invariably small number of the truly educated and intellectual leaders of the nation out of whose soil it has arisen and whose impulses it returns in this way — and it thereby acts on teachers and educators through the many branches of the university and school system."

Historiography in general thus had for Kantorowicz an explicitly pedagogical function, and pedagogy in Germany was a national affair, a matter of state — which to Kantorowicz meant in both the official and the secret sense. And it was to this most important source of history's legitimacy that Kantorowicz turned in his concluding statements. Now more than ever, he argued, after Germany had lost the war and suffered the indignities of revolution, civil strife, economic ruin, and social turmoil, "in the hopelessness after the collapse when doubt prevailed and faith in the inner truth of the nation had been universally shaken," history needed what Kantorowicz called "a new goal." Citing Friedrich Schiller as support for where that goal was to be found, he insisted, "While the political empire totters, the spiritual one has acquired an increasingly solid and perfect form." Instead of apologizing for the origin of his inspiration in writing history, Kantorowicz, while mildly mocking the scholarly pretensions of his more staid auditors, announced his allegiance to George as an article of faith:

> And thus, gentlemen, I can finally give an answer to the question posed to me about the scientific value of the historical works of the George school. Their value lies merely in the fact that they serve this belief in the day of the Germans, in the genius of the nation. This belief, handed down to be sure

not from science but from poetry, is the dogma that dominates and determines all of the works of this school and has hardly ever been recognized by the science that otherwise analyzes so finely. For it is not, as many would so like to believe, an aesthetic or phenomenological or any other such dogma that reigns here, but rather it is merely the dogma of the worthy future of the nation and of its honor that infuses these works. [. . .] And above all: only through this belief in the more authentic Germany did those works perhaps themselves become art.

It could hardly be stated more clearly. Kantorowicz's book, like all of the *Geistbücher,* was meant to recover the past for the sake of the future. And not just for any future but specifically for the future of Germany. *Frederick II* was a prescription in historical guise, an instruction manual on the language, character, and style — in short, on the spirit — of heroic, messianic leadership. It was a spiritual guidebook for the German people, not so much to orient them in the past but to conduct them toward things to come. It was, in other words, a model textbook for the "George school," a phrase that should be taken two ways. It circumscribed, on the one hand, the collective attitude and shared tenets of those who belonged within George's circle. But, on the other hand, it also described the actual experience of reading the books it produced: they aspired to educate, to train, to instruct, in short to "school" their readers in the manner of thinking and being they represented — an ambition their often spellbinding rhetoric went a long way toward fulfilling. To read a book by one of George's followers was thus akin to undergoing a rite of initiation. As with all institutions, however, admittance entailed both privileges and obligations. *Frederick II* had revealed the secret truth of Germany's destiny to its readers, but in return for that knowledge they were charged with the implicit pledge to hail the reincarnation of the ruler if — or rather when — he reappeared.

At the same time that Kantorowicz's book appeared in 1927, Max Kommerell was just completing his own contribution to the "George school" library. Ever since he had met George in mid-April 1922, Kommerell had been one of his most devoted companions, traveling across Germany to help the Master when he was ill and, when necessary, arranging for living quarters in Berlin, Munich, Basel, and in Kommerell's native Cannstatt, near Stuttgart. He also served as George's amanuensis, writing out letters in a near-perfect imitation of the Master's hand. Although Kommerell was often accompanied by his friend, Hans Anton, Kommerell knew that he was the favorite child, and he reveled in his standing. George obviously enjoyed Kommerell's presence as much for his attentiveness as for the pure pleasure of listening to him talk. Kommerell was by all accounts a captivating conversationalist. Ludwig Thormaehlen, who did not even like Kommerell very much, conceded that "everyone listened to him agog, there was never a lull in the conversation when he was present. Any fact, whether it was historical or personal, he elevated in vivid form to the level of luminous eloquence. It was wonderful how he linked ideas and explored the depths of connections. In that he resembled Friedrich Gundolf when he was younger." That no doubt constituted no small part of Kommerell's attractiveness: he filled the now vacant spot where Gundolf had stood for so long. (Although not in every respect: it was far better to listen to Kommerell than to look at him.) George even talked to them both in similar ways. When Kommerell would get too carried away expatiating on some notion or the other, George would say to him, as he had often done to Gundolf, "Now that's enough, you're talking nonsense!" But George loved these displays of verbal acrobatics and sought only to channel them in useful directions.

In mid-October of 1928, Kommerell, at the age of twenty-six, published his first book, *The Poet as Leader in German Classicism (Der Dichter als Führer in der deutschen Klassik)*. Like Kantorowicz's work, it appeared with Bondi. It also sported a line drawing featuring architectural ornaments — in this case Ionic columns — that was embossed on both the cover and title page and accompanied by the *Blätter* emblem. (The physical similarity between the books by Kommerell and Kantorowicz was carried over to every aspect of design and was in strict accordance with George's wishes. In a letter from late July, George instructed Bondi that he wanted the layout of the "new book" to be exactly like that of *Frederick II:* "Not only the finished book: one page of the new book must have precisely the same effect as a page of F II.") In its five principal sections, Kommerell's book traces the emergence of a distinctly German sensibility in the works and lives of what Kommerell took to be the main representatives of German classical literature: Klopstock, Goethe, Schiller, Jean Paul, and Hölderlin. Not incidentally, they were all, with the possible exception of Schiller, canonical poets in George's pantheon. Indeed, the entire book is a prose paean to George's notion of the poet's station and task, the poet's role as spiritual leader — *Führer* — to his people, and as the true but hidden sovereign who sees and articulates the collective fate of the *Volk*. In this way, then, Kommerell's book is itself also a canonical work, hewing to the official doctrine of the circle and pursuing the same greater objective of inculcating its readers with its values.

Yet, the book not only adheres to the circle's standard paradigm, it also matches its predecessors in the profundity of its psychological judgment, the subtlety of its philosophical refinement, and its stunning stylistic bravura. Sometimes the page almost seems to pulsate with intelligence, as if it were physically communicating the dynamic vigor of Kommerell's thought. It makes for thrilling but not easy reading: Kommerell's language is rhapsodic, lyrical even in its cadence, highly metaphorical, and allusive; and Kommerell invented words or retrieved ancient and arcane ones with an audacity bordering on George's own. Yet the words never substitute for thinking. Rather they embellish it, giving it more density and weight, but the radiance of the thought itself is still blinding.

Reading *The Poet as Leader* is an intensely exciting intellectual experience, no doubt — and for that very reason a deeply unsettling one. One feels even more powerfully than in the work of Kantorowicz or Gundolf the seductive pull in the direction of a particular, and politically motivated, goal. As in those previous books, the ultimate focus in Kommerell's work is not on the past but on the present and the future. But more explicitly than either Kantorowicz or Gundolf had done, Kommerell placed the fortunes of Germany at the core of his every analysis, making everything reflect the heroic struggle to recapture its former glory. And the language Kommerell used here is drenched in the vocabulary of martial conflict, constantly invoking "blood," "thunder," "weapons," "flames," and "death." The final chapter, on Hölderlin, ends with a virtuoso finale devoted to the poet's turn toward patriotic themes before he fell into madness (which, in typical fashion, Kommerell portrayed as a "sacrifice" Hölderlin made for his countrymen). In the concluding section, titled *Das Volk,* Kommerell interpreted the hundred and twenty-five years that had elapsed since the onset of Hölderlin's insanity — marking the end of the classical period in the early nineteenth century — as Germany's dark and fallow era, which only now was being revived through the advent of an even greater poet. And, Kommerell wrote in the closing words of the book, once the day had come when this poet, like his classical precursors, will have fully awakened his people to their calling,

> then what had once been divided in strife will become one and will act in one mind, and the *Volk* that is as diffident before the hardly believable scope of its inheritance, while facing the weight of its further destiny, will be helped by its name-giving poets to comprehend the privilege of a second golden age, the Present of masterly rule, the timelessly inexhaustible dream that continues to be woven in the midst of the worst of times, namely, the lack of confidence in the people's desire for life, *and* to fathom a fervent and grave Tomorrow in which the youth feels the birth of the new Fatherland in ardent union and in the clashing of weapons that had previously been buried all too deeply.

As murky as the passage is, anyone who had read George's poems and the writings of his followers with any attention or care would know what Kommerell was talking about here. One of Kommerell's most perceptive critics had understood him all too well. For more than two decades, Walter Benjamin had watched from a distance as George transformed himself from the plangent poet of *The Year of the Soul* into the remorseless judge of *The Star of the Covenant.*

Benjamin never lost his admiration for George's extraordinary poetic facility, but he also could not accept him, even from afar, as his personal Master, or as the authentic leader of Germany. As Benjamin's own political commitments solidified — in the meantime he had discovered Marxism — and as signs began to accumulate that the solutions offered by George and his circle were beginning to gain a broader and worrisome currency, Benjamin felt that the danger they posed went beyond private bewitchment. In 1929 he wrote an extended review that laid forth the reasons why he thought it was imperative to resist the siren's song that Kommerell and, through him, George had composed.

Benjamin began by acknowledging the unusual situation in which he found himself, as a critic "from the other side" of the political spectrum, in discussing a work whose many exceptional qualities he both recognized and affirmed. Even the title of his review mirrored this paradox: "Against a Masterpiece." It is an apt formulation: Benjamin well knew that Kommerell's book was as much the author's own as it was his Master's, that Kommerell's book very much belonged to what Benjamin also identified as "the George school." Benjamin stated outright that no one could question "the quality of the work, its stylistic form, the authority of the author." He generously praised the "extraordinary precision and boldness of his vision," adding that the "wealth of genuinely anthropological insights" was, simply, "amazing." "Rarely," Benjamin asserted, "has literary history been written thus." But in terms of what he called "its secret intention," Benjamin saw that the book's undeniable merits did not — could not — offset the perils it harbored; indeed, they were magnified by those very attributes. Once more underscoring the ambivalent nature of Kommerell's achievement, Benjamin declared, in ironic provocation, "If there were a German conservatism that took pride in itself, then it would have to view this book as its magna carta." Since, according to Benjamin, there was in fact no such creditable conservative movement in Germany — "there has not been one for eighty years," he polemically claimed — it was up to him, who maintained an opposite political stance, to give Kommerell's work the assessment it deserved.

In doing so, Benjamin looked past the surface discussion of the individual poets presented in the book and went straight to its actual inner purpose: "With a radicality that none of its predecessors in the circle attained, the book argues for an esoteric history of German literature." And even literature itself was not the real point, either. Instead, the book offered "in truth the history of salvation" — *Heilsgeschichte* — "of the Germans." It contained, Benjamin wrote, "a doctrine of true Germandom," which traced the providential rise of Germany as a whole toward its intended destiny. The difficulty was what that destiny foresaw. In particular, Benjamin shuddered at the profusion of images of violence in the book. Citing a characteristic phrase, Benjamin showed that Kommerell wanted his readers to submit to "the hardest hammer and the hottest forge of our future fate." Kommerell's entire book, Benjamin realized, sought to stage "a Germanic twilight of the gods," a pitched and bloody battle illuminated by the glistening "Lechter sun" — the spinning sign of the swastika — which in the interim, as Benjamin chillingly put it, "had armed itself."

Was all of this no more than "flowery figurative language," Benjamin rhetorically asked, the florid outpourings of an overstimulated but harmless littérateur? Benjamin was forced to answer his own question, "Alas, no." He knew that Kommerell, and all of George's followers, literally meant everything they said. Kommerell's talk of sacrifice and death, his worship of sharp blades and flashing lances, and his glorification of the inexorable German conquest, were not mere figures of speech but rather the solemn tenets of a shared and lived faith. Benjamin ended his review by repudiating the portrait of Hölderlin that Kommerell drew at the conclusion of his own work. "Hölderlin was not of the sort that rises from the dead," Benjamin insisted, "and the land whose prophets have visions that rise above corpses is not his." Hölderlin was not a covert warrior-king but a poet, and the land over which Kommerell prophesied that Hölderlin's spirit would reign bore little resemblance to the Germany Benjamin recognized as his own. But, in 1929, Benjamin's Germany — the liberal, humanistic, civilized Germany — was already in the process of disappearing, and it was uncertain what would arise in its place. One thing was certain, Benjamin said, "This land cannot become Germany again until it has been cleansed, and not cleansed in the name of Germany, much less in that of the secret one, which is after all only the arsenal of the official one, in which the magic cap that makes the wearer invisible hangs next to the steel helmet."

Walter Benjamin had written his review of Kommerell's book on *The Poet as Leader* while living in the Tuscan town of San Gimignano, where he had retreated in the summer of 1929 to escape the lowering atmosphere he had alluded to in his essay. It appeared, somewhat belatedly, on August 15, 1930. A month later, on September 14, the National Socialist party, having previously been ignored as a noisy but peripheral group, won a stunning electoral triumph. Seemingly out of nowhere, it leapt from a paltry twelve seats in the parliament to an astounding 107, or 18.3 per cent, becoming overnight the second largest party in the Reichstag. Soon, Germany would have the *Führer* it was being persuaded from all sides it needed.

CHAPTER 41
The New Reich

For four years, from the middle of 1924 to the autumn of 1928, George was largely consumed with the administrative details of bringing the works of others into being. He was most heavily involved with the books by Kommerell and Kantorowicz, and it was in them he placed his greatest hopes. He had not given up on Wolters, though, and George continued to try to goad him into completing the *Blätter* history. When George received the page proofs for *Frederick II* in February of 1927, he told Edith Landmann that he "wanted to send them as soon as possible to Wolters." Kantorowicz's book could serve him as a model, George said, for "Wolters also has to learn how to narrate so calmly, without looking backward and forward to larger connections."

But there were other projects that occupied George's attention in varying degrees as well. Berthold Vallentin, apparently undiscouraged by the abysmal failure of his *Napoleon,* had produced a new work in 1927, *Heroic Masks,* that contained, among other things, fictional "conversations" between Napoleon and various contemporaries. Although Bondi published it, this time George withheld the *Blätter* emblem. When George received his copy, he claimed that he didn't understand parts of it and that generally the invented conversations just sounded too much like Vallentin to be convincing. "Napoleon," George noticed, "speaks too cleverly, he thinks and feels too much." In the same year, the indefatigable Gundolf had finished yet another book, which he likewise published with Bondi but also minus the emblem. It was, for Gundolf, a comparatively short study of the German-Swiss Renaissance alchemist and physician known as Paracelsus, whose given name was ever more flamboyant:

{ 675 }

Philippus Aureolus Theophrastus Bombastus von Hohenheim. Although Paracelsus, who lived from 1493 to 1541, had been an outstanding chemist and had made important medical advances (he performed, for example, pioneering studies on syphilis and its possible cures), and despite the fact that the book is dedicated to Walter Kempner, who would be George's last physician, George was not impressed by it. He told Vallentin that he found the book "very superfluous and wondered what was going to become of Gundolf with such publications. He is now happily at the stage of imitating himself, like Hofmannsthal."

There was hardly a more withering comparison George could have made, and it highlights the gulf that now yawned between him and his former favorite. (Earlier that year, in a private conversation about the breakup with Gundolf, George had confided to Edith Landmann that he "was now over it.") But not all of George's energies were altruistically concentrated on the works of others — assuming one may speak of altruism when all of those works were in one way or another extensions of himself. Indeed, it was out of concern that his own writings survive in a form of his own choosing that in 1926 George had begun to consider assembling a collected edition of his published works. Since he had stopped writing poetry several years before, he could now safely call it "complete." And by overseeing the edition himself, he could also make certain there would never be any future confusion about variant readings or competing versions of individual works. It would be both final and definitive.

Naturally, Bondi would publish the complete edition, but a number of ticklish issues had to be resolved first. George may have had numerous spiritual offspring, but he needed to designate a legal heir. Several of his friends worried that, on George's death, the rights to his works would remain in the hands of Bondi and his own heirs, which could conceivably lead to an undesirable situation. The suggestion was thus made that a "foundation" be formed that would administer all legal and other matters pertaining to the poet's estate. George, to whom all of this sounded much too bourgeois, hesitated. As his primary legal advisor, Ernst Morwitz urged him to try to see the utility of it. "The foundation is necessary," he wrote George in November 1926, "to separate the copyright from your person, so that it becomes independent upon death and will not transfer to heirs." But there were other advantages such an arrangement would bring even before that unthinkable event. The foundation could act as a kind of agent on George's behalf, but he would still retain all of the decision-making power in his own hands, thus giving him all of the benefits of third-party representation with none of its drawbacks. In addition, and even more important, by transferring power of attorney to the foundation, George would be assured that the integrity of his estate would be guaranteed in perpetuity. Morwitz agreed with Julius Landmann, who also served as George's informal legal consultant on occasion and who had particularly argued for its long-term value. "Landmann correctly emphasized that through the organization of the foundation you would also obtain an external security for the continued existence of your work after your death that would be possible to obtain through an heir or executor, for the simple reason that the foundation would endure ad infinitum independently of individual persons."

Still, George was not sure he wanted to release control over his work, even if he continued to retain the right to manage it in all but name. It seemed to run counter to everything he had done and believed all his life, and he was understandably reluctant to commit himself to the plan. After all, the main issue was the work itself, and to him putting that into the shape he wanted was the predominant consideration. The foundation question could be settled later. Money, certainly, held little interest for him, and whatever more favorable conditions a foundation might entail in that regard made little difference to George. Here, too, however, his counselors attempted to prevail on him. In August 1927 Julius Landmann sent him a three-page, single-spaced typewritten letter imploring him not to let Bondi take material advantage of him. Knowing George's distaste for such matters, and in his impatience to get through to George, Landmann even became slightly sharp at one point, telling him that adopting "the posture of an unworldly idealist in the handling of a business affair [is] unworthy of the Master. In my house I learned: to let oneself be cheated is just as bad as cheating others oneself." Landmann urged George to press for an increase in the royalty percentage he received from the current and standard fifteen percent to twenty and to secure for himself a guaranteed annual income of six thousand marks. Anything less, either in the offering or in the taking, would, Landmann proclaimed, "contradict good manners."

George, though, regarded the entire topic as tedious. Not that there were insubstantial sums involved. His property and income tax assessment for 1928 indicates that his taxable assets amounted to a very considerable total of 29,500 Reichsmark. But he was so indifferent to money that did not even maintain a bank account, preferring to let Georg Bondi manage the proceeds that came in from the sales of his books. Whenever George needed money, he simply wrote to Bondi, who then arranged for a transfer of funds. In his memoirs, Bondi said that the only time George had ever had a bank account was during the period of inflation. On Bondi's advice, who felt uncomfortable watching the money disappear under his supervision, George opened one with the Darmstadt branch of the Deutsche Bank. But George had an "insurmountable aversion" to signing the payment orders and thus commissioned

Gundolf to endorse them in his stead. George claimed that Gundolf could imitate his handwriting so convincingly that even he could not tell it apart from his own. The scrupulous employees of the Deutsche Bank, however, trained to detect forgery, could. One day, George received an envelope in the mail containing one of the counterfeit payment slips Gundolf had submitted on his behalf attached to the laconic note, "We request your personal signature." Exasperated, George closed the account and never opened another one again.

Without having come to a decision about the foundation, George went ahead and concluded a deal with Bondi in November to publish an edition of his complete works. Morwitz and especially Landmann must have been disappointed by the terms. As Bondi informed Friedrich Gundolf, who had also inquired about the possibility of an increase in his royalty, the costs of producing books had more than doubled since 1914, but if prices were raised accordingly, the books would be unsellable. Thus, in order to make them affordable at all, Bondi said, most publishers set a price about twenty-five percent lower than would ordinarily be needed to cover costs. "This artificially low retail price is naturally only possible if the author agrees to a royalty of fifteen percent at the most," Bondi told Gundolf, and then played his trump. "I may also mention, by the way, that I had to deal with the same question with George in the final contract for the complete edition. Several friends of George had proposed a twenty percent royalty. But in view of the facts George also accepted the fifteen percent royalty." The seemingly casual reference to George was a shrewd stroke: Bondi knew that Gundolf would never presume he was worthy of better provisions than the Master. Fifteen percent it was.

At the end of the month, the first volume of what would be the complete edition of George's works already appeared, *The Primer* (*Die Fibel*). It contained all the juvenilia George wanted to preserve and present to the public. Like all subsequent volumes in the set, it was covered in dark blue buckram against which the embossed gold letters in his special typeface gleamed like stars in a night sky. This is not an arbitrary association: blue and gold were George's favorite colors and laden with Cosmic significance. According to Bachofen, Apollo, the solar god of poetry and prophecy, the crown deity of the father principle, was born out of the maternal obscurity of night, which his own brilliance then outshone. Or, as George told Edith Landmann a few years later, one should not take the Cosmics too seriously, but also not too unseriously: "They are necessary, just as the dark mysteries are necessary for Apollo the God of light." The only ornament is the seal designed by Lechter with the gothic monstrance set against the words "Blätter für die Kunst." Otherwise, the books present an austere, sober aspect: with the words of each poem surrounded by ample amounts of the heavy cream-colored paper, the impression is deliberately monumental in its simplicity and uniformity, with each page looking more like an engraved stone tablet than the printed leaf of a book.

Whatever George may have sacrificed in the percentage of royalties he earned was more than made up for in the sheer numbers published and sold. Six thousand copies of *The Primer* were printed for the collected edition. It was then, and still is, an enormous amount for a book of poetry, even more so for a poet's least accomplished or representative work. For the next volume in the series, the perennial favorite among all of George's works, *The Year of the Soul,* which was published in February 1928, the tally would be even higher. By the time George died five years later, a staggering thirty-one thousand copies of *The Year of the Soul* were in print. In June 1928, the third volume appeared, which gathered together his first three books, the *Hymns, Pilgrimages,* and *Algabal.* But George was most concerned with another volume that would come out later that year, in October. It was, for one thing, the only volume in the edition that had not been previously published. Not for fourteen years, not since *The Star of the Covenant* in 1914, had George produced a new book of poetry. Now, precisely two times seven years later — the preoccupation with the number seven was another lingering legacy of his Cosmic past — George brought out his last work, his poetic testament, his final bequest to his time and his people: *The New Reich.*

With very few exceptions, most of the poems in the new book had been written during and immediately after the war. One, the first poem in the book, "Goethe's Last Night in Italy," went as far back as 1908. Two simple "Songs" that open the third and concluding section of the volume were the most recent, having been composed shortly before it went to press in 1928. Thus, in terms of its contents and much of its tone, the book has the feel of a retrospective that sums up George's achievement during the previous two decades. Given the divergent origins of its parts, it will come as no surprise that *The New Reich* also lacks the rigid structure of George's most tightly organized books and possesses little of their thematic unity. What coherence there is results from the common motifs of violence, upheaval, destruction, and loss, tempered by the faint prospect of eventual renewal that had predominated in the works he had written during this period. In this category belong the major poems that had first appeared in the *Blätter.* Included are "The Burning of the Temple," "To the Dead," as well as numerous individual eulogies to friends killed in the conflict, in addition to George's ferocious denunciation, "The War." As in all of his books, however, no one mood predominates, and interspersed among the more dour verses are words of devotion to George's god and poems in celebration of beauty and youth. But at the center of *The New Reich,* both physically and conceptually, are two poems that, although written in the early twenties, were until then unknown even among his intimates: "Falkenstein Castle" and "Secret Germany." Both present the poet in the full guise of prophet, projecting a future — and perhaps a not too distant one after all — in which the country will be delivered from its malaise.

But the volume received its name from a poem that had already appeared in 1921, "The Poet in Times of Turmoil," which George had dedicated to the memory of Bernhard Uxkull, who had committed suicide in the final months of the war with his friend Adalbert Cohrs. Its principal themes are classically Georgean. The poem argues that, in more peaceful times, when people think the poet's function is only to "intone lovely dreams / And bring beauty into the work-a-day world," the poet's work is tolerated if misunderstood. In a period of unrest and strife, however, when "fate pounds with loud hammer blows" and the poet raises his voice to warn, he is not even heard, much less heeded:

> He sounds like raw metal and is ignored . .
> When all are struck by blindness · he the only seer
> Unveils in vain the nearby peril . .

Deaf to the poet sounding the alarm, the people run headlong into their own ruin. Here George recalled the examples of earlier prophets who had been disastrously disregarded: Cassandra, who futilely cautioned the Trojans from taking the wooden horse into their city; and Jeremiah, who was not believed when he foretold the destruction of Jerusalem by Nebuchadnezzar, the king who carried the Israelites back to Babylon as slaves. Like them, the poet can only watch on as what he predicted inexorably and mercilessly comes to pass: "He sighs and remains silent." Later, when the people have finally realized their error and approach him for comfort and wisdom, the poet turns down their belated request with scorn: "Of what use is the voice of heaven here when there is no ear / For that of the most common sense?" Filled with disgust over their unbroken search for material gain and sensual gratification, the poet warns that the worst has not yet come: "An even sharper plowshare must slash the soil / An even thicker haze must threaten the air." At that, the poet retreats to "melancholy regions" where his one concern is to ensure "that the marrow does not rot · the germ is not stifled. / He fans the holy embers that spread / And form into bodies." There, in his refuge, isolated from the corrupt and uncomprehending world, the poet, accompanied by those "who are chosen for the highest goal," prepares and educates a new young generation, which is "beautiful and grave / Glad of its singularity." Together they work toward the fulfillment of a single purpose: to help bring forth their savior, the one who will redeem them all, "the Man"

> Who will break the chains sweep order
> Onto fields of rubble · flog home those gone astray
> Into the eternal realm of right · where what is great is great again
> Master once more master · discipline once more discipline · he fixes
> The true symbol onto the people's banner
> Through the storm and horrible signals of the red dawn
> He leads his loyal horde to the work
> Of the wakeful day and plants the New Reich.

It is not difficult to discern, because it is so thinly disguised, the autobiographical background to the pseudo-mythic events described in the poem. What is less easy to accommodate is its unabashedly prophetic conclusion. Having returned to liberate his people, the great hero will create order at home through discipline and force, banishing all who are unwelcome from its borders, and lead his legions on to the battle that will found their new empire. This is a story George and his followers had told many times before, most recently in Kantorowicz's historical reworking of the tale through the person of Frederick II. But what had been portrayed as a relic of the distant past and as a remote possibility in the future is brought forcibly into the here and now in the poem. To underscore this sudden actuality, the verb tense shifts in the middle of the passage from the future to the present, making it seem that the vision conjured forth is happening as we read it. And the act that yanks us into the present moment is the attaching of "the true" symbol onto the flag that will lead the troops into battle and flutter above the new realm.

In his otherwise informative commentary on the poem, Ernst Morwitz becomes uncharacteristically perfunctory on what the "true symbol" is supposed to be. "What this symbol is," he tersely wrote, "is not stated." Yet Morwitz did acknowledge that in another poem in *The New Reich* the swastika plays a crucial role. Curiously, the reference to it is much more abstruse than in "The Poet in Times of Turmoil," even if the meaning associated with the swastika is no less disconcerting. The poem, entitled "The Hanged Man," reproduces the thoughts of a criminal up to the moment of his execution. He is full of disdain for the hypocritical masses who point to him while he is being lead to the gallows as if they were superior to him. He says he laughs at both their "revulsion" and "pity": what they do not admit to themselves is that they need him in order to appear virtuous. Even as the noose is placed around his neck, the condemned man predicts his eventual triumph:

> As victor I will one day penetrate your brain
> I the one buried in a shallow grave . . and in your seed
> I will continue as a hero in whose name songs are sung
> As a god . . and before you know what was happening · I will bend
> This rigid beam into a wheel.

In the last line George was making a very recondite allusion indeed. Morwitz informs us that Ulfilas, the fourth-century bishop who first translated the Bible into a Germanic language, had used *galga* to render the word "cross." Now, it happens that the word in German for "gallows" is *Galgen,* and the one for swastika is *Hakenkreuz,* or "hooked cross," which brings the linguistic chain full circle, so to speak. Morwitz insisted, that is, that "there exists no doubt" that George meant to combine the associations connected with the gallows and the swastika into a single potent image. George had considered before, in a short poem in *The Seventh Ring,* that the person who one day would rise up and take the reins of power in hand may not be an obvious "hero" in the Romantic sense but rather a criminal who had sat in jail among murderers. There, too, George had meant to mock the complacent pretensions of those people who flatter themselves that just because they are not overtly bad they are therefore good and, conversely, that those who are evil cannot prevail in the world. But it is more than a little unnerving that here a similar scenario is again imagined, only now the contemptuous outlaw-turned-hero conquers by using the swastika not just as an abstract symbol but as an instrument of death.

The two central poems of the book, "Falkenstein Castle" and "Secret Germany," are equally prophetic in their stance. The first, Morwitz also tells us, is dedicated to himself, having been inspired by a walk he took with the Master in the summer of 1922 from Königstein in the Taunus forest to the ruined fortress of Falkenstein that sits high atop a ridge nearby. From their vantage point, the poet and his companion survey the surrounding countryside below — the Rhine is visible in the distance — and they both begin to reflect on the fortunes of their native land. The younger man is pessimistic and sees nothing but misery and despair to come, but the older one is more hopeful, saying, "I already detect an audible sound through the sleepy air." He admits that "the ear was still unaccustomed" to hearing it, but "the golden tone" was unmistakable. That "sound" is the almost imperceptible noise of the old German empire as Frederick had known it — the vast territory of middle Europe extending below the Alps, eastward to the cedars of Lebanon and down to the Gulf of Naples — being reconstituted again under a single aegis and speaking a single language:

> The mighty breath comes through resounding with purer metal
> Rising over the mountains of rock all the way to the vault of cedars
> All the way to the glittering gulf without the confusion of languages . .
> With the procession of figures floods back toward the north
> The fable of blood and desire a fable of fire and radiance:
> The pageantry of our emperors the roaring of our warriors.

The "sound" the poet hears, in other words, is that of a marching army — presumably the same one that will raise the standard with the "true symbol" over the new empire.

In "Secret Germany" George is less specific about what fate held in store, but the focus is still on what lies ahead. It is one of George's most dense and compact poems, with almost every word supported by an architecture of semantic linkages all but invisible to anyone not completely immersed in his universe. (And even then one could have difficulties: the poem contains the word "yurt," which is the name of a collapsible tent made of animal skins or felt used by the Kirghiz or other Mongol nomads of Central Asia. Only one of George's friends, Morwitz recalled, had ever encountered the word before and knew what it meant.) As its title implies, the poem as a whole commemorates the poet's discovery of the only Germany he had ever sanctioned, the spiritual realm he had founded and now viewed as his proper home. It begins with an account of the world the poet faced before he had become aware of other possibilities. It was a place consumed by "insatiable greed," one in which everything, from the North Pole to the Equator, had been subjected to the cold light of rational inquiry, exposed "without shame," leaving no mystery — or secret — unexposed. The poet depicts himself lying on a "southern sea / Deeply careworn" in this world shorn of wonder and enchantment, when he is surprised by a Pan-like figure, who was sent by the gods to instruct him to return to his "sacred homeland" to find there what no one else could see. Once there, with an "eye sharpened" by the secret knowledge bestowed on him in the south, he would realize the miracle of the "sun-dream." Morwitz discloses that this last phrase also contains a Cosmic remnant. "By the word 'sun dream,' " Morwitz elucidated, George "suggested that spiritual filiation" — *geistige Sohnschaft* — "involved an Apollonian, patriarchal function as opposed to the matriarchal physical birth."

 Back home — in Munich, to be precise, which is referred to only as "the City" — the poet encounters his god — also unnamed but we know it is Maximin — and sets to putting into practice the secret knowledge of spiritual procreation entrusted to him. Other early companions also make their appear-

always at such a remove as to be all but unrecognizable: Karl
...led merely "the ball thrower" and "the uncatchable catcher,"
... is apostrophized as "Him of the pale golden locks," and so on.
...cludes with the poet reminding his "brothers" — now a sizable
...t it is still true today what had been true at the beginning of his
external world is nothing but "rotten leaves in the autumn wind /
...e end and of death." What is truly vital cannot be seen or touched
and lies below the surface unperceived by the masses, waiting for the right
moment to emerge:

> Only what rests in protective sleep
> Where no one yet feels and disturbs it
> Deep within the innermost shaft
> Of the consecrated earth —
> A miracle indecipherable today
> Becomes destiny tomorrow.

However that destiny may ultimately take shape, it was one in which George increasingly thought he would no longer play an active part. He felt that his work was done: he had transformed the "sun dream" into reality, engendered spiritual sons who were already continuing what he had begun. In one of the three poems, called "prayers," to Maximin, the poet candidly states that his powers are spent, that "my song does not correspond to the true course anymore." But he is not saddened, he says, for

> Now I see hundreds of noble brows
> On which your shimmer was secretly shed
> Praising your being with their magnificence —
> An obedient worker who has completed his task
> I do not want to lament any longer with poetic words:
> Since You are the greater one I must surrender.

The final poem of the book, and thus the last poem George ever published (even though it had been written a decade before and first appeared in the *Blätter* of 1919), also owed its inspiration to Bernhard von Uxkull's death. As it happens, it is also one of George's most moving elegies, managing to convey both tenderness and grief at once and combining the suffering of mourning over Uxkull's physical loss with the restorative knowledge that nothing can ever take him away again now. Its spare, repetitive simplicity only serves to heighten its emotional force:

> You slender and pure like a flame
> You like the morning gentle and light

You radiant shoot of a noble trunk
You like a spring secret and clean

You accompany me on sunny meadows
Make me shudder in the evening mist
Illuminate my path in the shade
You cool wind you hot breath

You are my wish and my thought
I breath you in with every draught
I drink you in with every pull
I kiss you in with every scent

You radiant shoot of a noble trunk
You like a spring secret and clean
You slender and pure like a flame
You like the morning gentle and light.

To celebrate the publication of the new work, George summoned his friends to Berlin in November 1928 for a ceremonial reading in Thormaehlen's studio. In all, there were fifteen or sixteen participants, including Kommerell, Johann Anton (and his brother Walter), the three Stauffenberg brothers, Ernst Morwitz, the sculptor Alexander Zschokke, Albrecht von Blumenthal, and several new acquaintances, the youngest being the nineteen-year-old Frank Mehnert, a friend of the Stauffenbergs. Morwitz began by reading the first several poems in the book, followed by Erich Boehringer, who recited "The Poet in Times of Turmoil" and the one after it. George himself read "Falkenstein Castle" and, finally, "Secret Germany." After he had finished, and without permitting any other conversation to arise, the Master slowly dismissed each person in the order in which he had come, alone or in groups.

The impact of the reading on those present, especially of the two final and previously unknown poems, must have been considerable. They had just listened to, and were aware that they had been the first to be privileged to do so, the dire forebodings of the man they all unquestioningly regarded as a prophet and a sage. True, not all of his vision was cheerless, and the new *Reich* he foresaw was to be understood as a glorious end. But achieving it would involve great sacrifice and would come — when it did come — at great cost. How great was hinted at in the second poem Erich Boehringer had read aloud that day. The poem, which eulogized those whom the war had consumed, is dedicated, as its title states, "To a Young *Führer* in the First World War." George had written it soon after the armistice was signed, when soldiers were beginning to return home after fighting in what was generally referred to as the Great War, or, more hopefully, the war to end all wars. Few thought then, before the Versailles treaty talks had even begun, that there would be, that there *could* be another one, that the war they were only just leaving behind them would have been merely "the First." Obviously, George thought otherwise.

CHAPTER 42
Fame

When George published *The New Reich* at the end of 1928, it was greeted as much more than a merely literary event. It was treated as nothing less than a matter of national importance. In the time that had elapsed since the appearance of *The Star of the Covenant* almost a decade and a half before, George had grown for countless numbers of Germans into something far greater than a poet. He represented to many of his countrymen the quintessence of a new German culture; he was seen as offering a model of acting and being, as providing answers to questions about the value and nature of existence, and as giving new content to old hopes and beliefs. It is more than doubtful that everyone who thought of him in this way had actually read, much less understood, all of his works or those of his followers. But in some ways that was irrelevant. By the late 1920s, the very name of Stefan George had acquired an aura of mystery and almost magical power, and even many of those who were unfamiliar with his poetry unavoidably knew something about it and him and were fascinated by the phenomenon. George, that is, had become famous, not only in Germany, but throughout Europe and much of the rest of the world as well, and his first public utterances since the end of the war had the effect of an official and much anticipated pronouncement.

As extraordinary as this entire development itself, perhaps, is the very fact that it happened at all. It certainly could have turned out otherwise. For here was a person who had once contemplated literally turning his back on his country forever and emigrating to Mexico, whose religious sensibilities, cultural and linguistic predilections, even his sexual orientation had made him an outsider to his own society, and someone who still now spoke of the necessity, indeed the inevitability of destroying major portions of that very society, now being hailed as its paragon. Few people pointed out these contradictions, and most preferred to focus solely on the ideas he proclaimed of leadership, heroic greatness, national renewal, and spiritual, as well as racial, purity. These were qualities anyone could recognize and myriads eagerly endorsed. Many who did ignored or blocked out the darker elements of George's world, while misjudging the dangers of the ones they consciously adopted. To a large extent, as we have witnessed, this response was not simply accidental, but also the result of a long-term and calculated campaign. In his own works and through those of his disciples, George had intentionally set out to inculcate and reinforce within his readers a receptivity to the ideals they collectively preached. To be sure, George and his circle were not the only proponents of such principles in Germany; far from it. But by the end of the decade George had achieved a level of visibility and consequence unmatched by any other comparable individual or group. As we know, not everyone viewed him or his movement as entirely wholesome. Yet, whether one approved of his prestige or not, George and everything he stood for had become a force to be reckoned with at those levels of society where opinions were formed, decisions were made, and the fortunes of the country were decided.

Although George became widely known only in the 1920s, a discerning few had always held his poetic abilities in high regard. As early as 1905, for instance, a journalist had evaluated several of his translations and wrote that "among Germany's linguistic artists Stephan George is probably the greatest at the moment." The comment was favorable enough that one could almost overlook the misspelling of his name. Of course, even then there were critics too. The following year, Georg Simmel had sent a clipping to George that he had seen in another newspaper where some wag had recorded the "literary opinions of a housewife." This amateur literary critic, the reporter wrote, had said that "Stefan George's poems are like oysters: many people love them with a passion, others are made sick by them." But overall the positive notices predominated, so that by 1912, the slightly hedging tone of earlier reviews had disappeared and more people confidently claimed, as did one writer for the *Breslauer Zeitung,* that "Stefan George is undoubtedly the greatest artist of words among living German poets." Not long thereafter, that final qualification vanished as well and in many people's minds George took a rightful place next to other immortals, becoming the equal of Goethe, Shakespeare, Dante, and Virgil.

Soon, he became even more. Once his disciples began to publish works of their own, promulgating his view of the world and contributing to its further dissemination, his function as a poet gradually receded before, or was folded into, other roles. It was as if the acknowledged preeminence he had achieved as a poet was transferred onto these other spheres and, if it were possible, magnified even further. And, increasingly, everything connected with George was being seen as having a significance that transcended his own or others' individual affairs. In an article from early 1924 devoted to defining, as it was titled, "The Prophetic Content of George's Work," the author stated that "between Nietzsche and George stretches the plain of a fifty-year empire, a spiritual tension invisibly mounted in the air between the *[Untimely] Meditations* on one end and the *Star [of the Covenant]* on the other, which has been unleashing itself since the war and will determine the coming generations in Germany." Later that same year, the literary historian Fritz Strich gave a public lecture on the poet. Although Strich held severe reservations about George's power and influence, he realized there was no denying its reality. "George!" Strich had exclaimed. "Today the youth of Germany, above all students, swear by this name, not by that of a poet, but rather that of a prophet. Is he the incarnation of the divine or only of the logos? That is in all seriousness the question debated as if in a senate." Strich rehearsed the "doctrine" associated with George while stressing how vital the mechanisms propagating it were to his success. "This doctrine is lent the broadest reverberations through George's disciples," Strich explained, "who today occupy important chairs in German universities. Through these interpreters and exegetes [. . .] the humanities, particularly history, have been stamped with George's sign. Goethe, Shakespeare, Nietzsche, Leibniz, Napoleon, Frederick II have been interpreted and reinterpreted in the spirit of George." Strich himself deplored this evolution as an expression of "enormous presumptuousness" and an example of "boundless hubris," but he could not refute that George had already made an indelible mark on the intellectual life of his time.

Others, including those more favorably disposed toward him, said much the same thing. Commenting in early 1928 on the publication of George's collected works, but before *The New Reich* had appeared, a critic named Peter Hamecher looked backward over George's long career and marveled at the metamorphosis that had occurred in the meantime. "How far back lies the time," Hamecher mused, "when a translator in an anthology of French poetry was able to speak of 'the newest German magical lyricist Stefan George'!" Now he was far more than that. "Today George's work is as good as complete, and the poet has placed his figure in his work in such symbolic greatness that it is no longer the concern of a circle but the affair of the nation. He is today the judge and arbiter of our time, and the person who once began alone and remote, in deliberate and extreme rejection of the day, has become the leader and awakener of a youth to which the best belong."

George's followers themselves also began to be accorded the kind of consideration that most scholars and writers can only secretly hope for. Another critic by the name of Fritz Cronheim saluted the publication of one of Wolters's patriotic compendia in 1926 with words of highest praise. "A new epoch of development has dawned," Cronheim declared, "in the educational work of the spiritual movement, among whose leaders Friedrich Wolters numbers, and which until recently had addressed itself to a closed circle, a more restricted community, [and this new epoch is one] of public action, so that the fruits of a necessary inner labor on the form of Germans and on German education shall be made generally usable through an act of national pedagogical character." The sentence is long and rather belabored, but the point is simple: Wolters's work, as part of a larger "spiritual movement," was important not just in itself, but in what it meant to the country as a whole. And, as the sales of Kantorowicz's, Bertram's, and Gundolf's books demonstrated, many others agreed. In November of the same year, someone referred to Gundolf, not atypically, as "the pride and summit of German literary scholarship in the present day." Even the firm of Georg Bondi earned its share of tributes. In late 1926, in an article discussing German publishing houses, the author singled out Bondi as representing "one of the greatest cultural treasures we have today with respect to publishing." Reminding the few readers who did not already know it that "Bondi is the publisher of Stefan George and his circle," the writer commended Bondi for having dedicated himself to the crucial task of making George's works available at a time when others may not have taken the risk. "One should remind oneself how George stood alone. Today the most important parts of the German character have been imbued by his substance. He not only created poetic language anew, but he also essentially helped to give new life to the spirit."

What is most curious about George's leap into celebrity, though, is that it occurred alongside an almost total ignorance of his person. No one except for the relatively few people he called his friends knew anything about his private life, and even they knew only what he chose to reveal to them. All the others had was what was contained in his poetry and in the mythogenetic works of the circle and little more. It was common knowledge that George had grown up in Bingen, that he traveled extensively, and that he had no fixed address. Otherwise Stefan George was little more than a phantom, seen occasionally on the streets of the cities he frequented and in the few photographs published as frontispieces to his books. In an article from 1927, Ludwig Marcuse remarked on this peculiar discrepancy between George's public prominence and private elusiveness, noting that "there is no other instance today of anonymity coexisting with world fame." There had always been rumors, of course, but they only fueled George's mystique, for no one who could have reliably confirmed or denied the stories would have ever deigned to do so.

One predictable effect of this scarcity of information about George was that anything bearing some connection to him had become highly prized. First editions of George's early books, rare in the first place since so few copies were ever printed, became extremely valuable collector's items. Walter Benjamin, an impassioned bibliophile and perpetually ambivalent admirer of George, told a friend that he had tried, and failed, to buy a first edition of *The Seventh Ring* at an auction in 1918. Benjamin said that, even though another friend of his had bought a copy of it a few years before for forty-five marks and he himself had offered seventy-five at the auction, another bidder had secured it at a price of more than four hundred marks. In the case of handwritten manuscripts or letters, the figures went even higher. In 1922, a newspaper article that addressed the question, "What are the letters of German writers worth?" revealed that "in general the autographs of Gerhart Hauptmann are valued most highly. Fifty to one hundred marks are paid for letters written by his hand." However, "yet another living poet is rated much more highly, namely Stefan George, since very few of his writings are in circulation. A one-page letter of his recently went for seven hundred marks, and the demand is very considerable."

To a large degree, this dearth of manuscripts for sale arose from George's careful management of his correspondence. Aside from the fact that he wrote few letters in the first place and even fewer containing anything that might be considered interesting, the recipients were often instructed to return the letters to him or to destroy them. George could not control everyone or everything, however, and sometimes letters did emerge despite his best efforts. Wherever possible, George sought to regain possession of them when they appeared on the market. In 1925, for example, Karl Wolfskehl reported that he had discovered a "pile of autographs" at a Munich dealer's shop, including "a small bundle of St. G., above all a four-line poem 'to B' in original handwriting. Then a few envelopes, also a postcard to St. G. from Greece and a long poem to St. G." Wolfskehl asked for instructions. He said that the dealer "is prepared to let me have the fascicle but is aware of its great value. Whatever happens one should take the poem away from him." Wolfskehl also tried his best to find out where the dealer had obtained the items, but to no avail. "Even at my insistent questioning he remained silent about the origin of the things." Yet, even if George was successful in recovering the odd letter or poem, others inevitably slipped through, which were then all the more valuable as a result. Notably, despite his evident irritation over his books and papers being handled like precious commodities, George did not regard the whole business entirely without humor. That year he told Edith Landmann he had learned of an antiquarian bookseller who owned the first editions of *The Tapestry of Life* and of other works but refused to sell them because he had heard that George was very ill. George found this act of speculative hoarding highly amusing. "He thinks," George said of the book dealer, "once that guy's dead then the prices for his books will absolutely go through the roof. It's almost worth living just to outfox someone like that."

As George's fame grew, there grew alongside it the seemingly irrepressible desire not only to possess something touched by his hands, but also to have his name, and thus his authority, attached in some way to oneself or to the organization to which one belonged. By 1924 there were stirrings in some quarters about nominating him for the Nobel Prize. George himself reacted with customary skepticism. The following year, he offhandedly mentioned to Edith Landmann that "the Austrians" — who exactly is uncertain — had suggested him for the Nobel Prize, but George considered it merely a cynical, self-interested gesture. "They think," he said, meaning the unnamed Austrians, "if he doesn't get it" — meaning himself — "then it won't be our turn yet."

As it turned out, although his name would come up regularly as a possible candidate over the next few years, George never did receive the Nobel Prize. But a few years later he was bestowed with an honor that, for many Germans, constituted an even greater distinction. In 1926, the city council of Frankfurt am Main, the birthplace of Germany's other great poet, Johann Wolfgang von Goethe, decided to inaugurate a prize in honor of its celebrated native son, to be awarded annually to a German of unusual accomplishment in any field. On July 28, 1927, the board of trustees charged with choosing the winners elected George as the person who should receive the first Goethe Prize.

Precisely one month later, on August 28, the day of Goethe's birth, an elaborate ceremony took place in his ancestral house in Frankfurt. With all of the city dignitaries assembled, a solemn declaration substantiating George's selection was read aloud and carefully distributed to all of the newspapers to be reprinted. The document announcing the award is, considering what might have been said, relatively well-informed and fairly dignified in its restraint. It praises George as a poet who had "preserved for us the linguistic spirit of Goethe, Novalis, and Hölderlin in times of confusion" and commends him for having also "demonstrated the eternal meaning of poetry in new, individual forms." George had, the text continued, advanced the "faith in the spiritual vocation of the word" by recognizing the existence of "beauty beyond the merely descriptive." The committee also emphasized George's role as a "teacher and guide of a generation of men of poetry and science," who demanded "discipline of the person and rigor in poetic creation," and "who had newly instructed a generation trained to think materialistically to see the word symbol as the goal of great poetry." Finally, as a person "who had formed himself uniquely through the spirit," he had "selfishly raised himself up to his own individual figure through personal discipline and singular freedom and yet, like a priest, maintained humility before what is holy and great." It was this man, then, who the city fathers, in their collective wisdom, had been deemed worthy of being the very first recipient of the prize named after the person regarded as the greatest German who had ever lived.

The award ceremony appears to have gone off without a hitch. As expected, it received enormous attention in the press, with virtually every major German newspaper carrying the news of the event, often on the first page. (One reporter could not, however, help noting how ironic it was that "the most democratic city in Germany had placed a wreath on the head of the most aristocratic poet of the nation.") The item also had wide coverage in the foreign press, and there was even a brief though factually challenged notice in *The New York Times,* which announced that the prize had been given "to a Berlin poet, Steppan George."

The entire ceremony had been a success except for one detail: the prizewinner himself had not shown up to accept the award or made any public acknowledgement of it. Officially, George excused his absence by saying he was feeling ill and was thus prevented from attending. Privately, however, he showed little interest in the prize itself, and anyone who knew George — or his poetry — would have also known that it was unthinkable that he would participate in such an event. George had, after all, included a poem in *The Seventh Ring* called "Goethe-Day" that ridiculed precisely such efforts to "honor" the poet, which were really only attempts to exploit the name of Goethe for base purposes. George had been inspired to write the poem by the festivities organized in Frankfurt in 1899 to commemorate the 150th anniversary of Goethe's birth. "You call him yours and are thankful and rejoice," George had written then, "You full of all of his drives, to be sure / But only in the lower registers of animals." It is doubtful that George had significantly changed his mind about the legitimacy of the Frankfurt City Council to honor anyone, let alone him.

Nevertheless, as George told Vallentin several weeks after the formalities were over, since they had already given him the prize — albeit, as George insisted, "against his will" — he was reluctant to turn it down "so as not to cause renewed gossip." One of George's major reservations about keeping it had to do with his concern about who would be the next year's recipient. If it were some "littérateur," some second-rate literary hack — a category that as far as George was concerned encompassed just about every living writer in Germany — then he would certainly be forced to return the prize after the fact. Julius Landmann, considering this problem, had proposed an ingenious solution. "There was actually no other choice," Landmann had said, "but for the Master to receive the prize again next year." Yet there was another consideration. The prize came with a cash award of ten thousand marks, an amount not to be dismissed lightly. Not that George was interested in the money, of course; but he also thought that one should not be irresponsible. He thus decided, Vallentin revealed, that "he would let the money sit and next year, if he did not like how the city of Frankfurt assigned the prize, he would award the prize he received to someone else himself." Fortunately, the next winner was neither a poet nor unambiguously German, but the Alsatian musician, philosopher, and physician Albert Schweitzer. As George put it to Edith Landmann the next September, after the prize had been announced: "That this lamb received the Goethe Prize saves me a lot of money. Now I don't need to give mine up."

Based on his experience with all the commotion surrounding the Goethe Prize, George could easily predict the clamor that would more than likely accompany his sixtieth birthday the following year. In mid-June 1928, he thus repaired to Switzerland, retreating to the tiny village of Spiez on Lake Thun at the foot of the Bernese Alps. There, in splendid seclusion, he spent the next two months with Wilhelm Stein, who were possibly joined by another friend named Robert von Steiger. Almost no one knew where he was, and the few who did were sworn to secrecy. Since George needed to correct the proofs of *The New Reich,* he had given his address to Bondi but had impressed on his publisher that he should share it with no one. On June 21, Bondi obediently assured him that "I will not give anyone your secret address and will treat it as strictly confidential; I will write the address myself on the proofs sent to you." Such precautions may appear excessive, but as George's renown grew, so did the number of people who would try almost anything to get close to him. George knew that his birthday would only intensify the swarms of unbidden curiosity seekers and unwelcome well-wishers.

As expected, inquiries began to come into Bondi's office weeks before the day and the harried publisher diligently fended them all off. In one instance, though, he was unsure if he had acted appropriately, and on June 30 Bondi wrote to George with the following news: "The president of Germany had someone call me today to find out your address since he intends to congratulate you on July 12. I answered that you were abroad and had not left an address but that letters addressed to me are occasionally forwarded to you." And, indeed, in a telegram dated July 11, President Paul von Hindenburg sent his wishes to the poet:

Dear Herr Stephan George!
On the occasion of your sixtieth birthday tomorrow I express my heartiest congratulations. May you be granted many more years of poetic creativity and personal health.
With best regards!
von Hindenburg

George seems to have been genuinely flattered by the note, even if he was under no illusion that the eighty-one-year-old former general turned reluctant politician was actually a secret admirer of his poetry. If nothing else, the misspelling of his name would have banished any such fantasy. But it was a sign of George's perceived importance that at least someone in the government had thought it politically expedient to have the president convey his private thoughts to the poet. For his part, George sincerely admired Hindenburg and credited him with having single-handedly prevented an even worse outcome to the war. Indeed, in his poem "The War," George had referred explicitly to Hindenburg in one stanza, in which he was declared to have "saved" the empire. As George told Vallentin in August, he thus decided to write Hindenburg and "personally answered his congratulatory letter in a few sentences. He owed it to the old man," George explained, "since Hindenburg was after all the only contemporary figure who appeared in his poems." George accordingly told Hindenburg that he was grateful for having been given the opportunity "to address a few personal words in addition to the poetic ones to the man who stands out in the immense world turmoil of our time as the sole symbolic figure."

It was, as always with George, ambiguous praise. Anyone who knew the poet might have justifiably thought he was extolling Hindenburg as much for his historical achievements as for being the only person outside of George's circle to have been included as a "symbolic figure" in his poetry. In response to Hindenburg's congratulations, in other words, George had merely returned the compliment.

Yet George could not be bothered to respond to the avalanche of letters, telegrams, and newspaper accounts that showered down from all over Germany and Europe during the next few days and weeks. Several tributes also came from other German government agencies and officials. "In profound reverence," one typical missive read, "the Prussian Academy of Arts, Section for Poetry, offers Stephan George on his sixtieth birthday thanks and best wishes for his great work and life." Another, from the minister for culture, Dr. Carl Heinrich Becker, who at least got the great man's name right, sent effusive "greetings, congratulations and thanks to the creative former of language and poet, to the Master and *Führer* of a burgeoning spiritual youth, who admonishes a new humanity in rigor and discipline." All of this made little impression on George, who again suspected that there was probably some ulterior motive in these homages. As he told Vallentin, he did not answer the telegram from the culture minister personally and instead "merely had him thanked through Bondi. Undoubtedly he wants something else from us." If George saw anything positive in all of the accolades raining down on him, it was that they demonstrated that both he and his movement had now become unassailable. He said, still to Vallentin, "that with the exception of a few scribblings that were impossible even with respect to their niveau, the world had adjusted itself to us to such a degree that it no longer dared to find fault with anything essential about us." George declared that it was "very important that this acknowledgement had been made so universally." As with everything else, George's birthday also served him as an instrument of his power, acting as a gauge that usefully measured — and broadcast — his newly acquired invulnerability.

Arriving as a kind of crowning finale within this charged atmosphere of celebratory excitement and public acclaim, George's final book of poetry appeared three months later. It was, as he knew it would be, a sensation. Everyone understood that *The New Reich* marked the culmination of his creative life. "When Stefan George's sixtieth birthday was celebrated last year," one reviewer wrote, "one was able to experience how the entirety of spiritual Germany, indeed, what is more, all of spiritual Europe, acknowledged in rare and appropriate unanimity this singular figure as one who is great and is a leader for the German spiritual world." *The New Reich,* the reviewer continued, validated that perception as it made the implicit demand that it be translated into real, concrete results. "The pedagogical effect and power of spiritual leadership that must radiate from this book, as from all books of the circle, cannot be valued highly enough and for that reason one would like to know that this work is in the hands of the youth now coming into maturity." For, the article went on, George's work "is after all the most visible manifestation of that unbroken spiritual will through whose existence we obtain the guarantee of the existence of a pure, indestructible spiritual world in the middle of the maelstrom of this godless and soulless present."

Other reviewers also recognized that, as Peter Hamecher put it, "George's new book is an eminently political book." True, Hamecher qualified his judgment by saying he meant the word political "not in the sense of the day, but in the sense of the eternal powers." But in fact the whole point of *The New Reich* was that here, for the first time, the timeless and the transitory, the universal and the particular — the secret and actual Germany — were supposed to merge into a single entity. Another critic underscored the gap between George's *Reich* and political reality as well, not, however, in order to argue that they should remain distinct, but rather to lament that they had not yet achieved a unity. "That the poet wants to go beyond his formed work and arrive at a formed *Reich*," the reviewer wrote, "that he announces his vision as a 'seer,' that he stands up against his time, judging and rejecting it, that he hopes to erect a greater future, [all of] that is, within the spiritual realm, duty and greatness. But [. . .] it is painful, when one speaks so concretely and unmetaphorically of a new *Reich,* to know that for the time being it doesn't exist anywhere and unfortunately will also most probably not come or come in this way."

Everywhere in Germany in the late 1920s there were already great and constantly growing numbers of intellectuals, academics, public figures, and politicians, but many more private, ordinary readers, intelligent and educated citizens who, like this reviewer, longed for a new *Reich* to come into being and who saw George's vision of it giving them the best hope for a future they could embrace. Only hindsight would prove how misguided that desire had been. But George's fame, which was both the product and the affirmation of this widespread agreement with his vision, made the wish to turn that vision into reality all but irresistible.

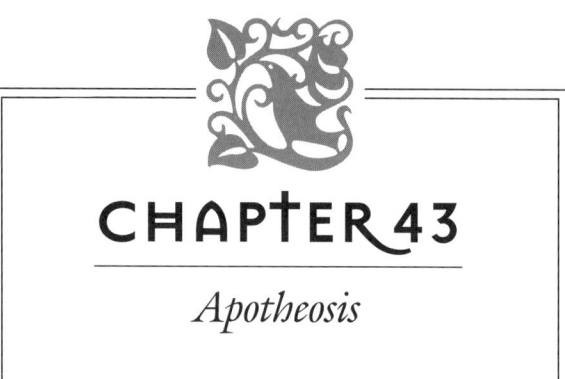

CHAPTER 43
Apotheosis

After seemingly endless interruptions and distractions, Friedrich Wolters finally settled down in the summer of 1926 to writing the history of the *Blätter*. It was an enormous and complex undertaking, made even more daunting by the knowledge that its primary subject was not only impatiently waiting its completion but would also submit the finished product to minute scrutiny before allowing it to be sent out into the world. Despite his other duties as a professor of history at Kiel, Wolters worked steadily on the project over the next three years, gradually amassing a manuscript of over 1,200 typewritten pages. Along the way there were the usual slowdowns and minor blocks any writer has to contend with. In early January 1927, Wolters informed George that "I am working on the *Blätter* book full of good spirits — just one thing is amiss: I am suffering from Achmed and sometimes sink to the level of El-Rey!" Wolters was an impassioned cigarette smoker and needed their stimulation to work. The two brands of tobacco he named were obviously of an inferior sort, and he turned to George, who was likewise addicted to the habit, for a "Masterly" donation of higher quality fare. George, no doubt thinking it would be a prudent investment, sent along a small supply, while warning Wolters that his store of Zara — their favorite brand — was running low and that haste was therefore all the more of the essence. When the shipment arrived, Wolters was doubly inspired to press on. "I am happy," he wrote George, "when the fine odor wafts through the rooms because it brings back to me a physical memory, as it were, and makes me believe for a moment that the Master himself is here again."

Fortified by such nicotine-induced recollections, Wolters made constant if occasionally faltering progress, and by March of 1928 he was already halfway through. Not surprisingly, he found some parts more challenging than others. "The chapters on the Cosmics," he told George, which were "twice as long as the others — cost me a great deal of trouble." When it was at last finished the following summer, Wolters had another experience familiar to all writers. While reading through his manuscript in its entirety, a feeling of revulsion rose up in him. "Looking through the whole work," he dismally confided to George in June of 1929, "put me in a not very cheery mood. I find the first book inadequate and too detailed with respect to individual matters." He wanted to rewrite the whole thing. Yet if he were to do so, it would create another delay of several months or more, and they both wanted to book to appear as soon as possible. "But," Wolters moaned, "what should I do?"

All the while, George had been watching carefully as the manuscript took shape and actively furthering its advancement in any way he could, such as by meeting with Wolters in Kiel and Berlin to help him resolve particularly troublesome portions or to address factual questions that came up in the course of writing. George also frequently spoke about the gradual gestation of the long-awaited book to his other friends. Of paramount significance to George was that the book capitalize on the favorable circumstances created by his own newly won celebrity. In February 1928, he had said to Vallentin that "this book is very important and useful now," for it would establish "how things were" — *was gewesen sei* — "and what effects the movement had produced." Yet it was here, contained in the buried allusion to Leopold von Ranke's famous dictum that the historian's task consisted in the narration of "how things really were" — *wie es eigentlich gewesen* — where Wolters's "history" of the *Blätter* stood in greatest contrast to the way history in any conventional sense was usually written.

One of the reasons Wolters had such difficulties in writing his book must have been that he was trying to pursue two distinct, and two strictly opposed, goals at once. On the one hand, he wanted to tell the story of George's life and works, of his triumphs and defeats, of his friendships and his enemies — in other words, to tell how things really were. On the other, Wolters was engaged in an overtly hagiographic exercise, enshrouding the image of the Master in the language of worship and devotion. From the beginning, George appears in Wolters's book as the flawless hero, the supreme Poet, the wise Master, the omnipotent Ruler, the Prophet of a new God, a figure always fated to assume the position of preeminence that his fellow countrymen were finally beginning to acknowledge. Wolters uncritically described George as if he actually were the poetic persona George's own poems and the works of his followers portrayed him to be. In this respect, it was not history Wolters was writing at all but myth fitted out in historical garb.

Of course, one could claim that much the same was true of all the supposedly "historical" works produced by the circle. But Wolters had to contend with something his colleagues had by and large been spared. Although George had energetically participated in the publication and even in the writing of the books by Gundolf, Bertram, Vallentin, Kantorowicz, and Kommerell, his contribution had been usually limited to revisions of their tone or style and only rarely had he intervened in their essence. In Wolters's book, George *was* the essence, and he wielded his authority accordingly. "Wolters has difficulty comprehending what has to remain occult in the state," George thus told Edith Landmann in September 1928. There was much he wanted to be left unsaid or at most vaguely alluded to, and that desire often conflicted with Wolters's historical instincts, weak though they were. Wolters had thus been forced to disclose and conceal at the same time, always keenly aware of the Master's critical eye looking over his shoulder. It would be enough to cause anyone to become unsteady.

Once George received the completed manuscript, he thus set about making numerous revisions, corrections, and above all extensive cuts. George eliminated entire people — one whole page devoted to Botho Graef, the brother of Sabine Lepsius, for example, was crossed out with the penciled remark, "All of Botho can disappear!" — and George removed information about others he considered superfluous. Concerning one relatively minor figure, whose date and place of birth Wolters had conscientiously recorded, George made the comment that "it is not so important that he had to be born somewhere." George likewise deleted many other details about various people in his life by indicating in the margin, "For you: private matter." That is, George had given Wolters certain kinds of information to aid him in giving the book its shape, but the details themselves were to remain hidden from uninvited inspection. And with regard to himself, George took particular care to alter any passage that could be taken as calling his own Germanness into question. To give only one illustration of his procedure, he objected to Wolters's description of the George household as one in which both German and French were freely mixed. Wolters had originally written that "the bilingualism which the members of the family had preserved referred to France." George changed this sentence to read only, "Many different memories pointed to France." The new wording was not in itself untrue, but its deliberate obscurity amounts to a distortion by omission nonetheless.

In a conversation with Vallentin in August of 1929, George described his editorial actions as stemming from purely pragmatic motivations. Briefly put, George thought the manuscript was simply too long. The cuts were necessary, he told Vallentin, "in order to force the book into a single volume." Moreover, he continued, "it would also only do the work good." After all, he explained, "when a wall in a chapel was placed at the disposal of a Renaissance artist for him to paint a picture on it, he also could not say: the wall is too small for me, I have to have ten more meters, otherwise I can't execute this idea of mine." There were other reasons as well that made a two-volume work less than desirable. If there are two volumes, George said, "readers are only encouraged to say subsequently: the first volume is better than the second one, the second one is disappointing. In addition two volumes were an obstacle to sales." But it was clear that, beyond such external considerations, many of the changes were designed to tailor the historical record so that it conformed to the image of himself George wanted to convey.

The final result, then, more than in any other previous instance, bore the direct imprint of George's active involvement. It presented his life in just the way he wanted it depicted. Wolters's book may have offered an apotheosis of George, but it was at least in equal measure an act of self-glorification on George's part. That this ideal portrait did not conform in every respect to reality, however, created unavoidable tensions within the book, strains between the requirements of fact and legend-making that were noticed and criticized even by George's friends. Ludwig Thormaehlen, who was among a group of people who read the manuscript before it went to press — and who appeared to have been unaware of the extent to which George had participated in the very creation of the book — mentioned that several people had recommended making this or that passage "more precise" and that Wolters formulate some things, as Thormaehlen tactfully put it, "with less rhetorical verve." George would hear nothing of it, saying that "the moment in which such a work appeared was more important than that it be written for eternity." Such works, George went on, were like the circle's other "polemical writings" — in particular the *Yearbooks* — and were thus primarily "meant for their temporal effect, their task was of the moment. A synthesis of this sort, describing George and his circle from a broader historical perspective, would after all come from some quarter at some point. So he, the poet, preferred to still be able to have an influence on what was evitable and to make sure that the accents and emphases were correctly placed. Accuracy in every detail, completeness and even less style were not so crucial. If one paid attention to all of that, such an undertaking would never be finished." The main issue, for George, was to get the book out where it could have an impact.

To the last, George had thus remained a committed polemicist, a cultural agitator, a resourceful politician of the spirit, ready to use whatever means available and necessary to advance his broader aims. If historical truth stood in the way of those goals, he was more than prepared to sacrifice it. Indeed, the concept of truth itself was a malleable one in George's mind. In early 1929, as Wolters was putting the final touches on his manuscript, George told Edith Landmann that "all truth must be equivocal. If it can be understood only in one way, then it is quickly done with. If it allows various interpretations it has a more lasting effect." That might be a sound principle when dealing with poetry, but history was a different matter. Yet George equated the painstaking documentation of sources, fidelity to known facts, and verifiable conclusions that constitute the basic tools of the historian's craft with empty and soul-killing *Wissenschaft*. He was after something else. And, in any case, he believed, as he had told Vallentin the year before, "what is not said is often much truer than what is said." At least as far as Wolters's history was concerned, a truer word was never spoken.

Given all of George's hopes for a project that had been fifteen years in the making and in which he had personally invested so much, it came as a bitter disappointment that the book aroused almost universal displeasure when it was published in November 1929. A few stubborn loyalists, such as Vallentin, professed their undivided admiration for the work. But almost everyone else, while recognizing it had some undeniable merits, found that in total it failed to live up to its promise. Edgar Salin, who was so disappointed by Wolters's book that he broke ranks and published a critical review of it, claimed in his memoirs that even before the publication of the *Blätter* history it had been an "open, frequently discussed question" whether Wolters had the stuff of a good historian in him. Salin reported that Julius Landmann, who had known Wolters since 1914 and, as an economic historian himself, was familiar with Wolters's previous work, "had always disputed" that Wolters had the ability to do the topic justice. Landmann had bluntly predicted that "Wolters would either drown in the material" or "he would sacrifice the accuracy of the subject matter to an animated rendering." When it appeared, the book confirmed their worst fears. As Salin put it, "We saw disquieting twists of fact that hardly corresponded to the demand for pure truthfulness, which must be made of all genuine historiography."

Most other readers reacted similarly. Although he had distanced himself from George several years before, Ernst Glöckner still followed George's career with interest, and he looked forward with some anticipation to the first authorized biography to appear of the man he formerly regarded as his Master. In January 1930, after having read most of it, Glöckner told Bertram that it "is an uncanny book, since everything that is seen and expressed is correct — except that it rests on false assumptions, so that, as one is driven from page to page, one desperately and repeatedly wishes that things really were as they are portrayed, and that the poets existed of whom there is so much talk, and that the god were present who is worshipped. I have never seen such a moving and sad testament."

Although Glöckner had once occupied a meaningful place in George's life, his name never appears in Wolters's book, and Glöckner probably never expected to be included. But there were others whose connection to George went deeper and had lasted longer who received only slightly better treatment. For understandable if not excusable reasons, Friedrich Gundolf was relegated to the status of a minor character. His friend Edgar Salin wrote that "we were offended that Wolters's 'history' completely ignored Gundolf's towering importance as the first disciple." Gundolf himself, who had also no doubt anticipated some kind of demotion in the official chronicle, confined his objections to a principled defense of the historical method. Writing to Wolfskehl, Gundolf said that even though he respected the amount of work Wolters had done and his collection and arrangement of materials, all of that still did not counterbalance the book's defects. "The Jesuitical shifting between the truth or the sincerity of faith," Gundolf wrote, "and the deception of propaganda goes too much against my nature and against the spirit of my requirements as a historian or thinker for me to be very happy about the sovereign skill with which he mainly carries out his task." As for the description of himself, Gundolf, who had dark blond hair, was surprised to find that Wolters had changed its color. "What kind of move is this? My head surrounded by a 'mane of blue-black hair'!! Not to know or to falsify the truth after decades-long friendship. In itself trivial, and I wouldn't mind black hair, but almost every individual passage I have read is the same: unreliable, mythologized, stylized, dressed up or retouched." Gundolf acknowledged that, like George, he also did not think that history was an exact science. But Gundolf still believed that a distinction existed between what was verifiably true and what was demonstrably false. "I know," he told Wolfskehl, "that nineteen out of twenty histories of the world are not more credible than that, even if most of them are lies told with less talent and much of them intended with a worse conscience and less purity of heart. But the mistrust and horror I feel toward all hagiographies and church histories have been further increased by this important book."

If Gundolf had suspected that there was some veiled stratagem behind the change in hair color Wolters had given him, he was almost certainly right. In his letter to Wolfskehl, Gundolf had also rather elusively complained, but without specifying what provoked his protest, that "I am annoyed to see the highest culture besmirched by ephemeral political and racial silliness." What Gundolf meant by "racial silliness" was made more explicit in Wolfskehl's own response to the book. While Wolters — or rather, through him, George — had given Wolfskehl more of the credit due to him as George's oldest friend and collaborator, Wolfskehl also came in for his fair share of criticism. In one passage, after commending the laudable traits of Wolfskehl's overflowing personality, Wolters had modulated his praise by writing that Wolfskehl "also had, like all subjugated or long suppressed races, the urge to dissolve everything that is solid, to subvert everything that is powerful, to overtax everything that is youthful and healthy, which cannot tolerate the ancient poisons, and he expressed that urge all the more dangerously the more expert and cunning his agile spirit, the more active and insistent his always lively will was."

That was not only unjust to the person, it was also a patently anti-Semitic slur. Wolfskehl, whose family had been in Germany for centuries, was overcome by indignation and distress when he read the passage about himself. On November 21, he confronted Wolters about the insult, telling him that "I have been choking on it for days: how can you call Karl Wolfskehl 'a subjugated and long suppressed race'?" Wolfskehl wanted to be, deserved to be, judged on his own account, not according to the accidental circumstances of his birth. Whether he was Jewish or not should have been irrelevant. "I don't know how the Jews have fared," Wolfskehl wrote, but *"that does not belong here."* And even if one were to mention his ancestry, the picture would not resemble the one Wolters drew. But, Wolfskehl continued, "I don't think about the fact that in me flows the blood of the most settled, the most distinguished Jewish families, on my father's side as well as my mother's side and maternal forebears'. *That does not matter here!* I am of free birth because I am of free birth! That has determined my path and steadied my stance, every one of my actions has been based on it. That led me to the Master. No one who is subjugated or suppressed, no one in whom even a hint lingers or is stained by the marks of former subjugation or suppression reaches the Master. Wolters have your eyes ever seen me? I am of free birth."

While attempting to mitigate the worst implications of his own words, Wolters remained basically unapologetic in his response. Assuring Wolfskehl that he had indeed seen him for what he was and that he now spoke as "a free man to a free man," Wolters explained that in his characterization he had sought to uncover the "essential qualities of a thousand-year heritage, whose existence no one of us can deny without becoming absurd." But Wolters also insisted that "if I had felt even the trace of a fear that you would be bothered by that expression, it would have been left out." Most revealingly, Wolters also told Wolfskehl that he had not been the only person to have read, and approved of, the passage. "I checked through every word of the book with the M[aster] precisely with a view toward something that could offend a friend. That there could have possibly been something in the expression you take exception to never even occurred to us." It was hard to decide which was worse: that Wolters and George had intentionally denigrated him with an anti-Semitic smear — and, despite Wolters's protestations, there was no other way to describe it — or that neither one of them had even noticed that the description was offensive and demeaning to their long-time friend.

Displaying the nobility of spirit that Wolters had implicitly wanted to disavow in him or at least to depreciate, Wolfskehl accepted his explanation substituting for an apology and, loyal to the end, he thereafter spoke only in the terms of highest admiration about the book. "It is after all a splendid achievement," Wolfskehl wrote to Gundolf, so much so, he added, that he could overlook a few defects. "To be sure," Wolfskehl said, "K. W. is seen and evaluated on p. 243 quite negatively but, despite the tossed-in racial reference, with such dignity, warmth, and inner love that I will gladly resign myself to this view."

As we have seen, others were not so willing to acquiesce in Wolters's slanted depiction of themselves. But when some took their concerns to George — not knowing, perhaps, how much of the book echoed his own standpoint, even his own words — they were met with little sympathy. In January of 1930, Edith Landmann questioned the fairness of the way Gundolf was presented, but George ascribed the portrait to larger imperatives. "Such a thing is a political book; Hofmannsthal, too, whose importance was very great, doesn't come out correspondingly." When Frau Landmann pointed out that Hofmannsthal, unlike Gundolf, had "revealed" his true nature in the meantime, George agreed. "Yes, Gundolf hasn't yet, but that can still happen. One has to make provisions." Similarly, when she, also a Jew, mentioned some of the complaints that had been made about the book's anti-Semitism, George was less than palliative. "No, but you can't deny it: one can't praise everything about you people, either. The others are railed at as well, after all, and Wilamowitz is certainly not Jewish. On the contrary, he isn't Jewish enough! Yes, we are very hard to please!" Knowing full well what George thought of Wilamowitz, Edith Landmann could not have found much comfort in the comparison. George was plainly saying that the Jews should not feel so bad about being roughed up here and there since no one else, including Wilamowitz, got off more lightly.

The response outside the circle to Wolters's book was hardly less discouraging. One article deplored the "canonization" Wolters had tried to perform in it as well as his "complete lack of humor and decency." Another simply called it "embarrassing." Notably, however, almost everyone, even those most dismissive of Wolters, exempted George himself from any criticism. A reviewer for the *Deutsche Allgemeine Zeitung* discounted the book but asserted that "the effect that radiates from the person and the work of George today is already immense and cannot yet be assessed for the future." And Peter Hamecher, who had written such a favorable notice of *The New Reich* two years before, judged Wolters's efforts to have been largely redundant. For, Hamecher asked, what had been Wolters's intention? "To correct foolish opinions, distorted statements, stupid gossip. As if this were still worth the trouble today!" In Hamecher's view, Wolters had merely reiterated the obvious and seemed to believe that the public still needed to have George "explained" to them. Not true, Hamecher wrote: "George has long since ceased to belong solely to the inner Circle; rather, he belongs to all of Germany, and if we ponder his incomprehensible mythic appearance, we do not need the spectacles of the initiated to do so. Yet we want to forget Wolters's foolish biography with its corrections and reprimands, which only distort the image of the Master, and to contemplate with a reverential bow the mythos of George! He is the living!"

When the winter semester ended in March of 1930, Wolters and his wife headed south with the aim of stopping in the Engadine in Switzerland, where they hoped to recuperate from the normal stresses of the university term and from the added tensions that had accumulated over the last several years while completing the *Blätter* history. The almost uniformly negative reception of the work, which had been the most ambitious undertaking of Wolters's life and the one into which he had poured his best blood, must have also caused him no little anguish and made the journey seem even more necessary. When they arrived in Munich in early March, however, Wolters suddenly fell seriously ill, so much so that he was admitted to the hospital. He was diagnosed with a coronary thrombosis; a clot had formed near his already weakened heart, which was aggravated by a flare-up of the rheumatism that had plagued him since the war. Karl Wolfskehl rushed to the hospital where Wolters was being treated and reported to George on his condition. "The main thing is that the heart holds out," Wolfskehl relayed. "A mild relapse of his rheumatic illness causes pain without being an objective complication. The doctors prescribe absolute rest but are not without confidence." Several days later, the danger seemed to have passed. Relieved by the turnaround, Wolfskehl also sent this news to George, saying, "How happy I am! It just could not have been! In his wonderful book W. committed himself to life and it to him! I am reading it again and again! For the first time there is once more a great monument that fills the eyes of the outside world against its will, a testament not only of growth but also of legitimate claims, of unity — for the first time since the *Yearbook*!"

A month later, in the night of April 14–15, Friedrich Wolters died in Munich at the age of fifty-three.

Wolters's history of the *Blätter* would claim another victim that year. Max Kommerell, whose own work, *The Poet as Leader,* Wolters had recommended to Wolfskehl as "probably the most brilliant book of the last few years," did not hold the book written by his former teacher in equally high regard. Publicly, Kommerell maintained appearances, writing a moving eulogy to Wolters in which he extolled his personal warmth, generosity, and integrity. But in private Kommerell made no secret of his distaste for Wolters's last work. It was, he said in June of 1930, quite simply an "awful book." His friend Hans Anton, however, wanted no part in what he considered disloyalty to their former mentor, and he told Kommerell so, accusing him of dishonoring the dead. Standing firm against Anton's accusations of disrespect, Kommerell defended his rejection of the book. "You confront me," he told Anton, "with a reminder that it is my duty to respect F. W.! You speak of desecrating a corpse, etc., compare me with Jews, etc. My dear child! When he was alive, I respected and loved F. W. but never in such a way that I subordinated myself to him, and if you say that I must start with the assumption of the fact of his superiority, then I have nothing to do with that." Kommerell merely wanted to be able to exercise his critical judgment, no more, and not even openly, but only among the people to whom he was closest. He agreed that Wolters had died nobly, in the service of the cause, and that in itself deserved recognition. "And it would be reason enough to remain silent about the weaknesses of his work since he has been dead such a short time. And I am silent — in public." But, Kommerell wrote, he could not pretend that the serious defects of the book did not exist. Like Gundolf, he felt its most egregious fault was the sanctimonious tone, the hagiographic sermonizing that brooked no dissent. Kommerell could not accept that Wolters "gave the entire foundation the appearance of a church in his book, dealt with important antagonisms with the small gestures of a sect, distorted the veneration of the great man (in the last chapters) into a kind of devotion that has to arouse shivers of shame in finer spirits and which, as another form of violation, t. M. had to reject!"

It was this last argument — that "the Master" should have prevented or at least tempered the fawning hero worship directed at himself — that actually lay at the heart of Kommerell's objections, and Kommerell knew it. "Basically," he admitted to Anton, "my deepest reproach concerns the administration that approves of this. And this has nothing to do with the fact that all books, mine as well, have flaws: no, it's a matter of practices! — yes, indeed, Hans! Practices! — with which my name is too important to me to identify myself." In spite of the guarded circumlocution, it was obvious what "administration" of which "practices" Kommerell meant. When he took his misgivings to George himself, saying that long stretches of Wolters's book simply did not correspond to the truth, George coolly answered, "This is not about truth here, it is about the state." And that was a sacrifice Kommerell was no longer willing to make.

The conflict between Kommerell and George had actually been a long time in the making and, some thought, even foreseen by George himself. Almost from the start of their association, Kommerell had been a disruptive element in the circle. As early as 1924, he had begun to act aggressively toward George's other friends whenever they assembled. Both Kurt Hildebrandt and Thormaehlen attributed Kommerell's hostility to his feelings of jealousy or envy over certain privileges enjoyed by the other — and invariably better-looking — members of George's entourage. In particular, Ernst Morwitz, George's friend, legal counsel, and confidant for two and a half decades, served as the frequent target of Kommerell's most abusive attacks. Even though Morwitz was no dullard, he was no match for Kommerell's incisive, nimble mind and his verbal virtuosity. Relentlessly, Kommerell would try to trip up Morwitz in some contradiction, force him to reveal his ignorance about some arcane fact, or expose some belief Morwitz held as being childish or naive. When George was a witness to these confrontations, however, he appears not to have intervened and he perhaps even found them entertaining. In 1926, George mentioned the ongoing scuffles to Edith Landmann, saying that "criticizing had become a habit in the state. Everyone is being accused of something, and once that's out in the open, that person runs around forever with his adjective. But it doesn't do any harm. It adds some spice." On another occasion, George shrugged off any suggestion that such altercations were necessarily a bad thing. "Wherever there are people," he said, "there are conflicts." Still, George was fully aware of Kommerell's quarrelsome, even malicious tendencies and once frankly told Frau Landmann, "Beware of him." To Kommerell himself, after kissing him on the head, George once said, half in disapproval, half in admiration, "You are an evil genius."

George's other friends were at a loss to explain why the Master, who was so strict with everyone else, showed such leniency toward someone who was not only short and ugly but ill-mannered as well. More than uncivil, Kommerell's behavior often bordered on the bizarre. Thormaehlen noted that Kommerell sustained himself largely from a large sack of fresh nuts he kept next to his bed, with his only other major source of nutrition apparently being milk. "The less aggressive friends of the poet, as well as the poet himself," Thormaehlen took care to point out, "usually preferred wine." When Kommerell did venture into other culinary arenas, the results could be varied. Kommerell once stayed with Thormaehlen in the studio apartment he had in Berlin, taking advantage of the meals prepared by the woman Thormaehlen had cook for him. One day, Thormaehlen received a reprimand from the manager of the apartment block where his studio was located. Complaints had been made by passersby, who reported that bones and other inedibles were being thrown down on them from the windows of Thormaehlen's rooms. When he asked Kommerell whether he was the culprit, Kommerell laughed and said yes, adding that he had got a kick out of his little game. Thormaehlen, who was not insensitive to the attractions of throwing refuse onto the bourgeoisie, nevertheless requested that Kommerell refrain from pulling such stunts in the future.

And still George treated Kommerell with an indulgence that smacked of coddling. It was Thormaehlen again, having had many opportunities to watch them interact, who suspected that George was consciously protecting Kommerell so that he could focus undisturbed on fulfilling his dream of becoming a leading scholar in the field of literary studies. Thormaehlen felt that George thus shielded Kommerell, whose belligerence Thormaehlen was convinced stemmed from a fundamental lack of confidence and self-esteem, from anything — including censuring his conduct — that might distract Kommerell from attaining his goal. And it was the very people Kommerell had injured the most who were also the most appalled that, once Kommerell had got what he so badly wanted, he turned his back on the person who they thought had been instrumental in helping him get it. After receiving his doctorate in 1925, Kommerell went on to obtain the *venia legendi,* the coveted right to teach at a university, by completing his habilitation thesis at Frankfurt in the spring of 1930. A few months later, he categorically renounced his allegiance to George and his "state." To Ernst Morwitz, these two events were intimately related. Thirty years later, after both George and Kommerell were long dead, Morwitz was still filled with bitterness toward his tormentor of old, who, Morwitz wrote in 1960, "found it opportune to break with the poet after he had achieved with the help of his spirit the object of his ambition (venia legendi)."

The actual rupture took place over what Hans Anton initially viewed as a triumph. Although George had not resolved the issue of establishing a foundation in his name before proceeding with the edition of his complete works, the matter had been only temporarily postponed. On June 17, 1930, Kommerell received a letter from Anton informing him that the "following matter" had recently come up: "The foundation for the continuance of the work of Stefan George will be instituted in the summer. The foundation's board will consist of Robert [Boehringer] you and — me. Thus the both of us have an absolute majority." Not only would he and Kommerell effectively have control over the foundation, Anton pointed out, but also, and just as gratifying, "the previous universal heir and executor Ernst [Morwitz] is now eliminated." It is unknown what caused George to remove Morwitz from the position, but it is easy to imagine that there must have been a considerable amount of jockeying going on behind the scenes. In any event, Anton wrote that the Master wanted to know when Kommerell would be in Frankfurt next "since he would like to discuss the entire matter with you."

Instead of feeling satisfaction at having decisively outmaneuvered Morwitz, Kommerell realized that it was time to come clean about something that by then had been gnawing at him for six months. In the previous December of 1929, while Kommerell was in Berlin, there seems to have been yet another confrontation between him and other members of the circle. Although neither Kommerell nor anyone else ever revealed what the nature of the dispute had been, it had clearly escalated to an open clash. Increasingly heated words were exchanged until, as Kommerell noted in his diary, "I found myself expected to hear and to accept a comment that it was my duty to myself to reject." What this "comment" was or who made it Kommerell kept to himself, but it was so serious "that I saw my relationship to St. G. changed by it." Suddenly, Kommerell perceived everything in a different light. "The entire way of coexisting as it had taken shape rested on such a complete abandonment of one's personal sense of self that I can consider it appropriate and bearable to a boy at most, never to a man." From that moment on, Max Kommerell, who was then about to turn twenty-eight, no longer wanted to be a "disciple" to a "Master," the subordinate member of a hierarchical organization, but an independent and free human being.

Thus, when Anton's letter arrived the following summer bearing the news of his imminent installation onto the foundation's board, Kommerell felt obligated to tell George about his change of heart. Explaining his delay in doing so by saying that some communities managed to stay intact despite "great inner conflicts" if only those conflicts were "not expressed," Kommerell attributed his silence to a final hope, now dashed, that life could go on as before. "For that reason," he told George, "I did not write during the half-year since my departure from Berlin what I now consider it a dictate of honesty to write." Putting it most simply, Kommerell said that "I am no longer the same person." He knew what the consequences would be, but "I do not wish to speak about what I am paying for all of this and will pay in the future. I am determined to let my Self grow in the direction in which its growth takes it." It was as simple as that.

Or should have been. Kommerell had unburdened himself even earlier to Hans Anton, who was now desperately caught between his Master and his friend. Anton tried to reason with Kommerell, but as Kommerell wrote in his diary, "Hans did not disguise the fact that he regarded me as someone whose mind had become ill and who had the choice only between a complete reversal or ruin." For the rest of the year, Anton struggled to convince Kommerell it was not too late to return to the fold and of the fallout if he did not. Anton predicted that, after a couple of years outside of the state, Kommerell would inevitably turn into a "harmless scientist." Anton said he could imagine scenes in which, one day in the future, "we will ride past you somewhere — and you will only ask yourself 'didn't I know them once? Why aren't I with them?'" Without the leavening exposure to the Master, Anton warned, "you will become a littérateur — which I do not wish for the one dearest and closest to me." Throughout, Anton tried to reassure Kommerell that his own feelings toward him had not changed. "You know," he told Kommerell, "how I am attached to you." However, Anton added, "Don't make me be ashamed of it."

Finally, the strain of attempting to reconcile the opposing camps was too much for Anton and he stopped communicating with Kommerell entirely. On Sunday, February 22, after waiting through a painful period of silence, Kommerell tried again to reestablish contact. "With great sadness I notice that you have given no answer to my last letter to you. Wednesday is my twenty-ninth birthday. Will I have to remain without a word from you then too?" Kommerell told him that he thought of him "daily," and plaintively wondered, "Do you refuse to be with me?"

Hans Anton did mark Kommerell's birthday but not in a way that brought anyone joy. That day, February 25, 1931, Anton traveled alone to Freiburg in southwestern Germany. From there, he wrote to Kommerell that for over a month "I felt myself threatened by something like insanity. I noticed that I occasionally acted, spoke wrongly. I had, so to speak, lost my grip on myself." Since then his psychic condition had further deteriorated, until "in the end I also did not understand the external world anymore." Anton did not know what to do, where to turn. Nothing seemed right anymore, and "it is horrible to see you disappear further and further." Seeing no other way out and his world coming apart, Anton killed himself in Freiburg on the day Kommerell turned twenty-nine.

Whereas George had reacted to Kommerell's apostasy with outward calm — Thormaehlen said, "It seemed to me as if the poet had expected it for a long time" — the suicide of Hans Anton affected him deeply. Someone who was with George when he received the news recalled that it was "a terrifying sight, how he — yes, I have to say: raced through the almost empty room, although he did not make rapid strides at all. But in this back and forth from the bench past the head of the long table across to the window and then back again, without pause, speaking to himself, more for himself than for me, turning his head back and forth, the same question over and over: 'How could that happen, how was that permitted to happen.' " However it had happened, George knew whom to blame. Thenceforth, Kommerell, who had often gone by the nickname Puck in observance of his rascally prankishness, was now referred to solely as "the toad" — *die Kröte*.

That same year Kommerell sealed his defection by marrying Eva Otto, whom he had met only shortly before. (When George heard of Kommerell's engagement he is said to have "laughed like twelve savages.") Kommerell may have liberated himself from George, but George did not let him go easily. Thirteen years later, in the early summer of 1943 and one year before Kommerell was to die of cancer at the age of forty-two, he told a friend about a bad dream he had recently had. Kommerell was teaching a course that semester on Rilke and George, and he said the experience was having a negative effect on his unconscious life. In most of his dreams, Kommerell wrote, it seemed "that I had still not freed myself, that I had let myself be enchanted and captured again, etc." But one dream in particular had given him a start. In it, "Wolters was holding a George service in a swimming pool (we all stood around naked) and praised him for having introduced the new Eros and for having got rid of the old one. At the same time, however, that very thing was taking place at the edge of the basin in a kind of cult ceremony: George killed a dragon-man who had just slept with his dragon-wife, cut off his genitals and threw them into the swimming pool."

It is an alarming yet remarkably rich image. Not only does it convey the duress experienced, even after the passing of many years, by anyone who dared to act counter to the Master's mandates, it also gestures toward an avenue of escape. Kommerell would have remembered from his Greek mythology that, according to one legend, Aphrodite (from *aphros,* or "foam") was born out of the sea after Cronus had castrated her father, Uranus, the first supreme god, and had flung his severed organ into the waves from which she then emerged. Out of violence sprang love, or at least one version of it. For Uranus had also given his name to that kind of love which George had early discovered as his own and which Kommerell, by marrying, had effectively rejected. The birth of Aphrodite meant, then, for Kommerell, that one era in his life had ended and that a new one could finally begin.

CHAPTER 44
Revolution II

George absorbed Wolters's death and Kommerell's desertion with an equanimity that stands in arresting contrast to the place they had formerly occupied in his life. It was as if he thought that their disappearance were somehow natural, to be as little lamented as the setting of the sun or the passing of a season. They had done their work for the state, had fulfilled their duty, and had simply moved on. Far from displaying sorrow or regret over their disappearance, George seemed to accept these newest losses as additional signs that his own work was done as well, that his own life had reached its natural limit, that his purpose had been achieved. All that remained now for him to do was to wait for the next inevitable stage to commence.

This imperturbability, almost impassiveness, emerges perhaps most strikingly over another death that took place in 1931. Ever since Friedrich Gundolf had married Elisabeth Salomon on November 4, 1926, Gundolf had continuously suffered from a variety of physical complaints. In March of the following year, he told his brother, Ernst, of the countless "minor maladies that plague me in my legs, skin, bowels, and stomach. I am now taking an assortment of pills according to a daily schedule." That summer, while vacationing in St. Moritz, Gundolf's condition dramatically worsened. A doctor he consulted speculated that he had "an ulcer." Seven days later it became apparent that Gundolf had something more serious. ("I haven't kept down a single bite," he told his brother, "and yesterday I fell down in the middle of the room.") His wife, Elli, urged him to look up a local stomach specialist, and after conducting several X-rays, the doctor discovered a "tumor" blocking the exit of Gundolf's stomach, "which did not let any food pass through." The doctor advised an immediate operation. "Otherwise," Gundolf wrote Ernst, "I will starve to death."

As he convalesced, Gundolf was unable to communicate with his brother for almost a month. Finally, on October 2, Gundolf told Ernst that "today I took a walk in the hospital's garden for the first time, with the help of Elli and a nurse." Only after the fact had his physician informed him how dangerous the operation had been. "Two kilograms of my stomach were cut out," Gundolf said, adding that the doctor estimated that "ninety percent die" of such a procedure. He had been lucky, but he felt not only luck had helped. "I am thinking night and day about the Master," he revealed to Ernst, "and notice that I know most of his poems by heart."

Gundolf had never disavowed George, not even in the most excruciating period when he was being forced to decide between his Master or his wife, and he had never wavered in his public posture. But the struggle he had fought with George had put enormous pressure on the feelings of steadfast devotion that had formed the center of Gundolf's emotional and intellectual life for almost three decades. His brush with death, however, renewed his hope that there still might be a chance George would change his mind and take him in again. From the hospital in Switzerland, Gundolf wrote a poem to George, titled, "To my Master," beseeching him to do so. The concluding two strophes read:

> Take me as if on the bier
> With a lowered glance of forgiveness.
> I am Your Child . . feel what I was
> Even in the nighttime cry of disunion
> May Your first kiss burn once more
> Your creative kiss on the one who is pale
> I live because live I must
> Through You, for You, in Your Sign.

It was all in vain. His brother, while trying to be as gentle as possible, cautioned Gundolf not to harbor unrealistic expectations. "I certainly believe that the Master heard about the danger you were in not without sympathy, but I have little hope that a change could now occur in his outward behavior, which is determined by outward affairs." George received the poem in silence.

It was Wolters's book that finally gave Gundolf the incentive to take the step he probably never imagined possible for himself. In 1930, Gundolf published a volume of poems, dedicated simply "To my wife," that concluded with a brief verse that, though short, signaled a seismic shift in his view of himself and the world.

> My youth was governed
> Dully, then willingly by the Master
> Until a Stronger One unleashed me:
> I stride more truly as an orphan,
> Without staff, track or rope
> Knowing only God and Love
> Through the rock-strewn vale
> Along the path drawn by death.

When Julius Landmann read these lines, he could hardly believe that Gundolf could have really meant what they appear to state so obviously. In a letter to Gundolf that November, Landmann confessed that "I am having difficulty comprehending that you are now formally and publicly announcing your break" with George. It seemed inconceivable to Landmann "how a force, which had decisively determined a person and had taken shape within him, could ever be felt to belong to the past." Saying he had spoken with no one else about the matter except with Gundolf's brother, Ernst, Landmann nevertheless stated that he had "the distinct impression that many of the friends will not be able to reconcile this renunciation with the image that you have built up in us over all these years."

In response, Gundolf calmly assured Landmann that the poem did not signify "a renunciation of George's work and person." However, "after Wolters's outrageously awful book, which is mendacious through and through, was published as the official or officious circle doctrine and history under George's sign, thus with his approval and thus unfortunately also as the presumed 'source' of his ecclesiastical history, I had to demonstrate in the most quiet and succinct form possible that I no longer have anything in common with the George orthodoxy or with Wolters's clericalism and sycophancy." Gundolf also explained that many students and others had been approaching him about Wolters's book, under the reasonable assumption that Gundolf agreed with it. In his role as a public figure, Gundolf argued, "I cannot, even for the sake of honesty, promote or tolerate the illusion that I share this dogmatism." Even more bluntly, "I do not belong to it and I have to say that."

Gundolf's freedom, hard bought though it was, lasted less than a year. Although the operation in 1927 had provided relief, he never fully recovered his strength. On July 7, 1931, he fell ill again. Five days later, Friedrich Gundolf died in Heidelberg at the age of fifty-one precisely on the day of George's birthday. Whether it was a last wordless reproach, a final pathetic gesture of fealty, or merely bizarre coincidence, Gundolf died, after all, under the sign of the man who had governed most of his conscious life. George himself passed over the event without a word.

The grim harvest was not yet over. Later the same year, Julius Landmann finally gave up fighting against a depression that had long tormented him and he put an end to his life. Although Julius Landmann wrote few letters to George and left no record of his conversations or meetings with the Master, he had counted, along with his wife, Edith, among George's most trusted and loyal friends ever since they had met just before the war. Although joined to George through friendship, they both regarded George as far more than just a friend. As one of their sons, Michael, later explained, "For my parents, George was not the eminent representative of modern literature. He belonged, in accordance with his own self-understanding, to a completely different dimension. His books were 'sacred books.'" The Landmanns had a special cabinet built to hold their collection of first editions of George's works, along with the entire series of *Die Blätter für die Kunst,* and the poetic works of his friends. It also contained a work by Michael's younger brother, Georg Peter, who had written out George's poem "The War" horizontally on a single, long piece of paper and rolled it together on two wooden rods like an ancient papyrus roll or the Torah. This was a natural association to the Landmanns, for as Michael also wrote, "in the circle of his disciples George enjoyed a reverence similar to that of an oriental wise man, a Brahman or a Hasidic rabbi." It was only right, they thought, that his works should be housed in something like a shrine.

People who did not know Julius Landmann personally wondered what he and George could have had to say to each other. True, Landmann was a professor of economics (and a very distinguished one at that: when the great economic and social theorist Werner Sombart retired from his chair at the University of Berlin in 1931, Landmann was recruited to replace him). But, as George said after his death and in explanation of the long and close attachment to a person who seemed so different from his other friends, Landmann was, quite simply, "a phenomenon." Although Landmann originally came from Galicia and spoke Polish natively, he learned German by reading voraciously, a habit he retained throughout his life (his spoken German always betrayed a slight accent, though, and as his son noted, "to the end he counted in Polish.") Equipped with a tenacious memory, Julius Landmann read, and seemed to know, everything. During his doctoral examination in his secondary subject — German literature — the questioner asked him whether he could name a hymn from Luther's time. Landmann responded by delivering a lecture on the development of the German hymn in the sixteenth century, even reciting the opening verses of numerous hymns. This performance presaged later tendencies in Landmann. It often happened that, when someone would ask him a question, he would fall silent, sometimes for ten minutes, half an hour or even longer. To the uninitiated, it appeared that he either did not want to or could not reply. In reality, he was inwardly composing his response, which would then come in the form of a detailed, cogent, and lengthy lecture. When a German visitor in Basel made a casual remark criticizing the plan to build a new energy plant near the city, Landmann instructed him in an hour-long speech on the economic necessity of the plant, complete with a battery of statistical information.

George clearly enjoyed these demonstrations of intellectual vibrancy. "What a person of profound and precise knowledge," George once admiringly exclaimed of him. Yet Landmann was no dry technocrat: he remained a lifelong reader of literature and poetry, and he was an impassioned, expert gardener, as well as an equally knowledgeable oenophile. His cellar was expansive and richly stocked — he once joked that he would spend a semester's sabbatical in search of the "best Burgundy" he could find — and he delighted in presenting his guests with rare but appropriate wines during meals. And, owing to his singular gift for cultivating friendships, there always seemed to be guests at the Landmanns' house. "We run a small, thriving hotel!" he once quipped. Of even temperament (which masked an underlying despair), grave but not dull, unfailingly courteous, Landmann provided excellent company — and, to George, frequently good advice. On rare occasions, Landmann exhibited a more deeply submerged sarcastic irascibility; of a philosopher he once said for example that, although the man was bright, he seldom showed his intelligence. But these flashes of flint must have made him even more appealing to George, who loved a good insult almost as much as he loved a good wine.

It was all the more bitter that Julius Landmann, who had turned only fifty-four in August of 1931, gave up the battle against his melancholy that November. George, who had last seen him in May in Berlin, had told Landmann that he "was his dearest friend — the last of the old guard." In George's condolence letter to Edith, he also wrote, "Thus we have also lost him, who understood like no other how to be a friend."

And still the series of deprivations did not cease. Early the next year, in the spring of 1932, Berthold Vallentin, who had known George even longer than Julius Landmann — although he and Vallentin had both been born in the same year, 1877 — suffered a massive stroke. It left him almost completely paralyzed and at times delusional. Vallentin vegetated in a semiconscious condition for over a year until a second stroke finally put an end to his misery on February 13, 1933. Two weeks later, his distraught wife Diana, after two unsuccessful attempts, followed her husband through suicide. George commented on this event to Edith Landmann as well, saying that life "had no longer been possible for her," adding that he was "happy for her that she had found the courage" to depart it. Since Diana had been Jewish (her maiden name was Rabinowicz), there were several reasons for her to despair over the impossibility of life in 1933. Their only son, Stefan — named after the poet, their revered Master — survived his parents by only a few years. In 1939, on the shore of Lake Maggiore in Italy, he, too, voluntarily put an end to his life.

Perhaps it was only understandable that in his last years George preferred the company of his most recent, and youngest, friends. Aside from the obvious attractions their youth lent them, they also carried no weighty baggage, did not stir any painful memories and, most reassuringly, were not likely to die any time soon. There was certainly no shortage of candidates eager to vie for the honor of being his companion. To the end, George was constantly sought out by young men who for a variety of motives wanted to be in his presence.

Predictably, their first encounter with him sometimes failed to produce results that satisfied both parties. A friend of Ernst Kantorowicz named Gerhart Ladner recalled his opportunity to meet the Master as one such failure. After Eka — that was Kantorowicz's nickname — had injudiciously revealed that he knew George well, Ladner pressed for an interview. Ladner, who earned a living working at an indifferent job, had secret aspirations to be a poet. Kantorowicz informed Ladner that before his request could be considered he would have to submit a sample of his work and a letter to the Master. On December 10, 1930, much to his own happy astonishment, Ladner was summoned to meet George in Berlin.

At five in the afternoon, Kantorowicz took Ladner to Thormaehlen's studio where George was staying. After introducing him by saying simply, "This is Ladner," Kantorowicz left the room and Ladner was alone with the Master. "What leads you to me?" was the first thing George wanted to know. Ladner launched into a long complaint about how he was drowning in his job, which did not leave him any time or energy to write, and that he was unsure even if he really was or should be a poet. George listened for awhile, then interrupted him. "What you are telling me there is nothing special at all," he abruptly said. "Those questions are a dime a dozen; all educated young people have them today. You don't even see the real questions yet. All of that has nothing to do with them. Everyone has to do something, after all. Even those who are with me, who have their assigned place with me and think now they can stay a while where they are, I say even to them that they have to do something. If your friend Eka had spent so much time thinking about what he should do he would never have written his book." That was bracing enough, but George was not yet finished. He next took up the issue of whether Ladner had the makings of a poet. The verdict was crushing. "You sent me poems," George said. "They are not all that bad. But you would have surely noticed yourself that one can not build a life on them. Or do you want to be like those people out there who make an entire book out of one poem that appeared in the *Blätter*? I'm sure you don't want that."

Steadying himself after this barrage but feeling that he had not received the answers he was looking for, Ladner unadvisedly returned to his original questions. Suddenly, George became furious. "So, you all come running to me and sit there a little while and chatter on to me about this and that. What is supposed to come of me, then? Something like that is possible only in a very few exceptional cases. My time would be entirely eaten up. What was it that you were actually thinking? Did you just want to see what the fabled creature looks like? You expected something completely different and now you are disappointed. But I can't help you. I'm not a monarch after all who can say a couple of friendly words to everyone."

George went on for about fifteen minutes in this vein until finally Ladner had had enough and indicated his defiance by looking at George full in the face, something the Master was not used to seeing. Quickly bringing the session to a close, George mockingly said that "it's all well and good to go straight to the highest authority, but there is also a little profanation in that. When you understand that you will have already taken a large step forward." On showing Ladner out, George gave him a final word of advice. "Look," he said, "there are many people around me. Some stand closer, others farther away. Everyone has to resign himself to his lot. And if something else arises again — but it must be something important — then write me a nice little letter." And with that, George ushered the devastated Ladner out through the door and locked it behind him. Needless to say, they never met again.

For the more fortunate ones — the ones who were invited to stand closer — the experience of meeting George was less traumatic but equally overpowering. The same month he had met Gerhart Ladner in 1930, another friend of George, the Swiss Robert von Steiger, had brought the Master some poems by Steiger's cousin, Michael Stettler, who lived in Bern and was then seventeen years old. George was entranced by the verses. "Finally another poetic talent," he said and expressed his wish to meet the author sometime soon. It was not until the following year, however, when George was staying in southern Switzerland near Locarno, that Stettler got the chance to fulfill that wish. One day in mid-November, 1931, as Stettler was discussing the possibility of visiting George, Stettler's friend and mentor, Wilhelm Stein, the author of the ill-fated *Raphael* and the person who had introduced Stettler to George's poetry, told his younger friend simply, "Just go then!" On an impulse, Stettler did. Without telling anyone, including his parents, about his plans, the now eighteen-year-old Stettler set out early the next morning to Locarno. After finding the correct address, he let himself through the garden gate and stood below the window of the house where George lived, waiting to be noticed. When a girl inquisitively looked out of the kitchen window, he said, "Can I be shown up?" A few moments later, George's companion, Frank Mehnert, emerged and stood before him. To Stettler's plain declaration, "I am Michael," Mehnert answered, as if he had been expecting him, "Ah, you have come from Bern!"

Once it became clear that Stettler wanted to see the Master, Mehnert told him that he was resting and that Stettler should return in an hour for tea. When he did, he was shown into the room where George stood waiting for him. At once, George took him by the arm and, while asking questions, listening to the responses, nodding and turning his head toward his guest, they paced back and forth in the room. After the tea, they took a walk, still arm in arm. When a car rushed toward them at one point, Stettler pressed George's arm closer to his and noticed "the grateful counterpressure of his hand as a mute reply." As evening fell, they returned to the house; Mehnert rolled down the shutters, lit candles, and the conversation continued over red wine and George's favorite cigarettes.

The next morning, Stettler, who spent the night in a nearby hotel, returned to undergo the ritual all prospective disciples had to pass through. George wanted him to read aloud. As always, the subject was allowed to choose his weapon. Stettler picked a poem from *The Year of the Soul*. "The result," Stettler confessed, "was bad, and the poet did not conceal it." Later on in the afternoon, George had Mehnert show Stettler how it was done. Mehnert also read from *The Year of the Soul,* with occasional corrections in emphasis or intonation from the Master himself. "The reading had a deep and lasting effect on me," Stettler wrote, but not as profound as the words George spoke to him while taking leave of him that evening. "Come, you tall one," George said, leading him to the door, "you are mine!"

For two more enchanted days, all three went on more walks through the village, with George in the middle and Mehnert and Stettler on either side clasping each arm, while George told them stories about his life and his friends. During these excursions, George wore a black cape and his trademark blue beret. Mehnert also wore one — George liked for his friends to wear a beret as well — and, after Stettler begged him for it, Mehnert let Stettler wear it for the rest of his stay. On the last day, Mehnert made photographs of everyone, and George let Stettler know that he would like to receive a letter from him now and again. "Not that much has to be in it," George said, "but it would be bad if you didn't have something to say at all."

On returning home in Bern, Stettler, who felt as if he had just made some miraculous trip to another planet, discovered that in his absence a veritable manhunt had been going on to find him. Worried about the sudden and unexplained disappearance of their son, his parents had enlisted the police in both Bern and Zurich, who had begun making inquiries that quickly led them to Stettler's "mentor," Wilhelm Stein. Suspecting something unspeakable was going on, they raised suspicions about the nature of the relationship between the forty-five-year-old Stein and a boy less than half his age. Michael Stettler arrived at his house just in time to prevent the police, who no doubt had a number of questions they wanted to ask, from calling on the Master himself.

Even in old age, then, George remained a powerful seducer, able to win the devotion of ardent young men — and to provoke the outrage and fears of the bourgeois he had detested all his life. But he always had to have a favorite, one person who was the primary focus of his attention and concern. After Gundolf there had been a succession of such privileged companions, but they were all now dead or too old or otherwise unsuitable. Fortunately, someone had appeared just in time to fill the void created by Kommerell's decampment. Until the end of George's life in December 1933, his constant companion, his caretaker and cook, his secretary and protector, was Frank Mehnert, the person who had met Stettler at the door. Typically, George had also devised a nickname for Mehnert, calling him, presumably in homage to having been vanquished by him, "Victor" Frank.

A friend of the Stauffenberg brothers, Mehnert had first come to George's notice in 1924, when he was fifteen. George happened to see him one day as Mehnert accompanied the Stauffenbergs to the train station in Stuttgart. Although they did not speak to each other, George pronounced him a "rare bird" and had one of the brothers give Mehnert an orange as a present from the Master. They met the following year, and over the next few years Mehnert was often present in Berlin for readings, and he sometimes went to Königstein or Basel to be with George. But it was only after Kommerell had begun to make his retreat in 1929 that Mehnert assumed the mantle of first disciple.

Mehnert answered all of the criteria George placed on his most favored intimates. Michael Stettler, who wrote a brief biographical sketch of Mehnert in the 1960s, said that "it seems to me beyond any doubt that Mehnert's youthful figure embodied for George the type most close to Maximin and as such the youth he dreamt of." Of medium build, with a slender but sturdy frame, Mehnert's face conformed to the familiar pattern: a regular oval, with full lips and almond-shaped eyes under gently arched brows, the bottom cupped by a firm chin. His parents, although German, lived in Moscow, where he was born in 1909. This gave Mehnert a slightly exotic air, and many people who met him thought they could detect something vaguely aristocratic about him. His manner enforced this sense: he was usually reserved, composed in his demeanor, and intensely proud, almost arrogant. Whenever he was around Kommerell, who tried his usual ploys on him, probing for intellectual weaknesses and baiting him with taunts or trick questions, Mehnert refused to allow himself to become ruffled. This cool unflappability only made Kommerell more rabid, but to no effect. Mehnert merely watched and calmly listened, as if he were biding his time, which then duly came once Kommerell disappeared.

It was thus natural that it was Mehnert who accompanied George when he went to southern Switzerland in October 1931 for what had been for many years his annual sojourn in the Helvetian Republic. This time, George stayed in a place he had never been before but which he may have discovered in 1926 when he had made a brief journey by himself to Locarno. There, on the shore of Lake Maggiore, surrounded by the Lepontine Alps, he had found a house for rent in a hamlet called Minusio, which lies adjacent to Locarno. The two-story structure, converted from an old mill, had a terrace overlooking a wild overgrown garden filled with grape vines, fruit trees, and cypresses, which offered a view that extended over the lake to the opposite shore. With the Italian border a mere six miles away, the weather could be expected to be mild even in winter. It seemed perfect in every way; Minusio provided a beautiful, comfortable, and well-hidden retreat.

With Mehnert to attend to his needs and to provide him company, George settled into something approaching contentment. He did not leave Minusio until the next April, totaling seven months, the longest period he had ever spent anywhere during his entire adult life. After returning to Berlin that May, where he remained for most of the next six months, George went back to Minusio, with Mehnert in tow, in November 1932 for a second winter and then again in October of the following year. It was as if, after a life of virtually continuous motion, George had finally found a place where he felt he could find rest and calm and perhaps even a measure of happiness.

Meanwhile, the world outside was gearing itself up for a cataclysm. After the Nazi party had won its stunning victory in the September elections of 1930, things had gone from bad to worse in Germany. Earlier that year, in March, President Hindenburg had responded to the collapse of the last Social Democratic government by appointing a young, forty-five-year-old Catholic politician named Heinrich Brüning to the office of chancellor. While not without talent and intelligence, Brüning, who lacked a majority in parliament, had neither the experience nor the political means to govern a country that was rapidly becoming ungovernable. The ascendance of the radical, chauvinistic Nazis made foreign creditors nervous, causing many to recall the loans that had made the German economic recovery possible after 1924. In the early summer of 1931, just over a year after Brüning had assumed office, banks began to hemorrhage money. Between June 8 and 12 alone, the losses in foreign exchange by the *Reichsbank* amounted to over five hundred million marks, which was to climb to two billion by the middle of July. Faced with no other alternative, the government began to slash the salaries of civil servants and eliminate inessential jobs. The economy, already hard hit by the worldwide depression following the New York stock market crash in 1929, almost seized up entirely. By the end of 1932, industrial production had fallen by forty-two percent compared to three years before, and unemployment had reached more than eight million, affecting almost half of the total work force. Everywhere people were beginning to go hungry again, many could not afford clothes or fuel, and some even lost their homes. It seemed to many as if Germany's darkest time had returned.

In this atmosphere of misery and desperation, the Nazis were able to capitalize on the general feeling among German citizens that they had been betrayed yet again, this time by the democratic government of the Weimar Republic. But the Nazis did not come to power by popular vote. Instead, they levered themselves into position through intrigue, political backroom maneuvering, and overt intimidation. Behind Brüning's back, the Nazis organized a shadow cabinet, designed to be put into place as soon as Brüning had been removed. At the same time, they contrived to persuade the now eighty-five-year-old Hindenburg that they would be better able to lead the country out of the crisis if only given free hand. In May 1932, Hindenburg confronted Brüning with demands fed to the aging president by Brüning's opponents. As they had planned, Brüning and his cabinet resigned, leaving the Nazis tantalizingly close to their goal. Still pretending they cared about parliamentary procedure, the Nazis conducted a vigorous election campaign that summer and won their biggest success yet, attracting 37.2 percent of the vote in the July elections. And, even though the party experienced a setback in November, when it gained only 33.1 percent, Nazi operatives continued to pursue their underhanded machinations. Finally, in January of the next year, the stage was set for their ultimate coup. After several intense private meetings with the president, Adolf Hitler and the members of his proposed cabinet convinced Hindenburg that the Nazi party under the leadership of Hitler as chancellor of Germany would restore the nation to its health. On January 30, 1933, foolishly believing he was acting to save Germany, Hindenburg handed over the country to the man who would come close to destroying it.

There are two persistent myths surrounding George in connection with the events that took place during the last year of his life. One is that he utterly rejected the Nazis, supposedly put off by the coarse, brutal hoodlums who filled the party's ranks. The other is that he went to Switzerland in exile to express his revulsion toward the National Socialists and everything they stood for. Neither tale is true. They are legends created by George's apologists, who have been understandably anxious to shield their Master from the taint of later Nazi crimes. But they are fabrications nonetheless. As usual, the truth is more messy and less edifying.

George attentively followed political developments to the end of his life and in conversations he often commented on the evolving political situation in the disintegrating Weimar Republic. Like so many other Germans, George had long hoped, indeed had prophesized, that a strong figure would emerge to take the reins of power in hand. And, like an increasingly large number of his countrymen as well, George also hoped that the values he and his movement represented would guide that future leader's actions. As early as February of 1928, George had told Vallentin that he feared "the terrible German fate" may once again occur, "that namely the ideas of the movement would not be brought to practical effect, but that the ideas of the movement would be taken up abroad and put into effect there, as had already happened before." For that not to happen, George argued, one thing was essential. "It always depends on a great man of action" — *Täterperson* — "to pick up such ideas and translate them into political effectiveness." As an example of the kind of person he meant, George mentioned Mussolini.

As we have seen, even before the war, George had become steadily more politicized and he had actively explored numerous ways to turn his ideas into reality. Every publication, every project connected with him since the *Yearbooks* had an implicit, and as time passed increasingly overt, political purpose. And George was supremely sensitive to the impact he had, or sought to have, on his environment. But he also realized that his was a spiritual empire, which was by nature small and select, and that someone else would have to transfer that spiritual reality into the concrete political realm. In the same conversation with Vallentin in early 1928, George thus said of himself that his "effect was a subterranean one. However his effect on the public at large may later manifest itself was of no concern to him. He could only have an effect on individual young people and he would have to leave it to them as to how the matter developed further." But George did envision that effect eventually being spread out over the whole country. Saying that, beginning with the first stage of those who were closest to him, then radiating out "from the first stage to the second one with a thousand people and to the third with ten thousand until the tenth one," his spirit would finally reach everyone. But, he stressed again, "the effect in the external world can be brought about only by a political person, a 'doer'" — *Täter* — "who will one day politically assemble the ideas of the movement into a body and use them to move the nation."

George's major concern was that the Germans themselves may be incapable of producing such a person or of recognizing him if he ever did come along. Mussolini was a case in point. Here was a man who seemed to embody many of the ideas George and his circle had expressed over the years, but those ideas had perversely — or perhaps all too typically — found their realization not in a German but in an Italian. "Foreigners," George thus pessimistically concluded, still to Vallentin, "were possibly in a better position than the Germans to see the new type of person we are creating." In September of 1930, following the Nazi's first triumph at the polls, George also mentioned to Vallentin "the current domestic political situation, which in his assessment looks very grim," saying, "What had seemed good until now was a lie, and the real true face of our situation will soon show itself." As the last half of this comment reveals, George, again like most Germans, attributed the major portion of the country's woes to the democratic government itself. Earlier that year, in a conversation with Edith Landmann, George had also spoken of "the impossible political circumstances," adding "how it had become merely ridiculous" for anyone "to stand by this democracy." Yet the question of what would replace it, and who would lead the country once that happened, was by no means clear. In April 1931, George and Vallentin once more talked about the unending "current political crisis." Vallentin expressed regret that Brüning had not been able to achieve very much and said that "on neither side did a person stand out who could take action and do something." George agreed, concluding that "it is very doubtful whether there is a person today capable of mastering the muddled situation."

Two years before the Nazis seized power, no one — including George — could have predicted that they would soon assume total control over the country. Nor had Adolf Hitler yet emerged as the obvious or most desirable person to fill the role that George and countless others had imagined was necessary to the rescue of the nation. When the Nazis did take over, however, George maintained his habitual reticence and at first publicly said nothing either in favor of or against them. In fact, this public neutrality seemed to have been something like an official policy, for he also gave the same advice to Kurt Hildebrandt — that is, that one should say nothing either for or against "the party" — even though Hildebrandt went ahead and joined the Nazi party in April 1933. Robert Boehringer, too, reported that "I never heard a word from the poet that would allow the persecutors or the persecuted to claim him for themselves."

Yet George did make private statements to others that more than imply he took a definite stance toward the new regime. In the memoirs Michael Landmann published in 1980 — he had been twenty in 1933 — Landmann wrote that, for all of the reverence he still felt for George even after the passage of nearly fifty years, "I cannot speak of George without discussing the problem of his attitude toward Nazism, which still haunts me to this day." Landmann emphasized that George closely followed the political fortunes of his country, indeed that "he perceived the destiny of Germany to be his own." And there was no doubt in Landmann's mind that although George "condemned the excesses, was repelled by the plebian, mass-like character of the movement, he still welcomed the change as such." To Landmann's mother, Edith, and clearly to her distress, George said in September of that year that "it was at least the first time that views he had advocated were being echoed by the outside world." Even George's estimation of Hitler was not perceptibly negative; on the contrary. When someone suggested that history was no longer being made by individuals but rather by impersonal, anonymous forces, George responded, "Hitler will show all of you what all a single person can do." Not even the bestial treatment of Jews caused George to denounce the Nazis or their leader. After Edith Landmann objected to George's apparent endorsement of the party by pointing out and lamenting "the brutality of its forms," he patronizingly said to her, "In the political realm things are simply different." The Jews, George thought, deserved no special exemption from this fundamental law. "I want to tell you something," he said to Edith Landmann in some of the last words she heard from him. "When I think of what Germany faces in the next fifty years, this whole Jewish thing in particular is not so important to me." To Hildebrandt, George was even more blunt. Perhaps feeling pestered by his other Jewish friends about his refusal to condemn the Nazis, George told Hildebrandt irritably, "The Jews should not be surprised if I side more with the Nazis."

As for the German people themselves, it seemed self-evident to a great many of those who knew or cared about George's poetry that the Third Reich was the realization of the New Reich he had proclaimed and that Hitler was the *Führer* George and his disciples had incessantly described and invoked. Journalists all over Germany rushed to make this connection, arguing that even though George's poetry may still be the preserve of a small elite, its influence was enormous. "There are probably few poets," one article published on his birthday in 1933 read, "who have exerted such a great effect on their time, even though their work is actually unknown to broad segments of the population." However, the author went on, this popular ignorance of George's work is irrelevant "if one knows that today at almost every German university there is a professor who consciously or unconsciously transmits something of the spirit of Stefan George to the youth, if one is of the opinion that the German language, as we confront it not only in literature but also even in political rallies, is unthinkable without George." In September, the *Dresdner Nachrichten* ran an essay, titled "Stefan George as Prophet of the new Reich," that advocated making George's poetry more widely accessible as a matter of great political significance. "May his work enter the consciousness of our people" — *Volk* — "more clearly and openly, not for the sake of the poet — for he needs no applause — but so that the same problem will be approached from another direction with which Adolf Hitler is wrestling today: *turning the Germans into a* Volk." More straightforwardly, the ever dependable

Peter Hamecher announced in October that "one can call George's world of ideas national-socialistic. The notion of the *Führer* plays a significant role in it. The *Führer* is the one who sets the tone, the measure, the form."

To be sure, many of these panegyrics may have arisen from cynical opportunism on the part of journalists who wanted to curry favor with the new rulers. Too, during the so-called *Gleichschaltung,* or "synchronization," everything the Nazis did not want to eliminate as corrupt, decadent, or unfit to survive was made to appear as if it either anticipated or mirrored the Nazis themselves. But the fact remains that an overwhelming number of people thought that George and his "world of ideas" stood in such close proximity to the world of the Nazis that they would not be running any risks to say so. Indeed, several senior Nazi party officials themselves were eager to enlist the most famous German poet of the day in the service of their cause and to adorn themselves with his name. The most dramatic attempt to win his co-operation occurred slightly more than three months after they had taken power.

On May 5, 1933, Ernst Morwitz wrote to George with what he called "an urgent matter." It had transpired that the new minister for science, art, and education, Bernhard Rust, had assigned an assistant by the name of Dr. Kurt Zierold the task of finding out how to establish contact with the notoriously elusive poet. Zierold eventually got in touch with Morwitz and, after making prior arrangements by telephone, appeared one day at Morwitz's apartment. The government wanted to know, Morwitz wrote in his report to George of Zierold's visit, "whether you would participate in some fashion in the Writers' Academy that is to be reorganized or synchronized." What "synchronization" meant in this instance was that all of the members of the academy who were ideologically, racially, or otherwise undesirable had been pressured to resign or expelled and thus needed to be replaced. So far, the outcasts included the former president of the academy, Heinrich Mann, as well as his brother Thomas, Alfred Döblin, Georg Kayser, Jacob Wassermann, Franz Werfel, and many others. To bring Stefan George into the reassembled academy would be a masterstroke. "The minister," Morwitz continued, "wants to describe you to the press as forefather of the current government, they would grant you membership in the academy or also an honorary post *without* any obligations on your part, the president of the Reich or the chancellor would personally send the invitation to you, they would also offer you an honorary stipend." The minister of culture clearly knew how chary George could be and absolutely wanted to avoid the public embarrassment of being turned down. Thus, Morwitz relayed that Zierold had driven home that "before anything could happen, they would have to have your consent since they want under *no* circumstances to receive a refusal — on the other hand the matter is pressing since the reorganization of the academy has to occur in the next few days."

Morwitz had often represented George before in legal issues and in assorted negotiations with Bondi. He thus had the authority to give Zierold a preliminary response in the name of the poet, even though Morwitz had underscored, as he assured George, that he could say nothing definitive "without your instructions." Morwitz did tell Zierold, however, that George would never sit at the same table with the "littérateurs" in the new academy (he specifically named Gottfried Benn and Guido Kolbenheyer), but that he may look favorably on a purely honorary association. Money also held no attraction. Somewhat more positively, Morwitz told George that he had suggested to Zierold "that one ought to mention you in a more spiritual fashion if it were in fact necessary at all to speak of you in public. The minister could say to the press," Morwitz had helpfully proposed, "that the government sees you as a forerunner — you could not prevent that since everyone may interpret your works according to their desire. The minister could go even further and say that he hesitated to incorporate you against your will since you have the right to give to posterity the image of your life, which until now has avoided the public, in the way you see fit." Morwitz indicated that this seemed to "impress the gentleman, especially since I had put it into his mouth as if they were his own thoughts." It seems Zierold was slightly puzzled that George may refuse such a high honor and mentioned the precedent of the Goethe Prize, which George had obviously accepted. Morwitz had a ready answer here, too, and "I responded with the story of the surprise attack that had taken place then." Apparently satisfied, Zierold bade his leave and retreated to wait for the poet's reply.

As remarkable as Morwitz's letter is — laying bare as it does his highly conscious manipulation of information and the effort to put what we would today call the desired "spin" on George's public image — George's own response is more extraordinary still. Knowing full well, as Morwitz had told him, that the minister intended to pass George's words on to the press and that his letter thus had the status of an official, public pronouncement, even that it would quite literally be viewed as a press release, George wrote a note to Morwitz indicating that "it is important to me · dear Ernst · that this is communicated verbatim to the appropriate address":

> In short: I can accept no post · even an honorary one · in the so-called academy just as little as I can accept a stipend . . That this academy now stands under a national sign is only to be welcomed and can perhaps later lead to favorable results — for almost half a century I have administered German

literature and German spirit without an academy · indeed had there been one probably against it.

Now for the positive: I absolutely do not deny being the forefather of the new national movement and also do not push aside my spiritual collaboration. What I could do for it I have done · the youth that gathers around me today is of the same opinion as I am . . The fiction of my standing to one side has accompanied me all my life — only the untrained eye sees it so. The laws of the spiritual and the political realms are certainly very different — where they meet and where spirit descends to be common knowledge, that is an extremely complicated process · I cannot tell the gentlemen of the government what they should think about my work and how they estimate its importance for themselves.

For those whose primary interest it has been to exonerate the poet from any involvement with National Socialism, this letter — or rather, since it has been reproduced in full only once before, only a selected portion of it — has been taken to indicate George's fundamental repudiation of Nazism. Because he refused the offer to join the academy, so goes the logic, he refused the government behind it. But even a forgiving reading of the letter in its entirety will not support that conclusion. Even in the first, "negative" paragraph George specifically welcomed the "reorganization" of the academy under "national" auspices — in other words, he subscribed, if only implicitly, to the ouster of the Jews, Communists, and all other untouchables from its body. And in the second "positive" section George categorically acknowledged an affinity between his own thinking and the ideology of the new regime; not only that, he claimed to be its sire. George did also point out, as he had to Edith Landmann, that the transition from the spiritual to the political was not easy and would not necessarily be pretty. But that was to be expected. George, who never denied his anarchist roots, had always regarded politics as violent; in fact, he thought violence essential to political action. Yet, as he had also repeatedly told Vallentin, what others did with his ideas was not his concern. It had been his task to envision the Secret Germany; it was the job of others to make it real.

But almost more significant than George's acknowledgement that he was the "forefather" of the "new national movement" — quite apart from the issue whether that was really true or not — was the fact that he made the statement at all. Apart from the letter to Hindenburg in 1928 thanking the president for the birthday wishes he had sent, George had never before communicated directly with anyone who represented any German government. On the contrary, he went out of his way to avoid all contact with officials or bureaucrats of any sort. The first honor he had ever allowed to be bestowed on him had been the Goethe Prize, and even then he neither accepted it personally nor even conveyed in any way his acknowledgement of the award to the city officials who granted it to him. Of course George had refused to be a member of the academy; it was purely delusional to imagine George would have even considered joining it. Anyone who knew him would have known it was unthinkable that George would belong to any organization he had not created himself and that was not wholly under his jurisdiction. But he had given the government something far more valuable — and without precedent in George's entire life — than agreeing to sit on the academy: he had for the first time recognized a Germany outside of his own and, as explicitly as he would ever do, he had given that Germany his blessing.

George's letter is dated May 10. That evening, in several large cities across Germany, in Berlin, Munich, Frankfurt, Dresden, and Breslau, among others, organized groups of students belonging to the National Socialist party burned large piles of books by "un-German" writers, including the works of the authors who had been purged from the academy. Seven days earlier, on May 3, Ernst Bertram had introduced his lecture course on the history of German literature at the University of Cologne with a speech called "German Awakening." Bertram celebrated the recent political developments and exhorted his students to take active part in the transformations taking place. "In the enormous political-spiritual breakthrough battle, in the midst of which we now stand," Bertram told his students, "our *Volk* requires all its spiritual powers and consciousness, and especially these." In particular, Bertram said, "no spiritual movement in Germany will ever remain vital for long that does not succeed in conquering the German university from the inside out." In urging his listeners to join the struggle, Bertram reminded them that the stakes were high: "If *this* battle fails," he warned, then it would mean "the end of the White World, chaos or a planet of termites." It was necessary, therefore, "always to remind ourselves that we are in the middle of a war (perhaps in a battle of life and death for our highest Germanic-German values)." Bertram predicted that in future history books, "this war of liberation by the German *Volk* for its inner and external right to live will stand as an event without parallel: as a revolution." He also stated what this "revolution" sought to overcome: it was "against false Enlightenment, against the whole arrogance of western civilization and civilized dogmatism." These were qualities, Bertram asserted, that had nothing to do with the true German spirit, with the inner character of the German *Volk*. And, he added, "What a *Volk* has truly experienced and recognized as its irreconcilably mortal enemy, it should be allowed to destroy." This was the lesson taught, Bertram concluded, by the poet of *The Star of the Covenant* and *The New Reich*, by "the prophet of a *Volk*," who had "chosen the old Germanic and pre-Germanic sacred symbol of the turning sun cross as the symbol of his hopes." Bertram had thus sought to give the credit for the ongoing "revolution" to George — for, Bertram intoned, "he called forth and summoned the present and the future and he thus also belongs among the fathers of today and tomorrow" — and Bertram incited his students to go out and destroy whatever opposed that revolution in his name. It is unknown whether any of the students who heard this speech also participated in the book burnings a week later, but if any did, they would have done so believing in part that they were thereby helping to fulfill George's vision.

It was one thing for George to claim his own paternity of the movement, but it was quite another for someone like Bertram to do so. When George learned of the speech, he was in a quandary about what to do. As Michael Landmann reported it, George ostensibly said that "if I remain silent about what Bertram said in favor of the Nazis, then it will be misinterpreted as agreement. If I publicly express my disapproval, then I will thereby expose my friends to danger." Again, this statement has frequently been offered as evidence that George really disapproved of Nazism but was afraid of speaking openly for the reasons he mentioned. But a much more plausible reading of his words, given all we know about George's many other remarks, about his long and never cozy relationship with Bertram, and indeed about George's whole life, would put matters in a different light. George never permitted anyone to speak on his behalf unless he approved of the person and of the words in advance. He did not want Bertram, whom he had not seen in over a decade, now using his name without authorization. But to publicly condemn or rebuke him, George realized, could produce unwelcome consequences. George had not specified which "friends" would be exposed to what kind of "danger" should he have spoken out against Bertram, and some have concluded that he must have meant his Jewish friends. Yet he just as well might have had his many friends in mind who had joined the Nazi party and whose position might have become very uncomfortable indeed had their Master uttered something that might, by the wrong people, be taken as criticism of the new government.

Thus in the end George said nothing, allowing people to interpret his stance however it suited them and also sparing his friends — Nazis or Jews — any unpleasant awkwardness. For, in addition to Ernst Bertram himself, many former and current associates of George fit the former description: Walter Elze, Kurt Hildebrandt, Woldemar von Uxkull, and Albrecht von Blumenthal had all signed on to the Nazi cause. Frank Mehnert and Max Kommerell also both toyed with the idea of joining — "I am," Kommerell wrote at the time, "despite everything, happy about the Nazis" — and Ludwig Thormaehlen energetically urged those still wavering to enlist. Not everyone had that option, of course, and it was George's Jewish friends who were made to feel the pain of his silence most acutely. Ernst Kantorowicz was the only surviving Jew among George's close friends who taught at a university — Kantorowicz had become a professor at Frankfurt in 1930 — and he watched with increasing disgust as the new government moved to cleanse the university of people like himself. On April 7 the so-called Law for the Restoration of Professional Civil Service was passed. It stipulated that all civil servants — and all professors fell into that category — "whose previous political activity did not offer proof that they had always unreservedly come to the defense of the national state [. . .] are to be dismissed from service." With that, those whose political sympathies were not demonstrably in line with the National Socialists were to be terminated. Likewise, the law ordered that "civil servants who are not of Aryan descent are to be placed in retirement." The only exception made was for those "who fought at the front during the World War for the German empire or for its allies or whose fathers or sons fell in the World War."

Kantorowicz, who had distinguished himself as a soldier in the war, was, though a Jew, thus exempted from immediate dismissal. But he was nevertheless nauseated by the law and all it implied. Two weeks later, on April 20, 1933 — the date, as Kantorowicz surely knew, of Hitler's birthday — he sent the following letter to the minister of science, art, and education. The letter is long, but it deserves to be cited in full as an example of how it was possible not to be silent, how not to hedge one's words in evasive circumlocution, how not to flirt with the henchmen:

> Although as a volunteer in the war from August 1914, as a soldier at the front for the duration of the war, as a fighter after the war against Poland, the Spartacists, and the Soviet Republic in Posen, Berlin, and Munich I do not have to face removal from service because of my Jewish descent; although on the basis of my publications on the Staufer Emperor Frederick II, I do not need a certificate of my convictions from either the day before yesterday, yesterday or today in a Germany that has again taken a national direction; although my attitude, which has a foundation beyond all prevailing trends and events of the day and is fundamentally positive toward a nationally governed Empire, was not able to be shaken by the most recent occurrences, and although I most certainly do not expect any disruption of my teaching duties from the students, so that any potential considerations that might be made with respect to the undisturbed academic operation of the entire university are not applicable to me, I nevertheless see myself as a Jew forced to draw my conclusions from what has happened and to suspend my teaching activities in the coming summer semester. For as long as every German Jew can be regarded — as is the case in the current time of revolution — almost as a "traitor" purely because of his origins; as long as

every Jew is deemed inferior as such on racial grounds; as long as the fact of even having Jewish blood in one's veins by definition indicates defective convictions; as long as every German Jew sees himself exposed to daily violations of his honor without the possibility of obtaining personal or legal satisfaction; as long as academic civil rights are refused to Jewish students, the use of the German language being permitted to them only as a 'foreign language,' as the announcements posted in the university building itself by the German Student Body also demand; as long as Jews in their capacity as leaders of seminars are officially expected to take active part in actions that are hostile toward Jews, and as long as every Jew, precisely because he fully affirms a national Germany, inescapably comes under the suspicion of acting out of fear or merely of seeking personal advantage in announcing his convictions, or of seeking out benefices and of wishing to secure his economic existence; as long therefore as every German and truly nationally minded Jew, in order to avoid that kind of suspicion, has to hide his national convictions in shame rather than being able to reveal them without inhibition: then it seems incompatible with the dignity of a university professor to remain responsibly in his office, which is based solely on inner truth, and it also seems a violation of the students' sense of shame to resume teaching in silence as if nothing had happened.

It was an honorable, courageous — and potentially dangerous — gesture of political defiance and moral probity. Symptomatically, Kantorowicz appeared to be concerned less about any repercussions his deed might bring on himself and worried more about how it might affect George. In June, Kantorowicz reported to George that reliable sources had informed him that, within the Ministry, "my request had been extraordinarily unpleasant because people were afraid my suspension would prevent t[he] M[aster] from joining the Writers' Academy!!" Kantorowicz, who was quite happy to be the cause of some discomfort to the Nazis, still did not want to make life more difficult for his Master. For his part, George did seem to regret that Kantorowicz had been forced — more by his own convictions than by any external coercion — to leave his academic post. George is said to have written to Kantorowicz on learning of his decision: "You should *certainly not* believe that I am doing fine when my best friends are doing so poorly." It was small consolation.

Kantorowicz need not have fretted over the possible effect his actions may have had on George's situation. In the time since George had written the letter to Morwitz containing the text to be transmitted to the minister, a new snag had developed. Apparently, after receiving George's message, the minister had asked for further clarification and requested whether only part of George's letter could be released to the public. On May 15, five days after the original communication, George sent another letter to Morwitz, to be acted on the same way. "You can imagine," George wrote, "that I both have nothing to add and cannot find it acceptable that isolated sentences be published. If I make my convictions known to the gentlemen then that can be important for them · but I do not see what right the so-called public is supposed to have to be given a glimpse of something where it is impossible for it to know anything of the entire context." Morwitz understood the message and ten days later reported back that, after he had delivered the final version of George's statement, he had managed to obtain the promise that it would not be published, since everyone had recognized that "publication was not advisable for all involved." Nevertheless, Morwitz confirmed that "they were pleased about the positive and they wish for this reason not to let the connection be severed. The possibility was very lightly touched upon of perhaps consulting you for advice should the occasion arise, they asked me to maintain absolute discretion toward *all third parties*. For my part, I kept all possibilities open for you on the positive side. When you come to Berlin yourself perhaps they will approach you with new plans."

Thus, even after George had turned down the invitation to join the academy and then forbade the publication of his declaration unless it was in its entirety, the Ministry still wanted to preserve cordial relations with the poet. Judging by Morwitz's words, George seemed interested in keeping the door open as well. Perhaps it was in anticipation of discussing the "new plans" Morwitz had vaguely alluded to that George traveled to Berlin on July 8 to spend his birthday in the capital. This, too, stands in profound contrast to his habit of the last few years, which was to flee to some remote hideaway in order to escape the predictable onslaught. Instead, he went to the one place where he would almost be guaranteed to be besieged by well-wishers from the new government — an especially likely probability given that George was to turn sixty-five, lending the birthday greater symbolic significance. There were even rumors of an official ceremony being planned in his honor, something that George would have ordinarily avoided like the plague. And still he made the journey to Berlin. Thormaehlen noted that "the poet had conflicting opinions about what was to be expected." But, again, for George merely to make himself available for such an event was unprecedented.

For whatever reason, the ceremony did not occur, but George did receive many letters, presents, accolades, and homages in his honor. One was from the propaganda minister of the Reich, Dr. Joseph Goebbels, who sent his "most devoted greetings and warmest congratulations to the poet and prophet, the master of the word, the good German on his sixty-fifth birthday." Goebbels had long been an admirer of George — and of his first disciple, Gundolf. In the early 1920s, after reading Gundolf's books and attending his lectures in Heidelberg, Goebbels, even though he was already a convinced anti-Semite, had wanted to study under the famous scholar. But since Gundolf had been relieved of the obligation to advise doctoral students as a result of the deal he had struck with the university after receiving the offer from Berlin, he thus referred Goebbels to his colleague, Professor Waldberg. But Gundolf had probably taken just one look at the clubfooted, gaunt young man to be convinced that Goebbels was not his — or George's — type. Nor was Goebbels the only high official within the party hierarchy who esteemed the work of George and even of some of his Jewish followers. Hitler owned in his personal library the translation of Shakespeare by Gundolf, and he was — as were both Hermann Göring and Heinrich Himmler — a devotee of Kantorowicz's *Frederick II*. When Hitler surprised one of his generals reading the book during the war, the officer feared that Hitler would object. Instead, the *Führer* said that he had read the book twice.

Kantorowicz himself observed George's birthday by sending him a letter that demonstrated his unfaltering loyalty to both George and their shared beliefs. Kantorowicz admitted to the probability that he would no longer be permitted to accompany his Master on his future journey. But such was his allegiance to George that, if the Germany that so plainly had no more use for the likes of Kantorowicz were truly the one George had envisaged, then Kantorowicz was prepared to accept both it and the fate it held in store for him. Thus, on George's last birthday, Kantorowicz made this extraordinary wish:

> "May Germany become what the Master has dreamt of!" And if current events are not merely the grimace of that desired ideal but really are the true path to its fulfillment, then I wish that everything may turn out for the best — and then it is of no consequence whether the individual will — rather: may — march along — or steps to one side instead of cheering. "Imperium transendat homine," Frederick II said, and I would be the last person to contradict him. If the fates block one's entrance to the "Reich" — and as a "Jew or Colored Person," as the new linguistic coupling states, one is necessarily excluded from the state founded on race alone — then one will have to summon *amor fati* and make one's decisions accordingly.

The next day, Kantorowicz was informed by the dean of his faculty that his name would not be included in the university's course catalogue for the fall semester. Although Kantorowicz stayed in Germany until 1938, when he finally emigrated to England, he never taught at a German university again.

On July 25, after the public and private tributes to him had died down, George traveled to Wasserburg on Lake Constance, where he was joined by Frank Mehnert, Berthold Stauffenberg, and for a time by his brother Claus, as well as several other younger friends of George. One of his most recent acquaintances, Willi Dette, was also there and remembered that "the Master was in a good mood." There followed four weeks of swimming, long walks, and conversations, or simply sitting by the lake, watching the sail boots glide over the silver-blue water. Everyone, including George, seemed happy and relaxed. At the end of August, when the weather turned and it became too humid, George crossed Lake Constance into Switzerland and stayed in Heiden near Sankt Gallen. Before September was out George had traveled farther south, alone this time, and by month's end he was back in Minusio, somewhat earlier than the previous two years.

The second myth concerning George's behavior during this time, as tenacious and ill-founded as the first, is that he went to Switzerland in exile, thus physically renouncing the new regime in his native land. George himself of course did not explicate his actions for others' benefit — he never did — but that reticence only made it easier for others to fill his silence with whatever version best served their own purposes. One of the earliest and most influential exponents of this fiction was Ernst Morwitz. After fleeing to the United States in the 1930s, Morwitz set about translating a selection of George's poems into English, which he published in 1943. In the preface Morwitz introduced the poet to the English-speaking world. Writing about the final year of George's life, Morwitz flatly asserted that "as an unambiguous protest against totalitarian compulsion and the increasing misinterpretation and misapplication of his ideas and words, he left his country and spent the rest of his life as a voluntary exile in Switzerland." Ever since, owing either to Morwitz's authority as one of George's closest friends or to the desire, for whatever reason, to believe it was true — or simply because of ignorance — this claim has been endlessly repeated as if it were an unshakeable fact.

Yet nothing supports the view that George went to Switzerland in order to quit Germany as an exile; indeed everything we know contradicts that assumption. To begin with, Germany itself, either in its national-socialistic incarnation or in any other of the political guises it had worn during George's life, had never been a place that he had been particularly anxious to identify with, much less live in. His itinerant life had been only one expression of his lifelong abhorrence toward most of what people called Germany. There was thereafter nothing inherently unusual in his leaving Germany in September of 1933. And with regard to Switzerland in particular, the journey was part of a natural and long-established pattern of movement. George had been going there virtually every year since just after the turn of the century. It was, we remember, while he was in Switzerland that George had learned of the outbreak of the first war. And in 1926, long before anyone was thinking of the Nazis as a serious political movement, he had even thought of settling permanently in Basel. What is more, George did not even consider Switzerland to be an essentially foreign country. Frank Mehnert — who was much closer to George in his final years than Morwitz, even though Mehnert, too, was not wholly impartial concerning George's legacy — wrote in 1937 that "the Master had always felt that to a certain extent Switzerland belonged" to the greater German cultural sphere. George thought, Mehnert continued, that Switzerland, "even if it led a separate existence with regard to constitutional law, had never entirely ceased to be a part of the *Reich* in spiritual terms," and George frequently said that he did not regard his sojourns in Switzerland in a strict sense as being "abroad." And we also know that this was to be his third consecutive winter in Minusio, which he treasured not because it was outside of Germany but above all for its seclusion and relative warmth. (The previous winter had been uncomfortably chilly, however, even bringing some snow. George had caught cold and complained about the treacherous weather, from which, he said, he "will have to escape on a yacht, probably all the way to Egypt next time.")

More to the point, however, George clearly felt no urge and certainly had no need to seek political exile, in Switzerland or anywhere else. The hopeful notion that George went into exile rests on the assumption that he vehemently objected to the Nazi dictatorship, and, as we have seen, that is simply not true. Not that he thought everything in the new Germany was rosy, but then he had never had a particularly cheery view of the future in the first place. In fact, every other indication would suggest, instead, that George thought he had less reason to avoid the current Germany than all the other states that had gone by that name in the past. But he had always lived according to his own rules and in response to his own desires, and nothing as inconsequential as a change in government was going to change what he did or where he went.

Almost immediately after his arrival in Minusio in late September 1933, George came down with a sudden and violent relapse of his old ailment. Robert Boehringer, who came to visit on October 3, found him in bed, looking tired and weak. George had been running a fever, he had lost his appetite and, although he was not in great pain, he felt a constant sensation of burning and itching. Alerted by Boehringer, Frank Mehnert came down from Berlin a few days later to look after the Master full time. Karl Wolfskehl — who *was* in exile, in nearby Locarno — had discovered George's whereabouts and also wanted to see him. Wolfskehl had already written several times asking for permission to visit, but so far he had not even received an answer to his letters. On October 20, worried that matters might be grave, Wolfskehl pleaded with George to give him an audience. "Master, my heart trembles, I am in great distress, why am I permitted to hear nothing, why can't I see you? I am going through terrible things and I am being tossed back and forth, but Master I am standing by you and I raise my hand and I beg you [. . .] Externally things are not well and I am almost blind. Master I beg you." George finally responded to this anguished cry with an answer dictated to Mehnert.

> Dear Karl: a fate is at work here that neither one of us can do anything about. We have been living for weeks now in the closest proximity and all the messages have duly arrived. But no sooner had I arrived here than I had to take to bed with a very nasty bladder infection. Each day I hoped that my condition would improve to such a degree that I could call you. But to this day there has been no trace of any noticeable improvement. I must therefore ask you to have a little more patience [. . .] I could not yet conduct a conversation. I thus ask you to wait for any news.

Wolfskehl, who would soon leave Europe entirely to settle in faraway New Zealand, never saw George alive again.

Under Mehnert's supervision, who was aided by a woman named Clothilde Schlayer who did most of the cooking and cleaning, George was slowly nursed back to reasonably good health in the following weeks. By the beginning of November he was eating again, drinking a little wine with his meals and even indulging in the occasional cigarette. His mood also brightened and he again took an active interest in some of the new publications that were appearing. Kommerell — "the Toad" — had just completed a book on Jean Paul, which George had Mehnert read aloud to him. George said he "wants to ascertain approximately what the mental state of the Toad is in order to know what can still be expected of it." Ernst Morwitz's book on George's poetry was also about to come out, and George read carefully through the proofs, commenting on passages he particularly liked. Clothilde Schlayer, who had been born in Barcelona, regularly bought Spanish illustrated magazines into the house and, as George convalesced, he delighted in leafing through pictures of Spanish cities and countryside, and he sometimes would even puzzle through an article.

As November passed and George showed steady improvement, Robert Boehringer consulted the urologist in Basel, Dr. Suter, who had examined George in early 1924. Asked for his opinion, Suter indicated that he could provide a reliable diagnosis of the patient's condition only if George would come to the clinic personally. Boehringer tried to persuade George to go to Basel but without success.

On November 26, a Sunday, after a heavy meal of roast duck, mashed potatoes, and a little more wine than usual — although watered down with San Pelligrino — George was finishing his dessert of rice pudding as Mehnert began to clear the table. When Mehnert looked up, he saw what he initially took to be a familiar sight. George had slumped down while still sitting in his armchair and his head sank slowly forward in a series of jerks. At first, Mehnert was not overly concerned, since George "had often made a similar gesture when he was tired, the gesture of someone who goes to sleep while sitting." But in the next instant Mehnert became frightened as he saw some uneaten rice pudding running out of George's half-open mouth. Thinking that George was going to vomit, Mehnert called for Frau Schlayer to bring a pot. Mehnert anxiously asked George if he were unwell, if the food had not agreed with him, while Frau Schlayer, who could see that George had fallen unconscious, said only, "No questions now."

After Mehnert had carried him to bed and began to undress him — his underclothes had become soaked with sweat and urine when he had fainted — George suddenly revived. Asked if he felt nauseous, George said not at all, he felt fine. Mehnert left him to try to sleep and went down to finish cleaning up. When Mehnert looked in on him later, George was still awake, now complaining of pains in his side. In the meantime, Frau Schlayer had called a doctor from the local clinic, who came and prescribed an analgesic and black coffee. The rest of the afternoon and early evening was uneventful — tea as usual at 4:00 and for dinner George had some porridge and applesauce. At 9:30 p.m., Mehnert heard him gagging and then vomit into the earthenware pot by his bed. After George had settled down again he seemed to fall asleep. Around eleven, another sound came from George's room, as if he were moving. When Mehnert went in he saw that George was again unconscious and shivering violently. The fit lasted for slightly more than half an hour as Mehnert and Frau Schlayer helplessly stood by. They called the doctor again, who did not seem overly concerned and merely prescribed a sedative. George then slept until two in the morning, woke up, vomited a second time and had another shivering fit. Terrified now, Mehnert knelt by the bed and did the only thing he could: he clasped George to try to warm him with his own body.

Later that morning, on Monday, they took George to the Clinica Sant'Agnese in neighboring Locarno. George's breathing had become labored and he was constantly slipping in and out of consciousness. Fearing the worst, Mehnert began sending telegrams to George's other friends. On Wednesday, November 29, Robert Boehringer, who was on a business trip in Paris, received a message at his hotel: "Health worsened since Sunday, condition cause for concern. Presence desired." When Boehringer arrived the next day, he was so alarmed that he conferred with Mehnert about who else should be alerted. Over the following three or four days, as George showed small signs that perhaps not all hope was lost, a number of friends arrived in the lakeside village. George could still speak and seemed to know what was going on around him, but he hardly slept and appeared exhausted. On December 1, his heart began to fail, and the following day his pulse became progressively weaker and his breathing turned into a tortured gasping for air. On December 3, his friends gathered in George's room and one by one silently stepped forward. George appeared to recognize each one, but he said nothing, exclaiming only at one point, "You children" and "Don't say a word." Then, muttering "enough, enough," he raised up his hands horizontally, as if he wanted more space around him. Everyone retreated to the walls of the darkened room and, at 1:15 in the morning of December 4, George stopped breathing.

That same day many German newspapers announced the terrible event with front-page headlines. Almost all of them took the opportunity to draw an explicit connection between George and the current political situation. "All of Germany," one evening paper reported, "will learn with the most profound shock the news of the death of Stefan George, who fulfilled the highest mission of the poet: to be a *spiritual* Führer. He gave the Germans not only a poetry of the highest order, he was also the prophet of a view of the world and of humanity that is being realized just in these months. In any case, it is no coincidence that his last great poetic work, which appeared in 1928, was titled *The New Reich*." The *Berliner Tageblatt* solemnly declared that "the death of Stefan George can be nothing other than the heaviest blow for everyone affected by his death, and that is the [entire] German nation." Others were more pithy still. The Nazi party organ, *Der Angriff*, ran a banner in bold letters with the words "George the Prophet — Hitler the *Führer*."

As the news of his death spread around the globe — every major national newspaper in Europe and many local ones featured an article discussing George, often accompanied by a photograph of the poet — German government officials sought to take advantage of the world's attention by joining in the public displays of mourning. In a telegram, which was also distributed to the press, to George's sole surviving relative, his sister Anna, Goebbels himself wrote on December 5 to "express my sincerest condolence on the terrible loss you have experienced through the death of your brother, the great poet, Stefan George. With you, all of spiritual Germany is deeply saddened." Two days later, Goebbels made another announcement. "On the occasion of the sudden demise of the German poet Stefan George," it read, "the minister for the education of the people and propaganda has decided that the planned prize in the amount of twelve thousand Reichsmark, to be awarded annually by the Imperial Ministry for the Education of the People and Propaganda to the best book of the previous year, shall carry the name 'Stefan-George-Prize.'" Not by accident, the amount was even greater than the award attached to the Goethe Prize. And now that George could no longer protest the publication of excerpts from the letter he had written in response to the offer to join the Writers' Academy, the minister of science, art, and education, Bernhard Rust, likewise used the occasion to send a telegram to George's sister, which he also simultaneously made available to newspapers. Following Rust's expressions of his condolences to Anna, he wrote, "With Stefan George not only one of the greatest poets of our people has passed, but also the spiritual pioneer and prophet of the new Germany. He, who only recently in a letter explicitly professed being a spiritual forefather of the new national movement, will always remain alive within us."

The memory of George may have been vivid, but the question of what to do with his mortal remains was pressing. Frank Mehnert revealed that "there existed no instructions from the poet about the place where he wished to be buried." At the end of 1931, two years before George died, Robert Boehringer had gently touched on the subject in conversation with George in Mehnert's presence. George refused to talk about it, saying only, "I am making no provisions for that. You all will know what to do then." During his illness in October 1933, George had darkly said to Boehringer that "this will come to no good end." But even then George had still not indicated what he wanted to happen in the event of his death. His apparent recovery in November had also made it seem indelicate to pursue the matter. As Mehnert wrote, "No one of us who saw the Master in the weeks before his final severe illness [. . .] could conceive of the possibility of his imminent death." Once the rapid decline had begun, no one dared bring up the unthinkable even as it loomed before them.

Once George had died, though, a decision had to be made. As the two people closest to George, Boehringer and Mehnert agreed that the choice came down to Bingen or Minusio. Mehnert claimed that "we were in principle agreed that the German poet should rest in German soil." Boehringer, however, noted that George "had occasionally said that a person should be buried where he dies." Yet they both realized that transporting the body would be "unpleasant" and, moreover, "undignified." Boehringer and Mehnert thus concluded that the person who should decide was George's sister, whom they then notified of the dilemma, indicating that "we were of the opinion that she was most entitled to determine the Master's final resting place." This solution, however, proved short-lived. Anna responded that she wanted to leave the decision to her brother's friends. After more consultations, Boehringer and Mehnert finally came to an acceptable agreement. Several considerations — none of them political — had helped them arrive at their conclusion that Minusio was, if not the best place, then at least an appropriate one for the Master to be buried. They had asked themselves, "Was not this simple resting place in the middle of the great, southern, and cheerful landscape precisely what corresponded to the conduct of his entire life? Should we correct fate, which had so arranged it that he closed his eyes here? Did not many great Germans lie south of the Alps? Was there in Germany one place of which one could say that this and no other was preordained to be the resting place of the poet?" Minusio, then, it would be.

The friends who had gathered in Minusio observed the local custom of keeping a standing vigil in pairs next to the body of the deceased. Those who participated in the wake were Michael Stettler, Robert Steiger, Frank Mehnert, the three Stauffenberg brothers — Claus, Berthold, and Alexander — Walter Anton, Ernst Kantorowicz, Wilhelm Stein, Albrecht Blumenthal, Ernst Morwitz, Robert Boehringer, and Ludwig Thormaehlen. On the morning of December 6, after being joined by Karl Wolfskehl and his wife, Hanna, as well as by George's housekeeper, Clothilde Schlayer, they all gathered around the coffin set up in a small chapel at the cemetery. After some poems were read from *The Seventh Ring,* they all filed out behind the six people carrying the coffin and two others bearing a wreath and sprigs of laurel. At the grave, more poems were read, this time from *The Star of the Covenant,* the wreath and flowers were laid on the coffin and then everyone departed. That afternoon, in the company of Robert Boehringer, the German envoy, Ernst von Weizsäcker, placed a wreath on the grave. The wreath, adorned with a ribbon displaying a swastika, remained there until it withered and died.

Earlier that year, in June of 1933, Walter Benjamin had written to his friend Gershom Scholem from the Spanish island of Ibiza where Benjamin had taken refuge from the people hailing George as their spiritual ancestor. Ironically, Benjamin had been asked to write a review of a book about George that had just appeared. He would do it, he informed Scholem, but it would not be easy to speak about George "now and in front of a German audience." Still, Benjamin felt it would give him the opportunity to say something he now thought was especially important. For, as he told Scholem, "this much I believe I have realized: if ever God has punished a prophet by fulfilling his prophecy, then that is the case with George." Only time would tell how right Benjamin had been.

CHAPTER 45
Epilogue

Not long after George had died, his name began to appear less frequently in newspapers and scholarly publications. Partly this was a normal development. The Nazis had much more urgent matters to attend to than burnishing the image of a dead poet, however revered he may have been. The Nazis were interested in deeds, not words, and in any case those who bothered to think that far could have imagined they were performing the greatest possible homage to the poet by concentrating on transforming his ideas into action.

Yet there were other reasons for the lowering silence as well. It was inevitable that many of the ardent Nazis who claimed George as their own without having actually read his works or even knowing very much about him would, on later doing their homework, discover some troubling facts. The early, decadent, French-inspired works made some shift uncomfortably in their chairs, as did the rather uncharitable remarks George made during the same period about his fellow Germans. But what most unsettled the party faithful was the exclusively male focus of George's erotic drive and, even more disturbing, the large number of Jews within his circle. No one could overlook these inconvenient details and as time went by they grew into something more than just an embarrassment. The "Stefan-George-Prize," so proudly introduced by Goebbels, was quietly forgotten, and by 1938 more articles and books appeared that condemned the unsavory aspects of George's "secret" Germany than lauded him as the "prophet" of the Third Reich.

Predictably, the distance the Nazis eventually put between themselves and George has been turned into yet another ostensible proof that they represented two entirely distinct phenomena, with nothing essentially in common to link them. Ultimately, however, it is not very important whether the Nazis affirmed an affinity between their worldview and George's or vice versa. As George had said in his first letter to Morwitz in response to the academy affair, whatever he could do for the "new national movement" he had already done long ago. What matters instead is whether, over the course of his lifetime, George's actions, words, and ideas had created an intellectual and psychological context that aided the Nazis in their subsequent rise to power, whether the values and attitudes George had always espoused had helped the Nazis be more readily accepted by many of the same Germans who venerated him, and whether he had, in his works and those of his followers, helped to prepare his countrymen to believe that their salvation lay in submitting themselves to the will and guidance of an all-powerful *Führer*, that national renewal would unavoidably entail terrible violence and suffering, that the deepest meaning of the German war to come would be to preserve and protect the "white race," and that those who were judged not worthy of surviving should be unflinchingly consigned to death. And the answer to all of these questions is — and can only be — yes.

No one person, not even Hitler, can be held singly responsible for everything that happened in Germany between 1933 and 1945. It was a collective effort, the work of millions of individual people caught up in a complex set of forces beyond anyone's full control. But it is equally true — if banal — that some forces and some people played a greater role than others in making Hitler and his regime possible. There is no such thing as a moral calculus, and when it comes to the crimes committed in Nazi Germany such a scale would be useless anyway. Still, in the final reckoning, the contribution performed by Stefan George and his circle to paving the way in the minds and hearts of his countrymen on which the Nazis rode to power is as significant as it has been underestimated, ignored, or denied.

An early attempt to expiate those crimes was undertaken, notably, by one of George's own disciples. Claus von Stauffenberg fought in the Second World War from the first campaigns on, taking part in the invasion of Poland in September 1939, and in the western offensive in France the following year. As a tank commander he earned a reputation as a highly effective leader, and he was known and valued for his organizational skills, discipline, and courage.

In 1942, however, during the murderous invasion of Russia, Stauffenberg watched with increasing dismay how the German high command, acting under direct instructions from Hitler, allowed millions of Russian prisoners to die miserable deaths in captivity. By February of that year, two million prisoners of war from the Red Army had already perished from hunger, physical abuse, illness, or exposure. Stauffenberg was appalled by this indifference toward human life — and also stunned that the initial sympathy among the Russian people for the Germans, whom the Russians had often greeted as liberators from the Stalinist terror, was being so senselessly squandered. But in the summer Stauffenberg heard something even worse. A close friend of his, Fritz-Dietlof von der Schulenburg, had told his wife as early as November of 1941 that there was a camp called Auschwitz where they were burning Jews in ovens. In May 1942, an officer working in Schulenburg's office, Lieutenant Herwarth von Bittenfeld — who let it be known that he thought Hitler was "the incarnation of the devil" and wanted him removed from power — gave Stauffenberg a detailed report about the mass murders of Jews. By the end of the summer, Stauffenberg needed to hear no more. Hitler, he now said with growing frequency, was "a fool and a criminal." One day in August 1942, during a horseback ride with a like-minded major named Oskar-Alfred Berger, Stauffenberg said abruptly, "They are shooting Jews on a massive scale. These crimes should not be permitted to continue."

Stauffenberg and the others soon formed a group of conspirators who had determined to remove Hitler from power. After two more agonizing years of careful preparations, doubts, interruptions — the war still had to be fought — and changes of plan, the chance to stop the man who was ordering the killing finally came on July 20, 1944 — barely a week after George's birthday. During a staff meeting at Hitler's headquarters in Eastern Prussia, Stauffenberg placed a briefcase filled with explosives under a large wooden map table. Stauffenberg then left the conference room. Although he had shoved the briefcase as close as possible to the spot where Hitler was standing, when the case detonated a few moments later, one of the thick wooden beams supporting the table shielded Hitler from the full force of the blast. Believing Hitler was dead, Stauffenberg flew immediately to Berlin where he hoped to begin reorganizing the leaderless country. However, Hitler emerged from the destroyed building dazed but largely unhurt and then initiated a bloodthirsty operation to hunt down and eliminate the conspirators. The same evening Stauffenberg was arrested in Berlin and executed by a firing squad. His last words were "Long live sacred Germany!"

Claus von Stauffenberg's death, as well as that of the many other members of the resistance who were subsequently caught and killed, was an honorable one in a dishonorable time, and he indisputably deserves the respect he now receives. He did not die in the name of democracy, though. He and several of his co-conspirators had drawn up a document in which they declared their shared ideals, the principles on which they imagined Germany should rest once the tyrant had been toppled. This "oath" asserted that they believed "in the future of the Germans," a people, it claimed, that represented a "fusion of Hellenic and Christian origins in its Germanic being." Allowed to cultivate their proper essence, the Germans, the document read, had a calling "to lead the community of the Western peoples to a more beautiful life." This projected "New Order" would involve all Germans, it continued, and would guarantee "rights and justice." At the same time, it announced that the conspirators "despise the lie of equality, however, and bow before the ranks assigned by nature." It ended, "We commit to join an inseparable community that through its attitude and actions serves the New Order and forms the fighters for the future leaders — *Führer* — which they will need."

To the end, then, Stauffenberg remained loyal to the ideals he had learned from Stefan George. We will never know if Stauffenberg ever considered whether those ideals themselves, and the man who had preached them, had helped to create the one he tried to destroy.

ABBREVIATIONS

AS
: Alfred Schuler. *Fragmente und Vorträge aus dem Nachlass*. Leipzig: Johann Ambrosius Barth, 1940.

AV
: Albert Verwey. *Mein Verhältnis zu Stefan George*. Strassburg: Heitz, 1936.

AvB
: Alexander von Bernus. *In Memoriam*. Edited by Otto Heuschele. Heidelberg: Lambert Schneider, 1966.

AV/SG
: Albert Verwey and Stefan George. *De documenten van hun vriendschap*. Bijeengebracht en toegelicht door Mea Nijland-Verwey. Amsterdam: Polak & Van Gennep, 1965.

BfdK
: *Blätter für die Kunst*. Edited by Carl August Klein and Stefan George. 1892–1919.

BV
: Berthold Vallentin. *Gespräche mit Stefan George*. Amsterdam: Castrum Peregrini, 1967.

CAK
: Carl August Klein. *Die Sendung Stefan Georges*. Berlin: Rabenpresse, 1935.

CP 1
: Percy Gothein. *Erste Begegnung mit dem Dichter*. In *Castrum Peregrini*. Vol. 1. Amsterdam: Castrum Peregrini, 1951.

CP 11
: Percy Gothein. *Die Halkyonischen Tage*. In *Castrum Peregrini*. Vol. 11. Amsterdam: Castrum Peregrini, 1951.

CP 21
: Percy Gothein. *Das Seelenfest*. In *Castrum Peregrini*. Vol. 21. Amsterdam: Castrum Peregrini, 1955.

CP 111–13
: *Stefan George: Dokumente seiner Wirkung. Aus dem Friedrich Gundolf Archiv der Universität London*. Edited by Lothar Helbing and Claus Victor Bock, with Karlhans Kluncker. In *Castrum Peregrini*. Vols. 111–13. Amsterdam: Castrum Peregrini, 1974.

CP 225
: Friedrich Wolters. *Frühe Aufzeichnungen nach Gesprächen mit Stefan George zur "Blättergeschichte."* Edited by Michael Philipp. In *Castrum Peregrini*. Vol. 225. Amsterdam: Castrum Peregrini, 1996.

EG
: Ernst Glöckner. *Begegnung mit Stefan George. Auszüge aus Briefen an Ernst Bertram und Tagebüchern.* Edited by Friedrich Adam. Heidelberg: Lothar Stiehm, 1972.

EL
: Edith Landmann. *Gespräche mit Stefan George.* Düsseldorf: Helmut Küpper, 1963.

EM 1
: Ernst Morwitz. *Kommentar zu dem Werk Stefan Georges.* Düsseldorf: Helmut Küpper, 1960.

EM 2
: Ernst Morwitz. *Kommentar zu den Prosa- Drama- und Jugend-Dichtungen Stefan Georges.* Düsseldorf: Helmut Küpper, 1962.

EM 3
: Ernst Morwitz. *Stefan George.* In *Poems,* translated by Carol North Valhope and Ernst Morwitz. New York: Pantheon, 1963.

ES
: Edgar Salin. *Um Stefan George. Erinnerung und Zeugnis.* 2d ed. Düsseldorf: Helmut Küpper, 1954.

FG 1
: Friedrich Gundolf. *Briefwechsel mit Herbert Steiner und Ernst Robert Curtius.* Edited by Lothar Helbing and Claus Victor Bock. Amsterdam: Castrum Peregrini, 1963.

FG 2
: Friedrich Gundolf. *Briefe. Neue Folge.* Edited by Lothar Helbing and Claus Victor Bock. Amsterdam: Castrum Peregrini, 1965.

FGA
: Friedrich Gundolf Archive, Institute of Germanic Studies, University of London.

FG/KW
: Friedrich Gundolf an Karl und Hanna Wolfskehl. *Briefwechsel.* 2 vols. Amsterdam: Castrum Peregrini, 1976–77.

Freundesgabe
: Robert Boehringer. *Eine Freundesgabe.* Edited by Erich Boehringer and Wilhelm Hoffmann. Tübingen: J. C. B. Mohr/Paul Siebeck, 1957.

FW
: Friedrich Wolters. *Stefan George und die Blätter für die Kunst. Deutsche Geistesgeschichte seit 1890.* Berlin: Georg Bondi, 1930.

GB
: Georg Bondi. *Erinnerungen an Stefan George.* Berlin: Georg Bondi, 1934.

GPL 1
  Georg Peter Landmann. *Stefan George und sein Kreis. Eine Bibliographie.* 2d ed. Hamburg: Dr. Ernst Hauswedell, 1976.

GPL 2
  Communications from Dr. Georg Peter Landmann as cited in H.-J. Seekamp, R. C. Ockenden, and M. Keilson, *Stefan George: Leben und Werk. Eine Zeittafel.* Amsterdam: Castrum Peregrini, 1972.

HB
  Hans Brasch. "Erinnerungen an Stefan George." In *Bewahrte Heimat*, edited by Georg Peter Landmann. Düsseldorf: Helmut Küpper, 1970.

HS
  Herbert Steiner. *Begegnung mit Stefan George.* Aurora, N.Y.: Wells Press, 1942.

HvH
  Hugo von Hofmannsthal. *Aufzeichnungen.* Edited by Herbert Steiner. Frankfurt: S. Fischer Verlag, 1959.

HvH Briefe
  Hugo von Hofmannsthal. *Briefe.* 2 vols. Aus dem Nachlass. Berlin: S. Fischer Verlag, 1935–1937.

HvH/LA
  Hugo von Hofmannsthal and Leopold Andrian. *Briefwechsel.* Edited by Walter H. Perl. Frankfurt: S. Fischer Verlag, 1968.

IC/SG
  Stefan George and Ida Coblenz. *Briefwechsel.* Edited by George Peter Landmann and Elisabeth Höpker-Herberg. Stuttgart: Klett-Cotta, 1983.

KB 1
  Kurt Breysig. *Stefan George. Gespräche, Dokumente.* Amsterdam: Castrum Peregrini, 1960.

KB 2
  Kurt Breysig. *Aus meinen Tagen und Träumen. Memoiren, Aufzeichnungen, Briefe, Gespräche.* Edited by Gertrud Breysig and Michael Landmann. Berlin: Walter de Gruyter, 1962.

KH 1
  Kurt Hildebrandt. *Erinnerungen an Stefan George und seinen Kreis.* Bonn: H. Bouvier, 1965.

KH 2
  Kurt Hildebrandt. *Das Werk Stefan Georges.* Hamburg: Dr. Ernst Hauswedell, 1960.

KS
  Kurt Singer. "Aus den Erinnerungen an Stefan George." *Neue Rundschau* 68, no. 2 (1957): 298–310.

KW
  Karl Wolfskehl. *Briefe und Aufsätze. München 1925–1933.* Edited by Margot Ruben. Hamburg: Claassen, 1966.

KW/AV
: *Wolfskehl und Verwey. Die Dokumente ihrer Freundschaft. 1897–1946.* Edited by Mea Nijland-Verwey. Heidelberg: Lambert Schneider, 1968.

KW Katalog
: *Karl Wolfskehl. Leben und Werk in Dokumenten. 1869–1969.* Edited by Manfred Schlösser. Darmstadt: Agora, 1969.

LA
: *Leopold Andrian und die Blätter für die Kunst.* Edited by Walter H. Perl. Hamburg: Dr. Ernst Hauswedell, 1960.

LC
: Ludwig Curtius. *Deutsche und antike Welt. Lebenserinnerungen.* Stuttgart: Deutsche Verlags-Anstalt, 1950.

LT
: Ludwig Thormaehlen. *Erinnerungen an Stefan George.* Hamburg: Dr. Ernst Hauswedell, 1962.

M
: Maximilian Kronberger. *Gedichte. Tagebücher. Briefe.* Edited by Georg Peter Landmann. Stuttgart: Klett-Cotta, 1987.

MK
: Max Kommerell. *Briefe und Aufzeichnungen 1919–1944.* Edited by Inge Jens. Olten and Freiburg/Br.: Walter-Verlag, 1967.

ML 1
: Michael Landmann. *Erinnerungen an Stefan George. Seine Freundschaft mit Edith und Julius Landmann.* Amsterdam: Castrum Peregrini, 1980.

ML 2
: Michael Landmann. *Figuren um Stefan George. Zehn Porträts.* Amsterdam: Castrum Peregrini, 1982.

MS
: Michael Stettler. *Begegnungen mit dem Meister.* Düsseldorf: Helmut Küpper, 1970.

RB 1
: Robert Boehringer. *Mein Bild von Stefan George.* 1st ed. Düsseldorf: Helmut Küpper, 1951.

RB 2
: Robert Boehringer. *Mein Bild von Stefan George.* 2d exp. ed. Düsseldorf: Helmut Küpper, 1967.

RB T
: *Tafelband* (illustrations to above).

SG
: Stefan George. *Gesamt-Ausgabe der Werke.* 18 vols. Berlin: Georg Bondi, 1927–34.

SG-Archiv
: Stefan George-Archiv. Württembergische Landesbibliothek, Stuttgart.

SG/FG
: Stefan George and Friedrich Gundolf. *Briefwechsel.* Edited by Robert Boehringer and Georg Peter Landmann. Düsseldorf: Helmut Küpper, 1962.

SG/FW
: Stefan George and Friedrich Wolters. *Briefwechsel. 1904–1930.* Edited by Michael Philipp. Amsterdam: Castrum Peregrini, 1998.

SG/HvH
: Stefan George and Hugo von Hofmannsthal. *Briefwechsel.* Edited by Robert Boehringer. 2d ed. Düsseldorf: Helmut Küpper, 1953.

SG Katalog
: *Stefan George. 1868–1968. Der Dichter und sein Kreis.* Eine Ausstellung des Deutschen Literaturarchivs im Schiller-Nationalmuseum Marbach a. N. Stuttgart: 1968.

SG/ML
: Stefan George and Melchior Lechter. *Briefe.* Edited by Günther Heintz. Stuttgart: Dr. Ernst Hauswedell, 1991.

SL
: Sabine Lepsius. *Stefan George. Geschichte einer Freundschaft.* Berlin: Die Runde, 1935.

SS
: Saladin Schmitt. *Die so gegangen sind. Seine Gedichte und sein Verhältnis zu Stefan George.* Edited by Robert Boehringer and Georg Peter Landmann. Düsseldorf: Helmut Küpper, 1964.

TM/EB
: Thomas Mann and Ernst Bertram. *Briefe aus den Jahren 1910–1955.* Edited by Inge Jens. Pfullingen: Neske, 1960.

VF
: Victor Frank. *Erinnerung an Frank. Ein Lebenszeugnis.* Edited by Michael Stettler. Düsseldorf: Helmut Küpper, 1968.

WS
: Wilhelm Stein. *Aufzeichnungen über George.* Aarau: AZ-Presse, 1963.

Y
: *Jahrbuch für die Geistige Bewegung.* 3 Vols. Berlin: 1910–11.

Z
: H.-J. Seekamp, R. C. Ockenden, and M. Keilson. *Stefan George: Leben und Werk. Eine Zeittafel.* Amsterdam: Castrum Peregrini, 1972.

notes

PREFACE

ix *"in the world"*: Eric Bentley, "The Story of Stefan George," first published in *Partisan Review* (1942), reprinted in Wuthenow, 142. Bentley was misquoting a remark by Friedrich Gundolf, who had said in 1910 that George was the most "important man in contemporary Germany." But the slip itself, and that Bentley would not have thought it hyperbolic, is noteworthy.

ix *"have become legends"*: Das illustrierte Blatt, 1929
ix *the post himself:* cf. KB 1, 27
xi *"in his work"*: FG 2, 137
xii *"them within himself"*: ES, 246
xii *"are no more"*: SG, 8:83
xiii *"public as judge"*: M, 61
xiii *"curiosity and indiscretion"*: BV, 17
xiii *in Latin:* "delendum": ES, 41
xiii *"later 'George-philologists' "*: KH 1, 74
xiv *"a little book!"*: EL, 151
xiv *"for such investigations"*: Kluncker, 8
xv *of George's Circle:* Michaël Defuster to Robert Norton, 28 May 1999
xv *"count the biographies"*: James Atlas, "The Dark Defile," *New York Times Book Review,* 30 April 1995, sec. 7, p. 6.
xv *"but little more"*: Russell A. Berman, "Cultural Studies and the Canon: Some Thoughts on Stefan George," *Profession* (1999): 174.

CHAPTER 1: BEGINNINGS

3 *Roman deity, Bacchus:* see RB 2, 19
3 *"call that divine!"*: SL, 41
4 *for each year:* see BV, 81–82
4 *his own way:* RB 2, 19
4 *from kissing her:* cf. SL, 40
4 *"taken care of"*: HS, 8
4 *"bottom of her"*: EL, 205
4 *"were very different"*: EL, 205
4 *"with damp eye"*: SG, 1:42
4 *"stay with me?"*: SG, 1:42

{ 753 }

5 *"the father's gaiety"*: AV, 29
5 *nun-like existence:* see IC/SG, 77
5 *"of my paths"*: SG, 4:5
5 *"especially great degree"*: RB 2, 20
5 *"in my life"*: SL, 41
5 *"the greatest triumphs"*: RB 2, 20
6 *"a good dancer"*: IC/SG, 77
6 *"Gospel of Fritz"*: EL, 45
6 *a French subject:* see Curtius, 102
7 *the old regime:* cf. Blanning
7 *Protestant "Prussian character"*: Engelhardt, 256
7 *"counting indirect taxes"*: Blanning, 161
8 *"our people's spirit"*: RB 2, 29–30
8 *"second native language"*: George to Wilhelm Ritter, May 1894, SG-Archiv
8 *gentler Gallic sibilants:* see Rouge, 21; David, 16; and Werner, 368
8 *as "Herr Shorsh"*: Curtius, 108; RB 2, 16
9 *being "entirely unliterary"*: EL, 44
9 *ready for him:* cf. RB 2, 21
9 *the annual event:* see Goethe, 10:401–428
10 *"stay on board!"*: EL, 85
10 *"completion of works"*: EL, 85
10 *"region in Germany"*: EL, 85
10 *in the sun:* cf. EL, 56
10 *"everything fishy, aquatic"*: EL, 188
10 *school for boys:* see EL, 31
10 *"of the occupants"*: SG, 12:10
11 *look for him:* see EL, 57
11 *of the domain:* see RB 2, 22
11 *was George himself:* EL, 184
11 *"now I knew!"*: EL, 194
12 *"odd man out"*: RB 2, 201
12 *forays into verse:* FW, 9. Wolters claims that George wrote verses in the margins of his school books in his "eighth and nineth year." They do not survive. KB 1, 13, states that George began to write at the age of six.
13 *"only to you"*: SG, 3:92–93
13 *"my eighteenth year"*: Curtius, 115
13 *arrived once again:* Much of the previous paragraph is based, in large part verbatim, on George's account in "Der kindliche Kalender," SG, 17:14–17.

CHAPTER 2: SCHOOL

15 *"of bodily harm"*: von Preuschen, 281
16 *"of sepulchral stillness"*: James, 645–647
16 *seven-week conflict:* see Nipperdey, 2:28
16 *"national greatness effective"*: Carr, 89

16 *a united Germany:* see Holborn, 229
17 *of its inhabitants:* Holborn, 233
17 *equipment, and chemicals:* Berghahn, 4
17 *"is now expected":* Pflanze, 2:119
18 *"my fifteenth year":* EL, 193
18 *was "nothing positive":* EL, 38
18 *"one?—The Prussians!":* EL, 165
18 *"increase its influence":* Gall, 2:13
19 *"theory into reality":* Pflanze, 2:187
19 *"Rome or Germany":* Pflanze, 2:187
19 *or political issues:* Friedrich, 217
20 *principal Catholic Church:* Rouge, 21
20 *other religious devotions:* Werner, 368
20 *"nothing at all!":* EL, 148
20 *"horde of opponents":* Werner, 368
21 *Greek as well:* KTB, 30; EM 1, 290
21 *even in mathematics:* Fuchs, 126
21 *"especially competent performance":* RB 2, 25
21 *"rejected us all":* Fuchs, 124
21 *their "natural cruelty":* EM 1, 143
21 *"French here, too":* Fuchs, 124
22 *poet Torquato Tasso:* FW, 14
22 *Defoe's* Robinson Crusoe: Rouge, 22
22 *"read through them":* EL, 124
22 *"only at thirty":* EL, 124
22 *his reading list:* Rouge, 22
22 *"names for things":* SG, 4:52
23 *International Auxiliary Language:* Rouge, 22, mentions these three artificial languages as being current at the time.
23 *"thin, harsh lips":* Fuchs, 125
23 *his fellow pupils:* EL, 48
23 *a "conceited fool":* Fuchs, 125
23 *"do that too' ":* Wendelin Seebacher to Anna George, 8 December 1933, SG-Archiv
23 *of Bismarck's* Kulturkampf: FW, 16
23 *classes with him:* Rouge, 22
24 *they be punctual:* Fuchs, 126
24 *"courtesy of kings":* Thormaehlen folder "Geheimnis," SG-Archiv
24 *a consecrated temple:* Fuchs, 127–28
24 *"him more deeply":* FW, 16
25 *"his class-mates":* Fuchs, 129–30
25 *purely Georgean themes:* see Oelmann, 294–310
25 *"holy penitential forest":* SG, 18:85
25 *his "sweet sojourn":* SG, 18:86
25 *"the right hour":* SG, 18:90

25 *"all her charms":* SG, 18:90
25 *"glances of love":* SG, 18:92
25 of *"impending sin":* SG, 18:92
26 *"in simple dress":* SG, 18:97
26 *"and so glad":* SG, 18:98
26 *"body and soul":* SG, 18:102
26 Aspara's *"vile temptations":* SG, 18:105
26 *"for all time":* SG, 18:107
27 *"of his capital":* James, 651
27 *fifty on Sundays:* Werner, 368
27 *at the "Olympus":* Werner, 368
28 *"deplorable, loathsome history":* see Egan, 188
28 *"suggestive and blasphemous":* Egan, 195
28 *of existing translations:* Werner, 368. Selections of these translations are included in the *Schlussband* of George's collected works, SG, 18:115–127.
28 *modern social dramas:* Fuchs, 126
28 *and the Galilean:* Rouge, 22
28 *by the host:* Rouge, 23
29 *"readers and listeners":* Rouge, 22
29 *"an ordained priest":* Fuchs, 130
29 *disseminating indecent literature:* see Killy, 12:117
29 *"poems for publication":* EL, 148; on the identity of the "older man" see Z, 6
29 *as Edmund Delorme:* on pseudonyms see EL, 49
30 *best. The Editors:* RB 2, 24
30 *drawn from Plutarch:* Rouge, 23
30 *"every other Monday":* RB T, 21
31 *"in our time":* Werner, 369
31 *"her" departing Etienne:* Rouge, 24; cf. also EL, 48–49, where George also alludes to this event

CHAPTER 3: FIRST TRAVELS
32 *to modern philology:* Z, 7; Rouge, 24; Werner, 369
32 *"suspected the danger":* Curtius, 112
32 *the Russian Czar:* Rudorff, 157
33 *in Paris alone:* Rudorff, 168
33 *"for no pity":* Rudorff, 165–66
33 *"long live anarchy!":* Rudorff, 163–64
34 *"under the earth":* KB 1, 20
34 *"and true today":* BV, 61
34 *"an upright soul":* Z, 7
34 *"Within gloomy halls":* SG, 1:123
34 *"peace of the pious":* SG, 1:123
34 *"shake my soul":* SG, 1:123–24
35 *of the book:* Rouge to George, 20 March and 1 April 1888, SG-Archiv

36 *"of great civilizations"*: cited from Ellman, 630
36 *with severe injuries*: see MacCarthy, 567–569
36 *"the Irish question"*: Rouge to George, 23 April 1888, SG-Archiv
36 *"much with oneself"*: EL, 79
36 *"fantastic, superbe, magnifique"*: George to Stahl, 18 May 1888, SG-Archiv
37 *"an exquisite thing"*: George to Stahl, 18 May 1888, SG-Archiv
37 *"spoken almost exclusively"*: FW, 17
37 *"I am living"*: George to Stahl, 18 May 1888, SG-Archiv
37 *"but* women *generally"*: George to Stahl, 5, 6, 7, 8, 14 August 1888, SG-Archiv
37 *"pleasant to me!"*: Rouge to George, 26 August–5 September 1888, SG-Archiv
37 *"closed against them"*: Moore, *Confessions*, 149
38 *"and trade successes"*: BV, 78
38 *"dirty, and Oriental"*: Moore, *Confessions*, 109–10
38 *"a foreign clime"*: Stahl to George, 23 April 1888, SG-Archiv
38 *"cosmopolitan in England"*: RB 2, 28
38 *"chest of drawers"*: George to Stahl, 5, 6, 7, 8, 14 August 1888, SG-Archiv
38 *"no encouragement whatsoever"*: RB 2, 28
38 *"'the great plan' "*: George to Stahl, 15–16 August 1888, SG-Archiv
38 *"finish the sentence"*: RB 2, 28
39 *"to reality anyway"*: RB 2, 28
39 *"mean that ironically"*: George to Stahl, 15–16 July 1888, SG-Archiv
39 *"notion of openness"*: Stahl to George, 17 July–1 August 1888, SG-Archiv
39 *"profit from it"*: Father to George, 6 June 1888, SG-Archiv
39 *"under massive pressure"*: George to Stahl, 21 September 1888, SG-Archiv
39 *"keep you company"*: Wellsted to George, 15 October 1888, SG-Archiv
40 *"boarder than you"*: RB 2, 273 n. 2
40 *"considering your genealogy"*: Caroline Mess to George, 9 September 1988, SG-Archiv
40 *"of its kind"*: RB 2, 29
40 *"drive to wander"*: RB 2, 28
40 *"of life's circumstances"*: RB 2, 29
41 *"nice feeling, no?"*: George to Stahl, 1 January 1889, SG-Archiv
41 *"to master it"*: EG, 81
41 *"that never lull"*: RB 2, 30
41 *"in a comedy?"*: RB 2, 30
42 *"thing about it"*: Stahl to George, 17–30 December 1888, SG-Archiv
42 *"a letter. EG"*: George to father, 8 March 1889, SG-Archiv
42 *"to stay here"*: SG, 1:80

CHAPTER 4: PARIS

44 *"of much use"*: Helen Kain to George, 8 May 1889, SG-Archiv
45 *"dark, handsome southerner"*: FW, 19
45 *"suited him well"*: Saint-Paul, 398

45 *"golden-brown hair"*: Saint-Paul, 398
45 *"slowly thawed out"*: Saint-Paul, 398
46 *"French poetic movement"*: Saint-Paul, 399
46 *tiny, makeshift stage*: cf. Rudorff, 149–51
47 *to anarchist ideas*: Rudorff, 169–72
47 *"and Jean Grave"*: Rudorff, 174
47 *"already very determined"*: Mockel, 386
48 *"them with beauty"*: Mockel, 389
48 *"on the walls"*: Symons, 183–84
48 *began to appear*: see Millan, 233
48 *"of our time"*: Symons, 184
48 *"cheerful and grave"*: Mockel, 390
49 *"simplicity, a priest"*: Symons, 185–86
49 *"listened to him"*: Symons, 187
49 *"was still alive"*: Mondor, 624–25
50 *was "very silent"*: Mockel, 389
50 *"the marvellous Word"*: Mockel, 389
50 *"has them, too"*: Mallarmé, Oeuvres, 257
50 *"of the enemy"*: Mallarmé, Oeuvres, 257
50 *"Theory of Ugliness"*: Mallarmé, Letters, 83
50 *Grave's* La Révolte: Rudorff, 170
51 *"address the crowd"*: Rudorff, 174
51 *"is a lie"*: Mallarmé, Letters, 75
51 *"to rare individuals"*: Mallarmé, Oeuvres, 259
51 *"remain an aristocrat"*: Mallarmé, Oeuvres, 259
51 *"poetry to ruin"*: Mallarmé, Oeuvres, 260
51 *"more, become disdainful"*: Mallarmé, Oeuvres, 260
51 *"readings to friends"*: Mallarmé, Letters, 65
52 *"ne rien faire"*: EL, 86
52 *"conduct of life"*: KB 1, 16
52 *"both impenitent noctambulists"*: Saint-Paul, 401
53 *"the Middle Ages"*: Richardson, 252
53 *"a fairy tale"*: Moore, Memoirs, 82
53 *"read poems well"*: CP 225, 24
54 *"For wild desires"*: SG, 1:96
54 *"haze of incense"*: SG, 1:96
54 *"a rapid death"*: SG, 1:96
54 *"enjoyed beyond measure"*: SG, 1:94
55 *"majesty of vice"*: SG, 1:94–95
55 *"of my childhood"*: SG, 1: *Anhang*
55 *had gone alone*: cf. Saint-Paul, 403, but also FW, 22, and BV, 108
55 *"but to Spain"*: EL, 104
56 *"foreign to us"*: BV, 62–63

56 *"entirely lacking there"*: EL, 108
56 *missed the ship:* see CP 225, 27

CHAPTER 5: BERLIN

57 *"stay in Paris"*: Saint-Paul, 404
58 *had been passed:* Masur, 62, 132
58 *"this terrible city"*: RB 2, 222
58 *"feels truly miserable"*: BV, 86
58 *"bad, uniformly artless"*: BV, 39
58 *"that surrounds one"*: SL, 24
59 *"of these Tuesdays"*: RB 2, 217
59 *"the natural sciences"*: Allgemeine Deutsche Biographie, 31:112
60 *"which surrounds us"*: Smith, 23–24
60 *"monk of doom"*: ES, 157
60 *nothing but Spanish:* FW, 23; SG, 3:27
60 *"race que vous"*: "I am the same race as you"; Muret
60 *"named Stéphane Mallarmé"*: Muret
61 *and Vielé-Griffin:* Muret
61 *"reflect on it"*: Muret
61 *"almost over-refined soul"*: FW, 28
61 *the moonlit countryside:* cf. FW, 28
61 *"meters oven pipe"*: RB 2, 37
61 *of George's "mission"*: Klein's book of memoirs, *Stefan Georges Sendung* (Stefan George's mission) was published in 1935, not quite two years after George's death.
61 *"a wordless bliss"*: CAK, 13
62 *"torture of doubt"*: CAK, 15
62 *"from me again"*: CAK, 16
62 *"never disappointed him"*: CAK, 16–17
62 *"the last day"*: CAK, 21
63 *"into a martyr"*: RB 2, 37–38
64 *"Italians, Mexicans, etc."*: RB 2, 37
64 *"of their son"*: Klein to George, 11 March 1890, SG-Archiv
64 *"remain in Germany"*: RB 2, 40
64 *going permanently "abroad"*: SG/HvH, 242
65 *"my dear Berlin"*: RB 2, 223–24
65 *"to our Circle"*: RB 2, 224
65 *"for your 'Cognicion' "*: Klein to George, 1 April 1890, SG-Archiv
65 *brooks, "virginal flowers"*: SG, 1:107
65 *"the Divine One"*: SG, 1:108
66 *"blossom and smile"*: SG, 1:108
66 *"a pure priestess"*: SG, 1:109
66 *his "bitter pain"*: SG, 1:109

66 *"I require you!"*: SG, 1:110
66 *"is mere trickery"*: SG, 1:110
66 *"purchase the answer"*: SG, 1:112
66 loathsome *"animal spasms"*: SG, 1:113
66 *"an ugly image"*: SG, 1:113
67 *"refrained from publication"*: Klein to George, 18 July 1890, SG-Archiv
67 *"at all erotic!"*: Klein to George, 18 July 1890, SG-Archiv. This sentence, but not the previous one, is reproduced in the *Zeittafel*.

CHAPTER 6: HYMNS

70 *"possession of everyone"*: Rouge to George, 30 August 1890, SG-Archiv
70 *"Etienne's particular 'sphere' "*: Rouge to George, 30 August 1890, SG-Archiv
71 *"pregnant, unique form"*: Rouge to George, 30 August 1890, SG-Archiv
71 *"say about them"*: Rouge to George, 30 August 1890, SG-Archiv
71 *"is certainly easier!"*: Rouge to George, 30 August 1890, SG-Archiv
72 *"above all effort"*: RB 2, 39
72 *"friend C[arl] R[ouge]"*: RB 2, 40
73 *"Monsieur Stéphane Mallarmé"*: RB 2, 217
73 *"poet of Germany"*: RB 2, 217
73 *"regards, Stéphane Mallarmé"*: RB 2, 202
74 to *"my ecstasy"*: RB 2, 202
74 *"the primordial Ideas"*: Moréas, 32–33
75 *"series of decipherments"*: Huret, 60
76 *"and pure genius"*: Mallarmé, *Letters*, 187
77 *"wrongfully with them"*: Huret, 62–63
78 *"l'art comme pouvoir"*: RB 2, 46
78 *"only expresses it"*: EL, 117
78 *"form of rule"*: EL, 45
79 to his calling: The following discussion of George's poetry is, if not in every detail, then most certainly in spirit, heavily indebted to the judicious and deeply informed interpretations of Claude David.
79 *"disturbance of thought"*: SG, 2:12
79 *"in the image"*: SG, 2:13
79 *"with guiding hand"*: SG, 2:13
80 *"was still king"*: SG, 2:27
80 *"brazenly desire it"*: SG, 2:42
80 a *"shadowy hall"*: SG, 2:14
80 to *"a turquoise"*: SG, 2:32
80 *"of heavengreen glass"*: SG, 2:40
80 *"stylus that resists"*: SG, 2:15
80 *"become your possession?"*: SG, 2:48
81 *"gloriously great deed"*: SG, 2:47
81 *"stream the indigo"*: SG, 2:47
81 *"the first crown"*: SG, 2:47

81 *"with dark undulations"*: SG, 2:34
81 *the "chaste sky"*: SG, 2:34
81 *secluded natural "altar"*: SG, 2:35
82 *"of secret mystery"*: SG, 2:35
82 *"tea and laurel"*: SG, 2:35
82 *"cheek white temple"*: SG, 2:22
82 *the "sweet body"*: SG, 2:23
82 *of "your portrait"*: SG, 2:23
82 *"how your eye"*: SG, 2:23
83 *"potentates of Europe"*: RB 2, 152

CHAPTER 7: *PILGRIMAGES*

85 *"to the harbor"*: George to Stahl, 11 December 1890, SG-Archiv
86 *the American metropolis*: Porfirio Peñafiel to George, 3 January 1891, SG-Archiv
86 *expressed "great astonishment"*: FW, 30
86 *"reputation of perfection"*: Mallarmé, *Letters*, 63
86 *"of Walt Whitman"*: Wellsted to George, 14 April 1891, SG-Archiv
87 *"than long phrases"*: Muret to George, 16 December 1890, SG-Archiv
87 *"you my opinion"*: Rozniecki to George, 28 December 1890, SG-Archiv
87 *"excited the palace"*: Sohnle, 96
88 *"for you French"*: RB 2, 217
88 *"were the originals"*: RB 2, 32
88 *"be very good"*: RB 2, 218
89 *"predominance of Naturalism"*: Sohnle, 96
89 *"a German monument"*: SG, 13–14:6
89 *"most obdurate matter"*: SG, 13–14:6
90 *that "true meadows"*: SG, 2:69
91 *"fought to gain"*: SG, 2:67
91 *"an honorable gown"*: SG, 2:67
92 *"the tree-trunk"*: SG, 2:70–71
92 *"expression of sorrow"*: SG, 2:72
92 *"in depraved splendor"*: SG, 2:73
92 *"still and stay!"*: SG, 2:60
92 *objects, including "tourmaline"*: SG, 2:55
92 *"diamond and emerald"*: SG, 2:67
92 *"heavy velvet"*: SG, 2:64
92 *"morocco"*: SG, 2:79
92 *"fiery-red gold"*: SG, 2:83
93 *"a strange green"*: SG, 2:82
93 *"by departing rays"*: SG, 2:82
93 *"with hesitant gait"*: SG, 2:82
94 *as "Your Prince"*: Klein to George, 1890/91, and 3 April 1891, SG-Archiv
94 *ongoing poetic "fertility"*: Klein to George, 25 March 1891, SG-Archiv

94 *"figure. Dear Master!"*: Klein to George, 9 June 1891, SG-Archiv
94 *"your mighty breast"*: Klein to George, 24 June 1891, SG-Archiv
94 *"the Canale grande"*: CAK, 18
94 *"since my youth"*: SG, 2:ii

CHAPTER 8: A CHILD IN PALE BLUE CLOTHES

95 *"newspapers and journals"*: Zweig, 47
95 *"the Burlington Magazine"*: Zweig, 47
95 *"and familiar circle"*: Zweig, 47
96 *"well-combed poodle"*: Fiechtner, 13
97 *"of sophisticated culture"*: Fiechtner, 15–16
98 *"during the day"*: Zweig, 54
98 *"the Poetic was"*: RB 2, 226–227
98 *"circle of Mallarmé"*: RB 2, 226
98 *of course, Mallarmé*: RB 2, 227
99 *"nighttime whispering wind"*: SG/HvH, 7
99 *"who passes by"*: SG/HvH, 7
99 *"place and time?"*: SG/HvH, 8
99 *"are you coming?"*: SG/HvH, 9
99 *"gaze has moved"*: SG/HvH, 10
99 *still in class*: Fiechtner, 59
99 *"in his absence"*: HvH, 94
100 *"even without touching"*: SG/HvH, 239
100 *"receive my letter?"*: SG/HvH, 10
102 *"who passes by"*: SG/HvH, 12–13
102 *"what frightens me"*: SG/HvH, 14
103 *"tactless pressing demands"*: SG/HvH, 14–15
103 *"in my apartment"*: SG/HvH, 15
103 *"with your life"*: SG/HvH, 15–16
104 *"with this explanation"*: SG/HvH, 16
104 *"when and where"*: SG/HvH, 16–17
104 *was, "very frightened"*: SG/HvH, 241
104 *"his own hands"*: SG/HvH, 241
105 *"do so himself"*: SG/HvH, 242
105 *"before doing so"*: SG/HvH, 243
105 *"was explicitly requested)"*: SG/HvH, 243
106 *"more than superficial"*: SG/HvH, 244
106 *"for a moment"*: SG/HvH, 244
106 *"too deeply offended"*: SG/HvH, 245
106 *"or written form"*: SG/HvH, 246
106 *"difficult to grasp"*: SG/HvH, 156
107 *"the same name"*: ES, 222

107 *"as much weariness"*: ES, 222
107 *finally manifested itself:* cf. EL, 53

CHAPTER 9: *ALGABAL* THE DECADENT
108 write *"after Halgabal"*: SG/HvH, 12
108 *"a revolutionary book"*: Curtius, 112
109 *"history attracted him"*: Gundolf, *George*, 80
109 *"of no importance"*: FW, 40, 38
110 *"and precious stones"*: Herodian, 39
110 *"enough for him"*: Herodian, 41
110 *"women than men"*: Herodian, 41
110 *"on his cheeks"*: Herodian, 57
110 *"his own beard"*: Lampridius, 169
110 *"to the sceptre"*: Gibbon, 1:144
110 *"vice with men"*: Lampridius, 115
110 *consulted most carefully:* on George's knowledge of the ancient sources, see Oswald
110 *"unusually large organs"*: Lampridius, 123
111 *"festival of Flora"*: Lampridius, 117
111 *"a bridal matron"*: Lampridius, 127
112 *Nero and Tiberius:* Carter, 31
112 *"Nero . . . Heliogabalus"*: Carter, 38
112 *androgyny and hermaphroditism:* see Carter, 39
113 *"didn't see it"*: C. Rouge to Stefan George, beginning 1 to 15 June 1888, SG-Archiv
113 *"our sexual love"*: Karl Heinrich Ulrichs, *Vier Briefe*, reprinted in Jonathan Katz et al., ed. *Documents of the Homosexual Rights Movement*, 47
113 *"examples throughout Creation"*: Katz, 50
113 *"variant of it"*: Katz, 50
114 *"nature in Uranians"*: Katz, 51
114 *"Lord, but Lady"*: Kennedy, 59
114 *"has no sexe!"*: Richard M. Meyer to George, 19 October 1897, SG-Archiv
114 *nature of homosexuality:* Jones, 94–95
115 *Schuler, in 1899:* Alfred Schuler to George, 3 November 1899, SG-Archiv
115 *cited and discussed:* cf. Kaufmann, "Heine und Platon"
115 *historical novel, L'Agonie:* Carter, 105–06
115 *"l'Amour Androgyne"*: Carter, 106
115 *"includes both sexes"*: Carter, 106
116 *and the Rosicrucians:* Rudorff, 188–89
116 *merely bemused visitors"* Rudorff, 188–89; see also Sohnle, 103–04
116 *ran into Verlaine:* Morwitz 2, 42; see also Sohnle, 117. Georg Fuchs also compared George to Péladan, cf. Fuchs, 132.
116 *"a symbolic figure"*: FW, 37
117 *"entice the master"*: SG, 2:90

117 *"he conceived them":* SG, 2:90
117 *"from his own":* SG, 2:91
117 *"light and weather":* SG, 2:91
117 *one we know:* On the following and other literary influences, see Meesen, Durzak, David, and Morwitz.
118 *to "extravagant caprices":* Huysmans, 90
118 *"of actual experience":* Huysmans, 101
118 *"had her day":* Huysmans, 103
118 *"whom he believes":* Huysmans, 104
119 *"dark black flower?":* SG, 2:96
119 *"secret of procreation":* Gundolf, *George,* 86
119 *"of Elagabalus reports":* Morwitz, 37
120 *"of a sister":* SG, 2:107
120 *a "double form":* SG, 2:101
120 *"a scornful gesture":* SG, 2:99
120 *"my purple train":* SG, 2:103
121 *"to the cross":* SG, 2:107
121 *the following spring:* see EM 1, 57; FW, 41

CHAPTER 10: *PAGES FOR ART*
122 *"also be imposed":* Oosterhuis, 56
123 *"makes bad metaphors":* Wuthenow, 11
123 *"to human immorality":* Kennedy, 187
124 *"would understand them":* IC/SG, 77
124 *"one there was":* IC/SG, 78
125 *"of his Muse":* IC/SG, 30
125 *"a long time":* IC/SG, 78
125 *"Verlaine, Baudelaire, Mallarmé":* IC/SG, 78–79
125 *"indescribably contemptuous arc":* IC/SG, 79
125 *"filled his soul":* Lessing, 307
126 *" 'Isi' had been":* SL, 37
126 *"was Ida Coblenz":* Bithell, 2
126 *"in his life":* RB 2, 64
126 *"was deeply shaken":* Bithell, 8
126 *"deeply impressed me":* IC/SG, 79
126 *"being almost repulsive":* Dehmel, 264
126 *"broken our alliance":* IC/SG, 80
127 *"of the food":* LA, 117–18
127 *"an aging hermaphrodite":* HvH/LA, 21
127 *"poetic and critical":* RB 2, 37
128 *"of our journal?":* Z, 12 April 1890
128 *"men in place":* Z, 16 September 1890
128 *"that to others!":* George to Klein, 30 September 1890, SG-Archiv
128 *"agreement prevented him":* SG/HvH, 26

128 *"George informed you"*: SG/HvH, 21
128 *"only besmirch you"*: SG/HvH, 21
129 *"a voice here"*: SG/HvH, 21
129 *"with the* Blätter?*"*: ES, 16
129 *called his "circle"*: ES, 304
129 *was being described:* The subtitle of Wolters's book can also be translated as "German Intellectual History since 1890." Part of the problem is the notorious word *Geist*, which can, and often does, simultaneously signify "spirit," "mind," "intellect," and "soul." But the phrase "intellectual history" conveys too much the sense of a dry academic discipline, which Wolters, who as much as anyone was aware of George's antipathy to *Wissenschaft* (another tough nut), surely did not mean.
129 *"welcome to me"*: SG/HvH, 22
130 *"as his equals"*: Fiechtner, 59
130 *"the same rank"*: Fiechtner, 59
130 *"popular critical essays"*: SG/HvH, 23
130 *"aid the other"*: SG/HvH, 24–25
130 *"is not Symbolism"*: Bahr, 114
131 *"into our undertaking"*: SG/HvH, 25–26
131 *that "certain agreement"*: SG/HvH, 26
131 *"our postal addresses"*: SG/HvH, 26–27
131 *" 'association of names' "*: SG/HvH, 27
131 *"oh-so professional level)"*: SG/HvH, 28–29
131 *"something worth knowing"*: SG/HvH, 29–30
132 *"very minor importance"*: SG/HvH, 30
132 *"theories of art"*: SG/HvH, 30
132 *"of minor importance?"*: SG/HvH, 31
132 *"or a quarter"*: SG/HvH, 31
132 *"to the journal"*: SG/HvH, 3

CHAPTER II: FORGING ALLIANCES
134 *"increase in number"*: EL, 49
134 *"and social matters"*: BfdK 1, 1:1
135 *"art for art"*: BfdK 1, 1:1
135 *"conception of reality"*: BfdK 1, 1:1
135 *"any naturalistic ties"*: RB 2, 202
135 *a "hairy lout"*: CAK, 47–48
135 *"renascence in art"*: BfdK 1, 1:2
136 *"an aging naturalism"*: Bahr, 48
136 *"for something new"*: Bahr, 111
136 *"have ever thought"*: SG/HvH, 51
136 *"sympathetic readers here"*: SG/HvH, 52
137 *"like-minded people"*: BfdK 1, 1:2
137 *"is his name"*: IC/SG, 78

137 *"enflames my enthusiasm"*: Karl Wolfskehl to George, 16 November 1892, SG-Archiv
137 *"Press for Art"*: George to Wolfskehl, 24 November 1892, SG-Archiv
138 *"once in centuries"*: KW Katalog, 74
138 *size thirteen feet:* ES, 219
138 *innovative accounting practices:* for these details, see KW Katalog, 144–45
139 *"for its maintenance?"*: SG/HvH, 45
139 *were suitably "qualified"*: SG/HvH, 45
139 *"me a little"*: SG/HvH, 46
139 *"semiannually three marks"*: SG/HvH, 47
139 *"of the* Blätter*?"*: Wolfskehl to George, 11 November 1895, SG-Archiv
139 *"through his works"*: IC/SG, 39
139 *"most talentless creations"*: IC/SG, 40
140 *some were "unsurpassed"*: SG/HvH, 119
140 *"baseness of soul"*: SG/HvH, 119–20
140 *"what poetic filth!"*: RB 2, 47
140 *"of the 'Lied' "*: Sohnle, 94
140 *"by their counsel"*: BfdK 1, 2:53
141 *"is the principal"*: RB 2, 220
141 *"of the editor"*: Sohnle, 94
141 *"of the foundation"*: SG/HvH, 52
141 *"you want it"*: SG/HvH, 53
142 *"a terra-cotta relief"*: SG/HvH, 66
142 *"of a family"*: SG/HvH, 66–67
142 *"irreplaceable to me"*: SG/HvH, 67
143 *"favorably disposed readership"*: SG/HvH, 68

CHAPTER 12: BECOMING GERMAN
144 *"transpositions were possible"*: RB 2, 55
144 *"creator, dear brother"*: Z, 22 March 1893
145 *"to disgust me"*: RB 2, 33
145 *"we are together"*: RB 2, 33
146 *"a golden boat"*: SG/HvH, 62
146 *"Verlaine, and Mallarmé"*: BfdK 1, 2:46
146 *his "great hero"*: Klein to George, undated letter ca. 1890/91, SG-Archiv
146 *"of a following"*: BfdK 1, 2:46
146 *"in German Romanticism"*: BfdK 1, 2:47
146 *"is a poet"*: BfdK 1, 2:50
147 *"pure Germanic symbolism"*: RB 2, 220
148 *"Baudelaire: but where?"*: George to Stuart Merrill, undated 1893/94, SG-Archiv

CHAPTER 13: A GROUP IS FORMED
150 *"a little taste"*: ES, 168
150 *"good to me"*: SG/HvH, 58

150 "skies of Berlin": SG/ML, 157
150 "jews and whores!": SG/ML, 240
151 "mop of hair": AS, 35
151 "un poète maudit": AS, 36
151 "understand a fifth": Lessing, 302
151 a pointed cowl: see LC, 246–47, and RB 2, 104
152 "a Roman feast": Huch, 26
152 a "blood light": Huch, 8
152 such reconstituted temple: see Lessing, 325
153 as a "Jew": Huch, 11
153 accorded this distinction: Huch, 14
153 "also a Jew?": RB 2, 106
153 "hermaphroditic double nature": Lessing, 323–24
153 "boys in lederhosen": Lessing, 322
153 "and half woman": ES, 192
154 the male genitals: see Huch, 43; Lessing, 323; and LC, 247
154 by "Jewish Christianity": LC, 247
154 extensive private collection: The source of this report is the afterword to Huch, 56.
154 buffoon and fantast: Lessing, 322
154 as "a lunatic": EL, 72
155 expel the Jews: see Nipperdey, 2:295
155 "are our misfortune": Nipperdey, 2:297
155 say instead "Molochitic": see Lessing, 423–24
155 "the 'Jewish people' ": Lessing, 421–22
155 "anti-realist, anti-Semite": LA, 118
155 "in the slightest": EL, 146
156 "their own business": Thormaehlen folder "Juden," SG-Archiv
156 "in the Yearbook": Curtius, 153
156 and his friends: ES, 244
156 "foreign to us": KB 1, 26
156 "them for? Art": EL, 72
156 "found a religion": KB 1, 15
157 "experience a loss": BfdK 2, 2:35
158 "its deepest stimulus": BfdK 2, 2:33
158 "a brilliant renascence": BfdK 1, 1:2
158 "realm of medicine": BfdK 2, 2:33
158 "to higher life": BfdK 2, 2:33
158 "and poetry itself": BfdK 2, 2:33
159 "maturity and depth": BfdK 2, 2:33
159 "entertainment but impression": BfdK 2, 2:33
159 "that of poetry": BfdK 1, 1:1
159 "of a mood": BfdK 2, 2:34
159 "of our neighbors": BfdK 2, 2:35
160 "at the time": EL, 54

161 *"the greatest regret"*: SG/HvH, 70
161 *"it in advance"*: SG/HvH, 71
161 *"are completely unbearable"*: HvH/LA, 21
161 *"impossible this time"*: LA, 28
161 *"the original version"*: LA, 28
161 *"wishes concerning changes"*: LA, 31
161 *"I am furious"*: LA, 114
162 *"am so fond"*: LA, 38
162 *"affection for you"*: LA, 40
162 *"group is formed"*: RB 2, 222
163 *"it any more"*: EL, 54

CHAPTER 14: SCHWABING

165 *"jerky Prussian elbow"*: Hollweck, 21
165 *apartments for rent:* Heisserer, 11
165 *"a Schwabing 'Schlawiner'"*: Heisserer, 11–12
165 Gil blas illustré: see Heisserer, 13
166 *"the tone here"*: Fuchs, 151
166 *"from rich admirers"*: Fuchs, 152
166 *"of Saint Peter's"*: Lessing, 305
166 *"of the paper"*: Lessing, 304
166 to his *"museum"*: Lessing, 304
166 *"in the mirror"*: Lessing, 306
166 *"were men-loving"*: Lessing, 307
166 *world of luxury:* Lessing, 304
166 *"imperious and careworn"*: Lessing, 305
167 *"at the time"*: Lessing, 306
167 *"organ for literature"*: Lessing, 308
167 *"is a writer"*: Lessing, 308
167 *"in German literature"*: Lessing, 309
168 *"to Herr Lessing!"*: Lessing, 307
168 *"in the Luitpold"*: Lessing, 307
168 *"a tree trunk"*: Lessing, 307
168 *"away from him"*: SL, 39
168 *"amidst loud shrieking"*: SL, 40
168 *"for buried treasure"*: SL, 40
169 like a *"gravedigger":* see Goldsmith, 73, and Morwitz, 229
169 *"entirely avant-garde"*: RB 2, 203
169 *"Baudelaire. I applaud"*: RB 2, 203.
170 *"in our endeavor"*: BfdK, 2, 3:96
171 *"lonely, desperately lonely"*: E. Rassenfosse to George, 2 June 1894, SG-Archiv
171 *"still so young!"*: George to E. Rassenfosse, undated, 1894/95, SG-Archiv, and RB 2, 54–55
172 *"doesn't die away"*: E. Rassenfosse to George, 22 April 1896, SG-Archiv

172 *"man and poet"*: RB 2, 65
172 *"husband too much"*: EM 1, 77
172 *dutiful acknowledgement remained:* see the thoughtful essay by Weevers
173 *"about our movement"*: Klein to Max Dessoir, 3 March 1895, SG-Archiv
173 *"movement into existence"*: Klein to Max Dessoir, 3 March 1895, SG-Archiv
173 *"to the people"*: Berlin um 1900, 268
173 *"cannot understand it"*: Dehmel, 182
174 *"from your pen"*: IC/SG, 55–56
174 *"on my behalf"*: IC/SG, 56–57
174 *"contributions in 'Pan' "*: IC/SG, 57
175 *"here in Germany"*: George to Wilhelm Ritter, December 1895, SG-Archiv

CHAPTER 15: A USABLE PAST

176 *"entirely different one"*: IC/SG, 59
176 *"works are together"*: IC/SG, 59
177 *"sought shelter there"*: SG, 3:7
178 *"our beloved cities"*: SG, 3:7
178 *"a beautiful goal"*: SG, 3:23
178 *"blond" and "lovely"*: SG, 3:24
178 *"and Most Supreme"*: SG, 3:24
179 *"On his brow"*: SG, 3:26
179 the *"divine nakedness"*: SG, 3:33
179 *"red like blood"*: SG, 3:90
179 *"drawn too taut"*: SG, 3:107
179 *"at my side"*: SG, 3:109
179 *"the other sex"*: Goldsmith, *Stefan George,* 71
179 *"pass by today"*: SG, 3:105
180 *"our warm blood"*: SG, 3:109
180 his *"steaming blade"*: SG, 3:91
180 *"and slender trunk"*: SG, 3:115
180 *"bridling their steeds"*: SG, 3:64
180 *"flaming swords"*: SG, 3:48
180 *"true heroic worth"*: SG, 3:47
180 *"and modest army"*: SG, 3:50
180 *"fame and blood"*: SG, 3:50
181 *"on the horizon"*: SG, 3:51
181 *ill-fated Antinous:* on these identifications, see EM 1, 69–79
182 *"back from it"*: Wuthenow, 7
182 *"a deep temple"*: Wuthenow, 8
182 *"violent, almost threatening"*: Wuthenow, 9
182 *"and cruel experiences"*: Wuthenow, 11, 13
182 *"existence than before"*: Wuthenow, 14
183 *"loyal to me"*: SG/HvH, 89
183 *"for your assistance"*: SG/HvH, 77

183 *"to the circle"*: SG/HvH, 77
183 *"your artistic efforts"*: SG/HvH, 78
183 *"way of feeling"*: SG/HvH, 85
183 *"my mother tongue!"*: SG/HvH, 83
184 *"owe worship, truly!"*: Wolfskehl to George, 25 March 1896, SG-Archiv
184 *"our awful age"*: Wolfskehl to George, 13 March 1896, SG-Archiv
184 *"entirely to us"*: ES, 170. Salin estimates the letter to have been written in the fall of 1897; it is conceivable, however, that it was written a year and a half earlier in response to the letter from Wolfskehl just cited, which Salin does not mention.
184 *"German Poets' Conference"*: SG/HvH, 253
185 *"addressing the masses"*: SG/HvH, 109–10
185 *"I am approaching"*: SG/HvH, 110
185 *professor Max Dessoir:* See the two letters from Dessoir to George, 16 and 24 February 1896, SG/HvH, 255, in which Dessoir writes that "I am keeping the journal plan in mind, but I am afraid that we cannot count on a satisfactory response from either a publisher or the readership under the present circumstances," and "I did speak with the publisher but found only slight interest. I fear that it will remain difficult to found such an undertaking in an appropriate manner."
185 *"my complete knowledge"*: SG/HvH, 256–57
185 *"interchanging friendly subjects?"*: Klein to George, 23 October 1896, SG-Archiv
186 *"send an objection"*: SG/HvH, 110
186 *"of language altogether?"*: SG/HvH, 112
187 *"you and me"*: SG/HvH, 113
187 *"other mysterious thing"*: HvH Briefe, 207
187 *"greatest spirits alive"*: SL, 11
187 *"southern German dialect"*: SL, 12–13
188 *"to the other"*: IC/SG, 63
188 *"still. Good bye"*: IC/SG, 63

CHAPTER 16: *THE YEAR OF THE SOUL*

190 *of his days:* cf. EM 1, 183–84
190 *"leftovers to guests"*: ES, 32
190 *before his output:* cf. EL, 187, where George says that later no one would believe that he had done everything he did for that very reason
191 *"the time being"*: BfdK 3, 1:1
191 *"sound and sun"*: BfdK 3, 1:2
191 *"paid no heed"*: BfdK 3, 1:20
191 *"creation, true creation"*: BfdK 3, 1:21
191 *"song of triumph"*: BfdK 3, 1:21
191 *"that preceded us"*: BfdK 3, 2:33
192 *"second-class cultural state"*: BfdK 3, 2:33
192 *"events at all"*: SG/HvH, 91
192 *"so-called German script"*: BfdK 3, 4:98

192 *"the northern element"*: Klages to George, 15 December 1895, SG-Archiv
192 *"the German Nation"*: BfdK 3, 2:35
193 *ancient Roman Limes:* This is pointed out as well by David, 135.
194 *"of the century"*: BfdK 4, 1–2:4
195 *"impress his audience"*: (London) *Daily Telegraph*, 31 December 1970
195 *"have ever encountered"*: Scott, *Years of Indiscretion*, 31
195 *"those beautiful boys"*: EL, 171
195 *"reciprocate his feelings"*: Scott, *Bone of Contention*, 103
195 *"loathing and disgust"*: Scott, *Bone of Contention*, 103–04
195 *"a painful association"*: Scott, *Bone of Contention*, 105
195 *George, strictly "platonic"*: Scott to George, 7 November 1904, SG-Archiv
196 *"taking any measures"*: Scott, *Die Tragödie Stefan Georges*, 31
196 *"of the publication"*: LA, 44
196 *"my particular case"*: LA, 44
196 *"poem of mine"*: LA, 45
197 *"spectators and listeners"*: LA, 46
197 *"laws and regulations"*: Scott, *Bone of Contention*, 75
197 *"feelings of democracy"*: Scott, *Bone of Contention*, 76
197 *"a slight lisp"*: Scott, *Bone of Contention*, 105
198 *"for the day!"*: Marguerite Hoffmann, 24
198 *still polular Péladan:* see Marguerite Hoffmann, 25
198 *"in my youth"*: ML 2, 13–14
198 *"read the* Blätter*"*: ML 2, 15
198 *"Stefan George myself"*: ML 2, 15
198 *"be his people"*: EL, 10
199 *"literature and poetry"*: AV/SG, 33
199 *"would be sacrilegious"*: Scott, *Bone of Contention*, 105–06
199 *in the air:* Scott, *My Years of Indiscretion*, 42
199 *" 'bloomer' in German"*: Scott, *Bone of Contention*, 106
199 *"all his friends"*: Scott, *My Years of Indiscretion*, 42
199 *"was greatly mistaken"*: Scott, *Bone of Contention*, 105
200 *"is animated form"*: ML 2, 12
200 *"history of art"*: Grautoff, 3
200 *of the works:* Grautoff, 17–18
200 *"up to now"*: SG/HvH, 109
201 *Germany as well:* see ES, 39
201 *"than in Germany"*: Grautoff, 102
201 *"of deep sounds!"*: Z, 2 October 1897
201 *"in recent times"*: Grautoff, 104
202 *"new master work"*: SG Katalog, 123
202 *"significance in it"*: EL, 37
202 *"some ideal year"*: RB 2, 206
203 *"your veto here"*: Sabine Lepsius to George, 10 November 1897, SG-Archiv
203 *largest auditorium available:* cf. Gassen, 21

204 *"any case harmless"*: Sabine Lepsius to George, 10 November 1897, SG-Archiv
204 *"bowed and left"*: FW, 124
205 *"in this book"*: SG, 4:7
206 *"words for you"*: SG, 4:14
206 *"onto the ground"*: SG, 4:15
206 *"the pallid surface"*: SG, 4:21
207 *"inhabit my dream"*: SG, 4:22
207 *"the diseased heart"*: SG, 4:31
207 *"the happy banner"*: SG, 4:33
207 *"a new adventure"*: SG, 4:36
208 *"nectar from umbels"*: SG, 4:40
208 *the young men:* The consensus is that the poems recall George's attachment to E. Rassenfosse (see EM 1, 118–119), but Claude David offers the (to my mind untenable) hypothesis that they were inspired by Cyril Scott (see David, 433).
208 *"of the real"*: BfdK 3, 1:21
208 *"as thankful guests!"*: SG, 4:38
208 *"a real one"*: SG, 4:43
209 *"has become late"*: SG, 4:118
209 *"an incomprehensible poem"*: Gundolf, *George*, 143

CHAPTER 17: GOING PUBLIC

211 *"greater public prominence"*: FW, 170
212 *"attack with advantage"*: Goldsmith, "The Growth of Stefan George's Reputation," 241
212 *"have it indecent"*: SG/HvH, 261
212 *"was considered ugly"*: SL, 27
213 *"also well proportioned"*: SL, 27–28
213 *"music of Bach"*: Gassen, 280
213 *"far too much"*: SL, 28
213 *"in the creation"*: Gassen, 235
214 *" 'to your seat' "*: Gassen, 249
214 *of abstract relations:* see ES, 191
214 *"word of it"*: KB 1, 36
214 *patterns of concepts:* cf. EL, 110
215 *"for a statue"*: Wuthenow, 37
215 *"pour le sentiment"*: Wuthenow, 31
215 *"principle of art"*: Wuthenow, 29–30
216 *"but rather timeless"*: Wuthenow, 31
216 *"become absolute ruler"*: Wuthenow, 32–33
216 *"as a poet"*: Wuthenow, 39
217 *"old was not"*: EL, 31
217 *"the thankless task"*: Wuthenow, 41

217 *whole "Parisian clique"*: Wuthenow, 41–42
217 *"of his gifts"*: Wuthenow, 42
218 *to be "nonsense"*: Wuthenow, 42
218 *"new-fashioned poets"*: Wuthenow, 45
218 *"for his congregation"*: Wuthenow, 45
218 *"the terrible Mallarmé"*: Wuthenow, 44
218 *"the same paper"*: Wuthenow, 47
218 *the "probable meaning"*: Wuthenow, 50
218 *"a silver platter"*: Wuthenow, 49
218 *"who made it?"*: Wuthenow, 50
218 *"flatly contradicted another"*: Scott, *Bone of Contention*, 76
218 *"babbling about art"*: Lessing, 310
219 *"to publish them"*: Bondi, 7
219 *"at the moment"*: Bondi, 7
219 *"in ideal costume"*: RB 2, 281
220 *"for this suggestion"*: Bondi to Klein, 7 June 1898, SG-Archiv
220 *"of the edition"*: Bondi to Klein, 7 June 1898, SG-Archiv
220 *"in my editions"*: Bondi, 9
221 *his fixed abode:* see Bondi, 11

CHAPTER 18: *THE TAPESTRY OF LIFE*

223 *"behest of t. M."*: SG/ML, 315
224 *"swindlers, and slanderers"*: Gundolf, *George*, 31
224 *"way to us"*: BfdK 4, 1–2:64
225 *"requesting of you"*: Z, 7 December 1897
225 *"of the* Blätter*"*: Z, 74
225 *"within a circle"*: BfdK 4, 1–2:3
225 *"idea can breathe"*: BfdK 4, 1–2:3
225 *"into his wreath"*: BfdK 4, 1–2:3
226 *"darkness holy night"*: BfdK 3, 5:142
226 *"a bright sun"*: BfdK 3, 5:141
226 *"trembling with secrets"*: BfdK 3, 5:141
226 *"in the twilight"*: BfdK 3, 5:141
226 *"all individual flames"*: BfdK 3, 5:142
227 *"of a work"*: BfdK 4, 1–2:35
227 *"the creative one"*: BfdK 4, 1–2:35
228 *"an apathetic omniscience?"*: BfdK 4, 1–2:38
228 *"shaping and forming"*: BfdK 4, 1–2:36
228 *"of this man"*: BfdK 4, 3:88
228 *"the other one"*: BfdK 4, 3:89
229 *"warriors with intoxication"*: BfdK 4, 3:89
229 *"lent a soul"*: BfdK 4, 3:90

{ NOTES }

229 *springs to mind:* cf. David, 220
230 *"of the temple":* SG/ML, 73
230 *book "cathedral-like":* Y, 1:28
231 *"the fresh roses":* SG, 5:12
232 *"you bless me":* SG, 5:13
232 *"you love me?":* SG, 5:15
233 *"the angel wants":* SG, 5:14
233 *"pilot to you":* SG, 5:18
233 *"forever our love":* SG, 5:18
234 *"to proclaim it":* SG, 5:21
234 *a "marching song":* EM 1, 175
234 *"all is drilling":* AV, 63
235 *"for his glory":* SG, 5:34
235 *"my noble Master":* SG, 5:51
235 *"my greatest Master":* SG, 5:51
235 *"a few brothers":* SG, 5:55
235 *"for your order":* SG, 5:55
235 *"most divine renunciation":* SG, 5:55
236 *"justify this treason?":* ES, 271
236 *"case of Nietzsche":* ES, 271–72
237 *"despise you all!":* SG, 5:49
237 *"hinted at them":* EM 1, 198
237 *"his future path":* EM 1, 198
237 *"the same time":* LA, 50
238 *"early May 1899":* cf. Z, 2 May 18
238 *"a young Roman":* Lessing, 313
238 *"beautiful Greek cameo":* SL, 32
238 *final, massive overdose:* see Lessing, 318
239 *"of all worlds":* RB 2, 248
239 *"most serious concerns":* RB 2, 93
239 *"will remember Him":* RB 2, 93
239 *sprigs of laurel:* see SL, 22
240 *"of a sermon":* SG Katalog, 144
240 Life, *"divine youth":* SG, 5:28

CHAPTER 19: THE DISCIPLE
265 *"hopes in him":* SG/FG, 27
265 *"life his eye":* Wolfskehl to George, 24 November 1900, SG-Archiv
266 *"you notice it?":* ES, 54
267 *"pairs in motion?":* ES, 54
267 *"noticed him either?!":* ES, 54
267 *"a little longer":* W/G 38–39

267 *it was "ugly"*: The name is, in German, unmistakably Jewish, although there is no evidence suggesting that it was this fact alone that prompted George to propose the alternative. Sabine Lepsius, who was also Jewish, commented neutrally on George's "aversion to ugly names." See SL, 25.
268 *word for graciousness*: cf. SL, 25
268 *"and slender frame"*: SL, 30
268 *as George's "page"*: Sabine Lepsius to George, 29 December 1900, SG-Archiv
268 *"this extraordinary appearance"*: Bondi, 10
268 *with their fingers*: see ES, 65
268 *to put them*: cf. EL, 103
269 *handling of language*: see ES, 79
269 *"inch a genius"*: EL, 39
269 *"Like a child"*: KH 1, 27
269 *soothing bird sounds*: cf. ES, 92
269 *the wailing child*: EL, 55
270 *"days and nights"*: KW/AV, 20
270 *"from you again"*: SG/FG, 29
270 *"thank for it"*: SG/FG, 29
270 *"devoted Friedrich Gundolf"*: SG/FG, 29
270 *"in consecutive order"*: SG/FG, 30
271 *at a stretch*: cf. SG/FG, 164
271 *"them to me"*: SG/FG, 29
271 *"than factual matters"*: George to Theodor Dienstbach, 19 October 1897, SG-Archiv
271 *"way of communicating"*: RB 2, 95
271 *as an "audience"*: SG/FG, 30
271 *"you in Bingen"*: SG/FG, 30
271 *"visit me now"*: SG/FG, 31
271 *"in the* Blätter*"*: SG/FG, 31
272 *"of the worst"*: AV/SG, 68
272 *"tell intelligent man"*: FG/KW, 1:44–45
272 *"the last time"*: FG/KW, 1:44
272 *"beautiful and unforgettable"*: SG/FG, 31
272 *"grateful to you"*: SG/FG, 32–32
272 *"above all industry"*: SG/FG, 33
273 *"sic fere dixit"*: "thus approximately he [i.e., George] spoke"
273 *"characteristic and strong"*: The photograph is by Curt Stöving (1863–1939), friend of Melchior Lechter. Reproduced in RB T, 75.
273 *"with slimy fingers"*: FG/KW, 1:49–50
274 *"you, dear Master"*: SG/FG, 37
274 *"motion and figure"*: SG/FG, 39
274 *"love and veneration"*: SG/FG, 40
276 *"in the matter?"*: SG/FG, 44

276 *"ghosts and fabrications"*: Wolfskehl to George, 20 November 1899, SG-Archiv
276 *"Master victory forever!"*: Wolfskehl to George, 2 December 1903 in response to *Tage und Thaten*, SG-Archiv
277 *"the best education"*: ES, 70

CHAPTER 20: THE ANTHOLOGIES
278 in the *"tasteful"*: SG/HvH, 109
279 *"and statesmanlike terms"*: AV, 25–26
279 *"to consolidate himself"*: AV, 26
280 *"wealth of feelings"*: BfdK 3, 2:59; also SG, 17:60
280 *"Paul's divine Germanness"*: FG/KW, 1:49
280 *"of carrying out"*: ES, 170
280 *"the J.-P. proofs"*: SG/FG, 44
280 him totally blind: see Z, 22 April 1895
280 *"decipher its contents!"*: ES, 332
281 *"of Wolfskehl Letters"*: ES, 332
281 *"in fact superficial"*: ES, 186. George, through Gundolf, was alluding to an essay by Klein that had appeared in the *Blätter* called "What is not in fact superficial"; see BfdK 1, 5:144–46.
281 *"completely illegible. Stefan"*: ES, 332
281 *"you both think"*: SG/FG, 50
281 *"the German scholars!!"*: SG/FG, 50
281 *"and faulty version"*: ES, 179
281 *"you have assumed"*: ES, 179
282 *"for 8 days"*: SG/ML, 113
282 *"J—P—work"*: SG/ML, 115
282 *"now at risk"*: SG/ML, 121
282 *"drawings are finished!"*: SG/ML, 122
282 *"on my deathbed"*: SG/ML, 128
282 *"a worthy garment"*: SG/ML, 136
282 *"blood of contempt"*: SG/ML, 136
283 *"positively astonishing incompetence"*: KW Katalog, 85–86
283 from publishing it: see FG/KW, 1:283, 397n
283 as the *"ARSch"*: FG/KW, 1:135
283 Insel the *"ARSCH-enal"*: FG/KW, 1:158
283 eight hundred copies: cf. Klein to George, 15 July 1898, SG-Archiv
285 *"and shallowly intellectualistic"*: BfdK 5:2
285 *"art and culture"*: BfdK 5:2
285 with *"inauthentic conglomerations"*: BfdK 5:2
285 *"ten conquered provinces"*: BfdK 5:3
286 *"feeling of life"*: BfdK 5:1
286 *"artificial and lifeless"*: BfdK 5:3
286 *"people's minds today"*: BfdK 5:4
287 *"make the doctrine"*: BfdK 5:1

287 *"too personally oriented"*: Klages to George, 15 December 1895, SG-Archiv
287 *in early 1899:* see Klages to George, 28 June 1899, SG-Archiv
288 *"be explained itself"*: Klages, 3
288 *"in philosophical writings"*: Klages, 3
288 *"the transpersonal sphere"*: Klages, 3–4
288 *certain "esoteric formulae"*: Klages, 4
288 *"formulas of science"*: Klages, 4
288 *"days of Romanticism"*: Klages, 7
288 *"labor called 'progress' "*: Klages, 8
288 *"out of atoms"*: Klages, 10
288 *"blasphemous word individualism"*: Klages, 13
288 *"has come before"*: Klages, 11
289 *"of thought falls"*: Klages, 11
289 *"in the blood"*: Klages, 12
289 *"into conceptual mummies"*: Klages, 17
289 *"tuned fundamental condition"*: Klages, 14
289 *"the circle: Spirit"*: Klages, 14
289 *"flights of birds"*: Klages, 23
289 "Germany's Protestant regions": Klages, 37
290 "George's poetry grows": Klages, 37
290 *"under the guillotine"*: Klages, 32
290 *"full of admiration"*: FG/KW, 1:121
290 *"is in ecstasy"*: FG/KW, 1:143
290 *"of their lives!"*: FG/KW, 1:142
290 *"have a 'tone'!"*: AV/SG, 105
291 *"WORTHY of him"*: SG/FG, 100
291 *"the poet George"*: cf. SG/FG, 100
291 *"most satisfying publication"*: Berliner-Tageblatt, 31 December 1900

CHAPTER 21: THE COSMIC CIRCLE
292 *"year in Berlin"*: FG/KW, 1:89
293 "Zeus of Schwabing": Von der Leyen, 106
293 *"away from Berlin"*: FG/KW, 1:84–85
293 *of the Curetes:* The Curetes were semidivine beings inhabiting Crete who protected the baby Zeus from Cronus by dancing about him and noisily clattering their weapons; they were often seen together with Corybants, who celebrated the Phrygian goddess Cybele in a state of wild abandon, accompanied by music and ecstatic dances. See the *Oxford Classical Dictionary.*
293 *"basis of life"*: FG/KW, 1:85
293 *a "delusional construction"*: FG/KW, 1:90
293 *"where we admire!"*: FG/KW, 1:93
294 *"easy to make"*: Wolfskehl to George, 17 June 1899, SG-Archiv
295 *"the Latin headings"*: Schuler to George, 20 June 1899, SG-Archiv
295 *a "castrated swastika"*: AS, 55

295 *expansively called "immortal"*: see AS, 221
296 *"high-flown nonsense"*: Bachofen, 2:1071; see also 2:1067
296 *"male-phallic principle"*: Bachofen, 1:47–48
296 *the "phallic master"*: Bachofen, 1:45
296 *"non-corporeal nature"*: Bachofen, 1:199
297 *"subordination to Man"*: Bachofen, 1:226
297 *the female "sex"*: Bachofen, 1:268
297 *"and intellectual perfection"*: Bachofen, 1:214
297 *"male, phallic nature"*: Bachofen, 1:44
297 *"ancient world itself"*: Bachofen, 1:58
298 *"became even older"*: LC, 252
299 *"was an Orphic"*: LC, 252
299 *"in the individual"*: AS, 168
299 *"would be dead"*: AS, 169
299 *"world-creating principle"*: AS, 169
299 *"sexes within it"*: AS, 170
300 *"numbers of boys"*: AS, 184
300 *"of the ancestors"*: AS, 193
300 *"of the dead"*: AS, 196
300 *"sperm in general"*: AS, 201
300 *"ideal sexual act"*: AS, 201
300 *"of the phallus"*: AS, 220
300 *"were totally unknown"*: AS, 219
300 *"as a symbol"*: SL, 48
301 *"purpose or goal"*: SL, 49
301 *"of physical life"*: Bachofen, 2:683
301 *"its original purity"*: Bachofen, 2:805
301 *"of approaching perfection"*: Bachofen, 2:805–06
302 *"worlds dazzling red?"*: SG, 4:86
302 *"it was stupendous!"*: FG/KW, 1:100
302 *"out everything foreign"*: AS, 73
303 *"lose his composure"*: AS, 73
303 *"robbing consciousness, transporting"*: AS, 73
303 *"up, inwardly restless"*: AS, 73
303 *"mysticism and occultism"*: cf. RB T, 201–02
303 *"about supernatural phenomena"*: EL, 36
303 *"of the spirit"*: EL, 36
304 *"that* not *insane?"*: SL, 49
304 *or Schuler's sense:* see Huch, 12
304 *"Yahweh or Baal"*: FG/KW, 1:174
305 *the following year:* see KW Katalog, 228
305 *"was a Zionist"*: AS, 56
305 *this "diplomatic mission"*: FG/KW, 1:119
305 *"more about that"*: FG/KW, 1:119

305 *"you about that"*: FG/KW, 1:157
305 *King of Damascus*: see SG/FG, 137
306 *"name was—Wolfskehl"*: AS, 75
306 *"punishable by death"*: von Reventlow, 108
306 *efforts in Jerusalem*: see Huch, 46
306 *the "cosmic meadow"*: Huch, 46
307 *"the Schwabing brewery"*: Huch, 46
307 *"place of spirits"*: ES, 192
307 *"you to Judas?"*: AS, 75
307 *"one-on-one"*: RB 2, 106
308 *"feeling of alienation"*: RB 2, 106–07
308 *"for the* Blätter*"*: RB 2, 107
308 *"repugnant to me!"*: RB 2, 107
308 *"human relationship impossible"*: RB 2, 107
308 *"regarded as* broken*"*: AS, 76
308 *"great personal danger"*: AS, 82
308 *"happened at all"*: David, 217–18
309 *in the leg*: see SG/FG, 171
309 *"revolver, the revolver!"*: Hanna Wolfskehl to George, 10 January 1906, SG-Archiv
309 *and transcribed lectures*: see Klages, foreword to AS, n.p.
309 *the first time*: see RB 2, 249–50

CHAPTER 22: BOYS: GOOD, BAD, AND DIVINE

310 *"to unprophetic minds"*: SG/FG, 146
310 *"out of fear"*: SG/FG, 146
310 *"it stirred up"*: SG/FG, 146
310 *"doubted Schuler's omniscience!"*: SG/FG, 146
311 *"world they combat"*: FG/KW, 1:159
311 *"and enticing insanity"*: FG/KW, 1:159
311 *"packages are arriving"*: SG/FG, 71
311 *"your loyal D."*: SG/FG, 73
311 *"forget me entirely!"*: SG/FG, 74
311 *"together in Munich!"*: SG/FG, 77
312 *"he did lie"*: cited in SG/FG, 95
312 *"relationship to it"*: SG/FG, 95
313 *whole felt "unwashed"*: SG/FG, 96
313 *"left with difficulty"*: SG/FG, 95
313 *"it may hang"*: SG/FG, 96
313 *"committed some stupidity"*: FG/KW, 1:122
313 *"censure me for"*: SG/FG, 102
314 *George's continuing "silence"*: SG/FG, 115
314 *"on your estimation"*: SG/FG, 116
315 *"of sunny down"*: SG, 6–7:66
315 *"the blossoming mouth"*: SG, 6–7:67

315 *"want to rejoice"*: SG, 6–7:68
315 *"upon my knees"*: SG, 6–7:69
315 *"the blue snow"*: SG, 6–7:70
315 *"of the lip"*: SG, 6–7:71
315 *"a foreign spirit"*: SG, 6–7:72
315 *"spent for you?"*: SG, 6–7:72
315 *"to a graveyard"*: SG, 6–7:74
315 only *"funeral bells"*: SG, 6–7:76
316 *"moved me... Farewell!"*: SG, 6–7:76
316 *"for the Master"*: SG/FG, 128
316 *"very great things"*: SG/FG, 132
316 be *"extraordinarily talented"*: SG/FG, 140
316 *"sloppy and uncleaned"*: SG/FG, 140
317 *"no way out"*: SG/FG, 143
317 *"friend my beloved!"*: SG/FG, 143
317 *"only disappoint us"*: SG/FG, 144
318 *"powerful verse form"*: Fischer, 86
318 *"your artistic existence"*: SG/HvH, 148–49
319 *"for business reasons"*: SG/HvH, 149–50
319 *"the evasive one"*: SG/HvH, 150
319 *"you alone responsible"*: SG/HvH, 150
320 *"made on me"*: SG/HvH, 151
320 *"come to you"*: SG/HvH, 152
320 *"tastelessness and crudity"*: SG/HvH, 153
321 *"genuine, fakes it"*: SG/HvH, 153–54
321 *"precisely the opposite"*: SG/HvH, 158
321 *"itself) with them"*: SG/HvH, 159
321 *"you knew them"*: SG/HvH, 159
321 *"your hopes on"*: SG/HvH, 160
322 *"an oral discussion"*: SG/HvH, 162
322 *"gloomily into myself"*: SG/HvH, 164–65
323 *"a certain rootlessness"*: SG/HvH, 166
323 *"which you intimate"*: SG/HvH, 169
323 Gundolf as *"ordinary"*: SG/HvH, 208
324 *"it is performed"*: SG/HvH, 224
324 *"real powder kegs"*: SG/HvH, 226
324 *"spiritual values again"*: SG/HvH, 226–27
324 *"misunderstand one another"*: SG/HvH, 227
324 *"claim for damages"*: SG/HvH, 227–28
325 *"absolutely no right"*: SG/HvH, 229
326 *"the New Man"*: Wolfskehl to George, 11 July 1902, SG-Archiv
327 *"speak to him"*: SG, 17:75
327 *"or approach him"*: HB, 34–35
327 *"inclinations and tendencies"*: M, 12

327 *"a single page"*: M, 12
327 *of his peers:* see M, 7
328 *and Aristotle's* Poetics: see M, 13–14
328 *"I was overjoyed"*: M, 25
328 *was "quite nice"*: M, 25
328 *"had now begun"*: M, 25–26
329 *"come and gone"*: M, 26, with some variations in SG, 6–7:101
329 *hermaphrodites and hetaerae:* see Reventlow, 110
329 *"and so on"*: Reventlow, 50
330 *sacrifice of children:* see *Scriptores Historiae Augustae,* 118–19
330 *he was "amazed"*: M, 35
330 *"beautiful naked boys"*: SL, 23
330 *"off your clothes!"*: Huch, 39
330 *"think, the Master!"*: Huch, 39
330 *"something for you!"*: Huch, 39
330 *own house again:* see Huch, 40
331 *in Dionysian abandon:* Fuchs, 134
331 *not his calling:* Huch, 52
331 *"Romans and Greeks?"*: Reventlow, 51
332 *"his aesthetic one"*: KW Katalog, 187
332 *and to Maximilian:* see the long note for p. 184 in ES, 331
332 *at their home:* see M, 46–47
332 *"into his house"*: M, 49
332 *"the arranged time"*: M, 50
333 *"there every Sunday)"*: M, 105
333 *"higher than love?"*: M, 51
333 *"to him again"*: Kronberger to Oskar Dietrich, 30 January 1904, SG-Archiv
334 *an "unpleasant shadow"*: M, 108
334 *"in my poems"*: M, 121
334 *"the Female Beloved"*: M, 128–29

CHAPTER 23: MAXIMIN

335 *in his hair:* KB 1, 15
335 *"and in despair"*: SG/FG, 153
336 *"through the images"*: ES, 196
336 *"the final chasms"*: SL, 9
336 *"over our friend"*: SL, 57
336 *"for the world"*: SL, 57
336 *"opinion it deserved"*: AV, 47
337 *"through his person"*: AV, 46
337 *"case with suspicion"*: SG/ML, 240–41
338 *"of supersexual Love"*: SG, 12:5
338 *"most secret marriage"*: SG, 6–7:118

339 *"in the dream"*: SG, 6–7:119
339 *"Whom I worship"*: SG, 6–7:96
339 *"a religious significance"*: Morwitz, 109
339 *"of earthly existence"*: FW, 314
340 *"a holy heart"*: SG, 6–7:98–99
340 *"down and pray!"*: SG, 6–7:100
340 *"among the living"*: SG, 6–7:102
340 *"from the forest"*: SG, 6–7:103
340 *"days are barren"*: SG, 6–7:104
340 *"god has lived!"*: SG, 6–7:105
341 *"the holy voice"*: SG, 6–7:122–23
342 *"a smaller surface"*: Curtius, 153
342 *"our immediate future"*: SG, 17:74
342 *"this entire race"*: SG, 17:74
343 *"commander's absolute power"*: SG, 17:75
343 his *"heroic soul"*: SG, 17:76
343 *"to be ruler"*: SG, 17:76
343 *"of our continents"*: SG, 17:78
344 *"conquer new realms"*: SG, 17:75
344 *"himself to mortals"*: SG, 17:78
344 *"and radiant beauty"*: SG, 17:81–82
345 *"for my blindness"*: SG/FG, 160–61
345 *"gentian to flower"*: Lepsius, 216 (also slightly modified in SL, 60–61)
345 *"we wandered around"*: SG/FG, 167
346 *"of Cosmic secrets"*: EM 1, 75
346 him *"the mollusk"*: LT, 84
347 *"think he's insane"*: SG/FG, 166
347 put it, *"impatient"*: RB 2, 7
347 *"in his hand"*: RB 2, 7
348 *"loyal like Gundolf"*: Robert Boehringer, 24 December 1905, SG-Archiv
348 Roman legal language: cf. LT, 20
349 of Fanny Ritter: cf. KH 1, 26
349 surrounding the city: cf. LT, 11
349 *"sheik or sultan"*: ES, 80
350 *"seeds have sprouted"*: ML 2, 49

CHAPTER 24: *THE SEVENTH RING*

351 *"year of misfortune"*: SG/FG, 154; see also FG/KW, 1:211
351 *"fate against him"*: FG/KW, 1:215
352 *"disbelief in magic"*: SG/FG, 159
352 *"the coming year"*: FG/KW, 2:21
352 *"if distant clan"*: FG/KW, 2:21
352 *"this a poem?"*: SS, 62
352 *"of its tone"*: SS, 62

353 *"one suspects it"*: SL, 11
354 *"flows through you"*: SG/FG, 147
354 *"being for another"*: Scott to George, 7 November 1904, SG-Archiv
354 his *"friend's abnormalities"*: Scott, *Bone of Contention*, 108
354 *"of ten women' "*: Scott to George, 7 November 1904, SG-Archiv
355 *"sustained in Munich"*: Scott, *Bone of Contention*, 109–10
355 *"translated them yourself!"*: Scott, *Bone of Contention*, 110
355 *"of the Seer"*: BfdK 7:11
355 *"perfect in itself"*: BfdK 7:5
356 *"that of catholicism"*: BfdK 7:8
356 *"aestheticians remain barbarians"*: BfdK 7:9
356 the *"mawkish bourgeoisie"*: BfdK 7:1
356 *"secret circles (cenacles)"*: BfdK 7:3
356 *"and aesthetic people"*: Verzeichnis der Erscheinungen der Blaetter fuer die Kunst, Berlin 1904
356 *"before the master"*: BfdK 7:5
357 *"the eternal fire"*: BfdK 7:11
358 *"and no further"*: BV, 31
359 *"such simple people!"*: SG/FG, 178
359 *"way life is"*: EL, 78
360 *"most powerful book"*: Borchardt, 289
361 *a logical choice*: Morwitz, 90
361 *seven individual components*: David, 202
361 *"sections of trees"*: EM 3, 28
361 *"over the five"*: Bachofen, 1:212
361 *"and intellectual perfection"*: Bachofen, 1:186
362 *"the Chosen One"*: SG, 6–7:48–49
363 *"the same thing"*: SG, 6–7:7
363 *"spreads molten fire"*: SG, 6–7:6–7
364 *"forced to die"*: SG/FG, 136
364 *"was born hell"*: SG, 6–7:9
365 *"an unrecognized king"*: SG, 6–7:10–11
365 *"him with praise"*: SG, 6–7:12
366 *"into the sea"*: SG, 6–7:30–31
366 *"to his toe"*: SG, 6–7:38
367 *"of the Heroes"*: SG, 6–7:63
368 *"from new love"*: SG, 6–7:21
368 *their marching song*: cf. EM 1, 250
368 *"do the deed"*: SG, 6–7:208
369 *"peacefully passed away"*: SG/FG, 182
369 *"do everything myself!"*: SG/ML, 280
369 *"trip to Switzerland"*: AV/SG, 147
369 *"it might be"*: AV, 53
370 *"among his enemies"*: AV, 55

370 *"to have style"*: LT, 26
370 *"of its victory"*: Mockel, 395
371 *"stand their faces"*: EL, 67
371 *"out its verdict?"*: ES, 262
371 *"sense his war"*: TM/EB, 49

CHAPTER 25: ADMISSION TO THE ORDER

395 *in the capital:* GB, 9
395 *"tennis tournament player"*: GB, 9
395 *"never seen him"*: BV, 26
395 *"in the circle"*: BV, 26
397 *"by such flames"*: Albert Rausch to George, May/June 1907, SG-Archiv. The lines Rausch quotes are from *The Year of the Soul;* cf. SG, 4:111.
397 *"forever with you"*: Morwitz to George, 29 January 1908, SG-Archiv
397 *"who selfishly desires"*: BfdK 5:10
397 stands totally *"naked"*: BfdK 5:11
398 *"vouch for you"*: BfdK 5:12
398 *"of all action"*: BfdK 5:15
398 *twice a week:* cf. Z, 11 February 1903
398 *"drama through verse"*: BfdK 4, 5:130
398 *"a solemn litany"*: RB 2, 8
399 *"a narrow range"*: HB, 30
399 *"some real work"*: BV, 44
399 *"have done it"*: LT, 21
399 *"that already existed"*: SG/HvH, 220
400 *"is entirely un-bourgeois"*: AV/SG, 129
400 *"to be read?"*: HS, 5
400 *"lowering the tone"*: EM 1, 111
402 *Master had ended:* ES, 16–18
402 *"the highest law"*: BfdK 8:2
403 *"never read otherwise"*: BfdK 8:3
403 *"generates substantial profit"*: BfdK 8:6
403 *"of our culture"*: LT, 23
403 *"time is impossible"*: AV, 59
403 *"his lyric art"*: KB 1, 15
403 *"theater I need"*: ES, 210
404 *"for the future"*: LT, 24

CHAPTER 26: THE *FÜHRER* AND HIS *REICH*

405 *"our secession painters"*: RB 2, 136
406 *"for the Whole"*: RB 2, 137
407 *"'mysterious systematic quality'"*: cf. Z, 13 July 1909
408 *"destruction and misinterpretation"*: FG 2, 91
408 *"Allegiance and Discipleship"*: Actually, the essay first appeared in the separate

publication of the third volume "selections" from the *Blätter* which came out in 1909. In this case, however, the volume also contained works published there for the first time, such as the piece by Gundolf.

409 *"and almost ridiculous":* BfdK 8:107
409 *"himself a Disciple":* BfdK 8: 109
410 *"of his power":* BfdK 8:110
410 *"the higher flame":* BfdK 8:111
410 *"a hyperactive vanity":* BfdK 8:111
410 *"sayer and doer":* BfdK 8:106
411 *"again to sacrifice":* BfdK 8:112
411 *of "false discipleship":* BfdK 8:107
411 *"the holy war":* BfdK 8:108–09
412 *"its resolute combativeness":* BV, 38
412 *the previous April:* cf. KH 1, 39
412 *"the entire work":* SG Katalog, 249
413 *"Master and Disciple":* KH 1, 39
413 *"and is perfect":* EL, 23
414 *"by the Ruler":* Wolters, 9–10
414 *"language or number":* Wolters, 11
414 *"of S[tefan] G[eorge]":* see Z, 3 May 1909
414 *"him more deeply":* Wolters, 12
415 *"in the child":* Wolters, 14
415 *"form of rule":* EL, 45
416 *"time to govern":* AvB, 40

CHAPTER 27: THE GLOBE ROOM

417 *"nimbus surrounded him":* AvB, 38
417 *"love seldom bridges":* ES, 205
417 *"seemed to me":* HB, 25
418 *"one, or mine":* AV, 60
418 *"only be poets":* AV, 62
418 *"a divine being":* AV, 62
419 *"exercise that influence":* AV, 63
419 *"a long shot":* AvB, 38
419 *"the coming war":* SG/FG, 198–99
419 *"Your masterly Goodness":* Ernst Schertel to George, 3 March 1910, SG-Archiv
420 *"beget in you":* Groppe, 343
420 *"property and wife":* Hermann Bodeck, 12 April 1911, SG-Archiv
420 *"and poetic days":* RB 1, 159
421 *in ancient Greece:* cf. LT, 51
421 *"Room in Munich":* EL, 132
421 *"of his being":* HB, 35
421 *"the entire furnishings":* LT, 51
422 *instantly recognized, "Maximin":* HS, 6

422 *"a distant land"*: LT, 51
422 *"many altars stand!"*: CP 21, 28
422 *"permitted to interfere"*: HB, 25
422 *what was read*: cf. LT, 56
423 *"inflected, barely modulated"*: HS, 7
423 *"of the nineties"*: FG 1, 71
423 *way to him*: BV, 37
423 *"unexpected distant impact"*: FG 1, 74
423 *"one should approach"*: FG 1, 80
423 *"to be sympathetic"*: FG 1, 82
424 *"you a standard"*: HS, 5
424 *"death-like face"*: HS, 6
424 *his own wedding*: HS, 8
425 *" 'made of him!' "*: HS, 8
425 *"in his image"*: HS, 9
425 *"of the visible"*: HS, 9
425 *"by the mahatmas"*: HS, 13
425 *"a primitive tribe"*: HS, 12–13
426 *"the first initiation"*: HS, 15
426 *"be shown around"*: HS, 14
426 *"and his courting"*: HS, 14
427 *"you — nothing more"*: SG, 8:106
427 *"the little wonder"*: EM 1, 398. The person in question was Jean-François Gravelet, a French acrobat who achieved notoriety in 1859 by being the first person to cross Niagara Falls on a tightrope.

CHAPTER 28: SECRET GERMANY

429 *"of his dangerousness"*: Y, 1:65
429 *he was "delighted"*: see KH 1, 48
429 *broadly "descriptive nature"*: SG/HvH, 79
429 *"important young scholars"*: SG/HvH, 110
429 *"often mentioned* Yearbook*"*: SG/HvH, 189
429 *"go to Berlin"*: SG/HvH, 196–97
429 *"works of combat"*: ES, 129
430 *"wary of them"*: EL, 182
430 *"to the people"*: LT, 36
431 *"weak and cowardly"*: KH 1, 49; the line from *The Tapestry of Life* is in SG, 5:33.
431 *"all hits home"*: KH 1, 49
431 *"name as necessary"*: KH 1, 49–50
431 *"the Master himself"*: KH 1, 49
431 *final page proofs*: cf. ES, 325 n. 3 to page 129
431 *"name very much"*: AV, 50
431 *"than through spirit?"*: KH 1, 49
432 *"will — an Idea"*: Y, 1:i

432 *"to celebrate illogicality"*: David, "Le *Jahrbuch für die geistige Bewegung*, 280–81
433 *called "our movement"*: Y, 1:1
433 *"accursed nineteenth century"*: Y, 1:7
433 *"we now stand"*: Y, 1:1
433 *"sound the same"*: Y, 1:6
434 *"Evil, Algabal was"*: EL, 100
434 *"and repulsive reality"*: Y, 1:14
434 *" 'reason,' 'freedom,' 'humanity' "*: Y, 1:7
434 *"have arisen organically"*: Y, 1:9
434 *"least embryonic form"*: Y, 1:9
434 *"the last time"*: Y, 1:14–15
434 *"may still hope"*: Y, 1:16
434 *"be of tomorrow"*: Y, 1:17
435 *"of our lives"*: Y, 1:18
435 *that predated George:* see Peter Hoffmann, 64
436 *out of favor:* see KH 1, 29–30
436 *"most profound belief"*: Y, 1:35
436 *"in Germany today"*: Y, 1:21
436 *"the coming faith"*: Y, 1:48
437 *"destroyed or converted"*: Y, 1:47–48
437 *"an ancient anguish"*: Y, 1:48
437 *"to accept it!"*: FG 1, 155–56
437 *"what is raw"*: Y, 1:70
437 *"bourgeois in costume"*: Y, 1:78
438 *"a fuss about"*: Y, 1:86
438 *Wit"—and "Wilamops"*: cf. Goldsmith, "Wilamowitz and the *Georgekreis*," 586
439 *"mouse-gray of impotence"*: Goldsmith, "Wilamowitz and the *Georgekreis*," 587–88
439 *"on Nietzsche's coattails"*: ES, 251
439 *"as latrine buckets!"*: EL, 95
439 *"a good figure"*: EL, 158
439 *"and glowing flame"*: SG/FG, 93
439 *"Plato for maids"*: KH 1, 55n
439 *"dementia praecox philologica"*: Gundolf to Hildebrandt, 4 February 1911, SG-Archiv
440 *"through something human"*: Curtius, 114
440 *"flesh and blood"*: ES, 45
440 *"by empty science"*: ES, 45
440 *"the critical yearbook?"*: SG/FW, 74
440 *" 'Guidelines' is excellent' "*: SG/FW, 75
441 *"to known laws"*: Y, 1:130
441 *"but from creation"*: Y, 1:132
441 *"are your boundaries!"*: Y, 1:140
441 *"the lowest procreation"*: Y, 1:140

441 *"in a system"*: Y, 1:144
441 *"of sensuous blood"*: Y, 1:145
442 *"what is living"*: Y, 1:145

CHAPTER 29: AFTER THE *YEARBOOK*

443 *"injured are howling!"*: SG/FG, 201
443 *"its very existence"*: Gundolf to Hildebrandt, 29 June 1910, SG-Archiv
444 *sent to him:* cf. Z, 7 March 1910
444 *"friendly as well"*: FG/KW, 2:86
444 *the "spiritual movement"*: cf. Z, 26 March 1910
444 *"point in history"*: SG/FG, 200
444 *"and to be"*: SG/FG, 200–201
445 *"and political importance"*: FG 1, 151–52
446 *"point of ideology"*: Albert Rausch to George, 26 December 1910, SG-Archiv
446 *"a new one"*: Wolters to Gundolf, 8 April 1910, FGA
446 *"but rather battle!"*: Wolters to Gundolf, 3 May 1911, FGA
447 *"then lost them"*: KB 1, 18
447 *"softly against mine"*: KB 1, 17
447 *"Only peripheral ones"*: KB 1, 18–19
447 *"We were friendly"*: KB 1, 21
448 *"Paris are perversions"*: Sabine Lepsius to Gundolf, 1 August 1910, FGA
449 *"be interpreted thus"*: FG 2, 66
449 *"profit and loss"*: FG 2, 66–68
449 *"in the* Yearbook*"*: FG 2, 69
450 *"place of women"*: Y, 1:82
450 *"nonworld or transworld"*: Y, 1:5
450 *"necessarily be inferior"*: BfdK 9:2
451 *"on this subject"*: Wolfskehl to George, 7 July 1910, SG-Archiv
451 *"not very important"*: FG/KW, 2:87
451 *under Paragraph 175:* see Hull, 132–42
452 *"of the group"*: Hull, 53
452 *in Harden's acquittal:* Hull, 138
452 *the late 1880s:* Hull, 138
452 *"done anything dirty"*: Hull, 138
452 *"Moltke, Maximilian Harden"*: BV, 25
452 *"of the scandalmongers"*: BV, 97
453 *"the Harden trials"*: FG 2, 67–68
453 *"for the war"*: FG 2, 71
453 *"a certain point"*: EL, 81
454 *"the right progeny"*: RB 2, 127
454 *"suited to it"*: EL, 157
454 *"in the background"*: RB 2, 137
454 *"instead of sewing"*: ES, 198
454 *"pleasant without it"*: EL, 56

455 *"doesn't involve her"*: EL, 80–81
455 *"easily dominates others"*: Thormaehlen folder "Geheimnis," SG-Archiv
455 *"emancipation of women"*: ML 1, 31
455 *"based liberal individualism"*: Evans, 3
455 *"that of women?"*: EL, 68
455 *"half past ten"*: cf. Z, 216
455 *"toward the unspiritual"*: SL, 80
456 *"children bursting in"*: SL, 84
456 was her *"conscientiousness"*: SL, 81
456 *"there for you"*: SL, 84
456 *"demonstratively to Reinhold"*: SL, 91–92
456 saying *"of course"*: SL, 93

CHAPTER 30: HEIDELBERG

457 *"here this winter"*: SG/FG, 204
457 *"have believed it"*: EG, 22
457 *"me to science"*: ES, 49
458 "teacher of science": Paulsen, 203
458 *"Riviera of Heidelberg"*: Marianne Weber, 362
458 easy, unconstrained manner: see Tompert, 11
458 doubled, reaching 2,668: Tompert, 17
459 Oxford in England: cf. Groppe, 568
459 *"days and nights"*: Groppe, 568
459 high as 10,000: Tompert, 36
459 *"the washing, sewing"*: Marianne Weber, 298
459 a *"millionaire's palace"*: Tompert, 38
460 *"now and again"*: Tompert, 30
460 *"amount to anything"*: Tompert, 39
460 unbecoming, indeed *"unprofessorial"*: Tompert, 39
460 *"be a professor"*: Tompert, 29
460 *"him than instruction"*: Paulsen, 213
460 *"never take it"*: Benz, 93
461 *"be very pleased"*: FG 1, 164
461 *"growing a beard"*: FG 1, 176
461 *"can go wrong"*: FG 1, 183
461 *"under my hands"*: SG/FG, 204
462 *"come from you"*: SG/FG, 206
462 *"theoretical 'Imperial' nature"*: SG/FG, 207
462 *"and remains good"*: SG/FG, 209
462 *"my dearest Gundel"*: SG/FG, 211
463 *"reverence and fidelity"*: SG/FG, 211
463 *"your brilliant work"*: FG 1, 194
463 *"fact applied metaphysics"*: FG 1, 194–95
464 *"never showy scholarship"*: Gothein, 199–200

464 *"who wrote it"*: Gothein, 201
465 *"Do you understand?"*: SG/FG, 224
465 *"the most talented"*: KH 1, 70
465 *to the others*: LT, 36
465 *"that you exist"*: EL, 29
466 *"something very beautiful"*: EL, 29
466 *"rest is 'education' "*: ES, 36
466 *"new elemental sound!"*: ES, 71
466 *be the Master*: cf. ES, 71
466 *"it is science"*: ES, 48
467 *"the vulgar aspects"*: SG/FG, 204–205
467 *make him "vain"*: SG/FG, 205
467 *"saying anything, either)"*: SG/FG, 205
467 *"this strange man"*: CP 1, 5
468 *"done something wrong"*: CP 1, 6
468 *only: "That's fine"*: CP 1, 6
468 *"of the others"*: CP 1, 6
468 *"hard to resist"*: SG/FG, 220
469 *"only about him!"*: SG/FG, 222
469 *"undisciplined and inchoate"*: SG/FG, 225
469 *"one of Greece"*: CP 1, 8–9
469 *was,* was *Greece*: see EM 1, 228
470 *"comment you've made"*: CP 1, 9
470 *"had been set"*: CP 1, 11–12
470 *"all the faithful"*: CP 1, 12
470 *"he who lost"*: CP 1, 14. The lines are part of a poem in *The Star of the Covenant* (*Der Stern des Bundes*), SG, 8:60.
471 *"that unavoidable picture"*: CP II, 7
471 *"loves the image"*: CP II, 8

CHAPTER 31. *THE STAR OF THE COVENANT*

472 *"of his mother"*: SG/FG, 226
473 *"richness of existence"*: FG 1, 196
473 *as "my Heidelberg"*: FG 1, 199
473 *"the very most"*: FG 2, 141
473 *modest three hundred*: Groppe, 589
473 *"never became one"*: ES, 64
473 *"I remain 'scientific' "*: FG 1, 235
474 *"reader's rapid pace"*: ES, 64
474 *"only too much"*: FG 1, 195
474 *"curiosity and reverence"*: cited after Groppe, 589
474 *win his approval*: ES, 25
475 *day and time*: cf. ES, 31
475 *"to walk by"*: Benjamin, *Schriften*, II/2, 622

475 *"the Secret Germany"*: ES, 12
476 *"in the shade"*: Gothein, 149
476 *"rather as will"*: SG/FG, 213
476 *"of this man"*: SG/FG, 229
476 *"become a myth"*: Gothein, 150
477 *"he may be"*: Marianne Weber, 464–65
477 *"on the grotesque"*: Max Weber, 6:559
477 *"quite simply absurd"*: Max Weber, 6:560
477 a *"foreign body"*: Max Weber, 6:562
478 *"had first fled"*: Max Weber, 6:561
478 *"dignity and geniality"*: Marianne Weber, 468
478 *"is their 'faith' "*: Marianne Weber, 469
478 *"to be present"*: Marianne Weber, 470
479 *"assumption was false"*: EL, 157
479 *"what we want"*: Marianne Weber, 470
479 *"destroy the body"*: Marianne Weber, 471
479 *"more polite form"*: EL, 157–58
480 *"would be solved"*: EL, 64
480 *"brings to fruition"*: EL, 197
480 *"for the Greeks"*: ES, 275
481 *"to modern life"*: Marianne Weber, 470
481 *"not a politician"*: EL, 157
481 *"of them together"*: Curtius, 113
481 *"new war plans"*: FG 1, 167
481 *"the right path"*: Y, 2:3
482 perpetrator had been: cf. ES, 208
482 *"on this way"*: Y, 3:iii
483 *"of heroic love"*: Y, 3:vii
483 *"modernizes the people"*: Y, 3:vii
483 *"feminine, corrosive ones"*: Y, 3:vi
483 *"World against World"*: Y, 3:viii
484 *"things upside down"*: EL, 44
484 *"freedom and justice"*: ES, 216
484 *"of American civilization"*: EL, 165
484 *"criteria of evaluation"*: EL, 56
484 *"ist ein Amerikaner!"*: Scott, *Die Tragödie*, 49
485 *"poison and fire"*: Y, 3:v
485 *"make war dispensable"*: Y, 2:25
485 *"acceptable to him"*: Y, 3:142
485 *"part of humanity"*: Y, 3:143
485 *"a necessary sacrifice"*: Y, 3:145
486 *"enslave its remnants"*: Y, 3:147
486 *"only for her"*: Y, 3:149
486 *"nor in censure"*: Y, 3:149–50

486 *"of your youth"*: Y, 3:151
486 *"the spiritual deed"*: Y, 3:153
487 *"inciting class hatred"*: KH 1, 78
488 *"and the occult"*: Z, 22 September 1909
488 *"mysticism and banality"*: Z, 235
488 *"(literary) new births"*: SG/FG, 245
488 *"Lechter's India book!"*: Curtius, 114
488 *"I'll choose Nero"*: EL, 99–100
488 *"a single syllable"*: ML 1, 60
488 *"the broader public"*: ML 2, 18
489 *"done with it"*: RB 2, 79
489 *"out of it!"*: ML 2, 19
489 *"of the person"*: Hans Hesse to SG, 17 May 1917, SG-Archiv
489 *"been very good"*: Marguerite Hoffmann, 49
490 *"by my nature"*: RB 2, 81
490 cried: *"That's Stefan!"*: EL, 123
490 would see him: see EL, 123–24
491 *"fully revealed themselves"*: LT, 106
491 *"of the Circle"*: ES, 239
492 *"end and middle"*: SG, 8:8
492 *"of my child"*: SG, 8:14
492 *"most secret marriage"*: SG, 6–7:118
492 *"fusion become flesh"*: SG, 8:9
493 *"dream became flesh"*: SG, 8:26
493 *"of the god"*: SG, 8:8
493 *"beautiful and glorious"*: SG, 8:16
493 *"and a beginning"*: SG, 8:27
493 *"night and nothingness"*: SG, 8:31
494 *"the holy war"*: SG, 8:31
494 *of later events:* thus FW, 401, and Gundolf, *George*, 251
495 *"think and are"*: SG, 8:33
495 *"nothing but decay"*: SG, 8:35
495 *"stone may stand"*: SG, 8:36
495 were *"dust-traps"*: ES, 37
495 *"it by heart!"*: ES, 267
496 *"free and naked"*: SG, 8:47; on the relation of Maximin to these lines, see EM 1, 365
496 *"of our people!"*: SG, 8:15
496 *"book of initiation"*: David, 286
496 *with Ernst Morwitz:* see EM 1, 365
496 *"in the wound"*: SG, 8:52
496 *"myself in you"*: SG, 8:59
497 *"same royal house"*: SG, 8:56
498 *"of the world"*: SG, 8:83

498 *"gave myself away"*: SG, 8:63
498 *"of your heart?"*: SG, 8:64
498 *"short and burning"*: SG, 8:72
498 *"of all coverings"*: SG, 8:71
499 *"trouble and danger"*: SG, 8:72
499 *"You toward death!"*: SG, 8:75
499 *"wreath of laurel"*: SG, 8:92
499 *"of their eyes"*: SG, 8:85
499 *"of the flame!"*: SG, 8:84
499 *"bond of ore"*: SG, 8:93
499 *"your own sword"*: SG, 8:93
500 *"to the monkey!"*: SG, 8:86
500 *"most characteristic secret"*: SG, 8:86
500 *"man and woman"*: SG, 8:96
500 *"has ripened us"*: SG, 8:114

CHAPTER 32: LEGENDS OF SUMMER

502 *flowers and greens:* see Zweig, 199
502 *"remember this summer!"*: Zweig, 203
502 *"looks simply beautiful"*: SG/FG, 251
503 *"great leisurely abandon"*: CP II, 18
503 *"harsh corporal punishment"*: CP II, 18–19
503 *"in fact necessary"*: CP II, 19
503 *"early Greek boy"*: CP II, 20
504 *"of this fussiness"*: SS, 88
504 *life-long companion:* for the information on Bertram and Glöckner, see EG, 14–15
504 *equally extravagant praise:* see BV, 33 and SS, 91
504 *"be a disciple"*: SS, 93
504 *was, "A werewolf!":* see EG, 224 n. 71
505 *a chosen jewel:* SS, 93
505 *as being "plain"*: ES, 244; see also 346
505 *was "unbelievably unfortunate"*: Z, 262
505 *"Too much* Geist*"*: EG, 32
505 *"an infinite abyss"*: EG, 23
506 *"and cursed myself"*: EG, 24
506 *"such things appear!"*: EG, 24
506 *"like a snake"*: EG, 24; see also 208 n. 8
506 *"that so quickly"*: EG, 25
507 *"is called silence"*: EG, 25
507 *"you read aloud"*: EG, 25
508 *"It was awful"*: EG, 26
508 *"what that means?"*: EG, 26
508 *"some personal interest"*: EG, 27
508 *"smiled on you"*: EG, 27

508 *find George "ridiculous"*: EG, 27
508 *"against the wall"*: EG, 28
508 *serious. "Terrible, terrible"*: EG, 29
508 *"already too determined"*: EG, 32
509 *"say to you"*: EG, 29
509 *"fear* and *cowardice"*: EG, 28
509 *added, "—and yet"*: EG, 33
509 *"surely means well"*: EG, 34
509 *"in his importance"*: EG, 47
509 *"is a prophet"*: EG, 48
510 *"read about him"*: BV, 81
510 *"sift through it"*: EL, 154
510 *"Cosmics and Maximin"*: ES, 331
510 *of the Covenant*: see SG, 8:73: "When you know me in my ultimate dignity / Have a sense of me in the rank assigned to me / Then will come the time when I give myself to you."
511 *"about it again"*: Glöckner to George, 1 August 1917, SG-Archiv
511 *"on his documents"*: BV, 34
511 *repertoire as well*: see LT, 99–100
512 *"be able to"*: CP 225, 57
512 *"of figurative truth"*: CP 225, 58
512 *"stood before me"*: Lessing, 309
512 *"in the summer"*: CP 225, 7
512 *the following year*: ES, 209; cf. also GPL 1, no. 387

CHAPTER 33: THE WAR AND SECRET GERMANY

514 *laid to rest*: see Zweig, 199–202
514 *with the Fatherland*: cf. Gilbert, 4
515 *"Germandom and Slavdom"*: cited from Hull, 241
515 *Holland and Belgium*: see Gilbert, 29
516 *last-minute alternative arrangements*: see EL, 12–19
517 *"war after all!"*: EL, 20
517 *" 'love and hate' "*: Tuchman, 124
517 *"from the trees"*: Tuchman, 119
517 *"value in itself"*: FG 2, 139
517 *"for our 'state' "*: SG/FG, 253
517 *"secret Germany, too"*: SG/FG, 254
517 *"to sixty hours"*: SG/FW, 103
517 *"along the route"*: SG/FW, 102
518 *"military trains don't"*: SG/FW, 102–103
518 *"papers with me)"*: SG/FG, 255
518 *"these days* HERE!*"*: SG/FG, 256
518 *"a German now"*: SG/FG, 258
518 *"not achieve it"*: FG 2, 143

518 *"of our Volk"*: FG/KW, 2:103
519 *"and its worth"*: SG/FW, 103–04
519 *"certainty of victory"*: SG/FW, 104
519 *"once brilliant world"*: SG/FW, 104
519 *"cross the border"*: SG/FG, 256
519 *"come ONLY AFTERWARD!!"*: SG/FG, 258
520 *"do the job"*: SG/FG, 260
520 *"later as well)"*: ES, 306 n. 1 to page 28
520 *"Gundolf as well"*: BV, 45
520 *"than before 1914?"*: ES, 27
521 *"if I could"*: SG/FG, 260
521 *"are absolutely unfit"*: FG/KW, 2:106
521 *"wounded in Kreuznach"*: SG/FG, 259
521 *"is he now?"*: SG/FG, 260
521 *"an impressive soldier"*: SG/FG, 262
521 *"are not there?"*: SG/FG, 260
522 *up in flames:* see Keegan, 82–83
522 *"abyss of hatred":* cited in Ullrich, 409
522 *"or of Attila?":* Romain Rolland, letter in *Frankfurter Zeitung,* 12 September 1914
523 *"necessity and conquest":* Karl Wolfskehl, letter in *Frankfurter Zeitung,* 12 September 1914
523 *"be our words":* Karl Wolfskehl, letter in *Frankfurter Zeitung,* 12 September 1914
523 *was a "blessing":* Friedrich Gundolf, "Tat und Wort im Krieg," *Frankfurter Zeitung,* 11 October 1914
524 *"enjoy the past":* Friedrich Gundolf, "Tat und Wort." It would appear significant that, without any explanation, this passage is left out of the only subsequent reproduction of the letter, published in Landmann.
524 *"decoration and enjoyment!":* Y, 3:6
524 *lost their vitality:* see SG, 8:35
524 *only "calorific value":* ES, 37
524 *"the secret Germany":* FG/KW, 2:108
525 *"such an article":* SG/FG, 266
525 *"Frf. Journal again!":* SG/FG, 267
525 *"of my essay":* SG/FG, 267
525 *"well-disposed bourgeoisie":* SG/FG, 268
525 *"do you think?":* SG/FG, 269–70
525 *"theosophists and suchlike":* SG/FG, 271
525 *"ineffectual and infertile":* EG, 56
525 *"by Wolfskehl, too":* TM/EB, 21
526 *"in public papers":* cited in Z, 254
526 *"the terrible events":* Gothein, 205
526 of the Covenant: ES, 28
526 *"a secret book":* SG, 8:5

{ NOTES }

527 *"by the poet"*: Johannes Nohl, "Deutschland und der Stern des Bundes," *Neue Zürcher Zeitung*, 31 December 1914.
527 *that an "outsider"*: SG/FW, 107
528 *"for an outsider"*: SG/FW, 108
528 *"that!' he said"*: EG, 73

CHAPTER 34: SURVIVING

529 *the heaviest artillery:* see Keegan, 310
530 *"worse in Belgium"*: SG/FW, 109
530 *made them necessary:* see Wolters to Gundolf, 12 September 1915, FGA
530 *fighting, Germany 241,000:* Keegan, 135–36
530 *age of twenty-two:* Keegan, 133
530 *"war must founder"*: FG I, 238
530 *"that is good"*: FG I, 240–41
531 *"be proven wrong"*: Robert Boehringer to George, 20 October 1914, SG-Archiv
531 *"in two nights"*: EG, 83
531 *"Sherlock Holmes novel"*: KH I, 101
531 *"to be something"*: BV, 94
531 Birth of Tragedy: see EG, 83
531 *"by this book"*: BV, 94
532 *"feeling of sorrow"*: SG/FG, 279
532 *summer of 1915:* EG, 62
532 *"by the war"*: EG, 61
533 *"depends on him"*: EG, 62–63
533 *do any work:* cf. EL, 28
533 *"to Germany's body"*: EL, 47
533 *"for the future"*: EG, 71
533 *"that exists, Ernst"*: EG, 71
534 *"end the war"*: Josef Liegle to George, 24 May 1916, SG-Archiv
534 *"peace—oh Master?"*: Hans Brasch to George, 24 September 1916, SG-Archiv
534 *"their own path"*: SG/FW, 124–25
534 *"Germany as well"*: EL, 32
534 *"the white race"*: HB, 29
535 *"a Chinese bishop"*: EL, 182
535 *"they think yellow"*: EL, 171
535 *"next fifty years"*: EL, 34
535 *"a rifle myself"*: ES, 260
535 *"Alexanderplatz in Berlin"*: HB, 29. In making this comment, George was perhaps playing a variation on a familar theme. Prince Metternich of Austria once similarly quipped that Asia began at the Rennweg, a road that leads eastward out of Vienna.
535 *"and European character"*: EL, 34
535 *"the 'phallic' element"*: BV, 61
535 *"worship of rot"*: EL, 168

535 *"cult of self-destruction"*: LT, 69
535 *"me feel ill"*: EL, 168
536 *"super-terrestrial reasons"*: SG/FG, 288
536 *"my intellectual abilities"*: FG 1, 270
536 *"any worry whatsoever"*: SG/FG, 289
537 *"a dozen professors"*: SG/FG, 290–91
537 *"the common soldier"*: SG/FG, 293
537 *"thunder of Verdun"*: SG/FG, 294–95
537 *"not yet comprehend"*: SG/FG, 295
537 *an enemy shell:* see ES, 124
537 *of his shoes:* see EM 1, 473
537 *"the Foreign Office"*: SG/FG, 296
538 *"and dirty jokes"*: FG 1, 271
538 *"a great deal"*: FG 1, 271–72
538 *"too after all"*: SG/FG, 300
539 *"the right one"*: SG/FG, 301
539 *"your own sword"*: SG, 8:93
540 *"and charming women"*: SL, 91
540 *"stay with him"*: KH 1, 70
540 *"as he said"*: EG, 70
540 *"out of it"*: SG/FG, 280
540 *in two years:* cf. Z, 272
541 *"cannot imagine. St. G."*: SG/FG, 304–05
541 *"loved very much"*: EL, 63
541 *"hardships of war"*: FG/KW, 1:139
542 *"me in court":* Gundolf to George, 13 January 1918, SG-Archiv. (This passage is left out of the letter reprinted in SG/FG, 313, with no indication of the omission.)
542 *"this first bleeding":* Gundolf to George, 25 February 1918, SG-Archiv (This passage, like the previous one, is also left out of the letter reprinted in SG/FG, 316–17, again with no indication of the omission.)
542 *that of 1914:* cf. Tucker, 209
542 *"children of whores"*: SL, 90
542 *"mutton and goat":* Julius Landmann to George, 1 May 1915, SG-Archiv
542 *"a mere 1,000":* cf. Tucker, 209
542 *"found any more":* Glöckner to George, 10 January 1917, SG-Archiv
543 *of hunger alone:* see Holborn, 460
543 *"sound too presumptuous"*: KB 1, 27
543 *"would do it"*: KB 1, 25–27
544 *"you are right"*: KB 1, 29
544 *"and more unfettered"*: KB 1, 39
544 *"be worth much"*: EL, 110
545 *"in its poverty"*: SG, 9:28
545 *"that moves you"*: SG, 9:29

{ NOTES }

545 *"else saw nothing"*: SG, 6–7:209
545 *"does not disappear"*: EL, 37
546 *"of Life itself?"*: SG, 9:29
546 *"sons and grandsons"*: SG, 9:29
547 *"be indiscriminately exterminated"*: SG, 9:30
547 *"and Semitic tribes"*: KH 2, 401
547 *"and black ones"*: Morwitz, 157–58
547 *and English armies*: cf. EM 1, 419
548 *"to be exterminated"*: ES, 262
548 *"will not die!"*: SG, 9:33
548 *"an entire river"*: SG, 9:30
548 *"right* this *time"*: EG, 96
548 *"is selling well"*: SG/FG, 309
549 *"merit and greatness"*: Gundolf, *Frankfurter Zeitung,* 10 October 1917, cited in SG Katalog, 267
549 *"a new world"*: SG Katalog, 268
550 *"well looked after"*: Boehringer to George, 25 February 1918, SG-Archiv
550 *"in those days"*: LT, 153
550 *"meat and fruit"*: Boehringer to George, 25 February 1918, SG-Archiv
550 *peelings and sawdust:* Much of this last paragraph is verbatim or close paraphrase from Gilbert, 395.
551 *"an ancient person"*: KS, 310
551 *"in modern literature"*: *Karlsruher Tageblatt,* 14 July 1918
551 *"to be sought"*: *Berliner Tageblatt,* 10 July 1918
551 *"few factual details"*: *Norddeutsche Allgemeine Zeitung,* 10 July 1918
552 *" 'effect on life'?"*: Anonymous to George, 12 July 1918, SG-Archiv
552 *Latin source texts:* see LT, 149
553 *to die alone:* see LT, 159 and 167–68
553 *"been shot off"*: EL, 187
553 *"I was frightened"*: EL, 66
553 *to his kidneys:* see LT, 168

CHAPTER 35: REVOLUTION I

572 *"of your realm"*: Carl Petersen to George, 29 December 29, 1918, SG-Archiv
573 *"the whole state"*: Craig, 395
573 *"and without victory"*: SG/FW, 147
574 *"chaos in Russia"*: EL, 64
574 *"along so slowly"*: EL, 64
574 *"prolongs peoples' suffering"*: EL, 65
574 *"a bad thing"*: EL, 94
574 *"behead its king"*: EL, 65
574 *"necessary and unavoidable"*: KS, 305
575 *"in the past"*: see Eyck, 1:58–59

575 *"before the war"*: KH 1, 105
578 *"bear any longer"*: WS, 8
575 *"Empire necessarily led"*: HB, 39
576 for *"masterly advice"*: SG/FW, 148
576 *"me away now"*: SG/FW, 149
576 *"for any activity"*: ES, 215
576 *"have one today"*: SG/ML, 317
576 *"the thousands first"*: EL, 78
576 *"can be done"*: EL, 78
577 *"victory over France!"*: Marguerite Hoffmann, 49
578 *"more and more"*: BfdK II, 12:5
578 *"fate is revealed"*: BfdK II, 12:6
578 *"a single day"*: BfdK II, 12:25
579 *"me · must die"*: BfdK II, 12:25
579 *"on the streets"*: BfdK II, 12:25
579 *"from the clutter"*: BfdK II, 12:26
579 *"stipulates the law"*: BfdK II, 12:30
579 *"it rises anew"*: BfdK II, 12:31
580 *"by this peace"*: EL, 70
580 *"shame and disgrace"*: EL, 193
580 *"our sacred lands"*: Wolters to Gundolf, 22 October 1918, SG-Archiv
581 *"the entire world"*: EG, 123–24
581 the Heidelberg castle: LT, 179
582 *"The Glorious Heroes!"*: SG, 9:114
582 *"little unrest there"*: EL, 90
582 *"we despise them"*: EL, 91
583 *"and very promising"*: BV, 48
583 *"of the present"*: BV, 54
583 *"knowledge and overview"*: BfdK II, 12:5
583 *"it has appeared"*: SG/FG, 311
584 an *"intellectual novel"*: Thomas Mann, *Die Forderungen des Tages* (Frankfurt a.M.: S. Fischer Verlag, 1986), 111
584 *"toward hero worship"*: Adolf von Grolman, "Methodische Probleme in Fr. Gundolfs 'Goethe,'" *Euphorion* (1921): 16–17
585 *"culture is restored"*: Y, 3:8
585 *"Geistbücher are politics"*: ES, 253
586 *"an appropriate symbol"*: CP 111–13, 180
586 *"do with politics"*: Sohnle, 200
587 *"history has achieved"*: TM/EB, 78
587 instituted Nietzsche Prize: Although administered by a separate jury chaired by the mayor of Weimar, the prize had been established by Nietzsche's opportunistic sister, Elizabeth Förster-Nietzsche, for whom no love was lost among George's friends. Gundolf, disgusted by her unscrupulous exploitation and

misrepresentation of her brother's legacy, called her the *Leichenschänderin*—a word that combines the equally unsavory meanings of one who desecrates a corpse and a necrophiliac—of Weimar. See SG/FG, 324.

587 *"on the literature"*: Walter Kaufmann, 15
588 *"sacrifice here, Ernst!"*: Raschel, 182
588 *"them to you"*: Raschel, 182
588 *"topic is permissible"*: Raschel, 183
588 *of his life:* see Raschel and also Frank Weber
588 *"very early on"*: EG, 75
589 *"the genuinely poetic"*: EL, 45
589 *"Nietzsche as well"*: EL, 64–65
589 *"as Nietzsche did"*: EL, 72
589 *"closer to him"*: EL, 100
589 *"doctrine, nor direction"*: EL, 115
589 *"didn't have one"*: EL, 145
590 *"validity in Nietzsche"*: KH 1, 107
590 *"the best kind"*: Raschel, 186
590 *"through your love"*: Raschel, 197–98
591 *"the whole atmosphere"*: Raschel, 202
591 *"in this instance"*: Raschel, 186
591 *"into the book"*: Raschel, 197
591 *"uneasiness about that"*: Raschel, 187
591 *"N's image today"*: Raschel, 203
591 *"is very good"*: Raschel, 203
591 *"the danger, boring"*: Raschel, 173
592 *"their same attire"*: Raschel, 191
592 *"this spiritual revolution"*: originally in Schmollers *Jahrbuch* 45 (1921), reprinted in Troeltsch, 653–77
592 *"against the revolution' "*: Troeltsch, 676
593 *"significance or consequence"*: Troeltsch, 677
593 *"been found already"*: Curtius, 115–16

CHAPTER 36: TREASON

594 *where he lived:* see LT, 168
594 *"ability to grow"*: EL, 69
595 *"is actually insanity"*: SG/FG, 276
595 *"does is right"*: BfdK II, 12:293
595 *"did not know"*: ES, 263
596 *"path with him"*: ES, 264
597 *"very pretty state"*: SG/FG, 326
598 *"the present one!"*: SG/FG, 327
598 true *"German Renaissance"*: EL, 125
599 *"my own feet"*: SG/FG, 325
600 *"brooding over Caesar"*: cited in Z, 298

601 *"and have faith!"*: BfdK 11, 12:60–64
601 *"in his expression"*: ES, 39
602 *"of a man"*: ES, 40
602 *"proofs to correct?"*: SG/FG, 332
602 *the assignment instead*: LT, 176
602 *"found him again"*: SG/FG, 334
603 *"of real love"*: LT, 154
603 *"know it entirely"*: EL, 160
603 *"piece of shit"*: see A. S. [probably Arthur Salz] to George, 14 July 1926, SG-Archiv, and Ernst Kantorowicz to George, 2 December 1931, SG-Archiv
604 *"can't change that"*: SG/FG, 334–35
604 *"me from sleeping"*: SG/FG, 336
604 *"the suffering party"*: SG/FG, 339
605 *"from existing conflicts"*: SG/FG, 339
606 *counter-revolutionary coup d'état*: Holborn, 579
607 *"Berlin frightens me"*: SG/FG, 339–40
607 *"course of things!"*: SG/FG, 340–41
608 *"be atoned for"*: ES, 57–58
608 *"what they want"*: Wolters to Gundolf, 11 March 1920, FGA
609 *"result for me"*: SG/FG, 341
609 *"sorts of vexations"*: SG/FG, 342
609 *down the invitation*: cf. Z, 308
609 *"years count double"*: ES, 46
610 *"is never thanked"*: SG, 9:29
610 *"than a poet"*: ES, 47–48
611 *was "making compromises"*: ES, 48
611 *"wasted and destroyed!"*: ES, 48
611 *"large bladder stone"*: SG/FG, 344
611 *and in Munich*: cf. Z, 311
611 *"of] the times"*: SG/FG, 343
611 *remaining to write*: SG/FG, 344
612 *"time since Plato"*: SG/FW, 158
612 *"if he does"*: Vossische Zeitung, 27 February 1920
613 *"of Gundolf's resonance"*: Vossische Zeitung, 27 February 1920
613 *"our literary heritage"*: Vossische Zeitung, 27 February 1920
613 *"the separation necessary"*: EL, 118
613 *"it was over"*: EL, 136
614 *"grave long ago"*: EL, 149
614 *"enlightenment or 'disenchantment'"*: SG/FG, 349
614 *"the worst names"*: SG/FG, 349–50
615 *"love Your Gundolf"*: SG/FG, 351
615 *a further operation*: cf. SG/FG, 356, and Z, 320
615 *"behind his back:"* EG, 169
615 *"responsibility" that "fate"*: SG/FG, 359

616 *"the same outcome"*: SG/FG, 359
616 *"to know about"*: SG/FG, 360
616 *"work and creation"*: SG/FG, 362
617 *"me. Your Gundolf"*: SG/FG, 371–72

CHAPTER 37: REGROUPING

618 *"in the clinic"*: George to urologist, 4 May 1921, SG-Archiv
619 *"a hundred thousand!"*: SG/FG, 286
619 *"physically oppressive torment"*: RB 2, 155
619 *"burden to George"*: RB 2, 155
620 *"noticing that already"*: EL, 119–20
620 *"agonizing for me"*: EG, 135
620 *"two years now"*: EG, 142
620 *"is however impossible"*: EG, 137
620 *"you cannot believe"*: EG, 138
621 *"on your side?"*: EG, 139
621 *"of my strength"*: Glöckner to George, 17 October 1920, SG-Archiv
621 *"the lowest sort"*: Thormaehlen folder "Literat", SG-Archiv
621 *"harm yourself immeasurably"*: EG, 143
622 *"are his words"*: EG, 144
622 *"life; respect it"*:, EG, 157–58
622 *"not to blame"*: EG, 160
622 *"again and again?"*: EG, 163
623 *"Jew after all"*: EG, 38
623 *"truly comforted me"*: EG, 39
623 *"deeper than George"*: EG, 162
623 *"mystery to me"*: EG, 163
623 *"nothing but Jews"*: EG, 164
623 *"to do so"*: EG, 165
623 *"clings to him"*: EG, 106
623 *"I thankfully revere"*: EG, 166–67
624 *"stand this tyrant"*: EG, 180
624 *"as its own"*: EG, 186–87
624 *dressed in field-grey:* Dschenfzig, 23
625 *"very well known"*: Grünewald, 21
625 *"fencer about him"*: RB 2, 168
625 *"pompous and dictatorial"*: Bowra, 286
625 *"a paradoxical jocularity"*: Gothein, 146–47
625 *in Bad Wildungen:* cf. ES, 308
626 *"[at] Wolfsbrunnenweg 12"*: SG/FW, 176
626 *"matter of principle"*: LT, 211
626 *"our unannounced visit"*: KH 1, 104
626 *"like such surprises"*: SG/FW, 174
627 *"he so desired"*: EL, 122

627 *"and stretch himself"*: RB 2, 171
627 *him a "dwarf"*: ES, 160
628 *"I can imagine"*: MK, 89
628 *"lot of Nietzsche"*: MK, 90–91
628 *"at the university"*: MK, 102
628 *"park almost daily"*: MK, 104
629 *"longed for that"*: MK, 104
629 *"the new Gundolf"*: EL, 118
629 *"here: Mein Kleinstes!"*: EL, 162

CHAPTER 38: REVIVAL

630 *"move them lightly"*: SG/FW, 157
631 *"Apollo in him"*: RB 2, 264
631 *him "the prince"*: RB 2, 264
631 *"him Prince Hans"*: EL, 118–19
631 *"look like me?"*: LT, 206
632 *"law and fate"*: MK, 73
632 *"had been lost"*: MK, 107
632 *"wrote the following"*: Kommerell to George, 22 August 1922, SG-Archiv
632 *"stronghold of reaction"*: Sieg, 55
633 *throughout North Hesse*: Koshar, 63
633 *"of anti-Semitism"*: Koshar, 121
633 *"year as last!"*: Dora Bondi to George, 13 April 1922, SG-Archiv
633 *"of the spirit"*: SG/FW, 159
633 *"and very existence"*: RB 2, 263
634 *"knows the tune"*: SG/FW, 170
634 *"a pied piper"*: SG/FW, 288 n. 283
634 *"with unfamiliar people"*: EL, 145
634 *40 billion marks*: Eyck, 1:130–31
634 *had been 4.2*: see Holborn, 596
635 *million to one*: see Mommsen, 133–34
635 *value in 1914*: Holborn, 598
635 *"Staff Reduction Decree"*: cited in SG/FW, 291 n. 308
635 *for "Masterly advice"*: SG/FW, 178
635 *"by the cutbacks"*: SG/FW, 179–80
635 *to as Reykjavik*: cf. EL, 189
635 *"have fish eyes"*: EL, 188
636 *"on the border"*: BV, 117
636 *"blond bread rolls"*: BV, 72
636 *"with each other"*: SG/FW, 180
636 *"if need be"*: ES, 145
636 *"for Physical Movement"*: RB 2, 145
637 *its value entirely*: see Gundolf to Bondi, 10 February 1923, SG-Archiv

637 *another 6 million:* see Gundolf to Bondi, 28 May 1923 and Bondi to Gundolf, 29 July 1923, SG-Archiv
637 *"sent last week":* Bondi to Gundolf, 23 September 1923, SG-Archiv
637 *totaling 29 billion:* Gundolf to Bondi, 31 October 1923, SG-Archiv
637 *"one hundred trillion":* Gundolf to Bondi, 8 December 1923, SG-Archiv
637 *"Sumatra* with pleasure": KW/AV, 160–61
638 *his own name:* cf. Z, 288
638 *"up with that":* EL, 109
638 *"am calling, calling":* Wolfskehl to George, 12 October 1923, SG-Archiv
638 *"have much life":* KW/AV, 193
638 *"would be unbearable":* KW/AV, 188
639 *"in his prime":* KW/AV, 193
639 *"becoming himself again":* EL, 126
639 *"without me, too":* EL, 131
640 *"concerns at all":* EL, 132
640 *"was in him":* EL, 133

CHAPTER 39: THE TIME OF TENTS
641 *"to Germany's body":* EL, 47
641 *agriculture and industry:* Holborn, 612
642 *a "second Versailles":* Holborn, 619
642 *the cultural elite:* cf. Kershaw, 258
643 *writing "rather rhapsodic":* WS, 10
643 *"that are right":* EL, 102
643 *"constantly in mind":* see CP 111–13, 250–51
643 *"interpretation of life":* FG 2, 191
643 *"big Napoleon book":* Gothein, 205–06
643 *"not on strike":* Gundolf to Bondi, 11 June 1919, SG-Archiv
644 *"to the world":* BV, 67
644 *"to its sales":* WS, 11
645 *"soon as possible":* SG/FW, 293 n. 324
646 *"to this work":* BV, 72–74
646 *weakened his heart:* cf. KH 1, 159
646 *"to Masterly intentions":* SG/FW, 190
647 *"wait so long":* BV, 76–77
647 *"disturbing and offensive":* ES, 144
647 *"on my time!":* EL, 176
647 *"commendation for it":* SG/FW, 189
648 *"to the eyes":* Bondi to Gundolf, 9 July 1924, SG-Archiv
648 *"of the vignette":* Bondi to Gundolf, 9 September 1924, SG-Archiv
648 *"now lack that":* BV, 74
648 *the last minute:* see Z, 25 September and 15 October 1924
649 *"praise in Bossuet":* Bondi to Gundolf, 19 September 1924, SG-Archiv
650 *"peoples and leaders":* Gundolf, *Caesar,* 7

650 *"Books are politics"*: ES, 253
650 *"power in Germany"*: Eduard Korrodi, "Stefan George und sein Kreis," *Neue Zürcher Zeitung,* 19 March 1925
651 *grant them victory:* Moritz Goldstein, "Literarische Umschau," *Vossische Zeitung,* 5 April 1925
652 *"forth just now"*: Richard Wolf, "Der neue Gundolf. Cäsar und die Jahrtausende," *Deutsche Allgemeine Zeitung,* 7 December 1924
652 *"Probationary Periods Commence"*: *Münchener Neueste Nachrichten,* 20 December 1924
653 *"with many bodies"*: ML 1, 64
653 *"makes too many"*: EL, 133–34
653 *"yet to come"*: EG, 170
653 *"not necessary anymore"*: EL, 147
653 *"is still possible"*: ML 1, 64
653 *"to repeat himself"*: ML 1, 18
653 *"write poems anymore!"*: Marguerite Hoffmann, 223
654 *"George remains intact"*: ML 1, 43
654 *"act like dynamite"*: EG, 170
654 *"life begins again"*: ML 1, 14
654 *"from not traveling"*: EL, 108
655 *"and that's it"*: EL, 197
655 *"live in them"*: CP II, 31
655 *"time of tents"*: EL, 179
655 *"one in Kiel"*: EL, 143
656 *"thing was Basel"*: EL, 156
656 *"too watery there"*: BV, 75
656 *"tone of conversation"*: RB 2, 163
657 *"roaring, merciless laughter"*: RB 2, 164
657 *"Unbelievably nasty, that"*: EL, 146
657 *"of this world"*: Peter Hoffmann, 52
658 had *"high connections"*: EL, 153; this story is also reproduced in LT, 214 and EM 1, 466.
658 *"them more often"*: EL, 162
658 *"of the soul"*: EL, 164
658 *an ancient legend:* cf. LT, 216 and 219
659 *king, and creator:* cf. Peter Hoffmann, 52

CHAPTER 40: STUPOR MUNDI

660 *"wonder of the world"*: Vaughn, 272
661 *"emperor but he"*: Abulafia, 433
661 *the Hohenstaufen lineage:* see Peter Hoffmann, 15
661 *"Agrigento and Selinunte"*: SG, 6–7:23
662 *"all an exception"*: BV, 50
662 *"haven't been poeticized"*: EL, 130

662 *"is entirely different"*: BV, 77
663 *"I am free"*: BV, 87
663 *"been achieved here"*: EL, 98
663 *"in our Italy"*: EL, 86
663 *he is entombed:* Peter Hoffmann, 62
664 *"high up there"*: Erika Wolters to George, 17 April 1924, SG-Archiv
664 *"to absorb it"*: Ernst Kantorowicz to George, 30 April 1924, SG-Archiv
664 *"the fascist dream"*: Ernst Kantorowicz to George, 30 April 1924, SG-Archiv
664 THE SECRET GERMANY: From the preliminary remark to Kantorowicz, 7
664 *was being written:* cf. KH 1, 126–27
665 *"in typewritten copy"*: George to Bondi, 12 July 1926, SG-Archiv
665 *"it with pleasure"*: Bondi to George, 22 July 1926, SG-Archiv
665 *"believe it possible"*: Bondi to George, 28 August 1926, SG-Archiv
665 *was "rather playful"*: Bondi to George, 14 January 1927, SG-Archiv
666 *"seen as misleading"*: Bondi to George, 24 January 1927, SG-Archiv
666 *"not do otherwise"*: George to Bondi, 31 January 1927, SG-Archiv
666 *"seven hundred pages"*: Cantor, 85–86
667 *"remarkable descriptive artistry"*: Baethgen, 2:542
667 *"in historical representation"*: Baethgen, 2:543
668 *"the George-Circle"*: Brackmann, 534
668 *"seeking the truth"*: Brackmann, 548–49
669 *the last minute:* cf. Grünewald, 90
669 *"and school system"*: Grünewald, 94–95
670 *themselves become art:* Grünewald, 96
671 *"he was younger"*: LT, 209
671 *"you're talking nonsense!"*: LT, 209
671 *"page of F II"*: George to Bondi, 26 July 1928, SG-Archiv
672 *all too deeply:* Kommerell, 483
673 *"for eighty years"*: Benjamin, *Gesammelte Schriften*, 3:252–53
674 *question: "Alas, no"*: Benjamin, *Gesammelte Schriften*, 3:254–55
674 *"the steel helmet"*: Benjamin, *Gesammelte Schriften*, 3:259
674 *in the Reichstag:* Kershaw, 333

CHAPTER 41: *THE NEW REICH*
675 *"to larger connections"*: EL, 173
675 *"feels too much"*: EL, 167
676 *"himself, like Hofmannsthal"*: BV, 95
676 *"now over it"*: EL, 166
677 *"of individual persons"*: Morwitz to George, 1 November 1926, SG-Archiv
677 *"contradict good manners"*: Julius Landmann to George, 19 August 1927, SG-Archiv
677 *of 29,500 Reichsmark:* SG-Archiv
678 *"your personal signature"*: GB, 13
678 *"fifteen percent royalty"*: Bondi to Gundolf, 4 December 1927, SG-Archiv

678 *"God of light"*: EL, 207
679 *were in print*: cf. GB, 28
679 *press in 1928:* cf. EM 1, 481–82
680 *"the nearby peril"*: SG, 9:36
680 *Babylon as slaves:* cf. EM 1, 427
681 *the New Reich"*: SG, 9:37–39
681 *"is not stated"*: EM 1, 431
682 *"into a wheel"*: SG, 9:69
682 *"exists no doubt"*: EM 1, 447
682 *jail among murderers:* see SG, 6–7:208
682 *a ridge nearby:* EM 1, 436
683 *"of our warriors"*: SG, 9:57
683 *what it meant:* cf. EM 1, 440
683 *"matriarchal physical birth"*: EM 1, 443
684 *and so on:* on these identifications, cf. EM 1, 443–44
684 *"Becomes destiny tomorrow"*: SG, 9:60–65
684 *"I must surrender"*: SG, 9:50
685 *"gentle and light"*: SG, 9:138
685 *or in groups:* cf. LT, 241

CHAPTER 42: FAME

688 *"at the moment"*: New York City, title of newspaper unknown, 30 July 1905, SG-Archiv
688 *"sick by them"*: George Simmel to George, 17 October 1906, SG-Archiv
688 *"living German poets"*: Breslauer Zeitung, 8 September 1912
689 *"generations in Germany"*: Anonymous, "Der Profetiegehalt von Georges Werk," Wissenschaftliche Beilage, in Braunschweigische Landeszeitung, 25 February 1924
689 *of "boundless hubris"*: Fritz Strich, Neue Zürcher Zeitung, 27 October 1924
689 *"the best belong"*: Peter Hamecher, "Stefan Georges Gesamtwerk," Der Tag, 13 January 1928
690 *"national pedagogical character"*: Fritz Cronheim, "Die neuen Publikationen des George Kreises," Literarische Rundschau, Berliner Tageblatt, 28 August 1926
690 *"the present day"*: C. A. P., "Literatur und Kunst," Hamburger Nachrichten, 15 November 1926
690 *"to the spirit"*: Paul Vois, "Deutsche Verleger," Deutsche Allgemeine Zeitung, 19 December 1926
690 *"with world fame"*: Ludwig Marcuse, "Stefan George. Zur Verleihung des Goethe-Preises," Thüringer Allgemeine Zeitung, 1 September 1927
691 *than four hundred marks:* cf. Benjamin, Gesammelte Briefe, 1:463
691 *"is very considerable"*: Anonymous, "Was sind Briefe deutscher Dichter wert?" Münchner Neueste Nachrichten, 11 February 1922
691 *"of the things"*: Wolfskehl to George, 8 October 1925, SG-Archiv
692 *"someone like that"*: EL, 135

692 *"our turn yet"*: EL, 135
693 *"holy and great"*: SG Katalog, 307
693 *"of the nation"*: Stefan Großmann, "Ich bemerke . . .", 3 September 1927, SG-Archiv
693 *"poet, Steppan George"*: New York Times, 29 August 1927
693 *"registers of animals"*: SG, 6–7:10
693 *"again next year"*: BV, 85
694 *"someone else himself"*: BV, 85
694 *"give mine up"*: EL, 189
694 Robert von Steiger: cf. LT, 240, and WS, 18 and Freundesgabe, 759
694 *"sent to you"*: Bondi to George, 21 June 1928, SG-Archiv
694 *"forwarded to you"*: Bondi to George, 30 June 1928, SG-Archiv
694 regards! von Hindenburg: SG Katalog, 301
695 *"saved" the empire*: SG, 9:29
695 *"in his poems"*: BV, 104
695 *"sole symbolic figure"*: SG Katalog, 302
695 *"work and life"*: Unsigned telegram, 12 July 1928, SG-Archiv
695 *"rigor and discipline"*: Telegram, 11 July 1928, SG-Archiv
696 *"made so universally"*: BV, 104
696 *"and soulless present"*: Otto Heuschele, "Das Reich Stefan Georges," in *Neckar Rundschau*, 2 January 1930
696 *"the eternal powers"*: Peter Hamecher, "Das neue Reich. Stefan Georges neues Gedichtwerk," in *Berliner Börse Zeitung*, 4 November 1928
696 *"in this way"*: Ernst Blass, "Das neue Buch von Stefan George," in *Berliner Tageblatt*, 13 December 1928

CHAPTER 43: APOTHEOSIS

698 *"level of El-Rey!"*: SG/FW, 216
698 *"is here again"*: SG/FW, 220
699 *"deal of trouble"*: SG/FW, 225
699 *"should I do"*: SG/FW, 234
699 *"movement had produced"*: BV, 101
700 *"in the state"*: EL, 190
700 *"pointed to France"*: SG/FW, 309
701 *"obstacle to sales"*: BV, 112
701 *"never be finished"*: LT, 249
701 *"more lasting effect"*: EL, 198
702 *"what is said"*: BV, 101
702 for the work: cf. BV, 112
702 *"an animated rendering"*: ES, 152
702 *"all genuine historiography*: ES, 155
702 *"and sad testament"*: EG, 192–93
703 *"the first disciple"*: ES, 155
703 *"and racial silliness"*: SG/FG, 387–88

703 *"lively will was"*: FW, 244
704 *"of free birth"*: KW, 39–40
704 *"occurred to us"*: KW, 40–41
705 *"to this view"*: KW, 297
705 *"hard to please!"*: EL, 204
705 *"humor and decency"*: Anonymous, "Das neue Ufer," *Kulturelle Beilage*, in *Germania*, 15 February 1930
705 *called it "embarrassing"*: Conrad Wandrey, "Friedrich Wolters: Stefan George und die Blätter für die Kunst," in *Die literarische Welt*, 3 January 1930
705 *"for the future"*: Anonymous, "Stefan George," *Deutsche Allgemeine Zeitung*, 25 March 1930
706 *"is the living!"*: Peter Hamecher, "Eine Biographie Stefan Georges," *Kunst Welt Wissen Unterhaltungsbeilage*, in *Berliner Börsen-Zeitung*, 26 March 1930
706 *"not without confidence"*: Wolfskehl to George, 13 March 1930, SG-Archiv
706 *"since the Yearbook!"*: Wolfskehl to George, 17 March 1930, SG-Archiv
706 *"last few years"*: ES, 159
706 *generosity and integrity*: see MK, 164–69
706 *an "awful book"*: MK, 171
707 *"to identify myself"*: MK, 195–96
707 *"about the state"*: MK, 200
707 *jealousy or envy*: see KH 1, 197 and LT, 243–44
708 *"adds some spice"*: EL, 151
708 *"there are conflicts"*: EL, 158
708 *"Beware of him"*: EL, 133
708 *"an evil genius"*: ML 1, 57
708 *"usually preferred wine"*: LT, 223
708 *in the future*: see LT, 231
709 *"ambition (venia legendi)"*: EM 1, 465
709 *"matter with you"*: MK, 172
710 *"to a man"*: MK, 182
710 *"growth takes it"*: MK, 170–71
710 *"reversal or ruin"*: MK, 186
710 *"ashamed of it"*: MK, 198–99
710 *"be with me?"*: MK, 204–05
711 *"further and further"*: MK, 207
711 *"a long time"*: LT, 244
711 *"permitted to happen"*: RB 2, 297
711 *"toad"*—die Kröte: LT, 243. Underscoring his continuing ambivalence toward Kommerell and his unbroken admiration of his intellectual gifts, George liked to remind his friends that, as Thormaehlen recorded, "according to popular belief the toad carries a precious stone in its head." Either George or Thormaehlen had apparently forgotten that, like Puck in *A Midsummer's Night Dream*, this nickname was also an allusion to another play by Shakespeare, namely *As You Like It*. There, the exiled Duke exclaims that "adversity, /

Which, like the toad, ugly and venomous, / Wears yet a precious jewel in his head" (2.1.12).
711 *"like twelve savages"*: MK, 225 and 226 n. 3
711 *"the swimming pool"*: MK, 415–16

CHAPTER 44: REVOLUTION II
713 *"a daily schedule"*: SG/FG, 377
713 had *"an ulcer"*: SG/FG, 378
714 *"starve to death"*: SG/FG, 379
714 *"poems by heart"*: SG/FG, 379–80
714 *"in Your Sign"*: SG/FG, 381
714 *"by outward affairs"*: SG/FG, 381
715 *"drawn by death"*: Gundolf, *Gedichte*, 107
715 *"all these years"*: SG/FG, 390
715 *"to say that"*: SG/FG, 390
716 *"were 'sacred books'"*: ML 1, 134
716 *"a Hasidic rabbi"*: ML 1, 133
716 *to replace him*: cf. ML 1, 78
716 *simply, "a phenomenon*: ML 1, 95
716 *"counted in Polish"*: ML 1, 75
716 *of numerous hymns*: cf. ML 1, 80
717 *of statistical information*: cf. ML 1, 91
717 *"and precise knowledge"*: ML 1, 94
717 *"small, thriving hotel!"*: ML 1, 83
717 *showed his intelligence*: cf. ML 1, 92
717 *"be a friend"*: EL, 208
717 *husband through suicide*: cf. Marguerite Hoffmann, 206
718 *"found the courage"*: EL, 208
718 *to his life*: cf. CP 111–13, 266–67
719 *"nice little letter"*: Ladner, 41–45
719 *"another poetic talent"*: LT, 253
720 *"say at all"*: MS, 13–22
721 *the Master himself*: cf. MS, 24
721 *from the Master*: LT, 238
721 *"he dreamt of"*: VF, 16
721 *to no effect*: cf. LT, 245
722 *himself to Locarno*: cf. EL, 154
722 *middle of July*: Holborn, 677–78
722 *eliminate inessential jobs*: Holborn, 682
723 *total work force*: Kershaw, 404
723 *the July elections*: Holborn, 698
725 *"we are creating"*: BV, 101–03
725 *"soon show itself"*: BV, 120
725 *"by this democracy"*: EL, 207

725 *"the muddled situation"*: BV, 135
725 *in April 1933*: cf. KH 1, 227, and Hildebrandt to George, 29 April 1933, SG-Archiv
725 *"him for themselves"*: RB 2, 182
725 *"change as such"*: ML 2, 48–49
726 *"the outside world"*: EL, 209
726 *"person can do"*: ML 2, 49
726 *"important to me"*: EL, 209
726 *"with the Nazis"*: from a conversation with George reported in a letter from Hildebrandt to Robert Boehringer, 17 April 1950, SG-Archiv
726 *"unthinkable without George"*: Anonymous, "Literarische Beilage," *Deutsche Allgemeine Zeitung*, 12 July 1933
726 *"into a Volk"*: Paul Niehaus, "Stefan George als Künder des neuen Reiches," in *Dresdner Nachrichten*, 28 September 1933
727 *"measure, the form"*: Peter Hamecher, "Stefan George," Beilage Kritische Gänge, *Berliner Börsen-Zeitung*, 29 October 1933
728 *"taken place then"*: Morwitz to George, 5 May 1933, SG-Archiv
729 *"importance for themselves"*: George to Morwitz, 10 May 1933, SG-Archiv
729 *be its sire*: There are those who argue that, since George acknowledged he was the forefather of the "movement" and not, as the minister had wanted him to say, of the new "government," George had cleverly sidestepped actually lending his support to the Nazis while simultaneously appearing to give it. Such semantic hairsplitting is not only unseemly, it is misinformed: the Nazis called themselves as frequently a "movement" as a "party," which to them sounded too conventional and too bourgeois. Munich, for example, the site of the failed beer-hall putsch in 1923 and the city where the Nazis emerged onto the political scene, was frequently referred to by the Nazis themselves as "The Capital of the Movement."
731 *"today and tomorrow"*: Ernst Bertram, "Deutscher Aufbruch," *Deutsche Zeitschrift* 46 (July 1933): 613–619
731 *"friends to danger"*: ML 2, 50
731 *the Nazi cause*: cf. Peter Hoffmann, 111
731 *"about the Nazis"*: Kommerell to Anton, 25 September 1930, SG-Archiv
731 *wavering to enlist*: KH 1, 230
732 *"the World War"*: Grünewald, 113–14
733 *nothing had happened*: Grünewald, 114–15
733 *"the Writers' Academy!!"*: Grünewald, 115
733 *"doing so poorly"*: from a letter by George to Kantorowicz, communicated by Hermann Bodeck to Kurt Hildebrandt, who cites it, making it third-hand information; see KH 1, 232
734 *"with new plans"*: Morwitz to George, 25 May 1933, SG-Archiv
734 *in his honor*: see LT, 283
734 *"to be expected"*: LT, 283
734 *"his sixty-fifth birthday"*: SG Katalog, 309
735 *colleague, Professor Waldberg*: cf. Reuth, 52–53

735 *Shakespeare by Gundolf*: Hitler's copy of the volumes, with his ex libris, are owned by the Stefan George-Archiv.
735 *the book twice*: Grünewald, 165
735 *"one's decisions accordingly"*: Kantorowicz to George, 10 July 1933, SG-Archiv
735 *the fall semester*: cf. Grünewald, 123
736 *"a good mood"*: LT, 285
736 *"exile in Switzerland"*: EM 3, 10
736 *permanently in Basel*: cf. EL, 156
737 *as being "abroad"*: Frank Mehnert, report on burial plans for George, SG-Archiv; cf. also VF, 83
737 *"Egypt next time"*: MS, 26
737 *tired and weak*: RB 2, 188–89
737 *burning and itching*: cf. Boehringer to Frank Mehnert, 5 October 1933, SG-Archiv
738 *"I beg you"*: Wolfskehl to George, 20 October 1933, SG-Archiv
738 *"for any news"*: George to Wolfskehl, 22 October 1933, SG-Archiv
738 *"expected of it"*: Frank Mehnert, "Krankheitstagebuch", SG-Archiv
738 *but without success*: cf. RB 2, 189
739 *"sleep while sitting"*: Frank Mehnert, "Krankheitstagebuch", SG-Archiv
739 *"no questions now"*: Frank Mehnert, "Krankheitstagebuch", SG-Archiv
739 *"concern. Presence desired"*: RB 2, 189
740 *George stopped breathing*: RB 2, 190–91; cf. also LT, 288
740 *" 'The New Reich' "*: 8-Uhr-Abendblatt, 4 December 1933
740 *"[entire] German nation"*: Franz Schauwecker, *Berliner Tageblatt*, 5 December 1933
740 *"Hitler the* Führer*"*: *Der Angriff*, 5 December 1933
740 *"is deeply saddened"*: cited from the newspaper, *Der Alemanne*, which reproduced the telegram on 5 December 1933
740 *" 'Stefan-George-Prize' "*: *Augsburger Postzeitung*, 7 December 1933
741 *"alive within us"*: *Hannoverscher Kurier*, 5 December 1933
741 *"to be buried"*: Frank Mehnert, folder with materials on death and burial, SG-Archiv
741 *"no good end"*: Frank Mehnert, folder with materials on death and burial, SG-Archiv
741 *"his imminent death"*: Frank Mehnert, folder with materials on death and burial, SG-Archiv
741 *"in German soil"*: Frank Mehnert, folder with materials on death and burial, SG-Archiv
741 *"where he dies"*: RB 2, 191
741 *"final resting place"*: Frank Mehnert, folder with materials on death and burial, SG-Archiv
741 *"of the poet?"*: Frank Mehnert, folder with materials on death and burial, SG-Archiv
742 *then everyone departed*: RB 2, 192
742 *withered and died*: In his diary, Frank Mehnert recorded that when he went to the cemetery the next morning, the attendant told him the *croce* was gone, and,

indeed, Mehnert discovered that the swastika, which had been glued to the ribbon, was missing. There were no signs it had been forcibly removed, and Mehnert speculated that moisture had caused it to fall off. But the swastika was nowhere to be found. There had been many visitors throughout the day, but the attendant said that a "big, fat man" who he thought was Dutch—an *Olandese*—had been there in the afternoon, and when he left the swastika had also vanished. Mehnert later found the man—he was a stranger—but the *Olandese* almost fell over with fright when he was confronted about the matter, and he convincingly protested his innocence. What happened to the swastika was never determined.

Sensitive to the symbolism of the situation and not wanting it to blow up into some sort of incident, Mehnert bought some material, fashioned a new swastika and sewed it the next day onto the ribbon, where it stayed until the wreath was discarded. Despite Mehnert's swift actions, the rumor spread that George's friends had removed the swastika. Indignantly, Mehnert noted how absurd it would have been for such a thing to have been done by, "of all people, friends of the poet who even before the war had used the swastika as a symbol on books!"

742 *"case with George"*: Benjamin, *Gesammelte Briefe*, 4:237

CHAPTER 45: EPILOGUE

745 *illness, or exposure:* cf. Peter Hoffmann, 248–49
745 *"of the devil"*: Peter Hoffman, 239
745 *"permitted to continue"*: Peter Hoffman, 251
745 *"live sacred Germany!"*: Peter Hoffman, 443
746 *"they will need"*: Peter Hoffman, 396–97

SELECTED BIBLIOGRAPHY

Abulafia, David. *Frederick II: A Medieval Emperor.* London: Penguin, 1988.
Bachofen, Johann Jakob. *Das Mutterrecht. Eine Untersuchung über die Gynaikokratie der alten Welt nach ihrer religiösen und rechtlichen Natur.* 2 vols. Basel: B. Schwabe, 1948.
Baethgen, Friedrich. *Mediaevalia. Aufsätze, Nachrufe, Besprechungen.* 2 vols. Stuttgart: Anton Hiersemann, 1960.
Bahr, Hermann. *Zur Überwindung des Naturalimus. Theoretische Schriften 1887–1904.* Edited by Gotthart Wunberg. Stuttgart: W. Kohlhammer, 1968.
Baudelaire, Charles. *Oeuvres complètes.* 2 vols. Paris: Gallimard, 1975–76.
Benjamin, Walter. *Gesammelte Briefe.* Edited by Christoph Gödde and Henri Lonitz. Frankfurt am Main: Suhrkamp, 1995.
——. *Gesammelte Schriften.* Edited by Rolf Tiedemann and Hermann Schweppenhäuser. Frankfurt am Main: Suhrkamp, 1991.
Benz, Richard. *Lebensmächte und Bildungs-Welten meiner Jugend. Dresdner und Heidelberger Erinnerungen.* Hamburg: Christian Wegner, 1950.
Berghahn, Volker R. *Imperial Germany, 1871–1914: Economy, Society, and Politics.* Providence: Berghahn Books, 1994.
Berlin um 1900: Ausstellung der Berlinischen Galerie in Verbindung mit der Akademie der Künste zu den Berliner Festwochen 1984. Berlin: Akademie der Künste, 1984.
Bithell, Jethro. "Stefan George and Ida Coblenz." In *German Studies. Presented to Leonard Ashley Willoughby by Pupils, Colleagues, and Friends on His Retirement,* 1–18. Oxford: Basil Blackwell, 1952.
Blanning, T. C. W. *The French Revolution in Germany: Occupation and Resistance in the Rhineland, 1792–1802.* Oxford: Oxford University Press, 1983.
Borchardt, Rudolf. *Gesammelte Werke.* Vol. 1, *Prosa.* Stuttgart: Ernst Klett, 1957.
Bowra, Cecil M. *Memories: 1898–1939.* London: Weidenfeld & Nicholson, 1966.
Brackmann, Albert. "Kaiser Friedrich II in 'mythischer Schau.'" *Historische Zeitschrift* 140 (1929): 534–49.
Bullock, Alan. *Hitler: A Study in Tyranny.* London: Odhams Books, 1964.
Burhan, Filiz Eda. "Vision and Visionaries: Nineteenth-Century Psychological Theory, the Occult Sciences, and the Formation of the Symbolist Aesthetic in France." Ph.D. diss., Princeton University, 1979.
Cantor, Norman F. *Inventing the Middle Ages: The Lives, Works, and Ideas of the Great Medievalists of the Twentieth Century.* New York: William Morrow, 1991.

Carr, William. *The Origins of the Wars of German Unification.* London: Longman, 1991.
Carter, A. E. *The Idea of Decadence in French Literature, 1830–1900.* Toronto: University of Toronto Press, 1958.
Craig, Gordon A. *Germany: 1866–1945.* New York: Oxford University Press, 1978.
Curtius, Ernst Robert. *Kritische Essays zur europäischen Literatur.* 2d exp. ed. Bern: Francke, 1954.
David, Claude. "Le *Jahrbuch für die geistige Bewegung* (1910–1911)." *Etudes Germaniques* 10 (1955): 276–99.
———. *Stefan George. Sein dichterisches Werk.* Munich: Carl Hanser, 1967.
Dehmel, Richard. *Dichtungen, Briefe, Dokumente.* Edited and with an afterword by Paul Johannes Schindler. Hamburg: Hoffmann und Campe, 1963.
Duthie, Enid Lowrie. *L'influence du symbolisme français dans le renouveau poétique de l'Allemagne. Les Blätter für die Kunst de 1892 à 1900.* Paris: n.p., 1933.
Dschenfzig, Theodor. *Stefan George und die Jugend.* Munich: F. Bruckmann, 1934.
Durzak, Manfred. *Der junge Stefan George. Kunsttheorie und Dichtung.* Munich: Wilhelm Fink, 1968.
Egan, Michael, ed. *Ibsen: The Critical Heritage.* London: Routledge and Kegan Paul, 1972.
Ellman, Richard. *Oscar Wilde.* New York: Vintage Books, 1988.
Engelhardt, Friedrich Rudolf. *Als Bingen zu Frankreich gehörte.* Bingen am Rhein: Verlag A. Engelhardt, 1979.
Evans, Richard J. *The Feminist Movement in Germany, 1894–1933.* London: Sage Publications, 1976.
Eyck, Erich. *A History of the Weimar Republic.* Translated by Harlan P. Hanson and Robert G. L. Waite. 2 vols. Cambridge: Harvard University Press, 1962.
Fiechtner, Helmut A., ed. *Hugo von Hofmannsthal. Die Gestalt des Dichters im Spiegel der Freunde.* Vienna: Humboldt Verlag, 1949.
Fischer, Samuel S., and Hedwig Fischer. *Briefwechsel mit Autoren.* Edited by Dierk Rodewald and Corinna Fiedler and with an introduction by Bernhard Zeller. Frankfurt am Main: S. Fischer Verlag, 1989.
Friedrich, Otto. *Blood and Iron: From Bismarck to Hitler. The von Moltke Family's Impact on German History.* New York: HarperCollins, 1995.
Fuchs, Georg. *Sturm und Drang in München um die Jahrhundertwende.* Munich: Georg D. W. Callwey, 1936.
Gall, Lothar. *Bismarck: The White Revolutionary.* Translated by J. A. Underwood. 2 vols. London: Allen & Unwin, 1986.
Gassen, Kurt, and Michael Landmann, eds. *Buch des Dankes an George Simmel. Briefe, Erinnerungen, Bibliographie. Zu seinem 100. Geburtstag am 1. März 1958.* Berlin: Duncker & Humblot, 1958.
Gay, Peter. *Freud: A Life for Our Time.* New York: W. W. Norton, 1988.
Gibbon, Edward. *The Decline and Fall of the Roman Empire.* Edited by J. B. Bury. 7 vols. London: Methuen, 1897.
Gilbert, Martin. *The First World War: A Complete History.* New York: Henry Holt, 1994.

Goethe, Johann Wolfgang von. *Werke. Hamburger Ausgabe.* Edited by Erich Trunz. 14 vols. Munich: Deutscher Taschenbuch Verlag, 1982.

Goldsmith, Ulrich K. "The Growth of Stefan George's Reputation: 1890–1900." *German Life and Letters* 13 (1959–60): 241–47.

———. *Stefan George: A Study of His Early Work.* Boulder: University of Colorado Press, 1959.

———. "Wilamowitz and the *Georgekreis:* New Documents." In *Wilamowitz nach 50 Jahren*, edited by William M. Calder III et al., 583–612. Darmstadt: Wissenschaftliche Buchgesellschaft, 1985.

Gothein, Marie Luise. *Eberhard Gothein. Ein Lebensbild.* Stuttgart: W. Kohlhammer, 1931.

Grautoff, Otto. *Die Entwicklung der modernen Buchkunst in Deutschland.* 2d ed. Leipzig: Hermann Seemann Nachfolger, 1902.

Grolman, Adolf von. "Methodische Probleme in Fr. Gundolfs 'Goethe.'" *Euphorion* (1921): 11–35.

Groppe, Carola. *Die Macht der Bildung. Das deutsche Bürgertum und der George-Kreis 1890–1933.* Cologne: Böhlau, 1997.

Grünewald, Eckhart. *Ernst Kantorowicz und Stefan George. Beiträge zur Biographie des Historikers bis zum Jahre 1938 und zu seinem Jugendwerk "Kaiser Friedrich der Zweite."* Wiesbaden: Franz Steiner, 1982.

Gundolf, Friedrich. *Caesar. Geschichte seines Ruhms.* Berlin: Georg Bondi, 1924.

———. *Gedichte.* Berlin: Georg Bondi, 1930.

———. *George.* Berlin: George Bondi, 1920.

Heisserer, Dirk. *Wo die Geister wandern. Eine Topographie der Schwabinger Bohème um 1900.* Munich: Diederichs, 1993.

Herodian. Edited by C. R. Whittaker. Vol. 2. Cambridge: Harvard University Press, 1970.

Hoffmann, Marguerite. *Mein Weg mit Melchior Lechter. Ein Künstler der Jahrhundertwende, der Freund Stefan Georges.* Amsterdam: Castrum Peregrini, 1966.

Hoffmann, Peter. *Claus Schenk Graf von Stauffenberg und seine Brüder.* Stuttgart: Deutsche Verlags-Anstalt, 1992.

Hofmannsthal, Hugo von. *Gesammelte Werke.* Vol. 2, *Prosa.* Frankfurt am Main: S. Fischer Verlag, 1951.

Holborn, Hajo. *A History of Modern Germany. 1840–1945.* Princeton: Princeton University Press, 1969.

Hollweck, Ludwig, ed. *Unser München. München im 20. Jahrhundert. Erinnerungen und Berichte, Bilder und Dokumente von 1900 bis heute.* Munich: Süddeutscher Verlag, 1967.

Huch, Roderich. *Alfred Schuler, Ludwig Klages und Stefan George. Erinnerungen an Kreise und Krisen der Jahrhundertwende in München-Schwabing.* Amsterdam: Castrum Peregrini, 1973.

Hull, Isabel V. *The Entourage of Kaiser Wilhelm II, 1888–1918.* Cambridge: Cambridge University Press, 1982.

Huret, Jules. *Enquête sur l'Évolution littéraire*. Paris: Bibliothèque-Charpentier, 1901.

Huysmans, J.-K. *À Rebours*. Paris: Gallimard, 1977.

James, Henry. *Collected Travel Writings: The Continent*. New York: Literary Classics of the United States, 1993.

Jones, James W. *"We of the Third Sex": Literary Representations of Homosexuality in Wilhelminian Germany*. New York: Peter Lang, 1990.

Kantorowicz, Ernst. *Kaiser Friedrich II*. Berlin: Georg Bondi, 1927.

Katz, Jonathan, et al. *Documents of the Homosexual Rights Movement in Germany, 1836–1927*. New York: Arno Press, 1975.

Kaufmann, Max. "Heine und Platen. Eine Revision ihrer literarischen Prozeßakten." *Zürcher Diskußionen* 2, 16–17 (1899): 1–13.

Kaufmann, Walter. *Nietzsche. Philosopher, Psychologist, Antichrist*. 4th ed. Princeton: Princeton University Press, 1974.

Keegan, John. *The First World War*. New York: Alfred A. Knopf, 1999.

Kennedy, Hubert. *Ulrichs: The Life and Works of Karl Heinrich Ulrichs, Pioneer of the Modern Gay Movement*. Boston: Alyson Publications, 1988.

Kershaw, Ian. *Hitler*. Vol. 1, *1889–1936: Hubris*. New York: W. W. Norton, 1999.

Killy, Walther, ed. *Literaturlexikon. Autoren und Werke deutscher Sprache*. Munich: Bertelsmann Lexikon Verlag, 1992.

Klages, Ludwig. *Stefan George*. Berlin: Georg Bondi, 1902.

Kommerell, Max. *Der Dichter als Führer in der deutschen Klassik*. Berlin: Georg Bondi, 1928.

Koshar, Rudy. *Social Life, Local Politics, and Nazism: Marburg, 1880–1935*. Chapel Hill: University of North Carolina Press, 1986.

Ladner, Gerhard B. "Erinnerungen an Stefan George." In *Erinnerungen*, edited by Herwig Wolfram and Walter Pohl, 41–46. Vienna: Verlag der österreichischen Akademie der Wissenschaften, 1994.

Lampridius, Aelius. "Antoninus Elagabalus." In *The Scriptores Historiae Augustae*, translated by David Magie, 104–77. London: William Heinemann, 1924.

Landmann, Georg Peter. *Der George-Kreis. Eine Auswahl aus seinen Schriften*. Stuttgart: Klett-Cotta, 1980.

Lepsius, Sabine. *Ein Berliner Künstlerleben um die Jahrhundertwende*. Munich: Gotthold Müller, 1972.

Lessing, Theodor. *Einmal und nie wieder*. Gütersloh: Bertelsmann, 1969.

Leyen, Friedrich von der. *Leben und Freiheit der Hochschule. Erinnerungen*. Cologne: Verlag der Löwe, 1960.

MacCarthy, Fiona. *William Morris: A Life for Our Time*. New York: Alfred A. Knopf, 1995.

Mallarmé, Stéphane. *Oeuvres complètes*. Edited by Henri Mondor and G. Jean-Aubry. Paris: Gallimard, 1945.

——. *Selected Letters*. Edited and translated by Rosemary Lloyd. Chicago: University of Chicago Press, 1988.

Masur, Gerhard. *Imperial Berlin*. New York: Basic Books, 1970.

Meesen, H. J. "Stefan George's *Algabal* und die französische Décadence." *Monatshefte* 39 (1947): 304–321.

Millan, Gordon. *A Throw of the Dice: The Life of Stéphane Mallarmé.* New York: Farrar Straus Giroux, 1994.

Mockel, Albert. "Quelques souvenirs sur Stefan George." *Revue d'Allemagne* (November/December 1928): 385–396.

Mommsen, Hans. *The Rise and Fall of Weimar Democracy.* Translated by Elborg Forster and Larry Eugene Jones. Chapel Hill: University of North Carolina Press, 1996.

Mondor, Henri. *Vie de Mallarmé.* Paris: Gallimard, 1941.

Moore, George. *Confessions of a Young Man.* Edited by Susan Dick. Montreal: McGill-Queen's University Press, 1972.

——. *Memoirs of My Dead Life.* New York: D. Appleton, 1929.

Moréas, Jean. "Le Symbolisme." In *Les premières armes du Symbolisme*, edited by Léon Vanier. Paris: n.p., 1889.

Morwitz, Ernst. *Die Dichtung Stefan Georges.* Berlin: Georg Bondi, 1934.

Muret, Maurice. "Le poète allemand Stefan George. Souvenirs personnels." *Journal des Débats* 2/3 (January 1934).

Nipperdey, Thomas. *Deutsche Geschichte: 1866–1918.* 2 vols. Munich: C. H. Beck, 1990.

Oelmann, Ute. "Das Eigene und das Fremde: Stefan Georges indische Romanze." *Jahrbuch des freien deutschen Hochstifts* (1992): 294–310.

Oosterhuis, Harry, ed. *Homosexuality and Male Bonding in Pre-Nazi Germany: The Youth Movement, the Gay Movement, and Male Bonding before Hitler's Rise.* Translated by Hubert Kennedy. London: Haworth Press, 1991.

Oswald, Victor A., Jr. "The Historical Content of Stefan George's *Algabal*." *Germanic Review* 23 (1948): 193–205.

Paulsen, Friedrich. *Die deutschen Universitäten und das Universitätsstudium.* Berlin: A. Asher, 1902.

Pflanze, Otto. *Bismarck and the Development of Germany.* 3 vols. Princeton: Princeton Unversity Press, 1990.

Preuschen, Max von. "Jugenderinnerungen eines alten Heiners." In *Darmstädter Geschichte(n).* Edited by Fritz Deppert and Karl-Eugen Schlapp. Darmstadt: H. L. Schlapp, 1980.

Raschel, Heinz. *Das Nietzsche-Bild im George-Kreis. Ein Beitrag zur Geschichte der deutschen Mythologeme.* Berlin: Walther de Gruyter, 1984.

Reuth, Ralf Georg. *Goebbels.* Munich: Piper, 1990.

Reventlow, Franziska Gräfin von. *Herrn Dames Aufzeichnungen oder Begebenheiten aus einem merkwürdigen Stadtteil.* Berlin: Buchverlag der Morgen, 1990.

Richardson, Joanna. *Verlaine.* London: Weidenfeld and Nicolson, 1971.

Rouge, Carl. "Schulerinnerungen an den Dichter Stefan George." *Volk und Scholle* 8, no. 1 (1930): 20–25.

Rudorff, Raymond. *The Belle Epoque: Paris in the Nineties.* New York: Saturday Review Press, 1972.

Saint-Paul, Albert. "Stefan George et le symbolisme français." *Revue d'Allemagne* (November/December 1928): 397–405.
Scott, Cyril M. *Bone of Contention: Life Story and Confessions.* London: Aquarian Press, 1969.
———. *My Years of Indiscretion.* London: Mills & Boon, 1924.
———. *Die Tragödie Stefan Georges. Ein Erinnerungsbild und ein Gang durch sein Werk.* Eltville am Rhein: Lothar Hempe, 1952.
Sieg, Ulrich. *Die Geschichte der Philosophie an der Universität Marburg von 1527 bis 1970.* Marburg: Hitzeroth, 1988.
Smith, Helmut Walser. *German Nationalism and Religious Conflict: Culture, Ideology, Politics, 1870–1914.* Princeton: Princeton University Press, 1995.
Sohnle, Werner Paul, ed. *Stefan George und der Symbolismus.* Exhibition catalogue. Stuttgart: Württembergische Landesbibliothek, 1983.
Symons, Arthur. *The Symbolist Movement in Literature.* New York: Haskell House, 1971.
Tompert, Helene. *Lebensformen und Denkweisen der akademischen Welt Heidelbergs im Wilhelminischen Zeitalter, vornehmlich im Spiegel zeitgenössischer Selbstzeugnisse.* Lübeck: Matthiesen Verlag, 1969.
Troeltsch, Ernst. *Aufsätze zur Geistesgeschichte und Religionssoziologie.* Tübingen: J.C.B. Mohr/Paul Siebeck, 1925.
Tuchman, Barbara. *The Guns of August.* New York: Macmillan, 1962.
Tucker, Spencer C. *The Great War: 1914–1918.* Bloomington: Indiana University Press, 1998.
Ullrich, Volker. *Die nervöse Grossmacht. Aufstieg und Untergang des deutschen Kaiserreichs: 1871–1918.* Frankfurt am Main: S. Fischer Verlag, 1997.
Vaughn, Richard, ed. and trans. *Chronicles of Matthew Paris: Monastic Life in the Thirteenth Century.* New York: St. Martin's Press, 1984.
Weber, Frank. *Die Bedeutung Nietzsches für Stefan George und seinen Kreis.* Frankfurt am Main: Peter Lang, 1989.
Weber, Marianne. *Max Weber. Ein Lebensbild.* Tübingen: J. C. B. Mohr/Paul Siebeck, 1926.
Weber, Max. *Gesamtausgabe.* Tübingen: J. C. B. Mohr/Paul Siebeck, 1994.
Weevers, Theodoor. "Albert Verwey and Stefan George—Their Conflicting Affinities." *German Life and Letters* 22 (1968–69): 79–89.
Werner, H. "Stefan George als Gymnasiast." *Deutsches Philologenblatt* 42 (1934): 368–70.
Winkler, Heinrich August. *Weimar 1918–1933. Geschichte der ersten deutschen Demokratie.* Munich: Beck, 1993.
Wolters, Friedrich. *Herrschaft und Dienst.* 2d ed. Berlin: Georg Bondi, 1923.
Wuthenow, Ralph-Rainer, ed. *Stefan George in seiner Zeit: Dokumente zur Wirkungsgeschichte.* Vol. 1. Stuttgart: Klett-Cotta, 1980.
Zweig, Stefan. *Die Welt von Gestern. Erinnerungen eines Europäers.* Frankfurt am Main: S. Fischer Verlag, 1953.

ACKNOWLEDGMENTS

It is my pleasant duty to acknowledge the contributions by a number of institutions and individuals toward enabling me to complete this book. It was essentially written in two intense year-long stints, the first made possible by the generosity of the John Simon Guggenheim Memorial Foundation, which gave me a fellowship allowing a year's leave from Vassar College in 1997–98. My former wife, Meredith Gill, an art historian then teaching at the University of Maryland had also received a grant from the Harvard Center for Italian Renaissance Studies at Villa I Tatti, Florence. This confluence permitted us to live for twelve months in a converted, fourteenth-century monastery in the hills above Florence, where the first half of the book was written. I was given permission to use the Biblioteca Berenson at Villa I Tatti, and for that privilege, as well as for the warm welcome extended to me, I thank the director Walter Kaiser and the head librarian Michael Rocke, who also read and gave useful comments on part of the manuscript.

I spent the summers of 1995 and 1996 at the Stefan George-Archiv in the Württembergische Landesbibliothek in Stuttgart. My work there was funded by a grant in 1995 from the American Philosophical Society and in the following year by the Alexander von Humboldt Foundation; for their support I am extremely grateful. My research in the Stefan George-Archiv would have been impossible without the interest, assistance, and steady encouragement of the director, Ute Oelmann, whom I am happy now to be able to call my friend. I thank, too, the former director of the Stuttgart library, Hans-Peter Geh, for having shown a lively interest in my project during its infancy. In addition, two other archivists, Sabine Ribbeck and especially Lore Frank, now retired, were enormously helpful in steering me toward documents that might have otherwise escaped my notice. In 1996 I also visited the Friedrich Gundolf Archive housed in the Institute of Germanic Studies at the University of London. I thank its director, William Abbey, for his kind assistance in making a number of materials available to me. While I was teaching at Vassar, I profited from the fine collection in the Thompson Memorial Library and of course from the labors of the Interlibrary Loan Office. I also benefited from the Milton S. Eisenhower Library at Johns Hopkins University; the Firestone Library at

Princeton; and the Theodore M. Hesburgh Library at the University of Notre Dame, where I joined as a professor of German and as the department chair in 1998. Although I was unable to write a word during my first year at Notre Dame because of my new duties, I returned to the manuscript in May of 1999 and made steady progress during the following academic year. I therefore thank my colleagues and students for their forbearance, and I hope that they had not felt too neglected as a result. I also appreciate the university's support of my work and in particular the material contribution the Institute for Scholarship in the Liberal Arts made toward bringing this book to publication.

I read portions of the manuscript at Princeton University, Vassar College, Colgate University, the University of Miami, the University of Notre Dame, Northwestern University, the University of Calgary, the University of Illinois, and Louisiana State University, and I received many useful comments and questions afterwards for which I am grateful. At Vassar, two student assistants, Alexandra Chan and Kaja Perina, helped me with photocopying, book ordering, filing, and so forth. Halfway through the first summer in the George-Archiv while I was transcribing unpublished letters, my computer failed, and I had to continue taking notes in the laborious, old-fashioned way, with pen and paper. Another student at Vassar, Vanessa Will, heroically transcribed all two hundred pages of what she pointedly called my "constantly deteriorating handwriting" and thus saved me the time and labor of doing so myself. At Notre Dame I was immeasurably aided by Elizabeth Campbell and Andreas Spahn, the latter of whom painstakingly checked all of the quotations against their originals. Friends and former colleagues at Vassar, especially Robert Pounder, Brian Lukacher, and Jennifer Church, were forced to learn more than they ever wanted to know about George, and I wish to apologize here for having put them through that unasked-for ordeal. Some students at Vassar, too, were subjected to more George than they probably cared for, and I am happy to say that, at least as far as Gideon Oliver, José Klein, and Adam Prince are concerned, it does not appear to have negatively affected our relationship, either. At Notre Dame I have called on the expertise of Albert Wimmer, who lent me sympathy and advice over some of the more creative linguistic inventions by George and his friends; Martin Bloomer provided help with some sticky Latin passages, a service Alain Toumayan performed for French; and Patrick Geary led me to the memoirs of Gerhard Ladner, who had an eventful encounter with George but not one that Ladner — or George, for that matter — would have wanted to repeat. Charles A. Miller informed me about a friend of Edith Landmann, Vera Lachmann, who knew George for over twenty years. Ms. Lachmann fled Nazi Germany in the 1930s, came to the United States, and made such an impression on Miller that he felt the need to tell me about her and her life when he happened to find out that I was working on this project. And I owe it, partially, to my work on George that I met William M. Calder III, the world's leading authority on one of George's antagonists, the great classical scholar Ulrich von Wilamowitz-Moellendorff. Bill Calder invited me to give a talk at his institution, the University of Illinois, and while I was there I stayed as a guest in his house, called, appropriately, the Villa Mowitz.

Although I had wanted to write a biography for many years, I was long uncertain about the subject I should choose. For over a year in the early 1990s, I collected information pertaining to Wilhelm von Humboldt, who was an extraordinary statesman, philosopher, and linguist, in addition to having been a fascinating personality. One biography of him in English, by Paul Sweet, is serviceable if not very inspiring, and Humboldt's life would still be well worth revisiting. But in the fall of 1993, I had a conversation with Richard Sieburth, who mentioned that there was not a single biography of George in English. The next day a little checking confirmed that fact — astonishing to me even then — and thus I had something to keep me occupied for the next seven years.

I have been the recipient of much good will and charitableness from my former teachers, now friends, at Princeton — Stanley Corngold, Theodore Ziolkowski and Walter Hinderer — who charmingly continue to be interested in the work of their onetime protégé. Colleagues elsewhere, such as Frederick Beiser and Wulf Koepke, have also lent me their endorsement for various grants and fellowships that supported my research, for which I am also very grateful. As one might expect, I have read many biographies in the course of writing one myself, and although I admire a number of them and learned a great deal from them all, the one I took most closely as a model in tone, style, and character is Peter Gay's *Freud*. I cannot say that I achieved his fluency and verve, but I would not be unhappy if my attempt to do so were recognized. And I am profoundly indebted to Cornell University Press for being willing, in these difficult times for academic publishers, to take on such a large book on a poet still so obscure. One could not ask for a more engaged, dedicated, or professional editor than Bernhard Kendler, and I am truly flattered that he and the Press have wanted to publish this biography. I owe a very special debt to Suzanne Marchand, who carefully read the entire manuscript for Cornell and, among other things, made detailed suggestions for cuts, something that without her sympathetic but firm judgment I probably would have found impossible to do myself.

Among the useful lessons one learns while writing a biography is that even the most purposeful life can take unexpected turns. In my own I discovered that the most elemental and transformative forces of all can arrive unannounced and change everything in an instant. That lesson love teaches best, and because of Amanda I know that now.

INDEX

Italic page numbers refer to photographs.

Aeschylus, 438
"After the Harvest" (George), 206–7
Albert, Henri, 140, 141
Algabal (George): and Andrian, 127; and androgynism, 120, 299; and Artaud, 113; and Coblenz, 174; and complete works, 679; and George's illness, 121, 122, 133; and German culture, 148; historical/literary origins of, 109; identification of George with, 116–17, 229; and Lechter, 198; and poet's purpose, 118; and political beliefs, 343; and Prussian condemnation of homosexuality, 123; publishing of, 176, 219; as revolutionary, 108, 116; and Schuler, 151–52, 153; second edition of, 284; *The Seventh Ring* compared to, 342; subterranean realm of, 117–19, 120; and Verwey, 172; and violence, 120–21, 180; and Weber, 477; *The Year of the Soul* compared to, 205
Anarchism: and *Algabal*, 113; and George, 33–34, 35, 39, 127, 156, 343, 358, 574, 729; and Lombard, 115, 116; and London, 36; prevalence of, 32–34; and symbolism, 47, 50–51, 74, 228
Andreae, Friedrich, 406
Andrian, Leopold von, *252*; and *Blätter für die Kunst*, 160, 161–62, 196, 324; and Hofmannsthal, 126, 127, 130, 160, 161; poem devoted to, 237–38;
relationship with George, 126–27, 155, 160–63, 196–97; and Schuler, 295
Androgynism, 115–16, 120, 289, 299, 344, 414–15
"Angelico, An" (George), 81
Ansorge, Conrad, 203
Ansorge, Margarethe, 203
Antique Fest (1903), *377*
Anti-Semitism: and *Blätter* history, 703–5; and Cosmic Circle, 304–8; and Dühring, 154–55; and George, 155–56, 547, 705, 726, 729; and Glöckner, 622–23; and Goebbels, 734; and Kapp, 606; and Klages, 150, 154, 155, 304, 305–6; and Marburg, 632–33; and Munich, 150–51; and Nazi Germany, 732–33, 745; and Schuler, 150, 152–53, 154, 155, 295, 304, 305–6, 309; toward Simmel, 213
Anton, Johann (Hans), *558*, *559*, 631–32, 663, 670, 685, 706–7, 709, 710–11
Anton, Karl, 631
Anton, Walter, 685, 742
Aristotle, 328
Artaud, Antonin, 113
Auerbach, Ida. *See* Coblenz, Ida "Isi"
Augustine, Saint, 597
Auschwitz, 745
Austria, 16
Austria-Hungary, 17, 18, 513, 514, 515
Axa, Zo d', 47

{ 825 }

Bachofen, Johann Jakob, 152, 226, 227, 295–98, 299, 301, 361, 362, 678
Baden, Max von, 573
Bahr, Hermann, 96–97, 130, 131–32, 135–36, 275
Bakunin, Mikhail Aleksandrovich, 34
"Battle, The" (George), 366
Baudelaire, Charles: and *Algabal*, 109, 117; and *Blätter für die Kunst*, 169, 198; and bourgeoisie, 50; and Gautier, 112; George's kinship with, 54, 125, 146, 147, 148; George's translation of, 48, 76, 88, 89, 284; and Hofmannsthal, 98; and symbolism, 47, 76; and *Yearbook for the Spiritual Movement*, 482
Bavarian Communists, 368
Bavarian Socialists, 575
Beaufront, Louis de, 23
Becker, Carl Heinrich, 605, 695
Belgium, 305, 516, 518, 521–24, 530
Benjamin, Walter, 475, 627, 672–74, 691, 742
Benn, Gottfried, 728
Berger, Erich, 406
Berger, Oskar-Alfred, 745
Bergson, Henri, 444, 546, 628
Berman, Russell, xv
Bernhardt, Sarah, 53
Bernus, Alexander von, 417, 419
Bertram, Ernst: and *Blätter* history, 702; essay on George, 504; and First World War, 525; George's editing of work, 700; and Glöckner, 503–4, 505, 509, 510, 532, 533, 548, 587–88, 590, 591–92, 620–24; and Gundolf, 457, 461; and Mann, 507; and Nazi Germany, 730–31; on Nietzsche, 587–88, 590–92; poem on George, 504–5; relationship with George, 506, 508, 731; and sales of Nietzsche book, 690; and Schmitt, 352. *See also Nietzsche: Essay in Mythology* (Bertram)
Bingen, 8–10, 243, 244, 245

Bismarck, Otto von, 16–20, 23, 59, 60, 122, 153, 598, 661
Bittenfeld, Herwarth von, 745
Blätter für die Kunst (*Pages for Art*): aesthetic manifesto in, 134–35; and Andrian, 160, 161–62, 196, 324; and anthologies of German literature, 278–83, 396; anthology from, 219; and Bertram, 504, 506; and Bondi, 220; and circle, 129, 130, 223–24, 225, 230, 356–57, 407, 420, 423; early conception of, 40; exclusiveness of, 136–37, 224, 276, 287, 358; final issue of, 577–78, 581, 582, 583; and First World War, 532; and George's desire for total control of German literature, 319–20; George's involvement in, 129, 131–33, 144, 169, 185, 189, 190, 223, 397, 511, 577–78, 581; and George's politics, 160, 285–87, 577; and German culture, 135, 157–60, 191–92, 193, 284–85, 287, 356; and Gundolf, 270, 271, 275–76, 316, 321, 323, 408–12, 463, 600–601, 602; history of, 129, 511, 512, 645, 646–47, 675, 698–706, 707, 714, 715; and Hofmannsthal, 128, 131–33, 134, 136, 137, 142–43, 144, 174, 183, 185, 187, 190, 276, 319, 320–21, 323; influence of, 211; international scope of, 170; and Klages, 151, 162, 192, 227–29, 287, 306, 355, 356; and Klein, 127–32, 139, 140–41, 146, 160, 161–62, 185–86, 190, 196, 577–78; maxims in, 134–35, 157, 158–59, 190–92, 194, 225, 284–87, 355–56, 357, 396–97, 450, 578; and modernity, 358; and new art, 129, 146, 157, 158, 159; new direction of, 286; omnibus issue of, 284; and Paul, 279–80; and Perls, 239; poetry selections from, 284; political program of, 160; and publishing strategy, 128, 129, 136, 212, 220, 577; and rationality, 227, 228, 303; and recitation of

poetry, 402–3; recruitment for, 129–30, 166, 169–70, 198, 265–66, 278; and Schmitt, 352; and Schuler, 294, 295; subscribers to, 224; and swastika, 586; and symbolism, 159; and Thormaehlen, 602; and Verwey, 172, 211, 595; as weapon of social change, 358; wider audience for, 175, 185, 212, 276, 287; and Wolfskehl, 137, 138–39, 162, 174, 190, 191, 208, 278; and Wolters, 349, 412, 511; and *Yearbook for the Spiritual Movement,* 429, 433, 434, 442

Blumenthal, Albrecht von, 658, 663, 685, 731, 742

Böckel, Otto, 632–33

Böcklin, Arnold, 125, 146, 177, 219, 290, 359

Bodeck, Hermann, 420

Boehringer, Erich, 521, 581, 618, 685

Boehringer, Robert: biography of George, 347; and Coblenz, 126; and collection on George, xiv, 347; and First World War, 521, 531; and foundation as legal heir, 709; and George's death, 741, 742; and George's illness, 737, 738, 739, 741; and George's political beliefs, 725; and Globe Room, 420; and Gundolf, 550; and Kommerell, 627; and Landmanns, 516; and Liegle, 619; and readings, 511; and recitation of poetry, 398; relationship with George, 347–48, 349, 352; and Verwey, 172; and women, 453–54; and *Yearbook for the Spiritual Movement,* 481

Bondi, Dora, 633

Bondi, Georg, *374*; and Bertram, 590–91; book on George, 287; and First World War, 525, 544; and Frederick II book, 664–66; and Friedemann, 531; and George's financial affairs, 677–78, 679; and George's sixtieth birthday, 694; and Gundolf, 268, 463, 583, 611, 615, 637, 647–48, 649, 665–66, 675, 678; and Harden, 452; and Hofmannsthal, 323, 324; and Jonas, 346; and Kantorowicz, 627; and Kommerell, 671; and publishing of George's works, 219–21, 282, 283, 676, 678; relationship with George, 221, 395, 549; and *Shakespeare and the German Spirit,* 396; and swastika, 586–87, 611, 615, 616; tributes to, 690; and Vallentin, 348, 643–44; and Wilamowitz-Moellendorff essay, 429; and Wolters, 512, 645

Books of Eclogues and Eulogies · of Legends and Songs and of the Hanging Gardens (Die Bücher der Hirten- und Preisgedichte · der Sagen und Sänge und der Hängenden Gärten) (George), 176, 177–81, 219, 229, 236, 237

Borchardt, Rudolf, 360, 436, 516

Bosnia-Herzegovina, 514

Bothwell (George), 30

Böttcher, Georg, 29

Bourgeoisie: and anarchism, 33, 50–51; and *Blätter für die Kunst,* 137, 285, 356; and Cosmic Circle, 331; and feminism, 455; and First World War, 520, 525, 546; George's avoidance of, 35; as George's enemy, 33, 127, 332, 412, 582, 658, 721; and George's pedagogical program, 277; and George's poetry, 364; and George's political ideas, 543; and George's relationship with Kronberger, 332; and George's typeface, 400; and Hildebrandt, 437, 449; and Ibsen, 28; and law, 197; and Mallarmé, 50–51; and Munich, 150; and symbolism, 74, 112, 118; and Thormaehlen, 708; transcendence of, 326, 415

Bowra, Cecil, 625

Brackmann, Albert, 667–68

Brasch, Hans, 417, 421, 422, 534, 619
Braune, Wilhelm, 460, 461
Breysig, Kurt, 348, 403, 446–47, 543–44
Britain, 38, 514–15, 530, 536, 547, 580, 641
Bruckmann, Elsa, 309–10
Bruckmann, Hugo, 309–10
Brüning, Heinrich, 722, 723, 725
Bunsen, Marie von, 203–4
Burke, Edmund, 592
Burkhardt, Jakob, 482
Burne-Jones, Edward, 35, 313
Burning of the Temple, The (George), 578–79, 679

Caesar, Julius, 647–51
Caesar: History of his Fame (Gundolf), 648–52, 663, 667
Café Griensteidl, 95–96, *251*
Cantor, Norman, 666
Carlyle, Thomas, 279
Carnival (1904), *379*
Catholicism: and Austrian monarchy, 90; and Bismarck, 18–20; and Britain, 38; and France, 43; and George's childhood friends, 23; and German culture, 19, 59, 148; and Holy Roman Empire, 193; influence of, on George, 13, 20, 52, 53, 54, 290; and internationalism, 534–35; and Prussia, 575; and symbolism, 78; and *The Tapestry of Life,* 232–33; and *Yearbook for the Spiritual Movement,* 482
Cazalis, Henri, 51, 86
Center Party, 19
Chamberlin, Houston Stewart, 309
Chavannes, Puvis de, 219
"Child's Kingdom, A" (George), 12–13
Circle, *555*; adversaries of, 407–8, 412; and *Algabal,* 108; and anti-Semitism, 156, 623; attention for, xv; and *Blätter für die Kunst,* 129, 130, 223–24, 225, 230, 356–57, 407, 420, 423; and

Blätter history, 701, 705, 715; and Bondi's publishing firm, 220; and composite style, 413; cultural influence of, x, xvi; fame of, 220, 668, 689–90, 695; and feminism, 455; and First World War, 521, 524, 525–26, 532, 597; and George as Master, 222–26, 233–36, 240, 277, 397–99, 408–15, 422, 619; and George's ambition, 229–30, 358; and George's political beliefs, 285, 357, 575, 650, 668, 673–74; and George's role, 408; and German culture, 224, 227; and Globe Room, 420–27; and Goldstein, 612–13; and hierarchy, 183, 225–26, 230, 275, 410, 623, 710; as higher social order, 356–57; and Hildebrandt, 406, 412–13; Hofmannsthal's relationship with, 320–21, 323, 423; and holy war, 412, 419, 430, 494, 520, 595; ideology of, 227, 356–58, 396–97, 406, 408–9, 420, 446, 571, 583, 585, 608, 624, 644, 688; and "The Induction into the Order," 397; instability in, 395–96, 405; Jews within, 156, 743; and Kantorowicz, 626, 630; and Klages, 150–51, 154, 287, 291; and Kommerell, 630, 707–8, 709, 710; and living against the world, 357–58; and national identity, 669–70; and Nazi Germany, 744; and perceptions of George, 138; and portrayals of George as poetic priest, 326; and rationality, 226–28; and recitation of poetry, 124–25, 398–402, 422, 424, 428; recruitment for, 265–67, 347–50, 352, 354, 355, 396–97, 400–402, 406–7, 419, 420, 423–25, 631, 633–34; and Salomon, 604–5; and Schuler, 151, 154; as secret circle, 356; and Secret Germany, x, 527; and secret of the ring, 425; and *The Seventh Ring,* 361; and spiritual state, 349; and *The Star of the Covenant,* 491–92,

499–500, 539; and swastika, 585–86, 591–92; systematization of, 223–26; and trains, 636–37; unity in, 405–8; values of, 230, 546, 671; and Versailles Treaty, 580–81; and will, 230, 400; and Wolfskehl, 154, 293, 406; and Wolters, 405–6, 616; and women, 478, 540; and *Yearbook for the Spiritual Movement,* 434, 442, 482, 483. *See also* Cosmic Circle; *specific disciples of George*

Clemen, Paul, 538

Coblenz, Ida "Isi," *254*; and Dehmel, 139, 173–74; George's poetic portrait of, 181; relationship with George, 124–26, 127, 137, 176, 188, 207

"Cognicion" ("Erkenntnis") (George), 65–67

Cohen, Hermann, 628

Cohrs, Adalbert, *390*, 552–53, 680

Conrad, M. G., 66–67

"Consecration" ("Weihe") (George), 70, 71, 79–80, 231

Constant, Alphonse Louis, 76

"Conversation" ("Gespräch") (George), 124

Correspondence: and Boehringer, 347; and Coblenz, 188; and Cosmic Circle, 332, 510; and French influence, 8; of George in Berlin, 58–59, 64, 65; and George's experience of love, 171; and George's linguistic experimentation, 63; and George's travels, 36, 37, 38–41; and *Hymns,* 86–88; and Kommerell, 670; and literary group, 38–39, 70–72; and privacy issues, xiii, 38–39, 100, 105, 271, 332, 352, 510, 539, 691; value of George's letters, 691. *See also specific disciples of George*

Cosmic Circle, *377*; and anti-Semitism, 304–8; and Bachofen, 361; and *Blätter für die Kunst* history, 699; and *Blätter für die Kunst* maxims, 355;

breaking up of, 307–9, 311, 316–17, 350, 362, 429; and correspondence, 332, 510; and George's complete works, 678, 679; and Gundolf, 306, 311–12; and Klages, 301, 303, 306, 311, 312, 346, 589; and Kronberger, 329, 330, 331; and Schuler, 294, 301–4, 306, 308, 309, 311–12, 329, 331, 589; and "Secret Germany," 683; and *The Seventh Ring,* 362, 364; and swastika, 314; and Wolfskehl, 294–95, 301, 304, 307, 312, 329, 330, 362, 589. *See also* Circle

Cronheim, Fritz, 690

Curtius, Ernst Robert: and Eick, 437; and First World War, 530–31; and George's political program, 481; and George's travels, 32; and Gundolf, 461, 463, 473, 474, 536, 538; and Lechter, 488; relationship with George, 406, 440; and Spirit Books, 593; and *Yearbook for the Spiritual Movement,* 444–45

Curtius, Ludwig, 298

D'Annunzio, Gabriele, 98, 144, 318

Dante: and faith, 597; George compared to, 21, 477, 612, 688; as George's idol, 6; George's translation of, 89, 284, 396, 511; and George's use of "we," 342; Goethe compared to, 217; and Gundolf, 651; Hofmannsthal compared to, 97; and Lechter, 198; and love, 301, 326; and poet's role, 543; and *The Seventh Ring,* 359, 361, 364; and Wilamowitz, 439

"Dante and the Time-Poem" (George), 364

Darmstadt, 15–16

David, Claude, 308, 432, 496

Dawes, Charles G., 641

Dawes Plan, 641–42

"Dead City, The" (George), 365–66

"Deed, The" (George), 180–81, 236
Defoe, Daniel, 22
Dehmel, Richard, 3–4, 139–40, 141, 173–75, 176, 188, 207, 318, 320
Delaroche, 73
Dernburg, Friedrich, 438
"Der Täter" (George), 236
Deschamps, Léon, 46, 47
Dessoir, Max, 172–73, 175, 185
Dette, Willi, 735
Die Blumen des Bösen (George), 89
Dietrich, Oskar, 345
Dilthey, Wilhelm, 407, 444, 546
Dio, Cassius, 109, 115
"Disciple, The" ("Der Jünger") (George), 235
Döblin, Alfred, 727
Dohna-Schlobitten, Eberhard Count, 451
Donnay, August, 170
Douglas, Lord Alfred, 48
Drawings in Gray (*Zeichnungen in Grau*) (George), 54
Droysen, Johann, 16
Dühring, Eugen, 154–55
Dujardin, Edouard, 45
Dumas, Alexandre, 6
Dürer, Albrecht, 229
Duse, Eleonora, 424

Ebert, Friedrich, 573
Edward, Georg, 137–38
Eick, Hugo, 432, 437
Einstein, Albert, 606
Eisner, Kurt, 575
Elagabalus (Roman emperor), 109–14, 115, 118, 120–21, 330
Elisabeth of Austria (empress), 32–33, 359, 513
Elze, Walter, 559, 628, 630, 633, 645, 731
Engels, Friedrich, 155
Enlightenment, 227, 411, 730
Ensor, James, 170
"Entrueckung" (George), 340–41

"Entry" (George), 366–67, 368
Erdmannsdörffer, Bernhard, 459
"Erkenntnis" ("Knowledge") (George), 134
Eulenburg, Philipp Count zu, 451–52, 453
Evans, Richard, 455

"Falkenstein Castle" (George), 680, 682–83, 685
Fehlig, Maria, 663
Feminism, 455, 482
Fierens-Gevaert, Hippolyte, 47, 51
First World War: casualties of, 529–32, 552; and circle, 521, 524, 525–26, 532, 597; events leading to, 513–16; and food shortages, 542–43, 549, 550; and France, 370–71, 514, 515, 530, 531–32, 536; and fuel shortages, 549–50; George's reaction to, 516, 519–28, 532–39, 542–53, 574; and German empire, 514–15, 517–19, 521–22, 530, 536, 543, 550–53; and German Jews, 305; and Gundolf, 517, 518–20, 521, 523–25, 530–32, 536–40, 594, 595, 597; and Hildebrandt, 521, 525, 594; and Kantorowicz, 624–25; public reaction to, 517, 519; and *The Star of the Covenant*, 501, 523, 526–27; and United States, 550, 580; and Wolfskehl, 520, 521, 522–23, 525, 532, 594, 595; and Wolters, 517–18, 519, 520, 521, 525, 529–30, 534, 594
Fischer, Kuno, 458, 459–60
Fischer, Samuel, 318
Fliess, Wilhelm, 299
France: and anarchism, 33; and Catholicism, 43; and Elagabalus, 111–12; and First World War, 370–71, 514, 515, 530, 531–32, 536; and Johann Baptist George, 6–7; and German empire, 17–18; and German reparations, 641–42; influence of, 8; and miscegenation, 547, 548; occupation

of Alsace-Lorraine, 7–8, 17; occupation of Ruhr, 371, 645; and Versailles Treaty, 580
Franckenstein, Clemens von, 187, 195, 237
Franco-Prussian War, 17, 58
Franz Ferdinand (archduke of Austria), 513–14, 515
Franz Josef (emperor of Austria), 513
Frederick Barbarossa, 661
Frederick II (Kantorowicz), *562*, 664–70, 671, 675, 681, 735
Frederick II of Hohenstaufen (Holy Roman Emperor), 9, 660–67
French drama, 396
Freud, Sigmund, 227, 299
Friedemann, Heinrich, *388*, 531, 535, 594
Friedrich-Wilhelm University, 57, 59
Fuchs, Georg, 23, 24, 29, 201–2, 331

Gadamer, Hans-Georg, 628
"Gardens Close, The" (George), 80
Gardiner, Alan H., 395
Gärtner, Johannes, 23
Gauguin, Paul, 48
Gautier, Théophile, 112
George, Anton, 7–8
George, Eva Schmitt, 4, 6, 11, *242*
George, Friedrich Johann Baptist, 6, 35, 90, 124
George, Jakob, 7
George, Johann Baptist, 6–8, 425
George, Stefan, *245, 248, 253, 254, 255, 256, 373, 377, 379, 386, 391, 555, 559, 560, 561, 564, 565, 566, 567*; attitude toward universities, 439–40, 610–11; chronology of life, xiii–xiv; critical acclaim for, 211, 214–17, 688–89, 696; death of, 739–42; early childhood of, 3–14; education of, 14, 20–31, 57, 59, 65, 90, 150; fame of, 86, 687–88, 690, 692, 694, 697, 699; and First World War, 516, 519–28, 532–39, 542–53, 574; foundation as legal heir, 676–77, 709, 710; homosexuality of, 24–25, 34–35, 42, 44, 98–100, 122, 166, 207–8, 354, 439, 450–51, 452, 510–11, 688, 712, 743; illnesses of, 121, 122, 133, 532–33, 551, 553, 575, 609, 611, 615, 618, 622, 639–40, 641, 693, 737–40; as leader/master, x, xi–xiv, 27, 62, 72, 94, 129, 138, 162, 184, 216, 222–26, 233–36, 240, 270, 272, 275, 277, 326, 397–99, 408–15, 422, 432, 442, 464–65, 494, 571, 595, 659, 673, 681, 699, 707, 710, 712; legacy of, 181, 344, 346, 737; and longing for companionship, 27, 28, 93–94, 222–23, 325–26, 335, 338–39; photographs of, 331, 690; as poet, x, xi, 12, 25–29, 43–47, 49–50, 52, 53–54, 56, 65, 69–70, 73, 79, 80, 83, 87, 91, 92, 117, 118, 123, 127, 145, 167, 168, 189–90, 205–10, 217, 218, 231–32, 240, 342, 653–54; political beliefs/program of, ix, x–xi, xvi, 47, 113, 160, 201, 279, 285, 324, 343, 349–50, 357, 368, 369, 403, 408, 415–16, 445, 478, 481, 486–87, 543–49, 571, 574–76, 586–87, 650, 667, 668, 671, 672, 673–74, 724–27, 729, 734; privacy of, xi, xii, xiii–xiv, 38–39, 86, 100, 105, 123, 190, 271, 332, 352, 353, 510, 539, 551, 690–91, 700; private religion of, 156–57, 199, 294, 339–44, 358, 367, 368, 422, 468–69, 477, 480, 492–93, 496, 498–99, 508, 510–11, 612, 683–84, 721; as prophet, 371, 494, 501, 520, 522–23, 545, 546, 547, 548, 571, 572, 582, 593, 594, 595, 610, 611, 680, 681, 682–83, 685, 689, 696, 699, 726, 740, 742; public prominence of, 211–12, 214, 216, 222, 291, 397, 417, 551–52, 571; self-deification of, 120, 339, 354, 428, 492–93, 510–11; self-perceived role of, 353–54, 417–19, 576, 699; travels of, 5, 35–42, 43, 55–56, 64, 90, 93, 125, 127, 144, 149, 189, 345–46, 369–70,

George, Stefan (*continued*) 516–18, 654–55, 690, 736. *See also* Circle; Correspondence; Publishing strategy; Secret Germany; Will; *specific works*
George, Stephan, I (Etienne), 7–8
George, Stephan, II, 3–4, 6, 8, 11, 35, *241, 242,* 368–69
George (Gundolf), 611–13, 650
Gérardy, Paul, 134, 162, 170, 174, 183, 184, *253,* 424
German culture: and anthologies of German literature, 278, 279, 280; and anti-Semitism, 154; and Bertram, 730; and *Blätter für die Kunst,* 135, 157–60, 191–92, 193, 284–85, 287, 356; and Catholicism, 19, 59, 148; and circle, 224, 227; George as incarnation of, 64, 371, 687; George's image of, 156, 192–93, 194, 279, 435; and George's new art, 146–48, 149, 150, 157, 158, 178, 212, 217, 279, 370; and George's political beliefs, 201, 279; George's visibility in, 224; and Greece, 193–94; and Italy, 663; past appropriated as, 178, 194, 202, 670; and Protestantism, 60, 63; and purifying German language, 157, 158; and rationality, 227; and *The Star of the Covenant,* 527; and Switzerland, 737; and *Yearbook for the Spiritual Movement,* 430, 433
German empire: collapse of, 573–75, 597; and First World War, 514–15, 517–19, 521–22, 530, 536, 543, 550–53; formation of, 16–17, 19; George's attitude toward, 17–18, 209, 278
German gesture, 286
German Jews, 154–56, 304–5
German Poets' Conference, 184
German reparations, 641
German youth: and Bertram, 588; and First World War, 520–21, 532, 536; George's contact with at Heidelberg, 475; George's influence on, 418–19, 657, 689, 695, 696, 724, 726, 729; and Gundolf, 462; and rationality, 441, 442; and *The Star of the Covenant,* 526; and Weimar Republic, 572; and *Yearbook for the Spiritual Movement,* 443, 444, 486
Ghil, René, 47
Gibbon, Edward, 110
Gide, André, 370
Globe Room, *384,* 420–27, 471, 490, 497, 508, 509, 549, 638, 656
Glöckner, Ernst, *388;* and Bertram, 503–4, 505, 509, 510, 532, 533, 548, 587–88, 590, 591–92, 620–24; and *Blätter* history, 702; and First World War, 525, 528; and Friedemann, 531; and Gundolf, 615; and Mann, 507; relationship with George, 505–11, 532, 533, 542, 587–88, 590, 620–24, 653; and "Secret Germany," 684; and Versailles Treaty, 581; and "The War," 548; and women, 540
Goebbels, Joseph, 734, 740, 743
Goethe, Johann Wolfgang von: and Bingen, 9; George compared to, 48, 215, 216–17, 290, 364, 370, 549, 612, 668; George on, 598; as George's idol, 6; George's poem on, 364–65; and German culture, 191; Hofmannsthal compared to, 98, 107; and Italy, 55, 193, 663; and Kommerell, 671; and Kronberger, 328; and Lechter, 198; and Mauthner, 217; and Rolland, 522; and theater, 27; Wolters on, 647
Goethe (Gundolf), 269, *387,* 583, 584–85, 586, 587, 592, 596, 644, 666
"Goethe-Day" (George), 693
Goethe Prize, 692–94, 728, 730, 740
Goethe's Century (*Das Jahrhundert Goethes*) (George and Wolfskehl), 328, 402

"Goethe's Last Night in Italy" (George), 679
Gogol, Nikolay, 22
Goldstein, Moritz, 612, 650–51
Göring, Hermann, 735
Görtz, Emil Count von, 451
Gothein, Eberhard, 266, 269, 459, 464, 466–68, 476, 536, 539
Gothein, Marie Luise, 464, 466–68, 471, 526, 625
Gothein, Percy, 467–71, 472, 498, 502–3, 521, 531, 581, 655
Grainger, Percy, 195
Grautoff, Otto, 200, 201
Grave, Jean, 47, 50
"Graves in Speyer, The" (George), 661
Great War. *See* First World War
Greece/Greek culture: and *Books of Eclogues and Eulogies,* 177; George as embodiment of Greek inheritance, 408; and George as Master, 270; and German culture, 193–94; and Globe Room, 421; and Gothein, 469, 503; and homosexuality, 450; and *The Tapestry of Life,* 233; and "The War," 548; and Wilamowitz, 428–29, 437–39, 449
Grimm, Jacob, 59
Gundelfinger, Friedrich. *See* Gundolf, Friedrich
Gundelfinger, Sigmund, 267
Gundolf, Ernst, 345, 511, 604, 615–16, 626–27, 665, 713–15
Gundolf, Friedrich, *375*; and *Algabal,* 108–9, 119; anti-Zionism of, 304, 305; and Bertram, 588, 591; and biography of George, xi, 611–13; and *Blätter für die Kunst,* 270, 271, 275–76, 316, 321, 323, 408–12, 463, 600–601, 602; and *Blätter* history, 702–3, 704, 705, 707, 714, 715; and blond wonder phrase, 427; and book on Caesar, 648–52, 663, 667; and book royalties, 637; and book sales, 690; and circle, 224, 226, 267–70, 406; and Cosmic Circle, 306, 311–12; and First World War, 517, 518–20, 521, 523–25, 530–32, 536–40, 594, 595, 597; and Frederick II, 661; and George's bank account, 677–78; George's editing works of, 700; George's naming of, 267, 268; and Goebbels, 734–35; and Gothein, 467–69, 502; and holy war, 494; and homosexuality, 452; and Huch, 330; illnesses of, 550, 713–16; in Italy, 663; as Jewish, 304, 305, 623; and Klages, 290, 291, 311, 312, 346, 364, 436; and Kommerell, 627–28, 629, 671; and Lechter, 268, 488; and Lepsius, 268, 447–49, 538–39, 540; and master/disciple treatise, 408–12, 413, 414; and Paul anthology, 280; personality of, 268–69; photographs of, 331; productivity in writing, 647; and recruitment for circle, 400–401, 406, 419, 423–25; relationship with George, 35, 270–76, 311–18, 325, 329, 344–45, 350, 352, 354, 359, 369, 410, 462–66, 472, 474–75, 518, 534, 538–41, 596–617, 618, 620, 626, 647–48, 676, 714–16, 721; and Salomon, 550, 598–601, 603–5, 609, 611, 613, 614, 615, 616, 617, 713; and Schröder, 283; and Stein, 643; and swastika, 586; and "To the Dead," 581; and University of Heidelberg, 268–69, 457–66, 472–75, 481, 502; and Vallentin, 411–12, 465, 615, 643, 648, 676; on war, 485, 530–31; and "The War," 548–49; and Weber, 476, 478; and Wilamowitz, 439; and Wolfskehl, 267, 271, 272, 273, 275, 276–77, 278, 280–81, 292–93, 305, 311, 313, 351–52, 518, 524, 703, 704; and Wolters, 530, 580, 608–9, 611–12, 616; and women, 317, 540–42, 550; and year of misfortune, 351; and *The Year of the Soul,* 209; and *Yearbook for the Spiritual*

Gundolf, Friedrich (*continued*)
  Movement, 429, 430, 431, 432, 435–37, 443–45, 452–53, 481, 485, 524, 584–85. See also *Caesar: History of his Fame* (Gundolf); *Goethe* (Gundolf); *Shakespeare and the German Spirit* (Gundolf)

Haan, Wiesi de, 345, 444
Haeften, Hans von, 538
Hamecher, Peter, 689, 696, 705, 727
"Hanged Man, The" (George), 681–82
Harden, Maximilian, 451–52, 453
Hardt, Ernst, 266
Hauptmann, Gerhart, 522, 691
Hebbel, Friedrich, 435
Hegel, Georg Wilhelm Friedrich, 59
Heidegger, Martin, 628
Heine, Heinrich, 22, 25, 115, 363, 435
Heiseler, Henry, 334
Hellingrath, Norbert von, *389*, 406, 511, 521, 537, 594
Helmholtz, Hermann, 238
Henry, Emile, 33
Hentschel, Albert, 306–7
Hermaphrodism, 113, 120, 127, 153, 299–300, 301, 309, 344, 493
Herodian, 109, 110
Herzen, Alexander, 34, 482
Herzl, Theodor, 305
Hesse, Hans, 489
Heyer, Wolfgang, 400–402, 521, 594
Hierarchy: and circle, 183, 225–26, 230, 275, 410, 623, 710; and master relationship, 223, 410
Hildebrandt, Kurt, *383*; and circle, 406, 412–13; and First World War, 521, 525, 594; and Friedemann, 531; and George's political beliefs, 725, 726; and Gundolf, 465; and Kommerell, 707; and National Socialist party, 725, 731; and Nietzsche book, 590; and race issues, 547; relationship with George, 626; and Wilamowitz-Moellendorff essay, 428–29, 432, 437–38, 443, 444, 449–50; and women, 540; and *Yearbook for the Spiritual Movement,* 431, 437, 443, 481, 487
Hilsdorf, Jacob, 467
Himmler, Heinrich, 735
Hindenburg, Paul von, 694–95, 722, 723, 729
Hirschfeld, Magnus, 114–15
Hitler, Adolf, 309, 642, 652, 723, 725, 726–27, 735, 744, 745
Hofmann, Ludwig von, 219
Hofmannsthal, Hugo von, *252*; and Andrian, 126, 127, 130, 160, 161; and *Blätter für die Kunst,* 128, 131–33, 134, 136, 137, 142–43, 144, 174, 183, 185, 187, 190, 276, 319, 320–21, 323; and *Blätter* history, 705; Borchardt's speech on, 436; and circle, 320–21, 323, 423; and Dehmel, 139–40, 174; essays on George, 123, 182–83, 408; Gundolf compared to, 676; and Klein, 128–31, 132, 139, 141, 161; and Munich, 150; poetry of, 97–98; relationship with George, 98–107, 108, 122, 124, 131–33, 141–43, 183–87, 188, 200, 212, 275, 318–25, 333, 350, 399–400; and *Yearbook for the Spiritual Movement,* 429
Holbein, Hans, 285, 290
Hölderlin, Friedrich, 290, 406, 435, 473, 477, 511, 588, 628, 671, 672, 674, 692
Holten, Otto von, 359, 423, 429
Holy Roman Empire, 193, 201
Homer, 216, 439
Homosexuality: and Elagabalus, 110–11, 112, 113–14, 115; and Gautier, 112; of George, 24–25, 34–35, 42, 44, 98–100, 122, 166, 207–8, 354, 439, 450–51, 452, 510–11, 688, 712, 743; George's belief in Shakespeare's homosexuality, 338; and

hermaphrodism, 299–300; and Loeffler, 123; and Paragraph 175, 114, 122, 123, 451; and Schuler, 153, 299–300; and Spohr, 114–15; and Ulrichs, 113–14, 123; and *Yearbook for the Spiritual Movement,* 448, 449, 452–53, 483
Huch, Roderich, 306–7, 330
Hull, Isabel, 451–52
Hülsen, Georg von, 451
Humanity, 108, 343, 364, 482, 485
Huret, Jules, 75
Hutten, Ulrich von, 473
Huysmans, Joris-Karl, 112, 116, 118, 198, 238
Hymns (*Hymnen*) (George): *Algabal* compared to, 117; and Coblenz, 124–25, 126, 174; and George's complete works, 679; George's reaction to, 191; and German culture, 148; and Gundolf, 444; and Hofmannsthal, 100, 103; and Mallarmé, 73–74, 83–84; muse in, 342; publishing of, 75, 85, 86, 90, 91, 94, 176, 219, 284; and Saint-Paul, 73, 87–89; second edition of, 284; themes of, 78–83, 92; and Weber, 477; writing of, 68–69

Ibsen, Henrik, 27–28, 30, 31, 61
"In the Park" (George), 70, 71, 80
"Incorporation" (George), 338, 340
Indianism, 488
"Induction in the Order, The" (George), 397–99, 578
Industrialism, 482
International Court of Arbitration, 514
"Invitation" (George), 70
Italian Fascists, 664
Ivan the Terrible (czar of Russia), 535

James, Henry, 15–16, 27
Jellinek, Dora, 477
Jonas, Paul, 346

Kahler, Fine von, 602
Kahn, Gustave, 45
Kain, Helen, 44
Kandinksy, Wassily, 165
Kant, Immanuel, 75, 411, 628
Kantorowicz, Ernst: and circle, 626, 630; and First World War, 624–25; on Frederick II, 664–70, 681; and George's death, 742; in Italy, 663; as Jew with university position, 732–33; and Ladner, 718; relationship with George, 627, 675, 700, 735; and sales of book on Frederick II, 690. See also *Frederick II* (Kantorowicz)
Kantorowicz, Gertrud, 203, 267–68, 455, 489, 625
Kapp, Wolfgang, 606
Kapp Putsch, 606
Karl (archduke of Austria), 513
Karo, Georg, 622–23
Kassner, Marianne, 600
Kassner, Rudolf, 425–27
Kaufmann, Walter, 587
Kayser, Georg, 727
Kempner, Walter, 676
Kessler, Harry, 239–40
Khnopff, Fernand, 170
Klages, Ludwig, *376, 377*; and anti-Semitism, 150, 154, 155, 304, 305–6; and *Blätter für die Kunst,* 151, 162, 192, 227–29, 287, 306, 355, 356; book on George, 287–91, 326, 327; and Cosmic Circle, 301, 303, 306, 311, 312, 346, 589; George's poetic portrait of, 181; and George's role, 408; and Gundolf, 290, 291, 311, 312, 346, 364, 436; and Hofmannsthal, 321; and Huch, 330; and humanity, 364; and Lessing, 166; photographs of, 346; and rationality, 227–28, 288; relationship with George, 151, 154, 155, 192–93, 287, 301, 303, 307–8, 309, 316, 317, 333, 337, 346; and Schuler, 294, 302–3; and Schwabing, 165; and war

Klages, Ludwig (*continued*)
glorification, 228–29; and Wolfskehl, 290, 293, 305–6, 351
Klee, Paul, 165
Klein, Carl August: and *Blätter für die Kunst,* 127–32, 139, 140–41, 146, 160, 161–62, 185–86, 190, 196, 577–78; and Bondi, 219; and Dessoir, 172–73, 175; first meeting with George, 61–62; as George's disciple, 62, 64, 94; George's masquerading as, 198; and George's new art, 146; and George's poetry, 65, 66; and naturalism, 135; and Nietzsche, 588; poems devoted to, 237
Kleist, Heinrich von, 615, 648
Klinger, Max, 125, 146, 173
Klopstock, Friedrich Gottlieb, 671
Kohnstamm, Oskar, 351
Kolbenheyer, Guido, 728
Kommerell, Eva Otto, 711
Kommerell, Max, *557, 559*; and Anton, 631–32, 670, 706–7, 709–11; and circle, 630, 707–8, 709, 710; and German classical literature, 671–74; and Gundolf, 627–28, 629, 671; in Italy, 663; and Mehnert, 721–22; and Nazi Germany, 731; and Paul, 738; relationship with George, 629, 670–71, 675, 685, 700, 707, 708–12, 713; and Thormaehlen, 670–71, 707, 708–9, 711; and Wolters, 628, 706–7. *See also The Poet as Leader in German Classicism* (*Der Dichter als Führer in der deutschen Klassik*) (Kommerell)
Korrodi, Edouard, 650
Krehl, Rudolf, 609
Kriebel, Hermann, 652
Kronberger, Alfred, 327
Kronberger, Johanna, 327
Kronberger, Maximilian, *378, 379, 380*; and correspondence, 332, 510; and Cosmic Circle, 329, 330, 331; divinity of, 339–42, 344, 358, 367, 368, 422, 468–69, 477, 492, 496, 498–99, 510–11, 612, 683–84, 721; early interests in poetry, 327, 328; as embodiment of "New Man," 326; George's book in commemoration of, 337, 338–45, 358–59; George's initial interest in, 326–27; photographs of, 327, 331, 421–22, 471; relationship with George, 332–35; and *The Seventh Ring,* 342, 359, 360, 367–68, 492; unexpected illness and death of, 334, 335–37, 350, 429, 520; and Wolfskehl, 328, 345
Kropotkin, Pyotr Alekseyevich, 47
Kubin, Alfred, 165
Kulturkampf, 19–20, 23, 59

Ladner, Gerhart, 718–19
Lampridius, 109, 110–11, 115
Landmann, Edith, *385*; and Anton, 631; and *Blätter* history, 705; and Breysig, 544; and Frederick II, 662; and George's complete works, 678; and George's legacy, 598; and George's political beliefs, 576, 582, 725–26, 729; and George's travels, 655; and George's view of truth, 701; and George's works on the market, 691–92; and Globe Room, 638; and Goethe Prize, 694; and Gundolf, 541, 611, 613–14, 705; and Kommerell, 629, 708; and Liegle, 619; and Nietzsche, 589; and noble backgrounds of followers, 658; and privacy issues, xiv; relationship with George, 516, 534–35, 545, 553, 574, 626–27, 639, 640, 654, 716, 717; and Salomon, 603; and Spirit Books, 653; and Stein, 643; and Wolters, 647, 657, 675, 700
Landmann, Georg Peter, 716
Landmann, Julius, *385*; and George's legal heir as foundation, 677; and Goethe Prize, 693; and Gundolf, 715; intellect of, 716–17; relationship

with George, 516, 534, 542, 545, 574, 654, 655, 716, 717; and Wolters, 576, 702
Landmann, Michael, 652–53, 716, 725–26, 731
Langen, Albert, 165
Language: and coining new words, xvi; and George as Master, 414–15; George's linguistic experimentation, 22–25, 55, 61, 63, 149, 355, 672; George's proficiency in foreign languages, 21–22; George's study of, 35, 37, 39, 42; George's study of Latin and Greek, 21; and George's study of philology, 59; and German culture, 157, 158; Hofmannsthal's crisis with, 186; and *Hymns*, 87; influence of French language, 8, 21, 700; Latin language, 21, 157; and symbolism, 121; and words of German origin, 157
Law: George's lack of respect for, 196–97, 220, 324; and Moritz, 346; and *The Star of the Covenant*, 491–92
Law for the Restoration of Professional Civil Service, 732
Leccheni, Luigi, 33
Lechter, Melchior, *258;* background of, 197–98; and *Blätter für die Kunst,* 170, 198–99; and book decoration, 199–201; and circle, 406; and George's complete works, 678; George's decision to not use designs of, 487–90; and George's political beliefs, 576; and Gundolf, 268, 488; illness of, 351, 358; and Klages, 290; and Lepsius, 204; and *Maximin,* 337, 345; and mysticism, 303, 488, 586; and Paul anthology, 280, 281–82, 284; relationship with George, 223, 655; and *The Seventh Ring,* 368, 369, 489; and swastika, 585–86; and *The Tapestry of Life,* 230, 283; and title page design, 220; travel to India, 405; and Treuge, 396; and Wolfskehl,

293; and *The Year of the Soul,* 201–2, 204, 283; and *Yearbook for the Spiritual Movement,* 429
Lenin, Vladimir Ilyich, 165
Lenz, Gustav, 21, 44–46
Leo XIII (pope), 359
Lepsius, Reinhold, 187, 204, 237, *261,* 267, 290, 336, 455, 456
Lepsius, Sabine, *260;* and Berlin, 58; and Coblenz, 126; and Gundolf, 268, 447–49, 538–39, 540; and Klages, 390; and mania, 303–4; nickname for, 267; poem devoted to, 237; and public readings, 203–5, 212, 214, 224, 238, 239–40, 330; relationship with George, 58, 168–69, 187–88, 238, 300–301, 336, 345, 353, 455–56; and Simmel, 203, 212–13, 214, 455; and Wolfskehl, 293; and *Yearbook for the Spiritual Movement,* 447–50, 452–53
Lerberghe, Charles von, 170
Lessing, Gotthold Ephraim, 27
Lessing, Theodor, 166–68, 218, 238
Liberalism, 410, 482, 485
Lichtenberg, Georg Christoph, 218
Liebenberg Round Table, 451
Lieder, Waclaw, 162, 181, 184
Liegle, Josef, 533–34, 618–20
Lipps, Theodor, 238
Loeffler, Friedrich Berthold, 123
Lombard, Jean, 115, 116
Louÿs, Pierre, 49
Löwith, Karl, 628
Ludwig III (king of Bavaria), 575
Ludwig-Georg-Gymnasium, 14, 20–21, 30, 61, *244*
Luther, Martin, 60, 152–53, 285, 300, 598, 651
Lytton, Bulwer, 37

Maeterlinck, Maurice, 48, 144, 170, 178
Mallachow, Agathe, 540–42, 596
Mallarmé, Stéphane, *250;* and *Blätter für die Kunst,* 135, 169; and confrater-

Mallarmé, Stéphane (*continued*)
nal affiliation, 184; death of, 203; George's comments on, 52, 60–61; George's kinship with, 125, 146, 147, 424, 433; George's translation of, 140; and Hofmannsthal, 98, 100; and *Hymns,* 73–74, 83–84; influence on George, 58–59, 69, 71, 73–74, 84, 86, 89, 90; introduction to George, 47–48; legacy to George, 222, 223; and *Mardistes,* 48–50, 52, 53, 78; and Mauthner, 217, 218; and men's friendship, 354; and naturalism, 76–77; and publishing, 86; and Saint-Paul, 45; and symbolism, 46, 47, 50, 51–52, 75, 76, 77–78, 83, 159; and *The Year of the Soul,* 202
Manet, Edouard, 48
Mann, Heinrich, 727
Mann, Thomas, 165, 345, 371, 507, 525, 584, 587, 621–22, 727
Manuel (George), 30, 38
Marcks, Erich, 459
Marcuse, Ludwig, 690
Marées, Hans von, 219
Marr, Wilhelm, 154
Materialism, 482, 484, 495
Mauclair, Camille, 49
Mauthner, Fritz, 217–18
Maximin. *See* Kronberger, Maximilian
Maximin (George), 337, 338–45, 358–59, *380,* 420
May laws of 1873, 19
Mayer-Oehler, August, 266
Mehnert, "Viktor" Frank, *565, 566, 567;* and Kommerell, 721–22; and National Socialist party, 731; and *The New Reich,* 685; relationship with George, 720, 721, 735, 736–39, 741, 742; and Stettler, 720, 721
Meinecke, Friedrich, 573
Merrill, Stuart, 45, 47, 48, 61, 147–48
Mess, Caroline, 39–40
Mexico, 64, 127

Meyer, Estella, 203
Meyer, Richard M., 114, 203, 219
Miscegenation, 547
Mockel, Albert, 45, 47, 48, 50, 87, 88, 170, 370
Modernity, 301, 358, 480, 482, 494, 495, 636
Molière, 41
Moltke, Helmuth von, 515
Moltke, Kuno von, 452
"Monastery, The" (George), 235
Moore, George, 37–38
Moréas, Jean, 45, 46, 74, 140
Morisot, Berthe, 48
Morris, William, 200, 278
Morwitz, Ernst, *381;* and *Algabal,* 119; and blond wonder phrase, 427; and Bondi, 395; and circle, 406; and correspondence, 510; and First World War, 521, 594; and George's death, 742; and George's legal heir as foundation, 676–77, 709; and George's poems devoted to individuals, 237; and George's poetry, 653, 738; and George's residence in Switzerland, 736; and Gundolf, 462, 602, 603–4; as Jewish, 346, 623; and Kommerell, 707–8, 709; and Lechter, 488; and Nazi Germany, 727–28, 733–34, 744; and *The New Reich,* 685; and Paris travels, 370; and race issues, 547; and recitation of poetry, 400; relationship with George, 346–47, 349, 352, 397, 417, 496, 511, 549, 656; and *The Seventh Ring,* 361; and *The Star of the Covenant,* 496–98; and swastika, 681–82; and "To the Dead," 581
Motke, Helmuth von, 451
Mühsam, Erich, 165
Munich, 150–51, 164–65
Muret, Maurice, 60–61, 63, 64, 65, 86–87
Mussolini, Benito, 724–25

Napoleon (Vallentin), 644, 665, 675
Napoleon I, 7, 78, 348, 631, 643, 651, 662
National identity, 669
National Socialist party: and burning of "un-German" writers' books, 730; and civil servants' political sympathies, 732; electoral victory of 1930, 349–50, 674, 722; and George's political program, 586, 727, 729; and Hildebrandt, 725, 731; and Hindenburg, 723; rise of, 722–23; and swastika, 586. *See also* Nazi Germany
Natorp, Paul, 531, 628
Naturalism, 76–77, 89, 121, 125, 135–36, 158, 174, 358, 412
Nazi Germany: and anti-Semitism, 732–33, 745; George's relationship to, 723, 725, 726, 727–30, 731, 733–37, 740, 741, 744; Secret Germany's relationship to, xvii, 729, 730, 743–44; silence of, concerning George, 743. *See also* National Socialist party
"Newland Love Feasts" (George), 71
New Reich, The (George), 182, 240, 679–86, 687, 694, 696–97, 730, 740
Nietzsche, Friedrich: Friedemann compared to, 531; George compared to, 146, 290, 433–34, 549, 589, 689; George on, 32, 235–36, 588–90; as George's idol, 6; George's poem on, 359, 365, 588–89; and German culture, 191, 193; and Goldstein, 651; Ibsen compared to, 28; and Klages, 228, 229, 289; and Kommerell, 628; and Lechter, 198; and philosophy of life, 546; and Schuler, 152, 299; and *The Star of the Covenant*, 491, 689; and Wilamowitz, 438, 439; and Wolfskehl, 226, 227; and *Yearbook for the Spiritual Movement*, 433, 482, 486
Nietzsche: Essay in Mythology (Bertram), 587–88, 590–92, 620, 623, 644, 666, 690

Nobel Prize, 692
Nohl, Johannes, 527–28
Nordau, Max, 116, 136
Norton, Kurt, 69
Novalis (Friedrich von Hardenberg), 588, 592, 628, 692

Oberg, Erich, 114
Oelmann, Ute, xiv
"Of an Encounter" (George), 82
"Of Hanging Gardens" (George), 179–80, 182
Ottilie, Anna Maria, 5, 345, 740–41

Paracelsus, 675–76
Parnassians, 75
Paschal, Léon, 170
Pater, Walter, 35
Paul, Jean, 22, 273, 279–83, 290, 671, 738
Paulsen, Friedrich, 457–58, 460
Péladan, Joséphin, 76, 116, 198
Peñafiel, Antonio, 55, 60
Peñafiel, Julio, 55, 60, 64, 65, 86
Peñafiel, Porfirio, 55, 60, 64, 65, 86
Percy, Thomas, 313
Pericles, 486
Perls, Richard, 238–40, 270
Petrarch, 22, 326, 651
Phraortes (George), 30
Pilgrimages (*Pilgerfahrten*) (George): *Algabal* compared to, 117; and Coblenz, 174; and George's complete works, 679; and German culture, 147, 148; and Hofmannsthal, 100, 103; publishing of, 91, 176, 219, 284; second edition of, 284; themes of, 91–93; and Verwey, 172; and Weber, 477
"Pilgrims in the Snow" (George), 206, 207
Platen, August von, 94, 115
Plato, 6, 21, 75, 277, 300–301, 349, 425, 440, 531

Poet as Leader in German Classicism, The (Der Dichter als Führer in der deutschen Klassik) (Kommerell), 563, 671–74, 706
"Poet in Times of Turmoil, The" (George), 680, 685
"Poison of Night" (George), 54
"Prayers" (George), 340
Preuschen, Margarete von, 351
"Priests" (George), 54–55
Primer, The (Die Fibel) (George), 28, 284, 678, 679
"Prince Indra" (George), 25–26, 28, 94
Princip, Gavrilo, 513
"Prologue" (George), 232–35, 430–31
Protestantism: and Bismarck, 18, 20; and *Blätter für die Kunst*, 285; and Britain, 38; George's attitude toward, 300, 412; and German culture, 60, 63; and Klages, 289; and Marburg, 632; and Prussia, 193; and Vatican Council of 1870, 19; and Weber, 476, 478; and *Yearbook for the Spiritual Movement*, 482, 483
Prussia, 16–19, 59, 123, 149, 193, 194, 285, 412, 484, 517–18, 520, 575
Publishing strategy: and *Algabal*, 176, 284; and *Blätter für die Kunst*, 128, 129, 136, 212, 220, 577; and Bondi, 219–21, 282, 283, 676, 678; and book decoration, 200–202; and First World War, 532; and Fischer, 318; George's ambiguity toward, 182, 491; George's control over, 88; and *Hymns*, 85, 86, 91, 176, 219, 284; and *Pilgrimages*, 91, 176, 219, 284; and Spirit Books, 653; and wider availability of works, 176–77, 488–89, 491, 526; and *The Year of the Soul*, 176, 203, 219, 283–84
"Pupil, The" (George), 34

Raab, Philip, 20, 31
Racial purity, 547–48, 688, 735, 744
Ranke, Leopold von, 699

Raphael (Stein), 643, 644, 665, 719
Rassenfosse, Armand, 170
Rassenfosse, Edmond, 170–72, 181, 208, 253
Rathenau, Walter, 538, 539
Rationality: and *Blätter für die Kunst*, 227, 228, 303; and circle, 226–28; and Gundolf, 463; and Klages, 227–28, 288; and Schuler, 152, 302; and Wolters, 431, 441, 442, 457; and *Yearbook for the Spiritual Movement*, 482
Rausch, Albert, 397, 419, 445–46
Redon, Odilon, 48
Régnier, Henri de, 45, 47, 140, 178
Reichstadt, Duc de, 631
Renoir, Auguste, 48
Revelation, book of, 367, 368
Reventlow, Franziska von, 306, 329, 331–32
Richter, Friedrich. *See* Paul, Jean
Rickert, Heinrich, 477
Rilke, Rainer Maria, 165, 203, 224–25, 711
Rimbaud, Arthur, 53
Ringleb, Heinrich, 640, 641
Rochus, Saint, 9, 13
Rodin, Auguste, 370
Rohde, Erwin, 459
Rolland, Romain, 521, 522, 523, 524
Römer, Robert, 19
Roses and Thistles: An Illustrated Journal, 29–30, 127, 246
Rossetti, Dante Gabriel, 35, 98, 178, 270, 511
Rouge, Carl, 247; and beauty of sin in antiquity, 113; befriending of, 23; and *Blätter für die Kunst*, 134; and George's poetry, 70–72; and George's travels, 35, 36, 37; and literary group, 38, 39, 40, 41–42; and poetry readings, 29; and *Roses and Thistles*, 30, 127
Rousseau, Jean-Jacques, 168

Rozniecki, Stanislaus, 68, 81, 87
Rudolf (crown prince of Austria), 513
Russia, 514, 515, 519, 535–36, 574, 744–45
Russian Revolution, 550
Rust, Bernhard, 727, 740–41

Sade, Marquis de, 111–12
Saint-Paul, Albert, *249*; and *Blätter für die Kunst,* 140–41, 162; and George's 1908 trip to Paris, 370; and George's moving to Berlin, 57, 58–59, 60; George's poetic portrait of, 181; and George's trip to Spain, 55; and George's writing in French, 145, 146, 148; and *Hymns,* 73, 87–89; and symbolism, 45–46, 47, 52, 53
Salin, Edgar, *381*; and *Blätter* history, 702; and correspondence, 510; and First World War, 517, 520, 521, 526; and George's life, xi–xii; and Gundolf, 473–74, 517, 601, 607–8; and Kommerell, 627; and privacy issues, xiii, 510; and recruitment for circle, 266–67, 400–402; relationship with George, 417, 608, 609–10; and *The Star of the Covenant,* 491–92, 526; and trains, 636; and University of Heidelberg, 475; and Verwey, 595–96; and Wolters, 647; and *Yearbook for the Spiritual Movement,* 429–30
Salomé, Lou-Andreas, 203, 224
Salomon, Elisabeth, 550, 598–601, 603–5, 609, 611, 613–17, 713, 714
Salten, Felix, 100
Salz, Arthur, 613, 614
Savigny, Friedrich Carl von, 295–96
Scherer, Wilhelm, 59–60, 63
Schertel, Ernst, 419–20
Schiller, Friedrich, 22, 27, 31, 435, 439, 628, 669, 671
Schlageter, Albert Leo, 645
Schlayer, Clothilde, 738, 739, 742
Schlegel, August Wilhelm von, 271

Schleyer, Johann Martin, 22
Schlieffen, Alfred von, 515
Schlieffen Plan, 515–16
Schliemann, Heinrich, 295
Schmidt, Erich, 59, 203, 292, 605
Schmitt, Saladin, 352
Schnitzler, Arthur, 97–98
Schoenberg, Arnold, 341
Scholem, Gershom, 742
Schopenhauer, Arthur, 76
Schröder, Rudolf Alexander, 282–83
Schulenburg, Fritz-Dietlof von der, 745
Schuler, Alfred, *377*; and *Algabal,* 151–52, 153; and anti-Semitism, 150, 152–53, 154, 155, 295, 304, 305–6, 309; and Bachofen, 295, 297–98, 299; and Bruckmann, 309–10; and Carnival celebration, 298–99; and Cosmic Circle, 294, 301–4, 306, 308, 309, 311–12, 329, 331, 589; George's poem dedicated to, 302; and Gundolf, 311, 312; and hermaphrodism, 299–300; relationship with George, 154, 155, 156, 294–95, 300, 301–3, 304, 307, 308, 309, 317, 333, 337; and Schwabing, 165, 294; and Spohr, 115; and swastika, 153, 294–95, 309, 310, 585; and Wolfskehl, 293–94, 302, 305–6, 308, 309, 311, 351
Schweitzer, Albert, 694
Scott, Cyril Meir, 194–97, 199, 208, 218, *258*, 354–55
Scott, Walter, 22
Second World War, 744
Secret Germany: and Benjamin, 674; and circle, x, 527; and First World War, 517, 520, 522–24, 527, 534; and Frederick II, 664; George as leader of, x, xii–xiii, 729; and Hellenic dream, 548; history of, 435; ideology of, xi, xvii; and Marburg, 630–31; and *The New Reich,* 696; and open discussion of ideas, 448–49; public acceptance of, 572; relationship with

Secret Germany (*continued*)
  Nazi Germany, xvii, 729, 730, 743–44; and *The Star of the Covenant*, 491; and University of Heidelberg, 475; and Wolfskehl, 434–35, 573
"Secret Germany" (George), 680, 682, 683–84, 685
Seebacher, Wendelin, 23
Serbia, 513, 515
Seventh Ring, The (George), *380*; *Algabal* compared to, 342; first edition of, 691; and First World War, 371, 545; and Frederick II, 661; and George's engagement in world, 408; and George's funeral, 742; and George's homosexuality, 450; and German cities, 360; and Kronberger, 342, 359, 360, 367–68, 492; and Lechter, 368, 369, 489; and Nietzsche, 588–89; and outlaw-turned-hero, 682; and poetic honors, 693; and poetic portraits of friends, 182, 360; publishing of, 240, 359, 368–69; second "public" edition of, 396; and Simmel, 407; themes of, 360–67; and war, 494; and Weber, 477; and *Yearbook for the Spiritual Movement*, 445
Shakespeare and the German Spirit (Gundolf), 271, *387*, 396, 463–65, 469, 735
Shakespeare, William: George's translations of, 89, 326, 337–38, 396, 416, 511, 532, 586; and George's view of drama, 403; Goethe compared to, 217, 612, 688; Gundolf's translations of, 270–71, 396, 416; and Kommerell, 628; and Lechter, 198; and love, 301, 326; and theater, 27
Shelley, Percy Bysshe, 98
Sieburg, Friedrich, 474
Simmel, Georg: essay on George, 214–17, 408; and George's critics, 688; and George's linguistic experimentation, 213, 214, 269; and George's single-mindedness, 412; and Gundolf, 268; intellectualism of, 213–14, 460; and Lepsius, 203, 212–13, 214, 455; relationship with George, 218, 407; and Weber, 475, 476
Simmel, Gertrud, 214, 268
Simon, Julius, 11–12
Socialism, 514
Socrates, 301
"Solstice Procession" (George), 362
Sombart, Werner, 716
"Songs" (George), 679
"Songs of Dream and Death, The" (George), 237
Sophocles, 438
"Sorrowful Dances" (George), 209
Spirit Books, 585–87, 592, 642, 650, 652–54, 665, 666, 670, 671. See also specific books
Spohr, Max, 114–15
Stahl, Arthur, *247*; befriending of, 23; ending of friendship with, 72–73; and George in Berlin, 63–64; and George's poetry, 70; and George's travels, 36, 37, 40–41; and *Hymns*, 85; and literary group, 38–39, 40, 41–42; and *Roses and Thistles*, 29–30, 127
Star of the Covenant, The (*Der Stern des Bundes*) (George): and Benjamin, 672; and Bertram, 730; and circle, 491–92, 499–500, 539; and First World War, 501, 523, 526–27; and George as Master, xii; and George's funeral, 742; and George's intentions, 487; and Glöckner, 510; and holy war, 494–95, 595; and initiation, 496; meaning of, 490–91, 492; and Morwitz, 496–98; and *The New Reich*, 687; and Nietzsche, 491, 689; and possession of artworks, 524; publishing of, 487, 490; review of, 526–27; and Steiner, 425, 498; *The*

Tapestry of Life compared to, 232, 492; and women, 500
Stauffenberg, Alexander von, *560*, 657–58, 660, 663, 685, 721, 742
Stauffenberg, Berthold von, *560*, 657–58, 660, 663, 685, 721, 735, 742
Stauffenberg, Claus von, *560*, 657–58, 660, 685, 721, 735, 742, 744–46
Stauffenberg, Franz Schenk von, 19, 657
Stefan George und die Blätter für die Kunst (Wolters), 129, 511, 512, *562*, 645, 646–47, 675, 698–706, 707, 714, 715
Stefan George-Archiv, xiv
Stefan-George-Prize, 740, 743
Steiger, Robert von, 694, 719, 742
Stein, Wilhelm, 642–43, 644, 694, 719, 721, 742
Steinberg, Manja, 317
Steiner, Herbert, 406, 423–27, 498
Stettler, Michael, *565*, 719–21, 742
"Strand" (George), 81–82
Strauss, Richard, 106, 341
Strich, Fritz, 689
Supersensory love, 337–39
Swastika: and Benjamin, 674; and Bertram, 730–31; and Bondi, 586–87, 611, 615, 616; and circle, 585–86, 591–92; and Cosmic Circle, 314; and George's funeral, 742; and *The New Reich*, 681–82; and Schuler, 153, 294–95, 309, 310, 585; and Spirit Books, 585, 586–87, 642, 652, 665, 671; as true symbol on flag, 681, 683
Swedenborg, Emanuel, 76
Swinburne, Algernon Charles, 35, 98, 511
Symbolism: and *Algabal*, 113, 118, 121; and anarchism, 47, 50–51, 74, 228; and Bahr, 130, 136; and *Blätter für die Kunst*, 159; and French symbolists, 45–53, 73, 83–84, 86–89, 99, 169, 222; and Gautier, 112; and George, 60, 68, 73, 76, 78, 80, 81, 86, 87, 89, 127, 145, 169, 177, 222, 336, 571; ideology of, 73–78; as international movement, 48, 514; and Maeterlinck, 144; and Mallarmé, 46, 47, 50, 51–52, 75, 76, 77–78, 83, 159; and nature, 169; and Simmel, 216; and *The Year of the Soul,* 212
Symons, Arthur, 48–49

Tapestry of Life, The (George): and Boehringer, 348; and Catholicism, 232–33; and disciples, 430–31; first edition of, 691–92; and George as Master, 233–36, 240, 408; and Lechter, 230, 283; and *Maximin*, 340, 342; and poetic portraits of friends, 237–38; and public reading, 330; publishing of, 229; second edition of, 284; *The Seventh Ring* compared to, 359; *The Star of the Covenant* compared to, 232, 492; structure of, 232; themes of, 230–36; and violence, 236–37; *The Year of the Soul* compared to, 230, 232
Tasso, Torquato, 22
Tertullian, 597
Thackeray, William Makepeace, 37
Thiersch, Paul, 406, 481
Thompson, Vance, 53
Thormaehlen, Ludwig, *557*; and Anton, 631; and *Blätter für die Kunst,* 602; and *Blätter* history, 701; and circle, 406; and First World War, 521, 594; and George's death, 742; and George's political beliefs, 734; and George's space, 656; and Gundolf, 465; and Kantorowicz, 626; and Kommerell, 670–71, 707, 708–9, 711; and National Socialist party, 731; and *The New Reich,* 685; and readings, 511; relationship with George, 549; and Salomon, 550, 603; and *The Star of the Covenant,* 491; and Stauffenberg, 658; and "To the Dead," 581;

{ INDEX } 843

Thormaehlen, Ludwig (*continued*)
and *Yearbook for the Spiritual Movement,* 429, 430
Tieck, Ludwig, 271
Tiersch, Paul, 429
"Time-Poem" ("Das Zeitgedicht") (George), 363
"To a Young Führer in the First World War" (George), 685–86
"To the Dead" (George), 581–82, 679
Tolstoy, Leo, 168
Tönnies, Ferdinand, 475
Treitschke, Heinrich von, 155
Treuge, Lothar, 345, 396
Troeltsch, Ernst, 592–93
Turgenev, Ivan, 22

Ulrichs, Karl Heinrich, 113–14, 115, 123
United States, 482–83, 484, 489, 550, 580, 641–42
Universal Exposition, Paris, 44, 46
Uxkull, Bernhard von, *390,* 552–53, 680, 684–85
Uxkull, Woldemar von, 581, 658, 731

Vaillant, Auguste, 33
Vallentin, Berthold, *382;* and *Blätter* history, 699, 700, 702; and Breysig, 447; and circle, 406; and correspondence, 510; and First World War, 520, 525, 594; and Frederick II, 662–63; George's editing of work, 700; and George's political beliefs, 724–25, 729; and Goethe Prize, 693–94; and Gundolf, 411–12, 465, 615, 643, 648, 676; and Hindenburg, 695; and homosexuality, 452; illness of, 717; and Kiel, 635–36; and Lechter, 488; and moving the state, 656; and Napoleon, 643, 644, 665, 675; and readings, 511; and recitation of poetry, 399; relationship with George, 348–49, 352, 395, 403, 423, 542; and Russians, 535; and "To the Dead," 581; and Wolters, 645, 646; and *Yearbook for the Spiritual Movement,* 430–31, 432, 437, 481, 583. *See also Napoleon* (Vallentin)
Vallentin, Diana Rabinowicz, 348–49, 663, 717–18
Vallentin, Stefan, 718
Vatican Council of 1870, 19
Verhaeren, Emile, 47, 48, 170
Verlaine, Paul, *249;* and Dehmel, 140, 141; George's kinship with, 89, 125, 146, 147; George's translation of, 140; and Hofmannsthal, 98; and Péladan, 116; and symbolism, 45, 46, 52–53, 86
Versailles Treaty, 579–82, 641, 686
Verwey, Albert, *257, 377;* and *Blätter für die Kunst,* 172, 211, 595; and First World War, 595; and George as Master, 234; and George's Rhine poems, 360; and George's typeface, 400; and George's view of poet's role, 417–19; and George's view on drama, 403, 418; and German culture, 279; and Gundolf, 269, 271–72; and Klages, 290; and Lechter, 198; and Ottilie, 5; relationship with George, 336–37, 369–70, 595; and *The Tapestry of Life,* 237; and Wolfskehl, 525, 637, 638–39; and *Yearbook for the Spiritual Movement,* 431
Verwey, Kitty, 172, 237, 272
"Victory of Summer" (George), 206, 207–9
Vielé-Griffin, Francis, 45, 47, 48, 61
Villiers de L'Isle-Adam, August de, 45, 50, 117
Violence: and *Algabal,* 120–21, 180; and anarchism, 33–34; and George's political beliefs, 574, 729; Hofmannsthal's observance of, 100, 182; and *The New Reich,* 679; and "Of Hanging Gardens," 180; and *The Poet as Leader,* 673; and *The Star of the*

Covenant, 493, 494, 499; and *The Tapestry of Life,* 236–37; and "The War," 548
Virgil, 688
Volhard, Ewald, *559,* 628, 630
Vollmoeller, Karl Gustav, 203, 266, 484
Von der Leyen, Friedrich, 450–51

Wagner, Richard, 27, 76, 146, 169, 235–36, 589
Wahl, Philipp, 23
Waldhausen, Balduin, 516
Walloth, Wilhelm, 29, 67, 115
Walzel, Oskar, 551
Wandrey, Conrad, 652
"War, The" ("Der Krieg") (George), 544–49, 610, 679, 695, 716
Wassermann, Jacob, 727
Weber, Alfred, 459, 476, 536
Weber, Marianne, 459, 476, 477, 478–81
Weber, Max, 269, 407, 459, 460, 475–81
Wedekind, Frank, 165
Weigel, Hermann, 23, 30
Weimar Republic, xi, 572, 642, 722–23, 724
Weizsäcker, Ernst von, 742
Wellsted, Tom, 39, 40, 86
Wenghöfer, Walter, 594
Werfel, Franz, 727
Werner, Bruno, 549
Whistler, James, 48
Wilamowitz-Moellendorff, Ulrich von, 428–29, 432, 437–39, 449–50, 705
Wilde, Oscar, 35–36, 38, 48, 123
Wilhelm I (emperor of Germany), 16, 36
Wilhelm II (emperor of Germany), 451–52, 515, 523, 553, 573, 661
Will: and *Algabal,* 108, 120; and *Blätter für die Kunst,* 129, 144; and *Books of Eclogues and Eulogies,* 181; and circle, 230, 400; and dependent relationships, 274–75; and drama, 403; and external influences, 74; and friendships, 188; and George's poetry, xii, 88, 92–93, 167, 363; and George's translations, 89; Hofmannsthal's observance of, 100; and *Hymns,* 83; and linguistic experimentation, 63; and longing for companionship, 222–23; and nature, 169; and new humanity, 108; and publishing, 86; and symbolism, 78
Wilson, Woodrow, 580
Winckelmann, Johann Joachim, 193, 348
Windelband, Wilhelm, 459
Wirtschaft zur Traube (Tavern of the Grape), *243*
Wittgenstein, Ludwig, 217
Wolff, Kurt, 591
Wölfflin, Heinrich, 407, 444
Wolfskehl, Hanna, 269, 302, 304, 309, 335–36, 403, 424, 454, 637, 742
Wolfskehl, Karl, *374, 377, 379;* and *Blätter für die Kunst,* 137, 138–39, 162, 174, 190, 191, 208, 278; and *Blätter* history, 703–5; and circle, 154, 293, 406; and correspondence, 510, 691; and Cosmic Circle, 294–95, 301, 304, 307, 312, 329, 330, 362, 589; and Dehmel, 174; and economic troubles, 637, 638–39; and First World War, 520, 521, 522–23, 525, 532, 594, 595; and George as leader of New Man, 326; and George's death, 742; and George's political beliefs, 576; and George's role in circle, 408; and Globe Room, 420–21, 424; and Gundolf, 267, 271, 272, 273, 275, 276–77, 278, 280–81, 292–93, 305, 311, 313, 351–52, 518, 524, 703, 704; and Hofmannsthal, 107, 321; and holy war, 494; in Italy, 638–39, 663; as Jewish, 138, 154, 304, 305, 307, 623; and Klages, 290, 293, 305–6, 351; and Kronberger, 328, 345; marriage of,

Wolfskehl, Karl (*continued*) 269; and mysticism, 303, 488; and nonrationality, 226–27; and Paul anthology, 280–81; and Perls, 239; photographs of, 331; publishing of, 396; and recruitment for circle, 265, 267; relationship with George, 137–38, 154, 184, 188, 191, 265, 276–77, 278, 281, 292, 293, 307, 350, 465, 466, 638, 737–38; and Schuler, 293–94, 302, 305–6, 308, 309, 311, 351; and Secret Germany, 434–35, 573; and "Secret Germany," 684; and Simmel, 214; and travel to India, 405; and Wolters, 704, 706; and year of misfortune, 351; and *The Year of the Soul*, 203; and *Yearbook for the Spiritual Movement*, 429, 430, 432–35, 450–51, 482; and Zionist movement, 305. *See also Goethe's Century (Das Jahrhundert Goethes)* (George and Wolfskehl)

Wolfskehl, Otto, 138, 267

Wolfskehl, Renate, 269, 637

Wolters, Erika, 520, 663–64

Wolters, Friedrich, *382, 556, 559*; and *Algabal*, 109; and biography of George, 109, 129, 339, 349, 511–12, 645–46, 675, 698–706; and Breysig, 446–47; and chaotic situation in Germany, 575–76; and circle, 405–6, 616; critical acclaim for, 690; and First World War, 517–18, 519, 520, 521, 525, 529–30, 534, 594; and Friedemann, 531; and Gundolf, 530, 580, 608–9, 611–12, 616; and history of movement, 511, 512; and holy war, 494; illnesses of, 581, 706; and Kantorowicz, 625; and Kiel, 635; and Kommerell, 628, 706–7; and Lechter, 488, 489; and Marburg, 630–34; and Nohl, 527–28; and recitation of poetry, 399; and recruitment for circle, 631, 633–34; relationship with George, 349, 350, 352, 516, 583, 626, 654, 657, 698, 713; and sovereignty/service treatise, 412–14, 436, 489, 511; travel to Italy, 663; and United States, 580; and Volhard, 630; and Wolfskehl, 704, 706; and women, 540; and *Yearbook for the Spiritual Movement*, 430, 431, 440–41, 444, 446, 481, 485–86, 511, 519. *See also Stefan George und die Blätter für die Kunst* (Wolters)

Women: and First World War, 546; George's attitude toward, 207, 208, 453–55, 540–42, 546, 603; and *The Star of the Covenant*, 500; and Marianne Weber, 476, 478, 479; and Max Weber, 476, 479; and *The Year of the Soul*, 207, 208, 453; and *Yearbook for the Spiritual Movement*, 448, 449–50, 453, 482, 483, 486

"Wrestler, The" (George), 179

Writers' Academy, 727–29, 730, 733

Year of the Soul, The (Das Jahr der Seele) (George), *259*; and Benjamin, 672; and Coblenz, 126; dedication of, to sister, 5, 207; and George's complete works, 679; and George's poetic persona, 206–7; and Lechter, 201–2, 204, 283; and linguistic experimentation, 22; and Mauthner, 218; organization of, 205, 206–9; and poetic portraits of friends, 182, 205, 209, 237; and public reading, 203–5, 212; publishing of, 176, 203, 219, 283–84; recitation of, 401; and Rilke, 224; second edition of, 283–84, 302; and Stettler, 720; and substitute realm within poetry, 210; *The Tapestry of Life* compared to, 230, 232; and "Time-Poem," 363; and women, 207, 208, 453

Yearbook for the Spiritual Movement (*Jahrbuch für die geistige Bewegung*), 384; as critical journal, 187; and First World War, 532; and George as Master, 442; George's involvement in, 431–32, 511; and Gundolf, 429, 430, 431, 432, 435–37, 443–45, 452–53, 481, 485, 524, 584–85; and image of George, 435–37; and Kommerell, 628; and meaning of George to world, 432, 436; and politics, 583, 724; public response to, 443–56, 457, 481, 482; publishing of, 429; revival of, 583; and sciences, 440–42, 446, 482; and Secret Germany, 434–35; and swastika, 586; and United States, 482–83; and war/combat orders, 432, 436–37, 439, 446, 453, 481, 484–86; and Weber, 478; and Wolfskehl, 429, 430, 432–35, 450–51, 482; and Wolters, 430, 431, 440–41, 444, 446, 481, 485–86, 511, 519; and women, 448, 449–50, 453, 482, 483, 486

Young, Owen D., 641

Zamenhof, Ludwik Lejzer, 22
Zierold, Kurt, 727–28
Zimmer-Zerny, Frieda, 181
Zola, Emile, 50
Zschokke, Alexander, 656–57, 685
Zweig, Stefan, 95, 473, 502, 513

OHIO UNIVERSITY LIBRARY
Please return this book as soon as you have finished with it. In order to avoid a fine it must be returned by the latest date stamped below. All books are subject to recall after two weeks or immediately if needed for reserve.

SEP 1 3 2004

OCT 2 0 2010

JUN 1 8 2004

CF